W9-BZR-165

# 2012 Scholarship Handbook

# 2012 Scholarship Handbook

## Fifteenth Edition

The College Board, New York

## About the College Board

The College Board is a mission-driven not-for-profit organization that connects students to college success and opportunity. Founded in 1900, the College Board was created to expand access to higher education. Today, the membership association is made up of more than 5,900 of the world's leading educational institutions and is dedicated to promoting excellence and equity in education. Each year, the College Board helps more than seven million students prepare for a successful transition to college through programs and services in college readiness and college success — including the SAT® and the Advanced Placement Program®. The organization also serves the education community through research and advocacy on behalf of students, educators and schools.

For further information, visit www.collegeboard.org.

Editorial inquiries concerning this book should be directed to Guidance Publications, The College Board, 45 Columbus Avenue, New York, NY 10023-6992; or telephone 212-713-8000.

Copies of this book are available from your local bookseller or may be ordered from College Board Publications, P.O. Box 869010, Plano, TX 75074-0998. The book may also be ordered online through the College Board Store at www.collegeboard.org. The price is $28.99.

© 2011 The College Board. College Board, ACCUPLACER, Advanced Placement, Advanced Placement Program, AP, CLEP, College-Level Examination Program, CSS/Financial Aid PROFILE, SAT, SpringBoard and the acorn logo are registered trademarks of the College Board. inspiring minds, My College QuickStart, MyRoad, SAT Preparation Booklet, SAT Preparation Center, SAT Reasoning Test, SAT Subject Tests, The Official SAT Online Course, The Official SAT Study Guide and The Official Study Guide for all SAT Subject Tests are trademarks owned by the College Board. PSAT/NMSQT is a registered trademark of the College Board and National Merit Scholarship Corporation. All other products and services may be trademarks of their respective owners.

ISBN: 978-0-87447-971-3

Printed in the United States of America

Distributed by Macmillan

The College Board is committed to publishing in a manner that both respects the environment and helps preserve its resources. We seek to achieve this through eco-friendly practices, including the use of soy inks, FSC and recycled paper, and biodegradable materials. When you see this symbol, be assured that we are working to reduce our ecological footprint.

# Contents

# Preface

Searching for scholarships has often been described as looking for a needle in a haystack. There are thousands of award programs available, but the typical student can expect to qualify for only a small number of them. This book is designed to point you toward programs that match your own personal and academic qualifications.

Compiled within this book are detailed descriptions of national and state-level award programs for undergraduate students. Most are available to all undergraduates, but some are restricted to entering freshmen, and others are only for continuing students — sophomores, juniors or seniors. Most awards are only available to U.S. citizens or permanent residents, but some are also available to students in other countries who plan to come to the United States for college.

The award program descriptions are based on information provided by the sponsors themselves, in response to the College Board's Annual Survey of Financial Aid Programs, conducted in the spring of 2011. A staff of editors verified the facts for every award program. While every effort was made to ensure that the information is correct and up to date, we urge you to confirm facts, especially deadline information, with the programs themselves. The award programs' websites are the best sources for current information.

We'd like to thank those who worked so hard to bring the *Scholarship Handbook 2012* to press: editors Rachael Mason, Rachel Korowitz, Elizabeth Blue and Christina Latimer, who compiled the data under the direction of project manager Andy Costello. In addition, we would like to thank the team of programmers and composers at Content Data Solutions, Inc., who converted the database into readable pages.

Tom Vanderberg
Senior Editor, Guidance Publications

# How to Use This Book

You may be tempted to go directly to the program descriptions and start browsing, but to get the most out of this book, start by reading the information and advice in the opening pages. They'll help you get a realistic perspective on financial aid and give you useful guidelines for understanding and taking advantage of your college funding options.

Your next step should be to complete the "Personal Characteristics Checklist" on page 13. This will help you think about all the ways you might qualify for scholarships and give you an idea of where you might start looking for awards you can apply for.

## Using the eligibility indexes

After your checklist is complete, use the eligibility indexes beginning on page 27 to find the award programs that correspond to your qualifications. You can also use the scholarship search program on www.collegeboard.org. This user-friendly program enables you to search with more criteria and with much greater speed than is possible with print indexes.

Please keep in mind that the eligibility indexes show programs for which *one* of the criteria is covered by the index. Most of these programs have additional requirements, such as financial need (as demonstrated on the FAFSA or CSS/Financial Aid PROFILE®), standardized test scores or GPA.

**Corporate/Employer:** Listed here are the many companies and businesses that offer scholarships to employees and/or employees' family members. You should check out any company that employs a member of your immediate family.

**Disabilities:** This category covers students with hearing or visual impairments, physical handicaps or learning disabilities.

**Field of Study/Intended Career:** This category, by far the longest, identifies broad major and career areas. If you don't see your specific area of interest, look for a more general area into which it might fit. In many cases, these awards require applicants to be already enrolled in college and to have declared a major in the relevant field.

**KNOW THE LINGO**

You'll find sidebars like this throughout the first part of this book highlighting and defining key terms. There's also a comprehensive glossary beginning on page 21.

**Gender:** Although the vast majority of awards are not gender-specific, there are more than 95 awards in this book exclusively for women, and more than 20 for men only.

**International Students:** Most awards in this book are available only to U.S. citizens or permanent residents. The programs in this category, however, are open to students from outside the United States.

**Military Participation:** Many of the awards in this category are for the children, descendants or spouses of members of the military, including the Reserves and National Guard, going back as far as the Civil War.

**Minority Status:** There are eight groups within this category, representing a wide range of awards.

**National/Ethnic Background:** The national/ethnic groups in this category are determined by the sponsoring organizations that responded to our annual survey.

**Organization/Civic Affiliation:** Many membership organizations and civic associations have generous higher education funding programs that are available for their members and/or their members' dependents or relatives. Check to see if any apply to your family.

**Religious Affiliation:** The 10 denominations in this category represent a broad range but, like the national/ethnic category, are determined by the respondents to our annual survey.

**Returning Adult:** This category includes awards for undergraduate, graduate and nondegree study. The age qualification varies, but most often is for students 25 years or older.

**State of Residence:** Each state has several award programs exclusively for state residents. Be sure to examine closely all those listed under your state.

**Study Abroad:** While most award programs for study abroad are for graduate students, a few are geared for undergraduates, and you will find them listed here.

**KEEP IN MIND**

This book does not describe local award programs that are restricted to a single community or school. For information about local programs for which you might qualify, talk to your school counselor or contact your local chamber of commerce.

Also not included in this are scholarships offered by colleges to their own students. For these "inside" awards, you should consult the financial aid offices at the colleges you are considering. Detailed financial aid information for more than 3,000 colleges can also be found in the College Board book *Getting Financial Aid 2012*.

# What's in the program descriptions?

The scholarship programs in this book are organized alphabetically by sponsor within three sections.

The scholarships section covers public and private scholarships and research grants for undergraduates. To be included, a scholarship program must grant at least $250 for the purpose of financing some aspect of higher education: tuition and fees, research, study abroad, travel expenses or other educational endeavors.

**PLANNING AHEAD**

Even if you qualify for a scholarship, you won't get it if you don't **apply on time**! Use the **planning worksheet on page 17** to keep track of deadlines, application requirements and notification dates for the programs you've selected.

The internships section covers public and private internships, providing opportunities either to earn money for education or to gain academic credit. To be included, paid internships must pay at least $100 per week and provide a viable path toward a future career. (The ESPN internship is an example of this; the Oscar Mayer Wienermobile is not.)

The loans section covers public and private education loan programs. Many have loan forgiveness options, usually in exchange for public or community service for a certain period of time.

Each program description contains all of the information provided by the sponsor and verified for accuracy by a staff of editors at the College Board. A typical description includes:

**Type of award:** Whether the award is a scholarship, grant, internship or loan; and whether it's renewable.

**Intended use:** Tells you the range and limitations of the award, such as level of study, full time or part time, at what kind of institution, and whether in the United States or abroad.

**Eligibility:** Indicates the characteristics you must have to be considered for an award — for example, U.S. citizenship, specific state of residence, disability, membership in a particular organization or minority status.

**Basis for selection:** May include major or career interest; personal qualities such as seriousness of purpose, high academic achievement or depth of character; or financial need.

**Application requirements:** Outlines what you must provide in support of your application, such as recommendations, essay, transcript, interview, proof of eligibility, a résumé or references.

**Additional information:** Gives you any facts or requirements not covered in the categories above — for example, which test scores to submit, GPA required, whether a particular type of student is given special consideration, when application forms are available, etc.

**Amount of award:** A single figure generally means the standard amount, but may indicate the maximum of a range of amounts. If a program awards different amounts, the range is provided.

**Number of awards:** Tells you how many awards are granted by the sponsor.

**Number of applicants:** Tells you how many students applied the previous year.

**Application deadline:** The date by which your application must be submitted; some scholarships have two deadlines for considering applications. Note: This information was obtained in spring 2011. Deadlines may have passed or changed. Check the sponsor's website for current deadlines.

**Notification begins:** The earliest date that an award notification is sent; in some cases, all go out on the same date; in others, notification is on a rolling basis. If there are two application deadlines, there are usually two notification dates.

**GOOD TO KNOW**

In addition to the eligibility indexes preceding the scholarship descriptions, there are two general indexes in the back of the book that list award programs by sponsor name and program name.

**KNOW THE LINGO**

**Academic internship** — An internship where you are not paid for your work, but rather earn college credit.

**Paid internship** — An internship where you are paid for your work.

**Total amount awarded:** Tells you how much money is disbursed in the current award year, including renewable awards.

**Contact:** Gives you all available information on where to get application forms and further information. Where the contact name and address are identical for several different scholarship programs sponsored by the same organization, this information will appear at the end of the last scholarship in that group.

While some descriptions don't include all these details because they were either not applicable or not supplied by the sponsor, in every case all essential information is provided. Readers are urged to verify all information (the sponsor's website is the best source) before submitting applications.

# Understanding Financial Aid

You shouldn't count on "outside scholarships" and summer internships like the ones in this book to pay for college. Rather, you should treat them as one possible source of aid, along with federal student aid and the scholarships and work-study jobs offered by colleges. In fact, outside scholarships account for only 4 percent of total student financial aid each year.

In order to get the most out of this book, you should first understand how to apply for the other 96 percent of total aid.

## What Is Financial Aid?

Financial aid is money given or loaned to you to help you pay for college. Different forms have different rules. The vast majority of aid comes from the federal government, and most of it consists of loans that you must pay back. However, some aid does not require repayment — which makes it the best kind.

If you qualify for financial aid, your college will put together an aid "package," usually with different types of aid bundled together. Most students qualify for some form of financial aid, so it makes sense to apply for it.

You'll apply for financial aid either at the same time or soon after you apply for admission. You may have to fill out more than one application. At the very least you will fill out the FAFSA, or federal government form, available on the Web at www.fafsa.ed.gov. You may also fill out another form, the CSS/Financial Aid PROFILE, which many colleges require. Some colleges and state aid agencies require their own financial aid forms, too. The colleges to which you apply will use the forms to figure out what your family can afford to pay and what your "need" is — that is, the difference between what you can pay and what the college actually costs. If the school wants you as a student but sees that you can't handle the whole bill, it will make you a financial aid offer to help you meet your need. If you accept, that financial aid package is your award.

**KNOW THE LINGO**

**Merit aid** — Aid awarded on the basis of academics, character or talent.

**Need-based aid** — Aid awarded on the basis of a family's inability to pay the full cost of attending a particular college.

**Non-need-based aid** — Aid awarded on some basis other than need or merit, such as grants with eligibility requirements related to field of study or state residence.

You will need to apply for financial aid every year that you are in college, mainly because your family's financial situation changes yearly. As a result, your financial aid package will probably be somewhat different from year to year.

Financial aid is a helping hand, not a free pass. In the United States, everyone has a right to a free public school education, but not to a free college education. The federal government and most colleges agree that students and their parents are the ones most responsible for paying for college. "The primary responsibility of paying for the student's education lies with the student and his or her parents," says Forrest M. Stuart, the director of financial aid at Furman University in Greenville, S.C. "Financial aid comes in to fill that gap, if you will, between what they can afford and what the college costs."

**GOOD TO KNOW**

For a more thorough explanation of student financial aid, read the College Board book *Getting Financial Aid 2012*, or read the articles in the "Pay for College" section of www.collegeboard.org.

# Types of Aid

Financial aid may come in many forms. However, all forms can be grouped into two major categories: gift aid and self-help aid.

## Gift Aid

Gift aid is free money, money that you don't have to pay back or work for. Naturally, this is the kind of aid most people want. It can take the form of grants or scholarships.

The terms "grant" and "scholarship" are often used interchangeably to mean free money. But here's the difference: A grant is usually given only on the basis of need, or your family's inability to pay the full cost of college. Scholarships are usually awarded only to those who have "merit," such as proven ability in academics, the arts or athletics. Once you're in college, you may have to maintain a minimum GPA or take certain courses to continue receiving a scholarship.

## Self-Help Aid

Self-help aid is money that requires a contribution from you. That can mean paying back the money (if the aid is a loan) or working for the money (if the aid is a work-study job).

The most common form of self-help aid is a loan. A loan is money that you have to pay back with interest. In light of that, you might not consider this aid at all. But it is — a loan means you don't have to pay the full price of college all at once: You can stretch the payments over time, as you would when buying a house or a car. Furthermore, some student loans are subsidized by the federal government, which means you don't have to pay the interest that comes due while you're in college.

Subsidized loans, which are awarded based on need and administered by the college, are the best kind. But you can also take out unsubsidized student loans and parent loans, which are not packaged by most colleges. However, be careful not to take on more debt than necessary. No matter what kind of loan you take out, you will have to pay it back.

Another form of self-help is work-study. This is financial aid in the form of a job. Since you earn the money through your work, this too may not seem like aid. But it is, because the federal work-study program pays most of your wages. And work-study jobs are usually available right on campus, with limits on your hours so that you won't be unduly distracted from studying.

# Who Gets Aid?

Grants and loans are not just for the poorest of the poor, nor are scholarships only for the smartest of the smart. The truth about who gets financial aid is somewhat different from what many people think.

## Those Who Need It

Most financial aid is based on need, not merit. There is money for merit, but most colleges in the United States focus their financial aid packages on meeting financial need.

However, there is a lot of confusion about what "need" means. "A lot of people think that they either have to be on welfare or Social Security — really poor — to get financial aid, and that's not correct," says Mary San Agustin, director of financial aid and scholarships at Palomar College in San Marcos, Calif. On the other hand, some wealthy families mistakenly think they are needy because their high living expenses leave them little money for college. "It's this expectation of, I pay my taxes, so my kid should be entitled to some federal financial aid regardless of how much money I make," says San Agustin.

*Need* simply means that your family can't afford to pay the full cost of a particular college. The *amount* of your need will vary from college to college, because it depends on the cost of attending an individual college. Whether your family has need is determined not by whether you think you are rich or poor, but by the financial aid forms you fill out.

## Those Who Don't

Despite the overall emphasis on need, many colleges do give away money on the basis of merit. They do this to attract the students they want most, and they may award this money even if it is more than the student needs. However, in many cases, the student both needs the money and has earned it on the basis of merit.

Don't think that only geniuses get merit aid. At many colleges a B average can put you in the running for merit money. Sometimes a separate application for merit aid is required to put you into consideration; sometimes your application for admission is enough. In either case, don't count yourself out by not applying; apply and let the college decide.

Grants are sometimes awarded based on neither need nor merit. For example, you may get a grant if you are in a certain field of study, are a resident of the state, or are a student from the same town as the college.

**KNOW THE LINGO**

**EFC (Expected Family Contribution)** — How much money a family is expected to pay for college, based on the family's ability to pay.

**Need** — The difference between your EFC and the cost of attending a particular college you've chosen. Financial aid is designed to meet your need, not your EFC.

**Gap** — The difference (if any) between the financial aid you need and the amount offered by a particular college.

## Part-Time Students

Some kinds of aid are only available to students enrolled in college full time — usually 12 or more credit hours of courses per semester. But part-time students are eligible for some financial aid. For example, federal loan programs require only that students be enrolled at least half time. Also, some employers offer tuition reimbursement benefits to students who work full time and go to college part time.

# Where the Money Comes From

Financial aid comes from three basic sources: governments (both federal and state), colleges and outside benefactors.

## From the Government

The lion's share of total financial aid awarded to undergraduates comes from the federal government. Fully 70 percent of all such aid is sent from Washington. The largest chunk of that consists of federal loans, which total $65.8 billion a year and represent 43 percent of all student aid. The loans take multiple shapes. Perkins loans are subsidized, with the lowest interest rate of any education loan. Stafford loans may be subsidized or unsubsidized. Both Perkins and Stafford loans are for students, but parents may take out a PLUS loan, which is not subsidized, to help pay for their children's education.

The federal government also funds several grants: the Pell Grant, the Supplemental Educational Opportunity Grant (SEOG), the Academic Competitiveness Grant and the SMART Grant. The Pell and SEOG grants are strictly need based, while the last two are based on both need and academic criteria. The government also funds the federal work-study program.

A much smaller piece of the financial aid pie (6 percent) comes from individual state governments. This is available in the form of grants, scholarships and loans. Most of this aid is for use only at colleges within the state, though a few states offer "portable" aid, which state residents can take with them to a college in another state.

## From the College

A great deal of financial aid comes from individual colleges, using their own "institutional" funds. In fact, colleges award nearly half of all grants. Many, though not all, award merit scholarships as well as need-based grants. They may also offer on-campus job opportunities and loans.

Private colleges give more financial aid than public ones, but their tuition is usually higher as well. Public colleges award less aid, but taxpayer support keeps their tuition lower.

### Outside Grants and Scholarships

Outside grants and scholarships come from sources other than the government or the college. These sources may include corporations like Coca-Cola or community groups like the Elks Club. Some are well known, such as National Merit Scholarship Corporation, but altogether they are the smallest piece of the financial aid pie: Only 4 percent of all student aid comes from outside sources. Pursue them, but don't expect them to outweigh the other aid you will get.

Bear in mind also that an outside scholarship is unlikely to expand the total aid you receive. If a college has already "met your full need" — that is, offered an aid package that covers the entire difference between what the college costs and what your family is expected to pay — it will not add an outside scholarship to that aid package. Rather, it will use your scholarship to substitute for some other piece of aid in the package. Think of your financial aid package as a barrel: When the barrel is full, no more can be added unless something is taken away. The last thing colleges will take away is whatever sum of money your family is expected to contribute.

# How Outside Awards Can Help

Even though outside scholarships rarely decrease the amount that your family is expected to pay out of pocket, it's still very worthwhile to pursue them. Why? Simply put, they expand your options for where you can go to college.

At some colleges, the first things taken away from a full-need package to make room for an outside scholarship are loans. Since that reduces the total amount you will have to pay back later, it makes that college more affordable. (Colleges vary in their policies on how they adjust packages for outside scholarships; you should call or e-mail the financial aid offices at the colleges you're considering to learn about their policies.)

There are also colleges that can't afford to offer every admitted student a financial aid package that meets the student's full need. If, for example, your need is $25,000 at a particular university, and the university's aid office can only offer you a combined total of $23,000 in grants, scholarships, work-study and subsidized federal loans, then there is a $2,000 "gap" in your aid package. Outside scholarships can help fill that gap.

Finally, there may be colleges where you don't have any financial need. For example, if your family's expected contribution to your college costs is $10,000, a state university that costs $10,000 a year to attend couldn't offer you any need-based aid. An outside merit scholarship, in this case, could decrease what your family pays below their expected contribution.

# FINANCIAL AID APPLICATION CALENDAR

## SOPHOMORE/JUNIOR YEARS

- Talk to your parents about college costs. Have realistic expectations, but understand how financial aid can expand your options.
- Take the PSAT/NMSQT® in October of each year. If you take it as a junior and meet other requirements, you will be entered into National Merit Scholarship Corporation competitions.
- Think about colleges you might want to apply to. If possible, visit some campuses in the spring of your junior year.
- Take the SAT® in the spring of your junior year.
- If you have a job, do your taxes each year (ask your parents for help). Knowing about tax forms and documents will be helpful when you have to fill out financial aid applications.
- Think about taking SAT Subject Tests™ near the end of courses in the subject areas you are studying.

## SENIOR YEAR

### SEPTEMBER

- Create a list of colleges you want to apply to. Start a checklist of their financial aid requirements and deadlines.
- If you're thinking about applying Early Decision to a college, ask whether it offers an early estimate of financial aid eligibility, and if so, what forms are required to receive one.
- Begin searching for outside scholarship programs available to seniors. Ask your school counselor about local scholarships offered by groups and businesses in your community.

### OCTOBER

- Ask your school counselor if there will be a family financial aid night at your school or elsewhere in your area this fall. If there is, be sure to attend; the event may be your single best source of information.
- Use the online calculators at **www.collegeboard.org** to estimate your family's Expected Family Contribution (EFC).
- If you need to fill out the CSS/Financial Aid PROFILE, you can do so on the PROFILE Online Web site starting Oct. 1.

### NOVEMBER

- Finalize the list of colleges that you'll apply to regular decision. Make sure you have all the financial aid forms you need.
- Starting Nov. 1, you can visit the FAFSA on the Web and get a sense of how the site works and what the application will ask for. But remember, you can't file the FAFSA until Jan. 1.

### DECEMBER

- You and your parents should save all end-of-year pay stubs for the year. You can use these to estimate income on aid forms.
- Apply for scholarships in time to meet application deadlines.
- Get PINs for the FAFSA for both yourself and one of your parents from **www.pin.ed.gov**.

### JANUARY

- You can file the FAFSA starting Jan. 1.
- If any colleges you're applying to have a financial aid priority date of Feb. 1, fill out the FAFSA (and PROFILE, if necessary) using estimated income information from your end-of-year pay stubs and last year's tax returns.
- Submit any other financial aid forms that may be required. Keep copies.

### FEBRUARY

- If you didn't file the FAFSA and other aid forms in January, do so now, using drafts of your family's income tax returns.
- Check your federal Student Aid Report (SAR) when you receive it, and correct it if necessary.
- You and your parents should consider filing your income tax returns early this year. Some colleges will request copies of your family's returns before finalizing offers.

### MARCH

- If necessary, write to colleges alerting them to special circumstances that affect your family's ability to pay for college.
- As you begin to receive letters of acceptance, check with aid offices to see if additional documentation (such as tax forms) must be submitted.

### APRIL

- Compare your financial aid award letters using the online tools at **www.collegeboard.org**.
- Write, e-mail or call the colleges that have offered you aid if you have any questions about the packages they've offered you.
- If you don't get enough aid to be able to attend a college, consider your options, which include appealing the award.

### MAY

- Be sure to accept the aid package from the college you want to attend by May 1.
- Be sure also to let other schools know you won't be attending.
- Plan now how you will cover your family's out-of-pocket expenses.
- Apply for loans if necessary.

# Finding and Applying for Scholarships

While you're researching and applying for colleges, you should also use this book to find scholarships that you qualify for and apply for them. In this chapter you'll find advice, as well as a calendar and worksheets to help keep you on track.

## When to Start Looking

It's never too early to start looking for scholarships. There are several programs that are open only to high school freshmen and sophomores, and some that are open only to juniors. There are other programs where you begin the work of applying up to a year before the final determination is made. For example, National Merit Scholarship Corporation competitions begin when students take the PSAT/NMSQT® in October of their junior year, and the competitions proceed in several rounds until fall of their senior year. If you're already a senior, though, don't despair — there are plenty of programs for entering freshmen that you can apply for during your senior year.

No matter what grade level you're in, the best time of the year to research programs is in the summer or early fall. That way you can be sure to find programs before their deadlines have passed, and with enough advance time to prepare a complete, competitive application. Remember that many scholarship programs require you to submit an essay as part of your application, and essays take time to write. Many programs also require recommendations; as a general rule, you should ask for recommendations at least four weeks in advance, and preferably more. Some programs even require you to perform additional academic work outside of school, such as writing a research paper or competing in a science fair.

You should let your school counselor know as early as possible that you're interested in applying for scholarships. He or she can help you think about your strengths as a student, which will make it easier to narrow down your scholarship search. Your counselor will also be able to recommend some programs you should apply for. (See "Thinking Locally" on page 14.)

**PLANNING AHEAD**

If you haven't already started looking for scholarships, start now. Today. Use this book to find a program you qualify for, and make a note of its application deadline and requirements. Then go to the program's website and download an application.

## Playing Catch-Up

If it's already the middle of your senior year, you've probably missed a lot of opportunities to apply for scholarships with October, November and December deadlines. But don't give up yet; there are plenty of scholarships with January, February and March deadlines.

The key to playing catch-up is to start working now, today. Find scholarships where the deadline hasn't passed. Get applications from the sponsors' websites. Talk to your school counselor immediately. The longer you wait, the less likely you are to win any awards.

The good news: Since you're already far into the college application process, you're now a pro at describing yourself to admission committees and scholarship review boards. You also have personal essays, academic writing samples and teacher recommendations ready to go.

# Choosing Where to Apply

There are so many scholarships, grants, fellowships, internships, fee waivers, work-study jobs and low-interest loans available for college-level study that just looking at the options can be daunting. (This book alone describes 2,100 national and state-level programs.) Fortunately, there are some easy ways to narrow the field of potential programs down to the ones where you have a good chance of winning an award.

The personal characteristics checklist on the next page highlights some of the common eligibility criteria for scholarship programs. You're not likely to find a scholarship that's targeted to every one of your characteristics, but you can use your answers on the checklist as a starting point for finding programs. The eligibility indexes on pages 27 to 69 will help you quickly match your characteristics to programs.

You'll probably find a few scholarship programs that match your characteristics. If you find a lot, you should consider narrowing your search — applying for scholarships is a lot of work! It's far better to send in four high-quality applications to programs that closely match your characteristics and interests than to send 16 hurried applications to a wide variety of programs.

# PERSONAL CHARACTERISTICS CHECKLIST

Are you **male** or **female**?

What is your **state of residence**?

Do you have a **learning or physical disability**? Many scholarships are offered to those who are disabled in any way, but some are for those with a specific disability.

**Military service** is the basis of many scholarships. Many of these awards are not just for those who have worn a uniform, but also for their spouses and children, or even descendants of a veteran. Talk to your family about its military history (was Grandpa in the Korean War?) Be sure to find out what branch of the military your family members served in, and, if possible, which unit(s) they served in.

List any family history of military service here:

You'll find scholarships for students with **minority status**, (e.g., African American, Alaska Native), and also for students with a particular **nationality or ethnic background** (e.g., Chinese, Greek).

If you belong to a minority, list it here:

List your ethnic and/or national origin(s) here:

What, if any, is your **religious affiliation**?

Are you an **international student** (a citizen of a foreign country, including Canada, seeking to study in the United States)?

The largest category of scholarships and internships is for students planning to study a particular college major (e.g., math, English, a foreign language) or prepare for a particular career (e.g., law, education, aviation). Even if you are "undecided" at this point, you should list all the **majors/careers** you are leaning toward.

☐ Do you want to **study abroad**? There are scholarships to help you pay for it — check here to remind yourself to seek them out.

"**Returning adult**" refers to students who have been out of high school a year or more before entering college. If that's you, look for scholarships designed to encourage your pursuit.

Years out of high school:

Your age:

Do you or any members of your family belong to a **national or local organization** or **civic association** (e.g., Kiwanis, Rotary, Elks Club)? Many such groups offer scholarships to members and/or their families. List here any that apply:

**Employers and corporations** often offer scholarship benefits to employees and/or their families. List the companies that you or someone in your family works for here:

## Narrowing Your Search

If you're having trouble narrowing down your scholarship search, consider the following:

**How many applicants are there each year?** Some of the better-known programs (such as the Coca-Cola Scholars Program) see hundreds of applicants for every award they give out! It can't hurt to apply for these programs, but you shouldn't invest so much effort in applying for them that you miss out on smaller programs where your chances may be better.

**Is this really for me?** If you couldn't get through *Atlas Shrugged* the first time, don't force yourself to read it and write an essay on its philosophical meaning for the Ayn Rand Institute contest — even if you're a great English student. Focus instead on programs that appeal to you or sound like fun.

**Can I live with the strings attached?** Many scholarship and internship programs have service requirements. Most notably, the Reserve Officers Training Corps (ROTC) program requires cadets to become military reserve officers upon graduation. And some summer internships will require you to move to another city.

KEEP IN MIND

**Don't let your scholarship search overshadow your other responsibilities** and application requirements. You still need to do well in school, get your college applications in on time, and submit the FAFSA and other financial aid forms by your colleges' priority dates.

## Thinking Locally

This book contains national and statewide financial aid programs offered by government agencies, charitable foundations and major corporations. But there are also thousands of small scholarship programs offered on a local level by civic clubs, parishes, memorial foundations and small businesses.

In many cases, these programs award just a few hundred dollars — enough to buy a semester's worth of textbooks. But since they are offered on a local level, your chances of receiving an award are much higher than they are for the big national competitions. So it pays to look for local scholarships.

Your school counselor may have files of local scholarship programs. There may even be a scholarship designated for graduates of your high school — you'll never know until you ask. You should also check with employers (either your parents' or your own); your church, temple or mosque; and any civic clubs that your family members are involved in.

## Avoiding Scholarship Scams

The Federal Trade Commission (FTC) developed Project $cholar$cam to alert students and families about potential scams and how to recognize them. Here are the FTC's seven basic warning signs:

- "This scholarship is guaranteed or your money back."
- "You can't get this information anywhere else."
- "May I have your credit card/bank account number to hold this scholarship?"
- "We'll do all the work for you."

**GOOD TO KNOW**

For more information about Project $cholar$cam, visit the FTC's website at **www.ftc.gov**.

- "The scholarship will cost some money."
- "You've been selected by a national foundation to receive a scholarship."
- "You're a finalist" in a competition you never entered.

Remember that no one can guarantee that you'll receive a grant or scholarship, and that you will have to do the work of submitting applications to be considered. Don't pay money for a service without a written document saying what you'll get for your money and what the company's refund policies are. And never, ever give your credit card number, Social Security number or bank account information to someone who called you unsolicited.

# Applying for Scholarships

This may mean not only filling out a form but also compiling supporting documents, such as transcripts, recommendations and an essay. Or you might need to provide evidence of leadership, patriotism, depth of character, desire to serve, or financial need. Get to know the requirements of each scholarship as early as possible so you can do any necessary extra work on time.

A few pointers to remember:

**Apply early!** Apply as early as possible to scholarship programs. If you can, do it in the fall of your senior year, even if the deadlines aren't until February or March. Very often, scholarship programs will have awarded all their funds for the year on a first-come, first-served basis before their stated deadline.

**Follow directions.** Read instructions carefully and do what they say. Scholarship programs receive hundreds and even thousands of applications. Don't lose out because of failure to submit a typewritten essay versus a handwritten one if required, or to provide appropriate recommendations. If you have a question about your eligibility for a particular scholarship or how to complete the application, contact the scholarship sponsors.

**Be organized.** It's a good idea to create a separate file for each scholarship and sort them by their due dates. Track application deadlines and requirements. Store in one place the different supporting documents you may need, such as transcripts, standardized test scores and letters of recommendation.

**Check your work.** Proofread your applications for spelling or grammar errors, fill in all blanks and make sure your handwriting is legible.

**Keep copies of everything.** If application materials get lost, having copies on file will make it easier to resend the application quickly.

**Reapply.** Some programs only offer money for the first year of college, but others must be renewed each subsequent year.

# SCHOLARSHIP APPLICATION PLANNER

| | PROGRAM 1 | PROGRAM 2 | PROGRAM 3 |
|---|---|---|---|
| PROGRAM/SPONSOR | *National Merit Scholarship* | *Young Epidemiology Scholars* | *First Bank* |
| ELIGIBILITY REQUIREMENTS | *Academic merit* | *Academic merit* | *Need, local residency* |
| TYPE OF AWARD | *Scholarship* | *Scholarship* | *Internship* |
| AMOUNT OF AWARD | *$2,500* | *$1,000 or more* | *$2,500* |
| CAN BE USED FOR | *Tuition/fees* | *Any expense* | *Any expense* |
| CAN BE USED AT | *First-choice college* | *Any college* | *In-state colleges* |
| DEADLINE | *Oct. 1 (give essay to English teacher for review)* | *Feb. 1* | *April 1* |
| FORMS REQUIRED | *NMSC application* | *Web form* | *Application (includes need analysis)* |
| TEST SCORES REQUIRED | *PSAT/NMSQT (already took), SAT (by December Senior year)* | *None* | *SAT* |
| ESSAY OR ACADEMIC SAMPLE | *Personal statement, academic transcript* | *Essay, research project* | *None required* |
| RECOMMENDATIONS | *Principal* | *None* | *One teacher (Mr. Filmer), Local branch manager* |
| NOTIFICATION BEGINS | *March* | *Not sure* | *May 15* |
| REQUIREMENTS TO KEEP AFTER FRESHMAN YEAR | *One-time payment only* | *One-time payment only* | *Based on performance during internship* |

*For a blank version of this worksheet that you can photocopy for your own use, see the next page.*

# SCHOLARSHIP APPLICATION PLANNER

| | PROGRAM 1 | PROGRAM 2 | PROGRAM 3 |
|---|---|---|---|
| PROGRAM/SPONSOR | | | |
| ELIGIBILITY REQUIREMENTS | | | |
| TYPE OF AWARD | | | |
| AMOUNT OF AWARD | | | |
| CAN BE USED FOR | | | |
| CAN BE USED AT | | | |
| DEADLINE | | | |
| FORMS REQUIRED | | | |
| TEST SCORES REQUIRED | | | |
| ESSAY OR ACADEMIC SAMPLE | | | |
| RECOMMENDATIONS | | | |
| NOTIFICATION BEGINS | | | |
| REQUIREMENTS TO KEEP AFTER FRESHMAN YEAR | | | |

# Sources of Information About State Grant Programs

### Alabama
Alabama Commission on Higher Education
P.O. Box 302000
Montgomery, AL 36130-2000
334-242-1998
www.ache.state.al.us

### Alaska
Alaska Commission on Postsecondary Education
P.O. Box 110505
Juneau, AK 99811-0505
800-441-2962
www.state.ak.us/acpe

### Arizona
Arizona Department of Education
1535 West Jefferson Street
Phoenix, AZ 85007
800-352-4558
www.ade.state.az.us

### Arkansas
Arkansas Department of Higher Education
114 East Capitol Avenue
Little Rock, AR 72201
501-371-2000
www.adhe.edu

### California
California Student Aid Commission
P.O. Box 419026
Rancho Cordova, CA 95741-9026
888-224-7268
www.csac.ca.gov

### Colorado
Colorado Department of Education
201 East Colfax Avenue
Denver, CO 80203-1799
303-866-6600
www.cde.state.co.us

### Connecticut
Connecticut Department of Higher Education
61 Woodland Street
Hartford, CT 06105-2326
860-947-1800
www.ctdhe.org

### Delaware
Delaware Higher Education Office
Carvel State Office Building, 5th floor
820 North French Street
Wilmington, DE 19801-3509
800-292-7935
www.doe.k12.de.us/dheo

### District of Columbia
Office of the State Superintendent of Education
810 First Street, NE, 9th Floor
Washington, DC 20002
202-727-6436
www.seo.dc.gov

### Florida
Florida Department of Education
Office of Student Financial Assistance
1940 North Monroe Street, Suite 70
Tallahassee, FL 32303-4759
888-827-2004
www.floridastudentfinancialaid.org

### Georgia
Georgia Student Finance Commission
2082 East Exchange Place
Tucker, GA 30084
800-505-4732
www.gsfc.org

### Hawaii
Hawaii State Department of Education
P.O. Box 2360
Honolulu, HI 96804
808-586-3230
www.doe.k12.hi.us

### Idaho
Idaho State Department of Education
650 West State Street
P.O. Box 83720
Boise, ID 83720-0027
800-432-4601
www.sde.idaho.gov

### Illinois
Illinois Student Assistance Commission
1755 Lake Cook Road
Deerfield, IL 60015-5209
800-899-4722
www.collegeillinois.org

### Indiana
State Student Assistance Commission of Indiana
W462 Indiana Government Center South
402 West Washington Street
Indianapolis, IN 46204
317-232-2350
www.in.gov/ssaci

### Iowa
Iowa College Student Aid Commission
603 E. 12th Street, FL 5th
Des Moines, IA 50319
877-272-4456
www.iowacollegeaid.gov

### Kansas
Kansas Board of Regents
1000 SW Jackson Street, Suite 520
Topeka, KS 66612-1368
785-296-3421
www.kansasregents.org

### Kentucky
KHEAA Student Aid Branch
P.O. Box 798
Frankfort, KY 40602
800-928-8926
www.kheaa.com

## Louisiana
Louisiana Office of Student Financial Assistance
P.O. Box 91202
Baton Rouge, LA 70821-9202
800-259-5626
www.osfa.la.gov

## Maine
Finance Authority of Maine
Education Assistance Division
P.O. Box 949
5 Community Drive
Augusta, ME 04332
800-228-3734
www.famemaine.com

## Maryland
Maryland Higher Education Commission
Office of Student Financial Assistance
839 Bestgate Road, Suite 400
Annapolis, MD 21401
800-974-0203
www.mhec.state.md.us

## Massachusetts
Massachusetts Department of Higher Education
Office of Student Financial Assistance
454 Broadway, Suite 200
Revere, MA 02151-3034
617-727-9420
www.osfa.mass.edu

## Michigan
Michigan Higher Education Assistance Authority
Office of Scholarships and Grants
P.O. Box 30462
Lansing, MI 48909-7962
888-447-2687
www.michigan.gov/mistudentaid

## Minnesota
Minnesota Office of Higher Education
1450 Energy Park Drive, Suite 350
St. Paul, MN 55108-5227
800-657-3866
www.ohe.state.mn.us

## Mississippi
Mississippi Office of Student Financial Aid
3825 Ridgewood Road
Jackson, MS 39211-6453
800-327-2980
www.ihl.state.ms.us/financialaid

## Missouri
Missouri Department of Higher Education
205 Jefferson Street
P.O. Box 1469
Jefferson City, MO 65102-1469
800-473-6757
www.dhe.mo.gov

## Montana
Montana Board of Regents
P.O. Box 203201
2500 Broadway Street
Helena, MT 59620-3201
406-444-6570
www.mus.edu

## Nebraska
Nebraska Coordinating Commission for Postsecondary Education
P.O. Box 95005
Lincoln, NE 68509-5005
402-471-2847
www.ccpe.state.ne.us

## Nevada
Nevada Department of Education
700 East Fifth Street
Carson City, NV 89701
775-687-9220
www.doe.nv.gov

## New Hampshire
New Hampshire Postsecondary Education Commission
3 Barrell Court, Suite 300
Concord, NH 03301-8543
603-271-2555
www.nh.gov/postsecondary

## New Jersey
New Jersey Higher Education Student Assistance Authority
P.O. Box 540
Trenton, NJ 08625
800-792-8670
www.hesaa.org

## New Mexico
New Mexico Higher Education Department
2048 Galisteo Street
Santa Fe, NM 87505
505-476-8400
www.hed.state.nm.us

## New York
New York State Higher Education Services Corporation
99 Washington Avenue
Albany, NY 12255
888-697-4372
www.hesc.state.ny.us

## North Carolina
North Carolina State Education Assistance Authority
P.O. Box 14103
Research Triangle Park, NC 27709
919-549-8614
www.ncseaa.edu

## North Dakota
North Dakota University System
10th Floor, State Capitol
600 East Boulevard Ave, Dept. 215
Bismarck, ND 58505-0230
701-328-2960
www.ndus.nodak.edu

## Ohio
Ohio Board of Regents
30 East Broad Street, 36th Floor
Columbus, OH 43215-3414
614-466-6000
http://regents.ohio.gov

## Oklahoma
Oklahoma State Regents for Higher Education
Tuition Aid Grant Program
655 Research Parkway, Suite 200
Oklahoma City, OK 73104
405-225-9100
www.okhighered.org

## Oregon
Oregon Student Assistance Commission
1500 Valley River Drive, Suite 100
Eugene, OR 97401
800-452-8807
www.osac.state.or.us

## Pennsylvania
Pennsylvania Higher Education Assistance Agency
1200 North Seventh Street
Harrisburg, PA 17102-1444
800-233-0557
www.pheaa.org

## Puerto Rico
Departmento de Educacion
P.O. Box 190759
San Juan, PR 00919-0759
787-759-2000
www.de.gobierno.pr

## Rhode Island
Rhode Island Higher Education Assistance Authority
560 Jefferson Boulevard, Suite 100
Warwick, RI 02886
401-736-1100
www.riheaa.org

## South Carolina
South Carolina Commission on Higher Education
1333 Main Street, Suite 200
Columbia, SC 29201
803-737-2260
www.che.sc.gov

## South Dakota
South Dakota Department of Education
Office of Finance and Management
800 Governors Drive
Pierre, SD 57501
605-773-3134
http://doe.sd.gov/

## Tennessee
Tennessee Student Assistance Corporation
404 James Robertson Parkway,
Suite 1510, Parkway Towers
Nashville, TN 37243-0820
800-342-1663
www.state.tn.us/tsac

## Texas
Texas Higher Education Coordinating Board
Hinson-Hazlewood College Student Loan Program
P.O. Box 12788
Austin, TX 78711-2788
800-242-3062
www.hhloans.com

## Utah
Utah Higher Education Assistance Authority
Board of Regents Building, The Gateway
60 South 400 West
Salt Lake City, UT 84101-1284
877-336-7378
www.uheaa.org

## Vermont
Vermont Student Assistance Corporation
P.O. Box 999
Winooski, VT 05404
800-798-8722
www.vsac.org

## Virginia
State Council of Higher Education for Virginia
James Monroe Building
101 North 14th Street
Richmond, VA 23219
804-225-2600
www.schev.edu

## Washington
Washington Higher Education Coordinating Board
917 Lakeridge Way SW
P.O. Box 43430
Olympia, WA 98504-3430
360-753-7800
www.hecb.wa.gov

## West Virginia
West Virginia Higher Education Policy Commission
Central Office, Higher Education Grant Program
1018 Kanawha Boulevard East, Suite 700
Charleston, WV 25301-2800
304-558-4614
http://wvhepcnew.wvnet.edu/

## Wisconsin
Wisconsin Higher Educational Aids Board
P. O. Box 7885
Madison, WI 53707
608-267-2206
www.heab.state.wi.us

## Wyoming
Wyoming Department of Education
2300 Capitol Avenue
Hathaway Building, Second Floor
Cheyenne, WY 82002-0050
307-777-7690
www.k12.wy.us

## Guam
University of Guam
Student Financial Aid Office
UOG Station
Mangilao, GU 96923
671-735-2284
www.uog.edu

## Virgin Islands
Financial Aid Office, Virgin Islands Board of Education
P.O. Box 11900
St. Thomas, VI 00801
340-774-4546

# Glossary

**ACT.** A college admission test given at test centers in the United States and other countries on specified dates. Please visit the organization's website for further information.

**Award letter.** A means of notifying admitted students of the financial aid being offered by the college or university. The award letter provides information on the types and amounts of aid offered, students' responsibilities and the conditions that govern the awards. Generally, the award letter gives students the opportunity to accept or decline the aid offered, and a deadline by which to respond.

**College Scholarship Service (CSS).** A unit of the College Board that assists postsecondary institutions, state scholarship programs and private scholarship organizations in the equitable and efficient distribution of student financial aid funds, mainly through its stewardship of the CSS/Financial Aid PROFILE and the Institutional Methodology.

**Competition.** An award based upon superior performance in relation to others in the competition. This book lists competitions based upon artistic talent, writing ability and other demonstrable talents.

**Cooperative education (co-op).** A career-oriented program in which students alternate between class attendance and employment in business, industry or government. Co-op students usually receive both academic credit and payment for their work. Under a cooperative plan, five years are normally required for completion of a bachelor's degree, but graduates have the advantage of about a year's practical work experience in addition to their studies.

**CSS code.** A four-digit College Board number that students use to designate colleges or scholarship programs to receive their CSS/Financial Aid PROFILE information. A complete list of all CSS codes can be viewed at the CSS/Financial Aid PROFILE section on collegeboard.org.

**CSS/Financial Aid PROFILE®.** A Web-based application service offered by the College Board and used by some colleges, universities and private scholarship programs to award their private financial aid funds. Students register for and complete the PROFILE on collegeboard.org. PROFILE provides a customized application for each registrant, based on the student's registration information and the requirements of the colleges and programs to which she or he is applying. The PROFILE is not a federal form and may not be used to apply for federal student aid.

**Curriculum Vitae (CV).** A type of résumé, from the Latin for "the course of one's life." Typically, a CV is used by applicants for fellowships or grants, or jobs in higher education, the sciences, or in a research capacity. The CV is typically longer than a résumé, and provides details about papers published, research conducted and more.

**Dependent student.** For federal financial aid purposes, the status that includes students who are under the age of 24; attend an undergraduate program; are not married; do not have children of their own; are not orphans, or wards of the court, veterans of the active-duty armed services; or certified as homeless. The term is used to define eligibility for certain financial aid programs, regardless of whether the student lives with a parent, receives financial support from a parent, or is claimed on a parents' tax returns. If a student is defined as a dependent, parental financial information must be supplied on the Free Application for Federal Student Aid (FAFSA) and institutional aid applications.

**Dependents.** Generally speaking, people who are dependent upon others (parents, relatives, a spouse) for food, clothing, shelter and other basics. For purposes of getting federal financial aid, students must meet strict criteria in order to be defined as dependents; in the view of federal aid programs, the family is the primary source of support for college. College students may have dependents (children dependent on them), and this too is taken into account by the federal government. Federal forms ask a series of questions about age, marital status, etc., to determine whether applicants are dependent on others or independent.

**Direct Loan Program.** *See* Federal Direct Loan Program.

**Expected Family Contribution (EFC).** The total amount students and their families are expected to pay toward college costs from their income and assets for one academic year.

**FAFSA.** *See* Free Application for Federal Student Aid.

**Federal code number.** A six-digit number that identifies a specific college to which students want their Free Application for Federal Student Aid form submitted. Also known as the Title IV number.

**Federal Direct Loan Program.** A program that allows participating schools to administer subsidized and unsubsidized Stafford and PLUS loans directly to student and parent borrowers. Direct loans have mostly the same terms and conditions as FFELP loans. Funds for these programs are provided by the federal government.

**Federal Family Education Loan Program (FFELP).** The subsidized and unsubsidized Federal Stafford Loan, PLUS Loan and Federal Loan Consolidation programs. Funds for these programs are provided by lenders, and the loans are guaranteed by the federal government.

**Federal Parent Loan for Undergraduate Students (PLUS).** A program that permits parents of undergraduate students to borrow up to the full cost of education, less any other financial aid the student may have received.

**Federal Pell Grant Program.** A federally sponsored and administered program that provides need-based grants to undergraduate students. Eligibility for Pell Grants is based on a student's expected family contribution, the total cost of attendance at the college, and whether the student is attending the college full time or part time.

**Federal Perkins Loan Program.** A federally funded campus-based program that provides low-interest loans, based on need, for undergraduate study. The combined cumulative total of loan funds available to an individual for undergraduate and graduate education is $40,000. Repayment need not begin until completion of the student's education, and may be deferred for limited periods of service in the military, Peace Corps or approved comparable organizations. The total debt may be forgiven by the federal government if the recipient enters a career of service as a public health nurse, law enforcement officer, public school teacher or social worker.

**Federal Stafford Loan.** A program that allows students to borrow money for education expenses from banks and other lending institutions (and sometimes from the colleges themselves). Subsidized Stafford loans are offered by colleges based on need. The federal government pays the interest on subsidized loans while the borrower is in college. Unsubsidized Stafford loans are non-need-based; anyone may apply for one, regardless of their ability to pay for college. The interest on unsubsidized loans begins accumulating immediately. For both programs, the amounts that may be borrowed depend on the student's year in school.

**Federal student aid.** A number of programs sponsored by the federal government that award students loans, grants or work-study jobs for the purpose of meeting their financial need. To receive any federal student aid, a student must demonstrate financial need by filing the Free Application for Federal Student Aid, be enrolled in college at least half time, and meet certain other eligibility requirements.

**Federal Supplemental Educational Opportunity Grant Program (SEOG).** A federal campus-based program that provides need-based grants for undergraduate study. Each college is given a certain total amount of SEOG money each year to distribute among its financial aid applicants, and each determines the amount to which the student is entitled.

**Federal Work-Study Program.** A campus-based financial aid program that allows students to meet some of their financial need by working on or off campus while attending school. The wages earned are used to help pay the student's education costs for the academic year. Job opportunities vary from campus to campus. The time commitment for a work-study job is usually between 10 and 15 hours each week.

**Financial aid.** Money awarded to students to help them pay for college. Financial aid comes in the form of gifts (scholarships and grants) and self-help aid (loans and work-study opportunities). Most aid is awarded on the basis of financial need, but some awards are non-need-based. Both need-based and non-need-based aid may be offered on the additional basis of merit.

**Financial aid award letter.** *See* award letter.

**Financial aid package.** The total financial aid offered to a student by a college, including all loans, grants, scholarships and work-study opportunities.

**Financial Aid PROFILE.** *See* CSS/Financial Aid PROFILE.

**Financial need.** The difference between the total cost of attending a college and a student's expected family contribution (EFC). Financial aid grants, loans and work-study will be offered by each college to fill the student's need.

**Free Application for Federal Student Aid (FAFSA).** A form completed by all applicants for federal student aid. The FAFSA is available on the Web at www.fafsa.ed.gov. In many states, completion of the FAFSA is also sufficient to establish eligibility for state-sponsored aid programs. There is no charge to students for completing the FAFSA. The FAFSA may be filed any time after Jan. 1 of the year for which one is seeking aid (e.g., after Jan. 1, 2011, for the academic year 2011-12).

**Full-time status.** Enrollment at a college or university for 12 or more credit hours per semester. Students must be enrolled full time to qualify for the maximum award available to them from federal grant programs.

**General Educational Development (GED).** A series of tests that individuals who did not complete high school may take through their state education system to qualify for a high school equivalency certificate.

**Gift.** Financial aid in the form of scholarships or grants that do not have to be repaid.

**Grade Point Average (GPA).** A system used by many schools for evaluating the overall scholastic performance of students. Grade points are determined by first multiplying the number of hours given for a course by the numerical value of the grade and then dividing the sum of all grade points by the total number of hours carried. The most common system of numerical values for grades is A = 4, B = 3, C = 2, D = 1, and E or F = 0.

**Grant.** A financial aid award that is given to a student and does not have to be paid back. The terms "grant" and "scholarship" are often used interchangeably to refer to gift aid, but often grants are awarded solely on the basis of financial need, while scholarships may require the student to demonstrate merit.

**Half-time status.** Enrollment at a college or university for at least six credit hours per semester, but less than the 12 credit hours required to qualify as full time. Students must be enrolled at least half time to qualify for federal student aid loan programs.

**High school transcript.** A formal document that shows all classes taken and grades earned in high school. It needs to be sent from the school to the scholarship sponsor, not from the applicant.

**Independent student.** For federal financial aid purposes, the status that generally includes students who are either 24 years old, married, a veteran or an orphan, a ward of the court, certified as homeless or have legal dependents (not including spouse). Independent students do not need to provide parental information to be considered for federal financial aid programs. However, private institutions may require independent students to provide parental information on their institutional forms in order to be considered for nonfederal sources of funding.

**Internship.** Any short-term, supervised work, usually related to a student's major, for which academic credit is earned. The work can be full or part time, on or off campus, paid or unpaid. Some majors require the student to complete an internship.

**Loan.** Money lent with interest for a specified period of time. This book includes several loan programs; some forgive the loan in exchange for public service, such as teaching in a rural area.

**Major.** The subject area in which students concentrate during their undergraduate study. At most colleges, students take a third to a half of their courses in the major; the rest of their course work is devoted to core requirements and electives. In liberal arts majors, students generally take a third of their courses in their chosen field, which they usually must choose by the beginning of their junior year. In career-related programs, such as nursing or engineering, students may take up to half of their courses in their major.

**Merit aid.** Financial aid awarded on the basis of academic qualifications, artistic or athletic talent, leadership qualities or similar qualities. Most merit aid comes in the form of scholarships. Merit aid may be non-need based, or the merit criteria may be in addition to a requirement that the student demonstrate financial need.

**National Science and Mathematics Access to Retain Talent (SMART) Grant.** A federal grant program for Pell Grant recipients who are in their third or fourth year of undergraduate study, have declared a major in the sciences, mathematics, engineering, technology or certain foreign languages, and have maintained a GPA of at least 3.0 in that major. The maximum annual award is $4,000, in addition to the student's Pell Grant.

**Need-based aid.** Financial aid (scholarships, grants, loans or work-study opportunities) given to students who have demonstrated financial need, calculated by subtracting the student's expected family contribution from a college's total cost of attendance. The largest source of need-based aid is the federal government, but colleges, states and private foundations also award need-based aid to eligible students.

**Nomination.** Being named as a candidate for an award or scholarship. Some scholarship programs require that a teacher or principal nominate students as applicants, and do not invite applications from students.

**Non-need-based aid.** Financial aid awarded without regard to the student's demonstrated ability to pay for college. Unsubsidized loans and scholarships awarded solely on the basis of merit are both non-need based. Some financial aid sponsors also offer non-need-based grants that are not tied to merit, but rather to other qualities, such as state of residence or participation in ROTC.

**Outside resources.** Student financial aid granted by a source other than the college that the college must take into account when assembling an aid package. Examples of common outside resources include scholarships from private foundations, employer tuition assistance and veterans' educational benefits.

**Parents' contribution.** The amount a student's parents are expected to pay toward college costs from their income and assets. It is derived from need analysis of the parents' overall financial situation. The parents' contribution and the student's contribution together constitute the total expected family contribution (EFC).

**Part-time status.** Enrollment at a college or university for 11 or fewer credit hours per semester.

**Pell Grant.** *See* Federal Pell Grant Program.

**Perkins Loan.** *See* Federal Perkins Loan Program.

**Permanent resident.** A non-U.S. citizen who has been given permission to make his or her permanent home in the United States. All permanent residents hold a "green card," and all holders of a green card are permanent residents. Permanent residents are eligible for numerous award programs.

**PLUS Loan.** *See* Federal Parent Loan for Undergraduate Students.

**Portfolio.** A physical collection of a student's work that demonstrates their skills and accomplishments. Portfolios may be physical or electronic. There are academic portfolios that include student-written papers and projects, and also portfolios that include created objects — art, photography, fashion illustrations and more. Some scholarship programs request a portfolio.

**Priority date.** The date by which applications for financial aid must be received to be given the strongest possible consideration. The college will consider the financial need of applicants who make the priority date before any other applicants. Qualified applicants who do not make the priority date are considered on a first-come, first-served basis, and are only offered financial aid if (and to the extent that) the college still has sufficient money left over after all the offers it has made.

**PROFILE.** *See* CSS/Financial Aid PROFILE®.

**PSAT/NMSQT® (Preliminary SAT/ National Merit Scholarship Qualifying Test).** A preparatory tool for the SAT that is administered by high schools to sophomores and juniors each year in October. The PSAT/NMSQT serves as the qualifying test for scholarships awarded by the National Merit Scholarship Corporation.

**Renewable.** A scholarship or loan that can be renewed after the first award. Typically students have to apply annually in order to receive the funds after the first year.

**Renewal FAFSA.** A simplified reapplication form for continuing students. The Renewal FAFSA allows the student to update the financial information and other items that have changed from the prior year's FAFSA, rather than completing the entire FAFSA for each award year.

**Reserve Officers' Training Corps (ROTC).** Programs conducted by certain colleges in cooperation with the United States Air Force, Army and Navy reserves. Participating students may receive a merit scholarship while they are in college, and will enter the reserves of their service branch as an officer upon graduation. Navy ROTC includes the Marine Corps. (The Coast Guard and Merchant Marine do not sponsor ROTC programs.) Local recruiting offices of the services themselves can supply detailed information about these programs, as can participating colleges.

**Residency requirements.** The minimum amount of time a student is required to have lived in a particular state or community in order to be eligible for scholarship, internship or loan programs offered to such residents. Can also refer to the minimum amount of time a student is required to have lived in a state to be eligible for in-state tuition at a public college or university.

**SAR.** *See* Student Aid Report.

**SAT®.** A college entrance exam that tests critical reading, writing and mathematics skills that is given on specified dates throughout the year at test centers in the United States and other countries. The SAT is used by most colleges and sponsors of financial aid programs.

**SAT Subject Tests™.** Admission tests in specific subjects that are given at test centers in the United States and other countries on specified dates throughout the year. The tests are used by colleges for help in both evaluating applicants for admission and determining course placement and exemption of enrolled first-year students.

**Scholarship.** A type of financial aid that doesn't have to be repaid. Grants are often based on financial need. Scholarships may be based on need, on need combined with merit, or solely on the basis of merit or some other qualification, such as minority status.

**Section 529 plans.** State-sponsored college savings programs commonly referred to as "529 plans" after the section of the Internal Revenue Code that provides the plan's tax breaks. There are two kinds: Section 529 college savings plans and Section 529 prepaid tuition plans.

**Self-help aid.** Student financial aid, such as loans and jobs, that requires repayment or employment.

**SEOG.** *See* Federal Supplemental Educational Opportunity Grant Program.

**SMART Grant.** *See* National Science and Mathematics Access to Retain Talent Grant.

**Stafford Loan.** *See* Federal Stafford Loan.

**Student Aid Report (SAR).** A report produced by the U.S. Department of Education and sent to students in response to their having filed the Free Application for Federal Student Aid (FAFSA). The SAR contains information the student provided on the FAFSA as well as the federally calculated expected family contribution.

**Student expense budget.** A calculation of the annual cost of attending college that is used to determine your financial need. Student expense budgets usually include tuition and fees, books and supplies, room and board, personal expenses and transportation. Sometimes additional expenses are included for students with special education needs, students who have a disability, or students who are married or have children.

**Student's contribution.** The amount you are expected to pay toward college costs from your income and assets. The amount is derived from need analysis of your resources. Your contribution and your parents' contribution together add up to the total expected family contribution.

**Subsidized Federal Stafford Loan.** *See* Federal Stafford Loan.

**Subsidized loan.** A loan awarded to a student on the basis of financial need. The federal government or the state awarding the loan pays the borrower's interest while the student is in college at least half time, thereby subsidizing the loan.

**Supplemental Educational Opportunity Grant.** *See* Federal Supplemental Educational Opportunity Grant Program.

**Tuition.** The price of instruction at a college. Tuition may be charged per term or per credit hour.

**Undergraduate.** A college student in the freshman, sophomore, junior or senior year of study, as opposed to a graduate student who has earned an undergraduate degree and is pursuing a master's, doctoral or professional degree.

**Unmet need.** The difference between a specific student's total available resources and the total cost for the student's attendance at a specific institution.

**Unsubsidized Federal Stafford Loan.** *See* Federal Stafford Loan.

**Unsubsidized loan.** An education loan that is non-need based and therefore not subsidized by the federal government; the borrower is responsible for accrued interest throughout the life of the loan.

**Verification.** A procedure whereby a school checks the information that the student reported on the FAFSA, usually by requesting a copy of the tax returns filed by the student and, if applicable, the student's spouse and parent(s). Colleges are required by federal regulations to verify a minimum percentage of financial aid applications.

**William D. Ford Federal Direct Loan Program.** *See* Federal Direct Loan Program.

**Work-Study.** An arrangement by which a student combines employment and college study. The employment may be an integral part of the academic program (as in cooperative education and internships) or simply a means of paying for college (as in the need-based Federal Work-Study Program).

# Eligibility Indexes

## Corporate/ Employer



## Disabilities

### Hearing impaired



### Learning disabled



### Physically challenged



### Visually impaired



## Field of Study/ Intended Career

### Agricultural science, business, and natural resources conservation

## Architecture and design

## Area and ethnic studies



## Arts, visual and performing

## Biological and biomedical sciences



## Biological and physical sciences

Eligibility Indexes



## Business/management/administration

## Communications

## Computer and information sciences

## Education

## Engineering and engineering technology

Eligibility Indexes

## English and literature



## Foreign languages



## Health professions and allied services

Eligibility Indexes

## Home economics



## Law



## Liberal arts and interdisciplinary studies



## Library science



## Mathematics

## Military science



## Mortuary science



## Philosophy, religion, and theology

## Protective services



## Social sciences and history



## Trade and industry

# Gender

## Female

## Male



# International Student

# Military Participation

## Air Force



## Army



## Coast Guard



## Marines



## Navy

## Reserves/National Guard



# Minority Status

## African American



## Alaskan native

## American Indian



## Asian American

## Hispanic American



## Mexican American

## Native Hawaiian/Pacific Islander



## Puerto Rican

# National/ethnic background

## Armenian



## Chinese



## Italian



## Japanese



## Jewish



## Polish



## Swiss



## Welsh



# Organization/civic affiliation

## American Legion

## American Legion Auxiliary



## American Legion, Boys State



## American Legion/Boys Scouts of America



## ASTA Arizona Chapter



## Boy Scouts of America



## Boy Scouts of America, Eagle Scouts



## Harness Racing Industry



## International Union of EESMF Workers, AFL-CIO



## Jaycees



## Knights of Columbus

### Learning for Life



### National Art Materials Trade Association



### Native Daughters of the Golden West



### New York State Grange



### Polish National Alliance of Brooklyn



### Reserve Officers Training Corps (ROTC)



### Screen Actor's Guild



### Society of Physics Students



### Society of Women Engineers



### Soil and Water Conservation Society



### Sons of Norway



### Transportation Clubs International



### United Food and Commerical Workers



### United Transportation Union



## Religious Affiliation

### Christian



### Eastern Orthodox



### Episcopal



### Jewish



### Lutheran



### Presbyterian



### Protestant



### Roman Catholic



### Unitarian Universalist



### United Methodist



## Returning Adult

Eligibility Indexes

# State of Residence



## Alabama



## Alaska



## Arizona



## Arkansas



## California

## Colorado



## Connecticut



## Delaware



## District of Columbia



## Florida



## Georgia

## Hawaii



Eligibility Indexes

## Idaho



## Illinois



## Indiana

## Iowa



## Kansas



## Kentucky



## Louisiana



## Maine



## Maryland



Eligibility Indexes

## Massachusetts



## Michigan



## Minnesota



## Mississippi

## Missouri



## Montana



## Nebraska



## Nevada



## New Hampshire

## New Jersey



## New Mexico



## New York



## North Carolina

## North Dakota



## Ohio



## Oklahoma



## Oregon

## Pennsylvania



## Puerto Rico



## Rhode Island



## South Carolina

## South Dakota



## Tennessee



## Texas



## U.S. Territories

## Utah



## Vermont



## Virgin Islands



## Virginia



## Washington



## West Virginia

## Wisconsin



## Wyoming



# Study Abroad

# Scholarships

## 10,000 Degrees

### Marin Education Undergraduate Scholarships

**Type of award:** Scholarship, renewable.
**Intended use:** For full-time undergraduate study at accredited 2-year or 4-year institution in United States.
**Eligibility:** Applicant must be residing in California.
**Basis for selection:** Applicant must demonstrate financial need.
**Additional information:** Must be resident of Marin County. Must be enrolled for minimum of twelve units per term. Applicants automatically considered for six other scholarships ranging from $1,500-5,000. Visit Website for more information.

| | |
|---|---|
| **Amount of award:** | $1,000-$5,000 |
| **Number of awards:** | 20 |

**Contact:**
Marin Education Fund
781 Lincoln Avenue
San Rafael, CA 94901
Phone: 415-459-4240
Fax: 415-459-0527
Web: www.marineducationfund.org

### New Leader Scholarship

**Type of award:** Scholarship, renewable.
**Intended use:** For full-time junior, senior or graduate study at postsecondary institution. Designated institutions: University of California, Berkeley; California State University East Bay; San Francisco State University; San Jose State University; Sonoma State University.
**Eligibility:** Applicant must be residing in California.
**Basis for selection:** Major/career interest in economics; health sciences; law; medicine; psychology; social work or sociology. Applicant must demonstrate financial need, high academic achievement, leadership and service orientation.
**Application requirements:** Interview, recommendations, essay, transcript. Financial statement.
**Additional information:** Preference given to recent immigrants and students of color. Applicants do not need to be Marin County residents to apply. Applicants should demonstrate commitment to giving back to their communities and plan to pursue career in public, legal, psychological, health, or social services. Graduate students may be considered if they have received scholarship as undergraduate and are attending California public universities. See Website (www.goldmanfamilyfund.com) for more information. Minimum 3.5 GPA.

| | |
|---|---|
| **Amount of award:** | $3,000-$7,000 |
| **Number of awards:** | 11 |
| **Number of applicants:** | 40 |
| **Application deadline:** | March 15 |
| **Total amount awarded:** | $50,000 |

**Contact:**
10,000 Degrees
New Leader Scholarship
781 Lincoln Avenue, Suite 140
San Rafael, CA 94901
Phone: 415-459-4240
Fax: 415-459-0527
Web: www.goldmanfamilyfund.org, www.10000degrees.org

## 1199SEIU Benefit Funds

### Joseph Tauber Scholarship

**Type of award:** Scholarship, renewable.
**Intended use:** For full-time undergraduate or non-degree study at accredited vocational, 2-year or 4-year institution in or outside United States.
**Basis for selection:** Applicant must demonstrate financial need.
**Application requirements:** Proof of eligibility. CSS profile.
**Additional information:** Must be receiving family coverage (Wage or Eligibility Class One) through benefit fund. Apply for pre-screening by deadline date; applications sent to qualified candidates. Visit Website for updates. Must apply for renewal. Amount of award varies.

| | |
|---|---|
| **Number of awards:** | 2,500 |
| **Number of applicants:** | 5,000 |
| **Application deadline:** | January 31 |
| **Notification begins:** | November 1 |
| **Total amount awarded:** | $4,500,000 |

**Contact:**
1199SEIU Child Care Funds Joseph Tauber Scholarship Program
330 West 42nd Street, 18th Floor
New York, NY 10036-6977
Phone: 646-473-8999
Fax: 646-473-6949
Web: www.1199seiubenefits.org

## Abbie Sargent Memorial Scholarship Fund

### Abbie Sargent Memorial Scholarship

**Type of award:** Scholarship, renewable.
**Intended use:** For undergraduate or graduate study at postsecondary institution.
**Eligibility:** Applicant must be residing in New Hampshire.
**Basis for selection:** Major/career interest in agriculture. Applicant must demonstrate financial need, high academic achievement and depth of character.

**Application requirements:** Recommendations, essay, transcript. Recent photo.
**Additional information:** Recipient may attend out-of-state university. Send SASE for application or download from Website. Number of awards varies.

| | |
|---|---|
| **Amount of award:** | $400-$1,000 |
| **Number of applicants:** | 17 |
| **Application deadline:** | March 15 |
| **Notification begins:** | June 1 |

**Contact:**
Abbie Sargent Memorial Scholarship
Attn: Melanie Phelps, Treasurer
295 Sheep Davis Road
Concord, NH 03301
Phone: 603-224-1934
Web: www.nhfarmbureau.org



# Academy of Interactive Arts & Sciences

## Mark Beaumont Scholarship Fund

**Type of award:** Scholarship.
**Intended use:** For full-time sophomore, junior or senior study in United States.
**Basis for selection:** Applicant must demonstrate financial need, depth of character, leadership and service orientation.
**Application requirements:** Recommendations, transcript. Two-page letter including information about your studies and how they will benefit the game industry and statement addressing service, leadership, character, and financial need.
**Additional information:** Minimum 3.3 GPA. Must intend to enter game industry in the area of business.

| | |
|---|---|
| **Amount of award:** | $2,500 |
| **Number of awards:** | 4 |
| **Application deadline:** | June 30 |

**Contact:**
Academy of Interactive Arts & Sciences
23622 Calabasas Road
Suite 300
Calabasas, CA 91302
Phone: 818-876-0826 ext. 206
Fax: 818-876-0850
Web: www.interactive.org/foundation/scholarships.asp

## Randy Pausch Scholarship Fund

**Type of award:** Scholarship.
**Intended use:** For full-time sophomore, junior or senior study at accredited postsecondary institution in United States.
**Basis for selection:** Applicant must demonstrate financial need, depth of character, leadership and service orientation.
**Application requirements:** Recommendations, transcript. Two-page letter including information about your studies and how they will benefit the game industry and statement addressing service, leadership, character, and financial need.
**Additional information:** Minimum 3.3 GPA. Must intend to enter game industry as developer of interactive entertainment.

| | |
|---|---|
| **Amount of award:** | $2,500 |
| **Number of awards:** | 4 |
| **Application deadline:** | June 30 |

**Contact:**
Academy of Interactive Arts & Sciences
23622 Calabasas Road
Suite 300
Calabasas, CA 91302
Phone: 818-876-0826 ext. 206
Fax: 818-876-0850
Web: www.interactive.org/foundation/scholarships.asp

# Academy of Television Arts & Sciences Foundation

## The Fred Rogers Memorial Scholarship

**Type of award:** Scholarship.
**Intended use:** For undergraduate or graduate study at accredited postsecondary institution.
**Basis for selection:** Major/career interest in education, early childhood; film/video; music or radio/television/film.
**Application requirements:** Recommendations. Project plan and budget.
**Additional information:** Applicant must have ultimate goal of working in children's media and must have studied or have experience in at least two of the following fields: early childhood education, child development/child psychology, film/television production, music, or animation. Download application from Website.

| | |
|---|---|
| **Amount of award:** | $10,000 |
| **Number of awards:** | 3 |
| **Number of applicants:** | 100 |
| **Application deadline:** | February 28 |
| **Total amount awarded:** | $30,000 |

**Contact:**
Academy of Television Arts & Sciences Foundation
Attn: Michele Fowble
5220 Lankershim Boulevard
North Hollywood, CA 91601-3109
Phone: 818-754-2802
Web: www.emmysfoundation.org

# ACFE Foundation

## Ritchie-Jennings Memorial Scholarship

**Type of award:** Scholarship.
**Intended use:** For full-time undergraduate or graduate study at accredited 4-year institution.
**Basis for selection:** Major/career interest in criminal justice/law enforcement; accounting; business or finance/banking.
**Application requirements:** Recommendations, essay, transcript.
**Additional information:** Award includes one-year ACFE Student Associate membership. Notifications of awards begin in end of April. Visit Website for additional information.

**Amount of award:** $1,000-$10,000
**Number of awards:** 30
**Number of applicants:** 150
**Application deadline:** January 31
**Notification begins:** April 15
**Total amount awarded:** $53,000

**Contact:**
ACFE Foundation Scholarships Program Coordinator
The Gregor Building
716 West Avenue
Austin, TX 78701-2727
Phone: 800-245-3321
Fax: 512-478-9297
Web: www.acfe.com/about/foundation.asp?copy=scholarship

# The Actuarial Foundation

## Actuarial Diversity Scholarships

**Type of award:** Scholarship, renewable.
**Intended use:** For full-time undergraduate or graduate study at accredited 2-year, 4-year or graduate institution.
**Eligibility:** Applicant must be Alaskan native, African American, Mexican American, Hispanic American, Puerto Rican, American Indian or Native Hawaiian/Pacific Islander. Applicant must be U.S. citizen, permanent resident or international student.
**Basis for selection:** Major/career interest in insurance/actuarial science or mathematics. Applicant must demonstrate high academic achievement.
**Application requirements:** Recommendations, essay, transcript, proof of eligibility. SAT/ACT scores.
**Additional information:** Must have at least one birth parent who is Black/African American, Hispanic, or Native American. Applicant must be admitted to institution offering actuarial science program or courses that will prepare student for actuarial career. Minimum 3.0 GPA. Minimum 28 ACT math score or 600 SAT math score. International students must have F1 visa. Visit Website for application, deadline, and more information.

**Amount of award:** $1,000-$3,000
**Number of awards:** 23
**Notification begins:** August 5

**Contact:**
The Actuarial Foundation
Actuarial Diversity Scholarship
475 North Martingale Road, Suite 600
Schaumburg, IL 60173-2226
Phone: 847-706-3535
Fax: 847-706-3599
Web: www.actuarialfoundation.org/programs/actuarial/scholarships.shtml

## Actuary of Tomorrow Stuart A. Robertson Memorial Scholarship

**Type of award:** Scholarship.
**Intended use:** For full-time sophomore, junior or senior study at accredited 4-year institution in United States.
**Basis for selection:** Major/career interest in accounting; mathematics or statistics. Applicant must demonstrate high academic achievement.
**Application requirements:** Recommendations, essay, transcript.
**Additional information:** Minimum 3.0 GPA. Must have successfully completed two actuarial exams. Must pursue course of study leading to career in actuarial science. Visit Website for essay topic and application.

**Amount of award:** $7,500
**Number of awards:** 1
**Application deadline:** June 1
**Notification begins:** August 1
**Total amount awarded:** $7,500

**Contact:**
The Actuarial Foundation
Attn: Actuary of Tomorrow Scholarship
475 N. Martingale Road, Suite 600
Schaumburg, IL 60173-2226
Phone: 847-706-3535
Fax: 847-706-3599
Web: www.actuarialfoundation.org/programs/actuarial/scholarships.shtml

## Woody Scholarship

**Type of award:** Scholarship.
**Intended use:** For full-time senior study at 4-year institution.
**Eligibility:** Applicant must be U.S. citizen or permanent resident.
**Basis for selection:** Major/career interest in insurance/actuarial science. Applicant must demonstrate high academic achievement and leadership.
**Application requirements:** Recommendations, essay, transcript, nomination by professor.
**Additional information:** Applicant must have passed at least one actuarial examination and must rank in the top quarter of class. Application is available on Website. Immediate relatives of members of the Board of Trustees of the Actuarial Foundation or boards of affiliated organizations are not eligible to apply. Limit one application per school.

**Amount of award:** $2,000
**Number of awards:** 13
**Application deadline:** June 22
**Notification begins:** August 30
**Total amount awarded:** $26,000

**Contact:**
The Actuarial Foundation
Attn: John Culver Wooddy Scholarship
475 N. Martingale Road, Suite 600
Schaumburg, IL 60173-2226
Phone: 847-706-3535
Fax: 847-706-3599
Web: www.actuarialfoundation.org/programs/actuarial/scholarships.shtml

# ADHA Institute for Oral Health

## Alice Hinchcliffe Williams, RDH, MS Graduate Scholarship

**Type of award:** Scholarship.
**Intended use:** For full-time sophomore, junior, senior or graduate study at 2-year or 4-year institution in United States.
**Eligibility:** Applicant must be residing in Virginia.
**Basis for selection:** Major/career interest in dental hygiene. Applicant must demonstrate financial need and high academic achievement.

Scholarships

**Application requirements:** Recommendations, essay. FAFSA.
**Additional information:** Applicant must be a Virginia resident and seeking a graduate degree in Dental Hygiene or accredited, degree studies related to the professional roles of the dental hygienist. Must have completed one year in a dental hygiene curriculum by award year; may apply during first year. Must be active ADHA or Student ADHA member with minimum 3.0 GPA. Download application from Website. All applications must be typed. Applying to more than one scholarship may void application. Amount of award varies.

**Number of awards:** 1
**Application deadline:** February 1

**Contact:**
ADHA Institute for Oral Health
Scholarship Award Program
444 N. Michigan Ave., Ste. 3400
Chicago, IL 60611-3980
Phone: 312-440-8900
Web: www.adha.org/institute



## Cadbury Community Outreach Scholarships

**Type of award:** Scholarship.
**Intended use:** For full-time undergraduate certificate, sophomore, junior or senior study at accredited 2-year or 4-year institution in United States.
**Basis for selection:** Major/career interest in dental hygiene. Applicant must demonstrate financial need, high academic achievement and service orientation.
**Application requirements:** Recommendations, essay. FAFSA. Additional essay required.
**Additional information:** Must have completed one year of dental hygiene curriculum by award year; may apply during first year. Must be active ADHA or Student ADHA member with minimum 3.0 dental hygiene GPA. Must display commitment to improving community's oral health. Download application from Website. All applications must be typed. Applying to more than one scholarship may void application. Amount of award varies.

**Number of awards:** 5
**Application deadline:** February 1

**Contact:**
ADHA Institute for Oral Health
Scholarship Award Program
444 N. Michigan Avenue, Suite 3400
Chicago, IL 60611-3980
Phone: 312-440-8900
Web: www.adha.org/institute

## Carol Bauhs Benson Memorial Scholarship

**Type of award:** Scholarship.
**Intended use:** For full-time sophomore, junior, senior or post-bachelor's certificate study at accredited 2-year or 4-year institution in United States.
**Eligibility:** Applicant must be residing in Wisconsin, South Dakota, Minnesota or North Dakota.
**Basis for selection:** Major/career interest in dental hygiene. Applicant must demonstrate financial need and high academic achievement.
**Application requirements:** Recommendations, essay. FAFSA.
**Additional information:** Must have completed one year in a dental hygiene curriculum by award year; may apply during first year. Must be active ADHA or Student ADHA member with minimum 3.0 GPA. Download application from Website. All applications must be typed. Applying to more than one scholarship may void application. Amount and number of award varies.

**Application deadline:** February 1

**Contact:**
ADHA Institute for Oral Health
Scholarship Award Program
444 N. Michigan Ave., Ste. 3400
Chicago, IL 60611-3980
Phone: 312-440-8900
Web: www.adha.org/institute

## Colgate "Bright Smiles, Bright Futures" Minority Scholarships

**Type of award:** Scholarship, renewable.
**Intended use:** For full-time undergraduate certificate, sophomore, junior or senior study in United States.
**Eligibility:** Applicant must be Asian American, African American, Mexican American, Hispanic American, Puerto Rican or American Indian.
**Basis for selection:** Major/career interest in dental hygiene. Applicant must demonstrate financial need and high academic achievement.
**Application requirements:** Recommendations, essay. FAFSA.
**Additional information:** Applicant must be member of ADHA or Student ADHA. Men considered a minority in this field and encouraged to apply. Applicant must have completed at least one year of certificate-level dental hygiene program; may apply during first year. Minimum 3.0 dental hygiene GPA. Download application from Website. All applications must be typed. Applying to more than one scholarship may void application. Amount of award varies.

**Number of awards:** 2
**Application deadline:** February 1

**Contact:**
ADHA Institute for Oral Health
Scholarship Award Program
444 N. Michigan Ave., Suite 3400
Chicago, IL 60611-3980
Phone: 312-440-8900
Web: www.adha.org/institute

## Crest Oral-B Dental Hygiene Scholarship

**Type of award:** Scholarship.
**Intended use:** For full-time sophomore, junior or senior study at accredited 4-year institution in United States.
**Basis for selection:** Major/career interest in dental hygiene. Applicant must demonstrate financial need, high academic achievement and seriousness of purpose.
**Application requirements:** Recommendations, essay. FAFSA.
**Additional information:** Applicant must have completed minimum one year dental hygiene curriculum; may apply during first year. Minimum 3.5 GPA in dental hygiene. Must demonstrate intent to encourage professional excellence and scholarship, promote quality research, and support dental hygiene through public and private education. Must be member of ADHA or Student ADHA. Download application from Website. All applications must be typed. Applying to more than one scholarship may void application. Amount of award varies.

**Number of awards:** 2
**Application deadline:** February 1

**Contact:**
ADHA Institute for Oral Health
Scholarship Award Program
444 N. Michigan Ave., Suite 3400
Chicago, IL 60611-3980
Phone: 312-440-8900
Web: www.adha.org/institute

## Dr. Esther Wilkins Scholarship

**Type of award:** Scholarship.
**Intended use:** For full-time sophomore, junior, senior or post-bachelor's certificate study at accredited 2-year or 4-year institution in United States.
**Basis for selection:** Major/career interest in dental hygiene. Applicant must demonstrate financial need and high academic achievement.
**Application requirements:** Recommendations, essay. FAFSA.
**Additional information:** Awarded to applicants pursuing additional degree necessary for career in dental hygiene education. Applicants must have completed an entry-level dental hygiene program. Must be active ADHA or Student ADHA member with minimum 3.0 GPA. Download application from Website. All applications must be typed. Applying to more than one scholarship may void application. Amount of award varies.

| | |
|---|---|
| **Number of awards:** | 1 |
| **Application deadline:** | February 1 |

**Contact:**
ADHA Institute for Oral Health
Scholarship Award Program
444 N. Michigan Ave., Ste. 3400
Chicago, IL 60611-3980
Phone: 312-440-8900
Web: www.adha.org/institute

## Hu-Friedy/Esther Wilkins Instrument Scholarships

**Type of award:** Scholarship.
**Intended use:** For full-time undergraduate certificate, sophomore, junior or senior study at accredited 2-year or 4-year institution in United States.
**Basis for selection:** Major/career interest in dental hygiene. Applicant must demonstrate financial need and high academic achievement.
**Application requirements:** Recommendations, essay. FAFSA.
**Additional information:** Must have completed one year of dental hygiene curriculum by award year; may apply during first year. Must be active ADHA or Student ADHA member with minimum 3.0 dental hygiene GPA. Download application from Website. Award given as $1,000 worth of Hu-Friedy dental hygiene instruments. All applications must be typed. Applying to more than one scholarship may void application.

| | |
|---|---|
| **Amount of award:** | $1,000 |
| **Number of awards:** | 5 |
| **Application deadline:** | February 1 |

**Contact:**
ADHA Institute for Oral Health
Scholarship Award Program
444 N. Michigan Avenue, Suite 3400
Chicago, IL 60611-3980
Phone: 312-440-8900
Web: www.adha.org/institute

## Johnson & Johnson Scholarships

**Type of award:** Scholarship.
**Intended use:** For full-time undergraduate certificate, sophomore, junior or senior study at accredited 2-year or 4-year institution in United States.
**Basis for selection:** Major/career interest in dental hygiene. Applicant must demonstrate financial need and high academic achievement.
**Application requirements:** Recommendations, essay. FAFSA.
**Additional information:** Must have completed one year of dental hygiene curriculum by award year; may apply during first year. Must be active ADHA or Student ADHA member with minimum 3.5 dental hygiene GPA. Visit Website for application. All applications must be typed. Applying to more than one scholarship may void application. Amount of award varies.

| | |
|---|---|
| **Number of awards:** | 5 |
| **Application deadline:** | February 1 |

**Contact:**
ADHA Institute for Oral Health
Scholarship Award Program
444 N. Michigan Avenue, Suite 3400
Chicago, IL 60611-3980
Phone: 312-440-8900
Web: www.adha.org/institute

## Karla Girts Memorial Community Outreach Scholarship

**Type of award:** Scholarship.
**Intended use:** For full-time sophomore, junior or senior study at accredited 2-year or 4-year institution in United States.
**Basis for selection:** Major/career interest in dental hygiene. Applicant must demonstrate financial need and high academic achievement.
**Application requirements:** Recommendations, essay. FAFSA. Additional essay required.
**Additional information:** Applicants must display a commitment to improving oral health within the geriatric population. Must have completed one year in a dental hygiene curriculum by award year; may apply during first year. Must be active ADHA or Student ADHA member with minimum 3.0 dental hygiene GPA. Download application from Website. All applications must be typed. Applying to more than one scholarship may void application. Amount of award varies.

| | |
|---|---|
| **Number of awards:** | 2 |
| **Application deadline:** | February 1 |

**Contact:**
ADHA Institute for Oral Health
Scholarship Award Program
444 N. Michigan Avenue, Suite 3400
Chicago, IL 60611-3980
Phone: 312-440-8900
Web: www.adha.org/institute

## Sigma Phi Alpha Undergraduate Scholarship

**Type of award:** Scholarship.
**Intended use:** For full-time undergraduate certificate, sophomore, junior or senior study at accredited 2-year or 4-year institution in United States. Designated institutions: Schools with active chapter of Sigma Phi Alpha Dental Hygiene Honor Society.

**Basis for selection:** Major/career interest in dental hygiene. Applicant must demonstrate financial need and high academic achievement.
**Application requirements:** Recommendations, essay. FAFSA.
**Additional information:** Must be member of Sigma Phi Alpha. Minimum 3.5 GPA in dental hygiene. Must be member of ADHA or Student ADHA. Must have completed at least one year of dental hygiene program. Visit Website for application. All applications must be typed. Applying to more than one scholarship may void application. Amount of award varies.

| | |
|---|---|
| **Number of awards:** | 1 |
| **Application deadline:** | February 1 |

**Contact:**
ADHA Institute for Oral Health
Scholarship Award Program
444 N. Michigan Avenue, Suite 3400
Chicago, IL 60611-3980
Phone: 312-440-8900
Web: www.adha.org/institute

### Wilma Motley Memorial California Merit Scholarship

**Type of award:** Scholarship.
**Intended use:** For full-time sophomore, junior, senior or graduate study at accredited 2-year or 4-year institution in United States.
**Basis for selection:** Major/career interest in dental hygiene. Applicant must demonstrate high academic achievement and leadership.
**Application requirements:** Recommendations, essay. FAFSA.
**Additional information:** Awarded to individuals pursuing associate/certificate in dental hygiene, baccalaureate degree, degree completion in dental hygiene, Registered Dental Hygienist in Alternative Practice (RDHAP), master's or doctorate degree in dental hygiene or related field. Applicants must either be a resident of California or attending a dental hygiene program in California. Must have completed one year in a dental hygiene curriculum by award year; may apply during first year. Must be active ADHA or Student ADHA member with minimum 3.0 GPA. Download application from Website. All applications must be typed. Applying to more than one scholarship may void application. Amount of award varies.

| | |
|---|---|
| **Number of awards:** | 3 |
| **Application deadline:** | February 1 |

**Contact:**
ADHA Institute for Oral Health
Scholarship Award Program
444 N. Michigan Ave., Ste. 3400
Chicago, IL 60611-3980
Phone: 312-440-8900
Web: www.adha.org/institute

## AFSA Scholarship Programs

### Air Force Sergeants Association Scholarship, Airmen Memorial Foundation, and Chief Master Sergeants of the Air Force Scholarship Programs

**Type of award:** Scholarship.
**Intended use:** For full-time undergraduate study at accredited postsecondary institution in United States.
**Eligibility:** Applicant must be single, no older than 23. Applicant must be dependent of active service person or veteran in the Air Force. May be dependent of retired member as well. Dependents of members of the Air National Guard or Air Force Reserve also eligible.
**Basis for selection:** Applicant must demonstrate high academic achievement, depth of character and leadership.
**Application requirements:** Recommendations, essay, transcript, proof of eligibility.
**Additional information:** Applicant must be under 23 years of age as of August 1 of award year. Applications available November 1 to March 31. Amount of award varies. See Website for application and eligibility requirements.

| | |
|---|---|
| **Amount of award:** | $1,000-$3,000 |
| **Number of awards:** | 44 |
| **Number of applicants:** | 154 |
| **Application deadline:** | March 31 |
| **Notification begins:** | July 1 |
| **Total amount awarded:** | $70,500 |

**Contact:**
AFSA Scholarship Programs
Attn: Nicholas Falcon,Scholarship Coordinator
5211 Auth Road
Suitland, MD 20746
Phone: 301-899-3500 ext. 230
Web: www.hqafsa.org

## AHIMA Foundation

### Student Merit Scholarships

**Type of award:** Scholarship.
**Intended use:** For full-time undergraduate or graduate study at accredited 2-year, 4-year or graduate institution.
**Basis for selection:** Major/career interest in information systems; health services administration or health-related professions. Applicant must demonstrate high academic achievement.
**Application requirements:** Recommendations, transcript. Enrollment verification form.
**Additional information:** Applicant must be member of AHIMA and enrolled in an undergraduate CAHIIM-accredited health information administration or health information technology program or a national accredited graduate level program. Minimum 3.5 GPA. Award is $1,000 for associate's degree, $1,500 for bachelor's degrees, $2,000 for master's degrees, and $2,500 for doctoral degrees. Apply online.

| | |
|---|---|
| **Amount of award:** | $1,000-$2,500 |
| **Number of awards:** | 64 |
| **Number of applicants:** | 146 |
| **Application deadline:** | September 30 |
| **Notification begins:** | November 30 |
| **Total amount awarded:** | $94,650 |

**Contact:**
AHIMA Foundation
233 North Michigan Avenue, 21st Floor
Chicago, IL 60601-5800
Phone: 312-233-1131
Web: www.ahimafoundation.org

# Air Force Aid Society

## General Henry H. Arnold Education Grant

**Type of award:** Scholarship.
**Intended use:** For full-time undergraduate study at accredited vocational, 2-year or 4-year institution in or outside United States.
**Eligibility:** Applicant must be spouse of active service person or deceased veteran who serves or served in the Air Force. Applicant may also be dependent child of active, retired or deceased Air Force service member. Veteran status alone not eligible. Sponsoring member must be active duty, retired due to length of service, retired Reserve with 20-plus qualifying years of service, or deceased while on active duty or in retired status. Dependent children of Title 32 AGR performing full-time active duty service are also eligible.
**Basis for selection:** Applicant must demonstrate financial need.
**Application requirements:** Proof of eligibility.
**Additional information:** Minimum 2.0 GPA.

| | |
|---|---|
| **Amount of award:** | $2,000 |
| **Number of awards:** | 3,000 |
| **Number of applicants:** | 4,200 |
| **Application deadline:** | March 11 |
| **Notification begins:** | June 1 |
| **Total amount awarded:** | $5,500,000 |

**Contact:**
Air Force Aid Society
Education Assistance Department
241 18th Street South, Suite 202
Arlington, VA 22202
Phone: 800-429-9475
Web: www.afas.org

# Air Force/ROTC

## Minority School Scholarships

**Type of award:** Scholarship.
**Intended use:** For undergraduate study at accredited 4-year institution in United States. Designated institutions: Historically black colleges/universities (HCBUs) and Hispanic Serving Institutions (HSIs) that offer Air Force ROTC.
**Eligibility:** Applicant must be at least 17. Applicant must be U.S. citizen.
**Basis for selection:** Applicant must demonstrate high academic achievement and depth of character.
**Application requirements:** Essay, transcript. One-page resume.
**Additional information:** Must maintain 2.5 GPA in college. Scholarship is Type 2: tuition is capped at $18,000 per year plus $900 per year for books. Must pass the AFOQ Test and the AFROTC Physical Fitness Test. Must pass physical examination and be certified as commission-qualified. Applicant does not need to be a minority to apply. Visit www.afrotc.com for deadline, online application, and full list of moral and other scholarship requirements and details for Air Force ROTC. Contact local ROTC recruiter for more information.

| | |
|---|---|
| **Amount of award:** | Full tuition |
| **Number of awards:** | 4 |

**Contact:**
AFROTC Admissions
551 E. Maxwell Blvd.
Maxwell AFB, AL 36112-5917
Phone: 866-423-7682
Fax: 334-953-4384
Web: www.afrotc.com

# Air Traffic Control Association, Inc.

## Air Traffic Control Full-Time Employee Student Scholarship

**Type of award:** Scholarship.
**Intended use:** For freshman, sophomore, junior, graduate or non-degree study at accredited postsecondary institution.
**Eligibility:** Applicant or parent must be employed by Aviation industry. Applicant must be returning adult student.
**Basis for selection:** Major/career interest in aviation. Applicant must demonstrate financial need.
**Application requirements:** Recommendations, essay, transcript.
**Additional information:** Applicant must work full-time in aviation-related field and be enrolled in coursework designed to enhance air traffic control or aviation skills. Must have minimum 30 semester or 45 quarter hours still to be completed before graduation. Award amount determined by ATCA Scholarship Program Board of Directors. Visit Website for application.

| | |
|---|---|
| **Number of awards:** | 1 |
| **Application deadline:** | May 1 |

**Contact:**
Air Traffic Control Association, Inc.
Attn: Scholarship Fund
1101 King Street, Suite 300
Alexandria, VA 22314
Phone: 703-299-2430
Fax: 703-299-2437
Web: www.atca.org

## Air Traffic Control Non-Employee Student Scholarship

**Type of award:** Scholarship.
**Intended use:** For freshman, sophomore, junior or graduate study at accredited 4-year or graduate institution.
**Basis for selection:** Major/career interest in aviation. Applicant must demonstrate financial need.
**Application requirements:** Recommendations, essay, transcript.
**Additional information:** Must have minimum 30 semester hours or 45 quarter hours still to be completed before graduation. Number of awards varies based on funding. Visit Website for application.

| | |
|---|---|
| **Amount of award:** | $1,500-$2,500 |
| **Number of applicants:** | 98 |
| **Application deadline:** | May 1 |
| **Total amount awarded:** | $17,000 |

**Contact:**
Air Traffic Control Association, Inc.
Attn: Scholarship Fund
1101 King Street, Suite 300
Alexandria, VA 22314
Phone: 703-299-2430
Fax: 703-299-2437
Web: www.atca.org

## Buckingham Memorial Scholarship

**Type of award:** Scholarship, renewable.
**Intended use:** For freshman, sophomore, junior or graduate study at accredited 4-year or graduate institution in United States.
**Eligibility:** Applicant must be U.S. citizen.
**Basis for selection:** Major/career interest in aviation. Applicant must demonstrate financial need.
**Application requirements:** Recommendations, essay, transcript.
**Additional information:** Must be child of a person serving, or having served, as an air traffic control specialist. Must have minimum of 30 semester or 45 quarter hours to be completed before graduation. Number of awards varies based on funding. Visit Website for application.

| | |
|---|---|
| **Application deadline:** | May 1 |

**Contact:**
Air Traffic Control Association, Inc.
Attn: Scholarship Fund
1101 King Street, Suite 300
Alexandria, VA 22314
Phone: 703-299-2430
Fax: 703-299-2437
Web: www.atca.org

## Gabe A. Hartl Scholarship

**Type of award:** Scholarship.
**Intended use:** For freshman, sophomore or junior study at 2-year, 4-year or graduate institution. Designated institutions: FAA-approved institutions.
**Basis for selection:** Major/career interest in aviation. Applicant must demonstrate financial need.
**Application requirements:** Recommendations, essay, transcript.
**Additional information:** Must have minimum of 30 semester or 45 quarter hours to be completed before graduation. Must be enrolled in air traffic control curriculum. Number of awards varies based on funding. Visit Website for application.

| | |
|---|---|
| **Application deadline:** | May 1 |

**Contact:**
Air Traffic Control Association, Inc.
Attn: Scholarship Fund
1101 King Street, Suite 300
Alexandria, VA 22314
Phone: 703-299-2430
Fax: 703-299-2437
Web: www.atca.org

# Aircraft Electronics Association Educational Foundation

## Bud Glover Memorial Scholarship

**Type of award:** Scholarship, renewable.
**Intended use:** For full-time undergraduate study at accredited vocational, 2-year or 4-year institution.
**Basis for selection:** Major/career interest in aviation; aviation repair or electronics. Applicant must demonstrate depth of character and seriousness of purpose.
**Application requirements:** Recommendations, essay, transcript, proof of eligibility.
**Additional information:** Minimum 2.5 GPA. Awards are announced at AEA Annual Convention and Trade Show each spring. Visit Website for more information.

| | |
|---|---|
| **Amount of award:** | $1,000 |
| **Number of awards:** | 1 |
| **Application deadline:** | February 15 |
| **Notification begins:** | April 1 |

**Contact:**
Aircraft Electronics Association Educational Foundation
3570 NE Ralph Powell Road
Lee's Summit, MO 64064
Phone: 816-347-8400
Fax: 816-347-8405
Web: www.aea.net/educationalfoundation

## David Arver Memorial Scholarship

**Type of award:** Scholarship, renewable.
**Intended use:** For full-time undergraduate study at accredited vocational or 2-year institution.
**Eligibility:** Applicant must be residing in Wisconsin, Michigan, Iowa, South Dakota, Minnesota, Kansas, Indiana, Nebraska, Illinois, North Dakota or Missouri.
**Basis for selection:** Major/career interest in aviation; aviation repair or electronics. Applicant must demonstrate depth of character and seriousness of purpose.
**Application requirements:** Recommendations, essay, transcript, proof of eligibility.
**Additional information:** Minimum 2.5 GPA. Awards are announced at AEA Annual Convention and Trade Show each spring. Visit Website for more information.

| | |
|---|---|
| **Amount of award:** | $1,000 |
| **Number of awards:** | 1 |
| **Application deadline:** | February 15 |
| **Notification begins:** | April 1 |
| **Total amount awarded:** | $1,000 |

**Contact:**
Aircraft Electronics Association Educational Foundation
3570 NE Ralph Powell Road
Lee's Summit, MO 64064
Phone: 816-347-8400
Fax: 816-347-8405
Web: www.aea.net/educationalfoundation

## Dutch and Ginger Arver Scholarship

**Type of award:** Scholarship, renewable.
**Intended use:** For full-time undergraduate study at accredited vocational, 2-year or 4-year institution.
**Basis for selection:** Major/career interest in aviation; electronics or aviation repair. Applicant must demonstrate depth of character and seriousness of purpose.
**Application requirements:** Recommendations, essay, transcript, proof of eligibility.
**Additional information:** Minimum 2.5 GPA. Awards are announced at AEA Annual Convention and Trade Show each spring. Visit Website for more information.

| | |
|---|---|
| **Amount of award:** | $1,000 |
| **Number of awards:** | 1 |
| **Application deadline:** | February 15 |
| **Notification begins:** | April 1 |
| **Total amount awarded:** | $1,000 |

**Contact:**
Aircraft Electronics Association Educational Foundation
3570 NE Ralph Powell Road
Lee's Summit, MO 64064
Phone: 816-347-8400
Fax: 816-347-8405
Web: www.aea.net/educationalfoundation

## Field Aviation Co. Inc. Scholarship

**Type of award:** Scholarship, renewable.
**Intended use:** For full-time undergraduate study at accredited vocational, 2-year or 4-year institution.
**Basis for selection:** Major/career interest in aviation; aviation repair or electronics. Applicant must demonstrate depth of character and seriousness of purpose.
**Application requirements:** Recommendations, essay, transcript, proof of eligibility.
**Additional information:** Minimum 2.5 GPA. Awards are announced at AEA Annual Convention and Trade Show each spring. Visit Website for more information.

| | |
|---|---|
| **Amount of award:** | $1,000 |
| **Number of awards:** | 1 |
| **Application deadline:** | February 15 |
| **Notification begins:** | April 1 |

**Contact:**
Aircraft Electronics Association Educational Foundation
3570 NE Ralph Powell Road
Lee's Summit, MO 64064
Phone: 816-347-8400
Fax: 816-347-8405
Web: www.aea.net/educationalfoundation

## Garmin Scholarship

**Type of award:** Scholarship, renewable.
**Intended use:** For full-time undergraduate study at accredited vocational, 2-year or 4-year institution.
**Basis for selection:** Major/career interest in aviation; aviation repair or electronics. Applicant must demonstrate depth of character and seriousness of purpose.
**Application requirements:** Recommendations, essay, transcript, proof of eligibility.
**Additional information:** Minimum 2.5 GPA. Awards are announced at AEA Annual Convention and Trade Show each spring. For more information, visit Website.

| | |
|---|---|
| **Amount of award:** | $2,000 |
| **Number of awards:** | 1 |
| **Application deadline:** | February 15 |
| **Notification begins:** | April 1 |
| **Total amount awarded:** | $2,000 |

**Contact:**
Aircraft Electronics Association Educational Foundation
3570 NE Ralph Powell Road
Lee's Summit, MO 64064
Phone: 816-347-8400
Fax: 816-347-8405
Web: www.aea.net/educationalfoundation

## Honeywell Avionics Scholarship

**Type of award:** Scholarship, renewable.
**Intended use:** For full-time undergraduate study at accredited vocational, 2-year or 4-year institution.
**Basis for selection:** Major/career interest in aviation; aviation repair or electronics.
**Application requirements:** Recommendations, essay, transcript, proof of eligibility.
**Additional information:** Minimum 2.5 GPA. Awards are announced at AEA Annual Convention and Trade Show each spring. Visit Website for additional information.

| | |
|---|---|
| **Amount of award:** | $1,000 |
| **Number of awards:** | 1 |
| **Application deadline:** | February 15 |
| **Notification begins:** | April 1 |
| **Total amount awarded:** | $1,000 |

**Contact:**
Aircraft Electronics Association Educational Foundation
3570 NE Ralph Powell Road
Lee's Summit, MO 64064
Phone: 816-347-8400
Fax: 816-347-8405
Web: www.aea.net/educationalfoundation

## Johnny Davis Memorial Scholarship

**Type of award:** Scholarship, renewable.
**Intended use:** For full-time undergraduate study at accredited vocational, 2-year or 4-year institution.
**Basis for selection:** Major/career interest in aviation; aviation repair or electronics. Applicant must demonstrate depth of character and seriousness of purpose.
**Application requirements:** Recommendations, essay, transcript, proof of eligibility.
**Additional information:** Minimum 2.5 GPA. Awards are announced at AEA Annual Convention and Trade Show each spring. Visit Website for additional information.

| | |
|---|---|
| **Amount of award:** | $1,000 |
| **Number of awards:** | 1 |
| **Application deadline:** | February 15 |
| **Notification begins:** | April 1 |
| **Total amount awarded:** | $1,000 |

**Contact:**
Aircraft Electronics Association Educational Foundation
3570 NE Ralph Powell Road
Lee's Summit, MO 64064
Phone: 816-347-8400
Fax: 816-347-8405
Web: www.aea.net/educationalfoundation

## L-3 Avionics Systems Scholarship

**Type of award:** Scholarship, renewable.
**Intended use:** For full-time undergraduate study at accredited vocational, 2-year or 4-year institution.
**Basis for selection:** Major/career interest in aviation; aviation repair or electronics. Applicant must demonstrate depth of character and seriousness of purpose.
**Application requirements:** Recommendations, essay, transcript, proof of eligibility.
**Additional information:** Applicant may be high school senior. Minimum 2.5 GPA. Awards are announced at AEA Annual Convention and Trade Show each spring. Visit Website for more information.

| | |
|---|---|
| **Amount of award:** | $2,500 |
| **Number of awards:** | 1 |
| **Application deadline:** | February 15 |
| **Notification begins:** | April 1 |
| **Total amount awarded:** | $2,500 |

**Contact:**
Aircraft Electronics Association Educational Foundation
3570 NE Ralph Powell Road
Lee's Summit, MO 64064
Phone: 816-347-8400
Fax: 816-347-8405
Web: www.aea.net/educationalfoundation

## Lee Tarbox Memorial Scholarship

**Type of award:** Scholarship, renewable.
**Intended use:** For full-time undergraduate study at accredited vocational, 2-year or 4-year institution.
**Basis for selection:** Major/career interest in aviation; aviation repair or electronics. Applicant must demonstrate depth of character and seriousness of purpose.
**Application requirements:** Recommendations, essay, transcript, proof of eligibility.
**Additional information:** Minimum 2.5 GPA. Awards are announced at AEA Annual Convention and Trade Show each spring. Visit Website for additional information.

| | |
|---|---|
| **Amount of award:** | $2,500 |
| **Number of awards:** | 1 |
| **Application deadline:** | February 15 |
| **Notification begins:** | April 1 |
| **Total amount awarded:** | $2,500 |

**Contact:**
Aircraft Electronics Association Educational Foundation
3570 NE Ralph Powell Road
Lee's Summit, MO 64064
Phone: 816-347-8400
Fax: 816-347-8405
Web: www.aea.net/educationalfoundation

## Lowell Gaylor Memorial Scholarship

**Type of award:** Scholarship, renewable.
**Intended use:** For full-time undergraduate study at accredited vocational, 2-year or 4-year institution.
**Basis for selection:** Major/career interest in aviation; aviation repair or electronics. Applicant must demonstrate depth of character and seriousness of purpose.
**Application requirements:** Recommendations, essay, transcript, proof of eligibility.
**Additional information:** Minimum 2.5 GPA. Awards are announced at AEA Annual Convention and Trade Show each spring. Visit Website for more information.

| | |
|---|---|
| **Amount of award:** | $1,000 |
| **Number of awards:** | 1 |
| **Application deadline:** | February 15 |
| **Notification begins:** | April 1 |

**Contact:**
Aircraft Electronics Association Educational Foundation
3570 NE Ralph Powell Road
Lee's Summit, MO 64064
Phone: 816-347-8400
Fax: 816-347-8405
Web: www.aea.net/educationalfoundation

## Mid-Continent Instrument Scholarship

**Type of award:** Scholarship, renewable.
**Intended use:** For full-time undergraduate study at accredited vocational, 2-year or 4-year institution.
**Basis for selection:** Major/career interest in aviation; electronics or aviation repair. Applicant must demonstrate depth of character and seriousness of purpose.
**Application requirements:** Recommendations, essay, transcript, proof of eligibility.
**Additional information:** Minimum 2.5 GPA. Awards are announced at AEA Annual Convention and Trade Show each spring. Visit Website for more information.

| | |
|---|---|
| **Amount of award:** | $1,000 |
| **Number of awards:** | 1 |
| **Application deadline:** | February 15 |
| **Notification begins:** | April 1 |
| **Total amount awarded:** | $1,000 |

**Contact:**
Aircraft Electronics Association Educational Foundation
3570 NE Ralph Powell Road
Lee's Summit, MO 64064
Phone: 816-347-8400
Fax: 816-347-8405
Web: www.aea.net/educationalfoundation

## Monte R. Mitchell Global Scholarship

**Type of award:** Scholarship, renewable.
**Intended use:** For full-time undergraduate study at accredited postsecondary institution in or outside United States. Designated institutions: Institutions with aviation maintenance technology, avionics, or aviation repair programs located in Europe or the United States.
**Eligibility:** Applicant must be U.S. citizen or European citizen.
**Basis for selection:** Major/career interest in aviation. Applicant must demonstrate depth of character and seriousness of purpose.
**Application requirements:** Essay, transcript.
**Additional information:** Applicant must have finished secondary school. Minimum 2.5 GPA. Scholarship given by Mid-Continent Instruments Company. Awards are announced at AEA Annual Convention and Trade Show each spring.

| | |
|---|---|
| **Amount of award:** | $1,000 |
| **Number of awards:** | 1 |
| **Application deadline:** | February 15 |
| **Notification begins:** | April 1 |

**Contact:**
Aircraft Electronics Association
3570 NE Ralph Powell Road
Lee's Summit, MO 64064
Phone: 816-347-8400
Fax: 816-347-8405
Web: www.aea.net/educationalfoundation

# Alabama Commission on Higher Education

## Alabama National Guard Educational Assistance Program

**Type of award:** Scholarship, renewable.
**Intended use:** For undergraduate or graduate study at postsecondary institution. Designated institutions: Public institutions in Alabama.
**Eligibility:** Applicant must be U.S. citizen residing in Alabama. Applicant must be in military service in the Reserves/National Guard. Must be active member in good standing with federally recognized unit of Alabama National Guard.
**Application requirements:** Proof of eligibility.
**Additional information:** Award to be used for tuition, books, fees, and supplies (minus any federal veterans benefits). Applications available from Alabama National Guard units. Funds are limited; apply early.

**Amount of award:** $25-$1,000
**Number of applicants:** 704
**Total amount awarded:** $424,665

**Contact:**
Alabama Commission on Higher Education
Phone: 334-242-2273
Fax: 334-242-2269
Web: www.ache.alabama.gov

### Alabama Student Assistance Program

**Type of award:** Scholarship, renewable.
**Intended use:** For full-time undergraduate study. Designated institutions: Eligible Alabama institutions.
**Eligibility:** Applicant must be residing in Alabama.
**Basis for selection:** Applicant must demonstrate financial need.
**Application requirements:** Proof of eligibility. FAFSA.
**Additional information:** Students urged to apply early. Applications available at college financial aid office.

**Amount of award:** $300-$5,000
**Number of applicants:** 7,457
**Total amount awarded:** $5,204,129

**Contact:**
Alabama Commission on Higher Education
Phone: 334-242-2273
Fax: 334-242-2269
Web: www.ache.alabama.gov

### Alabama Student Grant Program

**Type of award:** Scholarship, renewable.
**Intended use:** For undergraduate study at 2-year or 4-year institution. Designated institutions: Amridge University, Birmingham-Southern College, Concordia College, Faulkner University, Huntingdon College, Judson College, Miles College, Oakwood University, Samford University, South University, Spring Hill College, Stillman College, United States Sports Academy, University of Mobile.
**Eligibility:** Applicant must be residing in Alabama.
**Application requirements:** Proof of eligibility.
**Additional information:** For more information, contact financial aid office of participating colleges.

**Amount of award:** $1,200
**Number of applicants:** 7,217
**Application deadline:** February 15, September 15
**Total amount awarded:** $2,299,025

**Contact:**
Alabama Commission on Higher Education
Phone: 334-242-2273
Fax: 334-242-2269
Web: www.ache.alabama.gov

### Police/Firefighters' Survivors Educational Assistance Program

**Type of award:** Scholarship, renewable.
**Intended use:** For undergraduate study at vocational, 2-year or 4-year institution.
**Eligibility:** Applicant must be residing in Alabama. Applicant's parent must have been killed or disabled in work-related accident as firefighter or police officer.
**Application requirements:** Proof of eligibility.
**Additional information:** Grant covers full tuition, mandatory fees, books, and supplies. Also available to eligible spouses.

**Amount of award:** Full tuition
**Number of applicants:** 19
**Total amount awarded:** $105,521

**Contact:**
Alabama Commission on Higher Education
P.O. Box 302000
Montgomery, AL 36130-2000
Phone: 334-242-2273
Fax: 334-242-2269
Web: www.ache.alabama.gov

## Alabama Department of Education

### Robert C. Byrd Honors Scholarship

**Type of award:** Scholarship, renewable.
**Intended use:** For full-time undergraduate study at 2-year or 4-year institution in United States.
**Eligibility:** Applicant must be high school senior. Applicant must be U.S. citizen residing in Alabama.
**Basis for selection:** Applicant must demonstrate high academic achievement.
**Application requirements:** Nomination by high school guidance counselor. SAT/ACT scores.
**Additional information:** Contact high school guidance office or principal for information. Scholarship renewable up to four years if qualifications met. Number of scholarships varies. Visit Website for details.

**Amount of award:** $1,500
**Number of applicants:** 140
**Application deadline:** March 5

**Contact:**
Alabama State Department of Education
Robert C. Byrd Honors Scholarship
50 North Ripley Street, Box 302101
Montgomery, AL 36104
Phone: 334-242-8082
Web: www.alsde.edu

## Alabama Department of Postsecondary Education

### Alabama Junior/Community College Athletic Scholarship

**Type of award:** Scholarship, renewable.
**Intended use:** For freshman or sophomore study at 2-year institution. Designated institutions: Alabama public 2-year community colleges.
**Eligibility:** Applicant must be U.S. citizen or permanent resident.
**Basis for selection:** Competition/talent/interest in athletics/sports, based on athletic ability determined through tryouts.
**Additional information:** Renewal dependent on continued athletic participation. Contact individual institutions for specific requirements and amount of awards. Number of awards available varies by sport. Visit Website for participating institutions.

**Contact:**
Department of Postsecondary Education
P.O. Box 302130
Montgomery, AL 36130-2130
Phone: 334-293-4557
Fax: 334-293-4559
Web: www.accs.cc

### Institutional Scholarship Waivers

**Type of award:** Scholarship, renewable.
**Intended use:** For freshman or sophomore study at accredited 2-year institution. Designated institutions: Alabama public 2-year community or technical colleges.
**Eligibility:** Applicant must be U.S. citizen or permanent resident.
**Basis for selection:** Applicant must demonstrate high academic achievement.
**Additional information:** Focus of scholarship is determined by each institution. Application deadlines printed on application forms. Award may be renewed if student demonstrates academic excellence. Contact individual institutions for scholarship/waiver requirements. Number and amount of awards vary. Visit Website for participating institutions.
**Contact:**
Department of Postsecondary Education
P.O. Box 302130
Montgomery, AL 36130-2130
Phone: 334-293-4557
Fax: 334-293-4559
Web: www.accs.cc

## Alabama Department of Veterans Affairs

### G.I. Dependents' Scholarship Program

**Type of award:** Scholarship, renewable.
**Intended use:** For undergraduate or graduate study at postsecondary institution. Designated institutions: Alabama public institutions.
**Eligibility:** Applicant must be dependent of disabled veteran, deceased veteran or POW/MIA; or spouse of disabled veteran, deceased veteran or POW/MIA. Veteran must have served for at least 90 days continuous active federal duty during a wartime period, be rated with at least a 20% service-connected disability and must have resided in the state of Alabama for at least one year prior to enlistment or be rated with a 100% service connected disability and be a permanent resident of the State of Alabama for at least 5 years immediately prior to application for program.
**Application requirements:** Proof of eligibility.
**Additional information:** Children of veterans must submit application before their 26th birthday. Spouses of veterans have no age limit, but must not be remarried. Award for five academic years for children and three academic years for spouses (or part-time equivalent); covers tuition, textbooks, and laboratory fees. Unlimited number of awards available; no application deadline.

| | |
|---|---|
| **Amount of award:** | Full tuition |
| **Number of applicants:** | 2,417 |
| **Total amount awarded:** | $15,827,191 |

**Contact:**
Alabama Department of Veterans Affairs
P.O. Box 1509
Montgomery, AL 36102-1509
Phone: 334-242-5077
Fax: 334-353-4078
Web: www.va.alabama.gov/scholarship.htm

## Alcoa Foundation

### Alcoa Foundation Sons and Daughters Scholarship Program

**Type of award:** Scholarship, renewable.
**Intended use:** For full-time undergraduate study at accredited vocational, 2-year or 4-year institution in United States.
**Eligibility:** Applicant must be high school senior.
**Basis for selection:** Applicant must demonstrate high academic achievement, depth of character, leadership and service orientation.
**Application requirements:** Recommendations, essay, transcript, proof of eligibility. SAT/ACT scores (if attending four-year institution), school profile.
**Additional information:** Applicant must be child of US-based, full-time Alcoa employee. Four-year award renewable for three years. Two-year award renewable for one year. Deadline in January; see Website for details.

| | |
|---|---|
| **Amount of award:** | $1,500 |
| **Number of awards:** | 100 |
| **Number of applicants:** | 150 |
| **Total amount awarded:** | $57,000 |

**Contact:**
Alcoa Foundation Sons and Daughters Scholarship Program
P.O. Box 4030
Iowa City, IA 52243-4030
Phone: 800-525-6932
Fax: 319-337-1204
Web: www.act.org/alcoafoundation

## Alexander Graham Bell Association for the Deaf and Hard of Hearing

### AG Bell College Scholarship Awards

**Type of award:** Scholarship.
**Intended use:** For full-time undergraduate or graduate study at accredited 2-year, 4-year or graduate institution in or outside United States.
**Eligibility:** Applicant must be hearing impaired.
**Basis for selection:** Applicant must demonstrate high academic achievement.
**Application requirements:** Recommendations, essay, transcript, proof of eligibility.
**Additional information:** Applicant must have bilateral hearing loss in the moderate to profound range, diagnosed before the fourth birthday. Must use speech as primary form of communication, and be accepted or enrolled in mainstream

college/university. Number of awards granted varies. Visit Website for additional eligibility criteria.

| | |
|---|---|
| **Amount of award:** | $1,000-$10,000 |
| **Number of applicants:** | 144 |
| **Application deadline:** | March 1 |
| **Total amount awarded:** | $90,000 |

**Contact:**
AG Bell College Scholarship Program
3417 Volta Place, NW
Washington, DC 20007-2778
Phone: 202-337-5220
Web: www.agbell.org

# Alexia Foundation

## Alexia Foundation Grant and Scholarship

**Type of award:** Scholarship.
**Intended use:** For full-time undergraduate or graduate study in or outside United States or Canada. Designated institutions: Syracuse University London Program.
**Basis for selection:** Competition/talent/interest in photography.
**Application requirements:** Essay. 750-word proposal and 25-word summary, resume, portfolio of 10 to 20 photographs.
**Additional information:** Grand prize of full tuition scholarship to study photojournalism during fall semester at Syracuse University in London, plus $1,000 grant for completion of photo-story proposal. Additional awards will be given. Students who have completed more than three internships or who have a year of full-time professional experience are not eligible. Application must be submitted online. Check Website for number of awards available.

| | |
|---|---|
| **Amount of award:** | $2,100-$16,300 |
| **Application deadline:** | February 1 |

**Contact:**
Tom Kennedy/The Alexia Competition
S.I. Newhouse School of Communications
215 University Place
Syracuse, NY 13244-2100
Phone: 315-443-7388
Web: www.alexiafoundation.org

# Alliance for Young Artists and Writers

## Scholastic Art Portfolio Gold Award

**Type of award:** Scholarship.
**Intended use:** For undergraduate study at postsecondary institution.
**Eligibility:** Applicant must be high school senior.
**Basis for selection:** Competition/talent/interest in visual arts, based on originality, level of technical proficiency, and emergence of personal style or vision. Major/career interest in arts, general.
**Application requirements:** Portfolio. Signed registration form, artist's statement. Portfolio must contain eight works.
**Additional information:** Deadline varies. Contact sponsor or visit Website for more information.

| | |
|---|---|
| **Amount of award:** | $10,000 |
| **Number of awards:** | 8 |
| **Number of applicants:** | 36,000 |
| **Notification begins:** | March 1 |
| **Total amount awarded:** | $80,000 |

**Contact:**
Alliance for Young Artists & Writers
The Scholastic Art & Writing Awards
557 Broadway
New York, NY 10012
Phone: 212-343-6892
Fax: 212-389-3939
Web: www.artandwriting.org

## Scholastic Art Portfolio Silver With Distinction Award

**Type of award:** Scholarship.
**Intended use:** For undergraduate study at postsecondary institution.
**Eligibility:** Applicant must be high school senior.
**Basis for selection:** Competition/talent/interest in visual arts, based on originality, level of technical proficiency, and emergence of personal style or vision. Major/career interest in arts, general.
**Application requirements:** Portfolio. Signed registration form, artist's statement. Portfolio must contain eight works.
**Additional information:** Students nominated for scholarships offered by participating higher education institutions. Deadline varies. Contact sponsor or visit Website for more information.

| | |
|---|---|
| **Amount of award:** | $1,000 |
| **Number of awards:** | 20 |
| **Number of applicants:** | 54,000 |
| **Notification begins:** | March 1 |
| **Total amount awarded:** | $20,000 |

**Contact:**
Alliance for Young Artists & Writers
The Scholastic Art & Writing Awards
557 Broadway
New York, NY 10012
Phone: 212-343-6892
Fax: 212-389-3939
Web: www.artandwriting.org

## Scholastic Non-Fiction Writing Portfolio Gold Award

**Type of award:** Scholarship.
**Intended use:** For undergraduate study at postsecondary institution.
**Eligibility:** Applicant must be high school senior.
**Basis for selection:** Competition/talent/interest in writing/journalism, based on originality, level of technical proficiency, and emergence of personal voice or style. Major/career interest in English; journalism; literature or theater arts.
**Application requirements:** Table of contents, writer's statement. Portfolio must contain three to eight nonfiction works in the humor, journalism, personal essay/memoir and persuasive writing categories. Excerpts from longer works permitted. Entry form must be signed by student's parent and teacher, counselor, or principal.
**Additional information:** Deadline varies. Application fee varies by location and may be waived. Contact sponsor or visit Website for more information.

**Amount of award:** $10,000
**Number of awards:** 2
**Number of applicants:** 500
**Notification begins:** March 1
**Total amount awarded:** $20,000

**Contact:**
The Scholastic Art & Writing Awards
557 Broadway
New York, NY 10012
Phone: 212-343-6892
Fax: 212-389-3939
Web: www.artandwriting.org



## Scholastic Photography Portfolio Gold Award

**Type of award:** Scholarship.
**Intended use:** For undergraduate study at postsecondary institution.
**Eligibility:** Applicant must be high school senior.
**Basis for selection:** Competition/talent/interest in photography, based on originality, level of technical proficiency, and emergence of personal style or vision. Major/career interest in arts, general.
**Application requirements:** Portfolio. Signed registration form, artist's statement. Portfolio must contain eight works in form of prints.
**Additional information:** Deadline varies. Contact sponsor or visit Website for more information.

**Amount of award:** $10,000
**Number of awards:** 2
**Number of applicants:** 18,000
**Notification begins:** March 1
**Total amount awarded:** $20,000

**Contact:**
Alliance for Young Artists & Writers
The Scholastic Art & Writing Awards
557 Broadway
New York, NY 10012
Phone: 212-343-6892
Fax: 212-389-3939
Web: www.artandwriting.org

## Scholastic Photography Portfolio Silver Award

**Type of award:** Scholarship.
**Intended use:** For undergraduate study at postsecondary institution.
**Eligibility:** Applicant must be high school senior.
**Basis for selection:** Based on originality, level of technical proficiency, and emergence of personal style or vision. Major/career interest in arts, general; journalism; literature or theater arts.
**Application requirements:** Portfolio, recommendations. For art, portfolio must contain eight works in form of prints. Signed registration form. For writing, table of contents, writer's statement. Portfolio must contain three to eight works of narratives, individual poems, or dramatic scripts demonstrating diversity and talent. Excerpts from longer works permitted. Entry form must be signed by student's parent and teacher, counselor, or principal.
**Additional information:** Students nominated for scholarships offered by participating higher education institutions. Deadline varies. Application fee varies by location and may be waived. Contact sponsor or visit Website for more information.

**Amount of award:** $1,000
**Number of awards:** 30
**Number of applicants:** 5,000
**Notification begins:** March 1
**Total amount awarded:** $30,000

**Contact:**
Alliance for Young Artists & Writers
The Scholastic Art & Writing Awards
557 Broadway
New York, NY 10012
Phone: 212-343-6892
Fax: 212-389-3939
Web: www.artandwriting.org

## Scholastic Writing Portfolio Gold Award

**Type of award:** Scholarship.
**Intended use:** For undergraduate study at postsecondary institution.
**Eligibility:** Applicant must be high school senior.
**Basis for selection:** Competition/talent/interest in writing/journalism, based on originality, level of technical proficiency, and emergence of personal voice or style. Major/career interest in English; journalism; literature or theater arts.
**Application requirements:** Portfolio. Table of contents, writer's statement. Portfolio must contain three to eight works of narratives, individual poems, or dramatic scripts demonstrating diversity and talent. Excerpts from longer works permitted. Entry form must be signed by student's parent and teacher, counselor, or principal.
**Additional information:** Deadline varies. Application fee varies by location and may be waived. Contact sponsor or visit Website for more information.

**Amount of award:** $10,000
**Number of awards:** 5
**Number of applicants:** 4,500
**Notification begins:** March 1
**Total amount awarded:** $50,000

**Contact:**
Alliance for Young Artists & Writers
The Scholastic Art & Writing Awards
557 Broadway
New York, NY 10012
Phone: 212-343-6892
Fax: 212-389-3939
Web: www.artandwriting.org

# Alpha Beta Gamma International Business Honor Society

## Alpha Beta Gamma National Scholarship

**Type of award:** Scholarship.
**Intended use:** For full-time junior or senior study at accredited 4-year institution. Designated institutions: Participating four-year colleges.
**Basis for selection:** Major/career interest in business; business, international; business/management/administration; accounting

or computer/information sciences. Applicant must demonstrate high academic achievement and leadership.
**Application requirements:** Recommendations. Copy of ABG diploma.
**Additional information:** Must be initiated member of Alpha Beta Gamma. Awarded to enrollees of two-year schools who have been accepted at four-year schools to pursue baccalaureate degree in business or related professions. Some colleges have minimum GPA requirement. Amount of award varies by institution.

| | |
|---|---|
| **Amount of award:** | $500-$8,100 |
| **Number of awards:** | 300 |
| **Number of applicants:** | 400 |
| **Total amount awarded:** | $600,000 |

**Contact:**
Alpha Beta Gamma Scholarship Committee
75 Grasslands Road
Valhalla, NY 10595
Web: www.abg.org

# Alpha Mu Gamma, the National Collegiate Foreign Language Honor Society

## Alpha Mu Gamma Scholarships

**Type of award:** Scholarship.
**Intended use:** For full-time undergraduate, graduate or postgraduate study at 2-year, 4-year or graduate institution.
**Basis for selection:** Major/career interest in foreign languages. Applicant must demonstrate high academic achievement and seriousness of purpose.
**Application requirements:** Recommendations, essay, transcript. Photocopy of applicant's AMG full member certificate.
**Additional information:** Applicant must be full member of Alpha Mu Gamma. Three $1,000 awards granted for study of any foreign language; one $400 award for study of Esperanto or Spanish. May apply unlimited number of times. National office will not send out applications; forms must be requested from advisor of local AMG chapter.

| | |
|---|---|
| **Amount of award:** | $400-$1,000 |
| **Number of awards:** | 4 |
| **Number of applicants:** | 25 |
| **Application deadline:** | February 1 |
| **Notification begins:** | April 1 |
| **Total amount awarded:** | $3,400 |

**Contact:**
Advisor of local Alpha Mu Gamma chapter.
Web: www.lacitycollege.edu/academic/honor/amg/homepage.html

# Alumnae Panhellenic Association of Washington, D.C.

## Alumnae Panhellenic Association Women's Scholarship

**Type of award:** Scholarship, renewable.
**Intended use:** For sophomore, junior, senior or graduate study at 4-year or graduate institution.
**Eligibility:** Applicant must be female. Applicant must be residing in District of Columbia.
**Basis for selection:** Based on sorority involvement. Applicant must demonstrate high academic achievement and service orientation.
**Application requirements:** Recommendations, essay, transcript.
**Additional information:** Applicant must be member in good standing of sorority of National Panhellenic Conference and live or attend school in Washington, D.C., metro area. Send email for application request. Amount and number of awards varies.

| | |
|---|---|
| **Amount of award:** | $700 |
| **Number of applicants:** | 21 |
| **Application deadline:** | March 15 |
| **Notification begins:** | April 10 |
| **Total amount awarded:** | $1,950 |

Scholarships

# AMBUCS

## AMBUCS Scholars-Scholarship for Therapists

**Type of award:** Scholarship.
**Intended use:** For full-time junior, senior or master's study at accredited 4-year or graduate institution in United States. Designated institutions: Schools with programs accredited by appropriate health therapy association.
**Eligibility:** Applicant must be U.S. citizen.
**Basis for selection:** Major/career interest in occupational therapy; physical therapy or speech pathology/audiology. Applicant must demonstrate financial need, depth of character and service orientation.
**Additional information:** Award amount typically maximum $1,500, but one additional two-year award of $6,000 offered. Students must apply online; no paper applications accepted. Applicants may print online enrollment certificate. Additional documentation, including prior year's 1040 tax form, requested if applicant is selected as semifinalist.

| | |
|---|---|
| **Amount of award:** | $500-$6,000 |
| **Number of applicants:** | 1,246 |
| **Application deadline:** | April 15 |
| **Notification begins:** | June 20 |
| **Total amount awarded:** | $145,525 |

**Contact:**
AMBUCS Resource Center
P.O. Box 5127
High Point, NC 27262
Phone: 336-852-0052
Fax: 336-852-6830
Web: www.ambucs.org

# American Alpine Club

## Arthur K. Gilkey Memorial/William Putnam/Bedayn Research Grants

**Type of award:** Research grant.
**Intended use:** For undergraduate or graduate study.

**Basis for selection:** Major/career interest in science, general; biology; environmental science; forestry or atmospheric sciences/meteorology.
**Application requirements:** Research proposal. Curriculum vitae with biographical information.
**Additional information:** Research proposals evaluated on scientific or technical quality and contribution to scientific endeavor germane to mountain regions. Applications available from Website; must be submitted via email. Number of awards varies.

| | |
|---|---|
| **Amount of award:** | $200-$1,000 |
| **Number of applicants:** | 18 |
| **Application deadline:** | March 1 |
| **Notification begins:** | May 1 |
| **Total amount awarded:** | $10,000 |

**Contact:**
American Alpine Club
710 Tenth Street
Suite 100
Golden, CO 80401
Phone: 303-384-0110
Fax: 303-384-0111
Web: www.americanalpineclub.org/grants

# American Association for Cancer Research

## Gary J. Miller Undergraduate Prizes for Cancer and Cancer-Related Biomedical Research

**Type of award:** Scholarship.
**Intended use:** For full-time undergraduate or graduate study at 4-year institution.
**Basis for selection:** Competition/talent/interest in science project. Major/career interest in biochemistry; biology; chemistry; pharmacy/pharmaceutics/pharmacology; microbiology; engineering, chemical; epidemiology; oncology or science, general.
**Additional information:** Applicants compete in the annual Undergraduate Student Caucus and Poster Competition, where applicants exhibit a scientific poster concerning cancer or cancer-related biomedical research. First prize receives $1,500 in funding to support cost of participation in the next AACR Annual Meeting. Second place receives $300; third place receives $200. All applicants receive complimentary registration to the AACR Annual Meeting, where the competition takes place. Application deadline and Abstract submission deadlines in March. Visit Website for dates and details.

| | |
|---|---|
| **Amount of award:** | $200-$1,500 |
| **Number of awards:** | 3 |

**Contact:**
American Association for Cancer Research
615 Chestnut Street, 17th Floor
Philadelphia, PA 19106-4404
Phone: 215-440-9300
Fax: 215-440-9412
Web: www.aacr.org/ScienceEducation

## Thomas J. Bardos Science Education Awards for Undergraduate Students

**Type of award:** Research grant.
**Intended use:** For full-time junior study at 4-year institution.
**Basis for selection:** Major/career interest in biochemistry; biology; chemistry; pharmacy/pharmaceutics/pharmacology; microbiology; science, general; epidemiology or oncology. Applicant must demonstrate high academic achievement.
**Application requirements:** Recommendations, essay.
**Additional information:** Two-year award consists of $1,500 per year for travel expenses and registration fee waiver for AACR annual meeting. Selection based on qualifications and interest in research, mentor references, and selection committee's evaluation of potential professional benefit. Applicants not yet committed to cancer research welcome; those studying molecular biology and genetics or pathology also eligible. Awardees must attend scientific sessions at AACR meeting for at least four days and participate in required activities. Must submit two comprehensive reports each year. Contact AACR or visit Website for more information. Application deadline in December.

| | |
|---|---|
| **Amount of award:** | $3,000 |
| **Number of awards:** | 10 |
| **Number of applicants:** | 69 |

**Contact:**
American Association for Cancer Research
615 Chestnut Street, 17th Floor
Philadelphia, PA 19106-4404
Phone: 215-440-9300
Fax: 215-440-9412
Web: www.aacr.org/BardosAward

# American Association of University Women San Jose

## Local Scholarships for Women

**Type of award:** Scholarship, renewable.
**Intended use:** For junior or senior study at accredited 4-year institution in United States.
**Eligibility:** Applicant must be female. Applicant must be U.S. citizen or permanent resident residing in California.
**Basis for selection:** Applicant must demonstrate high academic achievement.
**Additional information:** Minimum 3.0 GPA. Number and amount of scholarships awarded depends upon funds available. Notification dates and deadlines will be posted each year online.

| | |
|---|---|
| **Amount of award:** | $500-$1,500 |
| **Number of awards:** | 5 |
| **Number of applicants:** | 18 |
| **Application deadline:** | April 8 |
| **Total amount awarded:** | $10,000 |

**Contact:**
American Association of University Women San Jose
Local Scholarship Committee
1165 Minnesota Ave.
San Jose, CA 95125
Phone: 408-294-2430
Web: www.aauwsanjose.org

# American Board of Funeral Service Education

## American Board of Funeral Service Education National Scholarship

**Type of award:** Scholarship.
**Intended use:** For full-time undergraduate study at 2-year or 4-year institution in United States.
**Eligibility:** Applicant must be U.S. citizen or permanent resident.
**Basis for selection:** Major/career interest in mortuary science. Applicant must demonstrate financial need, high academic achievement, depth of character, leadership and seriousness of purpose.
**Application requirements:** Recommendations, essay.
**Additional information:** Student must have completed at least one semester (or quarter) of study in funeral service or mortuary science at an education program accredited by American Board of Funeral Service Education. Visit Website for more information and application. Extracurricular activities are considered for eligibility. Number of awards varies.

| | |
|---|---|
| **Amount of award:** | $250-$1,000 |
| **Number of applicants:** | 200 |
| **Application deadline:** | March 1, September 1 |
| **Notification begins:** | May 1, November 1 |
| **Total amount awarded:** | $25,000 |

**Contact:**
American Board of Funeral Service Education
Attn: Scholarship Committee
3414 Ashland, Suite G
St. Joseph, MO 64506
Phone: 816-233-3747
Fax: 816-233-3793
Web: www.abfse.org

# American Center of Oriental Research

## Jennifer C. Groot Fellowship

**Type of award:** Research grant.
**Intended use:** For undergraduate or graduate study at 4-year or graduate institution.
**Eligibility:** Applicant must be U.S. citizen or Canadian citizen.
**Basis for selection:** Major/career interest in archaeology; Middle Eastern studies; ancient Near Eastern studies or ethnic/cultural studies.
**Application requirements:** Proof of acceptance on archaeological fieldwork in Jordan.
**Additional information:** Applicant must be accepted as staff member on archaeological project in Jordan with ASOR/CAP affiliation. Award used only for travel to project site in Jordan.

| | |
|---|---|
| **Amount of award:** | $1,800 |
| **Number of awards:** | 2 |
| **Number of applicants:** | 15 |
| **Application deadline:** | February 1 |
| **Notification begins:** | April 15 |
| **Total amount awarded:** | $4,500 |

**Contact:**
American Center of Oriental Research
Fellowship Committee
656 Beacon Street
Boston, MA 02215-2010
Phone: 617-353-6571
Fax: 617-353-6575
Web: www.bu.edu/acor

# American Chemical Society

## American Chemical Society Scholars Program

**Type of award:** Scholarship, renewable.
**Intended use:** For full-time undergraduate study at accredited 2-year or 4-year institution in United States.
**Eligibility:** Applicant must be African American, Mexican American, Hispanic American, Puerto Rican or American Indian. Applicant must be U.S. citizen or permanent resident.
**Basis for selection:** Major/career interest in chemistry; biochemistry; engineering, chemical; materials science; environmental science; forensics or food science/technology. Applicant must demonstrate financial need, high academic achievement, leadership, seriousness of purpose and service orientation.
**Application requirements:** Recommendations, transcript. SAR. ACT/SAT scores (for high school applicants).
**Additional information:** Other chemically-related majors also eligible. Minimum 3.0 GPA. Must be planning career in chemical sciences (pre-med, pharmacy, nursing, dentistry, veterinary medicine programs not eligible).

| | |
|---|---|
| **Amount of award:** | $1,000-$5,000 |
| **Number of awards:** | 100 |
| **Number of applicants:** | 670 |
| **Application deadline:** | March 1 |
| **Notification begins:** | May 31 |
| **Total amount awarded:** | $900,000 |

**Contact:**
ACS Scholars Program
1155 16th Street, NW
Washington, DC 20036
Phone: 800-227-5558 ext. 6250
Fax: 202-872-4361
Web: www.acs.org/scholars

# American Classical League

## Arthur Patch McKinlay Scholarship

**Type of award:** Scholarship.
**Intended use:** For non-degree study.
**Basis for selection:** Major/career interest in classics or education. Applicant must demonstrate financial need.
**Application requirements:** Recommendations. Study program proposal, including budget.
**Additional information:** Must be current member of American Classical League and for three years preceding application. Must be planning to teach classics in elementary or secondary school in upcoming school year. May apply for independent study program funding or support to attend American Classical

League Institute for first time. Number of awards varies year to year.

**Amount of award:** $1,500
**Number of applicants:** 20
**Application deadline:** January 15

**Contact:**
American Classical League Scholarship Awards
Miami University
422 Wells Mill Drive
Oxford, OH 45056
Phone: 513-529-7741
Fax: 513-529-7742
Web: www.aclclassics.org

### Maureen V. O'Donnell/Eunice C. Kraft Teacher Training Scholarships

**Type of award:** Scholarship.
**Intended use:** For junior, senior or graduate study at 4-year or graduate institution.
**Basis for selection:** Major/career interest in education or classics.
**Application requirements:** Recommendations.
**Additional information:** Must be member of ACL. Must be training for certification to teach Latin and have completed a substantial number of these courses. Must wait at least three years before reapplying. Number of awards varies.

**Amount of award:** $1,000
**Number of applicants:** 13
**Application deadline:** December 1

**Contact:**
The American Classical League
Miami University
422 Wells Mill Drive
Oxford, OH 45056
Phone: 513-529-7741
Fax: 513-529-7742
Web: www.aclclassics.org

## American College of Musicians

### National Guild of Piano Teachers $200 Scholarship

**Type of award:** Scholarship.
**Intended use:** For undergraduate, graduate or non-degree study.
**Basis for selection:** Major/career interest in music.
**Application requirements:** Nomination by piano teacher, who must be member of National Guild of Piano Teachers. Copies of ten inner report cards and stubs.
**Additional information:** Award to be used for piano study. Student must have been national winner for ten years, Paderewski Medal winner, and Guild High School Diploma recipient.

**Amount of award:** $200
**Number of awards:** 150
**Application deadline:** September 15
**Notification begins:** October 1

**Contact:**
American College of Musicians
Scholarship Committee
P.O. Box 1807
Austin, TX 78767-1807
Phone: 512-478-5775
Web: www.pianoguild.com

### National Guild of Piano Teachers Composition Contest

**Type of award:** Scholarship.
**Intended use:** For undergraduate, graduate or non-degree study.
**Basis for selection:** Competition/talent/interest in music performance/composition, based on composition for solo keyboard and keyboard ensemble.
**Application requirements:** Manuscript of composition.
**Additional information:** Teacher must be member of National Guild of Piano Teachers. Compositions rated on imagination, originality, and skill. Entry fees vary according to classification of student and length of composition. See Website for specific details.

**Amount of award:** $50-$150
**Number of awards:** 14
**Application deadline:** November 8

**Contact:**
American College of Musicians
P.O. Box 1807
Austin, TX 78767-1807
Phone: 512-478-5775
Web: www.pianoguild.com

## American Congress on Surveying and Mapping

### AAGS Joseph F. Dracup Scholarship Award

**Type of award:** Scholarship, renewable.
**Intended use:** For undergraduate study at 4-year institution.
**Basis for selection:** Major/career interest in surveying/mapping. Applicant must demonstrate high academic achievement and seriousness of purpose.
**Application requirements:** Recommendations, essay, transcript, proof of eligibility.
**Additional information:** Applicant must be member of American Congress on Surveying and Mapping. Preference will be given to applicants with significant focus on geodetic surveying. Students may also be enrolled in degree program related to surveying, such as geomatics or survey engineering. Visit Website for deadlines and additional information.

**Amount of award:** $2,000
**Number of awards:** 1
**Total amount awarded:** $2,000

**Contact:**
American Congress on Surveying and Mapping
6 Montgomery Village Avenue
Suite 403
Gaithersburg, MD 20879
Phone: 240-632-9716
Fax: 240-632-1321
Web: www.acsm.net

## ACSM Fellows Scholarship

**Type of award:** Scholarship.
**Intended use:** For junior or senior study at 4-year institution.
**Basis for selection:** Major/career interest in surveying/mapping or cartography. Applicant must demonstrate high academic achievement and seriousness of purpose.
**Application requirements:** Recommendations, essay, transcript, proof of eligibility.
**Additional information:** Applicant must be an ACSM member and be student in one of ACSM disciplines: surveying, mapping, geographic land sciences, or cartography. Student may also study related disciplines including geomatics or surveying engineering. Visit Website for deadlines and additional information.

| | |
|---|---|
| **Amount of award:** | $2,000 |
| **Number of awards:** | 1 |
| **Total amount awarded:** | $2,000 |

**Contact:**
American Congress on Surveying & Mapping
6 Montgomery Village Avenue
Suite 403
Gaithersburg, MD 20879
Phone: 240-632-9716
Fax: 240-632-1321
Web: www.acsm.net

## Berntsen International Scholarship in Surveying

**Type of award:** Scholarship, renewable.
**Intended use:** For undergraduate study at 4-year institution.
**Basis for selection:** Major/career interest in surveying/mapping. Applicant must demonstrate high academic achievement and seriousness of purpose.
**Application requirements:** Recommendations, essay, transcript, proof of eligibility.
**Additional information:** Applicant must be member of ACSM. Open to students in surveying or closely related programs such as geomatics or surveying engineering. Degree of financial need will be used, if necessary, to break ties after the primary criteria have been considered. Funded by Berntsen International Inc. of Madison, Wisconsin. Visit Website for deadlines and additional information.

| | |
|---|---|
| **Amount of award:** | $1,500 |
| **Number of awards:** | 1 |
| **Total amount awarded:** | $1,500 |

**Contact:**
American Congress on Surveying and Mapping
6 Montgomery Village Avenue
Suite 403
Gaithersburg, MD 20879
Phone: 240-632-9716
Fax: 240-632-1321
Web: www.acsm.net

## Berntsen International Scholarship in Surveying Technology

**Type of award:** Scholarship, renewable.
**Intended use:** For undergraduate certificate study at 2-year institution.
**Basis for selection:** Major/career interest in surveying/mapping or cartography. Applicant must demonstrate high academic achievement and seriousness of purpose.
**Application requirements:** Recommendations, essay, transcript, proof of eligibility.
**Additional information:** Applicant must be member of ACSM. Funded by Berntsen International Inc. of Madison, Wisconsin. Visit Website for deadlines and additional information.

| | |
|---|---|
| **Amount of award:** | $500 |
| **Number of awards:** | 1 |
| **Total amount awarded:** | $500 |

**Contact:**
American Congress on Surveying and Mapping
6 Montgomery Village Avenue
Suite 403
Gaithersburg, MD 20879
Phone: 240-632-9716
Fax: 240-632-1321
Web: www.acsm.net

## Cady McDonnell Memorial Scholarship

**Type of award:** Scholarship, renewable.
**Intended use:** For undergraduate study at 2-year or 4-year institution.
**Eligibility:** Applicant must be female. Applicant must be residing in Utah, Alaska, Washington, Arizona, Nevada, Wyoming, California, Montana, Oregon, New Mexico, Idaho, Colorado or Hawaii.
**Basis for selection:** Major/career interest in surveying/mapping or cartography. Applicant must demonstrate high academic achievement and seriousness of purpose.
**Application requirements:** Recommendations, essay, transcript, proof of eligibility. Proof of legal home residence.
**Additional information:** Applicant must be member of American Congress on Surveying and Mapping. Degree of financial need will be used, if necessary, to break ties after the primary criteria have been considered. Visit Website for deadlines and additional information.

| | |
|---|---|
| **Amount of award:** | $1,000 |
| **Number of awards:** | 1 |
| **Total amount awarded:** | $1,000 |

**Contact:**
American Congress on Surveying and Mapping
6 Montgomery Village Avenue
Suite 403
Gaithersburg, MD 20879
Phone: 240-632-9716
Fax: 240-632-1321
Web: www.acsm.net

## The Lowell H. and Dorothy Loving Undergraduate Scholarship

**Type of award:** Scholarship.
**Intended use:** For junior or senior study at accredited postsecondary institution.
**Basis for selection:** Major/career interest in surveying/mapping. Applicant must demonstrate high academic achievement and seriousness of purpose.
**Application requirements:** Recommendations, essay, transcript, proof of eligibility.
**Additional information:** Applicant must be ACSM member. In addition to basic surveying, applicant must take courses in at least two of the following: land surveying, geometric geodesy, photogrammetry/remote sensing; or analysis and design of spatial measurement. Visit Website for deadlines and additional information.

**Amount of award:** $2,500
**Number of awards:** 1
**Total amount awarded:** $2,500

**Contact:**
American Congress on Surveying and Mapping
6 Montgomery Village Avenue
Suite 403
Gaithersburg, MD 20879
Phone: 240-632-9716
Fax: 240-632-1321
Web: www.acsm.net



## Nettie Dracup Memorial Scholarship

**Type of award:** Scholarship, renewable.
**Intended use:** For undergraduate study at accredited 4-year institution.
**Eligibility:** Applicant must be U.S. citizen.
**Basis for selection:** Major/career interest in surveying/mapping. Applicant must demonstrate high academic achievement and seriousness of purpose.
**Application requirements:** Recommendations, essay, transcript, proof of eligibility.
**Additional information:** Applicant must be member of American Congress on Surveying and Mapping and enrolled in geodetic surveying program. Degree of financial need will be used, if necessary, to break ties after primary criteria have been considered. Visit Website for deadlines and additional information.

**Amount of award:** $2,000
**Number of awards:** 2
**Total amount awarded:** $4,000

**Contact:**
American Congress on Surveying and Mapping
6 Montgomery Village Avenue
Suite 403
Gaithersburg, MD 20879
Phone: 240-632-9716
Fax: 240-632-1321
Web: www.acsm.net

## NSPS Board of Governors Scholarship

**Type of award:** Scholarship, renewable.
**Intended use:** For junior study at 4-year institution.
**Basis for selection:** Major/career interest in surveying/mapping. Applicant must demonstrate high academic achievement and seriousness of purpose.
**Application requirements:** Recommendations, essay, transcript, proof of eligibility.
**Additional information:** Applicant must be member of American Congress on Surveying and Mapping. Minimum 3.0 GPA. Degree of financial need will be used, if necessary, to break ties after the primary criteria have been considered. Visit Website for deadlines and additional information.

**Amount of award:** $1,000
**Number of awards:** 1
**Total amount awarded:** $1,000

**Contact:**
American Congress on Surveying and Mapping
6 Montgomery Village Avenue
Suite 403
Gaithersburg, MD 20879
Phone: 240-632-9716
Fax: 240-632-1321
Web: www.acsm.net

## NSPS Scholarships

**Type of award:** Scholarship, renewable.
**Intended use:** For full-time undergraduate study at 4-year institution.
**Basis for selection:** Major/career interest in surveying/mapping. Applicant must demonstrate high academic achievement and seriousness of purpose.
**Application requirements:** Recommendations, essay, transcript, proof of eligibility.
**Additional information:** Applicant must be member of American Congress on Surveying and Mapping. Students may also be enrolled in related degree program such as geomatics or surveying engineering. Degree of financial need will be used, if necessary, to break ties after the primary criteria have been considered. Awarded by National Society of Professional Surveyors. Visit Website for deadlines and additional information.

**Amount of award:** $1,000
**Number of awards:** 2
**Total amount awarded:** $2,000

**Contact:**
American Congress on Surveying and Mapping
6 Montgomery Village Avenue
Suite 403
Gaithersburg, MD 20879
Phone: 240-632-9716
Fax: 240-632-1321
Web: www.acsm.net

## Schonstedt Scholarships in Surveying

**Type of award:** Scholarship, renewable.
**Intended use:** For undergraduate study at 4-year institution.
**Basis for selection:** Major/career interest in surveying/mapping. Applicant must demonstrate high academic achievement and seriousness of purpose.
**Application requirements:** Recommendations, essay, transcript, proof of eligibility.
**Additional information:** Applicant must be member of American Congress on Surveying and Mapping. Preference given to applicants with junior or senior standing. Degree of financial need will be used, if necessary, to break ties after primary criteria have been considered. Funded by Schonstedt Instrument Company of Kearneysville, West Virginia. Schonstedt donates magnetic locator to surveying program at each recipient's school. Visit Website for deadlines and additional information.

**Amount of award:** $1,500
**Number of awards:** 2

**Contact:**
American Congress on Surveying and Mapping
6 Montgomery Village Avenue
Suite 403
Gaithersburg, MD 20879
Phone: 240-632-9716
Fax: 240-632-1321
Web: www.acsm.net

## Tri-State Surveying & Photogrammetry Kris M. Kunze Scholarship

**Type of award:** Scholarship.
**Intended use:** For undergraduate study at postsecondary institution in United States.
**Basis for selection:** Major/career interest in business; business/management/administration or surveying/mapping. Applicant must demonstrate high academic achievement and seriousness of purpose.
**Additional information:** Applicant must be ACSM member. First priority: licensed professional land surveyors or certified photogrammetrists taking college business administration or management courses. Second priority: certified land survey interns taking college business administration or management courses. Third priority: full-time students in two or four-year surveying and mapping degree programs taking business administration or management courses. Visit Website for deadlines and additional information.

| | |
|---|---|
| **Amount of award:** | $1,000 |
| **Number of awards:** | 1 |
| **Total amount awarded:** | $1,000 |

**Contact:**
ACSM
6 Montgomery Village Avenue
Suite 403
Gaithersburg, MD 20879
Phone: 240-632-9716
Fax: 240-632-1321
Web: www.acsm.net

# American Council of Engineering Companies

## ACEC Scholarship

**Type of award:** Scholarship, renewable.
**Intended use:** For junior, senior, master's or doctoral study at postsecondary institution. Designated institutions: ABET-accredited engineering programs.
**Eligibility:** Applicant must be U.S. citizen residing in Alaska.
**Basis for selection:** Major/career interest in engineering. Applicant must demonstrate seriousness of purpose.
**Application requirements:** Recommendations, essay, transcript, nomination by Council Member Organization.
**Additional information:** Submit application through respective state member organization. Number and amount of award varies.

| | |
|---|---|
| **Number of applicants:** | 19 |

**Contact:**
American Council of Engineering Companies
1015 15th Street, NW
8th Floor
Washington, DC 20005-2605
Phone: 202-347-7474
Fax: 202-898-0068
Web: www.acec.org/awards/scholarships.cfm

# American Council of the Blind

## Floyd Qualls Memorial Scholarship

**Type of award:** Scholarship, renewable.
**Intended use:** For full-time undergraduate or graduate study at accredited postsecondary institution in United States.
**Eligibility:** Applicant must be visually impaired.
**Basis for selection:** Applicant must demonstrate high academic achievement, depth of character and leadership.
**Application requirements:** Interview, recommendations, essay, transcript, proof of eligibility.
**Additional information:** Applicant must be legally blind in both eyes. One award each for an entering freshman, other undergraduate, graduate, and vocational student, plus one discretionary award.

| | |
|---|---|
| **Amount of award:** | $2,500 |
| **Number of awards:** | 5 |
| **Number of applicants:** | 200 |
| **Application deadline:** | March 1 |
| **Notification begins:** | May 15 |
| **Total amount awarded:** | $12,500 |

**Contact:**
American Council of the Blind
2200 Wilson Boulevard
Suite 650
Arlington, VA 22201
Phone: 202-467-5081
Fax: 703-465-5085
Web: www.acb.org

# American Dental Assistants Association

## Juliette A. Southard/Oral-B Laboratories Scholarship

**Type of award:** Scholarship.
**Intended use:** For undergraduate study.
**Basis for selection:** Major/career interest in dental assistant. Applicant must demonstrate high academic achievement.
**Application requirements:** Recommendations, essay, transcript, proof of eligibility.
**Additional information:** Scholarships open to high school graduates and GED certificate holders. Must be ADAA member. Applicants must be enrolled in dental assisting program or be taking courses applicable to furthering career in dental assisting. Visit Website for application. All forms must be submitted via email.

| | |
|---|---|
| **Amount of award:** | $750 |
| **Number of awards:** | 10 |
| **Number of applicants:** | 30 |
| **Application deadline:** | March 1 |
| **Total amount awarded:** | $7,500 |

Scholarships

**Contact:**
American Dental Assistants Association
35 East Wacker Drive
Suite 1730
Chicago, IL 60601-2211
Phone: 312-541-1550
Fax: 312-541-1496
Web: www.dentalassistant.org

# American Dietetic Association Foundation

## Graduate, Baccalaureate or Coordinated Program Scholarships

**Type of award:** Scholarship, renewable.
**Intended use:** For full-time junior, senior or graduate study at accredited 4-year or graduate institution. Designated institutions: CADE-accredited/approved dietetics education programs.
**Eligibility:** Applicant must be U.S. citizen or permanent resident.
**Basis for selection:** Major/career interest in dietetics/nutrition. Applicant must demonstrate high academic achievement and seriousness of purpose.
**Application requirements:** Recommendations, proof of eligibility. GPA documentation signed by academic advisor.
**Additional information:** Applicant must be a member of the American Dietetic Association. Number and amount of awards varies. To be eligible, applicant must be enrolled in the approved program a minimum of four months during the academic year. Minority status considered. Must demonstrate or show promise of being a valuable, contributing member of the profession. See Website for more information and application.

| | |
|---|---|
| **Amount of award:** | $800-$10,000 |
| **Number of awards:** | 220 |
| **Number of applicants:** | 500 |
| **Application deadline:** | February 15 |
| **Notification begins:** | July 1 |
| **Total amount awarded:** | $264,000 |

**Contact:**
American Dietetic Association
Education Programs
120 South Riverside Plaza, Suite 2000
Chicago, IL 60606-6995
Web: www.eatright.org/students/careers/aid.aspx

# American Federation of State, County and Municipal Employees

## AFSCME Family Scholarship

**Type of award:** Scholarship, renewable.
**Intended use:** For full-time undergraduate study at accredited 4-year institution.
**Eligibility:** Applicant must be high school senior.
**Application requirements:** Recommendations, essay, transcript, proof of eligibility. SAT or ACT scores.
**Additional information:** Scholarships open to children and financially dependent grandchildren of active or retired AFSCME members.

| | |
|---|---|
| **Amount of award:** | $2,000 |
| **Number of awards:** | 10 |
| **Number of applicants:** | 650 |
| **Application deadline:** | December 31 |
| **Notification begins:** | August 1 |
| **Total amount awarded:** | $20,000 |

**Contact:**
AFSCME Family Scholarship Program
Attn: AFSCME Advantage
1625 L Street, NW
Washington, DC 20036
Phone: 202-429-1079
Web: www.afscme.org/family

## Jerry Clark Memorial Scholarship

**Type of award:** Scholarship, renewable.
**Intended use:** For full-time junior study at accredited 4-year institution.
**Basis for selection:** Major/career interest in political science/government; sociology; communications or ethnic/cultural studies.
**Application requirements:** Transcript, proof of eligibility.
**Additional information:** Scholarships open to children and financially dependent grandchildren of AFSCME members. Applicant must be a current college sophomore. Winners given opportunity to intern at International Union headquarters in Political Action department. Minimum 2.5 GPA.

| | |
|---|---|
| **Amount of award:** | $5,000 |
| **Number of awards:** | 2 |
| **Number of applicants:** | 30 |
| **Application deadline:** | April 30 |
| **Notification begins:** | August 1 |
| **Total amount awarded:** | $10,000 |

**Contact:**
Jerry Clark Memorial Scholarship Program
AFSCME, AFL-CIO, Attn: Education Department
1625 L Street, NW
Washington, DC 20036
Phone: 202-429-1250
Web: www.afscme.org

# American Floral Endowment

## Ball Horticultural Company Scholarship

**Type of award:** Scholarship.
**Intended use:** For junior or senior study at accredited 4-year institution in United States.
**Eligibility:** Applicant must be U.S. citizen or permanent resident.
**Basis for selection:** Major/career interest in horticulture.
**Application requirements:** Recommendations, transcript.
**Additional information:** Intended for students pursuing career in commercial floriculture. Minimum 3.0 GPA. Submit transcript and letters of recommendation via e-mail.

**Amount of award:** $500-$2,000
**Number of awards:** 1
**Number of applicants:** 1
**Application deadline:** May 1
**Notification begins:** January 1
**Total amount awarded:** $400

**Contact:**
American Floral Endowment
Attn: AFE Scholarship Applications
1601 Duke Street
Alexandria, VA 22314
Phone: 703-838-5211
Fax: 703-838-5212
Web: www.endowment.org

## Bettinger, Holden and Perry Memorial Scholarship

**Type of award:** Scholarship.
**Intended use:** For full-time undergraduate certificate, freshman, sophomore or non-degree study at accredited vocational, 2-year or 4-year institution in United States.
**Eligibility:** Applicant must be U.S. citizen or permanent resident.
**Basis for selection:** Major/career interest in horticulture. Applicant must demonstrate financial need and high academic achievement.
**Application requirements:** Recommendations, transcript.
**Additional information:** Minimum 3.0 GPA. Must intend to become floriculture grower or greenhouse manager. Number and amount of awards vary.

**Amount of award:** $500-$2,000
**Number of awards:** 1
**Number of applicants:** 1
**Application deadline:** May 1
**Notification begins:** January 1
**Total amount awarded:** $1,100

**Contact:**
American Floral Endowment
1601 Duke Street
Alexandria, VA 22314
Phone: 703-838-5211
Fax: 703-838-5212
Web: www.endowment.org

## Bioworks/IPM Sustainable Practices Scholarship

**Type of award:** Scholarship, renewable.
**Intended use:** For sophomore, junior or senior study at 2-year or 4-year institution.
**Eligibility:** Applicant must be U.S. citizen or permanent resident.
**Application requirements:** Recommendations, transcript.
**Additional information:** Applicant should major or show a career interest in floriculture, specifically in furthering the use of Integrated Pest Management (IPM) or sustainable practices. Minimum 3.0 GPA. E-mail is preferred method for submitting transcript and letters of recommendation.

**Amount of award:** $500-$2,000
**Number of awards:** 1
**Number of applicants:** 1
**Application deadline:** May 1
**Notification begins:** January 1
**Total amount awarded:** $900

**Contact:**
American Floral Endowment
1601 Duke Street
Alexandria, VA 22314
Phone: 703-838-5211
Fax: 703-838-5212
Web: www.endowment.org

## Bud Olman Memorial Scholarship

**Type of award:** Scholarship, renewable.
**Intended use:** For sophomore, junior or senior study at accredited postsecondary institution.
**Eligibility:** Applicant must be U.S. citizen or permanent resident.
**Basis for selection:** Major/career interest in horticulture.
**Application requirements:** Recommendations, transcript.
**Additional information:** For students pursuing a career in growing bedding plants. Minimum 3.0 GPA. E-mail is preferred method for submitting transcript and letters of recommendation.

**Amount of award:** $500-$2,000
**Number of awards:** 1
**Number of applicants:** 1
**Application deadline:** May 1
**Notification begins:** January 1
**Total amount awarded:** $300

**Contact:**
American Floral Endowment
1601 Duke Street
Alexandria, VA 22314
Phone: 703-838-5211
Fax: 703-838-5212
Web: www.endowment.org

## Earl Dedman Memorial Scholarship

**Type of award:** Scholarship.
**Intended use:** For full-time sophomore, junior or senior study at accredited 4-year institution in United States.
**Eligibility:** Applicant must be U.S. citizen or permanent resident residing in Wyoming, Oregon, Montana, Idaho or Washington.
**Basis for selection:** Major/career interest in horticulture.
**Application requirements:** Recommendations, transcript.
**Additional information:** Minimum 3.0 GPA. Career interest in becoming a greenhouse grower required. To apply for this scholarship, applicant must have interest in greenhouse production and potted plants. Applicant must be from the Northwestern area of the U.S. Number and amount of scholarships vary.

**Amount of award:** $500-$2,000
**Number of awards:** 1
**Number of applicants:** 1
**Application deadline:** May 1
**Notification begins:** January 1
**Total amount awarded:** $800

**Contact:**
American Floral Endowment
1601 Duke Street
Alexandria, VA 22314
Phone: 703-838-5211
Fax: 703-838-5212
Web: www.endowment.org

## Ed Markham International Scholarship

**Type of award:** Scholarship.
**Intended use:** For sophomore, junior, senior or graduate study at accredited 2-year, 4-year or graduate institution in United States or Canada.
**Eligibility:** Applicant must be U.S. citizen, permanent resident or Canadian citizen.
**Basis for selection:** Major/career interest in horticulture or marketing. Applicant must demonstrate financial need and high academic achievement.
**Application requirements:** Recommendations, transcript.
**Additional information:** Minimum 3.0 GPA. Must have interest in studying horticulture marketing through international travel. Operates in conjunction with the David Colegrave Foundation in London, England. Scholarship is part of annual exchange of students between U.S. and Europe, alternating between the two countries. U.S. students should apply in even number years (i.e. 2012, 2014, etc.). Number and amount of awards vary.

| | |
|---|---|
| **Amount of award:** | $500-$2,000 |
| **Number of awards:** | 1 |
| **Number of applicants:** | 1 |
| **Application deadline:** | May 1 |
| **Notification begins:** | January 1 |
| **Total amount awarded:** | $3,500 |

**Contact:**
American Floral Endowment
1601 Duke Street
Alexandria, VA 22314
Phone: 703-838-5211
Fax: 703-838-5212
Web: www.endowment.org

## Fran Johnson Non-Traditional Scholarship

**Type of award:** Scholarship.
**Intended use:** For full-time undergraduate or graduate study at accredited 4-year or graduate institution in United States.
**Eligibility:** Applicant must be returning adult student. Applicant must be U.S. citizen or permanent resident.
**Basis for selection:** Major/career interest in horticulture. Applicant must demonstrate financial need and high academic achievement.
**Application requirements:** Recommendations, transcript.
**Additional information:** Specific interest in bedding plants or floral crops required. Must be re-entering school after a minimum three-year absence. Number and amount of awards vary.

| | |
|---|---|
| **Amount of award:** | $500-$2,000 |
| **Number of awards:** | 1 |
| **Number of applicants:** | 1 |
| **Application deadline:** | May 1 |
| **Notification begins:** | January 1 |
| **Total amount awarded:** | $850 |

**Contact:**
American Floral Endowment
1601 Duke Street
Alexandria, VA 22314
Phone: 703-838-5211
Fax: 703-838-5212
Web: www.endowment.org

## Harold Bettinger Memorial Scholarship

**Type of award:** Scholarship.
**Intended use:** For full-time sophomore, junior or senior study at accredited 4-year institution in United States.
**Eligibility:** Applicant must be U.S. citizen or permanent resident.
**Basis for selection:** Major/career interest in horticulture; business or marketing. Applicant must demonstrate financial need and high academic achievement.
**Application requirements:** Recommendations, transcript.
**Additional information:** Minimum 3.0 GPA. To apply for this scholarship, applicant's major or minor must be in business and/or marketing with intent to apply it to a horticulture-related business. Amount of award varies.

| | |
|---|---|
| **Amount of award:** | $500-$2,000 |
| **Number of awards:** | 1 |
| **Number of applicants:** | 1 |
| **Application deadline:** | May 1 |
| **Notification begins:** | January 1 |
| **Total amount awarded:** | $1,500 |

**Contact:**
American Floral Endowment
1601 Duke Street
Alexandria, VA 22314
Phone: 703-838-5211
Fax: 703-838-5212
Web: www.endowment.org

## Jacob Van Namen Marketing Scholarship

**Type of award:** Scholarship.
**Intended use:** For sophomore, junior or senior study at accredited 2-year or 4-year institution in United States.
**Eligibility:** Applicant must be U.S. citizen or permanent resident.
**Basis for selection:** Major/career interest in marketing or agribusiness. Applicant must demonstrate financial need and high academic achievement.
**Application requirements:** Recommendations, transcript.
**Additional information:** Minimum 3.0 GPA. Applicant must have interest in agribusiness marketing and distribution of floral products. Number and amount of awards vary.

| | |
|---|---|
| **Amount of award:** | $500-$2,000 |
| **Number of awards:** | 1 |
| **Number of applicants:** | 1 |
| **Application deadline:** | May 1 |
| **Notification begins:** | January 1 |
| **Total amount awarded:** | $800 |

**Contact:**
American Floral Endowment
1601 Duke Street
Alexandria, VA 22314
Phone: 703-838-5211
Fax: 703-838-5212
Web: www.endowment.org

## James Bridenbaugh Memorial Scholarship

**Type of award:** Scholarship.
**Intended use:** For sophomore, junior or senior study at accredited postsecondary institution.
**Eligibility:** Applicant must be U.S. citizen or permanent resident.

**Basis for selection:** Major/career interest in horticulture.
**Application requirements:** Recommendations, transcript.
**Additional information:** For students pursuing career in floral design and marketing of fresh flowers and plants. Minimum 3.0 GPA. E-mail is preferred method for submitting transcripts and letters of recommendation.

| | |
|---|---|
| **Amount of award:** | $500-$2,000 |
| **Number of awards:** | 1 |
| **Number of applicants:** | 1 |
| **Application deadline:** | May 1 |
| **Notification begins:** | January 1 |
| **Total amount awarded:** | $350 |

**Contact:**
American Floral Endowment
Attn: AFE Scholarship Applications
1601 Duke Street
Alexandria, VA 22314
Phone: 703-838-5211
Fax: 703-838-5212
Web: www.endowment.org

## J.K. Rathmell, Jr. Memorial Scholarship for Work/Study Abroad

**Type of award:** Scholarship.
**Intended use:** For full-time junior, senior or graduate study at accredited 4-year or graduate institution outside United States.
**Eligibility:** Applicant must be U.S. citizen or permanent resident.
**Basis for selection:** Competition/talent/interest in study abroad. Major/career interest in horticulture or landscape architecture. Applicant must demonstrate financial need, high academic achievement, depth of character and seriousness of purpose.
**Application requirements:** Recommendations, transcript. Letter of invitation from host institution abroad.
**Additional information:** Minimum 3.0 GPA. Applicants must plan work/study abroad and submit specific plan for such. Preference given to those planning to work or study for six months or longer. Must have interest in floriculture, ornamental horticulture, or landscape architecture. Number and amount of awards vary.

| | |
|---|---|
| **Amount of award:** | $500-$2,000 |
| **Number of awards:** | 1 |
| **Number of applicants:** | 1 |
| **Application deadline:** | May 1 |
| **Notification begins:** | January 1 |
| **Total amount awarded:** | $2,500 |

**Contact:**
American Floral Endowment
1601 Duke Street
Alexandria, VA 22314
Phone: 703-838-5211
Fax: 703-838-5212
Web: www.endowment.org

## John L. Tomasovic, Sr. Scholarship

**Type of award:** Scholarship, renewable.
**Intended use:** For sophomore, junior or senior study at accredited postsecondary institution.
**Eligibility:** Applicant must be U.S. citizen or permanent resident.
**Basis for selection:** Major/career interest in horticulture. Applicant must demonstrate financial need and high academic achievement.
**Application requirements:** Recommendations, transcript.
**Additional information:** For horticulture students with financial need. 3.0-3.5 GPA required. E-mail is preferred method for submitting transcript and letters of recommendation.

| | |
|---|---|
| **Amount of award:** | $500-$2,000 |
| **Number of awards:** | 1 |
| **Number of applicants:** | 1 |
| **Application deadline:** | May 1 |
| **Notification begins:** | January 1 |
| **Total amount awarded:** | $650 |

**Contact:**
American Floral Endowment
1601 Duke Street
Alexandria, VA 22314
Phone: 703-838-5211
Fax: 703-838-5212
Web: www.endowment.org

## Long Island Flower Grower Association (LIFGA) Scholarship

**Type of award:** Scholarship, renewable.
**Intended use:** For sophomore, junior or senior study at 2-year or 4-year institution. Designated institutions: Institutions in the Long Island/New York area.
**Basis for selection:** Major/career interest in horticulture.
**Application requirements:** Recommendations, transcript.
**Additional information:** For students pursuing a career in ornamental horticulture. Minimum 3.0 GPA. E-mail is preferred method for submitting transcript and letters of recommendation.

| | |
|---|---|
| **Amount of award:** | $500-$2,000 |
| **Number of awards:** | 1 |
| **Number of applicants:** | 1 |
| **Application deadline:** | May 1 |
| **Notification begins:** | January 1 |
| **Total amount awarded:** | $1,000 |

**Contact:**
American Floral Endowment
1601 Duke Street
Alexandria, VA 22314
Phone: 703-838-5211
Fax: 703-838-5212
Web: www.endowment.org

## Mike and Flo Novovesky Scholarship

**Type of award:** Scholarship, renewable.
**Intended use:** For sophomore, junior or senior study at accredited postsecondary institution.
**Eligibility:** Applicant must be U.S. citizen or permanent resident.
**Basis for selection:** Major/career interest in horticulture. Applicant must demonstrate financial need.
**Application requirements:** Recommendations, transcript.
**Additional information:** For married students with financial need. Minimum 2.5 GPA. E-mail is preferred method for submitting transcript and letters of recommendation.

| | |
|---|---|
| **Amount of award:** | $500-$2,000 |
| **Number of awards:** | 1 |
| **Number of applicants:** | 1 |
| **Application deadline:** | May 1 |
| **Total amount awarded:** | $950 |

**Contact:**
American Floral Endowment
1601 Duke Street
Alexandria, VA 22314
Phone: 703-838-5211
Fax: 703-838-5212
Web: www.endowment.org

## National Greenhouse Manufacturing Association (NGMA) Scholarship

**Type of award:** Scholarship, renewable.
**Intended use:** For sophomore, junior or senior study at accredited 4-year institution.
**Eligibility:** Applicant must be U.S. citizen or permanent resident.
**Basis for selection:** Major/career interest in horticulture or bioengineering.
**Application requirements:** Recommendations, transcript.
**Additional information:** Minimum 3.0 GPA. E-mail is preferred method for submitting transcript and letters of recommendation.

| | |
|---|---|
| **Amount of award:** | $500-$2,000 |
| **Number of awards:** | 1 |
| **Number of applicants:** | 1 |
| **Application deadline:** | May 1 |
| **Notification begins:** | January 1 |
| **Total amount awarded:** | $450 |

**Contact:**
American Floral Endowment
1601 Duke Street
Alexandria, VA 22314
Phone: 703-838-5211
Fax: 703-838-5212
Web: www.endowment.org

## Seed Companies Scholarship

**Type of award:** Scholarship, renewable.
**Intended use:** For junior or senior study at accredited postsecondary institution.
**Eligibility:** Applicant must be U.S. citizen or permanent resident.
**Basis for selection:** Major/career interest in horticulture.
**Application requirements:** Recommendations, transcript.
**Additional information:** For students pursuing a career in the seed industry. Minimum 3.0 GPA. E-mail is preferred method for submitting transcript and letters of recommendation.

| | |
|---|---|
| **Amount of award:** | $500-$2,000 |
| **Number of awards:** | 1 |
| **Number of applicants:** | 1 |
| **Application deadline:** | May 1 |
| **Notification begins:** | January 1 |
| **Total amount awarded:** | $1,800 |

**Contact:**
American Floral Endowment
1601 Duke Street
Alexandria, VA 22314
Phone: 703-838-5211
Fax: 703-838-5212
Web: www.endowment.org

# American Foundation for Aging Research

## American Foundation for Aging Research Fellowship

**Type of award:** Research grant, renewable.
**Intended use:** For full-time undergraduate, master's, doctoral or first professional study in United States.
**Basis for selection:** Major/career interest in biochemistry or biomedical. Applicant must demonstrate high academic achievement.
**Application requirements:** Recommendations, transcript, proof of eligibility, research proposal.
**Additional information:** Applicants must be actively involved or planning active involvement in specific biomedical or biochemical research project in field of aging. AFAR areas of interest: cellular biology, immunobiology, cancer, neurobiology, biochemistry, molecular biophysics, genomics, and proteomics. Sociology, psychology, and health-related research (e.g., physical therapy/exercise physiology) not currently funded. Those granted awards utilize modern and innovative approaches/technologies. Also applicable toward Ph.D., MD, DVM, and DDS degrees. Number of awards varies. Call sponsor for information regarding deadline. Applicants must complete online pre-application in order to qualify for full application. Notification begins one month after paperwork is received.

| | |
|---|---|
| **Amount of award:** | $500-$2,000 |
| **Number of awards:** | 12 |
| **Number of applicants:** | 50 |
| **Total amount awarded:** | $18,000 |

**Contact:**
American Foundation for Aging Research
University at Albany, Biological Sciences
1400 Washington Ave.
Albany, NY 12222
Phone: 518-437-4448
Web: www.agingresearchfoundation.org

# American Foundation for the Blind

## Delta Gamma Foundation Florence Margaret Harvey Memorial Scholarship

**Type of award:** Scholarship.
**Intended use:** For undergraduate or graduate study at accredited postsecondary institution in United States.
**Eligibility:** Applicant must be visually impaired. Applicant must be U.S. citizen.
**Basis for selection:** Major/career interest in education, special or rehabilitation/therapeutic services.
**Application requirements:** Recommendations, essay, transcript, proof of eligibility.
**Additional information:** Applicant must be legally blind and studying in field of rehabilitation and/or education of blind or visually impaired persons.

**Amount of award:** $1,000
**Number of awards:** 1
**Application deadline:** April 30
**Total amount awarded:** $1,000
**Contact:**
American Foundation for the Blind Scholarship Committee
Attn: Tara Annis
1000 5th Avenue, Suite 350
Huntington, WV 25701
Phone: 800-232-5463
Web: www.afb.org/scholarships.asp

## Ferdinand Torres Scholarship

**Type of award:** Scholarship.
**Intended use:** For full-time undergraduate or graduate study at postsecondary institution in United States.
**Eligibility:** Applicant must be visually impaired. Applicant must be U.S. citizen or permanent resident.
**Basis for selection:** Applicant must demonstrate financial need.
**Application requirements:** Recommendations, essay, transcript, proof of eligibility. Student Aid Report (SAR).
**Additional information:** Applicant must be legally blind. Preference given to residents of New York City metropolitan area and new immigrants to the United States.
**Amount of award:** $2,500
**Number of awards:** 1
**Application deadline:** April 30
**Contact:**
American Foundation for the Blind Scholarship Committee
Attn: Tara Annis
1000 5th Avenue, Suite 350
Huntington, WV 25701
Phone: 800-232-5463
Web: www.afb.org/scholarships.asp

## Paul and Helen Ruckes Scholarship

**Type of award:** Scholarship, renewable.
**Intended use:** For full-time undergraduate or graduate study at accredited postsecondary institution in United States.
**Eligibility:** Applicant must be visually impaired. Applicant must be U.S. citizen.
**Basis for selection:** Major/career interest in engineering; computer/information sciences; physical sciences or life sciences.
**Application requirements:** Recommendations, essay, transcript, proof of eligibility.
**Additional information:** Applicant must be legally blind.
**Amount of award:** $1,000
**Number of awards:** 1
**Application deadline:** April 30
**Total amount awarded:** $1,000
**Contact:**
American Foundation for the Blind Scholarship Committee
Attn: Tara Annis
1000 5th Avenue, Suite 350
Huntington, WV 25701
Phone: 800-232-5463
Web: www.afb.org/scholarships.asp

## R.L. Gillette Scholarship

**Type of award:** Scholarship, renewable.
**Intended use:** For full-time undergraduate study at accredited 4-year institution in United States.
**Eligibility:** Applicant must be visually impaired. Applicant must be female. Applicant must be U.S. citizen.
**Basis for selection:** Major/career interest in literature or music.
**Application requirements:** Recommendations, essay, transcript, proof of eligibility. Creative writing sample or performance tape/CD not to exceed 30 minutes.
**Additional information:** Applicant must be legally blind.
**Amount of award:** $1,000
**Number of awards:** 2
**Application deadline:** April 30
**Total amount awarded:** $2,000
**Contact:**
American Foundation for the Blind Scholarship Committee
Attn: Tara Annis
1000 5th Avenue, Suite 350
Huntington, WV 25701
Phone: 800-232-5463
Web: www.afb.org/scholarships.asp

## Rudolph Dillman Memorial Scholarship

**Type of award:** Scholarship.
**Intended use:** For full-time undergraduate or graduate study at accredited postsecondary institution in United States.
**Eligibility:** Applicant must be visually impaired. Applicant must be U.S. citizen.
**Basis for selection:** Major/career interest in education, special or rehabilitation/therapeutic services.
**Application requirements:** Recommendations, essay, transcript, proof of eligibility. SAR (financial need applicants only).
**Additional information:** Applicant must be legally blind and studying in field of rehabilitation and/or education of blind or visually impaired persons. One scholarship specifically for student who submits evidence of economic need.
**Amount of award:** $2,500
**Number of awards:** 4
**Application deadline:** April 30
**Total amount awarded:** $10,000
**Contact:**
American Foundation for the Blind Scholarship Committee
Attn: Tara Annis
1000 5th Avenue, Suite 350
Huntington, WV 25701
Phone: 800-232-5463
Web: www.afb.org/scholarships.asp

# American Ground Water Trust

## Amtrol Scholarship

**Type of award:** Scholarship.
**Intended use:** For full-time freshman study at 4-year institution.
**Eligibility:** Applicant must be high school senior. Applicant must be U.S. citizen or permanent resident.
**Basis for selection:** Major/career interest in geology/earth sciences; engineering, environmental; environmental science; natural resources/conservation or hydrology. Applicant must demonstrate high academic achievement, leadership, seriousness of purpose and service orientation.

Scholarships

**Application requirements:** Recommendations, essay, transcript. Description of completed high school science project involving ground water resources or of non-school work experience related to environment and natural resources.
**Additional information:** Applicant must be entering field related to ground water, e.g., geology, hydrology, environmental science, or hydrogeology. Minimum 3.0 GPA required. Visit Website for application procedure and forms.

| | |
|---|---|
| **Amount of award:** | $3,000 |
| **Number of awards:** | 2 |
| **Number of applicants:** | 1 |
| **Application deadline:** | June 1 |
| **Notification begins:** | August 15 |

**Contact:**
American Ground Water Trust Scholarship
50 Pleasant Street, Suite 2
Concord, NH 03301-4073
Phone: 603-228-5444
Fax: 603-228-6557
Web: www.agwt.org

### Baroid Scholarship

**Type of award:** Scholarship.
**Intended use:** For full-time freshman study at accredited 4-year institution.
**Eligibility:** Applicant must be high school senior. Applicant must be U.S. citizen or permanent resident.
**Basis for selection:** Major/career interest in engineering, environmental; geology/earth sciences; environmental science or natural resources/conservation. Applicant must demonstrate high academic achievement, leadership, seriousness of purpose and service orientation.
**Application requirements:** Recommendations, essay, transcript. Description of previously completed high school science project involving ground water resources or of non-school work experience related to environment and natural resources.
**Additional information:** Must be entering field related to ground water, e.g., hydrology or hydrogeology. Minimum 3.0 GPA. Visit Website for application procedure and forms.

| | |
|---|---|
| **Amount of award:** | $2,000 |
| **Number of awards:** | 1 |
| **Number of applicants:** | 1 |
| **Application deadline:** | June 1 |
| **Notification begins:** | August 15 |

**Contact:**
American Ground Water Trust Scholarship
50 Pleasant Street, Suite 2
Concord, NH 03301-4073
Phone: 603-228-5444
Fax: 603-228-6557
Web: www.agwt.org

### Thomas M. Stetson Scholarship

**Type of award:** Scholarship.
**Intended use:** For full-time undergraduate study at accredited 4-year institution in United States. Designated institutions: Colleges and universities located west of the Mississippi River.
**Eligibility:** Applicant must be high school senior. Applicant must be U.S. citizen or permanent resident.
**Basis for selection:** Major/career interest in environmental science; natural resources/conservation or science, general. Applicant must demonstrate high academic achievement.
**Application requirements:** Recommendations, essay.
**Additional information:** Applicant must intend to pursue career in ground water related field. Minimum 3.0 GPA. Visit Website for application procedure and forms.

| | |
|---|---|
| **Amount of award:** | $1,500 |
| **Number of awards:** | 1 |
| **Application deadline:** | June 1 |
| **Notification begins:** | August 15 |
| **Total amount awarded:** | $1,500 |

**Contact:**
American Ground Water Trust
50 Pleasant Street
Concord, NH 03301
Phone: 603-228-5444
Fax: 603-228-6557
Web: www.agwt.org

## American Helicopter Society

### Arizona Chapter Vertical Flight Engineering Scholarship

**Type of award:** Scholarship.
**Intended use:** For full-time undergraduate or graduate study. Designated institutions: Schools of engineering in Arizona.
**Basis for selection:** Major/career interest in aviation or engineering. Applicant must demonstrate high academic achievement.
**Application requirements:** Recommendations, transcript. Resume.
**Additional information:** Award for students who demonstrate an interest in pursuing engineering careers in the fixed wing, rotorcraft, or VTOL aircraft industry. Recipients also receive one-year membership in AHS.

| | |
|---|---|
| **Amount of award:** | $1,500-$2,500 |
| **Number of awards:** | 1 |
| **Application deadline:** | October 10 |
| **Notification begins:** | November 26 |

**Contact:**
Ms. Pam Howard
The Boeing Company
Mail Stop M530-B111, 5000 East McDowell Road
Mesa, AZ 85215-9797
Phone: 480-891-5475
Web: www.vtol.org

### Vertical Flight Foundation Scholarship

**Type of award:** Scholarship.
**Intended use:** For full-time junior, senior, master's or doctoral study at accredited postsecondary institution.
**Basis for selection:** Major/career interest in aerospace; aviation or engineering. Applicant must demonstrate high academic achievement, depth of character and seriousness of purpose.
**Application requirements:** Recommendations, essay, transcript.
**Additional information:** Must demonstrate career interest in vertical flight engineering industry. Minimum 3.0 GPA required, 3.5 recommended. Number of awards varies based on funding.

| | |
|---|---|
| **Amount of award:** | $1,000-$4,000 |
| **Number of awards:** | 13 |
| **Number of applicants:** | 64 |
| **Application deadline:** | February 1 |
| **Notification begins:** | April 15 |
| **Total amount awarded:** | $32,000 |

**Contact:**
The Vertical Flight Foundation
217 North Washington Street
Alexandria, VA 22314-2538
Phone: 703-684-6777
Fax: 703-739-9279
Web: www.vtol.org

# American Hellenic Educational Progressive Association Educational Foundation

## AHEPA Educational Foundation Scholarships

**Type of award:** Scholarship.
**Intended use:** For full-time undergraduate or graduate study at accredited postsecondary institution.
**Basis for selection:** Applicant must demonstrate high academic achievement and service orientation.
**Application requirements:** Recommendations, transcript. Photo, financial information (when applicable).
**Additional information:** Applicant must be of Greek descent, or member/child of member (in good standing) of AHEPA, Daughters of Penelope, Sons of Pericles, or Maids of Athena. Minimum 3.0 GPA. High school seniors eligible to apply. Visit Website for details and application.

| | |
|---|---|
| **Amount of award:** | $2,000 |
| **Application deadline:** | March 31 |

**Contact:**
AHEPA Educational Foundation
1909 Q Street N.W., Suite 500
Washington, DC 20009
Phone: 202-232-6300
Fax: 202-232-2140
Web: www.ahepa.org

# American Hotel & Lodging Educational Foundation

## American Express Scholarship Competition

**Type of award:** Scholarship, renewable.
**Intended use:** For undergraduate study at accredited 2-year or 4-year institution.
**Basis for selection:** Major/career interest in hotel/restaurant management or hospitality administration/management.
**Application requirements:** Essay, transcript.
**Additional information:** Must work a minimum of 20 hours a week at hotel and have 12 months of hotel experience. Hotel must be member of American Hotel & Lodging Association. Dependents of hotel employees may also apply. Award must be used in hospitality management degree program. Visit Website to download application or apply online.

| | |
|---|---|
| **Amount of award:** | $500-$2,000 |
| **Number of applicants:** | 22 |
| **Application deadline:** | May 1 |
| **Notification begins:** | July 15 |
| **Total amount awarded:** | $9,000 |

**Contact:**
American Hotel & Lodging Educational Foundation
1201 New York Avenue, NW
Suite 600
Washington, DC 20005-3931
Phone: 202-289-3100
Fax: 202-289-3199
Web: www.ahlef.org

## American Hotel & Lodging Educational Foundation Incoming Freshman Scholarship Competition

**Type of award:** Scholarship.
**Intended use:** For full-time freshman study at 2-year or 4-year institution.
**Eligibility:** Applicant must be U.S. citizen or permanent resident.
**Basis for selection:** Major/career interest in hotel/restaurant management or hospitality administration/management.
**Additional information:** Award must be used in hospitality management program. Minimum 2.0 GPA. $1,000 awards go to Associate majors, $2,000 to Baccalaureate majors. Preference will be given to high school graduates of the Lodging Management Program (LMP). Visit Website to download application or apply online.

| | |
|---|---|
| **Amount of award:** | $1,000-$2,000 |
| **Number of applicants:** | 114 |
| **Application deadline:** | May 1 |
| **Notification begins:** | July 15 |
| **Total amount awarded:** | $15,000 |

**Contact:**
American Hotel & Lodging Educational Foundation
1201 New York Avenue, NW
Suite 600
Washington, DC 20005-3931
Phone: 202-289-3100
Fax: 202-289-3199
Web: www.ahlef.org

## Ecolab Scholarship Competition

**Type of award:** Scholarship.
**Intended use:** For full-time undergraduate study at 2-year or 4-year institution in United States.
**Basis for selection:** Major/career interest in hotel/restaurant management or hospitality administration/management.
**Application requirements:** Essay, transcript.
**Additional information:** Award must be used in hospitality management program. Applicant must maintain minimum 12 credit hours. Visit Website to download application or apply online.

| | |
|---|---|
| **Amount of award:** | $1,000-$2,000 |
| **Number of applicants:** | 513 |
| **Application deadline:** | May 1 |
| **Notification begins:** | July 15 |
| **Total amount awarded:** | $19,000 |

**Contact:**
American Hotel & Lodging Educational Foundation
1201 New York Avenue, NW
Suite 600
Washington, DC 20005-3931
Phone: 202-289-3100
Fax: 202-289-3199
Web: www.ahlef.org

### The Hyatt Hotels Fund for Minority Lodging Management Students Competition

**Type of award:** Scholarship, renewable.
**Intended use:** For sophomore, junior or senior study at 4-year institution.
**Eligibility:** Applicant must be Alaskan native, Asian American, African American, Mexican American, Hispanic American, Puerto Rican, American Indian or Native Hawaiian/Pacific Islander. Applicant must be U.S. citizen or permanent resident.
**Basis for selection:** Major/career interest in hotel/restaurant management or hospitality administration/management.
**Application requirements:** Recommendations, essay, transcript.
**Additional information:** Award must be used in hospitality management program. Must be enrolled in at least 12 credit hours for upcoming fall and spring semesters, or just fall semester if graduating in December. Visit Website to download application or apply online.

| | |
|---|---|
| **Amount of award:** | $2,000 |
| **Number of awards:** | 10 |
| **Number of applicants:** | 112 |
| **Application deadline:** | May 1 |
| **Notification begins:** | July 15 |
| **Total amount awarded:** | $20,000 |

**Contact:**
American Hotel & Lodging Educational Foundation
1201 New York Avenue, NW
Suite 600
Washington, DC 20005
Phone: 202-289-3100
Fax: 202-289-3199
Web: www.ahlef.org

## American Indian College Fund

### Austin Family Scholarship Endowment

**Type of award:** Scholarship, renewable.
**Intended use:** For full-time sophomore, junior or senior study at 4-year institution in United States. Designated institutions: University of Oklahoma (OU) or Southeastern Oklahoma State University (SOSU).
**Eligibility:** Applicant must be American Indian. Applicant must be U.S. citizen residing in Oklahoma.
**Basis for selection:** Applicant must demonstrate financial need.
**Application requirements:** Essay, proof of eligibility. Recent photo.
**Additional information:** Minimum 2.5 GPA. Must be a member or descendant of a tribe in Oklahoma.

| | |
|---|---|
| **Amount of award:** | $1,000 |
| **Number of awards:** | 5 |
| **Number of applicants:** | 316 |
| **Application deadline:** | May 31 |
| **Total amount awarded:** | $9,000 |

**Contact:**
American Indian College Fund
Austin Family Scholarship Endowment
8333 Greenwood Blvd
Denver, CO 80221
Phone: 800-776-3863
Web: www.collegefund.org

### Ford Motor Company/American Indian College Fund Corporate Scholars Program

**Type of award:** Scholarship, renewable.
**Intended use:** For full-time sophomore, junior or senior study at 4-year institution. Designated institutions: Participating colleges and universities.
**Eligibility:** Applicant must be Alaskan native or American Indian. Must have proof of tribal enrollment or ancestry. Applicant must be U.S. citizen.
**Basis for selection:** Major/career interest in computer/information sciences; engineering, electrical/electronic; accounting; finance/banking; information systems; marketing or business. Applicant must demonstrate financial need, high academic achievement, depth of character and leadership.
**Application requirements:** Recommendations, essay, transcript, proof of eligibility. Small color photo.
**Additional information:** Student must demonstrate leadership and commitment to the American Indian community and be attending a participating college or university. Award is up to $10,000 based on financial need. Minimum 3.0 GPA.

| | |
|---|---|
| **Amount of award:** | $10,000 |
| **Number of awards:** | 5 |
| **Number of applicants:** | 316 |
| **Application deadline:** | May 31 |
| **Notification begins:** | September 30 |
| **Total amount awarded:** | $50,000 |

**Contact:**
American Indian College Fund
Corporate Scholars Program
8333 Greenwood Blvd
Denver, CO 80221
Phone: 800-776-3863
Fax: 303-426-1200
Web: www.collegefund.org

### Foundation Scholarship

**Type of award:** Scholarship, renewable.
**Intended use:** For full-time undergraduate study in United States.
**Eligibility:** Applicant must be Alaskan native or American Indian. Applicant must be U.S. citizen.
**Basis for selection:** Applicant must demonstrate financial need.
**Application requirements:** Essay, proof of eligibility. Recent photo.
**Additional information:** Minimum 2.5 GPA. Applicant must be a resident of California or be a member or descendant of a California-based tribe.

| | |
|---|---|
| **Amount of award:** | $3,000 |
| **Number of awards:** | 4 |
| **Application deadline:** | May 31 |

**Contact:**
American Indian College Fund
Foundation Scholarship
8333 Greenwood Blvd.
Denver, CO 80221
Phone: 800-776-3863
Web: www.collegefund.org

## Morgan Stanley Scholars Program

**Type of award:** Scholarship, renewable.
**Intended use:** For full-time undergraduate study at 4-year institution.
**Eligibility:** Applicant must be Alaskan native or American Indian. Applicant must be U.S. citizen.
**Basis for selection:** Major/career interest in business; finance/banking; information systems; marketing or accounting. Applicant must demonstrate high academic achievement.
**Application requirements:** Recommendations, essay, transcript, proof of eligibility. Fall class schedule (when available), small color photograph. Personal Statement describing background and career/academic goals. Two essays, maximum 500 words each, on the topics: 1) How do you perceive yourself as a leader in your school and community? And 2) How will your education help the Native American community?
**Additional information:** Minimum 3.2 GPA.

| | |
|---|---|
| **Amount of award:** | $10,000 |
| **Number of awards:** | 5 |
| **Number of applicants:** | 316 |
| **Application deadline:** | May 31 |
| **Notification begins:** | September 30 |
| **Total amount awarded:** | $50,000 |

**Contact:**
American Indian College Fund
8333 Greenwood Blvd.
Denver, CO 80221
Phone: 800-776-3863
Web: www.collegefund.org

## Nissan North America, Inc. Scholarship

**Type of award:** Scholarship, renewable.
**Intended use:** For full-time undergraduate study at 4-year institution.
**Eligibility:** Applicant must be Alaskan native or American Indian. Applicant must be U.S. citizen.
**Basis for selection:** Applicant must demonstrate high academic achievement and leadership.
**Application requirements:** Recommendations, essay, transcript, proof of eligibility. Two short essays, fall class schedule (when available), and small color photograph.
**Additional information:** Minimum 2.5 GPA. For use at mainstream institution, not tribal college. Must have proof of American Indian/Alaskan Native enrollment or descent.

| | |
|---|---|
| **Amount of award:** | $5,000 |
| **Number of awards:** | 5 |
| **Number of applicants:** | 316 |
| **Application deadline:** | May 31 |
| **Notification begins:** | September 30 |
| **Total amount awarded:** | $25,000 |

**Contact:**
American Indian College Fund
8333 Greenwood Blvd.
Denver, CO 80221
Phone: 800-776-3863
Web: www.collegefund.org

## Sovereign Nations Scholarship Fund

**Type of award:** Scholarship.
**Intended use:** For full-time undergraduate study at 4-year or graduate institution.
**Eligibility:** Applicant must be Alaskan native or American Indian. Applicant must be U.S. citizen.
**Basis for selection:** Applicant must demonstrate financial need and high academic achievement.
**Application requirements:** Recommendations, essay, transcript, proof of eligibility. Two short essays, fall class schedule (when available), and small color photograph, proof of American Indian or Alaskan Native tribal enrollment or ancestry.
**Additional information:** Minimum 3.0 GPA. Must commit to working for tribe or Indian organization upon completion of degree. For use at mainstream institution, not tribal college.

| | |
|---|---|
| **Amount of award:** | $2,000 |
| **Number of awards:** | 13 |
| **Number of applicants:** | 316 |
| **Application deadline:** | May 31 |
| **Notification begins:** | September 30 |
| **Total amount awarded:** | $9,000 |

**Contact:**
American Indian College Fund
8333 Greenwood Blvd.
Denver, CO 80221
Phone: 800-776-3863
Web: www.collegefund.org

## Travelers Foundation

**Type of award:** Scholarship.
**Intended use:** For full-time undergraduate study in United States. Designated institutions: Mainstream colleges/universities in St. Paul-Minneapolis, MN; Seattle, WA; Spokane, WA; or Kansas City, KS.
**Eligibility:** Applicant must be Alaskan native or American Indian. Applicant must be U.S. citizen residing in Minnesota, Montana, Kansas or Washington.
**Basis for selection:** Major/career interest in accounting; business; computer/information sciences; engineering or mathematics. Applicant must demonstrate financial need and high academic achievement.
**Application requirements:** Essay, proof of eligibility. Recent photo.
**Additional information:** Minimum 2.5 GPA. May also major in computer technology. Applicant must commit to leadership development by attending a two-day Travelers career day.

| | |
|---|---|
| **Amount of award:** | $2,500 |
| **Number of awards:** | 2 |
| **Number of applicants:** | 316 |
| **Application deadline:** | May 31 |
| **Total amount awarded:** | $5,000 |

**Contact:**
American Indian College Fund
Travelers Foundation
8333 Greenwood Blvd.
Denver, CO 80221
Phone: 800-776-3863
Web: www.collegefund.org

Scholarships

### United Health Foundation Scholarship

**Type of award:** Scholarship, renewable.
**Intended use:** For full-time undergraduate study at 4-year institution. Designated institutions: Mainstream colleges/ universities in Arizona.
**Eligibility:** Applicant must be Alaskan native or American Indian. Applicant must be U.S. citizen residing in Arizona.
**Basis for selection:** Major/career interest in health-related professions; health education; health sciences or health services administration. Applicant must demonstrate financial need and high academic achievement.
**Application requirements:** Recommendations, essay, transcript, proof of eligibility. Two short essays, fall class schedule (when available), and small color photograph. Proof of American Indian/Alaskan Native tribal enrollment or ancestry.
**Additional information:** Minimum 3.0 GPA. Preference is given to tribal college graduates who are transferring.

| | |
|---|---|
| **Amount of award:** | $5,000 |
| **Number of awards:** | 4 |
| **Number of applicants:** | 316 |
| **Application deadline:** | May 31 |
| **Notification begins:** | September 30 |
| **Total amount awarded:** | $20,000 |

**Contact:**
American Indian College Fund
8333 Greenwood Blvd.
Denver, CO 80221
Phone: 800-776-3863
Web: www.collegefund.org

### Women's Self Worth Foundation Scholarship

**Type of award:** Scholarship, renewable.
**Intended use:** For freshman study at 4-year institution.
**Eligibility:** Applicant must be American Indian. Applicant must be female.
**Basis for selection:** Applicant must demonstrate high academic achievement and service orientation.
**Application requirements:** Essay, proof of eligibility.
**Additional information:** Awarded to mainstream students. Applicant must commit to volunteering 12 hours/year, submitting end-of-year confirmation of volunteer efforts, and completing degree within timeframe.

| | |
|---|---|
| **Amount of award:** | $4,000 |
| **Number of awards:** | 3 |
| **Number of applicants:** | 337 |
| **Application deadline:** | May 31 |
| **Total amount awarded:** | $12,000 |

**Contact:**
American Indian College Fund
8333 Greenwood Blvd.
Denver, CO 80221-4488
Phone: 303-426-8900
Fax: 303-426-1200
Web: www.collegefund.org

## American Indian Endowed Scholarship Program

### Washington State American Indian Endowed Scholarship

**Type of award:** Scholarship.
**Intended use:** For full-time undergraduate or graduate study at accredited vocational, 2-year, 4-year or graduate institution.
**Eligibility:** Applicant must be U.S. citizen residing in Washington.
**Basis for selection:** Applicant must demonstrate financial need, high academic achievement and service orientation.
**Application requirements:** Recommendations, essay, transcript, proof of eligibility. FAFSA.
**Additional information:** Must have close social and cultural ties to American Indian community within Washington State and strong commitment to return service to state's American Indian community. Applicants pursuing degree in theology not eligible.

| | |
|---|---|
| **Amount of award:** | $500-$2,000 |
| **Number of awards:** | 15 |
| **Application deadline:** | February 1 |
| **Notification begins:** | March 1 |

**Contact:**
American Indian Endowed Scholarship Program
Higher Education Coordinating Board
P.O. Box 43430
Olympia, WA 98504-3430
Phone: 360-753-7843
Web: www.hecb.wa.gov

## American Indian Science & Engineering Society

### A.T. Anderson Memorial Scholarship

**Type of award:** Scholarship.
**Intended use:** For full-time undergraduate or graduate study at accredited 2-year, 4-year or graduate institution in United States.
**Eligibility:** Applicant must be Alaskan native or American Indian. Must be member of American Indian tribe or be at least 1/4 American Indian/Alaskan Native blood.
**Basis for selection:** Major/career interest in science, general; engineering; medicine; natural resources/conservation; mathematics; physical sciences or technology. Applicant must demonstrate depth of character, leadership, seriousness of purpose and service orientation.
**Application requirements:** Recommendations, essay, transcript, proof of eligibility. Resume.
**Additional information:** Must be AISES member. Minimum 3.0 GPA. Undergraduate student award $1,000; graduate student award $2,000. Membership and scholarship applications available on Website.

| | |
|---|---|
| **Amount of award:** | $1,000-$2,000 |
| **Application deadline:** | June 15 |
| **Notification begins:** | October 1 |

**Contact:**
AISES Scholarships
P.O. Box 9828
Albuquerque, NM 87119-9828
Phone: 505-765-1052
Fax: 505-765-5608
Web: www.aises.org

### Burlington Northern Santa Fe Foundation Scholarship

**Type of award:** Scholarship, renewable.
**Intended use:** For full-time undergraduate study at accredited 4-year institution in United States.
**Eligibility:** Applicant must be Alaskan native or American Indian. Must be member of American Indian tribe or be at least 1/4 American Indian/Alaskan Native blood. Applicant must be high school senior. Applicant must be U.S. citizen residing in South Dakota, Texas, Minnesota, Washington, Kansas, Arizona, Oklahoma, California, Oregon, Montana, New Mexico, Colorado or North Dakota.
**Basis for selection:** Major/career interest in science, general; engineering; mathematics; physical sciences; medicine; natural sciences; business; health services administration; technology or education. Applicant must demonstrate financial need, depth of character, leadership, seriousness of purpose and service orientation.
**Application requirements:** Recommendations, essay, transcript, proof of eligibility. Resume.
**Additional information:** Applicant must be AISES member. Minimum 2.0 GPA. Award is renewable for four years (eight semesters) or until degree obtained, whichever comes first, assuming eligibility maintained. Membership and scholarship applications available on Website.

| | |
|---|---|
| **Amount of award:** | $2,500 |
| **Number of awards:** | 5 |
| **Application deadline:** | April 15 |
| **Notification begins:** | October 1 |

**Contact:**
AISES Scholarships
P.O. Box 9828
Albuquerque, NM 87119-9828
Phone: 505-765-1052
Fax: 505-765-5608
Web: www.aises.org

## American Institute For Foreign Study

### HACU (Hispanic Association of Colleges and Universities) Scholarships

**Type of award:** Scholarship.
**Intended use:** For undergraduate study in Australia, Austria, Botswana, Brazil, Costa Rica, Czech Republic, England, France, Germany, India, Ireland, Italy, New Zealand, Peru, Russia, South Africa, Spain, Turkey. Designated institutions: HACU member institutions.
**Eligibility:** Applicant must be Mexican American, Hispanic American or Puerto Rican.
**Basis for selection:** Competition/talent/interest in study abroad. Applicant must demonstrate high academic achievement and leadership.
**Application requirements:** Recommendations, essay, transcript. Disciplinary clearance.
**Additional information:** Scholarship intended for use at AIFS programs. Applicant must be involved in multicultural/ international activities. Deadlines are March 1 for summer, April 15 for fall, and September 15 for spring. Award amount is up to half of the AIFS all-inclusive program fee for summer and semester programs.

| | |
|---|---|
| **Number of awards:** | 3 |
| **Number of applicants:** | 15 |
| **Application deadline:** | March 1, April 15 |
| **Notification begins:** | April 1, May 15 |
| **Total amount awarded:** | $25,000 |

**Contact:**
AIFS College Division
9 West Broad Street
Stamford, CT 06902-3788
Phone: 800-727-2437
Fax: 203-399-5597
Web: www.aifsabroad.com

### International Semester Scholarship

**Type of award:** Scholarship.
**Intended use:** For undergraduate study in Australia, Austria, Botswana, Brazil, Costa Rica, Czech Republic, England, France, Germany, India, Ireland, Italy, New Zealand, Peru, Russia, South Africa, Spain, Turkey. Designated institutions: AIFS programs.
**Basis for selection:** Competition/talent/interest in study abroad. Applicant must demonstrate high academic achievement and leadership.
**Application requirements:** Recommendations, essay, transcript. Disciplinary clearance.
**Additional information:** Minimum 3.0 GPA. Must be involved in multicultural/international activities. Award amount is $500 for summer and $1,000 for semester program. Number of awards available is 40 for fall semester, 40 for spring semester, and 50 for summer. Application deadlines are March 1 for summer, April 15 for fall, and September 15 for spring.

| | |
|---|---|
| **Amount of award:** | $500-$1,000 |
| **Number of awards:** | 130 |
| **Number of applicants:** | 580 |
| **Application deadline:** | September 15, April 15 |
| **Notification begins:** | November 1, May 15 |
| **Total amount awarded:** | $130,000 |

**Contact:**
AIFS College Division
9 West Broad Street
Stamford, CT 06902-3788
Phone: 800-727-2437
Fax: 203-399-5597
Web: www.aifsabroad.com

### NAFEO (National Association for Equal Opportunity in Higher Education) Scholarships

**Type of award:** Scholarship.
**Intended use:** For undergraduate study in Australia, Austria, Botswana, Costa Rica, Czech Republic, England, France, India, Ireland, Italy, New Zealand, Russia, South Africa, Spain. Designated institutions: HCBUs or PBIs.
**Eligibility:** Applicant must be African American.

**Basis for selection:** Competition/talent/interest in study abroad. Applicant must demonstrate high academic achievement and leadership.
**Application requirements:** Recommendations, essay, transcript. Disciplinary clearance.
**Additional information:** Scholarship intended for use at AIFS programs. Applicant must be involved in multicultural/international activities. Deadlines are April 15 for fall and September 15 for spring. Award amount is up to half of the AIFS all-inclusive program fee for semester programs.

| | |
|---|---|
| **Number of awards:** | 2 |
| **Application deadline:** | April 15, September 15 |
| **Notification begins:** | May 15, November 1 |

**Contact:**
AIFS College Division
9 West Broad Street
Stamford, CT 06902-3788
Phone: 800-727-2437
Fax: 203-399-5597
Web: www.aifsabroad.com



# American Institute of Aeronautics and Astronautics

## AIAA Foundation Undergraduate Scholarship

**Type of award:** Scholarship, renewable.
**Intended use:** For full-time sophomore, junior or senior study in United States.
**Basis for selection:** Major/career interest in aerospace; engineering; mathematics or science, general. Applicant must demonstrate high academic achievement.
**Application requirements:** Recommendations, essay, transcript.
**Additional information:** Minimum 3.3 GPA. Must be AIAA member to apply. Not open to members of any AIAA national committees or subcommittees. Applicants must reapply for renewal.

| | |
|---|---|
| **Amount of award:** | $2,000-$2,500 |
| **Number of awards:** | 30 |
| **Number of applicants:** | 110 |
| **Application deadline:** | January 31 |
| **Notification begins:** | June 15 |
| **Total amount awarded:** | $61,000 |

**Contact:**
AIAA Student Programs
1801 Alexander Bell Drive
Suite 500
Reston, VA 20191-4344
Phone: 703-264-7500
Web: www.aiaa.org

# American Institute of Architects

## AIA/AAF Minority/Disadvantaged Scholarship

**Type of award:** Scholarship, renewable.
**Intended use:** For full-time freshman or sophomore study in United States. Designated institutions: NAAB-accredited institutions.
**Eligibility:** Applicant must be U.S. citizen or permanent resident.
**Basis for selection:** Major/career interest in architecture. Applicant must demonstrate financial need.
**Application requirements:** Recommendations, essay, transcript, proof of eligibility, nomination by high school guidance counselor, architect, or other individual who can speak to student's aptitude for architecture. Drawing.
**Additional information:** Check Website for deadline. Open to high school seniors, community college students and college freshmen who plan to enter programs leading to professional degree in architecture. Students who have completed full year of undergraduate course work not eligible. Renewable up to two years.

| | |
|---|---|
| **Amount of award:** | $3,000-$5,000 |
| **Number of awards:** | 5 |
| **Number of applicants:** | 120 |

**Contact:**
The American Institute of Architects
1735 New York Avenue, NW
Washington, DC 20006-5292
Phone: 202-626-7529
Fax: 202-626-7399
Web: www.aia.org/education/AIAS075223

# American Institute of Architects New Jersey

## AIA New Jersey Scholarship Foundation

**Type of award:** Scholarship, renewable.
**Intended use:** For full-time sophomore, junior, senior, master's or first professional study at accredited postsecondary institution. Designated institutions: Architectural schools.
**Eligibility:** Applicant must be residing in New Jersey.
**Basis for selection:** Major/career interest in architecture. Applicant must demonstrate financial need, high academic achievement, depth of character and seriousness of purpose.
**Application requirements:** $5 application fee. Portfolio, essay, transcript. FAFSA.
**Additional information:** Non-New Jersey residents attending architecture school in New Jersey also eligible. Applicant must have completed at least one year of architectural school at an accredited architecture program.

**Amount of award:** $2,500-$5,000
**Number of awards:** 5
**Number of applicants:** 35
**Application deadline:** June 3
**Notification begins:** August 1
**Total amount awarded:** $7,000

**Contact:**
AIA New Jersey Scholarship Foundation, Inc.
c/o Robert Zaccone
212 White Avenue
Old Tappan, NJ 07675
Phone: 609-393-5690
Fax: 609-393-9891
Web: www.aia-nj.org/about/scholarship.shtml

# American Institute of Certified Public Accountants

## Accountemps Student Scholarship

**Type of award:** Scholarship.
**Intended use:** For full-time junior, senior or graduate study at postsecondary institution in United States. Designated institutions: AACSB- and/or ACBSP-accredited institutions.
**Eligibility:** Applicant must be U.S. citizen or permanent resident.
**Basis for selection:** Major/career interest in accounting. Applicant must demonstrate financial need, high academic achievement, leadership and service orientation.
**Application requirements:** Recommendations, essay, transcript. Acceptance letter. Course schedule. List of scholarship or grant programs to which student has applied and/or been awarded.
**Additional information:** Minimum 3.0 GPA. Must be AICPA student affiliate member. Applicants may also study accounting-related fields, and must exhibit strong commitment to becoming a licensed CPA professional. Students selected to advance to second round selections notified in May. Award recipients must commit to performing eight hours of CPA-related community service per semester. AICPA and RHI/Accountemps staff and family members are ineligible.

**Amount of award:** $2,500
**Number of awards:** 5
**Number of applicants:** 340
**Application deadline:** April 1
**Notification begins:** August 1
**Total amount awarded:** $12,500

**Contact:**
American Institute of Certified Public Accountants
Elizabeth DeBragga
220 Leigh Farm Road
Durham, NC 27707
Phone: 919-402-4931
Web: www.thiswaytocpa.com/aicpascholarships

## Scholarship for Minority Accounting Students

**Type of award:** Scholarship, renewable.
**Intended use:** For full-time undergraduate or graduate study at postsecondary institution.
**Eligibility:** Applicant must be Alaskan native, Asian American, African American, Mexican American, Hispanic American, Puerto Rican, American Indian or Native Hawaiian/Pacific Islander. Applicant must be U.S. citizen or permanent resident.
**Basis for selection:** Major/career interest in accounting. Applicant must demonstrate high academic achievement, leadership and seriousness of purpose.
**Application requirements:** Recommendations, essay, transcript, proof of eligibility. Strategy plan for obtaining CPA, list of honors/activities/work experience.
**Additional information:** Applicants must have completed at least 30 semester hours or equivalent of college work, with at least six hours in accounting. Minimum 3.3 GPA. Applicants must be enrolled as accounting major, taxation major, finance major, or other related field. Application must be submitted online. Recipients must complete eight hours of community service per semester.

**Amount of award:** $3,000
**Number of awards:** 90
**Number of applicants:** 200
**Application deadline:** April 1
**Notification begins:** August 1
**Total amount awarded:** $254,000

**Contact:**
AICPA Scholarship for Minority Accounting Students
Elizabeth DeBragga
220 Leigh Farm Road
Durham, NC 27707
Phone: 919-402-4931
Web: www.thiswaytocpa.com/aicpascholarships

# American Institute of Polish Culture

## Harriet Irsay Scholarship

**Type of award:** Scholarship.
**Intended use:** For full-time undergraduate or graduate study.
**Eligibility:** Applicant must be U.S. citizen or permanent resident.
**Basis for selection:** Major/career interest in communications; education; film/video; history; humanities/liberal arts; international relations; journalism; polish language/studies; public relations or architecture. Applicant must demonstrate high academic achievement.
**Application requirements:** $10 application fee. Recommendations, essay, transcript. Detailed resume, 700-word article on any subject about Poland.
**Additional information:** Send SASE with application request or download from Website. Preference given to American students of Polish heritage.

**Amount of award:** $1,000
**Number of awards:** 15
**Application deadline:** July 1
**Notification begins:** August 9

**Contact:**
The American Institute of Polish Culture Scholarship Applications
1440 79th Street Causeway
Suite 117
Miami, FL 33141-3555
Phone: 305-864-2349
Fax: 305-865-5150
Web: www.ampolinstitute.org

# American Legion Alabama

## American Legion Alabama Oratorical Contest

**Type of award:** Scholarship.
**Intended use:** For undergraduate study at postsecondary institution.
**Eligibility:** Applicant or parent must be member/participant of American Legion. Applicant must be enrolled in high school. Applicant must be U.S. citizen residing in Alabama.
**Basis for selection:** Competition/talent/interest in oratory/debate, based on language style, voice, diction, delivery, originality, logic, breadth of knowledge, application of knowledge about topic, and skill in selecting examples and analogies.
**Application requirements:** Proof of eligibility.
**Additional information:** First place, $5,000; second place, $3,000; third place, $2,000. State finals held in March. Send business-size SASE for application.

| | |
|---|---|
| **Amount of award:** | $2,000-$5,000 |
| **Number of awards:** | 3 |
| **Total amount awarded:** | $10,000 |

**Contact:**
The American Legion, Department of Alabama
P.O. Box 1069
Montgomery, AL 36101-1069
Phone: 334-262-6638
Web: www.americanlegionalabama.org

## American Legion Alabama Scholarship

**Type of award:** Scholarship, renewable.
**Intended use:** For undergraduate study at postsecondary institution.
**Eligibility:** Applicant or parent must be member/participant of American Legion. Applicant must be U.S. citizen or permanent resident residing in Alabama. Applicant must be descendant of veteran; or dependent of veteran during Korean War, Persian Gulf War, WW I, WW II or Vietnam.
**Application requirements:** Recommendations, transcript, proof of eligibility. SAT/ACT scores.
**Additional information:** Four-year scholarships at Alabama colleges. Send business-size SASE for application.

| | |
|---|---|
| **Amount of award:** | $850 |
| **Number of awards:** | 130 |
| **Application deadline:** | April 1 |
| **Total amount awarded:** | $110,500 |

**Contact:**
The American Legion, Department of Alabama
P.O. Box 1069
Montgomery, AL 36101-1069
Phone: 334-262-6638
Web: www.americanlegionalabama.org

# American Legion Alabama Auxiliary

## American Legion Alabama Auxiliary Scholarship

**Type of award:** Scholarship, renewable.
**Intended use:** For undergraduate study at postsecondary institution. Designated institutions: Alabama state-supported colleges.
**Eligibility:** Applicant or parent must be member/participant of American Legion Auxiliary. Applicant must be U.S. citizen or permanent resident residing in Alabama. Applicant must be descendant of veteran; or dependent of veteran during Grenada conflict, Korean War, Lebanon conflict, Panama conflict, Persian Gulf War, WW I, WW II or Vietnam.
**Application requirements:** Proof of eligibility.
**Additional information:** Four-year scholarships at Alabama colleges. Previous one-year scholarship recipients can reapply. Grandchildren of veterans also eligible. Send SASE for application.

| | |
|---|---|
| **Amount of award:** | $850 |
| **Number of awards:** | 40 |
| **Application deadline:** | April 1 |
| **Total amount awarded:** | $34,000 |

**Contact:**
American Legion Auxiliary, Department of Alabama
120 North Jackson Street
Montgomery, AL 36104
Phone: 334-262-1176

# American Legion Alaska

## Alaska Boys State Scholarship

**Type of award:** Scholarship.
**Eligibility:** Applicant or parent must be member/participant of American Legion. Applicant must be residing in Alaska.
**Additional information:** Winner selected by the counselors.

| | |
|---|---|
| **Amount of award:** | $1,500 |

**Contact:**
Web: www.alaskalegion.org

## American Legion Alaska Oratorical Contest

**Type of award:** Scholarship.
**Intended use:** For undergraduate study at postsecondary institution.
**Eligibility:** Applicant or parent must be member/participant of American Legion. Applicant must be enrolled in high school. Applicant must be U.S. citizen or permanent resident residing in Alaska.
**Basis for selection:** Competition/talent/interest in oratory/debate, based on language style, voice, diction, delivery, originality, logic, breadth of knowledge, application of knowledge about topic, and skill in selecting examples and analogies.
**Application requirements:** Proof of eligibility.
**Additional information:** Awards: First place, $3,000; second place, $2,000; third and fourth place, $1,000. Must be high school student attending Alaska accredited institution. Must participate in local speech contests. Contest begins in November.

| | |
|---|---|
| **Amount of award:** | $1,000-$3,000 |
| **Number of awards:** | 4 |
| **Total amount awarded:** | $7,000 |

**Contact:**
American Legion, Department of Alaska
Department Adjutant
1550 Charter Circle
Anchorage, AK 99508
Phone: 907-278-8598
Fax: 907-278-0041
Web: www.alaskalegion.org

### American Legion Western District Postsecondary Scholarship

**Type of award:** Scholarship.
**Intended use:** For undergraduate study at vocational, 2-year or 4-year institution.
**Eligibility:** Applicant or parent must be member/participant of American Legion. Applicant must be high school senior. Applicant must be residing in Alaska.
**Basis for selection:** Applicant must demonstrate financial need, seriousness of purpose and service orientation.
**Application requirements:** Recommendations, essay, transcript.
**Additional information:** Minimum 2.0 GPA.

**Amount of award:** $750
**Application deadline:** February 15

**Contact:**
American Legion Western District Postsecondary Scholarship
Attn: Jim Scott
1124 Holmes Road
North Pole, AK 99705
Phone: 907-488-5310
Web: www.alaskalegion.org

## American Legion Alaska Auxiliary

### American Legion Alaska Auxiliary Scholarship

**Type of award:** Scholarship.
**Intended use:** For freshman study at postsecondary institution.
**Eligibility:** Applicant or parent must be member/participant of American Legion Auxiliary. Applicant must be at least 17, no older than 24, high school senior. Applicant must be U.S. citizen or permanent resident residing in Alaska. Applicant must be dependent of veteran during Grenada conflict, Korean War, Lebanon conflict, Panama conflict, Persian Gulf War, WW I, WW II or Vietnam.
**Application requirements:** Proof of eligibility.
**Additional information:** Scholarship to apply toward tuition, matriculation, laboratory, or similar fees. Must not have attended institution of higher education.

**Amount of award:** $1,500
**Application deadline:** March 15

**Contact:**
American Legion Auxiliary, Department of Alaska
1392 6th Avenue
Fairbanks, AK 99701
Web: www.alaskalegionauxiliary.org

### American Legion Alaska Auxiliary Western District Scholarship

**Type of award:** Scholarship.
**Intended use:** For undergraduate study at accredited vocational, 2-year, 4-year or graduate institution.
**Eligibility:** Applicant or parent must be member/participant of American Legion Auxiliary. Applicant must be returning adult student. Applicant must be residing in Alaska.
**Additional information:** For continuing education students who are furthering their education to enhance work skills for entry or re-entry into the work field.

**Amount of award:** $1,000

**Contact:**
American Legion Auxiliary, Department of Alaska
1392 6th Avenue
Fairbanks, AK 99701
Web: www.alaskalegionauxiliary.org

## American Legion Arizona

### American Legion Arizona Oratorical Contest

**Type of award:** Scholarship.
**Intended use:** For undergraduate study at postsecondary institution.
**Eligibility:** Applicant or parent must be member/participant of American Legion. Applicant must be enrolled in high school. Applicant must be U.S. citizen or permanent resident residing in Arizona.
**Basis for selection:** Competition/talent/interest in oratory/debate, based on language style, voice, diction, delivery, originality, logic, breadth of knowledge, application of knowledge about topic, and skill in selecting examples and analogies.
**Additional information:** Awards: First place, $1,500; second place, $800; third place, $500. For students enrolled in accredited Arizona high schools.

**Amount of award:** $500-$1,500
**Number of awards:** 3
**Application deadline:** January 15
**Total amount awarded:** $2,800

**Contact:**
American Legion Arizona, Oratorical Contest
4701 North 19th Avenue, Suite 200
Phoenix, AZ 85015-3799
Phone: 602-264-7706
Fax: 602-264-0029
Web: www.azlegion.org

## American Legion Arizona Auxiliary

### American Legion Arizona Auxiliary Health Care Occupation Scholarship

**Type of award:** Scholarship.
**Intended use:** For undergraduate or post-bachelor's certificate study at accredited vocational, 2-year or 4-year institution. Designated institutions: Arizona tax-supported institutions.

**Eligibility:** Applicant or parent must be member/participant of American Legion Auxiliary. Applicant must be U.S. citizen residing in Arizona.
**Basis for selection:** Major/career interest in health-related professions; health sciences or physical therapy. Applicant must demonstrate financial need, high academic achievement, depth of character and seriousness of purpose.
**Application requirements:** Recommendations, essay, transcript. Photograph of self.
**Additional information:** Must be resident of Arizona at least one year. Preference given to immediate family members of veterans.

| | |
|---|---|
| **Amount of award:** | $500 |

**Contact:**
American Legion Auxiliary, Department of Arizona
4701 North 19th Avenue, Suite 100
Phoenix, AZ 85015-3727
Phone: 602-241-1080
Fax: 602-604-9640
Web: www.azlegion.org/LadiesAuxiliary.htm

## American Legion Arizona Auxiliary Nurses' Scholarship

**Type of award:** Scholarship.
**Intended use:** For sophomore study. Designated institutions: Arizona institutions.
**Eligibility:** Applicant or parent must be member/participant of American Legion Auxiliary. Applicant must be U.S. citizen residing in Arizona.
**Basis for selection:** Major/career interest in nursing.
**Application requirements:** Recommendations, essay, transcript. Photograph of self.
**Additional information:** Must be pursuing RN degree. Must be Arizona resident for at least one year. Preference given to immediate family members of veterans.

| | |
|---|---|
| **Amount of award:** | $600 |
| **Application deadline:** | May 15 |

**Contact:**
American Legion Auxiliary, Department of Arizona
4701 North 19th Avenue, Suite 100
Phoenix, AZ 85015-3727
Phone: 602-241-1080
Fax: 602-604-9640
Web: www.azlegion.org/LadiesAuxiliary.htm

## Wilma D. Hoyal/Maxine Chilton Memorial Scholarship

**Type of award:** Scholarship.
**Intended use:** For full-time sophomore, junior or senior study. Designated institutions: University of Arizona, Arizona State University, Northern Arizona University.
**Eligibility:** Applicant or parent must be member/participant of American Legion Auxiliary. Applicant must be U.S. citizen residing in Arizona.
**Basis for selection:** Major/career interest in political science/government; education, special or public administration/service. Applicant must demonstrate financial need, high academic achievement, depth of character and seriousness of purpose.
**Application requirements:** Recommendations, transcript. Resume.
**Additional information:** For second-year or upper-division full-time students. Three $1,000 awards payable to three designated institutions in Arizona. Applicant must be state resident at least one year. Preference given to immediate family members of veterans.

| | |
|---|---|
| **Amount of award:** | $3,000 |
| **Number of awards:** | 3 |

**Contact:**
American Legion Auxiliary, Department of Arizona
4701 North 19th Avenue, Suite 100
Phoenix, AZ 85015-3727
Phone: 602-241-1080
Fax: 602-604-9640
Web: www.azlegion.org/LadiesAuxiliary.htm

# American Legion Arkansas

## American Legion Arkansas Oratorical Contest

**Type of award:** Scholarship.
**Intended use:** For undergraduate study at postsecondary institution.
**Eligibility:** Applicant or parent must be member/participant of American Legion. Applicant must be high school sophomore, junior or senior. Applicant must be U.S. citizen or permanent resident residing in Arkansas.
**Basis for selection:** Competition/talent/interest in oratory/debate, based on language style, voice, diction, delivery, originality, logic, breadth of knowledge, application of knowledge about topic, and skill in selecting examples and analogies.
**Application requirements:** Proof of eligibility.
**Additional information:** Oratorical Contest, State Division: first place, $2,000; second place, $1,500; third place, $1,000. Must apply to local Post.

| | |
|---|---|
| **Amount of award:** | $1,000-$2,000 |
| **Number of awards:** | 3 |
| **Application deadline:** | December 1 |
| **Total amount awarded:** | $4,500 |

**Contact:**
American Legion Arkansas
Department Adjutant
P.O. Box 3280
Little Rock, AR 72203
Phone: 501-375-1104
Fax: 501-375-4236
Web: www.arklegion.homestead.com

## American Legion Arkansas Scholarship

**Type of award:** Scholarship.
**Intended use:** For undergraduate study at postsecondary institution.
**Eligibility:** Applicant or parent must be member/participant of American Legion. Applicant must be residing in Arkansas.
**Application requirements:** Proof of eligibility.
**Additional information:** Four scholarships: amount to be determined. Must be child, grandchild, or great-grandchild of American Legion member.

| | |
|---|---|
| **Number of awards:** | 4 |

**Contact:**
American Legion Arkansas
Department Adjutant
P.O. Box 3280
Little Rock, AR 72203
Phone: 501-375-1104
Fax: 501-375-4236
Web: www.arklegion.homestead.com

# American Legion Arkansas Auxiliary

## American Legion Arkansas Auxiliary Scholarships

**Type of award:** Scholarship.
**Intended use:** For undergraduate study at postsecondary institution.
**Eligibility:** Applicant or parent must be member/participant of American Legion Auxiliary. Applicant must be high school senior. Applicant must be U.S. citizen residing in Arkansas. Applicant must be descendant of veteran; or dependent of veteran during Grenada conflict, Korean War, Lebanon conflict, Panama conflict, Persian Gulf War, WW I, WW II or Vietnam.
**Basis for selection:** Applicant must demonstrate financial need, high academic achievement, depth of character, leadership and patriotism.
**Application requirements:** Recommendations, essay, transcript, proof of eligibility. SAT/ACT scores.
**Additional information:** Academic Scholarship: one $500; Nurse Scholarship: one $500. Awards paid half first semester, half second semester. Student must be Arkansas resident attending Arkansas school. Include name of high school and SASE with application request.

| | |
|---|---|
| **Amount of award:** | $500 |
| **Number of awards:** | 2 |
| **Application deadline:** | March 1 |
| **Total amount awarded:** | $1,000 |

**Contact:**
American Legion Auxiliary, Department of Arkansas
Department Secretary
1415 West 7th St.
Little Rock, AR 72201
Phone: 501-374-5836
Web: www.arklegion.homestead.com/ArkAux.html

# American Legion Auxiliary, Department of Illinois

## Americanism Essay Contest Scholarship

**Type of award:** Scholarship.
**Intended use:** For undergraduate study at postsecondary institution.
**Eligibility:** Applicant must be enrolled in high school. Applicant must be residing in Illinois.
**Application requirements:** 500-word essay on selected topic.
**Additional information:** Award amount depends on placement and grade level. Open to students grade 7-12 enrolled at accredited Illinois junior high and high schools or home schooled. Deadline is first Friday in February. Submit essay to local American Legion Post, Auxiliary Unit, or Sons of American Legion Squadron.

| | |
|---|---|
| **Amount of award:** | $100-$1,200 |

**Contact:**
American Legion Auxiliary, Department of Illinois
P.O. Box 1426
Bloomington, IL 61702-1426
Web: www.illegion.org

# American Legion Auxiliary, Department of Maryland

## Past President's Parley Scholarship

**Type of award:** Scholarship.
**Intended use:** For undergraduate study at 2-year or 4-year institution.
**Eligibility:** Applicant must be female, at least 16, no older than 22. Applicant must be residing in Maryland. Must be daughter/step-daughter, granddaughter/step-granddaughter, great-granddaughter/step-great-granddaughter of ex-servicewoman or ex-serviceman.
**Basis for selection:** Major/career interest in nursing. Applicant must demonstrate financial need.
**Application requirements:** Recommendations.
**Additional information:** For RN degree only.

| | |
|---|---|
| **Amount of award:** | $2,000 |
| **Number of awards:** | 1 |
| **Application deadline:** | May 1 |
| **Total amount awarded:** | $2,000 |

**Contact:**
American Legion Auxiliary, Department of Maryland
Chairman, Past President's Parley Scholarship
1589 Sulphur Spring Road, Suite 105
Baltimore, MD 21227
Phone: 410-242-9519
Fax: 410-242-9553
Web: www.alamd.org

# American Legion California

## American Legion California Oratorical Contest

**Type of award:** Scholarship.
**Intended use:** For undergraduate study at postsecondary institution.
**Eligibility:** Applicant must be enrolled in high school. Applicant must be U.S. citizen or permanent resident residing in California.
**Basis for selection:** Competition/talent/interest in oratory/debate, based on language style, voice, diction, delivery, originality, logic, breadth of knowledge, application of knowledge about topic, and skill in selecting examples and analogies.

**Additional information:** Students selected by schools to participate in district contests, followed by area and departmental finals. Awards: First place, $1,200; second place, $1,000; third to sixth place, $700 each. Contact local Post for entry.

**Amount of award:** $700-$1,200
**Number of awards:** 6
**Total amount awarded:** $5,000

**Contact:**
American Legion California
401 Van Ness Avenue, Room 117
San Francisco, CA 94102-4587
Phone: 415-431-2400
Fax: 415-255-1571
Web: www.calegion.org

# American Legion California Auxiliary

## American Legion California Auxiliary General Scholarships

**Type of award:** Scholarship.
**Intended use:** For freshman study at postsecondary institution. Designated institutions: California colleges and universities.
**Eligibility:** Applicant or parent must be member/participant of American Legion Auxiliary. Applicant must be residing in California. Applicant must be dependent of veteran.
**Basis for selection:** Applicant must demonstrate financial need.
**Application requirements:** Recommendations, transcript, proof of eligibility. Cover letter.
**Additional information:** $7,500 in scholarships at the National level can be applied for through the Department of CA. See Website for application. Applications must be submitted to local Unit.

**Total amount awarded:** $7,500

**Contact:**
American Legion Auxiliary, Department of California
War Memorial Building
401 Van Ness Avenue, Room 113
San Francisco, CA 94102-4586
Phone: 415-861-5092
Fax: 415-861-8365
Web: www.calegionaux.org

# American Legion Colorado

## National High School Oratorical Contest

**Type of award:** Scholarship.
**Intended use:** For undergraduate study at postsecondary institution.
**Eligibility:** Applicant must be enrolled in high school. Applicant must be residing in Colorado.
**Basis for selection:** Competition/talent/interest in oratory/debate, based on language style, voice, diction, delivery, originality, logic, breadth of knowledge, application of knowledge about topic, and skill in selecting examples and analogies.
**Additional information:** Awards: First place, $2,500; second place, $2,000; third place, $1,500. Apply at local Post.

**Amount of award:** $500-$2,500
**Number of awards:** 3
**Total amount awarded:** $10,500

**Contact:**
American Legion, Department of Colorado
7465 East First Avenue, Suite D
Denver, CO 80230
Web: www.coloradolegion.org

# American Legion Colorado Auxiliary

## Department President's Scholarship

**Type of award:** Scholarship.
**Intended use:** For undergraduate study at postsecondary institution.
**Eligibility:** Applicant or parent must be member/participant of American Legion Auxiliary. Applicant must be high school senior. Applicant must be residing in Colorado. Applicant must be dependent of veteran during Grenada conflict, Korean War, Lebanon conflict, Panama conflict, Persian Gulf War, WW I, WW II or Vietnam.
**Additional information:** One $1,000 award and two $500 awards.

**Amount of award:** $500-$1,000
**Number of awards:** 3
**Application deadline:** April 4
**Total amount awarded:** $2,000

**Contact:**
American Legion Auxiliary, Department of Colorado
7465 East First Avenue, Suite D
Denver, CO 80230

## Department President's Scholarship for Junior Auxiliary Members

**Type of award:** Scholarship.
**Intended use:** For undergraduate study at postsecondary institution.
**Eligibility:** Applicant or parent must be member/participant of American Legion Auxiliary. Applicant must be high school senior. Applicant must be residing in Colorado. Applicant must be Colorado Junior Auxiliary member.

**Amount of award:** $1,000
**Number of awards:** 1
**Application deadline:** March 12
**Total amount awarded:** $1,000

**Contact:**
American Legion Auxiliary, Department of Colorado
7465 East First Avenue, Suite D
Denver, CO 80230

## Past President's Parley Nurse's Scholarship

**Type of award:** Scholarship.
**Intended use:** For undergraduate study at accredited 2-year or 4-year institution.

**Eligibility:** Applicant or parent must be member/participant of American Legion Auxiliary. Applicant must be residing in Colorado. Applicant must be veteran; or dependent of veteran; or spouse of veteran during Grenada conflict, Korean War, Lebanon conflict, Panama conflict, Persian Gulf War, WW I, WW II or Vietnam.
**Basis for selection:** Major/career interest in nursing.
**Additional information:** Number and amount of awards vary.

| | |
|---|---|
| **Amount of award:** | $500-$1,000 |
| **Application deadline:** | April 15 |

**Contact:**
American Legion Auxiliary, Department of Colorado
7465 East First Avenue, Suite D
Denver, CO 80230

### Violet Morrow Education Scholarship

**Type of award:** Scholarship.
**Intended use:** For undergraduate study at postsecondary institution.
**Eligibility:** Applicant or parent must be member/participant of American Legion Auxiliary. Applicant must be high school senior. Applicant must be residing in Colorado.
**Additional information:** Applicant must be relative of veteran who served in Armed Forces. Applicant must be senior in high school or in the first four years of college.

| | |
|---|---|
| **Application deadline:** | March 11 |

**Contact:**
American Legion Auxiliary, Department Headquarters
7465 East 1st Ave
Suite D
Denver, CO 80230

## American Legion Connecticut

### National High School Oratorical Contest

**Type of award:** Scholarship.
**Intended use:** For undergraduate study at postsecondary institution.
**Eligibility:** Applicant must be no older than 19, enrolled in high school. Applicant must be residing in Connecticut.
**Basis for selection:** Competition/talent/interest in oratory/debate, based on language style, voice, diction, delivery, originality, logic, breadth of knowledge, application of knowledge about topic, and skill in selecting examples and analogies.
**Additional information:** Awards: First place, $3,000; second-$2,000; third to seventh place, $1,000; all in Savings Bonds. Contest open only to students attending Connecticut high schools. Contact high school for more information.

| | |
|---|---|
| **Amount of award:** | $1,000-$3,000 |
| **Number of awards:** | 7 |
| **Total amount awarded:** | $10,000 |

**Contact:**
American Legion, Department of Connecticut
Department Oratorical Chairman
P.O. Box 208
Rocky Hill, CT 06067-0208
Phone: 860-436-9986
Web: www.ct.legion.org

## American Legion Connecticut Auxiliary

### Memorial Education Grant

**Type of award:** Scholarship.
**Intended use:** For undergraduate study at vocational, 2-year or 4-year institution.
**Eligibility:** Applicant or parent must be member/participant of American Legion Auxiliary. Applicant must be at least 16, no older than 23.
**Basis for selection:** Applicant must demonstrate financial need.
**Application requirements:** Recommendations, essay, transcript, proof of eligibility.
**Additional information:** Half of grants awarded to child/grandchild of Connecticut AL/ALA member or to a member of Connecticut ALA/Sons of the AL. No residency requirement. Other half awarded to child of Connecticut resident veteran.

| | |
|---|---|
| **Amount of award:** | $500 |
| **Number of awards:** | 4 |
| **Application deadline:** | March 1 |
| **Total amount awarded:** | $2,000 |

**Contact:**
American Legion Auxiliary, Department of Connecticut
P.O. Box 266
Rocky Hill, CT 06067-0266
Phone: 860-721-5945
Fax: 860-721-5828
Web: www.ct.legion.org/auxiliary.htm

### Past President's Parley Education Grant

**Type of award:** Scholarship, renewable.
**Intended use:** For undergraduate study at vocational, 2-year or 4-year institution.
**Eligibility:** Applicant or parent must be member/participant of American Legion Auxiliary. Applicant must be at least 16, no older than 23.
**Basis for selection:** Applicant must demonstrate financial need.
**Application requirements:** Recommendations, essay, transcript, proof of eligibility.
**Additional information:** Preference given to child or grandchild of ex-servicewoman who is a CT American Legion or American Legion Auxiliary member of at least five years or who was a member for the five years prior to her death. Second preference to child or grandchild of CT American Legion, American Legion Auxiliary, or Sons of American Legion member of at least five years, or who was a member for five years prior to death.

| | |
|---|---|
| **Amount of award:** | $500 |
| **Number of awards:** | 4 |
| **Application deadline:** | March 1 |
| **Total amount awarded:** | $2,000 |

**Contact:**
American Legion Auxiliary, Department of Connecticut
P.O. Box 266
Rocky Hill, CT 06067-0266
Phone: 860-721-5945
Fax: 860-721-5828
Web: www.ct.legion.org/auxiliary.htm

# American Legion Delaware Auxiliary

## Past President's Parley Nursing Scholarship

**Type of award:** Scholarship.
**Intended use:** For undergraduate study at postsecondary institution.
**Eligibility:** Applicant or parent must be member/participant of American Legion Auxiliary. Applicant must be residing in Delaware. Applicant must be dependent of veteran.
**Basis for selection:** Major/career interest in nursing.

| | |
|---|---|
| **Amount of award:** | $300 |
| **Number of awards:** | 1 |
| **Application deadline:** | February 28 |
| **Total amount awarded:** | $300 |

**Contact:**
American Legion Auxiliary, Department of Delaware
Attn: Tina Washington
25109 Prettyman Rd.
Georgetown, DE 19947

# American Legion District of Columbia

## National High School Oratorical Contest

**Type of award:** Scholarship.
**Intended use:** For undergraduate study at postsecondary institution.
**Eligibility:** Applicant must be no older than 20, enrolled in high school. Applicant must be U.S. citizen or permanent resident residing in District of Columbia.
**Basis for selection:** Competition/talent/interest in oratory/debate, based on language style, voice, diction, delivery, originality, logic, breadth of knowledge, application of knowledge about topic, and skill in selecting examples and analogies.
**Application requirements:** Proof of eligibility.
**Additional information:** Awards: First place, $800; second place, $500; third place, $200; fourth place, $100. All awards in U.S. Savings Bonds.

| | |
|---|---|
| **Amount of award:** | $100-$800 |
| **Number of awards:** | 4 |
| **Total amount awarded:** | $1,600 |

**Contact:**
The American Legion, Department of DC
3408 Wisconsin Avenue NW, Suite 218
Washington, DC 20016
Phone: 202-362-9151
Fax: 202-362-9152
Web: www.legiondc.org

# American Legion Florida

## American Legion Florida General Scholarship

**Type of award:** Scholarship.
**Intended use:** For undergraduate study at accredited postsecondary institution in United States.
**Eligibility:** Applicant or parent must be member/participant of American Legion. Applicant must be high school senior. Applicant must be residing in Florida. Must be child, grandchild, great-grandchild, or legally adopted child of member in good standing of American Legion Florida, or of a deceased U.S. veteran who would have been eligible for membership.
**Application requirements:** Proof of eligibility.
**Additional information:** Scholarships: First place, $2,500; second place, $1,500; third place, $1,000; fourth to seventh place, $500. Student must be attending FL high school. Parents must be FL residents.

| | |
|---|---|
| **Amount of award:** | $500-$2,500 |
| **Number of awards:** | 7 |
| **Application deadline:** | March 1 |
| **Total amount awarded:** | $7,000 |

**Contact:**
American Legion Florida, Department Headquarters
P.O. Box 547859
Orlando, FL 32854-7859
Phone: 407-295-2631 ext. 222
Web: www.floridalegion.org

## Eagle Scout of the Year

**Type of award:** Scholarship.
**Intended use:** For undergraduate study at accredited postsecondary institution in United States.
**Eligibility:** Applicant or parent must be member/participant of American Legion. Applicant must be male, enrolled in high school. Applicant must be residing in Florida.
**Application requirements:** Proof of eligibility.
**Additional information:** Applicant must be registered, active member of Boy Scout Troop, Varsity Scout Team, or Venturing Crew chartered to an American Legion Post, Auxiliary Unit, or Sons of American Legion Squadron; or be a registered, active member of a Boy Scout Troop, Varsity Scout Team, or Venturing Crew and be a son or grandson of American Legion member. Awards: First place, $2,500; second place, $1,500; third place, $1,000; fourth place, $500. Must have earned Eagle Award and religious emblem.

| | |
|---|---|
| **Amount of award:** | $500-$2,500 |
| **Number of awards:** | 4 |
| **Application deadline:** | March 1 |
| **Total amount awarded:** | $5,500 |

**Contact:**
American Legion Florida, Department Headquarters
P.O. Box 547859
Orlando, FL 32854-7859
Phone: 407-295-2631 ext. 222
Web: www.floridalegion.org

### High School Oratorical Contest

**Type of award:** Scholarship.
**Intended use:** For undergraduate study at postsecondary institution.
**Eligibility:** Applicant must be enrolled in high school. Applicant must be residing in Florida.
**Basis for selection:** Competition/talent/interest in oratory/debate, based on language style, voice, diction, delivery, originality, logic, breadth of knowledge, application of knowledge about topic, and skill in selecting examples and analogies.
**Additional information:** Awards: First place, $2,500; second place, $1,500; third place, $1,000; fourth to sixth place, $500. Parents must be FL residents.

| | |
|---|---|
| **Amount of award:** | $500-$2,500 |
| **Number of awards:** | 6 |
| **Application deadline:** | December 1 |
| **Total amount awarded:** | $6,500 |

**Contact:**
American Legion Florida, Department Headquarters
P.O. Box 547859
Orlando, FL 32854-7859
Phone: 407-295-2631 ext. 222
Web: www.floridalegion.org

## American Legion Florida Auxiliary

### American Legion Florida Auxiliary Memorial Scholarship

**Type of award:** Scholarship, renewable.
**Intended use:** For full-time undergraduate study at vocational, 2-year or 4-year institution.
**Eligibility:** Applicant or parent must be member/participant of American Legion Auxiliary. Applicant must be residing in Florida. Must be members or daughter/granddaughter of member with at least three years' membership in FL unit.
**Application requirements:** Recommendations, essay, transcript, proof of eligibility. Income tax forms.
**Additional information:** Must be members or daughter/granddaughter of member with at least three years' membership in FL unit. Up to $1,000 for junior colleges and vocational schools; $2,000 for four-year university. Must maintain minimum 2.5 GPA.

| | |
|---|---|
| **Amount of award:** | $1,000-$2,000 |

**Contact:**
American Legion Auxiliary, Department of Florida
Department Secretary
P.O. Box 547917
Orlando, FL 32854-7917
Fax: 407-299-6522
Web: www.alafl.org

### American Legion Florida Auxiliary Scholarships

**Type of award:** Scholarship, renewable.
**Intended use:** For undergraduate study at vocational, 2-year or 4-year institution.
**Eligibility:** Applicant or parent must be member/participant of American Legion Auxiliary. Applicant must be residing in Florida. Must be child or stepchild of honorably discharged U.S. military veteran and sponsored by local Auxiliary Unit.
**Application requirements:** Recommendations, essay, transcript, proof of eligibility. Income tax forms.
**Additional information:** Up to $1000 for junior colleges and vocational schools; $2,000 for four-year university. Must maintain minimum 2.5 GPA. Send application request by January 1.

| | |
|---|---|
| **Amount of award:** | $1,000-$2,000 |

**Contact:**
American Legion Auxiliary, Department of Florida
Department Secretary
P.O. Box 547917
Orlando, FL 32854-7917
Fax: 407-299-6522
Web: www.alafl.org

## American Legion Georgia

### American Legion Georgia Scholarship

**Type of award:** Scholarship.
**Intended use:** For undergraduate study at postsecondary institution.
**Eligibility:** Applicant or parent must be member/participant of American Legion Auxiliary. Applicant must be high school senior. Applicant must be residing in Georgia. Applicant must be dependent of veteran or deceased veteran.

| | |
|---|---|
| **Amount of award:** | $1,000 |
| **Number of awards:** | 6 |
| **Total amount awarded:** | $6,000 |

**Contact:**
American Legion Georgia, Department Headquarters
3035 Mt. Zion Road
Stockbridge, GA 30281-4101
Web: www.galegion.org

### Oratorical Contest

**Type of award:** Scholarship.
**Eligibility:** Applicant or parent must be member/participant of American Legion. Applicant must be residing in Georgia.

| | |
|---|---|
| **Amount of award:** | $450-$1,300 |
| **Number of awards:** | 4 |

**Contact:**
American Legion, Department of Georgia
3035 Mt Zion Rd
Stockbridge, GA 30281-4101
Web: www.galegion.org

Scholarships

# American Legion Georgia Auxiliary

## Past President's Parley Nurses Scholarship

**Type of award:** Scholarship.
**Intended use:** For undergraduate study at 2-year or 4-year institution.
**Eligibility:** Applicant or parent must be member/participant of American Legion Auxiliary. Applicant must be residing in Georgia. Applicant must be dependent of veteran or deceased veteran. Must be sponsored by local Auxiliary Unit.
**Basis for selection:** Major/career interest in nursing.
**Application requirements:** Proof of eligibility.
**Additional information:** Amount and number of scholarships determined by available funds.

**Application deadline:** May 1

**Contact:**
American Legion Georgia Auxiliary, Department Headquarters
3035 Mt. Zion Road
Stockbridge, GA 30281-4101
Web: www.galegionaux.org

# American Legion Hawaii

## American Legion Oratorical Contest

**Type of award:** Scholarship.
**Intended use:** For undergraduate study at postsecondary institution.
**Eligibility:** Applicant must be enrolled in high school. Applicant must be residing in Hawaii.
**Basis for selection:** Competition/talent/interest in oratory/debate, based on language style, voice, diction, delivery, originality, logic, breadth of knowledge, application of knowledge about topic, and skill in selecting examples and analogies.
**Additional information:** Awards: first place, $1000; second place, $500; third place, $100; fourth place, $50. Contest normally held in February.

**Amount of award:** $50-$1,000
**Number of awards:** 4
**Total amount awarded:** $1,650

**Contact:**
American Legion Hawaii, Department Headquarters
612 McCully Street
Honolulu, HI 96826
Phone: 808-946-6383
Fax: 808-947-3957
Web: www.50legion.org

# American Legion Idaho

## American Legion Idaho Scholarships

**Type of award:** Scholarship.
**Intended use:** For undergraduate study at postsecondary institution.
**Eligibility:** Applicant or parent must be member/participant of American Legion. Applicant must be residing in Idaho.
**Application requirements:** Proof of eligibility.
**Additional information:** Grandchildren of American Legion members and children and grandchildren of American Legion Auxiliary members in Idaho also eligible. Scholarships determined annually. See Website for more information.

**Application deadline:** July 1

**Contact:**
American Legion Idaho, Department Headquarters
901 Warren Street
Boise, ID 83706
Phone: 208-342-7061
Fax: 208-342-1964
Web: idlegion.home.mindspring.com

## Oratorical Contest

**Type of award:** Scholarship.
**Intended use:** For undergraduate study at postsecondary institution.
**Eligibility:** Applicant must be enrolled in high school. Applicant must be residing in Idaho.
**Basis for selection:** Competition/talent/interest in oratory/debate, based on language style, voice, diction, delivery, originality, logic, breadth of knowledge, application of knowledge about topic, and skill in selecting examples and analogies.
**Additional information:** Awards: First place, $750; second place, $500; third place, $250; fourth place, $100. Visit Website for more information.

**Amount of award:** $100-$750
**Number of awards:** 4
**Total amount awarded:** $1,600

**Contact:**
American Legion Idaho, Department Headquarters
901 Warren Street
Boise, ID 83706
Phone: 208-342-7061
Fax: 208-342-1964
Web: idlegion.home.mindspring.com

# American Legion Idaho Auxiliary

## American Legion Idaho Auxiliary Nurse's Scholarship

**Type of award:** Scholarship.
**Intended use:** For undergraduate study at 2-year or 4-year institution.
**Eligibility:** Applicant must be residing in Idaho. Applicant must be veteran; or dependent of veteran.
**Basis for selection:** Major/career interest in nursing.
**Additional information:** Applicant must be Idaho resident five years prior to application. Grandchildren of veterans also eligible. Submit application to local Auxiliary Unit.

**Amount of award:** $1,000
**Application deadline:** May 15

**Contact:**
American Legion Idaho Auxiliary, Department Headquarters
905 Warren Street
Boise, ID 83706-3825
Phone: 208-342-7066
Fax: 208-342-7066

# American Legion Illinois

## American Legion Illinois Boy Scout Scholarship

**Type of award:** Scholarship.
**Intended use:** For undergraduate study at postsecondary institution.
**Eligibility:** Applicant or parent must be member/participant of Boy Scouts of America. Applicant must be high school senior. Applicant must be residing in Illinois.
**Basis for selection:** Competition/talent/interest in writing/journalism.
**Application requirements:** Proof of eligibility. 500-word essay on American Legion, Americanism, and Boy Scout programs.
**Additional information:** Boy Scout Scholarship: $700. Runner-up awards: $200. Contact American Legion Department of Illinois, Post, County, District, or Division for application.

| | |
|---|---|
| **Amount of award:** | $200-$700 |
| **Application deadline:** | April 30 |

**Contact:**
American Legion, Department of Illinois
c/o Boy Scout Committee
P.O. Box 2910
Bloomington, IL 61702-2910
Web: www.illegion.org

## American Legion Illinois Oratorical Contest

**Type of award:** Scholarship.
**Intended use:** For undergraduate study at vocational, 2-year or 4-year institution.
**Eligibility:** Applicant must be enrolled in high school. Applicant must be U.S. citizen or permanent resident residing in Illinois.
**Basis for selection:** Competition/talent/interest in oratory/debate, based on language style, voice, diction, delivery, originality, logic, breadth of knowledge, application of knowledge about topic, and skill in selecting examples and analogies.
**Application requirements:** Proof of eligibility.
**Additional information:** Contest begins in January and starts at Post level, continuing to District level, to Division level, to Department level, and ending in National Competition. Awards: First place, $2,000; second place, $1,500; third place, $1,200; fourth and fifth place, $1,000. Applicants who wish to compete will be divided into 5 groups. First place in each of the 5 groups will advance to Departmental final. Second place in each group will receive $400 cash; third place will receive $300 cash; fourth place will receive $200 cash; fifth and sixth place will receive $100 each. First place winner of Department will proceed to national competition. Applications available in the fall. Contact local Post or Department Headquarters.

| | |
|---|---|
| **Amount of award:** | $1,000-$2,000 |

**Contact:**
American Legion, Department of Illinois
P.O. Box 2910
Bloomington, IL 61702-2910
Web: www.illegion.org

## American Legion Illinois Scholarships

**Type of award:** Scholarship.
**Intended use:** For undergraduate study at accredited vocational, 2-year or 4-year institution.
**Eligibility:** Applicant or parent must be member/participant of American Legion. Applicant must be high school senior. Applicant must be residing in Illinois.
**Basis for selection:** Applicant must demonstrate financial need and high academic achievement.
**Application requirements:** Proof of eligibility.
**Additional information:** Grandchildren of American Legion members also eligible. Applications available after December 15.

| | |
|---|---|
| **Amount of award:** | $1,000 |
| **Number of awards:** | 20 |
| **Application deadline:** | March 15 |
| **Total amount awarded:** | $20,000 |

**Contact:**
American Legion, Department of Illinois
P.O. Box 2910
Bloomington, IL 61702
Phone: 309-663-0361
Web: www.illegion.org

# American Legion Illinois Auxiliary

## Ada Mucklestone Memorial Scholarship

**Type of award:** Scholarship.
**Intended use:** For undergraduate study at postsecondary institution.
**Eligibility:** Applicant must be high school senior. Applicant must be residing in Illinois. Applicant must be descendant of veteran; or dependent of veteran during Grenada conflict, Korean War, Lebanon conflict, Panama conflict, Persian Gulf War, WW I, WW II or Vietnam.
**Basis for selection:** Applicant must demonstrate financial need, high academic achievement, depth of character and leadership.
**Application requirements:** Recommendations, essay, transcript, proof of eligibility. Copy of parents' most recent federal income tax return.
**Additional information:** Must be a resident of Illinois or a member in good standing of The American Legion Family, Department of Illinois. Awards: First place, $1,200; second place, $1,000; several $800. Nursing majors not eligible. Unit sponsorship required. Contact local Unit for application.

| | |
|---|---|
| **Amount of award:** | $800-$1,200 |
| **Application deadline:** | March 15 |

**Contact:**
American Legion Auxiliary, Department of Illinois
P.O. Box 1426
Bloomington, IL 61702-1426
Phone: 309-663-9366
Web: www.illegion.org/auxiliary

## Marie Sheehe Trade School Scholarship

**Type of award:** Scholarship.
**Intended use:** For undergraduate study at vocational institution.
**Eligibility:** Applicant must be residing in Illinois. Applicant must be descendant of veteran; or dependent of veteran during Grenada conflict, Korean War, Lebanon conflict, Panama conflict, Persian Gulf War, WW I, WW II or Vietnam.
**Basis for selection:** Applicant must demonstrate financial need, high academic achievement, depth of character and leadership.
**Application requirements:** Recommendations, essay, transcript, proof of eligibility. Copy of parents' most recent federal income tax return.
**Additional information:** Must be Illinois resident or member in good standing of American Legion Family, Department of Illinois. Unit sponsorship required. Contact local Unit for application.

| | |
|---|---|
| **Amount of award:** | $800 |
| **Number of awards:** | 1 |
| **Application deadline:** | March 15 |
| **Total amount awarded:** | $800 |

**Contact:**
American Legion Auxiliary, Department of Illinois
P.O. Box 1426
Bloomington, IL 61702-1426
Phone: 309-663-9366
Web: www.illegion.org/auxiliary

## Mildred R. Knoles Opportunity Scholarship

**Type of award:** Scholarship.
**Intended use:** For sophomore, junior or senior study at postsecondary institution.
**Eligibility:** Applicant must be residing in Illinois. Applicant must be veteran or descendant of veteran; or dependent of veteran during Grenada conflict, Korean War, Lebanon conflict, Panama conflict, Persian Gulf War, WW I, WW II or Vietnam.
**Basis for selection:** Applicant must demonstrate financial need, high academic achievement, depth of character and leadership.
**Application requirements:** Recommendations, essay, transcript, proof of eligibility. Copy of most recent federal income tax return.
**Additional information:** Must be resident of Illinois or member in good standing of the American Legion Family, Department of Illinois. Awards: one $1,200; several $800. Unit sponsorship required. Contact local Unit for application.

| | |
|---|---|
| **Amount of award:** | $800-$1,200 |
| **Application deadline:** | March 15 |

**Contact:**
American Legion Auxiliary, Department of Illinois
P.O. Box 1426
Bloomington, IL 61702-1426
Phone: 309-663-9366
Web: www.illegion.org/auxiliary

## Special Education Teaching Scholarships

**Type of award:** Scholarship.
**Intended use:** For sophomore or junior study at 4-year institution.
**Eligibility:** Applicant must be residing in Illinois. Applicant must be veteran or descendant of veteran; or dependent of veteran during Grenada conflict, Korean War, Lebanon conflict, Panama conflict, Persian Gulf War, WW I, WW II or Vietnam.
**Basis for selection:** Major/career interest in education, special. Applicant must demonstrate financial need.
**Application requirements:** Proof of eligibility.
**Additional information:** Unit sponsorship required. Contact local Unit for application.

| | |
|---|---|
| **Amount of award:** | $1,000 |
| **Application deadline:** | March 15 |
| **Total amount awarded:** | $1,000 |

**Contact:**
American Legion Auxiliary, Department of Illinois
P.O. Box 1426
Bloomington, IL 61702-1426
Phone: 309-663-9366
Web: www.illegion.org/auxiliary

## Student Nurse Scholarship

**Type of award:** Scholarship.
**Intended use:** For undergraduate study at 2-year or 4-year institution.
**Eligibility:** Applicant must be residing in Illinois.
**Basis for selection:** Major/career interest in nursing.
**Application requirements:** Proof of eligibility.
**Additional information:** Unit sponsorship required. Contact local Unit for application.

| | |
|---|---|
| **Amount of award:** | $1,000 |
| **Number of awards:** | 1 |
| **Application deadline:** | April 10 |
| **Total amount awarded:** | $1,000 |

**Contact:**
American Legion Auxiliary, Department of Illinois
P.O. Box 1426
Bloomington, IL 61702-1426
Phone: 309-663-9366
Web: www.illegion.org/auxiliary

# American Legion Indiana

## American Legion Americanism and Government Test

**Type of award:** Scholarship.
**Intended use:** For undergraduate study at postsecondary institution.
**Eligibility:** Applicant must be high school sophomore, junior or senior. Applicant must be residing in Indiana.
**Additional information:** Six state winners chosen annually (one male, one female in each grade). Test given during American Education Week in November. Visit Website for local chairperson's contact information.

| | |
|---|---|
| **Amount of award:** | $1,000 |
| **Number of awards:** | 6 |
| **Total amount awarded:** | $6,000 |

**Contact:**
American Legion Indiana, Department Headquarters
Americanism Office
777 North Meridian Street
Indianapolis, IN 46204
Phone: 317-630-1264
Web: www.indlegion.org

### American Legion Family Scholarship

**Type of award:** Scholarship.
**Intended use:** For undergraduate study at accredited vocational, 2-year or 4-year institution in United States.
**Eligibility:** Applicant or parent must be member/participant of American Legion. Applicant must be residing in Indiana. Applicant must be child or grandchild of current or deceased member of The American Legion Indiana, American Legion Indiana Auxiliary, or Sons of The American Legion.
**Application requirements:** Essay, transcript, proof of eligibility.
**Additional information:** Three awards of approximately $700-$1,000 each.

| | |
|---|---|
| **Amount of award:** | $700-$1,000 |
| **Number of awards:** | 3 |
| **Application deadline:** | April 1 |

**Contact:**
American Legion Indiana, Department Headquarters
Americanism Office
777 North Meridian Street
Indianapolis, IN 46204
Phone: 317-630-1264
Web: www.indlegion.org

### American Legion Indiana Oratorical Contest

**Type of award:** Scholarship.
**Intended use:** For undergraduate study at postsecondary institution.
**Eligibility:** Applicant must be enrolled in high school. Applicant must be residing in Indiana.
**Basis for selection:** Competition/talent/interest in oratory/debate, based on language style, voice, diction, delivery, originality, logic, breadth of knowledge, application of knowledge about topic, and skill in selecting examples and analogies.
**Application requirements:** Proof of eligibility.
**Additional information:** State awards: First place, $3,400; second to fourth place, $1,000. Zone awards: four winners receive $800 each; 7 participants receive $200 each. Must participate in local contests.

| | |
|---|---|
| **Amount of award:** | $200-$3,400 |
| **Number of awards:** | 15 |
| **Application deadline:** | December 1 |
| **Total amount awarded:** | $11,000 |

**Contact:**
American Legion Indiana, Department Headquarters
Americanism Office
777 North Meridian Street
Indianapolis, IN 46204
Phone: 317-630-1264
Web: www.indlegion.org

### Eagle Scout of the Year Scholarship

**Type of award:** Scholarship.
**Intended use:** For at postsecondary institution.
**Eligibility:** Applicant or parent must be member/participant of American Legion. Applicant must be residing in Indiana.
**Additional information:** Eagle Scout of the Year winner from IN submitted to the National Organization. Indiana awards the state winner a $1,000 scholarship and district winners receive a $200 scholarship. Applicant must attend U.S. postsecondary education institution for advance education beyond high school. Check website for details.

| | |
|---|---|
| **Amount of award:** | $200-$1,000 |
| **Application deadline:** | March 1 |

**Contact:**
Web: www.indlegion.org

## American Legion Indiana Auxiliary

### Edna M. Barcus Memorial Scholarship and Hoosier Scholarship

**Type of award:** Scholarship.
**Intended use:** For undergraduate study at postsecondary institution. Designated institutions: Indiana institutions.
**Eligibility:** Applicant or parent must be member/participant of American Legion Auxiliary. Applicant must be residing in Indiana. Applicant must be dependent of veteran.
**Basis for selection:** Applicant must demonstrate high academic achievement.
**Application requirements:** Send SASE for application.

| | |
|---|---|
| **Amount of award:** | $500 |
| **Application deadline:** | April 1 |

**Contact:**
American Legion Auxiliary, Department of Indiana
Department Secretary
777 North Meridian Street, Room 107
Indianapolis, IN 46204
Phone: 317-630-1390
Fax: 317-630-1277
Web: www.amlegauxin.org

### Past President's Parley Nursing Scholarship

**Type of award:** Scholarship.
**Intended use:** For undergraduate study.
**Eligibility:** Applicant or parent must be member/participant of American Legion Auxiliary. Applicant must be female. Applicant must be residing in Indiana.
**Basis for selection:** Major/career interest in nursing.
**Application requirements:** Send SASE for application.

| | |
|---|---|
| **Amount of award:** | $500 |
| **Application deadline:** | April 1 |
| **Total amount awarded:** | $500 |

**Contact:**
American Legion Auxiliary, Department of Indiana
Department Secretary
777 North Meridian Street, Room 107
Indianapolis, IN 46204
Phone: 317-630-1390
Fax: 317-630-1277
Web: www.amlegauxin.org

# American Legion Iowa

## American Legion Iowa Oratorical Contest

**Type of award:** Scholarship.
**Intended use:** For undergraduate study at postsecondary institution.
**Eligibility:** Applicant must be enrolled in high school. Applicant must be U.S. citizen or permanent resident residing in Iowa.
**Basis for selection:** Competition/talent/interest in oratory/debate, based on language style, voice, diction, delivery, originality, logic, breadth of knowledge, application of knowledge about topic, and skill in selecting examples and analogies.
**Application requirements:** Proof of eligibility.
**Additional information:** Awards: First place, $2,000; second place, $1,500; third place, $1000. Must enter Oratorical Contest at local level in September.

| | |
|---|---|
| **Amount of award:** | $1,000-$2,000 |
| **Number of awards:** | 3 |
| **Total amount awarded:** | $4,500 |

**Contact:**
American Legion Iowa, Department Headquarters
720 Lyon Street
Des Moines, IA 50309
Phone: 515-282-5068
Fax: 515-282-7583
Web: www.ialegion.org

## Boy Scout of the Year Scholarship

**Type of award:** Scholarship.
**Intended use:** For undergraduate study at postsecondary institution.
**Eligibility:** Applicant or parent must be member/participant of Boy Scouts of America, Eagle Scouts. Applicant must be male, at least 15. Applicant must be residing in Iowa.
**Basis for selection:** Applicant must demonstrate service orientation.
**Application requirements:** Recommendations, transcript, proof of eligibility.
**Additional information:** Must be registered, active member of Boy Scout Troop, Varsity Scout Team, or Venturing Crew chartered to American Legion Post, Auxiliary Unit, or Sons of American Legion Squadron; or be a registered, active member of Boy Scout Troop, Varsity Scout Team, or Venturing Crew and the son or grandson of an American Legion or Sons of American Legion member. Awards: First place, $2,000; second place, $1,500; third place, $1,000. Awarded on recommendation of Boy Scout Committee to Boy Scout who demonstrates outstanding service to religious institution, school, and community. Must have received Eagle Scout Award.

| | |
|---|---|
| **Amount of award:** | $1,000-$2,000 |
| **Number of awards:** | 3 |
| **Application deadline:** | February 1 |
| **Total amount awarded:** | $4,500 |

**Contact:**
American Legion Iowa, Department Headquarters
720 Lyon Street
Des Moines, IA 50309
Phone: 515-282-5068
Fax: 515-282-7583
Web: www.ialegion.org

# American Legion Iowa Auxiliary

## Department of Iowa Scholarships

**Type of award:** Scholarship.
**Intended use:** For undergraduate study at postsecondary institution. Designated institutions: Eligible Iowa postsecondary institutions.
**Eligibility:** Applicant must be residing in Iowa. Applicant must be veteran or descendant of veteran; or dependent of veteran or deceased veteran; or spouse of veteran or deceased veteran.
**Application requirements:** Recommendations, essay, transcript, proof of eligibility. Photo of self.

| | |
|---|---|
| **Amount of award:** | $300 |
| **Number of awards:** | 10 |
| **Application deadline:** | June 1 |
| **Total amount awarded:** | $3,000 |

**Contact:**
American Legion Auxiliary, Department of Iowa
Attn: Marlene Valentine
720 Lyon Street
Des Moines, IA 50309
Phone: 515-282-7987
Fax: 515-282-7583
Web: www.ialegion.org/ala

## Harriet Hoffman Memorial Scholarship

**Type of award:** Scholarship.
**Intended use:** For undergraduate study at postsecondary institution. Designated institutions: Eligible Iowa postsecondary institutions.
**Eligibility:** Applicant must be residing in Iowa. Applicant must be veteran or descendant of veteran; or dependent of veteran or deceased veteran; or spouse of veteran or deceased veteran.
**Basis for selection:** Major/career interest in education or education, teacher.
**Application requirements:** Recommendations, essay, transcript, proof of eligibility. Photo of self.

| | |
|---|---|
| **Amount of award:** | $400 |
| **Number of awards:** | 1 |
| **Application deadline:** | June 1 |
| **Total amount awarded:** | $400 |

**Contact:**
American Legion Auxiliary, Department of Iowa
Attn: Marlene Valentine
720 Lyon Street
Des Moines, IA 50309
Phone: 515-282-7987
Fax: 515-282-7583
Web: www.ialegion.org/ala

### Mary Virginia Macrea Memorial Scholarship

**Type of award:** Scholarship.
**Intended use:** For undergraduate study at postsecondary institution. Designated institutions: Eligible Iowa postsecondary institutions.
**Eligibility:** Applicant must be residing in Iowa. Applicant must be veteran or descendant of veteran; or dependent of veteran or deceased veteran; or spouse of veteran or deceased veteran.
**Basis for selection:** Major/career interest in nursing.
**Application requirements:** Recommendations, essay, transcript, proof of eligibility. Photo of self.

| | |
|---|---|
| **Amount of award:** | $400 |
| **Number of awards:** | 1 |
| **Application deadline:** | June 1 |
| **Total amount awarded:** | $400 |

**Contact:**
American Legion Auxiliary, Department of Iowa
Attn: Marlene Valentine
720 Lyon Street
Des Moines, IA 50309
Phone: 515-282-7987
Fax: 515-282-7583
Web: www.ialegion.org/ala

### Past President's Scholarship

**Type of award:** Scholarship.
**Intended use:** For undergraduate study at postsecondary institution.
**Eligibility:** Applicant must be residing in Iowa. Applicant must be veteran or descendant of veteran; or dependent of veteran or deceased veteran; or spouse of veteran or deceased veteran.
**Application requirements:** Recommendations, essay, transcript, proof of eligibility. Photo of self.
**Additional information:** Amount of award varies.

| | |
|---|---|
| **Application deadline:** | June 1 |

**Contact:**
American Legion Iowa Auxiliary
Attn: Marlene Valentine
720 Lyon Street
Des Moines, IA 50309
Phone: 515-282-7987
Fax: 515-282-7583
Web: www.ialegion.org/ala

## American Legion Kansas

### Albert M. Lappin Scholarship

**Type of award:** Scholarship.
**Intended use:** For freshman or sophomore study at accredited vocational, 2-year or 4-year institution. Designated institutions: Eligible colleges, universities, and trade schools in Kansas.
**Eligibility:** Applicant or parent must be member/participant of American Legion. Applicant must be high school senior. Applicant must be residing in Kansas.
**Application requirements:** Recommendations, essay, transcript, proof of eligibility. Income tax forms. Photo of self.
**Additional information:** Must be child of member of American Legion Kansas or American Legion Kansas Auxiliary whose parent has been a member for the past three years; or be a child of deceased member of either organization whose dues were paid-up at time of death.

| | |
|---|---|
| **Amount of award:** | $1,000 |
| **Number of awards:** | 1 |
| **Application deadline:** | February 15 |
| **Total amount awarded:** | $1,000 |

**Contact:**
American Legion Kansas
1314 Southwest Topeka Boulevard
Topeka, KS 66612-1886
Phone: 785-232-9315
Web: www.ksamlegion.org

### American Legion Music Scholarship

**Type of award:** Scholarship.
**Intended use:** For freshman or sophomore study at accredited vocational, 2-year or 4-year institution. Designated institutions: Eligible Kansas colleges and universities.
**Eligibility:** Applicant must be high school senior. Applicant must be residing in Kansas.
**Basis for selection:** Major/career interest in music. Applicant must demonstrate financial need.
**Application requirements:** Recommendations, transcript, proof of eligibility. Income tax forms. Photo of self.

| | |
|---|---|
| **Amount of award:** | $1,000 |
| **Number of awards:** | 1 |
| **Total amount awarded:** | $1,000 |

**Contact:**
American Legion Kansas
1314 Southwest Topeka Boulevard
Topeka, KS 66612-1886
Phone: 785-232-9315
Web: www.ksamlegion.org

### American Legion Oratorical Contest

**Type of award:** Scholarship.
**Intended use:** For undergraduate study at postsecondary institution.
**Eligibility:** Applicant must be enrolled in high school. Applicant must be residing in Kansas.
**Basis for selection:** Competition/talent/interest in oratory/debate, based on language style, voice, diction, delivery, originality, logic, breadth of knowledge, application of knowledge about topic, and skill in selecting examples and analogies.
**Additional information:** Awards: First place prize of $1,500 provided by National Organization; second place, $500; third place, $250, fourth place, $150. Additional awards: $1,500 first place award provided by Emporia State University Foundation; second place, $500; third place, $250; fourth place, $150 (renewable up to 4 years; must qualify for admission and attend Emporia State University).

| | |
|---|---|
| **Amount of award:** | $150-$1,500 |

Scholarships

**Contact:**
American Legion Kansas
1314 Southwest Topeka Boulevard
Topeka, KS 66612-1886
Phone: 785-232-9315
Web: www.ksamlegion.org

## Charles and Annette Hill Scholarship

**Type of award:** Scholarship.
**Intended use:** For freshman, sophomore or junior study at postsecondary institution.
**Eligibility:** Applicant or parent must be member/participant of American Legion. Applicant must be residing in Kansas. Must be descendent of member of American Legion Kansas who has been a member for the past three years; or be descendent of deceased member whose dues were paid-up at time of death.
**Basis for selection:** Major/career interest in science, general; engineering or business/management/administration. Applicant must demonstrate high academic achievement.
**Application requirements:** Recommendations, essay, transcript, proof of eligibility. Income tax forms. Photo of self.
**Additional information:** Minimum 3.0 GPA.

| | |
|---|---|
| **Amount of award:** | $1,000 |
| **Number of awards:** | 1 |
| **Application deadline:** | February 15 |
| **Total amount awarded:** | $1,000 |

**Contact:**
American Legion Kansas
1314 Southwest Topeka Blvd.
Topeka, KS 66612-1886
Phone: 785-232-9315
Web: www.ksamlegion.org

## Dr. Click Cowger Scholarship

**Type of award:** Scholarship.
**Intended use:** For freshman or sophomore study at accredited vocational, 2-year or 4-year institution. Designated institutions: Eligible Kansas colleges, universities, and trade schools.
**Eligibility:** Applicant must be male, high school senior. Applicant must be residing in Kansas.
**Basis for selection:** Competition/talent/interest in athletics/ sports.
**Application requirements:** Recommendations, essay, transcript, proof of eligibility. Income tax forms.
**Additional information:** For current players or those who have played in Kansas American Legion Baseball.

| | |
|---|---|
| **Amount of award:** | $500 |
| **Number of awards:** | 1 |
| **Application deadline:** | July 15 |
| **Total amount awarded:** | $500 |

**Contact:**
American Legion Kansas
1314 Southwest Topeka Boulevard
Topeka, KS 66612-1886
Phone: 785-232-9315
Web: www.ksamlegion.org

## Hugh A. Smith Scholarship

**Type of award:** Scholarship.
**Intended use:** For freshman or sophomore study at accredited vocational, 2-year or 4-year institution. Designated institutions: Eligible Kansas colleges, universities, and trade schools.
**Eligibility:** Applicant or parent must be member/participant of American Legion. Applicant must be high school senior. Applicant must be residing in Kansas. Applicant must be dependent of veteran or deceased veteran.
**Application requirements:** Recommendations, essay, transcript, proof of eligibility. Income tax forms. Photo of self.
**Additional information:** Must be child of member of American Legion Kansas or American Legion Kansas Auxiliary whose parent has been a member for the past three years; or be a child of deceased member of either organization whose dues were paid-up at time of death.

| | |
|---|---|
| **Amount of award:** | $500 |
| **Number of awards:** | 1 |
| **Application deadline:** | February 15 |
| **Total amount awarded:** | $500 |

**Contact:**
American Legion Kansas
1314 Southwest Topeka Boulevard
Topeka, KS 66612-1886
Phone: 785-232-9315
Web: www.ksamlegion.org

## John and Geraldine Hobble Licensed Practical Nursing Scholarship

**Type of award:** Scholarship.
**Intended use:** For freshman study at accredited postsecondary institution. Designated institutions: Kansas accredited schools that award LPN diplomas.
**Eligibility:** Applicant must be at least 18. Applicant must be residing in Kansas.
**Basis for selection:** Major/career interest in nursing. Applicant must demonstrate financial need.
**Application requirements:** Proof of eligibility.

| | |
|---|---|
| **Amount of award:** | $300 |
| **Number of awards:** | 1 |
| **Application deadline:** | February 15 |
| **Total amount awarded:** | $300 |

**Contact:**
American Legion Kansas
1314 Southwest Topeka Boulevard
Topeka, KS 66612-1886
Phone: 785-232-9315
Web: www.ksamlegion.org

## Rosedale Post 346 Scholarship

**Type of award:** Scholarship.
**Intended use:** For freshman or sophomore study at vocational, 2-year or 4-year institution.
**Eligibility:** Applicant or parent must be member/participant of American Legion. Applicant must be high school senior. Applicant must be residing in Kansas. Applicant must be dependent of veteran or deceased veteran. Must be child of member of American Legion Kansas or American Legion Kansas Auxiliary whose parent has been a member for the past three years; or be a child of deceased member of either organization whose dues were paid-up at time of death.
**Application requirements:** Recommendations, essay, transcript, proof of eligibility. Income tax forms. Photo of self.

| | |
|---|---|
| **Amount of award:** | $1,500 |
| **Number of awards:** | 2 |
| **Application deadline:** | February 15 |
| **Total amount awarded:** | $3,000 |

**Contact:**
American Legion Kansas
1314 Southwest Topeka Blvd.
Topeka, KS 66612-1886
Phone: 785-232-9315
Web: www.ksamlegion.org

### Ted and Nora Anderson Scholarship

**Type of award:** Scholarship.
**Intended use:** For freshman or sophomore study at accredited vocational, 2-year or 4-year institution. Designated institutions: Eligible colleges, universities, and trade schools in Kansas.
**Eligibility:** Applicant or parent must be member/participant of American Legion. Applicant must be high school senior. Applicant must be residing in Kansas. Applicant must be dependent of veteran or deceased veteran. Must be child of member of American Legion Kansas or American Legion Kansas Auxiliary whose parent has been a member for the past three years; or be a child of deceased member of either organization whose dues were paid-up at time of death.
**Application requirements:** Recommendations, essay, transcript, proof of eligibility. Photo of self.

| | |
|---|---|
| **Amount of award:** | $500 |
| **Number of awards:** | 4 |
| **Application deadline:** | February 15 |
| **Total amount awarded:** | $2,000 |

**Contact:**
American Legion Kansas
1314 Southwest Topeka Boulevard
Topeka, KS 66612-1886
Phone: 785-232-9315
Web: www.ksamlegion.org

## American Legion Kansas Auxiliary

### American Legion Kansas Auxiliary Department Scholarships

**Type of award:** Scholarship.
**Intended use:** For freshman study at postsecondary institution. Designated institutions: Kansas institutions.
**Eligibility:** Applicant must be residing in Kansas. Applicant must be dependent of veteran; or spouse of veteran or deceased veteran.
**Additional information:** Eight 2-year scholarships of $500, payable at $250 per year for two years. Applicants must be entering college for the first time. Spouses of deceased veterans must not be remarried.

| | |
|---|---|
| **Amount of award:** | $500 |
| **Number of awards:** | 8 |
| **Application deadline:** | April 1 |
| **Total amount awarded:** | $4,000 |

**Contact:**
American Legion Kansas Auxiliary
Department Secretary
1314 Southwest Topeka Boulevard
Topeka, KS 66612-1886
Phone: 785-232-1396
Web: www.kslegionaux.org

## American Legion Kentucky

### American Legion Department Oratorical Awards

**Type of award:** Scholarship.
**Intended use:** For undergraduate study at postsecondary institution.
**Eligibility:** Applicant must be enrolled in high school. Applicant must be residing in Kentucky.
**Basis for selection:** Competition/talent/interest in oratory/debate, based on language style, voice, diction, delivery, originality, logic, breadth of knowledge, application of knowledge about topic, and skill in selecting examples and analogies.
**Additional information:** Awards: First place, $1,000; second place, $800; third place, $600; and 11 $100 awards for District winners. Must be Kentucky Department Oratorical Contest participant.

| | |
|---|---|
| **Amount of award:** | $100-$1,000 |
| **Number of awards:** | 14 |
| **Total amount awarded:** | $3,500 |

**Contact:**
American Legion Kentucky, Department Headquarters
P.O. Box 2123
Louisville, KY 40201
Phone: 502-587-1414
Fax: 502-587-6356
Web: www.kylegion.org

## American Legion Kentucky Auxiliary

### American Legion Kentucky Auxiliary Mary Barrett Marshall Scholarship

**Type of award:** Scholarship.
**Intended use:** For undergraduate study at vocational, 2-year or 4-year institution. Designated institutions: Eligible postsecondary institutions in Kentucky.
**Eligibility:** Applicant or parent must be member/participant of American Legion Auxiliary. Applicant must be female. Applicant must be residing in Kentucky. Applicant must be descendant of veteran; or dependent of veteran; or spouse of veteran or deceased veteran during Grenada conflict, Korean War, Lebanon conflict, Panama conflict, Persian Gulf War, WW I, WW II or Vietnam.
**Application requirements:** Proof of eligibility. SASE.

| | |
|---|---|
| **Amount of award:** | $1,000 |
| **Number of awards:** | 1 |
| **Application deadline:** | April 1 |
| **Total amount awarded:** | $1,000 |

**Contact:**
American Legion Auxiliary, Department of Kentucky
Chairman Lois Smith
812 Madison Street
Rockport, IN 47635
Phone: 812-649-2163
Web: www.kyamlegionaux.org

Scholarships

## Laura Blackburn Memorial Scholarship

**Type of award:** Scholarship.
**Intended use:** For undergraduate study at postsecondary institution.
**Eligibility:** Applicant or parent must be member/participant of American Legion Auxiliary. Applicant must be high school senior. Applicant must be residing in Kentucky. Applicant must be descendant of veteran; or dependent of veteran during Grenada conflict, Korean War, Lebanon conflict, Panama conflict, Persian Gulf War, WW I, WW II or Vietnam.
**Application requirements:** Proof of eligibility.

| | |
|---|---|
| **Amount of award:** | $1,000 |
| **Number of awards:** | 1 |
| **Application deadline:** | March 31 |
| **Total amount awarded:** | $1,000 |

**Contact:**
American Legion Auxiliary, Department of Kentucky
Attn: Artie Eakins
3649 Rockhouse Road
Robards, KY 42452
Phone: 270-521-7183
Web: www.kyamlegionaux.org

# American Legion Maine

## Children and Youth Scholarships

**Type of award:** Scholarship.
**Intended use:** For undergraduate study at accredited postsecondary institution.
**Eligibility:** Applicant or parent must be member/participant of American Legion. Applicant must be high school senior. Applicant must be residing in Maine.
**Basis for selection:** Applicant must demonstrate financial need and depth of character.
**Application requirements:** Recommendations, transcript.
**Additional information:** High school seniors, college students, and veterans eligible. Students with GED may also apply.

| | |
|---|---|
| **Amount of award:** | $500 |
| **Number of awards:** | 7 |
| **Number of applicants:** | 300 |
| **Application deadline:** | May 1 |
| **Total amount awarded:** | $3,500 |

**Contact:**
American Legion Maine
Department Adjutant, State Headquarters
P.O. Box 900
Waterville, ME 04903-0900
Phone: 207-873-3229
Fax: 207-872-0501
Web: www.mainelegion.org

## Daniel E. Lambert Memorial Scholarship

**Type of award:** Scholarship.
**Intended use:** For undergraduate study at accredited vocational, 2-year or 4-year institution.
**Eligibility:** Applicant must be high school senior. Applicant must be U.S. citizen residing in Maine. Applicant must be descendant of veteran; or dependent of veteran.
**Basis for selection:** Applicant must demonstrate financial need and depth of character.
**Application requirements:** Recommendations, proof of eligibility.
**Additional information:** Must be child or grandchild of veteran.

| | |
|---|---|
| **Amount of award:** | $1,000 |
| **Number of awards:** | 1 |
| **Application deadline:** | May 1 |
| **Total amount awarded:** | $1,000 |

**Contact:**
American Legion Maine
Department Adjutant, State Headquarters
P.O. Box 900
Waterville, ME 04903-0900
Phone: 207-873-3229
Fax: 207-872-0501
Web: www.mainelegion.org

## James V. Day Scholarship

**Type of award:** Scholarship.
**Intended use:** For undergraduate study at vocational, 2-year or 4-year institution.
**Eligibility:** Applicant or parent must be member/participant of American Legion. Applicant must be high school senior. Applicant must be U.S. citizen residing in Maine.
**Basis for selection:** Applicant must demonstrate financial need, high academic achievement and depth of character.
**Application requirements:** Recommendations, essay, proof of eligibility.
**Additional information:** Must be in top half of graduating class. Grandchildren of current American Legion Post in Maine also eligible.

| | |
|---|---|
| **Amount of award:** | $500 |
| **Number of awards:** | 2 |
| **Application deadline:** | May 1 |
| **Total amount awarded:** | $1,000 |

**Contact:**
American Legion Maine
Department Adjutant, State Headquarters
P.O. Box 900
Waterville, ME 04903-0900
Phone: 207-873-3229
Fax: 207-872-0501
Web: www.mainelegion.org

# American Legion Maine Auxiliary

## American Legion Maine Auxiliary Scholarship

**Type of award:** Scholarship.
**Intended use:** For undergraduate study at vocational, 2-year or 4-year institution.
**Eligibility:** Applicant must be high school senior. Applicant must be residing in Maine. Applicant must be dependent of veteran.
**Basis for selection:** Applicant must demonstrate financial need.
**Application requirements:** Send SASE with application request.

**Amount of award:** $300
**Number of awards:** 2
**Application deadline:** April 5
**Total amount awarded:** $600

**Contact:**
American Legion Auxiliary, Department of Maine
Department Secretary
886B Kennedy Memorial Drive
Oakland, ME 04963

### President's Parley Nursing Scholarship

**Type of award:** Scholarship.
**Intended use:** For undergraduate study.
**Eligibility:** Applicant must be residing in Maine. Applicant must be descendant of veteran; or dependent of veteran during WW I or WW II.
**Basis for selection:** Major/career interest in nursing.
**Application requirements:** Proof of eligibility.
**Additional information:** Must be graduate of accredited high school.

**Amount of award:** $300
**Number of awards:** 1
**Total amount awarded:** $300

**Contact:**
American Legion Auxiliary, Department of Maine
Department Secretary
886B Kennedy Memorial Drive
Oakland, ME 04963

## American Legion Maryland

### Adler Science and Math Scholarship

**Type of award:** Scholarship.
**Intended use:** For undergraduate study at postsecondary institution.
**Eligibility:** Applicant must be at least 16, no older than 19. Applicant must be residing in Maryland. Applicant must be dependent of veteran.
**Basis for selection:** Major/career interest in science, general or mathematics.
**Application requirements:** Transcript.

**Amount of award:** $500
**Number of awards:** 1
**Total amount awarded:** $500

**Contact:**
American Legion Maryland
Attn: Department Adjutant
The War Memorial Building, 101 N Gay St.
Baltimore, MD 21202
Phone: 410-752-1405
Web: www.mdlegion.org

### American Legion Maryland Boys State Scholarship

**Type of award:** Scholarship.
**Intended use:** For undergraduate study at postsecondary institution.
**Eligibility:** Applicant or parent must be member/participant of American Legion, Boys State. Applicant must be male, at least 16, no older than 19. Applicant must be residing in Maryland.
**Additional information:** Applicant must be Maryland Boys State graduate.

**Amount of award:** $500
**Number of awards:** 5
**Application deadline:** May 1
**Total amount awarded:** $2,500

**Contact:**
American Legion Maryland
Attn: Department Adjutant
The War Memorial Building, 101 N Gay St.
Baltimore, MD 21202-1405
Phone: 410-752-1405
Web: www.mdlegion.org

### American Legion Maryland Oratorical Contest

**Type of award:** Scholarship.
**Intended use:** For undergraduate study at postsecondary institution.
**Eligibility:** Applicant must be at least 16, no older than 19. Applicant must be U.S. citizen or permanent resident residing in Maryland.
**Basis for selection:** Competition/talent/interest in oratory/debate, based on language style, voice, diction, delivery, originality, logic, breadth of knowledge, application of knowledge about topic, and skill in selecting examples and analogies.
**Additional information:** Awards: First place, $2,500; second place, $1,000; third through seventh place, $500 each. Must be an American Legion Oratorical Contest Department winner. Apply to nearest American Legion Post.

**Amount of award:** $500-$2,500
**Number of awards:** 7
**Application deadline:** October 1
**Total amount awarded:** $6,000

**Contact:**
American Legion Maryland
Attn: Department Adjutant
The War Memorial Building, 101 N Gay St.
Baltimore, MD 21202-1405
Phone: 410-752-1405
Web: www.mdlegion.org

### American Legion Maryland Scholarship

**Type of award:** Scholarship.
**Intended use:** For undergraduate study at postsecondary institution.
**Eligibility:** Applicant must be at least 16, no older than 19. Applicant must be residing in Maryland. Applicant must be dependent of veteran.
**Application requirements:** Transcript.
**Additional information:** Applicant must not have reached 20th birthday by January 1 of calendar year application is filed.

**Amount of award:** $500
**Number of awards:** 11
**Application deadline:** March 31
**Total amount awarded:** $5,500

**Contact:**
American Legion Maryland
Attn: Department Adjutant
The War Memorial Building, 101 N Gay St.
Baltimore, MD 21202-1405
Phone: 410-752-1405
Web: www.mdlegion.org

# American Legion Maryland Auxiliary

## American Legion Maryland Auxiliary Scholarship

**Type of award:** Scholarship.
**Intended use:** For undergraduate study at 2-year or 4-year institution.
**Eligibility:** Applicant must be female, high school senior. Applicant must be residing in Maryland. Applicant must be dependent of veteran.
**Basis for selection:** Major/career interest in arts, general; biomedical; business; education; health-related professions; health sciences; physical therapy; physician assistant; public administration/service or science, general.
**Additional information:** Other medical majors eligible. Nursing students not eligible.

| | |
|---|---|
| **Amount of award:** | $2,000 |
| **Number of awards:** | 1 |
| **Application deadline:** | May 1 |
| **Total amount awarded:** | $2,000 |

**Contact:**
American Legion Auxiliary, Department of Maryland
Department Secretary
1589 Sulphur Spring Road, Suite 105
Baltimore, MD 21227
Phone: 410-242-9519
Fax: 410-242-9553
Web: www.alamd.org

# American Legion Massachusetts

## American Legion Massachusetts General and Nursing Scholarships

**Type of award:** Scholarship.
**Intended use:** For freshman study at 2-year or 4-year institution.
**Eligibility:** Applicant or parent must be member/participant of American Legion. Applicant must be residing in Massachusetts. Applicant must be descendant of veteran; or dependent of veteran.
**Application requirements:** Recommendations, transcript, proof of eligibility.
**Additional information:** Grandchildren of American Legion Department of Massachusetts members also eligible. General Scholarships: Nine $1,000 awards; ten $500 awards. Nursing Scholarship: One $1,000 award.

| | |
|---|---|
| **Amount of award:** | $500-$1,000 |
| **Number of awards:** | 20 |
| **Application deadline:** | April 1 |
| **Total amount awarded:** | $15,000 |

**Contact:**
American Legion Massachusetts
Department Adjutant
State House, Room 546-2
Boston, MA 02133-1044
Web: www.masslegion.org

## Department of Massachusetts Oratorical Contest

**Type of award:** Scholarship.
**Intended use:** For undergraduate study at postsecondary institution.
**Eligibility:** Applicant must be no older than 19. Applicant must be residing in Massachusetts.
**Basis for selection:** Competition/talent/interest in oratory/debate, based on language style, voice, diction, delivery, originality, logic, breadth of knowledge, application of knowledge about topic, and skill in selecting examples and analogies.
**Application requirements:** Proof of eligibility.
**Additional information:** Awards: First place, $1,000; second place, $800; third place, $700; fourth place, $600.

| | |
|---|---|
| **Amount of award:** | $600-$1,000 |
| **Number of awards:** | 4 |
| **Application deadline:** | December 15 |
| **Total amount awarded:** | $3,100 |

**Contact:**
American Legion Massachusetts
Department Oratorical Chair
State House, Room 546-2
Boston, MA 02133-1044
Web: www.masslegion.org

# American Legion Massachusetts Auxiliary

## American Legion Massachusetts Auxiliary Scholarship

**Type of award:** Scholarship.
**Intended use:** For undergraduate study at vocational, 2-year or 4-year institution.
**Eligibility:** Applicant must be at least 16, no older than 22. Applicant must be residing in Massachusetts. Applicant must be descendant of veteran; or dependent of veteran or deceased veteran during Grenada conflict, Korean War, Lebanon conflict, Panama conflict, Persian Gulf War, WW I, WW II or Vietnam.
**Additional information:** One $750 award; ten $200 awards.

| | |
|---|---|
| **Amount of award:** | $200-$750 |
| **Number of awards:** | 11 |
| **Application deadline:** | March 1 |
| **Total amount awarded:** | $2,750 |

**Contact:**
American Legion Auxiliary, Department of Massachusetts
Department Secretary
State House, Room 546-2
Boston, MA 02133-1044
Web: www.masslegion-aux.org

### Past President's Parley Scholarship

**Type of award:** Scholarship.
**Intended use:** For undergraduate study at postsecondary institution.
**Eligibility:** Applicant must be residing in Massachusetts. Applicant must be dependent of veteran or deceased veteran.
**Basis for selection:** Major/career interest in nursing.
**Additional information:** Must be child of living or deceased veteran not eligible for Federal or Commonwealth scholarships.

| | |
|---|---|
| **Amount of award:** | $200 |
| **Number of awards:** | 1 |
| **Total amount awarded:** | $200 |

**Contact:**
American Legion Massachusetts Auxiliary
Department Secretary
State House, Room 546-2
Boston, MA 02133-1044
Web: www.masslegion-aux.org

## American Legion Michigan

### American Legion Michigan Oratorical Contest

**Type of award:** Scholarship.
**Intended use:** For undergraduate study at postsecondary institution.
**Eligibility:** Applicant must be enrolled in high school. Applicant must be U.S. citizen or permanent resident residing in Michigan.
**Basis for selection:** Competition/talent/interest in oratory/debate, based on ability to deliver an 8- to 10-minute speech on the U.S. Constitution.
**Additional information:** Awards: $1,500, $1,000, $800. Local contest in early February. Must be finalist in Zone Oratorical Contest. Contact local American Legion Post for more information.

| | |
|---|---|
| **Amount of award:** | $800-$1,500 |
| **Number of awards:** | 3 |
| **Total amount awarded:** | $3,300 |

**Contact:**
Deanna Clark American Legion Michigan
212 North Verlinden Avenue
Ste A
Lansing, MI 48915
Phone: 517-371-4720 ext. 11
Fax: 517-371-2401
Web: www.michiganlegion.org

### Guy M. Wilson Scholarship

**Type of award:** Scholarship.
**Intended use:** For undergraduate study at 2-year or 4-year institution. Designated institutions: Michigan institutions.
**Eligibility:** Applicant must be enrolled in high school. Applicant must be residing in Michigan. Applicant must be descendant of veteran; or dependent of veteran or deceased veteran.
**Basis for selection:** Applicant must demonstrate financial need.
**Application requirements:** Transcript, proof of eligibility.
**Additional information:** Minimum 2.5 GPA. Application should be filed at local American Legion Post. Deadline in mid-January.

| | |
|---|---|
| **Amount of award:** | $500 |

**Contact:**
Deanna Clark American Legion Michigan
212 North Verlinden Avenue
Ste A
Lansing, MI 48915
Phone: 517-371-4720 ext. 11
Fax: 517-371-2401
Web: www.michiganlegion.org

### William D. & Jewell W. Brewer Scholarship Trusts

**Type of award:** Scholarship.
**Intended use:** For undergraduate study at 2-year or 4-year institution.
**Eligibility:** Applicant must be residing in Michigan. Applicant must be descendant of veteran; or dependent of veteran or deceased veteran.
**Basis for selection:** Applicant must demonstrate financial need.
**Application requirements:** Transcript, proof of eligibility.
**Additional information:** Minimum 2.5 GPA. Application should be filed at local American Legion Post. Deadline in mid-January.

| | |
|---|---|
| **Amount of award:** | $500 |

**Contact:**
Deanna Clark American Legion Michigan
212 North Verlinden Avenue
Ste A
Lansing, MI 48915
Phone: 517-371-4720 ext. 11
Fax: 517-371-2401
Web: www.michiganlegion.org

## American Legion Michigan Auxiliary

### American Legion Michigan Auxiliary Memorial Scholarship

**Type of award:** Scholarship, renewable.
**Intended use:** For undergraduate study at postsecondary institution. Designated institutions: Michigan institutions.
**Eligibility:** Applicant must be female, at least 16, no older than 21. Applicant must be residing in Michigan. Applicant must be descendant of veteran; or dependent of veteran or deceased veteran during Grenada conflict, Korean War, Lebanon conflict, Panama conflict, Persian Gulf War, WW I, WW II or Vietnam. Applicant must be daughter, granddaughter, or great-granddaughter of honorably discharged or deceased veteran.
**Basis for selection:** Applicant must demonstrate financial need and high academic achievement.
**Application requirements:** Recommendations, transcript, proof of eligibility. FAFSA or copy of parents' income tax forms.
**Additional information:** Must be Michigan resident for at least one year. Visit Website for details and application.

Scholarships

**Amount of award:** $500
**Application deadline:** March 15
**Contact:**
American Legion Auxiliary, Department of Michigan
212 North Verlinden Avenue
Lansing, MI 48915
Phone: 517-267-8809 ext. 22
Fax: 517-371-2401
Web: www.michalaux.org

### Medical Career Scholarships

**Type of award:** Scholarship.
**Intended use:** For freshman study at postsecondary institution. Designated institutions: Michigan institutions.
**Eligibility:** Applicant must be high school senior. Applicant must be residing in Michigan. Applicant must be descendant of veteran; or dependent of veteran or deceased veteran; or spouse of veteran or deceased veteran during Grenada conflict, Korean War, Lebanon conflict, Panama conflict, Persian Gulf War, WW I, WW II or Vietnam. Applicant must be child, grandchild, great-grandchild, wife, or spouse of honorably discharged or deceased veteran.
**Basis for selection:** Major/career interest in nursing; physical therapy or respiratory therapy. Applicant must demonstrate financial need and high academic achievement.
**Application requirements:** Recommendations, transcript, proof of eligibility. FAFSA or copy of income tax form.
**Additional information:** For first-year training of men and women for the position of registered nurse, licensed practical nurse, physical therapist, or respiratory therapist. Applications available after November 15. Visit Website for details and application.
**Amount of award:** $500
**Application deadline:** March 15
**Total amount awarded:** $10,500
**Contact:**
American Legion Auxiliary, Department of Michigan
212 North Verlinden Avenue
Lansing, MI 48915
Phone: 517-267-8809 ext. 22
Fax: 517-371-2401
Web: www.michalaux.org

### National President's Scholarship

**Type of award:** Scholarship.
**Intended use:** For undergraduate study at postsecondary institution.
**Eligibility:** Applicant must be high school senior. Applicant must be residing in Michigan. Applicant must be descendant of veteran; or dependent of veteran during Grenada conflict, Korean War, Middle East War, Lebanon conflict, Panama conflict, Persian Gulf War, WW I, WW II or Vietnam.
**Application requirements:** Applicant must have completed 50 hours of community service during high school.
**Amount of award:** $1,000-$2,500
**Number of awards:** 1
**Application deadline:** March 1
**Contact:**
American Legion Auxiliary, Department of Michigan
212 North Verlinden Avenue
Lansing, MI 48915
Phone: 517-267-8809 ext. 22
Fax: 517-371-2401
Web: www.michalaux.org

## American Legion Minnesota

### American Legion Minnesota Legionnaire Insurance Trust Scholarship

**Type of award:** Scholarship.
**Intended use:** For undergraduate study at accredited vocational, 2-year or 4-year institution. Designated institutions: Minnesota colleges and universities and institutions in neighboring states with reciprocating agreements.
**Eligibility:** Applicant or parent must be member/participant of American Legion. Applicant must be U.S. citizen residing in Minnesota. Applicant must be veteran or descendant of veteran; or dependent of veteran.
**Basis for selection:** Applicant must demonstrate financial need and high academic achievement.
**Application requirements:** Recommendations, essay, transcript, proof of eligibility.
**Amount of award:** $500
**Number of awards:** 3
**Application deadline:** April 1
**Total amount awarded:** $1,500
**Contact:**
American Legion Minnesota
Education Committee
20 West 12th Street, Room 300A
St. Paul, MN 55155-2000
Phone: 651-291-1800
Web: www.mnlegion.org

### American Legion Minnesota Oratorical Contest

**Type of award:** Scholarship.
**Intended use:** For undergraduate study at accredited postsecondary institution.
**Eligibility:** Applicant must be enrolled in high school. Applicant must be U.S. citizen or permanent resident residing in Minnesota.
**Basis for selection:** Competition/talent/interest in oratory/debate, based on language style, voice, diction, delivery, originality, logic, breadth of knowledge, application of knowledge about topic, and skill in selecting examples and analogies.
**Additional information:** Awards: First place, $1,200; second place, $900; third place, $700; fourth place, $500.
**Amount of award:** $500-$1,200
**Number of awards:** 4
**Application deadline:** December 15
**Total amount awarded:** $3,300
**Contact:**
American Legion Minnesota
Education Committee
20 West 12th Street, Room 300A
St. Paul, MN 55155-2000
Phone: 866-259-9163
Web: www.mnlegion.org

### The Minnesota American Legion Memorial Scholarship

**Type of award:** Scholarship.
**Intended use:** For undergraduate study at accredited postsecondary institution. Designated institutions: Minnesota

colleges and universities and institutions in neighboring states with reciprocating agreement.
**Eligibility:** Applicant or parent must be member/participant of American Legion. Applicant must be residing in Minnesota.
**Basis for selection:** Applicant must demonstrate financial need.
**Application requirements:** Recommendations, essay, transcript, proof of eligibility.
**Additional information:** Grandchildren of American Legion or American Legion Auxiliary members also eligible.

| | |
|---|---|
| **Amount of award:** | $500 |
| **Number of awards:** | 6 |
| **Total amount awarded:** | $3,000 |

**Contact:**
American Legion Minnesota
Education Committee
20 West 12th Street, Room 300A
St. Paul, MN 55155-2000
Phone: 866-259-9163
Web: www.mnlegion.org

# American Legion Minnesota Auxiliary

## American Legion Minnesota Auxiliary Department Scholarship

**Type of award:** Scholarship.
**Intended use:** For undergraduate study at accredited postsecondary institution.
**Eligibility:** Applicant or parent must be member/participant of American Legion Auxiliary. Applicant must be residing in Minnesota. Applicant must be descendant of veteran; or dependent of veteran.

| | |
|---|---|
| **Amount of award:** | $1,000 |
| **Number of awards:** | 7 |
| **Application deadline:** | March 15 |
| **Total amount awarded:** | $7,000 |

**Contact:**
American Legion Auxiliary, Department of Minnesota
State Veterans Service Building
20 W 12th Street, Room 314
St. Paul, MN 55155-2069
Phone: 651-224-7634
Fax: 651-224-5243
Web: www.mnala.org

## Past President's Parley Health Care Scholarship

**Type of award:** Scholarship.
**Intended use:** For undergraduate study at accredited postsecondary institution.
**Eligibility:** Applicant or parent must be member/participant of American Legion Auxiliary. Applicant must be residing in Minnesota.
**Basis for selection:** Major/career interest in health-related professions.

| | |
|---|---|
| **Amount of award:** | $1,000 |
| **Number of awards:** | 10 |
| **Application deadline:** | March 15 |
| **Total amount awarded:** | $10,000 |

**Contact:**
American Legion Auxiliary, Department of Minnesota
State Veterans Service Building
20 W. 12th Street, Room 314
St. Paul, MN 55155-2069
Phone: 651-224-7634
Fax: 651-224-5243
Web: www.mnala.org

# American Legion Mississippi Auxiliary

## American Legion Mississippi Auxiliary Scholarship

**Type of award:** Scholarship.
**Intended use:** For undergraduate study at accredited postsecondary institution.
**Eligibility:** Applicant must be high school senior. Applicant must be residing in Mississippi. Applicant must be descendant of veteran; or dependent of veteran during Korean War, Lebanon conflict, Panama conflict, Persian Gulf War, WW I, WW II or Vietnam.
**Basis for selection:** Applicant must demonstrate financial need.

| | |
|---|---|
| **Amount of award:** | $500 |
| **Number of awards:** | 1 |
| **Application deadline:** | March 1 |
| **Total amount awarded:** | $500 |

**Contact:**
American Legion Mississippi Auxiliary, Department Headquarters
P.O. Box 1382
Jackson, MS 39215-1382
Phone: 601-353-3681
Fax: 601-353-3682
Web: www.missala.com

# American Legion Missouri

## Charles L. Bacon Memorial Scholarship

**Type of award:** Scholarship.
**Intended use:** For full-time undergraduate study at accredited 2-year or 4-year institution.
**Eligibility:** Applicant or parent must be member/participant of American Legion. Applicant must be single, no older than 20. Applicant must be U.S. citizen residing in Missouri.
**Basis for selection:** Applicant must demonstrate financial need.
**Additional information:** Applicants must be current member of American Legion, American Legion Auxiliary or the Sons of the American Legion, or descendent of any member.

| | |
|---|---|
| **Amount of award:** | $500 |
| **Number of awards:** | 2 |
| **Application deadline:** | April 20 |
| **Notification begins:** | July 1 |
| **Total amount awarded:** | $1,000 |

**Contact:**
American Legion Missouri
Attn: Education and Scholarship Committee
P.O. Box 179
Jefferson City, MO 65102-0179
Phone: 660-627-4713
Web: www.missourilegion.org

## Commander's Scholarship Fund

**Type of award:** Scholarship.
**Intended use:** For undergraduate study at postsecondary institution. Designated institutions: Vocational/technical colleges or universities in Missouri.
**Eligibility:** Applicant must be residing in Missouri. Applicant must be veteran who served in the Army, Air Force, Marines, Navy or Coast Guard. Applicant must have served in one of the U.S. Armed Forces branches for a minimum of 90 days and received honorable discharge.
**Application requirements:** Proof of eligibility. Letter of acceptance from college or university.
**Additional information:** Membership in The American Legion not required.

| | |
|---|---|
| **Amount of award:** | $1,000 |
| **Number of awards:** | 2 |
| **Application deadline:** | April 20 |
| **Total amount awarded:** | $2,000 |

**Contact:**
American Legion Missouri
Attn: Education and Scholarship Committee
P.O. Box 179
Jefferson City, MO 65102-0179
Phone: 660-627-4713
Web: www.missourilegion.org

## Erman W. Taylor Memorial Scholarship

**Type of award:** Scholarship.
**Intended use:** For full-time undergraduate study at accredited 2-year or 4-year institution.
**Eligibility:** Applicant must be single, no older than 20. Applicant must be U.S. citizen residing in Missouri. Applicant must be descendant of veteran who served in the Army, Air Force, Marines, Navy or Coast Guard. Must be child, grandchild, or great-grandchild of veteran who served 90 or more days of active duty in the Army, Navy, Air Force, Marines, or Coast Guard and has an honorable discharge.
**Basis for selection:** Major/career interest in education.
**Application requirements:** Copy of discharge certificate for veteran parent, grandparent; essay of 500 words or less on selected topic.

| | |
|---|---|
| **Amount of award:** | $500 |
| **Number of awards:** | 2 |
| **Notification begins:** | July 1 |
| **Total amount awarded:** | $1,000 |

**Contact:**
American Legion Missouri
Attn: Education and Scholarship Committee
P.O. Box 179
Jefferson City, MO 65102-0179
Phone: 660-627-4713
Web: www.missourilegion.org

## Joseph J. Frank Scholarship

**Type of award:** Scholarship.
**Intended use:** For full-time freshman study at accredited postsecondary institution.
**Eligibility:** Applicant or parent must be member/participant of American Legion. Applicant must be single, no older than 20. Applicant must be residing in Missouri. Applicant must be veteran or descendant of veteran; or dependent of veteran.
**Application requirements:** Proof of eligibility.
**Additional information:** Must be member or descendent of member of American Legion, American Legion Auxiliary, or Sons of the American Legion. Applicant must have attended a full session of The American Legion Boys State or Auxiliary Girls State program.

| | |
|---|---|
| **Amount of award:** | $500 |
| **Number of awards:** | 5 |
| **Total amount awarded:** | $2,500 |

**Contact:**
American Legion Missouri
Attn: Education and Scholarship Committee
P.O. Box 179
Jefferson City, MO 65102-0179
Phone: 660-627-4713
Web: www.missourilegion.org

## Lillie Lois Ford Boys' Scholarship

**Type of award:** Scholarship.
**Intended use:** For full-time undergraduate study at accredited postsecondary institution.
**Eligibility:** Applicant or parent must be member/participant of American Legion, Boys State. Applicant must be single, male, no older than 20. Applicant must be residing in Missouri. Applicant must be descendant of veteran who served in the Army, Air Force, Marines, Navy or Coast Guard. Must be child, grandchild, or great-grandchild of veteran who served at least 90 days active duty in Army, Navy, Air Force, Marines, or Coast Guard, and was honorably discharged.
**Basis for selection:** Applicant must demonstrate financial need.
**Application requirements:** Proof of eligibility.
**Additional information:** Must have attended complete session of American Legion Boys State or American Legion Department of Missouri Cadet Patrol Academy.

| | |
|---|---|
| **Amount of award:** | $1,000 |
| **Number of awards:** | 1 |
| **Application deadline:** | April 20 |
| **Notification begins:** | July 1 |
| **Total amount awarded:** | $1,000 |

**Contact:**
American Legion Missouri
Attn: Education and Scholarship Committee
P.O. Box 179
Jefferson City, MO 65102-0179
Phone: 660-627-4713
Web: www.missourilegion.org

## Lillie Lois Ford Girls' Scholarship

**Type of award:** Scholarship.
**Intended use:** For full-time undergraduate study at accredited postsecondary institution.
**Eligibility:** Applicant must be single, female, no older than 20. Applicant must be residing in Missouri. Applicant must be descendant of veteran who served in the Army, Air Force, Marines, Navy or Coast Guard. Must be child, grandchild, or great-grandchild of veteran who served at least 90 days active

duty in Army, Navy, Air Force, Marines, or Coast Guard, and was honorably discharged.
**Basis for selection:** Applicant must demonstrate financial need.
**Application requirements:** Proof of eligibility.
**Additional information:** Must have attended complete session of American Legion Auxiliary Girls State or American Legion Department of Missouri Cadet Patrol Academy.

| | |
|---|---|
| **Amount of award:** | $1,000 |
| **Number of awards:** | 1 |
| **Application deadline:** | April 20 |
| **Notification begins:** | July 1 |
| **Total amount awarded:** | $1,000 |

**Contact:**
American Legion Missouri
Attn: Education and Scholarship Committee
P.O. Box 179
Jefferson City, MO 65102
Phone: 660-627-4713
Web: www.missourilegion.org

### M.D. "Jack" Murphy Memorial Nurses Training Fund

**Type of award:** Scholarship, renewable.
**Intended use:** For full-time undergraduate study at 2-year or 4-year institution.
**Eligibility:** Applicant must be single, no older than 20. Applicant must be residing in Missouri. Applicant must be descendant of veteran who served in the Army, Air Force, Marines, Navy or Coast Guard. Must be child, grandchild, or great-grandchild of veteran who served at least 90 days active duty in Army, Navy, Air Force, Marines, or Coast Guard, and was honorably discharged.
**Basis for selection:** Major/career interest in nursing. Applicant must demonstrate financial need.
**Application requirements:** Proof of eligibility.
**Additional information:** Available to students training to be registered nurses. Applicant must have graduated in top 40% of high school class or have minimum "C" or equivalent standing from last college semester prior to applying for award.

| | |
|---|---|
| **Amount of award:** | $750 |
| **Number of awards:** | 1 |
| **Application deadline:** | April 20 |
| **Total amount awarded:** | $750 |

**Contact:**
American Legion Missouri
Attn: Education and Scholarship Committee
P.O. Box 179
Jefferson City, MO 65102-0179
Phone: 660-627-4713
Web: www.missourilegion.org

### Shane Dean Voyles Memorial Scholarship

**Type of award:** Scholarship.
**Intended use:** For full-time freshman study at accredited postsecondary institution.
**Eligibility:** Applicant must be high school senior. Applicant must be residing in Missouri.
**Basis for selection:** Applicant must demonstrate high academic achievement, leadership and service orientation.
**Application requirements:** Nomination by high school.
**Additional information:** Each school in Missouri may nominate one student for the award. Nominee selected based on leadership, athletic, and scholastic abilities.

| | |
|---|---|
| **Amount of award:** | $500 |
| **Number of awards:** | 1 |
| **Total amount awarded:** | $500 |

**Contact:**
American Legion Missouri
Attn: Education and Scholarship Committee
P.O. Box 179
Jefferson City, MO 65102-0179
Phone: 660-627-4713
Web: www.missourilegion.org

## American Legion Missouri Auxiliary

### American Legion Missouri Auxiliary Scholarship

**Type of award:** Scholarship.
**Intended use:** For undergraduate study at postsecondary institution.
**Eligibility:** Applicant must be high school senior. Applicant must be residing in Missouri. Applicant must be descendant of veteran; or dependent of veteran during Korean War, Lebanon conflict, Panama conflict, Persian Gulf War, WW I, WW II or Vietnam.
**Additional information:** Applicant must not have previously attended institution of higher learning.

| | |
|---|---|
| **Amount of award:** | $500 |
| **Number of awards:** | 2 |
| **Application deadline:** | March 1 |
| **Total amount awarded:** | $1,000 |

**Contact:**
American Legion Missouri Auxiliary
Department Secretary
600 Ellis Blvd.
Jefferson City, MO 65101-2204
Phone: 573-636-9133
Fax: 573-635-3467

### National President's Scholarship

**Type of award:** Scholarship.
**Eligibility:** Applicant or parent must be member/participant of American Legion Auxiliary. Applicant must be residing in Missouri. Applicant must be dependent of veteran.
**Additional information:** Applicant must be child of veteran who served in the Armed Forces during the eligibility dates of The American Legion. Applicant must complete 50 hours of community service during student's high school years.

| | |
|---|---|
| **Amount of award:** | $500 |
| **Number of awards:** | 1 |
| **Total amount awarded:** | $500 |

**Contact:**
American Legion Missouri Auxiliary
600 Ellis Blvd
Jefferson City, MO 65101-2204
Phone: 573-636-9133
Fax: 573-635-3467

### Past President's Parley Scholarship

**Type of award:** Scholarship.
**Intended use:** For undergraduate study at 2-year or 4-year institution.

Scholarships

**Eligibility:** Applicant must be residing in Missouri. Applicant must be descendant of veteran; or dependent of veteran.
**Basis for selection:** Major/career interest in nursing.
**Application requirements:** Recommendations.
**Additional information:** Applicant must not have previously attended institution of higher learning.

| | |
|---|---|
| **Amount of award:** | $500 |
| **Number of awards:** | 2 |

**Contact:**
American Legion Missouri Auxiliary
Department Secretary
600 Ellis Blvd
Jefferson City, MO 65101-2204
Phone: 573-636-9133
Fax: 573-635-3467

# American Legion Montana Auxiliary

## Aloha Scholarship

**Type of award:** Scholarship.
**Intended use:** For freshman study at postsecondary institution. Designated institutions: Accredited nursing schools.
**Eligibility:** Applicant or parent must be member/participant of American Legion Auxiliary. Applicant must be residing in Montana.
**Basis for selection:** Major/career interest in nursing.
**Application requirements:** Recommendations, proof of eligibility.
**Additional information:** Grandchildren of Auxiliary members also eligible.

| | |
|---|---|
| **Amount of award:** | $400 |
| **Number of awards:** | 1 |
| **Application deadline:** | April 1 |

**Contact:**
American Legion Montana Auxiliary
Department Secretary
P.O. Box 40
Townsend, MT 59644
Phone: 406-266-4566
Web: www.mtlegion.org/auxiliary

## American Legion Montana Auxiliary Scholarships (1)

**Type of award:** Scholarship.
**Intended use:** For undergraduate study at postsecondary institution.
**Eligibility:** Applicant must be high school senior. Applicant must be residing in Montana. Applicant must be dependent of veteran.
**Application requirements:** Essay, proof of eligibility. 500-word essay on any topic.
**Additional information:** Applicant must be high school senior or graduate who has not attended college. Must be state resident for at least two years.

| | |
|---|---|
| **Amount of award:** | $500 |
| **Number of awards:** | 2 |
| **Application deadline:** | April 1 |
| **Total amount awarded:** | $1,000 |

**Contact:**
American Legion Montana Auxiliary
Department Secretary
P.O. Box 40
Townsend, MT 59644
Phone: 406-266-4566
Fax: 406-266-4566
Web: www.mtlegion.org/auxiliary

## American Legion Montana Auxiliary Scholarships (2)

**Type of award:** Scholarship.
**Intended use:** For junior study at postsecondary institution.
**Eligibility:** Applicant must be residing in Montana. Applicant must be dependent of veteran.
**Application requirements:** Proof of eligibility. Essay stating interest in issues relating to children and youth.
**Additional information:** Must have completed sophomore year in college and be going into field relating to children and youth.

| | |
|---|---|
| **Amount of award:** | $500 |
| **Number of awards:** | 2 |
| **Application deadline:** | June 1 |
| **Total amount awarded:** | $1,000 |

**Contact:**
American Legion Montana Auxiliary
Department Secretary
P.O. Box 40
Townsend, MT 59644
Phone: 406-266-4566
Fax: 406-266-4566
Web: www.mtlegion.org/auxiliary

# American Legion National Headquarters

## American Legion Auxiliary National President's Scholarship

**Type of award:** Scholarship.
**Intended use:** For undergraduate study at postsecondary institution.
**Eligibility:** Applicant or parent must be member/participant of American Legion Auxiliary. Applicant must be high school senior. Applicant must be dependent of veteran during Grenada conflict, Korean War, Lebanon conflict, Panama conflict, Persian Gulf War, WW I, WW II or Vietnam.
**Basis for selection:** Applicant must demonstrate financial need, high academic achievement, depth of character, leadership and patriotism.
**Additional information:** Scholarships: five-$2,500; five-$2,000; five-$1,500; awarded annually. Applications available online, from Unit President of Auxiliary in local community, from Department Secretary, or from National Headquarters. See Website for details.

| | |
|---|---|
| **Amount of award:** | $1,500-$2,500 |
| **Number of awards:** | 15 |
| **Application deadline:** | March 1 |
| **Total amount awarded:** | $27,500 |

**Contact:**
American Legion Auxiliary
8945 North Meridian Street
Indianapolis, IN 46260-1189
Phone: 317-569-4500
Web: www.legion-aux.org

## American Legion Eagle Scout of the Year

**Type of award:** Scholarship.
**Intended use:** For undergraduate study at accredited postsecondary institution in United States.
**Eligibility:** Applicant or parent must be member/participant of Boy Scouts of America, Eagle Scouts. Applicant must be male, enrolled in high school. Applicant must be U.S. citizen.
**Basis for selection:** Applicant must demonstrate depth of character and service orientation.
**Application requirements:** Recommendations, transcript, proof of eligibility.
**Additional information:** Applicant must be registered, active member of Boy Scout Troop, Varsity Scout Team or Venturing Crew AND either chartered to American Legion Post/Auxiliary Unit OR son or grandson of American Legion or Auxiliary member. Awards: One $10,000 Eagle Scout of the Year; three runners-up get $2,500. Scholarships available upon graduation from accredited high school and must be used within four years of graduation date. Request application from State Department Headquarters.

| | |
|---|---|
| **Amount of award:** | $2,500-$10,000 |
| **Number of awards:** | 4 |
| **Total amount awarded:** | $17,500 |

**Contact:**
American Legion National Headquarters
Eagle Scout of the Year
P.O. Box 1055
Indianapolis, IN 46206-1055
Phone: 317-630-1249
Web: www.legion.org

## American Legion Legacy Scholarship

**Type of award:** Scholarship, renewable.
**Intended use:** For undergraduate study at postsecondary institution in United States.
**Eligibility:** Applicant must be high school senior. Applicant must be residing in Indiana. Applicant must be child (dependent, legally adopted, or from a spouse of prior marriage) of active duty personnel of the U.S. military or National Guard or military reservists who were federalized and died on active duty on or after September 11, 2001.
**Application requirements:** Transcript, proof of eligibility.
**Additional information:** Amount and number of awards vary. Previous scholarship recipients may reapply. Visit Website for details.

| | |
|---|---|
| **Application deadline:** | April 15 |

**Contact:**
American Legion National Headquarters
Education Programs Chair
P.O. Box 1055
Indianapolis, IN 46206-1055
Web: www.legion.org

## American Legion National High School Oratorical Contest

**Type of award:** Scholarship.
**Intended use:** For undergraduate study at postsecondary institution.
**Eligibility:** Applicant must be enrolled in high school. Applicant must be U.S. citizen or permanent resident.
**Basis for selection:** Competition/talent/interest in oratory/debate, based on language style, voice, diction, delivery, originality, logic, breadth of knowledge, application of knowledge about topic, and skill in selecting examples and analogies.
**Additional information:** Awards: State winners participating in regional level win $1,500; second-round participants not advancing to national finals receive additional $1,500. Finalists win $18,000 (first place), $16,000 (runner-up), and $14,000 (third place). Obtain oratorical contest rules from local Legion Post or state Department Headquarters.

| | |
|---|---|
| **Amount of award:** | $1,500-$18,000 |
| **Number of awards:** | 54 |

**Contact:**
American Legion National Headquarters
Education Programs Chair
P.O. Box 1055
Indianapolis, IN 46206-1055
Web: www.legion.org

## American Legion Scholarship for Non-Traditional Students

**Type of award:** Scholarship.
**Eligibility:** Applicant or parent must be member/participant of American Legion Auxiliary.
**Basis for selection:** Applicant must demonstrate financial need, depth of character and leadership.
**Additional information:** Applicant must be a non-traditional student returning to school after some period in which his or her formal education was interrupted or who is just beginning his or her education at a later point in life.

| | |
|---|---|
| **Amount of award:** | $1,000 |
| **Number of awards:** | 5 |
| **Application deadline:** | March 1 |
| **Total amount awarded:** | $1,000 |

**Contact:**
American Legion Auxiliary
8945 North Meridian Street
Indianapolis, IN 46260
Phone: 317-569-4500
Web: www.legion-aux.org

## Eight and Forty Lung and Respiratory Nursing Scholarship Fund

**Type of award:** Scholarship.
**Intended use:** For undergraduate, graduate or non-degree study.
**Eligibility:** Applicant must be returning adult student.
**Basis for selection:** Major/career interest in health education; health services administration or nursing.
**Application requirements:** Proof of eligibility.
**Additional information:** Applicant must be registered nurse. Program assists registered nurses with advanced preparation for positions in supervision, administration, or teaching. On completion of education, must have full-time employment

Scholarships

prospects related to pediatric lung and respiratory control in hospitals, clinics, or health departments. Contact Eight and Forty Scholarship Chairman or the American Legion Education Program for application.

**Amount of award:** $3,000
**Application deadline:** May 15
**Notification begins:** July 1
**Total amount awarded:** $3,000

**Contact:**
American Legion National Headquarters
Eight and Forty Scholarships
P.O. Box 1055
Indianapolis, IN 46206-1055
Web: www.legion.org

## Samsung American Legion Scholarship

**Type of award:** Scholarship.
**Intended use:** For undergraduate study at postsecondary institution in United States.
**Eligibility:** Applicant or parent must be member/participant of American Legion. Applicant must be high school junior. Applicant must be descendant of veteran; or dependent of veteran.
**Basis for selection:** Applicant must demonstrate financial need, high academic achievement and service orientation.
**Application requirements:** Essay, proof of eligibility.
**Additional information:** Applicant must have completed American Legion Boys State or Girls State program. Amount and number of awards vary. In 2007, 10 $20,000 and 90 $1,000 scholarships awarded. Visit Website for details.

**Contact:**
American Legion National Headquarters
Education Programs Chair
P.O. Box 1055
Indianapolis, IN 46206-1055
Web: www.legion.org

## Spirit of Youth Scholarship for Junior Members

**Type of award:** Scholarship.
**Intended use:** For undergraduate study at postsecondary institution.
**Eligibility:** Applicant or parent must be member/participant of American Legion Auxiliary. Applicant must be high school senior. Applicant must be U.S. citizen.
**Basis for selection:** Applicant must demonstrate financial need, high academic achievement, depth of character, leadership and patriotism.
**Application requirements:** Proof of eligibility.
**Additional information:** Must be Junior member of three years' standing, holding current membership card. Applications available online, from Unit President of Auxiliary in local community, from Department Secretary, or from National Headquarters. See Website for details.

**Amount of award:** $4,000
**Number of awards:** 5
**Application deadline:** March 1

**Contact:**
American Legion Auxiliary
8945 North Meridian Street
Indianapolis, IN 46260
Phone: 317-569-4500
Web: www.legion-aux.org

# American Legion Nebraska

## American Legion Nebraska Oratorical Contest

**Type of award:** Scholarship.
**Intended use:** For undergraduate study at postsecondary institution.
**Eligibility:** Applicant or parent must be member/participant of American Legion. Applicant must be enrolled in high school. Applicant must be residing in Nebraska.
**Basis for selection:** Competition/talent/interest in oratory/debate, based on language style, voice, diction, delivery, originality, logic, breadth of knowledge, application of knowledge about topic, and skill in selecting examples and analogies.
**Application requirements:** Proof of eligibility.
**Additional information:** Awards: First place, $1,000; second place, $600; third place, $400; fourth place, $200, plus one $100 award for first place in each District upon participation in area contest. Contact local American Legion post for more information.

**Amount of award:** $100-$1,000
**Application deadline:** November 1

**Contact:**
American Legion Nebraska, Department Headquarters
P.O. Box 5205
Lincoln, NE 68505-0205
Phone: 402-464-6338
Web: www.nebraskalegion.net

## Edgar J. Boschult Memorial Scholarship

**Type of award:** Scholarship.
**Intended use:** For full-time undergraduate study. Designated institutions: University of Nebraska.
**Eligibility:** Applicant or parent must be member/participant of American Legion. Applicant must be residing in Nebraska.
**Basis for selection:** Applicant must demonstrate financial need and high academic achievement.
**Additional information:** Must be student at University of Nebraska with high academic and ROTC standing, or military veteran attending University of Nebraska with financial need and acceptable scholastic standing.

**Amount of award:** $500
**Number of awards:** 4
**Application deadline:** March 1

**Contact:**
American Legion Nebraska, Department Headquarters
P.O. Box 5205
Lincoln, NE 68505-0205
Phone: 402-464-6338
Web: www.nebraskalegion.net

## Maynard Jensen American Legion Memorial Scholarship

**Type of award:** Scholarship.
**Intended use:** For full-time undergraduate study at vocational, 2-year or 4-year institution. Designated institutions: Nebraska institutions.
**Eligibility:** Applicant or parent must be member/participant of American Legion. Applicant must be residing in Nebraska.

Applicant must be descendant of veteran; or dependent of veteran, deceased veteran or POW/MIA.
**Basis for selection:** Applicant must demonstrate financial need and high academic achievement.

| | |
|---|---|
| **Amount of award:** | $500 |
| **Number of awards:** | 10 |
| **Application deadline:** | March 1 |
| **Total amount awarded:** | $5,000 |

**Contact:**
American Legion Nebraska, Department Headquarters
P.O. Box 5205
Lincoln, NE 68505-0205
Phone: 402-464-6338
Web: www.nebraskalegion.net

# American Legion Nebraska Auxiliary

## American Legion Nebraska President's Scholarship

**Type of award:** Scholarship.
**Intended use:** For undergraduate study at postsecondary institution.
**Eligibility:** Applicant must be residing in Nebraska.
**Additional information:** Given to Nebraska's entry for National President's Scholarship in event applicant does not win same.

| | |
|---|---|
| **Amount of award:** | $200 |

**Contact:**
American Legion Nebraska Auxiliary, Department Headquarters
P.O. Box 5227
Lincoln, NE 68505-0227
Web: www.nebraskalegionaux.net

## Averyl Elaine Keriakedes Memorial Scholarship

**Type of award:** Scholarship.
**Intended use:** For undergraduate study. Designated institutions: University of Nebraska-Lincoln.
**Eligibility:** Applicant must be female. Applicant must be residing in Nebraska. Applicant must be descendant of veteran; or dependent of veteran; or spouse of veteran.
**Basis for selection:** Major/career interest in education or social/behavioral sciences.
**Application requirements:** Recommendations, transcript, proof of eligibility.
**Additional information:** Applicant must plan to teach middle or junior high school social studies.

| | |
|---|---|
| **Amount of award:** | $500 |
| **Number of awards:** | 1 |
| **Total amount awarded:** | $500 |

**Contact:**
American Legion Nebraska Auxiliary, Department Headquarters
P.O. Box 5227
Lincoln, NE 68505-0227
Web: www.nebraskalegionaux.net

## Junior Member Scholarship

**Type of award:** Scholarship.
**Intended use:** For undergraduate study at postsecondary institution.
**Eligibility:** Applicant must be residing in Nebraska.
**Additional information:** Given to Nebraska's entry for Spirit of Youth Scholarship for Junior member, in event applicant does not win same.

| | |
|---|---|
| **Amount of award:** | $200 |

**Contact:**
American Legion Nebraska Auxiliary
Department Education Chairman
P.O. Box 5227
Lincoln, NE 68505-0227
Web: www.nebraskalegionaux.net

## Nurse Gift Tuition Scholarships

**Type of award:** Scholarship.
**Intended use:** For undergraduate study.
**Eligibility:** Applicant must be residing in Nebraska. Applicant must be descendant of veteran; or dependent of veteran; or spouse of veteran.
**Basis for selection:** Major/career interest in nursing. Applicant must demonstrate financial need.
**Application requirements:** Recommendations, essay, transcript, proof of eligibility.
**Additional information:** Awards given as funds permit.

| | |
|---|---|
| **Amount of award:** | $200-$400 |

**Contact:**
American Legion Nebraska Auxiliary, Department Headquarters
P.O. Box 5227
Lincoln, NE 68505-0227
Web: www.nebraskalegionaux.net

## Practical Nursing Scholarship

**Type of award:** Scholarship.
**Intended use:** For undergraduate study at 2-year or 4-year institution. Designated institutions: Schools of practical nursing.
**Eligibility:** Applicant must be residing in Nebraska. Applicant must be veteran or descendant of veteran; or dependent of veteran; or spouse of veteran.
**Basis for selection:** Major/career interest in nursing. Applicant must demonstrate financial need.
**Application requirements:** Recommendations, transcript, proof of eligibility.
**Additional information:** Must be Nebraska resident for at least three years, be accepted at school of practical nursing, and be veteran-connected.

| | |
|---|---|
| **Amount of award:** | $300 |

**Contact:**
American Legion Nebraska Auxiliary, Department Headquarters
P.O. Box 5227
Lincoln, NE 68505-0227
Web: www.nebraskalegionaux.net

## Roberta Marie Stretch Memorial Scholarship

**Type of award:** Scholarship.
**Intended use:** For undergraduate or master's study at 4-year institution.
**Eligibility:** Applicant must be residing in Nebraska. Applicant must be descendant of veteran; or dependent of veteran; or spouse of veteran.

**Application requirements:** Recommendations, transcript, proof of eligibility.
**Additional information:** Preference given to former Nebraska Girls State citizens.

| | |
|---|---|
| **Amount of award:** | $400 |

**Contact:**
American Legion Nebraska Auxiliary, Department Headquarters
P.O. Box 5227
Lincoln, NE 68505-0227
Web: www.nebraskalegionaux.net

## Ruby Paul Campaign Fund Scholarship

**Type of award:** Scholarship.
**Intended use:** For freshman study at accredited 2-year or 4-year institution.
**Eligibility:** Applicant or parent must be member/participant of American Legion Auxiliary. Applicant must be high school senior. Applicant must be residing in Nebraska. Must be Legion member, ALA member, Sons of the American Legion member of two years' standing, or child, grandchild, or great-grandchild of American Legion or ALA member of two years' standing.
**Basis for selection:** Applicant must demonstrate high academic achievement.
**Application requirements:** Recommendations, essay, transcript, proof of eligibility.
**Additional information:** Award varies with availability of funds. Applicant must be state resident for three years. Must have maintained "B" or better during last two semesters of high school. Must be accepted for fall term at college or university. Scholarships exclude applicants enrolled in nursing.

| | |
|---|---|
| **Amount of award:** | $100-$300 |
| **Application deadline:** | April 1 |

**Contact:**
American Legion Nebraska Auxiliary, Department Headquarters
P.O. Box 5227
Lincoln, NE 68505-0227
Web: www.nebraskalegionaux.net

## Student Aid Grant or Vocational Technical Scholarship

**Type of award:** Scholarship.
**Intended use:** For undergraduate study at vocational or 2-year institution in United States.
**Eligibility:** Applicant must be residing in Nebraska. Applicant must be descendant of veteran; or dependent of veteran; or spouse of veteran.
**Application requirements:** Recommendations, transcript, proof of eligibility.

| | |
|---|---|
| **Amount of award:** | $200-$300 |
| **Application deadline:** | April 1 |

**Contact:**
American Legion Nebraska Auxiliary, Department Headquarters
P.O. Box 5227
Lincoln, NE 68505-0227
Web: www.nebraskalegionaux.net

# American Legion Nevada

## American Legion Nevada Oratorical Contest

**Type of award:** Scholarship.
**Intended use:** For undergraduate study at postsecondary institution.
**Eligibility:** Applicant must be enrolled in high school. Applicant must be U.S. citizen or permanent resident residing in Nevada.
**Basis for selection:** Competition/talent/interest in oratory/debate, based on language style, voice, diction, delivery, originality, logic, breadth of knowledge, application of knowledge about topic, and skill in selecting examples and analogies.
**Additional information:** Awards: First place, $500; second place, $300; third place, $200; all in promissory notes.

| | |
|---|---|
| **Amount of award:** | $200-$500 |
| **Number of awards:** | 3 |
| **Application deadline:** | January 15 |
| **Total amount awarded:** | $1,000 |

**Contact:**
American Legion Nevada Oratorical Contest
737 Veterans Memorial Drive
Las Vegas, NV 89101
Web: www.nvlegion.org

# American Legion Nevada Auxiliary

## Past President's Parley Nurses' Scholarship

**Type of award:** Scholarship.
**Intended use:** For junior study at postsecondary institution.
**Eligibility:** Applicant must be residing in Nevada. Applicant must be veteran; or dependent of veteran.
**Basis for selection:** Major/career interest in nursing.
**Additional information:** $150 for each university. Applicant must have completed first two years of training.

| | |
|---|---|
| **Amount of award:** | $150 |

**Contact:**
American Legion Nevada Auxiliary
Past President Parley Chair Nancy Michalski
1025 Twin Berry Ct
Henderson, NV 89002

## President's Scholarship

**Type of award:** Scholarship.
**Intended use:** For undergraduate study at postsecondary institution.
**Eligibility:** Applicant must be residing in Nevada.
**Additional information:** President's Scholarship: $300 for winner of Department competition.

| | |
|---|---|
| **Amount of award:** | $300 |
| **Number of awards:** | 1 |

**Contact:**
American Legion Nevada Auxiliary, Department Secretary
4030 Bobolink Cir.
Reno, NV 89508

### Silver Eagle Indian Scholarship

**Type of award:** Scholarship.
**Intended use:** For undergraduate study at postsecondary institution.
**Eligibility:** Applicant must be American Indian. Applicant must be U.S. citizen residing in Nevada. Applicant must be child or grandchild of American Indian veteran.

**Amount of award:** $200

**Contact:**
American Legion Nevada Auxiliary, Department Secretary
4030 Bobolink Cir.
Reno, NV 89508

## American Legion New Hampshire

### Albert T. Marcoux Memorial Scholarship

**Type of award:** Scholarship.
**Intended use:** For freshman study at accredited postsecondary institution.
**Eligibility:** Applicant or parent must be member/participant of American Legion. Applicant must be residing in New Hampshire. Must be child of living or deceased New Hampshire American Legion or New Hampshire American Legion Auxiliary member.
**Basis for selection:** Applicant must demonstrate high academic achievement.
**Application requirements:** Recommendations, essay, transcript, proof of eligibility. Resume.
**Additional information:** Must be child of living or deceased Washington Legionnaire or Auxiliary member. Must be graduate of New Hampshire high school and state resident for three years.

**Amount of award:** $2,000
**Number of awards:** 1
**Total amount awarded:** $2,000

**Contact:**
American Legion New Hampshire
State House Annex
25 Capitol Street, Room 431
Concord, NH 03301-6312
Phone: 603-271-2211
Web: www.nhlegion.org

### American Legion New Hampshire Boys State Scholarship

**Type of award:** Scholarship.
**Intended use:** For undergraduate study at postsecondary institution.
**Eligibility:** Applicant or parent must be member/participant of American Legion, Boys State. Applicant must be male. Applicant must be residing in New Hampshire.
**Additional information:** Award given to participants of Boys State during Boys State graduation. Award amount varies. Apply during Boys State session.

**Contact:**
American Legion New Hampshire
State House Annex
25 Capitol Street, Room 431
Concord, NH 03301-6312
Phone: 603-271-2211
Web: www.nhlegion.org

### American Legion New Hampshire Oratorical Contest

**Type of award:** Scholarship.
**Intended use:** For undergraduate study at postsecondary institution.
**Eligibility:** Applicant must be enrolled in high school. Applicant must be residing in New Hampshire.
**Basis for selection:** Competition/talent/interest in oratory/debate, based on language style, voice, diction, delivery, originality, logic, breadth of knowledge, application of knowledge about topic, and skill in selecting examples and analogies.
**Application requirements:** Proof of eligibility.
**Additional information:** Awards: First place, $1,000; second place, $750; third place, $500; fourth place, $250; and four $100 awards.

**Amount of award:** $100-$1,000
**Number of awards:** 8
**Total amount awarded:** $2,900

**Contact:**
American Legion New Hampshire
State House Annex
25 Capitol Street, Room 431
Concord, NH 03301-6312
Phone: 603-271-2211
Web: www.nhlegion.org

### Christa McAuliffe Memorial Scholarship

**Type of award:** Scholarship.
**Intended use:** For freshman study at accredited 4-year institution.
**Eligibility:** Applicant must be residing in New Hampshire.
**Basis for selection:** Major/career interest in education. Applicant must demonstrate high academic achievement.
**Application requirements:** Recommendations, essay, transcript. Resume.
**Additional information:** Must be high school student or recent graduate of New Hampshire school entering first year of higher education; state resident for at least three years.

**Amount of award:** $2,000
**Number of awards:** 1
**Application deadline:** May 1
**Total amount awarded:** $2,000

**Contact:**
American Legion New Hampshire
State House Annex
25 Capitol Street, Room 431
Concord, NH 03301-6312
Phone: 603-271-2211
Web: www.nhlegion.org

## Department of New Hampshire Scholarship

**Type of award:** Scholarship.
**Intended use:** For freshman study at accredited 4-year institution.
**Eligibility:** Applicant or parent must be member/participant of American Legion. Applicant must be enrolled in high school. Applicant must be residing in New Hampshire.
**Basis for selection:** Applicant must demonstrate high academic achievement.
**Application requirements:** Recommendations, essay, transcript. Resume.
**Additional information:** Must be high school student or graduate from New Hampshire school entering first year of higher education; state resident for at least three years.

| | |
|---|---|
| **Amount of award:** | $2,000 |
| **Number of awards:** | 2 |
| **Application deadline:** | May 1 |
| **Total amount awarded:** | $4,000 |

**Contact:**
American Legion New Hampshire
State House Annex
25 Capitol Street, Room 431
Concord, NH 03301-6312
Phone: 603-271-2211
Web: www.nhlegion.org

## Department Vocational Scholarship

**Type of award:** Scholarship.
**Intended use:** For freshman study at vocational or 2-year institution.
**Eligibility:** Applicant or parent must be member/participant of American Legion. Applicant must be enrolled in high school. Applicant must be residing in New Hampshire.
**Basis for selection:** Applicant must demonstrate high academic achievement.
**Application requirements:** Recommendations, essay, transcript, proof of eligibility.
**Additional information:** Must be high school student or graduate from New Hampshire school entering first year of higher education in specific vocation; state resident for at least three years.

| | |
|---|---|
| **Amount of award:** | $2,000 |
| **Number of awards:** | 1 |
| **Total amount awarded:** | $2,000 |

**Contact:**
American Legion New Hampshire
State House Annex
25 Capitol Street, Room 431
Concord, NH 03301-6312
Phone: 603-271-2211
Web: www.nhlegion.org

## John A. High Child Welfare Scholarship

**Type of award:** Scholarship.
**Intended use:** For freshman study at postsecondary institution.
**Eligibility:** Applicant must be male, high school senior. Applicant must be residing in New Hampshire.
**Basis for selection:** Applicant must demonstrate financial need, high academic achievement, depth of character and patriotism.
**Application requirements:** Recommendations, essay, transcript.
**Additional information:** Parent must be member of American Legion New Hampshire or American Legion New Hampshire Auxiliary for three consecutive years.

| | |
|---|---|
| **Amount of award:** | $2,000 |
| **Number of awards:** | 1 |
| **Total amount awarded:** | $2,000 |

**Contact:**
American Legion New Hampshire
State House Annex
25 Capitol Street, Room 431
Concord, NH 03301-6312
Phone: 603-271-2211
Web: www.nhlegion.org

## Raymond K. Conley Memorial Scholarship

**Type of award:** Scholarship.
**Intended use:** For freshman study at vocational, 2-year or 4-year institution.
**Eligibility:** Applicant must be high school senior. Applicant must be residing in New Hampshire.
**Basis for selection:** Major/career interest in rehabilitation/therapeutic services.
**Application requirements:** Recommendations, essay, transcript.
**Additional information:** Three-year state residency required. Must have at least a 'B' average.

| | |
|---|---|
| **Amount of award:** | $2,000 |
| **Number of awards:** | 1 |
| **Application deadline:** | May 1 |
| **Total amount awarded:** | $2,000 |

**Contact:**
American Legion New Hampshire
State House Annex
25 Capitol Street, Room 431
Concord, NH 03301-6312
Phone: 603-271-2211
Web: www.nhlegion.org

# American Legion New Hampshire Auxiliary

## Adrienne Alix Scholarship

**Type of award:** Scholarship.
**Intended use:** For undergraduate study at postsecondary institution.
**Eligibility:** Applicant or parent must be member/participant of American Legion Auxiliary. Applicant must be returning adult student. Applicant must be residing in New Hampshire.
**Application requirements:** Recommendations, essay.
**Additional information:** Must be one of the following: Re-entering work force or upgrading skills; displaced from work force; or recently honorably discharged from military. Scholarship must be used for a refresher course or to advance applicant's knowledge of techniques needed in today's work force.

| | |
|---|---|
| **Amount of award:** | $1,000 |
| **Number of awards:** | 1 |
| **Application deadline:** | May 1 |
| **Total amount awarded:** | $1,000 |

**Contact:**
American Legion New Hampshire Auxiliary
Department Secretary
25 Capitol Street, Room 432
Concord, NH 03301-6312
Web: www.nhlegion.org

## Elsie B. Brown Scholarship Fund

**Type of award:** Scholarship.
**Intended use:** For freshman study at postsecondary institution.
**Eligibility:** Applicant or parent must be member/participant of American Legion Auxiliary. Applicant must be residing in New Hampshire. Applicant must be dependent of deceased veteran.
**Application requirements:** Recommendations, essay, transcript.

| | |
|---|---|
| **Amount of award:** | $150 |
| **Number of awards:** | 1 |
| **Application deadline:** | May 1 |
| **Total amount awarded:** | $150 |

**Contact:**
American Legion New Hampshire Auxiliary
Department Secretary
25 Capitol Street, Room 432
Concord, NH 03301-6312
Web: www.nhlegion.org

## Grace S. High Memorial Child Welfare Scholarship Fund

**Type of award:** Scholarship.
**Intended use:** For undergraduate study at postsecondary institution.
**Eligibility:** Applicant or parent must be member/participant of American Legion Auxiliary. Applicant must be female, high school senior. Applicant must be residing in New Hampshire. Daughters of deceased veterans also eligible.
**Basis for selection:** Applicant must demonstrate financial need.
**Application requirements:** Recommendations, essay, transcript, proof of eligibility.
**Additional information:** Applicant must be high school graduate and daughter of Legion or Auxiliary member. Parent must be member of American Legion New Hampshire or American Legion New Hampshire Auxiliary for at least three years.

| | |
|---|---|
| **Amount of award:** | $300 |
| **Number of awards:** | 2 |
| **Application deadline:** | May 1 |
| **Total amount awarded:** | $600 |

**Contact:**
American Legion Auxiliary, Department of New Hampshire
Department Secretary
25 Capitol Street, Room 432
Concord, NH 03301-6312
Web: www.nhlegion.org

## Marion J. Bagley Scholarship

**Type of award:** Scholarship.
**Intended use:** For undergraduate study at accredited postsecondary institution.
**Eligibility:** Applicant or parent must be member/participant of American Legion Auxiliary. Applicant must be residing in New Hampshire.
**Application requirements:** Recommendations, essay, transcript.
**Additional information:** Applicant must be high school graduate (or equivalent) or attending school of higher learning.

| | |
|---|---|
| **Amount of award:** | $1,000 |
| **Number of awards:** | 1 |
| **Application deadline:** | May 1 |
| **Total amount awarded:** | $1,000 |

**Contact:**
American Legion Auxiliary, Department of New Hampshire
Department Secretary
25 Capitol Street, Room 432
Concord, NH 03301-6312
Web: www.nhlegion.org

## Past President's Parley Nurses' Scholarship

**Type of award:** Scholarship.
**Intended use:** For undergraduate study at postsecondary institution.
**Eligibility:** Applicant or parent must be member/participant of American Legion Auxiliary. Applicant must be residing in New Hampshire.
**Basis for selection:** Major/career interest in nursing. Applicant must demonstrate financial need.
**Application requirements:** Recommendations, essay, transcript.
**Additional information:** Applicant must be high school graduate. Children of veteran given preference. One award to Registered Nurse study and one to Licensed Practical Nurse study.

| | |
|---|---|
| **Amount of award:** | $300-$400 |
| **Number of awards:** | 2 |
| **Application deadline:** | May 1 |

**Contact:**
American Legion Auxiliary, Department of New Hampshire
Department Secretary
25 Capitol Street, Room 432
Concord, NH 03301-6312
Web: www.nhlegion.org

# American Legion New Jersey

## American Legion New Jersey Oratorical Contest

**Type of award:** Scholarship.
**Intended use:** For undergraduate study at postsecondary institution.
**Eligibility:** Applicant must be enrolled in high school. Applicant must be residing in New Jersey.
**Basis for selection:** Competition/talent/interest in oratory/debate, based on language style, voice, diction, delivery, originality, logic, breadth of knowledge, application of knowledge about topic, and skill in selecting examples and analogies.
**Application requirements:** Proof of eligibility.
**Additional information:** Awards: First place, $4,000; second place, $2,500; third place, $2,000; fourth place, $1000; fifth place, $1000. See high school counselor for application.

| | |
|---|---|
| **Amount of award:** | $1,000-$4,000 |
| **Number of awards:** | 5 |
| **Total amount awarded:** | $10,500 |

**Contact:**
American Legion New Jersey
135 West Hanover Street
Trenton, NJ 08618
Phone: 609-695-5418
Web: www.njamericanlegion.org

### Department of New Jersey Scholarship

**Type of award:** Scholarship.
**Intended use:** For undergraduate study at 4-year institution.
**Eligibility:** Applicant or parent must be member/participant of American Legion. Applicant must be high school senior. Applicant must be residing in New Jersey.
**Additional information:** Applicant must be natural or adopted child of American Legion, Department of New Jersey member, or of a deceased member if parent was member at time of death. Contact local Post for application.

| | |
|---|---|
| **Amount of award:** | $1,000-$4,000 |
| **Number of awards:** | 8 |
| **Application deadline:** | February 15 |

**Contact:**
American Legion, Department of New Jersey
Department Adjutant
135 West Hanover Street
Trenton, NJ 08618
Phone: 609-695-5418
Web: www.njamericanlegion.org

## American Legion New Jersey Auxiliary

### American Legion New Jersey Auxiliary Department Scholarships

**Type of award:** Scholarship.
**Intended use:** For freshman study at 2-year or 4-year institution.
**Eligibility:** Applicant must be high school senior. Applicant must be residing in New Jersey. Must be child or grandchild of honorably discharged veteran of U.S. Armed Forces.
**Additional information:** Several awards offered. Amount and number of awards vary. Must be New Jersey resident for at least two years.
**Contact:**
American Legion Auxiliary, Department of New Jersey
Department Secretary
1540 Kuser Road, Suite A-8
Hamilton, NJ 08619
Phone: 609-581-9580
Fax: 609-581-8429

### Claire Oliphant Memorial Scholarship

**Type of award:** Scholarship.
**Intended use:** For freshman study at 2-year or 4-year institution.
**Eligibility:** Applicant must be high school senior. Applicant must be residing in New Jersey. Must be child of honorably discharged veteran of U.S. Armed Forces.
**Additional information:** Must be New Jersey resident for at least two years. Rules and applications distributed to all New Jersey high school guidance departments.

| | |
|---|---|
| **Amount of award:** | $1,800 |
| **Number of awards:** | 1 |
| **Application deadline:** | April 15 |
| **Total amount awarded:** | $1,800 |

**Contact:**
American Legion Auxiliary, Department of New Jersey
Department Secretary
1540 Kuser Road, Suite A-8
Hamilton, NJ 08619
Phone: 609-581-9580
Fax: 609-581-8429

### Past President's Parley Nurses' Scholarship

**Type of award:** Scholarship.
**Intended use:** For freshman study at 2-year or 4-year institution.
**Eligibility:** Applicant must be high school senior. Applicant must be residing in New Jersey. Must be child or grandchild of honorably discharged veteran of U.S. Armed Forces.
**Basis for selection:** Major/career interest in nursing.
**Additional information:** Applicant must be enrolled in nursing program. Must be New Jersey resident for at least two years. Award amount varies.
**Contact:**
American Legion Auxiliary, Department of New Jersey
Department Secretary
1540 Kuser Road, Suite A-8
Hamilton, NJ 08619
Phone: 609-581-9580
Fax: 609-581-8429

## American Legion New Mexico Auxiliary

### National President's Scholarship

**Type of award:** Scholarship.
**Intended use:** For undergraduate study at postsecondary institution.
**Eligibility:** Applicant must be residing in New Mexico.
**Additional information:** Awarded to Department winner of National President's Scholarship, if she does not win in Division. If she does, it will be given to second place winner in Department.

| | |
|---|---|
| **Amount of award:** | $150 |
| **Number of awards:** | 1 |
| **Application deadline:** | April 1 |
| **Total amount awarded:** | $150 |

**Contact:**
American Legion New Mexico Auxiliary
Attn: National President's Scholarship
1215 Mountain Road, NE
Albuquerque, NM 87102
Phone: 505-242-9918

### Past President's Parley Scholarship for Nurses

**Type of award:** Scholarship.
**Intended use:** For undergraduate study at postsecondary institution.
**Eligibility:** Applicant must be residing in New Mexico.
**Basis for selection:** Major/career interest in health-related professions; nursing or medicine.
**Application requirements:** Copy of school registration and letter of request for assistance.

| | |
|---|---|
| **Application deadline:** | May 1 |

**Contact:**
American Legion Auxiliary, Department of New Mexico
Attn: Nurses Scholarship
1215 Mountain Road, NE
Albuquerque, NM 87102
Phone: 505-242-9918

## American Legion New York

### American Legion New York Oratorical Contest

**Type of award:** Scholarship.
**Intended use:** For undergraduate study at postsecondary institution.
**Eligibility:** Applicant or parent must be member/participant of American Legion. Applicant must be no older than 20, enrolled in high school. Applicant must be residing in New York.
**Basis for selection:** Competition/talent/interest in oratory/debate, based on language style, voice, diction, delivery, originality, logic, breadth of knowledge, application of knowledge about topic, and skill in selecting examples and analogies.
**Application requirements:** Proof of eligibility.
**Additional information:** Awards: First place, $6,000; second place, $4,000; third place, $2,500; fourth and fifth place, $2,000. Scholarship payments are made directly to student's college and are awarded over a four-year period. Contact local Post for more information.

| | |
|---|---|
| **Amount of award:** | $2,000-$6,000 |
| **Number of awards:** | 5 |
| **Total amount awarded:** | $16,500 |

**Contact:**
American Legion, Department of New York
Department Adjutant
112 State Street, Suite 1300
Albany, NY 12207
Phone: 518-463-2215
Web: www.ny.legion.org

### Dr. Hannah K. Vuolo Memorial Scholarship

**Type of award:** Scholarship.
**Intended use:** For freshman study at accredited 2-year or 4-year institution.
**Eligibility:** Applicant or parent must be member/participant of American Legion. Applicant must be no older than 20, high school senior. Applicant must be descendant of veteran.
**Basis for selection:** Major/career interest in education, teacher.
**Additional information:** Applicant must be natural or adopted direct descendant of member or deceased member of American Legion, Department of New York.

| | |
|---|---|
| **Amount of award:** | $1,000 |
| **Number of awards:** | 1 |
| **Application deadline:** | May 1 |
| **Total amount awarded:** | $1,000 |

**Contact:**
American Legion, Department of New York
Department Adjutant
112 State Street, Suite 1300
Albany, NY 12207
Phone: 518-463-2215
Web: www.ny.legion.org

### New York American Legion Press Association Scholarship

**Type of award:** Scholarship.
**Intended use:** For full-time undergraduate study at accredited 4-year institution.
**Eligibility:** Applicant or parent must be member/participant of American Legion. Applicant must be residing in New York.
**Basis for selection:** Major/career interest in communications; journalism; graphic arts/design; film/video or radio/television/film.
**Additional information:** Applicant must be child of New York Legion or Auxiliary member; Sons of American Legion or American Legion Auxiliary Junior member; or graduate of New York American Legion Boys State or Girls State.

| | |
|---|---|
| **Amount of award:** | $1,000 |
| **Number of awards:** | 1 |
| **Application deadline:** | April 15 |

**Contact:**
New York American Legion Press Association
Scholarship Chairman
P.O. Box 650
East Aurora, NY 14052
Web: www.ny.legion.org

## American Legion New York Auxiliary

### American Legion New York Auxiliary Scholarship

**Type of award:** Scholarship.
**Intended use:** For undergraduate study at postsecondary institution.
**Eligibility:** Applicant must be U.S. citizen residing in New York. Applicant must be descendant of veteran; or dependent of veteran or deceased veteran during Grenada conflict, Korean War, Lebanon conflict, Panama conflict, Persian Gulf War, WW I, WW II or Vietnam.
**Basis for selection:** Applicant must demonstrate financial need, high academic achievement, depth of character, leadership and patriotism.
**Additional information:** May use other scholarships. Visit Website for application.

| | |
|---|---|
| **Amount of award:** | $1,000 |
| **Number of awards:** | 1 |
| **Application deadline:** | March 1 |
| **Total amount awarded:** | $1,000 |

**Contact:**
American Legion New York Auxiliary
112 State Street, Suite 1310
Albany, NY 12207-0003
Web: www.deptny.org

### Past President's Parley Student Scholarship in Medical Field

**Type of award:** Scholarship.
**Intended use:** For undergraduate study at 2-year or 4-year institution.
**Eligibility:** Applicant must be no older than 19, high school senior. Applicant must be U.S. citizen residing in New York. Applicant must be descendant of veteran; or dependent of veteran during Grenada conflict, Korean War, Lebanon conflict, Panama conflict, Persian Gulf War, WW I, WW II or Vietnam.
**Basis for selection:** Major/career interest in health-related professions. Applicant must demonstrate financial need, high academic achievement, depth of character, leadership and patriotism.
**Additional information:** Visit Website for application.

| | |
|---|---|
| **Amount of award:** | $1,500 |
| **Number of awards:** | 3 |
| **Application deadline:** | March 1 |

**Contact:**
American Legion New York Auxiliary
112 State Street, Suite 1310
Albany, NY 12207-0003
Phone: 518-463-1162
Web: www.deptny.org

## American Legion North Carolina

### American Legion Oratorical Contest

**Type of award:** Scholarship.
**Intended use:** For undergraduate study at postsecondary institution.
**Eligibility:** Applicant must be enrolled in high school. Applicant must be U.S. citizen or permanent resident residing in North Carolina.
**Basis for selection:** Competition/talent/interest in oratory/debate, based on language style, voice, diction, delivery, originality, logic, breadth of knowledge, application of knowledge about topic, and skill in selecting examples and analogies.
**Additional information:** Awards: First place, $2,000; second place, $750; third, fourth, and fifth place, $500. Visit Website for more information.

| | |
|---|---|
| **Amount of award:** | $500-$2,000 |
| **Number of awards:** | 5 |
| **Total amount awarded:** | $4,250 |

**Contact:**
American Legion North Carolina
Oratorical Contest
P.O. Box 26657
Raleigh, NC 27611-6657
Web: www.nclegion.org

### Colon Furr Scholarship

**Type of award:** Scholarship.
**Intended use:** For undergraduate study at 2-year or 4-year institution. Designated institutions: North Carolina schools granting LPN or RN degree.
**Eligibility:** Applicant must be residing in North Carolina.
**Basis for selection:** Major/career interest in nursing.
**Application requirements:** Nomination by North Carolina American Legion Post.
**Additional information:** Applicant must be accepted or enrolled in a one-year LPN program or a two, three, or four-year RN program. Contact local Post for application.

| | |
|---|---|
| **Amount of award:** | $600 |
| **Number of awards:** | 1 |
| **Total amount awarded:** | $600 |

**Contact:**
American Legion North Carolina
P.O. Box 26657
Raleigh, NC 27611-6657
Web: www.nclegion.org

## American Legion North Carolina Auxiliary

### Nannie W. Norfleet Scholarship

**Type of award:** Scholarship.
**Intended use:** For undergraduate study at postsecondary institution.
**Eligibility:** Applicant or parent must be member/participant of American Legion Auxiliary. Applicant must be high school senior. Applicant must be residing in North Carolina.
**Basis for selection:** Applicant must demonstrate financial need.
**Additional information:** Preference given to children of American Legion Auxiliary members.

| | |
|---|---|
| **Amount of award:** | $1,000 |
| **Number of awards:** | 1 |
| **Total amount awarded:** | $1,000 |

**Contact:**
American Legion North Carolina Auxiliary, Department Headquarters
P.O. Box 25726
Raleigh, NC 27611
Phone: 919-832-4051
Web: www.nclegion.org/auxil.htm

## American Legion North Dakota

### American Legion North Dakota Oratorical Contest

**Type of award:** Scholarship.
**Intended use:** For undergraduate study at postsecondary institution.
**Eligibility:** Applicant must be high school freshman, sophomore, junior or senior. Applicant must be residing in North Dakota.

**Basis for selection:** Competition/talent/interest in oratory/debate, based on language style, voice, diction, delivery, originality, logic, breadth of knowledge, application of knowledge about topic, and skill in selecting examples and analogies.
**Application requirements:** Proof of eligibility. For application, contact local American Legion Post or Department Headquarters after start of school year.
**Additional information:** State awards: First place, $400; second place, $300; third place, $200; fourth place, $100; East and West Divisional Contests: First place, $300; second place, $200; and 10 District Contests: First place, $300; second place, $200; third place, $100. Local contests begin in the fall.

**Amount of award:** $100-$400

**Contact:**
American Legion North Dakota, Department Headquarters
P.O. Box 2666
Fargo, ND 58108-2666
Phone: 701-293-3120
Fax: 701-293-9951
Web: www.ndlegion.org

### Hattie Tedrow Memorial Fund Scholarship

**Type of award:** Scholarship.
**Intended use:** For undergraduate study at vocational, 2-year or 4-year institution.
**Eligibility:** Applicant must be high school senior. Applicant must be residing in North Dakota. Applicant must be descendant of veteran; or dependent of veteran.
**Basis for selection:** Applicant must demonstrate high academic achievement.
**Application requirements:** Essay, proof of eligibility. SASE.
**Additional information:** Number and amount of awards based on availability of funds.

**Amount of award:** $2,000

**Contact:**
American Legion North Dakota
Hattie Tedrow Memorial Fund Scholarship
P.O. Box 1055
Indianapolis, IN 46206
Phone: 701-293-3120
Fax: 701-293-9951
Web: www.ndlegion.org

## American Legion North Dakota Auxiliary

### American Legion North Dakota Auxiliary Scholarships

**Type of award:** Scholarship.
**Intended use:** For undergraduate study at postsecondary institution. Designated institutions: North Dakota institutions.
**Eligibility:** Applicant must be residing in North Dakota.
**Basis for selection:** Applicant must demonstrate financial need.
**Additional information:** Obtain application from local American Legion Auxiliary Unit.

**Amount of award:** $500
**Number of awards:** 4
**Application deadline:** January 15

**Contact:**
American Legion North Dakota Auxiliary
Department Education Chairman
P.O. Box 1060
Jamestown, ND 58402-1060
Phone: 701-253-5992
Web: www.ndlegion.org

### Past President's Parley Scholarship

**Type of award:** Scholarship.
**Intended use:** For undergraduate study at 2-year or 4-year institution. Designated institutions: North Dakota hospital and nursing schools.
**Eligibility:** Applicant or parent must be member/participant of American Legion Auxiliary. Applicant must be residing in North Dakota.
**Basis for selection:** Major/career interest in nursing.
**Additional information:** Children, grandchildren or great-grandchildren of American Legion or Auxiliary member in good standing. Must be graduate of North Dakota high school. Apply to local American Legion Auxiliary Unit.

**Amount of award:** $350
**Application deadline:** May 15

**Contact:**
American Legion Auxiliary, Department of North Dakota
Chair of Dept. Parley Scholarship Committee
P.O. Box 1060
Jamestown, ND 58402-1060
Phone: 701-872-3865
Web: www.ndlegion.org

## American Legion Ohio

### American Legion Ohio Scholarships

**Type of award:** Scholarship.
**Intended use:** For undergraduate study at postsecondary institution.
**Eligibility:** Applicant or parent must be member/participant of American Legion. For Legion members; direct descendants of Legionnaires in good standing; direct descendants of deceased Legionnaires; spouses or children of deceased U.S. military persons who died on active duty or of injuries received on active duty.
**Additional information:** Number and amount of awards vary. Contact sponsor or visit Website for more information.

**Application deadline:** April 15

**Contact:**
American Legion, Department of Ohio
Department Scholarship Committee
P.O. Box 8007
Delaware, OH 43015-8007
Web: www.ohiolegion.com

### Department Oratorical Awards

**Type of award:** Scholarship.
**Intended use:** For undergraduate study at postsecondary institution.
**Eligibility:** Applicant or parent must be member/participant of American Legion. Applicant must be enrolled in high school. Applicant must be residing in Ohio.
**Basis for selection:** Competition/talent/interest in oratory/debate, based on language style, voice, diction, delivery,

originality, logic, breadth of knowledge, application of knowledge about topic, and skill in selecting examples and analogies.
**Additional information:** Awards: First place, $2,000; second place, $1000; third place, $600; fourth place, $400.

| | |
|---|---|
| **Amount of award:** | $400-$2,000 |
| **Number of awards:** | 4 |
| **Total amount awarded:** | $4,000 |

**Contact:**
American Legion Ohio
Department Scholarship Committee
P.O. Box 8007
Delaware, OH 43015-8007
Phone: 740-362-7478
Fax: 740-362-1429
Web: www.ohiolegion.com

# American Legion Ohio Auxiliary

## American Legion Ohio Auxiliary Past President's Parley Nurse's Scholarship

**Type of award:** Scholarship.
**Intended use:** For undergraduate study at 2-year or 4-year institution.
**Eligibility:** Applicant or parent must be member/participant of American Legion Auxiliary. Applicant must be residing in Ohio. Applicant must be descendant of veteran; or dependent of veteran; or spouse of veteran.
**Basis for selection:** Major/career interest in nursing.
**Additional information:** Awards: 15 $300 and two $750 scholarships.

| | |
|---|---|
| **Amount of award:** | $300-$750 |
| **Number of awards:** | 17 |
| **Application deadline:** | May 1 |
| **Total amount awarded:** | $6,000 |

**Contact:**
American Legion Ohio Auxiliary
Department Secretary
P.O. Box 2760
Zanesville, OH 43702-2760
Phone: 740-452-8245
Fax: 740-452-2620

## American Legion Ohio Auxiliary Scholarship

**Type of award:** Scholarship.
**Intended use:** For freshman study at postsecondary institution.
**Eligibility:** Applicant or parent must be member/participant of American Legion Auxiliary. Applicant must be high school senior. Applicant must be residing in Ohio. Applicant must be descendant of veteran; or dependent of veteran or deceased veteran during Grenada conflict, Korean War, Lebanon conflict, Persian Gulf War, WW I, WW II or Vietnam.
**Additional information:** Awards: one $1,500 and one $1,000.

| | |
|---|---|
| **Amount of award:** | $1,000-$1,500 |
| **Number of awards:** | 2 |
| **Application deadline:** | March 1 |
| **Total amount awarded:** | $2,500 |

**Contact:**
American Legion Ohio Auxiliary
Department Secretary
P.O. Box 2760
Zanesville, OH 43702-2760
Phone: 740-452-8245
Fax: 740-452-2620

# American Legion Oregon

## American Legion Department Oratorical Contest

**Type of award:** Scholarship.
**Intended use:** For undergraduate study at postsecondary institution.
**Eligibility:** Applicant must be enrolled in high school. Applicant must be U.S. citizen or permanent resident residing in Oregon.
**Basis for selection:** Competition/talent/interest in oratory/debate, based on language style, voice, diction, delivery, originality, logic, breadth of knowledge, application of knowledge about topic, and skill in selecting examples and analogies.
**Application requirements:** Proof of eligibility.
**Additional information:** Awards: First place, $500; second place, $400; third place, $300; fourth place, $200. Applications available at local high schools.

| | |
|---|---|
| **Amount of award:** | $200-$500 |
| **Number of awards:** | 4 |
| **Application deadline:** | December 1 |
| **Total amount awarded:** | $1,400 |

**Contact:**
American Legion Oregon
P.O. Box 1730
Wilsonville, OR 97070-1730
Phone: 503-685-5006
Fax: 503-685-5008

# American Legion Oregon Auxiliary

## American Legion Auxiliary Department of Oregon Scholarship

**Type of award:** Scholarship.
**Intended use:** For undergraduate study at postsecondary institution.
**Eligibility:** Applicant must be residing in Oregon. Applicant must be dependent of veteran or deceased veteran; or spouse of disabled veteran or deceased veteran.

| | |
|---|---|
| **Amount of award:** | $1,000 |
| **Number of awards:** | 1 |
| **Application deadline:** | March 10 |
| **Total amount awarded:** | $1,000 |

**Contact:**
American Legion Auxiliary, Department of Oregon
Chariman of Education
P.O. Box 1730
Wilsonville, OR 97070-1730

## American Legion Oregon Auxiliary Department Nurses Scholarship

**Type of award:** Scholarship.
**Intended use:** For undergraduate study at accredited 2-year or 4-year institution.
**Eligibility:** Applicant must be residing in Oregon. Applicant must be dependent of disabled veteran or deceased veteran; or spouse of disabled veteran or deceased veteran.
**Basis for selection:** Major/career interest in nursing. Applicant must demonstrate financial need, high academic achievement, depth of character, seriousness of purpose and service orientation.
**Application requirements:** Proof of eligibility.

| | |
|---|---|
| **Amount of award:** | $1,500 |
| **Number of awards:** | 1 |
| **Application deadline:** | May 15 |
| **Total amount awarded:** | $1,500 |

**Contact:**
American Legion Auxiliary, Department of Oregon
Chairman of Education
P.O. Box 1730
Wilsonville, OR 97070-1730

## National President's Scholarship

**Type of award:** Scholarship.
**Intended use:** For undergraduate study at postsecondary institution.
**Eligibility:** Applicant or parent must be member/participant of American Legion Auxiliary. Applicant must be high school senior. Applicant must be residing in Oregon. Applicant must be dependent of veteran during Grenada conflict, Korean War, Lebanon conflict, Panama conflict, Persian Gulf War, WW I, WW II or Vietnam.
**Additional information:** Three awards in each division of American Legion Auxiliary: First place, $2,500; second place, $2,000; and third place, $1,000.

| | |
|---|---|
| **Amount of award:** | $1,000-$2,500 |
| **Number of awards:** | 15 |
| **Application deadline:** | March 1 |

**Contact:**
American Legion Auxiliary, Department of Oregon
Chairman of Education
P.O. Box 1730
Wilsonville, OR 97070-1730

## Spirit of Youth Scholarship

**Type of award:** Scholarship.
**Intended use:** For undergraduate study at accredited vocational, 2-year or 4-year institution.
**Eligibility:** Applicant or parent must be member/participant of American Legion Auxiliary. Applicant must be residing in Oregon. Applicant must be dependent of deceased veteran; or spouse of disabled veteran or deceased veteran.
**Additional information:** Must be Junior member of The American Legion Auxiliary for past three years and hold current membership.

| | |
|---|---|
| **Amount of award:** | $1,000 |
| **Application deadline:** | March 1 |

**Contact:**
American Legion Auxiliary, Department of Oregon
Chairman of Education
P.O. Box 1730
Wilsonville, OR 97070-1730

# American Legion Pennsylvania

## American Legion High School Oratorical Contest

**Type of award:** Scholarship.
**Intended use:** For undergraduate study at postsecondary institution.
**Eligibility:** Applicant must be enrolled in high school. Applicant must be U.S. citizen or permanent resident residing in Pennsylvania.
**Basis for selection:** Competition/talent/interest in oratory/debate, based on language style, voice, diction, delivery, originality, logic, breadth of knowledge, application of knowledge about topic, and skill in selecting examples and analogies.
**Additional information:** Awards: First place, $7,500; second place, $5,000; third place, $4,000. Contact local American Legion Post for details and application.

| | |
|---|---|
| **Amount of award:** | $4,000-$7,500 |
| **Number of awards:** | 3 |
| **Application deadline:** | January 1 |
| **Total amount awarded:** | $16,500 |

**Contact:**
American Legion Pennsylvania
Scholarship Secretary
P.O. Box 2324
Harrisburg, PA 17105-2324
Phone: 717-730-9100
Web: www.pa-legion.com

## Joseph P. Gavenonis Scholarship

**Type of award:** Scholarship, renewable.
**Intended use:** For full-time undergraduate study at 4-year institution.
**Eligibility:** Applicant or parent must be member/participant of American Legion. Applicant must be high school senior. Applicant must be residing in Pennsylvania. Applicant must be child of living member in good standing of Pennsylvania American Legion, or child of deceased Pennsylvania American Legion member.
**Basis for selection:** Applicant must demonstrate financial need.
**Application requirements:** Transcript, proof of eligibility.
**Additional information:** Award is $1,000 per year for four years; renewal based on grades. Minimum GPA 2.5.

| | |
|---|---|
| **Amount of award:** | $1,000 |
| **Number of awards:** | 1 |
| **Application deadline:** | May 30 |
| **Total amount awarded:** | $4,000 |

**Contact:**
American Legion Pennsylvania
Dept. Adjutant, Attn: Scholarship Secretary
P.O. Box 2324
Harrisburg, PA 17105-2324
Phone: 717-730-9100
Web: www.pa-legion.com

### Robert W. Valimont Endowment Fund Scholarship

**Type of award:** Scholarship, renewable.
**Intended use:** For full-time undergraduate study at vocational or 2-year institution.
**Eligibility:** Applicant must be residing in Pennsylvania. Applicant must be dependent of active service person, veteran or deceased veteran.
**Basis for selection:** Applicant must demonstrate financial need.
**Application requirements:** Proof of eligibility.
**Additional information:** Parent must be member of American Legion, Pennsylvania. Award is $600 for first year; must reapply for second year. Minimum 2.5 GPA.

| | |
|---|---|
| **Amount of award:** | $600 |
| **Total amount awarded:** | $600 |

**Contact:**
American Legion Pennsylvania
Dept. Adjutant, Attn: Scholarship Secretary
P.O. Box 2324
Harrisburg, PA 17105-2324
Phone: 717-730-9100
Web: www.pa-legion.com

## American Legion Pennsylvania Auxiliary

### Scholarship for Children of Deceased or Totally Disabled Veterans

**Type of award:** Scholarship.
**Intended use:** For undergraduate study at postsecondary institution.
**Eligibility:** Applicant must be high school senior. Applicant must be residing in Pennsylvania. Applicant must be dependent of disabled veteran or deceased veteran.
**Basis for selection:** Applicant must demonstrate financial need.
**Additional information:** Award is $600 per year for four years.

| | |
|---|---|
| **Amount of award:** | $600 |
| **Number of awards:** | 1 |
| **Application deadline:** | March 15 |
| **Total amount awarded:** | $2,400 |

**Contact:**
American Legion Auxiliary, Department of Pennsylvania
Department Education Chairman
P.O. Box 1285
Camp Hill, PA 17105
Phone: 717-763-7545

### Scholarship for Children of Living Veterans

**Type of award:** Scholarship.
**Intended use:** For undergraduate study at postsecondary institution.
**Eligibility:** Applicant must be high school senior. Applicant must be residing in Pennsylvania. Applicant must be dependent of veteran.
**Basis for selection:** Applicant must demonstrate financial need.
**Additional information:** Award: $600 per year for four years.

| | |
|---|---|
| **Amount of award:** | $600 |
| **Number of awards:** | 1 |
| **Application deadline:** | March 15 |
| **Total amount awarded:** | $2,400 |

**Contact:**
American Legion Auxiliary, Department of Pennsylvania
Department Education Chairman
P.O. Box 1285
Camp Hill, PA 17105
Phone: 717-763-7545

## American Legion Press Club of New Jersey

### American Legion Press Club of New Jersey and Post 170—Arthur Dehardt Memorial Scholarship

**Type of award:** Scholarship.
**Intended use:** For freshman study at accredited 4-year institution.
**Eligibility:** Applicant or parent must be member/participant of American Legion. Applicant must be residing in New Jersey. Applicant must be child or grandchild of current member of New Jersey American Legion or Auxiliary, including Sons of American Legion and Auxiliary Juniors. Graduates from either American Legion New Jersey Boys State or Auxiliary Girls State programs also eligible.
**Basis for selection:** Major/career interest in communications; computer graphics; journalism or public relations.
**Application requirements:** Essay, proof of eligibility.

| | |
|---|---|
| **Amount of award:** | $500 |
| **Number of awards:** | 2 |
| **Application deadline:** | July 15 |
| **Total amount awarded:** | $1,000 |

**Contact:**
American Legion Press Club of New Jersey
Jack W. Kuepfer, Education Chairman
68 Merrill Road
Clifton, NJ 07012-1622
Phone: 973-473-5176
Web: www.njamericanlegion.org

## American Legion Puerto Rico Auxiliary

### American Legion Puerto Rico Auxiliary Nursing Scholarships

**Type of award:** Scholarship.
**Intended use:** For undergraduate study at 2-year or 4-year institution. Designated institutions: Eligible institutions in Puerto Rico.
**Eligibility:** Applicant must be residing in Puerto Rico.
**Basis for selection:** Major/career interest in nursing.
**Application requirements:** Interview.

**Additional information:** Two $250 awards for two consecutive years.

| | |
|---|---|
| **Amount of award:** | $250 |
| **Number of awards:** | 2 |
| **Application deadline:** | March 15 |

**Contact:**
American Legion Auxiliary, Department of Puerto Rico
Education Chairman
P.O. Box 11424
Caparra Heights Station, PR 00922-1424

# American Legion Rhode Island

## American Legion Rhode Island Oratorical Contest

**Type of award:** Scholarship.
**Eligibility:** Applicant must be enrolled in high school. Applicant must be U.S. citizen or permanent resident residing in Rhode Island.
**Basis for selection:** Competition/talent/interest in oratory/debate, based on language style, voice, diction, delivery, originality, logic, breadth of knowledge, application of knowledge about topic, and skill in selecting examples and analogies.
**Additional information:** Awards: First place, $500; second place, $250; third place, $100; fourth place, $50.

| | |
|---|---|
| **Amount of award:** | $50-$500 |
| **Number of awards:** | 4 |
| **Total amount awarded:** | $900 |

**Contact:**
American Legion of Rhode Island, Oratorical Contest
1005 Charles Street
North Providence, RI 02904
Web: www.ri.legion.org

# American Legion Rhode Island Auxiliary

## American Legion Rhode Island Auxiliary Book Award

**Type of award:** Scholarship.
**Intended use:** For undergraduate study at postsecondary institution.
**Eligibility:** Applicant or parent must be member/participant of American Legion Auxiliary. Applicant must be residing in Rhode Island. Applicant must be descendant of veteran; or dependent of veteran.
**Additional information:** Award: $500. Must be child or grandchild of veteran.

| | |
|---|---|
| **Amount of award:** | $500 |
| **Number of awards:** | 1 |
| **Application deadline:** | April 1 |
| **Total amount awarded:** | $500 |

**Contact:**
American Legion Auxiliary, Department of Rhode Island
Department Secretary
815 Sandy Lane #18
Warwick, RI 02889
Web: www.rialaux.com

# American Legion South Carolina

## American Legion South Carolina Department Oratorical Contest

**Type of award:** Scholarship.
**Intended use:** For undergraduate study at postsecondary institution.
**Eligibility:** Applicant must be enrolled in high school. Applicant must be residing in South Carolina.
**Basis for selection:** Competition/talent/interest in oratory/debate, based on language style, voice, diction, delivery, originality, logic, breadth of knowledge, application of knowledge about topic, and skill in selecting examples and analogies.
**Additional information:** Awards: First place, $3,500; second place, $2,000; third and fourth place, $500. Distributed over four-year period. Zone Contest winners: four $100 awards.

| | |
|---|---|
| **Amount of award:** | $100-$3,500 |
| **Number of awards:** | 8 |
| **Application deadline:** | January 29 |
| **Total amount awarded:** | $6,900 |

**Contact:**
American Legion South Carolina, Department Adjutant
P.O. Box 3309
Irmo, SC 29063
Phone: 803-612-1171
Fax: 803-213-9902
Web: www.scarolinalegion.org

# American Legion South Carolina Auxiliary

## American Legion South Carolina Auxiliary Scholarship

**Type of award:** Scholarship.
**Intended use:** For undergraduate study at postsecondary institution.
**Eligibility:** Applicant or parent must be member/participant of American Legion Auxiliary. Applicant must be high school senior. Applicant must be residing in South Carolina.
**Additional information:** Must be American Legion Auxiliary junior or senior member with at least three consecutive years' membership at time of application. Must have current membership card.

| | |
|---|---|
| **Amount of award:** | $500 |
| **Number of awards:** | 2 |
| **Application deadline:** | April 15 |
| **Total amount awarded:** | $1,000 |

Scholarships

**Contact:**
American Legion Auxiliary, Department of South Carolina
Department Secretary
1200 Main Street, Suite 400-B
Columbia, SC 29201
Phone: 803-799-6695
Fax: 803-799-7907

# American Legion South Dakota

## American Legion South Dakota Oratorical Contest

**Type of award:** Scholarship.
**Intended use:** For undergraduate study at postsecondary institution.
**Eligibility:** Applicant must be enrolled in high school. Applicant must be residing in South Dakota.
**Basis for selection:** Competition/talent/interest in oratory/debate, based on language style, voice, diction, delivery, originality, logic, breadth of knowledge, application of knowledge about topic, and skill in selecting examples and analogies.
**Application requirements:** Proof of eligibility.
**Additional information:** Awards: First place, $1,000; second place, $500; third place, $300; fourth and fifth place, $100. Redeemable within five years of date of award.

| | |
|---|---|
| **Amount of award:** | $100-$1,000 |
| **Number of awards:** | 5 |
| **Total amount awarded:** | $2,000 |

**Contact:**
American Legion, Department of South Dakota
Department Adjutant
P.O. Box 67
Watertown, SD 57201-0067
Phone: 605-886-3604

# American Legion South Dakota Auxiliary

## American Legion South Dakota Auxiliary Scholarships

**Type of award:** Scholarship.
**Intended use:** For undergraduate study at vocational, 2-year or 4-year institution.
**Eligibility:** Applicant or parent must be member/participant of American Legion Auxiliary. Applicant must be at least 16, no older than 22. Applicant must be residing in South Dakota. Applicant must be dependent of veteran.
**Additional information:** College scholarships: two $500; vocational scholarships: two $500.

| | |
|---|---|
| **Amount of award:** | $500 |
| **Number of awards:** | 4 |
| **Application deadline:** | March 1 |
| **Total amount awarded:** | $2,000 |

**Contact:**
American Legion South Dakota Auxiliary
Patricia Coyle, Department Secretary
P.O. Box 117
Huron, SD 57350-0117
Phone: 605-353-1793

## Scholarship for College or Vocational

**Type of award:** Scholarship.
**Intended use:** For undergraduate study at vocational, 2-year or 4-year institution.
**Eligibility:** Applicant or parent must be member/participant of American Legion Auxiliary. Applicant must be residing in South Dakota.
**Additional information:** Applicant must have been senior South Dakota American Legion Auxiliary member for three consecutive years including current year.

| | |
|---|---|
| **Amount of award:** | $400 |
| **Number of awards:** | 1 |
| **Application deadline:** | March 1 |
| **Total amount awarded:** | $400 |

**Contact:**
American Legion South Dakota Auxiliary
Patricia Coyle, Department Secretary
P.O. Box 117
Huron, SD 57350-0117
Phone: 605-353-1793

## Thelma Foster Junior American Legion Auxiliary Members Scholarship

**Type of award:** Scholarship.
**Intended use:** For undergraduate study at postsecondary institution.
**Eligibility:** Applicant or parent must be member/participant of American Legion Auxiliary. Applicant must be residing in South Dakota. Must be Junior American Legion member for at least three years, including current year.
**Additional information:** Must be high school senior or graduate of accredited high school.

| | |
|---|---|
| **Amount of award:** | $300 |
| **Number of awards:** | 1 |
| **Application deadline:** | March 1 |

**Contact:**
American Legion South Dakota Auxiliary
Patricia Coyle, Dept. Secretary
P.O. Box 117
Huron, SD 57350-0117
Phone: 605-353-1793

## Thelma Foster Senior American Legion Auxiliary Member Scholarship

**Type of award:** Scholarship.
**Intended use:** For undergraduate study at postsecondary institution.
**Eligibility:** Applicant or parent must be member/participant of American Legion Auxiliary. Applicant must be residing in South Dakota. Must be senior South Dakota American Legion Auxiliary member for past three years, including current year.

**Amount of award:** $300
**Number of awards:** 1
**Application deadline:** March 1
**Total amount awarded:** $300

**Contact:**
American Legion South Dakota Auxiliary
Patricia Coyle, Department Secretary
P.O. Box 117
Huron, SD 57350-0117
Phone: 605-353-1793

# American Legion Tennessee

## American Legion Tennessee Oratorical Contest

**Type of award:** Scholarship, renewable.
**Intended use:** For undergraduate study at vocational, 2-year or 4-year institution in United States.
**Eligibility:** Applicant must be enrolled in high school. Applicant must be residing in Tennessee.
**Basis for selection:** Competition/talent/interest in oratory/debate, based on language style, voice, diction, delivery, originality, logic, breadth of knowledge, application of knowledge about topic, and skill in selecting examples and analogies.
**Application requirements:** Proof of eligibility.
**Additional information:** Awards: First place, $3,000; second place, $2,000; third place, $1,000. First place winner eligible to enter National Contest. National winner receives $18,000 scholarship. Enter contest through local high school participating in Tennessee Oratorical Contest.

**Amount of award:** $1,000-$3,000
**Number of awards:** 3
**Application deadline:** January 1
**Total amount awarded:** $6,000

**Contact:**
American Legion Tennessee
3530 Central Pike
Suite #104
Hermitage, TN 37076
Phone: 615-391-5088
Web: www.tennesseelegion.org

## Eagle Scout of the Year Scholarship

**Type of award:** Scholarship.
**Intended use:** For undergraduate study at postsecondary institution in United States.
**Eligibility:** Applicant or parent must be member/participant of Boy Scouts of America, Eagle Scouts. Applicant must be male, at least 15, no older than 18, enrolled in high school. Applicant must be residing in Tennessee.
**Application requirements:** Nomination by Tennessee American Legion.
**Additional information:** Must be registered, active member of Boy Scout Troop, Varsity Scout Team, or Venturing Crew and either chartered to an American Legion Post, Auxiliary Unit or Sons of American Legion Squadron, or be son or grandson of American Legion or American Legion Auxiliary member.

**Amount of award:** $1,500
**Number of awards:** 1
**Total amount awarded:** $1,500

**Contact:**
American Legion Tennessee
3530 Central Pike
Suite #104
Hermitage, TN 37076
Phone: 615-391-5088
Web: www.tennesseelegion.org

# American Legion Tennessee Auxiliary

## Vara Gray Scholarship Fund

**Type of award:** Scholarship.
**Intended use:** For undergraduate study at vocational, 2-year or 4-year institution.
**Eligibility:** Applicant must be high school senior. Applicant must be residing in Tennessee. Applicant must be dependent of veteran.
**Application requirements:** Recommendations, essay, nomination by local American Legion Auxiliary Unit.

**Amount of award:** $500
**Number of awards:** 3
**Application deadline:** March 1
**Total amount awarded:** $1,500

**Contact:**
American Legion Tennessee Auxiliary, Department Headquarters
104 Point East Drive
Nashville, TN 37216
Phone: 615-226-8648
Fax: 615-226-8649

# American Legion Texas

## Texas Legion Oratorical Contest

**Type of award:** Scholarship.
**Intended use:** For undergraduate study at postsecondary institution.
**Eligibility:** Applicant must be no older than 18, enrolled in high school. Applicant must be residing in Texas.
**Basis for selection:** Competition/talent/interest in oratory/debate, based on language style, voice, diction, delivery, originality, logic, breadth of knowledge, application of knowledge about topic, and skill in selecting examples and analogies. Applicant must demonstrate patriotism.
**Application requirements:** Proof of eligibility.
**Additional information:** Awards: First place, $2,000; second place, $1,500; third place, $1,000; fourth place, $500. First place winner eligible to enter national contest.

**Amount of award:** $500-$2,000
**Number of awards:** 4
**Application deadline:** August 31
**Total amount awarded:** $5,000

**Contact:**
American Legion, Department of Texas
Oratorical Contest
P.O. Box 140527
Austin, TX 78714-0527
Phone: 512-472-4138
Fax: 512-472-0603
Web: www.txlegion.org

# American Legion Texas Auxiliary

## American Legion Texas Auxiliary General Education Scholarship

**Type of award:** Scholarship.
**Intended use:** For undergraduate study at postsecondary institution.
**Eligibility:** Applicant must be residing in Texas. Applicant must be descendant of veteran; or dependent of veteran during Grenada conflict, Korean War, Lebanon conflict, Panama conflict, Persian Gulf War, WW I, WW II or Vietnam.
**Basis for selection:** Applicant must demonstrate financial need and depth of character.
**Application requirements:** Recommendations, transcript. Resume listing statements of financial support from all their sources not listed on the application, extracurricular activities, and honors and awards received.
**Additional information:** Obtain application from local Unit. Unit sponsorship required.

| | |
|---|---|
| **Amount of award:** | $500 |
| **Application deadline:** | April 1 |

**Contact:**
American Legion Auxiliary, Department of Texas
P.O. Box 140407
Austin, TX 78721-0407
Phone: 512-476-7278
Web: www.alatexas.org

## American Legion Texas Auxiliary Medical Scholarship

**Type of award:** Scholarship.
**Intended use:** For undergraduate study at postsecondary institution.
**Eligibility:** Applicant must be residing in Texas. Applicant must be descendant of veteran; or dependent of veteran during Grenada conflict, Korean War, Lebanon conflict, Panama conflict, Persian Gulf War, WW I, WW II or Vietnam.
**Basis for selection:** Major/career interest in nursing; health sciences; health-related professions or medical assistant. Applicant must demonstrate depth of character and seriousness of purpose.
**Application requirements:** Recommendations.
**Additional information:** Obtain application from local Unit. Unit sponsorship required.

| | |
|---|---|
| **Amount of award:** | $1,000 |
| **Application deadline:** | June 1 |

**Contact:**
American Legion Auxiliary, Department of Texas
P.O. Box 140407
Austin, TX 78721-0407
Phone: 512-476-7278
Web: www.alatexas.org

# American Legion Utah Auxiliary

## American Legion Utah Auxiliary National President's Scholarship

**Type of award:** Scholarship.
**Intended use:** For undergraduate study at postsecondary institution.
**Eligibility:** Applicant must be high school senior. Applicant must be residing in Utah. Applicant must be descendant of veteran; or dependent of veteran during Grenada conflict, Korean War, Lebanon conflict, Panama conflict, Persian Gulf War, WW I, WW II or Vietnam.

| | |
|---|---|
| **Amount of award:** | $1,500 |
| **Number of awards:** | 1 |
| **Application deadline:** | February 15 |
| **Total amount awarded:** | $1,500 |

**Contact:**
American Legion Utah Auxiliary
Department Secretary
P.O. Box 148000
Salt Lake City, UT 84114-8000
Phone: 801-539-1015
Fax: 801-521-9191
Web: www.legion-aux.org

# American Legion Vermont

## American Legion Eagle Scout of the Year

**Type of award:** Scholarship.
**Intended use:** For undergraduate study.
**Eligibility:** Applicant or parent must be member/participant of Boy Scouts of America, Eagle Scouts. Applicant must be male, at least 15, no older than 18, enrolled in high school. Applicant must be residing in Vermont.
**Application requirements:** Recommendations.
**Additional information:** Must be registered, active member of Boy Scout Troop, Varsity Scout Troop, or Explorer Post. Awarded for outstanding service to school and community. Applicant must have received Eagle Scout Award.

| | |
|---|---|
| **Amount of award:** | $1,000 |
| **Number of awards:** | 1 |
| **Application deadline:** | March 1 |
| **Total amount awarded:** | $1,000 |

**Contact:**
American Legion of Vermont
Education and Scholarship Committee
P.O. Box 192
Montpelier, VT 05601
Phone: 802-223-0318
Web: www.legionvthq.com

## American Legion Vermont Scholarship

**Type of award:** Scholarship.
**Intended use:** For undergraduate study at postsecondary institution.
**Eligibility:** Applicant must be high school senior. Applicant must be U.S. citizen or permanent resident residing in Vermont.
**Application requirements:** Recommendations, transcript.
**Additional information:** Awards: Charles Barber, one $1,000 award; Ray Greenwood, one $1,500 award and ten $500 awards. Applicant must be senior at Vermont secondary school; senior from adjacent state whose parents are legal Vermont residents; or senior from adjacent state attending Vermont school.

| | |
|---|---|
| **Amount of award:** | $500-$1,500 |
| **Number of awards:** | 12 |
| **Application deadline:** | April 1 |
| **Total amount awarded:** | $7,500 |

**Contact:**
American Legion of Vermont
Education and Scholarship Committee
P.O. Box 192
Montpelier, VT 05601
Phone: 802-223-0318
Fax: 802-223-7131
Web: www.legionvthq.com

## National High School Oratorical Contest

**Type of award:** Scholarship.
**Intended use:** For undergraduate study at postsecondary institution.
**Eligibility:** Applicant must be enrolled in high school. Applicant must be U.S. citizen or permanent resident residing in Vermont.
**Basis for selection:** Competition/talent/interest in oratory/debate, based on language style, voice, diction, delivery, originality, logic, breadth of knowledge, application of knowledge about topic, and skill in selecting examples and analogies.
**Additional information:** No application required. Selection based on prepared oration. Request rules by January 1.

| | |
|---|---|
| **Amount of award:** | $2,000 |
| **Number of awards:** | 1 |
| **Total amount awarded:** | $2,000 |

**Contact:**
American Legion of Vermont
Education and Scholarship Committee
P.O. Box 192
Montpelier, VT 05601-0396
Phone: 802-223-0318
Web: www.legionvthq.com

# American Legion Virginia

## American Legion Virginia Oratorical Contest

**Type of award:** Scholarship.
**Intended use:** For undergraduate study at postsecondary institution.
**Eligibility:** Applicant must be enrolled in high school. Applicant must be residing in Virginia.
**Basis for selection:** Competition/talent/interest in oratory/debate, based on language style, voice, diction, delivery, originality, logic, breadth of knowledge, application of knowledge about topic, and skill in selecting examples and analogies.
**Application requirements:** Proof of eligibility.
**Additional information:** Awards: First place, $1,100; second place, $600; third place, $600.

| | |
|---|---|
| **Amount of award:** | $600-$1,100 |
| **Number of awards:** | 3 |
| **Application deadline:** | December 1 |
| **Total amount awarded:** | $2,300 |

**Contact:**
American Legion Virginia
Department Adjutant
1708 Commonwealth Ave.
Richmond, VA 23230
Phone: 804-353-6606
Fax: 804-358-1940
Web: www.valegion.org

# American Legion Virginia Auxiliary

## Anna Gear Junior Scholarship

**Type of award:** Scholarship.
**Intended use:** For undergraduate study at postsecondary institution.
**Eligibility:** Applicant or parent must be member/participant of American Legion Auxiliary. Applicant must be high school senior. Applicant must be residing in Virginia. Must be Junior member of American Legion Auxiliary for three years.

| | |
|---|---|
| **Amount of award:** | $1,000 |
| **Number of awards:** | 1 |
| **Application deadline:** | April 1 |
| **Total amount awarded:** | $1,000 |

**Contact:**
American Legion Auxiliary, Department of Virginia
Education Chairman
1708 Commonwealth Avenue
Richmond, VA 23230
Phone: 804-355-6410
Web: www.valegion.org

## Dr. Kate Waller Barrett Grant

**Type of award:** Scholarship.
**Intended use:** For undergraduate study at accredited vocational, 2-year or 4-year institution.
**Eligibility:** Applicant or parent must be member/participant of American Legion Auxiliary. Applicant must be high school

Scholarships

senior. Applicant must be residing in Virginia. Applicant must be dependent of veteran.
**Basis for selection:** Applicant must demonstrate financial need.

| | |
|---|---|
| **Amount of award:** | $1,000 |
| **Number of awards:** | 1 |
| **Application deadline:** | March 15 |
| **Total amount awarded:** | $1,000 |

**Contact:**
American Legion Auxiliary, Department of Virginia
Education Chairman
1708 Commonwealth Avenue
Richmond, VA 23230
Phone: 804-355-6410
Web: www.valegion.org



# American Legion Washington

## American Legion Department Oratorical Contest

**Type of award:** Scholarship.
**Intended use:** For undergraduate study at postsecondary institution.
**Eligibility:** Applicant must be enrolled in high school. Applicant must be residing in Washington.
**Basis for selection:** Competition/talent/interest in oratory/debate, based on language style, voice, diction, delivery, originality, logic, breadth of knowledge, application of knowledge about topic, and skill in selecting examples and analogies.
**Additional information:** Student participates in Post, District, Area, and Department contests.

| | |
|---|---|
| **Application deadline:** | January 15 |
| **Total amount awarded:** | $7,800 |

**Contact:**
American Legion Washington
Chairman, Department of Child Welfare
P.O. Box 3917
Lacey, WA 98509-3917
Phone: 360-491-4373
Fax: 360-491-7442
Web: www.walegion.org

## American Legion Washington Scholarships

**Type of award:** Scholarship.
**Intended use:** For undergraduate study at accredited vocational, 2-year or 4-year institution. Designated institutions: Eligible institutions in Washington State.
**Eligibility:** Applicant or parent must be member/participant of American Legion. Applicant must be high school senior. Applicant must be residing in Washington.
**Basis for selection:** Applicant must demonstrate financial need.
**Application requirements:** Recommendations.
**Additional information:** Must be child of living or deceased Washington Legionnaire or Auxiliary member. One $2,500 award and one $1,500 award.

| | |
|---|---|
| **Amount of award:** | $1,500-$2,500 |
| **Number of awards:** | 2 |
| **Application deadline:** | April 1 |
| **Total amount awarded:** | $4,000 |

**Contact:**
American Legion Washington
Chairman, Department of Child Welfare
P.O. Box 3917
Lacey, WA 98509-3917
Phone: 360-491-4373
Fax: 360-491-7442
Web: www.walegion.org

# American Legion Washington Auxiliary

## American Legion Washington Auxiliary Scholarships

**Type of award:** Scholarship.
**Intended use:** For undergraduate study at postsecondary institution.
**Eligibility:** Applicant must be high school senior. Applicant must be residing in Washington. Applicant must be dependent of disabled veteran or deceased veteran.
**Basis for selection:** Applicant must demonstrate financial need.
**Application requirements:** Recommendations, essay, transcript, proof of eligibility.
**Additional information:** Must be high school senior or high school graduate who has not attended institution of higher learning. Must submit application to Unit chairman.

| | |
|---|---|
| **Amount of award:** | $400 |
| **Number of awards:** | 2 |
| **Application deadline:** | March 1 |

**Contact:**
American Legion Washington Auxiliary
P.O. Box 5867
Lacey, WA 98509-5867
Phone: 360-456-5995
Fax: 360-491-7442
Web: www.walegion-aux.org

## Florence Lemcke Memorial Scholarship

**Type of award:** Scholarship.
**Intended use:** For undergraduate study at 2-year or 4-year institution.
**Eligibility:** Applicant must be high school senior. Applicant must be residing in Washington. Applicant must be dependent of veteran or deceased veteran.
**Basis for selection:** Major/career interest in arts, general; art/art history; architecture; dance; literature; music or theater arts. Applicant must demonstrate financial need and depth of character.
**Application requirements:** Recommendations, essay, transcript, proof of eligibility.
**Additional information:** For use in field of fine arts.

| | |
|---|---|
| **Amount of award:** | $300 |
| **Number of awards:** | 1 |
| **Application deadline:** | March 1 |
| **Total amount awarded:** | $300 |

**Contact:**
American Legion Washington Auxiliary
P.O. Box 5867
Lacey, WA 98509-5867
Phone: 360-456-5995
Fax: 360-491-7442
Web: www.walegion-aux.org

## Margarite McAlpin Nurse's Scholarship

**Type of award:** Scholarship.
**Intended use:** For undergraduate or graduate study at postsecondary institution.
**Eligibility:** Applicant must be residing in Washington. Applicant must be dependent of disabled veteran or deceased veteran. Grandchildren of deceased or disabled veterans also eligible.
**Basis for selection:** Major/career interest in nursing. Applicant must demonstrate financial need, high academic achievement and depth of character.
**Application requirements:** Recommendations, essay, transcript, proof of eligibility.
**Additional information:** Must submit application to local Unit chairman.

| | |
|---|---|
| **Amount of award:** | $300 |
| **Number of awards:** | 1 |
| **Application deadline:** | March 1 |
| **Total amount awarded:** | $300 |

**Contact:**
American Legion Washington Auxiliary
P.O. Box 5867
Lacey, WA 98509-5867
Phone: 360-456-5995
Fax: 360-491-7442
Web: www.walegion-aux.org

## Susan Burdett Scholarship

**Type of award:** Scholarship.
**Intended use:** For undergraduate study at postsecondary institution.
**Eligibility:** Applicant must be female. Applicant must be residing in Washington. Applicant must be dependent of disabled veteran or deceased veteran. Grandchildren of deceased or disabled veterans also eligible.
**Basis for selection:** Applicant must demonstrate financial need, high academic achievement, depth of character and leadership.
**Application requirements:** Recommendations, essay, transcript, proof of eligibility.
**Additional information:** Applicant must be former Evergreen Girls State Citizen (WA). Must submit application to local Unit chairman.

| | |
|---|---|
| **Amount of award:** | $300 |
| **Number of awards:** | 1 |
| **Application deadline:** | March 1 |
| **Total amount awarded:** | $300 |

**Contact:**
American Legion Washington Auxiliary
Education Scholarships
P.O. Box 5867
Lacey, WA 98509-5867
Phone: 360-456-5995
Fax: 360-491-7442
Web: www.walegion-aux.org

# American Legion West Virginia

## American Legion West Virginia Oratorical Contest

**Type of award:** Scholarship.
**Intended use:** For undergraduate study at postsecondary institution.
**Eligibility:** Applicant must be enrolled in high school. Applicant must be residing in West Virginia.
**Basis for selection:** Competition/talent/interest in oratory/debate, based on language style, voice, diction, delivery, originality, logic, breadth of knowledge, application of knowledge about topic, and skill in selecting examples and analogies.
**Additional information:** Nine district awards of $200; three section awards of $300. State winner receives $500 and four-year scholarship to West Virginia University or other state college under control of Board of Regents. Contest is held in January and February. Information may be obtained from local high school or American Legion Post.

| | |
|---|---|
| **Amount of award:** | $200-$500 |

**Contact:**
American Legion West Virginia
State Adjutant
2016 Kanawha Blvd. E, Box 3191
Charleston, WV 25332-3191
Phone: 304-343-7591
Fax: 304-343-7592
Web: www.wvlegion.org

## William F. Johnson Memorial Scholarship

**Type of award:** Scholarship.
**Intended use:** For full-time freshman study at postsecondary institution.
**Eligibility:** Applicant must be residing in West Virginia.
**Application requirements:** Essay, transcript. Must submit copy of transcript from first college semester to receive award.
**Additional information:** First place winner: $1,000; second place: $500, to be presented to recipients before start of second semester.

| | |
|---|---|
| **Amount of award:** | $500-$1,000 |
| **Number of awards:** | 1 |
| **Application deadline:** | May 15 |
| **Total amount awarded:** | $1,000 |

**Contact:**
American Legion, Department of West Virginia
State Adjutant
2016 Kanawha Blvd. E, Box 3191
Charleston, WV 25332-3191
Phone: 304-343-7591
Fax: 304-343-7592
Web: www.wvlegion.org

Scholarships

# American Legion West Virginia Auxiliary

## American Legion West Virginia Auxiliary Scholarship

**Type of award:** Scholarship.
**Intended use:** For undergraduate study at postsecondary institution. Designated institutions: West Virginia institutions.
**Eligibility:** Applicant must be no older than 22. Applicant must be residing in West Virginia. Applicant must be dependent of veteran.
**Application requirements:** Proof of eligibility.

**Number of awards:** 4
**Application deadline:** March 1

**Contact:**
American Legion West Virginia Auxiliary
Secretary/Treasurer Mary Rose Yoho
RR 1 Box 144A
Proctor, WV 26055-9616
Phone: 304-455-3449
Web: www.wvaux.org

# American Legion Wisconsin

## American Legion Wisconsin Eagle Scout of the Year Scholarship

**Type of award:** Scholarship.
**Intended use:** For undergraduate study at postsecondary institution.
**Eligibility:** Applicant or parent must be member/participant of American Legion/Boys Scouts of America. Applicant must be male, high school senior. Applicant must be residing in Wisconsin.
**Basis for selection:** Applicant must demonstrate high academic achievement.
**Additional information:** Applicant must be Boy Scout, Varsity Scout or Explorer. Applicant's group must be sponsored by Legion, Auxiliary, or Sons of American Legion, applicant's father or grandfather must be Legion or Auxiliary member.

**Amount of award:** $1,000
**Number of awards:** 1
**Application deadline:** March 1
**Total amount awarded:** $1,000

**Contact:**
American Legion Wisconsin
Program Secretary
P.O. Box 388
Portage, WI 53901
Phone: 608-745-1090
Fax: 608-745-0179
Web: www.wilegion.org

## Oratorical Contest Scholarships

**Type of award:** Scholarship.
**Intended use:** For undergraduate study at postsecondary institution.
**Eligibility:** Applicant must be enrolled in high school. Applicant must be residing in Wisconsin.
**Basis for selection:** Competition/talent/interest in oratory/debate, based on language style, voice, diction, delivery, originality, logic, breadth of knowledge, application of knowledge about topic, and skill in selecting examples and analogies.
**Additional information:** Awards: State winner, $2,000; three regional awards of $1,000 each; regional participants win $600 each.

**Amount of award:** $600-$2,000

**Contact:**
American Legion, Department of Wisconsin
Program Secretary
P.O. Box 388
Portage, WI 53901
Phone: 608-745-1090
Fax: 608-745-0179
Web: www.wilegion.org

## Schneider-Emanuel American Legion Scholarships

**Type of award:** Scholarship.
**Intended use:** For undergraduate study at 4-year institution in United States.
**Eligibility:** Applicant or parent must be member/participant of American Legion. Applicant must be residing in Wisconsin. Applicant must be veteran; or dependent of veteran.
**Basis for selection:** Applicant must demonstrate financial need, high academic achievement and depth of character.
**Application requirements:** Recommendations, transcript. ACT scores.
**Additional information:** Must be current member or child/grandchild of current member of American Legion, Auxiliary/Junior Auxiliary, or Sons of the American Legion, and have membership card at time of application.

**Amount of award:** $1,000
**Number of awards:** 3
**Application deadline:** March 1
**Total amount awarded:** $3,000

**Contact:**
American Legion, Department of Wisconsin
Program Secretary
P.O. Box 388
Portage, WI 53901
Phone: 608-745-1090
Fax: 608-745-0179
Web: www.wilegion.org

# American Legion Wisconsin Auxiliary

## American Legion Wisconsin Auxiliary Department President's Scholarship

**Type of award:** Scholarship.
**Intended use:** For undergraduate study at accredited postsecondary institution.
**Eligibility:** Applicant or parent must be member/participant of American Legion Auxiliary. Applicant must be residing in Wisconsin. Applicant must be descendant of veteran; or dependent of veteran; or spouse of veteran or deceased veteran. Mother of applicant or applicant must be Auxiliary member.

Grandchildren and great-grandchildren of veterans eligible if Auxiliary members.
**Basis for selection:** Applicant must demonstrate financial need.
**Application requirements:** Recommendations, essay, transcript, proof of eligibility.
**Additional information:** Minimum 3.5 GPA.

| | |
|---|---|
| **Amount of award:** | $1,000 |
| **Number of awards:** | 3 |
| **Application deadline:** | March 15 |
| **Total amount awarded:** | $3,000 |

**Contact:**
American Legion Wisconsin Auxiliary
Department Secretary
P.O. Box 140
Portage, WI 53901-0140
Phone: 608-745-0124
Fax: 608-745-1947
Web: www.amlegionauxwi.org

## American Legion Wisconsin Auxiliary H.S. and Angeline Lewis Scholarships

**Type of award:** Scholarship.
**Intended use:** For undergraduate or graduate study at accredited postsecondary institution.
**Eligibility:** Applicant or parent must be member/participant of American Legion Auxiliary. Applicant must be residing in Wisconsin. Applicant must be descendant of veteran; or dependent of veteran; or spouse of veteran or deceased veteran. Grandchildren and great-grandchildren of veterans eligible if members of Auxiliary.
**Basis for selection:** Applicant must demonstrate financial need.
**Application requirements:** Recommendations, essay, transcript, proof of eligibility.
**Additional information:** Minimum 3.5 GPA. One award for graduate study; five awards for undergraduate study.

| | |
|---|---|
| **Amount of award:** | $1,000 |
| **Number of awards:** | 6 |
| **Application deadline:** | March 15 |
| **Total amount awarded:** | $6,000 |

**Contact:**
American Legion Wisconsin Auxiliary
Department Secretary
P.O. Box 140
Portage, WI 53901-0140
Phone: 608-745-0124
Fax: 608-745-1947
Web: www.amlegionauxwi.org

## American Legion Wisconsin Auxiliary Merit and Memorial Scholarship

**Type of award:** Scholarship.
**Intended use:** For undergraduate study.
**Eligibility:** Applicant or parent must be member/participant of American Legion Auxiliary. Applicant must be residing in Wisconsin. Applicant must be descendant of veteran; or dependent of veteran; or spouse of veteran or deceased veteran. Grandchildren and great-grandchildren of veterans eligible if members of Auxiliary.
**Basis for selection:** Applicant must demonstrate financial need.
**Application requirements:** Recommendations, essay, transcript, proof of eligibility.
**Additional information:** Minimum 3.5 GPA.

| | |
|---|---|
| **Amount of award:** | $1,000 |
| **Number of awards:** | 7 |
| **Application deadline:** | March 15 |
| **Total amount awarded:** | $7,000 |

**Contact:**
American Legion Wisconsin Auxiliary
Department Secretary
P.O. Box 140
Portage, WI 53901-0140
Phone: 608-745-0124
Fax: 608-745-1947
Web: www.amlegionauxwi.org

## American Legion Wisconsin Auxiliary Past Presidents Parley Scholarship

**Type of award:** Scholarship.
**Intended use:** For undergraduate study at accredited vocational, 2-year or 4-year institution.
**Eligibility:** Applicant or parent must be member/participant of American Legion Auxiliary. Applicant must be residing in Wisconsin. Applicant must be descendant of veteran; or dependent of veteran or deceased veteran; or spouse of veteran or deceased veteran. Grandchildren or great-grandchildren of veterans eligible if Auxiliary member.
**Basis for selection:** Major/career interest in nursing. Applicant must demonstrate financial need.
**Application requirements:** Recommendations, essay, transcript, proof of eligibility.
**Additional information:** Minimum 3.5 GPA. Must be in or accepted to accredited school of nursing, accredited hospital, or university registered nursing program. Hospital, university, or technical school program acceptable.

| | |
|---|---|
| **Amount of award:** | $1,000 |
| **Number of awards:** | 2 |
| **Application deadline:** | March 15 |

**Contact:**
American Legion Wisconsin Auxiliary
Department Secretary
P.O. Box 140
Portage, WI 53901-0140
Phone: 608-745-0124
Fax: 608-745-1947
Web: www.amlegionauxwi.org

## Della Van Deuren Memorial Scholarship

**Type of award:** Scholarship.
**Intended use:** For undergraduate study.
**Eligibility:** Applicant or parent must be member/participant of American Legion Auxiliary. Applicant must be residing in Wisconsin. Applicant must be descendant of veteran; or dependent of veteran; or spouse of veteran or deceased veteran.
**Basis for selection:** Applicant must demonstrate financial need.
**Application requirements:** Recommendations, essay, transcript, proof of eligibility.
**Additional information:** Applicant's mother or applicant must be member of American Legion Auxiliary. Grandchildren and great-grandchildren of veterans are eligible if they are members of American Legion Auxiliary. Minimum 3.5 GPA. Applicant's school need not be in Wisconsin.

**Amount of award:** $1,000
**Number of awards:** 2
**Application deadline:** March 15
**Total amount awarded:** $2,000

**Contact:**
American Legion Wisconsin Auxiliary
Department Secretary
P.O. Box 140
Portage, WI 53901-0140
Phone: 608-745-0124
Fax: 608-745-1947
Web: www.amlegionauxwi.org



# American Legion Wyoming

## American Legion Wyoming E.A. Blackmore Memorial Scholarship

**Type of award:** Scholarship.
**Intended use:** For undergraduate study at postsecondary institution.
**Eligibility:** Applicant or parent must be member/participant of American Legion. Applicant must be residing in Wyoming.
**Basis for selection:** Applicant must demonstrate financial need and high academic achievement.
**Application requirements:** Recommendations, transcript, proof of eligibility. Resume. Photo of self.
**Additional information:** Must be child or grandchild of American Legion member in good standing, or child or grandchild of deceased American Legion member who was in good standing. Must rank in upper 20 percent of high school class.

**Amount of award:** $1,000
**Number of awards:** 1
**Application deadline:** May 15
**Total amount awarded:** $1,000

**Contact:**
American Legion Wyoming
Department Adjutant
1320 Hugur Ave.
Cheyenne, WY 82001
Phone: 307-634-3035
Fax: 307-635-7093
Web: www.wylegion.org

## American Legion Wyoming Oratorical Contest

**Type of award:** Scholarship.
**Intended use:** For undergraduate study at postsecondary institution.
**Eligibility:** Applicant must be enrolled in high school. Applicant must be U.S. citizen or permanent resident residing in Wyoming.
**Basis for selection:** Competition/talent/interest in oratory/debate, based on language style, voice, diction, delivery, originality, logic, breadth of knowledge, application of knowledge about topic, and skill in selecting examples and analogies.
**Application requirements:** Proof of eligibility.

**Number of awards:** 1
**Application deadline:** May 15
**Total amount awarded:** $2,000

**Contact:**
American Legion Wyoming
Department Adjutant
1320 Hugur Ave.
Cheyenne, WY 82001
Phone: 307-634-3035
Web: www.wylegion.org

# American Legion Wyoming Auxiliary

## American Legion Wyoming Auxiliary Past Presidents' Parley Scholarship

**Type of award:** Scholarship, renewable.
**Intended use:** For full-time undergraduate study at accredited 2-year or 4-year institution. Designated institutions: University of Wyoming or one of Wyoming community colleges.
**Eligibility:** Preference given to nursing students who are children of veterans.
**Basis for selection:** Major/career interest in health-related professions; medicine; nursing; occupational therapy; pharmacy/pharmaceutics/pharmacology; physical therapy; respiratory therapy or speech pathology/audiology. Applicant must demonstrate financial need and high academic achievement.
**Application requirements:** Recommendations.
**Additional information:** Must have completed one year or two semesters of study. Minimum 3.0 GPA. Preference given to Wyoming residents.

**Amount of award:** $300
**Number of awards:** 1
**Application deadline:** June 1
**Total amount awarded:** $600

**Contact:**
American Legion Wyoming Auxiliary
Department Secretary
P.O. Box 2198
Gillette, WY 82717-2198
Phone: 307-686-7137
Web: www.deptofwyala.org

# American Medical Technologists

## Medical Technologists Student Scholarship

**Type of award:** Scholarship.
**Intended use:** For full-time undergraduate or graduate study at accredited postsecondary institution in United States.
**Eligibility:** Applicant must be U.S. citizen or permanent resident.
**Basis for selection:** Major/career interest in medical assistant; dental assistant or health services administration. Applicant must demonstrate financial need.
**Application requirements:** Recommendations, essay, transcript. List of school activities.

**Additional information:** Scholarship is available only to high school graduates studying to become one of the following: medical assistant, dental assistant, medical administrative specialist, medical technologist, medical laboratory technician, medical laboratory assistant, allied health instructor, clinical laboratory consultant, or phlebotomy technician.

| | |
|---|---|
| **Amount of award:** | $500 |
| **Number of awards:** | 5 |
| **Number of applicants:** | 76 |
| **Application deadline:** | April 1 |
| **Total amount awarded:** | $2,500 |

**Contact:**
American Medical Technologists
10700 West Higgins Road, Suite 150
Rosemont, IL 60018
Phone: 847-823-5169
Fax: 847-823-0458
Web: www.amt1.com

# American Meteorological Society

## American Meteorological Society Named Undergraduate Scholarship

**Type of award:** Scholarship.
**Intended use:** For full-time senior study at accredited 4-year institution in United States.
**Eligibility:** Applicant must be U.S. citizen or permanent resident.
**Basis for selection:** Major/career interest in atmospheric sciences/meteorology; oceanography/marine studies or hydrology. Applicant must demonstrate high academic achievement and seriousness of purpose.
**Application requirements:** Recommendations, transcript.
**Additional information:** Minimum 3.25 GPA. Marine biology majors not eligible. Visit Website for more information and to download application. Number and amount of scholarships vary. Applicants must demonstrate financial need to be eligible for the Schroeder Scholarship. The Murphy Scholarship is awarded to students who, through curricular or extracurricular activities, have shown interest in weather forecasting or in the value and utilization of forecasts. The Glahn Scholarship is for a student who has shown strong interest in statistical meteorology. The Crow Scholarship is for a student who has shown strong interest in applied meteorology. Number and amount of awards varies.

| | |
|---|---|
| **Application deadline:** | February 10 |
| **Notification begins:** | May 1 |

**Contact:**
American Meteorological Society
Fellowship/Scholarship Program
45 Beacon Street
Boston, MA 02108-3693
Phone: 617-226-3907
Fax: 617-742-8718
Web: www.ametsoc.org

## American Meteorological Society/ Industry Minority Scholarship

**Type of award:** Scholarship.
**Intended use:** For full-time freshman study at accredited 4-year institution in United States.
**Eligibility:** Applicant must be Alaskan native, Asian American, African American, Mexican American, Hispanic American, Puerto Rican or American Indian. Applicant must be high school senior. Applicant must be U.S. citizen or permanent resident.
**Basis for selection:** Major/career interest in atmospheric sciences/meteorology; oceanography/marine studies or hydrology.
**Application requirements:** Recommendations, essay, transcript. SAT or ACT scores.
**Additional information:** Minimum 3.0 GPA. Award is $3,000 per year for freshman and sophomore years. Award is for minority students who have traditionally been underrepresented in the sciences, especially Hispanic, Native American, and African-American students. Marine biology majors ineligible. Number of awards varies. Visit Website to download application.

| | |
|---|---|
| **Amount of award:** | $6,000 |
| **Number of applicants:** | 40 |
| **Application deadline:** | February 10 |
| **Notification begins:** | May 1 |
| **Total amount awarded:** | $3,000 |

**Contact:**
American Meteorological Society
Fellowship/Scholarship Program
45 Beacon Street
Boston, MA 02108-3693
Phone: 617-226-3907
Fax: 617-742-8718
Web: www.ametsoc.org

## Father James B. Macelwane Annual Award

**Type of award:** Scholarship.
**Intended use:** For undergraduate study.
**Eligibility:** Applicant must be U.S. citizen or permanent resident.
**Basis for selection:** Major/career interest in atmospheric sciences/meteorology; oceanography/marine studies or hydrology.
**Application requirements:** Essay, transcript, proof of eligibility. Original paper plus three photocopies. Letter of application including contact information and stating paper's title and name of university where paper was written. Letter from university faculty stating author was undergraduate when paper was written and indicating elements of paper that are original contributions by the student. Abstract of maximum 250 words describing paper.
**Additional information:** Award intended to stimulate interest in meteorology among college students through submission of original papers concerned with some phase of atmospheric sciences. Student must have been undergraduate when paper was written. Submissions from women, minorities and disabled students who are traditionally underrepresented in atmospheric and related oceanic and hydrologic sciences encouraged. No more than two students from any one institution may enter papers in any one contest. Visit Website for application and additional information.

**Amount of award:** $1,000
**Number of awards:** 1
**Application deadline:** June 8
**Notification begins:** September 1
**Total amount awarded:** $1,000

**Contact:**
American Meteorological Society
Macelwane Award
45 Beacon Street
Boston, MA 02108-3693
Phone: 617-226-3907
Fax: 617-742-8718
Web: www.ametsoc.org



### Freshman Undergraduate Scholarship Program

**Type of award:** Scholarship, renewable.
**Intended use:** For full-time freshman study at accredited 4-year institution in United States.
**Eligibility:** Applicant must be high school senior. Applicant must be U.S. citizen or permanent resident.
**Basis for selection:** Major/career interest in atmospheric sciences/meteorology; oceanography/marine studies or hydrology. Applicant must demonstrate high academic achievement.
**Application requirements:** Recommendations, essay, transcript. SAT/ACT scores.
**Additional information:** Scholarships are renewable for the sophomore year, providing recipient plans to continue studies in the AMS-related sciences. Minimum 3.0 GPA. Award is $2,500 each for freshman and sophomore years.

**Amount of award:** $2,500
**Number of awards:** 14
**Number of applicants:** 159
**Application deadline:** February 10
**Notification begins:** May 1

**Contact:**
American Meteorological Society
Fellowship/Scholarship Program
45 Beacon Street
Boston, MA 02108-3693
Phone: 617-226-3907
Fax: 617-742-8718
Web: www.ametsoc.org

## American Morgan Horse Institute

### AMHI Educational Scholarships

**Type of award:** Scholarship.
**Intended use:** For undergraduate or non-degree study at vocational, 2-year or 4-year institution.
**Eligibility:** Applicant must be high school senior.
**Basis for selection:** Major/career interest in equestrian/equine studies. Applicant must demonstrate financial need, depth of character, leadership, seriousness of purpose and service orientation.
**Application requirements:** Recommendations, essay, transcript. List of horse-related activities, photo.
**Additional information:** Applicant must demonstrate achievement with registered Morgan horses. Award amount varies based on funding. Send SASE or visit Website for application.

**Number of awards:** 5
**Number of applicants:** 45
**Application deadline:** March 1
**Notification begins:** June 15
**Total amount awarded:** $15,000

**Contact:**
AMHI Scholarships
P.O. Box 837
Shelburne, VT 05482-0837
Web: www.morganhorseinstitute.com

### AMHI van Schaik Dressage Scholarship

**Type of award:** Scholarship.
**Intended use:** For non-degree study.
**Basis for selection:** Major/career interest in dressage or equestrian/equine studies. Applicant must demonstrate seriousness of purpose.
**Application requirements:** Recommendations, essay.
**Additional information:** Must be dressage rider using a registered Morgan horse and interested in advancing from lower levels of dressage to Fourth Level and above. Preference given to applicants who have competed their Morgan at First Level Test 4 or above and scored 60 percent or higher at recognized competition. Visit Website for application.

**Amount of award:** $1,000
**Number of awards:** 1
**Number of applicants:** 2
**Application deadline:** November 30
**Notification begins:** March 31
**Total amount awarded:** $1,000

**Contact:**
AMHI Scholarship
Attn: AMHI van Schaik Dressage Scholarship
P.O. Box 837
Shelburne, VT 05482-0837
Web: www.morganhorseinstitute.com

## American Museum of Natural History

### Young Naturalist Awards

**Type of award:** Scholarship, renewable.
**Intended use:** For freshman study.
**Basis for selection:** Competition/talent/interest in science project.
**Application requirements:** Essay. Original artwork/photographs.
**Additional information:** For students grades 7-12 in the U.S and Canada to plan and conduct scientific investigations and report them in an illustrated essay. Children of Alcoa Corporation or American Museum of Natural History employees or consultants are ineligible. Two winners per grade level receive the following: 7th grade, $500; 8th grade, $750; 9th grade, $1,000; 10th grade, $1,500; 11th grade, $2,000; 12th grade, $2,500. Also trip to New York City for award ceremony and tour of the museum. Up to 36 additional finalists receive $50 prize.

**Amount of award:** $50-$2,500
**Number of awards:** 48
**Application deadline:** March 1
**Notification begins:** March 21
**Contact:**
Young Naturalist Awards Administrator
American Museum of Natural History
Central Park West at 79th Street
New York, NY 10024-5192
Phone: 212-496-3498
Web: www.amnh.org/nationalcenter/youngnaturalistawards

# American Nuclear Society

## Accelerator Applications Division Scholarship

**Type of award:** Scholarship.
**Intended use:** For full-time junior study at accredited 4-year institution in United States.
**Basis for selection:** Major/career interest in physics; engineering or materials science. Applicant must demonstrate financial need and high academic achievement.
**Application requirements:** Recommendations, essay, transcript.
**Additional information:** Applicant must be an ANS student member. Must be sponsored by ANS organization. Visit Website for application. One request/application covers all Graduate and Undergraduate scholarships; check appropriate boxes on application form. Number of awards varies. Additional consideration given to applicants who are members of an under-represented class (female/minority), and have a record of service to ANS. Recipients will receive $1,000 for their junior year and $1,000 for their senior year for a total award of $2000 over a two-year period.
**Amount of award:** $2,000
**Application deadline:** February 1
**Contact:**
American Nuclear Society
555 North Kensington Avenue
La Grange Park, IL 60526
Phone: 708-352-6611
Fax: 708-352-0499
Web: www.ans.org

## Angelo S. Bisesti Scholarship

**Type of award:** Scholarship.
**Intended use:** For full-time junior or senior study at accredited 4-year institution in United States.
**Basis for selection:** Major/career interest in nuclear science or engineering, nuclear.
**Application requirements:** Recommendations, transcript.
**Additional information:** Applicant must be an ANS student member enrolled in a program leading to a degree in nuclear science, nuclear engineering or a nuclear related field. Must be sponsored by ANS organization. Visit Website for application. One request/application covers all Graduate and Undergraduate scholarships; check appropriate boxes on application form.
**Amount of award:** $2,000
**Number of awards:** 1
**Application deadline:** February 1
**Total amount awarded:** $2,000
**Contact:**
American Nuclear Society
555 North Kensington Avenue
La Grange Park, IL 60526
Phone: 708-352-6611
Fax: 708-352-0499
Web: www.ans.org

## ANS Incoming Freshman Scholarship

**Type of award:** Scholarship.
**Intended use:** For freshman or senior study at postsecondary institution.
**Basis for selection:** Major/career interest in engineering, nuclear. Applicant must demonstrate high academic achievement.
**Application requirements:** Recommendations, transcript, proof of eligibility. 500-word essay.
**Additional information:** For graduating high-school seniors who have enrolled, full-time, in college courses and are pursuing a degree in nuclear engineering or have the intent to pursue a degree in nuclear engineering.
**Amount of award:** $1,000
**Number of awards:** 4
**Application deadline:** April 1
**Contact:**
American Nuclear Society
555 North Kensington Avenue
La Grange Park, IL 60526
Phone: 708-352-6611
Fax: 708-352-0499
Web: www.ans.org

## ANS Undergraduate Scholarships

**Type of award:** Scholarship.
**Intended use:** For sophomore, junior or senior study at accredited 4-year institution in United States.
**Basis for selection:** Major/career interest in nuclear science or engineering, nuclear.
**Application requirements:** Recommendations, transcript.
**Additional information:** Maximum of four scholarships for entering sophomores in study leading to degree in nuclear science, nuclear engineering, or nuclear-related field; maximum of 21 scholarships for students who will be entering junior or senior year. Applicant must be an ANS student member and must be sponsored by ANS organization. Visit Website for application. One request/application covers all Graduate and Undergraduate scholarships; check appropriate boxes on application form.
**Amount of award:** $2,000
**Application deadline:** February 1
**Contact:**
American Nuclear Society
555 North Kensington Avenue
La Grange Park, IL 60526
Phone: 708-352-6611
Fax: 708-352-0499
Web: www.ans.org

## ANS Washington, DC Section Undergraduate Scholarship

**Type of award:** Scholarship.
**Intended use:** For full-time junior or senior study at accredited 4-year institution in United States.

**Basis for selection:** Major/career interest in engineering, nuclear.
**Application requirements:** Recommendations, transcript.
**Additional information:** Permanent address must be within 100 miles of Washington, DC. Applicant must be an ANS student member enrolled in a program leading to a degree in nuclear engineering, health physics, or nuclear-related studies; minor in nuclear engineering or health physics may be considered as meeting requirement. Must be sponsored by ANS organization. Visit Website for application. One request/application covers all Graduate and Undergraduate scholarships; check appropriate boxes on application form.

| | |
|---|---|
| **Amount of award:** | $2,500 |
| **Number of awards:** | 1 |
| **Application deadline:** | February 1 |

**Contact:**
American Nuclear Society
555 North Kensington Avenue
La Grange Park, IL 60526
Phone: 708-352-6611
Fax: 708-352-0499
Web: www.ans.org

## Charles (Tommy) Thomas Memorial Scholarship

**Type of award:** Scholarship.
**Intended use:** For full-time junior or senior study at accredited 4-year institution in United States.
**Basis for selection:** Major/career interest in nuclear science; engineering, nuclear; environmental science; engineering, environmental; ecology or natural resources/conservation.
**Application requirements:** Recommendations, essay, transcript.
**Additional information:** Applicant must be an ANS student member enrolled in a program leading to a degree in nuclear science, nuclear engineering or a nuclear related field. Must be sponsored by ANS organization. Visit Website for application. One request/application covers all Graduate and Undergraduate scholarships; check appropriate boxes on application form.

| | |
|---|---|
| **Amount of award:** | $3,000 |
| **Number of awards:** | 1 |
| **Application deadline:** | February 1 |

**Contact:**
American Nuclear Society
555 North Kensington Avenue
La Grange Park, IL 60526
Phone: 708-352-6611
Fax: 708-352-0499
Web: www.ans.org

## Decommissioning, Decontamination and Reutilization Scholarship

**Type of award:** Scholarship.
**Intended use:** For junior or senior study at accredited 4-year institution in United States.
**Eligibility:** Applicant must be U.S. citizen.
**Basis for selection:** Major/career interest in engineering, nuclear; environmental science; engineering, environmental or nuclear science.
**Application requirements:** Recommendations, essay, transcript.
**Additional information:** Applicant must be enrolled in curriculum of engineering or science associated with decommissioning/decontamination of nuclear facilities, management/characterization of nuclear waste, or restoration of environment. If awarded scholarship, student must join ANS and designate DDR Division as one professional division. Awardee must also provide support to DDR Division at next ANS meeting after receiving award (funding provided for travel to meeting but does not include food and lodging). Visit Website for application.

| | |
|---|---|
| **Amount of award:** | $2,000 |
| **Number of awards:** | 1 |
| **Application deadline:** | February 1 |

**Contact:**
American Nuclear Society
555 North Kensington Avenue
La Grange Park, IL 60526
Phone: 708-352-6611
Fax: 708-352-0499
Web: www.ans.org

## Delayed Education Scholarship for Women

**Type of award:** Scholarship.
**Intended use:** For undergraduate study at accredited 4-year institution in United States.
**Eligibility:** Applicant must be female, returning adult student.
**Basis for selection:** Major/career interest in nuclear science or engineering, nuclear. Applicant must demonstrate financial need and high academic achievement.
**Application requirements:** Recommendations, transcript.
**Additional information:** Must be a mature woman whose undergraduate studies in nuclear science, nuclear engineering, or a nuclear-related field have been delayed. Applicants must check the appropriate box on the Landis Scholarship form. Visit Website for application and requirements.

| | |
|---|---|
| **Amount of award:** | $5,000 |
| **Number of awards:** | 1 |
| **Application deadline:** | February 1 |

**Contact:**
American Nuclear Society
555 North Kensington Avenue
La Grange Park, IL 60526
Phone: 708-352-6611
Fax: 708-352-0499
Web: www.ans.org

## John and Muriel Landis Scholarship

**Type of award:** Scholarship.
**Intended use:** For undergraduate or graduate study at 4-year or graduate institution in United States.
**Basis for selection:** Major/career interest in nuclear science or engineering, nuclear. Applicant must demonstrate financial need.
**Application requirements:** Recommendations, transcript.
**Additional information:** Awarded to students with greater than average financial need. Consideration given to conditions or experiences that render student disadvantaged (poor high school/undergraduate preparation, etc.). Applicants should be planning career in nuclear science or nuclear engineering. Qualified high school seniors eligible to apply. Visit Website for application and requirements. Applicants must check the appropriate box on the Landis Scholarship form.

| | |
|---|---|
| **Amount of award:** | $5,000 |
| **Number of awards:** | 9 |
| **Application deadline:** | February 1 |

**Contact:**
American Nuclear Society
555 North Kensington Avenue
La Grange Park, IL 60526
Phone: 708-352-6611
Fax: 708-352-0499
Web: www.ans.org

## John R. Lamarsh Scholarship

**Type of award:** Scholarship.
**Intended use:** For full-time junior or senior study at accredited 4-year institution in United States.
**Basis for selection:** Major/career interest in nuclear science or engineering, nuclear.
**Application requirements:** Recommendations, transcript.
**Additional information:** Applicant must be an ANS student member enrolled in a program leading to a degree in nuclear science, nuclear engineering or a nuclear related field. Must be sponsored by ANS organization. Visit Website for application. One request/application covers all Graduate and Undergraduate scholarships; check appropriate boxes on application form.

**Amount of award:** $2,000
**Number of awards:** 1
**Application deadline:** February 1

**Contact:**
American Nuclear Society
555 North Kensington Avenue
La Grange Park, IL 60526
Phone: 708-352-6611
Fax: 708-352-0499
Web: www.ans.org

## Joseph R. Dietrich Scholarship

**Type of award:** Scholarship.
**Intended use:** For full-time junior or senior study at accredited 4-year institution in United States.
**Basis for selection:** Major/career interest in nuclear science; engineering, nuclear; chemistry or physics.
**Application requirements:** Recommendations, transcript.
**Additional information:** Applicant must be an ANS student member enrolled in a program leading to a degree in nuclear science, nuclear engineering or a nuclear related field. Must be sponsored by ANS organization. Visit Website for application. One request/application covers all Graduate and Undergraduate scholarships; check appropriate boxes on application form.

**Amount of award:** $2,000
**Number of awards:** 1
**Application deadline:** February 1

**Contact:**
American Nuclear Society
555 North Kensington Avenue
La Grange Park, IL 60526
Phone: 708-352-6611
Fax: 708-352-0499
Web: www.ans.org

## Operations and Power Division Scholarship

**Type of award:** Scholarship.
**Intended use:** For full-time junior or senior study at accredited 4-year institution in United States.
**Eligibility:** Applicant must be U.S. citizen or permanent resident.
**Basis for selection:** Major/career interest in nuclear science or engineering, nuclear.
**Application requirements:** Recommendations, transcript.
**Additional information:** Applicant must be an ANS student member enrolled in a program leading to a degree in nuclear science, nuclear engineering or a nuclear related field. Must be sponsored by ANS organization. Must have completed at least two full academic years of four-year nuclear science or engineering program. Visit Website for application. One request/application covers all Graduate and Undergraduate scholarships; check appropriate boxes on application form.

**Amount of award:** $2,500
**Number of awards:** 1
**Application deadline:** February 1

**Contact:**
American Nuclear Society
555 North Kensington Avenue
La Grange Park, IL 60526
Phone: 708-352-6611
Fax: 708-352-0499
Web: www.ans.org

## Pittsburgh Local Section Scholarship

**Type of award:** Scholarship.
**Intended use:** For full-time junior, senior or graduate study at accredited 4-year or graduate institution in United States.
**Basis for selection:** Major/career interest in nuclear science or engineering, nuclear.
**Application requirements:** Recommendations, transcript.
**Additional information:** Applicant must either attend school in Western Pennsylvania or have some affiliation with the region. Awards are $2,000 for undergraduates and $3,500 for graduate students. Applicant must be an ANS student member enrolled in a program leading to a degree in nuclear science, nuclear engineering or a nuclear related field. Must be sponsored by ANS organization. Visit Website for application. One request/application covers all Graduate and Undergraduate scholarships; check appropriate boxes on application form.

**Amount of award:** $2,000-$3,500
**Number of awards:** 2
**Application deadline:** February 1

**Contact:**
American Nuclear Society
555 North Kensington Avenue
La Grange Park, IL 60526
Phone: 708-352-6611
Fax: 708-352-0499
Web: www.ans.org

## Raymond DiSalvo Scholarship

**Type of award:** Scholarship.
**Intended use:** For full-time junior or senior study at accredited 4-year institution in United States.
**Basis for selection:** Major/career interest in nuclear science or engineering, nuclear.
**Application requirements:** Recommendations, transcript.
**Additional information:** Applicant must be an ANS student member enrolled in a program leading to a degree in nuclear science, nuclear engineering or a nuclear related field. Must be sponsored by ANS organization. Visit Website for application. One request/application covers all Graduate and Undergraduate scholarships; check appropriate boxes on application form.

**Amount of award:** $2,000
**Number of awards:** 1
**Application deadline:** February 1

**Contact:**
American Nuclear Society
555 North Kensington Avenue
La Grange Park, IL 60526
Phone: 708-352-6611
Fax: 708-352-0499
Web: www.ans.org

## Robert G. Lacy Scholarship

**Type of award:** Scholarship.
**Intended use:** For full-time junior or senior study at accredited 4-year institution in United States.
**Basis for selection:** Major/career interest in nuclear science or engineering, nuclear.
**Application requirements:** Recommendations, transcript.
**Additional information:** Applicant must be an ANS student member enrolled in a program leading to a degree in nuclear science, nuclear engineering or a nuclear related field. Must be sponsored by ANS organization. Visit Website for application. One request/application covers all Graduate and Undergraduate scholarships; check appropriate boxes on application form.

| | |
|---|---|
| **Amount of award:** | $2,000 |
| **Number of awards:** | 1 |
| **Application deadline:** | February 1 |

**Contact:**
American Nuclear Society
555 North Kensington Avenue
La Grange Park, IL 60526
Phone: 708-352-6611
Fax: 708-352-0499
Web: www.ans.org

## Robert T. (Bob) Liner Scholarship

**Type of award:** Scholarship.
**Intended use:** For full-time junior or senior study at accredited 4-year institution in United States.
**Basis for selection:** Major/career interest in nuclear science or engineering, nuclear.
**Application requirements:** Recommendations, transcript.
**Additional information:** Applicant must be an ANS student member enrolled in a program leading to a degree in nuclear science, nuclear engineering or a nuclear related field. Must be sponsored by ANS organization. Visit Website for application. One request/application covers all Graduate and Undergraduate scholarships; check appropriate boxes on application form.

| | |
|---|---|
| **Amount of award:** | $2,000 |
| **Number of awards:** | 1 |
| **Application deadline:** | February 1 |

**Contact:**
American Nuclear Society
555 North Kensington Avenue
La Grange Park, IL 60526
Phone: 708-352-6611
Fax: 708-352-0499
Web: www.ans.org

## Vogt Radiochemistry Scholarship

**Type of award:** Scholarship.
**Intended use:** For full-time undergraduate or graduate study at accredited 4-year or graduate institution.
**Basis for selection:** Major/career interest in chemistry or nuclear science.
**Application requirements:** Recommendations, transcript.
**Additional information:** Applicants must be enrolled in or proposing to undertake research in radioanalytical chemistry, analytical chemistry, or analytical applications of nuclear science. Applicant must be an ANS student member and must be sponsored by ANS organization. Visit Website for application and requirements. One request/application covers all Graduate and Undergraduate scholarships; check appropriate boxes on application form.

| | |
|---|---|
| **Amount of award:** | $3,000 |
| **Number of awards:** | 1 |
| **Application deadline:** | February 1 |

**Contact:**
American Nuclear Society
555 North Kensington Avenue
La Grange Park, IL 60526
Phone: 708-352-6611
Fax: 708-352-0499
Web: www.ans.org

## William R. and Mila Kimel Scholarship

**Type of award:** Scholarship.
**Intended use:** For full-time junior or senior study at accredited 4-year institution in United States.
**Basis for selection:** Major/career interest in engineering, nuclear.
**Application requirements:** Recommendations, transcript.
**Additional information:** Applicant must be an ANS student member enrolled in a program leading to a degree in nuclear science, nuclear engineering or a nuclear related field. Must be sponsored by ANS organization. Visit Website for application. One request/application covers all Graduate and Undergraduate scholarships; check appropriate boxes on application form. Number and amount of award varies.

| | |
|---|---|
| **Application deadline:** | February 1 |

**Contact:**
American Nuclear Society
555 North Kensington Avenue
La Grange Park, IL 60526
Phone: 708-352-6611
Fax: 708-352-0499
Web: www.ans.org

# American Physical Society

## Scholarship for Minority Undergraduate Physics Majors

**Type of award:** Scholarship, renewable.
**Intended use:** For full-time freshman, sophomore or junior study at 2-year or 4-year institution in United States. Designated institutions: Institutions with physics departments or provisions for procurement of physics degrees.
**Eligibility:** Applicant must be African American, Mexican American, Hispanic American, Puerto Rican or American Indian. Applicant must be U.S. citizen or permanent resident.
**Basis for selection:** Major/career interest in physics. Applicant must demonstrate high academic achievement.
**Application requirements:** Recommendations, essay, transcript, proof of eligibility. ACT/SAT scores.
**Additional information:** Must be high school senior or college freshman or sophomore to apply. Applications available early November. Visit Website for more information.

**Amount of award:** $2,000-$3,000
**Number of awards:** 25
**Number of applicants:** 100
**Application deadline:** February 4
**Notification begins:** May 15
**Total amount awarded:** $70,000
**Contact:**
American Physical Society
Minority Undergraduate Physics Scholarship
One Physics Ellipse
College Park, MD 20740
Phone: 301-209-3232
Fax: 301-209-3357
Web: www.aps.org/programs/minorities/honors/scholarship/

# American Public Power Association

## DEED Student Research Grants

**Type of award:** Research grant.
**Intended use:** For undergraduate or graduate study at accredited 2-year or 4-year institution in United States or Canada.
**Basis for selection:** Major/career interest in electronics; engineering, electrical/electronic or engineering, mechanical.
**Application requirements:** Transcript.
**Additional information:** Applicants must complete energy-related research project and be sponsored by DEED member utility.
**Amount of award:** $4,000
**Number of awards:** 10
**Number of applicants:** 26
**Application deadline:** February 15, October 15
**Notification begins:** April 1, November 1
**Total amount awarded:** $40,000
**Contact:**
American Public Power Association
Attn: DEED Administrator
1875 Connecticut Avenue, NW, Suite 1200
Washington, DC 20009-5715
Phone: 202-467-2960
Fax: 202-467-2910
Web: www.publicpower.org

# American Quarter Horse Foundation

## American Quarter Horse Foundation Scholarships

**Type of award:** Scholarship, renewable.
**Intended use:** For full-time undergraduate or first professional study in United States or Canada.
**Eligibility:** Applicant must be at least 17.
**Basis for selection:** Applicant must demonstrate financial need and high academic achievement.
**Application requirements:** Recommendations, transcript, proof of eligibility.
**Additional information:** Number of scholarships vary. Applicants must be current members of the American Quarter Horse Youth Association or American Quarter Horse Association, and must exhibit strong involvement. Visit Website for requirements, deadline, and scholarship criteria.
**Amount of award:** $500-$25,000
**Number of awards:** 130
**Number of applicants:** 200
**Application deadline:** December 1
**Notification begins:** May 1
**Total amount awarded:** $275,000
**Contact:**
American Quarter Horse Foundation
Scholarship Office
2601 I-40 East
Amarillo, TX 79104
Phone: 806-378-5040
Fax: 806-376-1005
Web: www.aqha.com/foundation

# American Radio Relay League (ARRL) Foundation, Inc.

## Androscoggin Amateur Radio Club Scholarship

**Type of award:** Scholarship.
**Intended use:** For undergraduate study at 2-year or 4-year institution.
**Basis for selection:** Competition/talent/interest in amateur radio. Major/career interest in computer/information sciences; electronics or engineering, electrical/electronic.
**Application requirements:** Transcript.
**Additional information:** Must be amateur radio operator with active Technician Class Amateur Radio License or higher. High school seniors are eligible to apply. Offered as either $1,000 award for a 4-year college student or two awards of $500 each for 2-year college students. Regional preference given to applicants in the Maine or New England Division, including Maine, New Hampshire, Vermont, Rhode Island, Massachusetts or Connecticut. Visit Website for application.
**Amount of award:** $500-$1,000
**Application deadline:** February 1
**Contact:**
American Radio Relay League (ARRL) Foundation, Inc.
225 Main Street
Newington, CT 06111
Phone: 860-594-0397
Fax: 860-594-0259
Web: www.arrlf.org

## ARRL Earl I. Anderson Scholarship

**Type of award:** Scholarship.
**Intended use:** For undergraduate or graduate study at accredited postsecondary institution in United States.
**Eligibility:** Applicant must be residing in Michigan, Indiana, Illinois or Florida.
**Basis for selection:** Competition/talent/interest in amateur radio. Major/career interest in engineering, electrical/electronic.
**Application requirements:** Transcript.

**Additional information:** Must be amateur radio operator holding any class license. Must be ARRL member. Major may be in other related technical field. Must be attending classes in Illinois, Indiana, Michigan, or Florida. High school seniors eligible to apply. Application may be obtained on Website, and will only be accepted via email.

| | |
|---|---|
| **Amount of award:** | $1,250 |
| **Number of awards:** | 3 |
| **Application deadline:** | February 1 |

**Contact:**
The ARRL Foundation, Inc. Scholarship Program
225 Main Street
Newington, CT 06111
Phone: 860-594-0397
Fax: 860-594-0259
Web: www.arrlf.org

## ARRL Scholarship Honoring Barry Goldwater, K7UGA

**Type of award:** Scholarship.
**Intended use:** For undergraduate or graduate study at accredited 4-year or graduate institution in or outside United States.
**Basis for selection:** Competition/talent/interest in amateur radio.
**Application requirements:** Transcript.
**Additional information:** Must be amateur radio operator with novice class license or higher. High school seniors are eligible to apply. Application may be obtained on Website, and will only be accepted via email.

| | |
|---|---|
| **Amount of award:** | $5,000 |
| **Number of awards:** | 1 |
| **Application deadline:** | February 1 |
| **Total amount awarded:** | $5,000 |

**Contact:**
The ARRL Foundation, Inc. Scholarship Program
225 Main Street
Newington, CT 06111
Phone: 860-594-0397
Fax: 860-594-0259
Web: www.arrlf.org

## The Bill, W2ONV, and Ann Salerno Memorial Scholarship

**Type of award:** Scholarship.
**Intended use:** For undergraduate study at accredited 4-year institution.
**Basis for selection:** Competition/talent/interest in amateur radio. Applicant must demonstrate financial need and high academic achievement.
**Application requirements:** Transcript.
**Additional information:** Minimum 3.7 GPA. Must be amateur radio operator with active Amateur Radio license. High school seniors are eligible to apply. Aggregate income of family household must be no greater than $100,000 per year. Visit Website for application.

| | |
|---|---|
| **Amount of award:** | $1,000 |
| **Number of awards:** | 2 |
| **Application deadline:** | February 1 |

**Contact:**
American Radio Relay League (ARRL) Foundation, Inc.
225 Main Street
Newington, CT 06111
Phone: 860-594-0397
Fax: 860-594-0259
Web: www.arrlf.org

## The Carole J. Streeter, KB9JBR, Scholarship

**Type of award:** Scholarship.
**Intended use:** For undergraduate study at accredited postsecondary institution.
**Eligibility:** Applicant must be U.S. citizen.
**Basis for selection:** Competition/talent/interest in amateur radio. Major/career interest in medicine.
**Application requirements:** Transcript.
**Additional information:** Must be amateur radio operator with any class of active Amateur Radio license with preference for basic Morse code capability. High school seniors are eligible to apply. Applicants should study medicine or related majors. Visit Website for application.

| | |
|---|---|
| **Amount of award:** | $750 |
| **Number of awards:** | 1 |
| **Application deadline:** | February 1 |

**Contact:**
American Radio Relay League (ARRL) Foundation, Inc.
225 Main Street
Newington, CT 06111
Phone: 860-594-0397
Fax: 860-594-0259
Web: www.arrlf.org

## Central Arizona DX Association Scholarship

**Type of award:** Scholarship.
**Intended use:** For undergraduate study at postsecondary institution.
**Eligibility:** Applicant must be residing in Arizona.
**Basis for selection:** Competition/talent/interest in amateur radio. Applicant must demonstrate high academic achievement.
**Application requirements:** Transcript.
**Additional information:** Minimum 3.2 GPA. Must be amateur radio operator with active Technician Class or higher license. High school seniors are eligible to apply. Graduating high school students will be considered before current college students. Visit Website for application.

| | |
|---|---|
| **Amount of award:** | $1,000 |
| **Number of awards:** | 1 |
| **Application deadline:** | February 1 |

**Contact:**
American Radio Relay League (ARRL) Foundation, Inc.
225 Main Street
Newington, CT 06111
Phone: 860-594-0397
Fax: 860-594-0259
Web: www.arrlf.org

## Challenge Met Scholarship

**Type of award:** Scholarship.
**Intended use:** For undergraduate study at accredited vocational, 2-year or 4-year institution.
**Eligibility:** Applicant must be learning disabled.

**Basis for selection:** Competition/talent/interest in amateur radio.
**Application requirements:** Transcript, proof of eligibility.
**Additional information:** Must be amateur radio operator holding any class license. Preference given to those with documented learning disabilities who put forth effort regardless of resulting grades. High school seniors are eligible to apply. Application may be obtained on Website, and will only be accepted via email. Number of awards varies.

| | |
|---|---|
| **Amount of award:** | $500 |
| **Application deadline:** | February 1 |

**Contact:**
The ARRL Foundation, Inc. Scholarship Program
225 Main Street
Newington, CT 06111
Phone: 860-594-0347
Fax: 860-594-0259
Web: www.arrlf.org

## Charles Clarke Cordle Memorial Scholarship

**Type of award:** Scholarship.
**Intended use:** For undergraduate or graduate study at postsecondary institution in United States. Designated institutions: Institutions in Alabama or Georgia.
**Eligibility:** Applicant must be residing in Alabama or Georgia.
**Basis for selection:** Competition/talent/interest in amateur radio. Major/career interest in electronics or communications.
**Application requirements:** Transcript.
**Additional information:** Minimum 2.5 GPA. Must hold active amateur radio license. Preference to students of majors listed or other related fields. High school seniors are eligible to apply. Application may be obtained from Website, and will only be accepted via email.

| | |
|---|---|
| **Amount of award:** | $1,000 |
| **Number of awards:** | 1 |
| **Application deadline:** | February 1 |
| **Total amount awarded:** | $1,000 |

**Contact:**
The ARRL Foundation, Inc. Scholarship Program
225 Main Street
Newington, CT 06111
Phone: 860-594-0397
Fax: 860-594-0259
Web: www.arrlf.org

## Charles N. Fisher Memorial Scholarship

**Type of award:** Scholarship.
**Intended use:** For undergraduate or graduate study at accredited postsecondary institution in United States.
**Eligibility:** Applicant must be residing in California or Arizona.
**Basis for selection:** Competition/talent/interest in amateur radio. Major/career interest in communications or electronics.
**Application requirements:** Transcript.
**Additional information:** Must hold active amateur radio license. Major may be in other fields related to those listed. California candidates must reside in Los Angeles, Orange County, San Diego, or Santa Barbara. High school seniors eligible to apply. Application may be obtained on Website, and will only be accepted via email.

| | |
|---|---|
| **Amount of award:** | $1,000 |
| **Number of awards:** | 1 |
| **Application deadline:** | February 1 |
| **Total amount awarded:** | $1,000 |

**Contact:**
The ARRL Foundation, Inc. Scholarship Program
225 Main Street
Newington, CT 06111
Phone: 860-594-0397
Fax: 860-594-0259
Web: www.arrlf.org

## Chicago FM Club Scholarship

**Type of award:** Scholarship.
**Intended use:** For undergraduate study at accredited vocational, 2-year or 4-year institution in United States.
**Eligibility:** Applicant must be U.S. citizen residing in Wisconsin, Indiana or Illinois.
**Basis for selection:** Competition/talent/interest in amateur radio.
**Application requirements:** Transcript.
**Additional information:** Student also eligible if within three months of becoming U.S. citizen. Must be amateur radio operator with technician class license or higher. Number of awards varies. High school seniors eligible to apply. Application may be obtained on Website, and will only be accepted via email.

| | |
|---|---|
| **Amount of award:** | $500 |
| **Application deadline:** | February 1 |

**Contact:**
The ARRL Foundation, Inc. Scholarship Program
225 Main Street
Newington, CT 06111
Phone: 860-594-0397
Fax: 860-594-0259
Web: www.arrlf.org

## The Dayton Amateur Radio Association Scholarships

**Type of award:** Scholarship.
**Intended use:** For undergraduate study at accredited 4-year institution in United States.
**Eligibility:** Applicant must be residing in North Carolina.
**Basis for selection:** Competition/talent/interest in amateur radio.
**Application requirements:** Transcript.
**Additional information:** Must be amateur radio operator holding any class license. High school seniors are eligible to apply. Application may be obtained on Website, and will only be accepted via email.

| | |
|---|---|
| **Amount of award:** | $1,000 |
| **Number of awards:** | 4 |
| **Application deadline:** | February 1 |

**Contact:**
The ARRL Foundation, Inc. Scholarship Program
225 Main Street
Newington, CT 06111
Phone: 860-594-0347
Fax: 860-594-0259
Web: www.arrlf.org

Scholarships

## Donald Riebhoff Memorial Scholarship

**Type of award:** Scholarship.
**Intended use:** For undergraduate or graduate study at accredited 4-year or graduate institution in United States.
**Basis for selection:** Competition/talent/interest in amateur radio. Major/career interest in international relations. Applicant must demonstrate financial need and high academic achievement.
**Application requirements:** Transcript.
**Additional information:** Must be amateur radio operator with active technician class license or higher. Must be ARRL member. High school seniors are eligible to apply. Application may be obtained on Website, and will only be accepted via email.

| | |
|---|---|
| **Amount of award:** | $1,000 |
| **Number of awards:** | 1 |
| **Application deadline:** | February 1 |

**Contact:**
The ARRL Foundation, Inc. Scholarship Program
225 Main Street
Newington, CT 06111
Phone: 860-594-0397
Fax: 860-594-0259
Web: www.arrlf.org

## Dr. James L. Lawson Memorial Scholarship

**Type of award:** Scholarship.
**Intended use:** For undergraduate or graduate study at 4-year or graduate institution in United States. Designated institutions: Any institution in New England or New York.
**Eligibility:** Applicant must be residing in Vermont, Connecticut, New York, New Hampshire, Maine, Massachusetts or Rhode Island.
**Basis for selection:** Competition/talent/interest in amateur radio. Major/career interest in communications or electronics.
**Application requirements:** Transcript.
**Additional information:** Must be amateur radio operator holding general class license or higher. Major may be in other fields related to those listed. High school seniors eligible to apply. Application may be obtained on Website, and will only be accepted via email.

| | |
|---|---|
| **Amount of award:** | $500 |
| **Number of awards:** | 1 |
| **Application deadline:** | February 1 |
| **Total amount awarded:** | $500 |

**Contact:**
The ARRL Foundation, Inc. Scholarship Program
225 Main Street
Newington, CT 06111
Phone: 860-594-0397
Fax: 860-594-0259
Web: www.arrlf.org

## Edmond A. Metzger Scholarship

**Type of award:** Scholarship.
**Intended use:** For undergraduate, graduate or non-degree study at 4-year or graduate institution in United States. Designated institutions: Schools in ARRL Central Division (Illinois, Indiana, Wisconsin).
**Eligibility:** Applicant must be residing in Wisconsin, Indiana or Illinois.
**Basis for selection:** Competition/talent/interest in amateur radio. Major/career interest in engineering, electrical/electronic.
**Application requirements:** Transcript.
**Additional information:** Must be amateur radio operator with novice class license or higher. Must be American Radio Relay League member. High school seniors eligible to apply. Application may be obtained on Website, and will only be accepted via email.

| | |
|---|---|
| **Amount of award:** | $500 |
| **Number of awards:** | 1 |
| **Application deadline:** | February 1 |
| **Total amount awarded:** | $500 |

**Contact:**
The ARRL Foundation, Inc. Scholarship Program
225 Main Street
Newington, CT 06111
Phone: 860-594-0397
Fax: 860-594-0259
Web: www.arrlf.org

## Eugene "Gene" Sallee, W4YFR Memorial Scholarship

**Type of award:** Scholarship.
**Intended use:** For undergraduate or graduate study at accredited postsecondary institution in United States.
**Eligibility:** Applicant must be residing in Georgia.
**Basis for selection:** Competition/talent/interest in amateur radio. Major/career interest in electronics or communications. Applicant must demonstrate financial need and high academic achievement.
**Application requirements:** Transcript.
**Additional information:** Must be amateur radio operator with active technician plus or higher class license. Minimum 3.0 GPA. Major may be in a related field. High school seniors are eligible to apply. Application may be obtained on Website, and will only be accepted via email.

| | |
|---|---|
| **Amount of award:** | $500 |
| **Number of awards:** | 1 |
| **Application deadline:** | February 1 |
| **Total amount awarded:** | $500 |

**Contact:**
The ARRL Foundation, Inc. Scholarship Program
225 Main Street
Newington, CT 06111
Phone: 860-594-0397
Fax: 860-594-0259
Web: www.arrlf.org

## Fred R. McDaniel Memorial Scholarship

**Type of award:** Scholarship.
**Intended use:** For undergraduate or graduate study at 4-year or graduate institution in United States. Designated institutions: Any colleges or universities in FCC fifth call district (Texas, Oklahoma, Arkansas, Louisiana, Mississippi, New Mexico).
**Eligibility:** Applicant must be residing in Oklahoma, Texas, Mississippi, Arkansas, New Mexico or Louisiana.
**Basis for selection:** Competition/talent/interest in amateur radio. Major/career interest in electronics or communications. Applicant must demonstrate high academic achievement.
**Application requirements:** Transcript.
**Additional information:** Preference for students with minimum 3.0 GPA. Must be amateur radio operator holding general class license or higher. Major may be in other fields related to those listed. High school students eligible to apply.

Application may be obtained from Website, and will only be accepted via email.

**Amount of award:** $500
**Number of awards:** 1
**Application deadline:** February 1
**Total amount awarded:** $500

**Contact:**
The ARRL Foundation, Inc. Scholarship Program
225 Main Street
Newington, CT 06111
Phone: 860-594-0397
Fax: 860-594-0259
Web: www.arrlf.org

## The Gary Wagner, K3OMI, Scholarship

**Type of award:** Scholarship.
**Intended use:** For undergraduate study at accredited 4-year institution.
**Eligibility:** Applicant must be U.S. citizen residing in Virginia, Tennessee, West Virginia, Maryland or North Carolina.
**Basis for selection:** Competition/talent/interest in amateur radio. Major/career interest in engineering. Applicant must demonstrate financial need.
**Application requirements:** Transcript.
**Additional information:** Must be amateur radio operator with an active Novice Class Amateur Radio License or higher. High school seniors are eligible to apply. Visit Website for application.

**Amount of award:** $1,000
**Number of awards:** 1
**Application deadline:** February 1

**Contact:**
American Radio Relay League (ARRL) Foundation, Inc.
225 Main Street
Newington, CT 06111
Phone: 860-594-0397
Fax: 860-594-0259
Web: www.arrlf.org

## General Fund Scholarship

**Type of award:** Scholarship.
**Intended use:** For undergraduate or graduate study at postsecondary institution.
**Basis for selection:** Competition/talent/interest in amateur radio.
**Application requirements:** Transcript.
**Additional information:** Must hold active amateur radio license. Number of awards varies. High school seniors eligible to apply. Application may be obtained on Website, and will only be accepted via email.

**Amount of award:** $2,000
**Application deadline:** February 1

**Contact:**
The ARRL Foundation, Inc. Scholarship Program
225 Main Street
Newington, CT 06111
Phone: 860-594-0397
Fax: 860-594-0259
Web: www.arrlf.org

## Gwinnett Amateur Radio Society Scholarship

**Type of award:** Scholarship.
**Intended use:** For undergraduate study at 4-year institution.
**Eligibility:** Applicant must be residing in Georgia.
**Basis for selection:** Competition/talent/interest in amateur radio.
**Application requirements:** Transcript.
**Additional information:** Must be amateur radio operator with active Amateur Radio license, any class. Applicants must be residents of Gwinnett County, GA or the state of GA. High school seniors are eligible to apply. Visit Website for application.

**Amount of award:** $500
**Number of awards:** 1
**Application deadline:** February 1

**Contact:**
American Radio Relay League (ARRL) Foundation, Inc.
225 Main Street
Newington, CT 06111
Phone: 860-594-0397
Fax: 860-594-0259
Web: www.arrlf.org

## Henry Broughton, K2AE Memorial Scholarship

**Type of award:** Scholarship.
**Intended use:** For undergraduate or graduate study at accredited 4-year or graduate institution in United States.
**Eligibility:** Applicant must be residing in New York.
**Basis for selection:** Competition/talent/interest in amateur radio. Major/career interest in engineering or science, general.
**Application requirements:** Transcript.
**Additional information:** Applicant must live within 70-mile radius of Schenectady, NY. Must be amateur radio operator with general class license. Major may be in other fields similar to those listed. High school seniors are eligible to apply. May offer additional awards if funding permits. Application may be obtained on Website, and will only be accepted via email.

**Amount of award:** $1,000
**Number of awards:** 1
**Application deadline:** February 1

**Contact:**
The ARRL Foundation, Inc. Scholarship Program
225 Main Street
Newington, CT 06111
Phone: 860-594-0397
Fax: 860-594-0259
Web: www.arrlf.org

## Irving W. Cook WA0CGS Scholarship

**Type of award:** Scholarship.
**Intended use:** For undergraduate or graduate study at postsecondary institution in United States.
**Eligibility:** Applicant must be residing in Kansas.
**Basis for selection:** Competition/talent/interest in amateur radio. Major/career interest in communications or electronics.
**Application requirements:** Transcript.
**Additional information:** Must hold active amateur radio license. Major may be in other fields related to those listed. High schools seniors eligible to apply. Application may be obtained on Website, and will only be accepted via email.

**Amount of award:** $1,000
**Number of awards:** 1
**Application deadline:** February 1
**Total amount awarded:** $1,000

**Contact:**
The ARRL Foundation, Inc. Scholarship Program
225 Main Street
Newington, CT 06111
Phone: 860-594-0397
Fax: 860-594-0259
Web: www.arrlf.org

## The K2TEO Martin J. Green, Sr. Memorial Scholarship

**Type of award:** Scholarship.
**Intended use:** For undergraduate or graduate study at postsecondary institution.
**Basis for selection:** Competition/talent/interest in amateur radio.
**Application requirements:** Transcript.
**Additional information:** Must be amateur radio operator with general class license or higher. Preference given to student from family of ham operators. High school seniors are eligible to apply. Application may be obtained on Website, and will only be accepted via email.

**Amount of award:** $1,000
**Number of awards:** 1
**Application deadline:** February 1
**Total amount awarded:** $1,000

**Contact:**
The ARRL Foundation, Inc. Scholarship Program
225 Main Street
Newington, CT 06111
Phone: 860-594-0397
Fax: 860-594-0259
Web: www.arrlf.org

## L. Phil and Alice J. Wicker Scholarship

**Type of award:** Scholarship.
**Intended use:** For undergraduate, graduate or non-degree study at 4-year or graduate institution in United States. Designated institutions: Schools in ARRL Roanoke Division (NC, SC, VA, WV).
**Eligibility:** Applicant must be residing in Virginia, West Virginia, North Carolina or South Carolina.
**Basis for selection:** Competition/talent/interest in amateur radio. Major/career interest in communications or electronics.
**Application requirements:** Transcript.
**Additional information:** Must be amateur radio operator holding general class license. Major may be in other fields related to those listed. High school seniors eligible to apply. Application may be obtained on Website, and will only be accepted via email.

**Amount of award:** $500
**Number of awards:** 1
**Application deadline:** February 1
**Total amount awarded:** $1,000

**Contact:**
The ARRL Foundation, Inc. Scholarship Program
225 Main Street
Newington, CT 06111
Phone: 860-594-0397
Fax: 860-594-0259
Web: www.arrlf.org

## The L.B. Cebik, W4RNL, and Jean Cebik, N4TZP, Memorial Scholarship

**Type of award:** Scholarship.
**Intended use:** For undergraduate study at 4-year institution in United States.
**Eligibility:** Applicant must be residing in New Jersey.
**Basis for selection:** Competition/talent/interest in amateur radio.
**Application requirements:** Transcript.
**Additional information:** Must be amateur radio operator holding technician class license or higher. High school seniors are eligible to apply. Application may be obtained on Website, and will only be accepted via email.

**Amount of award:** $1,000
**Number of awards:** 1
**Application deadline:** February 1

**Contact:**
The ARRL Foundation, Inc. Scholarship Program
225 Main Street
Newington, CT 06111
Phone: 860-594-0397
Fax: 860-594-0259
Web: www.arrlf.org

## Louisiana Memorial Scholarship

**Type of award:** Scholarship.
**Intended use:** For undergraduate study at 4-year or graduate institution in United States.
**Basis for selection:** Competition/talent/interest in amateur radio. Applicant must demonstrate high academic achievement.
**Application requirements:** Transcript.
**Additional information:** Must be resident of or student in Louisiana. Minimum 3.0 GPA. Must be amateur radio operator holding technician class license or higher. High school seniors eligible to apply. Application may be obtained on Website, and will only be accepted via email.

**Amount of award:** $750
**Number of awards:** 1
**Application deadline:** February 1

**Contact:**
The ARRL Foundation, Inc. Scholarship Program
225 Main Street
Newington, CT 06111
Phone: 860-594-0397
Fax: 860-594-0259
Web: www.arrlf.org

## Mary Lou Brown Scholarship

**Type of award:** Scholarship.
**Intended use:** For undergraduate or graduate study at 4-year or graduate institution in United States.
**Eligibility:** Applicant must be residing in Oregon, Montana, Alaska, Idaho or Washington.
**Basis for selection:** Competition/talent/interest in amateur radio. Applicant must demonstrate high academic achievement.
**Application requirements:** Transcript.
**Additional information:** Minimum 3.0 GPA and demonstrated interest in promoting Amateur Radio Service. Must be amateur radio operator with general class license. Number of awards varies based on funding. High school seniors eligible to apply. Application may be obtained on Website, and will only be accepted via email.

**Amount of award:** $2,500
**Application deadline:** February 1

**Contact:**
The ARRL Foundation, Inc. Scholarship Program
225 Main Street
Newington, CT 06111
Phone: 860-594-0397
Fax: 860-594-0259
Web: www.arrlf.org

## Mississippi Scholarship

**Type of award:** Scholarship.
**Intended use:** For undergraduate or graduate study at 4-year or graduate institution in United States. Designated institutions: Schools in Mississippi.
**Eligibility:** Applicant must be no older than 30. Applicant must be residing in Mississippi.
**Basis for selection:** Competition/talent/interest in amateur radio. Major/career interest in communications or electronics.
**Application requirements:** Transcript.
**Additional information:** Must hold active amateur radio license. Major may be in other fields related to those listed. High school seniors eligible to apply. Application may be obtained on Website, and will only be accepted via email.

**Amount of award:** $500
**Number of awards:** 1
**Application deadline:** February 1
**Total amount awarded:** $500

**Contact:**
The ARRL Foundation, Inc. Scholarship Program
225 Main Street
Newington, CT 06111
Phone: 860-594-0397
Fax: 860-594-0259
Web: www.arrlf.org

## New England FEMARA Scholarship

**Type of award:** Scholarship.
**Intended use:** For undergraduate, graduate or non-degree study at postsecondary institution in United States.
**Eligibility:** Applicant must be residing in Vermont, Connecticut, New Hampshire, Maine, Massachusetts or Rhode Island.
**Basis for selection:** Competition/talent/interest in amateur radio.
**Application requirements:** Transcript.
**Additional information:** Must be amateur radio operator holding technical class license or higher. Number of awards varies based on funding. High school seniors eligible to apply. Application may be obtained on Website, and will only be accepted via email.

**Amount of award:** $1,000
**Application deadline:** February 1

**Contact:**
The ARRL Foundation, Inc. Scholarship Program
225 Main Street
Newington, CT 06111
Phone: 860-594-0397
Fax: 860-594-0259
Web: www.arrlf.org

## Northern California DX Foundation Scholarship

**Type of award:** Scholarship.
**Intended use:** For undergraduate study at accredited vocational, 2-year or 4-year institution in United States.
**Eligibility:** Applicant must be residing in New York.
**Basis for selection:** Competition/talent/interest in amateur radio.
**Application requirements:** Transcript.
**Additional information:** Must be amateur radio operator holding technician class license or higher. Applicant must demonstrate interest and activity in DXing. High school seniors eligible to apply. Application may be obtained on Website, and will only be accepted via email.

**Amount of award:** $1,500
**Number of awards:** 2
**Application deadline:** February 1
**Total amount awarded:** $3,000

**Contact:**
The ARRL Foundation, Inc. Scholarship Program
225 Main Street
Newington, CT 06111
Phone: 860-594-0397
Fax: 860-594-0259
Web: www.arrlf.org

## Paul and Helen L. Grauer Scholarship

**Type of award:** Scholarship.
**Intended use:** For undergraduate or graduate study at 4-year or graduate institution in United States. Designated institutions: Schools in Midwest Division (Iowa, Kansas, Missouri, Nebraska).
**Eligibility:** Applicant must be residing in Iowa, Nebraska, Kansas or Missouri.
**Basis for selection:** Competition/talent/interest in amateur radio. Major/career interest in communications or electronics.
**Application requirements:** Transcript.
**Additional information:** Must be amateur radio operator with novice class license or higher. Major may be in other fields related to those listed. High school seniors are eligible to apply. Application may be obtained on Website, and will only be accepted via email.

**Amount of award:** $1,000
**Number of awards:** 1
**Application deadline:** February 1
**Total amount awarded:** $1,000

**Contact:**
The ARRL Foundation, Inc. Scholarship Program
225 Main Street
Newington, CT 06111
Phone: 860-594-0397
Fax: 860-594-0259
Web: www.arrlf.org

## PHD Amateur Radio Association Scholarship

**Type of award:** Scholarship.
**Intended use:** For undergraduate, graduate or non-degree study at postsecondary institution in United States.
**Eligibility:** Applicant must be residing in Iowa, Nebraska, Kansas or Missouri.

**Basis for selection:** Competition/talent/interest in amateur radio. Major/career interest in journalism; computer/information sciences or engineering, electrical/electronic.
**Application requirements:** Transcript.
**Additional information:** Must hold active amateur radio license. May be child of deceased radio amateur. High school seniors eligible to apply. Application may be obtained on Website, and will only be accepted via email.

| | |
|---|---|
| **Amount of award:** | $1,000 |
| **Number of awards:** | 1 |
| **Application deadline:** | February 1 |
| **Total amount awarded:** | $1,000 |

**Contact:**
The ARRL Foundation, Inc. Scholarship Program
225 Main Street
Newington, CT 06111
Phone: 860-594-0397
Fax: 860-594-0259
Web: www.arrlf.org



## The Ray, NØRP, & Katie, WØKTE, Pautz Scholarship

**Type of award:** Scholarship.
**Intended use:** For undergraduate study at accredited 4-year institution.
**Eligibility:** Applicant must be residing in Iowa, Nebraska, Kansas or Missouri.
**Basis for selection:** Competition/talent/interest in amateur radio. Major/career interest in electronics or computer/information sciences.
**Application requirements:** Transcript.
**Additional information:** Must be an ARRL member, and an amateur radio operator with active General Class or higher license. High school seniors are eligible to apply. Applicant should be majoring in electronics, computer science or related field. Visit Website for application.

| | |
|---|---|
| **Amount of award:** | $500-$1,000 |
| **Number of awards:** | 1 |
| **Application deadline:** | February 1 |

**Contact:**
American Radio Relay League (ARRL) Foundation, Inc.
225 Main Street
Newington, CT 06111
Phone: 860-594-0397
Fax: 860-594-0259
Web: www.arrlf.org

## Richard W. Bendicksen N7ZL Memorial Scholarship

**Type of award:** Scholarship.
**Intended use:** For undergraduate study at 4-year institution in United States.
**Eligibility:** Applicant must be residing in Nebraska.
**Basis for selection:** Competition/talent/interest in amateur radio.
**Application requirements:** Transcript.
**Additional information:** Must hold active amateur radio license. High school seniors eligible to apply. Application may be obtained on Website, and will only be accepted via email.

| | |
|---|---|
| **Amount of award:** | $2,000 |
| **Number of awards:** | 1 |
| **Application deadline:** | February 1 |

**Contact:**
The ARRL Foundation, Inc. Scholarship Program
225 Main Street
Newington, CT 06111
Phone: 860-594-0397
Fax: 860-594-0259
Web: www.arrlf.org

## Six Meter Club of Chicago Scholarship

**Type of award:** Scholarship.
**Intended use:** For undergraduate study at accredited postsecondary institution in United States. Designated institutions: Schools in Illinois, Indiana or Wisconsin.
**Eligibility:** Applicant must be residing in Wisconsin, Indiana or Illinois.
**Basis for selection:** Competition/talent/interest in amateur radio.
**Application requirements:** Transcript.
**Additional information:** Must hold active amateur radio license. Preference given to applicants with minimum 2.5 GPA. High school seniors eligible to apply. Application may be obtained on Website, and will only be accepted via email.

| | |
|---|---|
| **Amount of award:** | $500 |
| **Number of awards:** | 1 |
| **Application deadline:** | February 1 |
| **Total amount awarded:** | $500 |

**Contact:**
The ARRL Foundation, Inc. Scholarship Program
225 Main Street
Newington, CT 06111
Phone: 860-594-0397
Fax: 860-594-0259
Web: www.arrlf.org

## Ted, W4VHF, and Itice, K4LVV, Goldthorpe Scholarship

**Type of award:** Scholarship.
**Intended use:** For undergraduate study at 4-year institution.
**Basis for selection:** Competition/talent/interest in amateur radio. Applicant must demonstrate financial need and service orientation.
**Application requirements:** Transcript.
**Additional information:** Must be amateur radio operator with any active Amateur Radio License Class. High school seniors are eligible to apply. Visit Website for application.

| | |
|---|---|
| **Amount of award:** | $500 |
| **Number of awards:** | 1 |
| **Application deadline:** | February 1 |

**Contact:**
American Radio Relay League (ARRL) Foundation, Inc.
225 Main Street
Newington, CT 06111
Phone: 860-594-0397
Fax: 860-594-0259
Web: www.arrlf.org

## Tom and Judith Comstock Scholarship

**Type of award:** Scholarship.
**Intended use:** For undergraduate study at 2-year or 4-year institution in United States.
**Eligibility:** Applicant must be high school senior. Applicant must be residing in Oklahoma or Texas.

**Basis for selection:** Competition/talent/interest in amateur radio.
**Application requirements:** Transcript.
**Additional information:** Must hold active amateur radio license. High school seniors are also eligible to apply. Application may be obtained on Website, and will only be accepted via email.

| | |
|---|---|
| **Amount of award:** | $2,000 |
| **Number of awards:** | 1 |
| **Application deadline:** | February 1 |
| **Total amount awarded:** | $2,000 |

**Contact:**
The ARRL Foundation, Inc. Scholarship Program
225 Main Street
Newington, CT 06111
Phone: 860-594-0397
Fax: 860-594-0259
Web: www.arrlf.org

## William Bennett, W7PHO, Memorial Scholarship

**Type of award:** Scholarship.
**Intended use:** For undergraduate study at 4-year institution.
**Basis for selection:** Competition/talent/interest in amateur radio. Applicant must demonstrate high academic achievement.
**Application requirements:** Transcript.
**Additional information:** Minimum 3.0 GPA. Must be amateur radio operator with active General Class license or higher. High school seniors are eligible to apply. Applicants should be residents of the ARRL's Northwest, Pacific or Southwest Divisions. Visit Website for application.

| | |
|---|---|
| **Amount of award:** | $500 |
| **Number of awards:** | 1 |
| **Application deadline:** | February 1 |

**Contact:**
American Radio Relay League (ARRL) Foundation, Inc.
225 Main Street
Newington, CT 06111
Phone: 860-594-0397
Fax: 860-594-0259
Web: www.arrlf.org

## William R. Goldfarb Memorial Scholarship

**Type of award:** Scholarship, renewable.
**Intended use:** For undergraduate study at accredited 4-year institution in United States.
**Eligibility:** Applicant must be high school senior.
**Basis for selection:** Competition/talent/interest in amateur radio. Major/career interest in business; engineering; science, general; computer/information sciences; medicine or nursing. Applicant must demonstrate financial need.
**Application requirements:** Recommendations, transcript. FAFSA or Student Aid Report.
**Additional information:** Must hold active amateur radio license. Award amount varies based on applicant's qualifications, need, and other funding; $10,000 is the minimum award. Application may be obtained on Website, and will only be accepted via email.

| | |
|---|---|
| **Amount of award:** | $10,000 |
| **Number of awards:** | 1 |
| **Application deadline:** | February 1 |

**Contact:**
The ARRL Foundation, Inc. Scholarship Program
225 Main Street
Newington, CT 06111
Phone: 860-594-0397
Fax: 860-594-0259
Web: www.arrlf.org

## Yankee Clipper Contest Club, Inc. Youth Scholarship

**Type of award:** Scholarship.
**Intended use:** For undergraduate study at accredited 2-year or 4-year institution in United States.
**Eligibility:** Applicant must be residing in Vermont, New York, Maine, Pennsylvania, Massachusetts, Connecticut, New Hampshire, New Jersey or Rhode Island.
**Basis for selection:** Competition/talent/interest in amateur radio.
**Application requirements:** Transcript.
**Additional information:** Must be amateur radio operator holding active general class license or higher. Must be resident of or college/university student in area within 175-mile radius of YCCC Center in Erving, MA. This includes MA; RI; CT; Long Island, NY; and some of VT, NH, ME, PA, and NJ. High school seniors are eligible to apply. Application may be obtained on Website, and will only be accepted via email.

| | |
|---|---|
| **Amount of award:** | $1,200 |
| **Number of awards:** | 1 |
| **Application deadline:** | February 1 |

**Contact:**
The ARRL Foundation, Inc. Scholarship Program
225 Main Street
Newington, CT 06111
Phone: 860-594-0397
Fax: 860-594-0259
Web: www.arrlf.org

## Yasme Foundation Scholarship

**Type of award:** Scholarship, renewable.
**Intended use:** For undergraduate study at accredited 4-year institution in United States.
**Basis for selection:** Competition/talent/interest in amateur radio. Major/career interest in science, general or engineering. Applicant must demonstrate high academic achievement and service orientation.
**Application requirements:** Transcript.
**Additional information:** Must hold active amateur radio license technician class or higher. Preference given to high school applicants in top five to ten percent of class or college students in top ten percent of class. Participation in local amateur radio club and community service strongly preferred. Previous YASME winners must submit new application and transcript each year. Number of awards varies. Application may be obtained on Website, and will only be accepted via email.

| | |
|---|---|
| **Amount of award:** | $2,000 |
| **Application deadline:** | February 1 |

**Contact:**
The ARRL Foundation, Inc. Scholarship Program
225 Main Street
Newington, CT 06111
Phone: 860-594-0397
Fax: 860-594-0259
Web: www.arrlf.org

Scholarships

### You've Got a Friend in Pennsylvania Scholarship

**Type of award:** Scholarship.
**Intended use:** For undergraduate, graduate or non-degree study at postsecondary institution in United States.
**Eligibility:** Applicant must be residing in Pennsylvania.
**Basis for selection:** Competition/talent/interest in amateur radio.
**Application requirements:** Transcript.
**Additional information:** Must be amateur radio operator with general class license. Must be member of American Radio Relay League and maintain an "A" equivalent GPA. High school seniors eligible to apply. Application may be obtained from Website, and will only be accepted via email.

| | |
|---|---|
| **Amount of award:** | $2,000 |
| **Number of awards:** | 2 |
| **Application deadline:** | February 1 |
| **Total amount awarded:** | $4,000 |

**Contact:**
The ARRL Foundation, Inc. Scholarship Program
225 Main Street
Newington, CT 06111
Phone: 860-594-0397
Fax: 860-594-0259
Web: www.arrlf.org

### Zachary Taylor Stevens Memorial Scholarship

**Type of award:** Scholarship.
**Intended use:** For undergraduate study at accredited vocational, 2-year or 4-year institution in United States.
**Eligibility:** Applicant must be residing in Michigan, Ohio or West Virginia.
**Basis for selection:** Competition/talent/interest in amateur radio.
**Application requirements:** Transcript.
**Additional information:** Must be amateur radio operator holding technician class license or higher. Preference given to residents of Michigan, Ohio, and West Virginia. High school seniors eligible to apply. Application may be obtained on Website, and will only be accepted via email.

| | |
|---|---|
| **Amount of award:** | $750 |
| **Number of awards:** | 1 |
| **Application deadline:** | February 1 |

**Contact:**
The ARRL Foundation, Inc. Scholarship Program
225 Main Street
Newington, CT 06111
Phone: 860-594-0397
Fax: 860-594-0259
Web: www.arrlf.org

## American Respiratory Care Foundation

### Jimmy A. Young Memorial Education Recognition Award

**Type of award:** Scholarship, renewable.
**Intended use:** For undergraduate study at accredited postsecondary institution.
**Eligibility:** Applicant must be Alaskan native, Asian American, African American, Mexican American, Hispanic American, Puerto Rican, American Indian or Native Hawaiian/Pacific Islander.
**Basis for selection:** Competition/talent/interest in research paper. Major/career interest in respiratory therapy. Applicant must demonstrate high academic achievement.
**Application requirements:** Recommendations, transcript, proof of eligibility, nomination by school or program representative. Student may initiate request for sponsorship in absence of nomination. Original referenced paper on some aspect of respiratory care.
**Additional information:** Minimum 3.0 GPA. Award includes airfare, one night lodging, and registration for AARC International Respiratory Congress. Preference given to applicants of minority origin. Application available on Website. Application must be notarized.

| | |
|---|---|
| **Amount of award:** | $1,000 |
| **Number of awards:** | 1 |
| **Application deadline:** | June 15 |
| **Total amount awarded:** | $1,000 |

**Contact:**
American Respiratory Care Foundation
Attn: Education Recognition Award
9425 N. MacArthur Blvd., Suite 100
Irving, TX 75063-4706
Phone: 972-243-2272
Fax: 972-484-2720
Web: www.arcfoundation.org/awards

### Morton B. Duggan, Jr. Memorial Education Recognition Award

**Type of award:** Scholarship, renewable.
**Intended use:** For undergraduate study at accredited postsecondary institution.
**Basis for selection:** Competition/talent/interest in research paper. Major/career interest in respiratory therapy. Applicant must demonstrate high academic achievement.
**Application requirements:** Recommendations, transcript, proof of eligibility. Research paper on some aspect of respiratory care.
**Additional information:** Applicants accepted from all states, but preference given to applicants from Georgia and South Carolina. Minimum 3.0 GPA. Award includes airfare, one night lodging, and registration for the AARC International Respiratory Congress. Application available on Website. Application must be notarized.

| | |
|---|---|
| **Amount of award:** | $1,000 |
| **Number of awards:** | 1 |
| **Application deadline:** | June 15 |

**Contact:**
American Respiratory Care Foundation
Attn: Education Recogniton Award
9425 N. MacArthur Blvd., Suite 100
Irving, TX 75063-4706
Phone: 972-243-2272
Fax: 972-484-2720
Web: www.arcfoundation.org/awards

### NBRC/AMP Robert M. Lawrence, MD Education Recognition Award

**Type of award:** Scholarship.
**Intended use:** For junior or senior study at accredited 4-year institution.

**Basis for selection:** Competition/talent/interest in research paper. Major/career interest in respiratory therapy. Applicant must demonstrate high academic achievement.
**Application requirements:** Recommendations, essay, transcript, proof of eligibility. Original referenced paper on some aspect of respiratory care.
**Additional information:** Minimum 3.0 GPA. Award includes airfare, one night lodging, and registration for AARC International Respiratory Congress. Application available on Website. Application must be notarized.

| | |
|---|---|
| **Amount of award:** | $2,500 |
| **Number of awards:** | 1 |
| **Application deadline:** | June 15 |

**Contact:**
American Respiratory Care Foundation
Attn: Education Recognition Award
9425 N. MacArthur Blvd., Suite 100
Irving, TX 75063-4706
Phone: 972-243-2272
Fax: 972-484-2720
Web: www.arcfoundation.org/awards

## NBRC/AMP William W. Burgin, Jr. MD Education Recognition Award

**Type of award:** Scholarship.
**Intended use:** For sophomore study at accredited 2-year institution.
**Basis for selection:** Competition/talent/interest in research paper. Major/career interest in respiratory therapy. Applicant must demonstrate high academic achievement.
**Application requirements:** Recommendations, essay, transcript, proof of eligibility, nomination by school or educational program (or may apply directly). Original referenced paper on some aspect of respiratory care.
**Additional information:** Must be student in respiratory therapy associate's degree program. Minimum 3.0 GPA. Award includes one night lodging and registration for AARC International Respiratory Congress. Application available on Website. Application must be notarized.

| | |
|---|---|
| **Amount of award:** | $2,500 |
| **Number of awards:** | 1 |
| **Application deadline:** | June 15 |

**Contact:**
American Respiratory Care Foundation
Attn: Education Recognition Award
9425 N. MacArthur Blvd., Suite 100
Irving, TX 75063-4706
Phone: 972-243-2272
Fax: 972-484-2720
Web: www.arcfoundation.org/awards

# American Society for Enology and Viticulture

## American Society for Enology and Viticulture Scholarship Program

**Type of award:** Scholarship, renewable.
**Intended use:** For full-time junior, senior or graduate study at accredited 4-year or graduate institution.
**Eligibility:** Applicant must be U.S. citizen, permanent resident or Resident of Canada or Mexico.
**Basis for selection:** Major/career interest in agriculture; food science/technology or horticulture. Applicant must demonstrate financial need and high academic achievement.
**Application requirements:** Recommendations, essay, transcript. Student questionnaire, list of planned courses for upcoming year.
**Additional information:** Minimum 3.0 GPA for undergraduates, 3.2 GPA for graduate students. Applicants must be enrolled in major or graduate program emphasizing enology or viticulture, or in curriculum emphasizing science basic to wine and grape industry. Awards vary.

| | |
|---|---|
| **Number of applicants:** | 14 |
| **Application deadline:** | March 1 |

**Contact:**
ASEV Scholarship Committee
P.O. Box 1855
Davis, CA 95617-1855
Phone: 530-753-3142
Fax: 530-753-3318
Web: www.asev.org/scholarship-program

# American Society for Microbiology

## Undergraduate Research Fellowship (URF)

**Type of award:** Research grant.
**Intended use:** For full-time undergraduate study in United States.
**Eligibility:** Applicant must be U.S. citizen or permanent resident.
**Basis for selection:** Major/career interest in microbiology. Applicant must demonstrate high academic achievement and seriousness of purpose.
**Application requirements:** Recommendations, transcript.
**Additional information:** Applicant must demonstrate strong interest in pursuing graduate career (Ph.D. or M.D./Ph.D.) in microbiology. Students conduct research for 10-12 weeks in summer and present results at ASM General Meeting the following year. Fellowship offers up to $4,000 stipend and up to $1,000 to travel to ASM General Meeting (if abstract is accepted). Applicant must have ASM member at home institution willing to serve as faculty mentor. Students may not receive financial support for research from other scientific organizations during fellowship. Faculty member's department chair or dean must endorse research project. Number of awards varies. See Website for application.

| | |
|---|---|
| **Amount of award:** | $5,000 |
| **Number of applicants:** | 81 |
| **Application deadline:** | February 1 |
| **Notification begins:** | April 15 |

**Contact:**
American Society for Microbiology
ASM Undergraduate Research Fellowship Program
1752 N Street, NW
Washington, DC 20036
Phone: 202-942-9283
Fax: 202-942-9329
Web: www.asm.org/students

# American Society of Civil Engineers

## Eugene C. Figg Jr. Civil Engineering Scholarship

**Type of award:** Scholarship.
**Intended use:** For junior or senior study.
**Eligibility:** Applicant must be U.S. citizen.
**Basis for selection:** Major/career interest in engineering, civil. Applicant must demonstrate financial need, high academic achievement and leadership.
**Application requirements:** Recommendations, essay, transcript. One-page resume, detailed financial plan.
**Additional information:** Must be American Society of Civil Engineers member in good standing, be enrolled in ABET-accredited program, and have passion for bridges. Recipient eligible to interview for internship opportunity with Figg Engineering Group.

| | |
|---|---|
| **Amount of award:** | $3,000 |
| **Number of awards:** | 1 |
| **Application deadline:** | February 9 |
| **Notification begins:** | April 1 |
| **Total amount awarded:** | $3,000 |

**Contact:**
American Society of Civil Engineers
Attn: Student Services
1801 Alexander Bell Drive
Reston, VA 20191-4400
Phone: 800-548-2723 ext. 6106
Fax: 703-295-6222
Web: www.asce.org

## Freeman Fellowship

**Type of award:** Research grant.
**Intended use:** For undergraduate or graduate study.
**Basis for selection:** Major/career interest in engineering, civil.
**Application requirements:** Recommendations, essay, transcript, research proposal. One- to two-page resume. Detailed financial statement indicating how fellowship will finance applicant's research. Statement from institution where research will be conducted.
**Additional information:** Applicant must be American Society of Civil Engineers member in good standing. Grants are made toward expenses for experiments, observations, and compilations to discover new and accurate data that will be useful in engineering. Grant may be in form of prize for most useful paper relating to science/art of hydraulic construction. Travel grants available to ASCE members under 45, in recognition of achievement or promise. Visit Website for application and more information.

| | |
|---|---|
| **Amount of award:** | $2,000-$5,000 |
| **Application deadline:** | February 9 |
| **Notification begins:** | April 1 |

**Contact:**
American Society of Civil Engineers
Attn: Student Services
1801 Alexander Bell Drive
Reston, VA 20191-4440
Phone: 800-548-2723 ext. 6106
Fax: 703-295-6222
Web: www.asce.org

## Samuel Fletcher Tapman ASCE Student Chapter Scholarship

**Type of award:** Scholarship, renewable.
**Intended use:** For undergraduate study at accredited postsecondary institution.
**Basis for selection:** Major/career interest in engineering, civil. Applicant must demonstrate financial need, high academic achievement and leadership.
**Application requirements:** Recommendations, essay, transcript. One-page resume, detailed annual budget.
**Additional information:** Applicant must be enrolled in ABET-accredited program and be member in good standing of local American Society of Civil Engineers student chapter and national society. Membership applications may be submitted with scholarship application. One submission per student chapter. Visit Website for application and more information.

| | |
|---|---|
| **Amount of award:** | $3,000 |
| **Number of awards:** | 12 |
| **Application deadline:** | February 9 |
| **Notification begins:** | April 1 |

**Contact:**
American Society of Civil Engineers
Attn: Student Services
1801 Alexander Bell Drive
Reston, VA 20191-4440
Phone: 800-548-2723 ext. 6106
Fax: 703-295-6222
Web: www.asce.org

## Y.C. Yang Civil Engineering Scholarship

**Type of award:** Scholarship.
**Intended use:** For junior or senior study.
**Basis for selection:** Major/career interest in engineering, civil or engineering, structural. Applicant must demonstrate financial need, high academic achievement and leadership.
**Application requirements:** Recommendations, essay, transcript. One-page resume, detailed financial plan.
**Additional information:** Must be student at ABET-accredited institution, an ASCE student member in good standing, and have interest in structural engineering.

| | |
|---|---|
| **Amount of award:** | $2,000 |
| **Number of awards:** | 2 |
| **Application deadline:** | February 9 |
| **Notification begins:** | April 1 |

**Contact:**
American Society of Civil Engineers
Attn: Student Services
1801 Alexander Bell Drive
Reston, VA 20191-4400
Phone: 800-548-2723 ext. 6106
Fax: 703-295-6222
Web: www.asce.org

# American Society of Heating, Refrigerating, and Air-Conditioning Engineers, Inc.

## Alwin B. Newton Scholarship

**Type of award:** Scholarship.
**Intended use:** For full-time undergraduate study at accredited 4-year institution in or outside United States. Designated institutions: Schools with ABET-accredited programs.

**Basis for selection:** Major/career interest in engineering or air conditioning/heating/refrigeration technology. Applicant must demonstrate financial need, high academic achievement, depth of character and leadership.
**Application requirements:** Recommendations, transcript.
**Additional information:** For engineering students considering service to heating/ventilation/air-conditioning (HVAC) and/or refrigeration profession. Minimum 3.0 GPA.

| | |
|---|---|
| **Amount of award:** | $3,000 |
| **Number of awards:** | 1 |
| **Application deadline:** | December 1 |

**Contact:**
ASHRAE, Inc. - Scholarship Administrator
1791 Tullie Circle, NE
Atlanta, GA 30329-2305
Phone: 404-636-8400
Fax: 404-321-5478
Web: www.ashrae.org/students/page/1271

## ASHRAE General Scholarships

**Type of award:** Scholarship.
**Intended use:** For full-time undergraduate study at accredited 4-year institution in or outside United States. Designated institutions: Schools with ABET-accredited programs.
**Basis for selection:** Major/career interest in engineering or air conditioning/heating/refrigeration technology. Applicant must demonstrate financial need, high academic achievement, depth of character and leadership.
**Application requirements:** Recommendations, transcript.
**Additional information:** For engineering students considering service to heating/ventilation/air-conditioning (HVAC) and/or refrigeration profession. Minimum 3.0 GPA.

| | |
|---|---|
| **Amount of award:** | $3,000 |
| **Number of awards:** | 2 |
| **Application deadline:** | December 1 |

**Contact:**
ASHRAE, Inc. - Scholarship Administrator
1791 Tullie Circle, NE
Atlanta, GA 30329-2305
Phone: 404-636-8400
Fax: 404-321-5478
Web: www.ashrae.org/students/page/1271

## ASHRAE Memorial Scholarship

**Type of award:** Scholarship.
**Intended use:** For full-time undergraduate study at accredited 4-year institution in or outside United States. Designated institutions: Schools with ABET-accredited programs.
**Basis for selection:** Major/career interest in engineering or air conditioning/heating/refrigeration technology. Applicant must demonstrate financial need, high academic achievement, depth of character and leadership.
**Application requirements:** Recommendations, transcript.
**Additional information:** For engineering students considering service to heating/ventilation/air-conditioning (HVAC) and/or refrigeration profession. Minimum 3.0 GPA.

| | |
|---|---|
| **Amount of award:** | $3,000 |
| **Number of awards:** | 1 |
| **Application deadline:** | December 1 |

**Contact:**
ASHRAE, Inc. - Scholarship Administrator
1791 Tullie Circle, NE
Atlanta, GA 30329-2305
Phone: 404-636-8400
Fax: 404-321-5478
Web: www.ashrae.org/students/page/1271

## ASHRAE Region IV Benny Bootle Scholarship

**Type of award:** Scholarship.
**Intended use:** For full-time undergraduate study at accredited 4-year institution. Designated institutions: Schools with NAAB or ABET-accredited program located within the geographic boundaries of ASHRAE's Region IV (North Carolina, South Carolina, Georgia).
**Eligibility:** Applicant must be residing in North Carolina, Georgia or South Carolina.
**Basis for selection:** Major/career interest in air conditioning/heating/refrigeration technology; architecture or engineering. Applicant must demonstrate financial need, high academic achievement, depth of character and leadership.
**Application requirements:** Recommendations, transcript.
**Additional information:** Minimum 3.0 GPA. For engineering or architecture students considering service to heating/ventilation/air-conditioning (HVAC) and/or refrigeration profession. Visit www.abet.org and www.naab.org for list of ABET- and NAAB-accredited programs within Region IV.

| | |
|---|---|
| **Amount of award:** | $3,000 |
| **Number of awards:** | 1 |
| **Application deadline:** | December 1 |

**Contact:**
ASHRAE, Inc. - Scholarship Administrator
1791 Tullie Circle, NE
Atlanta, GA 30329-2305
Phone: 404-636-8400
Fax: 404-321-5478
Web: www.ashrae.org/students/page/1271

## ASHRAE Region VIII Scholarship

**Type of award:** Scholarship.
**Intended use:** For full-time undergraduate study in or outside United States. Designated institutions: Schools with ABET-accredited programs located within the geographic boundaries of ASHRAE's Region VIII (Arkansas, Oklahoma, Mexico, and parts of Louisiana and Texas).
**Eligibility:** Applicant must be residing in Oklahoma, Texas, Arkansas or Louisiana.
**Basis for selection:** Major/career interest in engineering or air conditioning/heating/refrigeration technology. Applicant must demonstrate financial need, high academic achievement, depth of character and leadership.
**Application requirements:** Recommendations, transcript.
**Additional information:** Minimum 3.0 GPA. For engineering students considering service to heating/ventilation/air-conditioning (HVAC) and/or refrigeration profession. Contact ASHRAE for information regarding Region VIII. Visit www.abet.org for ABET-accredited programs within the region.

| | |
|---|---|
| **Amount of award:** | $3,000 |
| **Number of awards:** | 1 |
| **Application deadline:** | December 1 |

**Contact:**
ASHRAE, Inc. - Scholarship Administrator
1791 Tullie Circle, NE
Atlanta, GA 30329-2305
Phone: 404-636-8400
Fax: 404-321-5478
Web: www.ashrae.org/students/page/1271

## Duane Hanson Scholarship

**Type of award:** Scholarship.
**Intended use:** For full-time undergraduate study at accredited 4-year institution in or outside United States. Designated institutions: Schools with ABET-accredited programs.
**Basis for selection:** Major/career interest in engineering or air conditioning/heating/refrigeration technology. Applicant must demonstrate financial need, high academic achievement, depth of character and leadership.
**Application requirements:** Recommendations, transcript.
**Additional information:** For engineering students considering service to heating/ventilation/air-conditioning (HVAC) and/or refrigeration profession. Minimum 3.0 GPA.

| | |
|---|---|
| **Amount of award:** | $3,000 |
| **Number of awards:** | 1 |
| **Application deadline:** | December 1 |

**Contact:**
ASHRAE, Inc. - Scholarship Administrator
1791 Tullie Circle, NE
Atlanta, GA 30329-2305
Phone: 404-636-8400
Fax: 404-321-5478
Web: www.ashrae.org/students/page/1271

## Engineering Technology Scholarships

**Type of award:** Scholarship.
**Intended use:** For full-time undergraduate study at accredited 2-year or 4-year institution. Designated institutions: Schools with ABET-accredited engineering technology programs.
**Basis for selection:** Major/career interest in engineering or air conditioning/heating/refrigeration technology. Applicant must demonstrate financial need, high academic achievement, depth of character and leadership.
**Application requirements:** Recommendations, transcript.
**Additional information:** For students pursuing bachelor's or associate's degree in engineering technology and intending to pursue career in heating/ventilation/air-conditioning (HVAC) and/or refrigeration profession. Minimum 3.0 GPA.

| | |
|---|---|
| **Amount of award:** | $3,000 |
| **Number of awards:** | 3 |
| **Application deadline:** | May 1 |

**Contact:**
ASHRAE, Inc. - Scholarship Administrator
1791 Tullie Circle, NE
Atlanta, GA 30329-2305
Phone: 404-636-8400
Fax: 404-321-5478
Web: www.ashrae.org/students/page/1271

## Frank M. Coda Scholarship

**Type of award:** Scholarship.
**Intended use:** For full-time undergraduate study at accredited 4-year institution in or outside United States. Designated institutions: Schools with ABET-accredited programs.
**Basis for selection:** Major/career interest in engineering or air conditioning/heating/refrigeration technology. Applicant must demonstrate financial need, high academic achievement, depth of character and leadership.
**Application requirements:** Recommendations, transcript.
**Additional information:** For engineering students considering service to heating/ventilation/air-conditioning (HVAC) and/or refrigeration profession. Minimum 3.0 GPA.

| | |
|---|---|
| **Amount of award:** | $5,000 |
| **Number of awards:** | 1 |
| **Application deadline:** | December 1 |

**Contact:**
ASHRAE, Inc. - Scholarship Administrator
1791 Tullie Circle, NE
Atlanta, GA 30329-2305
Phone: 404-636-8400
Fax: 404-321-5478
Web: www.ashrae.org/students/page/1271

## Henry Adams Scholarship

**Type of award:** Scholarship.
**Intended use:** For full-time undergraduate study at accredited 4-year institution in or outside United States. Designated institutions: Schools with ABET-accredited programs.
**Basis for selection:** Major/career interest in engineering or air conditioning/heating/refrigeration technology. Applicant must demonstrate financial need, high academic achievement, depth of character and leadership.
**Application requirements:** Recommendations, transcript.
**Additional information:** For engineering students considering service to heating/ventilation/air-conditioning (HVAC) and/or refrigeration profession. Minimum 3.0 GPA.

| | |
|---|---|
| **Amount of award:** | $3,000 |
| **Number of awards:** | 1 |
| **Application deadline:** | December 1 |

**Contact:**
ASHRAE, Inc. - Scholarship Administrator
1791 Tullie Circle, NE
Atlanta, GA 30329-2305
Phone: 404-636-8400
Fax: 404-321-5478
Web: www.ashrae.org/students/page/1271

## J. Richard Mehalick Scholarship

**Type of award:** Scholarship.
**Intended use:** For full-time undergraduate study at accredited 4-year institution in United States. Designated institutions: University of Pittsburgh.
**Basis for selection:** Major/career interest in engineering, mechanical or air conditioning/heating/refrigeration technology. Applicant must demonstrate financial need, high academic achievement, depth of character and leadership.
**Application requirements:** Recommendations, transcript.
**Additional information:** Must have minimum 3.0 GPA. For mechanical engineering students considering service to heating/ventilation/air-conditioning (HVAC) and/or refrigeration profession.

| | |
|---|---|
| **Amount of award:** | $3,000 |
| **Number of awards:** | 1 |
| **Application deadline:** | December 1 |

**Contact:**
ASHRAE, Inc. - Scholarship Administrator
1791 Tullie Circle, NE
Atlanta, GA 30329
Phone: 404-636-8400
Fax: 404-321-5478
Web: www.ashrae.org/students/page/1271

## Reuben Trane Scholarship

**Type of award:** Scholarship.
**Intended use:** For full-time undergraduate study at accredited 4-year institution in or outside United States. Designated institutions: Schools with ABET-accredited programs.

**Basis for selection:** Major/career interest in air conditioning/heating/refrigeration technology or engineering. Applicant must demonstrate financial need, high academic achievement, depth of character and leadership.
**Application requirements:** Recommendations, transcript.
**Additional information:** Minimum 3.0 GPA. Award is for two years; $5,000 given at beginning of each year. Must be considering service to heating/ventilation/air-conditioning (HVAC) and/or refrigeration profession.

| | |
|---|---|
| **Amount of award:** | $10,000 |
| **Number of awards:** | 4 |
| **Application deadline:** | December 1 |

**Contact:**
ASHRAE, Inc. - Scholarship Administrator
1791 Tullie Circle, NE
Atlanta, GA 30329-2305
Phone: 404-636-8400
Fax: 404-321-5478
Web: www.ashrae.org/students/page/1271

### Willis H. Carrier Scholarship

**Type of award:** Scholarship.
**Intended use:** For full-time undergraduate study at accredited 4-year institution in or outside United States. Designated institutions: ABET-accredited institutions.
**Basis for selection:** Major/career interest in engineering or air conditioning/heating/refrigeration technology. Applicant must demonstrate financial need, high academic achievement, depth of character and leadership.
**Application requirements:** Recommendations, transcript.
**Additional information:** For engineering students considering service to heating/ventilation/air-conditioning (HVAC) and/or refrigeration profession. Minimum 3.0 GPA.

| | |
|---|---|
| **Amount of award:** | $10,000 |
| **Number of awards:** | 2 |
| **Application deadline:** | December 1 |

**Contact:**
ASHRAE, Inc. - Scholarship Administrator
1791 Tullie Circle, NE
Atlanta, GA 30329-2305
Phone: 404-636-8400
Fax: 404-321-5478
Web: www.ashrae.org/students/page/1271

## American Society of Interior Designers Foundation, Inc.

### Joel Polsky Academic Achievement Award

**Type of award:** Scholarship.
**Intended use:** For undergraduate or graduate study at postsecondary institution.
**Basis for selection:** Competition/talent/interest in research paper, based on content, breadth of material, comprehensive coverage of topic, innovative subject matter, bibliography, and references. Major/career interest in interior design.
**Application requirements:** Photo.
**Additional information:** Award to recognize outstanding interior design research or thesis project addressing topics such as educational research, behavioral science, business practice, design process, theory, or other technical subjects.

| | |
|---|---|
| **Amount of award:** | $1,000 |
| **Number of awards:** | 1 |
| **Application deadline:** | March 1 |

**Contact:**
American Society of Interior Designers Foundation, Inc.
Joel Polsky Academic Achievement Award
608 Massachusetts Avenue, NE
Washington, DC 20002-6006
Phone: 202-546-3480
Fax: 202-546-3240
Web: www.asid.org

## American Society of Naval Engineers

### ASNE Scholarship

**Type of award:** Scholarship, renewable.
**Intended use:** For full-time senior or graduate study at accredited 4-year or graduate institution.
**Eligibility:** Applicant must be U.S. citizen.
**Basis for selection:** Major/career interest in engineering; engineering, civil; engineering, electrical/electronic; engineering, environmental; engineering, marine; engineering, mechanical; engineering, nuclear; engineering, structural or physical sciences. Applicant must demonstrate high academic achievement and seriousness of purpose.
**Application requirements:** Recommendations, essay, transcript.
**Additional information:** Graduate applicants must be members of American Society of Naval Engineers. Applicants' major/career interests may also include naval architecture, aeronautical and ocean engineering, or other programs leading to careers with relevant military and civilian organizations. Financial need may be considered. Award also includes one-year honorary student membership to Society.

| | |
|---|---|
| **Amount of award:** | $3,000-$4,000 |
| **Number of awards:** | 21 |
| **Application deadline:** | February 28 |
| **Notification begins:** | May 1 |

**Contact:**
American Society of Naval Engineers
1452 Duke Street
Alexandria, VA 22314-3458
Phone: 703-836-6727
Fax: 703-836-7491
Web: www.navalengineers.org

## American Water Ski Educational Foundation

### American Water Ski Educational Foundation Scholarship

**Type of award:** Scholarship, renewable.
**Intended use:** For full-time sophomore, junior or senior study at 2-year or 4-year institution.
**Eligibility:** Applicant must be U.S. citizen.

**Basis for selection:** Applicant must demonstrate financial need, high academic achievement, depth of character, leadership and seriousness of purpose.
**Application requirements:** Recommendations, essay, transcript. College freshmen should include both college and high school transcripts. Visit Website for current essay topic.
**Additional information:** Must be member of USA Water Ski Association.

| | |
|---|---|
| **Amount of award:** | $1,500-$3,000 |
| **Number of awards:** | 6 |
| **Number of applicants:** | 10 |
| **Application deadline:** | March 1 |
| **Notification begins:** | September 1 |
| **Total amount awarded:** | $11,000 |

**Contact:**
American Water Ski Educational Foundation
1251 Holy Cow Road
Polk City, FL 33868-8200
Phone: 863-324-2472
Fax: 863-324-3996
Web: www.waterskihalloffame.com

# American Welding Society Foundation, Inc.

## Airgas-Jerry Baker Scholarship

**Type of award:** Scholarship, renewable.
**Intended use:** For full-time undergraduate study at postsecondary institution.
**Eligibility:** Applicant must be at least 18. Applicant must be U.S. citizen or Canadian citizen.
**Basis for selection:** Major/career interest in welding.
**Application requirements:** Essay.
**Additional information:** Applicants must have minimum 2.8 overall GPA with 3.0 GPA in engineering courses. Priority given to individuals residing or attending school in Alabama, Georgia, or Florida. Applicant must show interest in welding engineering or welding engineering technology.

| | |
|---|---|
| **Amount of award:** | $2,500 |
| **Number of awards:** | 1 |
| **Number of applicants:** | 2 |
| **Application deadline:** | February 15 |
| **Notification begins:** | April 1 |
| **Total amount awarded:** | $2,500 |

**Contact:**
American Welding Society Foundation, Inc.
Attn: Scholarships
550 Northwest LeJeune Road
Miami, FL 33126
Phone: 800-443-9353 ext. 461
Web: www.aws.org/foundation/scholarships

## Airgas-Terry Jarvis Memorial Scholarship

**Type of award:** Scholarship.
**Intended use:** For full-time sophomore, junior or senior study at 4-year institution in United States or Canada.
**Eligibility:** Applicant must be at least 18. Applicant must be U.S. citizen or Canadian citizen.
**Basis for selection:** Major/career interest in welding.
**Application requirements:** Recommendations, essay, transcript, proof of eligibility.
**Additional information:** Must have interest in pursuing a minimum four-year degree in welding engineering or welding engineering technology. Minimum 2.8 GPA overall, with 3.0 GPA in engineering courses. Priority given to residents of Florida, Alabama, and Georgia. Applicant does not have to be a member of the American Welding Society.

| | |
|---|---|
| **Amount of award:** | $2,500 |
| **Number of awards:** | 1 |
| **Number of applicants:** | 2 |
| **Application deadline:** | February 15 |
| **Notification begins:** | April 1 |
| **Total amount awarded:** | $2,500 |

**Contact:**
American Welding Society Foundation, Inc.
Attn: Scholarships
550 Northwest LeJeune Road
Miami, FL 33126
Phone: 800-443-9353
Web: www.aws.org/foundation/scholarships

## American Welding Society District Scholarship Program

**Type of award:** Scholarship.
**Intended use:** For undergraduate study at accredited vocational, 2-year or 4-year institution in United States.
**Eligibility:** Applicant must be U.S. citizen.
**Basis for selection:** Major/career interest in welding. Applicant must demonstrate financial need, high academic achievement, depth of character, leadership and seriousness of purpose.
**Application requirements:** Recommendations, transcript, proof of eligibility. Personal statement, biography, and photo.

| | |
|---|---|
| **Amount of award:** | $200-$2,000 |
| **Number of awards:** | 150 |
| **Number of applicants:** | 350 |
| **Application deadline:** | March 1 |
| **Notification begins:** | July 1 |
| **Total amount awarded:** | $165,000 |

**Contact:**
American Welding Society Foundation, Inc.
Attn: Scholarships
550 Northwest LeJeune Road
Miami, FL 33126
Phone: 800-443-9353
Web: www.aws.org/foundation/scholarships

## Arsham Amirikian Engineering Scholarship

**Type of award:** Scholarship, renewable.
**Intended use:** For undergraduate study at accredited 4-year institution.
**Eligibility:** Applicant must be at least 18. Applicant must be U.S. citizen.
**Basis for selection:** Major/career interest in welding. Applicant must demonstrate financial need.
**Additional information:** Minimum 3.0 GPA. Must show interest in pursuing career in the application of the art of welding in civil and structural engineering.

| | |
|---|---|
| **Amount of award:** | $2,500 |
| **Number of awards:** | 1 |
| **Number of applicants:** | 13 |
| **Application deadline:** | February 15 |
| **Notification begins:** | April 1 |
| **Total amount awarded:** | $2,500 |

**Contact:**
American Welding Society Foundation, Inc.
Attn: Scholarships
550 Northwest LeJeune Road
Miami, FL 33126
Phone: 800-443-9353
Web: www.aws.org/foundation/scholarships

## D. Fred and Mariam L. Bovie Scholarship

**Type of award:** Scholarship, renewable.
**Intended use:** For full-time at 4-year institution. Designated institutions: The Ohio State University.
**Eligibility:** Applicant must be U.S. citizen.
**Basis for selection:** Major/career interest in welding or engineering, electrical/electronic.
**Application requirements:** Recommendations, essay, transcript, proof of eligibility. Statement of Unmet Financial Need.
**Additional information:** Award may be renewed for a maximum of four years. Membership in the American Welding Society is not required. Electrical engineering candidates will be considered if there are no qualified welding engineering candidates.

| | |
|---|---|
| **Amount of award:** | $3,000 |
| **Number of awards:** | 1 |
| **Number of applicants:** | 7 |
| **Application deadline:** | February 15 |

**Contact:**
American Welding Society Foundation, Inc.
Attn: Scholarships
550 Northwest LeJeune Road
Miami, FL 33126
Phone: 800-443-9353
Web; www.aws.org/foundation/scholarships

## D. Fred and Mariam L. Bovie Technical Scholarship

**Type of award:** Scholarship, renewable.
**Intended use:** For undergraduate study at postsecondary institution.
**Basis for selection:** Major/career interest in welding. Applicant must demonstrate financial need.
**Application requirements:** Recommendations, essay, transcript, proof of eligibility. Statement of Unmet Financial Need.
**Additional information:** Minimum 2.8 GPA. Applicant must be pursuing an associate's degree in welding, with a minimum of a two-year program. Award may be renewed for a maximum of four years. Membership in the American Welding Society is not required.

| | |
|---|---|
| **Amount of award:** | $2,000 |
| **Number of awards:** | 1 |
| **Number of applicants:** | 1 |
| **Application deadline:** | February 15 |
| **Total amount awarded:** | $2,000 |

**Contact:**
AWS Foundation, Inc.
Attn: Scholarships
550 Northwest LeJeune Road
Miami, FL 33126
Phone: 800-443-9353 ext. 250
Fax: 305-443-7559
Web: www.aws.org/foundation/scholarships

## Donald and Shirley Hastings National Scholarship

**Type of award:** Scholarship, renewable.
**Intended use:** For undergraduate study at 4-year institution in United States.
**Eligibility:** Applicant must be at least 18. Applicant must be U.S. citizen.
**Basis for selection:** Major/career interest in welding. Applicant must demonstrate financial need.
**Additional information:** Minimum 2.5 GPA. Must show interest in welding engineering or welding engineering technology. Priority given to Iowa, Ohio, or California residents.

| | |
|---|---|
| **Amount of award:** | $2,500 |
| **Number of awards:** | 1 |
| **Number of applicants:** | 17 |
| **Application deadline:** | February 15 |
| **Notification begins:** | April 1 |
| **Total amount awarded:** | $2,500 |

**Contact:**
American Welding Society Foundation, Inc.
Attn: Scholarships
550 Northwest LeJeune Road
Miami, FL 33126
Phone: 800-443-9353
Web: www.aws.org/foundation/scholarships

## Donald F. Hastings Scholarship

**Type of award:** Scholarship, renewable.
**Intended use:** For sophomore, junior or senior study at 4-year institution in United States.
**Eligibility:** Applicant must be at least 18. Applicant must be U.S. citizen.
**Basis for selection:** Major/career interest in welding. Applicant must demonstrate financial need and seriousness of purpose.
**Application requirements:** Recommendations, transcript, proof of eligibility.
**Additional information:** Priority given to residents of Ohio and California. Minimum 2.5 GPA.

| | |
|---|---|
| **Amount of award:** | $2,500 |
| **Number of awards:** | 1 |
| **Number of applicants:** | 16 |
| **Application deadline:** | February 15 |
| **Notification begins:** | April 1 |
| **Total amount awarded:** | $2,500 |

**Contact:**
American Welding Society Foundation, Inc.
Attn: Scholarships
550 Northwest LeJeune Road
Miami, FL 33126
Phone: 800-443-9353
Web: www.aws.org/foundation/scholarships

## Edward J. Brady Memorial Scholarship

**Type of award:** Scholarship, renewable.
**Intended use:** For sophomore, junior or senior study at 4-year institution.
**Eligibility:** Applicant must be at least 18. Applicant must be U.S. citizen or Canadian citizen.
**Basis for selection:** Major/career interest in welding or engineering. Applicant must demonstrate financial need and seriousness of purpose.

Scholarships

**Application requirements:** Recommendations, essay, transcript, proof of eligibility. Proposed curriculum; brief biography; proof of hands-on welding experience.
**Additional information:** Interest in pursuing minimum four-year degree in welding engineering or welding engineering technology. Minimum 2.5 GPA.

| | |
|---|---|
| **Amount of award:** | $2,500 |
| **Number of awards:** | 1 |
| **Number of applicants:** | 6 |
| **Application deadline:** | February 15 |
| **Notification begins:** | April 1 |
| **Total amount awarded:** | $2,500 |

**Contact:**
American Welding Society Foundation, Inc.
Attn: Scholarships
550 Northwest LeJeune Road
Miami, FL 33126
Phone: 800-443-9353
Web: www.aws.org/foundation/scholarships

## Howard E. and Wilma J. Adkins Memorial Scholarship

**Type of award:** Scholarship, renewable.
**Intended use:** For full-time junior or senior study at 4-year institution.
**Eligibility:** Applicant must be at least 18. Applicant must be U.S. citizen.
**Basis for selection:** Major/career interest in welding. Applicant must demonstrate high academic achievement and seriousness of purpose.
**Application requirements:** Recommendations, transcript, proof of eligibility.
**Additional information:** Applicant should have interest in pursuing four-year degree in welding engineering or welding engineering technology. Priority given to residents of Kentucky and Wisconsin. Minimum 3.2 GPA in engineering, scientific, and technical subjects; minimum overall 2.8 GPA.

| | |
|---|---|
| **Amount of award:** | $2,500 |
| **Number of awards:** | 1 |
| **Number of applicants:** | 14 |
| **Application deadline:** | February 15 |
| **Notification begins:** | April 1 |
| **Total amount awarded:** | $2,500 |

**Contact:**
American Welding Society Foundation Inc.
Attn: Scholarships
550 Northwest LeJeune Road
Miami, FL 33126
Phone: 800-443-9353
Web: www.aws.org/foundation/scholarships

## Jack R. Barckhoff Welding Management Scholarship

**Type of award:** Scholarship.
**Intended use:** For junior study at 4-year institution. Designated institutions: Ohio State University.
**Eligibility:** Applicant must be U.S. citizen.
**Basis for selection:** Major/career interest in welding. Applicant must demonstrate high academic achievement.
**Application requirements:** 300-to-500-word essay.
**Additional information:** Minimum 2.5 GPA.

| | |
|---|---|
| **Amount of award:** | $2,500 |
| **Number of awards:** | 2 |
| **Number of applicants:** | 4 |
| **Application deadline:** | February 15 |
| **Notification begins:** | April 1 |
| **Total amount awarded:** | $5,000 |

**Contact:**
American Welding Society Foundation
Attn: Scholarships
550 Northwest LeJeune Road
Miami, FL 33126
Phone: 800-443-9353
Web: www.aws.org/foundation/scholarships

## James A. Turner, Jr. Memorial Scholarship

**Type of award:** Scholarship, renewable.
**Intended use:** For full-time sophomore, junior or senior study at accredited 4-year institution.
**Eligibility:** Applicant must be at least 18. Applicant must be U.S. citizen.
**Basis for selection:** Major/career interest in welding or business/management/administration. Applicant must demonstrate financial need and seriousness of purpose.
**Application requirements:** Recommendations, transcript, proof of eligibility. Verification of employment, brief biography, financial aid report, proposed curriculum.
**Additional information:** Must have interest in pursuing management career in welding. Must work minimum ten hours per week at welding store.

| | |
|---|---|
| **Amount of award:** | $3,500 |
| **Number of awards:** | 1 |
| **Number of applicants:** | 4 |
| **Application deadline:** | February 15 |
| **Notification begins:** | April 1 |
| **Total amount awarded:** | $3,500 |

**Contact:**
American Welding Society Foundation, Inc.
Attn: Scholarships
550 Northwest LeJeune Road
Miami, FL 33126
Phone: 800-443-9353
Web: www.aws.org/foundation/scholarships

## John C. Lincoln Memorial Scholarship

**Type of award:** Scholarship, renewable.
**Intended use:** For sophomore, junior or senior study at 4-year institution.
**Eligibility:** Applicant must be at least 18. Applicant must be U.S. citizen.
**Basis for selection:** Major/career interest in welding. Applicant must demonstrate financial need and seriousness of purpose.
**Application requirements:** Recommendations, transcript, proof of eligibility.
**Additional information:** Minimum 2.5 GPA. Priority will be given to those individuals residing or attending school in Ohio or Arizona.

| | |
|---|---|
| **Amount of award:** | $3,500 |
| **Number of awards:** | 1 |
| **Number of applicants:** | 17 |
| **Application deadline:** | February 15 |
| **Notification begins:** | April 1 |
| **Total amount awarded:** | $3,500 |

**Contact:**
American Welding Society Foundation, Inc.
Attn: Scholarships
550 Northwest LeJeune Road
Miami, FL 33126
Phone: 800-443-9353
Web: www.aws.org/foundation/scholarships

## Matsuo Bridge Company Ltd of Japan Scholarship

**Type of award:** Scholarship.
**Intended use:** For junior, senior or graduate study at accredited 4-year or graduate institution in United States.
**Eligibility:** Applicant must be at least 18.
**Basis for selection:** Major/career interest in welding or engineering, civil.
**Application requirements:** Recommendations, transcript, proof of eligibility.
**Additional information:** For students interested in pursuing career in civil engineering, welding engineering, or welding engineering technology. Priority given to applicants residing in California, Texas, Oregon, or Washington. Applicant does not have to be member of American Welding Society but must agree to participate in AWS Foundation or Matsuo Bridge Company sponsored publicity. Minimum 3.0 GPA.

| | |
|---|---|
| **Amount of award:** | $2,500 |
| **Number of awards:** | 1 |
| **Number of applicants:** | 20 |
| **Application deadline:** | February 15 |
| **Notification begins:** | April 1 |
| **Total amount awarded:** | $2,500 |

**Contact:**
American Welding Society Foundation, Inc.
Attn: Scholarships
550 Northwest LeJeune Road
Miami, FL 33126
Phone: 800-443-9353
Web: www.aws.org/foundation/scholarships

## Miller Electric Manufacturing Company Ivic Scholarship

**Type of award:** Scholarship, renewable.
**Intended use:** For undergraduate study at accredited vocational, 2-year or 4-year institution in United States.
**Eligibility:** Applicant must be U.S. citizen.
**Basis for selection:** Major/career interest in welding. Applicant must demonstrate depth of character, leadership and seriousness of purpose.
**Additional information:** Competition based on AWS National Welding Trials and World Skills Competition.

| | |
|---|---|
| **Amount of award:** | $10,000 |
| **Number of awards:** | 1 |

**Contact:**
American Welding Society Foundation, Inc.
Attn: Scholarships
550 Northwest LeJeune Road
Miami, FL 33126
Phone: 800-443-9353
Web: www.aws.org/foundation/scholarships

## Miller Electric Mfg. Co. Scholarship

**Type of award:** Scholarship, renewable.
**Intended use:** For senior study at 4-year institution.
**Eligibility:** Applicant must be at least 18. Applicant must be U.S. citizen.
**Basis for selection:** Major/career interest in welding.
**Additional information:** Applicant must show interest in welding engineering or welding engineering technology, and have work experience in the welding equipment field. Applicant must have minimum 3.0 GPA.

| | |
|---|---|
| **Amount of award:** | $3,000 |
| **Number of awards:** | 2 |
| **Number of applicants:** | 19 |
| **Application deadline:** | February 15 |
| **Notification begins:** | April 1 |
| **Total amount awarded:** | $6,000 |

**Contact:**
American Welding Society Foundation, Inc.
Attn: Scholarships
550 Northwest LeJeune Road
Miami, FL 33126
Phone: 800-443-9353
Web: www.aws.org/foundation/scholarships

## Past Presidents Scholarship

**Type of award:** Scholarship.
**Intended use:** For junior, senior, master's or doctoral study at 4-year or graduate institution.
**Basis for selection:** Major/career interest in welding or engineering. Applicant must demonstrate financial need.
**Application requirements:** Essay. Essay should be 300-500 words.

| | |
|---|---|
| **Amount of award:** | $2,500 |
| **Number of awards:** | 1 |
| **Number of applicants:** | 2 |
| **Application deadline:** | February 15 |
| **Notification begins:** | April 1 |
| **Total amount awarded:** | $2,500 |

**Contact:**
American Welding Society Foundation, Inc.
Attn: Scholarships
550 Northwest LeJeune Road
Miami, FL 33126
Phone: 800-443-9353
Web: www.aws.org/foundation/scholarships

## Praxair International Scholarship

**Type of award:** Scholarship, renewable.
**Intended use:** For full-time sophomore, junior or senior study at 4-year institution.
**Eligibility:** Applicant must be at least 18. Applicant must be U.S. citizen or Canadian citizen.
**Basis for selection:** Major/career interest in welding. Applicant must demonstrate financial need, leadership and service orientation.
**Application requirements:** Recommendations, transcript, proof of eligibility.
**Additional information:** Applicant must have interest in pursuing minimum four-year degree in welding engineering or welding engineering technology. Minimum 2.5 GPA.

| | |
|---|---|
| **Amount of award:** | $2,500 |
| **Number of awards:** | 1 |
| **Number of applicants:** | 30 |
| **Application deadline:** | February 15 |
| **Notification begins:** | April 1 |
| **Total amount awarded:** | $2,500 |

**Contact:**
American Welding Society Foundation, Inc.
Attn: Praxair Scholarship
550 Northwest LeJeune Road
Miami, FL 33126
Phone: 800-443-9353
Web: www.aws.org/foundation/scholarships

## Robert L. Peaslee-Detroit Brazing and Soldering Division Scholarship

**Type of award:** Scholarship, renewable.
**Intended use:** For junior or senior study at 4-year institution.
**Eligibility:** Applicant must be at least 18. Applicant must be U.S. citizen.
**Basis for selection:** Major/career interest in welding.
**Application requirements:** Recommendations, essay, transcript.
**Additional information:** Applicant must have 3.0 GPA in engineering courses. Must show interest in pursuing degree in welding engineering or welding technology with emphasis on brazing and soldering application.

| | |
|---|---|
| **Amount of award:** | $2,500 |
| **Number of awards:** | 1 |
| **Number of applicants:** | 2 |
| **Application deadline:** | February 15 |
| **Notification begins:** | April 1 |
| **Total amount awarded:** | $2,500 |

**Contact:**
American Welding Society Foundation, Inc.
Attn: Scholarships
550 Northwest LeJeune Road
Miami, FL 33126
Phone: 800-443-9353
Web: www.aws.org/foundation/scholarships

## RWMA Scholarship

**Type of award:** Scholarship.
**Intended use:** For full-time junior study at 4-year institution.
**Eligibility:** Applicant must be U.S. citizen or Canadian citizens.
**Basis for selection:** Major/career interest in welding or engineering. Applicant must demonstrate high academic achievement.
**Application requirements:** 500-word-or-less essay.
**Additional information:** Minimum 3.0 GPA.

| | |
|---|---|
| **Amount of award:** | $2,500 |
| **Number of awards:** | 1 |
| **Number of applicants:** | 2 |
| **Application deadline:** | February 15 |
| **Notification begins:** | April 1 |

**Contact:**
American Welding Society Foundation, Inc.
Attn: Scholarships
550 Northwest LeJeune Road
Miami, FL 33126
Phone: 800-443-9353
Web: www.aws.org/foundation/scholarships

## William A. and Ann M. Brothers Scholarship

**Type of award:** Scholarship, renewable.
**Intended use:** For full-time undergraduate study at accredited 4-year institution.
**Eligibility:** Applicant must be at least 18. Applicant must be U.S. citizen.
**Basis for selection:** Major/career interest in welding. Applicant must demonstrate financial need.
**Additional information:** Applicant must have minimum 2.5 GPA. Priority will be given to those individuals residing or attending schools in Ohio.

| | |
|---|---|
| **Amount of award:** | $3,500 |
| **Number of awards:** | 1 |
| **Number of applicants:** | 16 |
| **Application deadline:** | February 15 |
| **Notification begins:** | April 1 |
| **Total amount awarded:** | $3,500 |

**Contact:**
American Welding Society Foundation
Attn: Scholarships
550 Northwest LeJeune Road
Miami, FL 33126
Phone: 800-443-9353 ext. 461
Web: www.aws.org/foundation/scholarships

## William B. Howell Memorial Scholarship

**Type of award:** Scholarship, renewable.
**Intended use:** For full-time undergraduate study at accredited 4-year institution in United States.
**Eligibility:** Applicant must be at least 18. Applicant must be U.S. citizen.
**Basis for selection:** Major/career interest in welding. Applicant must demonstrate financial need.
**Application requirements:** Recommendations, transcript, proof of eligibility.
**Additional information:** Minimum 2.5 GPA required. Priority given to residents of Florida, Michigan, and Ohio. Applicant does not have to be a member of the American Welding Society.

| | |
|---|---|
| **Amount of award:** | $2,500 |
| **Number of awards:** | 1 |
| **Number of applicants:** | 14 |
| **Application deadline:** | February 15 |
| **Notification begins:** | April 1 |
| **Total amount awarded:** | $2,500 |

**Contact:**
American Welding Society Foundation, Inc.
Attn: Scholarships
550 Northwest LeJeune Road
Miami, FL 33126
Phone: 800-443-9353
Web: www.aws.org

# Annie's Homegrown

## Annie's Homegrown Sustainable Agriculture Scholarships

**Type of award:** Scholarship.
**Intended use:** For full-time undergraduate or graduate study in United States.
**Basis for selection:** Major/career interest in agriculture. Applicant must demonstrate high academic achievement.
**Application requirements:** Recommendations, essay, transcript.

**Additional information:** Award amount varies. Application and more information available on Website.

**Amount of award:** $2,500-$10,000
**Number of awards:** 8
**Application deadline:** December 15
**Notification begins:** March 1
**Total amount awarded:** $75,000

**Contact:**
Annie's Homegrown Scholarship
564 Gateway Drive
Napa, CA 94558
Web: www.annies.com/sustainable_agriculture_scholarship

# Appaloosa Youth Foundation

## Appaloosa Youth Foundation Educational Scholarships

**Type of award:** Scholarship, renewable.
**Intended use:** For full-time undergraduate or graduate study at accredited postsecondary institution in United States.
**Eligibility:** Applicant must be U.S. citizen or permanent resident.
**Basis for selection:** Applicant must demonstrate high academic achievement, leadership and service orientation.
**Application requirements:** Recommendations, essay, transcript, proof of eligibility. Photo. SAT/ACT scores optional.
**Additional information:** Applicant must be member of Appaloosa Horse Club or Appaloosa Youth Association. Must be involved in the Appaloosa industry and have general knowledge and accomplishments in horsemanship. One scholarship requires intent to pursue equine-related studies. GPA of 3.5 for one scholarship, GPA of 2.5 for other scholarships. Application available online.

**Amount of award:** $1,000-$2,000
**Number of awards:** 7
**Application deadline:** June 1
**Notification begins:** July 15

**Contact:**
Appaloosa Youth Foundation Scholarship Committee
2720 Pullman Road
Moscow, ID 83843
Phone: 208-882-5578 ext. 264
Fax: 208-882-8150
Web: www.appaloosa.com

# Arkansas Department of Higher Education

## Academic Challenge Scholarship

**Type of award:** Scholarship, renewable.
**Intended use:** For full-time undergraduate study at postsecondary institution. Designated institutions: Approved Arkansas colleges and universities.
**Eligibility:** Applicant must be high school senior. Applicant must be U.S. citizen or permanent resident residing in Arkansas.
**Basis for selection:** Applicant must demonstrate financial need.
**Application requirements:** Transcript. ACT scores and FAFSA.
**Additional information:** Award is renewable up to four years, provided student maintains minimum 2.5 GPA and at least 30 credit hours per academic year. Applications available online or from the Department of Higher Education.

**Amount of award:** $2,500-$5,000
**Application deadline:** June 1

**Contact:**
Arkansas Department of Higher Education
114 East Capitol Avenue
Little Rock, AR 72201-3818
Phone: 501-371-2000
Web: www.adhe.edu

## Governor's Scholars Program

**Type of award:** Scholarship, renewable.
**Intended use:** For full-time undergraduate study at postsecondary institution. Designated institutions: Approved Arkansas colleges and universities.
**Eligibility:** Applicant must be high school senior. Applicant must be U.S. citizen or permanent resident residing in Arkansas.
**Basis for selection:** Applicant must demonstrate high academic achievement and leadership.
**Additional information:** Governor's Distinguished Scholars must have at least 32 ACT or 1410 SAT and minimum 3.5 GPA or have been selected as National Merit or National Achievement Finalist. Governor's Distinguished Scholars receive award equal to tuition, fees, room, and board up to $10,000 per year. One Governor's Scholarship award per county given to applicants who do not meet Governor's Distinguished Scholars criteria. Governor's Scholars must have minimum 3.5 GPA or 27 ACT or 1220 SAT and receive award of $4,000. Awards renewable up to four years if Distinguished Scholars maintain minimum 3.25 GPA and Governor's Scholars maintain minimum 3.0 GPA and at least 30 credit hours per year. Visit Website for more information.

**Amount of award:** $4,000-$10,000
**Number of awards:** 375
**Application deadline:** February 1

**Contact:**
Arkansas Department of Higher Education
Attn: Governor's Scholars Program
114 East Capitol Avenue
Little Rock, AR 72201-3818
Phone: 501-371-2000
Web: www.adhe.edu

## Law Enforcement Officers' Dependents Scholarship

**Type of award:** Scholarship, renewable.
**Intended use:** For undergraduate study at accredited vocational, 2-year or 4-year institution in United States. Designated institutions: Public schools in Arkansas.
**Eligibility:** Applicant must be U.S. citizen or permanent resident residing in Arkansas.
**Application requirements:** Proof of eligibility.
**Additional information:** Applicant must be dependent or spouse of one of the following who was killed or permanently disabled in line of duty: law enforcement officer; firefighter; sheriff; constable; game warden; certain state highway, forestry, correction, or park employees; EMT; Department of Community Punishment employee. Dependent child applicant

Scholarships

may be no older than 23; no age restriction for spouse, but must not be remarried. Award is for tuition, fees, and room and is for up to eight semesters. Must maintain 2.0 GPA. Visit Website for more information and application.

**Amount of award:** Full tuition
**Application deadline:** June 1, November 1

**Contact:**
Arkansas Department of Higher Education
114 East Capitol Avenue
Little Rock, AR 72201-3818
Phone: 501-371-2000
Web: www.adhe.edu

## Military Dependents Scholarship Program

**Type of award:** Scholarship, renewable.
**Intended use:** For full-time undergraduate study at vocational, 2-year or 4-year institution in United States. Designated institutions: Public schools in Arkansas.
**Eligibility:** Applicant must be U.S. citizen or permanent resident residing in Arkansas. Applicant must be dependent of disabled veteran or POW/MIA; or spouse of disabled veteran or POW/MIA who served in the Army, Air Force, Marines, Navy, Coast Guard or Reserves/National Guard. Parent/spouse may also have been killed in action or killed on ordinance delivery. All incidents must have occurred while on active duty after 1/1/60. Parent/spouse must be AR resident or must have been at time of enlistment. Dependent must have been born, adopted, or in legal custody of veteran under whom he/she is applying.
**Application requirements:** Proof of eligibility.
**Additional information:** Award for tuition, fees, room, and board. Renewable up to four years. Must maintain 2.0 GPA. Visit Website for more information and application.

**Amount of award:** Full tuition
**Application deadline:** June 1, November 1

**Contact:**
Arkansas Department of Higher Education
Attn: Military Dependents Scholarship Program
114 East Capitol Avenue
Little Rock, AR 72201-3818
Phone: 501-371-2000
Web: www.adhe.edu

## Second Effort Scholarship

**Type of award:** Scholarship, renewable.
**Intended use:** For undergraduate study at postsecondary institution.
**Eligibility:** Applicant must be at least 18, returning adult student. Applicant must be U.S. citizen or permanent resident residing in Arkansas.
**Basis for selection:** Applicant must demonstrate high academic achievement.
**Additional information:** Applicant must not have graduated from high school. Must have scored in top ten on GED test in previous calendar year. Students do not apply for this award; top ten scorers are contacted directly by Arkansas Department of Higher Education. Award renewable up to four years (or equivalent if student is enrolled part-time), provided student maintains minimum 2.5 GPA.

**Amount of award:** $1,000
**Number of awards:** 10

**Contact:**
Arkansas Department of Higher Education
114 East Capitol Avenue
Little Rock, AR 72201-3818
Phone: 501-371-2000
Web: www.adhe.edu

## Workforce Improvement Grant

**Type of award:** Scholarship.
**Intended use:** For undergraduate study at postsecondary institution. Designated institutions: Not-for-profit institutions in AR.
**Eligibility:** Applicant must be at least 24, returning adult student. Applicant must be U.S. citizen or permanent resident residing in Arkansas.
**Basis for selection:** Applicant must demonstrate financial need.
**Application requirements:** FAFSA.
**Additional information:** Must be Arkansas resident at least six months before applying. Students enrolled part time will have grants prorated. Must have unmet need after any Pell Grant awarded. Application deadline determined by each institution for its students. Students apply by completing FAFSA. Must have graduated high school or have GED.

**Amount of award:** $2,000

**Contact:**
Arkansas Department of Higher Education
144 East Capitol Avenue
Little Rock, AR 72201-3818
Phone: 501-371-2000
Web: www.adhe.edu

# Armed Forces Communications and Electronics Association

## AFCEA Cyber Studies Scholarship

**Type of award:** Scholarship..
**Intended use:** For full-time undergraduate study at accredited 2-year or 4-year institution in United States.
**Eligibility:** Applicant must be U.S. citizen.
**Basis for selection:** Major/career interest in computer/information sciences; information systems or engineering, computer. Applicant must demonstrate high academic achievement.
**Application requirements:** Recommendations, transcript.
**Additional information:** Minimum 3.0 GPA. Candidates must major in a field directly related to the support of U.S. cyber enterprises with relevance to the mission of AFCEA, such as cyber security, cyber attack, computer science, information technology, or electronic engineering. Distance-learning programs are eligible. Visit Website for application and details.

**Amount of award:** $5,000
**Number of awards:** 10
**Application deadline:** May 15

**Contact:**
Armed Forces Communications and Electronics Association
Attn: Mr. Fred H. Rainbow
4400 Fair Lakes Court
Fairfax, VA 22033-3899
Phone: 703-631-6149
Fax: 703-631-4693
Web: www.afcea.org

## AFCEA General Emmett Paige Scholarship

**Type of award:** Scholarship.
**Intended use:** For full-time sophomore, junior or senior study at accredited 4-year institution in United States.
**Eligibility:** Applicant must be U.S. citizen. Applicant must be in military service or veteran; or dependent of active service person or veteran; or spouse of active service person or veteran.
**Basis for selection:** Major/career interest in aerospace; computer/information sciences; engineering, chemical; physics; mathematics; engineering, electrical/electronic; education; technology or information systems. Applicant must demonstrate high academic achievement, depth of character, leadership, patriotism, seriousness of purpose and service orientation.
**Application requirements:** Recommendations, transcript, proof of eligibility. Copy of discharge form DD214, certificate of service, or facsimile of applicant's current DOD or Coast Guard identification card.
**Additional information:** Veterans enrolled as freshmen eligible to apply, but all other applicants must be in at least their sophomore year. Must have minimum 3.0 GPA. Majors directly related to support of U.S. intelligence enterprises or national security with relevance to the mission of AFCEA also eligible. Visit Website for application and deadline.

| | |
|---|---|
| **Amount of award:** | $2,000 |
| **Number of awards:** | 10 |
| **Application deadline:** | March 1 |
| **Notification begins:** | June 1 |
| **Total amount awarded:** | $20,000 |

**Contact:**
AFCEA Educational Foundation
Attn: Mr. Fred H. Rainbow
4400 Fair Lakes Court
Fairfax, VA 22033-3899
Phone: 703-631-6149
Fax: 703-631-4693
Web: www.afcea.org/scholarships

## AFCEA General John A. Wickham Scholarship

**Type of award:** Scholarship.
**Intended use:** For full-time sophomore or junior study at accredited 4-year institution in United States.
**Eligibility:** Applicant must be U.S. citizen.
**Basis for selection:** Major/career interest in aerospace; engineering, computer; computer/information sciences; physics; mathematics; engineering, electrical/electronic; engineering, chemical; education; technology or information systems. Applicant must demonstrate high academic achievement, depth of character, leadership, patriotism, seriousness of purpose and service orientation.
**Application requirements:** Recommendations, transcript.
**Additional information:** Majors directly related to support of U.S. intelligence enterprises or national security with relevance to mission of AFCEA also eligible. Minimum 3.5 GPA. Visit Website for application and deadline.

| | |
|---|---|
| **Amount of award:** | $2,000 |
| **Number of awards:** | 12 |
| **Application deadline:** | May 1 |
| **Notification begins:** | June 1 |
| **Total amount awarded:** | $30,000 |

**Contact:**
AFCEA Educational Foundation
Attn: Mr. Fred H. Rainbow
4400 Fair Lakes Court
Fairfax, VA 22033-3899
Phone: 800-336-4583 ext. 6149
Fax: 703-631-4693
Web: www.afcea.org/scholarships

## AFCEA ROTC Scholarship

**Type of award:** Scholarship.
**Intended use:** For full-time sophomore or junior study at accredited 4-year institution in United States.
**Eligibility:** Applicant must be U.S. citizen.
**Basis for selection:** Major/career interest in aerospace; engineering; computer/information sciences; education; physics; mathematics; technology; electronics; foreign languages or international studies. Applicant must demonstrate financial need, high academic achievement, depth of character, leadership, patriotism, seriousness of purpose and service orientation.
**Application requirements:** Recommendations, transcript, nomination by professor of military science, naval science, aerospace studies, or designated commanding officer.
**Additional information:** Applicant must be enrolled in ROTC. Majors directly related to support of U.S. national security enterprises with relevance to mission of AFCEA also eligible.

| | |
|---|---|
| **Amount of award:** | $2,000 |
| **Number of awards:** | 50 |
| **Application deadline:** | March 1 |
| **Notification begins:** | June 1 |
| **Total amount awarded:** | $112,000 |

**Contact:**
Armed Forces Communications and Electronics Association
Mr. Fred H. Rainbow
4400 Fair Lakes Court
Fairfax, VA 22033-3899
Phone: 703-631-6149
Fax: 703-631-4693
Web: www.afcea.org/scholarships

## AFCEA Young Entrepreneur Scholarship

**Type of award:** Scholarship.
**Intended use:** For half-time sophomore, junior or senior study at accredited 2-year, 4-year or graduate institution in United States.
**Eligibility:** Applicant must be no older than 40. Applicant must be U.S. citizen.
**Basis for selection:** Major/career interest in engineering, electrical/electronic; engineering, computer; engineering, chemical; computer/information sciences; physics; mathematics or business. Applicant must demonstrate high academic achievement.
**Application requirements:** Recommendations, transcript.
**Additional information:** Minimum 3.0 GPA. Applicant must be employed by a small business, and must be working toward a degree in the following C4I-related fields of electrical, computer, chemical, systems or communications engineering;

computer science; physics; mathematics; technology management; computer information systems; management information systems or related fields. Graduate students who apply must have completed at least two postgraduate-level classes prior to deadline date. Student enrolled in on-line or distance-learning programs are eligible as long as all other criteria are met. Visit Website for application.

**Amount of award:** $2,000
**Number of awards:** 1
**Number of applicants:** 2
**Application deadline:** June 1

**Contact:**
Armed Forces Communications and Electronics Association
4400 Fair Lakes Court
Fairfax, VA 22033-3899
Phone: 703-631-6119
Web: www.afcea.org

## Disabled War Veterans Scholarship

**Type of award:** Scholarship, renewable.
**Intended use:** For undergraduate study at accredited 2-year or 4-year institution in United States.
**Eligibility:** Applicant must be in military service or disabled while on active duty during Middle East War. Must be disabled because of wounds received during service in Enduring Freedom—Afghanistan or Iraqi Freedom Operations.
**Basis for selection:** Major/career interest in aerospace; computer/information sciences; education; engineering, computer; engineering, electrical/electronic; information systems; mathematics; military science; physics or technology. Applicant must demonstrate financial need, high academic achievement and leadership.
**Application requirements:** Recommendations, transcript.
**Additional information:** Students of accredited distance-learning programs also eligible. Majors directly related to the support of U.S. intelligence or national security enterprises with relevance to the mission of AFCEA also eligible. Visit Website for application and deadline.

**Amount of award:** $2,500
**Number of awards:** 6
**Application deadline:** April 1
**Notification begins:** November 1

**Contact:**
AFCEA Educational Foundation
Attn: Mr. Fred H. Rainbow
440 Fair Lakes Court
Fairfax, VA 22033
Phone: 703-631-6149
Fax: 703-631-4693
Web: www.afcea.org/scholarships

## Intelligence Scholarships

**Type of award:** Scholarship, renewable.
**Intended use:** For full-time sophomore, junior or graduate study at accredited 4-year or graduate institution in United States.
**Eligibility:** Applicant must be U.S. citizen.
**Basis for selection:** Major/career interest in international relations or foreign languages. Applicant must demonstrate financial need, high academic achievement and leadership.
**Application requirements:** Recommendations, transcript.
**Additional information:** Minimum 3.0 GPA. Must be majoring in field directly related to support of U.S. intelligence or homeland security enterprises. Visit Website for deadline and application.

**Amount of award:** $2,250-$5,000
**Number of awards:** 6
**Application deadline:** November 1

**Contact:**
AFCEA Educational Foundation
Attn: Mr. Fred H. Rainbow
4400 Fair Lakes Court
Fairfax, VA 22033
Phone: 703-631-6149
Fax: 703-631-4693
Web: www.afcea.org/scholarships

## MG Eugene C. Renzi/ManTech International Corporation Scholarship for Math and Science Teachers

**Type of award:** Scholarship, renewable.
**Intended use:** For full-time sophomore, junior or senior study at accredited postsecondary institution in United States.
**Eligibility:** Applicant must be U.S. citizen.
**Basis for selection:** Major/career interest in education. Applicant must demonstrate high academic achievement.
**Application requirements:** Recommendations, transcript.
**Additional information:** Award for students who intend to teach science, mathematics, or information technology at a U.S. middle or secondary school. Graduate students must be enrolled in at least two (semester-equivalent) classes. Minimum 3.0 GPA. Application available online.

**Amount of award:** $2,500
**Number of awards:** 1
**Number of applicants:** 1
**Application deadline:** May 1
**Total amount awarded:** $2,500

**Contact:**
AFCEA Educational Foundation
Mr. Fred H. Rainbow
4400 Fair Lakes Court
Fairfax, VA 22033-3899
Phone: 703-631-6149
Fax: 703-631-4693
Web: www.afcea.org/scholarships

## STEM Teacher Scholarships

**Type of award:** Scholarship.
**Intended use:** For full-time junior, senior or graduate study at accredited postsecondary institution in United States.
**Eligibility:** Applicant must be U.S. citizen.
**Basis for selection:** Major/career interest in education. Applicant must demonstrate high academic achievement.
**Application requirements:** Recommendations, transcript.
**Additional information:** Minimum 3.0 GPA. Intended for students pursuing an education degree for the purpose of teaching science, technology, engineering or mathematics at a U.S. middle or secondary school. Each graduating recipient receives a $1,000 AFCEA Science Teaching Tools grant per year for 3 years, on the condition they remain teaching a STEM subject.

**Amount of award:** $5,000
**Number of awards:** 35
**Application deadline:** May 1

**Contact:**
AFCEA Educational Foundation
Mr. Fred H. Rainbow
4400 Fair Lakes Court
Fairfax, VA 22033-3899
Phone: 703-631-6149
Fax: 703-631-4693
Web: www.afcea.org/scholarships

### VADM Samuel L. Gravely Jr. USN (Ret.) Memorial Scholarship

**Type of award:** Scholarship.
**Intended use:** For junior or senior study at accredited 2-year or 4-year institution in United States. Designated institutions: Historically black colleges and universities.
**Basis for selection:** Major/career interest in aerospace; engineering, electrical/electronic; engineering, computer; information systems; computer/information sciences; physics or mathematics. Applicant must demonstrate financial need, high academic achievement and leadership.
**Application requirements:** Recommendations, transcript.
**Additional information:** Distance-learning or online programs affiliated with HCBUs are eligible. Majors directly related to the support of U.S. intelligence or homeland security enterprises with relevance to the mission of AFCEA are also eligible. Special consideration given to military enlisted candidates/military veterans.

| | |
|---|---|
| **Amount of award:** | $5,000 |
| **Number of awards:** | 2 |
| **Application deadline:** | September 1 |

**Contact:**
AFCEA Educational Foundation
Mr. Fred H. Rainbow
4400 Fair Lakes Court
Fairfax, VA 22033-3899
Phone: 703-631-6149
Fax: 703-631-4693
Web: www.afcea.org/scholarships

### William E. "Buck" Bragunier Scholarship for Outstanding Leadership

**Type of award:** Scholarship.
**Intended use:** For full-time sophomore or junior study at accredited 4-year institution. Designated institutions: Colleges or universities in the greater San Diego, California geographical area.
**Eligibility:** Applicant must be U.S. citizen residing in California.
**Basis for selection:** Major/career interest in aerospace; computer/information sciences; engineering, chemical; engineering, electrical/electronic; information systems; mathematics; physics or technology. Applicant must demonstrate leadership.
**Application requirements:** Recommendations, transcript.
**Additional information:** Minimum 3.5 GPA. Applicants qualified for General Wickham Scholarship are eligible. Distance learning programs not eligible. Majors directly related to the support of U.S. intelligence enterprises or national security with relevance to the mission of AFCEA will also be eligible.

| | |
|---|---|
| **Amount of award:** | $2,000 |
| **Number of awards:** | 1 |
| **Application deadline:** | May 1 |
| **Notification begins:** | June 1 |

**Contact:**
AFCEA Educational Foundation
Attn: Mr. Fred H. Rainbow
4400 Fair Lakes Court
Fairfax, VA 22033
Phone: 800-336-4583 ext. 6149
Fax: 703-631-4693
Web: www.afcea.org/scholarships

## Armenian General Benevolent Union (AGBU)

### International Scholarships

**Type of award:** Scholarship, renewable.
**Intended use:** For full-time undergraduate study at postsecondary institution outside United States or Canada.
**Eligibility:** Applicant must be international student.
**Basis for selection:** Applicant must demonstrate financial need, high academic achievement and service orientation.
**Application requirements:** Recommendations, transcript, proof of eligibility. Resume, passport-size photograph. Copy of Bursar's receipt, copy of financial award letter.
**Additional information:** Minimum 3.0 GPA. Awarded to students of Armenian descent enrolled in institutions in their countries of residence. Some selected fields of graduate study may also be considered. Number of awards varies. Not for use in the U.S., the U.K. or France.

| | |
|---|---|
| **Amount of award:** | $500-$2,000 |
| **Number of applicants:** | 400 |
| **Application deadline:** | May 31 |
| **Total amount awarded:** | $400,000 |

**Contact:**
Armenian General Benevolent Union (AGBU)
55 East 59th Street
7th Floor
New York, NY 10022
Phone: 212-319-6383
Fax: 212-319-6507
Web: www.agbu.org

### Performing Arts Fellowships

**Type of award:** Scholarship, renewable.
**Intended use:** For full-time undergraduate or graduate study.
**Eligibility:** Applicant must be Armenian.
**Basis for selection:** Competition/talent/interest in performing arts. Major/career interest in performing arts. Applicant must demonstrate financial need, high academic achievement and service orientation.
**Application requirements:** Recommendations, transcript. Resume, one passport-size photograph, enrollment verification/acceptance letter, bursar's receipt, financial award letter, most recent federal tax return (U.S. applicants only), CD of or link to most current recording (if applicable).
**Additional information:** Minimum 3.5 GPA. Number of awards varies based on funding. Excludes Armenian citizens studying in Armenia. Visit Website for application.

| | |
|---|---|
| **Amount of award:** | $1,000-$5,000 |
| **Number of applicants:** | 40 |
| **Application deadline:** | May 15 |
| **Notification begins:** | August 31 |
| **Total amount awarded:** | $64,500 |

**Contact:**
Armenian General Benevolent Union
Attn: Scholarship Program
55 E. 59th Street, 7th Floor
New York, NY 10022-1112
Phone: 212-319-6383
Fax: 212-319-6507
Web: www.agbu.org

# ARMY Emergency Relief

## MG James Ursano Scholarship Program

**Type of award:** Scholarship, renewable.
**Intended use:** For full-time undergraduate study at accredited postsecondary institution.
**Eligibility:** Applicant must be single, no older than 22. Applicant must be dependent of active service person, veteran or deceased veteran who serves or served in the Army.
**Basis for selection:** Applicant must demonstrate financial need, high academic achievement and leadership.
**Application requirements:** Transcript, proof of eligibility. Student Aid Report (SAR).
**Additional information:** Applicant must be registered in DEERS. Must maintain 2.0 GPA. Number of awards varies. Application must be submitted via Website; supporting documentation should be emailed.

| | |
|---|---|
| **Amount of award:** | $500-$3,500 |
| **Number of applicants:** | 6,700 |
| **Application deadline:** | April 1 |
| **Total amount awarded:** | $10,000,000 |

**Contact:**
ARMY Emergency Relief
MG James Ursano Scholarship Program
200 Stovall Street
Alexandria, VA 22332-0600
Phone: 703-428-0035
Fax: 703-325-7183
Web: www.aerhq.org

# The Art Institutes

## Best Teen Chef Culinary Scholarship Competition

**Type of award:** Scholarship.
**Intended use:** For undergraduate study at 2-year or 4-year institution in United States. Designated institutions: Art Institute schools offering culinary arts programs.
**Eligibility:** Applicant must be high school senior. Applicant must be U.S. citizen, Canadian citizen (excluding Quebec).
**Basis for selection:** Competition/talent/interest in culinary arts, based on meal preparation ability and originality. Major/career interest in culinary arts or hotel/restaurant management.
**Application requirements:** Essay, transcript. Recipe.
**Additional information:** Award amount varies depending on placement in competition. First-place winner will compete in national event slated for May. Minimum high school GPA of 2.0. Visit Website for deadline and application.

| | |
|---|---|
| **Number of applicants:** | 265 |

**Contact:**
The Art Institutes
210 Sixth Avenue, 33rd Floor
Pittsburgh, PA 15222-2603
Phone: 888-624-0300
Fax: 412-562-1732
Web: www.artinstitutes.edu/btc

# Arthur and Doreen Parrett Scholarship Trust Fund

## Arthur and Doreen Parrett Scholarship

**Type of award:** Scholarship, renewable.
**Intended use:** For full-time sophomore, junior, senior, master's, doctoral or first professional study at accredited postsecondary institution.
**Eligibility:** Applicant must be residing in Washington.
**Basis for selection:** Major/career interest in science, general; engineering; dentistry or medicine. Applicant must demonstrate financial need and high academic achievement.
**Application requirements:** Recommendations, transcript.
**Additional information:** Applicants must have completed first year of college. Include SASE with inquiries, and information will be forwarded.

| | |
|---|---|
| **Amount of award:** | $2,500-$3,600 |
| **Number of awards:** | 10 |
| **Number of applicants:** | 50 |
| **Application deadline:** | January 31 |

**Contact:**
Arthur and Doreen Parrett Scholarship Trust Fund
c/o U.S. Bank - Trust Dept.
1420 5th Avenue, Suite 2100
Seattle, WA 98101

# The ASCAP Foundation

## Morton Gould Young Composer Awards

**Type of award:** Scholarship, renewable.
**Intended use:** For non-degree study.
**Eligibility:** Applicant must be no older than 29.
**Basis for selection:** Competition/talent/interest in music performance/composition. Major/career interest in music.
**Application requirements:** Reproduction of original score, biographical and educational information, list of compositions to date, SASE, CD of composition (if available).
**Additional information:** Number of awards varies. Applicant must not have reached 30th birthday by January 1 and may submit only one composition. International applicants must have student visa.

| | |
|---|---|
| **Amount of award:** | $750-$2,500 |
| **Number of applicants:** | 730 |
| **Application deadline:** | March 1 |
| **Notification begins:** | April 1 |
| **Total amount awarded:** | $45,000 |

**Contact:**
ASCAP Foundation Morton Gould Young Composer Awards
c/o Frances Richard
One Lincoln Plaza
New York, NY 10023
Phone: 212-621-6329
Web: www.ascapfoundation.org

## Rudolf Nissim Prize

**Type of award:** Scholarship.
**Intended use:** For non-degree study.
**Basis for selection:** Competition/talent/interest in music performance/composition. Major/career interest in music.
**Application requirements:** Bound copy of score of one original concert work, composer biography, SASE.
**Additional information:** Award for work requiring a conductor that has not been performed professionally. Applicant must be concert composer member of ASCAP. Visit Website for specific application requirements and details.

| | |
|---|---|
| **Amount of award:** | $5,000 |
| **Number of awards:** | 1 |
| **Number of applicants:** | 230 |
| **Application deadline:** | November 15 |
| **Notification begins:** | January 15 |
| **Total amount awarded:** | $5,000 |

**Contact:**
Frances Richard
c/o The ASCAP Foundation/Rudolf Nissim Prize
One Lincoln Plaza
New York, NY 10023
Phone: 212-621-6329
Web: www.ascapfoundation.org

# ASCO Numatics

## Industrial Automation Engineering College Scholarships

**Type of award:** Scholarship.
**Intended use:** For full-time junior, senior or graduate study at accredited 4-year or graduate institution in United States.
**Eligibility:** Applicant must be U.S. citizen or permanent resident.
**Basis for selection:** Major/career interest in engineering; engineering, electrical/electronic or engineering, mechanical. Applicant must demonstrate high academic achievement and leadership.
**Additional information:** For students planning to pursue careers in industrial automation-related disciplines. Minimum 3.2 GPA. Asco Numatics employees and their families are ineligible. Application details and forms available on Website.

| | |
|---|---|
| **Amount of award:** | $5,000 |
| **Number of awards:** | 2 |
| **Application deadline:** | June 1 |
| **Total amount awarded:** | $10,000 |

**Contact:**
ASCO Numatics
50 Hanover Road
Florham Park, NJ 07932
Phone: 973-966-2000
Fax: 973-966-2628
Web: www.asconumatics.com/scholarship

# Asian American Journalists Association

## Broadcast News Grants

**Type of award:** Scholarship.
**Intended use:** For full-time undergraduate study at 4-year institution.
**Eligibility:** Applicant must be at least 18.
**Basis for selection:** Major/career interest in journalism or radio/television/film. Applicant must demonstrate financial need.
**Application requirements:** Recommendations, essay. Resume, proof of age, statement of financial need, and internship verification. Submit original plus three copies of all materials.
**Additional information:** Applicant must have already secured summer broadcast internship at TV or radio network, and must be committed to AAJA's mission. Application may be downloaded from Website. AAJA membership encouraged for all applicants and required for awardees. Recent college graduates also eligible.

| | |
|---|---|
| **Amount of award:** | $1,000-$2,500 |
| **Number of awards:** | 2 |
| **Application deadline:** | May 16 |

**Contact:**
Asian American Journalists Association
Broadcast News Grants
5 Third Street, Suite 1108
San Francisco, CA 94103
Phone: 415-346-2051 ext. 102
Fax: 415-346-6343
Web: www.aaja.org

## Print & Online News Grants

**Type of award:** Scholarship.
**Intended use:** For full-time undergraduate study.
**Eligibility:** Applicant must be at least 18.
**Basis for selection:** Major/career interest in journalism. Applicant must demonstrate financial need and seriousness of purpose.
**Application requirements:** Recommendations, essay. Resume, proof of age, statement of financial need, and internship verification. Submit original plus three copies of all material.
**Additional information:** Applicant may also be recent college graduate. Must have already secured summer internship at print or online company before applying. Must be committed to AAJA's mission. Application may be downloaded from Website. AAJA membership encouraged for all applicants and required for selected interns.

| | |
|---|---|
| **Amount of award:** | $1,000 |
| **Number of awards:** | 1 |
| **Application deadline:** | May 16 |

**Contact:**
Asian American Journalists Association
Print & Online News Grants
5 Third Street, Suite 1108
San Francisco, CA 94103
Phone: 415-346-2051 ext. 102
Fax: 415-346-6343
Web: www.aaja.org

### Stanford Chen Internship Grant

**Type of award:** Scholarship.
**Intended use:** For junior, senior or graduate study at 4-year or graduate institution.
**Basis for selection:** Major/career interest in journalism. Applicant must demonstrate financial need and seriousness of purpose.
**Application requirements:** Recommendations, essay. Resume, statement of financial need, and internship verification. Original plus three copies of all application materials.
**Additional information:** Applicant must have already secured internship with small- to medium-size media company (print companies with daily circulation under 100,000 and broadcast markets smaller than top 50). Application may be downloaded from Website. AAJA membership is encouraged for all applicants and required for selected recipients.

| | |
|---|---|
| **Amount of award:** | $1,750 |
| **Number of awards:** | 1 |
| **Application deadline:** | April 23 |
| **Total amount awarded:** | $1,750 |

**Contact:**
Asian American Journalists Association
Stanford Chen Internship Grant
5 Third Street, Suite 1108
San Francisco, CA 94103
Phone: 415-346-2051 ext. 102
Fax: 415-346-6343
Web: www.aaja.org

## Asian American Journalists Association, Texas Chapter

### AAJA Texas Student Scholarship

**Type of award:** Scholarship.
**Intended use:** For undergraduate or graduate study.
**Basis for selection:** Major/career interest in journalism. Applicant must demonstrate high academic achievement and seriousness of purpose.
**Application requirements:** Recommendations, essay, transcript. Resume, work samples.
**Additional information:** Applicant must be resident of or attending school in Texas, Arkansas, Louisiana, Oklahoma, or New Mexico. Must display awareness of Asian-American issues. Visit Website for application.

| | |
|---|---|
| **Amount of award:** | $1,000 |
| **Number of awards:** | 2 |
| **Application deadline:** | May 31 |
| **Notification begins:** | June 30 |
| **Total amount awarded:** | $1,000 |

**Contact:**
Scott Nishimura Fort Worth Star-Telegram
P.O. Box 1870
Fort Worth, TX 76101
Phone: 817-390-7808
Web: www.aajatexas.org

## ASM Materials Education Foundation

### ASM Outstanding Scholars Awards

**Type of award:** Scholarship, renewable.
**Intended use:** For full-time sophomore, junior or senior study at accredited 4-year institution in or outside United States.
**Basis for selection:** Major/career interest in engineering, materials or materials science. Applicant must demonstrate high academic achievement.
**Application requirements:** Recommendations, essay, transcript. Photograph. Resume optional.
**Additional information:** May also major in metallurgy or related science or engineering disciplines if applicant demonstrates strong interest in materials science. Must be student member of Material Advantage. International student members may apply. Visit Website for application and full details.

| | |
|---|---|
| **Amount of award:** | $2,000 |
| **Number of awards:** | 3 |
| **Number of applicants:** | 100 |
| **Application deadline:** | May 1 |
| **Notification begins:** | July 15 |
| **Total amount awarded:** | $6,000 |

**Contact:**
ASM Materials Education Foundation
Scholarship Program
9639 Kinsman Road
Materials Park, OH 44073-0002
Phone: 440-338-5151
Fax: 440-338-4634
Web: www.asmfoundation.org

### Edward J. Dulis Scholarship

**Type of award:** Scholarship, renewable.
**Intended use:** For junior or senior study at accredited 4-year institution in United States or Canada.
**Basis for selection:** Major/career interest in engineering, materials or materials science. Applicant must demonstrate financial need and high academic achievement.
**Application requirements:** Recommendations, essay, transcript. Photograph. Resume optional.
**Additional information:** Applicant may also major in metallurgy or related science or engineering field if interested in materials science. Must be student member of Material Advantage. Visit Website for application and full details.

| | |
|---|---|
| **Amount of award:** | $1,500 |
| **Number of awards:** | 1 |
| **Application deadline:** | May 1 |
| **Notification begins:** | July 15 |

**Contact:**
ASM Materials Education Foundation
Scholarship Program
9639 Kinsman Road
Materials Park, OH 44073-0002
Phone: 440-338-5151
Fax: 440-338-4634
Web: www.asmfoundation.org

### George A. Roberts Scholarships

**Type of award:** Scholarship, renewable.
**Intended use:** For junior or senior study at accredited 4-year institution in United States or Canada.

**Basis for selection:** Major/career interest in engineering, materials or materials science. Applicant must demonstrate financial need and high academic achievement.
**Application requirements:** Recommendations, essay, transcript. Photograph, resume optional.
**Additional information:** Applicant may also major in metallurgy or related science or engineering field if interested in materials science. Must be student member of Material Advantage. Visit Website for application and full details.

| | |
|---|---|
| **Amount of award:** | $6,000 |
| **Number of awards:** | 7 |
| **Application deadline:** | May 1 |
| **Notification begins:** | July 15 |
| **Total amount awarded:** | $42,000 |

**Contact:**
ASM Materials Education Foundation
Scholarship Program
9639 Kinsman Road
Materials Park, OH 44073-0002
Phone: 440-338-5151
Fax: 440-338-4634
Web: www.asmfoundation.org

## John M. Haniak Scholarship

**Type of award:** Scholarship, renewable.
**Intended use:** For junior or senior study at accredited 4-year institution in United States or Canada.
**Basis for selection:** Major/career interest in engineering, materials or materials science. Applicant must demonstrate financial need and high academic achievement.
**Application requirements:** Recommendations, essay, transcript. Photograph. Resume optional.
**Additional information:** Applicant may also major in metallurgy or related science or engineering field if interested in materials science. Must be student member of Material Advantage. Visit Website for application and full details.

| | |
|---|---|
| **Amount of award:** | $1,500 |
| **Number of awards:** | 1 |
| **Application deadline:** | May 1 |
| **Notification begins:** | July 15 |

**Contact:**
ASM Materials Education Foundation
Scholarship Program
9639 Kinsman Road
Materials Park, OH 44073-0002
Phone: 440-338-5151
Fax: 440-338-4634
Web: www.asmfoundation.org

## Ladish Co. Foundation Scholarships

**Type of award:** Scholarship.
**Intended use:** For sophomore, junior or senior study at accredited 4-year institution. Designated institutions: Wisconsin institutions.
**Eligibility:** Applicant must be residing in Wisconsin.
**Basis for selection:** Major/career interest in engineering or materials science. Applicant must demonstrate high academic achievement, depth of character and seriousness of purpose.
**Application requirements:** Recommendations, essay, transcript. Photo.
**Additional information:** Applicant must be a Material Advantage student member, and must have intended or declared major in metallurgy, materials science engineering, or related science or engineering disciplines. Visit Website for application and details.

| | |
|---|---|
| **Amount of award:** | $2,500 |
| **Number of awards:** | 2 |
| **Application deadline:** | May 1 |
| **Notification begins:** | July 15 |

**Contact:**
ASM Materials Education Foundation
Undergraduate Scholarship Program
9639 Kinsman Road
Materials Park, OH 44073-0002
Phone: 440-338-5151
Fax: 440-338-4634
Web: www.asmfoundation.org

## Lucille & Charles A. Wert Scholarship

**Type of award:** Scholarship, renewable.
**Intended use:** For junior or senior study at accredited 4-year institution in United States or Canada.
**Basis for selection:** Major/career interest in engineering, materials or materials science. Applicant must demonstrate financial need and high academic achievement.
**Application requirements:** Recommendations, essay, transcript. Photograph, resume optional.
**Additional information:** Applicant may also major in metallurgy or related science or engineering field if interested in materials science. Must be student member of Material Advantage. Scholarship provides recipient with one-year full tuition up to $10,000. Visit Website for application and full details.

| | |
|---|---|
| **Amount of award:** | $10,000 |
| **Number of awards:** | 1 |
| **Application deadline:** | May 1 |
| **Notification begins:** | July 15 |

**Contact:**
ASM Materials Education Foundation
Scholarship Program
9639 Kinsman Road
Materials Park, OH 44073-0002
Phone: 440-338-5151
Fax: 440-338-4634
Web: www.asmfoundation.org

## William & Mary Dyrkacz Scholarships

**Type of award:** Scholarship.
**Intended use:** For sophomore, junior or senior study at accredited 4-year institution.
**Basis for selection:** Major/career interest in engineering or materials science. Applicant must demonstrate financial need, high academic achievement, depth of character and seriousness of purpose.
**Application requirements:** Recommendations, essay, transcript. Photo.
**Additional information:** Applicant must be a Material Advantage student member, and must have intended or declared major in metallurgy, materials science engineering, or related science or engineering disciplines. Visit Website for application and details.

| | |
|---|---|
| **Amount of award:** | $6,000 |
| **Number of awards:** | 4 |
| **Application deadline:** | May 1 |
| **Notification begins:** | July 15 |

**Contact:**
ASM Materials Education Foundation
Undergraduate Scholarship Program
9639 Kinsman Road
Materials Park, OH 44073-0002
Phone: 440-338-5151
Fax: 440-338-4634
Web: www.asmfoundation.org

### William Park Woodside Founder's Scholarship

**Type of award:** Scholarship, renewable.
**Intended use:** For junior or senior study at accredited 4-year institution in United States or Canada.
**Basis for selection:** Major/career interest in engineering, materials or materials science. Applicant must demonstrate financial need and high academic achievement.
**Application requirements:** Recommendations, essay, transcript. Photograph. Resume optional.
**Additional information:** May also have major in metallurgy or related science or engineering discipline if applicant demonstrates strong interest in materials science. Must be Material Advantage student member. Scholarship provides recipient with one-year full tuition, up to $10,000. Visit Website for application and full details.

| | |
|---|---|
| **Amount of award:** | $10,000 |
| **Number of awards:** | 1 |
| **Application deadline:** | May 1 |
| **Notification begins:** | July 15 |
| **Total amount awarded:** | $10,000 |

**Contact:**
ASM Materials Education Foundation
Scholarship Program
9639 Kinsman Road
Materials Park, OH 44073-0002
Phone: 440-338-5151
Fax: 440-338-4634
Web: www.asmfoundation.org

## ASME Auxiliary, Inc.

### Agnes Malakate Kezios Scholarship

**Type of award:** Scholarship.
**Intended use:** For senior study at 4-year institution in United States. Designated institutions: Schools with ABET-accredited mechanical engineering programs.
**Eligibility:** Applicant must be U.S. citizen.
**Basis for selection:** Major/career interest in engineering, mechanical. Applicant must demonstrate financial need, high academic achievement and depth of character.
**Application requirements:** Recommendations, transcript.
**Additional information:** For student in final year of undergraduate program in mechanical engineering. American Society of Mechanical Engineers participation preferred. Download application from Website or send SASE or e-mail to request application.

| | |
|---|---|
| **Amount of award:** | $2,000 |
| **Number of awards:** | 1 |
| **Application deadline:** | March 15 |

**Contact:**
Sara Sahay
ASME Auxiliary - Undergraduate Scholarships
170 East Opel Drive
Glastonbury, CT 06033
Web: www.asme.org/Education/College/FinancialAid/

### Allen J. Baldwin Scholarship

**Type of award:** Scholarship.
**Intended use:** For senior study at 4-year institution in United States. Designated institutions: Schools with ABET-accredited mechanical engineering programs.
**Eligibility:** Applicant must be U.S. citizen.
**Basis for selection:** Major/career interest in engineering, mechanical. Applicant must demonstrate financial need, high academic achievement and depth of character.
**Application requirements:** Recommendations, transcript.
**Additional information:** For student in final year of undergraduate study in mechanical engineering. American Society of Mechanical Engineers participation preferred. Download application from Website or send SASE or e-mail to request application.

| | |
|---|---|
| **Amount of award:** | $2,000 |
| **Number of awards:** | 1 |
| **Application deadline:** | March 15 |

**Contact:**
Sara Sahay
ASME Auxiliary - Undergraduate Scholarships
170 East Opel Drive
Glastonbury, CT 06033
Web: www.asme.org/Education/College/FinancialAid/

### Berna Lou Cartwright Scholarship

**Type of award:** Scholarship.
**Intended use:** For senior study at 4-year institution in United States. Designated institutions: Schools with ABET-accredited mechanical engineering programs.
**Eligibility:** Applicant must be U.S. citizen.
**Basis for selection:** Major/career interest in engineering, mechanical. Applicant must demonstrate financial need, high academic achievement and depth of character.
**Application requirements:** Recommendations, transcript.
**Additional information:** For student in final year of undergraduate program in mechanical engineering. American Society of Mechanical Engineers participation preferred. Download application from Website or send SASE or email to request application.

| | |
|---|---|
| **Amount of award:** | $2,000 |
| **Number of awards:** | 1 |
| **Application deadline:** | March 15 |

**Contact:**
Sara Sahay
ASME Auxiliary - Undergraduate Scholarships
170 East Opel Drive
Glastonbury, CT 06033
Web: www.asme.org/Education/College/FinancialAid/

### Charles B. Scharp Scholarship

**Type of award:** Scholarship.
**Intended use:** For senior study at 4-year institution in United States. Designated institutions: Schools with ABET-accredited mechanical engineering programs.
**Eligibility:** Applicant must be U.S. citizen.

**Basis for selection:** Major/career interest in engineering, mechanical. Applicant must demonstrate financial need, high academic achievement and depth of character.
**Application requirements:** Recommendations, transcript.
**Additional information:** For student in final year of undergraduate program in mechanical engineering. ASME participation preferred. Download application from Website or send SASE or email to request application.

| | |
|---|---|
| **Amount of award:** | $2,000 |
| **Number of awards:** | 1 |
| **Application deadline:** | March 15 |

**Contact:**
Sara Sahay
ASME Auxiliary - Undergraduate Scholarships
170 East Opel Drive
Glastonbury, CT 06033
Web: www.asme.org/Education/College/FinancialAid/

## Sylvia W. Farny Scholarship

**Type of award:** Scholarship.
**Intended use:** For senior study at 4-year institution in United States. Designated institutions: Schools with ABET-accredited mechanical engineering programs.
**Eligibility:** Applicant must be U.S. citizen.
**Basis for selection:** Major/career interest in engineering, mechanical. Applicant must demonstrate financial need, high academic achievement and depth of character.
**Application requirements:** Recommendations, transcript.
**Additional information:** For student in final year of undergraduate study in mechanical engineering. American Society of Mechanical Engineers participation preferred. Download application from Website or send SASE or email to request application.

| | |
|---|---|
| **Amount of award:** | $2,000 |
| **Number of awards:** | 1 |
| **Application deadline:** | March 15 |

**Contact:**
Sara Sahay
ASME Auxiliary - Undergraduate Scholarships
170 East Opel Drive
Glastonbury, CT 06033
Web: www.asme.org/Education/College/FinancialAid/

# ASME Foundation

## Allen Rhodes Memorial Scholarship

**Type of award:** Scholarship.
**Intended use:** For sophomore, junior or senior study at accredited 4-year institution. Designated institutions: Schools with ABET-accredited program.
**Basis for selection:** Major/career interest in engineering, mechanical. Applicant must demonstrate high academic achievement.
**Application requirements:** Recommendations, essay, transcript.
**Additional information:** For student with specific interest in oil and gas industry. Preference given to students enrolled at Villanova University. Applicant must be ASME student member in good standing. Mechanical engineering technology and other related majors also eligible. Apply online.

| | |
|---|---|
| **Amount of award:** | $1,500 |
| **Number of awards:** | 1 |
| **Number of applicants:** | 138 |
| **Application deadline:** | March 15 |
| **Notification begins:** | June 30 |
| **Total amount awarded:** | $1,500 |

**Contact:**
ASME
Attn: Beth Lefever
Three Park Avenue, 22nd Floor
New York, NY 10016-5990
Phone: 800-843-2763
Web: www.asme.org

## American Electric Power Scholarship

**Type of award:** Scholarship.
**Intended use:** For junior or senior study at accredited 4-year institution. Designated institutions: Schools with ABET-accredited programs.
**Basis for selection:** Major/career interest in engineering, mechanical. Applicant must demonstrate high academic achievement.
**Application requirements:** Recommendations, essay, transcript.
**Additional information:** Applicant must be American Society of Mechanical Engineers student member in good standing. Preference given to students interested in power engineering or who reside or attend school in American Electric Power service area of Arkansas, Indiana, Kentucky, Louisiana, Michigan, Ohio, Oklahoma, Tennessee, Texas, Virginia, and West Virginia. Apply online.

| | |
|---|---|
| **Amount of award:** | $2,500 |
| **Number of awards:** | 1 |
| **Number of applicants:** | 138 |
| **Application deadline:** | March 15 |
| **Notification begins:** | June 15 |
| **Total amount awarded:** | $1,500 |

**Contact:**
ASME
Attn: Beth Lefever
Three Park Avenue, 22nd Floor
New York, NY 10016-5990
Phone: 800-843-2763
Web: www.asme.org/education/college/financialaid

## ASME Auxiliary/FIRST Clarke Scholarship

**Type of award:** Scholarship.
**Intended use:** For full-time freshman study at accredited 4-year institution. Designated institutions: Schools with ABET-accredited programs.
**Eligibility:** Applicant must be high school senior.
**Basis for selection:** Major/career interest in engineering, mechanical. Applicant must demonstrate financial need, high academic achievement and leadership.
**Application requirements:** Transcript, nomination by ASME member, ASME Auxiliary member, or student member active with FIRST. Financial data worksheet.
**Additional information:** Applicant must be active on FIRST team. One nomination per member. Applicant may also enroll in mechanical engineering technology program. Recipient announced at FIRST National Championship. Visit Website for more information and to download forms.

Scholarships

**Amount of award:** $5,000
**Number of awards:** 5
**Number of applicants:** 36
**Application deadline:** March 15
**Total amount awarded:** $25,000

**Contact:**
ASME
Attn: RuthAnn Bigley
Three Park Avenue, 22nd Floor
New York, NY 10016-5990
Phone: 212-591-7650
Fax: 212-591-7739
Web: www.asme.org/education/college/financialaid



## The ASME Foundation Hanley Scholarship

**Type of award:** Scholarship.
**Intended use:** For sophomore, junior or senior study at accredited 4-year institution. Designated institutions: Schools with ABET-accredited programs.
**Basis for selection:** Major/career interest in engineering, mechanical. Applicant must demonstrate financial need and high academic achievement.
**Application requirements:** Recommendations, essay, transcript.
**Additional information:** Must be American Society of Mechanical Engineers student member in good standing. Apply online.

**Amount of award:** $2,500
**Number of awards:** 1
**Number of applicants:** 138
**Application deadline:** March 15
**Notification begins:** June 15

**Contact:**
ASME
Attn: Beth Lefever
Three Park Avenue, 22nd Floor
New York, NY 10016-5990
Phone: 800-843-2763
Web: www.asme.org/education/college/financialaid

## ASME Foundation Scholarships

**Type of award:** Scholarship.
**Intended use:** For sophomore, junior or senior study at accredited 4-year institution. Designated institutions: Schools with ABET-accredited programs.
**Basis for selection:** Major/career interest in engineering, mechanical. Applicant must demonstrate high academic achievement.
**Application requirements:** Recommendations, essay, transcript.
**Additional information:** Applicant must be student member of American Society of Mechanical Engineers. Apply online.

**Amount of award:** $1,500
**Number of awards:** 17
**Number of applicants:** 138
**Application deadline:** March 15
**Notification begins:** June 15
**Total amount awarded:** $24,000

**Contact:**
ASME
Attn: Beth Lefever
Three Park Avenue, 22nd Floor
New York, NY 10016-5990
Phone: 800-843-2763
Web: www.asme.org/education/college/financialaid

## ASME Metropolitan Section John Rice Memorial Scholarship

**Type of award:** Scholarship.
**Intended use:** For junior or senior study at 4-year institution. Designated institutions: City College/CUNY, College of Staten Island, Columbia University, Cooper Union, Manhattan College, NYC Technology College of City University, Polytechnic Institute of New York University (Brooklyn), SUNY/Maritime College.
**Basis for selection:** Based on potential contribution to the mechanical engineering profession. Major/career interest in engineering, mechanical. Applicant must demonstrate high academic achievement, depth of character, leadership and seriousness of purpose.
**Application requirements:** Recommendations, essay, transcript.
**Additional information:** Applicant must be a current ASME student member in good standing. Awarded to student attending a school within ASME Met Section.

**Amount of award:** $2,500
**Number of awards:** 1
**Number of applicants:** 138
**Application deadline:** March 1
**Total amount awarded:** $1,000

**Contact:**
ASME Centers Administrator
Attn: Beth Lefever
Three Park Avenue, 22nd Floor
New York, NY 10016-5990
Phone: 800-843-2763
Web: www.asme.org

## ASME Power Division Scholarship

**Type of award:** Scholarship.
**Intended use:** For sophomore, junior or senior study at accredited 4-year institution. Designated institutions: Schools with ABET-accredited programs.
**Basis for selection:** Major/career interest in engineering, mechanical. Applicant must demonstrate financial need and high academic achievement.
**Application requirements:** Recommendations, essay, transcript.
**Additional information:** Applicant must be American Society of Mechanical Engineers student member in good standing and demonstrate special interest in area of fuels, combustion, or the power industry. Apply online.

**Amount of award:** $2,700
**Number of awards:** 1
**Number of applicants:** 138
**Application deadline:** March 15
**Notification begins:** June 15
**Total amount awarded:** $2,500

**Contact:**
ASME
Attn: Beth Lefever
Three Park Avenue, 22nd Floor
New York, NY 10016-5990
Phone: 800-843-2763
Web: www.asme.org/education/college/financialaid

## Frank and Dorothy Miller ASME Auxiliary Scholarships

**Type of award:** Scholarship.
**Intended use:** For full-time sophomore, junior or senior study at accredited 4-year institution in United States. Designated institutions: Schools with ABET-accredited programs.
**Eligibility:** Applicant must be U.S. citizen, permanent resident or resident of Canada or Mexico.
**Basis for selection:** Major/career interest in engineering, mechanical. Applicant must demonstrate depth of character and leadership.
**Application requirements:** Recommendations, essay, transcript.
**Additional information:** Applicant must be student member of American Society of Mechanical Engineers. Apply online.

| | |
|---|---|
| **Amount of award:** | $2,000 |
| **Number of awards:** | 2 |
| **Number of applicants:** | 138 |
| **Application deadline:** | March 15 |
| **Notification begins:** | June 15 |

**Contact:**
ASME
Attn: Beth Lefever
Three Park Avenue, 22nd Floor
New York, NY 10016-5990
Phone: 800-843-2763
Web: www.asme.org/education/college/financialaid

## F.W. "Beich" Beichley Scholarship

**Type of award:** Scholarship.
**Intended use:** For junior or senior study at accredited 4-year institution in United States. Designated institutions: Schools with ABET-accredited programs.
**Basis for selection:** Major/career interest in engineering, mechanical. Applicant must demonstrate financial need, high academic achievement, depth of character and leadership.
**Application requirements:** Recommendations, essay, transcript.
**Additional information:** Applicant must be member of American Society of Mechanical Engineers. Apply online.

| | |
|---|---|
| **Amount of award:** | $2,500 |
| **Number of awards:** | 1 |
| **Number of applicants:** | 138 |
| **Application deadline:** | March 15 |
| **Notification begins:** | June 15 |

**Contact:**
ASME
Attn: Beth Lefever
Three Park Avenue, 22nd Floor
New York, NY 10016-5990
Phone: 800-843-2763
Web: www.asme.org/education/college/financialaid

## Garland Duncan Scholarships

**Type of award:** Scholarship.
**Intended use:** For junior or senior study at accredited 4-year institution. Designated institutions: Schools with ABET-accredited programs.
**Basis for selection:** Major/career interest in engineering, mechanical. Applicant must demonstrate financial need, high academic achievement and leadership.
**Application requirements:** Recommendations, essay, transcript.
**Additional information:** Applicant must be member of American Society of Mechanical Engineers. Apply online.

| | |
|---|---|
| **Amount of award:** | $5,000 |
| **Number of awards:** | 2 |
| **Number of applicants:** | 138 |
| **Application deadline:** | March 15 |
| **Notification begins:** | June 15 |
| **Total amount awarded:** | $7,000 |

**Contact:**
ASME
Attn: Beth Lefever
Three Park Avenue, 22nd Floor
New York, NY 10016-5990
Phone: 800-843-2763
Web: www.asme.org/education/college/financialaid

## International Gas Turbine Institute (IGTI) Scholarship

**Type of award:** Scholarship.
**Intended use:** For sophomore, junior, senior or graduate study at accredited 4-year or graduate institution.
**Basis for selection:** Major/career interest in aerospace or engineering, mechanical. Applicant must demonstrate high academic achievement.
**Application requirements:** Recommendations, essay, transcript.
**Additional information:** Applicant must be American Society of Mechanical Engineers student member in good standing at the time of application. Applicants must be enrolled in baccalaureate or graduate program in their respective country. Preference given to students with work experience or research ties to gas turbine industry.

| | |
|---|---|
| **Amount of award:** | $4,000 |
| **Number of awards:** | 1 |
| **Number of applicants:** | 138 |
| **Application deadline:** | March 15 |
| **Notification begins:** | June 15 |
| **Total amount awarded:** | $4,000 |

**Contact:**
ASME
Attn: Beth Lefever
Three Park Avenue, 22nd Floor
New York, NY 10016-5990
Phone: 800-843-2763
Web: www.asme.org/education/college/financialaid

## John & Elsa Gracik Scholarships

**Type of award:** Scholarship.
**Intended use:** For sophomore, junior or senior study at accredited 4-year institution in United States. Designated institutions: Schools with ABET-accredited programs.
**Eligibility:** Applicant must be U.S. citizen.
**Basis for selection:** Major/career interest in engineering, mechanical. Applicant must demonstrate financial need, high academic achievement, depth of character and leadership.
**Application requirements:** Recommendations, essay, transcript.
**Additional information:** Applicant must be member of American Society of Mechanical Engineers. Apply online.

| | |
|---|---|
| **Amount of award:** | $1,600 |
| **Number of awards:** | 18 |
| **Number of applicants:** | 138 |
| **Application deadline:** | March 15 |
| **Notification begins:** | June 15 |

**Contact:**
ASME
Attn: Beth Lefever
Three Park Avenue, 22nd Floor
New York, NY 10016-5990
Phone: 800-843-2763
Web: www.asme.org/education/college/financialaid

## Kenneth Andrew Roe Mechanical Engineering Scholarship

**Type of award:** Scholarship.
**Intended use:** For junior or senior study at accredited 4-year institution in United States. Designated institutions: Schools with ABET-accredited programs or equivalent.
**Eligibility:** Applicant must be U.S. citizen, permanent resident or resident of Canada or Mexico.
**Basis for selection:** Major/career interest in engineering, mechanical. Applicant must demonstrate high academic achievement, depth of character and leadership.
**Application requirements:** Recommendations, essay, transcript.
**Additional information:** Applicant must be member of American Society of Mechanical Engineers. Apply online.

| | |
|---|---|
| **Amount of award:** | $10,000 |
| **Number of awards:** | 1 |
| **Number of applicants:** | 138 |
| **Application deadline:** | March 15 |
| **Notification begins:** | June 15 |
| **Total amount awarded:** | $10,000 |

**Contact:**
ASME
Attn: Beth Lefever
Three Park Avenue, 22nd Floor
New York, NY 10016-5990
Phone: 800-843-2763
Web: www.asme.org/education/college/financialaid

## Melvin R. Green Scholarships

**Type of award:** Scholarship.
**Intended use:** For junior or senior study at accredited 4-year institution. Designated institutions: Schools with ABET-accredited programs.
**Basis for selection:** Major/career interest in engineering, mechanical. Applicant must demonstrate financial need, high academic achievement and leadership.
**Application requirements:** Recommendations, essay, transcript.
**Additional information:** Applicant must be student member of American Society of Mechanical Engineers. Apply online.

| | |
|---|---|
| **Amount of award:** | $4,000 |
| **Number of awards:** | 2 |
| **Number of applicants:** | 138 |
| **Application deadline:** | March 15 |
| **Notification begins:** | June 15 |

**Contact:**
ASME
Attn: Beth Lefever
Three Park Avenue, 22nd Floor
New York, NY 10016-5990
Phone: 800-843-2763
Web: www.asme.org/education/college/financialaid

## Nuclear Engineering Division (NED) Scholarship

**Type of award:** Scholarship.
**Intended use:** For junior or senior study at accredited 4-year institution. Designated institutions: ABET-accredited organizations.
**Basis for selection:** Based on potential contribution to the nuclear engineering profession. Major/career interest in engineering, nuclear. Applicant must demonstrate financial need, high academic achievement, depth of character, leadership and seriousness of purpose.
**Application requirements:** Recommendations, essay, transcript.
**Additional information:** Applicant must be a current ASME student member in good standing, and must demonstrate a particular interest in the design, analysis, development, testing, operation, and maintenance of reactor systems and components, nuclear fusion, heat transport, nuclear fuels technology, and radioactive waste.

| | |
|---|---|
| **Amount of award:** | $5,000 |
| **Number of awards:** | 3 |
| **Number of applicants:** | 138 |
| **Application deadline:** | March 1 |
| **Total amount awarded:** | $15,000 |

**Contact:**
ASME Centers Administrator
Attn: Beth Lefever
Three Park Avenue, 22nd Floor
New York, NY 10016-5990
Phone: 800-843-2763
Web: www.asme.org

## Stephen T. Kugle Scholarship

**Type of award:** Scholarship.
**Intended use:** For junior or senior study at 4-year institution in United States. Designated institutions: Public colleges or universities in District E (Arizona, Arkansas, Colorado, Louisiana, New Mexico, Oklahoma, Texas, Utah, and Wyoming).
**Eligibility:** Applicant must be U.S. citizen.
**Basis for selection:** Major/career interest in engineering, mechanical.
**Application requirements:** Recommendations, essay, transcript.
**Additional information:** Applicant must be American Society of Mechanical Engineers student member in good standing and U.S. citizen by birth. Minimum 3.0 GPA. Students from University of Texas at Arlington not eligible. Apply online.

| | |
|---|---|
| **Amount of award:** | $2,500 |
| **Number of awards:** | 1 |
| **Number of applicants:** | 138 |
| **Application deadline:** | March 15 |
| **Notification begins:** | June 15 |

**Contact:**
ASME
Attn: Beth Lefever
Three Park Avenue, 22nd Floor
New York, NY 10016-5990
Phone: 800-843-2763
Web: www.asme.org/education/college/financialaid

## William J. and Marijane E. Adams, Jr. Scholarship

**Type of award:** Scholarship.
**Intended use:** For sophomore, junior or senior study at accredited 4-year institution in United States. Designated institutions: Schools with ABET-accredited programs in California, Nevada, and Hawaii.
**Eligibility:** Applicant must be residing in California, Hawaii or Nevada.
**Basis for selection:** Major/career interest in engineering, mechanical. Applicant must demonstrate financial need and high academic achievement.
**Application requirements:** Recommendations, essay, transcript.
**Additional information:** Minimum 2.5 GPA. Applicant must be member of American Society of Mechanical Engineers. Award designated for student with special interest in product development and design. Apply online.

| | |
|---|---|
| **Amount of award:** | $3,500 |
| **Number of awards:** | 1 |
| **Number of applicants:** | 138 |
| **Application deadline:** | March 15 |
| **Notification begins:** | June 15 |
| **Total amount awarded:** | $2,500 |

**Contact:**
ASME
Attn: Beth Lefever
Three Park Avenue, 22nd Floor
New York, NY 10016-5990
Phone: 800-843-2763
Web: www.asme.org/education/college/financialaid

## Willis F. Thompson Memorial Scholarship

**Type of award:** Scholarship.
**Intended use:** For sophomore, junior, senior or graduate study at accredited 4-year institution. Designated institutions: Schools with ABET-accredited programs.
**Basis for selection:** Major/career interest in engineering, mechanical. Applicant must demonstrate high academic achievement.
**Application requirements:** Recommendations, essay, transcript.
**Additional information:** Applicant must be American Society of Mechanical Engineers student member in good standing. Preference given to students who demonstrate interest in advancing field of power generation. Apply online.

| | |
|---|---|
| **Amount of award:** | $5,000 |
| **Number of awards:** | 3 |
| **Number of applicants:** | 138 |
| **Application deadline:** | March 15 |
| **Notification begins:** | June 15 |

**Contact:**
ASME
Attn: Beth Lefever
Three Park Avenue, 22nd Floor
New York, NY 10016-5990
Phone: 800-843-2763
Web: www.asme.org/education/college/financialaid

# Associated Builders and Contractors, Inc.

## Trimmer Education Foundation Student Scholarships

**Type of award:** Scholarship, renewable.
**Intended use:** For sophomore, junior or senior study at 2-year or 4-year institution.
**Basis for selection:** Major/career interest in construction management or construction. Applicant must demonstrate financial need and high academic achievement.
**Application requirements:** Recommendations, transcript. Resume, photocopy of first page of Student Aid Report.
**Additional information:** Minimum 3.0 GPA in major; minimum 2.85 GPA overall. Must be current member of Associated Builders and Contractors student chapter or employed by ABC member firm. Architecture and most engineering students excluded. Number and amount of awards varies based on funding.

| | |
|---|---|
| **Number of applicants:** | 45 |
| **Application deadline:** | May 21 |
| **Notification begins:** | June 15 |
| **Total amount awarded:** | $60,000 |

**Contact:**
Associated Buliders and Contractors
Attn: Jamie VanVoorhis
4250 North Fairfax Drive, 9th Floor
Arlington, VA 22203-1607
Phone: 703-812-2000
Web: www.abc.org

# Associated General Contractors Education and Research Foundation

## AGC Education and Research Undergraduate Scholarship

**Type of award:** Scholarship, renewable.
**Intended use:** For full-time sophomore, junior or senior study at accredited 4-year institution. Designated institutions: ABET or ACCE accredited institutions.
**Eligibility:** Applicant must be U.S. citizen or permanent resident.
**Basis for selection:** Major/career interest in engineering, civil; engineering, construction or construction.
**Application requirements:** Recommendations, essay, transcript.
**Additional information:** Must be enrolled in or planning to enroll in an ABET- or ACCE- acctedited full-time, four- or five-year university program of construction or civil engineering. Applications are available July 1 from AGC Website. Seniors with one full academic year of coursework remaining are eligible. Number of awards varies.

**Amount of award:** $2,500-$7,500
**Number of awards:** 50
**Number of applicants:** 380
**Application deadline:** November 1
**Notification begins:** February 1
**Total amount awarded:** $350,000

**Contact:**
Association of General Contractors Education and Research Foundation
Attn: Melinda Patrician, Director
2300 Wilson Boulevard, Suite 400
Arlington, VA 22201
Phone: 703-837-5342
Fax: 703-837-5451
Web: www.agcfoundation.org

### James L. Allhands Essay Competition

**Type of award:** Scholarship, renewable.
**Intended use:** For full-time senior study at accredited 4-year institution. Designated institutions: ABET- or ACCE-accredited universities with construction or construction-related engineering programs.
**Basis for selection:** Competition/talent/interest in research paper, based on advancement of technological, educational, or vocational expertise in the construction industry. Major/career interest in engineering, civil; engineering, construction or construction.
**Application requirements:** Essay abstract, letter from faculty sponsor.
**Additional information:** First prize is $1,000, plus all-expenses-paid trip to AGC convention; winner's faculty sponsor receives $500 and all-expenses-paid trip to convention. Second prize is $500. Third prize is $300. Application material must be emailed. Only five submittals from each college/university are accepted. See Website for essay topic and guidelines.

**Amount of award:** $300-$1,000
**Number of awards:** 3
**Number of applicants:** 50
**Application deadline:** November 1
**Total amount awarded:** $2,300

**Contact:**
AGC Education and Research Foundation
Attn: Melinda Patrician Director of Programs
2300 Wilson Boulevard, Suite 400
Arlington, VA 22201
Phone: 703-837-5342
Fax: 703-837-5451
Web: www.agc.org

## Associated General Contractors of Maine Education Foundation

### AGC of Maine Scholarship Program

**Type of award:** Scholarship.
**Intended use:** For full-time undergraduate study at accredited postsecondary institution in United States. Designated institutions: Schools in Maine.
**Eligibility:** Applicant must be U.S. citizen residing in Maine.
**Basis for selection:** Major/career interest in construction. Applicant must demonstrate financial need and high academic achievement.
**Application requirements:** Interview, recommendations, essay, transcript.
**Additional information:** Number of awards varies. Application deadline at end of March; check Website for exact date.

**Amount of award:** $1,500-$3,000
**Number of applicants:** 30
**Total amount awarded:** $24,000

**Contact:**
AGC of Maine
P.O. Box 5519
Augusta, ME 04332-5519
Phone: 207-622-4741
Web: www.agcmaine.org

## Associated Press Los Angeles

### APTRA-Clete Roberts Memorial Journalism Scholarship

**Type of award:** Scholarship.
**Intended use:** For sophomore, junior, senior or graduate study at 4-year or graduate institution in United States. Designated institutions: Colleges and universities in California, Nevada, Hawaii, Arizona, New Mexico, Idaho, Washington, Colorado, Utah, Montana, Wyoming and Alaska.
**Basis for selection:** Major/career interest in journalism or radio/television/film. Applicant must demonstrate financial need, high academic achievement and seriousness of purpose.
**Application requirements:** Essay. May submit examples of broadcast-related work.
**Additional information:** Open to students pursuing career in broadcast journalism. Applications must be typed and mailed; no e-mailed or faxed submissions accepted. Application deadline in December; see Website for exact date and more information.

**Amount of award:** $1,500
**Number of awards:** 1
**Notification begins:** January 1

**Contact:**
AP Los Angeles
Jeff Wilson
221 S. Figueroa St., Suite 300
Los Angeles, CA 90012
Web: www.aptra.com

### Kathryn Dettman Memorial Journalism Scholarship

**Type of award:** Scholarship.
**Intended use:** For sophomore, junior, senior or graduate study at 4-year or graduate institution in United States. Designated institutions: Colleges and universities in California, Nevada, Hawaii, Arizona, New Mexico, Idaho, Washington, Colorado, Utah, Montana, Wyoming and Alaska.
**Basis for selection:** Competition/talent/interest in writing/journalism. Major/career interest in journalism or radio/television/film. Applicant must demonstrate financial need, high academic achievement and seriousness of purpose.

**Application requirements:** Essay. May submit examples of broadcast-related work.
**Additional information:** Open to students pursuing career in broadcast journalism. Applications must be typed and mailed; no e-mailed or faxed submissions accepted. Application deadline in December; see Website for exact date and more information.

| | |
|---|---|
| **Amount of award:** | $1,500 |
| **Number of awards:** | 1 |
| **Total amount awarded:** | $1,500 |

**Contact:**
AP Los Angeles
Jeff Wilson
221 S. Figueroa St., Suite 300
Los Angeles, CA 90012
Web: www.aptra.com

# Association for Library and Information Science Education

## ALISE Bohdan S. Wynar Research Paper Competition

**Type of award:** Scholarship.
**Intended use:** For undergraduate or graduate study.
**Basis for selection:** Competition/talent/interest in research paper, based on any aspect of library and information science using any methodology. Major/career interest in library science.
**Application requirements:** Paper must not exceed 35 double-spaced pages with one-inch margins and 12-point font. Two title pages, one with and one without author name(s) and institution.
**Additional information:** Research papers prepared by joint investigators eligible; at least one author must be member of Association for Library and Information Science Education. Winners expected to present papers at ALISE Annual Conference. Can submit only one paper per competition and may not submit same paper to other ALISE competitions. Paper cannot have been published, though may be accepted for publication. Papers completed in pursuit of master's and doctoral degrees not eligible, though data and spinoffs from such papers are eligible, as are papers generated through other grants and funding. Visit Website for detailed explanation of requirements.

| | |
|---|---|
| **Amount of award:** | $2,500 |
| **Number of awards:** | 2 |
| **Number of applicants:** | 12 |
| **Application deadline:** | July 15 |
| **Notification begins:** | October 1 |
| **Total amount awarded:** | $5,000 |

**Contact:**
ALISE
65 E. Wacker Place, Suite 1900
Chicago, IL 60601-7246
Phone: 312-795-0996
Fax: 312-419-8950
Web: www.alise.org

## ALISE Research Grant

**Type of award:** Research grant.
**Intended use:** For non-degree study.
**Basis for selection:** Major/career interest in library science. Applicant must demonstrate high academic achievement.
**Application requirements:** Research proposal.
**Additional information:** Must be member of Association for Library and Information Science Education. Proposal must not exceed 20 double-spaced pages. Award to support research broadly related to education for library and information science. Visit Website for detailed explanation of proposal requirements. More than one grant may be awarded; however, total amount of funding for all grants not to exceed $5,000. Award cannot be used to support doctoral dissertation. Awardee(s) must present preliminary report at ALISE Annual Conference.

| | |
|---|---|
| **Amount of award:** | $5,000 |
| **Application deadline:** | October 1 |
| **Total amount awarded:** | $5,000 |

**Contact:**
ALISE
65 E. Wacker Place, Suite 1900
Chicago, IL 60601-7246
Phone: 312-795-0996
Fax: 312-419-8950
Web: www.alise.org

## ALISE/Dialog Methodology Paper Competition

**Type of award:** Scholarship.
**Intended use:** For undergraduate or graduate study.
**Basis for selection:** Competition/talent/interest in research paper, based on description and discussion of a research method or technique. Major/career interest in library science.
**Application requirements:** Paper must not exceed 25 double-spaced pages with one-inch margins and 12-point font. Two title pages, one with and one without author name and institution. 200-word abstract.
**Additional information:** Papers prepared by joint authors eligible; at least one author must be member of Association for Library and Information Science Education. Papers completed in pursuit of master's or doctoral degrees are eligible, as are papers generated as result of research grant or other source of funding. Papers that stress findings are ineligible. Winners expected to present papers at ALISE Annual Conference. May submit only one paper per competition and may not submit same paper to multiple ALISE competitions.

| | |
|---|---|
| **Amount of award:** | $500 |
| **Number of awards:** | 1 |
| **Number of applicants:** | 10 |
| **Application deadline:** | July 15 |
| **Notification begins:** | October 1 |
| **Total amount awarded:** | $500 |

**Contact:**
ALISE
65 E. Wacker Place, Suite 1900
Chicago, IL 60601-7246
Phone: 312-795-0996
Fax: 312-419-8950
Web: www.alise.org

# Association for Women in Architecture Foundation

## Women in Architecture Scholarship

**Type of award:** Scholarship, renewable.
**Intended use:** For full-time sophomore, junior, senior or graduate study at 4-year or graduate institution.
**Eligibility:** Applicant must be female.
**Basis for selection:** Major/career interest in architecture; interior design; landscape architecture; urban planning; engineering, structural; engineering, civil; engineering, electrical/electronic or engineering, mechanical. Applicant must demonstrate high academic achievement.
**Application requirements:** Portfolio, recommendations, essay, transcript. SASE.
**Additional information:** Must be California resident or attending accredited California school to qualify. Students may also be studying in the following majors: land planning, environmental design, architectural rendering and illustrating. Must have completed minimum of 18 units in major by application due date. Applications may be downloaded from Website. Applications due in mid-April; see Website for exact date.

| | |
|---|---|
| **Amount of award:** | $1,000 |
| **Number of awards:** | 5 |
| **Application deadline:** | April 15 |
| **Total amount awarded:** | $5,000 |

**Contact:**
Association for Women in Architecture Foundation
AWAF Scholarship
22815 Frampton Avenue
Torrance, CA 90501-5034
Phone: 310-534-8466
Fax: 310-257-6885
Web: www.awa-la.org/scholarships.php

# Association for Women in Communications

## Seattle Professional Chapter Scholarship

**Type of award:** Scholarship.
**Intended use:** For junior, senior or graduate study at accredited 4-year or graduate institution in United States. Designated institutions: Washington state colleges.
**Eligibility:** Applicant must be residing in Washington.
**Basis for selection:** Major/career interest in communications; journalism; radio/television/film; film/video; graphic arts/design; advertising; public relations or marketing. Applicant must demonstrate financial need and high academic achievement.
**Application requirements:** Transcript. Cover letter, resume, two work samples.
**Additional information:** Additional majors may include multimedia design, photography, or technical communication. Selection based on demonstrated excellence in communications and positive contributions to communications on campus or in community. Application deadline in April; check Website for exact date. Amount and number of awards varies.

| | |
|---|---|
| **Application deadline:** | April 15 |

**Contact:**
AWC Seattle Professional Chapter
Attn: Pam Love, Scholarship Chair
3417 30th Ave W.
Seattle, WA 98199
Web: www.seattleawc.org

# Association of American Geographers

## Anne U. White Fund

**Type of award:** Research grant, renewable.
**Intended use:** For non-degree study.
**Basis for selection:** Major/career interest in geography.
**Application requirements:** Research proposal.
**Additional information:** Fund enables Association of American Geographers member to engage in useful field study jointly with his/her partner. Must have been member for at least two years at time of application. Report summarizing results and documenting expenses underwritten by grant must be submitted within 12 months of receiving award.

| | |
|---|---|
| **Amount of award:** | $1,500 |
| **Number of awards:** | 2 |
| **Application deadline:** | December 31 |
| **Notification begins:** | March 1 |

**Contact:**
Association of American Geographers
Attn: Anne U. White Fund
1710 16th Street, NW
Washington, DC 20009-3198
Phone: 202-234-1450
Fax: 202-234-2744
Web: www.aag.org/grantsawards

## Darrel Hess Community College Geography Scholarship

**Type of award:** Scholarship, renewable.
**Intended use:** For at 2-year institution in United States.
**Basis for selection:** Major/career interest in geography. Applicant must demonstrate financial need and high academic achievement.
**Application requirements:** Recommendations, essay, transcript.
**Additional information:** Applicants eligible if currently enrolled in a US community college, junior college, city college, or similar two-year educational institution at the time of submission of application. Applicant must have completed at least two transfer courses in geography and plan to transfer to a four-year institution as a geography major during the coming academic year. AAG membership strongly encouraged, but not required.

| | |
|---|---|
| **Amount of award:** | $1,000 |
| **Number of awards:** | 4 |
| **Application deadline:** | December 31 |

**Contact:**
Association of American Geographers
1710 16th Street NW
Washington, DC 20009-3198
Phone: 202-234-1450
Fax: 202-234-2744
Web: www.aag.org/grantsawards

## Marble-Boyle Award

**Type of award:** Scholarship, renewable.
**Intended use:** For full-time senior study at accredited postsecondary institution in United States or Canada.
**Basis for selection:** Major/career interest in computer/information sciences or geography.
**Application requirements:** Recommendations, essay, transcript. Cover letter.
**Additional information:** Applicant must demonstrate reasonable intent to embark upon a career or further education that will make use of joint geographic science and computer science knowledge. AAG membership strongly encouraged, but not required. Award consists of $700 cash prize and $200 credit for books published by the ESRI Press. ESRI will provide priority consideration to awardees interested in participating in ESRI Summer Intern Program. Awardees also eligible to compete for an additional research fellowship award offered biannually by MicroGIS Foundation for Spatial Analysis (MFSA).

| | |
|---|---|
| **Amount of award:** | $700 |
| **Number of awards:** | 3 |
| **Application deadline:** | October 15 |

**Contact:**
Association of American Geographers
1710 16th Street NW
Washington, DC 20009-3198
Phone: 202-234-1450
Fax: 202-234-2744
Web: www.aag.org/grantsawards

# The Association of Insurance Compliance Professionals

## AICP Heartland Chapter Scholarship

**Type of award:** Scholarship, renewable.
**Intended use:** For full-time undergraduate or graduate study at postsecondary institution.
**Eligibility:** Applicant must be residing in Iowa, South Dakota, Minnesota, Nebraska, Kansas, North Dakota or Missouri.
**Basis for selection:** Major/career interest in accounting; business; business/management/administration; economics; finance/banking; mathematics or statistics.
**Application requirements:** Recommendations, transcript. Resume, short narrative describing current and future interest to pursue education/career in the insurance field.
**Additional information:** Must be a Heartland member in good standing; a spouse (including domestic partner or civil union partner), son, daughter, grandson, granddaughter (including step or custodial) of a Heartland member in good standing; or be sponsored by current Heartland AICP member in good standing. Must be a permanent resident in the Heartland territory region. Minimum 2.75 GPA. Applicants with major/career interest in risk management also eligible. Part-time enrollment allowed only for Heartland members; must be enrolled for at least six hours or half-time as defined by the institution. Graduate students working towards an MBA in insurance, risk management, or mathematics, with an actuarial emphasis, are also eligible. Mathematics majors' studies should have emphasis in actuarial science.

| | |
|---|---|
| **Amount of award:** | $500 |
| **Number of awards:** | 1 |
| **Application deadline:** | May 15 |
| **Notification begins:** | May 31 |
| **Total amount awarded:** | $500 |

**Contact:**
Bonnie Blue
Principal Life Insurance Company
711 High Street, K-005-E81
Des Moines, IA 50392-0002
Phone: 515-247-0657
Fax: 515-246-2497
Web: www.aicp.net

## AICP Scholarship

**Type of award:** Scholarship, renewable.
**Intended use:** For full-time sophomore, junior, senior or master's study.
**Basis for selection:** Major/career interest in business; business/management/administration; economics; finance/banking; insurance/actuarial science; mathematics or statistics.
**Application requirements:** Recommendations, transcript. Resume, short narrative describing current and future interest to pursue education/career in the insurance field.
**Additional information:** Minimum 2.75 GPA. Applicant must be at least a second-semester sophomore. Applicants with major/career interest in risk management also eligible.

| | |
|---|---|
| **Amount of award:** | $1,000 |
| **Number of awards:** | 3 |
| **Number of applicants:** | 32 |
| **Application deadline:** | June 1 |
| **Notification begins:** | July 1 |
| **Total amount awarded:** | $3,000 |

**Contact:**
Association of Insurance Compliance Professionals
12100 Sunset Hills Road, Suite 130
Reston, VA 20190
Phone: 703-234-4074
Fax: 703-435-4390
Web: www.aicp.net

# Association of State Dam Safety Officials

## ASDSO Undergraduate Scholarship

**Type of award:** Scholarship.
**Intended use:** For full-time senior study in United States.
**Eligibility:** Applicant must be U.S. citizen.
**Basis for selection:** Major/career interest in engineering, civil. Applicant must demonstrate financial need and high academic achievement.
**Application requirements:** Recommendations, essay, transcript.
**Additional information:** Must be planning to pursue career in dams or dam safety. Minimum 2.5 GPA.

| | |
|---|---|
| **Amount of award:** | $5,000 |
| **Number of awards:** | 2 |
| **Number of applicants:** | 60 |
| **Application deadline:** | March 31 |
| **Notification begins:** | June 1 |
| **Total amount awarded:** | $10,000 |

**Contact:**
Association of State Dam Safety Officials
450 Old Vine Street, 2nd Floor
Lexington, KY 40507
Phone: 859-257-5140
Fax: 859-323-1958
Web: www.damsafety.org



# AXA Achievement Scholarship

## AXA Achievement Scholarship in Association with U.S. News & World Report

**Type of award:** Scholarship.
**Intended use:** For full-time undergraduate study at accredited 2-year or 4-year institution in United States.
**Eligibility:** Applicant must be high school senior. Applicant must be U.S. citizen.
**Application requirements:** Recommendations.
**Additional information:** Fifty-two students, to be known as AXA Achievers, will be selected to receive $10,000 scholarships, one from each state, the District of Columbia and Puerto Rico. From among the state recipients, ten students will be named national AXA Achievers. They will be selected to receive national awards at $15,000 each for a total of $25,000 per national recipient. Must demonstrate achievement in a non-academic activity or project. Consideration will also be given to other extracurricular activities in school and community, work experience, and the applicant's academic record over the past four years. Visit Website for more information, application, and deadline date. Questions about the application process may be directed to Scholarship America's toll-free number or by e-mail to axaachievement@scholarshipamerica.org.

| | |
|---|---|
| **Amount of award:** | $10,000-$25,000 |
| **Number of awards:** | 52 |
| **Total amount awarded:** | $670,000 |

**Contact:**
AXA Achievement Scholarship
Scholarship Managent Services
One Scholarship Way
Saint Peter, MN 56082
Phone: 800-537-4180
Web: www.axa-achievement.com

# Ayn Rand Institute

## Atlas Shrugged Essay Contest

**Type of award:** Scholarship.
**Intended use:** For undergraduate study.
**Basis for selection:** Competition/talent/interest in writing/journalism, based on an outstanding grasp of the philosophic meaning of "Atlas Shrugged."
**Application requirements:** Essay between 800 and 1,600 words, typewritten and double-spaced.
**Additional information:** Student must be enrolled in full-time college degree program or 12th grade at time of entry. See Website for rules, guidelines, and topic questions.

| | |
|---|---|
| **Amount of award:** | $50-$10,000 |
| **Number of awards:** | 49 |
| **Number of applicants:** | 1,917 |
| **Application deadline:** | September 17 |
| **Notification begins:** | November 27 |
| **Total amount awarded:** | $24,000 |

**Contact:**
The Ayn Rand Institute
Atlas Shrugged Essay Contest
P.O. Box 57044
Irvine, CA 92619-7044
Phone: 949-222-6550
Fax: 949-222-6558
Web: www.aynrand.org/contests

## The Fountainhead Essay Contest

**Type of award:** Scholarship.
**Intended use:** For undergraduate study.
**Eligibility:** Applicant must be high school junior or senior.
**Basis for selection:** Competition/talent/interest in writing/journalism, based on an outstanding grasp of the philosophic meaning of "The Fountainhead."
**Application requirements:** Essay between 800 and 1,600 words, typewritten and double-spaced.
**Additional information:** Rules, guidelines, and topic questions on Website.

| | |
|---|---|
| **Amount of award:** | $50-$10,000 |
| **Number of awards:** | 236 |
| **Number of applicants:** | 5,399 |
| **Application deadline:** | April 26 |
| **Notification begins:** | July 26 |
| **Total amount awarded:** | $43,250 |

**Contact:**
Ayn Rand Institute
"The Fountainhead" Essay Contest
P.O. Box 57044
Irvine, CA 92619-7044
Phone: 949-222-6550
Fax: 949-222-6558
Web: www.aynrand.org/contests

## "Anthem" Essay Contest

**Type of award:** Scholarship.
**Intended use:** For undergraduate study.
**Eligibility:** Applicant must be high school freshman or sophomore.
**Basis for selection:** Competition/talent/interest in writing/journalism, based on outstanding grasp of the philosophic meaning of "Anthem."
**Application requirements:** Essay between 600 and 1,200 words, typewritten and double-spaced.
**Additional information:** Eighth-grade students may also apply. Rules, guidelines, and topic questions on Website.

**Amount of award:** $30-$2,000
**Number of awards:** 236
**Number of applicants:** 13,420
**Application deadline:** March 20
**Notification begins:** July 26
**Total amount awarded:** $14,000

**Contact:**
Ayn Rand Institute
"Anthem" Essay Contest
P.O. Box 57044
Irvine, CA 92619-7044
Phone: 949-222-6550
Fax: 949-222-6558
Web: www.aynrand.org/contests

### "We the Living" Essay Contest

**Type of award:** Scholarship.
**Intended use:** For undergraduate study.
**Eligibility:** Applicant must be high school sophomore, junior or senior.
**Basis for selection:** Competition/talent/interest in writing/journalism, based on outstanding grasp of the philosophic meaning of "We the Living."
**Application requirements:** Essay between 700 and 1,500 words, typewritten and double-spaced.
**Additional information:** Rules, guidelines, and topic questions on Website.

**Amount of award:** $25-$3,000
**Number of awards:** 111
**Application deadline:** May 5

**Contact:**
Ayn Rand Institute
"We the Living" Essay Contest
P.O. Box 57044
Irvine, CA 92619-7044
Phone: 949-222-6550
Fax: 949-222-6558
Web: www.aynrandnovels.com/contests

## Barry M. Goldwater Scholarship and Excellence In Education Foundation

### Barry M. Goldwater Scholarship

**Type of award:** Scholarship, renewable.
**Intended use:** For full-time junior or senior study at accredited 2-year or 4-year institution in United States.
**Eligibility:** Applicant must be U.S. citizen, permanent resident or U.S. national.
**Basis for selection:** Major/career interest in engineering; mathematics; natural sciences or engineering, computer. Applicant must demonstrate high academic achievement and seriousness of purpose.
**Application requirements:** Recommendations, essay, transcript, nomination by Goldwater faculty representative. Permanent resident nominees must include letter of intent to obtain U.S. citizenship and photocopy of Permanent Resident Card.
**Additional information:** Bulletin of information, nomination materials, application, and list of faculty representatives available on Website. Applicants must be legal residents of state in which they are candidates. Residents of District of Columbia, Puerto Rico, Guam, American Samoa, Virgin Islands, and Commonwealth of Northern Mariana Islands also eligible. Must have minimum 3.0 GPA and rank in top 25 percent of class. Application deadline in late January; check Website for exact date.

**Amount of award:** $7,500
**Number of awards:** 300
**Number of applicants:** 1,097
**Application deadline:** January 31
**Notification begins:** April 1
**Total amount awarded:** $2,407,500

**Contact:**
Barry M. Goldwater Scholarship and Excellence in Education Foundation
6225 Brandon Avenue
Suite 315
Springfield, VA 22150-2519
Phone: 703-756-6012
Fax: 703-756-6015
Web: www.act.org/goldwater

## Best Buy

### Best Buy \@15 Scholarship Program

**Type of award:** Scholarship.
**Intended use:** For full-time undergraduate study at accredited postsecondary institution in United States.
**Eligibility:** Applicant must be enrolled in high school. Applicant must be U.S. citizen, permanent resident or resident of Puerto Rico.
**Basis for selection:** Applicant must demonstrate high academic achievement and service orientation.
**Additional information:** Apply online. See Website for more information.

**Amount of award:** $1,000
**Number of awards:** 1,200
**Application deadline:** February 15
**Total amount awarded:** $1,000,000

**Contact:**
Web: www.bestbuyinc.com/community_relations

## Bethesda Lutheran Communities

### Developmental Disability Scholastic Achievement Scholarship

**Type of award:** Scholarship.
**Intended use:** For full-time junior or senior study at accredited 4-year institution in United States.
**Eligibility:** Applicant must be Lutheran.
**Basis for selection:** Major/career interest in social work; education; psychology; mental health/therapy; education, special; education, early childhood; education, teacher; speech pathology/audiology; occupational therapy or health-related professions. Applicant must demonstrate high academic achievement, seriousness of purpose and service orientation.

**Application requirements:** Recommendations, essay, transcript, proof of eligibility.
**Additional information:** Preference given to those interested in working with persons with mental retardation. Minimum 3.0 GPA.

| | |
|---|---|
| **Amount of award:** | $3,000 |
| **Number of awards:** | 2 |
| **Number of applicants:** | 6 |
| **Application deadline:** | April 15 |
| **Notification begins:** | June 1 |
| **Total amount awarded:** | $6,000 |

**Contact:**
Bethesda Lutheran Communities
Attn: Pam Bergen
600 Hoffmann Drive
Watertown, WI 53094
Phone: 920-206-4410
Fax: 920-206-7706 Attn: Pam Bergen
Web: www.bethesdalutherancommunities.org

# BioCommunications Association, Inc.

## Endowment Fund For Education (EFFE)

**Type of award:** Scholarship.
**Intended use:** For full-time sophomore, junior, senior or graduate study at accredited vocational or 4-year institution.
**Basis for selection:** Major/career interest in arts, general; biomedical; communications or science, general.
**Application requirements:** Portfolio, recommendations, essay, transcript, proof of eligibility.
**Additional information:** For students pursuing careers in scientific/biomedical visual communications and scientific/ biomedical photography.

| | |
|---|---|
| **Amount of award:** | $500 |
| **Number of awards:** | 2 |
| **Application deadline:** | April 30 |
| **Notification begins:** | June 1 |

**Contact:**
BioCommunications Association, Inc.
220 Southwind Lane
Hillsborough, NC 27278-7907
Phone: 919-245-0906
Fax: 919-245-0906
Web: www.bca.org

# Blinded Veterans Association

## Kathern F. Gruber Scholarship Program

**Type of award:** Scholarship, renewable.
**Intended use:** For full-time undergraduate or graduate study at accredited postsecondary institution in United States.
**Eligibility:** Applicant must be U.S. citizen. Applicant must be dependent of disabled veteran; or spouse of disabled veteran who served in the Army, Air Force, Marines, Navy or Coast Guard.
**Application requirements:** Recommendations, essay, transcript.
**Additional information:** Dependent children and spouses of blinded U.S. Armed Forces veterans are eligible, as well as blinded active duty members of the U.S. Armed Forces. Veteran must meet definition of blindness used by Blinded Veterans Association; blindness may be service-connected or non-service-connected. Katherine Gruber scholarships are awarded for one year only. The number of scholarships a recipient may receive under this program is limited to four.

| | |
|---|---|
| **Amount of award:** | $2,000 |
| **Number of awards:** | 6 |
| **Number of applicants:** | 15 |
| **Application deadline:** | April 16 |
| **Notification begins:** | January 1 |
| **Total amount awarded:** | $12,000 |

**Contact:**
Kathern F. Gruber Scholarship Program
Blinded Veterans Association
477 H Street NW
Washington, DC 20001-2694
Phone: 202-371-8880
Fax: 202-371-8258
Web: www.bva.org

# BlueScope Foundation, N.A.

## Bluescope Foundation Scholarship

**Type of award:** Scholarship, renewable.
**Intended use:** For full-time undergraduate study at accredited 4-year institution.
**Eligibility:** Applicant must be high school senior.
**Basis for selection:** Applicant must demonstrate financial need, high academic achievement, depth of character, leadership and service orientation.
**Application requirements:** Recommendations, essay, transcript. SAT/ACT scores, financial report.
**Additional information:** Applicant's parent must be employed by BlueScope Steel. Contact human resources office at workplace for information and application. Renewable up to four years.

| | |
|---|---|
| **Amount of award:** | $3,000 |
| **Number of awards:** | 8 |
| **Number of applicants:** | 46 |
| **Application deadline:** | February 15 |
| **Notification begins:** | April 30 |
| **Total amount awarded:** | $24,000 |

**Contact:**
BlueScope Foundation, N.A.
P.O. Box 419917
Kansas City, MO 64141-6917
Phone: 816-968-3208
Fax: 816-627-8993

# BMI Foundation, Inc.

## BMI Student Composer Awards

**Type of award:** Scholarship.
**Intended use:** For undergraduate or graduate study at accredited postsecondary institution.
**Eligibility:** Applicant must be no older than 27. Applicant must be Citizen of a Western hemisphere country.
**Basis for selection:** Competition/talent/interest in music performance/composition, based on composition of classical music. Major/career interest in music.
**Application requirements:** Manuscript/recording of score, which must be submitted under a pseudonym. SASE.
**Additional information:** Application deadline in early February. Check Website for exact date and application. Must be enrolled in accredited public, private, or parochial secondary schools; accredited colleges or conservatories of music; or engaged in private study of music with recognized and established teachers (other than relatives).

| | |
|---|---|
| **Amount of award:** | $500-$5,000 |
| **Notification begins:** | May 1 |
| **Total amount awarded:** | $20,000 |

**Contact:**
Ralph N. Jackson
BMI Student Composer Awards
7 World Trade Center, 250 Greenwich St.
New York, NY 10007-0030
Web: www.bmifoundation.org

## John Lennon Scholarships

**Type of award:** Scholarship.
**Intended use:** For undergraduate or graduate study.
**Eligibility:** Applicant must be at least 15, no older than 24.
**Basis for selection:** Competition/talent/interest in music performance/composition, based on best song of any genre with original music and lyrics. Major/career interest in music or performing arts.
**Application requirements:** Music and lyrics of original song, CD and three typed lyric sheets.
**Additional information:** Current students and alumnae at select schools may apply directly to Foundation; others must contact the National Association for Music Education chapter advisor at their college. Visit Website for application and more information.

| | |
|---|---|
| **Amount of award:** | $5,000-$10,000 |
| **Number of awards:** | 3 |
| **Application deadline:** | January 31 |
| **Total amount awarded:** | $20,000 |

**Contact:**
BMI Foundation, Inc.
John Lennon Scholarship Competition
7 World Trade Center, 250 Greenwich St.
New York, NY 10007-0030
Web: www.bmifoundation.org

## peermusic Latin Scholarship

**Type of award:** Scholarship.
**Intended use:** For undergraduate or graduate study at postsecondary institution in United States.
**Eligibility:** Applicant must be at least 16, no older than 24.
**Basis for selection:** Competition/talent/interest in music performance/composition, based on best song or instrumental work in any Latin genre with original music and lyrics. Major/career interest in music.
**Application requirements:** CD of original song and three typed lyric sheets. Should not include name of student or school.
**Additional information:** Application deadline in early February. Check Website for exact date and application.

| | |
|---|---|
| **Amount of award:** | $5,000 |
| **Number of awards:** | 1 |

**Contact:**
BMI Foundation, Inc.
Porfirio Pilfna/peermusic Latin Scholarship
7 World Trade Center, 250 Greenwich St.
New York, NY 10007-0030
Web: www.bmifoundation.org

# Boeing Company

## Historically Black Colleges and Minority Institutions Scholarships

**Type of award:** Scholarship.
**Intended use:** For undergraduate study at 4-year institution in United States.
**Eligibility:** Applicant must be African American.
**Additional information:** Boeing provides scholarship funds to selected schools including historically black colleges and universities and minority institutions. Boeing does not provide scholarship funds directly to students. For more information, contact college financial aid office or college advisor.
**Contact:**
Web: www.boeing.com/educationrelations/index.html

# Boy Scouts of America Patriots' Path Council

## Frank D. Visceglia Memorial Scholarship

**Type of award:** Scholarship, renewable.
**Intended use:** For full-time freshman study at accredited 4-year institution.
**Eligibility:** Applicant must be male, high school senior. Applicant must be U.S. citizen or permanent resident residing in New Jersey.
**Additional information:** Applicant must be an Eagle Scout. Preference given to Scouts whose service projects relate to the environment or economy. Application available online.

| | |
|---|---|
| **Amount of award:** | $1,000 |
| **Number of awards:** | 1 |
| **Number of applicants:** | 20 |
| **Application deadline:** | June 1 |
| **Notification begins:** | August 1 |
| **Total amount awarded:** | $1,000 |

**Contact:**
The Frank D. Visceglia Memorial Scholarship Program
Attn: Dennis Kohl
222 Columbia Turnpike
Florham Park, NJ 07932
Phone: 973-765-9322
Fax: 973-765-9142
Web: www.advancement.ppbsa.org/scholarship.htm

# Boys and Girls Clubs of Greater San Diego

## Spence Reese Scholarship

**Type of award:** Scholarship, renewable.
**Intended use:** For full-time undergraduate study at accredited 4-year institution in United States.
**Eligibility:** Applicant must be male, high school senior.
**Basis for selection:** Major/career interest in engineering; law; medicine or political science/government. Applicant must demonstrate financial need and high academic achievement.
**Application requirements:** Recommendations, transcript. SAT/ACT scores, college acceptance letter.
**Additional information:** One award in each of four eligible majors. Award is renewable for four years of study. Application available on Website.

| | |
|---|---|
| **Amount of award:** | $4,000 |
| **Number of awards:** | 4 |
| **Number of applicants:** | 40 |
| **Application deadline:** | April 1 |
| **Notification begins:** | January 1 |
| **Total amount awarded:** | $32,000 |

**Contact:**
Boys and Girls Clubs of Greater San Diego
Attn: Spence Reese Scholarship Committee
4635 Clairemont Mesa Blvd.
San Diego, CA 92117
Phone: 858-866-0591 ext. 201
Web: www.sdyouth.org/scholarships.htm

# Brandon Goodman Scholarship

## BG Scholarship

**Type of award:** Scholarship.
**Intended use:** For undergraduate study at vocational, 2-year or 4-year institution.
**Eligibility:** Applicant must be U.S. citizen or permanent resident.
**Basis for selection:** Applicant must demonstrate financial need and service orientation.
**Application requirements:** Essay.
**Additional information:** 2.0 minimum GPA.

| | |
|---|---|
| **Amount of award:** | $400 |
| **Number of awards:** | 12 |

**Contact:**
Brandon Goodman Scholarship
Phone: 949-547-9427
Fax: 949-716-6102
Web: www.bgscholarship.com/scholarship

# Broadcast Education Association

## Abe Voron Scholarship

**Type of award:** Scholarship.
**Intended use:** For full-time junior, senior or graduate study at 4-year or graduate institution. Designated institutions: BEA Institutional Member schools.
**Basis for selection:** Major/career interest in radio/television/film. Applicant must demonstrate high academic achievement, depth of character and seriousness of purpose.
**Application requirements:** Recommendations, essay, transcript.
**Additional information:** Award intended for study in radio only. Should be able to show evidence of potential to be outstanding electronic media professional. Application available from campus faculty or online.

| | |
|---|---|
| **Amount of award:** | $5,000 |
| **Number of awards:** | 1 |
| **Application deadline:** | October 12 |
| **Total amount awarded:** | $5,000 |

**Contact:**
Broadcast Education Association (BEA)
1771 N Street, N.W.
Washington, DC 20036-2891
Phone: 202-429-3935
Web: www.beaweb.org

## Alexander M. Tanger Scholarship

**Type of award:** Scholarship.
**Intended use:** For full-time junior, senior or graduate study at 4-year or graduate institution in United States. Designated institutions: BEA Institutional Member schools.
**Basis for selection:** Major/career interest in radio/television/film. Applicant must demonstrate high academic achievement, depth of character and seriousness of purpose.
**Application requirements:** Recommendations, essay, transcript.
**Additional information:** Must show evidence of potential in electronic media. Application available from campus faculty or on Website.

| | |
|---|---|
| **Amount of award:** | $5,000 |
| **Number of awards:** | 1 |
| **Application deadline:** | October 12 |
| **Total amount awarded:** | $5,000 |

**Contact:**
Broadcast Education Association (BEA)
1771 N Street, N.W.
Washington, DC 20036-2891
Phone: 202-429-3935
Web: www.beaweb.org

## Helen J. Sioussat/Fay Wells Scholarship

**Type of award:** Scholarship.
**Intended use:** For full-time junior, senior or graduate study at 4-year or graduate institution. Designated institutions: BEA Institutional Member schools.
**Basis for selection:** Major/career interest in radio/television/film. Applicant must demonstrate high academic achievement, depth of character and seriousness of purpose.

**Application requirements:** Recommendations, essay, transcript.
**Additional information:** Should be able to show evidence of potential in electronic media. Application available from campus faculty or on Website.

| | |
|---|---|
| **Amount of award:** | $1,250 |
| **Number of awards:** | 2 |
| **Application deadline:** | October 12 |
| **Total amount awarded:** | $2,500 |

**Contact:**
Broadcast Education Association (BEA)
1771 N Street, N.W.
Washington, DC 20036-2891
Phone: 202-429-3935
Web: www.beaweb.org

## Richard Eaton Foundation Award

**Type of award:** Scholarship.
**Intended use:** For full-time junior, senior or graduate study at 4-year or graduate institution. Designated institutions: BEA Institutional Member schools.
**Basis for selection:** Major/career interest in radio/television/film. Applicant must demonstrate high academic achievement, depth of character and seriousness of purpose.
**Application requirements:** Recommendations, essay, transcript.
**Additional information:** Must show evidence of potential in electronic media. Application available from campus faculty or on Website.

| | |
|---|---|
| **Amount of award:** | $2,000 |
| **Number of awards:** | 1 |
| **Application deadline:** | October 12 |

**Contact:**
Broadcast Education Association (BEA)
1771 N Street, NW
Washington, DC 20036-2891
Phone: 202-429-3935
Web: www.beaweb.org

## Two Year Community College BEA Award

**Type of award:** Scholarship.
**Intended use:** For full-time undergraduate study at 2-year or 4-year institution. Designated institutions: BEA Institutional Member schools.
**Basis for selection:** Major/career interest in radio/television/film. Applicant must demonstrate high academic achievement, depth of character and seriousness of purpose.
**Application requirements:** Recommendations, essay, transcript.
**Additional information:** Scholarship for use at two-year community college, or, if applicant has already graduated from BEA two-year campus, can be used at four-year school. Should show evidence of potential in electronic media. Application available from campus faculty or on Website.

| | |
|---|---|
| **Amount of award:** | $1,500 |
| **Number of awards:** | 2 |
| **Application deadline:** | October 12 |
| **Total amount awarded:** | $3,000 |

**Contact:**
Broadcast Education Association (BEA)
1771 N Street, N.W.
Washington, DC 20036-2891
Phone: 202-429-3935
Web: www.beaweb.org

## Vision Award

**Type of award:** Scholarship.
**Intended use:** For full-time junior, senior or graduate study at 4-year or graduate institution. Designated institutions: BEA Institutional Member schools.
**Basis for selection:** Major/career interest in radio/television/film. Applicant must demonstrate high academic achievement, depth of character and seriousness of purpose.
**Application requirements:** Recommendations, essay, transcript.
**Additional information:** Must show evidence of potential in electronic media. Application available from campus faculty or on Website.

| | |
|---|---|
| **Amount of award:** | $1,500 |
| **Number of awards:** | 1 |
| **Application deadline:** | October 12 |
| **Total amount awarded:** | $1,500 |

**Contact:**
Broadcast Education Association (BEA)
1771 N Street, N.W.
Washington, DC 20036-2891
Phone: 202-429-3935
Web: www.beaweb.org

## Walter S. Patterson Scholarship

**Type of award:** Scholarship.
**Intended use:** For full-time junior, senior or graduate study at 4-year or graduate institution. Designated institutions: BEA Institutional Member schools.
**Basis for selection:** Major/career interest in radio/television/film. Applicant must demonstrate high academic achievement, depth of character and seriousness of purpose.
**Application requirements:** Recommendations, essay, transcript.
**Additional information:** Award intended for study in radio only. Should be able to show evidence of potential in electronic media. Application available from campus faculty or on Website.

| | |
|---|---|
| **Amount of award:** | $2,750 |
| **Number of awards:** | 2 |
| **Application deadline:** | October 12 |
| **Total amount awarded:** | $5,500 |

**Contact:**
Broadcast Education Association (BEA)
1771 N Street, N.W.
Washington, DC 20036-2891
Phone: 202-429-3935
Web: www.beaweb.org

# Brown and Caldwell

## Dr. W. Wes Eckenfelder Jr. Scholarship

**Type of award:** Scholarship.
**Intended use:** For full-time junior, senior or graduate study at accredited 4-year or graduate institution in United States.
**Eligibility:** Applicant must be U.S. citizen or permanent resident.
**Basis for selection:** Major/career interest in engineering, civil; engineering, chemical; engineering, environmental; environmental science; biology; ecology or environmental

science. Applicant must demonstrate high academic achievement and seriousness of purpose.
**Application requirements:** Recommendations, essay, transcript. Resume.
**Additional information:** Minimum 3.0 GPA. Visit Website for additional information.

| | |
|---|---|
| **Amount of award:** | $5,000 |
| **Number of awards:** | 1 |
| **Number of applicants:** | 150 |
| **Application deadline:** | March 1 |
| **Notification begins:** | April 1 |
| **Total amount awarded:** | $3,000 |

**Contact:**
Brown and Caldwell
Attn: HR/Scholarship Program
P.O. Box 8045
Walnut Creek, CA 94596
Phone: 800-727-2224
Web: www.brownandcaldwell.com/_Index_scholarships.htm

### Minority Scholarship Program

**Type of award:** Scholarship.
**Intended use:** For full-time junior study at accredited 4-year institution in United States.
**Eligibility:** Applicant must be Alaskan native, Asian American, African American, Mexican American, Hispanic American, Puerto Rican, American Indian or Native Hawaiian/Pacific Islander. Applicant must be U.S. citizen or permanent resident.
**Basis for selection:** Major/career interest in engineering, civil; engineering, chemical; engineering, environmental; environmental science; biology; ecology or geology/earth sciences.
**Application requirements:** Recommendations, essay, transcript. Resume.
**Additional information:** Award includes optional paid summer internship at Brown and Caldwell office. Minimum cumulative 3.0 GPA.

| | |
|---|---|
| **Amount of award:** | $5,000 |
| **Number of awards:** | 5 |
| **Number of applicants:** | 50 |
| **Application deadline:** | March 31 |
| **Notification begins:** | April 30 |
| **Total amount awarded:** | $12,000 |

**Contact:**
Brown and Caldwell
Attn: HR/Scholarship Program
P.O. Box 8045
Walnut Creek, CA 94596
Phone: 800-727-2224
Web: www.brownandcaldwell.com/_Index_scholarships.htm

## Brown Foundation

### Teacher Quest Scholarship Program

**Type of award:** Scholarship, renewable.
**Intended use:** For junior or senior study at accredited 4-year institution.
**Eligibility:** Applicant must be Alaskan native, Asian American, African American, Mexican American, Hispanic American, Puerto Rican or American Indian.
**Basis for selection:** Major/career interest in education or education, teacher. Applicant must demonstrate high academic achievement and leadership.
**Application requirements:** Recommendations.
**Additional information:** Minimum 3.0 GPA. Visit Website for application.

| | |
|---|---|
| **Amount of award:** | $2,000 |
| **Number of awards:** | 4 |
| **Number of applicants:** | 200 |
| **Application deadline:** | April 1 |
| **Notification begins:** | June 1 |
| **Total amount awarded:** | $10,000 |

**Contact:**
Brown Foundation Scholarship Committee
1515 SE Monroe
Topeka, KS 66615
Phone: 785-235-3939
Fax: 785-235-1001
Web: www.brownvboard.org

## Building Industry Association

### BIA Cares of San Diego Scholarship

**Type of award:** Scholarship.
**Intended use:** For full-time sophomore, junior or senior study at postsecondary institution.
**Eligibility:** Applicant must be residing in California.
**Basis for selection:** Major/career interest in engineering, civil; real estate; construction; finance/banking; landscape architecture; engineering, construction; advertising; accounting; architecture or engineering, structural. Applicant must demonstrate financial need, high academic achievement and seriousness of purpose.
**Application requirements:** Interview, essay, proof of eligibility.
**Additional information:** For residents of San Diego who have either graduated from a San Diego County high school or are attending college in San Diego and are interested in careers in the building industry. Also open to students pursuing major/career as developer, contractor, soils engineer, designer, land planner, framer, plumber, electrician, or other related profession. Number and amount of awards varies. See Website for application and deadline.
**Contact:**
Building Industry Association of San Diego
c/o Nancy Diamond
9201 Spectrum Center Blvd., Suite 110
San Diego, CA 92123
Phone: 858-450-1221
Web: www.biasandiego.org/biacares.php

## Bureau of Indian Education

### Higher Education Grant Program

**Type of award:** Scholarship, renewable.
**Intended use:** For full-time undergraduate study at accredited 2-year or 4-year institution in United States.
**Eligibility:** Applicant must be American Indian. Member or at least one-quarter degree descendent of member of federally recognized tribe.

**Basis for selection:** Applicant must demonstrate financial need.
**Application requirements:** Proof of eligibility.
**Additional information:** Contacts or inquiries for these funds should be directed to the tribe or prospective Education Line Office relative to the person's tribal headquarters. The Higher Education scholarships are not awarded through the D.C. offices. Award amount based on student's financial need. No application deadline.

| | |
|---|---|
| **Number of awards:** | 12,000 |
| **Total amount awarded:** | $25,000,000 |

**Contact:**
Bureau of Indian Education
Division of Post Secondary Education
215 Dean A McGee, Suite 610
Oklahoma City, OK 73102
Phone: 405-605-6001
Fax: 405-605-6010
Web: www.bie.edu

# Bureau of Indian Education-Oklahoma Area Education Office

## Osage Tribal Education Committee Award

**Type of award:** Scholarship.
**Intended use:** For undergraduate or graduate study at accredited postsecondary institution in United States.
**Eligibility:** Applicant must be American Indian. Must be member of Osage Tribe.
**Application requirements:** Transcript, proof of eligibility.
**Additional information:** Minimum 2.0 GPA. Part-time students funded at half rate. Application deadlines: July 1 for fall semester and December 31 for spring (funds permitting). Contact Oklahoma Area Education Office for application and additional information.

| | |
|---|---|
| **Number of applicants:** | 204 |
| **Application deadline:** | July 1, December 31 |

**Contact:**
Bureau of Indian Affairs - Oklahoma Area Education Office
200 N.W. 4th Street
Suite 4049
Oklahoma City, OK 73102
Phone: 405-605-6051 ext. 304

# California Association of Realtors Scholarship Foundation

## C.A.R. Scholarship

**Type of award:** Scholarship, renewable.
**Intended use:** For undergraduate or graduate study at 2-year or 4-year institution. Designated institutions: California colleges/universities.
**Eligibility:** Applicant must be U.S. citizen residing in California.
**Basis for selection:** Major/career interest in real estate. Applicant must demonstrate financial need.
**Application requirements:** Recommendations, essay, transcript, proof of eligibility. Photocopy of valid CA driver's license or ID card.
**Additional information:** Must be California resident of at least one year before applying. Awarded to all eligible applicants. Students attending two-year colleges receive up to $2,000; four-year college/university students receive up to $4,000. Applications deadlines are in May, September, and December, with notification about six weeks later. May receive one award per year, maximum two years. Minimum 2.6 GPA. Must have completed minimum 12 college-level course units within last four years; at least two courses in real estate or real-estate related. Must be enrolled in one real estate course at the time of submission of application. Visit Website for application, exact deadlines, and other information.

| | |
|---|---|
| **Amount of award:** | $2,000-$4,000 |
| **Number of applicants:** | 20 |
| **Total amount awarded:** | $18,600 |

**Contact:**
California Association of Realtors Scholarship Foundation
525 South Virgil Avenue
Los Angeles, CA 90020
Phone: 213-739-8243
Fax: 213-739-7286
Web: www.car.org/aboutus

# California Farm Bureau Federation

## California Farm Bureau Scholarship

**Type of award:** Scholarship, renewable.
**Intended use:** For full-time undergraduate study at accredited 4-year institution. Designated institutions: Colleges/universities in California.
**Eligibility:** Applicant must be U.S. citizen residing in California.
**Basis for selection:** Major/career interest in agriculture; agribusiness; engineering, agricultural or veterinary medicine. Applicant must demonstrate high academic achievement, leadership and seriousness of purpose.
**Application requirements:** Recommendations, transcript.
**Additional information:** Must be preparing for career in agricultural industry. Visit Website for application. Number of awards varies.

| | |
|---|---|
| **Amount of award:** | $1,500-$5,000 |
| **Application deadline:** | March 1 |
| **Notification begins:** | June 1 |
| **Total amount awarded:** | $165,750 |

**Contact:**
California Farm Bureau Scholarship Foundation
2300 River Plaza Drive
Sacramento, CA 95833
Phone: 916-561-5500
Web: www.cfbf.com/programs/scholar

# California Masonic Foundation

## California Masonic Foundation Scholarship

**Type of award:** Scholarship, renewable.
**Intended use:** For full-time undergraduate study at accredited 2-year or 4-year institution.
**Eligibility:** Applicant must be high school senior. Applicant must be U.S. citizen residing in California.
**Basis for selection:** Applicant must demonstrate financial need and high academic achievement.
**Application requirements:** Essay.
**Additional information:** Minimum 3.0 GPA. Must have been California resident for at least one year. While not required, some preference is given to applicants with Masonic relatives and/or involvement in Masonic youth orders. Visit Website for more information and application.

| | |
|---|---|
| **Amount of award:** | $2,500-$10,000 |
| **Number of awards:** | 50 |
| **Number of applicants:** | 1,300 |
| **Application deadline:** | February 15 |
| **Notification begins:** | May 1 |
| **Total amount awarded:** | $962,000 |

**Contact:**
California Masonic Foundation
1111 California Street
San Francisco, CA 94108-2284
Web: www.freemason.org

# California Student Aid Commission

## Cal Grant A & B Entitlement Award Program

**Type of award:** Scholarship, renewable.
**Intended use:** For undergraduate study at postsecondary institution. Designated institutions: Qualifying California postsecondary schools.
**Eligibility:** Applicant must be high school senior. Applicant must be U.S. citizen or permanent resident residing in California.
**Basis for selection:** Applicant must demonstrate financial need and high academic achievement.
**Application requirements:** FAFSA, GPA verification form.
**Additional information:** Applicants who graduated in the last year also eligible. Awards given to all eligible applicants. Minimum 3.0 GPA for Cal Grant A; minimum 2.0 GPA for Cal Grant B. Cal Grant A provides tuition and fees. Cal Grant B awards up to $1,551 the first year and $1,551 plus tuition and fees for years two through four. Visit Website or contact CSAC for more details.

| | |
|---|---|
| **Amount of award:** | $1,551-$10,302 |
| **Number of applicants:** | 192,270 |
| **Application deadline:** | March 2 |
| **Notification begins:** | March 31 |
| **Total amount awarded:** | $678,300,000 |

**Contact:**
California Student Aid Commission
Student Support Services Branch
P.O. Box 419027
Rancho Cordova, CA 95741-9027
Phone: 888-224-7268
Fax: 916-464-8002
Web: www.calgrants.org

## Cal Grant A and B Competitive Awards

**Type of award:** Scholarship, renewable.
**Intended use:** For undergraduate study at postsecondary institution. Designated institutions: Qualifying California postsecondary schools.
**Eligibility:** Applicant must be U.S. citizen or permanent resident residing in California.
**Basis for selection:** Applicant must demonstrate financial need and high academic achievement.
**Application requirements:** FAFSA, GPA verification form.
**Additional information:** Minimum 3.0 GPA for Cal Grant A; minimum 2.0 GPA for Cal Grant B. Cal Grant A pays tuition and fees. Cal Grant B awards up to $1,551 first year and $1,551 plus tuition and fees for years two through four. Students with no available GPA can submit SAT, ACT, or GED scores. Visit Website or contact CSAC for more details.

| | |
|---|---|
| **Amount of award:** | $1,551-$7,788 |
| **Number of awards:** | 22,500 |
| **Number of applicants:** | 62,295 |
| **Application deadline:** | March 2, September 2 |
| **Notification begins:** | April 30, October 31 |
| **Total amount awarded:** | $129,400,000 |

**Contact:**
California Student Aid Commission
Student Support Services Branch
P.O. Box 419027
Rancho Cordova, CA 95741-9027
Phone: 888-224-7268
Fax: 916-464-8002
Web: www.calgrants.org

## Cal Grant C Award

**Type of award:** Scholarship, renewable.
**Intended use:** For undergraduate study at vocational or 2-year institution. Designated institutions: Qualifying California postsecondary institutions.
**Eligibility:** Applicant must be U.S. citizen or permanent resident residing in California.
**Basis for selection:** Applicant must demonstrate financial need.
**Application requirements:** FAFSA, GPA verification form.
**Additional information:** Funding is available for up to two years, and vocational program must be at least four months in length. Visit Website or contact CSAC for more details.

| | |
|---|---|
| **Amount of award:** | $576-$2,592 |
| **Number of awards:** | 7,761 |
| **Number of applicants:** | 15,875 |
| **Application deadline:** | March 2 |
| **Notification begins:** | May 30 |
| **Total amount awarded:** | $9,200,000 |

**Contact:**
California Student Aid Commission
Student Support Services Branch
P.O. Box 419027
Rancho Cordova, CA 95741-9027
Phone: 888-224-7268
Fax: 916-464-8002
Web: www.calgrants.org

## California Chafee Grant Program

**Type of award:** Scholarship, renewable.
**Intended use:** For undergraduate or graduate study at accredited postsecondary institution.
**Eligibility:** Applicant must be no older than 21.
**Basis for selection:** Applicant must demonstrate financial need.
**Application requirements:** FAFSA.
**Additional information:** Must be current or former foster youth from any state attending a California college or current foster youth from California attending any college. Must have been eligible for foster care between 16th and 18th birthdays. Must not have reached 22nd birthday by July 1st of award year. Must be enrolled at least half time in course of study lasting at least one year. Renewable through 23rd birthday. Apply early.

| | |
|---|---|
| **Amount of award:** | $5,000 |
| **Number of awards:** | 3,025 |
| **Number of applicants:** | 9,141 |
| **Notification begins:** | July 1 |
| **Total amount awarded:** | $11,661,294 |

**Contact:**
California Student Aid Commission
Attn: Specialized Programs Operations Branch
P.O. Box 419029
Rancho Cordova, CA 95741-9029
Phone: 888-224-7268
Fax: 916-464-7977
Web: www.chafee.csac.ca.gov

## California Child Development Grant Program

**Type of award:** Scholarship.
**Intended use:** For undergraduate study at accredited 2-year or 4-year institution. Designated institutions: California postsecondary institutions.
**Eligibility:** Applicant must be U.S. citizen or permanent resident residing in California.
**Basis for selection:** Major/career interest in education, early childhood. Applicant must demonstrate financial need.
**Application requirements:** Recommendations, nomination by postsecondary institution or employing agency. FAFSA.
**Additional information:** Recipients attending two-year institutions receive up to $1,000 annually; those attending four-year institutions receive up to $2,000 annually. Recipients must maintain at least half-time enrollment in approved course of study leading to Child Development Permit in one of following levels: Teacher, Master Teacher, Site Supervisor or Program Director. Must maintain satisfactory academic progress, meet federal Selective Service filing requirements, and commit to one year of full-time employment in licensed child care center for every year they receive the grant. Deadlines and notification dates vary. Visit Website for application and more information.

| | |
|---|---|
| **Amount of award:** | $1,000-$2,000 |
| **Number of awards:** | 100 |
| **Number of applicants:** | 1,017 |
| **Application deadline:** | June 15 |
| **Notification begins:** | February 1 |
| **Total amount awarded:** | $302,838 |

**Contact:**
California Student Aid Commission
Attn: Child Development Grant Program
P.O. Box 419029
Rancho Cordova, CA 95741-9029
Phone: 888-224-7268 opt. 3
Fax: 916-464-7977
Web: www.csac.ca.gov

## California Robert C. Byrd Honors Scholarship

**Type of award:** Scholarship, renewable.
**Intended use:** For full-time undergraduate study at accredited postsecondary institution in United States.
**Eligibility:** Applicant must be high school senior. Applicant must be U.S. citizen or permanent resident residing in California.
**Basis for selection:** Applicant must demonstrate high academic achievement.
**Application requirements:** Nomination by high school.
**Additional information:** Current high school students should contact high school guidance counselor for application instructions. GED students may apply directly to the Commission. Renewable up to four years.

| | |
|---|---|
| **Amount of award:** | $1,500 |
| **Number of awards:** | 804 |
| **Number of applicants:** | 1,287 |
| **Application deadline:** | April 1 |
| **Notification begins:** | May 16 |
| **Total amount awarded:** | $1,206,000 |

**Contact:**
California Student Aid Commission
Attn: Robert C. Byrd Honors Scholarship
P.O. Box 419029
Rancho Cordova, CA 95741-9029
Phone: 888-224-7268
Fax: 916-464-7977
Web: www.csac.ca.gov

## Law Enforcement Personnel Dependents (LEPD) Grant Program

**Type of award:** Scholarship, renewable.
**Intended use:** For undergraduate study at accredited 2-year or 4-year institution. Designated institutions: California postsecondary institutions.
**Eligibility:** Applicant must be U.S. citizen residing in California. Applicant's parent must have been killed or disabled in work-related accident as firefighter, police officer or public safety officer.
**Basis for selection:** Applicant must demonstrate financial need.
**Application requirements:** SAR, birth certificate (not required for spouse), death certificate, findings of Workers' Compensation Appeals Board.
**Additional information:** Applicant must be dependent or spouse of California peace or law enforcement officer, officer or employee of Department of Corrections or Department of Youth Authority in California, or California firefighter, who

was killed or 100 percent disabled in performance of duty. Number of awards varies.

**Amount of award:** $1,551-$11,259
**Number of awards:** 63
**Number of applicants:** 12
**Notification begins:** February 1
**Total amount awarded:** $54,571

**Contact:**
California Student Aid Commission
LEPD Program
P.O. Box 419029
Rancho Cordova, CA 95741-9029
Phone: 888-224-7268 opt. 3
Fax: 916-464-7977
Web: www.csac.ca.gov

# California Teachers Association

## California Teachers Association Martin Luther King, Jr., Memorial Scholarship

**Type of award:** Scholarship.
**Intended use:** For undergraduate or graduate study at accredited postsecondary institution.
**Eligibility:** Applicant must be Alaskan native, Asian American, African American, Mexican American, Hispanic American, Puerto Rican, American Indian or Native Hawaiian/Pacific Islander. Applicant must be residing in California.
**Basis for selection:** Major/career interest in education; education, early childhood; education, special or education, teacher. Applicant must demonstrate financial need.
**Application requirements:** Recommendations, essay, transcript, proof of eligibility.
**Additional information:** Must be active California Teachers Association (CTA) member, active Student CTA member, or dependent child of an active, retired, or deceased CTA member. Amount of award and number of awards varies. To receive funds, must show proof of registration in approved credential or degree program. Must pursue teaching-related career in public education. Application must be typed and mailed. Check Website for deadline and additional information.

**Contact:**
CTA Scholarship Committee Human Rights Department
c/o Janeya Collins
P.O. Box 921
Burlingame, CA 94011-0921
Phone: 650-552-5446
Fax: 650-552-5001
Web: www.cta.org

## CTA Scholarship for Dependent Children

**Type of award:** Scholarship, renewable.
**Intended use:** For full-time undergraduate or graduate study at accredited postsecondary institution.
**Eligibility:** Applicant must be residing in California.
**Basis for selection:** Major/career interest in education. Applicant must demonstrate high academic achievement, depth of character, leadership, seriousness of purpose and service orientation.
**Application requirements:** Recommendations, essay, transcript, proof of eligibility.
**Additional information:** Applicant must be dependent child of active, retired, or deceased member of California Teachers Association. Minimum 3.5 high school GPA. Awards based on overall achievement in four categories: 1) involvement in and sensitivity to human, social, and civic issues; 2) characteristics such as responsibility, reliability, and integrity; 3) academic and vocational potential; and 4) special and personal achievements. Application deadline between end of January and beginning of February; visit Website for exact date and the most current information. Number of awards varies.

**Amount of award:** $5,000

**Contact:**
CTA Scholarship Committee Human Rights Department
c/o Janeya Collins
P.O. Box 921
Burlingame, CA 94011-0921
Phone: 650-552-5446
Fax: 650-552-5001
Web: www.cta.org

## CTA Scholarships for Members

**Type of award:** Scholarship, renewable.
**Intended use:** For undergraduate or graduate study at accredited postsecondary institution.
**Eligibility:** Applicant must be residing in California.
**Basis for selection:** Major/career interest in education; education, early childhood; education, special or education, teacher. Applicant must demonstrate high academic achievement, depth of character, leadership, seriousness of purpose and service orientation.
**Application requirements:** Recommendations, essay, transcript, proof of eligibility.
**Additional information:** Scholarships awarded based on overall achievement in four categories: 1) involvement in and sensitivity to human, social, and civic issues; 2) characteristics such as responsibility, reliability, and integrity; 3) academic and vocational potential; and 4) special and personal achievements. Applicant must be active member of California Teachers Association (including members working on emergency credential). Application deadline is between end of January and beginning of February; visit Website for exact date and the most up-to-date information. Number of awards varies.

**Amount of award:** $3,000
**Number of awards:** 5

**Contact:**
CTA Scholarship Committee Human Rights Department
c/o Janeya Collins
P.O. Box 921
Burlingame, CA 94011-0921
Phone: 650-552-5446
Fax: 650-552-5001
Web: www.cta.org

## GLBT "Guy DeRosa" Safety in Schools Grant and Scholarship Program

**Type of award:** Scholarship.
**Intended use:** For undergraduate study at 2-year or 4-year institution.
**Application requirements:** Essay, proof of eligibility.
**Additional information:** Awards support projects and presentations that promote understanding and respect for GLBT persons and GLBT educators. Must be active California

Teachers Association (CTA) member, active Student CTA member, or a public school student or district nominated by a CTA or SCTA member. Number of awards varies. Both grants and scholarships available. Check Website for deadline and additional information. Application must be typed and mailed.

| | |
|---|---|
| **Amount of award:** | $2,000 |

**Contact:**
California Teachers Association
c/o Janeya Collins
P.O. Box 921
Burlingame, CA 94011-0921
Phone: 650-552-5446
Fax: 650-552-5001
Web: www.cta.org

### L. Gordon Bittle Memorial Scholarship for SCTA

**Type of award:** Scholarship, renewable.
**Intended use:** For full-time undergraduate, graduate or non-degree study at accredited postsecondary institution.
**Basis for selection:** Major/career interest in education; education, early childhood; education, special or education, teacher. Applicant must demonstrate high academic achievement, depth of character and service orientation.
**Application requirements:** Recommendations, essay, transcript.
**Additional information:** Applicant must be active member of Student CTA. Minimum 3.5 high school GPA. Must pursue career in public education. Not available to CTA members currently working in schools. May be enrolled in teacher credential program. Application deadline is between end of January and beginning of February; visit Website for exact date and more information.

| | |
|---|---|
| **Amount of award:** | $3,000 |
| **Number of awards:** | 3 |

**Contact:**
CTA Scholarship Committee Human Rights Department
c/o Janeya Collins
P.O. Box 921
Burlingame, CA 94011-0921
Phone: 650-552-5446
Fax: 650-552-5001
Web: www.cta.org

## CAP Charitable Foundation

### Ron Brown Scholar Program

**Type of award:** Scholarship, renewable.
**Intended use:** For full-time undergraduate study at accredited 4-year institution in United States.
**Eligibility:** Applicant must be African American. Applicant must be high school senior. Applicant must be U.S. citizen or permanent resident.
**Basis for selection:** Applicant must demonstrate financial need, high academic achievement, depth of character, leadership, seriousness of purpose and service orientation.
**Application requirements:** Recommendations, essay, transcript.
**Additional information:** In addition to financial assistance, scholars get other benefits: summer internships, career guidance, placement opportunities, mentors, and leadership training. Scholarships may be used to pursue any academic discipline. Award is $10,000 per year for four years. Earlier deadline is for those who wish to have their information forwarded to select colleges and scholarship programs.

| | |
|---|---|
| **Amount of award:** | $40,000 |
| **Number of awards:** | 10 |
| **Number of applicants:** | 6,185 |
| **Application deadline:** | November 1, January 9 |
| **Notification begins:** | April 1 |
| **Total amount awarded:** | $480,000 |

**Contact:**
Ron Brown Scholar Program
1160 Pepsi Place, Suite 206
Charlottesville, VA 22901
Phone: 434-964-1588
Fax: 434-964-1589
Web: www.ronbrown.org

## Carl's Jr. Restaurants

### Carl N. & Margaret Karcher Founders' Scholarship

**Type of award:** Scholarship.
**Intended use:** For full-time freshman study at accredited vocational, 2-year or 4-year institution.
**Eligibility:** Applicant must be no older than 21, high school senior. Applicant must be residing in Utah, Texas, Alaska, Washington, Arizona, Nevada, Oklahoma, California, Oregon, Idaho, New Mexico, Colorado or Hawaii.
**Application requirements:** Transcript.
**Additional information:** High school graduates also eligible. Employees, affiliates, and franchisees of Carl Karcher Enterprises, Inc., Scholarship America, affiliated agencies and their immediate families are ineligible. Application available on Website.

| | |
|---|---|
| **Amount of award:** | $1,000 |
| **Number of awards:** | 60 |
| **Number of applicants:** | 5,000 |
| **Application deadline:** | February 1 |
| **Total amount awarded:** | $60,000 |

**Contact:**
Carl N. & Margaret Karcher Founders' Scholarship
c/o Scholarship America
One Scholarship Way, P.O. Box 297
St. Peter, MN 56082
Phone: 507-931-1682
Web: www.carlsjr.com/promotions

## Catching the Dream

### MESBEC Scholarships

**Type of award:** Scholarship, renewable.
**Intended use:** For full-time undergraduate or graduate study at accredited postsecondary institution in United States.
**Eligibility:** Applicant must be Alaskan native or American Indian. Must be at least one-quarter Native American and enrolled member of federally recognized, state recognized, or terminated tribe. Applicant must be U.S. citizen or permanent resident.

Scholarships

**Basis for selection:** Major/career interest in mathematics; engineering; science, general; business; education; computer/ information sciences; health sciences or medicine. Applicant must demonstrate high academic achievement, depth of character, leadership, seriousness of purpose and service orientation.
**Application requirements:** Recommendations, essay, transcript, proof of eligibility.
**Additional information:** Deadlines are March 15 for summer funding, April 15 for fall, September 15 for spring.

| | |
|---|---|
| **Amount of award:** | $500-$5,000 |
| **Number of awards:** | 180 |
| **Number of applicants:** | 150 |
| **Application deadline:** | April 15, September 15 |
| **Total amount awarded:** | $300,000 |

**Contact:**
Catching the Dream
8200 Mountain Road NE
Suite 203
Albuquerque, NM 87110
Phone: 505-262-2351
Fax: 505-262-0534
Web: www.catchingthedream.org

## Native American Leadership in Education Scholarship

**Type of award:** Scholarship, renewable.
**Intended use:** For full-time undergraduate or graduate study at accredited postsecondary institution in United States.
**Eligibility:** Applicant must be American Indian. Must be at least one-quarter Native American and enrolled member of federally recognized, state recognized, or terminated tribe. Applicant must be U.S. citizen or permanent resident.
**Basis for selection:** Major/career interest in education. Applicant must demonstrate high academic achievement, depth of character, leadership, seriousness of purpose and service orientation.
**Application requirements:** Recommendations, essay, transcript, proof of eligibility.
**Additional information:** Deadlines are March 15 for summer funding, April 15 for fall, September 15 for spring.

| | |
|---|---|
| **Amount of award:** | $500-$5,000 |
| **Number of awards:** | 30 |
| **Number of applicants:** | 40 |
| **Application deadline:** | April 15, September 15 |
| **Total amount awarded:** | $100,000 |

**Contact:**
Catching the Dream
8200 Mountain Road NE
Suite 203
Albuquerque, NM 87110
Phone: 505-262-2351
Fax: 505-262-0534
Web: www.catchingthedream.org

## Tribal Business Management Scholarship

**Type of award:** Scholarship, renewable.
**Intended use:** For full-time undergraduate, graduate or postgraduate study at accredited postsecondary institution in United States.
**Eligibility:** Applicant must be Alaskan native or American Indian. Must be at least one-quarter Native American and enrolled member of federally recognized, state recognized, or terminated tribe. Applicant must be U.S. citizen or permanent resident.
**Basis for selection:** Major/career interest in business; economics; finance/banking; hotel/restaurant management; accounting; marketing or business/management/administration. Applicant must demonstrate high academic achievement, depth of character, leadership, seriousness of purpose and service orientation.
**Application requirements:** Recommendations, essay, transcript, proof of eligibility.
**Additional information:** Scholarships are for fields of study directly related to tribal business development and management. Application deadlines are March 15 for summer semester, April 15 for fall semester, September 15 for spring semester.

| | |
|---|---|
| **Amount of award:** | $500-$5,000 |
| **Number of awards:** | 15 |
| **Number of applicants:** | 30 |
| **Application deadline:** | April 15, September 15 |
| **Total amount awarded:** | $50,000 |

**Contact:**
Catching the Dream
8200 Mountain Road NE
Suite 203
Albuquerque, NM 87110
Phone: 505-262-2351
Fax: 505-262-0534
Web: www.catchingthedream.org

# Catholic United Financial

## Post-High School Tuition Scholarship

**Type of award:** Scholarship.
**Intended use:** For full-time freshman or sophomore study at accredited vocational, 2-year or 4-year institution in United States.
**Basis for selection:** Applicant must demonstrate leadership and service orientation.
**Application requirements:** Essay, proof of eligibility.
**Additional information:** Must have been member of Catholic United Financial for two years prior to application deadline. Award is $300 awards for students attending non-Catholic schools and $500 for those attending Catholic colleges. Visit Website for application. Number of awards varies.

| | |
|---|---|
| **Amount of award:** | $300-$500 |
| **Number of awards:** | 486 |
| **Number of applicants:** | 565 |
| **Application deadline:** | February 15 |
| **Notification begins:** | April 1 |
| **Total amount awarded:** | $162,600 |

**Contact:**
Catholic United Financial Scholarship Program
3499 Lexington Avenue North
St. Paul, MN 55126
Phone: 651-490-0170
Web: www.catholicunited.org

# CCNMA:Latino Journalists of California

## CCNMA Scholarships

**Type of award:** Scholarship, renewable.
**Intended use:** For full-time undergraduate or graduate study at accredited postsecondary institution.
**Eligibility:** Applicant must be Mexican American, Hispanic American or Puerto Rican.
**Basis for selection:** Competition/talent/interest in writing/journalism. Major/career interest in journalism. Applicant must demonstrate financial need, high academic achievement, seriousness of purpose and service orientation.
**Application requirements:** Interview, recommendations, essay, transcript. Proof of full-time enrollment. Samples of work: newspaper clips, photographs, audio or television tapes.
**Additional information:** Must be a Latino resident of California attending school in or out of state, or nonresident attending school in California. Number of awards varies.

| | |
|---|---|
| **Amount of award:** | $500-$2,000 |
| **Number of applicants:** | 100 |
| **Application deadline:** | April 1 |
| **Notification begins:** | June 1 |
| **Total amount awarded:** | $8,000 |

**Contact:**
CCNMA:Latino Journalists of California
727 W. 27th Street
Room 201
Los Angeles, CA 90007-3212
Phone: 213-821-0075
Fax: 213-743-1838
Web: www.ccnma.org

# Center for Architecture

## Center for Architecture Design Scholarship

**Type of award:** Scholarship.
**Intended use:** For undergraduate or graduate study. Designated institutions: Schools in New York State.
**Basis for selection:** Major/career interest in architecture; design; engineering, civil; engineering, electrical/electronic; engineering, environmental; engineering, mechanical; landscape architecture or urban planning. Applicant must demonstrate financial need and high academic achievement.
**Application requirements:** Portfolio, recommendations, nomination by Dean of school. Cover page with full contact information, SASE required for return of work samples. Must apply both online and hard copy and can be hand-delivered.
**Additional information:** Single or multiple awards up to $5,000. Number of awards varies. Graduate students eligible if from a different undergraduate background.

| | |
|---|---|
| **Amount of award:** | $5,000 |
| **Number of applicants:** | 27 |
| **Application deadline:** | March 15 |
| **Notification begins:** | May 31 |
| **Total amount awarded:** | $2,000 |

**Contact:**
Center for Architecture Foundation
Attn: Design Scholarship
536 LaGuardia Place
New York, NY 10012
Phone: 212-358-6133
Web: www.cfafoundation.org/cfadesign

## Center for Architecture Design Scholarship

**Type of award:** Scholarship.
**Intended use:** For undergraduate study at accredited postsecondary institution in United States. Designated institutions: New York State institutions.
**Basis for selection:** Major/career interest in architecture; design or engineering. Applicant must demonstrate financial need and high academic achievement.
**Application requirements:** Recommendations by dean or chair of school attended. Portfolio.
**Additional information:** Number of awards varies. Applicant may also study related disciplines, including planning, architectural engineering, civil engineering, electrical engineering, environmental engineering, mechanical engineering, structural engineering, architectural design, environmental design, furniture design, industrial design, interior design, landscape design, sustainable design, and urban design. Graduate students eligible if undergraduate degree is in a field other than architecture.

| | |
|---|---|
| **Amount of award:** | $5,000 |
| **Application deadline:** | March 15 |

**Contact:**
Center for Architecture Foundation
536 LaGuardia Place
New York, NY 10012
Phone: 212-358-6133
Web: www.cfafoundation.org/cfadesign

## Eleanor Allwork Scholarship

**Type of award:** Scholarship.
**Intended use:** For undergraduate or graduate study at accredited postsecondary institution. Designated institutions: NAAB-accredited schools in the State of New York.
**Eligibility:** Applicant must be U.S. citizen, permanent resident or international student residing in New York.
**Basis for selection:** Major/career interest in architecture. Applicant must demonstrate financial need and high academic achievement.
**Application requirements:** Portfolio, recommendations, nomination by Dean of architecture school. Cover page with full contact information, SASE required for return of work samples. Must apply both online and hard copy and can be hand-delivered.
**Additional information:** Number of awards varies. Single or multiple awards up to $10,000. Graduate students eligible if from a different undergraduate background and currently completing their first architectural degree.

| | |
|---|---|
| **Amount of award:** | $10,000 |
| **Number of applicants:** | 30 |
| **Application deadline:** | March 15 |
| **Notification begins:** | May 31 |
| **Total amount awarded:** | $15,000 |

**Contact:**
Center for Architecture Foundation
Attn: Eleanor Allwork Scholarship
536 LaGuardia Place
New York, NY 10012
Phone: 212-358-6133
Web: www.cfafoundation.org/allwork

# Central Intelligence Agency

## CIA Undergraduate Scholarship Program

**Type of award:** Scholarship, renewable.
**Intended use:** For full-time freshman or sophomore study at accredited 4-year institution in United States.
**Eligibility:** Applicant must be at least 18, high school senior. Applicant must be U.S. citizen.
**Basis for selection:** Major/career interest in engineering; computer/information sciences; foreign languages; international relations; human resources or finance/banking. Applicant must demonstrate financial need, high academic achievement, depth of character, patriotism and seriousness of purpose.
**Application requirements:** Recommendations, transcript. SAT/ACT scores, resume, FAFSA or SAR.
**Additional information:** Applicant may have wide range of majors in addition to those listed. High school applicants must be 18 by April 1 of senior year. Minimum 3.0 GPA; 1500 SAT (1000 Math and Reading, 500 Writing), or 21 ACT required. Household income must not exceed $70,000 for family of four or $80,000 for family of five or more. Scholars work at CIA offices in Washington, D.C. metro area during summer breaks and receive annual salary in addition to up to $18,000 per school year for tuition, fees, books, and supplies. Must commit to employment with Agency after college graduation for period 1.5 times length of scholarship. Number of awards varies. Apply online. Deadline in October; check site for exact date.

| | |
|---|---|
| **Amount of award:** | $18,000 |
| **Application deadline:** | October 15 |

**Contact:**
Phone: 800-368-3886
Web: www.cia.gov

# C.G. Fuller Foundation c/o Bank of America

## C.G. Fuller Foundation Scholarship

**Type of award:** Scholarship, renewable.
**Intended use:** For full-time undergraduate study at 4-year institution. Designated institutions: Colleges and universities in South Carolina.
**Eligibility:** Applicant must be high school senior. Applicant must be residing in South Carolina.
**Basis for selection:** Applicant must demonstrate financial need, high academic achievement and leadership.
**Application requirements:** Transcript. Financial statement, recent photograph, copy of parents' most recent 1040 tax return, SAT or ACT scores.
**Additional information:** Contact Bank of America office for application; submit to financial aid office of college or university you plan to attend. Minimum 3.0 GPA and 1100 SAT or 24 ACT. Number of awards varies with changes in funding. Parents' adjusted gross income must be $60,000 or less. Award is $1,000 per semester, renewable for four years.

| | |
|---|---|
| **Amount of award:** | $1,000 |
| **Number of applicants:** | 50 |
| **Application deadline:** | March 15 |
| **Notification begins:** | August 1 |

**Contact:**
C.G. Fuller Foundation Scholarship c/o Bank of America
#SC3-240-04-17
P.O. Box 448
Columbia, SC 29202-0448

# ChairScholars Foundation, Inc.

## National ChairScholars Scholarship

**Type of award:** Scholarship, renewable.
**Intended use:** For full-time undergraduate study at postsecondary institution.
**Eligibility:** Applicant must be physically challenged. Applicant must be no older than 21. Applicant must be U.S. citizen or permanent resident.
**Basis for selection:** Applicant must demonstrate financial need and service orientation.
**Application requirements:** Recommendations, essay, transcript. Photograph, parent's IRS Form 1040 from last year, SAT and ACT scores.
**Additional information:** Applicant must have a serious physical disability but does not have to be confined to a wheelchair. Applicant must be unable to attend college without financial aid; no household income above $85,000. Applicant must have at least a B+ average. If applicant has obtained any other scholarships already, he or she must inform ChairScholars. Award is renewable up to four years, for maximum $20,000.

| | |
|---|---|
| **Amount of award:** | $1,000-$5,000 |
| **Number of awards:** | 15 |
| **Number of applicants:** | 85 |
| **Application deadline:** | February 15 |
| **Notification begins:** | March 27 |
| **Total amount awarded:** | $320,000 |

**Contact:**
ChairScholars Foundation, Inc.
16101 Carencia Lane
Odessa, FL 33556
Phone: 813-926-0544
Fax: 813-920-7661
Web: www.chairscholars.org

## New York Metropolitan Area Scholarship Program

**Type of award:** Scholarship, renewable.
**Eligibility:** Applicant must be physically challenged. Applicant must be high school senior.
**Basis for selection:** Applicant must demonstrate financial need.
**Application requirements:** Recommendations, essay, transcript. Recent photograph. Parent's or guardian's federal

income tax return. Physician's documentation of disability. Notification of receipt of other scholarships.
**Additional information:** College freshmen also eligible. Minimum "C" average. Available to physically disabled students in the New York Metropolitan area: five boroughs of New York City, part of Long Island, northern and central New Jersey. Visit Website for details and application.

| | |
|---|---|
| **Amount of award:** | $2,000-$5,000 |
| **Number of awards:** | 6 |
| **Number of applicants:** | 4 |
| **Application deadline:** | February 28 |
| **Total amount awarded:** | $32,000 |

**Contact:**
ChairScholars Foundation, Inc.
16101 Carencia Lane
Odessa, FL 33556
Phone: 813-926-0544
Fax: 813-920-7661
Web: www.chairscholars.org

# Charles & Lucille King Family Foundation, Inc.

## Charles & Lucille King Family Foundation Scholarships

**Type of award:** Scholarship, renewable.
**Intended use:** For full-time junior or senior study at accredited 4-year institution in United States.
**Basis for selection:** Major/career interest in communications or radio/television/film.
**Application requirements:** Recommendations, transcript. Personal statement. Application form with financial information.
**Additional information:** Download application from Website.

| | |
|---|---|
| **Amount of award:** | $3,500 |
| **Application deadline:** | March 15 |

**Contact:**
Charles & Lucille King Family Foundation, Inc.
1212 Avenue of the Americas
7th Floor
New York, NY 10036
Phone: 212-682-2913
Web: www.kingfoundation.org

# The Charles A. and Anne Morrow Lindbergh Foundation

## Lindbergh Grant

**Type of award:** Research grant.
**Intended use:** For undergraduate or non-degree study at postsecondary institution.
**Basis for selection:** Major/career interest in agriculture; aviation; biomedical; education; environmental science; health sciences or natural resources/conservation.
**Application requirements:** Research proposal.
**Additional information:** Applicant research or educational project should address balance between technological advancement and environmental preservation. Citizens of all countries are eligible. Deadline is second Thursday in June.

| | |
|---|---|
| **Amount of award:** | $1,000-$10,580 |
| **Number of awards:** | 10 |
| **Number of applicants:** | 200 |
| **Notification begins:** | April 15 |

**Contact:**
The Charles A. and Anne Morrow Lindbergh Foundation
2150 Third Avenue North
Suite 310
Anoka, MN 55303-2200
Phone: 763-576-1596
Fax: 763-576-1664
Web: www.lindberghfoundation.org

# Charleston Women in International Trade

## Charleston Women in International Trade Scholarship

**Type of award:** Scholarship.
**Intended use:** For undergraduate study at accredited postsecondary institution in United States.
**Eligibility:** Applicant must be U.S. citizen residing in South Carolina.
**Basis for selection:** Applicant must demonstrate financial need and seriousness of purpose.
**Application requirements:** Recommendations, transcript, proof of eligibility. Two-page (minimum length), double-spaced essay explaining the importance of international trade and state your goals for working in the international business environment. Must also explain why you believe you should be awarded this scholarship. Listing of courses/work experience relevant to interest in international trade; extracurricular activities, civic and community involvement. List of relevant courses/work experience. Financial aid/tuition information.
**Additional information:** Applicant must be pursuing degree specific to international trade or related course of study. To apply, complete application on Website.

| | |
|---|---|
| **Amount of award:** | $3,000 |
| **Number of awards:** | 2 |
| **Application deadline:** | February 28 |
| **Notification begins:** | January 1 |
| **Total amount awarded:** | $6,000 |

**Contact:**
Pam Everitt, CWIT Awards Chairperson
P.O. Box 31258
Charleston, SC 29417
Phone: 843-577-8678
Web: www.cwitsc.org

# Chicago Scholars Foundation

## Chicago Scholars Program

**Type of award:** Scholarship, renewable.
**Intended use:** For freshman study at postsecondary institution.

**Eligibility:** Applicant must be high school junior. Applicant must be residing in Illinois.
**Basis for selection:** Applicant must demonstrate financial need, high academic achievement and service orientation.
**Application requirements:** Recommendations, essay, transcript.
**Additional information:** Applicant must live or go to high school within Chicago city limits. Award provides five years' support, including a year of college prep, a $5,000 merit scholarship, summer programming, and internship opportunities. Visit Website for more information.

| | |
|---|---|
| **Amount of award:** | $1,250 |
| **Number of awards:** | 50 |
| **Number of applicants:** | 131 |
| **Application deadline:** | February 28 |
| **Notification begins:** | May 1 |
| **Total amount awarded:** | $224,283 |

**Contact:**
Chicago Scholars Foundation
55 E. Jackson Boulevard
Suite 1010
Chicago, IL 60604
Phone: 312-784-3300
Fax: 312-784-3301
Web: www.chicagoscholars.org

# Choctaw Nation of Oklahoma

## Choctaw Nation Higher Education Program

**Type of award:** Scholarship, renewable.
**Intended use:** For undergraduate or graduate study at accredited 2-year, 4-year or graduate institution in United States.
**Eligibility:** Applicant must be American Indian. Must be enrolled member of Choctaw Tribe and have Certificate of Degree of Indian Blood (CDIB) and tribal membership card.
**Application requirements:** Transcript. Proof of Choctaw descent. FAFSA. School enrollment verification via submission of class schedule.
**Additional information:** Program made up of two awards: a grant or a scholarship. The $1,600 grant is based on financial need. The $2,000 scholarship is for applicants with minimum 2.5 GPA. Grant will assist with any unmet need up to award amount. Must reapply for renewal. Number of awards varies. May only receive either grant or scholarship.

| | |
|---|---|
| **Amount of award:** | $1,600-$2,000 |
| **Number of applicants:** | 5,000 |
| **Application deadline:** | October 1, March 1 |
| **Notification begins:** | July 15 |

**Contact:**
Choctaw Nation of Oklahoma
Higher Education Department
P.O. Box 1210
Durant, OK 74702-1210
Phone: 800-522-6170
Fax: 580-924-1267
Web: www.choctawnation.com

# Christian Record Services

## Christian Record Services Scholarship

**Type of award:** Scholarship, renewable.
**Intended use:** For full-time undergraduate study at postsecondary institution in United States.
**Eligibility:** Applicant must be visually impaired.
**Basis for selection:** Applicant must demonstrate financial need and high academic achievement.
**Application requirements:** Recommendations. Photo and bio.
**Additional information:** Applicants must be totally or legally blind. Awardees must reapply yearly.

| | |
|---|---|
| **Amount of award:** | $500 |
| **Number of awards:** | 10 |
| **Application deadline:** | April 1 |
| **Notification begins:** | May 15 |
| **Total amount awarded:** | $5,000 |

**Contact:**
Christian Record Services
4444 South 52 Street
Lincoln, NE 68516
Phone: 402-488-0981
Fax: 402-488-7582
Web: www.christianrecord.org

# City University of New York

## Peter F. Vallone Academic Scholarship

**Type of award:** Scholarship, renewable.
**Intended use:** For full-time undergraduate study. Designated institutions: CUNY branches.
**Eligibility:** Applicant must be residing in New York.
**Application requirements:** FAFSA.
**Additional information:** Students are considered as part of the admissions process; no separate application. Applicants must have a B average or better and have successfully completed at least 12 College Preparatory Initiative (Regents level) year-long courses. Must graduate from New York City high school. Award amount varies yearly.

| | |
|---|---|
| **Amount of award:** | $500 |
| **Number of awards:** | 7,500 |
| **Number of applicants:** | 13,000 |
| **Notification begins:** | August 1 |
| **Total amount awarded:** | $7,500,000 |

**Contact:**
City University of New York Office of Financial Aid
1114 Avenue of the Americas, FL15
New York, NY 10036
Phone: 212-290-5600
Web: www.cuny.edu/financialaid

# The Coca-Cola Foundation

## Coca-Cola All-State Community Colleges Academic Team Scholarship

**Type of award:** Scholarship.
**Intended use:** For undergraduate study at 2-year institution in United States. Designated institutions: Community colleges.
**Eligibility:** Applicant must be U.S. citizen or permanent resident.
**Basis for selection:** Applicant must demonstrate high academic achievement, depth of character and service orientation.
**Application requirements:** Nomination by college at which student is enrolled or is planning to enroll.
**Additional information:** Applicant/nominee must have done community service within past 12 months. Minimum 3.5 GPA for all coursework completed in last five years. Minimum 30 credit hours at community college in past five years. Must be planning to enroll in at least two courses during next term. Children and grandchildren of Coca-Cola employees not eligible. Program administered by Phi Theta Kappa Honor Society. Award notification begins in March. Visit Website for college credit requirements and nomination information.

| | |
|---|---|
| **Amount of award:** | $1,000-$2,000 |
| **Number of awards:** | 350 |
| **Number of applicants:** | 1,600 |
| **Total amount awarded:** | $500,000 |

**Contact:**
Scholarship Programs Department
Phi Theta Kappa Honor Society
1625 Eastover Drive
Jackson, MS 39211
Phone: 601-987-5741
Web: www.coca-colascholars.org or www.ptk.org/schol/aaat/announce.htm

## Coca-Cola Scholars Program

**Type of award:** Scholarship, renewable.
**Intended use:** For full-time undergraduate study at accredited 4-year institution in United States.
**Eligibility:** Applicant must be high school senior. Applicant must be U.S. citizen or permanent resident.
**Basis for selection:** Applicant must demonstrate high academic achievement, depth of character, leadership, seriousness of purpose and service orientation.
**Additional information:** Applicant may also be temporary resident in legalization program, refugee, asylee, Cuban/Haitian entrant, or Humanitarian Parole. Must be attending high school in United States or territories. Minimum 3.0 GPA required at the end of junior year high school. Award is for four years, $2,500 or $5,000 per year. Notification begins December 1 for semifinalists; mid-February for finalists. Children and grandchildren of Coca-Cola employees not eligible.

| | |
|---|---|
| **Amount of award:** | $10,000-$20,000 |
| **Number of awards:** | 250 |
| **Number of applicants:** | 75,000 |
| **Application deadline:** | October 31 |
| **Notification begins:** | December 7 |
| **Total amount awarded:** | $3,000,000 |

**Contact:**
Coca-Cola Scholars Foundation
Phone: 800-306-2653
Web: www.coca-colascholars.org

# The College Board

## Young Epidemiology Scholars Student Competition

**Type of award:** Scholarship.
**Intended use:** For undergraduate study at 4-year institution in United States.
**Eligibility:** Applicant must be high school junior or senior. Applicant must be U.S. citizen or permanent resident.
**Basis for selection:** Major/career interest in epidemiology; sociology; health sciences or mathematics.
**Application requirements:** An individual research project that applies epidemiological principles to health-related area.
**Additional information:** See Website for online registration and more information.

| | |
|---|---|
| **Amount of award:** | $1,000-$50,000 |
| **Number of awards:** | 120 |
| **Number of applicants:** | 639 |
| **Application deadline:** | February 1 |
| **Notification begins:** | March 31 |
| **Total amount awarded:** | $457,000 |

**Contact:**
The College Board
YES Program
11955 Democracy Drive
Reston, VA 20190
Phone: 877-358-6777
Fax: 703-935-7727
Web: www.collegeboard.com/yes

# Colorado Commission on Higher Education

## Colorado Student Grant

**Type of award:** Scholarship.
**Intended use:** For undergraduate study at postsecondary institution. Designated institutions: Eligible Colorado institutions.
**Eligibility:** Applicant must be residing in Colorado.
**Basis for selection:** Applicant must demonstrate financial need.
**Application requirements:** FAFSA.
**Additional information:** Contact college financial aid office or visit Website for additional information. International students must be working toward becoming permanent resident of U.S.

| | |
|---|---|
| **Amount of award:** | $850-$5,000 |
| **Total amount awarded:** | $68,237,460 |

**Contact:**
Colorado Commission on Higher Education
1560 Broadway
Suite 1600
Denver, CO 80202
Phone: 303-866-2723
Web: highered.colorado.gov

### Colorado Work-Study Program

**Type of award:** Scholarship.
**Intended use:** For undergraduate study at postsecondary institution. Designated institutions: Eligible post-secondary institutions in Colorado.
**Eligibility:** Applicant must be residing in Colorado.
**Additional information:** Part-time employment program for students who need work experience or who can prove financial need. International students must be working toward becoming permanent resident of U.S. Amount of award cannot exceed need. Institutions must award 70% of work-study allocations to students with documented need; remaining 30% may be awarded to students without need. Contact college financial aid office or visit Website for additional information.

| | |
|---|---|
| **Total amount awarded:** | $18,061,358 |

**Contact:**
Colorado Commission on Higher Education
1560 Broadway
Suite 1600
Denver, CO 80202
Phone: 303-866-2723
Web: highered.colorado.gov

## Colorado Masons Benevolent Fund Association

### Colorado Masons Scholarship

**Type of award:** Scholarship, renewable.
**Intended use:** For full-time undergraduate study at accredited vocational, 2-year or 4-year institution. Designated institutions: Institutions of higher learning in Colorado.
**Eligibility:** Applicant must be high school senior. Applicant must be residing in Colorado.
**Basis for selection:** Applicant must demonstrate financial need, high academic achievement and depth of character.
**Additional information:** Applicant must be graduating senior at public high school in Colorado and attending an institution of higher learning in Colorado. Scholarship is renewable for up to four years. Number of awards varies. Visit Website for application and details.

| | |
|---|---|
| **Amount of award:** | $7,000 |
| **Number of applicants:** | 456 |
| **Application deadline:** | March 1 |
| **Total amount awarded:** | $279,000 |

**Contact:**
Tom J. Cox, PGM Scholarship Administrator
2445 So. Quebec St.
Denver, CO 80231
Phone: 303-290-8544
Web: www.cmbfa.org

## Colorado Society of CPAs Educational Foundation

### General Scholarship

**Type of award:** Scholarship, renewable.
**Intended use:** For junior, senior or graduate study at accredited 4-year or graduate institution in United States. Designated institutions: Colorado colleges/universities with accredited accounting programs.
**Eligibility:** Applicant must be residing in Colorado.
**Basis for selection:** Major/career interest in accounting. Applicant must demonstrate high academic achievement.
**Application requirements:** Essay, transcript.
**Additional information:** Must have completed six semester hours in accounting. Must be at least half-time student. Minimum 3.0 GPA. International students must have work visa. Visit Website for application and deadline.

| | |
|---|---|
| **Amount of award:** | $2,500 |

**Contact:**
CSCPA
7979 East Tufts Avenue
Suite 1000
Denver, CO 80237-2847
Phone: 800-523-9082 or 303-773-2877
Web: www.cocpa.org/student-center/scholarships.html

### Mark J. Smith Scholarship

**Type of award:** Scholarship.
**Intended use:** For junior, senior or graduate study at accredited 4-year or graduate institution in United States. Designated institutions: Colorado colleges and universities with accredited accounting programs.
**Eligibility:** Applicant must be residing in Colorado.
**Basis for selection:** Major/career interest in accounting. Applicant must demonstrate financial need and high academic achievement.
**Application requirements:** Essay, transcript.
**Additional information:** Must be student from single-parent household. Must have completed six semester hours in accounting. Must be at least half-time student. Minimum 3.0 GPA. International students must have work visa. Visit Website for application and deadline.

| | |
|---|---|
| **Amount of award:** | $2,500 |
| **Number of awards:** | 1 |

**Contact:**
CSCPA
7979 East Tufts Avenue
Suite 1000
Denver, CO 80237-2847
Phone: 800-523-9082 or 303-773-2877
Web: www.cocpa.org/student-center/scholarships.html

## Columbus Citizens Foundation

### College Scholarship Program

**Type of award:** Scholarship, renewable.
**Intended use:** For full-time undergraduate study at accredited 4-year institution in United States or Canada.
**Eligibility:** Applicant must be high school senior. Applicant must be Italian. Applicant must be residing in Vermont, New York, Maine, Delaware, Maryland, Pennsylvania, Massachusetts, District of Columbia, Connecticut, New Hampshire, New Jersey or Rhode Island.
**Basis for selection:** Applicant must demonstrate financial need, high academic achievement and service orientation.
**Application requirements:** $25 application fee. Interview, recommendations, essay, transcript. Parent/guardian's most recent state and federal income tax returns, family tree.

**Additional information:** Applicant must be Italian American. Minimum 3.25 GPA. Family's taxable income must not exceed $25,000 per household dependent. Applicants who reach semifinalist round must travel to New York City for interview at own expense. Applications available on Website in first week of December each year; deadline is in February. Number and amount of awards varies. Special attention given to students pursuing a degree in culinary arts or engineering. Special attention given to students attending Bowling Green State University, Fordham University, Hobart and William Smith College, Iona College, Long Island University at C.W. Post, Marist College, New York Institute of Technology School of Architecture, Rhode Island School of Design, Villanova University, Wagner College.

**Application deadline:** February 13
**Notification begins:** May 1

**Contact:**
Columbus Citizens Foundation College Scholarship Program
8 East 69th Street
New York, NY 10021-4906
Phone: 212-249-9923
Fax: 212-517-7619
Web: www.columbuscitizensfd.org

# Congressional Black Caucus Foundation, Inc.

## The CBC Spouses Cheerios Brand Health Initiative Scholarship

**Type of award:** Scholarship, renewable.
**Intended use:** For full-time undergraduate study at accredited 4-year institution.
**Eligibility:** Applicant must be U.S. citizen or permanent resident.
**Basis for selection:** Major/career interest in engineering; health-related professions; medicine or technology. Applicant must demonstrate financial need and service orientation.
**Application requirements:** Recommendations, essay, transcript, proof of eligibility. Resume, recent photo, copy of Student Aid Report (SAR).
**Additional information:** Minimum 2.5 GPA. Award amount set annually. Visit Website for application and details.

**Application deadline:** June 1

**Contact:**
Congressional Black Caucus Foundation
1720 Massachusetts Avenue, NW
Washington, DC 20036
Phone: 202-263-2800
Fax: 202-775-0773
Web: www.cbcfinc.org

## The CBC Spouses Education Scholarship

**Type of award:** Scholarship, renewable.
**Intended use:** For full-time undergraduate or graduate study at accredited 4-year or graduate institution in United States.
**Eligibility:** Applicant must be U.S. citizen or permanent resident.
**Basis for selection:** Applicant must demonstrate financial need and service orientation.
**Application requirements:** Recommendations, essay, transcript. Resume, recent photo, copy of Student Aid Report (SAR).
**Additional information:** Minimum 2.5 GPA. Award amount varies. Selection made at district level. Visit Website for application and details.

**Application deadline:** June 1

**Contact:**
Congressional Black Caucus Foundation
1720 Massachusetts Avenue, NW
Washington, DC 20036
Phone: 202-263-2800
Fax: 202-775-0773
Web: www.cbcfinc.org

## The CBC Spouses Performing Arts Scholarship Program

**Type of award:** Scholarship, renewable.
**Intended use:** For full-time undergraduate study at accredited 4-year institution.
**Basis for selection:** Major/career interest in performing arts. Applicant must demonstrate financial need and service orientation.
**Application requirements:** Recommendations, essay, transcript, proof of eligibility. Resume, recent photograph, copy of Student Aid Report (SAR), two-minute performance sample.
**Additional information:** Minimum 2.5 GPA. Check Website for application and details.

**Amount of award:** $3,000
**Application deadline:** April 27

**Contact:**
Congressional Black Caucus Foundation
1720 Massachusetts Avenue, NW
Washington, DC 20036
Phone: 202-263-2800
Fax: 202-775-0773
Web: www.cbcfinc.org

## The CBC Spouses Visual Arts Scholarship

**Type of award:** Scholarship.
**Intended use:** For undergraduate study at 4-year institution in United States.
**Basis for selection:** Major/career interest in arts, general. Applicant must demonstrate financial need and service orientation.
**Application requirements:** Recommendations, essay, transcript. Recent photo of applicant, resume, copy of Student Aid Report (SAR), up to five artwork samples. High school seniors must submit college acceptance letter.
**Additional information:** Minimum 2.5 GPA. Check Website for application and details.

**Amount of award:** $3,000
**Application deadline:** April 27

**Contact:**
Congressional Black Caucus Foundation
1720 Massachusetts Avenue, NW
Washington, DC 20036
Phone: 202-263-2800
Fax: 202-775-0773
Web: www.cbcfinc.org

### Environmental Studies Scholarship

**Type of award:** Scholarship.
**Intended use:** For full-time junior study at accredited 4-year institution.
**Eligibility:** Applicant must be U.S. citizen or permanent resident.
**Basis for selection:** Major/career interest in environmental science.
**Application requirements:** Recommendations, essay. Resume, photograph. Student Aid Report.
**Additional information:** Minimum 2.5 GPA. Awarded to minority and female college students pursuing a degree in environmental science or other related fields, and intending to seek work in an underserved community.

| | |
|---|---|
| **Amount of award:** | $10,000 |
| **Number of awards:** | 2 |
| **Number of applicants:** | 30 |
| **Application deadline:** | March 15 |
| **Total amount awarded:** | $20,000 |

**Contact:**
Congressional Black Caucus Foundation, Inc.
1720 Massachusetts Avenue, NW
Washington, DC 20036
Phone: 202-263-2800
Fax: 202-775-0773
Web: www.cbcfinc.org/scholarships

### Louis Stokes Health Scholars

**Type of award:** Scholarship.
**Intended use:** For full-time undergraduate study at vocational, 2-year or 4-year institution.
**Eligibility:** Applicant must be U.S. citizen or permanent resident.
**Basis for selection:** Major/career interest in health-related professions. Applicant must demonstrate financial need and high academic achievement.
**Application requirements:** Recommendations, essay. Resume, photograph. Student Aid Report.
**Additional information:** High school seniors also eligible to apply. Minimum 3.0 GPA. For students entering the health workforce. Preference given to students demonstrating an interest in underserved communities. Students currently attending two-year institutions strongly encouraged to apply.

| | |
|---|---|
| **Amount of award:** | $5,000-$8,000 |
| **Number of awards:** | 10 |
| **Number of applicants:** | 130 |
| **Application deadline:** | March 15 |
| **Total amount awarded:** | $90,000 |

**Contact:**
Congressional Black Caucus Foundation, Inc.
1720 Massachusetts Avenue, NW
Washington, DC 20036
Phone: 202-263-2800
Fax: 202-775-0773
Web: www.cbcfinc.org/scholarships

## Congressional Hispanic Caucus Institute

### Congressional Hispanic Caucus Institute Scholarship Awards

**Type of award:** Scholarship.
**Intended use:** For full-time undergraduate or graduate study at 2-year, 4-year or graduate institution.
**Eligibility:** Applicant must be U.S. citizen or permanent resident.
**Basis for selection:** Applicant must demonstrate financial need, leadership and service orientation.
**Application requirements:** Recommendations, essay. One-page resume, SAR.
**Additional information:** Community college students receive $1,000; students enrolled at four-year colleges or universities receive $2,500; students enrolled in graduate programs receive $5,000. Apply online.

| | |
|---|---|
| **Amount of award:** | $1,000-$5,000 |
| **Number of awards:** | 150 |
| **Application deadline:** | April 16 |

**Contact:**
Congressional Hispanic Caucus Institute
911 2nd Street NE
Washington, DC 20002
Phone: 202-543-1771
Fax: 202-546-2143
Web: www.chci.org/scholarships

## Connecticut Building Congress, Inc.

### CBC Scholarship

**Type of award:** Scholarship, renewable.
**Intended use:** For undergraduate or master's study at 4-year institution in United States.
**Eligibility:** Applicant must be high school senior. Applicant must be residing in Connecticut.
**Basis for selection:** Major/career interest in engineering, construction; architecture; construction management; surveying/mapping or construction. Applicant must demonstrate financial need and high academic achievement.
**Application requirements:** Essay, transcript. Student Aid Report or FAFSA.
**Additional information:** Must be involved in extracurricular activities and exhibit potential. Applicant may attend school outside of Connecticut. Number of awards and amount at discretion of Board of Directors. Renewable based on academic performance and available funds.

| | |
|---|---|
| **Amount of award:** | $500-$2,000 |
| **Number of awards:** | 3 |
| **Number of applicants:** | 60 |
| **Application deadline:** | March 31 |
| **Notification begins:** | May 1 |
| **Total amount awarded:** | $2,500 |

**Contact:**
Connecticut Building Congress
c/o DiBlasi Associates
500 Purdy Hill Road Suite 101
Monroe, CT 06468
Web: www.cbc-ct.org/pages/scholarship.htm

# Connecticut Department of Higher Education

## Connecticut Aid for Public College Students

**Type of award:** Scholarship, renewable.
**Intended use:** For undergraduate study at 2-year or 4-year institution. Designated institutions: Connecticut public colleges and universities.
**Eligibility:** Applicant must be U.S. citizen residing in Connecticut.
**Basis for selection:** Applicant must demonstrate financial need.
**Application requirements:** FAFSA.
**Additional information:** Awards up to amount of unmet financial need, determined by the college. Deadline based on financial aid deadline. Apply at financial aid office at Connecticut public college.

| | |
|---|---|
| **Number of awards:** | 16,674 |
| **Total amount awarded:** | $30,208,469 |

**Contact:**
Contact school's financial aid office, or:
Connecticut Department of Higher Education
61 Woodland Street
Hartford, CT 06105-2391
Phone: 800-842-0229
Fax: 860-947-1311
Web: www.ctdhe.org

## Connecticut Aid to Dependents of Deceased/POW/MIA Veterans

**Type of award:** Scholarship.
**Intended use:** For undergraduate or graduate study. Designated institutions: Connecticut public colleges and universities.
**Eligibility:** Applicant must be U.S. citizen residing in Connecticut. Applicant must be dependent of deceased veteran or POW/MIA; or spouse of deceased veteran or POW/MIA. Death must be service-related. Parent/spouse must have been Connecticut resident prior to enlistment.
**Application requirements:** Proof of eligibility.
**Additional information:** Visit Website for more information.

| | |
|---|---|
| **Amount of award:** | Full tuition |
| **Number of awards:** | 5 |

**Contact:**
Contact financial aid office of Connecticut public college, or:
Connecticut Department of Higher Education
61 Woodland Street
Hartford, CT 06105-2391
Phone: 800-842-0229
Fax: 860-947-1310
Web: www.ctdhe.org

## Connecticut Capitol Scholarship Program

**Type of award:** Scholarship, renewable.
**Intended use:** For undergraduate study at 2-year or 4-year institution. Designated institutions: Connecticut colleges and universities; eligible institutions in Maine, Massachusetts, New Hampshire, Pennsylvania, Rhode Island, Vermont, and Washington, D.C.
**Eligibility:** Applicant must be high school senior. Applicant must be U.S. citizen or permanent resident residing in Connecticut.
**Basis for selection:** Applicant must demonstrate financial need and high academic achievement.
**Application requirements:** FAFSA.
**Additional information:** Must rank in top 20 percent of class, or have minimum 1800 SAT score or minimum 27 ACT score. May be used at institutions in Connecticut or at institutions in states with reciprocity agreements with Connecticut.

| | |
|---|---|
| **Amount of award:** | $500-$3,000 |
| **Number of awards:** | 5,500 |
| **Number of applicants:** | 4,969 |
| **Application deadline:** | February 15 |
| **Total amount awarded:** | $9,465,259 |

**Contact:**
High school guidance office for application, or:
Connecticut Department of Higher Education
61 Woodlawn St.
Hartford, CT 06105-2391
Phone: 800-842-0229
Fax: 860-947-1311
Web: www.ctdhe.org

## Connecticut Independent College Student Grant

**Type of award:** Scholarship, renewable.
**Intended use:** For undergraduate study in United States. Designated institutions: Private institutions in Connecticut.
**Eligibility:** Applicant must be U.S. citizen residing in Connecticut.
**Basis for selection:** Applicant must demonstrate financial need.
**Application requirements:** FAFSA and any other financial aid forms required by the college.
**Additional information:** Award based on financial need. Deadline determined by financial aid deadline at each college.

| | |
|---|---|
| **Amount of award:** | $8,341 |
| **Number of awards:** | 6,121 |
| **Total amount awarded:** | $23,441,546 |

**Contact:**
Contact school's financial office, or:
Connecticut Department of Higher Education
61 Woodland Street
Hartford, CT 06105-2391
Phone: 800-842-0229
Fax: 860-947-1311
Web: www.ctdhe.org

## Connecticut Minority Teacher Incentive Grant

**Type of award:** Scholarship.
**Intended use:** For full-time junior or senior study. Designated institutions: Eligible Connecticut colleges and universities.
**Eligibility:** Applicant must be Alaskan native, Asian American, African American, Mexican American, Hispanic American, Puerto Rican, American Indian or Native Hawaiian/Pacific Islander. Applicant must be residing in Connecticut.
**Basis for selection:** Major/career interest in education; education, special or education, teacher.
**Application requirements:** Nomination by college or university's Education Dean, or other appropriate official.
**Additional information:** Must be enrolled in Connecticut college or university teacher preparation program. Grants up to $5,000/year for two years; loan reimbursement of $2,500/year

for up to four years of teaching in Connecticut public school. Visit Website for more information.

**Amount of award:** $2,500-$5,000
**Number of awards:** 82
**Number of applicants:** 30
**Application deadline:** October 1
**Total amount awarded:** $276,000

**Contact:**
Minority Teaching Incentive Grant/Weisman Scholarship Program
Connecticut Department of Higher Education
61 Woodland Street
Hartford, CT 06105-2326
Phone: 860-947-1857
Fax: 860-947-1838
Web: www.ctdhe.org

## Connecticut Robert C. Byrd Honors Scholarship

**Type of award:** Scholarship, renewable.
**Intended use:** For full-time undergraduate study.
**Eligibility:** Applicant must be high school senior. Applicant must be U.S. citizen or permanent resident residing in Connecticut.
**Basis for selection:** Applicant must demonstrate high academic achievement.
**Additional information:** Applicant must rank in top two percent of high school graduating class; have minimum 2100 SAT score, or minimum 32 ACT score. File applications through high school guidance office.

**Amount of award:** $1,500
**Number of awards:** 322
**Number of applicants:** 1,051
**Application deadline:** April 1
**Total amount awarded:** $455,812

**Contact:**
Connecticut Department of Higher Education
61 Woodland Street
Hartford, CT 06105-2391
Phone: 800-842-0229
Fax: 860-947-1838
Web: www.ctdhe.org

## Connecticut Tuition Waiver for Senior Citizens

**Type of award:** Scholarship.
**Intended use:** For undergraduate study at 2-year or 4-year institution. Designated institutions: Connecticut public colleges and universities.
**Eligibility:** Applicant must be returning adult student. Applicant must be U.S. citizen residing in Connecticut.
**Application requirements:** Proof of eligibility.
**Additional information:** Waivers approved on space available basis. Apply through financial aid office of institution.

**Amount of award:** Full tuition
**Number of awards:** 1,621
**Total amount awarded:** $779,199

**Contact:**
Financial aid office of Connecticut public colleges, or:
Connecticut Department of Higher Education
61 Woodland St.
Hartford, CT 06105-2391
Phone: 800-842-0229
Fax: 860-947-1310
Web: www.ctdhe.org

## Connecticut Tuition Waiver for Veterans

**Type of award:** Scholarship, renewable.
**Intended use:** For undergraduate or graduate study. Designated institutions: Connecticut public colleges and universities.
**Eligibility:** Applicant must be U.S. citizen residing in Connecticut. Applicant must be veteran. Must have been Connecticut resident at time of enlistment. Active members of Connecticut Army or Air National Guard also eligible.
**Application requirements:** Proof of eligibility.
**Additional information:** Visit Website for more information.

**Amount of award:** Full tuition
**Number of awards:** 3,232
**Total amount awarded:** $5,026,345

**Contact:**
Financial aid office of Connecticut public colleges, or:
Connecticut Department of Higher Education
61 Woodland St.
Hartford, CT 06105-2326
Phone: 800-842-0229
Fax: 860-947-1310
Web: www.ctdhe.org

## Connecticut Tuition Waiver for Vietnam MIA/POW Dependents

**Type of award:** Scholarship.
**Intended use:** For undergraduate study. Designated institutions: Connecticut public colleges and universities.
**Eligibility:** Applicant must be U.S. citizen residing in Connecticut. Applicant must be dependent of POW/MIA; or spouse of POW/MIA. Open to spouse or dependent of veteran who is POW/MIA after 1/1/60.
**Application requirements:** Proof of eligibility.
**Additional information:** Apply at financial aid office of institution. Awarded through Connecticut public colleges. Visit Website for more information.

**Amount of award:** Full tuition

**Contact:**
Financial aid office at Connecticut public college, or:
Connecticut Department of Higher Education
61 Woodland St.
Hartford, CT 06105-2326
Phone: 800-842-0229
Fax: 860-947-1310
Web: www.ctdhe.org

## Weisman Scholarship

**Type of award:** Scholarship, renewable.
**Intended use:** For full-time junior or senior study. Designated institutions: Eligible Connecticut colleges and universities.
**Eligibility:** Applicant must be Alaskan native, Asian American, African American, Mexican American, Hispanic American, Puerto Rican, American Indian or Native Hawaiian/Pacific Islander. Applicant must be residing in Connecticut.
**Basis for selection:** Major/career interest in education or education, teacher.
**Application requirements:** Nomination by college or university's Education Dean, or appropriate official.
**Additional information:** Must be enrolled in Connecticut teacher preparation program and intend to teach math or science in middle or high school. Loan reimbursement up to $2,500 per year for up to four years of teaching science or math in Connecticut public middle or high school. Visit Website for more information.

**Amount of award:** $2,500-$5,000
**Number of awards:** 8
**Number of applicants:** 30
**Application deadline:** October 1
**Total amount awarded:** $25,000

**Contact:**
Connecticut Department of Higher Education
61 Woodland Street
Hartford, CT 06105-2326
Phone: 800-842-0229
Fax: 860-947-1838
Web: www.ctdhe.org

# Consortium of Information and Telecommunication Executives

## CITE Scholarship

**Type of award:** Scholarship.
**Intended use:** For full-time undergraduate study at accredited 4-year institution in United States.
**Eligibility:** Applicant must be African American. Applicant must be high school senior. Applicant must be U.S. citizen.
**Basis for selection:** Major/career interest in accounting; advertising; business; communications; computer/information sciences; engineering, electrical/electronic; engineering, industrial; finance/banking; marketing or mathematics. Applicant must demonstrate financial need and high academic achievement.
**Application requirements:** Recommendations, essay, transcript. College acceptance letter, proof of parents' income.
**Additional information:** Minimum 3.0 GPA. Applicant must reside in area where there is a CITE chapter. Family income must be $75,000 or less. Recipient must attend a scholarship event to accept award. Deadline in spring; see Website for date and details.

**Amount of award:** $3,000
**Number of awards:** 1
**Total amount awarded:** $3,000

**Contact:**
Web: www.forcite.org

# Costume Society of America

## Adele Filene Student Travel Award

**Type of award:** Scholarship.
**Intended use:** For undergraduate or graduate study in United States.
**Eligibility:** Applicant must be U.S. citizen or international student.
**Basis for selection:** Major/career interest in ethnic/cultural studies; art/art history; arts, general; history or fashion/fashion design/modeling.
**Application requirements:** One faculty recommendation, budget. Must submit additional essay.
**Additional information:** Award only for those who have paper or research poster accepted for presentation at the national meeting. Award is for travel expenses to the meeting. Must be student member of Costume Society of America. Major/career interests may include apparel design, historic costume, and fashion merchandising. Number of awards varies.

**Amount of award:** $500
**Application deadline:** March 1

**Contact:**
Costume Society of America
Attn: Chair Christina Bates
Fax: 819-776-8300
Web: www.costumesocietyamerica.com/GrantsAwards/adelefilene.html

## Stella Blum Student Research Grant

**Type of award:** Research grant.
**Intended use:** For undergraduate or graduate study at vocational, 2-year, 4-year or graduate institution in United States.
**Eligibility:** Applicant must be U.S. citizen, permanent resident or international student.
**Basis for selection:** Major/career interest in art/art history; arts, general; history; museum studies or performing arts.
**Application requirements:** Recommendations, transcript. References and written proposal researching North American costumes. The proposal should be typed, double-spaced, no more than 1,000 words. Must also submit a brief abstract, no more than 50 words. Must provide seven copies of all documents.
**Additional information:** Must be member of Costume Society of America researching a North American costume topic as part of degree requirement. Award is $2,000 for research and $500 for expenses to present at national meeting.

**Amount of award:** $2,500
**Number of awards:** 1
**Application deadline:** May 1
**Notification begins:** August 1
**Total amount awarded:** $2,500

**Contact:**
Costume Society of America
Attn: Chair Ann Wass
5903 60th Ave
Riverdale, MD 20737
Phone: 800-CSA-9447 or 908-359-1471
Fax: 908-450-1118
Web: www.costumesocietyamerica.com/GrantsAwards/stellablum.html

# Council on International Educational Exchange

## CIEE International Study Programs (CIEE-ISP) Scholarships

**Type of award:** Scholarship.
**Intended use:** For full-time undergraduate study at accredited 4-year institution. Designated institutions: CIEE Member or CIEE Academic Consortium Member institutions.
**Basis for selection:** Competition/talent/interest in study abroad. Applicant must demonstrate financial need and high academic achievement.
**Application requirements:** Essay, transcript.
**Additional information:** Available to CIEE Study Center program applicants only. Program application is used in

consideration of scholarship applicants. Visit Website for details and application.

**Amount of award:** $1,000-$2,000
**Application deadline:** April 1, November 1
**Notification begins:** May 1, December 1

**Contact:**
CIEE
Attn: Scholarship Committee
300 Fore Street
Portland, ME 04101
Phone: 800-40-STUDY
Fax: 207-221-4299
Web: www.ciee.org/study/scholarships.aspx

## Jennifer Ritzmann Scholarship for Studies in Tropical Biology

**Type of award:** Scholarship.
**Intended use:** For full-time undergraduate study at accredited 4-year institution. Designated institutions: CIEE Study Center program in Monteverde, Costa Rica.
**Basis for selection:** Major/career interest in biology. Applicant must demonstrate financial need and high academic achievement.
**Application requirements:** Essay, transcript.
**Additional information:** Award is for students applying to the Monteverde, Costa Rica semester program only. Visit Website for more information.

**Amount of award:** $1,000
**Number of awards:** 2
**Application deadline:** April 1, November 1
**Notification begins:** May 1, December 1

**Contact:**
CIEE
Attn: Scholarship Committee
300 Fore Street
Portland, ME 04101
Phone: 800-40-STUDY
Fax: 207-221-4299
Web: www.ciee.org/study/scholarships.aspx

## John E. Bowman Travel Grants

**Type of award:** Scholarship.
**Intended use:** For full-time undergraduate study at accredited 4-year institution. Designated institutions: CIEE Member or CIEE Academic Consortium member institutions.
**Basis for selection:** Competition/talent/interest in study abroad. Applicant must demonstrate financial need and high academic achievement.
**Application requirements:** Essay, transcript.
**Additional information:** Applicant must participate in CIEE study abroad program in Africa, Asia, Eastern Europe, or Latin America. Visit Website for details and application.

**Amount of award:** $1,000
**Application deadline:** April 1, November 1
**Notification begins:** May 1, December 1

**Contact:**
CIEE Attn: Scholarship Committee
Attn: Scholarship Committee
300 Fore Street
Portland, ME 04101
Phone: 800-40-STUDY
Fax: 207-221-4299
Web: www.ciee.org/study/scholarships.aspx

## Peter Wollitzer Scholarships for Study in Asia

**Type of award:** Scholarship.
**Intended use:** For full-time undergraduate study at accredited 4-year institution. Designated institutions: CIEE Academic Consortium Board Member institutions: Arizona State University; Brown University; Fordham University; Pacific Lutheran University; Princeton University; Purdue University; Reed College; Oberlin College; University of North Carolina, Charlotte; University of Tulsa; Washington University.
**Basis for selection:** Competition/talent/interest in study abroad. Applicant must demonstrate financial need and high academic achievement.
**Application requirements:** Essay, transcript.
**Additional information:** Applicant must participate in a CIEE Study Center program in Asia (includes Cambodia, China, India, Japan, Korea, Taiwan, Thailand, and Vietnam). Award is $500 for summer program, $2,000 for spring and fall semesters.

**Amount of award:** $500-$2,000
**Number of awards:** 4
**Application deadline:** April 1, November 1
**Notification begins:** May 1, December 1

**Contact:**
CIEE Attn: Scholarship Committee
Attn: Scholarship Committee
300 Fore Street
Portland, ME 04101
Phone: 800-40-STUDY
Fax: 207-221-4299
Web: www.ciee.org/study/scholarships.aspx

## Robert B. Bailey Scholarship

**Type of award:** Scholarship.
**Intended use:** For full-time undergraduate or graduate study at accredited 4-year institution. Designated institutions: CIEE Member or CIEE Academic Consortium member institutions.
**Basis for selection:** Competition/talent/interest in study abroad. Applicant must demonstrate financial need and high academic achievement.
**Application requirements:** Essay, transcript.
**Additional information:** Available to CIEE Study Center applicants only. Must be self-identified as belonging to underrepresented group. Program application is used in consideration of scholarship applicants. Visit Website for details and application.

**Amount of award:** $500-$1,500
**Application deadline:** April 1, November 1
**Notification begins:** May 1, December 1

**Contact:**
CIEE
Attn: Scholarship Committee
300 Fore Street
Portland, ME 04101
Phone: 800-40-STUDY
Fax: 207-221-4299
Web: www.ciee.org/study/scholarships.aspx

## U.S. Department of Education Fulbright-Hays Project Abroad Scholarship for Programs in China

**Type of award:** Scholarship.
**Intended use:** For junior, senior, graduate or postgraduate study at postsecondary institution. Designated institutions:

CIEE Study Centers at Peking University (Beijing), Nanjing University, East China Normal University (Shanghai), and National Chengchi University (Taipei).
**Eligibility:** Applicant must be U.S. citizen or permanent resident.
**Basis for selection:** Major/career interest in Asian studies; foreign languages; education or public administration/service. Applicant must demonstrate financial need and high academic achievement.
**Application requirements:** Essay, transcript, proof of eligibility.
**Additional information:** Must be applicant for CIEE programs in Beijing, Shanghai, Nanjing, or Taipei. Must plan to pursue advanced study or career related to China in the areas of academia or public affairs. Must have completed two years, or equivalent, of college-level Mandarin Chinese. Program application taken into consideration for scholarship. Visit Website for details and application.

| | |
|---|---|
| **Amount of award:** | $1,000-$8,000 |
| **Application deadline:** | April 1, November 1 |
| **Notification begins:** | May 1, December 1 |

**Contact:**
CIEE Attn: Scholarship Committee
Attn: Scholarship Committee
300 Fore Street
Portland, ME 04101
Phone: 800-40-STUDY
Fax: 207-221-4299
Web: www.ciee.org/study/scholarships.aspx

# Courage Center

## Scholarship for People with Disabilities

**Type of award:** Scholarship.
**Intended use:** For full-time undergraduate study at accredited vocational, 2-year or 4-year institution.
**Eligibility:** Applicant must be visually impaired, hearing impaired or physically challenged. Applicant must be U.S. citizen residing in Minnesota.
**Basis for selection:** Applicant must demonstrate financial need.
**Application requirements:** Interview, essay.
**Additional information:** If not Minnesota resident, student must be participant in Courage Center services.

| | |
|---|---|
| **Amount of award:** | $500-$1,000 |
| **Number of awards:** | 20 |
| **Number of applicants:** | 20 |
| **Application deadline:** | May 31 |
| **Notification begins:** | July 31 |
| **Total amount awarded:** | $10,500 |

**Contact:**
Courage Center Vocational Services
3915 Golden Valley Road
Minneapolis, MN 55422
Phone: 763-520-0553
Fax: 763-520-0861
Web: www.couragecenter.org/ContentPages/Resources.aspx

# Courage to Grow

## Courage to Grow Scholarship

**Type of award:** Scholarship.
**Intended use:** For undergraduate or graduate study at vocational, 2-year, 4-year or graduate institution in United States.
**Eligibility:** Applicant must be U.S. citizen.
**Basis for selection:** Applicant must demonstrate financial need.
**Application requirements:** Essay, transcript.
**Additional information:** High school seniors may also apply. Minimum 2.0 GPA. Program awards one $500 scholarship every month; deadline date is last day of each month. Visit Website for application and details.

| | |
|---|---|
| **Amount of award:** | $6,000 |
| **Number of awards:** | 12 |
| **Number of applicants:** | 1,000 |
| **Total amount awarded:** | $6,000 |

**Contact:**
Courage to Grow Scholarship
PO Box 2507
Chelan, WA 98816
Phone: 509-731-3056
Web: www.couragetogrowscholarship.com

# The Cynthia E. Morgan Memorial Scholarship Fund

## The Cynthia E. Morgan Memorial Scholarship Fund

**Type of award:** Scholarship.
**Intended use:** For undergraduate or graduate study at accredited vocational, 2-year or 4-year institution. Designated institutions: Maryland vocational school, college, or university.
**Eligibility:** Applicant must be high school junior or senior. Applicant must be residing in Maryland.
**Basis for selection:** Major/career interest in medicine; nursing; pharmacy/pharmaceutics/pharmacology; dietetics/nutrition; occupational therapy; physical therapy; physician assistant or speech pathology/audiology. Applicant must demonstrate financial need and high academic achievement.
**Application requirements:** Essay, transcript, proof of eligibility.
**Additional information:** Must be first person in immediate family to attend college. Must be entering or planning on entering medical or medical-related field.

| | |
|---|---|
| **Amount of award:** | $1,000 |
| **Application deadline:** | February 25 |
| **Notification begins:** | March 15 |

**Contact:**
The Cynthia E. Morgan Memorial Scholarship Fund
5516 Maudes Way
White Marsh, MD 21162
Web: www.cemsfund.com

# Cystic Fibrosis Foundation

## Cystic Fibrosis Student Traineeship

**Type of award:** Research grant, renewable.
**Intended use:** For full-time senior, master's or doctoral study at accredited 4-year or graduate institution in United States.
**Basis for selection:** Major/career interest in medical specialties/research.
**Application requirements:** Recommendations, research proposal.
**Additional information:** Trainees must work with faculty sponsor on research project related to cystic fibrosis. Applications accepted throughout the year, but should be submitted at least two months prior to anticipated start date of project.

| | |
|---|---|
| **Amount of award:** | $1,500 |

**Contact:**
Cystic Fibrosis Foundation
Office of Grants Management
6931 Arlington Road
Bethesda, MD 20814
Phone: 301-951-4422
Fax: 301-841-2605
Web: www.cff.org

# The Dallas Foundation

## Dallas Architectural Foundation - Humphries/HKS Scholarship

**Type of award:** Scholarship, renewable.
**Intended use:** For undergraduate study at 4-year institution in or outside United States.
**Eligibility:** Applicant must be high school senior. Applicant must be U.S. citizen residing in Texas.
**Basis for selection:** Major/career interest in architecture.
**Application requirements:** Portfolio, recommendations, essay, transcript, nomination.
**Additional information:** Applicant must be enrolled in Skyline High School Architecture Cluster. Funds must be used in the year awarded. Visit Website for application.

| | |
|---|---|
| **Amount of award:** | $2,000 |
| **Number of awards:** | 1 |
| **Application deadline:** | March 31 |
| **Total amount awarded:** | $2,000 |

**Contact:**
The Dallas Architectural Foundation
1909 Woodall Rodgers Freeway
Suite 100
Dallas, TX 75201
Phone: 214-742-3242
Web: www.dallasfoundation.org or www.DallasCFA.com

## Dallas Architectural Foundation - Swank Travelling Fellowship

**Type of award:** Scholarship.
**Intended use:** For senior or graduate study at accredited postsecondary institution.
**Eligibility:** Applicant must be U.S. citizen residing in Texas.
**Basis for selection:** Major/career interest in architecture.
**Application requirements:** Portfolio, recommendations, essay, transcript. Resume, budget statement.
**Additional information:** Applicant must be permanent resident of the Dallas-Fort Worth area. Fellowship established to assist architecture students or recent graduates in broadening their architectural knowledge through travel. Funds must be used for travel and study costs, and within the same calendar year. Recipient must agree to present program of results to the Dallas Architectural Foundation board. Visit Website for application.

| | |
|---|---|
| **Amount of award:** | $2,000 |
| **Number of awards:** | 1 |
| **Number of applicants:** | 5 |
| **Application deadline:** | March 31 |
| **Total amount awarded:** | $2,000 |

**Contact:**
Dallas Architectural Foundation
1909 Woodall Rodgers Freeway
Suite 100
Dallas, TX 75201
Phone: 214-742-3242
Web: www.dallasfoundation.org

## Dr. Dan J. and Patricia S. Pickard Scholarship

**Type of award:** Scholarship, renewable.
**Intended use:** For freshman study at 2-year or 4-year institution.
**Eligibility:** Applicant must be African American. Applicant must be male. Applicant must be residing in Texas.
**Basis for selection:** Applicant must demonstrate financial need and service orientation.
**Application requirements:** Recommendations, essay, transcript. FAFSA or SAR.
**Additional information:** Must be graduating from high school in Dallas County. Minimum 2.5 GPA. Visit Website for application.

| | |
|---|---|
| **Amount of award:** | $1,000 |
| **Application deadline:** | April 1 |

**Contact:**
The Dallas Foundation
900 Jackson Street, Suite 705
Dallas, TX 75202
Phone: 214-741-9898
Web: www.dallasfoundation.org

## Dr. Don and Rose Marie Benton Scholarship

**Type of award:** Scholarship, renewable.
**Intended use:** For undergraduate or graduate study at accredited postsecondary institution in United States.
**Eligibility:** Applicant must be residing in Texas.
**Application requirements:** Nomination by member of the Scholarship Committee at Trinity River Mission.
**Additional information:** Award amount varies; maximum is $1,500. Number of awards varies. Applicant or parent must be affiliated with Trinity River Mission. Must reside in Dallas county.

| | |
|---|---|
| **Amount of award:** | $1,500 |
| **Number of awards:** | 3 |
| **Application deadline:** | April 1 |

**Contact:**
Trinity River Mission
Attn: Ms. Dolores Sosa Green
2060 Singleton Blvd., Suite 104
Dallas, TX 75212
Phone: 214-744-5648
Web: www.dallasfoundation.org

## Hirsch Family Scholarship

**Type of award:** Scholarship.
**Intended use:** For freshman study at accredited vocational, 2-year or 4-year institution in United States.
**Eligibility:** Applicant must be high school senior.
**Basis for selection:** Applicant must demonstrate financial need and high academic achievement.
**Application requirements:** Recommendations, essay, transcript. List of extracurricular activities, community service, and work experience; FAFSA.
**Additional information:** Applicant must be the dependent child of an active employee of Eagle Materials, Performance Chemicals and Ingredients, Martin Fletcher, Hadlock Plastics, Highlander Partners and any of their majority-owned subsidiaries. Past recipients are encouraged to apply each year.

**Amount of award:** $1,000-$5,000
**Application deadline:** April 1

**Contact:**
The Dallas Foundation
900 Jackson Street, Suite 705
Dallas, TX 75202
Phone: 214-741-9898
Web: www.dallasfoundation.org

## Jere W. Thompson, Jr. Scholarship Fund

**Type of award:** Scholarship, renewable.
**Intended use:** For full-time junior or senior study at accredited 4-year institution in United States. Designated institutions: Texas institutions.
**Eligibility:** Applicant must be U.S. citizen or permanent resident residing in Texas.
**Basis for selection:** Major/career interest in engineering, civil or engineering, construction. Applicant must demonstrate financial need and seriousness of purpose.
**Application requirements:** Recommendations, essay, transcript, proof of eligibility. FAFSA or SAR.
**Additional information:** Applicant must be college sophomore. Award amount varies; maximum is $2,000 per semester, renewable for three additional semesters if student maintains 3.0 GPA and submits grade report within 45 days after the end of the semester. Recipients will be given opportunity for paid internship with one of scholarship's sponsors between junior and senior year. Preference may be given to residents of Collin, Dallas, Denton, or Tarrant counties. Visit Website for program profile and application.

**Amount of award:** $2,000
**Number of awards:** 1
**Application deadline:** April 1

**Contact:**
The Dallas Foundation
900 Jackson Street, Suite 705
Dallas, TX 75202
Phone: 214-741-9898
Web: www.dallasfoundation.org

## The Mayor's Chesapeake Energy Scholarship

**Type of award:** Scholarship, renewable.
**Intended use:** For undergraduate study at accredited vocational, 2-year or 4-year institution.
**Eligibility:** Applicant must be Alaskan native, Asian American, African American, Mexican American, Hispanic American, Puerto Rican, American Indian or Native Hawaiian/Pacific Islander. Applicant must be high school senior. Applicant must be U.S. citizen or permanent resident residing in Texas.
**Basis for selection:** Applicant must demonstrate high academic achievement and service orientation.
**Application requirements:** Recommendations, essay, transcript. FAFSA or SAR.
**Additional information:** Must be a graduating senior of eligible high schools in Dallas Independent School District. Must be active member of Education is Freedom (EIF Dallas). Must be female or member of minority group. Minimum 3.0 GPA. Must have taken SAT or ACT. Children and grandchildren of Chesapeake Energy employees not eligible. Visit Website for application.

**Amount of award:** $20,000
**Application deadline:** April 15

**Contact:**
The Dallas Foundation
900 Jackson Street, Suite 705
Dallas, TX 75202
Phone: 214-741-9898
Web: www.dallasfoundation.org

## The Tommy Tranchin Award

**Type of award:** Scholarship.
**Intended use:** For non-degree study at postsecondary institution.
**Eligibility:** Applicant must be physically challenged or learning disabled. Applicant must be high school freshman, sophomore, junior or senior. Applicant must be residing in Texas.
**Application requirements:** Recommendations, essay. Description and budget for proposed activity.
**Additional information:** Award for student with physical, emotional, or intellectual disability who wants to participate in an activity that furthers development in an area in which he/she excels or shows promise. Funds may be used for program expenses, travel, other related expenses. Must be high school student in North Texas. Award is up to $1,500. Visit Website for application. Deadline in mid-March.

**Contact:**
The Dallas Foundation
900 Jackson Street, Suite 705
Dallas, TX 75202
Phone: 214-741-9898
Web: www.dallasfoundation.org

# Data Processing Management Association/ Portland Chapter

## DPMA/PC Scholarship

**Type of award:** Scholarship, renewable.
**Intended use:** For undergraduate study in United States. Designated institutions: Institutions in Oregon or Washington.

**Eligibility:** Applicant must be high school senior. Applicant must be residing in Oregon or Washington.
**Basis for selection:** Major/career interest in computer/information sciences. Applicant must demonstrate financial need, high academic achievement and seriousness of purpose.
**Application requirements:** Recommendations, transcript. List and description of past and current IT-related activities, and of IT career goals. Explanation of reasons for applying for scholarship.
**Additional information:** Applicants must graduate from high school in Oregon or Clark County in Washington. Renewable for $500 each year if awardee maintains a minimum "B" GPA and remains in a technology-related program. Check Website for application deadline.

| | |
|---|---|
| **Amount of award:** | $1,000 |
| **Number of awards:** | 1 |
| **Number of applicants:** | 17 |
| **Application deadline:** | May 31 |
| **Notification begins:** | June 15 |
| **Total amount awarded:** | $4,000 |

**Contact:**
DPMA/PC Scholarship
Attn: Scholarship Chair
P.O. Box 61493
Vancouver, WA 98666
Web: www.dpmapc.com/scholarship.htm

# Daughters of Union Veterans of the Civil War 1861-1865

## Grand Army of the Republic Living Memorial Scholarship

**Type of award:** Scholarship.
**Intended use:** For sophomore, junior or senior study at accredited 4-year institution in United States.
**Eligibility:** Applicant must be descendant of veteran during Civil War. Must be lineal descendant of Union Veteran of Civil War of 1861-1865.
**Basis for selection:** Applicant must demonstrate depth of character, leadership, patriotism, seriousness of purpose and service orientation.
**Application requirements:** Transcript. Two letters of reference, ancestor's military record.
**Additional information:** Must be of good moral character and have firm belief in US Government. Must have satisfactory scholastic standing. Request for information and application honored only with SASE. Number of awards varies.

| | |
|---|---|
| **Amount of award:** | $200-$500 |
| **Application deadline:** | April 30 |
| **Notification begins:** | August 30 |
| **Total amount awarded:** | $1,500 |

**Contact:**
Daughters of Union Veterans of the Civil War 1861-1865
P.O. Box 211
Springfield, IL 62704-0211

# Davidson Institute

## Davidson Fellows Scholarship

**Type of award:** Scholarship.
**Intended use:** For undergraduate study at accredited postsecondary institution in United States.
**Eligibility:** Applicant must be U.S. citizen or permanent resident.
**Basis for selection:** Major/career interest in literature; music; philosophy; mathematics; science, general or technology.
**Application requirements:** Three nominator forms, three copies of a 15-minute DVD or VHS videotape. Signed statement of commitment that, if named a Davidson Fellow, the applicant and a parent or guardian will attend the award reception in Washington, D.C.
**Additional information:** Applicants awarded for accomplishment that is recognized as significant by experts in that field and has a positive contribution to society. Applicant must be under the age of 18 as of October 1 of the year of application. Applications are accepted in the following categories: science, technology, mathematics, music, literature, philosophy, and "outside the box." Work may be exceptionally creative application of existing knowledge, new idea with high impact, innovative solution with broad-range implications, important advancement that can be replicated and built upon, interdisciplinary discovery, prodigious performance, or another demonstration of extraordinary accomplishment. Application deadline is first Wednesday in February.

| | |
|---|---|
| **Amount of award:** | $10,000-$50,000 |
| **Number of awards:** | 20 |
| **Notification begins:** | July 1 |
| **Total amount awarded:** | $460,000 |

**Contact:**
Davidson Institute for Talent Development
9665 Gateway Drive
Suite B
Reno, NV 89521
Phone: 775-852-3483 ext. 423
Fax: 775-852-2184
Web: www.davidsongifted.org/fellows

# Davis-Roberts Scholarship Fund

## Davis-Roberts Scholarship

**Type of award:** Scholarship, renewable.
**Intended use:** For full-time undergraduate study at 2-year or 4-year institution.
**Eligibility:** Applicant must be U.S. citizen residing in Wyoming.
**Basis for selection:** Applicant must demonstrate financial need.
**Application requirements:** Recommendations, essay, transcript. Applicant's photograph.
**Additional information:** Applicant must be member of Job's Daughters or DeMolay.

Amount of award: $300-$1,000
Number of awards: 10
Number of applicants: 12
Application deadline: June 15
Notification begins: August 31
Total amount awarded: $4,000

**Contact:**
Davis-Roberts Scholarship Fund
c/o Gary D. Skillern
P.O. Box 20645
Cheyenne, WY 82003
Phone: 307-632-0491

# Delaware Higher Education Commission

## B. Bradford Barnes Scholarship

**Type of award:** Scholarship, renewable.
**Intended use:** For full-time freshman study at 4-year institution. Designated institutions: University of Delaware.
**Eligibility:** Applicant must be high school senior. Applicant must be U.S. citizen or permanent resident residing in Delaware.
**Basis for selection:** Applicant must demonstrate high academic achievement.
**Application requirements:** Essay, transcript. FAFSA.
**Additional information:** Must rank in top 25 percent of high school class. Combined score of 1800 on the SAT. Awards full tuition, fees, room, board, and books. Visit Website for deadline.

Amount of award: Full tuition
Number of awards: 1
Number of applicants: 35

**Contact:**
Delaware Higher Education Commission
820 North French Street
Wilmington, DE 19801
Phone: 302-577-5240
Fax: 302-577-6765
Web: www.doe.k12.de.us/programs/dhec/how_to_apply/financial_aid

## Charles L. Hebner Memorial Scholarship

**Type of award:** Scholarship, renewable.
**Intended use:** For full-time undergraduate study at 4-year institution. Designated institutions: University of Delaware, Delaware State University.
**Eligibility:** Applicant must be high school senior. Applicant must be U.S. citizen or permanent resident residing in Delaware.
**Basis for selection:** Major/career interest in humanities/liberal arts; social/behavioral sciences or political science/government. Applicant must demonstrate high academic achievement.
**Application requirements:** Essay, transcript. FAFSA.
**Additional information:** Applicant must rank in top half of graduating class. Minimum combined score of 1350 on SAT. Preference given to political science majors. Award covers tuition, fees, room, board, and books. Visit Website for deadline information.

Amount of award: Full tuition
Number of awards: 2
Number of applicants: 65

**Contact:**
Delaware Higher Education Commission
820 North French Street
Wilmington, DE 19801
Phone: 302-577-5240
Fax: 302-577-6765
Web: www.doe.k12.de.us/programs/dhec/how_to_apply/financial_aid

## Delaware Scholarship Incentive Program

**Type of award:** Scholarship.
**Intended use:** For full-time undergraduate study at accredited 2-year or 4-year institution. Designated institutions: Nonprofit, regionally accredited institutions in Delaware or Pennsylvania.
**Eligibility:** Applicant must be U.S. citizen or permanent resident residing in Delaware.
**Basis for selection:** Applicant must demonstrate financial need.
**Application requirements:** Transcript. FAFSA.
**Additional information:** Minimum 2.5 GPA. Full-time undergraduate and graduate students whose majors are not offered at a Delaware public college will be considered. Visit Website for deadline.

Amount of award: $700-$2,200
Number of awards: 1,670
Number of applicants: 11,000
Total amount awarded: $1,455,000

**Contact:**
Delaware Higher Education Commission
820 North French Street
Wilmington, DE 19801
Phone: 302-577-5240
Fax: 302-577-6765
Web: www.doe.k12.de.us/programs/dhec/how_to_apply/financial_aid

## Diamond State Scholarship

**Type of award:** Scholarship, renewable.
**Intended use:** For full-time freshman study at accredited vocational, 2-year or 4-year institution in United States. Designated institutions: Nonprofit, regionally accredited institutions.
**Eligibility:** Applicant must be high school senior. Applicant must be U.S. citizen or permanent resident residing in Delaware.
**Basis for selection:** Applicant must demonstrate high academic achievement.
**Application requirements:** Essay, transcript. SAT scores.
**Additional information:** Must rank in top 25 percent of high school class. Minimum combined score of 1800 on SAT. Visit Website for deadline.

Amount of award: $1,250
Number of awards: 12
Number of applicants: 174
Total amount awarded: $35,000

Scholarships

**Contact:**
Delaware Higher Education Commission
820 North French Street
Wilmington, DE 19801
Phone: 302-577-5240
Fax: 302-577-6765
Web: www.doe.k12.de.us/programs/dhec/how_to_apply/financial_aid

## Educational Benefits for Children of Deceased Veterans and Others

**Type of award:** Scholarship, renewable.
**Intended use:** For undergraduate study at postsecondary institution.
**Eligibility:** Applicant must be at least 16, no older than 24. Applicant must be U.S. citizen or permanent resident residing in Delaware.
**Additional information:** Must live in Delaware for at least three years before applying. Must apply at least four weeks before classes begin. Award prorated when major not available at a Delaware public college. Award for maximum of four years. Must be child of one of the following: member of armed forces whose death was service-related, who is or was a POW, or is officially MIA; state police officer whose death was service-related; or state employee of the Department of Transportation routinely employed in job-related activities on the state highway system whose death was job-related. Visit Website for deadline.

| | |
|---|---|
| **Amount of award:** | Full tuition |
| **Number of applicants:** | 2 |

**Contact:**
Delaware Higher Education Commission
820 North French Street
Wilmington, DE 19801
Phone: 302-577-5240
Fax: 302-577-6765
Web: www.doe.k12.de.us/high-ed

## Herman M. Holloway, Sr. Memorial Scholarship

**Type of award:** Scholarship, renewable.
**Intended use:** For full-time freshman study at 4-year institution. Designated institutions: Delaware State University.
**Eligibility:** Applicant must be high school senior. Applicant must be U.S. citizen or permanent resident residing in Delaware.
**Basis for selection:** Applicant must demonstrate high academic achievement.
**Application requirements:** Essay, transcript. FAFSA.
**Additional information:** Applicants must rank in upper half of class and have combined score of at least 1350 on SAT. Awards full tuition, fees, room, board, and books. Visit Website for deadline information.

| | |
|---|---|
| **Amount of award:** | Full tuition |
| **Number of awards:** | 1 |
| **Number of applicants:** | 60 |

**Contact:**
Delaware Higher Education Commission
820 North French Street
Wilmington, DE 19801
Phone: 302-577-5240
Fax: 302-577-6765
Web: www.doe.k12.de.us/programs/dhec/how_to_apply/financial_aid

## Robert C. Byrd Honors Scholarship

**Type of award:** Scholarship, renewable.
**Intended use:** For full-time undergraduate study at accredited postsecondary institution in United States. Designated institutions: Nonprofit, regionally accredited schools.
**Eligibility:** Applicant must be high school senior. Applicant must be U.S. citizen or permanent resident residing in Delaware.
**Basis for selection:** Applicant must demonstrate high academic achievement.
**Application requirements:** Essay, transcript. SAT scores.
**Additional information:** Applicant must be in top 25 percent of graduating class or GED recipient with score of at least 300. Minimum combined score of 1800 on SAT. Program dependent on federal funding. Renewable up to three years. Visit Website for deadline information.

| | |
|---|---|
| **Amount of award:** | $1,500 |
| **Number of awards:** | 20 |
| **Number of applicants:** | 176 |

**Contact:**
Delaware Higher Education Commission
820 North French Street
Wilmington, DE 19801
Phone: 302-577-5240
Fax: 302-577-6765
Web: www.doe.k12.de.us/programs/dhec/how_to_apply/financial_aid

# Discover Financial Services

## Discover Scholarship Program

**Type of award:** Scholarship.
**Intended use:** For undergraduate study at accredited postsecondary institution.
**Eligibility:** Applicant must be high school junior. Applicant must be U.S. citizen or permanent resident.
**Basis for selection:** Applicant must demonstrate leadership and service orientation.
**Application requirements:** Recommendations, essay, transcript. Community service verification.
**Additional information:** Applicant must have minimum cumulative 2.75 GPA for ninth and tenth grades and must have faced significant roadblock or challenge. Submit application online at International Scholarship and Tuition Services Website. More information at www.discoverfinancial.com/community.

| | |
|---|---|
| **Amount of award:** | $25,000 |
| **Number of awards:** | 10 |
| **Number of applicants:** | 10,000 |
| **Application deadline:** | January 31 |
| **Notification begins:** | May 1 |
| **Total amount awarded:** | $400,000 |

**Contact:**
Phone: 866-756-7932
Web: www.discoverfinancial.com/community

# Distinguished Young Women (Formerly California's Junior Miss)

## California's Distinguished Young Woman Competition

**Type of award:** Scholarship.
**Intended use:** For undergraduate study at accredited 2-year or 4-year institution in United States.
**Eligibility:** Applicant must be single, female, high school junior. Applicant must be U.S. citizen residing in California.
**Basis for selection:** Competition/talent/interest in poise/talent/fitness. Applicant must demonstrate high academic achievement.
**Additional information:** Local competitions held from January to May; state competition held in late July or early August. Awards not limited to state Junior Miss finalists; winners of various judged categories also receive awards. Winner of state-level Junior Miss program will receive $15,000; other prizes of varying amounts may be awarded on local level. Participants must never have been pregnant. Minimum 3.0 GPA. Check Website for details.

| | |
|---|---|
| **Amount of award:** | $500-$15,000 |
| **Number of awards:** | 20 |
| **Number of applicants:** | 280 |
| **Application deadline:** | January 1 |
| **Notification begins:** | May 15 |
| **Total amount awarded:** | $30,000 |

**Contact:**
Distinguished Young Women (Formerly California's Junior Miss)
P.O. Box 2719
Bakersfield, CA 93303
Web: www.distinguishedyw.org

# Distinguished Young Women, Inc.

## Distinguished Young Women Scholarship

**Type of award:** Scholarship.
**Intended use:** For undergraduate or graduate study.
**Eligibility:** Applicant must be single, female, high school junior or senior. Applicant must be U.S. citizen.
**Basis for selection:** Competition/talent/interest in poise/talent/fitness, based on scholastic evaluation, skill in creative and performing arts, physical fitness, presence and composure, and panel interview.
**Additional information:** Must compete in state of legal residence. State winners expected to compete at higher levels. Must never have been married or pregnant. Only high school seniors can compete in finals but students are encouraged to begin application process during sophomore year. Scholarship funds can be used for undergraduate work or deferred for graduate and professional studies. Visit Website for application deadline information, as it varies from state to state.

| | |
|---|---|
| **Amount of award:** | $100-$50,000 |
| **Number of applicants:** | 6,000 |

**Contact:**
Distinguished Young Women
Contestant Inquiry
751 Government Street
Mobile, AL 36602
Phone: 800-256-5435
Fax: 251-431-0063
Web: www.distinguishedyw.org

# District of Columbia Higher Education Financial Services

## DC Tuition Assistance Grant Program (DCTAG)

**Type of award:** Scholarship, renewable.
**Intended use:** For undergraduate study at 2-year or 4-year institution in United States. Designated institutions: DCTAG-eligible institutions that can participate in Title IV programs.
**Eligibility:** Applicant must be no older than 24. Applicant must be U.S. citizen or permanent resident residing in District of Columbia.
**Application requirements:** Transcript, proof of eligibility. Student Aid Report, FAFSA, current utility bill.
**Additional information:** Parents or guardian of applicant must be DC resident for 12 months prior to enrollment and throughout college. Award may not be used at proprietary institutions. Awards vary, visit Website for details.

| | |
|---|---|
| **Amount of award:** | $2,500-$10,000 |
| **Application deadline:** | June 30 |

**Contact:**
Higher Education Financial Services
810 First St. NE
Third Floor
Washington, DC 20002
Phone: 202-727-2824
Web: www.dconeapp.dc.gov

## District of Columbia Leveraging Educational Assistance Partnership Program

**Type of award:** Scholarship, renewable.
**Intended use:** For undergraduate study at 2-year or 4-year institution in or outside United States. Designated institutions: Postsecondary institutions certified to participate in Title IV Student Aid Programs.
**Eligibility:** Applicant must be no older than 23. Applicant must be U.S. citizen or permanent resident residing in District of Columbia.
**Basis for selection:** Applicant must demonstrate financial need.
**Application requirements:** Transcript, proof of eligibility. Student Aid Report, FAFSA, current utility bill.
**Additional information:** Must be D.C. resident for 12 months prior to application and throughout college. Must be eligible for Pell Grant. Award may not be used at proprietary institutions. Apply online.

| | |
|---|---|
| **Amount of award:** | $1,500-$5,000 |
| **Application deadline:** | June 30 |

Scholarships

**Contact:**
Higher Education Financial Services
810 First St. NE
Third Floor
Washington, DC 20002
Phone: 202-727-2824
Web: www.dconeapp.dc.gov

# Dolphin Scholarship Foundation

## Dolphin Scholarship

**Type of award:** Scholarship, renewable.
**Intended use:** For full-time undergraduate study at accredited 4-year institution.
**Eligibility:** Applicant must be single, no older than 23. Applicant must be U.S. citizen. Must be child/stepchild of member or former member of U.S. Navy who served in, or in support of, Submarine Force.
**Basis for selection:** Applicant must demonstrate financial need, high academic achievement and service orientation.
**Application requirements:** Recommendations, essay, transcript, proof of eligibility. SAT/ACT scores.
**Additional information:** Applicant must be high school senior or college student. Applicant must demonstrate commitment to extracurricular activities and community service.

| | |
|---|---|
| **Amount of award:** | $3,400 |
| **Number of awards:** | 114 |
| **Number of applicants:** | 231 |
| **Application deadline:** | March 15 |
| **Notification begins:** | April 30 |
| **Total amount awarded:** | $445,250 |

**Contact:**
Dolphin Scholarship Foundation
4966 Euclid Road
Suite 109
Virginia Beach, VA 23462
Phone: 757-671-3200 ext. 111
Fax: 757-671-3330
Web: www.dolphinscholarship.org

## Laura W. Bush Scholarship

**Type of award:** Scholarship, renewable.
**Intended use:** For undergraduate study at accredited 4-year institution.
**Eligibility:** Applicant must be no older than 23. Must be child/stepchild of member or former member of U.S. Navy submarine force who served on the USS Texas (SSN775).
**Basis for selection:** Applicant must demonstrate financial need, high academic achievement, depth of character, leadership, seriousness of purpose and service orientation.
**Application requirements:** SAT/ACT scores.
**Additional information:** Applicant must be unmarried high school senior or college student. Sponsor must be qualified in submarines and have served on active duty in the Submarine Force for a minimum of 8 years or must have served on active duty in direct submarine support activities for a minimum of 10 years. Visit Website for application and details.

| | |
|---|---|
| **Amount of award:** | $3,400 |
| **Number of awards:** | 3 |
| **Number of applicants:** | 3 |
| **Application deadline:** | March 15 |
| **Notification begins:** | May 15 |
| **Total amount awarded:** | $10,200 |

**Contact:**
Dolphin Scholarship Foundation
4966 Euclid Road, Suite 109
Virginia Beach, VA 23462
Phone: 757-671-3200 ext. 111
Fax: 757-671-3330
Web: www.dolphinscholarship.org

# Eastern Orthodox Committee on Scouting

## Boy and Girl Scouts Scholarship

**Type of award:** Scholarship.
**Intended use:** For full-time freshman study at accredited 4-year institution in United States.
**Eligibility:** Applicant must be high school senior. Applicant must be Eastern Orthodox. Applicant must be U.S. citizen.
**Basis for selection:** Applicant must demonstrate depth of character and service orientation.
**Application requirements:** Four letters of recommendation with application, one from each of following groups: religious institution, school, community leader, and head of Scouting unit.
**Additional information:** Eligible applicant must be registered member of Boy or Girl Scouts unit; Eagle Scout or Gold Award recipient; active member of Eastern Orthodox Church; have received Alpha Omega Religious Scout Award; have demonstrated practical citizenship in his or her church, school, Scouting unit, and community. Offers one $1,000 scholarship and one $500 scholarship upon acceptance to four-year accredited college or university.

| | |
|---|---|
| **Amount of award:** | $500-$1,000 |
| **Number of awards:** | 2 |
| **Number of applicants:** | 120 |
| **Application deadline:** | May 1 |
| **Total amount awarded:** | $1,500 |

**Contact:**
EOCS Scholarship Committee
862 Guy Lombardo Avenue
Freeport, NY 11520
Phone: 516-868-4050
Web: www.eocs.org

# Edmund F. Maxwell Foundation

## Edmund F. Maxwell Foundation Scholarship

**Type of award:** Scholarship, renewable.
**Intended use:** For full-time freshman study. Designated institutions: Private colleges and universities.

**Eligibility:** Applicant must be U.S. citizen or permanent resident residing in Washington.
**Basis for selection:** Applicant must demonstrate financial need, high academic achievement, depth of character, leadership, seriousness of purpose and service orientation.
**Application requirements:** Essay, transcript. Financial aid worksheet.
**Additional information:** Must be resident of western Washington. Combined reading and math SAT scores must be greater than 1200. Applicants encouraged to apply early in year. Visit Website for application and more information.

| | |
|---|---|
| **Amount of award:** | $5,000 |
| **Application deadline:** | April 30 |
| **Notification begins:** | June 1 |

**Contact:**
The Edmund F. Maxwell Foundation
P.O. Box 22537
Seattle, WA 98122-0537
Web: www.maxwell.org

# Elie Wiesel Foundation for Humanity

## Elie Wiesel Prize in Ethics

**Type of award:** Scholarship.
**Intended use:** For full-time junior or senior study at accredited 4-year institution in United States.
**Basis for selection:** Competition/talent/interest in writing/journalism.
**Application requirements:** Proof of eligibility. Letter from college/university verifying full-time junior or senior status. Sponsorship by faculty member. Submit three copies of essay concerning an ethical dilemma, issue, or question related to the contest's annual topic. In 3,000 to 4,000 words, students are encouraged to raise questions, single out issues, and identify dilemmas.
**Additional information:** First prize is $5,000; second prize is $2,500; third prize is $1,500; two honorable mentions are $500 each. See Website for more information.

| | |
|---|---|
| **Amount of award:** | $500-$5,000 |
| **Number of awards:** | 5 |
| **Number of applicants:** | 300 |
| **Application deadline:** | December 1 |
| **Notification begins:** | May 31 |
| **Total amount awarded:** | $10,000 |

**Contact:**
Elie Wiesel Prize in Ethics
The Elie Wiesel Foundation for Humanity
555 Madison Avenue, 20th Floor
New York, NY 10022
Phone: 212-490-7788
Fax: 212-490-6006
Web: www.eliewieselfoundation.org

# Elizabeth Greenshields Foundation

## The Elizabeth Greenshields Grant

**Type of award:** Scholarship, renewable.
**Intended use:** For undergraduate, graduate or non-degree study at postsecondary institution.
**Basis for selection:** Major/career interest in arts, general.
**Application requirements:** Jpeg on CD.
**Additional information:** For artists (fine arts) in early stages of careers creating representational or figurative works through painting, drawing, printmaking, or sculpture. Must make a commitment to making art a lifetime career. Applications are welcome throughout the year. All award amounts are in Canadian dollars. Funds may be used for any art-related purpose.

| | |
|---|---|
| **Amount of award:** | $12,500 |
| **Number of awards:** | 50 |
| **Number of applicants:** | 1,000 |

**Contact:**
Elizabeth Greenshields Foundation
1814 Sherbrooke Street West, Suite 1
Montreal
Quebec, Canada, H3H 1E4
Phone: 514-937-9225
Web: elizabethgreenshieldsfoundation.ca

# Elks National Foundation

## Elks Most Valuable Student Scholarship

**Type of award:** Scholarship.
**Intended use:** For full-time undergraduate study at accredited postsecondary institution in United States.
**Eligibility:** Applicant must be high school senior. Applicant must be U.S. citizen.
**Basis for selection:** Applicant must demonstrate financial need, high academic achievement and leadership.
**Application requirements:** Transcript. Counselor report, SAT/ACT scores, income range.
**Additional information:** Applications available starting September 1 from local Benevolent and Protective Order of Elks Lodge; also available on Website or by sending SASE to foundation. Application deadline is in November. Award is distributed over four years. Membership in Elks not required, but application must be endorsed by and submitted to local Elks Lodge for entry into competition. Judging occurs at lodge, district, and state level before reaching national competition.

| | |
|---|---|
| **Amount of award:** | $4,000-$60,000 |
| **Number of awards:** | 500 |
| **Number of applicants:** | 20,000 |
| **Application deadline:** | December 1 |
| **Notification begins:** | April 15 |
| **Total amount awarded:** | $2,296,000 |

**Contact:**
Elks National Foundation
2750 North Lakeview Avenue
Chicago, IL 60614-1889
Phone: 773-755-4732
Fax: 773-755-4733
Web: www.elks.org/enf/scholars

### Elks National Foundation Legacy Awards

**Type of award:** Scholarship.
**Intended use:** For full-time undergraduate study at accredited postsecondary institution in United States.
**Eligibility:** Applicant must be high school senior. Applicant must be U.S. citizen.
**Basis for selection:** Applicant must demonstrate high academic achievement and leadership.
**Application requirements:** Essay, transcript. SAT/ACT scores.
**Additional information:** Application deadline in mid-January. Applicant must be child or grandchild of Elks member who has been paid-up and in good standing for two consecutive years. Application available September 1 from Website. Eligible applicants from Guam, Panama, Puerto Rico, and the Philippines may attend schools in those countries. Visit Website for additional information.

| | |
|---|---|
| **Amount of award:** | $4,000 |
| **Number of awards:** | 250 |
| **Application deadline:** | February 1 |
| **Notification begins:** | April 15 |
| **Total amount awarded:** | $1,000,000 |

**Contact:**
Elks National Foundation
2750 North Lakeview Avenue
Chicago, IL 60614-1889
Phone: 773-755-4732
Fax: 773-755-4733
Web: www.elks.org/enf/scholars

## Engineers Foundation of Ohio

### Engineers Foundation of Ohio Scholarships

**Type of award:** Scholarship.
**Intended use:** For freshman study at accredited 4-year institution in United States. Designated institutions: ABET-accredited schools in Ohio and University of Notre Dame.
**Eligibility:** Applicant must be high school senior. Applicant must be U.S. citizen residing in Ohio.
**Basis for selection:** Major/career interest in engineering. Applicant must demonstrate high academic achievement.
**Application requirements:** Essay, transcript.
**Additional information:** Minimum 3.0 GPA. Must have minimum 600 SAT (Math) and 500 SAT (Reading or Composition) or 29 ACT Math and 25 ACT English. EFO offers scholarships per year with various requirements; see Website for specifics. Some awards renewable.

| | |
|---|---|
| **Amount of award:** | $500-$2,500 |
| **Application deadline:** | December 15 |

**Contact:**
Engineers Foundation of Ohio
400 South Fifth Street
Suite 300
Columbus, OH 43215-5430
Phone: 614-223-1177
Fax: 614-223-1131
Web: www.ohioengineer.com

## The Entomological Foundation

### The Entomological Foundation BioQuip Undergraduate Scholarship

**Type of award:** Scholarship.
**Intended use:** For full-time junior or senior study at 4-year institution. Designated institutions: Institutions in United States, Canada, or Mexico.
**Basis for selection:** Competition/talent/interest in study abroad. Major/career interest in entomology; zoology; biology or science, general. Applicant must demonstrate financial need.
**Application requirements:** Recommendations, essay, transcript. Letter of nomination, three statements from school officials attesting to entomological interests, character, aptitude, financial need.
**Additional information:** Applicant must have been enrolled as undergraduate student in entomology in the fall prior to application deadline. If student's college or university does not offer a degree in entomology, student must be preparing to become an entomologist through his/her studies. By September 1 following application deadline, student must accumulate at least 90 credit hours and either complete two junior-level entomology courses or a research project in entomology. See Website for more information.

| | |
|---|---|
| **Amount of award:** | $2,000 |
| **Number of awards:** | 1 |
| **Number of applicants:** | 72 |
| **Application deadline:** | July 1 |
| **Notification begins:** | September 30 |
| **Total amount awarded:** | $2,000 |

**Contact:**
The Entomological Foundation
9332 Annapolis Road, Suite 210
Lanham, MD 20706
Phone: 301-731-4535
Web: www.entfdn.org

### Stan Beck Fellowship

**Type of award:** Scholarship, renewable.
**Intended use:** For undergraduate or graduate study at 4-year or graduate institution. Designated institutions: Colleges or universities in the United States, Mexico, or Canada.
**Basis for selection:** Major/career interest in entomology; biology or zoology. Applicant must demonstrate financial need.
**Application requirements:** Recommendations, essay, transcript, proof of eligibility. Letter of nomination, letters of support demonstrating applicant's need or challenge.
**Additional information:** Award amount varies. Need is based on physical limitations or economic, minority, or environmental conditions. Applications must be submitted electronically. See Website for additional information.

| | |
|---|---|
| **Application deadline:** | July 1 |

**Contact:**
The Entomological Foundation
9332 Annapolis Road, Suite 210
Lanham, MD 20706
Phone: 301-731-4535
Web: www.entfdn.org

# The Environmental Institute for Golf

## GCSAA Legacy Awards

**Type of award:** Scholarship.
**Intended use:** For full-time undergraduate or graduate study at accredited postsecondary institution.
**Basis for selection:** Applicant must demonstrate high academic achievement, leadership and service orientation.
**Application requirements:** Essay, transcript, proof of eligibility. Letter of acceptance from college or university (high school seniors).
**Additional information:** Applicant's parent or grandparent must have been a Golf Course Superintendents Association of America (GCSAA) member for five or more consecutive years and must be current active member in one of the following classifications: A, Superintendent Member, C, Retired-A, Retired-B, or AA Life. Children or grandchildren of deceased members also eligible if member was active at time of death. Award limited to one student per family. Children of Syngenta Professional Products employees, The Environmental Institute for Golf's Board of Trustees, and GCSAA staff not eligible. Past winners are ineligible to apply the following year. They may re-apply after a one-year hiatus.

| | |
|---|---|
| **Amount of award:** | $1,500 |
| **Application deadline:** | April 15 |
| **Notification begins:** | June 15 |

**Contact:**
Golf Course Superintendents Association of America
Scholarship Program
1421 Research Park Drive
Lawrence, KS 66049-3859
Phone: 785-832-4445 or 800-472-7878 ext. 4445
Web: www.gcsaa.org

## GCSAA Scholars Competition

**Type of award:** Scholarship.
**Intended use:** For sophomore, junior or senior study at accredited 2-year or 4-year institution.
**Basis for selection:** Major/career interest in turf management. Applicant must demonstrate high academic achievement and leadership.
**Application requirements:** Recommendations, essay, transcript, proof of eligibility.
**Additional information:** Must be member of Golf Course Superintendents Association of America. Must be planning career in golf course management or closely related profession. First and second place winners receive all-expense paid trip to GCSAA-sponsored Golf Industry Show. Children of GCSAA Environmental Institute for Golf's Board of Trustees, GCSAA Board of Directors, and GCSAA staff not eligible. Visit Website for details and application.

| | |
|---|---|
| **Amount of award:** | $500-$6,000 |
| **Number of awards:** | 28 |
| **Application deadline:** | June 1 |
| **Notification begins:** | August 1 |

**Contact:**
Golf Course Superintendents Association of America
Scholarship Program
1421 Research Park Drive
Lawrence, KS 66049-3859
Phone: 785-832-4445 or 800-472-7878 ext. 4445
Web: www.gcsaa.org

## GCSAA Student Essay Contest

**Type of award:** Scholarship.
**Intended use:** For undergraduate or graduate study at postsecondary institution.
**Basis for selection:** Competition/talent/interest in writing/journalism, based on essay focusing on golf course management. Major/career interest in turf management.
**Application requirements:** Essay, proof of eligibility.
**Additional information:** Must be member of Golf Course Superintendents Association of America. Must be pursuing degree in turf grass science, agronomy, or any other field related to golf course management. First prize is $2000; second prize, $1500; third prize, $1000. Visit Website for details.

| | |
|---|---|
| **Amount of award:** | $1,000-$2,000 |
| **Number of awards:** | 3 |
| **Application deadline:** | March 31 |

**Contact:**
Golf Course Superintendents Association of America
Student Essay Contest
1421 Research Park Drive
Lawrence, KS 66049-3859
Phone: 800-472-7878 ext. 4445
Web: www.gcsaa.org

# Epilepsy Foundation

## Behavioral Sciences Student Fellowship

**Type of award:** Research grant.
**Intended use:** For undergraduate or graduate study in United States.
**Basis for selection:** Major/career interest in social/behavioral sciences; sociology; social work; psychology; anthropology; nursing; economics; rehabilitation/therapeutic services or political science/government.
**Application requirements:** Recommendations, research proposal. Research proposal.
**Additional information:** Three-month fellowship for epilepsy study project. Professor or advisor must supervise student's project. Other appropriate fields include vocational rehabilitation, counseling, and subjects relevant to epilepsy research or practice. Women and minorities are especially encouraged to apply. Visit Website for application instructions and for more information.

| | |
|---|---|
| **Amount of award:** | $3,000 |
| **Application deadline:** | March 1 |
| **Notification begins:** | May 31 |
| **Total amount awarded:** | $3,000 |

**Contact:**
Epilepsy Foundation
8301 Professional Place
Landover, MD 20785-2267
Phone: 301-459-3700
Fax: 301-577-2684
Web: www.epilepsyfoundation.org/grants

# Epilepsy Foundation of San Diego County

## Epilepsy Foundation of San Diego County Scholarship

**Type of award:** Scholarship.
**Intended use:** For undergraduate study at vocational, 2-year or 4-year institution.
**Eligibility:** Applicant must be residing in California.
**Basis for selection:** Applicant must demonstrate financial need and high academic achievement.
**Additional information:** Two categories of eligibility: 1) Student being treated for epilepsy who is or will be enrolled in a college, university, or trade school in the Fall. 2) Full-time college or university student involved in an epilepsy research project in health or social science with minimum 3.0 GPA. All applicants must be residents of San Diego or Imperial counties, but may be attending school outside the area.

| | |
|---|---|
| **Amount of award:** | $250-$2,000 |
| **Number of awards:** | 6 |
| **Number of applicants:** | 8 |
| **Application deadline:** | June 1 |
| **Total amount awarded:** | $4,000 |

**Contact:**
Epilepsy Foundation of San Diego County
2055 El Cajon Boulevard
San Diego, CA 92104
Phone: 619-296-0161
Web: www.epilepsysandiego.org

# EqualityMaine Foundation

## The Joel Abromson Memorial Scholarship

**Type of award:** Scholarship.
**Intended use:** For freshman study at postsecondary institution.
**Eligibility:** Applicant must be high school senior. Applicant must be U.S. citizen or permanent resident residing in Maine.
**Basis for selection:** Competition/talent/interest in gay/lesbian, based on involvement and leadership in promoting equality for lesbian, gay, bisexual, and transgender people in schools and community. Applicant must demonstrate depth of character and service orientation.
**Application requirements:** Recommendations, essay. Cover letter. Acceptance letter from chosen higher education institution.
**Additional information:** Visit Website for essay question and additional information.

| | |
|---|---|
| **Amount of award:** | $1,000 |
| **Application deadline:** | April 15 |
| **Total amount awarded:** | $3,000 |

**Contact:**
EqualityMaine
P.O. Box 1951
Portland, ME 04104
Phone: 207-761-3732
Fax: 207-761-3752
Web: www.equalitymaine.org

# ESA Foundation

## ESA Foundation Scholarship Program

**Type of award:** Scholarship, renewable.
**Intended use:** For undergraduate or graduate study at vocational, 2-year, 4-year or graduate institution.
**Basis for selection:** Applicant must demonstrate financial need, high academic achievement, depth of character, leadership and service orientation.
**Application requirements:** $5 application fee. Recommendations, essay, transcript.
**Additional information:** Individual scholarships have specific requirements; visit Website for details and application form.

| | |
|---|---|
| **Amount of award:** | $500-$7,500 |
| **Number of awards:** | 160 |
| **Number of applicants:** | 8,000 |
| **Application deadline:** | February 1 |
| **Notification begins:** | June 1 |
| **Total amount awarded:** | $160,906 |

**Contact:**
ESA Foundation
P.O. Box 270517
Fort Collins, CO 80527
Phone: 970-223-2824
Fax: 970-223-4456
Web: www.esaintl.com/esaf/scholarship_application.html

# Executive Women International

## Executive Women International Scholarship

**Type of award:** Scholarship, renewable.
**Intended use:** For full-time undergraduate study at accredited 4-year institution in United States.
**Eligibility:** Applicant must be high school junior.
**Basis for selection:** Applicant must demonstrate high academic achievement, depth of character, leadership, seriousness of purpose and service orientation.
**Application requirements:** Interview, recommendations, essay.
**Additional information:** Applicant must reside within boundaries of participating Executive Women International chapter. Scholarship awarded each academic year, for up to five consecutive years, until student completes degree. Applicants must have sponsoring teacher at their school. Must have a major/career interest in a professional field.

**Amount of award:** $1,000-$10,000
**Application deadline:** April 30
**Notification begins:** June 1

**Contact:**
Executive Women International
7414 South State St.
Midvale, UT 84047
Phone: 801-355-2800
Fax: 801-355-2852
Web: www.ewiconnect.com

# Experimental Aircraft Association

## David Alan Quick Scholarship

**Type of award:** Scholarship.
**Intended use:** For junior or senior study at accredited 4-year institution.
**Basis for selection:** Major/career interest in aerospace or engineering. Applicant must demonstrate financial need.
**Application requirements:** Recommendations, essay. Resume, financial information.
**Additional information:** Must be Experimental Aircraft Association member. Awarded to student pursuing degree in aerospace or aeronautical engineering. Apply online.

**Amount of award:** $500
**Number of awards:** 1
**Application deadline:** February 28

**Contact:**
EAA Scholarship Department
P.O. 2683
Oshkosh, WI 54903-2683
Phone: 920-426-6823
Web: www.youngeagles.org/programs/scholarships

## Hansen Scholarship

**Type of award:** Scholarship, renewable.
**Intended use:** For undergraduate study at accredited vocational, 2-year or 4-year institution.
**Basis for selection:** Major/career interest in aerospace; aviation or engineering. Applicant must demonstrate financial need, high academic achievement, depth of character, leadership and service orientation.
**Application requirements:** Recommendations, essay. Resume, financial information.
**Additional information:** Must be Experimental Aircraft Association member to apply. Student should be pursuing degree in aerospace engineering or aeronautical engineering. Visit Website for details and application.

**Amount of award:** $1,000
**Number of awards:** 1
**Application deadline:** February 28

**Contact:**
EAA Scholarship Department
P.O. 2683
Oshkosh, WI 54903-2683
Phone: 920-426-6823
Web: www.youngeagles.org/programs/scholarships

## H.P. "Bud" Milligan Aviation Scholarship

**Type of award:** Scholarship, renewable.
**Intended use:** For undergraduate study at accredited vocational, 2-year or 4-year institution.
**Basis for selection:** Major/career interest in aviation. Applicant must demonstrate financial need, depth of character, leadership and service orientation.
**Application requirements:** Recommendations, essay. Resume, financial information.
**Additional information:** Must be Experimental Aircraft Association member. Complete application online.

**Amount of award:** $500
**Number of awards:** 1
**Application deadline:** February 28

**Contact:**
EAA Scholarship Department
P.O. 2683
Oshkosh, WI 54903-2683
Phone: 920-426-6823
Web: www.youngeagles.org/programs/scholarships

## Hudner Medal of Honor Scholarship

**Type of award:** Scholarship.
**Intended use:** For undergraduate study at postsecondary institution.
**Eligibility:** Applicant must be residing in Wisconsin.
**Basis for selection:** Major/career interest in aviation; military science or public administration/service. Applicant must demonstrate financial need, leadership and service orientation.
**Application requirements:** Recommendations, essay. Resume, financial information.
**Additional information:** Must be an Experimental Aircraft Association member and have strong record of involvement with Experimental Aircraft Association. Must express intent to serve the country through military or public service. Winner must attend award presentation dinner. Special consideration given to Wisconsin or nearby resident. Recommendation from Experimental Aircraft Association member strongly desired. Apply online.

**Amount of award:** $500
**Number of awards:** 1
**Application deadline:** February 28

**Contact:**
EAA Scholarship Department
P.O. 2683
Oshkosh, WI 54903-2683
Phone: 920-426-6823
Web: www.youngeagles.org/programs/scholarships

## Payzer Scholarship

**Type of award:** Scholarship.
**Intended use:** For undergraduate study at accredited postsecondary institution.
**Basis for selection:** Major/career interest in engineering; mathematics; physical sciences; biology or aviation. Applicant must demonstrate financial need, depth of character, leadership and service orientation.
**Application requirements:** Recommendations, essay. Resume, financial information.
**Additional information:** Must be current Experimental Aircraft Association member or recommended by EAA member. Applicant must intend to pursue career in engineering,

Scholarships

mathematics, or physical/biological sciences. Complete application online.

**Amount of award:** $5,000
**Number of awards:** 1
**Application deadline:** February 28

**Contact:**
EAA Scholarship Department
P.O. 2683
Oshkosh, WI 54903-2683
Phone: 920-426-6823
Web: www.youngeagles.org/programs/scholarships

### Richard Lee Vernon Aviation Scholarship

**Type of award:** Scholarship.
**Intended use:** For undergraduate study at postsecondary institution.
**Basis for selection:** Major/career interest in aviation. Applicant must demonstrate financial need.
**Application requirements:** Recommendations, essay. Resume, financial information.
**Additional information:** Must be Experimental Aircraft Association member. Awarded to a student pursuing training leading to professional aviation occupation. Apply online.

**Amount of award:** $500
**Number of awards:** 1
**Application deadline:** February 28

**Contact:**
EAA Scholarship Department
P.O. 2683
Oshkosh, WI 54903-2683
Phone: 920-426-6823
Web: www.youngeagles.org/programs/scholarships

## Explorers Club

### Explorers Club Youth Activity Fund

**Type of award:** Research grant.
**Intended use:** For undergraduate study at postsecondary institution.
**Basis for selection:** Competition/talent/interest in research paper, based on proposal's scientific and practical merit, investigator's competence, and budget's appropriateness. Major/career interest in natural sciences. Applicant must demonstrate seriousness of purpose.
**Application requirements:** Recommendations, proof of eligibility, research proposal. One-page description of project.
**Additional information:** For research project in the natural sciences under supervision of qualified scientist or institution. For full-time high school students or undergraduates only. Recipients of grants must provide one- to two-page report on their exploration or research within year of receiving the grant. Photographs are encouraged. Request application form from club. See Website for more details and deadline.

**Amount of award:** $500-$1,500
**Number of applicants:** 52

**Contact:**
The Explorers Club c/o Annie Lee
46 East 70th Street
New York, NY 10021
Phone: 212-628-8383
Fax: 212-288-4449
Web: www.explorers.org

## Federal Employee Education and Assistance Fund

### Federal Employee Education and Assistance Fund Scholarship

**Type of award:** Scholarship.
**Intended use:** For undergraduate, master's or doctoral study at accredited 2-year, 4-year or graduate institution.
**Eligibility:** Applicant or parent must be employed by Federal/U.S. Government.
**Basis for selection:** Applicant must demonstrate high academic achievement.
**Application requirements:** Recommendations, essay, transcript. List of community service/extracurricular activities.
**Additional information:** Current civilian federal and postal employees with minimum three years' service by the end of August of the application year and their dependents are eligible. Applicant must have completed community service activities. Minimum 3.0 GPA. Employee applicants eligible for part-time study; dependents must enroll full-time. Visit Website for application materials beginning in January.

**Amount of award:** $500-$2,000
**Number of applicants:** 3,578
**Application deadline:** March 25
**Notification begins:** September 30
**Total amount awarded:** $490,000

**Contact:**
Federal Employee Education and Assistance Fund
3333 S. Wadsworth Blvd.
Suite 300
Lakewood, CO 80227
Phone: 800-323-4140
Web: www.feea.org

## Finance Authority of Maine

### Maine Robert C. Byrd Honors Scholarship

**Type of award:** Scholarship, renewable.
**Intended use:** For full-time undergraduate study at 2-year or 4-year institution.
**Eligibility:** Applicant must be high school senior. Applicant must be U.S. citizen residing in Maine.
**Basis for selection:** Applicant must demonstrate high academic achievement.
**Application requirements:** Essay, transcript. High school profile from guidance office with SAT scores, list of scholastic achievements, awards and honors. FAFSA.

**Additional information:** Information available through Maine high school guidance offices and Finance Authority of Maine. See Website for details.

| | |
|---|---|
| **Amount of award:** | $1,500 |
| **Number of awards:** | 27 |
| **Number of applicants:** | 448 |
| **Application deadline:** | May 1 |
| **Notification begins:** | June 1 |
| **Total amount awarded:** | $40,500 |

**Contact:**
Finance Authority of Maine
5 Community Drive
P.O. Box 949
Augusta, ME 04332-0949
Phone: 800-228-3734
Fax: 207-623-0095
Web: www.famemaine.com

# Financial Service Centers of New York

## Rewarding Young Leaders in Our Community Scholarship

**Type of award:** Scholarship.
**Intended use:** For freshman study at postsecondary institution.
**Eligibility:** Applicant must be U.S. citizen or permanent resident.
**Basis for selection:** Applicant must demonstrate high academic achievement, leadership and service orientation.
**Application requirements:** Essay, transcript. Written verification of community involvement.
**Additional information:** Applicant must have contributed at least 50 hours of volunteer service per year in high school.

| | |
|---|---|
| **Amount of award:** | $500-$7,500 |
| **Number of awards:** | 16 |
| **Total amount awarded:** | $40,000 |

**Contact:**
Financial Service Centers of New York
Mr. Sanford Herman, Chairman
286 Madison Avenue, Suite 907
New York, NY 10017
Phone: 212-268-1911
Web: www.fscny.org/scholar.htm

# First Catholic Slovak Ladies Association

## First Catholic Slovak Ladies Association Scholarship Program

**Type of award:** Scholarship.
**Intended use:** For full-time undergraduate or graduate study at accredited postsecondary institution in United States or Canada.
**Basis for selection:** Applicant must demonstrate high academic achievement, leadership and service orientation.
**Application requirements:** Recommendations, essay, transcript, proof of eligibility. SAT/ACT scores. Photograph of candidate encouraged.
**Additional information:** Applicant must be member of First Catholic Slovak Ladies Association for at least three years prior to date of application, and on a $1,000 legal reserve certificate, a $5,000 term certificate, or have an annuity certificate. Minimum 2.5 GPA. Visit Website for more information.

| | |
|---|---|
| **Amount of award:** | $1,250-$1,750 |
| **Number of awards:** | 135 |
| **Number of applicants:** | 384 |
| **Application deadline:** | March 1 |
| **Notification begins:** | May 15 |
| **Total amount awarded:** | $177,750 |

**Contact:**
First Catholic Slovak Ladies Association
Director of Fraternal Scholarship Aid
24950 Chagrin Boulevard
Beachwood, OH 44122
Phone: 800-464-4642
Fax: 216-464-9260
Web: www.fcsla.org

# First Marine Division Association

## First Marine Division Association Scholarship

**Type of award:** Scholarship, renewable.
**Intended use:** For full-time undergraduate study at accredited vocational, 2-year or 4-year institution in United States.
**Eligibility:** Applicant must be no older than 22. Applicant must be U.S. citizen. Applicant must be dependent of disabled veteran or deceased veteran who served in the Marines. Must have served specifically in any unit part of, attached to, or in support of First Marine Division.
**Basis for selection:** Applicant must demonstrate depth of character and seriousness of purpose.
**Application requirements:** Essay, proof of eligibility. Veteran sponsor's DD214 if available (if not, applicant must complete Standard Form 180). Death certificate or affidavit proving veteran's 100 percent and permanent disability. Copy of applicant's birth certificate. Photograph. See Website for other required information.
**Additional information:** Number of awards varies. Visit Website for application deadline and details.

| | |
|---|---|
| **Amount of award:** | $1,750 |
| **Total amount awarded:** | $39,750 |

**Contact:**
First Marine Division Association
403 North Freeman St.
Oceanside, CA 92054
Phone: 760-967-8561
Fax: 760-967-8567
Web: www.1stmarinedivisionassociation.org/scholarships.php

Scholarships

# Fisher Communications, Inc.

## Fisher Broadcasting Company Scholarship for Minorities

**Type of award:** Scholarship.
**Intended use:** For full-time sophomore, junior or senior study at accredited vocational, 2-year or 4-year institution in United States.
**Eligibility:** Applicant must be Alaskan native, Asian American, African American, Mexican American, Hispanic American, Puerto Rican, American Indian or Native Hawaiian/Pacific Islander. Applicant must be U.S. citizen.
**Basis for selection:** Major/career interest in radio/television/ film; journalism or marketing. Applicant must demonstrate financial need and high academic achievement.
**Application requirements:** Recommendations, essay, transcript, proof of eligibility. Estimated expense/income worksheet.
**Additional information:** Must have career interest in broadcast communications. Amount of award varies each year. Minimum 2.5 GPA. For use at schools in Washington, California, Oregon, Idaho, and Montana, or for students with permanent addresses in those states who attend school out of state.

| | |
|---|---|
| **Number of applicants:** | 25 |
| **Application deadline:** | April 30 |
| **Notification begins:** | July 30 |
| **Total amount awarded:** | $12,950 |

**Contact:**
Fisher Communications Inc. Minority Scholarship
Attn: Human Resources
140 4th Ave. N.
Seattle, WA 98109
Web: www.fsci.com/scholarship.html

# Florida Department of Education

## Access to Better Learning and Education (ABLE) Grant Program

**Type of award:** Scholarship, renewable.
**Intended use:** For full-time undergraduate study at accredited postsecondary institution in United States. Designated institutions: Eligible private Florida colleges and universities.
**Eligibility:** Applicant must be U.S. citizen or permanent resident residing in Florida.
**Basis for selection:** Applicant must demonstrate financial need.
**Additional information:** Each participating institution determines application procedures, deadlines, and student eligibility. The amount of ABLE award plus all other scholarships and grants specifically designated for payment of tuition and fees cannot exceed the total amount of tuition and fees charged by the institution. May not be enrolled in program of study leading to degree in theology or divinity.

| | |
|---|---|
| **Amount of award:** | $945 |

**Contact:**
Office of Student Financial Assistance
325 West Gaines Street
Suite 1314
Tallahassee, FL 32399-0400
Phone: 888-827-2004
Web: www.floridastudentfinancialaid.org

## Florida Academic Scholars Award

**Type of award:** Scholarship, renewable.
**Intended use:** For undergraduate study at postsecondary institution in United States. Designated institutions: Eligible Florida post-secondary institutions.
**Eligibility:** Applicant must be high school senior. Applicant must be U.S. citizen or permanent resident residing in Florida.
**Basis for selection:** Applicant must demonstrate high academic achievement and service orientation.
**Additional information:** Applicant must have minimum 3.5 GPA, taken 16 credits of college preparatory academic courses, completed 75 hours of community service, and scored at least 1270 on SAT or 28 on ACT (excluding writing sections). Applicant with highest academic ranking in each county will receive Academic Top Scholars award of $1,500. Application available online, and must be completed before high school graduation. Check Website for additional information and requirements.

| | |
|---|---|
| **Amount of award:** | Full tuition |

**Contact:**
Office of Student Financial Assistance
325 West Gaines Street
Suite 1314
Tallahassee, FL 32399-0400
Phone: 888-827-2004
Web: www.floridastudentfinancialaid.org

## Florida Gold Seal Vocational Scholars Award

**Type of award:** Scholarship, renewable.
**Intended use:** For undergraduate study at vocational, 2-year or 4-year institution. Designated institutions: Eligible Florida post-secondary institutions.
**Eligibility:** Applicant must be high school senior. Applicant must be U.S. citizen or permanent resident residing in Florida.
**Basis for selection:** Applicant must demonstrate high academic achievement.
**Additional information:** Minimum 3.0 GPA in core credits, 3.5 GPA in minimum of three vocational credits. Specific CPT, SAT, or ACT test scores required. Check Website for additional information and requirements. Applications available online and must be completed before high school graduation.
**Contact:**
Office of Student Financial Assistance
325 West Gaines Street
Suite 1314
Tallahassee, FL 32399-0400
Phone: 888-827-2004
Web: www.floridastudentfinancialaid.org

## Florida Medallion Scholars Award

**Type of award:** Scholarship, renewable.
**Intended use:** For undergraduate study at 2-year or 4-year institution. Designated institutions: Eligible Florida post-secondary institutions.
**Eligibility:** Applicant must be high school senior. Applicant must be U.S. citizen or permanent resident residing in Florida.

**Basis for selection:** Applicant must demonstrate high academic achievement.
**Additional information:** Minimum 3.0 GPA. Minimum composite score of 970 on SAT or 20 on ACT (excluding writing sections). Must have taken 16 credits of college preparatory academic courses. Applications available online, and must be completed before high school graduation. Check Website for additional information and requirements.
**Contact:**
Office of Student Financial Assistance
325 West Gaines Street
Suite 1314
Tallahassee, FL 32399-0400
Phone: 888-827-2004
Web: www.floridastudentfinancialaid.org

## Florida Student Assistance Grant Program

**Type of award:** Scholarship, renewable.
**Intended use:** For full-time undergraduate study at 2-year or 4-year institution. Designated institutions: Eligible Florida postsecondary institutions.
**Eligibility:** Applicant must be U.S. citizen or permanent resident residing in Florida.
**Basis for selection:** Applicant must demonstrate financial need.
**Application requirements:** Proof of eligibility. FAFSA.
**Additional information:** Each participating institution determines application deadlines, student eligibility, and award amounts. Applications available from participating schools' financial aid offices. Visit Website for more information.
**Amount of award:** $200-$2,235
**Contact:**
Office of Student Financial Assistance
325 West Gaines Street
Suite 1314
Tallahassee, FL 32399-0400
Phone: 888-827-2004
Web: www.floridastudentfinancialaid.org

## Jose Marti Scholarship Challenge Grant Fund

**Type of award:** Scholarship, renewable.
**Intended use:** For full-time freshman or graduate study at 2-year, 4-year or graduate institution in United States. Designated institutions: Florida public or eligible private institutions.
**Eligibility:** Applicant must be Mexican American, Hispanic American or Puerto Rican. Applicant must be U.S. citizen or permanent resident residing in Florida.
**Basis for selection:** Applicant must demonstrate financial need and high academic achievement.
**Application requirements:** FAFSA.
**Additional information:** Minimum 3.0 GPA. Must be of Spanish culture, born in Mexico or Hispanic country of the Caribbean, Central America, or South America, or child of same. Award number is limited to the amount of available funds. First priority given to renewal applicants, second priority to graduating high school seniors, third priority to graduate students. Applications available from high school guidance office or college financial aid office. Visit Website for more information.
**Amount of award:** $2,000
**Application deadline:** April 1
**Contact:**
Office of Student Financial Assistance
325 West Gaines Street
Suite 1314
Tallahassee, FL 32399-0400
Phone: 888-827-2004
Web: www.floridastudentfinancialaid.org

## Mary McLeod Bethune Scholarship

**Type of award:** Scholarship, renewable.
**Intended use:** For full-time undergraduate study at 4-year institution in United States. Designated institutions: Bethune-Cookman University, Edward Waters College, Florida A&M University, and Florida Memorial University.
**Eligibility:** Applicant must be U.S. citizen or permanent resident residing in Florida.
**Basis for selection:** Applicant must demonstrate financial need and high academic achievement.
**Additional information:** Minimum 3.0 high school GPA. Deadlines established by participating institutions. Award funds contingent upon matching contributions raised by the eligible institutions. Applications can be obtained from any of four designated institutions' financial aid offices. Visit Website for more information.
**Amount of award:** $3,000
**Contact:**
Office of Student Financial Assistance
325 West Gaines Street
Suite 1314
Tallahassee, FL 32399-0400
Phone: 888-827-2004
Web: www.floridastudentfinancialaid.org

## Robert C. Byrd Honors Scholarship Program

**Type of award:** Scholarship, renewable.
**Intended use:** For full-time undergraduate study at 2-year or 4-year institution in United States.
**Eligibility:** Applicant must be high school senior. Applicant must be U.S. citizen or permanent resident residing in Florida.
**Basis for selection:** Applicant must demonstrate high academic achievement.
**Application requirements:** Proof of eligibility, nomination by high school principal, adult education director, or school district superintendent.
**Additional information:** Nomination based on cumulative unweighted GPA multiplied by ACT score. Applicants are ranked with members of designated geographic region. Number and award amount determined annually.
**Amount of award:** $1,500
**Application deadline:** April 15
**Contact:**
Office of Student Financial Assistance
325 West Gaines Street
Suite 1314
Tallahassee, FL 32399-0400
Phone: 888-827-2004
Web: www.floridastudentfinancialaid.org

Scholarships

## Rosewood Family Scholarship Program

**Type of award:** Scholarship, renewable.
**Intended use:** For full-time undergraduate study at vocational, 2-year or 4-year institution in United States. Designated institutions: Public post-secondary institutions.
**Eligibility:** Applicant must be Alaskan native, Asian American, African American, Mexican American, Hispanic American, Puerto Rican, American Indian or Native Hawaiian/Pacific Islander. Applicant must be U.S. citizen or permanent resident.
**Basis for selection:** Applicant must demonstrate financial need.
**Application requirements:** Transcript. FAFSA. If not Florida resident, copy of Student Aid Report (SAR) must be sent to OSFA and postmarked by May 15th.
**Additional information:** Applicant must be descendent of African-American Rosewood families affected by the incidents of January, 1923; renewal applicants given priority. Award covers annual cost of tuition and fees up to $4,000 per semester for up to eight semesters. Visit Website for more information.

| | |
|---|---|
| **Amount of award:** | $4,000 |
| **Number of awards:** | 25 |
| **Application deadline:** | April 1 |

**Contact:**
Office of Student Financial Assistance
325 West Gaines Street
Suite 1314
Tallahassee, FL 32399-0400
Phone: 888-827-2004
Web: www.floridastudentfinancialaid.org

## Scholarships for Children and Spouses of Deceased or Disabled Veterans and Servicemembers

**Type of award:** Scholarship, renewable.
**Intended use:** For undergraduate study at postsecondary institution. Designated institutions: Eligible Florida postsecondary institutions.
**Eligibility:** Applicant must be at least 16, no older than 22. Applicant must be U.S. citizen or permanent resident residing in Florida. Applicant must be dependent of disabled veteran, deceased veteran or POW/MIA; or spouse of disabled veteran or deceased veteran.
**Application requirements:** Proof of eligibility.
**Additional information:** Child applicant must be between ages of 16 and 22. Spouse of deceased service member must not be remarried. Service members must be certified by Florida Department of Veterans Affairs. Award for students of eligible private schools based on average cost of Florida public tuition/fees. Award amount varies. Visit Website for additional information.

| | |
|---|---|
| **Application deadline:** | April 1 |

**Contact:**
Office of Student Financial Assistance
325 West Gaines Street
Suite 1314
Tallahassee, FL 32399-0400
Phone: 888-827-2004
Web: www.floridastudentfinancialaid.org

## William L. Boyd, IV, Florida Resident Access Grant Program

**Type of award:** Scholarship, renewable.
**Intended use:** For full-time undergraduate study at accredited 4-year institution. Designated institutions: Eligible private, nonprofit Florida colleges and universities.
**Eligibility:** Applicant must be U.S. citizen or permanent resident residing in Florida.
**Application requirements:** Proof of eligibility.
**Additional information:** Applicant must not have previously received bachelor's degree and may not use award for study of divinity or theology. Amount of award plus all other scholarships and grants may not exceed total amount of tuition. Contact financial aid office of eligible institutions for application and more information.

| | |
|---|---|
| **Amount of award:** | $2,425 |

**Contact:**
Office of Student Financial Assistance
325 West Gaines Street
Suite 1314
Tallahassee, FL 32399-0400
Phone: 888-827-2004
Web: www.floridastudentfinancialaid.org

# Foundation for Surgical Technology

## Foundation Student Scholarship

**Type of award:** Scholarship.
**Intended use:** For undergraduate study in United States.
**Basis for selection:** Major/career interest in surgical technology. Applicant must demonstrate financial need and high academic achievement.
**Application requirements:** Recommendations, transcript, proof of eligibility.
**Additional information:** Applicant must be enrolled in surgical technology program accredited by CAAHEP or ABHES and be eligible to sit for the NBSTSA national surgical technologist certifying examination. Award amount varies. Visit Website for application.

| | |
|---|---|
| **Number of awards:** | 23 |
| **Number of applicants:** | 200 |
| **Application deadline:** | March 1 |
| **Notification begins:** | June 15 |
| **Total amount awarded:** | $23,500 |

**Contact:**
The Foundation for Surgical Technology
Attn: Scholarship Department
6 West Dry Creek Circle, Suite 200
Littleton, CO 80120
Phone: 303-694-9130
Fax: 303-694-9169
Web: www.ast.org/educators/scholarships.aspx

# Foundation of the National Student Nurses Association, Inc.

## National Student Nurses Association Scholarship

**Type of award:** Scholarship.
**Intended use:** For full-time undergraduate study at accredited 2-year or 4-year institution. Designated institutions: State-approved schools of nursing or pre-nursing.
**Eligibility:** Applicant must be U.S. citizen or permanent resident.
**Basis for selection:** Major/career interest in nursing. Applicant must demonstrate financial need, high academic achievement and service orientation.
**Application requirements:** $10 application fee. Essay, transcript, proof of eligibility. National Student Nurses Association members must submit proof of membership.
**Additional information:** All applicants considered for following scholarships: General Scholarships, Career Mobility Scholarships, Breakthrough to Nursing Scholarships, Specialty Scholarships, and Promise of Nursing Scholarships. Applicants must be enrolled in nursing or pre-nursing program, and may hold alien registration. Awards granted for use in summer, fall of the same year and only spring of following academic year. Number of awards varies. Application deadline in January. Applications available from May through January. See Website for deadline and application.

| | |
|---|---|
| **Amount of award:** | $1,000-$2,500 |
| **Number of applicants:** | 212 |
| **Total amount awarded:** | $120,000 |

**Contact:**
Foundation of the National Student Nurses Association, Inc.
45 Main Street
Suite 606
Brooklyn, NY 11201
Phone: 718-210-0705
Fax: 718-797-1186
Web: www.nsna.org

# Francis Ouimet Scholarship Fund

## The Ouimet Scholarship

**Type of award:** Scholarship, renewable.
**Intended use:** For full-time undergraduate study at postsecondary institution.
**Basis for selection:** Competition/talent/interest in athletics/sports. Applicant must demonstrate financial need and high academic achievement.
**Application requirements:** Interview, recommendations, essay, transcript. FAFSA and CSS Profile, SAT scores. Photo.
**Additional information:** Applicants must have worked on golf course in Massachusetts for at least two years. Contact the Ouimet Fund office in June to be put on application mailing list for awards for following school year, or sign up for application online.

| | |
|---|---|
| **Amount of award:** | $1,500-$8,000 |
| **Number of awards:** | 350 |
| **Number of applicants:** | 364 |
| **Application deadline:** | December 1 |
| **Notification begins:** | August 31 |
| **Total amount awarded:** | $1,460,000 |

**Contact:**
Francis Ouimet Scholarship Fund
William F. Connell Golf House & Museum
300 Arnold Palmer Blvd.
Norton, MA 02766
Phone: 774-430-9090
Fax: 774-430-9091
Web: www.ouimet.org

# Fred G. Zahn Foundation

## Fred G. Zahn Scholarship Fund

**Type of award:** Scholarship, renewable.
**Intended use:** For undergraduate study at accredited 2-year or 4-year institution in United States. Designated institutions: Institutions in Washington state.
**Eligibility:** Applicant must be residing in Washington.
**Basis for selection:** Applicant must demonstrate financial need, high academic achievement and depth of character.
**Application requirements:** Essay, transcript. Student Aid Report.
**Additional information:** Must have graduated from Washington state high school. Preference to juniors and seniors with minimum 3.75 GPA. May obtain application and more information at eligible Washington state institutions.

| | |
|---|---|
| **Amount of award:** | $1,500 |
| **Application deadline:** | April 15 |
| **Notification begins:** | June 15 |

**Contact:**
Fred G. Zahn Scholarship Fund
c/o US Trust/Bank of America
P.O. Box 830259
Dallas, TX 75283-0259
Phone: 866-461-7282
Fax: 800-658-6507

# Freedom From Religion Foundation

## Herbert Buschong Scholarship

**Type of award:** Scholarship.
**Intended use:** For freshman study at postsecondary institution.
**Eligibility:** Applicant must be high school senior.
**Basis for selection:** Competition/talent/interest in writing/journalism, based on best-written essays.
**Application requirements:** Essay, proof of eligibility. Essay should be 500-750 words, stapled, typed, double-spaced with standard margins. Include autobiographical paragraph giving both campus and permanent address, phone numbers, and e-mail. Identify high school and college/university to be attended. Include intended major and other interests.
**Additional information:** Applicant must be college-bound high school senior. Essay topics and requirements change

annually and are announced in February. Students are requested not to inquire before then. Visit Website for more information. First place receives $2,000; second place, $1,000; third place, $500; fourth place, $300; honorable mention(s), $200. Essays must be submitted via postal mail and email.

**Amount of award:** $200-$2,000
**Application deadline:** June 1
**Notification begins:** August 1

**Contact:**
Freedom From Religion Foundation
High School Essay Contest
P.O. Box 750
Madison, WI 53701
Phone: 608-256-8900
Web: www.ffrf.org



### Michael Hakeem Memorial Award

**Type of award:** Scholarship.
**Intended use:** For full-time undergraduate or graduate study at postsecondary institution. Designated institutions: North American institutions.
**Eligibility:** Applicant must be no older than 24.
**Basis for selection:** Competition/talent/interest in writing/journalism, based on best-written essays.
**Application requirements:** Essay. Essay should be 750-1000 words, typed, stapled, double-spaced with standard margins. Include autobiographical paragraph giving both campus and permanent addresses, phone numbers, and e-mail. Identify college/university, major, and interests. Essay on free thought concerning religion; essay most suitable for atheistic and agnostic student.
**Additional information:** Applicant must be currently enrolled college student. Essay topics and requirements change annually and are announced in February. Check Website for current topic. Students are requested not to inquire before then. Visit Website for more information. First place receives $2,000; second place, $1,000; third place, $500; fourth place, $300; honorable mention(s), $200. Essays must be submitted via postal mail and email.

**Amount of award:** $200-$2,000
**Application deadline:** June 15
**Notification begins:** September 1

**Contact:**
Freedom From Religion Foundation
College Essay Competition
P.O. Box 750
Madison, WI 53701
Phone: 608-256-8900
Web: www.ffrf.org

## Garden Club of America

### Award in Desert Studies

**Type of award:** Scholarship.
**Intended use:** For junior, senior or graduate study at accredited postsecondary institution in United States.
**Basis for selection:** Major/career interest in horticulture; botany; environmental science or landscape architecture.
**Application requirements:** Recommendations, essay. Resume, itemized budget, research/project proposal.
**Additional information:** Projects must pertain to arid environment, preference given to projects that generate scientifically sound water and plant management. Visit www.dbg.org for application information.

**Amount of award:** $4,000
**Application deadline:** January 15
**Notification begins:** March 31

**Contact:**
Desert Botanical Garden
Attn: Cathy Babcock, Director of Horticulture
1201 N. Galvin Parkway
Phoenix, AZ 85008
Phone: 480-481-8162
Web: www.gcamerica.org or www.desertbotanical.org

### Caroline Thorn Kissel Summer Environmental Studies Scholarship

**Type of award:** Scholarship.
**Intended use:** For undergraduate or graduate study at postsecondary institution.
**Eligibility:** Applicant must be U.S. citizen residing in New Jersey.
**Basis for selection:** Major/career interest in environmental science.
**Application requirements:** Recommendations, essay.
**Additional information:** Must be either New Jersey resident or non-resident studying in New Jersey. All application elements must be mailed together in one envelope. Visit Website for application and deadline.

**Amount of award:** $2,000
**Number of awards:** 1

**Contact:**
Garden Club of America
Connie Yates
14 East 60th Street
New York, NY 10022-1002
Phone: 212-753-8287
Fax: 212-753-0134
Web: www.gcamerica.org

### Field Botany Scholarships

**Type of award:** Scholarship.
**Intended use:** For undergraduate or master's study at accredited postsecondary institution in United States.
**Basis for selection:** Major/career interest in botany or horticulture.
**Application requirements:** Recommendations, essay, transcript.
**Additional information:** One application for two awards: GCA Scholarship in Field Botany and Joan K. and Rachel M. Hunt Summer Scholarship in Field Botany. Submit application via U.S. Mail with all information in one envelope. Visit Website for application.

**Amount of award:** $2,000
**Application deadline:** February 1

**Contact:**
Garden Club of America
Ms. Connie Yates
14 East 60th Street
New York, NY 10022-1002
Phone: 212-753-8287
Fax: 212-753-0134
Web: www.gcamerica.org

## Francis M. Peacock Native Bird Habitat Scholarship

**Type of award:** Scholarship.
**Intended use:** For senior or graduate study at postsecondary institution.
**Basis for selection:** Major/career interest in ornithology.
**Application requirements:** Project proposal of no more than five pages.
**Additional information:** Grant for advanced study of U.S. winter/summer habitat of threatened or endangered native birds. Awarded in cooperation with the Cornell Lab of Ornithology. Second semester juniors may apply for senior year. No phone calls. To apply, contact: www.birds.cornell.edu/about/jobs.html.

| | |
|---|---|
| **Amount of award:** | $4,000 |
| **Number of awards:** | 1 |
| **Application deadline:** | January 15 |
| **Notification begins:** | March 31 |
| **Total amount awarded:** | $4,000 |

**Contact:**
Cornell Lab of Ornithology
Scott Sutcliffe
159 Sapsucker Woods Road
Ithaca, NY 14850
Fax: 212-753-8287
Web: www.gcamerica.org

## Garden Club of America Summer Environmental Awards

**Type of award:** Scholarship.
**Intended use:** For freshman, sophomore or junior study at 4-year institution.
**Basis for selection:** Major/career interest in environmental science or ecology.
**Application requirements:** Recommendations, essay, transcript.
**Additional information:** Three awards for summer study in field of ecology and environmental studies: The Mary T. Carothers Scholarship, The Clara Carter Higgins/GCA Scholarship, and The Elizabeth Gardner Norweb Scholarship. Application must be sent via mail.

| | |
|---|---|
| **Amount of award:** | $2,000 |
| **Number of awards:** | 3 |
| **Application deadline:** | February 10 |

**Contact:**
Garden Club of America Awards for Summer Environmental Studies
Connie Yates
14 East 60th Street
New York, NY 10022-1002
Phone: 212-753-8287
Fax: 212-753-0134
Web: www.gcamerica.org

## Katharine M. Grosscup Scholarship

**Type of award:** Scholarship.
**Intended use:** For sophomore, junior, senior or graduate study at accredited 4-year or graduate institution in United States. Designated institutions: Kentucky, Indiana, Michigan, Ohio, Pennsylvania, West Virginia institutions.
**Basis for selection:** Major/career interest in horticulture. Applicant must demonstrate financial need and high academic achievement.
**Application requirements:** Interview, recommendations, essay, transcript.
**Additional information:** Minimum 3.5 GPA. Several scholarships available. Preference given to students who are residents of Pennsylvania, Ohio, West Virginia, Michigan, Indiana and, Kentucky. Major can be in related field. Please do not contact by phone. Application available on Website, and must be submitted via mail.

| | |
|---|---|
| **Amount of award:** | $3,000 |
| **Application deadline:** | February 1 |

**Contact:**
Katharine M. Grosscup Scholarship Committee/
Cleveland Botanical Garden
11030 East Boulevard
Cleveland, OH 44106
Fax: 216-721-2056
Web: www.gcamerica.org

## The Loy McCandless Marks Scholarship

**Type of award:** Scholarship.
**Intended use:** For junior, senior or graduate study at accredited 4-year or graduate institution in United States.
**Eligibility:** Applicant must be U.S. citizen.
**Basis for selection:** Major/career interest in botany; horticulture or landscape architecture.
**Application requirements:** Recommendations, essay, transcript. Budget.
**Additional information:** For study and research at appropriate foreign institution specializing in study of tropical plants. Visit Website for application. Award only given in even-numbered years.

| | |
|---|---|
| **Amount of award:** | $4,000 |
| **Number of awards:** | 1 |
| **Application deadline:** | January 15 |

**Contact:**
Garden Club of America
Connie Yates
14 East 60th Street
New York, NY 10022-1002
Phone: 212-753-8287
Fax: 212-753-0134
Web: www.gcamerica.org

## Zeller Summer Scholarship in Medicinal Botany

**Type of award:** Scholarship.
**Intended use:** For undergraduate or graduate study at accredited postsecondary institution in United States.
**Basis for selection:** Major/career interest in botany.
**Application requirements:** Recommendations, essay, transcript.
**Additional information:** Mail all application materials together in one envelope.

| | |
|---|---|
| **Amount of award:** | $2,000 |
| **Number of awards:** | 1 |
| **Application deadline:** | February 1 |

**Contact:**
Garden Club of America
Ms. Connie Yates
14 East 60th Street
New York, NY 10022-1002
Phone: 212-753-8287
Fax: 212-753-0134
Web: www.gcamerica.org

# Georgia Student Finance Commission

## Accel Program Grant

**Type of award:** Scholarship.
**Intended use:** For undergraduate study at accredited vocational, 2-year or 4-year institution.
**Eligibility:** Applicant must be high school junior or senior. Applicant must be U.S. citizen or permanent resident residing in Georgia.
**Application requirements:** Must submit completed application to high school for each participating term.
**Additional information:** Assistance for high school students to take college level coursework for credit in both high school and college. Must be approved by both high school and college as a dual credit enrollment student. Awards are pro-rated for students taking less than 12 hours per semester. Students must apply on or before the last day of school term or student's withdrawal date, whichever is first. Visit Website for application, deadline, amount of award, and number of awards available.

| | |
|---|---|
| **Number of applicants:** | 3,739 |
| **Total amount awarded:** | $5,764,625 |

**Contact:**
Georgia Student Finance Commission
2082 East Exchange Place
Suite 100
Tucker, GA 30084
Phone: 800-505-4732
Fax: 770-724-9004
Web: www.gacollege411.org

## Georgia Hope Grant - GED Recipient

**Type of award:** Scholarship.
**Intended use:** For undergraduate study at accredited vocational, 2-year or 4-year institution. Designated institutions: HOPE-eligible colleges and universities in Georgia.
**Eligibility:** Applicant must be U.S. citizen or permanent resident residing in Georgia.
**Application requirements:** Proof of eligibility.
**Additional information:** Must have received GED from Georgia Department of Technical and Adult Education after June 30, 1993. Submit HOPE voucher upon enrollment. Students receiving GED from DTAE receive voucher automatically. Visit Website for application, deadline, amount of award, and number of awards available.

| | |
|---|---|
| **Number of applicants:** | 4,947 |
| **Total amount awarded:** | $2,467,836 |

**Contact:**
Georgia Student Finance Commission
2082 East Exchange Place
Suite 100
Tucker, GA 30084
Phone: 800-505-4732
Fax: 770-724-9004
Web: www.gacollege411.org

## Georgia Hope Grant - Public Technical Institution

**Type of award:** Scholarship, renewable.
**Intended use:** For undergraduate study at accredited vocational, 2-year or 4-year institution. Designated institutions: Branches and affiliates of the Georgia Department of Technical and Adult Education and branches of the University System of Georgia.
**Eligibility:** Applicant must be U.S. citizen or permanent resident residing in Georgia. Applicant may also be dependent child of military personnel stationed in Georgia.
**Additional information:** Must be enrolled, matriculated technical certificate or diploma student. Visit Website for application, deadline, amount of award, and number of awards available.

| | |
|---|---|
| **Number of applicants:** | 114,288 |
| **Total amount awarded:** | $128,700,000 |

**Contact:**
Georgia Student Finance Commission
2082 East Exchange Place
Suite 100
Tucker, GA 30084
Phone: 800-505-4732
Fax: 770-724-9004
Web: www.gacollege411.org

## Georgia Hope Scholarship - Private Institution

**Type of award:** Scholarship, renewable.
**Intended use:** For undergraduate study at accredited 2-year or 4-year institution. Designated institutions: Eligible Georgia private colleges and universities.
**Eligibility:** Applicant must be U.S. citizen or permanent resident residing in Georgia.
**Basis for selection:** Applicant must demonstrate high academic achievement.
**Additional information:** Visit Website for application, deadline, amount of award, and number of awards available.

| | |
|---|---|
| **Number of applicants:** | 13,980 |
| **Total amount awarded:** | $43,300,000 |

**Contact:**
Georgia Student Finance Commission
2082 East Exchange Place
Suite 100
Tucker, GA 30084
Phone: 800-505-4732
Fax: 770-724-9004
Web: www.gacollege411.org

## Georgia Hope Scholarship - Public College or University

**Type of award:** Scholarship, renewable.
**Intended use:** For undergraduate study at accredited 2-year or 4-year institution. Designated institutions: Eligible Georgia public colleges and universities.
**Eligibility:** Applicant must be U.S. citizen or permanent resident residing in Georgia.
**Basis for selection:** Applicant must demonstrate high academic achievement.
**Application requirements:** Proof of eligibility.
**Additional information:** Minimum 3.0 GPA. Must be designated HOPE scholar. Visit Website for application, deadline, amount of award, and number of awards available.

**Number of applicants:** 89,751
**Total amount awarded:** $348,100,000

**Contact:**
Georgia Student Finance Commission
2082 East Exchange Place
Suite 100
Tucker, GA 30084
Phone: 800-505-4732
Fax: 770-724-9004
Web: www.gacollege411.org

## Georgia Law Enforcement Personnel Dependents Grant

**Type of award:** Scholarship, renewable.
**Intended use:** For full-time undergraduate study at accredited vocational, 2-year or 4-year institution. Designated institutions: Georgia colleges and public technical institutions.
**Eligibility:** Applicant must be U.S. citizen or permanent resident residing in Georgia. Applicant's parent must have been killed or disabled in work-related accident as firefighter, police officer or public safety officer.
**Application requirements:** Proof of eligibility.
**Additional information:** Must complete preliminary document that verifies claim with parent's former employer and doctors. Parent must have been permanently disabled or killed in the line of duty as Georgia police officer, firefighter, emergency medical technician, or corrections officer. Visit Website for application, deadline, amount of award, and number of awards available.

**Total amount awarded:** $64,270

**Contact:**
Georgia Student Finance Commission
2082 East Exchange Place
Suite 100
Tucker, GA 30084
Phone: 800-505-4732
Fax: 770-724-9004
Web: www.gacollege411.org

## Georgia LEAP Grant

**Type of award:** Scholarship, renewable.
**Intended use:** For undergraduate study at vocational, 2-year or 4-year institution.
**Eligibility:** Applicant must be U.S. citizen or permanent resident residing in Georgia.
**Basis for selection:** Applicant must demonstrate financial need.
**Application requirements:** FAFSA.
**Additional information:** Must submit application on or before the last day of school term. Must apply for and be eligible to receive Federal Pell Grant. Visit Website for application, deadline, amount of award, and number of awards available.

**Total amount awarded:** $1,475,500

**Contact:**
Georgia Student Finance Commission
2082 East Exchange Place
Suite 100
Tucker, GA 30084
Phone: 800-505-4732
Fax: 770-724-9004
Web: www.gacollege411.org

## Georgia Robert C. Byrd Scholarship

**Type of award:** Scholarship, renewable.
**Intended use:** For full-time undergraduate study at accredited 2-year or 4-year institution in United States.
**Eligibility:** Applicant must be high school senior. Applicant must be U.S. citizen or permanent resident residing in Georgia.
**Basis for selection:** Applicant must demonstrate high academic achievement.
**Application requirements:** Essay, transcript, proof of eligibility. SAT/ACT scores.
**Additional information:** Obtain application from high school guidance office and submit to Georgia Department of Education. Visit Website for deadline, amount of award, and number of awards available.

**Total amount awarded:** $1,023,545

**Contact:**
Georgia Student Finance Commission
2082 East Exchange Place
Suite 100
Tucker, GA 30084
Phone: 800-505-4732
Fax: 770-724-9004
Web: www.gacollege411.org

## Georgia Tuition Equalization Grant

**Type of award:** Scholarship, renewable.
**Intended use:** For full-time undergraduate study at accredited 2-year or 4-year institution. Designated institutions: GSFC approved institutions.
**Eligibility:** Applicant must be U.S. citizen or permanent resident residing in Georgia.
**Application requirements:** Proof of eligibility. Mileage affidavit (for out-of-state schools only).
**Additional information:** Must be enrolled at eligible private college or university in Georgia, or be a junior or senior with no Georgia public college within 50 miles of home and enrolled at eligible public college outside Georgia. Amount of award determined by Georgia General Assembly appropriations. Application deadlines set by schools. Visit Website for list of approved institutions, application, amount of award, and number of awards available.

**Total amount awarded:** $31,242,792

**Contact:**
Georgia Student Finance Commission
2082 East Exchange Place
Suite 100
Tucker, GA 30084
Phone: 800-505-4732
Fax: 770-724-9004
Web: www.gacollege411.org

# Glamour Magazine

## Top 10 College Women Competition

**Type of award:** Scholarship.
**Intended use:** For full-time junior study at accredited 4-year institution in United States or Canada.
**Eligibility:** Applicant must be female.
**Basis for selection:** Applicant must demonstrate high academic achievement, leadership and service orientation.

**Application requirements:** Recommendations, essay, transcript. List of activities, black-and-white or color photograph.
**Additional information:** See Website for deadline, application, and details. Not applicable in Quebec.

| | |
|---|---|
| **Amount of award:** | $3,000-$20,000 |
| **Number of awards:** | 10 |

**Contact:**
Glamour's Top 10 College Women Competition
4 Times Square
16th Floor
New York, NY 10036-6593
Fax: 212-286-6922
Web: www.glamour.com/about/top-10-college-women

# Golden Apple

## Golden Apple Scholars of Illinois Program

**Type of award:** Scholarship.
**Intended use:** For undergraduate study at 4-year institution in United States. Designated institutions: Participating Illinois universities.
**Eligibility:** Applicant must be high school senior. Applicant must be U.S. citizen residing in Illinois.
**Basis for selection:** Major/career interest in education; education, early childhood; education, special or education, teacher. Applicant must demonstrate high academic achievement.
**Application requirements:** Transcript. SAT/ACT scores.
**Additional information:** Must obtain teacher's certification and teach for five years in Illinois school of need. Must participate in Summer Institutes. Must be high school senior or college sophomore. Scholars receive $2,000 stipend for attending Summer Institute program. Recipients may receive a maximum of $23,000 over four years. Visit Website for application and nomination forms.

| | |
|---|---|
| **Number of awards:** | 110 |
| **Number of applicants:** | 105 |
| **Application deadline:** | November 15 |
| **Notification begins:** | April 1 |
| **Total amount awarded:** | $492,500 |

**Contact:**
Golden Apple
8 South Michigan Avenue
Suite 700
Chicago, IL 60603
Phone: 312-407-0006
Fax: 312-407-0344
Web: www.goldenapple.org

# Golden Key International Honour Society

## Business Achievement Awards

**Type of award:** Scholarship.
**Intended use:** For undergraduate or graduate study at accredited postsecondary institution.
**Basis for selection:** Major/career interest in business. Applicant must demonstrate high academic achievement.
**Application requirements:** Recommendations, transcript. Business-related paper/report (must not exceed 10,000 words).
**Additional information:** Open to Golden Key members only. First-place winner receives $2,000; second place, $1,500; third place, $1,000. Visit Website for application.

| | |
|---|---|
| **Amount of award:** | $1,000-$2,000 |
| **Number of awards:** | 3 |
| **Application deadline:** | March 1 |

**Contact:**
Phone: 800-377-2401
Web: www.goldenkey.org

## Community Service Award

**Type of award:** Scholarship.
**Intended use:** For undergraduate or graduate study at accredited postsecondary institution.
**Basis for selection:** Applicant must demonstrate service orientation.
**Application requirements:** Recommendations, essay. List of extracurricular activities.
**Additional information:** Only Golden Key members who were enrolled as students during previous academic year eligible to apply. Winner and charity of winner's choice will each receive $1,000. Visit Website for application. Number of awards varies.

| | |
|---|---|
| **Amount of award:** | $1,000 |
| **Application deadline:** | March 1 |

**Contact:**
Phone: 800-377-2401
Web: www.goldenkey.org

## Education Achievement Awards

**Type of award:** Scholarship.
**Intended use:** For undergraduate or graduate study at accredited postsecondary institution.
**Basis for selection:** Major/career interest in education. Applicant must demonstrate high academic achievement.
**Application requirements:** Recommendations, essay, transcript. An education-related paper (no more than 10,000 words).
**Additional information:** Open to Golden Key members only. First-place winner receives $2,000; second place, $1,500; third place, $1,000. Visit Website for application.

| | |
|---|---|
| **Amount of award:** | $1,000-$2,000 |
| **Number of awards:** | 3 |
| **Application deadline:** | March 1 |

**Contact:**
Phone: 800-377-2401
Web: www.goldenkey.org

## Engineering/Technology Achievement Awards

**Type of award:** Scholarship.
**Intended use:** For undergraduate or graduate study at accredited postsecondary institution.
**Basis for selection:** Major/career interest in engineering or technology. Applicant must demonstrate high academic achievement.
**Application requirements:** Recommendations, essay, transcript. An engineering-related paper (no more than 10,000 words).

**Additional information:** Open to Golden Key members only. First-place winner receives $2,000; second place, $1,500; third place, $1,000. Visit Website for application.

**Amount of award:** $1,000-$2,000
**Number of awards:** 3
**Application deadline:** March 1

**Contact:**
Phone: 800-377-2401
Web: www.goldenkey.org

## GEICO Life Scholarship

**Type of award:** Scholarship.
**Intended use:** For undergraduate study at accredited 4-year institution.
**Eligibility:** Applicant must be returning adult student.
**Basis for selection:** Applicant must demonstrate high academic achievement.
**Application requirements:** Recommendations, essay, transcript. Essay should be no more than 500 words and describe educational goals, other commitments, and obstacles overcome to achieve academic excellence.
**Additional information:** Only Golden Key members eligible to apply. Applicants must have completed at least 12 credit hours since returning to school. Visit Website for details and application. Number of awards varies.

**Amount of award:** $1,000
**Application deadline:** April 1

**Contact:**
Phone: 800-377-2401
Web: www.goldenkey.org

## Literary Achievement Awards

**Type of award:** Scholarship.
**Intended use:** For undergraduate or graduate study at accredited postsecondary institution.
**Basis for selection:** Competition/talent/interest in writing/journalism.
**Application requirements:** Original composition, not to exceed 1,500 words.
**Additional information:** Open to Golden Key members only. Previously published works not accepted. Four contest categories: fiction, non-fiction, poetry, and news writing. Only one entry per category per member. Visit Website for details and application.

**Amount of award:** $1,000
**Number of awards:** 4
**Application deadline:** March 1
**Total amount awarded:** $4,000

**Contact:**
Phone: 800-377-2401
Web: www.goldenkey.org

## Regional Student Leader of the Year Award

**Type of award:** Scholarship.
**Intended use:** For undergraduate or graduate study at accredited postsecondary institution in United States.
**Basis for selection:** Applicant must demonstrate high academic achievement and leadership.
**Application requirements:** Recommendations, essay, transcript. List of personal Golden Key involvement and other extracurricular activities.
**Additional information:** Open to Golden Key members only. Applicant must be active member in good standing. Winners at regional level will be considered for International Student Leader Award. Visit Website for details and application.

**Amount of award:** $1,000
**Number of awards:** 13
**Application deadline:** April 1

**Contact:**
Phone: 800-377-2401
Web: www.goldenkey.org

## Research Grants

**Type of award:** Research grant.
**Intended use:** For undergraduate or graduate study.
**Basis for selection:** Applicant must demonstrate high academic achievement.
**Application requirements:** Transcript. Budget summary and description of proposed research.
**Additional information:** Only Golden Key members eligible to apply. Grant for members to travel to professional conferences and student research symposia, or to conduct thesis research. At least four awards will be presented for the October 15 deadline, at least six for the April 1 deadline. Number of awards varies. Visit Website for details and application.

**Amount of award:** $1,000
**Application deadline:** April 1, October 15

**Contact:**
Phone: 800-377-2401
Web: www.goldenkey.org

## Study Abroad Scholarships

**Type of award:** Scholarship.
**Intended use:** For undergraduate or graduate study at postsecondary institution.
**Basis for selection:** Competition/talent/interest in study abroad, based on relevance of study abroad program to major field of study. Applicant must demonstrate high academic achievement.
**Application requirements:** Transcript, proof of eligibility. Description of planned academic program at host university. One-page statement of relevance of program to degree.
**Additional information:** Only Golden Key members eligible to apply. At least three awards presented for the October 15 deadline and at least seven for the April 1 deadline. Number of awards varies. Visit Website for details and application.

**Amount of award:** $1,000
**Application deadline:** April 1, October 15

**Contact:**
Phone: 800-377-2401
Web: www.goldenkey.org

## Visual and Performing Arts Achievement Awards

**Type of award:** Scholarship.
**Intended use:** For undergraduate or graduate study at accredited postsecondary institution.
**Basis for selection:** Competition/talent/interest in visual arts, based on quality of work submitted.
**Application requirements:** Digital images of visual work; digital file of performance (ten minute maximum).
**Additional information:** Open to Golden Key members only. At least one award in each of nine categories: painting, drawing, mixed media, sculpture, photography, computer-generated art/illustration/graphic design, instrumental performance, vocal performance, and dance. One entry per member per category. Visit Website for details and application.

**Amount of award:** $1,000
**Application deadline:** March 1

**Contact:**
Phone: 800-377-2401
Web: www.goldenkey.org

# Grange Insurance Association

## Grange Insurance Scholarship

**Type of award:** Scholarship.
**Intended use:** For full-time undergraduate or graduate study at accredited vocational, 2-year, 4-year or graduate institution.
**Eligibility:** Applicant must be U.S. citizen or permanent resident residing in Wyoming, California, Oregon, Idaho, Washington or Colorado.
**Basis for selection:** Applicant must demonstrate financial need, high academic achievement, depth of character, leadership, patriotism, seriousness of purpose and service orientation.
**Application requirements:** Essay, transcript. Cover letter.
**Additional information:** Applicant must be one of the following: current GIA policyholder (or child of GIA policyholder), Grange member (or child of Grange member), or child of current GIA company employee. Previous recipients also eligible to apply. Application must be postmarked by deadline.

| | |
|---|---|
| **Amount of award:** | $1,000-$1,500 |
| **Number of awards:** | 26 |
| **Number of applicants:** | 129 |
| **Application deadline:** | March 1 |
| **Notification begins:** | April 15 |
| **Total amount awarded:** | $26,000 |

**Contact:**
Grange Insurance Association
Scholarship Committee
P.O. Box 21089
Seattle, WA 98111-3089
Phone: 800-247-2643 ext. 2200
Web: www.grange.com

# Great Minds in Stem

## Great Minds in Stem Scholars Program

**Type of award:** Scholarship, renewable.
**Intended use:** For full-time undergraduate or graduate study at 2-year, 4-year or graduate institution.
**Basis for selection:** Major/career interest in engineering; mathematics; science, general or technology. Applicant must demonstrate high academic achievement and leadership.
**Application requirements:** Recommendations, essay. Resume.
**Additional information:** Minimum 3.0 GPA. Include SASE with application request, or download application from Website. Amount of award varies.

| | |
|---|---|
| **Amount of award:** | $500-$5,000 |
| **Number of awards:** | 80 |
| **Application deadline:** | April 30 |
| **Notification begins:** | August 1 |
| **Total amount awarded:** | $250,000 |

**Contact:**
Great Minds in Stem
Student Scholarship Committee
3900 Whiteside Street
Los Angeles, CA 90063
Phone: 323-262-0997
Web: www.greatmindsinstem.org

# Greater Kanawha Valley Foundation

## Greater Kanawha Valley Scholarship Program

**Type of award:** Scholarship, renewable.
**Intended use:** For full-time undergraduate or graduate study at 4-year or graduate institution.
**Eligibility:** Applicant must be residing in West Virginia.
**Basis for selection:** Applicant must demonstrate high academic achievement and depth of character.
**Application requirements:** Recommendations, transcript. First page of parents' federal income tax return.
**Additional information:** Minimum 20 ACT score. Foundation offers more than 80 scholarships, each with specific eligibility criteria. Visit Website for complete listing, and to apply.

| | |
|---|---|
| **Amount of award:** | $1,000 |
| **Number of awards:** | 565 |
| **Number of applicants:** | 750 |
| **Application deadline:** | January 15 |
| **Notification begins:** | May 15 |
| **Total amount awarded:** | $865,000 |

**Contact:**
The Greater Kanawha Valley Foundation
P.O. Box 3041
Charleston, WV 25331
Phone: 304-346-3620
Web: www.tgkvf.org

# Greenhouse Scholars

## Greenhouse Scholars Program

**Type of award:** Scholarship, renewable.
**Intended use:** For full-time undergraduate study at 4-year institution.
**Eligibility:** Applicant must be high school senior. Applicant must be U.S. citizen or permanent resident residing in Colorado.
**Basis for selection:** Based on commitment to community, ability to persevere through difficult circumstances, strong sense of accountability. Applicant must demonstrate financial need, high academic achievement and leadership.
**Application requirements:** Transcript. Three letters of recommendation, ACT scores.
**Additional information:** The Greenhouse Scholars Program is a scholarship and mentorship program for under-resourced, high-achieving students. The program uses a 'Whole Person' approach to address the intellectual, academic, professional, and financial needs of students. Minimum 3.5 GPA. Renewable

for four years. Visit Website for application and more information.

| | |
|---|---|
| **Amount of award:** | $1,000-$5,000 |
| **Number of awards:** | 15 |
| **Number of applicants:** | 150 |
| **Application deadline:** | January 20 |
| **Notification begins:** | February 22 |
| **Total amount awarded:** | $90,000 |

**Contact:**
Greenhouse Scholars
1011 Walnut Street, Third Floor
Boulder, CO 80302
Phone: 303-464-7811
Fax: 303-464-7796
Web: www.greenhousescholars.org

# Harness Tracks of America

## Harness Tracks of America Scholarship Fund

**Type of award:** Scholarship.
**Intended use:** For full-time undergraduate or graduate study at accredited postsecondary institution.
**Eligibility:** Applicant or parent must be member/participant of Harness Racing Industry.
**Basis for selection:** Applicant must demonstrate financial need and high academic achievement.
**Application requirements:** Essay, transcript, proof of eligibility. FAFSA and U.S. or Canadian tax return.
**Additional information:** Must be child of licensed driver, trainer, breeder, owner or caretaker of harness horses or be personally active in harness racing industry. Children of deceased industry members also eligible. Recommendations not required but considered if included with application. Awards based on financial need, academic excellence, and active harness racing involvement. Visit Website for more information.

| | |
|---|---|
| **Amount of award:** | $5,000 |
| **Number of awards:** | 5 |
| **Number of applicants:** | 39 |
| **Application deadline:** | May 15 |
| **Notification begins:** | September 15 |
| **Total amount awarded:** | $25,000 |

**Contact:**
Harness Tracks of America
4640 East Sunrise Drive
Suite 200
Tucson, AZ 85718
Phone: 520-529-2525
Fax: 520-529-3235
Web: www.harnesstracks.com

# Havana National Bank

## McFarland Charitable Foundation Scholarship

**Type of award:** Scholarship, renewable.
**Intended use:** For full-time undergraduate study at accredited vocational, 2-year or 4-year institution in United States.
**Basis for selection:** Major/career interest in nursing. Applicant must demonstrate seriousness of purpose.
**Application requirements:** Interview, recommendations, transcript, proof of eligibility. Letter of acceptance to RN program.
**Additional information:** Award recipients must contractually obligate themselves to return to Havana, Illinois, and work as registered nurses for two years for each year of funding. Reverts to loan if work obligation is not met. Two co-signers are required. To fund RN programs only. Number of awards and amounts varies.

| | |
|---|---|
| **Amount of award:** | $1,000-$20,000 |
| **Number of applicants:** | 6 |
| **Application deadline:** | May 15 |
| **Notification begins:** | June 15 |
| **Total amount awarded:** | $75,000 |

**Contact:**
Havana National Bank
112 South Orange
P.O. Box 200
Havana, IL 62644-0200
Phone: 309-543-3361
Web: www.havanabank.com

# Hawaii Community Foundation

## 100th Infantry Battalion Memorial Scholarship Fund

**Type of award:** Scholarship.
**Intended use:** For full-time undergraduate or graduate study at 2-year or 4-year institution in United States.
**Eligibility:** Applicant must be U.S. citizen or permanent resident. Applicant must be descendant of veteran. Must be direct descendant of a 100th Infantry Battalion World War II veteran.
**Basis for selection:** Applicant must demonstrate financial need, high academic achievement, depth of character and service orientation.
**Application requirements:** Recommendations, essay, transcript, proof of eligibility. SAR, Personal Statement. Essay on topic: "What is the legacy of the 100th Infantry Battalion of WWII and how will you contribute to forwarding this legacy?" Name World War II 100th Battalion and your relationship to individual.
**Additional information:** Must be direct descendant of a 100th Infantry Battalion World War II veteran and be willing to promote its legacy. Minimum 3.5 GPA. Applicant does not have to reside in Hawaii.

| | |
|---|---|
| **Application deadline:** | March 1 |

**Contact:**
Hawaii Community Foundation Scholarships
1164 Bishop Street
Suite 800
Honolulu, HI 96813
Phone: 888-731-3863
Fax: 808-521-6286
Web: www.hawaiicommunityfoundation.org

## A & B Ohana Scholarship

**Type of award:** Scholarship, renewable.
**Intended use:** For full-time undergraduate study at 2-year or 4-year institution in United States.
**Eligibility:** Applicant must be residing in Hawaii.
**Basis for selection:** Applicant must demonstrate financial need and high academic achievement.
**Application requirements:** Recommendations, essay, transcript. Name and title of parent who is Alexander & Baldwin employee, SAR.
**Additional information:** Minimum 2.7 GPA. Must be dependent child of full-time employee of Alexander & Baldwin, Inc. Employee must have completed one year of full-time continuous service by application deadline. Must attend college or university with 501c3 status. If attending community college, award amount will be lower.

**Application deadline:** March 1

**Contact:**
Hawaii Community Foundation
827 Fort Street Mall
Honolulu, HI 96813
Phone: 888-731-3863
Fax: 808-521-6286
Web: www.hawaiicommunityfoundation.org

## ABC Stores Jumpstart Scholarship

**Type of award:** Scholarship.
**Intended use:** For undergraduate or graduate study at accredited 2-year, 4-year or graduate institution in United States.
**Eligibility:** Applicant must be residing in Hawaii or Nevada.
**Basis for selection:** Applicant must demonstrate financial need, high academic achievement and depth of character.
**Application requirements:** Recommendations, essay, transcript. SAR, FAFSA, Personal Statement. Name of ABC Stores Employee and relationship (i.e., mother).
**Additional information:** Must be resident of Hawaii, Nevada, Guam or Saipan. Minimum 2.7 GPA. Applicants must have permanent address in Hawaii. Amount of award may change yearly. Applicant must be employee or dependent of ABC Stores or Company Island Gourmet Markets employee.

**Application deadline:** March 1

**Contact:**
Hawaii Community Foundation Scholarships
827 Fort Street Mall
Honolulu, HI 96813
Phone: 888-731-3863
Fax: 808-521-6286
Web: www.hawaiicommunityfoundation.org

## ABC Stores Vocational Education Scholarship

**Type of award:** Scholarship.
**Intended use:** For full-time undergraduate study at postsecondary institution in United States. Designated institutions: University of Hawaii system community colleges.
**Eligibility:** Applicant must be residing in Hawaii.
**Basis for selection:** Applicant must demonstrate financial need and high academic achievement.
**Application requirements:** Recommendations, essay, transcript. SAR.
**Additional information:** Minimum 2.7 GPA. Must be employee or relative of employee of ABC Stores or Company Island Gourmet Markets. Must enroll in an AS or AA career and technical degree program within University of Hawaii community college system.

**Application deadline:** March 1

**Contact:**
Hawaii Community Foundation
827 Fort Street Mall
Honolulu, HI 96813
Phone: 888-731-3863
Fax: 808-521-6286
Web: www.hawaiicommunityfoundation.org

## Aiea General Hospital Association Scholarship

**Type of award:** Scholarship, renewable.
**Intended use:** For full-time undergraduate study at accredited 2-year, 4-year or graduate institution in United States.
**Eligibility:** Applicant must be U.S. citizen or permanent resident residing in Hawaii.
**Basis for selection:** Major/career interest in health-related professions. Applicant must demonstrate financial need, high academic achievement and depth of character.
**Application requirements:** Recommendations, essay, transcript. FAFSA and SAR.
**Additional information:** Minimum 2.7 GPA. Applicant must be resident of Leeward Oahu ZIP Codes: 96701, 96706, 96707, 96782, 96792, or 96797. Amount and number of awards vary.

**Number of awards:** 26
**Application deadline:** March 1

**Contact:**
Hawaii Community Foundation Scholarships
827 Fort Street Mall
Honolulu, HI 96813
Phone: 888-731-3863
Fax: 808-521-6286
Web: www.hawaiicommunityfoundation.org

## Allan Eldin & Agnes Sutorik Geiger Scholarship Fund

**Type of award:** Scholarship.
**Intended use:** For full-time undergraduate or graduate study at accredited 2-year or 4-year institution in United States.
**Eligibility:** Applicant must be U.S. citizen residing in Hawaii.
**Basis for selection:** Major/career interest in veterinary medicine. Applicant must demonstrate financial need, high academic achievement and depth of character.
**Application requirements:** Recommendations, essay, transcript. SAR, FAFSA, Personal Statement.
**Additional information:** Minimum 3.0 GPA. Applicants must have permanent address in Hawaii. Applicants taking up mainland residency must have relatives living in Hawaii. Amount of award may change yearly.

**Application deadline:** March 1

**Contact:**
Hawaii Community Foundation Scholarships
827 Fort Street Mall
Honolulu, HI 96813
Phone: 888-731-3863
Fax: 808-521-6286
Web: www.hawaiicommunityfoundation.org

## Alma White-Delta Kappa Gamma Scholarship

**Type of award:** Scholarship.
**Intended use:** For full-time junior, senior or graduate study at accredited postsecondary institution in United States.
**Eligibility:** Applicant must be U.S. citizen or permanent resident residing in Hawaii.
**Basis for selection:** Major/career interest in education. Applicant must demonstrate financial need, high academic achievement and depth of character.
**Application requirements:** Recommendations, essay, transcript. FAFSA and SAR. Official letter confirming enrollment in education program.
**Additional information:** Applicants must have permanent address in Hawaii. Applicants taking up mainland residency must have relatives living in Hawaii. Amount and number of awards vary and may change yearly.
**Number of awards:** 10
**Application deadline:** March 1
**Contact:**
Hawaii Community Foundation Scholarships
827 Fort Street Mall
Honolulu, HI 96813
Phone: 888-731-3863
Fax: 808-521-6286
Web: www.hawaiicommunityfoundation.org

## Ambassador Minerva Jean Falcon Hawaii Scholarship

**Type of award:** Scholarship.
**Intended use:** For full-time undergraduate study at 2-year or 4-year institution. Designated institutions: 2-year or 4-year colleges in Hawaii.
**Eligibility:** Applicant must be Native Hawaiian/Pacific Islander. Applicant must be residing in Hawaii.
**Basis for selection:** Applicant must demonstrate financial need and high academic achievement.
**Application requirements:** Recommendations, essay, transcript. SAR.
**Additional information:** Minimum 2.7 GPA. Must be graduate of Hawaii high school. Must be of Filipino ancestry.
**Application deadline:** March 1
**Contact:**
Hawaii Community Foundation
827 Fort Street Mall
Honolulu, HI 96813
Phone: 888-731-3863
Fax: 808-521-6286
Web: www.hawaiicommunityfoundation.org

## American Institute of Graphic Arts (AIGA) Honolulu Chapter Scholarship Fund

**Type of award:** Scholarship.
**Intended use:** For full-time undergraduate study at 2-year, 4-year or graduate institution.
**Eligibility:** Applicant must be residing in Hawaii.
**Basis for selection:** Major/career interest in arts, general or graphic arts/design. Applicant must demonstrate financial need and high academic achievement.
**Application requirements:** Recommendations, essay, transcript. SAR.
**Additional information:** Minimum 2.7 GPA. Must major in graphic design, visual communication, or commercial arts.
**Application deadline:** March 1
**Contact:**
Hawaii Community Foundation
827 Fort Street Mall
Honolulu, HI 96813
Phone: 888-731-3863
Fax: 808-521-6286
Web: www.hawaiicommunityfoundation.org

## Arthur Jackman Memorial Scholarship

**Type of award:** Scholarship.
**Intended use:** For full-time undergraduate study at vocational institution in United States. Designated institutions: Vocational institutions in Hawaii.
**Eligibility:** Applicant must be residing in Hawaii.
**Basis for selection:** Applicant must demonstrate financial need and high academic achievement.
**Application requirements:** Recommendations, essay, transcript. SAR.
**Additional information:** Minimum 2.7 GPA.
**Application deadline:** March 1
**Contact:**
Hawaii Community Foundation
827 Fort Street Mall
Honolulu, HI 96813
Phone: 888-731-3863
Fax: 808-521-6286
Web: www.hawaiicommunityfoundation.org

## Bal Dasa Scholarship Fund

**Type of award:** Scholarship.
**Intended use:** For full-time undergraduate study at accredited 2-year or 4-year institution in United States.
**Eligibility:** Applicant must be U.S. citizen or permanent resident residing in Hawaii.
**Basis for selection:** Applicant must demonstrate financial need, high academic achievement and depth of character.
**Application requirements:** Essay, transcript. FAFSA and SAR.
**Additional information:** Must be graduate of Waipahu High School. Award amount varies yearly. Applicants taking up mainland residency must have relatives living in Hawaii.
**Number of awards:** 1
**Application deadline:** March 1
**Contact:**
Hawaii Community Foundation Scholarships
827 Fort Street Mall
Honolulu, HI 96813
Phone: 888-731-3863
Fax: 808-521-6286
Web: www.hawaiicommunityfoundation.org

## Blossom Kalama Evans Memorial Scholarship

**Type of award:** Scholarship, renewable.
**Intended use:** For full-time junior, senior or graduate study at accredited 4-year or graduate institution in United States.
**Eligibility:** Applicant must be Native Hawaiian/Pacific Islander. Applicant must be U.S. citizen or permanent resident residing in Hawaii.

**Basis for selection:** Major/career interest in Hawaiian studies. Applicant must demonstrate financial need, high academic achievement and depth of character.
**Application requirements:** Transcript. FAFSA and SAR. Personal essay stating how applicant's knowledge will be used to serve the needs of the Native Hawaiian community.
**Additional information:** Minimum 2.7 GPA. Students must be of Hawaiian ancestry. Applicants must have permanent address in Hawaii. Applicants who take up mainland residency must have relatives living in Hawaii. Amount and number of awards vary.
**Number of awards:** 9
**Application deadline:** March 1
**Contact:**
Hawaii Community Foundation Scholarships
827 Fort Street Mall
Honolulu, HI 96813
Phone: 888-731-3863
Fax: 808-521-6286
Web: www.hawaiicommunityfoundation.org

## Booz Allen Scholarship

**Type of award:** Scholarship.
**Intended use:** For full-time undergraduate study at accredited 2-year or 4-year institution.
**Eligibility:** Applicant must be residing in Hawaii.
**Basis for selection:** Applicant must demonstrate financial need and high academic achievement.
**Application requirements:** Recommendations, essay, transcript. SAR.
**Additional information:** Minimum 3.0 GPA.
**Application deadline:** March 1
**Contact:**
Hawaii Community Foundation
827 Fort Street Mall
Honolulu, HI 96813
Phone: 888-731-3863
Fax: 808-521-6286
Web: www.hawaiicommunityfoundation.org

## Camille C. Chidiac Fund

**Type of award:** Scholarship.
**Intended use:** For full-time undergraduate study at accredited 2-year or 4-year institution in United States.
**Eligibility:** Applicant must be high school senior. Applicant must be U.S. citizen or permanent resident residing in Hawaii.
**Basis for selection:** Applicant must demonstrate financial need, high academic achievement and depth of character.
**Application requirements:** Essay, transcript. FAFSA and SAR. Essay must state why it is important for Hawaii students to be internationally aware.
**Additional information:** Applicant must be student at Ka'u High School. Amount of scholarship varies yearly. Applicants taking up mainland residency must have relatives living in Hawaii.
**Number of awards:** 1
**Application deadline:** March 1
**Contact:**
Hawaii Community Foundation Scholarships
827 Fort Street Mall
Honolulu, HI 96813
Phone: 888-731-3863
Fax: 808-521-6286
Web: www.hawaiicommunityfoundation.org

## Candon, Todd, & Seabolt Scholarship Fund

**Type of award:** Scholarship.
**Intended use:** For junior or senior study at 4-year institution in United States.
**Eligibility:** Applicant must be U.S. citizen residing in Hawaii.
**Basis for selection:** Major/career interest in accounting or finance/banking.
**Application requirements:** Recommendations, essay, transcript. SAR.
**Additional information:** Minimum 3.2 GPA.
**Number of awards:** 1
**Application deadline:** March 1
**Contact:**
Hawaii Community Foundation Scholarships
827 Fort Street Mall
Honolulu, HI 96813
Phone: 888-731-3863
Fax: 808-521-6286
Web: www.hawaiicommunityfoundation.org

## Castle & Cooke Mililani Technology Park Scholarship Fund

**Type of award:** Scholarship.
**Intended use:** For full-time freshman study at accredited 2-year or 4-year institution in United States.
**Eligibility:** Applicant must be high school senior. Applicant must be U.S. citizen or permanent resident residing in Hawaii.
**Basis for selection:** Major/career interest in science, general; engineering or computer/information sciences. Applicant must demonstrate financial need and high academic achievement.
**Application requirements:** Essay, transcript. FAFSA and SAR.
**Additional information:** Applicants must be graduating senior from Leilehua, Mililani, or Waialua high schools. Preference given to majors in technology fields. Applicants must have permanent address in Hawaii. Applicants taking up mainland residency must have relatives living in Hawaii. Amount and number of awards vary and may change yearly.
**Number of awards:** 10
**Application deadline:** March 1
**Contact:**
Hawaii Community Foundation Scholarships
827 Fort Street Mall
Honolulu, HI 96813
Phone: 888-731-3863
Fax: 808-521-6286
Web: www.hawaiicommunityfoundation.org

## Castle & Cooke W. Y. Yim Scholarship Fund

**Type of award:** Scholarship.
**Intended use:** For full-time undergraduate or graduate study at accredited 2-year or 4-year institution in United States.
**Eligibility:** Applicant must be U.S. citizen residing in Hawaii.
**Basis for selection:** Applicant must demonstrate financial need, high academic achievement and depth of character.
**Application requirements:** Recommendations, essay, transcript. SAR, FAFSA, Personal Statement. Castle & Cooke employee name, position, and relationship to applicant.
**Additional information:** Minimum 3.0 GPA. Must be a dependent of current employee with at least one year of service with Castle & Cooke Hawaii affiliated company. Applicants must have permanent address in Hawaii. Applicants taking up

mainland residency must have relatives living in Hawaii. Amount of award may change yearly.

**Application deadline:** March 1

**Contact:**
Hawaii Community Foundation Scholarships
827 Fort Street Mall
Honolulu, HI 96813
Phone: 888-731-3863
Fax: 808-521-6286
Web: www.hawaiicommunityfoundation.org

## Cayetano Foundation Scholarship

**Type of award:** Scholarship.
**Intended use:** For full-time undergraduate study at accredited 2-year or 4-year institution.
**Eligibility:** Applicant must be high school senior. Applicant must be residing in Hawaii.
**Basis for selection:** Applicant must demonstrate financial need, high academic achievement and depth of character.
**Application requirements:** Recommendations, essay, transcript. FAFSA and SAR. SAT scores. Personal statement should describe community service. In personal essay imagine yourself in your late 50s: Reflect on your adult life, list the major accomplishments in your life, and explain why you consider them to be significant. Also include, on a separate piece of paper, your name, the occupations of your parents and your yearly income.
**Additional information:** Minimum 3.5 GPA. Preference given to students with greatest financial need. Applicants must have permanent Hawaii address. Applicants taking up mainland residency must have relatives living in Hawaii.

**Number of awards:** 14
**Application deadline:** March 1

**Contact:**
Hawaii Community Foundation Scholarships
827 Fort Street Mall
Honolulu, HI 96813
Phone: 888-731-3863
Fax: 808-521-6286
Web: www.hawaiicommunityfoundation.org

## Community Scholarship Fund

**Type of award:** Scholarship, renewable.
**Intended use:** For full-time undergraduate or graduate study at accredited 2-year or 4-year institution in United States.
**Eligibility:** Applicant must be U.S. citizen or permanent resident residing in Hawaii.
**Basis for selection:** Major/career interest in arts, general; architecture; education; humanities/liberal arts or social/behavioral sciences. Applicant must demonstrate financial need, high academic achievement, depth of character and service orientation.
**Application requirements:** Essay, transcript. FAFSA and SAR.
**Additional information:** Minimum 3.0 GPA. Must show potential for fulfilling a community need; demonstrate accomplishment, motivation, initiative, vision, and intention of returning to or staying in Hawaii to work. Must have permanent address in Hawaii. Applicants taking up mainland residency must have relatives living in Hawaii. Amount and number of awards vary and may change yearly.

**Application deadline:** March 1

**Contact:**
Hawaii Community Foundation Scholarships
827 Fort Street Mall
Honolulu, HI 96813
Phone: 888-731-3863
Fax: 808-521-6286
Web: www.hawaiicommunityfoundation.org

## Cora Aguda Manayan Fund

**Type of award:** Scholarship, renewable.
**Intended use:** For full-time undergraduate or graduate study in United States.
**Eligibility:** Applicant must be of Filipino ancestry. Applicant must be U.S. citizen or permanent resident residing in Hawaii.
**Basis for selection:** Major/career interest in health-related professions. Applicant must demonstrate financial need, high academic achievement and depth of character.
**Application requirements:** Essay, transcript. FAFSA and SAR.
**Additional information:** Preference given to students studying in Hawaii. Applicants must have permanent address in Hawaii. Applicants who take up mainland residency must have relatives living in Hawaii. Amount and number of awards vary.

**Number of awards:** 10
**Application deadline:** March 1

**Contact:**
Hawaii Community Foundation Scholarships
827 Fort Street Mall
Honolulu, HI 96813
Phone: 888-731-3863
Fax: 808-521-6286
Web: www.hawaiicommunityfoundation.org

## CPB Works For You Scholarship

**Type of award:** Scholarship.
**Intended use:** For undergraduate study at 2-year or 4-year institution.
**Eligibility:** Applicant must be residing in Hawaii.
**Basis for selection:** Applicant must demonstrate financial need and high academic achievement.
**Application requirements:** Recommendations, essay, transcript. SAR, Name and position of CPB employee.
**Additional information:** Minimum 2.7 GPA. Must be active status employee or dependent child (no older than 25) of active status employee of CPB or CPHL with minimum one year of service by application deadline. Part-time awards will be less than full-time awards.

**Application deadline:** March 1

**Contact:**
Hawaii Community Foundation
827 Fort Street Mall
Honolulu, HI 96813
Phone: 888-731-3863
Fax: 808-521-6286
Web: www.hawaiicommunityfoundation.org

## Dan & Pauline Lutkenhouse & Hawaii Tropical Botanical Garden Scholarship

**Type of award:** Scholarship.
**Intended use:** For full-time undergraduate study at accredited postsecondary institution.
**Eligibility:** Applicant must be residing in Hawaii.

**Basis for selection:** Major/career interest in agriculture; science, general; medicine or nursing. Applicant must demonstrate financial need and high academic achievement.
**Application requirements:** Recommendations, essay, transcript. SAR.
**Additional information:** Minimum 2.7 GPA. Must be resident of Hilo Coast and Hamakua Coast, north of Wailuki River.
**Application deadline:** March 1
**Contact:**
Hawaii Community Foundation
827 Fort Street Mall
Honolulu, HI 96813
Phone: 888-731-3863
Fax: 808-521-6286
Web: www.hawaiicommunityfoundation.org



## David L. Irons Memorial Scholarship Fund

**Type of award:** Scholarship.
**Intended use:** For full-time undergraduate study at accredited 2-year or 4-year institution in United States.
**Eligibility:** Applicant must be high school senior. Applicant must be U.S. citizen or permanent resident residing in Hawaii.
**Basis for selection:** Applicant must demonstrate financial need, high academic achievement and depth of character.
**Application requirements:** Essay, transcript. FAFSA and SAR. Essay must respond to following questions: 1) How would you spend a free day? 2) Who is a hero of yours, and what is an overriding quality that makes this person your hero?
**Additional information:** Applicant must be student at Punahou School. Applicants taking up mainland residency must have relatives living in Hawaii. Amount of award may change yearly.
**Number of awards:** 1
**Application deadline:** March 1
**Contact:**
Hawaii Community Foundation Scholarships
827 Fort Street Mall
Honolulu, HI 96813
Phone: 888-731-3863
Fax: 808-521-6286
Web: www.hawaiicommunityfoundation.org

## Dolly Ching Scholarship Fund

**Type of award:** Scholarship.
**Intended use:** For full-time undergraduate study at accredited postsecondary institution in United States. Designated institutions: Institutions in University of Hawaii system.
**Eligibility:** Applicant must be high school senior. Applicant must be U.S. citizen or permanent resident residing in Hawaii.
**Basis for selection:** Applicant must demonstrate financial need, high academic achievement, depth of character and service orientation.
**Application requirements:** Recommendations, essay, transcript. FAFSA and SAR.
**Additional information:** Minimum 2.7 GPA. Must be resident of Kauai. Amount and number of awards vary.
**Number of awards:** 1
**Application deadline:** March 1
**Contact:**
Hawaii Community Foundation Scholarships
827 Fort Street Mall
Honolulu, HI 96813
Phone: 888-731-3863
Fax: 808-521-6286
Web: www.hawaiicommunityfoundation.org

## Doris & Clarence Glick Classical Music Scholarship

**Type of award:** Scholarship.
**Intended use:** For full-time undergraduate study at accredited 2-year or 4-year institution in United States.
**Eligibility:** Applicant must be residing in Hawaii.
**Basis for selection:** Major/career interest in music. Applicant must demonstrate financial need, high academic achievement and depth of character.
**Application requirements:** Essay, transcript. FAFSA and SAR. Describe in personal statement how program of study relates to classical music.
**Additional information:** Must major in music, with emphasis on classical music. Applicants must have permanent address in Hawaii. Applicants taking up mainland residency must have relatives living in Hawaii. Amount and number of awards vary and may change yearly.
**Number of awards:** 4
**Application deadline:** March 1
**Contact:**
Hawaii Community Foundation Scholarships
827 Fort Street Mall
Honolulu, HI 96813
Phone: 888-731-3863
Fax: 808-521-6286
Web: www.hawaiicommunityfoundation.org

## Dr. Alvin and Monica Saake Scholarship

**Type of award:** Scholarship.
**Intended use:** For full-time junior, senior or graduate study at accredited 2-year, 4-year or graduate institution.
**Eligibility:** Applicant must be residing in Hawaii.
**Basis for selection:** Major/career interest in physical education; athletic training; sports/sports administration; physical therapy or occupational therapy. Applicant must demonstrate financial need, high academic achievement and depth of character.
**Application requirements:** Essay, transcript. FAFSA and SAR.
**Additional information:** Must be majoring in kinesiology, leisure science, physical education, athletic training, exercise science, sports medicine, physical therapy, or occupational therapy. Applicant must have permanent Hawaii address. Applicants taking up mainland residency must have relatives living in Hawaii.
**Number of awards:** 12
**Application deadline:** March 1
**Contact:**
Hawaii Community Foundation Scholarships
827 Fort Street Mall
Honolulu, HI 96813
Phone: 888-731-3863
Fax: 808-521-6286
Web: www.hawaiicommunityfoundation.org

## Dr. and Mrs. Moon Park Scholarship

**Type of award:** Scholarship.
**Intended use:** For full-time undergraduate or graduate study at accredited 2-year or 4-year institution in United States.
**Eligibility:** Applicant must be U.S. citizen residing in Hawaii.
**Basis for selection:** Applicant must demonstrate financial need and high academic achievement.

**Application requirements:** Recommendations, essay, transcript. SAR, FAFSA, Personal Statement. Clinical Laboratories of Hawaii, LLC employee name and relationship to applicant.
**Additional information:** Minimum 3.0 GPA. Must be an employee or child dependent with minimum one year of service of Clinical Laboratories of Hawaii, LLP and/or Pan Pacific Pathologies, LLC. Applicants must have permanent address in Hawaii. Applicants taking up mainland residency must have relatives living in Hawaii. Amount of award may change yearly.

**Application deadline:** March 1

**Contact:**
Hawaii Community Foundation Scholarships
827 Fort Street Mall
Honolulu, HI 96813
Phone: 888-731-3863
Fax: 808-521-6286
Web: www.hawaiicommunityfoundation.org

## Dr. Hans & Clara Zimmerman Foundation Education Scholarship

**Type of award:** Scholarship.
**Intended use:** For full-time undergraduate or graduate study at accredited 2-year or 4-year institution in United States.
**Eligibility:** Applicant must be U.S. citizen or permanent resident residing in Hawaii.
**Basis for selection:** Major/career interest in education or education, teacher. Applicant must demonstrate financial need, high academic achievement, depth of character and leadership.
**Application requirements:** Recommendations, essay, transcript. FAFSA and SAR. Recommendations must include an evaluation of applicant's "classroom teaching effectiveness." Personal statement describing applicant's community service projects or activities. Essay must also answer question "What is your teaching philosophy and how is it applied in classroom today?" (with one example). Applicants disqualified if they fail to address essay topic in personal statement.
**Additional information:** Minimum 2.8 GPA. Must major in education with an emphasis on classroom teaching. Preference given to nontraditional students with at least two years of teaching experience. Preference given to students of Hawaiian ethnicity. Applicants must have permanent address in Hawaii. Amount and number of awards vary and may change yearly.

**Number of awards:** 28
**Application deadline:** March 1

**Contact:**
Hawaii Community Foundation Scholarships
827 Fort Street Mall
Honolulu, HI 96813
Phone: 888-731-3863
Fax: 808-521-6286
Web: www.hawaiicommunityfoundation.org

## Dr. Hans and Clara Zimmerman Foundation Health Scholarship

**Type of award:** Scholarship, renewable.
**Intended use:** For full-time junior, senior or graduate study at accredited postsecondary institution in United States.
**Eligibility:** Applicant must be U.S. citizen or permanent resident residing in Hawaii.
**Basis for selection:** Major/career interest in health sciences; health-related professions or medicine. Applicant must demonstrate financial need, high academic achievement and depth of character.
**Application requirements:** Transcript. FAFSA and SAR. Personal statement including description of applicant's community service projects or activities.
**Additional information:** Minimum 3.0 GPA. Applicants must have permanent address in Hawaii. Applicants who take up mainland residency must have relatives living in Hawaii. Sports medicine and some psychology majors ineligible. Amount and number of awards vary.

**Number of awards:** 190
**Application deadline:** March 1

**Contact:**
Hawaii Community Foundation Scholarships
827 Fort Street Mall
Honolulu, HI 96813
Phone: 888-731-3863
Fax: 808-521-6286
Web: www.hawaiicommunityfoundation.org

## Eastside & Northshore Kauai Scholarship Fund

**Type of award:** Scholarship.
**Intended use:** For full-time undergraduate or graduate study at accredited 2-year or 4-year institution in United States.
**Eligibility:** Applicant must be U.S. citizen residing in Hawaii.
**Basis for selection:** Applicant must demonstrate financial need, high academic achievement and depth of character.
**Application requirements:** Recommendations, essay, transcript. SAR, FAFSA, Personal Statement.
**Additional information:** Minimum 2.5 GPA. Must be resident of one of the following East and Northshore Kaua'i areas: Anahola (96703), Kapa'a (96746), Kilauea (96754), Hanalei (96714), Princeville (96722), Kealia (96751), Wailua (96746).

**Application deadline:** March 1

**Contact:**
Hawaii Community Foundation Scholarships
827 Fort Street Mall
Honolulu, HI 96813
Phone: 888-731-3863
Fax: 808-521-6286
Web: www.hawaiicommunityfoundation.org

## Edward Payson and Bernice Pi'ilani Irwin Scholarship Trust Fund

**Type of award:** Scholarship.
**Intended use:** For full-time junior, senior or graduate study at accredited 4-year institution in United States.
**Eligibility:** Applicant must be U.S. citizen or permanent resident residing in Hawaii.
**Basis for selection:** Major/career interest in journalism or communications. Applicant must demonstrate financial need, high academic achievement and depth of character.
**Application requirements:** Essay, transcript. FAFSA and SAR.
**Additional information:** Must have permanent address in Hawaii. Applicants who take up mainland residency must have relatives living in Hawaii. Amount and number of awards vary and may change yearly.

**Application deadline:** March 1

**Contact:**
Hawaii Community Foundation Scholarships
827 Fort Street Mall
Honolulu, HI 96813
Phone: 888-731-3863
Fax: 808-521-6286
Web: www.hawaiicommunityfoundation.org

## E.E. Black Scholarship

**Type of award:** Scholarship, renewable.
**Intended use:** For full-time undergraduate study at accredited postsecondary institution in United States.
**Eligibility:** Applicant must be U.S. citizen or permanent resident residing in Hawaii.
**Basis for selection:** Applicant must demonstrate financial need, high academic achievement and depth of character.
**Application requirements:** Essay, transcript. FAFSA and SAR. Name of Tesoro employee and relationship.
**Additional information:** Minimum 3.0 GPA. Must be dependent of an employee of Tesoro Hawaii or its subsidiaries. Applicants must have permanent address in Hawaii. Applicants who take up mainland residency must have relatives living in Hawaii. Amount and number of awards vary.

**Number of awards:** 11
**Application deadline:** March 1

**Contact:**
Hawaii Community Foundation Scholarships
827 Fort Street Mall
Honolulu, HI 96813
Phone: 888-731-3863
Fax: 808-521-6286
Web: www.hawaiicommunityfoundation.org

## Elena Albano "Maka'alohilohi" Scholarship Fund

**Type of award:** Scholarship.
**Intended use:** For full-time undergraduate or graduate study at 2-year or 4-year institution in United States.
**Eligibility:** Applicant must be U.S. citizen residing in Hawaii.
**Basis for selection:** Applicant must demonstrate financial need, high academic achievement and depth of character.
**Application requirements:** Recommendations, essay, transcript. SAR, FAFSA, Personal Statement. Two letters of recommendation from mentors, teachers, counselors, or other mental health professionals.
**Additional information:** Minimum 2.7 GPA. Must be in recovery from mental health/behavioral/psychological disability. Must be resident of Maui county. Preference given to students of Hawaiian ancestry and renewal applicants. Applicants must have permanent address in Hawaii. Applicants taking up mainland residency must have relatives living in Hawaii. Amount of award may change yearly.

**Application deadline:** March 1

**Contact:**
Hawaii Community Foundation Scholarships
827 Fort Street Mall
Honolulu, HI 96813
Phone: 888-731-3863
Fax: 808-521-6286
Web: www.hawaiicommunityfoundation.org

## Ellen Hamada Fashion Design Scholarship

**Type of award:** Scholarship.
**Intended use:** For full-time undergraduate study at 2-year institution in United States. Designated institutions: University of Hawaii community colleges.
**Eligibility:** Applicant must be residing in Hawaii.
**Basis for selection:** Major/career interest in fashion/fashion design/modeling. Applicant must demonstrate financial need and high academic achievement.
**Application requirements:** Recommendations, essay, transcript. SAR.
**Additional information:** Minimum 2.7 GPA.

**Application deadline:** March 1

**Contact:**
Hawaii Community Foundation
827 Fort Street Mall
Honolulu, HI 96813
Phone: 888-731-3863
Fax: 808-521-6286
Web: www.hawaiicommunityfoundation.org

## Ellison Onizuka Memorial Scholarship

**Type of award:** Scholarship.
**Intended use:** For full-time undergraduate study at accredited 2-year or 4-year institution in United States.
**Eligibility:** Applicant must be high school senior. Applicant must be U.S. citizen or permanent resident residing in Hawaii.
**Basis for selection:** Major/career interest in aerospace. Applicant must demonstrate financial need and depth of character.
**Application requirements:** Recommendations, transcript. SAT scores, FAFSA, SAR and personal statement describing extracurricular activities, club affiliations, and community service projects.
**Additional information:** Applicants must have permanent address in Hawaii. Applicants who take up mainland residency must have relatives living in Hawaii. Amount and number of awards vary.

**Number of awards:** 5
**Application deadline:** March 1

**Contact:**
Hawaii Community Foundation Scholarships
827 Fort Street Mall
Honolulu, HI 96813
Phone: 888-731-3863
Fax: 808-521-6286
Web: www.hawaiicommunityfoundation.org

## Esther Kanagawa Memorial Art Scholarship

**Type of award:** Scholarship.
**Intended use:** For full-time undergraduate or graduate study at accredited 2-year or 4-year institution in United States.
**Eligibility:** Applicant must be U.S. citizen or permanent resident residing in Hawaii.
**Basis for selection:** Major/career interest in arts, general. Applicant must demonstrate financial need, high academic achievement and depth of character.
**Application requirements:** Essay, transcript. FAFSA and SAR.
**Additional information:** Must major in fine art, drawing, painting, sculpture, ceramics, or photography. Applicants must have permanent address in Hawaii. Applicants taking up mainland residency must have relatives living in Hawaii. Amount of award varies yearly.

**Number of awards:** 2
**Application deadline:** March 1

**Contact:**
Hawaii Community Foundation Scholarships
827 Fort Street Mall
Honolulu, HI 96813
Phone: 888-731-3863
Fax: 808-521-6286
Web: www.hawaiicommunityfoundation.org

## F. Koehnen Ltd. Scholarship Fund

**Type of award:** Scholarship.
**Intended use:** For full-time undergraduate or graduate study at accredited 4-year institution in United States.
**Eligibility:** Applicant must be U.S. citizen residing in Hawaii.
**Basis for selection:** Applicant must demonstrate financial need, high academic achievement and depth of character.
**Application requirements:** Recommendations, essay, transcript. SAR, FAFSA, Personal Statement. Name of employee, retail establishment and phone number of human resources department of retail establishment.
**Additional information:** Minimum 2.5 GPA. Must be graduate of high school on island of Hawaii. Must be son, daughter or grandchild of employee of retail establishment on island of Hawaii.

**Application deadline:** March 1

**Contact:**
Hawaii Community Foundation Scholarships
827 Fort Street Mall
Honolulu, HI 96813
Phone: 888-731-3863
Fax: 808-521-6286
Web: www.hawaiicommunityfoundation.org

## Filipino Nurses' Organization of Hawaii Scholarship

**Type of award:** Scholarship.
**Intended use:** For full-time undergraduate study at accredited 2-year or 4-year institution in United States.
**Eligibility:** Applicant must be of Filipino ancestry. Applicant must be U.S. citizen or permanent resident residing in Hawaii.
**Basis for selection:** Major/career interest in nursing. Applicant must demonstrate financial need, high academic achievement, depth of character and service orientation.
**Application requirements:** Essay, transcript. FAFSA and SAR.
**Additional information:** Must have permanent address in Hawaii. Applicants taking up mainland residency must have relatives living in Hawaii. Amount of award may vary yearly.

**Number of awards:** 2
**Application deadline:** March 1

**Contact:**
Hawaii Community Foundation Scholarships
827 Fort Street Mall
Honolulu, HI 96813
Phone: 888-731-3863
Fax: 808-521-6286
Web: www.hawaiicommunityfoundation.org

## Financial Women International Scholarship

**Type of award:** Scholarship.
**Intended use:** For full-time junior, senior or graduate study at accredited 2-year or 4-year institution in United States.
**Eligibility:** Applicant must be female. Applicant must be U.S. citizen or permanent resident residing in Hawaii.
**Basis for selection:** Major/career interest in business. Applicant must demonstrate financial need, high academic achievement and depth of character.
**Application requirements:** Essay, transcript. FAFSA and SAR.
**Additional information:** Minimum 3.5 GPA. Applicant must have permanent address in Hawaii. Applicants taking up mainland residency must have relatives living in Hawaii. Amount of award may change yearly.

**Number of awards:** 1
**Application deadline:** March 1

**Contact:**
Hawaii Community Foundation Scholarships
827 Fort Street Mall
Honolulu, HI 96813
Phone: 888-731-3863
Fax: 808-521-6286
Web: www.hawaiicommunityfoundation.org

## Fletcher & Fritzi Hoffmann Education Fund

**Type of award:** Scholarship.
**Intended use:** For full-time undergraduate study at accredited vocational, 2-year or 4-year institution. Designated institutions: College or vocational school on island of Hawaii.
**Eligibility:** Applicant must be U.S. citizen or permanent resident residing in Hawaii.
**Basis for selection:** Applicant must demonstrate financial need, high academic achievement and depth of character.
**Application requirements:** Essay, transcript. FAFSA and SAR. Personal statement must include information on family's history and roots in the Hamakua area.
**Additional information:** Minimum 2.7 GPA. Preference given to applicants whose families worked in sugar plantation industry and Honoka'a high school graduates. Must be longtime resident of Hamakua Coast in Hawaii. Amount of award may change yearly.

**Number of awards:** 1
**Application deadline:** March 1

**Contact:**
Hawaii Community Foundation Scholarships
827 Fort Street Mall
Suite 80
Honolulu, HI 96813
Phone: 888-731-3863
Fax: 808-521-6286
Web: www.hawaiicommunityfoundation.org

## Friends of Hawaii Public Housing Scholarship

**Type of award:** Scholarship.
**Intended use:** For full-time undergraduate study at postsecondary institution.
**Eligibility:** Applicant must be residing in Hawaii.
**Basis for selection:** Applicant must demonstrate financial need and high academic achievement.
**Application requirements:** Recommendations, essay, transcript. SAR. Must include name of public housing complex in your personal statement.
**Additional information:** Minimum 2.7 GPA. Must be resident of public housing complex in Hawaii.

**Application deadline:** March 1

**Contact:**
Hawaii Community Foundation
827 Fort Street Mall
Honolulu, HI 96813
Phone: 888-731-3863
Fax: 808-521-6286
Web: www.hawaiicommunityfoundation.org

## GEAR UP Scholars Program

**Type of award:** Scholarship.
**Intended use:** For full-time undergraduate study at accredited postsecondary institution.
**Eligibility:** Applicant must be residing in Hawaii.
**Basis for selection:** Applicant must demonstrate financial need and high academic achievement.
**Application requirements:** Recommendations, essay, transcript. SAR.
**Additional information:** Minimum 3.0 GPA. Must have graduated high school between 2006 and 2009. Must be Gear Up scholar and earn State of Hawaii Board of Education Recognition Diploma.

**Application deadline:** March 1

**Contact:**
Hawaii Community Foundation
827 Fort Street Mall
Honolulu, HI 96813
Phone: 888-731-3863
Fax: 808-521-6286
Web: www.hawaiicommunityfoundation.org

## George Mason Business Scholarship Fund

**Type of award:** Scholarship.
**Intended use:** For full-time senior study at accredited 4-year institution. Designated institutions: Universities and colleges in Hawaii.
**Eligibility:** Applicant must be residing in Hawaii.
**Basis for selection:** Major/career interest in business or business/management/administration. Applicant must demonstrate financial need, high academic achievement and depth of character.
**Application requirements:** Essay, transcript. FAFSA and SAR. Essay must state why you have chosen business as an intended career and how you expect to make a difference in the business world.
**Additional information:** Minimum 3.0 GPA. Applicant must have permanent Hawaii address.

**Number of awards:** 1
**Application deadline:** March 1

**Contact:**
Hawaii Community Foundation Scholarships
827 Fort Street Mall
Honolulu, HA 96813
Phone: 888-731-3863
Fax: 808-521-6286
Web: www.hawaiicommunityfoundation.org

## Gerrit R. Ludwig Scholarship

**Type of award:** Scholarship.
**Intended use:** For full-time undergraduate or graduate study at accredited 2-year, 4-year or graduate institution.
**Eligibility:** Applicant must be residing in Hawaii.
**Basis for selection:** Major/career interest in classics or arts, general. Applicant must demonstrate financial need, high academic achievement and depth of character.
**Application requirements:** Essay, transcript. FAFSA and SAR.
**Additional information:** Minimum 2.5 GPA. Preference given to applicants pursuing a degree in fine arts or classics. Must be graduate from East Hawaii public school: Hilo, Honoka'a, Kea'au, Laupahoehoe, Pahoa, and Waiakea. Applicants taking up mainland residency must have relatives living in Hawaii.

**Number of awards:** 3
**Application deadline:** March 1

**Contact:**
Hawaii Community Foundation Scholarships
827 Fort Street Mall
Honolulu, HI 96813
Phone: 888-731-3863
Fax: 808-521-6286
Web: www.hawaiicommunityfoundation.org

## Good Eats Scholarship Fund

**Type of award:** Scholarship.
**Intended use:** For full-time undergraduate or graduate study at accredited vocational, 2-year or 4-year institution in United States.
**Eligibility:** Applicant must be U.S. citizen residing in Hawaii.
**Basis for selection:** Major/career interest in culinary arts; agriculture or food production/management/services. Applicant must demonstrate depth of character.
**Application requirements:** Recommendations, essay, transcript. SAR, FAFSA, personal statement discussing activities that demonstrate interest in food production and preparation.
**Additional information:** Minimum 2.7 GPA. Must pursue post high school studies in culinary arts or agriculture. Must demonstrate interest in food production and preparation.

**Contact:**
Hawaii Community Foundation Scholarships
827 Fort Street Mall
Honolulu, HI 96813
Phone: 888-731-3863
Fax: 808-521-6286
Web: www.hawaiicommunityfoundation.org

## Grace Pacific Outstanding Scholars Fund

**Type of award:** Scholarship.
**Intended use:** For full-time undergraduate or graduate study at accredited 2-year or 4-year institution in United States.
**Eligibility:** Applicant must be high school senior. Applicant must be U.S. citizen residing in Hawaii.
**Basis for selection:** Applicant must demonstrate financial need, high academic achievement and depth of character.
**Application requirements:** Recommendations, essay, transcript. SAR, FAFSA, Personal Statement.
**Additional information:** Minimum 2.7 GPA. Must be former participant of Grace Pacific Outstanding Keiki Scholars Program. Applicants must have permanent address in Hawaii. Applicants taking up mainland residency must have relatives living in Hawaii. Amount of award may change yearly.

**Application deadline:** March 1

**Contact:**
Hawaii Community Foundation Scholarships
827 Fort Street Mall
Honolulu, HI 96813
Phone: 888-731-3863
Fax: 808-521-6286
Web: www.hawaiicommunityfoundation.org

## Guy Marshall Scholarship Fund

**Type of award:** Scholarship.
**Intended use:** For full-time freshman study at accredited 2-year or 4-year institution in United States.
**Eligibility:** Applicant must be U.S. citizen residing in Hawaii.
**Basis for selection:** Applicant must demonstrate financial need, high academic achievement and depth of character.
**Application requirements:** Recommendations, essay, transcript. SAR, FAFSA, Personal Statement.
**Additional information:** Minimum 2.7 GPA. Must plan to attend college in continental United States. Must be graduate of Hawaii high school.
**Application deadline:** March 1
**Contact:**
Hawaii Community Foundation Scholarships
827 Fort Street Mall
Honolulu, HI 96813
Phone: 888-731-3863
Fax: 808-521-6286
Web: www.hawaiicommunityfoundation.org

## Haseko Training Fund

**Type of award:** Scholarship.
**Intended use:** For full-time undergraduate study at accredited 2-year institution.
**Eligibility:** Applicant must be residing in Hawaii.
**Basis for selection:** Applicant must demonstrate financial need and high academic achievement.
**Application requirements:** Recommendations, essay, transcript. SAR.
**Additional information:** Minimum 2.7 GPA. Must be Ewa Beach resident. Must enroll in AS or AAS career and technical degree program within University of Hawaii community college system. Preference given to student in marine-related program.
**Application deadline:** March 1
**Contact:**
Hawaii Community Foundation
827 Fort Street Mall
Honolulu, HI 96813
Phone: 888-731-3863
Fax: 808-521-6286
Web: www.hawaiicommunityfoundation.org

## Hawaii Pacific Gerontological Society Nursing Scholarship Fund

**Type of award:** Scholarship.
**Intended use:** For full-time undergraduate or graduate study at accredited 2-year or 4-year institution in United States.
**Eligibility:** Applicant must be U.S. citizen residing in Hawaii.
**Basis for selection:** Major/career interest in nursing. Applicant must demonstrate financial need, high academic achievement and depth of character.
**Application requirements:** Recommendations, essay, transcript. SAR, FAFSA, Personal Statement.
**Additional information:** Minimum 2.7 GPA. Must pursue an LN or RN degree with interest in geriatric nursing.
**Application deadline:** March 1
**Contact:**
Hawaii Community Foundation Scholarships
827 Fort Street Mall
Honolulu, HI 96813
Phone: 888-731-3863
Fax: 808-521-6286
Web: www.hawaiicommunityfoundation.org

## Hawaii Pizza Hut Scholarship Fund

**Type of award:** Scholarship.
**Intended use:** For full-time undergraduate study at accredited 2-year or 4-year institution in United States.
**Eligibility:** Applicant must be U.S. citizen residing in Hawaii.
**Basis for selection:** Applicant must demonstrate financial need, high academic achievement and depth of character.
**Application requirements:** Recommendations, essay, transcript. SAR, FAFSA, Personal Statement.
**Additional information:** GPA must be between 2.5 and 3.5.
**Application deadline:** March 1
**Contact:**
Hawaii Community Foundation Scholarships
827 Fort Street Mall
Honolulu, HI 96813
Phone: 888-731-3863
Fax: 808-521-6286
Web: www.hawaiicommunityfoundation.org

## Hawaii Society of Certified Public Accountants Scholarship Fund

**Type of award:** Scholarship.
**Intended use:** For full-time junior, senior or graduate study at 4-year institution in United States. Designated institutions: Four-year colleges and universities in Hawaii.
**Eligibility:** Applicant must be U.S. citizen residing in Hawaii.
**Basis for selection:** Major/career interest in accounting. Applicant must demonstrate financial need, high academic achievement and depth of character.
**Application requirements:** Recommendations, essay, transcript. SAR, FAFSA, Personal statement should include description of extracurricular activities, involvement in professional, civic and social organizations, and employment history.
**Additional information:** Minimum 3.0 GPA. Must have already completed two or more 300-level accounting courses.
**Application deadline:** March 1
**Contact:**
Hawaii Community Foundation Scholarships
827 Fort Street Mall
Honolulu, HI 96813
Phone: 888-731-3863
Fax: 808-521-6286
Web: www.hawaiicommunityfoundation.org

## Hawaiian Homes Commission Scholarship

**Type of award:** Scholarship.
**Intended use:** For full-time undergraduate study at accredited postsecondary institution.
**Eligibility:** Applicant must be Native Hawaiian/Pacific Islander. Applicant must be residing in Hawaii.
**Basis for selection:** Applicant must demonstrate financial need and high academic achievement.
**Application requirements:** Recommendations, essay, transcript. SAR.
**Additional information:** Minimum 2.0 GPA for undergraduates, 3.0 GPA for graduate students. Must be at least fifty percent Hawaiian and Department of Hawaiian Home Lands (DHHL) lessee. Applicants not required to be resident of Hawaii.
**Application deadline:** March 1

**Contact:**
Hawaii Community Foundation
827 Fort Street Mall
Honolulu, HI 96813
Phone: 888-731-3863
Fax: 808-521-6286
Web: www.hawaiicommunityfoundation.org

## Henry A. Zuberano Scholarship

**Type of award:** Scholarship.
**Intended use:** For full-time undergraduate study at accredited 2-year or 4-year institution.
**Eligibility:** Applicant must be residing in Hawaii.
**Basis for selection:** Major/career interest in political science/government; international relations; business, international or public administration/service. Applicant must demonstrate financial need, high academic achievement and depth of character.
**Application requirements:** Essay, transcript. FAFSA and SAR.
**Additional information:** Applicant must have permanent Hawaii address. Applicants taking up mainland residency must have relatives living in Hawaii.
**Number of awards:** 9
**Application deadline:** March 1
**Contact:**
Hawaii Community Foundation Scholarships
827 Fort Street Mall
Honolulu, HI 96813
Phone: 888-731-3863
Fax: 808-521-6286
Web: www.hawaiicommunityfoundation.org

## Herbert & Ollie Brook Fund

**Type of award:** Scholarship.
**Intended use:** For full-time undergraduate or graduate study at accredited 2-year or 4-year institution in United States.
**Eligibility:** Applicant must be U.S. citizen residing in Hawaii.
**Basis for selection:** Applicant must demonstrate financial need, high academic achievement and depth of character.
**Application requirements:** Recommendations, essay, transcript. SAR, FAFSA, Personal Statement.
**Additional information:** Minimum 2.7 GPA. Must be high school senior in Maui County. Preference given to those who plan to return to Maui County after completing education to contribute to community.
**Application deadline:** March 1
**Contact:**
Hawaii Community Foundation Scholarships
1164 Bishop Street
Suite 800
Honolulu, HI 96813
Phone: 888-731-3863
Fax: 808-521-6286
Web: www.hawaiicommunityfoundation.org

## Hew-Shinn Scholarship Fund

**Type of award:** Scholarship.
**Intended use:** For full-time undergraduate study at accredited vocational or 2-year institution in United States.
**Eligibility:** Applicant must be residing in Hawaii.
**Basis for selection:** Applicant must demonstrate financial need and high academic achievement.
**Application requirements:** Recommendations, essay, transcript. SAR.
**Additional information:** Minimum 2.7 GPA. Must be enrolled in vocational program in the University of Hawaii Community College system. Residents of Maui County may also attend vocational school on mainland.
**Application deadline:** March 1
**Contact:**
Hawaii Community Foundation Scholarships
827 Fort Street Mall
Honolulu, HI 96813
Phone: 888-731-3863
Fax: 808-521-6286
Web: www.hawaiicommunityfoundation.org

## Hideko & Zenzo Matsuyama Scholarship Fund

**Type of award:** Scholarship.
**Intended use:** For full-time undergraduate or graduate study at 2-year or 4-year institution in United States.
**Eligibility:** Applicant must be U.S. citizen residing in Hawaii.
**Basis for selection:** Applicant must demonstrate financial need, high academic achievement and depth of character.
**Application requirements:** Recommendations, essay, transcript. SAR, FAFSA, Personal Statement.
**Additional information:** Minimum 3.0 GPA. Must be graduate of high school in Hawaii or have received GED in Hawaii. Preference given to students of Japanese ancestry born in Hawaii.
**Application deadline:** March 1
**Contact:**
Hawaii Community Foundation Scholarships
827 Fort Street Mall
Honolulu, HI 96813
Phone: 888-731-3863
Fax: 808-521-6286
Web: www.hawaiicommunityfoundation.org

## Hilo Chinese School Scholarship

**Type of award:** Scholarship.
**Intended use:** For full-time undergraduate or graduate study at accredited 2-year or 4-year institution in United States.
**Eligibility:** Applicant must be U.S. citizen residing in Hawaii.
**Basis for selection:** Applicant must demonstrate financial need, high academic achievement and depth of character.
**Application requirements:** Recommendations, essay, transcript. SAR, FAFSA, Personal Statement.
**Additional information:** Minimum 2.5 GPA. Must be resident of Hawaii island. Preference given to descendants of Hilo Chinese School alumni and students of Chinese ancestry.
**Application deadline:** March 1
**Contact:**
Hawaii Community Foundation Scholarships
827 Fort Street Mall
Honolulu, HI 96813
Phone: 888-731-3863
Fax: 808-521-6286
Web: www.hawaiicommunityfoundation.org

## Hoku Scholarship Fund

**Type of award:** Scholarship.
**Intended use:** For full-time undergraduate or graduate study at accredited 2-year, 4-year or graduate institution.
**Eligibility:** Applicant must be residing in Hawaii.
**Basis for selection:** Major/career interest in physics; astronomy; mathematics; engineering; technology or computer/

information sciences. Applicant must demonstrate financial need and high academic achievement.
**Application requirements:** Recommendations, essay, transcript. SAR. Personal statement should include description of interest and intent to pursue observatory career.
**Additional information:** Minimum 3.0 GPA. Must intend to pursue an observatory career.
**Application deadline:** March 1
**Contact:**
Hawaii Community Foundation Scholarships
827 Fort Street Mall
Honolulu, HI 96813
Phone: 888-731-3863
Fax: 808-521-6286
Web: www.hawaiicommunityfoundation.org

## Hokuli'a Foundation Scholarship Fund

**Type of award:** Scholarship.
**Intended use:** For full-time undergraduate or graduate study at accredited 2-year or 4-year institution in United States.
**Eligibility:** Applicant must be U.S. citizen residing in Hawaii.
**Basis for selection:** Major/career interest in health-related professions; education or social work. Applicant must demonstrate financial need, high academic achievement, depth of character and service orientation.
**Application requirements:** Recommendations, essay, transcript. SAR, FAFSA, Personal Statement should include record of community service and how future career will benefit Hawaii residents.
**Additional information:** Minimum 2.7 GPA. Must be resident of South or North Kona. Preference given to students demonstrating emphasis in advancing native Hawaiian culture.
**Application deadline:** March 1
**Contact:**
Hawaii Community Foundation Scholarships
827 Fort Street Mall
Honolulu, HI 96813
Phone: 888-731-3863
Fax: 808-521-6286
Web: www.hawaiicommunityfoundation.org

## Hon Chew Hee Scholarship Fund

**Type of award:** Scholarship.
**Intended use:** For full-time undergraduate or graduate study at accredited 2-year or 4-year institution in United States.
**Eligibility:** Applicant must be U.S. citizen residing in Hawaii.
**Basis for selection:** Major/career interest in art/art history. Applicant must demonstrate financial need, high academic achievement and depth of character.
**Application requirements:** Recommendations, essay, transcript. SAR, FAFSA, Personal Statement. Two letters of recommendation required. One from an art instructor, one from a non-related person.
**Additional information:** Minimum 2.7 GPA. Major in fine arts with preference given to students focusing on painting, drawing, sculpting, ceramics, printmaking, and textiles.
**Application deadline:** March 1
**Contact:**
Hawaii Community Foundation Scholarships
827 Fort Street Mall
Honolulu, HI 96813
Phone: 888-731-3863
Fax: 808-521-6286
Web: www.hawaiicommunityfoundation.org

## Ho'omaka Hou Scholarship

**Type of award:** Scholarship.
**Intended use:** For full-time undergraduate or graduate study at accredited 2-year or 4-year institution in United States.
**Eligibility:** Applicant must be U.S. citizen residing in Hawaii.
**Basis for selection:** Applicant must demonstrate financial need, high academic achievement and depth of character.
**Application requirements:** Recommendations, essay, transcript. SAR, FAFSA, Personal Statement should describe problems and how they were overcome.
**Additional information:** Minimum 2.7 GPA. Applicant must have overcome substance abuse.
**Application deadline:** March 1
**Contact:**
Hawaii Community Foundation Scholarships
827 Fort Street Mall
Honolulu, HI 96813
Phone: 888-731-3863
Fax: 808-521-6286
Web: www.hawaiicommunityfoundation.org

## Ian Doane Smith Scholarship Fund

**Type of award:** Scholarship.
**Intended use:** For full-time undergraduate or graduate study at accredited 2-year or 4-year institution in United States.
**Eligibility:** Applicant must be high school senior. Applicant must be U.S. citizen residing in Hawaii.
**Basis for selection:** Applicant must demonstrate financial need, high academic achievement, depth of character and service orientation.
**Application requirements:** Recommendations, essay, transcript. SAR, FAFSA, Personal Statement must detail community service and experiences with surfing or soccer.
**Additional information:** Minimum 2.7 GPA. Must resident of island of Maui. Must be active in soccer and/or surfing.
**Application deadline:** March 1
**Contact:**
Hawaii Community Foundation Scholarships
827 Fort Street Mall
Honolulu, HI 96813
Phone: 888-731-3863
Fax: 808-521-6286
Web: www.hawaiicommunityfoundation.org

## Ichiro & Masako Hirata Scholarship

**Type of award:** Scholarship.
**Intended use:** For full-time junior, senior or graduate study at accredited postsecondary institution.
**Eligibility:** Applicant must be residing in Hawaii.
**Basis for selection:** Major/career interest in education. Applicant must demonstrate financial need and high academic achievement.
**Application requirements:** Recommendations, essay, transcript. SAR.
**Additional information:** Minimum 3.0 GPA.
**Application deadline:** March 1
**Contact:**
Hawaii Community Foundation
827 Fort Street Mall
Honolulu, HI 96813
Phone: 888-731-3863
Fax: 808-521-6286
Web: www.hawaiicommunityfoundation.org

## Ida M. Pope Memorial Scholarship

**Type of award:** Scholarship.
**Intended use:** For full-time undergraduate or graduate study at accredited 2-year or 4-year institution in United States.
**Eligibility:** Applicant must be Native Hawaiian/Pacific Islander. Applicant must be female. Applicant must be U.S. citizen residing in Hawaii.
**Basis for selection:** Major/career interest in health-related professions; science, general or education. Applicant must demonstrate depth of character.
**Application requirements:** Recommendations, essay, transcript. SAR, FAFSA, Personal Statement. Birth certificate.
**Additional information:** Minimum 3.5 GPA.

**Application deadline:** March 1

**Contact:**
Hawaii Community Foundation Scholarships
827 Fort Street Mall
Honolulu, HI 96813
Phone: 888-731-3863
Fax: 808-521-6286
Web: www.hawaiicommunityfoundation.org

Scholarships

## Isemoto Contracting Co., Ltd. Scholarship Fund

**Type of award:** Scholarship.
**Intended use:** For full-time sophomore, junior, senior or graduate study at accredited 2-year or 4-year institution in United States.
**Eligibility:** Applicant must be U.S. citizen residing in Hawaii.
**Basis for selection:** Major/career interest in engineering; nursing or education. Applicant must demonstrate financial need, high academic achievement and depth of character.
**Application requirements:** Recommendations, essay, transcript. SAR, FAFSA, Personal Statement.
**Additional information:** Minimum 2.7 GPA. Must be graduate of high school on island of Hawaii. Must be accepted as upper classman to a school of engineering, teacher education program, or nursing program.

**Application deadline:** March 1

**Contact:**
Hawaii Community Foundation Scholarships
827 Fort Street Mall
Honolulu, HI 96813
Phone: 888-731-3863
Fax: 808-521-6286
Web: www.hawaiicommunityfoundation.org

## Jean Estes Epstein Charitable Foundation Scholarship

**Type of award:** Scholarship, renewable.
**Intended use:** For full-time freshman study at accredited postsecondary institution in United States. Designated institutions: Schools in the continental United States.
**Eligibility:** Applicant must be residing in Hawaii.
**Basis for selection:** Applicant must demonstrate financial need and high academic achievement.
**Application requirements:** Recommendations, essay, transcript. SAR. Personal statement must include personal and career goals.
**Additional information:** Minimum 3.0 GPA. Must be graduate of Hawaii public high school. Must attend college in the continental United States.

**Application deadline:** March 1

**Contact:**
Hawaii Community Foundation
827 Fort Street Mall
Honolulu, HI 96813
Phone: 888-731-3863
Fax: 808-521-6286
Web: www.hawaiicommunityfoundation.org

## Jean Fitzgerald Scholarship Fund

**Type of award:** Scholarship, renewable.
**Intended use:** For full-time freshman study at accredited 2-year or 4-year institution in United States.
**Eligibility:** Applicant must be female, high school senior. Applicant must be U.S. citizen or permanent resident residing in Hawaii.
**Basis for selection:** Applicant must demonstrate financial need, high academic achievement and depth of character.
**Application requirements:** Essay, transcript. FAFSA and SAR.
**Additional information:** Applicant must be active tennis player; preference may be given to USTA/Hawaii Pacific Section members. Applicants must have permanent address in Hawaii. Applicants who take up mainland residency must have relatives living in Hawaii. Amount and number of awards vary.

**Number of awards:** 2
**Application deadline:** March 1
**Total amount awarded:** $7,000

**Contact:**
Hawaii Community Foundation Scholarships
827 Fort Street Mall
Honolulu, HI 96813
Phone: 888-731-3863
Fax: 808-521-6286
Web: www.hawaiicommunityfoundation.org

## Jean Ileialoha Beniamina Scholarship for Ni'ihau Students Fund

**Type of award:** Scholarship.
**Intended use:** For full-time undergraduate or graduate study at accredited postsecondary institution.
**Eligibility:** Applicant must be residing in Hawaii.
**Basis for selection:** Applicant must demonstrate financial need and high academic achievement.
**Application requirements:** Recommendations, essay, transcript. SAR. Essay describing family descent and connection to Ni'ihau and addressing proficiency in Hawaiian language and listing courses taken in Hawaiian.
**Additional information:** Minimum 2.7 GPA. Must be resident of Kauai or Ni'ihau Island. Preference given to current Ni'ihau residents or Kauai residents who are one two generations removed from Ni'ihau Island. Preference given to students fluent in Hawaiian language.

**Application deadline:** March 1

**Contact:**
Hawaii Community Foundation
827 Fort Street Mall
Honolulu, HI 96813
Phone: 888-731-3863
Fax: 808-521-6286
Web: www.hawaiicommunityfoundation.org

## Johanna Drew Cluney Scholarship

**Type of award:** Scholarship.
**Intended use:** For undergraduate study at accredited vocational or 2-year institution in United States. Designated institutions: Community colleges in the University of Hawaii system.
**Eligibility:** Applicant must be residing in Hawaii.
**Basis for selection:** Applicant must demonstrate financial need and high academic achievement.
**Application requirements:** Recommendations, essay, transcript. SAR.
**Additional information:** Minimum 2.7 GPA. Must be enrolled in University of Hawaii Community College system.
**Application deadline:** March 1
**Contact:**
Hawaii Community Foundation
827 Fort Street Mall
Honolulu, HI 96813
Phone: 888-731-3863
Fax: 808-521-6286
Web: www.hawaiicommunityfoundation.org

## John & Anne Clifton Scholarship Fund

**Type of award:** Scholarship.
**Intended use:** For full-time undergraduate study at accredited 2-year or 4-year institution in United States. Designated institutions: Community colleges in the University of Hawaii system.
**Eligibility:** Applicant must be residing in Hawaii.
**Basis for selection:** Applicant must demonstrate financial need and high academic achievement.
**Application requirements:** Recommendations, essay, transcript. SAR.
**Additional information:** Minimum 2.7 GPA. Must be enrolled in the University of Hawaii Community College system.
**Application deadline:** March 1
**Contact:**
Hawaii Community Foundation
827 Fort Street Mall
Honolulu, HI 96813
Phone: 888-731-3863
Fax: 808-521-6286
Web: www.hawaiicommunityfoundation.org

## John Dawe Dental Education Fund

**Type of award:** Scholarship, renewable.
**Intended use:** For full-time undergraduate or graduate study at accredited postsecondary institution in United States.
**Eligibility:** Applicant must be U.S. citizen or permanent resident residing in Hawaii.
**Basis for selection:** Major/career interest in dentistry; dental hygiene or dental assistant. Applicant must demonstrate financial need, high academic achievement and depth of character.
**Application requirements:** Recommendations, essay, transcript, proof of eligibility. FAFSA and SAR. Must submit Dawe Supplemental Financial Form (download from Website). Letter from their school confirming enrollment in the dental hygiene or dentistry program.
**Additional information:** Applicants must have permanent address in Hawaii. Applicants taking up mainland residency must have relatives living in Hawaii. Amount and number of awards vary.
**Number of awards:** 6
**Application deadline:** March 1
**Contact:**
Hawaii Community Foundation Scholarships
827 Fort Street Mall
Honolulu, HI 96813
Phone: 888-731-3863
Fax: 808-521-6286
Web: www.hawaiicommunityfoundation.org

## Joseph & Alice Duarte Memorial Fund

**Type of award:** Scholarship.
**Intended use:** For full-time undergraduate or graduate study at accredited 2-year or 4-year institution in United States.
**Eligibility:** Applicant must be U.S. citizen residing in Hawaii.
**Basis for selection:** Applicant must demonstrate financial need, high academic achievement and depth of character.
**Application requirements:** Recommendations, essay, transcript. SAR, FAFSA, Personal Statement.
**Additional information:** Minimum 2.7 GPA. Must be from North or South Kona districts of Hawaii. Preference given to graduates of Holualoa Elementary School.
**Application deadline:** March 1
**Contact:**
Hawaii Community Foundation Scholarships
827 Fort Street Mall
Honolulu, HI 96813
Phone: 888-731-3863
Fax: 808-521-6286
Web: www.hawaiicommunityfoundation.org

## Juliette M. Atherton Scholarship - Minister's Sons and Daughters

**Type of award:** Scholarship.
**Intended use:** For full-time undergraduate or graduate study at accredited postsecondary institution.
**Eligibility:** Applicant must be Protestant. Applicant must be residing in Hawaii.
**Basis for selection:** Applicant must demonstrate financial need and high academic achievement.
**Application requirements:** Recommendations, essay, transcript. SAR. Personal statement must include minister's current position, name of church/parish, denomination, place/ date of ordination, name of seminary attended.
**Additional information:** Minimum 2.7 GPA. Must be dependent son or daughter of ordained and active Protestant minister in established denomination in Hawaii.
**Application deadline:** March 1
**Contact:**
Hawaii Community Foundation
827 Fort Street Mall
Honolulu, HI 96813
Phone: 888-731-3863
Fax: 808-521-6286
Web: www.hawaiicommunityfoundation.org

## Ka'iulani Home for Girls Trust Scholarship

**Type of award:** Scholarship, renewable.
**Intended use:** For full-time freshman or sophomore study at accredited postsecondary institution in United States.
**Eligibility:** Applicant must be Native Hawaiian/Pacific Islander. Applicant must be female. Applicant must be U.S. citizen or permanent resident residing in Hawaii.

**Basis for selection:** Applicant must demonstrate financial need, high academic achievement and depth of character.
**Application requirements:** Essay, transcript, proof of eligibility. FAFSA and SAR, birth certificate.
**Additional information:** Minimum 3.3 GPA. Must be of Hawaiian ancestry. First time applicants must be freshmen or sophomores. Juniors and seniors who are past recipients also eligible. Must have permanent address in Hawaii. Applicants taking up mainland residency must have relatives living in Hawaii. Amount and number of awards vary and may change yearly.

| | |
|---|---|
| **Number of awards:** | 222 |
| **Application deadline:** | March 1 |

**Contact:**
Hawaii Community Foundation Scholarships
827 Fort Street Mall
Honolulu, HI 96813
Phone: 888-731-3863
Fax: 808-521-6286
Web: www.hawaiicommunityfoundation.org

## Ka'a'awa Community Fund

**Type of award:** Scholarship.
**Intended use:** For full-time undergraduate or graduate study at accredited 2-year or 4-year institution in United States.
**Eligibility:** Applicant must be U.S. citizen or permanent resident residing in Hawaii.
**Basis for selection:** Applicant must demonstrate financial need, high academic achievement and depth of character.
**Application requirements:** Essay, transcript. FAFSA and SAR.
**Additional information:** Must be resident of the Ka'a'awa area on Windward O'ahu. Preference given to long-time residents. Amount and number of awards vary and may change yearly.

**Application deadline:** March 1

**Contact:**
Hawaii Community Foundation Scholarships
827 Fort Street Mall
Honolulu, HI 96813
Phone: 888-731-3863
Fax: 808-521-6286
Web: www.hawaiicommunityfoundation.org

## Kahala Nui Residents Scholarship Fund

**Type of award:** Scholarship.
**Intended use:** For full-time undergraduate or graduate study at accredited 2-year or 4-year institution.
**Eligibility:** Applicant must be U.S. citizen residing in Hawaii.
**Basis for selection:** Applicant must demonstrate financial need, high academic achievement and depth of character.
**Application requirements:** Recommendations, essay, transcript. SAR, FAFSA, personal statement.
**Additional information:** Minimum 2.7 GPA. Applicant must be an employee or a dependent of an employee of Kahala Senior Living Community, Inc. for at least 6 months prior to application deadline. Amount of award varies.

**Application deadline:** March 1

**Contact:**
Hawaii Community Foundation Scholarships
827 Fort Street Mall
Honolulu, HI 96813
Phone: 888-731-3863
Fax: 808-521-6286
Web: www.hawaiicommunityfoundation.org

## Kahiau Scholarship Fund

**Type of award:** Scholarship.
**Intended use:** For full-time undergraduate or graduate study at accredited 2-year or 4-year institution in United States.
**Eligibility:** Applicant must be U.S. citizen residing in Hawaii.
**Basis for selection:** Applicant must demonstrate financial need, high academic achievement and depth of character.
**Application requirements:** Recommendations, essay, transcript. SAR, FAFSA, personal statement.
**Additional information:** Minimum 2.7 GPA. Amount of award varies. Applicant must be a graduate from Kohala High School. Applicant's family must have lived in the North Kohala community for at least two generations. Applicant must be attending an out-of-state college or university, or a four-year university on O'ahu.

**Application deadline:** March 1

**Contact:**
Hawaii Community Foundation Scholarships
827 Fort Street Mall
Honolulu, HI 96813
Phone: 888-731-3863
Fax: 808-521-6286
Web: www.hawaiicommunityfoundation.org

## Kalihi Education Coalition Scholarship Fund

**Type of award:** Scholarship.
**Intended use:** For full-time undergraduate or graduate study at accredited postsecondary institution.
**Eligibility:** Applicant must be residing in Hawaii.
**Basis for selection:** Applicant must demonstrate financial need and high academic achievement.
**Application requirements:** Recommendations, essay, transcript. SAR.
**Additional information:** Minimum 3.0 GPA. Must either be a graduate or undergraduate student who is a resident of Kalihi-Palama with one of following zip codes: 96817, 96819, or be current graduating senior from Damien High School, Farrington High School, or Kamehameha School (Kapalama campus).

**Application deadline:** March 1

**Contact:**
Hawaii Community Foundation
827 Fort Street Mall
Honolulu, HI 96813
Phone: 888-731-3863
Fax: 808-521-6286
Web: www.hawaiicommunityfoundation.org

## Kaneta Foundation Scholarship

**Type of award:** Scholarship.
**Intended use:** For full-time undergraduate study at accredited postsecondary institution in United States.
**Eligibility:** Applicant must be Christian. Applicant must be residing in Hawaii.
**Basis for selection:** Applicant must demonstrate financial need and high academic achievement.
**Application requirements:** Recommendations, essay, transcript. SAR. SAT and ACT scores, one letter from pastor or minister, one letter from teacher or counselor. Personal statement should include description of family dynamic, adversities overcome, and community service.
**Additional information:** Minimum 3.0 GPA. Must be in good standing at any Christian church in Hawaii. Must be 2011 high school graduate.

**Application deadline:** March 1
**Contact:**
Hawaii Community Foundation
827 Fort Street Mall
Honolulu, HI 96813
Phone: 888-731-3863
Fax: 808-521-6286
Web: www.hawaiicommunityfoundation.org

## Kaneta Foundation Vocational Education Scholarship

**Type of award:** Scholarship.
**Intended use:** For undergraduate study at accredited 2-year institution in United States. Designated institutions: Community colleges of University of Hawaii.
**Eligibility:** Applicant must be residing in Hawaii.
**Basis for selection:** Major/career interest in culinary arts. Applicant must demonstrate financial need and high academic achievement.
**Application requirements:** Recommendations, essay, transcript.
**Additional information:** Minimum 2.7 GPA.
**Application deadline:** March 1
**Contact:**
Hawaii Community Foundation
827 Fort Street Mall
Honolulu, HI 96813
Phone: 888-731-3863
Fax: 808-521-6286
Web: www.hawaiicommunityfoundation.org

## Kapolei Community & Business Scholarship

**Type of award:** Scholarship.
**Intended use:** For full-time undergraduate study at accredited 2-year or 4-year institution in United States.
**Eligibility:** Applicant must be high school senior. Applicant must be U.S. citizen or permanent resident residing in Hawaii.
**Basis for selection:** Applicant must demonstrate financial need, high academic achievement and depth of character.
**Application requirements:** Essay, transcript. FAFSA and SAR.
**Additional information:** Must major in computer studies or international studies. Applicant must be a senior from Campbell, Nanakuli, or Waianae high schools. Applicants taking up mainland residency must have relatives living in Hawaii. Amount of award may vary yearly.
**Number of awards:** 4
**Application deadline:** March 1
**Contact:**
Hawaii Community Foundation Scholarships
827 Fort Street Mall
Honolulu, HI 96813
Phone: 888-731-3863
Fax: 808-521-6286
Web: www.hawaiicommunityfoundation.org

## Kawasaki-McGaha Scholarship Fund

**Type of award:** Scholarship.
**Intended use:** For full-time undergraduate study at postsecondary institution. Designated institutions: Hawaii Pacific University.
**Eligibility:** Applicant must be permanent resident residing in Hawaii.
**Basis for selection:** Major/career interest in computer/information sciences or international studies. Applicant must demonstrate financial need, high academic achievement and depth of character.
**Application requirements:** Essay, transcript. FAFSA and SAR.
**Additional information:** Applicants must have permanent address in Hawaii. Applicants taking up mainland residency must have relatives living in Hawaii. Amount and number of awards vary and may change yearly.
**Number of awards:** 2
**Application deadline:** March 1
**Contact:**
Hawaii Community Foundation Scholarships
827 Fort Street Mall
Honolulu, HI 96813
Phone: 888-731-3863
Fax: 808-521-6286
Web: www.hawaiicommunityfoundation.org

## Kazuma and Ichiko Hisanaga Scholarship Fund

**Type of award:** Scholarship.
**Intended use:** For full-time undergraduate study at accredited 2-year or 4-year institution in United States. Designated institutions: NAIA or Division III school in the contiguous United States.
**Eligibility:** Applicant must be high school senior. Applicant must be U.S. citizen residing in Hawaii.
**Basis for selection:** Applicant must demonstrate financial need, high academic achievement, depth of character, leadership and service orientation.
**Application requirements:** Recommendations, essay, transcript. SAR, FAFSA, Personal statement detailing sports involvement, leadership experience and community service. One recommendation letter must be from high school athletic director, or post-secondary counselor or administrator.
**Additional information:** Minimum 3.0 GPA. Amount of award varies. Applicant must be a graduating senior at Hilo High School; if Hilo has no eligible applicants from Hilo High School, seniors from other Hawai'i Island high schools will be considered in the following order: Waiakea High School, St. Joseph High School, other Hawai'i Island high schools. Applicant must be an athlete that participated in more than one varsity high school sport. Must have served as the captain of a varsity sports team, a student government leader or an officer of an extracurricular program.
**Application deadline:** March 1
**Contact:**
Hawaii Community Foundation Scholarships
827 Fort Street Mall
Honolulu, HI 96813
Phone: 888-731-3863
Fax: 808-521-6286
Web: www.hawaiicommunityfoundation.org

## King Kekaulike High School Scholarship

**Type of award:** Scholarship.
**Intended use:** For full-time undergraduate study at accredited 2-year or 4-year institution in United States.
**Eligibility:** Applicant must be high school senior. Applicant must be U.S. citizen or permanent resident residing in Hawaii.

**Basis for selection:** Applicant must demonstrate financial need, high academic achievement, depth of character and service orientation.
**Application requirements:** Essay, transcript. FAFSA and SAR. Additional 500-word essay on how well Na Ali'i 3 R's (Respect, Relevance, and Rigor) relate to your future goals.
**Additional information:** Minimum 2.8 GPA and three or more hours of community service required. Applicant must be student at King Kekaulike High School. Children of KKHS staff members not eligible. Amount of award may change yearly. Applicants taking up mainland residency must have relatives living in Hawaii.

**Number of awards:** 1
**Application deadline:** March 1

**Contact:**
Hawaii Community Foundation Scholarships
827 Fort Street Mall
Honolulu, HI 96813
Phone: 888-731-3863
Fax: 808-521-6286
Web: www.hawaiicommunityfoundation.org

## K.M. Hatano Scholarship

**Type of award:** Scholarship, renewable.
**Intended use:** For full-time undergraduate study at accredited 4-year institution in United States. Designated institutions: Institutions in Hawaii.
**Eligibility:** Applicant must be high school senior. Applicant must be U.S. citizen or permanent resident residing in Hawaii.
**Basis for selection:** Applicant must demonstrate financial need, high academic achievement and depth of character.
**Application requirements:** Essay, transcript. FAFSA and SAR.
**Additional information:** Applicant must be high school graduate of Maui, including Lanai or Molokai counties. Must attend college in Hawaii. Applicant must have permanent address in Hawaii. Applicants taking up mainland residency must have relatives living in Hawaii. Amount and number of awards vary and may change yearly.

**Number of awards:** 8
**Application deadline:** March 1

**Contact:**
Hawaii Community Foundation Scholarships
827 Fort Street Mall
Honolulu, HI 96813
Phone: 888-731-3863
Fax: 808-521-6286
Web: www.hawaiicommunityfoundation.org

## Kohala Ditch Education Fund

**Type of award:** Scholarship.
**Intended use:** For full-time undergraduate study at accredited 2-year or 4-year institution in United States.
**Eligibility:** Applicant must be high school senior. Applicant must be U.S. citizen or permanent resident residing in Hawaii.
**Basis for selection:** Applicant must demonstrate financial need, high academic achievement and depth of character.
**Application requirements:** Essay, transcript. FAFSA and SAR.
**Additional information:** Applicant must be student at Kohala High School. Amount of award may change yearly. Applicants taking up mainland residency must have relatives living in Hawaii.

**Number of awards:** 3
**Application deadline:** March 1

**Contact:**
Hawaii Community Foundation Scholarships
827 Fort Street Mall
Honolulu, HI 96813
Phone: 888-731-3863
Fax: 808-521-6286
Web: www.hawaiicommunityfoundation.org

## Koloa Scholarship

**Type of award:** Scholarship, renewable.
**Intended use:** For full-time undergraduate or graduate study at accredited vocational, 2-year or 4-year institution in United States.
**Eligibility:** Applicant must be U.S. citizen or permanent resident residing in Hawaii.
**Basis for selection:** Applicant must demonstrate financial need, high academic achievement and depth of character.
**Application requirements:** Recommendations, transcript. FAFSA and SAR. Personal essay explaining personal understanding of meaning of "aloha," how it has played a part in personal development and how applicant hopes to use chosen field to further this meaning among family and community. Must include how long applicant has lived in Koloa area, list of books or other publications read on Hawaii's history, and list of relatives born in Koloa District, including relationship to applicant, and place and approximate year of birth.
**Additional information:** Minimum 2.0 GPA. Applicant must be resident of one of the following Kauai areas in Hawaii: Koloa, including Omao and Poipu (96756), Lawai (96765), or Kalaheo (96741). Applicants taking up mainland residency must have relatives living in Hawaii. Amount of award varies and may change yearly.

**Number of awards:** 4
**Application deadline:** March 1

**Contact:**
Hawaii Community Foundation Scholarships
827 Fort Street Mall
Honolulu, HI 96813
Phone: 888-731-3863
Fax: 808-521-6286
Web: www.hawaiicommunityfoundation.org

## Korean University Club Scholarship Fund

**Type of award:** Scholarship.
**Intended use:** For full-time undergraduate or graduate study at accredited 2-year or 4-year institution in United States.
**Eligibility:** Applicant must be U.S. citizen residing in Hawaii.
**Basis for selection:** Applicant must demonstrate financial need, high academic achievement and depth of character.
**Application requirements:** Recommendations, essay, transcript. SAR, FAFSA, Personal Statement.
**Additional information:** Minimum 2.7 GPA. Must be of Korean ancestry.

**Application deadline:** March 1

**Contact:**
Hawaii Community Foundation Scholarships
827 Fort Street Mall
Honolulu, HI 96813
Phone: 888-731-3863
Fax: 808-521-6286
Web: www.hawaiicommunityfoundation.org

## Kurt W. Schneider Memorial Scholarship Fund

**Type of award:** Scholarship.
**Intended use:** For full-time undergraduate study at accredited 2-year or 4-year institution in United States.
**Eligibility:** Applicant must be high school senior. Applicant must be U.S. citizen or permanent resident residing in Hawaii.
**Basis for selection:** Major/career interest in tourism/travel. Applicant must demonstrate financial need, high academic achievement and depth of character.
**Application requirements:** Essay, transcript. FAFSA and SAR.
**Additional information:** Applicant must be student at Lana'i High School. Preference given to travel industry management majors. Applicants taking up mainland residency must have relatives living in Hawaii. Amount of award may change yearly.

**Number of awards:** 1
**Application deadline:** March 1
**Contact:**
Hawaii Community Foundation Scholarships
827 Fort Street Mall
Honolulu, HI 96813
Phone: 888-731-3863
Fax: 808-521-6286
Web: www.hawaiicommunityfoundation.org

## Laheenae Rebecca Hart Gay Scholarship

**Type of award:** Scholarship.
**Intended use:** For full-time undergraduate or graduate study at accredited 2-year or 4-year institution in United States.
**Eligibility:** Applicant must be U.S. citizen residing in Hawaii.
**Basis for selection:** Major/career interest in arts, general. Applicant must demonstrate financial need, high academic achievement and depth of character.
**Application requirements:** Recommendations, essay, transcript. SAR, FAFSA, Personal Statement.
**Additional information:** Minimum 2.7 GPA. Amount of award varies. Scholarship does not apply to study of video, film, performing arts or the culinary arts.

**Application deadline:** March 1
**Contact:**
Hawaii Community Foundation Scholarships
827 Fort Street Mall
Honolulu, HI 96813
Phone: 888-731-3863
Fax: 808-521-6286
Web: www.hawaiicommunityfoundation.org

## Laura N. Dowsett Fund

**Type of award:** Scholarship, renewable.
**Intended use:** For full-time junior, senior or graduate study at accredited 2-year, 4-year or graduate institution in United States.
**Eligibility:** Applicant must be U.S. citizen or permanent resident residing in Hawaii.
**Basis for selection:** Major/career interest in occupational therapy. Applicant must demonstrate financial need, high academic achievement and depth of character.
**Application requirements:** Essay, transcript. FAFSA and SAR.
**Additional information:** Minimum 2.7 GPA. Applicants must have permanent address in Hawaii. Applicants who take up mainland residency must have relatives living in Hawaii. Amount and number of awards vary.

**Number of awards:** 2
**Application deadline:** March 1
**Contact:**
Hawaii Community Foundation Scholarships
827 Fort Street Mall
Honolulu, HI 96813
Phone: 888-731-3863
Fax: 808-521-6286
Web: www.hawaiicommunityfoundation.org

## Laura Rowe Burdick Scholarship Fund

**Type of award:** Scholarship.
**Intended use:** For full-time undergraduate study at accredited 2-year or 4-year institution in United States.
**Eligibility:** Applicant must be high school senior. Applicant must be U.S. citizen residing in Hawaii.
**Basis for selection:** Applicant must demonstrate financial need, high academic achievement, depth of character and service orientation.
**Application requirements:** Recommendations, essay, transcript. SAR, FAFSA, Personal Statement.
**Additional information:** Minimum 2.7 GPA. Amount of award varies. Applicant must be a high school senior in Maui County. Preference given to applicants who want to return to Maui County after completing their education or training in order to contribute to the community that formed them.

**Application deadline:** March 1
**Contact:**
Hawaii Community Foundation Scholarships
827 Fort Street Mall
Honolulu, HI 96813
Phone: 888-731-3863
Fax: 808-521-6286
Web: www.hawaiicommunityfoundation.org

## Logan Nainoa Fujimoto Memorial Scholarship

**Type of award:** Scholarship.
**Intended use:** For full-time undergraduate study at accredited vocational institution in United States. Designated institutions: Vocational schools with automotive technology programs.
**Eligibility:** Applicant must be residing in Hawaii.
**Basis for selection:** Applicant must demonstrate financial need and high academic achievement.
**Application requirements:** Recommendations, essay, transcript. SAR.
**Additional information:** Minimum 2.7 GPA. Preference given to students attending Universal Technical Institute. Must be concentrating in Automotive Technology.

**Application deadline:** March 1
**Contact:**
Hawaii Community Foundation
827 Fort Street Mall
Honolulu, HI 96813
Phone: 888-731-3863
Fax: 808-521-6286
Web: www.hawaiicommunityfoundation.org

## Makinney & Pietsch Familes Scholarship Fund

**Type of award:** Scholarship.
**Intended use:** For full-time undergraduate or graduate study at accredited postsecondary institution.
**Eligibility:** Applicant must be residing in Hawaii.
**Basis for selection:** Applicant must demonstrate financial need and high academic achievement.
**Application requirements:** Recommendations, essay, transcript. SAR, name and job title of Guaranty employee.
**Additional information:** Minimum 2.7 GPA. Must be full-time employee of at least one year or qualified dependent of Title Guaranty of Hawaii, Incorporated and Title Guaranty Escrow Services, Inc.

**Application deadline:** March 1

**Contact:**
Hawaii Community Foundation
827 Fort Street Mall
Honolulu, HI 96813
Phone: 888-731-3863
Fax: 808-521-6286
Web: www.hawaiicommunityfoundation.org

## Margaret Jones Memorial Nursing Scholarship

**Type of award:** Scholarship, renewable.
**Intended use:** For full-time junior, senior or graduate study at accredited 4-year or graduate institution in United States. Designated institutions: University of Hawaii, Manoa; University of Hawaii, Hilo; Hawaii Pacific University; or PhD programs in Hawaii or mainland U.S.
**Eligibility:** Applicant must be U.S. citizen or permanent resident residing in Hawaii.
**Basis for selection:** Major/career interest in nursing. Applicant must demonstrate financial need, high academic achievement and depth of character.
**Application requirements:** Essay, transcript. FAFSA and SAR.
**Additional information:** Minimum 3.0 GPA. Applicants must be enrolled in BSN, MSN, or doctoral nursing program. Preference may be given to members of Hawaii Nurses Association. Applicants must have permanent address in Hawaii. Applicant taking up mainland residency must have relatives living in Hawaii. Amount and number of awards vary and change yearly.

**Number of awards:** 13
**Application deadline:** March 1

**Contact:**
Hawaii Community Foundation Scholarships
827 Fort Street Mall
Honolulu, HI 96813
Phone: 888-731-3863
Fax: 808-521-6286
Web: www.hawaiicommunityfoundation.org

## Marion Maccarrell Scott Scholarship

**Type of award:** Scholarship, renewable.
**Intended use:** For full-time undergraduate or graduate study at accredited postsecondary institution in United States. Designated institutions: Institutions on U.S. mainland.
**Eligibility:** Applicant must be U.S. citizen or permanent resident residing in Hawaii.
**Basis for selection:** Applicant must demonstrate financial need, high academic achievement and depth of character.
**Application requirements:** Essay, transcript. FAFSA and SAR. Essay (2-3 typed pages, double-spaced) must demonstrate commitment to international understanding and world peace.
**Additional information:** Minimum 2.8 GPA. Must be graduate of Hawaii public high school and attend accredited mainland U.S. college or university. Applicant must have permanent address in Hawaii. Applicants taking up mainland residency must have relatives living in Hawaii. Amount and number of awards vary and may change yearly.

**Number of awards:** 331
**Application deadline:** March 1

**Contact:**
Hawaii Community Foundation Scholarships
827 Fort Street Mall
Honolulu, HI 96813
Phone: 888-731-3863
Fax: 808-521-6286
Web: www.hawaiicommunityfoundation.org

## Mary Josephine Bloder Scholarship

**Type of award:** Scholarship.
**Intended use:** For full-time undergraduate study at accredited 2-year or 4-year institution in United States.
**Eligibility:** Applicant must be high school senior. Applicant must be U.S. citizen or permanent resident residing in Hawaii.
**Basis for selection:** Applicant must demonstrate financial need, high academic achievement and depth of character.
**Application requirements:** Recommendations, essay, transcript. FAFSA and SAR. One of the two letters of recommendation must be from Lahainaluna High School science teacher.
**Additional information:** Must be student at Lahainaluna High School. Preference given to boarding students. Must have high GPA in sciences. Applicants taking up mainland residency must have relatives living in Hawaii. Amount and number of awards vary and may change yearly.

**Application deadline:** March 1

**Contact:**
Hawaii Community Foundation Scholarships
827 Fort Street Mall
Honolulu, HI 96813
Phone: 888-731-3863
Fax: 808-521-6286
Web: www.hawaiicommunityfoundation.org

## Mildred Towle Scholarship - Study Abroad

**Type of award:** Scholarship, renewable.
**Intended use:** For full-time junior, senior or graduate study at accredited postsecondary institution outside United States.
**Eligibility:** Applicant must be residing in Hawaii.
**Basis for selection:** Applicant must demonstrate financial need, high academic achievement and depth of character.
**Application requirements:** Essay, transcript. FAFSA and SAR. Essay must include intended country and semester of study.
**Additional information:** Minimum 3.0 GPA. Award for Hawaii residents studying abroad while enrolled at U.S. institution. Amount and number of awards vary and may change yearly.

**Number of awards:** 6
**Application deadline:** March 1

**Contact:**
Hawaii Community Foundation Scholarships
827 Fort Street Mall
Honolulu, HI 96813
Phone: 888-731-3863
Fax: 808-521-6286
Web: www.hawaiicommunityfoundation.org

## Mildred Towle Scholarship for African-Americans

**Type of award:** Scholarship.
**Intended use:** For undergraduate study at postsecondary institution. Designated institutions: Hawaii post-secondary institutions.
**Eligibility:** Applicant must be African American. Applicant must be U.S. citizen.
**Application requirements:** Recommendations, essay, transcript. SAR.
**Additional information:** Minimum 3.0 GPA. Must attend school in Hawaii. Hawaii residency not required.
**Number of awards:** 11
**Total amount awarded:** $11,000
**Contact:**
Hawaii Community Foundation Scholarships
827 Fort Street Mall
Honolulu, HI 96813
Phone: 888-731-3863
Fax: 808-521-6286
Web: www.hawaiicommunityfoundation.org

## Nick Van Pernis Scholarship

**Type of award:** Scholarship.
**Intended use:** For full-time undergraduate study at accredited 2-year or 4-year institution in United States.
**Eligibility:** Applicant must be U.S. citizen or permanent resident residing in Hawaii.
**Basis for selection:** Major/career interest in oceanography/marine studies; bioengineering; health sciences or education, early childhood. Applicant must demonstrate financial need, high academic achievement, depth of character and service orientation.
**Application requirements:** Essay, transcript. FAFSA and SAR. Essay must include record of community service and description of how student's education and career will benefit Hawaii residents.
**Additional information:** Must be graduate of public or private school in the North Kona, South Kona, North Kohala, South Kohala, or Ka'u districts. Applicants taking up mainland residency must have relatives living in Hawaii. Amount and number of awards may vary yearly.
**Application deadline:** March 1
**Contact:**
Hawaii Community Foundation Scholarships
827 Fort Street Mall
Honolulu, HI 96813
Phone: 888-731-3863
Fax: 808-521-6286
Web: www.hawaiicommunityfoundation.org

## Office of Hawaiian Affairs Scholarship Fund

**Type of award:** Scholarship.
**Intended use:** For undergraduate or graduate study at accredited 2-year or 4-year institution in United States.
**Eligibility:** Applicant must be Native Hawaiian/Pacific Islander. Applicant must be U.S. citizen.
**Basis for selection:** Applicant must demonstrate financial need, high academic achievement and depth of character.
**Application requirements:** Recommendations, essay, transcript, proof of eligibility. SAR, FAFSA, Personal Statement.
**Additional information:** Minimum 2.0 GPA for undergraduate students, 3.0 GPA for graduate students. Applicant must be of Hawaiian ancestry; ancestry must be verified through OHA's Hawaiian Registry Program. Amount of award varies.
**Application deadline:** March 1
**Contact:**
Hawaii Community Foundation Scholarships
827 Fort Street Mall
Honolulu, HI 96813
Phone: 888-731-3863
Fax: 808-521-6286
Web: www.hawaiicommunityfoundation.org

## Oscar and Rosetta Fish Fund

**Type of award:** Scholarship.
**Intended use:** For full-time undergraduate or graduate study at 2-year or 4-year institution. Designated institutions: Any University of Hawaii campus, excluding Manoa.
**Eligibility:** Applicant must be U.S. citizen or permanent resident residing in Hawaii.
**Basis for selection:** Major/career interest in business. Applicant must demonstrate financial need, high academic achievement and depth of character.
**Application requirements:** Essay, transcript. FAFSA and SAR.
**Additional information:** Must have permanent address in Hawaii. Amount and number of awards vary and may change yearly.
**Application deadline:** March 1
**Contact:**
Hawaii Community Foundation Scholarships
827 Fort Street Mall
Honolulu, HI 96813
Phone: 888-731-3863
Fax: 808-521-6286
Web: www.hawaiicommunityfoundation.org

## Ouida Mundy Hill Memorial Fund

**Type of award:** Scholarship.
**Intended use:** For full-time undergraduate study at accredited vocational or 2-year institution in United States. Designated institutions: Community colleges in the University of Hawaii system.
**Eligibility:** Applicant must be residing in Hawaii.
**Basis for selection:** Applicant must demonstrate financial need and high academic achievement.
**Application requirements:** Recommendations, essay, transcript. SAR.
**Additional information:** Minimum 2.7 GPA. Must be enrolled in vocational education program.
**Application deadline:** March 1
**Contact:**
Hawaii Community Foundation
827 Fort Street Mall
Honolulu, HI 96813
Phone: 888-731-3863
Fax: 808-521-6286
Web: www.hawaiicommunityfoundation.org

## Paul and Betty Honzik Scholarship

**Type of award:** Scholarship.
**Intended use:** For full-time undergraduate or graduate study at postsecondary institution.
**Eligibility:** Applicant must be Presbyterian. Applicant must be residing in Hawaii.
**Basis for selection:** Applicant must demonstrate financial need and high academic achievement.
**Application requirements:** Recommendations, essay, transcript. SAR, letter of reference from church or pastor.
**Additional information:** Minimum 3.0 GPA. Must be member in good standing of Presbyterian Church in Hawaii. May attend four-year college or seminary.
**Application deadline:** March 1
**Contact:**
Hawaii Community Foundation
827 Fort Street Mall
Honolulu, HI 96813
Phone: 888-731-3863
Fax: 808-521-6286
Web: www.hawaiicommunityfoundation.org

## Paulina L. Sorg Scholarship

**Type of award:** Scholarship.
**Intended use:** For full-time junior, senior or graduate study at accredited 2-year or 4-year institution in United States.
**Eligibility:** Applicant must be U.S. citizen residing in Hawaii.
**Basis for selection:** Major/career interest in physical therapy. Applicant must demonstrate financial need and depth of character.
**Application requirements:** Recommendations, essay, transcript. SAR, FAFSA, Personal Statement.
**Additional information:** Minimum 2.7 GPA. Amount of award varies.
**Application deadline:** March 1
**Contact:**
Hawaii Community Foundation Scholarships
827 Fort Street Mall
Honolulu, HI 96813
Phone: 888-731-3863
Fax: 808-521-6286
Web: www.hawaiicommunityfoundation.org

## Perry & Sally Sorenson Scholarship for Dependents of Hospitality Workers

**Type of award:** Scholarship.
**Intended use:** For full-time undergraduate or graduate study at accredited 2-year or 4-year institution in United States.
**Eligibility:** Applicant must be U.S. citizen residing in Hawaii.
**Basis for selection:** Applicant must demonstrate financial need, high academic achievement and depth of character.
**Application requirements:** Recommendations, essay, transcript, proof of eligibility. SAR, FAFSA, personal statement, name of Outrigger employee/position at company.
**Additional information:** Minimum 2.7 GPA. Amount of award varies. Applicant must be a dependent of an employee currently employed by Outrigger Enterprises in Hawaii working in a hospitality industry position.
**Application deadline:** March 1
**Contact:**
Hawaii Community Foundation Scholarships
827 Fort Street Mall
Honolulu, HI 96813
Phone: 888-731-3863
Fax: 808-521-6286
Web: www.hawaiicommunityfoundation.org

## Perry & Sally Sorenson Scholarship for Foster Youth

**Type of award:** Scholarship.
**Intended use:** For full-time undergraduate or graduate study at accredited 4-year or graduate institution in United States.
**Eligibility:** Applicant must be at least 18, no older than 25. Applicant must be U.S. citizen residing in Hawaii.
**Basis for selection:** Applicant must demonstrate financial need, high academic achievement and depth of character.
**Application requirements:** Recommendations, essay, transcript. SAR, FAFSA, Personal Statement.
**Additional information:** Minimum 2.0 GPA. Amount of award varies. Applicant must be permanently or temporarily separated from birth parent(s) and aged out of the foster care system in the state of Hawaii.
**Application deadline:** March 1
**Contact:**
Hawaii Community Foundation Scholarships
827 Fort Street Mall
Honolulu, HI 96813
Phone: 888-731-3863
Fax: 808-521-6286
Web: www.hawaiicommunityfoundation.org

## Peter Papworth Scholarship

**Type of award:** Scholarship.
**Intended use:** For full-time sophomore, junior, senior or graduate study at accredited 2-year or 4-year institution in United States.
**Eligibility:** Applicant must be U.S. citizen residing in Hawaii.
**Basis for selection:** Applicant must demonstrate financial need, high academic achievement and depth of character.
**Application requirements:** Recommendations, essay, transcript. SAR, FAFSA, Personal Statement.
**Additional information:** Applicant must be a graduate of Campbell High School. Minimum 2.7 GPA. Amount of award varies.
**Application deadline:** March 1
**Contact:**
Hawaii Community Foundation Scholarships
827 Fort Street Mall
Honolulu, HI 96813
Phone: 888-731-3863
Fax: 808-521-6286
Web: www.hawaiicommunityfoundation.org

## PRSA-Hawaii/Roy Leffingwell Public Relations Scholarship

**Type of award:** Scholarship.
**Intended use:** For full-time junior, senior or graduate study at accredited 2-year or 4-year institution in United States.
**Eligibility:** Applicant must be U.S. citizen or permanent resident residing in Hawaii.
**Basis for selection:** Major/career interest in public relations; communications or journalism. Applicant must demonstrate

financial need, high academic achievement and depth of character.
**Application requirements:** Essay, transcript. FAFSA and SAR.
**Additional information:** Must intend to pursue career in public relations. Award amount varies.

**Number of awards:** 1
**Application deadline:** March 1

**Contact:**
Hawaii Community Foundation Scholarships
827 Fort Street Mall
Honolulu, HI 96813
Phone: 888-731-3863
Fax: 808-521-6286
Web: www.hawaiicommunityfoundation.org

## Ray Yoshida Kauai Fine Arts Scholarship

**Type of award:** Scholarship.
**Intended use:** For full-time undergraduate study at accredited 2-year or 4-year institution in United States.
**Eligibility:** Applicant must be high school senior. Applicant must be U.S. citizen residing in Hawaii.
**Basis for selection:** Major/career interest in arts, general. Applicant must demonstrate financial need, high academic achievement and depth of character.
**Application requirements:** Recommendations, essay, transcript. SAR, FAFSA, Personal Statement.
**Additional information:** Minimum 2.7 GPA. Amount of award varies. Applicant must be a high school senior from a school on the island of Kauai, and must pursue studies in Fine Arts.

**Application deadline:** March 1

**Contact:**
Hawaii Community Foundation Scholarships
827 Fort Street Mall
Honolulu, HI 96813
Phone: 888-731-3863
Fax: 808-521-6286
Web: www.hawaiicommunityfoundation.org

## Raymond F. Cain Scholarship Fund

**Type of award:** Scholarship.
**Intended use:** For full-time undergraduate or graduate study at accredited 2-year or 4-year institution in United States.
**Eligibility:** Applicant must be U.S. citizen residing in Hawaii.
**Basis for selection:** Major/career interest in landscape architecture. Applicant must demonstrate financial need, high academic achievement and depth of character.
**Application requirements:** Recommendations, essay, transcript. SAR, FAFSA, Personal Statement.
**Additional information:** Minimum 2.7 GPA. Amount of award varies.

**Application deadline:** March 1

**Contact:**
Hawaii Community Foundation Scholarships
827 Fort Street Mall
Honolulu, HI 96813
Phone: 888-731-3863
Fax: 808-521-6286
Web: www.hawaiicommunityfoundation.org

## Rich Meiers Health Administration Fund

**Type of award:** Scholarship.
**Intended use:** For full-time junior, senior or graduate study at accredited 2-year or 4-year institution in United States. Designated institutions: Hawaii institutions.
**Eligibility:** Applicant must be U.S. citizen residing in Hawaii.
**Basis for selection:** Major/career interest in health services administration. Applicant must demonstrate financial need, high academic achievement and depth of character.
**Application requirements:** Recommendations, essay, transcript. SAR, FAFSA, Personal Statement.
**Additional information:** Minimum 2.7 GPA. Amount of award varies. Majors may also include hospital administration, health care administration and long-term care administration.

**Application deadline:** March 1

**Contact:**
Hawaii Community Foundation Scholarships
827 Fort Street Mall
Honolulu, HI 96813
Phone: 888-731-3863
Fax: 808-521-6286
Web: www.hawaiicommunityfoundation.org

## Richie Gregory Fund

**Type of award:** Scholarship.
**Intended use:** For full-time undergraduate or graduate study at accredited 2-year or 4-year institution in United States.
**Eligibility:** Applicant must be U.S. citizen residing in Hawaii.
**Basis for selection:** Major/career interest in arts, general. Applicant must demonstrate financial need, high academic achievement and depth of character.
**Application requirements:** Recommendations, essay, transcript. SAR, FAFSA, Personal Statement.
**Additional information:** Minimum 2.7 GPA. Amount of award varies. Applicant must major in Art.

**Application deadline:** March 1

**Contact:**
Hawaii Community Foundation Scholarships
827 Fort Street Mall
Honolulu, HI 96813
Phone: 888-731-3863
Fax: 808-521-6286
Web: www.hawaiicommunityfoundation.org

## Robanna Fund

**Type of award:** Scholarship.
**Intended use:** For full-time undergraduate study at accredited 2-year or 4-year institution in United States.
**Eligibility:** Applicant must be U.S. citizen residing in Hawaii.
**Basis for selection:** Major/career interest in health-related professions. Applicant must demonstrate financial need, high academic achievement and depth of character.
**Application requirements:** Recommendations, essay, transcript. SAR, FAFSA, Personal Statement.
**Additional information:** Minimum 2.7 GPA. Amount of award varies.

**Application deadline:** March 1

**Contact:**
Hawaii Community Foundation Scholarships
827 Fort Street Mall
Honolulu, HI 96813
Phone: 888-731-3863
Fax: 808-521-6286
Web: www.hawaiicommunityfoundation.org

## Ron Bright Scholarship

**Type of award:** Scholarship.
**Intended use:** For full-time undergraduate study at accredited 2-year or 4-year institution in United States.
**Eligibility:** Applicant must be high school senior. Applicant must be U.S. citizen or permanent resident residing in Hawaii.
**Basis for selection:** Major/career interest in education. Applicant must demonstrate financial need, high academic achievement and depth of character.
**Application requirements:** Essay, transcript. FAFSA and SAR. Grades from first semester of 12th grade.
**Additional information:** Must attend one of the following Windward Oahu high schools: Castle, Kahuku, Kailua, Kalaheo, or Olomana. Preference given to students with extracurricular activities in the performing arts. Must have permanent address in Hawaii. Applicants taking up mainland residency must have relatives living in Hawaii. Amount and number of awards vary and may change yearly.

**Application deadline:** March 1

**Contact:**
Hawaii Community Foundation Scholarships
827 Fort Street Mall
Honolulu, HI 96813
Phone: 888-731-3863
Fax: 808-521-6286
Web: www.hawaiicommunityfoundation.org

## Rosemary & Nellie Ebrie Fund

**Type of award:** Scholarship.
**Intended use:** For full-time undergraduate or graduate study at accredited 2-year or 4-year institution in United States.
**Eligibility:** Applicant must be Native Hawaiian/Pacific Islander. Applicant must be U.S. citizen or permanent resident residing in Hawaii.
**Basis for selection:** Applicant must demonstrate financial need, high academic achievement and depth of character.
**Application requirements:** Essay, transcript. FAFSA and SAR.
**Additional information:** Must be of Hawaiian ancestry. Must be long-term resident born and currently living on the island of Hawaii. Applicants taking up mainland residency must have relatives living in Hawaii. Amount of award may change yearly.

**Number of awards:** 15
**Application deadline:** March 1

**Contact:**
Hawaii Community Foundation Scholarships
827 Fort Street Mall
Honolulu, HI 96813
Phone: 888-731-3863
Fax: 808-521-6286
Web: www.hawaiicommunityfoundation.org

## Safeway Foundation Hawaii Scholarship Fund

**Type of award:** Scholarship.
**Intended use:** For full-time undergraduate or graduate study at accredited 2-year or 4-year institution in United States. Designated institutions: Hawaii institutions.
**Eligibility:** Applicant must be U.S. citizen residing in Hawaii.
**Basis for selection:** Applicant must demonstrate financial need, high academic achievement and depth of character.
**Application requirements:** Recommendations, essay, transcript. SAR, FAFSA, Personal Statement.
**Additional information:** Minimum 3.0 GPA. Must be resident of Kauai. Amount of award varies. Preference for current and past employees of Safeway Hawaii and their dependents.

**Application deadline:** March 1

**Contact:**
Hawaii Community Foundation Scholarships
827 Fort Street Mall
Honolulu, HI 96813
Phone: 888-731-3863
Fax: 808-521-6286
Web: www.hawaiicommunityfoundation.org

## Sarah Rosenberg Teacher Education Scholarship

**Type of award:** Scholarship.
**Intended use:** For full-time senior study at accredited postsecondary institution.
**Eligibility:** Applicant must be residing in Hawaii.
**Basis for selection:** Major/career interest in education. Applicant must demonstrate financial need and high academic achievement.
**Application requirements:** Recommendations, essay, transcript. SAR.
**Additional information:** Minimum 2.7 GPA.

**Application deadline:** March 1

**Contact:**
Hawaii Community Foundation
827 Fort Street Mall
Honolulu, HI 96813
Phone: 888-731-3863
Fax: 808-521-6286
Web: www.hawaiicommunityfoundation.org

## Senator Richard M. & Dr. Ruth Matsuura Scholarship Fund

**Type of award:** Scholarship.
**Intended use:** For full-time undergraduate or graduate study at accredited 2-year or 4-year institution in United States.
**Eligibility:** Applicant must be U.S. citizen residing in Hawaii.
**Basis for selection:** Applicant must demonstrate financial need, high academic achievement and depth of character.
**Application requirements:** Recommendations, essay, transcript. SAR, FAFSA, Personal Statement.
**Additional information:** Applicant must be a graduate of Hilo High School or Waiakea High School and a resident of the island of Hawaii. Minimum 2.7 GPA. Amount of award varies.

**Application deadline:** March 1

**Contact:**
Hawaii Community Foundation Scholarships
827 Fort Street Mall
Honolulu, HI 96813
Phone: 888-731-3863
Fax: 808-521-6286
Web: www.hawaiicommunityfoundation.org

## Shirley McKown Scholarship Fund

**Type of award:** Scholarship.
**Intended use:** For full-time junior, senior or graduate study at accredited 4-year institution in United States.
**Eligibility:** Applicant must be U.S. citizen or permanent resident residing in Hawaii.
**Basis for selection:** Major/career interest in advertising; journalism or public relations. Applicant must demonstrate depth of character.

**Application requirements:** Essay, transcript. FAFSA and SAR.
**Additional information:** Minimum 3.0 GPA. Applicants must have permanent address in Hawaii. Applicants taking up mainland residency must have relatives living in Hawaii.
**Number of awards:** 1
**Application deadline:** March 1
**Contact:**
Hawaii Community Foundation Scholarships
827 Fort Street Mall
Honolulu, HI 96813
Phone: 888-731-3863
Fax: 808-521-6286
Web: www.hawaiicommunityfoundation.org

## Shuichi, Katsu and Itsuyo Suga Scholarship

**Type of award:** Scholarship.
**Intended use:** For full-time undergraduate or graduate study at accredited 2-year or 4-year institution in United States.
**Eligibility:** Applicant must be U.S. citizen or permanent resident residing in Hawaii.
**Basis for selection:** Major/career interest in mathematics; physics; science, general; computer/information sciences or technology. Applicant must demonstrate financial need, high academic achievement and depth of character.
**Application requirements:** Essay, transcript. FAFSA and SAR.
**Additional information:** Minimum 3.0 GPA. Applicants must have permanent address in Hawaii. Applicants taking up mainland residency must have relatives living in Hawaii. Amount of award may change yearly.
**Number of awards:** 9
**Application deadline:** March 1
**Contact:**
Hawaii Community Foundation Scholarships
827 Fort Street Mall
Honolulu, HI 96813
Phone: 888-731-3863
Fax: 808-521-6286
Web: www.hawaiicommunityfoundation.org

## Takehiko Hasegawa Academic Scholarship

**Type of award:** Scholarship.
**Intended use:** For full-time undergraduate or graduate study at accredited 2-year or 4-year institution in United States.
**Eligibility:** Applicant must be U.S. citizen residing in Hawaii.
**Basis for selection:** Applicant must demonstrate financial need, high academic achievement and depth of character.
**Application requirements:** Recommendations, essay, transcript. SAR, FAFSA, Personal statement.
**Additional information:** Minimum GPA of 3.8. Must be a resident of the Island of Kaua'i. Amount of award varies.
**Application deadline:** March 1
**Contact:**
Hawaii Community Foundation Scholarships
827 Fort Street Mall
Honolulu, HI 96813
Phone: 888-731-3863
Fax: 808-521-6286
Web: www.hawaiicommunityfoundation.org

## Thz Fo Farm Fund

**Type of award:** Scholarship.
**Intended use:** For full-time undergraduate or graduate study at accredited postsecondary institution in United States.
**Eligibility:** Applicant must be Chinese. Applicant must be U.S. citizen or permanent resident residing in Hawaii.
**Basis for selection:** Major/career interest in gerontology. Applicant must demonstrate financial need, high academic achievement and depth of character.
**Application requirements:** FAFSA and SAR.
**Additional information:** Minimum 2.7 GPA. Applicants must have permanent address in Hawaii. Applicants who take up mainland residency must have relatives living in Hawaii. Amount of award varies.
**Number of awards:** 6
**Contact:**
Hawaii Community Foundation Scholarships
827 Fort Street Mall
Honolulu, HI 96813
Phone: 888-731-3863
Fax: 808-521-6286
Web: www.hawaiicommunityfoundation.org

## Times Supermarket Shop & Score Scholarship

**Type of award:** Scholarship.
**Intended use:** For full-time undergraduate study at accredited postsecondary institution in United States.
**Eligibility:** Applicant must be high school senior. Applicant must be residing in Hawaii.
**Basis for selection:** Applicant must demonstrate financial need and high academic achievement.
**Application requirements:** Recommendations, essay, transcript. SAR.
**Additional information:** Minimum 2.7 GPA. Must be graduating senior of any high school on Oahu participating in Times Shop and Score program.
**Application deadline:** March 1
**Contact:**
Hawaii Community Foundation
827 Fort Street Mall
Honolulu, HI 96813
Phone: 888-731-3863
Fax: 808-521-6286
Web: www.hawaiicommunityfoundation.org

## Tommy Lee Memorial Scholarship Fund

**Type of award:** Scholarship.
**Intended use:** For full-time undergraduate study at accredited 2-year or 4-year institution in United States.
**Eligibility:** Applicant must be high school senior. Applicant must be U.S. citizen or permanent resident residing in Hawaii.
**Basis for selection:** Applicant must demonstrate financial need, high academic achievement and depth of character.
**Application requirements:** Recommendations, essay, transcript. FAFSA and SAR.
**Additional information:** Must be high school senior residing in the Waialua or Haleiwa area. Applicants taking up mainland residency must have relatives living in Hawaii. Amount of award may change yearly.
**Number of awards:** 4
**Application deadline:** March 1

**Contact:**
Hawaii Community Foundation Scholarships
827 Fort Street Mall
Honolulu, HI 96813
Phone: 888-731-3863
Fax: 808-521-6286
Web: www.hawaiicommunityfoundation.org

## The Tongan Cultural Society Scholarship

**Type of award:** Scholarship.
**Intended use:** For full-time undergraduate or graduate study at accredited 2-year or 4-year institution in United States. Designated institutions: Hawaii institutions.
**Eligibility:** Applicant must be U.S. citizen residing in Hawaii.
**Basis for selection:** Applicant must demonstrate financial need, high academic achievement and depth of character.
**Application requirements:** Recommendations, essay, transcript. SAR, FAFSA, Personal Statement.
**Additional information:** Must be of primarily Tongan ancestry. Must attend school in Hawaii. Minimum 2.7 GPA. Amount of awards varies.

**Application deadline:** March 1

**Contact:**
Hawaii Community Foundation Scholarships
827 Fort Street Mall
Honolulu, HI 96813
Phone: 888-731-3863
Fax: 808-521-6286
Web: www.hawaiicommunityfoundation.org

## Toraji & Toki Yoshinaga Scholarship

**Type of award:** Scholarship.
**Intended use:** For full-time sophomore study at accredited 2-year or 4-year institution. Designated institutions: Brigham Young University-Hawaii, Chaminade University, Hawaii Pacific University, Heald College.
**Eligibility:** Applicant must be U.S. citizen or permanent resident residing in Hawaii.
**Basis for selection:** Applicant must demonstrate financial need, high academic achievement and depth of character.
**Application requirements:** Essay, transcript. FAFSA and SAR.
**Additional information:** Minimum 2.7 GPA. Applicants must have permanent address in Hawaii. Applicants taking up mainland residency must have relatives living in Hawaii. Amount of award may change yearly.

**Number of awards:** 2
**Application deadline:** March 1

**Contact:**
Hawaii Community Foundation Scholarships
827 Fort Street Mall
Honolulu, HI 96813
Phone: 888-731-3863
Fax: 808-521-6286
Web: www.hawaiicommunityfoundation.org

## Troy Barboza Educational Fund Hero Award

**Type of award:** Scholarship.
**Intended use:** For full-time undergraduate or graduate study at accredited postsecondary institution.
**Eligibility:** Applicant must be residing in Hawaii.
**Basis for selection:** Applicant must demonstrate financial need and high academic achievement.
**Application requirements:** Recommendations, essay, transcript, proof of eligibility. SAR.
**Additional information:** Minimum 2.7 GPA. Must be private citizen that performed heroic act for welfare of others.

**Application deadline:** March 1

**Contact:**
Hawaii Community Foundation
827 Fort Street Mall
Honolulu, HI 96813
Phone: 888-731-3863
Fax: 808-521-6286
Web: www.hawaiicommunityfoundation.org

## Troy Barboza Educational Fund Scholarship

**Type of award:** Scholarship.
**Intended use:** For full-time undergraduate or graduate study at accredited postsecondary institution in United States.
**Eligibility:** Applicant must be residing in Hawaii. Applicant's parent must have been killed or disabled in work-related accident as firefighter, police officer or public safety officer.
**Basis for selection:** Applicant must demonstrate financial need and high academic achievement.
**Application requirements:** Recommendations, essay, transcript. SAR.
**Additional information:** Minimum 2.7 GPA. Must be public employee or dependent of public employee injured in line of duty.

**Application deadline:** March 1

**Contact:**
Hawaii Community Foundation
827 Fort Street Mall
Honolulu, HI 96813
Phone: 888-731-3863
Fax: 808-521-6286
Web: www.hawaiicommunityfoundation.org

## Vicki Willder Scholarship Fund

**Type of award:** Scholarship.
**Intended use:** For full-time undergraduate study at accredited 2-year or 4-year institution in United States.
**Eligibility:** Applicant must be U.S. citizen or permanent resident residing in Hawaii.
**Basis for selection:** Major/career interest in culinary arts or tourism/travel. Applicant must demonstrate financial need, high academic achievement and depth of character.
**Application requirements:** Essay, transcript. FAFSA and SAR.
**Additional information:** Applicant must be employee or dependent of employee of Kamehameha Schools food services department or a graduate of Kamehameha Schools. Preference given to students majoring in culinary arts or travel industry management. Applicants taking up mainland residency must have relatives living in Hawaii. Amount and number of awards vary and may change yearly.

**Number of awards:** 13
**Application deadline:** March 1

**Contact:**
Hawaii Community Foundation Scholarships
827 Fort Street Mall
Honolulu, HI 96813
Phone: 888-731-3863
Fax: 808-521-6286
Web: www.hawaiicommunityfoundation.org

## Victoria S. and Bradley L. Geist Foundation Scholarship

**Type of award:** Scholarship.
**Intended use:** For full-time undergraduate or graduate study at accredited postsecondary institution.
**Eligibility:** Applicant must be residing in Hawaii.
**Basis for selection:** Applicant must demonstrate financial need and high academic achievement.
**Application requirements:** Recommendations, essay, transcript, proof of eligibility. SAR, confirmation letter from DHS or Family Foster program case worker.
**Additional information:** Minimum 2.7 GPA. Must be currently or formerly placed in foster care in Hawaii. Deadlines are June 1st for fall and spring; October 1st for spring.
**Application deadline:** June 1, October 1
**Contact:**
Hawaii Community Foundation
827 Fort Street Mall
Honolulu, HI 96813
Phone: 888-731-3863
Fax: 808-521-6286
Web: www.hawaiicommunityfoundation.org

## Walter H. Kupau Memorial Fund

**Type of award:** Scholarship.
**Intended use:** For full-time undergraduate study at accredited 2-year or 4-year institution in United States.
**Eligibility:** Applicant must be U.S. citizen or permanent resident residing in Hawaii.
**Basis for selection:** Applicant must demonstrate financial need, high academic achievement and depth of character.
**Application requirements:** Essay, transcript. FAFSA and SAR. Name and social security number of Local 745 member, along with relationship to applicant.
**Additional information:** Applicant must be descendant of Hawaii Carpenter's Union Local 745 member in good standing; preference given to descendants of retired members. Applicant must have permanent address in Hawaii. Applicants taking up mainland residency must have relatives living in Hawaii. Amount and number of awards vary.
**Number of awards:** 5
**Application deadline:** March 1
**Contact:**
Hawaii Community Foundation Scholarships
827 Fort Street Mall
Honolulu, HI 96813
Phone: 888-731-3863
Fax: 808-521-6286
Web: www.hawaiicommunityfoundation.org

## Will J. Henderson Scholarship Fund in Hawaii

**Type of award:** Scholarship.
**Intended use:** For full-time undergraduate or graduate study at accredited vocational, 2-year or 4-year institution in United States. Designated institutions: Institutions approved by the Hawaii Community Foundation.
**Eligibility:** Applicant must be U.S. citizen residing in Hawaii.
**Basis for selection:** Applicant must demonstrate financial need, high academic achievement and depth of character.
**Application requirements:** Recommendations, essay, transcript. SAR, FAFSA, Personal Statement, name/job title of parent employed by Queen's Medical Center.
**Additional information:** Minimum 2.0 GPA. Amount of award varies. Applicant must be a child dependent of a current employee at Queen's Medical Center, and must attend or plan to attend an institution approved by the Hawaii Community Foundation.
**Application deadline:** March 1
**Contact:**
Hawaii Community Foundation Scholarships
827 Fort Street Mall
Honolulu, HI 96813
Phone: 888-731-3863
Fax: 808-521-6286
Web: www.hawaiicommunityfoundation.org

## William James & Dorothy Bading Lanquist Fund

**Type of award:** Scholarship.
**Intended use:** For full-time undergraduate or graduate study at accredited 2-year or 4-year institution in United States.
**Eligibility:** Applicant must be U.S. citizen or permanent resident residing in Hawaii.
**Basis for selection:** Major/career interest in physical sciences. Applicant must demonstrate financial need, high academic achievement and depth of character.
**Application requirements:** Essay, transcript. FAFSA and SAR.
**Additional information:** Must major in the physical sciences or related fields, excluding biological and social sciences. Must have permanent address in Hawaii. Applicants taking up mainland residency must have relatives living in Hawaii. Amount and number of awards vary and may change yearly.
**Application deadline:** March 1
**Contact:**
Hawaii Community Foundation Scholarships
827 Fort Street Mall
Honolulu, HI 96813
Phone: 888-731-3863
Fax: 808-521-6286
Web: www.hawaiicommunityfoundation.org

# Helicopter Association International

## Bill Sanderson Aviation Maintenance Technician Scholarship Award

**Type of award:** Scholarship.
**Intended use:** For undergraduate or non-degree study at vocational institution. Designated institutions: U.S. helicopter airframe and engine manufacturers; aviation maintenance schools.
**Basis for selection:** Major/career interest in aviation repair.
**Application requirements:** Recommendations.
**Additional information:** For students who wish to study helicopter maintenance. Award includes full tuition to aviation maintenance program and stipend of $650-1600. Applicant must be about to graduate from FAA-approved Part 147 Aviation Maintenance Technician School, or a recent recipient of Airframe and Powerplant (A&P) certificate or international equivalent. Applications and deadline information available on Website.

**Amount of award:** $600-$1,600
**Number of awards:** 7
**Number of applicants:** 45
**Contact:**
Bill Sanderson Aviation Maintenance Technician Scholarship
Helicopter Association International
1635 Prince Street
Alexandria, VA 22314-2818
Phone: 703-683-4646
Fax: 703-683-4745
Web: www.rotor.com

# Herschel C. Price Educational Foundation

## Herschel C. Price Educational Scholarship

**Type of award:** Scholarship, renewable.
**Intended use:** For undergraduate or graduate study at accredited 2-year, 4-year or graduate institution in United States.
**Eligibility:** Applicant must be U.S. citizen.
**Basis for selection:** Applicant must demonstrate financial need and high academic achievement.
**Application requirements:** Interview, transcript.
**Additional information:** Applicant must reside in West Virginia or attend West Virginia college or university. Achievement in community activities also considered. Preference given to undergraduates. Limited number of applications available by written request in January and February for fall term or August for spring term. Limited number of applications available.
**Amount of award:** $250-$5,000
**Number of awards:** 175
**Number of applicants:** 275
**Application deadline:** April 1, October 1
**Notification begins:** May 15, November 15
**Total amount awarded:** $157,500
**Contact:**
Herschel C. Price Educational Foundation
P.O. Box 412
Huntington, WV 25708-0412
Phone: 304-529-3852

# Higher Education Services Corporation (HESC)

## NYC World Trade Center Memorial Scholarship

**Type of award:** Scholarship, renewable.
**Intended use:** For full-time undergraduate study at postsecondary institution. Designated institutions: Approved New York State institutions.
**Basis for selection:** Applicant must demonstrate financial need.
**Application requirements:** Proof of eligibility. FAFSA, TAP.
**Additional information:** Applicants must be children, spouses and financial dependents of deceased or severely and permanently disabled victims of the Sept. 11, 2001 terrorist attacks on the United States or the subsequent rescue and recovery operations; this includes victims at the World Trade Center site, at the Pentagon, or on flights 11, 77, 93, or 175. Applicants may also be survivors of the terrorist attacks who are severely and permanently disabled as a result of injuries sustained in the attacks or the subsequent rescue and recovery operations. Applicant must have graduated from high school in the United States, earned a GED, or passed a federally approved "Ability to Benefit" test as defined by the Commissioner of the State Education Department. Applicant must have "C" minimum grade average, and must not be in default on a student loan guaranteed by HESC or on any repayment of state awards. Award covers up to four years of full-time undergraduate study (or five years in an approved five-year bachelor's degree program). Award is equivalent of full tuition at public institution.
**Amount of award:** Full tuition
**Application deadline:** June 30
**Contact:**
New York State Higher Education Services Corporation
99 Washington Avenue
Albany, NY 12255
Phone: 888-697-4372
Web: www.hesc.com/content.nsf/SFC/0/NYS_World_Trade_Center_Memorial_Scholarship

# Hispanic College Fund

## Google Hispanic College Fund Scholarship Program

**Type of award:** Scholarship.
**Intended use:** For junior, senior, master's or doctoral study at postsecondary institution in or outside United States. Designated institutions: Institutions in the United States or Puerto Rico.
**Eligibility:** Applicant must be Hispanic American. Applicant must be U.S. citizen or permanent resident.
**Basis for selection:** Major/career interest in computer/information sciences or engineering, computer. Applicant must demonstrate financial need.
**Application requirements:** Recommendations, essay, transcript. Proof of family income, proof of citizenship status, resume.
**Additional information:** Minimum 3.5 GPA. Visit Website for application and more information.
**Amount of award:** $10,000
**Number of awards:** 20
**Number of applicants:** 18
**Total amount awarded:** $180,000
**Contact:**
Hispanic College Fund
1300 L Street NW, Suite 975
Washington, DC 20005
Phone: 800-644-4223
Fax: 202-296-3774
Web: www.hispanicfund.org

## HCF Scholarship Program

**Type of award:** Scholarship.
**Intended use:** For full-time undergraduate or graduate study at accredited postsecondary institution. Designated institutions: Institutions in the United States and Puerto Rico.
**Eligibility:** Applicant must be Hispanic American. Applicant must be U.S. citizen or permanent resident.
**Basis for selection:** Applicant must demonstrate financial need.
**Application requirements:** Recommendations, essay, transcript, proof of eligibility. Resume, proof of family income, proof of citizenship status.
**Additional information:** Minimum 3.0 GPA. Deadline in February. Check Website for details.

| | |
|---|---|
| **Amount of award:** | $500-$10,000 |
| **Number of applicants:** | 1,151 |
| **Application deadline:** | March 1 |
| **Total amount awarded:** | $1,000,000 |

**Contact:**
Hispanic College Fund
1300 L Street NW, Suite 975
Washington, DC 20005
Phone: 800-644-4223
Fax: 202-296-3774
Web: www.hispanicfund.org

## Marriott Scholars Program

**Type of award:** Scholarship.
**Intended use:** For full-time freshman or sophomore study at accredited postsecondary institution in United States. Designated institutions: Colleges in U.S. and Puerto Rico.
**Eligibility:** Applicant must be Mexican American, Hispanic American or Puerto Rican. Applicant must be U.S. citizen or permanent resident.
**Basis for selection:** Major/career interest in culinary arts; food production/management/services; hospitality administration/ management or hotel/restaurant management. Applicant must demonstrate financial need.
**Application requirements:** Recommendations, essay, transcript. Resume, proof of family income, proof of citizenship status, financial aid verification.
**Additional information:** Must plan to pursue a degree in hospitality management or related field. Minimum 3.0 GPA. Visit Website for deadline.

| | |
|---|---|
| **Amount of award:** | $9,000 |

**Contact:**
Hispanic College Fund
1300 L Street NW, Suite 975
Washington, DC 20005
Phone: 800-644-4223
Fax: 202-296-3774
Web: www.hispanicfund.org

## Scholarships for Students of Puerto Rican Descent

**Type of award:** Scholarship.
**Intended use:** For full-time undergraduate study at 4-year institution. Designated institutions: Colleges and universities in the United States and Puerto Rico.
**Eligibility:** Applicant must be Puerto Rican. Applicant must be U.S. citizen.
**Application requirements:** Recommendations, essay, transcript. Resume, proof of family income, proof of citizenship, birth certificate.
**Additional information:** Minimum 3.0 GPA. Must be Puerto Rican or of Puerto Rican descent. Preference given to students who live in Puerto Rico.

| | |
|---|---|
| **Amount of award:** | $500-$5,000 |

**Contact:**
Hispanic College Fund
1300 L Street NW, Suite 975
Washington, DC 20005
Phone: 800-644-4223
Fax: 202-296-3774
Web: www.hispanicfund.org

# Hispanic Heritage Foundation

## Hispanic Heritage Youth Awards Program

**Type of award:** Scholarship.
**Intended use:** For full-time undergraduate study at postsecondary institution.
**Eligibility:** Applicant must be Hispanic American. Applicant must be high school junior. Applicant must be U.S. citizen or permanent resident.
**Basis for selection:** Applicant must demonstrate high academic achievement, depth of character, leadership and service orientation.
**Application requirements:** Recommendations, essay, transcript, proof of eligibility.
**Additional information:** Applicant must have at least one parent of Hispanic/Latino ancestry. Foundation offers regional and national awards in a number of categories; amount of award and application deadlines vary by year. Awards may also be used for education related expenses, or to establish a community service effort in the student's community. Applications due in June or July. Visit Website for application and updates regarding Youth Awards Program.

| | |
|---|---|
| **Amount of award:** | $1,000 |
| **Number of awards:** | 160 |
| **Number of applicants:** | 13,000 |
| **Total amount awarded:** | $210,000 |

**Contact:**
Hispanic Heritage Foundation
Hispanic Heritage Youth Awards
1775 Wiehle Ave, Suite 400
Reston, VA 20190
Phone: 703-871-4846
Fax: 703-773-5000
Web: www.hispanicheritage.org

# Hispanic Scholarship Fund

## General College Scholarship

**Type of award:** Scholarship.
**Intended use:** For full-time undergraduate or graduate study at 2-year, 4-year or graduate institution in or outside United States. Designated institutions: Colleges in United States, Puerto Rico, U.S. Virgin Islands, and Guam.

**Eligibility:** Applicant must be Mexican American, Hispanic American or Puerto Rican. Applicant must be U.S. citizen or permanent resident.
**Basis for selection:** Applicant must demonstrate financial need, high academic achievement, seriousness of purpose and service orientation.
**Application requirements:** Recommendations, essay, transcript, proof of eligibility. FAFSA and SAR. Copy of permanent resident card or passport stamped I-551 (if applicable).
**Additional information:** Minimum 3.0 GPA. Must be pursuing first undergraduate or graduate degree. Visit Website or contact via e-mail for application deadlines and tips on how to apply.

| | |
|---|---|
| **Amount of award:** | $1,000-$5,000 |
| **Application deadline:** | April 1 |

**Contact:**
General Selection Committee Hispanic Scholarship Fund
55 Second Street
Suite 1500
San Francisco, CA 94105
Phone: 877-473-4636
Fax: 415-808-2302
Web: www.hsf.net

## Macy's College Scholarship Program

**Type of award:** Scholarship.
**Intended use:** For full-time junior or senior study at accredited 4-year institution in United States. Designated institutions: Baruch College, Columbia University, New York University, Pennsylvania State University, Syracuse University, Texas A&M University, The Ohio State University, University of Arizona, University of California - Berkeley, University of Florida, University of Georgia, University of Maryland - College Park, University of Southern California, University of Texas - Austin, University of Washington.
**Eligibility:** Applicant must be Mexican American, Hispanic American or Puerto Rican. Applicant must be U.S. citizen or permanent resident.
**Basis for selection:** Applicant must demonstrate financial need and high academic achievement.
**Application requirements:** FAFSA.
**Additional information:** Minimum 3.0 GPA.

| | |
|---|---|
| **Amount of award:** | $5,000 |

**Contact:**
Hispanic Scholarship Fund
55 Second Street
Suite 1500
San Francisco, CA 94105
Phone: 877-473-4636
Fax: 415-808-2302
Web: www.hsf.net

## Marathon Oil Corporation College Scholarship

**Type of award:** Scholarship, renewable.
**Intended use:** For junior or master's study at 4-year institution.
**Eligibility:** Applicant must be Alaskan native, African American, Hispanic American, American Indian or Native Hawaiian/Pacific Islander. Applicant must be U.S. citizen or permanent resident.
**Basis for selection:** Major/career interest in engineering, chemical; engineering, civil; engineering, electrical/electronic; engineering, mechanical; engineering, petroleum; geology/earth sciences; geophysics; accounting or marketing. Applicant must demonstrate leadership and seriousness of purpose.
**Application requirements:** Recommendations, essay, transcript. Resume and FAFSA.
**Additional information:** Other acceptable fields of study are global procurement or supply chain management, environmental health and safety, energy management, petroleum land management, transportation and logistics, and geotechnical engineering. Must be sophomore, or be graduating senior enrolling in master's program in geology or geophysics. Must agree to participate in a possible paid summer internship. Minimum 3.0 GPA. See Website for application and further requirements.

| | |
|---|---|
| **Amount of award:** | $15,000 |
| **Number of awards:** | 20 |
| **Application deadline:** | August 15 |

**Contact:**
HSF/ Marathon Oil Corporation Scholarship Committee
55 Second Street
Suite 1500
San Francisco, CA 94105
Phone: 877-473-4636
Fax: 415-808-2302
Web: www.hsf.net

## MassMutual Multicultural College Scholarship

**Type of award:** Scholarship.
**Intended use:** For full-time sophomore, junior or senior study at accredited postsecondary institution in United States.
**Eligibility:** Applicant must be Asian American, African American, Mexican American, Hispanic American, Puerto Rican or Native Hawaiian/Pacific Islander. Applicant must be U.S. citizen or permanent resident.
**Basis for selection:** Major/career interest in accounting; business; economics; engineering; finance/banking; marketing; mathematics or statistics. Applicant must demonstrate financial need, high academic achievement and leadership.
**Application requirements:** FAFSA.
**Additional information:** Minimum 3.0 GPA. Must have a permanent address or plan to attend school in one of the following cities: Atlanta, Chicago, New Jersey, Denver, Miami, San Antonio, Houston, Los Angeles, or San Francisco. Visit Website for deadline.

| | |
|---|---|
| **Amount of award:** | $5,000 |

**Contact:**
Hispanic Scholarship Fund
55 Second Street
Suite 1500
San Francisco, CA 94105
Phone: 877-473-4636
Fax: 415-808-2302
Web: www.hsf.net

## McNamara Family Creative Arts Project Grant

**Type of award:** Scholarship.
**Intended use:** For full-time undergraduate or graduate study at accredited 4-year or graduate institution in United States.
**Eligibility:** Applicant must be Mexican American, Hispanic American or Puerto Rican. Applicant must be U.S. citizen or permanent resident.

**Basis for selection:** Major/career interest in arts, general; communications; film/video or performing arts. Applicant must demonstrate financial need and high academic achievement.
**Application requirements:** FAFSA.
**Additional information:** Minimum 3.0 GPA. Grant intended to assist students in completing an art project. Must be majoring in Arts, including but not limited to media, film, performing arts, communications, or writing. Visit Website for deadline.

**Amount of award:** $15,000
**Application deadline:** December 15

**Contact:**
Hispanic Scholarship Fund
55 Second Street
Suite 1500
San Francisco, CA 94105
Phone: 877-473-4636
Fax: 415-808-2302
Web: www.hsf.net

## Nissan Community College Transfer Scholarship

**Type of award:** Scholarship.
**Intended use:** For full-time undergraduate or graduate study at accredited postsecondary institution in United States. Designated institutions: Accredited four-year postsecondary institutions in United States, Puerto Rico, U.S. Virgin Islands, and Guam.
**Eligibility:** Applicant must be Mexican American, Hispanic American or Puerto Rican. Applicant must be U.S. citizen or permanent resident.
**Basis for selection:** Major/career interest in business or engineering. Applicant must demonstrate financial need and high academic achievement.
**Application requirements:** Recommendations, essay, transcript, proof of eligibility. FAFSA and copy of permanent resident card or passport stamped I-551 (if applicable).
**Additional information:** Must have permanent address or attend school in one of the following locations: Atlanta, Georgia; Chicago, Illinois; Dallas/Fort Worth, Texas; Denver, Colorado; Los Angeles, California; Miami/Ft. Lauderdale, Florida; Nashville, Tennessee; New York City/New Jersey metropolitan area; San Antonio, Texas; San Diego, California; Washington, D.C. Must be enrolled part-time or full-time at community college and plan to transfer to four-year institution in fall or spring of next academic year. Minimum 3.0 GPA. Visit Website or contact via e-mail for more information.

**Amount of award:** $2,500
**Application deadline:** January 31

**Contact:**
Community College Transfer Program Hispanic Scholarship Fund
55 Second Street
Suite 1500
San Francisco, CA 94105
Phone: 877-473-4636
Fax: 415-808-2302
Web: www.hsf.net

## Procter & Gamble Scholarship

**Type of award:** Scholarship.
**Intended use:** For full-time undergraduate study at accredited 4-year institution in United States.
**Eligibility:** Applicant must be Mexican American, Hispanic American or Puerto Rican. Applicant must be U.S. citizen or permanent resident.
**Basis for selection:** Major/career interest in engineering; mathematics; science, general or technology.
**Application requirements:** FAFSA.
**Additional information:** Minimum 3.0 GPA.

**Amount of award:** $2,500
**Application deadline:** February 28

**Contact:**
Hispanic Scholarship Fund
55 Second Street
Suite 1500
San Francisco, CA 94105
Phone: 877-473-4636
Fax: 415-808-2302
Web: www.hsf.net

## Wal-Mart Stores, Inc. High School Scholarship

**Type of award:** Scholarship.
**Intended use:** For full-time freshman study at accredited 4-year institution in United States.
**Eligibility:** Applicant must be Mexican American, Hispanic American or Puerto Rican. Applicant must be high school senior. Applicant must be U.S. citizen or permanent resident.
**Basis for selection:** Applicant must demonstrate financial need and high academic achievement.
**Application requirements:** FAFSA.
**Additional information:** Minimum 3.0 GPA. Must reside in one of the following areas: Baltimore, Boston, Chicago, Detroit, Los Angeles, Miami, Minneapolis/Twin Cities, New York, Philadelphia, Portland, Sacramento, San Diego, San Francisco, Seattle, or Washington, D.C.

**Amount of award:** $2,500
**Application deadline:** January 31

**Contact:**
Hispanic Scholarship Fund
55 Second Street
Suite 1500
San Francisco, CA 94105
Phone: 877-473-4636
Fax: 415-808-2302
Web: www.hsf.net

# Hopi Tribe Grants and Scholarship Program

## Hopi BIA Higher Education Grant

**Type of award:** Scholarship, renewable.
**Intended use:** For undergraduate or graduate study at accredited 2-year, 4-year or graduate institution.
**Eligibility:** Applicant must be American Indian. Must be enrolled member of the Hopi Tribe.
**Basis for selection:** Applicant must demonstrate financial need.
**Additional information:** Entering freshmen must have minimum 2.0 GPA for high school coursework or minimum composite score of 45% on GED Exam. Continuing students must have minimum 2.0 GPA for all graduate coursework. Four deadlines per year: November 1st (for winter quarter), December 1st (for spring), May 1st (for summer), and July 1st (for fall). Must reapply each academic year or semester.

**Amount of award:** $3,000
**Number of applicants:** 150
**Application deadline:** December 1, July 1
**Contact:**
Hopi Tribe Grants and Scholarship Program
P.O. Box 123
Kykotsmovi, AZ 86039
Phone: 800-762-9630
Fax: 928-734-9575

## Hopi Education Award

**Type of award:** Scholarship, renewable.
**Intended use:** For undergraduate or graduate study at accredited 2-year, 4-year or graduate institution.
**Eligibility:** Applicant must be American Indian. Must be enrolled member of the Hopi Tribe.
**Basis for selection:** Applicant must demonstrate financial need.
**Additional information:** Entering freshmen must have minimum 2.5 GPA for high school coursework or minimum composite score of 45 percent on the GED Exam. Continuing students must have minimum 2.5 GPA for all college work. $3,000 may be awarded each semester. Four deadlines per year: November 1st (for winter quarter), December 1st (for spring), May 1st (for summer), and July 1st (for fall). Must reapply each academic year or semester.
**Amount of award:** $1,000-$6,000
**Number of applicants:** 140
**Application deadline:** December 1, July 1
**Contact:**
Hopi Tribe Grants and Scholarship Program
P.O. Box 123
Kykotsmovi, AZ 86039
Phone: 800-762-9630
Fax: 928-734-9575

## Hopi Tribal Priority Award

**Type of award:** Scholarship, renewable.
**Intended use:** For full-time junior, senior or graduate study at accredited 4-year or graduate institution.
**Eligibility:** Applicant must be American Indian. Must be enrolled member of the Hopi Tribe.
**Basis for selection:** Applicant must demonstrate high academic achievement, depth of character, leadership and seriousness of purpose.
**Application requirements:** Recommendations, transcript, proof of eligibility.
**Additional information:** Award is based on amount of college cost. Preference given to those majoring in fields considered to be of tribal priority. Applicant must have college submit financial needs analysis to determine amount of award.
**Amount of award:** Full tuition
**Number of awards:** 5
**Number of applicants:** 2
**Application deadline:** July 1
**Contact:**
Hopi Tribe Grants and Scholarship Program
P.O. Box 123
Kykotsmovi, AZ 86039
Phone: 800-762-9630
Fax: 928-734-9575

# Horatio Alger Association

## Horatio Alger Ak-Sar-Ben Scholarship Program

**Type of award:** Scholarship.
**Intended use:** For full-time undergraduate study at accredited 2-year or 4-year institution in United States.
**Eligibility:** Applicant must be high school senior. Applicant must be U.S. citizen residing in Iowa or Nebraska.
**Basis for selection:** Applicant must demonstrate financial need, high academic achievement, seriousness of purpose and service orientation.
**Application requirements:** Essay, transcript. Letter of support, income statement.
**Additional information:** Minimum 2.0 GPA. Program assists high school seniors who have faced and overcome great obstacles and have participated in co-curricular and community activities. Must plan to pursue bachelor's degree. See Website for application and list of eligible Iowa counties.
**Amount of award:** $5,000
**Number of awards:** 50
**Application deadline:** October 30
**Contact:**
Horatio Alger Association
99 Canal Center Plaza, Suite 320
Alexandria, VA 22314
Phone: 703-684-9444
Fax: 703-684-9445
Web: www.horatioalger.org/scholarships

## Horatio Alger Al and Cathy Annexstad Scholarship Fund

**Type of award:** Scholarship.
**Intended use:** For full-time undergraduate study at accredited 2-year or 4-year institution in United States.
**Eligibility:** Applicant must be high school senior. Applicant must be U.S. citizen residing in Minnesota.
**Basis for selection:** Applicant must demonstrate financial need, high academic achievement and service orientation.
**Application requirements:** Essay, transcript. Letter of support, income statement.
**Additional information:** Minimum 2.0 GPA. Program assists high school seniors who have faced and overcome great obstacles and have participated in co-curricular and community activities. Must plan to pursue bachelor's degree.
**Amount of award:** $5,000
**Number of awards:** 10
**Application deadline:** October 30
**Contact:**
Horatio Alger Association
99 Canal Center Plaza, Suite 320
Alexandria, VA 22314
Phone: 703-684-9444
Fax: 703-684-9445
Web: www.horatioalger.org/scholarships

## Horatio Alger Arizona Scholarship

**Type of award:** Scholarship.
**Intended use:** For full-time freshman study at 2-year or 4-year institution in United States.
**Eligibility:** Applicant must be high school senior. Applicant must be U.S. citizen residing in Arizona.

**Basis for selection:** Applicant must demonstrate financial need, high academic achievement, seriousness of purpose and service orientation.
**Application requirements:** Essay, transcript. Letter of support, income statement.
**Additional information:** Minimum 2.0 GPA. Program assists high school seniors who have faced and overcome great obstacles and have participated in co-curricular and community activities. Must plan to pursue bachelor's degree.

| | |
|---|---|
| **Amount of award:** | $5,000 |
| **Number of awards:** | 10 |
| **Application deadline:** | October 30 |

**Contact:**
Horatio Alger Association
99 Canal Center Plaza, Suite 320
Alexandria, VA 22314
Phone: 703-684-9444
Fax: 703-684-9445
Web: www.horatioalger.org/scholarships

## Horatio Alger Delaware Scholarship Program

**Type of award:** Scholarship.
**Intended use:** For full-time undergraduate study at accredited 2-year or 4-year institution in United States.
**Eligibility:** Applicant must be high school senior. Applicant must be U.S. citizen residing in Delaware.
**Basis for selection:** Applicant must demonstrate financial need, high academic achievement and service orientation.
**Application requirements:** Essay, transcript. Letter of support, income statement.
**Additional information:** Minimum 2.0 GPA. Program assists high school seniors who have faced and overcome great obstacles and have participated in co-curricular and community activities. Must plan to pursue bachelor's degree. See Website for application.

| | |
|---|---|
| **Amount of award:** | $5,000 |
| **Number of awards:** | 5 |
| **Application deadline:** | October 30 |

**Contact:**
Horatio Alger Association
99 Canal Center Drive, Suite 320
Alexandria, VA 22314
Phone: 703-684-9444
Fax: 703-684-9445
Web: www.horatioalger.org/scholarships

## Horatio Alger District of Columbia, Maryland and Virginia Scholarship Program

**Type of award:** Scholarship.
**Intended use:** For full-time undergraduate study at accredited 2-year or 4-year institution in United States.
**Eligibility:** Applicant must be high school senior. Applicant must be U.S. citizen residing in District of Columbia.
**Basis for selection:** Applicant must demonstrate financial need, high academic achievement, seriousness of purpose and service orientation.
**Application requirements:** Essay, transcript. Letter of support, income statement.
**Additional information:** Minimum 2.0 GPA. Applicant must reside in D.C. metro area. Program assists high school seniors who have faced and overcome great obstacles and have participated in co-curricular and community activities. See Website for list of eligible counties. Must plan to pursue bachelor's degree. See Website for application.

| | |
|---|---|
| **Amount of award:** | $2,500 |
| **Number of awards:** | 25 |
| **Application deadline:** | October 30 |

**Contact:**
Horatio Alger Association
99 Canal Center Plaza, Suite 320
Alexandria, VA 22314
Phone: 703-684-9444
Fax: 703-684-9445
Web: www.horatioalger.com/scholarships/

## Horatio Alger Franklin Scholarship

**Type of award:** Scholarship.
**Intended use:** For full-time undergraduate study at accredited 2-year or 4-year institution in United States.
**Eligibility:** Applicant must be high school senior. Applicant must be U.S. citizen residing in Pennsylvania.
**Basis for selection:** Applicant must demonstrate financial need, high academic achievement, seriousness of purpose and service orientation.
**Application requirements:** Essay, transcript. Letter of support, income statement, additional essays about Benjamin Franklin.
**Additional information:** Minimum 2.0 GPA. Program assists high school seniors who have faced and overcome great obstacles and have participated in co-curricular and community activities. Must plan to pursue bachelor's degree. Visit Website for application.

| | |
|---|---|
| **Amount of award:** | $10,000 |
| **Number of awards:** | 25 |
| **Application deadline:** | October 30 |

**Contact:**
Horatio Alger Association
99 Canal Center Plaza, Suite 320
Alexandria, VA 22314
Phone: 703-684-9444
Fax: 703-684-9445
Web: www.horatioalger.org/scholarships

## Horatio Alger Georgia Scholarship Program

**Type of award:** Scholarship.
**Intended use:** For full-time undergraduate study at accredited 2-year or 4-year institution in United States.
**Eligibility:** Applicant must be high school senior. Applicant must be U.S. citizen residing in Georgia.
**Basis for selection:** Applicant must demonstrate financial need, high academic achievement, seriousness of purpose and service orientation.
**Application requirements:** Essay, transcript. Letter of support, income statement.
**Additional information:** Minimum 2.0 GPA. Program assists high school seniors who have faced and overcome great obstacles and have participated in co-curricular and community activities. Preference given to students who reside in Walker and Catoosa counties. Must plan to pursue bachelor's degree. Visit Website for application.

| | |
|---|---|
| **Amount of award:** | $5,000 |
| **Number of awards:** | 50 |
| **Application deadline:** | October 30 |

**Contact:**
Horatio Alger Assocation
99 Canal Center Plaza, Suite 320
Alexandria, VA 22314
Phone: 703-684-9444
Fax: 703-684-9445
Web: www.horatioalger.org/scholarships

## Horatio Alger Idaho Scholarship Program

**Type of award:** Scholarship.
**Intended use:** For full-time undergraduate study in United States. Designated institutions: University of Idaho, North Idaho College, and Lewis-Clark State College (Coeur d'Alene or Lewiston).
**Eligibility:** Applicant must be high school senior. Applicant must be U.S. citizen residing in Idaho.
**Basis for selection:** Applicant must demonstrate financial need, high academic achievement, depth of character and service orientation.
**Application requirements:** Essay, transcript. Letter of support, income statement.
**Additional information:** Program assists high school seniors who have faced and overcome great obstacles and have participated in co-curricular and community activities. Must attend high school in Benewah, Boundary, Bonner, Kootenai, Latah, or Shoshone counties. Must plan to pursue bachelor's degree. See Website for application, county eligibility, and additional information.

| | |
|---|---|
| **Amount of award:** | $5,000 |
| **Number of awards:** | 25 |
| **Application deadline:** | October 30 |

**Contact:**
Horatio Alger Association
99 Canal Center Plaza, Suite 320
Alexandria, VA 22314
Phone: 703-684-9444
Fax: 703-684-9445
Web: www.horatioalger.org/scholarships

## Horatio Alger Illinois Scholarship Program

**Type of award:** Scholarship.
**Intended use:** For full-time undergraduate study at accredited 2-year or 4-year institution in United States.
**Eligibility:** Applicant must be high school senior. Applicant must be U.S. citizen residing in Illinois.
**Basis for selection:** Applicant must demonstrate financial need, high academic achievement and service orientation.
**Application requirements:** Essay, transcript. Letter of support, income statement.
**Additional information:** Minimum 2.0 GPA. Program assists high school seniors who have faced and overcome great obstacles and have participated in co-curricular and community activities. Must plan to pursue bachelor's degree. Visit Website for application.

| | |
|---|---|
| **Amount of award:** | $5,000 |
| **Number of awards:** | 20 |
| **Application deadline:** | October 30 |

**Contact:**
Horatio Alger Association
99 Canal Center Plaza, Suite 320
Alexandria, VA 22314
Phone: 703-684-9444
Fax: 703-684-9445
Web: www.horatioalger.org/scholarships

## Horatio Alger Louisiana Scholarship Program

**Type of award:** Scholarship.
**Intended use:** For full-time undergraduate study at accredited 2-year or 4-year institution in United States. Designated institutions: Louisiana colleges and universities.
**Eligibility:** Applicant must be high school senior. Applicant must be U.S. citizen residing in Louisiana.
**Basis for selection:** Applicant must demonstrate financial need, high academic achievement, seriousness of purpose and service orientation.
**Application requirements:** Essay, transcript. Letter of support, income statement.
**Additional information:** Minimum 2.0 GPA. Program assists high school seniors who have faced and overcome great obstacles and have participated in co-curricular and community activities. Must plan to pursue bachelor's degree. See Website for application.

| | |
|---|---|
| **Amount of award:** | $10,500 |
| **Number of awards:** | 50 |
| **Application deadline:** | October 30 |

**Contact:**
Horatio Alger Association
99 Canal Center Plaza, Suite 320
Alexandria, VA 22314
Phone: 703-684-9444
Fax: 703-684-9445
Web: www.horatioalger.org/scholarships

## Horatio Alger Missouri Scholarship Program

**Type of award:** Scholarship.
**Intended use:** For full-time undergraduate study at accredited 2-year or 4-year institution in United States.
**Eligibility:** Applicant must be high school senior. Applicant must be U.S. citizen residing in Missouri.
**Basis for selection:** Applicant must demonstrate financial need, high academic achievement, seriousness of purpose and service orientation.
**Application requirements:** Essay, transcript. Letter of support, income statement.
**Additional information:** Minimum 2.0 GPA. Program assists high school seniors who have faced and overcome great obstacles and have participated in co-curricular and community activities. Must plan to pursue bachelor's degree. See Website for application.

| | |
|---|---|
| **Amount of award:** | $5,000 |
| **Number of awards:** | 10 |
| **Application deadline:** | October 30 |

**Contact:**
Horatio Alger Association
99 Canal Center Plaza, Suite 320
Alexandria, VA 22314
Phone: 703-684-9444
Fax: 703-684-9445
Web: www.horatioalger.org/scholarships

## Horatio Alger Montana Scholarship Program

**Type of award:** Scholarship.
**Intended use:** For full-time undergraduate study in United States. Designated institutions: University of Montana institutions.
**Eligibility:** Applicant must be high school senior. Applicant must be U.S. citizen residing in Montana.
**Basis for selection:** Applicant must demonstrate financial need, high academic achievement and service orientation.
**Application requirements:** Essay, transcript. Letter of support, income statement.
**Additional information:** Minimum 2.0 GPA. Program assists high school seniors who have faced and overcome great obstacles and have participated in co-curricular and community activities. Must plan to pursue bachelor's degree. See Website for application.

| | |
|---|---|
| **Amount of award:** | $5,000 |
| **Number of awards:** | 50 |
| **Application deadline:** | October 30 |

**Contact:**
Horatio Alger Association
99 Canal Center Plaza, Suite 320
Alexandria, VA 22314
Phone: 703-684-9444
Fax: 703-684-9445
Web: www.horatioalger.org/scholarships

## Horatio Alger National Scholarship

**Type of award:** Scholarship.
**Intended use:** For full-time undergraduate study at accredited 2-year or 4-year institution in United States.
**Eligibility:** Applicant must be high school senior. Applicant must be U.S. citizen.
**Basis for selection:** Based on co-curricular and community activities. Applicant must demonstrate financial need, high academic achievement, seriousness of purpose and service orientation.
**Application requirements:** Essay, transcript. Letter of support, income statement.
**Additional information:** Minimum 2.0 GPA. Program assists high school seniors who have faced and overcome great obstacles and have participated in co-curricular and community activities. Must plan to pursue bachelor's degree. Visit Website for application.

| | |
|---|---|
| **Amount of award:** | $20,000 |
| **Number of awards:** | 104 |
| **Application deadline:** | October 30 |

**Contact:**
Horatio Alger Association
99 Canal Center Plaza, Suite 320
Alexandria, VA 22314
Phone: 703-684-9444
Fax: 703-684-9445
Web: www.horatioalger.org/scholarships

## Horatio Alger North Dakota Scholarship Program

**Type of award:** Scholarship.
**Intended use:** For full-time undergraduate study at accredited 2-year or 4-year institution in United States.
**Eligibility:** Applicant must be high school senior. Applicant must be U.S. citizen residing in North Dakota.
**Basis for selection:** Applicant must demonstrate financial need, high academic achievement, seriousness of purpose and service orientation.
**Application requirements:** Essay, transcript. Letter of support, income statement.
**Additional information:** Minimum 2.0 GPA. Program assists high school seniors who have faced and overcome great obstacles and have participated in co-curricular and community activities. Must plan to pursue bachelor's degree. Visit Website for application.

| | |
|---|---|
| **Amount of award:** | $5,000 |
| **Number of awards:** | 25 |
| **Application deadline:** | October 30 |

**Contact:**
Horatio Alger Association
99 Canal Center Plaza, Suite 320
Alexandria, VA 22314
Phone: 703-684-9444
Fax: 703-684-9445
Web: www.horatioalger.org/scholarships

## Horatio Alger Northern California Scholarship Program

**Type of award:** Scholarship.
**Intended use:** For full-time undergraduate study at accredited 2-year or 4-year institution in United States.
**Eligibility:** Applicant must be high school senior. Applicant must be U.S. citizen residing in California.
**Basis for selection:** Applicant must demonstrate financial need, high academic achievement, seriousness of purpose and service orientation.
**Application requirements:** Essay, transcript. Letter of support, income statement.
**Additional information:** Minimum 2.0 GPA. Program assists high school seniors who have faced and overcome great obstacles and have participated in co-curricular and community activities. Applicant should have strong commitment to use college degree in service to others. Must plan to pursue bachelor's degree. See Website for application.

| | |
|---|---|
| **Amount of award:** | $4,000 |
| **Number of awards:** | 37 |
| **Application deadline:** | October 30 |

**Contact:**
Horatio Alger Association
99 Canal Center Plaza, Suite 320
Alexandria, VA 22314
Phone: 703-684-9444
Fax: 703-684-9445
Web: www.horatioalger.org/scholarships

## Horatio Alger Pennsylvania Scholarship Program

**Type of award:** Scholarship.
**Intended use:** For full-time undergraduate study at accredited 2-year or 4-year institution in United States.
**Eligibility:** Applicant must be high school senior. Applicant must be U.S. citizen residing in Pennsylvania.
**Basis for selection:** Applicant must demonstrate financial need, high academic achievement and service orientation.
**Application requirements:** Essay, transcript. Letter of support, income statement.
**Additional information:** Minimum 2.0 GPA. Program assists high school seniors who have faced and overcome great obstacles and have participated in co-curricular and community

activities. Must plan to pursue bachelor's degree. See Website for application.

**Amount of award:** $5,000
**Number of awards:** 50
**Application deadline:** October 30

**Contact:**
Horatio Alger Association
99 Canal Center Drive, Suite 320
Alexandria, VA 22314
Phone: 703-684-9444
Fax: 703-684-9445
Web: www.horatioalger.org/scholarships



## Horatio Alger South Dakota Scholarship Program

**Type of award:** Scholarship.
**Intended use:** For full-time undergraduate study at accredited 2-year or 4-year institution in United States.
**Eligibility:** Applicant must be high school senior. Applicant must be U.S. citizen residing in South Dakota.
**Basis for selection:** Applicant must demonstrate financial need, high academic achievement, seriousness of purpose and service orientation.
**Application requirements:** Essay, transcript. Letter of support, income statement.
**Additional information:** Minimum 2.0 GPA. Program assists high school seniors who have faced and overcome great obstacles and have participated in co-curricular and community activities. Must plan to pursue bachelor's degree. See Website for application and more information.

**Amount of award:** $5,000
**Number of awards:** 25
**Application deadline:** October 30

**Contact:**
The Horatio Alger Association
99 Canal Center Plaza, Suite 320
Alexandria, VA 22314
Phone: 703-684-9444
Fax: 703-684-9445
Web: www.horatioalger.org/scholarships

## Horatio Alger Texas Ft. Worth Scholarship Program

**Type of award:** Scholarship.
**Intended use:** For full-time undergraduate study at accredited 2-year or 4-year institution in United States.
**Eligibility:** Applicant must be high school senior. Applicant must be U.S. citizen residing in Texas.
**Basis for selection:** Applicant must demonstrate financial need, high academic achievement, seriousness of purpose and service orientation.
**Application requirements:** Essay, transcript. Letter of support, income statement.
**Additional information:** Minimum 2.0 GPA. Applicant must reside in Forth Worth, Texas. Program assists high school seniors who have faced and overcome great obstacles and have participated in co-curricular and community activities. Must plan to pursue bachelor's degree. Visit Website for application.

**Amount of award:** $5,000
**Number of awards:** 12
**Application deadline:** October 30

**Contact:**
Horatio Alger Assocation
99 Canal Center Plaza, Suite 320
Alexandria, VA 22314
Phone: 703-684-9444
Fax: 703-684-9445
Web: www.horatioalger.org/scholarships

## Horatio Alger Texas Scholarship Program

**Type of award:** Scholarship.
**Intended use:** For full-time undergraduate study at accredited 2-year or 4-year institution in United States.
**Eligibility:** Applicant must be high school senior. Applicant must be U.S. citizen residing in Texas.
**Basis for selection:** Applicant must demonstrate financial need, high academic achievement, depth of character and service orientation.
**Application requirements:** Essay, transcript. Letter of support, income statement.
**Additional information:** Program assists high school seniors who have faced and overcome great obstacles and have participated in co-curricular and community activities. Must plan to pursue bachelor's degree. See Website for application.

**Amount of award:** $5,000
**Number of awards:** 7
**Application deadline:** October 30

**Contact:**
Horatio Alger Association
99 Canal Center Plaza, Suite 320
Alexandria, VA 22314
Phone: 703-684-9444
Fax: 703-684-9445
Web: www.horatioalger.org/scholarships

## Horatio Alger Utah Scholarship Program

**Type of award:** Scholarship.
**Intended use:** For full-time undergraduate study at accredited 2-year or 4-year institution in United States.
**Eligibility:** Applicant must be high school senior. Applicant must be U.S. citizen residing in Utah.
**Basis for selection:** Applicant must demonstrate financial need, high academic achievement, seriousness of purpose and service orientation.
**Application requirements:** Essay, transcript. Letter of support, income statement.
**Additional information:** Minimum 2.0 GPA. Program assists high school seniors who have faced and overcome great obstacles and have participated in co-curricular and community activities. Must plan to pursue bachelor's degree. Visit Website for application.

**Amount of award:** $5,000
**Number of awards:** 25
**Application deadline:** October 30

**Contact:**
Horatio Alger Association
99 Canal Center Plaza, Suite 320
Alexandria, VA 22314
Phone: 703-684-9444
Fax: 703-684-9445
Web: www.horatioalger.org/scholarships

## Horatio Alger Wyoming Scholarship Program

**Type of award:** Scholarship.
**Intended use:** For full-time undergraduate study at accredited 2-year or 4-year institution in United States.
**Eligibility:** Applicant must be high school senior. Applicant must be U.S. citizen residing in Wyoming.
**Basis for selection:** Applicant must demonstrate financial need, high academic achievement, seriousness of purpose and service orientation.
**Application requirements:** Essay, transcript. Letter of support, income statement.
**Additional information:** Minimum 2.0 GPA. Program assists high school seniors who have faced and overcome great obstacles and have participated in co-curricular and community activities. Must plan to pursue bachelor's degree. Visit Website for application.

| | |
|---|---|
| **Amount of award:** | $5,000 |
| **Number of awards:** | 25 |
| **Application deadline:** | October 30 |

**Contact:**
Horatio Alger Association
99 Canal Center Plaza, Suite 320
Alexandria, VA 22314
Phone: 703-684-9444
Fax: 703-684-9445
Web: www.horatioalger.org/scholarships

# Horticultural Research Institute

## Carville M. Akehurst Memorial Scholarship

**Type of award:** Scholarship.
**Intended use:** For full-time junior, senior or graduate study at accredited 2-year, 4-year or graduate institution.
**Eligibility:** Applicant must be residing in Virginia, West Virginia or Maryland.
**Basis for selection:** Major/career interest in horticulture or landscape architecture. Applicant must demonstrate high academic achievement.
**Application requirements:** Recommendations, essay, transcript. Resume.
**Additional information:** Minimum 2.7 overall GPA and minimum 3.0 in major. Must have junior standing in four-year curriculum or senior standing in two-year curriculum. Preference given to applicants who plan to work within industry following graduation. Previous winners eligible for additional funding. Visit Website for application and more information.

| | |
|---|---|
| **Amount of award:** | $2,000 |
| **Number of awards:** | 1 |
| **Number of applicants:** | 10 |
| **Application deadline:** | May 31 |
| **Total amount awarded:** | $2,000 |

**Contact:**
Horticultural Research Institute
1000 Vermont Avenue NW
Suite 300
Washington, DC 20005-4914
Phone: 202-789-2900
Fax: 202-478-7288
Web: www.hriresearch.org

## Horticultural Research Institute Spring Meadow Scholarship

**Type of award:** Scholarship.
**Intended use:** For full-time undergraduate or graduate study at accredited vocational, 2-year, 4-year or graduate institution.
**Basis for selection:** Major/career interest in horticulture or landscape architecture.
**Application requirements:** Recommendations, essay, transcript. Resume.
**Additional information:** Must have minimum 2.25 overall GPA, and minimum 2.7 in major. Must be enrolled in accredited landscape, horticulture or related program. Must be interested in woody plant production, propagation, and breeding or horticulture sales and marketing. Preference given to those who plan to work in industry following graduation. Visit Website for application and more information.

| | |
|---|---|
| **Amount of award:** | $1,500 |
| **Number of awards:** | 1 |
| **Number of applicants:** | 69 |
| **Application deadline:** | May 31 |
| **Total amount awarded:** | $1,500 |

**Contact:**
Horticultural Research Institute
1000 Vermont Avenue NW
Suite 300
Washington, DC 20005-4914
Phone: 202-789-2900
Fax: 202-478-7288
Web: www.hriresearch.org

## Muggets Scholarship

**Type of award:** Scholarship, renewable.
**Intended use:** For full-time undergraduate or graduate study at vocational, 2-year, 4-year or graduate institution in United States. Designated institutions: California state colleges and universities.
**Eligibility:** Applicant must be residing in California.
**Basis for selection:** Major/career interest in landscape architecture or horticulture.
**Application requirements:** Recommendations, essay, transcript. Cover letter and resume.
**Additional information:** Students enrolled in vocational agricultural programs also eligible. Preference given to applicants who plan to work within the industry after graduation. Minimum 2.5 GPA overall; minimum 2.7 GPA in major. Visit Website for application.

| | |
|---|---|
| **Amount of award:** | $1,000 |
| **Number of awards:** | 1 |
| **Application deadline:** | May 31 |

**Contact:**
Endowment Program Administrator, Horticultural Research Institute
1000 Vermont Ave. NW
Suite 300
Washington, DC 20005-4914
Phone: 202-789-5980 ext. 3014
Fax: 202-478-7288
Web: www.hriresearch.org

### Timothy and Palmer W. Bigelow, Jr. Scholarship

**Type of award:** Scholarship.
**Intended use:** For full-time undergraduate or graduate study at accredited 2-year, 4-year or graduate institution.
**Eligibility:** Applicant must be residing in Vermont, New Hampshire, Connecticut, Maine, Massachusetts or Rhode Island.
**Basis for selection:** Major/career interest in landscape architecture or horticulture. Applicant must demonstrate financial need, high academic achievement, depth of character and seriousness of purpose.
**Application requirements:** Recommendations, essay, transcript. Resume and cover letter.
**Additional information:** Minimum 2.25 GPA for undergraduates and 3.0 GPA for graduate students. Must be enrolled in accredited landscape or horticulture program. Applicant must have senior standing in two-year program, junior standing in four-year program, or graduate standing. Applicant must be resident of one of the six New England states, but need not attend institution there. Preference given to applicants who plan to work with industry after graduation. Preference also given to applicants who demonstrate financial need. Visit Website for application.

| | |
|---|---|
| **Amount of award:** | $2,000 |
| **Number of awards:** | 1 |
| **Number of applicants:** | 8 |
| **Application deadline:** | May 31 |
| **Notification begins:** | July 1 |
| **Total amount awarded:** | $2,000 |

**Contact:**
Horticultural Research Institute
1000 Vermont Ave. NW
Suite 300
Washington, DC 20005-4914
Phone: 202-789-2900 ext. 3014
Fax: 202-478-7288
Web: www.hriresearch.org

## Houston Livestock Show and Rodeo

### Area Go Texan Scholarships

**Type of award:** Scholarship.
**Intended use:** For undergraduate study at postsecondary institution. Designated institutions: Texas colleges and universities.
**Eligibility:** Applicant must be high school senior. Applicant must be U.S. citizen residing in Texas.
**Basis for selection:** Applicant must demonstrate financial need, high academic achievement, depth of character, leadership and service orientation.
**Application requirements:** Recommendations, essay, transcript, proof of eligibility. Class standing and photograph. SAT/ACT scores. FAFSA.
**Additional information:** Scholarships awarded to one eligible public high school student from each of 60 Area Go Texan counties. Minimum 1350 SAT combined score (reading and math), or minimum 19 ACT score. Applicant must attend public high school and be in top third of graduating class. Applicant cannot receive more than $40,000 from financial aid or other scholarships. Contact sponsor or visit Website for eligible counties, deadline, and application.

| | |
|---|---|
| **Amount of award:** | $16,000 |
| **Number of awards:** | 70 |
| **Total amount awarded:** | $1,050,000 |

**Contact:**
Houston Livestock Show and Rodeo
Office of Education Programs
P.O. Box 20070
Houston, TX 77225-0070
Phone: 832-667-1000
Web: www.hlsr.com

### Metropolitan Scholarships

**Type of award:** Scholarship, renewable.
**Intended use:** For undergraduate study at accredited 4-year institution in United States. Designated institutions: Colleges and universities in Texas.
**Eligibility:** Applicant must be high school senior. Applicant must be U.S. citizen residing in Texas.
**Basis for selection:** Applicant must demonstrate financial need, high academic achievement, depth of character and leadership.
**Application requirements:** Recommendations, essay, transcript. SAT/ACT Scores. FAFSA.
**Additional information:** Must be graduating from Houston-area public school districts in Brazoria, Chambers, Fort Bend, Galveston, Harris, Liberty, Montgomery, and Waller Counties. Must be in top quarter of graduating class and have minimum 1350 SAT (reading and math) or 19 ACT score.

| | |
|---|---|
| **Amount of award:** | $16,000 |
| **Number of awards:** | 221 |

**Contact:**
Houston Livestock Show and Rodeo
Office of Education Programs
P.O. Box 20070
Houston, TX 77225-0070
Phone: 832-667-1000
Web: www.hlsr.com

### Opportunity Scholarship

**Type of award:** Scholarship, renewable.
**Intended use:** For full-time undergraduate study at 4-year institution. Designated institutions: Texas colleges and universities.
**Eligibility:** Applicant must be high school senior. Applicant must be U.S. citizen residing in Texas.
**Basis for selection:** Applicant must demonstrate financial need, high academic achievement, depth of character, leadership and service orientation.
**Application requirements:** Recommendations, transcript, proof of eligibility. Up to three references. FAFSA. Two-page essay must describe importance of college and career goals. Class standing and photograph. SAT/ACT scores.
**Additional information:** Must have minimum 1210 SAT (reading and math) or 17 ACT. Must be graduating in top half of class from specified Texas school districts in Brazoria,

Chambers, Fort Bend, Galveston, Harris, Liberty, Montgomery, or Waller counties. Visit Website for list of eligible districts, application, and more information. For applications, contact guidance counselor or Office of Education Programs.

| | |
|---|---|
| **Amount of award:** | $16,000 |
| **Number of awards:** | 106 |
| **Total amount awarded:** | $1,500,000 |

**Contact:**
Houston Livestock Show and Rodeo
Office of Education Programs
P.O. Box 20070
Houston, TX 77225-0070
Phone: 832-667-1000
Web: www.hlsr.com

### School Art Scholarships

**Type of award:** Scholarship, renewable.
**Intended use:** For undergraduate study at accredited 4-year institution in United States. Designated institutions: Colleges and universities in Texas.
**Eligibility:** Applicant must be high school senior. Applicant must be U.S. citizen or international student residing in Texas.
**Basis for selection:** Applicant must demonstrate financial need, high academic achievement, depth of character and leadership.
**Application requirements:** Recommendations, essay, transcript, proof of eligibility. SAT/ACT scores. FAFSA.
**Additional information:** Must be high school senior who was judged by School Art Committee judges or who was selected to compete in Quick Draw competition. Must be in top quarter of class and have minimum 1350 SAT (reading and math) or 19 ACT score. Visit Website for deadline.

| | |
|---|---|
| **Amount of award:** | $16,000 |
| **Number of awards:** | 15 |

**Contact:**
Houston Livestock Show and Rodeo
Office of Education Programs
P.O. Box 20070
Houston, TX 77225-0070
Phone: 832-667-1000
Web: www.hlsr.com

## ICMA Retirement Corporation

### Vantagepoint Public Employee Memorial Scholarship Fund

**Type of award:** Scholarship.
**Intended use:** For full-time undergraduate or graduate study at accredited postsecondary institution.
**Basis for selection:** Applicant must demonstrate financial need, high academic achievement, leadership and service orientation.
**Application requirements:** Recommendations, essay, transcript, proof of eligibility. Statement of goals and aspirations, official letter from deceased employee's place of work certifying employee died in line of duty.
**Additional information:** High school seniors and graduates, as well as current undergraduate or graduate students eligible. Must be child or spouse of deceased local or state government employee who has died in the line of duty. Work experience, goals and aspirations, and unusual personal or family circumstances also factored into selection. Award amount varies; maximum is $10,000 (tuition and fees only). Visit Website for complete information and application.

| | |
|---|---|
| **Amount of award:** | $10,000 |
| **Number of awards:** | 7 |
| **Number of applicants:** | 40 |
| **Application deadline:** | March 15 |
| **Notification begins:** | June 1 |
| **Total amount awarded:** | $90,000 |

**Contact:**
Vantagepoint Public Employee Memorial Scholarship Program
c/o Scholarship America
One Scholarship Way
St. Peter, MN 56082
Phone: 800-473-2950
Web: www.vantagescholar.org

## Idaho State Board of Education

### Grow Your Own Teacher Scholarship Program

**Type of award:** Scholarship.
**Intended use:** For undergraduate study at 2-year or 4-year institution. Designated institutions: Boise State University, Idaho State University, Lewis-Clark State College, College of Southern Idaho.
**Eligibility:** Applicant must be residing in Idaho.
**Basis for selection:** Major/career interest in education.
**Application requirements:** FAFSA.
**Additional information:** Program established to aid students becoming bilingual education, ESL and Native American teachers. Minimum 3.0 GPA. Award for part-time students based on credit hours. Contact college of education at intended institution of matriculation for more information.

| | |
|---|---|
| **Amount of award:** | $3,000 |
| **Application deadline:** | February 15 |

**Contact:**
Idaho State Board of Education
650 West State Street
P.O. Box 83720
Boise, ID 83720-0037
Phone: 208-332-1574
Web: www.boardofed.idaho.gov/scholarships

### Idaho Governor's Cup Scholarship

**Type of award:** Scholarship, renewable.
**Intended use:** For full-time undergraduate study at postsecondary institution. Designated institutions: Idaho colleges and universities.
**Eligibility:** Applicant must be high school senior. Applicant must be residing in Idaho.
**Basis for selection:** Applicant must demonstrate high academic achievement, leadership and service orientation.
**Application requirements:** Recommendations, essay, transcript. SAT/ACT scores. Documentation of volunteer work, leadership, and public service.
**Additional information:** Minimum 2.8 GPA. Must have demonstrated commitment to public service. For more information, contact high school guidance counselor or Idaho State Board of Education.

**Amount of award:** $3,000
**Number of awards:** 12
**Application deadline:** January 15
**Contact:**
Idaho State Board of Education
650 West State Street
P.O. Box 83720
Boise, ID 83720-0037
Phone: 208-332-1574
Web: www.boardofed.idaho.gov/scholarships

## Idaho Robert C. Byrd Scholarship

**Type of award:** Scholarship, renewable.
**Intended use:** For full-time freshman study at 2-year or 4-year institution.
**Eligibility:** Applicant must be high school senior. Applicant must be U.S. citizen or permanent resident residing in Idaho.
**Basis for selection:** Applicant must demonstrate high academic achievement.
**Application requirements:** Transcript, proof of eligibility. Statement of Selective Service registration status.
**Additional information:** Maximum award is $1,500 per year, renewable for up to four years. Visit Website or contact high school counselor for application, deadlines and more information.
**Amount of award:** $1,500
**Application deadline:** January 15
**Contact:**
Idaho State Board of Education
650 West State Street
P.O. Box 83720
Boise, ID 83720-0037
Phone: 208-332-1574
Web: www.boardofed.idaho.gov/scholarships

## Leveraging Educational Assistance State Partnership Program (LEAP)

**Type of award:** Scholarship, renewable.
**Intended use:** For undergraduate or graduate study at vocational, 2-year, 4-year or graduate institution. Designated institutions: Eligible Idaho public and private colleges and universities.
**Eligibility:** Applicant must be U.S. citizen or permanent resident.
**Basis for selection:** Applicant must demonstrate financial need.
**Application requirements:** FAFSA.
**Additional information:** Formerly the Idaho State Student Incentive Grant. Institution makes recommendations to Idaho State Board of Education. Visit Website for list of eligible institutions. Contact financial aid office of institution for materials or additional information.
**Amount of award:** $400-$5,000
**Contact:**
Financial aid offices at Idaho colleges
Phone: 208-332-1574
Web: www.boardofed.idaho.gov

## Robert R. Lee Promise Category A Scholarship

**Type of award:** Scholarship, renewable.
**Intended use:** For full-time freshman study at postsecondary institution. Designated institutions: Idaho state-funded colleges and universities.
**Eligibility:** Applicant must be high school senior. Applicant must be residing in Idaho.
**Additional information:** Applicant must be graduating senior of Idaho high school or equivalent. Academic applicants must have minimum 28 ACT and 3.5 GPA, and be in top ten percent of graduating class. Applicants for professional-technical programs must have minimum 2.8 GPA and take COMPASS exam. Apply online or contact Idaho State Board of Education for application.
**Amount of award:** $3,000
**Number of awards:** 25
**Number of applicants:** 3,000
**Application deadline:** January 15
**Total amount awarded:** $75,000
**Contact:**
Dana Kelly, Idaho State Board of Education
650 West State Street
P.O. Box 83720
Boise, ID 83720-0037
Phone: 208-332-1574
Web: www.boardofed.idaho.gov/scholarships

## Robert R. Lee Promise Category B Scholarship

**Type of award:** Scholarship, renewable.
**Intended use:** For full-time freshman study at postsecondary institution. Designated institutions: Boise State University, College of Southern Idaho, Eastern Idaho Technical College, Idaho State University, Lewis-Clark State College, North Idaho College, University of Idaho, Northwest Nazarene University, BYU-Idaho, The College of Idaho, College of Western Idaho.
**Eligibility:** Applicant must be no older than 21. Applicant must be residing in Idaho.
**Additional information:** Minimum 3.0 GPA or ACT score of 20. Must be younger than 22 on July 1 of academic term of award. Must have completed high school, or equivalent, in Idaho. For more information, contact college or university.
**Amount of award:** $600
**Contact:**
Dana Kelly, Idaho State Board of Education
650 West State Street
P.O. Box 83720
Boise, ID 83720-0037
Phone: 208-332-1574
Web: www.boardofed.idaho.gov/scholarships

# Illinois Department of Veterans' Affairs

## MIA/POW Scholarship

**Type of award:** Scholarship, renewable.
**Intended use:** For full-time undergraduate study at accredited postsecondary institution in United States. Designated institutions: Illinois state-supported schools.
**Eligibility:** Applicant must be U.S. citizen. Applicant must be dependent of disabled veteran, deceased veteran or POW/MIA; or spouse of disabled veteran, deceased veteran or POW/MIA.
**Application requirements:** Proof of eligibility.
**Additional information:** Available to dependents of veterans who have been declared prisoners of war, missing in action, become permanently disabled, or have died due to service

related disability. Veteran must have been Illinois resident within six months of entering service.

**Amount of award:** Full tuition

**Contact:**
Illinois Department of Veterans' Affairs
833 South Spring Street
P.O. Box 19432
Springfield, IL 62794-9432
Phone: 217-782-6641
Web: www.veterans.illinois.gov/benefits

# Illinois State Board of Education

## Illinois General Assembly Legislative Scholarships

**Type of award:** Scholarship, renewable.
**Intended use:** For undergraduate study at accredited postsecondary institution in United States. Designated institutions: Illinois state-supported universities.
**Eligibility:** Applicant must be U.S. citizen residing in Illinois.
**Application requirements:** Nomination by member of Illinois General Assembly.
**Additional information:** Each member of General Assembly annually awards two scholarships from his or her district. Contact your County Clerk's Election office to determine the name and phone number of your legislators. Student must be resident of legislative district of the awarding legislator.

**Amount of award:** Full tuition

**Contact:**
Contact your state senator and state representative for application.
Web: www.isbe.state.il.us

# Illinois Student Assistance Commission

## Bonus Incentive Grant (BIG)

**Type of award:** Scholarship.
**Intended use:** For undergraduate study at 2-year or 4-year institution in United States. Designated institutions: Approved Illinois public and private colleges, universities, and hospital schools.
**Eligibility:** Applicant must be U.S. citizen or permanent resident residing in Illinois.
**Additional information:** Bonus Incentive Grants are non-need based grants available to beneficiaries of Illinois College Savings Bonds, if at least 70 percent of bond proceeds are used for costs at eligible institution. Must have owned bond for at least 12 consecutive months. Grant amounts range from $40 to $440 per bond. Grants can be used for educational purposes only. Not for use at religious institutions, for divinity programs, or for studies in preparation for the priesthood, regardless of denomination or faith. Contact sponsor for more information, or visit Website.

**Amount of award:** $40-$440
**Number of awards:** 262
**Total amount awarded:** $206,440

**Contact:**
Illinois Student Assistance Commission
ISAC College Zone Counselor
1755 Lake Cook Road
Deerfield, IL 60015
Phone: 800-899-ISAC
Web: www.collegeillinois.org

## Grant Program for Dependents of Correctional Officers

**Type of award:** Scholarship, renewable.
**Intended use:** For freshman study at 2-year or 4-year institution in United States. Designated institutions: ISAC-approved institutions in Illinois.
**Eligibility:** Applicant must be U.S. citizen or permanent resident. Applicant's parent must have been killed or disabled in work-related accident as public safety officer.
**Application requirements:** Proof of eligibility.
**Additional information:** Must be child or spouse of Illinois corrections officer killed or at least 90 percent disabled in line of duty. Award is equal to full tuition and mandatory fees at public Illinois institutions; at private schools a corresponding amount is awarded. Applicant need not be Illinois resident at time of enrollment. Beneficiaries may receive the equivalent of eight semesters or 12 quarters of assistance. Contact ISAC or visit Website for additional information.

**Amount of award:** Full tuition
**Number of awards:** 86
**Total amount awarded:** $710,192

**Contact:**
Illinois Student Assistance Commission
ISAC College Zone Counselor
1755 Lake Cook Road
Deerfield, IL 60015
Phone: 800-899-ISAC
Web: www.collegeillinois.org

## Grant Program for Dependents of Police or Fire Officers

**Type of award:** Scholarship, renewable.
**Intended use:** For undergraduate or graduate study at 2-year, 4-year or graduate institution. Designated institutions: ISAC-approved institutions in Illinois.
**Eligibility:** Applicant must be U.S. citizen or permanent resident. Applicant's parent must have been killed or disabled in work-related accident as firefighter or police officer.
**Application requirements:** Proof of eligibility.
**Additional information:** Grant for tuition and fees for spouses and children of Illinois policemen or firemen killed or at least 90 percent disabled in line of duty. Award amount adjusted annually. Applicant need not be Illinois resident at time of enrollment. Beneficiaries may receive the equivalent of eight semesters or 12 quarters of assistance. Contact ISAC or visit Website for additional information.

**Amount of award:** Full tuition
**Number of awards:** 86
**Application deadline:** October 1
**Total amount awarded:** $710,192

**Contact:**
Illinois Student Assistance Commission
ISAC College Zone Counselor
1755 Lake Cook Road
Deerfield, IL 60015
Phone: 800-899-ISAC
Web: www.collegeillinois.org

Scholarships

## Higher Education License Plate (HELP) Program

**Type of award:** Scholarship.
**Intended use:** For undergraduate study at accredited postsecondary institution in United States. Designated institutions: Participating Illinois universities.
**Eligibility:** Applicant must be U.S. citizen.
**Application requirements:** FAFSA.
**Additional information:** Provides grants to students who attend Illinois colleges for which collegiate license plates are available. Contact your college to determine if it participates in the HELP program. Number and amount of awards contingent on number of license plates sold.

| | |
|---|---|
| **Number of awards:** | 274 |
| **Total amount awarded:** | $68,425 |

**Contact:**
Illinois Student Assistance Commission
1755 Lake Cook Road
Deerfield, IL 60015
Phone: 800-899-ISAC
Web: www.collegeillinois.org

## Illinois Future Teacher Corps

**Type of award:** Scholarship, renewable.
**Intended use:** For junior, senior or graduate study at accredited 2-year or 4-year institution. Designated institutions: Approved Illinois public and private four-year colleges and universities offering teacher program, and certain other degree-granting institutions.
**Eligibility:** Applicant must be U.S. citizen or permanent resident residing in Illinois.
**Basis for selection:** Major/career interest in education; education, teacher or education, early childhood. Applicant must demonstrate financial need and high academic achievement.
**Application requirements:** FAFSA and Teacher Education Program Application.
**Additional information:** Scholarships for students planning to pursue careers as preschool, elementary school, and secondary school teachers in Illinois. Priority given to students with financial need, minority students, and students planning to teach in teacher shortage discipline and/or hard-to-staff school. Must fulfill teaching commitment or scholarship becomes loan. Minimum 2.5 GPA. See Website for application.

| | |
|---|---|
| **Amount of award:** | $5,000-$10,000 |
| **Number of awards:** | 267 |
| **Application deadline:** | March 1 |
| **Total amount awarded:** | $1,868,103 |

**Contact:**
Illinois Student Assistance Commission
ISAC College Zone Counselor
1755 Lake Cook Road
Deerfield, IL 60015
Phone: 800-899-ISAC
Web: www.collegeillinois.org

## Illinois National Guard Grant

**Type of award:** Scholarship, renewable.
**Intended use:** For undergraduate or graduate study at 2-year or 4-year institution. Designated institutions: Approved Illinois institutions.
**Eligibility:** Applicant must be residing in Illinois. Applicant must be in military service in the Reserves/National Guard. Must have served at least one year of active duty in Illinois National Guard or Naval Militia.
**Application requirements:** Proof of eligibility.
**Additional information:** Available to enlisted and company grade officers up to rank of captain who have either served one year active duty; are currently on active duty status; or have been active for at least five consecutive years and have been called to federal active duty for at least six months and be within 12 months after discharge date. Applied toward tuition and certain fees. Recipients may use award for eight semesters or 12 quarters (or the equivalent). Award amount varies. Deadlines: 10/1 for full year, 3/1 for second/third term, 6/15 for summer term. Applications available from ISAC or National Guard units. Contact ISAC or National Guard units or visit Website for additional information.

| | |
|---|---|
| **Number of awards:** | 1,931 |
| **Application deadline:** | October 1 |
| **Total amount awarded:** | $4,729,653 |

**Contact:**
Illinois Student Assistance Commission
ISAC College Zone Counselor
1755 Lake Cook Road
Deerfield, IL 60015
Phone: 800-899-ISAC
Web: www.collegeillinois.org

## Illinois Veteran Grant (IVG) Program

**Type of award:** Scholarship, renewable.
**Intended use:** For undergraduate or graduate study at postsecondary institution.
**Eligibility:** Applicant must be U.S. citizen or permanent resident residing in Illinois. Applicant must be veteran. Must have been Illinois resident or Illinois college student six months prior to entering service and must have returned to Illinois to reside within six months of leaving service. Must have served one year of federal active duty or have served in a foreign country in a time of hostilities in that country.
**Application requirements:** Proof of eligibility.
**Additional information:** Provides payment of tuition and mandatory fees to qualified Illinois veterans or military service members. Grant is available for equivalent of four academic years of full-time enrollment for undergraduate and graduate study. Recipient not required to enroll for minimum number of credit hours each term. One-time application only. See Website for additional information and application.

| | |
|---|---|
| **Amount of award:** | Full tuition |
| **Number of awards:** | 11,450 |
| **Total amount awarded:** | $16,812,105 |

**Contact:**
Illinois Student Assistance Commission
ISAC College Zone Counselor
1755 Lake Cook Road
Deerfield, IL 60015
Phone: 800-899-ISAC
Web: www.collegeillinois.org

## Minority Teachers of Illinois Scholarship

**Type of award:** Scholarship, renewable.
**Intended use:** For undergraduate or graduate study at postsecondary institution. Designated institutions: ISAC-approved institutions in Illinois.
**Eligibility:** Applicant must be Alaskan native, Asian American, African American, Mexican American, Hispanic American, Puerto Rican or American Indian. Applicant must be U.S. citizen or permanent resident residing in Illinois.

**Basis for selection:** Major/career interest in education, teacher or education.
**Application requirements:** Teacher Education Program application.
**Additional information:** Minimum 2.5 GPA. Applicant should be in course of study leading to teacher certification. Recipient must sign commitment to teach one year in Illinois for each year assistance is received. Must teach at nonprofit Illinois preschool, elementary school, or secondary school with at least 30 percent minority enrollment. If teaching commitment is not fulfilled, scholarship converts to loan, and entire amount, plus interest, must be paid. Contact ISAC or visit Website for additional information.

| | |
|---|---|
| **Amount of award:** | $5,000 |
| **Number of awards:** | 459 |
| **Application deadline:** | March 1 |
| **Total amount awarded:** | $2,158,821 |

**Contact:**
Illinois Student Assistance Commission
ISAC College Zone Counselor
1755 Lake Cook Road
Deerfield, IL 60015
Phone: 800-899-ISAC
Web: www.collegeillinois.org

## Monetary Award Program (MAP)

**Type of award:** Scholarship, renewable.
**Intended use:** For undergraduate study at 2-year or 4-year institution. Designated institutions: ISAC/MAP-approved institutions in Illinois.
**Eligibility:** Applicant must be U.S. citizen or permanent resident residing in Illinois.
**Basis for selection:** Applicant must demonstrate financial need.
**Application requirements:** FAFSA.
**Additional information:** Must reapply every year for renewal. Contact ISAC or visit Website for application, deadlines, and additional information. Amount of award dependent on legislative action and available funding in any given year.

| | |
|---|---|
| **Amount of award:** | $4,968 |
| **Number of awards:** | 141,380 |
| **Number of applicants:** | 773,930 |
| **Total amount awarded:** | $390,465,309 |

**Contact:**
Illinois Student Assistance Commission
ISAC College Zone Counselor
1755 Lake Cook Road
Deerfield, IL 60015
Phone: 800-899-ISAC
Web: www.collegeillinois.org

## Robert C. Byrd Honors Scholarship Program

**Type of award:** Scholarship, renewable.
**Intended use:** For full-time undergraduate study at accredited postsecondary institution in United States.
**Eligibility:** Applicant must be high school senior. Applicant must be U.S. citizen or permanent resident residing in Illinois.
**Basis for selection:** Applicant must demonstrate high academic achievement.
**Additional information:** Names of qualifying students submitted by high school guidance counselors. Student must be high school senior and enrolled, or accepted for enrollment, as full-time undergraduate. May not be used for military service academies. Eligibility based on standardized test scores, high school rank, and GPA.

| | |
|---|---|
| **Amount of award:** | $1,500 |
| **Number of awards:** | 1,322 |
| **Total amount awarded:** | $1,955,876 |

**Contact:**
Illinois Student Assistance Commission
ISAC College Zone Counselor
1755 Lake Cook Road
Deerfield, IL 60015
Phone: 800-899-ISAC
Web: www.collegeillinois.org

## Silas Purnell Illinois Incentive for Access

**Type of award:** Scholarship.
**Intended use:** For freshman study at postsecondary institution. Designated institutions: ISAC-approved institutions.
**Eligibility:** Applicant must be U.S. citizen or permanent resident residing in Illinois.
**Basis for selection:** Applicant must demonstrate financial need.
**Application requirements:** FAFSA.
**Additional information:** Applicant must have been determined by federal needs calculation to have an expected family contribution (EFC) of $0. Must meet Monetary Award Program eligibility requirements. Contact ISAC or visit Website for additional information.

| | |
|---|---|
| **Amount of award:** | $500 |
| **Number of awards:** | 18,874 |
| **Application deadline:** | September 30 |
| **Total amount awarded:** | $4,718,500 |

**Contact:**
Illinois Student Assistance Commission
ISAC College Zone Counselor
1755 Lake Cook Road
Deerfield, IL 60015
Phone: 800-899-ISAC
Web: www.collegeillinois.org

## Special Education Teacher Tuition Waiver

**Type of award:** Scholarship, renewable.
**Intended use:** For undergraduate or graduate study at postsecondary institution in United States. Designated institutions: Eligible four-year institutions in Illinois: Chicago State University, Eastern Illinois University, Governors State University, Illinois State University, Northeastern Illinois University, Northern Illinois University, Southern Illinois University (Carbondale and Edwardsville), University of Illinois (Chicago, Springfield, Urbana), and Western Illinois University.
**Eligibility:** Applicant must be U.S. citizen or permanent resident residing in Illinois.
**Basis for selection:** Major/career interest in education, special.
**Additional information:** Must be Illinois high school graduate and rank in upper half of graduating class. Must not already hold valid teaching certificate in special education. Recipients must teach in Illinois for two years, or scholarship becomes loan. See Website for application and more details.

| | |
|---|---|
| **Amount of award:** | Full tuition |
| **Number of awards:** | 244 |
| **Application deadline:** | March 1 |
| **Notification begins:** | July 1 |

**Contact:**
Illinois Student Assistance Commission
1755 Lake Cook Road
Deerfield, IL 60015
Phone: 800-899-ISAC
Web: www.collegeillinois.org

### Student-to-Student (STS) Program

**Type of award:** Scholarship, renewable.
**Intended use:** For undergraduate study at postsecondary institution. Designated institutions: Participating institutions in Illinois.
**Eligibility:** Applicant must be U.S. citizen or permanent resident residing in Illinois.
**Basis for selection:** Applicant must demonstrate financial need.
**Additional information:** Voluntary student contributions are matched, dollar for dollar, by ISAC, and paid to participating institutions. Need-based grants are then made available to students through procedures established by campus financial aid administrator and local student government. Deadline for application set by individual schools. Recipient must attend school on at least half-time basis. Must reapply for renewal. Contact college or university financial aid office, or visit ISAC Website for additional information.

| | |
|---|---|
| **Number of awards:** | 3,012 |
| **Total amount awarded:** | $948,281 |

**Contact:**
Illinois Student Assistance Commission
ISAC College Zone Counselor
1755 Lake Cook Road
Deerfield, IL 60015
Phone: 800-899-ISAC
Web: www.collegeillinois.org

## Institute for Humane Studies

### Humane Studies Fellowship

**Type of award:** Scholarship.
**Intended use:** For full-time junior, senior or graduate study at postsecondary institution.
**Basis for selection:** Applicant must demonstrate high academic achievement.
**Application requirements:** $25 application fee. Recommendations, essay, transcript. Test scores (GRE, LSAT, GMAT, SAT, ACT, etc.), resume and writing sample. Sample is typically draft dissertation or academic paper; 30 page maximum.
**Additional information:** Applicants should have demonstrated interest in the principles, practices, and institutions necessary to a free society. Amounts awarded take into account the cost of tuition at the recipient's institution and any other funds received. Number of fellowships awarded each year varies. IHS begins accepting applications online in September.

| | |
|---|---|
| **Amount of award:** | $2,000-$15,000 |
| **Number of awards:** | 180 |
| **Number of applicants:** | 760 |
| **Application deadline:** | December 31 |
| **Notification begins:** | April 20 |
| **Total amount awarded:** | $650,000 |

**Contact:**
Institute for Humane Studies at George Mason University
3301 N. Fairfax Drive
Suite 440
Arlington, VA 22201
Phone: 800-697-8799
Fax: 703-993-4890
Web: www.theihs.org

## Institute of Food Technologists

### Institute of Food Technologists Freshman Scholarship

**Type of award:** Scholarship, renewable.
**Intended use:** For full-time freshman study at 4-year institution in United States or Canada. Designated institutions: Educational institutions with approved programs in food science/technology.
**Eligibility:** Applicant must be high school senior.
**Basis for selection:** Major/career interest in food science/ technology. Applicant must demonstrate high academic achievement.
**Application requirements:** Recommendations, essay, transcript. SAT/ACT report. Essay should be one page statement regarding applicant's desire to become food scientist/ technologist.
**Additional information:** IFT Scholarship recipients must join IFT student association. Applicant must be high school senior or high school graduate entering college for first time. Minimum 3.0 GPA required. Must have a well-rounded personality. Must enroll in IFT-approved program. Program descriptions and application available on Website. All inquiries and completed applications should be directed to department head of approved school.

| | |
|---|---|
| **Amount of award:** | $1,000 |
| **Number of awards:** | 16 |
| **Application deadline:** | March 15 |
| **Notification begins:** | April 15 |
| **Total amount awarded:** | $16,000 |

**Contact:**
Scholarship Department Institute of Food Technologists
525 W. Van Buren, Suite 1000
Chicago, IL 60607
Phone: 312-782-8424
Fax: 312-782-8348
Web: www.ift.org

### Institute of Food Technologists Junior/Senior Scholarship

**Type of award:** Scholarship, renewable.
**Intended use:** For full-time junior or senior study at 4-year institution in United States or Canada. Designated institutions: Educational institutions with approved programs in food science/technology.
**Basis for selection:** Major/career interest in food science/ technology. Applicant must demonstrate high academic achievement.
**Application requirements:** Recommendations, transcript.
**Additional information:** Applicant must have minimum 3.0 GPA and must be enrolled in IFT-approved program. Program

description and application available through Website or via fax. All other inquiries and completed applications should be directed to department head of approved school. Previous scholarship recipients must be IFT members to reapply.

| | |
|---|---|
| **Amount of award:** | $1,000-$2,500 |
| **Number of awards:** | 42 |
| **Notification begins:** | April 15 |
| **Total amount awarded:** | $50,000 |

**Contact:**
Scholarship Department
Institute of Food Technologists
525 W. Van Buren, Suite 1000
Chicago, IL 60601
Phone: 312-782-8424
Fax: 312-782-8348
Web: www.ift.org

### Institute of Food Technologists Sophomore Scholarship

**Type of award:** Scholarship, renewable.
**Intended use:** For full-time sophomore study at 4-year institution in United States or Canada. Designated institutions: Educational institutions with approved programs in food science/technology.
**Basis for selection:** Major/career interest in food science/technology. Applicant must demonstrate high academic achievement.
**Application requirements:** Recommendations, essay, transcript, proof of eligibility. SAT/ACT report. Essay must be one-page statement regarding desire to continue studies in food science/technology. Non-food majors must submit one page explaining desire to become food scientist/technologist.
**Additional information:** Applicant must be college freshman. Scholarship recipients must be member of IFT student association. Must have minimum 3.0 GPA. Must be enrolled in or plan to enroll in IFT-approved program. Program descriptions and application available through Website or via fax. All inquiries and completed applications should be directed to the department head of approved school. Previous scholarship recipients must be IFT members to reapply.

| | |
|---|---|
| **Amount of award:** | $1,000 |
| **Number of awards:** | 15 |
| **Application deadline:** | March 1 |
| **Notification begins:** | April 15 |
| **Total amount awarded:** | $15,000 |

**Contact:**
Institute of Food Technologists
Scholarship Department
525 West Van Buren, Suite 1000
Chicago, IL 60607
Phone: 312-782-8424
Fax: 312-782-8348
Web: www.ift.org

## Institute of Real Estate Management Foundation

### Diversity Outreach Scholarship

**Type of award:** Scholarship.
**Intended use:** For full-time junior, senior, master's or doctoral study at 4-year or graduate institution.
**Eligibility:** Applicant must be Alaskan native, Asian American, African American, Mexican American, Hispanic American, Puerto Rican or American Indian. Applicant must be U.S. citizen.
**Basis for selection:** Major/career interest in real estate; business or business/management/administration. Applicant must demonstrate high academic achievement, depth of character, leadership and seriousness of purpose.
**Application requirements:** Interview, recommendations, essay, transcript. Resume.
**Additional information:** Must have 3.0 GPA in major. Must intend to enter the field of real estate management. Award notification is made on an ongoing basis.

| | |
|---|---|
| **Amount of award:** | $2,500-$5,000 |
| **Number of awards:** | 3 |
| **Number of applicants:** | 5 |
| **Total amount awarded:** | $4,500 |

**Contact:**
Institute of Real Estate Management Foundation
Scholarship and Grant Program
430 North Michigan Avenue
Chicago, IL 60611-4090
Phone: 312-329-6008
Fax: 312-410-7908
Web: www.irem.org

## Insurance Scholarship Foundation of America

### ISFA Education Foundation College Scholarship

**Type of award:** Scholarship.
**Intended use:** For junior, senior or graduate study at accredited 4-year or graduate institution.
**Basis for selection:** Major/career interest in insurance/actuarial science.
**Application requirements:** Recommendations, essay, transcript.
**Additional information:** Applicant must have major or minor in insurance, risk management, or actuarial science with a minimum 3.0 GPA. Must have completed or be currently enrolled in two insurance, actuarial science, or risk-management-related courses, a minimum of three credit hours each. Postmark dates have no bearing on application deadline. Visit Website for application.

| | |
|---|---|
| **Amount of award:** | $500-$5,000 |
| **Number of awards:** | 168 |
| **Number of applicants:** | 428 |
| **Application deadline:** | January 15 |
| **Total amount awarded:** | $214,595 |

**Contact:**
NAIW Education Foundation
Insurance Scholarship Foundation of America
14286-19 Beach Boulevard, Suite 353
Jacksonville, FL 32250
Phone: 866-379-4732
Fax: 828-891-2667
Web: www.inssfa.org

# International Association of Fire Fighters

## W.H. McClennan Scholarship

**Type of award:** Scholarship, renewable.
**Intended use:** For full-time undergraduate study at accredited vocational, 2-year or 4-year institution.
**Eligibility:** Applicant's parent must have been killed or disabled in work-related accident as firefighter.
**Basis for selection:** Applicant must demonstrate financial need, high academic achievement, depth of character, seriousness of purpose and service orientation.
**Application requirements:** Recommendations, essay, transcript, proof of eligibility. IA77 McClennan application.
**Additional information:** Open to children of firefighters who were killed in the line of duty and were members in good standing of IAFF at the time of deaths. Minimum 2.0 GPA.

| | |
|---|---|
| **Amount of award:** | $2,500 |
| **Number of applicants:** | 50 |
| **Application deadline:** | February 1 |
| **Notification begins:** | August 1 |
| **Total amount awarded:** | $127,500 |

**Contact:**
W. H. McClennan Scholarship/International Association of Fire Fighters
1750 New York Ave., NW
3rd Floor, Dept. of Education
Washington, DC 20006
Phone: 202-737-8484
Fax: 202-737-8418
Web: www.iaff.org/scholarships

# International Buckskin Horse Association, Inc.

## Buckskin Horse Association Scholarship

**Type of award:** Scholarship, renewable.
**Intended use:** For full-time undergraduate study at accredited postsecondary institution in United States.
**Eligibility:** Applicant must be high school senior. Applicant must be U.S. citizen.
**Basis for selection:** Applicant must demonstrate financial need, high academic achievement, depth of character, leadership and seriousness of purpose.
**Application requirements:** Portfolio, recommendations, proof of eligibility.
**Additional information:** Available to children of association members. Parent must have been member for at least 2 years.

| | |
|---|---|
| **Amount of award:** | $500-$1,000 |
| **Number of awards:** | 12 |
| **Number of applicants:** | 8 |
| **Application deadline:** | February 1 |
| **Notification begins:** | September 15 |
| **Total amount awarded:** | $7,500 |

**Contact:**
International Buckskin Horse Association, Inc.
P.O. Box 268
Shelby, IN 46377
Phone: 219-552-1013
Fax: 219-552-1013
Web: www.ibha.net

# International Executive Housekeepers Association

## IEHA Educational Foundation Scholarship

**Type of award:** Scholarship.
**Intended use:** For undergraduate or non-degree study at accredited postsecondary institution.
**Basis for selection:** Major/career interest in hospitality administration/management.
**Application requirements:** Essay, transcript. Letter from school official verifying enrollment. Class schedule and coursework curriculum. Original and three copies of prepared manuscript on housekeeping (maximum 2,000 words, double-spaced).
**Additional information:** Applicant must be member of International Executive Housekeepers Association. Scholarship will be awarded to student submitting best original manuscript on housekeeping within any industry segment (e.g., hospitality, healthcare, education, rehabilitation centers, government buildings). Other major/career interest: facilities management. Can be used for IEHA certification program. No set limit on number of awards granted.

| | |
|---|---|
| **Amount of award:** | $800 |
| **Number of awards:** | 15 |
| **Application deadline:** | January 10 |
| **Notification begins:** | June 1 |
| **Total amount awarded:** | $8,000 |

**Contact:**
International Executive Housekeepers Association
Educational Foundation Scholarships
1001 Eastwind Drive, Suite 301
Westerville, OH 43081-3361
Phone: 800-200-6342
Fax: 614-895-1248
Web: www.ieha.org

# International Foodservice Editorial Council

## Foodservice Communicators Scholarship

**Type of award:** Scholarship.
**Intended use:** For full-time undergraduate or master's study at accredited postsecondary institution in United States.
**Basis for selection:** Major/career interest in food science/technology; food production/management/services; culinary arts; communications; public relations or journalism. Applicant must demonstrate financial need, high academic achievement,

depth of character, leadership, seriousness of purpose and service orientation.
**Application requirements:** Recommendations, transcript, proof of eligibility.
**Additional information:** Applicant must pursue academic study in editorial or public relations within the food service industry. Writing ability considered. Applications may be requested by e-mail or downloaded from Website. Four to six awards granted each year for total of $8,000 to $15,000.

| | |
|---|---|
| **Amount of award:** | $1,000-$3,750 |
| **Number of awards:** | 4 |
| **Number of applicants:** | 85 |
| **Application deadline:** | March 15 |
| **Notification begins:** | July 1 |
| **Total amount awarded:** | $17,000 |

**Contact:**
International Foodservice Editorial Council (IFEC)
P.O. Box 491
Hyde Park, NY 12538
Phone: 845-229-6973
Fax: 845-229-6973
Web: www.ifeconline.com

# International Furnishings and Design Association Educational Foundation

## IFDA Leaders Commemorative Scholarship

**Type of award:** Scholarship.
**Intended use:** For undergraduate study at postsecondary institution in United States.
**Eligibility:** Applicant must be U.S. citizen or permanent resident.
**Basis for selection:** Major/career interest in design or interior design. Applicant must demonstrate depth of character, leadership and service orientation.
**Application requirements:** Portfolio, recommendations, essay, transcript. Copies of two examples of original design work, recommendation from professor on official school stationery.
**Additional information:** Must have completed four courses in interior design (or related field) at post-secondary level. Student must be involved with volunteer or community service and held leadership positions during past five years. See Website for further requirements and application.

| | |
|---|---|
| **Amount of award:** | $1,500 |
| **Number of awards:** | 1 |
| **Number of applicants:** | 25 |
| **Application deadline:** | March 31 |
| **Total amount awarded:** | $1,500 |

**Contact:**
IFDA Educational Foundation, Director of Grants/Scholarships
Attn: Merry Mabbett Dean
10765 SW Canterbury Lane, #101
Tigard, OR 97244
Web: www.ifdaef.org

## International Furnishings and Design Association Student Member Scholarships

**Type of award:** Scholarship.
**Intended use:** For full-time undergraduate or graduate study at accredited postsecondary institution in United States.
**Basis for selection:** Major/career interest in architecture or interior design. Applicant must demonstrate high academic achievement, depth of character, seriousness of purpose and service orientation.
**Application requirements:** Recommendations, essay, transcript. Two to three examples of student work, four copies of each element of application. Recommendation from IFPA member. Recommendation from professor or instructor on official school stationery.
**Additional information:** Must be member of IFDA. Must have completed four courses in interior design (or related field) at post-secondary level. Must have completed at least one semester of postsecondary school. Furniture design majors also eligible. See Website for further requirements and application.

| | |
|---|---|
| **Amount of award:** | $2,000 |
| **Number of awards:** | 1 |
| **Number of applicants:** | 2 |
| **Application deadline:** | March 31 |
| **Notification begins:** | July 31 |
| **Total amount awarded:** | $2,000 |

**Contact:**
IFDA Educational Foundation
Attn: Merry Mabbett Dean
10765 SW Canterbury Lane, #101
Tigard, OR 97244
Web: www.ifdaef.org

## Marketing Internship Scholarship

**Type of award:** Scholarship.
**Intended use:** For undergraduate study at postsecondary institution in United States.
**Eligibility:** Applicant must be U.S. citizen or permanent resident.
**Basis for selection:** Major/career interest in marketing or public relations.
**Application requirements:** Recommendations, essay. Letter from internship supervisor at university or institution, letter from employer on company letterhead confirming responsibilities, outline of how one would promote product through marketing, list of four completed courses in marketing or related subjects, list of awards, extracurricular and volunteer work.
**Additional information:** Must be member of IFDA. Available to full time college students or someone entering job market. IFDA does not provide internships or internship information. Internship must directly involve marketing, promoting or advertising design industry. Internship must last two to six months. Must have completed four courses in marketing or related subjects. See Website for further requirements and application.

| | |
|---|---|
| **Amount of award:** | $1,500 |
| **Number of awards:** | 1 |
| **Number of applicants:** | 12 |
| **Total amount awarded:** | $1,500 |

Scholarships

**Contact:**
IFDA Educational Foundation, Director of Grants/Scholarships
Attn: Merry Mabbett Dean
10765 SW Canterbury Lane, #101
Tigard, OR 97244
Web: www.ifdaef.org

### Part-Time Student Scholarship

**Type of award:** Scholarship.
**Intended use:** For half-time undergraduate study at postsecondary institution in United States.
**Basis for selection:** Major/career interest in interior design.
**Application requirements:** Portfolio, recommendations, essay, transcript. Two examples of the student's original work. Resume. Four copies of all application materials.
**Additional information:** Applicants must have completed four courses in interior design or related field. Must be currently enrolled in at least two interior design-related courses. Visit Website for application and additional information.

| | |
|---|---|
| **Amount of award:** | $1,500 |
| **Number of awards:** | 1 |
| **Number of applicants:** | 10 |
| **Application deadline:** | March 31 |
| **Notification begins:** | July 31 |
| **Total amount awarded:** | $1,500 |

**Contact:**
IFDA Educational Foundation, Director of Grants/Scholarships
Attn: Merry Mabbett Dean
10765 SW Canterbury Lane, #101
Tigard, OR 97224
Web: www.ifdaef.org

### Ruth Clark Furniture Design Scholarship

**Type of award:** Scholarship.
**Intended use:** For full-time undergraduate or graduate study at postsecondary institution in United States.
**Eligibility:** Applicant must be U.S. citizen or permanent resident.
**Basis for selection:** Major/career interest in design.
**Application requirements:** Portfolio, recommendations, essay, transcript. Letter from instructor on official school stationery. Five examples of original furniture designs.
**Additional information:** Must be member of IFDA. Must have completed four courses in interior design (or related field) at post-secondary level. Must be major in design with focus on residential upholstered and/or wood furniture design. See Website for further requirements and application.

| | |
|---|---|
| **Amount of award:** | $3,000 |
| **Number of awards:** | 1 |
| **Number of applicants:** | 12 |
| **Application deadline:** | March 31 |
| **Notification begins:** | July 31 |
| **Total amount awarded:** | $3,000 |

**Contact:**
IFDA Educational Foundation, Director of Grants/Scholarships
Attn: Merry Mabbett Dean
10765 SW Canterbury Lane, #101
Tigard, OR 97244
Web: www.ifdaef.org

## International Order of the King's Daughters and Sons

### Health Career Scholarship

**Type of award:** Scholarship, renewable.
**Intended use:** For full-time junior, senior, master's or first professional study at accredited 4-year or graduate institution in United States or Canada.
**Eligibility:** Applicant must be U.S. citizen or Canadian citizen.
**Basis for selection:** Major/career interest in medicine; dentistry; pharmacy/pharmaceutics/pharmacology; nursing; health sciences; health-related professions; physical therapy or occupational therapy. Applicant must demonstrate financial need, high academic achievement, depth of character, leadership, seriousness of purpose and service orientation.
**Application requirements:** Recommendations, essay, transcript, proof of eligibility.
**Additional information:** To request application, student must write to director stating field and present level of study and include business-size SASE. Pre-med students not eligible. R.N., M.D. and D.D.S. students must have completed first year. Number of scholarships varies year to year.

| | |
|---|---|
| **Amount of award:** | $1,000 |
| **Application deadline:** | April 1 |

**Contact:**
International Order of the King's Daughters and Sons
Director, Health Careers Department
P.O. Box 1040
Chautauqua, NY 14722-1040
Phone: 716-357-4951
Fax: 716-357-3762
Web: www.iokds.org

### North American Indian Scholarship

**Type of award:** Scholarship, renewable.
**Intended use:** For full-time undergraduate study at accredited 2-year or 4-year institution in United States.
**Eligibility:** Applicant must be American Indian. Applicant must be U.S. citizen.
**Basis for selection:** Applicant must demonstrate financial need, depth of character, leadership, seriousness of purpose and service orientation.
**Application requirements:** Recommendations, essay, transcript, proof of eligibility. Written documentation of tribal registration and other requirements.
**Additional information:** Offers scholarships with no restrictions as to tribal affiliations or Indian blood quantum. For more information, send SASE to director of North American Indian Department.

| | |
|---|---|
| **Amount of award:** | $650 |
| **Number of awards:** | 30 |
| **Application deadline:** | April 1 |
| **Notification begins:** | July 1 |
| **Total amount awarded:** | $19,500 |

**Contact:**
International Order of the King's Daughters and Sons
Director, North American Indian Dept.
P.O. Box 1040
Chautauqua, NY 14722-1040
Phone: 716-357-4951
Fax: 716-357-3762
Web: www.iokds.org

# Intertribal Timber Council

## Truman D. Picard Scholarship

**Type of award:** Scholarship, renewable.
**Intended use:** For full-time undergraduate or graduate study at accredited 2-year, 4-year or graduate institution in United States.
**Eligibility:** Applicant must be Alaskan native or American Indian. Must be enrolled member of a federally recognized tribe. Applicant must be U.S. citizen.
**Basis for selection:** Major/career interest in natural resources/conservation; forestry; wildlife/fisheries or agriculture. Applicant must demonstrate financial need, high academic achievement, depth of character, leadership, seriousness of purpose and service orientation.
**Application requirements:** Recommendations, transcript, proof of eligibility. Resume, and two-page (maximum) letter of application.
**Additional information:** Applicants must be Native American and pursuing higher education in natural resources. Check Website for application deadline dates.

| | |
|---|---|
| **Amount of award:** | $1,500-$2,000 |
| **Number of applicants:** | 60 |
| **Notification begins:** | November 1 |
| **Total amount awarded:** | $64,500 |

**Contact:**
Intertribal Timber Council
Education Committee
1112 NE 21st Avenue, Ste. 4
Portland, OR 97232-2114
Phone: 503-282-4296
Fax: 503-282-1274
Web: www.itcnet.org

# Iowa College Student Aid Commission

## All Iowa Opportunity Scholarship

**Type of award:** Scholarship.
**Intended use:** For undergraduate study at accredited 2-year or 4-year institution in United States. Designated institutions: Eligible Iowa colleges and universities.
**Eligibility:** Applicant must be high school senior. Applicant must be U.S. citizen residing in Iowa.
**Application requirements:** FAFSA.
**Additional information:** Minimum 2.5 GPA. Awards of up to average tuition and fee rate of Regents University for current academic year. Priority given to students who participated in federal TRIO programs, students who graduated from alternative high schools, and homeless youth.

| | |
|---|---|
| **Application deadline:** | March 1 |

**Contact:**
Iowa College Student Aid Commission
200 10th Street, Fourth Floor
Des Moines, IA 50309-3609
Phone: 877-272-4456
Fax: 515-725-3401
Web: www.iowacollegeaid.gov

## Governor Terry E. Branstad Iowa State Fair Scholarship

**Type of award:** Scholarship.
**Intended use:** For undergraduate study at postsecondary institution in United States. Designated institutions: Iowa colleges and universities.
**Eligibility:** Applicant must be high school senior. Applicant must be U.S. citizen residing in Iowa.
**Basis for selection:** Applicant must demonstrate financial need.
**Application requirements:** Recommendations, essay. Proof of involvement in Iowa State Fair.
**Additional information:** Must be graduating senior from Iowa state high school who has been actively involved with the Iowa State Fair. Visit Website for application.

| | |
|---|---|
| **Amount of award:** | $500-$1,000 |
| **Number of awards:** | 4 |
| **Application deadline:** | May 1 |

**Contact:**
Iowa College Student Aid Commission
200 10th Street, Fourth Floor
Des Moines, IA 50309-3609
Phone: 877-272-4456
Fax: 515-725-3401
Web: www.iowacollegeaid.gov

## Iowa Farm Bureau Federation Scholarship

**Type of award:** Scholarship.
**Intended use:** For freshman, sophomore or junior study at accredited 2-year or 4-year institution in United States. Designated institutions: Iowa colleges and universities.
**Eligibility:** Applicant must be U.S. citizen residing in Iowa.
**Basis for selection:** Major/career interest in agriculture; agricultural economics; horticulture; economics; education; forestry or veterinary medicine. Applicant must demonstrate financial need and high academic achievement.
**Application requirements:** Recommendations, essay, transcript.
**Additional information:** Must be child of Iowa Farm Bureau member. Must be working toward degree in agriculture-related field. Visit Website for application.

| | |
|---|---|
| **Amount of award:** | $1,200 |
| **Application deadline:** | March 1 |

**Contact:**
Iowa College Student Aid Commission
200 10th Street, Fourth Floor
Des Moines, IA 50309-3609
Phone: 877-272-4456
Fax: 515-725-3401
Web: www.iowacollegeaid.gov

## Iowa Grant

**Type of award:** Scholarship, renewable.
**Intended use:** For undergraduate study at vocational, 2-year or 4-year institution. Designated institutions: Approved Iowa institutions.
**Eligibility:** Applicant must be U.S. citizen or permanent resident residing in Iowa.
**Basis for selection:** Applicant must demonstrate financial need.
**Application requirements:** FAFSA.
**Additional information:** Award amount adjusted for part-time study. Eligible colleges and universities receive Iowa grant

allocations and award grants to students with greatest financial need.

**Amount of award:** $1,000
**Notification begins:** March 20
**Total amount awarded:** $1,029,784

**Contact:**
Iowa College Student Aid Commission
603 East 12th Street, 5th Floor
Des Moines, IA 50319
Phone: 877-272-4456
Fax: 515-725-3401
Web: www.iowacollegeaid.gov

## Iowa National Guard Educational Assistance Program

**Type of award:** Scholarship, renewable.
**Intended use:** For undergraduate study at accredited postsecondary institution.
**Eligibility:** Applicant must be U.S. citizen residing in Iowa. Applicant must be in military service in the Reserves/National Guard.
**Application requirements:** National Guard application.
**Additional information:** Applicant must be in military service in the Iowa Reserves/National Guard. Selection is based on National Guard designation. Award varies yearly. Maximum award is 80 percent of tuition for students at public institutions; for students at private institutions, award is equal to average tuition rate at Iowa Regents Universities. Must apply through National Guard unit.

**Number of awards:** 1,217
**Number of applicants:** 1,326
**Application deadline:** August 31
**Total amount awarded:** $4,111,816

**Contact:**
Iowa National Guard Headquarters
Military Personnel Office
77000 NW Beaver Drive
Johnston, IA 50131-1902
Web: www.iowacollegeaid.gov

## Iowa Robert C. Byrd Honor Scholarship

**Type of award:** Scholarship.
**Intended use:** For full-time undergraduate or graduate study at accredited 2-year or 4-year institution in United States.
**Eligibility:** Applicant must be high school senior. Applicant must be U.S. citizen or permanent resident residing in Iowa.
**Basis for selection:** Applicant must demonstrate high academic achievement, leadership and service orientation.
**Application requirements:** Recommendations, essay, transcript, proof of eligibility. AP scores.
**Additional information:** Eligible applicants must have completed three years of social studies, math (beyond general math and pre-Algebra) and science (beyond general science), two years of the same foreign language, and four years of English. Must have minimum 28 ACT or 1860 SAT, and 3.5 GPA. Must rank in top ten percent of class. Award amount varies; maximum is $1,500.

**Amount of award:** $1,500
**Number of awards:** 249
**Number of applicants:** 297
**Application deadline:** May 1
**Notification begins:** July 15
**Total amount awarded:** $366,000

**Contact:**
Todd Brown, Byrd Scholarship Competition
Iowa College Student Aid Commission
200 Tenth Street, Fourth Floor
Des Moines, IA 50309-3609
Phone: 877-272-4456
Fax: 515-725-3401
Web: www.iowacollegeaid.gov

## Iowa Tuition Grant

**Type of award:** Scholarship, renewable.
**Intended use:** For undergraduate study at accredited 2-year or 4-year institution. Designated institutions: Private colleges in Iowa.
**Eligibility:** Applicant must be U.S. citizen or permanent resident residing in Iowa.
**Basis for selection:** Applicant must demonstrate financial need.
**Application requirements:** Proof of eligibility. FAFSA.

**Amount of award:** $3,700
**Number of awards:** 17,531
**Number of applicants:** 33,889
**Application deadline:** July 1
**Total amount awarded:** $53,637,612

**Contact:**
Iowa College Student Aid Commission
200 Tenth Street, Fourth Floor
Des Moines, IA 50309-3609
Phone: 877-272-4456
Fax: 515-725-3401
Web: www.iowacollegeaid.gov

## Iowa Vocational-Technical Tuition Grant

**Type of award:** Scholarship, renewable.
**Intended use:** For undergraduate study at vocational or 2-year institution. Designated institutions: Iowa community colleges.
**Eligibility:** Applicant must be U.S. citizen or permanent resident residing in Iowa.
**Basis for selection:** Applicant must demonstrate financial need.
**Application requirements:** Proof of eligibility. FAFSA.
**Additional information:** Only vocational-technical career majors considered.

**Amount of award:** $1,200
**Number of awards:** 3,397
**Number of applicants:** 19,611
**Application deadline:** January 1
**Total amount awarded:** $2,776,222

**Contact:**
Iowa College Student Aid Commission
200 Tenth Street, Fourth Floor
Des Moines, IA 50309-3609
Phone: 877-272-4456
Fax: 515-725-3401
Web: www.iowacollegeaid.gov

## Robert D. Blue Scholarship

**Type of award:** Scholarship.
**Intended use:** For undergraduate study at postsecondary institution in United States. Designated institutions: Iowa colleges and universities.
**Eligibility:** Applicant must be U.S. citizen residing in Iowa.

**Basis for selection:** Applicant must demonstrate financial need, high academic achievement, depth of character, leadership and seriousness of purpose.
**Application requirements:** Recommendations, essay, transcript.
**Additional information:** Visit Website for application.

| | |
|---|---|
| **Amount of award:** | $500-$1,000 |
| **Application deadline:** | May 10 |

**Contact:**
Robert D. Blue Scholarship
Michael L. Fitzgerald, Treasurer of State
State Capitol Building
Des Moines, IA 50309-3609
Phone: 515-242-5270
Fax: 515-725-3401
Web: www.iowacollegeaid.gov

# Italian Catholic Federation

## Italian Catholic Federation Scholarship

**Type of award:** Scholarship, renewable.
**Intended use:** For full-time freshman study at accredited 2-year or 4-year institution.
**Eligibility:** Applicant must be high school senior. Applicant must be Italian. Applicant must be Roman Catholic. Applicant must be U.S. citizen residing in California, Illinois, Arizona or Nevada.
**Basis for selection:** Applicant must demonstrate financial need and high academic achievement.
**Application requirements:** Recommendations, essay, transcript.
**Additional information:** Minimum 3.2 GPA. Also open to non-Italian students whose parents or grandparents are members of Federation. First year's scholarship award is $400. Larger amounts available for advanced scholarships.

| | |
|---|---|
| **Amount of award:** | $400 |
| **Number of awards:** | 200 |
| **Number of applicants:** | 491 |
| **Application deadline:** | March 15 |
| **Notification begins:** | May 1 |
| **Total amount awarded:** | $85,200 |

**Contact:**
Italian Catholic Federation
8393 Capwell Drive
Suite 110
Oakland, CA 94621
Phone: 510-633-9058
Fax: 510-633-9758
Web: www.icf.org

# IUE-CWA

## Bruce van Ess Scholarship

**Type of award:** Scholarship.
**Intended use:** For full-time undergraduate study at accredited vocational, 2-year or 4-year institution.
**Eligibility:** Applicant or parent must be member/participant of International Union of EESMF Workers, AFL-CIO.
**Basis for selection:** Applicant must demonstrate depth of character, leadership, seriousness of purpose and service orientation.
**Application requirements:** Proof of GPA, short statement on civic contributions. 500-word essay on importance of labor movement.
**Additional information:** Available to all IUE-CWA members and employees (including retired or deceased members and employees) and their children and grandchildren. Apply online.

| | |
|---|---|
| **Amount of award:** | $2,500 |
| **Number of awards:** | 1 |
| **Application deadline:** | March 31 |
| **Total amount awarded:** | $2,500 |

**Contact:**
IUE Department of Education
Web: www.iue-cwa.org

## David J. Fitzmaurice Scholarship

**Type of award:** Scholarship.
**Intended use:** For full-time undergraduate study at accredited vocational, 2-year or 4-year institution.
**Eligibility:** Applicant or parent must be member/participant of International Union of EESMF Workers, AFL-CIO.
**Basis for selection:** Major/career interest in engineering. Applicant must demonstrate depth of character, leadership, seriousness of purpose and service orientation.
**Application requirements:** Proof of GPA, 150-word essay on civic contributions, 500-word essay on importance of labor movement.
**Additional information:** Available to children and grandchildren of all IUE-CWA members and employees (including retired or deceased members and employees). Applicant must be in engineering program. Apply online.

| | |
|---|---|
| **Amount of award:** | $2,000 |
| **Number of awards:** | 1 |
| **Application deadline:** | March 31 |
| **Total amount awarded:** | $2,000 |

**Contact:**
IUE Department of Education
Web: www.iue-cwa.org

## James B. Carey Scholarship

**Type of award:** Scholarship.
**Intended use:** For full-time undergraduate study at accredited postsecondary institution in United States.
**Eligibility:** Applicant or parent must be member/participant of International Union of EESMF Workers, AFL-CIO.
**Basis for selection:** Applicant must demonstrate depth of character, leadership, seriousness of purpose and service orientation.
**Application requirements:** Recommendations, transcript, proof of eligibility. 150-word essay on civic contributions, 500-word essay on importance of labor movement.
**Additional information:** Available to children and grandchildren of all IUE-CWA members and employees (including retired or deceased members and employees) and their children and grandchildren. Must be accepted or enrolled in college, university, nursing school, or technical school. Apply online.

| | |
|---|---|
| **Amount of award:** | $1,000 |
| **Number of awards:** | 9 |
| **Application deadline:** | March 31 |
| **Total amount awarded:** | $9,000 |

**Contact:**
IUE Department of Education
Web: www.iue-cwa.org

Scholarships

## Paul Jennings Scholarship

**Type of award:** Scholarship.
**Intended use:** For full-time undergraduate study in United States.
**Eligibility:** Applicant must be high school senior.
**Basis for selection:** Applicant must demonstrate depth of character, leadership and service orientation.
**Application requirements:** Transcript, proof of eligibility. 150-word essay on civic contributions, 500-word essay on importance of labor movement.
**Additional information:** Award available to children and grandchildren of IUE-CWA members who are now or have been local union elected officials. Families of full-time union officers or employees not eligible. Must be accepted or enrolled in college, university, nursing school, or technical school. Apply online.

| | |
|---|---|
| **Amount of award:** | $3,000 |
| **Number of awards:** | 1 |
| **Application deadline:** | March 31 |
| **Total amount awarded:** | $3,000 |

**Contact:**
IUE Department of Education
Web: www.iue-cwa.org

## Robert L. Livingston Scholarship

**Type of award:** Scholarship.
**Intended use:** For full-time undergraduate study at accredited vocational, 2-year or 4-year institution.
**Basis for selection:** Applicant must demonstrate depth of character, leadership, seriousness of purpose and service orientation.
**Application requirements:** Proof of GPA, short statement which includes applicant's civic contributions, career objectives, and extracurricular activities.
**Additional information:** Open to dependents of IUE-CWA Automotive Conference Board members (active, retired or deceased). Dependents of IUE-CWA Division employees ineligible. Apply online.

| | |
|---|---|
| **Amount of award:** | $1,500 |
| **Number of awards:** | 2 |
| **Application deadline:** | March 31 |
| **Total amount awarded:** | $3,000 |

**Contact:**
IUE Department of Education
Web: www.iue-cwa.org

## Sal Ingrassia Scholarship

**Type of award:** Scholarship.
**Intended use:** For full-time undergraduate study at accredited vocational, 2-year or 4-year institution.
**Eligibility:** Applicant or parent must be member/participant of International Union of EESMF Workers, AFL-CIO.
**Basis for selection:** Applicant must demonstrate depth of character, leadership, seriousness of purpose and service orientation.
**Application requirements:** Proof of GPA, 150-word essay on civic contributions, 500-word essay on relationship to labor movement.
**Additional information:** Available to all IUE-CWA members and employees (including retired or deceased members and employees) and their children and grandchildren. Apply online.

| | |
|---|---|
| **Amount of award:** | $2,500 |
| **Number of awards:** | 1 |
| **Application deadline:** | March 31 |
| **Total amount awarded:** | $2,500 |

**Contact:**
IUE Department of Education
Web: www.iue-cwa.org

## Willie Rudd Scholarship

**Type of award:** Scholarship.
**Intended use:** For full-time undergraduate study at accredited vocational, 2-year or 4-year institution.
**Eligibility:** Applicant or parent must be member/participant of International Union of EESMF Workers, AFL-CIO.
**Basis for selection:** Applicant must demonstrate depth of character, leadership, seriousness of purpose and service orientation.
**Application requirements:** Proof of GPA, 150-word essay on civic contributions, 500-word essay on importance of labor movement.
**Additional information:** Available to all IUE-CWA members and employees and their children and grandchildren (including retired or deceased members and employees). Apply online.

| | |
|---|---|
| **Amount of award:** | $1,000 |
| **Number of awards:** | 1 |
| **Application deadline:** | March 31 |
| **Total amount awarded:** | $1,000 |

**Contact:**
IUE Department of Education
Web: www.iue-cwa.org

# Jackie Robinson Foundation

## Mentoring and Leadership Curriculum

**Type of award:** Scholarship, renewable.
**Intended use:** For full-time undergraduate study at accredited 4-year institution in United States.
**Eligibility:** Applicant must be Alaskan native, Asian American, African American, Mexican American, Hispanic American, Puerto Rican or American Indian. Applicant must be high school senior. Applicant must be U.S. citizen.
**Basis for selection:** Applicant must demonstrate financial need, high academic achievement, leadership and service orientation.
**Application requirements:** Interview, recommendations, essay, transcript. SAT/ACT scores.
**Additional information:** Applicants must have minimum SAT score of 1000 or ACT score of 21. Award amount varies up to $6,000. Applications available online and must be submitted via website.

| | |
|---|---|
| **Amount of award:** | $6,000 |
| **Number of awards:** | 50 |
| **Number of applicants:** | 3,000 |
| **Application deadline:** | March 15 |
| **Notification begins:** | June 1 |
| **Total amount awarded:** | $1,800,000 |

**Contact:**
Jackie Robinson Foundation
Attn: Scholarship Programs
One Hudson Sq., 75 Varick Street, 2nd floor
New York, NY 10013-1917
Phone: 212-290-8600
Fax: 212-290-8081
Web: www.jackierobinson.org

# James Beard Foundation

## American Restaurant Scholarship

**Type of award:** Scholarship.
**Intended use:** For undergraduate study in United States. Designated institutions: Licensed or accredited culinary schools.
**Basis for selection:** Major/career interest in culinary arts. Applicant must demonstrate financial need.
**Application requirements:** Recommendations, transcript. Financial statement, resume.
**Additional information:** Must plan to enroll in licensed or accredited culinary school.

| | |
|---|---|
| **Amount of award:** | $4,000 |
| **Number of awards:** | 1 |
| **Application deadline:** | May 15 |

**Contact:**
Scholarship America
1 Scholarship Way
St. Peter, MN 56082
Phone: 507-931-1682
Web: www.jamesbeard.org

## Bern Laxer Memorial Scholarship

**Type of award:** Scholarship.
**Intended use:** For undergraduate study at accredited postsecondary institution. Designated institutions: Licensed or accredited culinary schools.
**Eligibility:** Applicant must be residing in Florida.
**Basis for selection:** Major/career interest in culinary arts; hospitality administration/management or food science/technology. Applicant must demonstrate financial need.
**Application requirements:** Recommendations, essay, transcript, proof of eligibility. Proof of residency, financial statement, resume.
**Additional information:** Must have at least one year of culinary experience and have high school diploma or equivalent. One scholarship granted annually in one of the following categories: culinary studies, hospitality management, and viticulture/oenology. Recipients who reapply will be given priority consideration over new applicants. May be received for a maximum of four years, but applicant must maintain a B-GPA.

| | |
|---|---|
| **Amount of award:** | $2,500 |
| **Number of awards:** | 1 |
| **Application deadline:** | May 15 |
| **Total amount awarded:** | $7,500 |

**Contact:**
Scholarship America
1 Scholarship Way
St. Peter, MN 56082
Phone: 507-931-1682
Web: www.jamesbeard.org

## Blackberry Farm Scholarship

**Type of award:** Scholarship.
**Intended use:** For undergraduate study at accredited postsecondary institution. Designated institutions: Licensed or accredited culinary institutions.
**Basis for selection:** Major/career interest in culinary arts; food production/management/services; food science/technology; hospitality administration/management or hotel/restaurant management. Applicant must demonstrate financial need, high academic achievement, leadership, seriousness of purpose and service orientation.
**Application requirements:** Recommendations, essay, transcript. Resume, financial statement.
**Additional information:** Must plan to enroll in licensed or accredited culinary school.

| | |
|---|---|
| **Amount of award:** | $2,525 |
| **Number of awards:** | 1 |
| **Application deadline:** | May 15 |
| **Total amount awarded:** | $7,700 |

**Contact:**
Scholarship America
1 Scholarship Way
St. Peter, MN 56082
Phone: 507-931-1682
Web: www.jamesbeard.org

## Bob Zappatelli Memorial Scholarship

**Type of award:** Scholarship.
**Intended use:** For undergraduate study at accredited postsecondary institution.
**Basis for selection:** Major/career interest in culinary arts; food production/management/services; food science/technology; hospitality administration/management or hotel/restaurant management.
**Application requirements:** Recommendations, essay, transcript.
**Additional information:** Must plan to enroll in culinary school. Preference given to Benchmark employees or relatives of employees. Must have experience in food and beverage industry.

| | |
|---|---|
| **Amount of award:** | $3,000 |
| **Number of awards:** | 1 |
| **Application deadline:** | May 15 |
| **Total amount awarded:** | $5,000 |

**Contact:**
Scholarship America
1 Scholarship Way
St. Peter, MN 56082
Phone: 504-931-1682
Web: www.jamesbeard.org

## Chefs of Louisiana Cookery Scholarship

**Type of award:** Scholarship.
**Intended use:** For undergraduate study at postsecondary institution. Designated institutions: Culinary schools in Louisiana.
**Eligibility:** Applicant must be U.S. citizen residing in Louisiana.
**Basis for selection:** Major/career interest in culinary arts; food production/management/services; food science/technology; hospitality administration/management or hotel/restaurant management. Applicant must demonstrate financial need.
**Application requirements:** Recommendations, essay, transcript.
**Additional information:** Must plan to enroll in Louisiana culinary school.

| | |
|---|---|
| **Amount of award:** | $4,000 |
| **Number of awards:** | 2 |
| **Application deadline:** | May 15 |

Scholarships

**Contact:**
Scholarship America
1 Scholarship Way
St. Peter, MN 56082
Phone: 504-931-1682
Web: www.jamesbeard.org

## Christian Wolffer Scholarship

**Type of award:** Scholarship.
**Intended use:** For undergraduate study at accredited postsecondary institution. Designated institutions: Licensed or accredited culinary schools.
**Eligibility:** Applicant must be residing in New York.
**Basis for selection:** Major/career interest in culinary arts; food production/management/services or food science/technology. Applicant must demonstrate high academic achievement.
**Application requirements:** Recommendations, essay, transcript, proof of eligibility. Proof of residency, financial statement, resume.
**Additional information:** Minimum 3.0 GPA. Must be enrolled or planning to enroll in accredited culinary or wine studies program.

| | |
|---|---|
| **Amount of award:** | $2,000 |
| **Number of awards:** | 1 |
| **Application deadline:** | May 15 |
| **Total amount awarded:** | $5,000 |

**Contact:**
Scholarship America
1 Scholarship Way
St. Peter, MN 56082
Phone: 507-931-1682
Web: www.jamesbeard.org

## Clat Triplette Scholarship

**Type of award:** Scholarship.
**Intended use:** For undergraduate study at accredited postsecondary institution.
**Basis for selection:** Major/career interest in culinary arts; food production/management/services or food science/technology. Applicant must demonstrate financial need.
**Application requirements:** Recommendations, transcript, proof of eligibility. Proof of residency, financial statement, resume, 250 word essay on James Beard.
**Additional information:** Applicants must be enrolled or planning to enroll in accredited baking or pastry studies program at licensed or accredited culinary school.

| | |
|---|---|
| **Amount of award:** | $5,000 |
| **Number of awards:** | 2 |
| **Application deadline:** | May 15 |
| **Total amount awarded:** | $12,000 |

**Contact:**
Scholarship America
1 Scholarship Way
St. Peter, MN 56082
Phone: 507-931-1682
Web: www.jamesbeard.org

## Dana Campbell Memorial Scholarship

**Type of award:** Scholarship.
**Intended use:** For undergraduate study at 4-year institution in United States.
**Eligibility:** Applicant must be residing in Texas, Arkansas, Delaware, Maryland, Louisiana, South Carolina, Georgia, Florida, Oklahoma, Virginia, West Virginia, Mississippi, Kentucky, Alabama, North Carolina or Missouri.
**Basis for selection:** Major/career interest in food production/management/services; culinary arts or journalism.
**Additional information:** Must have career interest in food journalism. Must be in second or third year of study in journalism or food-related curriculum.

| | |
|---|---|
| **Amount of award:** | $2,000 |
| **Number of awards:** | 1 |
| **Application deadline:** | May 15 |

**Contact:**
James Beard Foundation Scholarship Program
One Scholarship Way
Saint Peter, MN 56082
Phone: 507-931-1682
Web: www.jamesbeard.org

## Deseo at the Westin Scholarship

**Type of award:** Scholarship.
**Intended use:** For undergraduate study at postsecondary institution.
**Eligibility:** Applicant must be residing in Arizona.
**Basis for selection:** Major/career interest in culinary arts; food production/management/services or food science/technology. Applicant must demonstrate financial need.
**Application requirements:** Recommendations, essay, transcript, proof of eligibility. Proof of residency, financial statement, resume.
**Additional information:** Applicants must have participated in Arizona Careers Through Culinary Arts program and be recommended by Arizona C-CAP.

| | |
|---|---|
| **Amount of award:** | $3,750 |
| **Number of awards:** | 1 |
| **Application deadline:** | May 15 |
| **Total amount awarded:** | $6,250 |

**Contact:**
Scholarship America
1 Scholarship Way
St. Peter, MN 56082
Phone: 507-931-1682
Web: www.jamesbeard.org

## Girl and the Goat Scholarship

**Type of award:** Scholarship.
**Intended use:** For undergraduate study at accredited postsecondary institution. Designated institutions: Licensed or accredited culinary schools.
**Basis for selection:** Major/career interest in culinary arts. Applicant must demonstrate financial need.
**Application requirements:** Recommendations, transcript. Financial statement, resume.
**Additional information:** Must plan to enroll in licensed or accredited culinary school.

| | |
|---|---|
| **Amount of award:** | $3,750 |
| **Number of awards:** | 1 |
| **Application deadline:** | May 15 |

**Contact:**
Scholarship America
1 Scholarship Way
St. Peter, MN 56082
Phone: 507-931-1682
Web: www.jamesbeard.org

## Kitchen Table Bistro Scholarship

**Type of award:** Scholarship.
**Intended use:** For undergraduate study at accredited postsecondary institution. Designated institutions: Licensed or accredited culinary schools.
**Basis for selection:** Major/career interest in culinary arts. Applicant must demonstrate financial need.
**Application requirements:** Recommendations, essay, transcript. Financial statement, resume.
**Additional information:** Must plan to attend licensed or accredited culinary school.

| | |
|---|---|
| **Amount of award:** | $3,750 |
| **Number of awards:** | 1 |
| **Application deadline:** | May 15 |

**Contact:**
Scholarship America
1 Scholarship Way
St. Peter, MN 56082
Phone: 507-931-1682
Web: www.jamesbeard.org

## La Quinta Resort and Spa PGA West Scholarship

**Type of award:** Scholarship.
**Intended use:** For undergraduate study at accredited postsecondary institution.
**Basis for selection:** Major/career interest in culinary arts; food production/management/services or food science/technology. Applicant must demonstrate financial need.
**Application requirements:** Recommendations, essay, transcript, proof of eligibility. Financial statement, resume.
**Additional information:** Must plan to attend culinary school.

| | |
|---|---|
| **Amount of award:** | $3,750 |
| **Number of awards:** | 1 |
| **Application deadline:** | May 15 |

**Contact:**
Scholarship America
1 Scholarship Way
St. Peter, MN 56082
Phone: 507-931-1682
Web: www.jamesbeard.org

## La Toque Scholarship in Wine Studies

**Type of award:** Scholarship.
**Intended use:** For undergraduate study at postsecondary institution. Designated institutions: Licensed or accredited culinary schools.
**Basis for selection:** Major/career interest in culinary arts or food production/management/services. Applicant must demonstrate financial need.
**Application requirements:** Recommendations, essay, transcript, proof of eligibility. Proof of residency, financial statement, resume.
**Additional information:** Applicants must be enrolled in or be planning to enroll in an accredited wine studies program.

| | |
|---|---|
| **Amount of award:** | $3,000 |
| **Number of awards:** | 1 |
| **Application deadline:** | May 15 |
| **Total amount awarded:** | $6,000 |

**Contact:**
Scholarship America
1 Scholarship Way
St. Peter, MN 56082
Phone: 507-931-1682
Web: www.jamesbeard.org

## Palm Desert Food & Wine Festival Scholarship

**Type of award:** Scholarship.
**Intended use:** For undergraduate study at accredited postsecondary institution.
**Basis for selection:** Major/career interest in culinary arts.
**Additional information:** Must plan to attend licensed or accredited culinary school. Preference given to residents of Riverside, CA.

| | |
|---|---|
| **Amount of award:** | $5,000 |
| **Number of awards:** | 1 |
| **Application deadline:** | May 15 |

**Contact:**
James Beard Foundation Scholarship
One Scholarship Way
St. Peter, MN 56082
Phone: 507-931-1682
Web: www.jamesbeard.org

## The Peter Cameron/Housewares Charity Foundation Scholarship

**Type of award:** Scholarship.
**Intended use:** For undergraduate study at accredited postsecondary institution. Designated institutions: Licensed or accredited culinary schools.
**Eligibility:** Applicant must be high school senior.
**Basis for selection:** Major/career interest in culinary arts; food production/management/services or food science/technology. Applicant must demonstrate financial need and high academic achievement.
**Application requirements:** Recommendations, essay, transcript, proof of eligibility. Financial statement, resume.
**Additional information:** Minimum 3.0 GPA.

| | |
|---|---|
| **Amount of award:** | $4,000 |
| **Number of awards:** | 1 |
| **Application deadline:** | May 15 |
| **Total amount awarded:** | $4,000 |

**Contact:**
Scholarship America
1 Scholarship Way
St. Peter, MN 56082
Phone: 507-931-1682
Web: www.jamesbeard.org

## Peter Kump Memorial Scholarship

**Type of award:** Scholarship.
**Intended use:** For undergraduate study at accredited postsecondary institution. Designated institutions: Licensed or accredited culinary schools.
**Eligibility:** Applicant must be high school senior.
**Basis for selection:** Major/career interest in culinary arts; food production/management/services or food science/technology. Applicant must demonstrate financial need and high academic achievement.
**Application requirements:** Recommendations, essay, transcript, proof of eligibility. Proof of residency, financial statement, resume.

**Additional information:** Minimum 3.0 GPA. Minimum one year substantiated culinary experience.

| | |
|---|---|
| **Amount of award:** | $4,000 |
| **Number of awards:** | 3 |
| **Application deadline:** | May 15 |
| **Total amount awarded:** | $12,000 |

**Contact:**
Scholarship America
1 Scholarship Way
St. Peter, MN 56082
Phone: 507-931-1682
Web: www.jamesbeard.org



## Spencer's Scholarship

**Type of award:** Scholarship.
**Intended use:** For undergraduate, graduate or non-degree study at postsecondary institution in or outside United States or Canada.
**Basis for selection:** Major/career interest in culinary arts.
**Application requirements:** Recommendations, essay, transcript. Resume, financial statement.
**Additional information:** Must plan to enroll in licensed or accredited culinary school. Visit Website for application and additional information.

| | |
|---|---|
| **Amount of award:** | $5,000 |
| **Number of awards:** | 1 |
| **Application deadline:** | May 15 |

**Contact:**
Scholarship America
1 Scholarship Way
St. Peter, MN 56082
Phone: 507-931-1682
Web: www.jamesbeard.org

## Steve Scher Memorial Scholarship for Aspiring Restaurateurs

**Type of award:** Scholarship.
**Intended use:** For undergraduate study at accredited postsecondary institution.
**Basis for selection:** Major/career interest in culinary arts. Applicant must demonstrate financial need.
**Application requirements:** Essay. Detail work experience; list of top three favorite restaurants and explaining why they have earned that ranking.
**Additional information:** Must be enrolled in culinary or hospitality management program. Must be high school graduate. One scholarship will be granted for study in restaurant management at the French Culinary Institute; the other to an institution of the applicant's choice.

| | |
|---|---|
| **Amount of award:** | $5,000 |
| **Number of awards:** | 2 |
| **Application deadline:** | May 15 |
| **Total amount awarded:** | $10,000 |

**Contact:**
James Beard Foundation Scholarship Program
One Scholarship Way
St. Peter, MN 56082
Phone: 507-931-1682
Web: www.jamesbeard.org

## Studio at the Montage Resort & Spa Scholarship

**Type of award:** Scholarship.
**Intended use:** For undergraduate study at accredited postsecondary institution. Designated institutions: Licensed or accredited culinary schools.
**Basis for selection:** Major/career interest in culinary arts. Applicant must demonstrate financial need.
**Application requirements:** Recommendations, essay, transcript. Financial statement, resume.
**Additional information:** Must plan to attend licensed or accredited culinary school.

| | |
|---|---|
| **Amount of award:** | $2,500 |
| **Number of awards:** | 2 |
| **Application deadline:** | May 15 |
| **Total amount awarded:** | $10,000 |

**Contact:**
Scholarship America
1 Scholarship Way
St. Peter, MN 56082
Phone: 507-931-1682
Web: www.jamesbeard.org

## Sunday Supper Atlanta Scholarship

**Type of award:** Scholarship.
**Intended use:** For undergraduate study at accredited postsecondary institution.
**Basis for selection:** Major/career interest in culinary arts. Applicant must demonstrate financial need.
**Additional information:** Applicants must plan to enroll in accredited culinary school.

| | |
|---|---|
| **Amount of award:** | $2,500-$5,000 |
| **Number of awards:** | 3 |
| **Application deadline:** | May 15 |
| **Total amount awarded:** | $11,500 |

**Contact:**
James Beard Foundation Scholarship Program
One Scholarship Way
Saint Peter, MN 56082
Phone: 507-931-1682
Web: www.jamesbeard.org

## T.J. Bartalotta Scholarship

**Type of award:** Scholarship.
**Intended use:** For undergraduate study at accredited postsecondary institution.
**Basis for selection:** Major/career interest in culinary arts. Applicant must demonstrate financial need.
**Additional information:** Must attend a licensed or accredited culinary school. Preference given to residents of Wisconsin or those studying in Wisconsin culinary arts program.

| | |
|---|---|
| **Amount of award:** | $3,750 |
| **Number of awards:** | 1 |
| **Application deadline:** | May 15 |

**Contact:**
James Beard Foundation Scholarship Program
One Scholarship Way
St. Peter, MN 56082
Phone: 507-931-1682
Web: www.jamesbeard.org

### Zov's Bistro Scholarship

**Type of award:** Scholarship.
**Intended use:** For undergraduate study at accredited postsecondary institution. Designated institutions: Licensed or accredited culinary schools.
**Basis for selection:** Major/career interest in culinary arts. Applicant must demonstrate financial need.
**Application requirements:** Recommendations, essay, transcript. Financial statement, resume.
**Additional information:** Must plan to enroll in licensed or accredited culinary school.

| | |
|---|---|
| **Amount of award:** | $4,000 |
| **Number of awards:** | 2 |
| **Application deadline:** | May 15 |

**Contact:**
Scholarship America
1 Scholarship Way
St. Peter, MN 56082
Phone: 507-931-1682
Web: www.jamesbeard.org

## James F. Byrnes Foundation

### James F. Byrnes Scholarship

**Type of award:** Scholarship, renewable.
**Intended use:** For full-time at accredited 4-year institution.
**Eligibility:** Applicant must be high school senior. Applicant must be U.S. citizen residing in South Carolina.
**Basis for selection:** Applicant must demonstrate financial need, high academic achievement, depth of character, leadership, patriotism, seriousness of purpose and service orientation.
**Application requirements:** Interview, essay, transcript. SAT/ACT scores, photograph, autobiography (three typed pages maximum) describing home situation, death of parent/s, desire for college education, college ambitions, reasons financial assistance is needed, how college will be financed, etc. Two non-relative references (one from current guidance counselor or teacher).
**Additional information:** Applicant must be high school senior. Applicant must have minimum 2.5 GPA. One or both parents of applicant must be deceased. Visit Website for additional information.

| | |
|---|---|
| **Amount of award:** | $3,250 |
| **Number of awards:** | 6 |
| **Number of applicants:** | 126 |
| **Application deadline:** | February 15 |
| **Notification begins:** | April 20 |

**Contact:**
James F. Byrnes Foundation
P.O. Box 6781
Columbia, SC 29260-6781
Phone: 803-254-9325
Fax: 803-254-9354
Web: www.byrnesscholars.org

## Japanese American Association of New York

### Japanese American General Scholarship

**Type of award:** Scholarship.
**Intended use:** For full-time freshman study at accredited 2-year or 4-year institution in United States.
**Eligibility:** Applicant must be high school senior. Applicant must be Japanese. Applicant must be U.S. citizen or permanent resident residing in Connecticut, New York or New Jersey.
**Basis for selection:** Applicant must demonstrate financial need, high academic achievement and service orientation.
**Application requirements:** Essay, transcript. SAT scores, photograph. Letter of recommendation from a JAA member if no one in family is a member.
**Additional information:** Open to Japanese students who hold green cards and Asian-Americans of Japanese descent. Two awards given are need-based. Contact sponsor or visit Website for future competitions and deadlines.

| | |
|---|---|
| **Amount of award:** | $1,000-$6,000 |
| **Number of awards:** | 13 |
| **Number of applicants:** | 30 |
| **Application deadline:** | May 2 |
| **Notification begins:** | May 20 |
| **Total amount awarded:** | $44,500 |

**Contact:**
Japanese American Association of New York
15 West 44 Street
New York, NY 10036
Phone: 212-840-6942
Fax: 212-840-0616
Web: www.jaany.org

### Japanese American Music Scholarship Competition

**Type of award:** Scholarship.
**Intended use:** For undergraduate or graduate study at postsecondary institution.
**Eligibility:** Applicant must be Japanese. Applicant must be U.S. citizen or permanent resident.
**Basis for selection:** Competition/talent/interest in music performance/composition, based on piano performance. Major/career interest in music.
**Application requirements:** Photograph.
**Additional information:** Open to Japanese students who hold green cards and Asian-Americans of Japanese descent. Awards given every other year. Contact sponsor or visit Website for future competitions and deadlines.

| | |
|---|---|
| **Amount of award:** | $1,500 |
| **Number of awards:** | 3 |
| **Total amount awarded:** | $4,500 |

**Contact:**
Japanese American Association of New York
15 West 44 Street
New York, NY 10036
Phone: 212-840-6942
Fax: 212-840-0616
Web: www.jaany.org

Scholarships

# Jaycee War Memorial Fund

## Charles R. Ford Scholarship

**Type of award:** Scholarship.
**Intended use:** For undergraduate study at postsecondary institution.
**Eligibility:** Applicant or parent must be member/participant of Jaycees. Applicant must be returning adult student. Applicant must be U.S. citizen.
**Basis for selection:** Applicant must demonstrate financial need, high academic achievement and leadership.
**Application requirements:** $10 application fee.
**Additional information:** Must be active member of Jaycees who wishes to return to college or university to complete education. To receive application, send business-size SASE with application fee between July 1 and February 1. Make check or money order payable to the Jaycee War Memorial Fund. Visit Website for more information.

| | |
|---|---|
| **Amount of award:** | $2,500 |
| **Number of awards:** | 1 |
| **Application deadline:** | February 1 |
| **Notification begins:** | May 15 |

**Contact:**
Jaycee War Memorial Fund
Ford Scholarship
7447 S. Lewis Ave.
Tulsa, OK 74136
Phone: 918-584-2481
Fax: 918-584-4422
Web: www.usjaycees.org

## Jaycee War Memorial Scholarship

**Type of award:** Scholarship.
**Intended use:** For full-time undergraduate study at accredited vocational, 2-year or 4-year institution.
**Eligibility:** Applicant must be U.S. citizen.
**Basis for selection:** Applicant must demonstrate financial need, high academic achievement and leadership.
**Application requirements:** $10 application fee.
**Additional information:** To receive application, send business-size SASE with application fee between July 1 and February 1. Make check or money order payable to the Jaycee War Memorial Fund. Visit Website for additional information.

| | |
|---|---|
| **Amount of award:** | $1,000 |
| **Number of awards:** | 10 |
| **Application deadline:** | February 1 |
| **Notification begins:** | May 15 |
| **Total amount awarded:** | $25,000 |

**Contact:**
Jaycee War Memorial Scholarship
Jycee War Memorial Scholarship
7447 S. Lewis Ave.
Tulsa, OK 74136
Phone: 918-584-2481
Fax: 918-584-4422
Web: www.usjaycees.org

## Thomas Wood Baldridge Scholarship

**Type of award:** Scholarship.
**Intended use:** For full-time undergraduate study at accredited 2-year or 4-year institution.
**Eligibility:** Applicant or parent must be member/participant of Jaycees. Applicant must be U.S. citizen.
**Basis for selection:** Applicant must demonstrate financial need, high academic achievement and leadership.
**Application requirements:** $10 application fee.
**Additional information:** Applicant must be member or have immediate family who is Jaycee member. To receive application, send business-size SASE along with application fee between July 1 and February 1. Make check or money order payable to the Jaycee War Memorial Fund. Visit Website for additional information.

| | |
|---|---|
| **Amount of award:** | $3,000 |
| **Number of awards:** | 1 |
| **Application deadline:** | February 1 |
| **Notification begins:** | May 15 |
| **Total amount awarded:** | $3,000 |

**Contact:**
Jaycee War Memorial Fund
Baldridge Scholarship
7447 S. Lewis Ave.
Tulsa, OK 74136
Phone: 918-584-2481
Fax: 918-584-4422
Web: www.usjaycees.org

# Jeannette Rankin Foundation

## Jeanette Rankin Foundation Scholarship

**Type of award:** Scholarship.
**Intended use:** For undergraduate study at accredited vocational, 2-year or 4-year institution in United States.
**Eligibility:** Applicant must be female, at least 35. Applicant must be U.S. citizen.
**Basis for selection:** Applicant must demonstrate financial need, depth of character and seriousness of purpose.
**Application requirements:** Recommendations, essay.
**Additional information:** Applicant must be 35+ as of March 1 and meet low-income guidelines. Must display courage and attainable goals. Download application from Website from November through mid-February, or send SASE with application request.

| | |
|---|---|
| **Amount of award:** | $2,000 |
| **Number of applicants:** | 850 |
| **Application deadline:** | March 1 |
| **Notification begins:** | June 30 |
| **Total amount awarded:** | $160,000 |

**Contact:**
Jeannette Rankin Foundation
1 Huntington Road, # 701
Athens, GA 30606
Phone: 706-208-1211
Web: www.rankinfoundation.org

# Jewish Vocational Service

## Jewish Vocational Service Scholarship Fund

**Type of award:** Scholarship, renewable.
**Intended use:** For full-time undergraduate or graduate study at accredited postsecondary institution in United States.
**Eligibility:** Applicant must be Jewish. Applicant must be U.S. citizen or permanent resident residing in California.
**Basis for selection:** Applicant must demonstrate financial need.
**Application requirements:** Recommendations, essay, transcript. FAFSA and tax returns.
**Additional information:** Minimum 2.7 GPA. Must be Jewish and legal, permanent resident of Los Angeles County with verifiable financial need. Number of awards varies. Visit Website for electronic application.

| | |
|---|---|
| **Amount of award:** | $1,000-$5,000 |
| **Number of applicants:** | 400 |
| **Notification begins:** | June 15 |
| **Total amount awarded:** | $340,000 |

**Contact:**
JVS Scholarship Fund
c/o Cathy Kersh
6505 Wilshire Blvd., Suite 200
Los Angeles, CA 90048
Phone: 323-761-8888 ext. 8868
Fax: 323-761-8580
Web: www.jvsla.org

# Jewish War Veterans of the United States of America

## Jewish War Veterans of the United States of America Bernard Rotberg Memorial Scholarship

**Type of award:** Scholarship.
**Intended use:** For freshman study at accredited 4-year institution.
**Eligibility:** Applicant must be high school senior. Applicant must be Jewish.
**Basis for selection:** Applicant must demonstrate financial need and high academic achievement.
**Additional information:** Applicant must be direct descendant of Jewish War Veterans member. Must be in upper 25 percent of high school class; must have participated in extracurricular activities in school as well as in Jewish community. SAT scores and recommendations encouraged. Visit Website for application and more information.

| | |
|---|---|
| **Amount of award:** | $1,000 |
| **Number of awards:** | 1 |

**Contact:**
Jewish War Veterans of the United States of America
National Scholarship Committee
1811 R Street NW
Washington, DC 20009
Phone: 202-265-6280
Fax: 202-234-5662
Web: www.jwv.org

## Jewish War Veterans of the United States of America JWV Grant

**Type of award:** Research grant.
**Intended use:** For freshman study at accredited vocational or 4-year institution.
**Eligibility:** Applicant must be high school senior. Applicant must be Jewish.
**Basis for selection:** Applicant must demonstrate financial need and high academic achievement.
**Additional information:** Applicant must be direct descendant of JWV member. Must be in upper 25 percent of high school class; must have participated in extracurricular activities in school as well as in Jewish community. SAT and recommendations encouraged. Visit Website for application and more information.

| | |
|---|---|
| **Amount of award:** | $500 |
| **Number of awards:** | 1 |

**Contact:**
Jewish War Veterans of the United States of America
National Scholarship Committee
1811 R Street NW
Washington, DC 20009
Phone: 202-265-6280
Fax: 202-234-5662
Web: www.jwv.org

## Jewish War Veterans of the United States of America XX Olympiad Memorial Award

**Type of award:** Scholarship.
**Intended use:** For undergraduate study at accredited 4-year institution.
**Eligibility:** Applicant must be high school senior.
**Basis for selection:** Applicant must demonstrate high academic achievement, leadership and service orientation.
**Application requirements:** SAT scores.
**Additional information:** Selection based on merit with focus on athletic achievement. Application deadline March - May. Visit Website for application and more information.

| | |
|---|---|
| **Amount of award:** | $200-$1,000 |
| **Number of awards:** | 1 |

**Contact:**
Jewish War Veterans of the United States of America
National Scholarship Committee
1811 R Street NW
Washington, DC 20009
Phone: 202-265-6280
Fax: 202-234-5662
Web: www.jwv.org

## Louis S. Silvey Grant

**Type of award:** Research grant.
**Intended use:** For freshman study at accredited 4-year institution.
**Eligibility:** Applicant must be high school senior. Applicant must be Jewish.
**Basis for selection:** Applicant must demonstrate financial need and high academic achievement.
**Additional information:** Applicant must be direct descendant of JWV member. Must be in upper 25 percent of high school class; must have participated in extracurricular activities in school as well as in Jewish community. SAT and recommendations encouraged. Visit Website for application and more information.

**Amount of award:** $750
**Number of awards:** 1
**Contact:**
Jewish War Veterans of the United States of America
National Scholarship Committee
1811 R Street NW
Washington, DC 20009
Phone: 202-265-6280
Fax: 202-234-5662
Web: www.jwv.org



# Kansas Board of Regents

## Kansas Comprehensive Grant

**Type of award:** Scholarship, renewable.
**Intended use:** For full-time undergraduate study at accredited 4-year institution. Designated institutions: Kansas post-secondary institutions.
**Eligibility:** Applicant must be U.S. citizen or permanent resident.
**Basis for selection:** Applicant must demonstrate financial need.
**Application requirements:** Proof of eligibility. FAFSA.
**Additional information:** Up to $1,100 for those attending public institutions; up to $3,000 for those attending private institutions.

| | |
|---|---|
| **Number of awards:** | 10,682 |
| **Number of applicants:** | 23,855 |
| **Application deadline:** | April 1 |
| **Notification begins:** | May 1 |
| **Total amount awarded:** | $16,395,672 |

**Contact:**
Kansas Board of Regents
1000 SW Jackson Street
Suite 520
Topeka, KS 66612-1368
Phone: 785-296-3517
Fax: 785-296-0983
Web: www.kansasregents.org

## Kansas Ethnic Minority Scholarship

**Type of award:** Scholarship, renewable.
**Intended use:** For full-time undergraduate study at postsecondary institution. Designated institutions: Kansas post-secondary institutions.
**Eligibility:** Applicant must be Alaskan native, Asian American, African American, Mexican American, Hispanic American, Puerto Rican or American Indian. Applicant must be U.S. citizen or permanent resident.
**Basis for selection:** Applicant must demonstrate financial need and high academic achievement.
**Application requirements:** $12 application fee. Proof of eligibility. State of Kansas Student Aid Application. FAFSA.
**Additional information:** Minimum 3.0 GPA.

| | |
|---|---|
| **Amount of award:** | $1,850 |
| **Number of awards:** | 167 |
| **Number of applicants:** | 671 |
| **Application deadline:** | May 1 |
| **Total amount awarded:** | $299,276 |

**Contact:**
Kansas Board of Regents
1000 SW Jackson Street
Suite 520
Topeka, KS 66612-1368
Phone: 785-296-3517
Fax: 785-296-0983
Web: www.kansasregents.org

## Kansas Nursing Service Scholarship

**Type of award:** Scholarship, renewable.
**Intended use:** For full-time undergraduate study at postsecondary institution. Designated institutions: Kansas postsecondary schools with approved nursing programs.
**Eligibility:** Applicant must be U.S. citizen or permanent resident.
**Basis for selection:** Major/career interest in nursing. Applicant must demonstrate financial need.
**Application requirements:** $12 application fee. State of Kansas Student Aid Application. FAFSA.
**Additional information:** Must obtain sponsorship from adult-care home licensed under the Adult Care Home Licensure Act; state agency that employs LPNs or RNs; or state-licensed medical care facility, psychiatric hospital, home health agency or local health department. Must agree to work in Kansas one year for each year that scholarship is received. If recipient does not meet obligation, award becomes loan.

| | |
|---|---|
| **Amount of award:** | $2,500-$3,500 |
| **Number of awards:** | 203 |
| **Number of applicants:** | 356 |
| **Application deadline:** | May 1 |
| **Total amount awarded:** | $525,072 |

**Contact:**
Kansas Board of Regents
1000 SW Jackson Street
Suite 520
Topeka, KS 66612-1368
Phone: 785-296-3518
Fax: 785-296-0983
Web: www.kansasregents.org

## Kansas ROTC Service Scholarship

**Type of award:** Scholarship.
**Intended use:** For full-time undergraduate study at postsecondary institution.
**Eligibility:** Applicant or parent must be member/participant of Reserve Officers Training Corps (ROTC). Applicant must be residing in Kansas.
**Additional information:** Applicant must be Kansas resident enrolled in Kansas ROTC program. Must be full-time undergraduate with at least 12 credit hours. Scholarship limited to eight semesters. Award amount may be up to tuition and costs of average four-year regents institution; average award is $1,650.

| | |
|---|---|
| **Number of awards:** | 22 |
| **Number of applicants:** | 22 |
| **Application deadline:** | August 1 |
| **Total amount awarded:** | $159,622 |

**Contact:**
Kansas Board of Regents Director of Student Financial Assistance
1000 SW Jackson Street
Suite 520
Topeka, KS 66612-1368
Phone: 785-296-3518
Fax: 785-296-0983
Web: www.kansasregents.org

## Kansas State Scholarship

**Type of award:** Scholarship, renewable.
**Intended use:** For full-time undergraduate study at postsecondary institution.
**Basis for selection:** Applicant must demonstrate financial need and high academic achievement.
**Application requirements:** $12 application fee. Proof of eligibility. FAFSA.
**Additional information:** Applicant must be Kansas resident, high school senior or undergraduate, and must be designated State Scholar in senior year of high school. Must be enrolled in Kansas school. Must have high GPA (average: 3.9) and ACT scores (average: 29).

| | |
|---|---|
| **Amount of award:** | $1,000 |
| **Number of awards:** | 970 |
| **Number of applicants:** | 2,211 |
| **Application deadline:** | May 1 |
| **Total amount awarded:** | $1,000,503 |

**Contact:**
Kansas Board of Regents
1000 SW Jackson Street
Suite 520
Topeka, KS 66612-1368
Phone: 785-296-3517
Fax: 785-296-0983
Web: www.kansasregents.org

## Kansas Teacher Service Scholarship

**Type of award:** Scholarship, renewable.
**Intended use:** For full-time undergraduate or post-bachelor's certificate study at 4-year or graduate institution.
**Basis for selection:** Major/career interest in education, teacher or education, special. Applicant must demonstrate high academic achievement.
**Application requirements:** $12 application fee. Recommendations, transcript, proof of eligibility. FAFSA. Personal statement.
**Additional information:** Applicant must be Kansas resident enrolled in Kansas school that offers education degree. Must identify a "hard-to fill" or "underserved" area. Scholarships are competitive; selection based on ACT score, GPA, high school rank, transcript and recommendation. Preference given to juniors and seniors, or currently licensed teachers pursuing licensure or endorsement in hard-to-fill disciplines.

| | |
|---|---|
| **Amount of award:** | $5,000 |
| **Number of awards:** | 386 |
| **Number of applicants:** | 766 |
| **Application deadline:** | May 1 |
| **Total amount awarded:** | $1,540,499 |

**Contact:**
Kansas Board of Regents
1000 SW Jackson Street
Suite 520
Topeka, KS 66612-1368
Phone: 785-296-3517
Fax: 785-296-0983
Web: www.kansasregents.org

## Kansas Vocational Education Scholarship

**Type of award:** Scholarship, renewable.
**Intended use:** For full-time undergraduate study at vocational or 2-year institution. Designated institutions: Kansas institutions.
**Eligibility:** Applicant must be U.S. citizen or permanent resident.
**Application requirements:** $12 application fee. Essay, proof of eligibility.
**Additional information:** Applicant must be Kansas resident and graduate of Kansas high school. Must take vocational test given on first Saturday of November or March and complete Vocational Education application. Renewals awarded first; remaining scholarships offered to those with highest exam scores.

| | |
|---|---|
| **Amount of award:** | $500 |
| **Number of awards:** | 258 |
| **Number of applicants:** | 357 |
| **Application deadline:** | May 1, February 1 |
| **Notification begins:** | May 15 |
| **Total amount awarded:** | $120,000 |

**Contact:**
Kansas Board of Regents
1000 SW Jackson Street
Suite 520
Topeka, KS 66612-0983
Phone: 785-296-3518
Fax: 785-296-0983
Web: www.kansasregents.org

## National Guard Educational Assistance Program

**Type of award:** Scholarship, renewable.
**Intended use:** For undergraduate study at postsecondary institution. Designated institutions: Kansas institutions.
**Eligibility:** Applicant must be U.S. citizen residing in Kansas.
**Additional information:** Award amount varies. Requires service obligation.

| | |
|---|---|
| **Number of awards:** | 277 |
| **Number of applicants:** | 376 |
| **Application deadline:** | August 1 |
| **Total amount awarded:** | $899,291 |

**Contact:**
Kansas Board of Regents Attn: Diane Lindeman
1000 SW Jackson Street
Suite 520
Topeka, KS 66612-1368
Phone: 785-296-3518
Fax: 785-296-0983
Web: www.kansasregents.org

# Kappa Kappa Gamma Foundation

## Kappa Kappa Gamma Scholarship

**Type of award:** Scholarship, renewable.
**Intended use:** For full-time undergraduate or graduate study at 4-year or graduate institution in United States.
**Basis for selection:** Applicant must demonstrate financial need and high academic achievement.
**Application requirements:** Recommendations, transcript.
**Additional information:** Applicant must be active member in good standing of Kappa Kappa Gamma fraternity, with minimum 3.0 GPA. Recipients must reapply each year. Must be U.S. citizen or permanent resident from Canada.

| | |
|---|---|
| **Amount of award:** | $500-$3,000 |
| **Number of awards:** | 141 |
| **Number of applicants:** | 427 |
| **Application deadline:** | February 1 |
| **Total amount awarded:** | $448,529 |

**Contact:**
Kappa Kappa Gamma Foundation
P.O. Box 38
Columbus, OH 43216-0038
Phone: 614-228-6515
Fax: 614-228-6303
Web: www.kappa.org

# KarMel Scholarship Committee

## KarMel Scholarship

**Type of award:** Scholarship.
**Intended use:** For undergraduate or graduate study at postsecondary institution in United States.
**Eligibility:** Applicant must be U.S. citizen.
**Basis for selection:** Competition/talent/interest in gay/lesbian, based on artistic or written ability on Gay/Lesbian subject. Applicant must demonstrate depth of character, leadership and seriousness of purpose.
**Application requirements:** Artistic work or writing samples.
**Additional information:** Open to high school seniors, undergraduates, and graduate students. Applicant need not be gay/lesbian/bi to apply for scholarship, but must submit works that include gay/lesbian/bi content. Scholarship is divided into two categories: Best "Written" Gay/Lesbian/Bi Themed Work and Best "Artistic" Gay/Lesbian/Bi Themed Work. Applicant may submit up to three works in both categories. Written work of any length will be accepted. All applicants may submit work via e-mail or postal mail. Visit Website for more information.

| | |
|---|---|
| **Amount of award:** | $50-$400 |
| **Number of awards:** | 35 |
| **Number of applicants:** | 1,300 |
| **Application deadline:** | March 31 |
| **Notification begins:** | July 31 |
| **Total amount awarded:** | $3,000 |

**Contact:**
KarMel Scholarship Committee
P.O. Box 70382
Sunnyvale, CA 94086
Web: www.karenandmelody.com

# Kentucky Higher Education Assistance Authority (KHEAA)

## Early Childhood Development Scholarship

**Type of award:** Scholarship.
**Intended use:** For half-time undergraduate study at 2-year or 4-year institution. Designated institutions: Approved Kentucky institutions.
**Eligibility:** Applicant must be U.S. citizen or permanent resident residing in Kentucky.
**Basis for selection:** Major/career interest in education, early childhood. Applicant must demonstrate financial need.
**Application requirements:** FAFSA and ECDS application.
**Additional information:** Part-time students working at least twenty hours in childcare facility eligible. Must agree to service commitment. To apply register through Zip Access on Website. Must reapply for each term. Deadlines: July 15 for fall, November 15 for spring, April 15 for summer.

| | |
|---|---|
| **Amount of award:** | $1,800 |
| **Number of awards:** | 1,140 |
| **Number of applicants:** | 1,800 |
| **Application deadline:** | July 15, November 15 |
| **Total amount awarded:** | $1,261,000 |

**Contact:**
Kentucky Higher Education Assistance Authority
P.O. Box 798
Frankfort, KY 40602-0798
Phone: 800-928-8926
Fax: 502-696-7373
Web: www.kheaa.com

## Go Higher Grant

**Type of award:** Scholarship.
**Intended use:** For undergraduate study at postsecondary institution in United States. Designated institutions: Kentucky colleges and universities.
**Eligibility:** Applicant must be at least 24. Applicant must be U.S. citizen or permanent resident residing in Kentucky.
**Basis for selection:** Applicant must demonstrate financial need.
**Application requirements:** FAFSA and Go Higher Grant application.
**Additional information:** For less than half-time adult students who are at least 24 years old.

| | |
|---|---|
| **Amount of award:** | $1,000 |
| **Number of awards:** | 235 |
| **Number of applicants:** | 880 |
| **Total amount awarded:** | $235,000 |

**Contact:**
Kentucky Higher Education Assistance Authority (KHEAA)
P.O. Box 798
Frankfort, KY 40602-0798
Phone: 800-928-8926
Web: www.kheaa.com

## Kentucky College Access Program Grant (CAP)

**Type of award:** Scholarship, renewable.
**Intended use:** For undergraduate study at postsecondary institution.
**Eligibility:** Applicant must be U.S. citizen or permanent resident residing in Kentucky.
**Basis for selection:** Applicant must demonstrate financial need.
**Application requirements:** FAFSA.
**Additional information:** Applicant ineligible if family contribution exceeds the maximum Pell EFC, which is currently $5,273. May be used at eligible schools. Visit Website for additional information.

| | |
|---|---|
| **Amount of award:** | $50-$1,900 |
| **Number of awards:** | 40,000 |
| **Number of applicants:** | 269,800 |
| **Total amount awarded:** | $63,300,000 |

**Contact:**
Kentucky Higher Education Assistance Authority (KHEAA)
Grant Programs
P.O. Box 798
Frankfort, KY 40602-0798
Phone: 800-928-8926
Fax: 502-696-7373
Web: www.kheaa.com

## Kentucky Educational Excellence Scholarship (KEES)

**Type of award:** Scholarship, renewable.
**Intended use:** For undergraduate study at accredited vocational, 2-year or 4-year institution in United States. Designated institutions: Participating public and private postsecondary institutions in Kentucky and selected out-of-state institutions if program of study not offered in Kentucky.
**Eligibility:** Applicant must be enrolled in high school. Applicant must be U.S. citizen or permanent resident residing in Kentucky.
**Basis for selection:** Applicant must demonstrate high academic achievement.
**Additional information:** Scholarship is earned each year of high school. Minimum annual high school GPA of 2.5. Supplemental award is given for highest ACT score (or SAT equivalent) achieved by high school graduation, based on minimum ACT score of 15. Recipient must be enrolled in postsecondary program at least half-time. Visit Website or contact via e-mail for additional information.

| | |
|---|---|
| **Amount of award:** | $125-$2,500 |
| **Number of awards:** | 67,900 |
| **Number of applicants:** | 67,900 |
| **Total amount awarded:** | $93,800,000 |

**Contact:**
Kentucky Higher Education Assistance Authority (KHEAA)
P.O. Box 798
Frankfort, KY 40602-0798
Phone: 800-928-8926
Fax: 502-696-7373
Web: www.kheaa.com

## Kentucky Teacher Scholarship

**Type of award:** Scholarship, renewable.
**Intended use:** For full-time undergraduate or graduate study at accredited 2-year, 4-year or graduate institution. Designated institutions: Participating Kentucky institutions.
**Eligibility:** Applicant must be U.S. citizen residing in Kentucky.
**Basis for selection:** Major/career interest in education, teacher; education, early childhood or education, special. Applicant must demonstrate financial need.
**Application requirements:** FAFSA and Kentucky teacher scholarship application.
**Additional information:** Must enroll in course of study leading to initial Kentucky teacher certification. Loan forgiveness for teaching in Kentucky schools: one semester for each semester of financial assistance, two semesters if service is in teacher shortage area. Scholarship becomes loan if recipient does not complete education program or fulfill teaching obligation. Visit Website for application (see ZipAccess) and additional information.

| | |
|---|---|
| **Amount of award:** | $300-$5,000 |
| **Number of awards:** | 175 |
| **Number of applicants:** | 1,975 |
| **Application deadline:** | May 1 |
| **Notification begins:** | May 30 |
| **Total amount awarded:** | $600,000 |

**Contact:**
Kentucky Higher Education Assistance Authority (KHEAA)
Teacher Scholarship Program
P.O. Box 798
Frankfort, KY 40602-0798
Phone: 800-928-8926
Fax: 502-696-7373
Web: www.kheaa.com

## Kentucky Tuition Grant

**Type of award:** Scholarship, renewable.
**Intended use:** For full-time undergraduate study at 2-year or 4-year institution. Designated institutions: Eligible private institutions in Kentucky.
**Eligibility:** Applicant must be U.S. citizen residing in Kentucky.
**Basis for selection:** Applicant must demonstrate financial need.
**Application requirements:** FAFSA.
**Additional information:** Visit Website for additional information.

| | |
|---|---|
| **Amount of award:** | $200-$3,000 |
| **Number of awards:** | 12,500 |
| **Number of applicants:** | 43,000 |
| **Total amount awarded:** | $32,400,000 |

**Contact:**
Kentucky Higher Education Assistance Authority
Grant Programs
P.O. Box 798
Frankfort, KY 40602-0798
Phone: 800-928-8926
Fax: 502-696-7373
Web: www.kheaa.com

## Mary Jo Young Scholarship

**Type of award:** Scholarship.
**Intended use:** For non-degree study at postsecondary institution.

**Eligibility:** Applicant must be enrolled in high school. Applicant must be residing in Kentucky.
**Basis for selection:** Applicant must demonstrate financial need.
**Additional information:** Provides college tuition assistance to disadvantaged high school students taking dual credit college courses or AP courses through the Kentucky Virtual High School. Eligibility for free or reduced lunch through high school required. Award amounts are: $375 per semester if taking one course; $750 per semester if taking two courses.

| | |
|---|---|
| **Number of awards:** | 450 |
| **Number of applicants:** | 1,400 |
| **Application deadline:** | May 1 |
| **Total amount awarded:** | $330,000 |

**Contact:**
Kentucky Higher Education Assistance Authority (KHEAA)
P.O. Box 798
Frankfort, KY 40602-0798
Phone: 800-928-8926
Fax: 502-696-7373
Web: www.kheaa.com

## Robert C. Byrd Honors Scholarship

**Type of award:** Scholarship, renewable.
**Intended use:** For undergraduate study at 2-year or 4-year institution in United States.
**Eligibility:** Applicant must be high school senior. Applicant must be U.S. citizen residing in Kentucky.
**Basis for selection:** Applicant must demonstrate high academic achievement.
**Application requirements:** Recommendation from school official or GED coordinator, who must certify eligibility on KHEAA Website.
**Additional information:** Applicant must be high school senior, home school senior, or GED graduate. Minimum 3.5 GPA, and minimum 23 ACT score or minimum 1060 SAT score; or 2700 GED score. Maximum award is $1,500 per year, renewable for four years. See Website or school counselor for more information. Apply through ZipAccess on Website.

| | |
|---|---|
| **Amount of award:** | $1,500 |
| **Number of awards:** | 380 |
| **Number of applicants:** | 1,800 |
| **Application deadline:** | February 1 |
| **Notification begins:** | May 30 |
| **Total amount awarded:** | $568,000 |

**Contact:**
Kentucky Higher Education Assistance Authority
P.O. Box 798
Frankfort, KY 40602-0798
Phone: 800-928-8926
Fax: 502-696-7373
Web: www.kheaa.com

# The Kim and Harold Louie Family Foundation

## The Louie Foundation Scholarship

**Type of award:** Scholarship.
**Intended use:** For full-time undergraduate study at vocational, 2-year or 4-year institution.
**Eligibility:** Applicant must be U.S. citizen or permanent resident.
**Basis for selection:** Applicant must demonstrate financial need and high academic achievement.
**Application requirements:** Recommendations, transcript, proof of eligibility. Proof of acceptance to college, personal essays, SAR, proof of citizenship or legal residency.
**Additional information:** Minimum 3.0 GPA; SAT score of 1700 or ACT score of 24. Special consideration will be noted for applicants whose parents did not attend college, whose parents are United States veterans, who have overcome significant adversity, or who are first-generation immigrants to the United States.

| | |
|---|---|
| **Number of awards:** | 25 |
| **Number of applicants:** | 400 |
| **Application deadline:** | March 1 |
| **Total amount awarded:** | $100,000 |

**Contact:**
The Kim and Harold Louie Family Foundation - 'Scholarship
102 Fey Drive
Burlingame, CA 94010
Phone: 650-491-3434
Fax: 650-490-3153
Web: www.louiefamilyfoundation.org

# Knights of Columbus

## Fourth Degree Pro Deo and Pro Patria Scholarship

**Type of award:** Scholarship, renewable.
**Intended use:** For full-time freshman study at 4-year institution in United States. Designated institutions: Catholic colleges and universities.
**Eligibility:** Applicant or parent must be member/participant of Knights of Columbus. Applicant must be high school senior. Applicant must be Roman Catholic. Applicant must be U.S. citizen.
**Basis for selection:** Applicant must demonstrate high academic achievement.
**Application requirements:** Recommendations, essay, transcript, proof of eligibility.
**Additional information:** Must be Knights of Columbus member in good standing; child of such a member or deceased member; or member in good standing of Columbian Squires. There are 12 scholarships designated for students at the Catholic University of America in Washington, DC; 50 scholarships available to students entering other Catholic colleges in the United States. Scholarships are renewable for up to four years, pending satisfactory academic performance. Obtain application from Department of Scholarships, Knights of Columbus, in New Haven, CT.

| | |
|---|---|
| **Amount of award:** | $1,500 |
| **Number of awards:** | 62 |
| **Application deadline:** | March 1 |
| **Notification begins:** | May 1 |

**Contact:**
Knights of Columbus
Department of Scholarships
P.O. Box 1670
New Haven, CT 06507-0901
Phone: 203-752-4332
Fax: 203-752-4103
Web: www.kofc.org

## Matthews/Swift Educational Trust - Military Dependants

**Type of award:** Scholarship, renewable.
**Intended use:** For full-time undergraduate study at 4-year institution in United States. Designated institutions: Catholic colleges and universities.
**Eligibility:** Applicant or parent must be member/participant of Knights of Columbus. Applicant must be Roman Catholic. Applicant must be veteran; or dependent of disabled veteran or deceased veteran who served in the Army, Air Force, Marines, Navy, Coast Guard or Reserves/National Guard. Veterans of Iraq, Afghanistan and Pakistan conflicts and their dependents are also eligible. Parent must have been active Knights of Columbus member who died or became totally disabled while serving in the military during hostile action.
**Application requirements:** Proof of eligibility.
**Additional information:** Applicant's parent must have been killed or wounded by hostile action while serving in military, resulting in permanent and total disability. Application must be filed within two years of death or determination of disability. Award pays tuition up to $25,000 for bachelor's degree at Catholic college. No application deadline.

**Amount of award:** $25,000

**Contact:**
Knights of Columbus
Department of Scholarships
P.O. Box 1670
New Haven, CT 06507-0901
Phone: 203-752-4332
Fax: 203-752-4103
Web: www.kofc.org

## Matthews/Swift Educational Trust - Police/Firefighters

**Type of award:** Scholarship, renewable.
**Intended use:** For full-time undergraduate study at 4-year institution in United States. Designated institutions: Catholic colleges and universities.
**Eligibility:** Applicant or parent must be member/participant of Knights of Columbus. Applicant must be Roman Catholic.
**Application requirements:** Proof of eligibility.
**Additional information:** Parent must have been active Knights of Columbus member who died as the result of criminal violence while performing duties as full-time firefighter or law enforcement officer. Application must be filed within two years of death or determination of disability. Award pays tuition up to $25,000 for bachelor's degree at Catholic college. No application deadline.

**Amount of award:** $25,000

**Contact:**
Knights of Columbus
Department of Scholarships
P.O. Box 1670
New Haven, CT 06507-0901
Phone: 203-752-4332
Fax: 203-752-4103
Web: www.kofc.org

# Kosciuszko Foundation

## Kosciuszko Foundation Year Abroad Program

**Type of award:** Scholarship, renewable.
**Intended use:** For sophomore, junior, senior or graduate study at 4-year or graduate institution in Poland. Designated institutions: Jagiellonian University, Institute of Polish Diaspora and Ethnic Studies (formerly the Polonia Institute, Krakow).
**Eligibility:** Applicant must be U.S. citizen.
**Basis for selection:** Competition/talent/interest in study abroad. Major/career interest in Polish language/studies. Applicant must demonstrate high academic achievement.
**Application requirements:** $50 application fee. Recommendations, essay, transcript. Certificate of proficiency in Polish, two passport-sized photos with full name on reverse side of each. Graduates must submit copies of degree diplomas, Polish Ministry of Education application completed in English.
**Additional information:** Must have interest in Polish subjects and/or involvement in Polish-American community. Scholarship covers tuition and stipend for housing and living expenses for one academic year or semester. Airfare not included. Minimum 3.0 GPA. Visit Website for more information and application. Applications available from October 1 to December 30.

**Amount of award:** Full tuition
**Number of applicants:** 12
**Total amount awarded:** $11,475

**Contact:**
Kosciuszko Foundation
Year Abroad Program
15 East 65th Street
New York, NY 10065
Phone: 212-734-2130 ext.210
Fax: 212-628-4552
Web: www.kosciuszkofoundation.org

## Massachusetts Federation of Polish Women's Clubs Scholarships

**Type of award:** Scholarship.
**Intended use:** For full-time sophomore, junior or senior study at postsecondary institution in United States.
**Eligibility:** Applicant must be Polish. Applicant must be U.S. citizen or permanent resident.
**Basis for selection:** Applicant must demonstrate financial need and high academic achievement.
**Application requirements:** $35 application fee. Recommendations, essay, transcript, proof of eligibility. Proof of Polish ancestry. Two passport-sized photos with full name printed on reverse side of each. SASE.
**Additional information:** Applicant must be member of Massachusetts Federation of Polish Women's Clubs. Children and grandchildren of federation members also eligible. Minimum 3.0 GPA. Selection based on academic excellence, motivation, and interest in Polish subjects and involvement in Polish-American community. Only one member per immediate family may receive Massachusetts Federation of Polish Women's Scholarship during any given academic year. Visit Website for more information and application.

**Amount of award:** $1,250
**Number of applicants:** 3
**Application deadline:** January 5
**Notification begins:** May 1
**Total amount awarded:** $7,000

**Contact:**
Kosciuszko Foundation
15 East 65th Street
New York, NY 10065
Phone: 212-734-2130 ext.210
Fax: 212-628-4552
Web: www.kosciuszkofoundation.org

## The Polish American Club of North Jersey Scholarships

**Type of award:** Scholarship, renewable.
**Intended use:** For full-time undergraduate or graduate study at accredited postsecondary institution in United States.
**Eligibility:** Applicant must be Polish. Applicant must be U.S. citizen or permanent resident.
**Basis for selection:** Applicant must demonstrate financial need and high academic achievement.
**Application requirements:** $35 application fee. Recommendations, essay, transcript, proof of eligibility. Proof of Polish ancestry. Two passport-sized photos with full name printed on reverse side of each. SASE.
**Additional information:** Applicant must be an active member of Polish American Club of North Jersey. Children and grandchildren of Polish American Club of North Jersey members also eligible. Minimum 3.0 GPA. Only one member per immediate family may receive a Polish American Club of North Jersey Scholarship during any given academic year. Selection based on academic excellence, motivation, and interest in Polish subjects and involvement in the Polish-American community. Number of awards varies. Applications available October 1 through December 30. Visit Website for application and more information.

**Amount of award:** $500-$2,000
**Number of applicants:** 7
**Application deadline:** January 5
**Notification begins:** May 1
**Total amount awarded:** $7,200

**Contact:**
Kosciuszko Foundation
15 East 65th Street
New York, NY 10065
Phone: 212-734-2130 ext.210
Fax: 212-628-4552
Web: www.kosciuszkofoundation.org

## The Polish National Alliance of Brooklyn, USA, Inc. Scholarships

**Type of award:** Scholarship, renewable.
**Intended use:** For full-time undergraduate study at accredited postsecondary institution in United States.
**Eligibility:** Applicant or parent must be member/participant of Polish National Alliance of Brooklyn. Applicant must be Polish. Applicant must be U.S. citizen or permanent resident.
**Basis for selection:** Applicant must demonstrate financial need and high academic achievement.
**Application requirements:** $35 application fee. Recommendations, essay, transcript, proof of eligibility. Proof of Polish ancestry. Two passport-sized photos with full name printed on reverse side of each. SASE.
**Additional information:** Applicant must be member in good standing of Polish National Alliance of Brooklyn, USA, Inc. Minimum 3.0 GPA. Only one member per immediate family may receive scholarship during any given academic year. Selection based on academic excellence, motivation, and interest in Polish subjects and involvement in the Polish-American community. Applications available October 1 through December 30. Visit Website for application and more information.

**Amount of award:** $2,000
**Number of awards:** 3
**Number of applicants:** 7
**Application deadline:** January 5
**Notification begins:** May 15
**Total amount awarded:** $6,000

**Contact:**
Kosciuszko Foundation
15 East 65th Street
New York, NY 10065
Phone: 212-734-2130 ext.210
Fax: 212-628-4552
Web: www.kosciuszkofoundation.org

# The Lagrant Foundation

## Lagrant Scholarships

**Type of award:** Scholarship.
**Intended use:** For full-time sophomore, junior, senior or graduate study at accredited 4-year or graduate institution.
**Eligibility:** Applicant must be Alaskan native, African American, Mexican American, Hispanic American, Puerto Rican, American Indian or Native Hawaiian/Pacific Islander. Applicant must be U.S. citizen or permanent resident.
**Basis for selection:** Major/career interest in advertising; marketing or public relations.
**Application requirements:** Recommendations, essay, transcript. Resume.
**Additional information:** Minimum 2.75 GPA for undergraduates; 3.2 GPA for graduate students. Scholarship winners receive trip to New York City to take part in Annual Scholarship Recognition Reception and Award Program. Students attend welcome dinner and workshop with networking opportunities. Travel expenses paid by TLF. Visit Website for application.

**Amount of award:** $5,000-$10,000
**Number of awards:** 20
**Number of applicants:** 150
**Application deadline:** February 24
**Notification begins:** April 15
**Total amount awarded:** $125,000

**Contact:**
The Lagrant Foundation
600 Wilshire Boulevard, Suite 1520
Los Angeles, CA 90017-3247
Phone: 323-469-8680
Fax: 323-469-8683
Web: www.lagrantfoundation.org

# Lambda Alpha National Collegiate Honors Society for Anthropology

## Senior Scholarship

**Type of award:** Scholarship.
**Intended use:** For senior study in United States.
**Eligibility:** Applicant must be U.S. citizen or permanent resident.
**Basis for selection:** Major/career interest in anthropology. Applicant must demonstrate high academic achievement and seriousness of purpose.
**Application requirements:** Recommendations, transcript, nomination by faculty sponsor from department of anthropology. Curriculum vitae, writing sample.
**Additional information:** Applicant must be member of Lambda Alpha. Institution must have a chartered Lambda Alpha chapter. Apply in senior year.

| | |
|---|---|
| **Amount of award:** | $5,000 |
| **Number of awards:** | 1 |
| **Number of applicants:** | 16 |
| **Application deadline:** | March 1 |
| **Notification begins:** | May 1 |
| **Total amount awarded:** | $5,000 |

**Contact:**
Lambda Alpha National Collegiate Honors Society for Anthropology
Department of Anthropology, Attn: B.K. Swartz
Ball State University
Muncie, IN 47306-0435
Phone: 765-285-5297
Web: www.lambdaalpha.com

# Landscape Architecture Foundation

## ASLA Council of Fellows Scholarship

**Type of award:** Scholarship.
**Intended use:** For junior or senior study at accredited 4-year institution in United States.
**Eligibility:** Applicant must be U.S. citizen or permanent resident.
**Basis for selection:** Applicant must demonstrate financial need.
**Application requirements:** Recommendations, essay. Photo in jpg format; two letters of recommendation, at least one from a faculty member, 500-word essay about how applicant will contribute to the profession of landscape architecture; 250-word statement describing financial need; SAR.
**Additional information:** Two scholarships awarded; one specifically available to students of under-represented populations. Applicants seeking consideration for diversity scholarship should indicate specific cultural or ethnic group. Each winner will receive a one-year student ASLA membership and airfare to attend ASLA meeting where award is presented.

| | |
|---|---|
| **Amount of award:** | $4,000 |
| **Number of awards:** | 2 |
| **Application deadline:** | February 15 |
| **Total amount awarded:** | $8,000 |

**Contact:**
Landscape Architecture Foundation
818 18th Street
Suite 810
Washington, DC 20006
Phone: 202-331-7070
Fax: 202-898-1185
Web: www.lafoundation.org

## Courtland Paul Scholarship

**Type of award:** Scholarship.
**Intended use:** For junior or senior study at accredited postsecondary institution. Designated institutions: Schools accredited by the Landscape Architecture Accreditation Board.
**Eligibility:** Applicant must be U.S. citizen.
**Basis for selection:** Major/career interest in landscape architecture. Applicant must demonstrate financial need and seriousness of purpose.
**Application requirements:** Recommendations, essay. Cover sheet, personal profile.
**Additional information:** All application materials must be sent together in one email, except for the recommendation letters which must be sent by email from the author. Minimum 'C' GPA. Award must be used for tuition and/or books within the school year of the award.

| | |
|---|---|
| **Amount of award:** | $5,000 |
| **Number of awards:** | 1 |
| **Number of applicants:** | 37 |
| **Application deadline:** | February 15 |

**Contact:**
Landscape Architecture Foundation
818 18th Street
Suite 810
Washington, DC 20006
Phone: 202-331-7070
Fax: 202-898-1185
Web: www.lafoundation.org

## David T. Woolsey Scholarship

**Type of award:** Scholarship.
**Intended use:** For full-time junior, senior or graduate study at accredited 4-year or graduate institution.
**Eligibility:** Applicant must be permanent resident residing in Hawaii.
**Basis for selection:** Major/career interest in landscape architecture. Applicant must demonstrate service orientation.
**Application requirements:** Recommendations, essay. Photo. Cover Letter. Three 8.5 x 11 work samples as jpg or pdf. Personal profile, proof of Hawaii residency.
**Additional information:** Applicant must be enrolled in landscape architecture program at accredited college or university. Visit Website for more information.

| | |
|---|---|
| **Amount of award:** | $2,000 |
| **Number of awards:** | 1 |
| **Application deadline:** | February 15 |

**Contact:**
Landscape Architecture Foundation
818 18th Street
Suite 810
Washington, DC 20006
Phone: 202-331-7070
Fax: 202-898-1185
Web: www.lafoundation.org

## The EDSA Minority Scholarship

**Type of award:** Scholarship.
**Intended use:** For junior, senior or graduate study at postsecondary institution.
**Eligibility:** Applicant must be Alaskan native, Asian American, African American, Mexican American, Hispanic American, Puerto Rican, American Indian or Native Hawaiian/Pacific Islander.
**Basis for selection:** Major/career interest in landscape architecture. Applicant must demonstrate financial need and seriousness of purpose.
**Application requirements:** Recommendations, transcript. Cover letter, personal profile, 500-word essay describing design effort you plan to pursue and its contribution to the advancement of the profession and your ethnic heritage, three work samples (jpg or pdf).
**Additional information:** Visit Website for more information.

| | |
|---|---|
| **Amount of award:** | $5,000 |
| **Number of awards:** | 1 |
| **Number of applicants:** | 7 |
| **Application deadline:** | February 15 |

**Contact:**
Landscape Architecture Foundation
818 18th Street
Suite 810
Washington, DC 20006
Phone: 202-331-7070
Fax: 202-898-1185
Web: www.lafoundation.org

## Landscape Forms Design for People Scholarship

**Type of award:** Scholarship.
**Intended use:** For full-time senior study at postsecondary institution. Designated institutions: Schools with LAAB-accredited program.
**Basis for selection:** Major/career interest in landscape architecture. Applicant must demonstrate financial need and seriousness of purpose.
**Application requirements:** Portfolio, recommendations, transcript. Cover sheet, personal profile, 300-word essay describing qualities essential to great and successful public spaces, three work samples (jpg or pdf).
**Additional information:** Must show proven contribution to design of public spaces that promote social interaction.

| | |
|---|---|
| **Amount of award:** | $3,000 |
| **Number of awards:** | 1 |
| **Number of applicants:** | 17 |
| **Application deadline:** | February 15 |

**Contact:**
Landscape Architecture Foundation
818 18th Street
Suite 810
Washington, DC 20006
Phone: 202-331-7070
Fax: 202-898-1185
Web: www.lafoundation.org

## Peridian International Inc./Rae L. Price FASLA Scholarship

**Type of award:** Scholarship.
**Intended use:** For junior or senior study at postsecondary institution. Designated institutions: UCLA Extension or Cal Poly Pomona.
**Eligibility:** Applicant must be U.S. citizen.
**Basis for selection:** Major/career interest in landscape architecture. Applicant must demonstrate financial need and high academic achievement.
**Application requirements:** Recommendations, essay. Photo in jpg format.
**Additional information:** Award restricted to tuition, books, and program required supplies. Minimum 'B' GPA.

| | |
|---|---|
| **Amount of award:** | $5,000 |
| **Application deadline:** | February 15 |

**Contact:**
Landscape Architecture Foundation
818 18th Street
Suite 810
Washington, DC 20006
Phone: 202-331-7070
Fax: 202-898-1185
Web: www.lafoundation.org

## Rain Bird Intelligent Use of Water Company Scholarship

**Type of award:** Scholarship.
**Intended use:** For full-time junior or senior study at accredited 4-year institution.
**Basis for selection:** Major/career interest in landscape architecture; horticulture; hydrology or urban planning. Applicant must demonstrate high academic achievement.
**Application requirements:** Essay. Photo, personal profile. Cover letter explaining enclosures and interests. 300-word essay stating career goals and how applicant will continue advancement of landscape architecture.
**Additional information:** Visit Website for more information.

| | |
|---|---|
| **Amount of award:** | $2,500 |
| **Number of awards:** | 1 |
| **Number of applicants:** | 30 |
| **Application deadline:** | February 15 |

**Contact:**
Landscape Architecture Foundation
818 18th Street
Suite 810
Washington, DC 20006
Phone: 202-331-7070
Fax: 202-898-1185
Web: www.lafoundation.org

## Steven G. King Play Environments Scholarship

**Type of award:** Scholarship.
**Intended use:** For full-time junior, senior or graduate study. Designated institutions: LAAB-accredited schools.
**Basis for selection:** Major/career interest in landscape architecture. Applicant must demonstrate financial need and seriousness of purpose.
**Application requirements:** Recommendations, transcript. Cover sheet, personal profile, 300- to 500-word essay explaining value of play and of integrating playgrounds into recreation environments, plan or details of play environment of applicant's design (jpg or pdf).

**Additional information:** Must have demonstrated interest in park and playground planning.

| | |
|---|---|
| **Amount of award:** | $5,000 |
| **Number of awards:** | 1 |
| **Number of applicants:** | 9 |
| **Application deadline:** | February 15 |

**Contact:**
Landscape Architecture Foundation
818 18th Street
Suite 810
Washington, DC 20006
Phone: 202-331-7070
Fax: 202-898-1185
Web: www.lafoundation.org

# Latin American Educational Foundation

## Latin American Educational Scholarship

**Type of award:** Scholarship, renewable.
**Intended use:** For full-time undergraduate or non-degree study at accredited postsecondary institution in United States.
**Eligibility:** Applicant must be Mexican American, Hispanic American or Puerto Rican. Applicant must be residing in Colorado.
**Basis for selection:** Applicant must demonstrate financial need, high academic achievement, leadership and service orientation.
**Application requirements:** Recommendations, essay, transcript. Previous year's tax return.
**Additional information:** Minimum 3.0 GPA. SAT/ACT scores required for high school seniors. Must be Hispanic American or actively involved in Hispanic American community. Recipients must fulfill ten hours of community service during the award year. Applicants must reapply each year.

| | |
|---|---|
| **Amount of award:** | $750-$2,000 |
| **Number of awards:** | 100 |
| **Number of applicants:** | 350 |
| **Application deadline:** | March 15 |
| **Notification begins:** | June 15 |
| **Total amount awarded:** | $200,000 |

**Contact:**
Latin American Education Foundation
561 Santa Fe Drive
Denver, CO 80214
Phone: 303-446-0541 ext. 12
Fax: 303-446-0526
Web: www.laef.org

# League of United Latin American Citizens

## GE Foundation/LULAC Scholarship Program

**Type of award:** Scholarship, renewable.
**Intended use:** For full-time sophomore study at accredited 2-year or 4-year institution in United States.
**Eligibility:** Applicant must be Alaskan native, Asian American, African American, Mexican American, Hispanic American, Puerto Rican, American Indian or Native Hawaiian/Pacific Islander. Applicant must be U.S. citizen or permanent resident.
**Basis for selection:** Major/career interest in business or engineering. Applicant must demonstrate high academic achievement, seriousness of purpose and service orientation.
**Application requirements:** Recommendations, essay, transcript, proof of eligibility.
**Additional information:** Must be minority student with minimum 3.25 GPA who is entering sophomore year in the fall. Recipients may be offered temporary summer or internship positions with GE businesses; however, the students are under no obligation to accept GE employment. Application available on Website.

| | |
|---|---|
| **Amount of award:** | $5,000 |
| **Number of awards:** | 11 |
| **Application deadline:** | August 13 |
| **Notification begins:** | August 15 |
| **Total amount awarded:** | $55,000 |

**Contact:**
League of United Latin American Citizens
Attn: GE Scholarship
2000 L Street NW, Suite 610
Washington, DC 20036
Phone: 202-835-9646
Fax: 202-835-9685
Web: www.lnesc.org

## LULAC National Scholarship Fund Honors Awards

**Type of award:** Scholarship.
**Intended use:** For full-time undergraduate or graduate study at accredited vocational, 2-year, 4-year or graduate institution in United States.
**Eligibility:** Applicant must be Mexican American, Hispanic American or Puerto Rican. Applicant must be U.S. citizen or permanent resident.
**Basis for selection:** Applicant must demonstrate high academic achievement.
**Application requirements:** Essay, transcript, proof of eligibility. Verification of admittance to institution. SAT/ACT scores.
**Additional information:** Students are ineligible for scholarship if related to scholarship committee member, council president, or individual contributor to the local funds of the council. Minimum 3.25 GPA. Entering freshmen must have scored at least 23 on ACT or 1100 (reading and math) on SAT. Submit application to local participating LULAC council. See Website for application and list of participating LULAC councils. Local LULAC council may require additional information and personal interview.

| | |
|---|---|
| **Amount of award:** | $500-$2,000 |
| **Application deadline:** | March 31 |
| **Notification begins:** | May 15 |

**Contact:**
League of United Latin American Citizens
2000 L Street NW, Suite 610
Washington, DC 20036
Phone: 202-835-9646
Fax: 202-835-9685
Web: www.lnesc.org

### LULAC National Scholarship Fund National Scholastic Achievement Awards

**Type of award:** Scholarship.
**Intended use:** For full-time undergraduate or graduate study at accredited 2-year, 4-year or graduate institution in United States.
**Eligibility:** Applicant must be Hispanic American. Applicant must be U.S. citizen or permanent resident.
**Basis for selection:** Applicant must demonstrate high academic achievement.
**Application requirements:** Essay, transcript, proof of eligibility. Verification of admittance to institution. SAT/ACT scores.
**Additional information:** Students are ineligible for scholarship if related to scholarship committee member, council president, or individual contributor to the local funds of the council. Entering freshmen must have scored at least 29 on ACT or 1350 (reading and math) on SAT. Minimum 3.5 GPA. Minimum amount of award is $1,000. See Website for list of participating LULAC councils. Local LULAC council may require additional information and personal interview.

| | |
|---|---|
| **Amount of award:** | $2,000 |
| **Application deadline:** | March 31 |
| **Notification begins:** | May 15 |

**Contact:**
League of United Latin American Citizens
2000 L Street NW, Suite 610
Washington, DC 20036
Phone: 202-835-9646
Fax: 202-835-9685
Web: www.lnesc.org

### LULAC National Scholarshp Fund General Awards

**Type of award:** Scholarship.
**Intended use:** For undergraduate or graduate study at accredited vocational, 2-year, 4-year or graduate institution in United States.
**Eligibility:** Applicant must be Mexican American, Hispanic American or Puerto Rican. Applicant must be U.S. citizen or permanent resident.
**Basis for selection:** Applicant must demonstrate financial need, high academic achievement, depth of character, leadership and service orientation.
**Application requirements:** Verification of admittance to institution.
**Additional information:** Academic performance considered, however motivation, sincerity, and integrity will also be considered in selection process. Students are ineligible for scholarship if related to scholarship committee member, council president, or individual contributor to the local funds of the council. Submit application to local participating LULAC council. See Website for application and list of participating councils. Local council may require additional information and personal interview.

| | |
|---|---|
| **Amount of award:** | $250-$1,000 |
| **Application deadline:** | March 31 |
| **Notification begins:** | May 15 |
| **Total amount awarded:** | $750,000 |

**Contact:**
League of United Latin American Citizens
2000 L Street NW, Suite 610
Washington, DC 20036
Phone: 202-835-9646
Fax: 202-835-9685
Web: www.lnesc.org

## Learning for Life

### Captain James J. Regan Memorial Scholarship

**Type of award:** Scholarship.
**Intended use:** For full-time undergraduate study at accredited postsecondary institution.
**Eligibility:** Applicant or parent must be member/participant of Learning for Life. Applicant must be U.S. citizen or permanent resident.
**Basis for selection:** Major/career interest in criminal justice/law enforcement. Applicant must demonstrate high academic achievement, leadership and seriousness of purpose.
**Application requirements:** Essay, transcript, proof of eligibility. Certification from post advisor, head of participating organization, Learning for Life representative. Three letters of recommendation (two from outside of law enforcement). Additional essay (minimum of 250 words) on "How Will Technology Affect Law Enforcement in the 21st Century?" Black-and-white photo (preferably in uniform). Must submit original and four copies of all materials.
**Additional information:** Program open to Learning for Life's Law Enforcement Explorers. Visit Website for application and more information.

| | |
|---|---|
| **Amount of award:** | $500 |
| **Number of awards:** | 2 |
| **Application deadline:** | March 31 |
| **Total amount awarded:** | $1,000 |

**Contact:**
National Law Enforcement Scholarships and Awards
1325 West Walnut Hill Lane
P.O. Box 152079
Irving, TX 75015
Phone: 972-580-2433
Fax: 972-580-2502
Web: www.learning-for-life.org/exploring

### Sheryl A. Horak Law Enforcement Explorer Scholarship

**Type of award:** Scholarship.
**Intended use:** For full-time undergraduate study at accredited 2-year or 4-year institution.
**Eligibility:** Applicant or parent must be member/participant of Learning for Life. Applicant must be high school senior. Applicant must be U.S. citizen or permanent resident.
**Basis for selection:** Major/career interest in criminal justice/law enforcement. Applicant must demonstrate high academic achievement, leadership and service orientation.
**Application requirements:** Transcript. Certification from post advisor, head of participating organization, Learning for Life representative. Three letters of recommendation (two from outside of law enforcement). Essay (500 words minimum) on

"Why I Want to Pursue a Career in Law Enforcement." Black-and-white photo (preferably in uniform). Must submit original and two copies of all materials.
**Additional information:** Program open to Learning for Life's Law Enforcement Explorers. Number of awards granted varies. Visit Website for application and more information.

| | |
|---|---|
| **Amount of award:** | $1,000 |
| **Application deadline:** | March 31 |

**Contact:**
National Law Enforcement Scholarships and Awards
1325 West Walnut Hill Lane
P.O. Box 152079
Irving, TX 75015
Phone: 972-580-2433
Fax: 972-580-2502
Web: www.learning-for-life.org/exploring

# Life and Health Insurance Foundation for Education

## LIFE Lessons Scholarship Program

**Type of award:** Scholarship.
**Intended use:** For undergraduate study at postsecondary institution in United States.
**Eligibility:** Applicant must be at least 17, no older than 24. Applicant must be U.S. citizen or permanent resident.
**Basis for selection:** Competition/talent/interest in writing/journalism, based on 500-word essay or 3-minute video describing how applicant has experienced personal and financial challenges caused by death of parent or legal guardian.
**Application requirements:** Proof of eligibility. Essay of 500 words or 3-minute video describing personal and financial challenges caused by death of a parent.
**Additional information:** Applicant must have experienced the death of a parent or legal guardian. Apply online, or e-mail or call to receive paper application. Employees of Life and Health Insurance Foundation for Education ("LIFE" or "Sponsor"), Weber Shandwick, and their respective parents, affiliates, subsidiaries, and advertising, and promotion agencies, and any such employee's immediate family members and those living in their same households, whether or not related, are not eligible. Applications due in late Feb or early March; visit Website for exact dates.

| | |
|---|---|
| **Amount of award:** | $1,000-$10,000 |
| **Number of awards:** | 59 |
| **Total amount awarded:** | $105,000 |

**Contact:**
Life and Health Insurance Foundation for Education
Attn: Life Lessons Scholarship
1655 North Fort Meyer Drive, Suite 610
Arlington, VA 22209
Phone: 202-464-5000 ext. 4446
Fax: 202-464-5011
Web: www.lifehappens.org/life-lessons

# Liggett-Stashower, Inc.

## David L. Stashower Scholarship

**Type of award:** Scholarship.
**Intended use:** For senior study at 4-year institution. Designated institutions: Ohio colleges and universities.
**Eligibility:** Applicant must be residing in Ohio.
**Basis for selection:** Major/career interest in advertising; graphic arts/design; public relations or communications. Applicant must demonstrate high academic achievement.
**Application requirements:** Recommendations, essay, transcript. Optional: Portfolio of work, writing samples, or other form of appropriate communication.
**Additional information:** Award includes trip to Cleveland in August for awards ceremony at Liggett-Stashower.

| | |
|---|---|
| **Amount of award:** | $2,000 |
| **Number of awards:** | 2 |
| **Number of applicants:** | 23 |
| **Total amount awarded:** | $4,000 |

**Contact:**
Scholarship Award Committee Liggett-Stashower, Inc
LS Brand Building
1240 Huron Road
Cleveland, OH 44115
Phone: 216-348-8500
Web: www.liggett.com

# Lighthouse International

## Lighthouse College-Bound Award

**Type of award:** Scholarship.
**Intended use:** For full-time freshman study at accredited 2-year or 4-year institution in United States.
**Eligibility:** Applicant must be visually impaired. Applicant must be high school senior. Applicant must be U.S. citizen residing in Virginia, Vermont, West Virginia or South Carolina.
**Basis for selection:** Applicant must demonstrate high academic achievement.
**Application requirements:** Recommendations, essay, transcript, proof of eligibility. Official documentation of legal blindness. Recommendations required from two people other than family members. Personal essay should be 400-600 words. Letter of acceptance to college.
**Additional information:** Applicant must be legally blind. College-bound high school seniors or recent high school graduates now planning to begin college may apply. Must reside in United States or U.S. territory. Previous SCA recipients and Lighthouse members and employees are ineligible. Application deadline in late February or early March; visit Website for exact dates.

| | |
|---|---|
| **Amount of award:** | $10,000 |
| **Number of awards:** | 1 |
| **Number of applicants:** | 65 |
| **Total amount awarded:** | $5,000 |

Scholarships

**Contact:**
Lighthouse International
Scholarship Awards Program
111 East 59 Street
New York, NY 10022-1202
Phone: 212-821-9200
Fax: 212-821-9707
Web: www.lighthouse.org/sca

### Lighthouse Undergraduate Award

**Type of award:** Scholarship.
**Intended use:** For full-time undergraduate study at postsecondary institution in United States.
**Eligibility:** Applicant must be visually impaired. Applicant must be U.S. citizen.
**Basis for selection:** Applicant must demonstrate high academic achievement.
**Application requirements:** Recommendations, essay, transcript, proof of eligibility. Official documentation of legal blindness. Recommendations required from two people other than family members. Personal essay of 400-600 words.
**Additional information:** Applicant must be legally blind. Must reside in United States or U.S. territory. Previous SCA recipients and Lighthouse members and employees are ineligible. Application deadline in late February or early March; visit Website for exact dates.

| | |
|---|---|
| **Amount of award:** | $10,000 |
| **Number of awards:** | 1 |
| **Number of applicants:** | 65 |
| **Total amount awarded:** | $5,000 |

**Contact:**
Lighthouse International
Scholarship Awards Program
111 East 59 Street
New York, NY 10022-1202
Phone: 212-821-9200
Fax: 212-821-9707
Web: www.lighthouse.org

## Los Padres Foundation

### Los Padres Foundation College Tuition Assistance Program

**Type of award:** Scholarship, renewable.
**Intended use:** For full-time undergraduate or graduate study at 4-year or graduate institution in United States.
**Eligibility:** Applicant must be Mexican American, Hispanic American or Puerto Rican. Applicant must be high school senior. Applicant must be U.S. citizen or permanent resident residing in New York or New Jersey.
**Basis for selection:** Applicant must demonstrate financial need, seriousness of purpose and service orientation.
**Additional information:** Primarily for Latin American or Puerto Rican students in New York or New Jersey metropolitan area. Applicant must have minimum 3.0 GPA and proof of low income. Applicant must be first generation in family to attend college. Award is renewable up to four years. Must complete 100 hours of community service by June 1st of first college year. Application available at financial aid office, high school counselor's office, and online.

| | |
|---|---|
| **Amount of award:** | $2,000 |
| **Number of applicants:** | 30 |
| **Application deadline:** | January 12 |

**Contact:**
Los Padres Foundation
CTA Program
P.O. Box 8421
McLean, VA 22106
Phone: 877-843-7555
Fax: 866-810-1361
Web: www.lospadresfoundation.org

### Second Chance Program

**Type of award:** Scholarship.
**Intended use:** For undergraduate study at accredited postsecondary institution.
**Eligibility:** Applicant must be Mexican American, Hispanic American or Puerto Rican. Applicant must be U.S. citizen or permanent resident residing in New York, Puerto Rico or New Jersey.
**Basis for selection:** Applicant must demonstrate financial need.
**Application requirements:** Transcript, proof of eligibility. Proof of low income.
**Additional information:** Applicant must have high school diploma or GED and be out of high school for more than a year prior to submitting and never attended a postsecondary institution. Awardees must complete 100 hours of non-faith-based community service by June 1 of the first year in program. Must meet low-income federal guidelines.

| | |
|---|---|
| **Amount of award:** | $2,000 |
| **Application deadline:** | October 26 |

**Contact:**
Los Padres Foundation
Second Chance Program
P.O. Box 8421
McLean, VA 22106
Phone: 877-843-7555
Fax: 866-810-1361
Web: www.lospadresfoundation.org

## Louisiana Department of Veterans Affairs

### Louisiana Veterans Affairs Educational Assistance for Dependent Children

**Type of award:** Scholarship, renewable.
**Intended use:** For full-time undergraduate, graduate or non-degree study at vocational, 2-year, 4-year or graduate institution. Designated institutions: Louisiana public institutions.
**Eligibility:** Applicant must be at least 16, no older than 25. Applicant must be residing in Louisiana. Applicant must be dependent of disabled veteran or deceased veteran. Deceased veteran must have died of wartime injuries.
**Application requirements:** Proof of eligibility. Certification of eligibility.
**Additional information:** Award is a tuition waiver at all Louisiana state-supported schools. Veteran must have been Louisiana resident for at least two years prior to entering

service. Disability must be at least 90 percent as rated by U.S. Department of Veterans Affairs to qualify. Applicant also eligible if disability rating is 60 percent or more but employability rating is 100 percent unemployable. Waiver available for five year period before applicant turns 25. Award amounts vary.

| | |
|---|---|
| **Amount of award:** | Full tuition |

**Contact:**
Louisiana Department of Veterans Affairs
P.O. Box 94095, Capitol Station
Baton Rouge, LA 70804-9095
Phone: 225-922-0500 ext. 203
Fax: 225-922-0511
Web: www.vetaffairs.la.gov

### Louisiana Veterans Affairs Educational Assistance for Surviving Spouse

**Type of award:** Scholarship, renewable.
**Intended use:** For full-time undergraduate, graduate or non-degree study at postsecondary institution. Designated institutions: Louisiana public institutions.
**Eligibility:** Applicant must be single. Applicant must be residing in Louisiana. Applicant must be spouse of deceased veteran. Veteran must have been a Louisiana resident at least 12 months prior to entering service.
**Application requirements:** Proof of eligibility. Certification of eligibility.

| | |
|---|---|
| **Amount of award:** | Full tuition |

**Contact:**
Louisiana Department of Veterans Affairs
P.O. Box 94095, Capitol Station
Baton Rouge, LA 70804-9095
Phone: 225-922-0500 ext. 203
Fax: 225-922-0511
Web: www.vetaffairs.la.gov

## Louisiana Office of Student Financial Assistance

### Leveraging Educational Assistance Partnership (LEAP)

**Type of award:** Scholarship, renewable.
**Intended use:** For full-time undergraduate study.
**Eligibility:** Applicant must be U.S. citizen or permanent resident residing in Louisiana.
**Basis for selection:** Applicant must demonstrate financial need.
**Application requirements:** FAFSA.
**Additional information:** Must be Louisiana resident for at least one year prior to application. Minimum 2.0 GPA or minimum 45 GED score or 20 ACT score.

| | |
|---|---|
| **Amount of award:** | $200-$2,000 |
| **Number of awards:** | 4,810 |
| **Number of applicants:** | 4,810 |
| **Application deadline:** | July 1 |
| **Total amount awarded:** | $1,950,000 |

**Contact:**
Louisiana Office of Student Financial Assistance
P.O. Box 91202
Baton Rouge, LA 70821-9202
Phone: 225-219-7295
Fax: 225-208-1206
Web: www.osfa.la.gov

### Louisiana Go Grants

**Type of award:** Scholarship, renewable.
**Intended use:** For undergraduate study at postsecondary institution.
**Eligibility:** Applicant must be residing in Louisiana.
**Basis for selection:** Applicant must demonstrate financial need.
**Application requirements:** FAFSA.
**Additional information:** Financial aid for nontraditional and low to moderate income students. Must receive Pell grant to qualify.

| | |
|---|---|
| **Amount of award:** | $200-$2,000 |
| **Number of awards:** | 11,000 |
| **Number of applicants:** | 22,397 |
| **Total amount awarded:** | $26,429,108 |

**Contact:**
Louisiana Office of Student Financial Assistance
P.O. Box 91202
Baton Rouge, LA 70821-9202
Phone: 800-259-5626 ext 1012
Fax: 225-922-0790
Web: www.osfa.la.gov

### Louisiana Rockefeller Wildlife Scholarship

**Type of award:** Scholarship, renewable.
**Intended use:** For full-time undergraduate or graduate study at 4-year or graduate institution.
**Eligibility:** Applicant must be U.S. citizen residing in Louisiana.
**Basis for selection:** Major/career interest in wildlife/fisheries; forestry or oceanography/marine studies. Applicant must demonstrate high academic achievement.
**Application requirements:** FAFSA, Rockefeller State Wildlife Application.
**Additional information:** Minimum 2.5 GPA for undergraduate students or 3.0 for graduate students.

| | |
|---|---|
| **Amount of award:** | $1,000 |
| **Number of awards:** | 60 |
| **Number of applicants:** | 45 |
| **Application deadline:** | July 1 |
| **Total amount awarded:** | $48,669 |

**Contact:**
Louisiana Office of Student Financial Assistance
P.O. Box 91202
Baton Rouge, LA 70821-9202
Phone: 800-259-5626 ext. 1012
Fax: 225-922-0790
Web: www.osfa.la.gov

### Louisiana Taylor Opportunity Program for Students (TOPS) Award

**Type of award:** Scholarship, renewable.
**Intended use:** For full-time undergraduate study at postsecondary institution. Designated institutions: Eligible Louisiana postsecondary institutions.
**Eligibility:** Applicant must be U.S. citizen or permanent resident residing in Louisiana.
**Basis for selection:** Applicant must demonstrate high academic achievement.
**Application requirements:** FAFSA. SAT or ACT scores.
**Additional information:** Open to Louisiana residents who will be first-time, full-time freshmen at Louisiana public or LAICU private postsecondary institutions no later than fall following first anniversary of high school graduation. Must have no criminal convictions. Must have completed 17.5 units college-prep TOPS core curriculum. Individual requirements for awards below; please send one inquiry, only, for all award levels: TOPS OPPORTUNITY AWARD: Equal to tuition at public institution (or weighted average tuition at LAICU member institution). Must have minimum 2.5 GPA, minimum ACT score based on state's prior year average (never below 20) or minimum SAT of 940. TOPS PERFORMANCE AWARDS: Equal to tuition at public institution (or weighted average tuition at LAICU member institution) plus $400/yr stipend. Minimum 3.0 GPA, minimum ACT score of 23 or SAT score of 1050. TOPS HONORS AWARDS: Equal to tuition at public institution (or weighted average tuition at LAICU member institution) plus $800/yr stipend. Minimum 3.0 GPA, ACT score of 27 or SAT score of 1210. Contact Public Information Rep for more details.

| | |
|---|---|
| **Amount of award:** | Full tuition |
| **Number of applicants:** | 30,845 |
| **Application deadline:** | July 1 |
| **Notification begins:** | June 1 |
| **Total amount awarded:** | $130,005,445 |

**Contact:**
Louisiana Office of Student Financial Assistance
P.O. Box 91202
Baton Rouge, LA 70821-9202
Phone: 800-259-5626 ext. 1012
Fax: 225-922-0790
Web: www.osfa.la.gov

## Louisiana State Department of Education

### Robert C. Byrd Honors Scholarship

**Type of award:** Scholarship, renewable.
**Intended use:** For full-time undergraduate study at vocational, 2-year or 4-year institution.
**Eligibility:** Applicant must be U.S. citizen or permanent resident residing in Louisiana.
**Basis for selection:** Applicant must demonstrate high academic achievement.
**Application requirements:** Proof of eligibility. FAFSA.
**Additional information:** Minimum 3.5 GPA and 23 ACT or 970 SAT score (reading and math) or 620 GED score. Must have received high school diploma or GED in Louisiana. Award amount varies; maximum is $1,500 per year, renewable for up to four years. Must be registered with the Selective Service, if required. Students at military academies not eligible. Award may be used for tuition for schools outside Louisiana.

| | |
|---|---|
| **Amount of award:** | $1,500 |

**Contact:**
Louisiana State Department of Education
P.O. Box 94064
Baton Rouge, LA 70804
Phone: 225-342-2098 or 877-453-2721
Fax: 225-342-3432
Web: www.doe.state.la.us/lde/students.html

## Maine Division of Veterans Services

### Maine Veterans Services Dependents Educational Benefits

**Type of award:** Scholarship.
**Intended use:** For undergraduate or master's study at vocational, 2-year or 4-year institution.
**Eligibility:** Applicant must be at least 16, no older than 26. Applicant must be residing in Maine. Applicant must be dependent of disabled veteran; or spouse of disabled veteran. Must apply for program prior to 22nd birthday, or before 26th birthday if applicant was enrolled in the U.S. Armed Forces. Age limits apply to child applicants only, not spouses.
**Application requirements:** Proof of eligibility. Proof of veteran's disability, birth certificate. Stepchildren must provide parent's marriage certificate. Adopted children must provide adoption certificate or proof of paternity to natural parent. Spouse must provide marriage certificate.
**Additional information:** Applicant must have graduated from high school and must be dependent of permanently and totally disabled veteran. Veteran must have been resident of Maine prior to enlistment or resident of Maine for five years preceding application for aid. Provides tuition at all branches of University of Maine system, all State of Maine vocational-technical colleges, and Maine Maritime Academy for eight semesters to be used within six years. Must maintain "C" average to continue receiving benefits. Award must be used within ten years.

| | |
|---|---|
| **Amount of award:** | Full tuition |

**Contact:**
Maine Division of Veterans Services
117 State House Station
Augusta, ME 04333-0117
Phone: 207-626-4464
Fax: 207-626-4471
Web: www.mainebvs.org

## Maine Innkeepers Association

### Maine Innkeepers Association Scholarship

**Type of award:** Scholarship.
**Intended use:** For full-time undergraduate or graduate study at accredited vocational, 4-year or graduate institution in United

States. Designated institutions: Institutions with fully accredited programs in hotel administration or culinary arts.
**Eligibility:** Applicant must be U.S. citizen or permanent resident residing in Maine.
**Basis for selection:** Major/career interest in culinary arts; hotel/restaurant management or hospitality administration/ management. Applicant must demonstrate financial need and high academic achievement.
**Application requirements:** Recommendations, essay, transcript.
**Additional information:** Applicant must be Maine resident who is high school senior or college undergraduate. Deadline in early April; visit Website for exact date.

| | |
|---|---|
| **Amount of award:** | $500-$2,500 |
| **Number of awards:** | 11 |
| **Number of applicants:** | 30 |
| **Application deadline:** | April 8 |
| **Notification begins:** | January 1 |
| **Total amount awarded:** | $9,200 |

**Contact:**
Maine Innkeepers Association
Scholarship Chairperson
304 US Route 1
Freeport, ME 04032
Phone: 207-865-6100
Fax: 207-865-6120
Web: www.maineinns.com

# Maine Metal Products Association Education Fund

## Maine Metal Products Association Scholarship

**Type of award:** Scholarship.
**Intended use:** For undergraduate study at postsecondary institution.
**Eligibility:** Applicant must be permanent resident residing in Maine.
**Basis for selection:** Major/career interest in engineering; welding or manufacturing. Applicant must demonstrate financial need, high academic achievement, depth of character, leadership, seriousness of purpose and service orientation.
**Application requirements:** Recommendations, essay, transcript, proof of eligibility.
**Additional information:** Applicant must have career interest in Maine precision machining technology or manufacturing technology industry or related majors. Amount of award varies based on need and fund account. Visit Website for more information.

| | |
|---|---|
| **Number of applicants:** | 12 |
| **Application deadline:** | May 1 |
| **Total amount awarded:** | $8,350 |

**Contact:**
Angel Kimball
Manufacturers Association of Maine
386 Bridgton Road
Westbrook, ME 04092
Phone: 207-854-2153
Fax: 207-854-3865
Web: www.mainemfg.com

# Maine Restaurant Association

## Russ Casey Scholarship

**Type of award:** Scholarship.
**Intended use:** For undergraduate or graduate study at accredited 2-year, 4-year or graduate institution. Designated institutions: New England colleges and universities.
**Eligibility:** Applicant must be U.S. citizen residing in Maine.
**Basis for selection:** Major/career interest in culinary arts.
**Application requirements:** Transcript. Two recommendations from high school or college teachers, one from restaurant owner/manager or allied member of Maine Restaurant Association. Cover letter detailing applicant's interest in and connection to food service industry in 300 words or less.
**Additional information:** Open to Maine students pursuing career in food service industry.

| | |
|---|---|
| **Amount of award:** | $1,000-$1,500 |
| **Number of awards:** | 8 |
| **Application deadline:** | April 1 |
| **Total amount awarded:** | $10,000 |

**Contact:**
Chairman, Scholarship Committee Maine Restaurant Association
P.O. Box 5060
5 Wade Street
Augusta, ME 04332
Phone: 207-623-2178
Fax: 207-623-8377
Web: www.mainerestaurant.com

# Maine Society of Professional Engineers

## Maine Society of Professional Engineers Scholarship Program

**Type of award:** Scholarship.
**Intended use:** For freshman study at 4-year institution in United States. Designated institutions: ABET-accredited engineering schools.
**Eligibility:** Applicant must be high school senior. Applicant must be permanent resident residing in Maine.
**Basis for selection:** Major/career interest in engineering or engineering, civil.
**Application requirements:** Recommendations, essay, transcript. SAT/ACT scores.
**Additional information:** Applicant must intend to earn a degree in engineering and to enter the practice of engineering after graduation. Must go to ABET-accredited school. Money awarded only after successful completion of first semester. Must be resident of Maine but awardees do not have to attend school in Maine.

| | |
|---|---|
| **Amount of award:** | $1,500-$2,500 |
| **Number of awards:** | 2 |
| **Number of applicants:** | 40 |
| **Application deadline:** | March 1 |
| **Notification begins:** | May 30 |
| **Total amount awarded:** | $5,000 |

**Contact:**
Colon Hewett
Maine Society of Professional Engineers
P.O. Box 318
Winthrop, ME 04364
Phone: 207-449-0339
Web: www.mespe.org

# Maine State Society of Washington, DC

## Maine State Society of Washington, DC, Foundation Scholarship Program

**Type of award:** Scholarship.
**Intended use:** For full-time sophomore, junior or senior study at accredited 4-year institution. Designated institutions: Maine institutions.
**Eligibility:** Applicant must be no older than 25. Applicant must be U.S. citizen.
**Basis for selection:** Applicant must demonstrate high academic achievement and seriousness of purpose.
**Application requirements:** Portfolio, essay, transcript, proof of eligibility.
**Additional information:** Applicant must have been born in Maine or have been legal resident of Maine for at least four years or have at least one parent who was born in Maine or who has been legal resident of Maine for at least four years. Applicant must currently attend college in Maine, with a minimum GPA of 3.0 for latest academic year. Requests for applications must include SASE. Visit Website for application.

| | |
|---|---|
| **Amount of award:** | $1,000 |
| **Number of applicants:** | 79 |
| **Application deadline:** | April 1 |
| **Notification begins:** | May 15 |
| **Total amount awarded:** | $12,500 |

**Contact:**
Maine State Society of Washington DC Foundation Scholarship Program
4718 Columbia Road
Annandale, VA 22003
Phone: 703-256-4524
Web: www.mainestatesociety.org/MSSFoundation.htm

# Manomet Center for Conservation Sciences

## Kathleen S. Anderson Award

**Type of award:** Research grant.
**Intended use:** For junior, senior or graduate study in or outside United States. Designated institutions: Institutions in Western Hemisphere.
**Basis for selection:** Major/career interest in ornithology. Applicant must demonstrate leadership and seriousness of purpose.
**Application requirements:** Recommendations, research proposal.
**Additional information:** Research grant: Either one $1,000 award or two $500 awards. Kathleen Anderson is asked to choose winner from five finalists submitted by Manomet staff. Apply via email only.

| | |
|---|---|
| **Amount of award:** | $500-$1,000 |
| **Number of awards:** | 2 |
| **Number of applicants:** | 20 |
| **Application deadline:** | December 1 |
| **Notification begins:** | March 1 |
| **Total amount awarded:** | $1,000 |

**Contact:**
Manomet Center for Conservation Sciences
c/o Jennie Robbins
P.O. Box 1770
Manomet, MA 02345
Phone: 508-224-6521
Fax: 508-224-9220
Web: www.manomet.org

# Marine Corps Scholarship Foundation

## Marine Corps Scholarship

**Type of award:** Scholarship, renewable.
**Intended use:** For undergraduate study at accredited vocational, 2-year or 4-year institution in United States.
**Eligibility:** Applicant must be U.S. citizen. Applicant must be dependent of active service person or veteran in the Marines. Must be child of active Marine, Marine reservist, or Marine who has received honorable discharge.
**Basis for selection:** Applicant must demonstrate financial need.
**Application requirements:** Essay, transcript, proof of eligibility. FAFSA, Tax return.
**Additional information:** Gross family income must not exceed $86,000. Open to high school seniors and undergraduates attending post-high school vocational/technical institutions.

| | |
|---|---|
| **Amount of award:** | $500-$10,000 |
| **Number of awards:** | 1,000 |
| **Number of applicants:** | 1,405 |
| **Application deadline:** | March 1 |
| **Total amount awarded:** | $3,500,000 |

**Contact:**
Marine Corps Scholarship Foundation
121 S. Afaph Street
Alexandria, VA 22314
Phone: 800-292-7777 or 703-549-2977
Fax: 703-549-9474
Web: www.mcsf.org

# Maryland Higher Education Commission Office of Student Financial Assistance

## Charles W. Riley Fire and Emergency Medical Services Tuition Reimbursement Program

**Type of award:** Scholarship, renewable.
**Intended use:** For undergraduate study at postsecondary institution.

**Eligibility:** Applicant must be U.S. citizen or permanent resident residing in Maryland.
**Basis for selection:** Major/career interest in fire science/technology or medical emergency.
**Application requirements:** Transcript, proof of eligibility.
**Additional information:** Applicant must be active career/volunteer firefighter or ambulance/rescue squad member serving the Maryland community while taking courses, and must agree to continue to serve for one year after completing courses. Must maintain satisfactory academic progress and remain enrolled in eligible program to renew award.

| | |
|---|---|
| **Amount of award:** | Full tuition |
| **Number of awards:** | 108 |
| **Number of applicants:** | 207 |
| **Application deadline:** | July 1 |
| **Total amount awarded:** | $340,979 |

**Contact:**
Maryland Higher Ed. Commission Office of Student Financial Assistance
Reimbursement of Firefighters
839 Bestgate Road, Suite 400
Annapolis, MD 21401-3013
Phone: 800-974-1024
Fax: 410-260-3200
Web: www.mhec.state.md.us/financialaid/descriptions

## Howard P. Rawlings Guaranteed Access Grant

**Type of award:** Scholarship, renewable.
**Intended use:** For full-time undergraduate study at accredited postsecondary institution.
**Eligibility:** Applicant must be high school senior. Applicant must be U.S. citizen or permanent resident residing in Maryland.
**Basis for selection:** Applicant must demonstrate financial need.
**Application requirements:** Proof of eligibility. FAFSA.
**Additional information:** Applicant must be high school senior who has completed college preparatory program or has graduated prior to the academic year and provide written documentation explaining why he or she was unable to attend college within one year of graduation from high school. Minimum 2.5 GPA. Must meet Guaranteed Access Family Grant income requirements; award equals 100% of student's financial need.

| | |
|---|---|
| **Amount of award:** | $400-$13,700 |
| **Number of awards:** | 1,156 |
| **Number of applicants:** | 2,808 |
| **Application deadline:** | March 1 |
| **Total amount awarded:** | $10,862,060 |

**Contact:**
Maryland Higher Ed. Commission Office of Student Financial Assistance
Guaranteed Access Grant
839 Bestgate Road, Suite 400
Annapolis, MD 21401-3103
Phone: 800-974-1024
Fax: 410-260-3200
Web: www.mhec.state.md.us/financialaid/descriptions

## Maryland Delegate Scholarship

**Type of award:** Scholarship, renewable.
**Intended use:** For undergraduate or graduate study at vocational, 2-year, 4-year or graduate institution.
**Eligibility:** Applicant must be high school senior. Applicant must be U.S. citizen or permanent resident residing in Maryland.
**Application requirements:** Proof of eligibility, nomination by local state delegate. FAFSA.
**Additional information:** Applicant's parents (if applicant is dependent) must be Maryland residents. Rolling application deadline. Certain vocational programs eligible. Out-of-state institutions eligible only if major not offered in Maryland. Each state delegate makes awards to students. If OSFA makes awards for delegates, applicant must demonstrate financial need. Non-U.S. citizens living in Maryland may be eligible. Applicants must reapply yearly for renewal and maintain satisfactory academic progress.

| | |
|---|---|
| **Amount of award:** | $200-$19,000 |
| **Number of awards:** | 5,510 |
| **Notification begins:** | July 1 |
| **Total amount awarded:** | $4,736,357 |

**Contact:**
Maryland Higher Ed. Commission Office of Student Financial Assistance
Delegate Scholarship
839 Bestgate Road, Suite 400
Annapolis, MD 21401-3013
Phone: 800-974-1024
Fax: 410-260-3200
Web: www.mhec.state.md.us/financialaid/descriptions

## Maryland Distinguished Scholar: Achievement

**Type of award:** Scholarship, renewable.
**Intended use:** For full-time undergraduate study at 2-year or 4-year institution. Designated institutions: Eligible Maryland institutions.
**Eligibility:** Applicant must be high school junior. Applicant must be U.S. citizen or permanent resident residing in Maryland.
**Basis for selection:** Applicant must demonstrate high academic achievement.
**Application requirements:** Transcript, nomination by high school. SAT scores from tests taken in January of junior year or earlier. PSAT or ACT scores may be submitted if student has not taken SAT 1.
**Additional information:** Applicant's parents (if applicant is dependent) must be Maryland residents. Applications must be submitted to high school guidance office in February of junior year. Guidance counselor submits talent nominations in March. Applicant must have minimum 3.7 GPA. Students not funded initially will be placed on waiting list; funds may not be available to award all eligible students. Award automatically renewed up to three additional years if annual minimum 3.0 GPA and other eligibility requirements maintained.

| | |
|---|---|
| **Amount of award:** | $3,000 |
| **Number of awards:** | 1,245 |
| **Number of applicants:** | 5,227 |
| **Notification begins:** | June 30 |
| **Total amount awarded:** | $3,638,250 |

**Contact:**
Maryland Higher Ed. Commission Office of Student Financial Assistance
Distinguished Scholar Program
839 Bestgate Road, Suite 400
Annapolis, MD 21401-3013
Phone: 800-974-1024
Fax: 410-260-3200
Web: www.mhec.state.md.us/financialaid/descriptions

## Maryland Distinguished Scholar: National Merit and National Achievement Finalists

**Type of award:** Scholarship, renewable.
**Intended use:** For full-time undergraduate study at 2-year or 4-year institution in United States. Designated institutions: Eligible Maryland institutions.
**Eligibility:** Applicant must be high school junior. Applicant must be U.S. citizen or permanent resident residing in Maryland.
**Basis for selection:** Applicant must demonstrate high academic achievement.
**Additional information:** Applicant's parents (if applicant is dependent) must be Maryland residents. Applicant must be National Merit Finalist or National Achievement Finalist. Award automatically offered to students in these scholarship programs when they have been selected as finalists and indicate they will attend a Maryland institution. Award automatically renewed up to three additional years if annual minimum 3.0 GPA and other eligibility requirements maintained.

| | |
|---|---|
| **Amount of award:** | $3,000 |
| **Number of awards:** | 1,245 |
| **Number of applicants:** | 5,227 |
| **Total amount awarded:** | $3,638,250 |

**Contact:**
Maryland Higher Ed. Commission Office of Student Financial Assistance
Distinguished Scholar Program
839 Bestgate Road, Suite 400
Annapolis, MD 21401-3013
Phone: 800-974-1024
Fax: 410-260-3200
Web: www.mhec.state.md.us/financialaid/descriptions

## Maryland Distinguished Scholar: Talent in the Arts

**Type of award:** Scholarship, renewable.
**Intended use:** For full-time undergraduate study at 2-year or 4-year institution. Designated institutions: Eligible Maryland schools.
**Eligibility:** Applicant must be high school junior. Applicant must be U.S. citizen or permanent resident residing in Maryland.
**Basis for selection:** Competition/talent/interest in performing arts. Major/career interest in performing arts; theater arts or music. Applicant must demonstrate high academic achievement.
**Application requirements:** Audition, nomination by designated magnet high schools in spring of junior year. Audition or portfolio review.
**Additional information:** Awards for dance, drama, visual arts, and vocal and instrumental music. Winners determined by panel of judges. Applicant's parents (if applicant is dependent) must be Maryland residents. Students not funded initially will be placed on waiting list; funds may not be available to award all eligible students. Award automatically renewed if annual minimum 3.0 GPA and other eligibility requirements maintained.

| | |
|---|---|
| **Amount of award:** | $3,000 |
| **Number of awards:** | 1,245 |
| **Number of applicants:** | 5,227 |
| **Total amount awarded:** | $3,638,250 |

**Contact:**
Maryland Higher Ed. Commission Office of Student Financial Assistance
Distinguished Scholar Program
839 Bestgate Road, Suite 400
Annapolis, MD 21401-3013
Phone: 800-974-1024
Fax: 410-260-3200
Web: www.mhec.state.md.us/financialaid/descriptions

## Maryland Educational Assistance Grant

**Type of award:** Scholarship, renewable.
**Intended use:** For full-time undergraduate study at 2-year or 4-year institution. Designated institutions: Maryland institutions.
**Eligibility:** Applicant must be U.S. citizen or permanent resident residing in Maryland.
**Basis for selection:** Applicant must demonstrate financial need.
**Application requirements:** Proof of eligibility.
**Additional information:** Applicant's parents (if applicant is dependent) must be Maryland resident. Applicants are ranked by Expected Family Contribution (EFC); those with lowest EFC are awarded first. Award may be renewed if eligibility maintained and FAFSA is submitted by March 1 each year. Funds may not be available to award all eligible students each year.

| | |
|---|---|
| **Amount of award:** | $400-$3,000 |
| **Number of awards:** | 28,219 |
| **Number of applicants:** | 103,000 |
| **Application deadline:** | March 1 |
| **Notification begins:** | April 15 |
| **Total amount awarded:** | $63,234,000 |

**Contact:**
Maryland Higher Ed. Commission Office of Student Financial Assistance
Educational Assistance Grant
839 Bestgate Road, Suite 400
Annapolis, MD 21401-3013
Phone: 800-974-1024
Fax: 410-260-3200
Web: www.mhec.state.md.us/financialaid/descriptions

## Maryland Edward T. Conroy Memorial Scholarship Program

**Type of award:** Scholarship, renewable.
**Intended use:** For undergraduate or graduate study at postsecondary institution. Designated institutions: Eligible Maryland institutions.
**Eligibility:** Applicant must be U.S. citizen. Applicant must be veteran or disabled while on active duty; or dependent of veteran, disabled veteran or deceased veteran; or spouse of disabled veteran, deceased veteran or POW/MIA who served in the Army during Vietnam. If applicant is dependent of disabled US Armed Forces veteran, the veteran must be declared 100% disabled as direct result of military service. Applicant may also be dependent or surviving spouse of victim of September 11, 2001 attacks. Also open to dependent or surviving spouse (not remarried) of Maryland resident who was public safety employee or volunteer who died or was 100% disabled in the line of duty.
**Additional information:** Must be Maryland resident unless spouse or child of Maryland state or local public safety employee killed in line of duty. Parent, veteran, POW, public

safety employee, or volunteer specified above must have been resident of Maryland at time of death or when declared disabled. Amount of award may be equal to tuition and fees, but may not exceed $9,000. Visit Website for more information and application.

**Amount of award:** $9,000
**Number of awards:** 121
**Number of applicants:** 72
**Application deadline:** July 15
**Total amount awarded:** $649,392

**Contact:**
Maryland Higher Ed. Commission Office of Student Financial Assistance
Edward T. Conroy Memorial Grant Program
839 Bestgate Road, Suite 400
Annapolis, MD 21401-3013
Phone: 800-974-1024
Fax: 410-260-3200
Web: www.mhec.state.md.us/financialaid/descriptions

## Maryland Jack F. Tolbert Memorial Grant

**Type of award:** Scholarship, renewable.
**Intended use:** For full-time undergraduate study at vocational institution. Designated institutions: Private career schools in Maryland.
**Eligibility:** Applicant must be U.S. citizen or permanent resident residing in Maryland.
**Basis for selection:** Applicant must demonstrate financial need.
**Application requirements:** Nomination by financial aid counselor at private career school. FAFSA.
**Additional information:** Applicant's parents (if applicant is dependent) must be Maryland residents. Applicant must enroll for minimum of 18 hours per week. Award amount varies; maximum is $500.

**Amount of award:** $500
**Number of awards:** 522
**Application deadline:** March 1
**Total amount awarded:** $261,000

**Contact:**
Maryland Higher Ed. Commission Office of Student Financial Assistance
Jack F. Tolbert Memorial Grant
839 Bestgate Road, Suite 400
Annapolis, MD 21401-3013
Phone: 800-974-0203
Fax: 410-260-3200
Web: www.mhec.state.md.us/financialaid/descriptions

## Maryland Part-Time Grant Program

**Type of award:** Scholarship, renewable.
**Intended use:** For half-time undergraduate study at accredited postsecondary institution. Designated institutions: Accredited institutions in Maryland.
**Eligibility:** Applicant must be enrolled in high school. Applicant must be residing in Maryland.
**Basis for selection:** Applicant must demonstrate financial need.
**Additional information:** Applicant's parents (if applicant is dependent) must be Maryland residents. Must be taking 6 to 11 semester credit hours. Apply through financial aid office of Maryland institution. Applicants simultaneously enrolled in secondary school and an institution of higher education are also eligible. To renew award, student must maintain satisfactory academic progress and submit FAFSA by March 1 each year; may receive award up to eight years.

**Amount of award:** $200-$2,000
**Number of awards:** 8,667
**Application deadline:** March 1
**Total amount awarded:** $5,964,385

**Contact:**
Maryland Higher Ed. Commission Office of Student Financial Assistance
Part-Time Grant Program
839 Bestgate Road, Suite 400
Annapolis, MD 21401-3013
Phone: 800-974-1024
Fax: 410-260-3200
Web: www.mhec.state.md.us/financialaid/descriptions

## Maryland Senatorial Scholarship

**Type of award:** Scholarship, renewable.
**Intended use:** For undergraduate or graduate study at postsecondary institution. Designated institutions: Maryland colleges and universities.
**Eligibility:** Applicant must be residing in Maryland.
**Basis for selection:** Applicant must demonstrate financial need.
**Application requirements:** Nomination by local state senator. FAFSA.
**Additional information:** Applicant and parents (if applicant is dependent) must be Maryland residents. SAT or ACT required for freshmen at four-year institutions unless applicant graduated from high school five years prior to aid application or has earned 24 college credit hours. Out-of-state institutions eligible only if major not offered in Maryland. Contact state senator's office for more information. Award automatically renewed if satisfactory academic progress is maintained. Full-time students may be awarded four years total, part-time students eight years total.

**Amount of award:** $400-$9,000
**Number of awards:** 6,874
**Application deadline:** March 1
**Total amount awarded:** $5,769,725

**Contact:**
Maryland Higher Ed. Commission Office of Student Financial Assistance
Senatorial Scholarship Program
839 Bestgate Road, Suite 400
Annapolis, MD 21401-3013
Phone: 800-974-1024
Fax: 410-260-3200
Web: www.mhec.state.md.us/financialaid/descriptions

## Maryland Tuition Reduction for Non-Resident Nursing Students

**Type of award:** Scholarship, renewable.
**Intended use:** For undergraduate study at postsecondary institution.
**Eligibility:** Applicant must be U.S. citizen.
**Basis for selection:** Major/career interest in nursing.
**Additional information:** Must be resident of state other than Maryland and accepted into Maryland degree-granting nursing program at two- or four-year public institution. Awardees fulfill service obligation in Maryland following graduation; two years for two-year program, four years for four-year program. Service must begin within six months of graduation. Award amount varies; college may reduce tuition so that non-residents pay tuition charged to Maryland resident.

**Number of applicants:** 51

**Contact:**
Maryland Higher Ed. Commission Office of Student Financial Assistance
Out-of-State Nursing Program
839 Bestgate Road, Suite 400
Annapolis, MD 21401-3013
Phone: 800-974-1024
Fax: 410-260-3200
Web: www.mhec.state.md.us/financialaid/descriptions

### Tuition Waiver for Foster Care Recipients

**Type of award:** Scholarship, renewable.
**Intended use:** For undergraduate study at 2-year or 4-year institution. Designated institutions: Eligible Maryland public institutions.
**Eligibility:** Applicant must be no older than 20. Applicant must be residing in Maryland.
**Application requirements:** FAFSA.
**Additional information:** Applicant must have resided in Maryland foster care home at time of high school graduation or completion of GED. Also open to applicants who resided in Maryland foster care home on 14th birthday and were subsequently adopted. The Department of Human Resources must confirm applicant's eligibility. Applicant must be enrolled as a degree-seeking student before age of 21. Award renewal possible if satisfactory academic progress and enrollment in eligible program maintained.

| | |
|---|---|
| **Amount of award:** | Full tuition |
| **Application deadline:** | March 1 |

**Contact:**
Maryland Higher Ed. Commission Office of Student Financial Assistance
839 Bestgate Road, Suite 400
Annapolis, MD 21401-3013
Phone: 800-974-1024
Fax: 410-260-3200
Web: www.mhec.state.md.us/financialaid/descriptions

## Massachusetts Board of Higher Education

### Massachusetts Christian A. Herter Memorial Scholarship Program

**Type of award:** Scholarship, renewable.
**Intended use:** For full-time undergraduate study at accredited vocational, 2-year or 4-year institution. Designated institutions: Massachusetts institutions.
**Eligibility:** Applicant must be high school sophomore or junior. Applicant must be U.S. citizen or permanent resident residing in Massachusetts.
**Basis for selection:** Applicant must demonstrate financial need, depth of character and seriousness of purpose.
**Application requirements:** Interview, recommendations, essay, transcript, nomination by high school principal, counselor, teacher, or social service agency.
**Additional information:** Program provides grant assistance for students from low income or disadvantaged backgrounds who have had to overcome adverse circumstances. Selection made during sophomore and junior years in high school. Award amount is up to half of student's demonstrated financial need. Minimum 2.5 GPA.

| | |
|---|---|
| **Amount of award:** | $15,000 |
| **Number of awards:** | 25 |
| **Number of applicants:** | 200 |
| **Application deadline:** | April 1 |
| **Total amount awarded:** | $900,000 |

**Contact:**
Office of Student Financial Assistance
Massachusetts Board of Higher Education
454 Broadway, Suite 200
Revere, MA 02151
Phone: 617-727-9420
Fax: 617-727-0667
Web: www.osfa.mass.edu

### Massachusetts Gilbert Matching Student Grant

**Type of award:** Scholarship, renewable.
**Intended use:** For full-time undergraduate study at accredited 2-year or 4-year institution. Designated institutions: Independent colleges or hospital schools of nursing in Massachusetts.
**Eligibility:** Applicant must be U.S. citizen or permanent resident residing in Massachusetts.
**Basis for selection:** Major/career interest in nursing. Applicant must demonstrate financial need.
**Additional information:** Deadline depends on institution. Applicant must be dependent of parent who has been a Massachusetts resident for at least 12 months prior to start of academic year. Must not have received prior bachelor's degree.

| | |
|---|---|
| **Amount of award:** | $200-$2,500 |
| **Total amount awarded:** | $18,600,000 |

**Contact:**
Apply to college financial aid office.
Phone: 617-727-9420
Fax: 617-727-0667
Web: www.osfa.mass.edu

### Massachusetts MASSgrant Program

**Type of award:** Scholarship, renewable.
**Intended use:** For full-time undergraduate study at accredited vocational, 2-year or 4-year institution. Designated institutions: Schools in Massachusetts, Connecticut, Maine, New Hampshire, Vermont, Rhode Island, Pennsylvania or Washington, DC.
**Eligibility:** Applicant must be U.S. citizen or permanent resident residing in Vermont, Maine, Pennsylvania, Massachusetts, District of Columbia, Connecticut, New Hampshire or Rhode Island.
**Basis for selection:** Applicant must demonstrate financial need.
**Application requirements:** FAFSA.
**Additional information:** Applicant must have expected family contribution of $5,273 or less and be eligible for Title IV financial aid. Applicant must maintain satisfactory academic progress. Must not have received prior bachelor's degree. Award amount varies.

| | |
|---|---|
| **Number of awards:** | 28,553 |
| **Number of applicants:** | 250,000 |
| **Application deadline:** | May 1 |
| **Notification begins:** | June 15 |
| **Total amount awarded:** | $24,000,000 |

**Contact:**
Office of Student Financial Assistance
Massachusetts Board of Higher Education
454 Broadway, Suite 200
Revere, MA 02151
Phone: 617-727-9420
Fax: 617-727-0667
Web: www.osfa.mass.edu

## Massachusetts Public Service Grant Program

**Type of award:** Scholarship, renewable.
**Intended use:** For full-time undergraduate study at accredited 2-year or 4-year institution. Designated institutions: Massachusetts colleges and universities.
**Eligibility:** Applicant must be U.S. citizen or permanent resident residing in Massachusetts.
**Application requirements:** Proof of eligibility.
**Additional information:** Awards available for children or widowed spouse of deceased firefighters, police officers, or corrections officers who died from injuries received performing his or her duties. Children of veterans killed in action or Vietnam POWs also eligible. Award in form of entitlement grant. Applicant must be resident of Massachusetts at least one year prior to start of school. For recipients attending Massachusetts public college or university, award shall equal cost of tuition. Must not have received a prior bachelor's degree. Recipients attending Massachusetts independent college or university, award will be equivalent to highest tuition amount paid to public institution.

| | |
|---|---|
| **Amount of award:** | Full tuition |
| **Application deadline:** | May 1 |
| **Notification begins:** | June 1 |
| **Total amount awarded:** | $22,665 |

**Contact:**
Office of Student Financial Assistance
Massachusetts Board of Higher Education
454 Broadway, Suite 200
Revere, MA 02151
Phone: 617-727-9420
Fax: 617-727-0667
Web: www.osfa.mass.edu

## Paul Tsongas Scholarship Program

**Type of award:** Scholarship.
**Intended use:** For undergraduate study at postsecondary institution. Designated institutions: Massachusetts state colleges.
**Eligibility:** Applicant must be U.S. citizen or permanent resident residing in Massachusetts.
**Basis for selection:** Applicant must demonstrate financial need.
**Additional information:** Minimum 3.75 GPA and SAT score of 1200 (reading and math). Tuition waiver for full tuition and related fees. For renewal, must maintain 3.3 GPA.

| | |
|---|---|
| **Amount of award:** | Full tuition |
| **Number of awards:** | 45 |

**Contact:**
Contact State College financial aid office.
Phone: 617-727-9420
Fax: 617-727-0667
Web: www.osfa.mass.edu

# Massachusetts Democratic Party

## John F. Kennedy Scholars Award

**Type of award:** Scholarship.
**Intended use:** For junior or senior study at 4-year institution.
**Eligibility:** Applicant must be U.S. citizen or permanent resident residing in Massachusetts.
**Basis for selection:** Major/career interest in political science/government or public administration/service. Applicant must demonstrate financial need, high academic achievement, leadership, seriousness of purpose and service orientation.
**Additional information:** Awarded to one male and one female at Massachusetts Democratic State Convention. Preference given to registered Democrats and students with 3.0 GPA or higher. Visit Website or contact local chairperson for more information and important dates.

| | |
|---|---|
| **Amount of award:** | $1,500 |
| **Number of awards:** | 2 |
| **Number of applicants:** | 10 |
| **Application deadline:** | April 13 |
| **Total amount awarded:** | $3,000 |

**Contact:**
Massachusetts Democratic Party
MDP Office, Attn: Stacy Monahan
56 Roland Street, Suite 203
Boston, MA 02129
Phone: 617-776-2676
Fax: 617-776-2579
Web: www.massdems.org

# Massachusetts Department of Education

## Massachusetts Robert C. Byrd Honors Scholarship

**Type of award:** Scholarship, renewable.
**Intended use:** For full-time undergraduate study at accredited postsecondary institution.
**Eligibility:** Applicant must be high school senior. Applicant must be U.S. citizen or permanent resident residing in Massachusetts.
**Basis for selection:** Applicant must demonstrate high academic achievement, leadership and service orientation.
**Application requirements:** Nomination by high school.
**Additional information:** Minimum 3.5 GPA or class rank in top five percent required. Must have paid employment. Military academy students are ineligible. Students are nominated by high school. See guidance officer for additional information and application procedure. Number of awards varies.

| | |
|---|---|
| **Amount of award:** | $1,500 |
| **Number of applicants:** | 235 |
| **Application deadline:** | June 1 |



Scholarships

**Contact:**
Massachusetts Department of Education
Sally Teixeira
75 Pleasant Street
Malden, MA 02148-4906
Phone: 781-338-6304
Web: www.doe.mass.edu

# McKee Scholars

## John McKee Scholarship

**Type of award:** Scholarship, renewable.
**Intended use:** For undergraduate study at vocational or 4-year institution.
**Eligibility:** Applicant must be male, no older than 19, enrolled in high school. Applicant must be U.S. citizen residing in Pennsylvania.
**Basis for selection:** Applicant must demonstrate financial need and high academic achievement.
**Application requirements:** Interview, transcript. SAT/ACT scores.
**Additional information:** For male applicants whose fathers are dead, missing, permanently absent, or dysfunctional. Applicant must be a resident of Philadelphia, Bucks, Chester, Montgomery or Delaware counties. Award allotment after initial award year is based on upheld academic standards. Application available on Website.

| | |
|---|---|
| **Amount of award:** | $1,000-$5,500 |
| **Number of awards:** | 70 |
| **Number of applicants:** | 70 |
| **Application deadline:** | February 1 |
| **Total amount awarded:** | $320,000 |

**Contact:**
John McKee Scholarship Committee
Attn: Robert J. Stern
P.O. Box 144
Merion Station, PA 19066
Phone: 484-323-1348
Fax: 610-640-1965
Web: www.mckeescholars.org

# McNeil Consumer Healthcare

## Tylenol Future Care Scholarship

**Type of award:** Scholarship.
**Intended use:** For sophomore, junior or graduate study at vocational, 2-year, 4-year or graduate institution.
**Eligibility:** Applicant must be U.S. citizen or permanent resident.
**Basis for selection:** Major/career interest in nursing; health-related professions; medicine or pharmacy/pharmaceutics/pharmacology.
**Additional information:** Must have completed at least one year of school and have at least one year remaining. Employees and relatives of employees of McNeil Consumer Healthcare not eligible.

| | |
|---|---|
| **Amount of award:** | $5,000-$10,000 |
| **Number of awards:** | 40 |
| **Total amount awarded:** | $250,000 |

**Contact:**
Web: www.tylenol.com/scholarship

# Menominee Indian Tribe of Wisconsin

## Menominee Adult Vocational Training Grant

**Type of award:** Scholarship, renewable.
**Intended use:** For undergraduate or non-degree study at accredited vocational or 2-year institution in United States.
**Eligibility:** Applicant must be American Indian. Applicant must be enrolled member of Menominee Indian tribe of Wisconsin.
**Basis for selection:** Applicant must demonstrate financial need.
**Application requirements:** FAFSA and Menominee Tribal Grant Application.
**Additional information:** Award also applicable toward associate's degree. Must apply through college financial aid office.

| | |
|---|---|
| **Amount of award:** | $550-$2,200 |
| **Number of applicants:** | 100 |
| **Application deadline:** | October 30, March 1 |

**Contact:**
Menominee Indian Tribe of Wisconsin
P.O. Box 910
Keshena, WI 54135
Phone: 715-799-5118 or 715-799-5110
Fax: 715-799-5102
Web: www.menominee-nsn.gov

## Menominee Higher Education Grant

**Type of award:** Scholarship, renewable.
**Intended use:** For undergraduate study at accredited 2-year or 4-year institution in United States.
**Eligibility:** Applicant must be American Indian. Applicant must be enrolled member of Menominee Indian tribe.
**Basis for selection:** Applicant must demonstrate financial need.
**Application requirements:** FAFSA and Menominee Tribal Grant Application.
**Additional information:** Applications and deadline dates available through Tribal Education office.

| | |
|---|---|
| **Amount of award:** | $550-$2,200 |
| **Number of applicants:** | 200 |
| **Application deadline:** | October 30, March 1 |

**Contact:**
Menominee Indian Tribe of Wisconsin
P.O. Box 910
Keshena, WI 54135
Phone: 715-799-5118 or 715-799-5110
Fax: 715-799-5102
Web: www.menominee-nsn.gov/education/educationhome.asp

# The Merchants Exchange

## The Merchants Exhange Scholarship Fund

**Type of award:** Scholarship, renewable.
**Intended use:** For junior or senior study at postsecondary institution.
**Basis for selection:** Major/career interest in international relations. Applicant must demonstrate high academic achievement and depth of character.
**Application requirements:** Recommendations, transcript.
**Additional information:** Scholarship is for students from the Pacific Northwest studying maritime affairs/international trade. Minimum 2.5 GPA. Financial need may be considered if all other factors are equal. Visit Website for application.

| | |
|---|---|
| **Amount of award:** | $1,500 |
| **Number of awards:** | 7 |
| **Number of applicants:** | 5 |
| **Application deadline:** | May 31 |

**Contact:**
The Merchants Exchange
200 SW Market, Suite 190
Portland, OR 97201
Phone: 503-220-2092
Web: www.pdxmex.com

# Michigan Higher Education Assistance Authority

## Children of Veterans Tuition Grant

**Type of award:** Scholarship, renewable.
**Intended use:** For undergraduate study at postsecondary institution. Designated institutions: Michigan institutions.
**Eligibility:** Applicant must be at least 16, no older than 25. Applicant must be U.S. citizen or permanent resident residing in Michigan. Applicant must be dependent of disabled veteran or deceased veteran.
**Additional information:** Veteran must have been killed in action, been listed as MIA, or been permanently disabled due to service-related injuries. Veteran must have been a Michigan resident before entering military service or must have established residency in Michigan after entering military service.

| | |
|---|---|
| **Amount of award:** | $1,400-$2,800 |
| **Number of awards:** | 399 |
| **Total amount awarded:** | $859,930 |

**Contact:**
Michigan Higher Education Assistance Authority
Office of Scholarships and Grants
P.O. Box 30462
Lansing, MI 48909-7962
Phone: 888-447-2687
Web: www.michigan.gov/osg

## Michigan Competitive Scholarship

**Type of award:** Scholarship, renewable.
**Intended use:** For undergraduate study at postsecondary institution. Designated institutions: Michigan institutions.
**Eligibility:** Applicant must be U.S. citizen or permanent resident residing in Michigan.
**Basis for selection:** Applicant must demonstrate financial need.
**Application requirements:** FAFSA and qualifying ACT score.

| | |
|---|---|
| **Amount of award:** | $100-$1,512 |
| **Number of awards:** | 27,885 |
| **Application deadline:** | March 1 |
| **Total amount awarded:** | $37,071,451 |

**Contact:**
Michigan Higher Education Assistance Authority
Office of Scholarships and Grants
P.O. Box 30462
Lansing, MI 48909-7962
Phone: 888-447-2687
Web: www.michigan.gov/osg

## Michigan Robert C. Byrd Honors Scholarship

**Type of award:** Scholarship, renewable.
**Intended use:** For full-time undergraduate study at accredited postsecondary institution in United States.
**Eligibility:** Applicant must be high school senior. Applicant must be U.S. citizen or permanent resident residing in Michigan.
**Basis for selection:** Applicant must demonstrate high academic achievement.
**Application requirements:** Nomination by high school principal.

| | |
|---|---|
| **Amount of award:** | $1,500 |
| **Number of awards:** | 230 |
| **Total amount awarded:** | $1,399,500 |

**Contact:**
Michigan Higher Education Assistance Authority
Office of Scholarships and Grants
P.O. Box 30462
Lansing, MI 48909-7962
Phone: 888-447-2687
Web: www.michigan.gov/osg

## Michigan Tuition Grant

**Type of award:** Scholarship, renewable.
**Intended use:** For undergraduate, master's or doctoral study at 2-year, 4-year or graduate institution. Designated institutions: Michigan institutions.
**Eligibility:** Applicant must be U.S. citizen or permanent resident residing in Michigan.
**Basis for selection:** Applicant must demonstrate financial need.
**Application requirements:** FAFSA.
**Additional information:** Theology or religious education students ineligible.

| | |
|---|---|
| **Amount of award:** | $100-$1,512 |
| **Number of awards:** | 35,518 |
| **Application deadline:** | July 1 |
| **Total amount awarded:** | $53,088,352 |

**Contact:**
Michigan Higher Education Assistance Authority
Office of Scholarships and Grants
P.O. Box 30462
Lansing, MI 48909-7962
Phone: 888-447-2687
Web: www.michigan.gov/osg

### Tuition Incentive Program

**Type of award:** Scholarship, renewable.
**Intended use:** For undergraduate study at postsecondary institution. Designated institutions: Michigan institutions.
**Eligibility:** Applicant must be U.S. citizen or permanent resident residing in Michigan.
**Basis for selection:** Applicant must demonstrate financial need.
**Application requirements:** Proof of eligibility.
**Additional information:** Eligibility determined by Medicaid status. Provides tuition assistance for up to 24 semesters or 36 term credits for first two years. Up to $2,000 total assistance for third and fourth years.

| | |
|---|---|
| **Number of awards:** | 12,041 |
| **Total amount awarded:** | $21,798,128 |

**Contact:**
Michigan Higher Education Assistance Authority
Office of Scholarships and Grants
P.O. Box 30462
Lansing, MI 48909-7962
Phone: 888-447-2687
Web: www.michigan.gov/osg

## Michigan Society of Professional Engineers

### Michigan Society of Professional Engineers Scholarships for High School Seniors

**Type of award:** Scholarship.
**Intended use:** For undergraduate study at accredited 4-year institution. Designated institutions: ABET-accredited schools in Michigan.
**Eligibility:** Applicant must be high school senior. Applicant must be U.S. citizen residing in Michigan.
**Basis for selection:** Major/career interest in engineering. Applicant must demonstrate high academic achievement, depth of character, leadership and service orientation.
**Application requirements:** Recommendations, essay, transcript. ACT scores.
**Additional information:** Minimum 3.0 GPA and 26 ACT score. Application must be postmarked by third Friday of February. Contact guidance counselor or local MSPE chapter for application and specific eligibility requirements. Applications must be submitted to local MSPE chapter.

| | |
|---|---|
| **Amount of award:** | $1,000 |
| **Number of awards:** | 20 |
| **Number of applicants:** | 450 |
| **Notification begins:** | April 1 |
| **Total amount awarded:** | $35,000 |

**Contact:**
Scholarship Coordinator Local MSPE Chapter
P.O. Box 15276
Lansing, MI 48901
Phone: 517-487-9388
Fax: 517-487-0635
Web: www.michiganspe.org

## Microscopy Society of America

### Microscopy Society of America Undergraduate Research Scholarship

**Type of award:** Research grant.
**Intended use:** For full-time junior or senior study at postsecondary institution.
**Basis for selection:** Major/career interest in science, general; biology; physics; chemistry; natural sciences or engineering, materials. Applicant must demonstrate seriousness of purpose.
**Application requirements:** Recommendations. Resume, budget, research proposal, letter from laboratory supervisor, letter from MSA member (may be same as supervisor or professor). Four hard copies of all application materials if not submitting electronically.
**Additional information:** Award for students interested in pursuing microscopy as career or major research tool. Applicant should be sponsored by MSA member. Must supply abstract of research project. Funds must be spent within year of award date, but in special cases may be extended to cover additional research during summer semester following graduation. Visit Website for more information and application.

| | |
|---|---|
| **Amount of award:** | $3,000 |
| **Number of awards:** | 6 |
| **Number of applicants:** | 20 |
| **Application deadline:** | December 31 |
| **Notification begins:** | April 1 |
| **Total amount awarded:** | $9,000 |

**Contact:**
Microscopy Society of America
Undergraduate Research Scholarship
12100 Sunset Hills Road, Suite 130
Reston, VA 20190
Phone: 800-538-3672
Fax: 703-435-4390
Web: www.microscopy.org

## Microsoft Corporation

### Microsoft General Scholarship

**Type of award:** Scholarship.
**Intended use:** For full-time undergraduate study at 4-year institution. Designated institutions: Colleges and universities in the United States, Canada, and Mexico.
**Basis for selection:** Major/career interest in computer/information sciences; engineering, computer; mathematics or physics. Applicant must demonstrate financial need and high academic achievement.
**Application requirements:** Recommendations, essay, transcript. Resume.
**Additional information:** Minimum 3.0 GPA. Scholarship will cover up to 100 percent of tuition for one academic year. All recipients required to complete salaried summer internship of 12 weeks or more at Microsoft in Redmond, Washington. Applicant must be enrolled in degree-granting program in computer science, computer engineering, or related technical

discipline, with demonstrated interest in computer science. See Website for important dates, more information and application.

| | |
|---|---|
| **Amount of award:** | Full tuition |
| **Application deadline:** | February 1 |
| **Notification begins:** | March 20 |
| **Total amount awarded:** | $500,000 |

**Contact:**
Microsoft Scholarship Program
Microsoft Corporation
One Microsoft Way
Redmond, WA 98052-8303
Web: www.microsoft.com/college/en/us/collegescholarship.aspx

# Midwestern Higher Education Compact

## Midwest Student Exchange Program

**Type of award:** Scholarship, renewable.
**Intended use:** For full-time undergraduate, master's, doctoral or first professional study at accredited 2-year, 4-year or graduate institution in United States. Designated institutions: Participating institutions in Illinois, Indiana, Kansas, Michigan, Minnesota, Missouri, Nebraska, North Dakota, and Wisconsin.
**Eligibility:** Applicant must be residing in Wisconsin, Michigan, Minnesota, Kansas, Indiana, Nebraska, Illinois, Missouri or North Dakota.
**Application requirements:** Proof of eligibility.
**Additional information:** Reduced tuition rate for Illinois, Indiana, Kansas, Michigan, Minnesota, Missouri, Nebraska, North Dakota, and Wisconsin residents attending participating out-of-state institutions in one of eight other states in designated institutions or programs of study. For information, contact high school counselor or college admissions officer. For list of participating institutions and programs, and for individual state contact information, visit Website.

| | |
|---|---|
| **Amount of award:** | $4,194 |
| **Number of applicants:** | 3,330 |
| **Total amount awarded:** | $13,966,861 |

**Contact:**
Midwestern Higher Education Compact
Attn: Amber Cameron
1300 S. Second St., Suite 130
Minneapolis, MN 55454-1079
Phone: 612-625-4368
Fax: 612-626-8290
Web: www.mhec.org/MidwestStudentExchangeProgram

# Military Officers Association of America

## General John Paul Ratay Educational Fund Grants

**Type of award:** Scholarship.
**Intended use:** For undergraduate study at postsecondary institution.
**Eligibility:** Applicant must be U.S. citizen. Applicant must be dependent of veteran.
**Additional information:** Grants available to children of surviving spouse of retired officers. Must be seeking first undergraduate degree. Students cannot receive both an MOAA loan and Ratay grant.

| | |
|---|---|
| **Amount of award:** | $4,000 |
| **Application deadline:** | March 1 |

**Contact:**
Military Officers Association of America
201 N. Washington Street
Alexandria, VA 22314
Phone: 703-549-2311
Web: www.moaa.org/education

## MOAA American Patriot Scholarship Program

**Type of award:** Scholarship, renewable.
**Intended use:** For undergraduate study at postsecondary institution.
**Eligibility:** Applicant must be no older than 23. Applicant must be dependent of disabled veteran or deceased veteran.
**Basis for selection:** Applicant must demonstrate financial need.
**Additional information:** Must be dependent of an active duty uniformed service member (including Drilling Reserve and National Guard). Minimum 3.0 GPA. Military academy cadets are ineligible. Must be seeking first undergraduate degree. Amount and number of awards given vary.

| | |
|---|---|
| **Amount of award:** | $2,500 |
| **Number of awards:** | 50 |
| **Number of applicants:** | 60 |
| **Application deadline:** | March 1 |
| **Total amount awarded:** | $300,000 |

**Contact:**
MOAA Scholarship Fun
American Patriot Scholarships Department 889
201 North Washington Street
Alexandria, VA 22314-2529
Phone: 800-234-6622 ext. 169
Web: www.moaa.org/education

# Military Order of the Purple Heart

## Military Order of the Purple Heart Scholarship

**Type of award:** Scholarship, renewable.
**Intended use:** For full-time undergraduate or graduate study at postsecondary institution.
**Eligibility:** Applicant must be U.S. citizen. Applicant must be descendant of veteran or disabled while on active duty; or dependent of disabled veteran or deceased veteran; or spouse of disabled veteran or deceased veteran. Applicant must be either a recipient of the Purple Heart or a descendent, spouse or widow of a recipient of the Purple Heart, a veteran killed in action, or a veteran who died of wounds incurred during service.
**Basis for selection:** Applicant must demonstrate high academic achievement.
**Application requirements:** $15 application fee. Recommendations, essay, transcript, proof of eligibility.

**Additional information:** Applicant must either be a recipient of the Purple Heart or descendant of recipient of the Purple Heart, or descendant or spouse of veteran killed in action or who died of wounds. Must have minimum unweighted 2.75 GPA. Deadline in mid-late February. Contact the Military Order of the Purple Heart for applications, deadline information, award amounts, and other details.

| | |
|---|---|
| **Amount of award:** | $3,000 |
| **Number of awards:** | 83 |
| **Number of applicants:** | 400 |
| **Application deadline:** | February 15 |
| **Total amount awarded:** | $250,000 |

**Contact:**
Military Order of the Purple Heart
Scholarship Coordinator
5413-B Backlick Road
Springfield, VA 22151
Phone: 703-642-5360
Fax: 703-642-2054
Web: www.PurpleHeart.org



# Milk Processor's Education Program

## Scholar Athlete Milk Mustache of the Year Awards

**Type of award:** Scholarship.
**Intended use:** For undergraduate study at postsecondary institution.
**Eligibility:** Applicant must be high school senior. Applicant must be U.S. citizen.
**Basis for selection:** Competition/talent/interest in athletics/sports. Applicant must demonstrate high academic achievement, leadership and service orientation.
**Application requirements:** Essay. A description, in 75 words or less, of how drinking milk is part of applicant's life and training regimen.
**Additional information:** Minimum 3.2 GPA. Must be participant in high school sport or club sport. In addition to scholarship, winners receive spot in SAMMY Hall of Fame located in Milk House at Disney's Wide World of Sports and trip to Disney World to be honored in special ceremony. SAMMY award winners will be selected based on four criteria: academic performance, athletic excellence, leadership skills, and community service. Visit Website for application and more information.

| | |
|---|---|
| **Amount of award:** | $7,500 |
| **Number of awards:** | 25 |

**Contact:**
Visit Website for more information.
Web: www.bodybymilk.com/sammy_scholarship.php

# Minnesota Department of Veterans Affairs

## Minnesota Educational Assistance for Surviving Spouse or Dependent

**Type of award:** Scholarship, renewable.
**Intended use:** For full-time undergraduate study at accredited vocational, 2-year or 4-year institution. Designated institutions: Approved Minnesota public institutions.
**Eligibility:** Applicant must be residing in Minnesota. Applicant must be dependent of deceased veteran; or spouse of deceased veteran. Parent or spouse must have been in Minnesota at time of entry on active duty (and for six months prior). Veteran's death must have been on active duty or service-connected condition.
**Application requirements:** Proof of eligibility.
**Additional information:** All recipients also receive $750 stipend. Applicant must be resident of Minnesota for two years prior to application. Adopted children eligible. Step-children and foster children not eligible. Available until recipient obtains bachelor's degree or equivalent. Information also available from institution or county veterans service office.

| | |
|---|---|
| **Amount of award:** | Full tuition |

**Contact:**
Minnesota Department of Veterans Affairs
Veterans Service Building, 2nd Floor
20 West 12 Street
St. Paul, MN 55155-2079
Phone: 651-296-2562
Fax: 651-296-3954
Web: www.mdva.state.mn.us/education

## Minnesota Educational Assistance for Veterans

**Type of award:** Scholarship.
**Intended use:** For undergraduate or graduate study at postsecondary institution. Designated institutions: Approved Minnesota institutions.
**Eligibility:** Applicant must be U.S. citizen residing in Minnesota. Applicant must be veteran. Applicant must have been Minnesota resident at time of entry into active duty and for six months immediately preceding entry. Must have served 181 consecutive days of active duty.
**Application requirements:** Proof of eligibility. Military Service DD Form 214.
**Additional information:** Applicant must have exhausted eligible federal educational benefits prior to the delimiting date or within the eligibility period in which benefits were available. Grant is one-time award. Contact county veterans service officer or institution for more information.

| | |
|---|---|
| **Amount of award:** | $750 |

**Contact:**
Minnesota Department of Veterans Affairs
Veterans Service Building, 2nd Floor
20 West 12 Street
St. Paul, MN 55155-2079
Phone: 651-296-2562
Fax: 651-296-3954
Web: www.mdva.state.mn.us/education

# Minnesota Office of Higher Education

## Minnesota Achieve Scholarship

**Type of award:** Scholarship.
**Intended use:** For undergraduate study at postsecondary institution.
**Eligibility:** Applicant must be residing in Minnesota.
**Application requirements:** Transcript. FAFSA. Must qualify for Pell or state grant.

**Additional information:** Applicant must have graduated from Minnesota high school after January 1, 2008. Must have completed one of four eligible rigorous high school course programs and meet other academic requirements.

| | |
|---|---|
| **Amount of award:** | $1,200-$4,022 |
| **Number of applicants:** | 6,000 |
| **Total amount awarded:** | $9,315,372 |

**Contact:**
Minnesota Office of Higher Education
1450 Energy Park Drive, Suite 350
Saint Paul, MN 55108-5227
Phone: 800-657-3866
Fax: 651-642-0675
Web: www.getreadyforcollege.org/achieve

## Minnesota GI Bill

**Type of award:** Scholarship, renewable.
**Intended use:** For undergraduate or graduate study at postsecondary institution. Designated institutions: Eligible Minnesota institutions.
**Eligibility:** Applicant must be residing in Minnesota. Applicant must be in military service or veteran; or dependent of disabled veteran or deceased veteran; or spouse of disabled veteran or deceased veteran who serves or served in the Army, Air Force, Marines, Navy, Coast Guard or Reserves/National Guard.
**Additional information:** Applicant must be a veteran, or spouse or child of military personnel who died or became permanently disabled on or since September 11, 2001. Applicant may also be non-veteran who has served a total of five years in the United States military with any part of service occurring after September 11, 2001.

| | |
|---|---|
| **Amount of award:** | $100-$3,000 |
| **Number of applicants:** | 1,384 |
| **Total amount awarded:** | $958,316 |

**Contact:**
Minnesota Office of Higher Education
1450 Energy Park Drive, Suite 350
St. Paul, MN 55108-5227
Phone: 800-657-3866
Web: www.getreadyforcollege.org/military

## Minnesota Indian Scholarship Program

**Type of award:** Scholarship.
**Intended use:** For undergraduate or graduate study in United States. Designated institutions: Eligible Minnesota institutions.
**Eligibility:** Applicant must be American Indian. Applicant must be residing in Minnesota.
**Application requirements:** Proof of one-fourth or more Indian ancestry. FAFSA.
**Additional information:** Applicant must be at least one-quarter American Indian. Undergraduates must be enrolled at least three-quarters time and graduate students must be enrolled at least half-time. Must be eligible for Pell grant or Minnesota state grant. Awards made on first-come, first-served basis.

| | |
|---|---|
| **Amount of award:** | $4,000-$6,000 |
| **Number of applicants:** | 2,403 |
| **Application deadline:** | July 1 |
| **Total amount awarded:** | $1,950,000 |

**Contact:**
Minnesota Office of Higher Education
1450 Energy Park Drive, Suite 350
St. Paul, MN 55108-5227
Phone: 800-657-3866
Web: www.getreadyforcollege.org/indianscholarship

## Minnesota Post-Secondary Child Care Grant

**Type of award:** Scholarship, renewable.
**Intended use:** For undergraduate study at accredited postsecondary institution. Designated institutions: Eligible Minnesota schools.
**Eligibility:** Applicant must be no older than 22. Applicant must be U.S. citizen or permanent resident residing in Minnesota.
**Basis for selection:** Applicant must demonstrate financial need.
**Additional information:** Apply at college's financial aid office. Award amount prorated upon enrollment. Award based on family income and size. Eligibility limited to applicants with children 12 years or younger; maximum of $2600 per eligible child per academic year. Applicant cannot be receiving Aid to Families With Dependent Children, Minnesota Family Investment Program, or tuition reciprocity, or be in default of loan. Those with bachelor's degree or eight semesters or 12 quarters of credit, or equivalent, are not eligible. Applicant must be enrolled at least half-time in nonsectarian program and must be in good academic standing. Deadlines established by individual institution.

| | |
|---|---|
| **Number of applicants:** | 2,866 |
| **Total amount awarded:** | $6,246,159 |

**Contact:**
Minnesota Office of Higher Education
1450 Energy Park Drive, Suite 350
St. Paul, MN 55108-5227
Phone: 800-657-3866
Web: www.getreadyforcollege.org

## Minnesota Public Safety Officers Survivors Program

**Type of award:** Scholarship.
**Intended use:** For undergraduate study at accredited 2-year or 4-year institution. Designated institutions: Eligible Minnesota schools.
**Eligibility:** Applicant must be residing in Minnesota. Applicant's parent must have been killed or disabled in work-related accident as firefighter, police officer or public safety officer.
**Application requirements:** Proof of eligibility. Eligibility certificate.
**Additional information:** Must be enrolled in degree or certificate program at institution participating in State Grant Program. Applicant must be the surviving spouse or dependent child of a public safety officer killed in the line of duty. Also eligible if parent or spouse, not officially employed in public safety, was killed while assisting public safety officer or offering emergency medical assistance. Maximum age for dependent's child is 22 unless called for active military service, in which case maximum age is 29. Obtain eligibility certificate from Nancy Reissner, Department of Public Safety, 211 Transportation Building, St. Paul, MN 55155. Apply through financial aid office. Award covers tuition and fees up to $10,488 at four-year college and $5,808 at two-year college.

| | |
|---|---|
| **Number of applicants:** | 13 |
| **Total amount awarded:** | $78,328 |

**Contact:**
Minnesota Office of Higher Education
1450 Energy Park Drive, Suite 350
St. Paul, MN 55108-5227
Phone: 800-657-3866
Web: www.getreadyforcollege.org

### Minnesota State Grant Program

**Type of award:** Scholarship, renewable.
**Intended use:** For undergraduate study at accredited vocational, 2-year or 4-year institution.
**Eligibility:** Applicant must be U.S. citizen or permanent resident residing in Minnesota.
**Basis for selection:** Applicant must demonstrate financial need.
**Application requirements:** Proof of eligibility. FAFSA.
**Additional information:** Applicant must not have completed four years of college. If not Minnesota high school graduate and parents not residents of Minnesota, applicant must be resident of Minnesota for at least one year without being enrolled half-time or more. Cannot be in default on loans or delinquent on child-support payments. FAFSA used as application for Minnesota State Grant. Application deadline is 30 days from term start date.

| | |
|---|---|
| **Amount of award:** | $100-$9,444 |
| **Number of awards:** | 103,509 |
| **Number of applicants:** | 150,000 |
| **Total amount awarded:** | $168,600,000 |

**Contact:**
Minnesota Office of Higher Education
1450 Energy Park Drive, Suite 350
St. Paul, MN 55108-5227
Phone: 800-657-3866
Web: www.getreadyforcollege.org

## Miss America Organization

### Allman Medical Scholarships

**Type of award:** Scholarship, renewable.
**Intended use:** For undergraduate or graduate study at postsecondary institution.
**Eligibility:** Applicant must be female.
**Basis for selection:** Major/career interest in medicine. Applicant must demonstrate financial need and high academic achievement.
**Application requirements:** Recommendations, essay, transcript, proof of eligibility. MCAT scores.
**Additional information:** Must be pursuing a degree in medicine. Must have competed in Miss America system at local, state, or national level after 1998. Notification begins in August.

| | |
|---|---|
| **Application deadline:** | June 30 |

**Contact:**
Miss America Organization Attn: Scholarship Department
222 New Road, Suite 700
Attn: Scholarships
Linwood, NJ 08221
Phone: 609-653-8700
Web: www.missamerica.org/scholarships

### Eugenia Vellner Fischer Award for the Performing Arts

**Type of award:** Scholarship.
**Intended use:** For undergraduate or graduate study at postsecondary institution.
**Eligibility:** Applicant must be female.
**Basis for selection:** Major/career interest in performing arts. Applicant must demonstrate financial need and high academic achievement.
**Application requirements:** Recommendations, essay, transcript, proof of eligibility.
**Additional information:** Must be pursuing degree in the performing arts, such as dance or music. Must have competed in Miss America system in local, state, or national level after 1998. Visit Website for more information.

| | |
|---|---|
| **Application deadline:** | June 30 |
| **Notification begins:** | September 1 |

**Contact:**
Miss America Organization
Attn: Scholarships
222 New Road, Suite 700
Linwood, NJ 08221
Phone: 609-653-8700
Web: www.missamerica.org

### Miss America Competition Awards

**Type of award:** Scholarship.
**Intended use:** For undergraduate, graduate or non-degree study at accredited postsecondary institution.
**Eligibility:** Applicant must be single, female, at least 17, no older than 24. Applicant must be U.S. citizen.
**Basis for selection:** Competition/talent/interest in poise/talent/fitness. Applicant must demonstrate depth of character, leadership, patriotism, seriousness of purpose and service orientation.
**Application requirements:** Proof of eligibility.
**Additional information:** Local winners go on to compete at state level, and state winners compete for Miss America. Contestants will apply their talent, intelligence, and speaking ability, and demonstrate their commitment to community service. Cash and tuition-based scholarships available at every level of competition. Deadlines for local competitions vary. Contact the Miss America Organization for more information or visit Website.

| | |
|---|---|
| **Amount of award:** | $1,000-$50,000 |
| **Total amount awarded:** | $40,000,000 |

**Contact:**
Miss America Organization
Attn: Scholarships
222 New Road, Suite 700
Linwood, NJ 08221
Phone: 609-653-8700
Web: www.missamerica.org/scholarships

## Mississippi Office of Student Financial Aid

### Leveraging Educational Assistance Partnership Program (LEAP)

**Type of award:** Scholarship, renewable.
**Intended use:** For full-time undergraduate study at accredited 2-year or 4-year institution. Designated institutions: Mississippi institutions.
**Eligibility:** Applicant must be enrolled in high school. Applicant must be U.S. citizen or permanent resident residing in Mississippi.
**Basis for selection:** Applicant must demonstrate financial need and high academic achievement.

**Application requirements:** Recommendations, proof of eligibility. FAFSA.
**Additional information:** Must meet general requirements for participation in federal student aid program. Award amount varies. Apply to college financial aid office.

| | |
|---|---|
| **Number of awards:** | 7,730 |
| **Number of applicants:** | 9,800 |
| **Total amount awarded:** | $14,819,446 |

**Contact:**
Mississippi Student Financial Aid
3825 Ridgewood Road
Jackson, MS 39211-6453
Phone: 800-327-2980
Web: www.mississippi.edu/riseupms/financialaid-state.php

## Mississippi Eminent Scholars Grant

**Type of award:** Scholarship, renewable.
**Intended use:** For full-time undergraduate study at accredited vocational, 2-year or 4-year institution. Designated institutions: Eligible Mississippi institutions.
**Eligibility:** Applicant must be residing in Mississippi.
**Basis for selection:** Applicant must demonstrate high academic achievement.
**Application requirements:** Transcript. State of Mississippi tax return.
**Additional information:** Applicant may be high school senior. Must be Mississippi resident for at least one year. Minimum 3.5 GPA or rank in top 25 percent of class. Must have minimum ACT score of 29.

| | |
|---|---|
| **Amount of award:** | $2,500 |
| **Number of awards:** | 1,829 |
| **Application deadline:** | September 15 |
| **Total amount awarded:** | $4,337,024 |

**Contact:**
Mississippi Office of Student Financial Aid
3825 Ridgewood Road
Jackson, MS 39211-6453
Phone: 800-327-2980
Web: www.mississippi.edu/riseupms

## Mississippi Higher Education Legislative Plan

**Type of award:** Scholarship, renewable.
**Intended use:** For full-time freshman or sophomore study at accredited 2-year or 4-year institution. Designated institutions: Eligible Mississippi institutions.
**Eligibility:** Applicant must be U.S. citizen residing in Mississippi.
**Basis for selection:** Applicant must demonstrate financial need.
**Application requirements:** FAFSA. Household verification form.
**Additional information:** Minimum 2.5 GPA or must rank in top 50 percent of class. Must be legal resident of Mississippi for at least two years. Must have graduated from high school within two years of application. Preference given to early applicants. Covers tuition and fees up to ten semesters. Visit Website for application and more details.

| | |
|---|---|
| **Amount of award:** | Full tuition |
| **Application deadline:** | March 31 |
| **Total amount awarded:** | $1,753,252 |

**Contact:**
Mississippi Office of Student Financial Aid
3825 Ridgewood Road
Jackson, MS 39211-6453
Phone: 800-327-2980
Web: www.mississippi.edu/riseupms

## Mississippi Tuition Assistance Grant

**Type of award:** Scholarship, renewable.
**Intended use:** For full-time undergraduate study at accredited vocational, 2-year or 4-year institution. Designated institutions: Eligible Mississippi institutions.
**Eligibility:** Applicant must be U.S. citizen residing in Mississippi.
**Application requirements:** FAFSA and Student Aid Report.
**Additional information:** Applicant must be resident of Mississippi for at least one year. Must be receiving less than full Federal Pell Grant. Must have minimum 2.5 GPA or rank in top 50 percent of class. Award is up to $500 per year for freshmen and sophomores; up to $1,000 per year for juniors and seniors. Recipients must maintain minimum 2.5 GPA to reapply. Applicants must not be in default on an educational loan. Apply online.

| | |
|---|---|
| **Amount of award:** | $500-$1,000 |
| **Number of awards:** | 26,295 |
| **Application deadline:** | September 15 |
| **Total amount awarded:** | $15,286,070 |

**Contact:**
Mississippi Office of Student Financial Aid
3825 Ridgewood Road
Jackson, MS 39211-6453
Phone: 800-327-2980
Web: www.mississippi.edu/riseupms

## Nissan Scholarship

**Type of award:** Scholarship, renewable.
**Intended use:** For full-time undergraduate study at 2-year or 4-year institution. Designated institutions: Mississippi public institutions.
**Eligibility:** Applicant must be high school senior. Applicant must be residing in Mississippi.
**Basis for selection:** Applicant must demonstrate financial need, high academic achievement, leadership, seriousness of purpose and service orientation.
**Application requirements:** Recommendations, transcript. FAFSA, 200-word essay. Resume. SAT/ACT scores.
**Additional information:** Must be graduating from Mississippi high school in current year. Must have 20 ACT score or 940 SAT score (reading and math). Minimum 2.0 GPA. Visit Website for more information and application. Number and amount of awards vary.

| | |
|---|---|
| **Amount of award:** | Full tuition |
| **Application deadline:** | March 1 |

**Contact:**
Mississippi Office of Student Financial Aid
3825 Ridgewood Road
Jackson, MS 39211-6453
Phone: 800-327-2980
Web: www.mississippi.edu/riseupms

# Missouri Department of Elementary and Secondary Education

## Missouri Robert C. Byrd Honors Scholarship

**Type of award:** Scholarship, renewable.
**Intended use:** For undergraduate study at accredited 4-year institution in United States. Designated institutions: Eligible Missouri institutions.
**Eligibility:** Applicant must be high school senior. Applicant must be U.S. citizen or permanent resident residing in Missouri.
**Basis for selection:** Applicant must demonstrate high academic achievement.
**Application requirements:** Seventh semester transcripts.
**Additional information:** Applicant must be completing high school or GED in year of application. Must score in 90th percentile on ACT. Final selection at each congressional district level based on SAT/ACT scores and GPA. Award amount varies; contact sponsor for more information. Applicant's high school guidance counselor must sign and verify application form. Applications may be renewed for total of four years.

| | |
|---|---|
| **Amount of award:** | $1,500 |
| **Number of applicants:** | 700 |
| **Application deadline:** | April 15 |
| **Notification begins:** | October 1 |
| **Total amount awarded:** | $750,000 |

**Contact:**
Missouri Department of Elementary and Secondary Education
Robert C. Byrd Honors Scholarship
P.O. Box 480
Jefferson City, MO 65102
Phone: 573-751-1668
Fax: 573-526-3580
Web: www.dese.mo.gov

# Missouri Department of Higher Education

## Access Missouri Financial Assistance Program

**Type of award:** Scholarship, renewable.
**Intended use:** For full-time undergraduate study at vocational, 2-year or 4-year institution. Designated institutions: Approved Missouri institutions.
**Eligibility:** Applicant must be U.S. citizen or permanent resident residing in Missouri.
**Basis for selection:** Applicant must demonstrate financial need.
**Application requirements:** FAFSA.
**Additional information:** Must be used only toward first baccalaureate degree and may not be used towards theology or divinity studies. Eligibility based on Expected Family Contribution (EFC), with individuals with EFC of $12,000 or less eligible. Award amounts vary. No paper application. Students must apply for renewal each year.

| | |
|---|---|
| **Amount of award:** | $300-$4,600 |
| **Number of awards:** | 49,228 |
| **Number of applicants:** | 99,881 |
| **Application deadline:** | April 1 |
| **Total amount awarded:** | $82,957,041 |

**Contact:**
Missouri Department of Higher Education
P.O. Box 1469
Jefferson City, MO 65102-1469
Phone: 800-473-6757, option 4
Fax: 573-751-6635
Web: www.dhe.mo.gov

## Marguerite Ross Barnett Memorial Scholarship

**Type of award:** Scholarship, renewable.
**Intended use:** For half-time undergraduate study at accredited vocational, 2-year or 4-year institution in United States. Designated institutions: Participating Missouri schools.
**Eligibility:** Applicant must be at least 18. Applicant must be U.S. citizen or permanent resident residing in Missouri.
**Basis for selection:** Applicant must demonstrate financial need.
**Application requirements:** Proof of eligibility. FAFSA.
**Additional information:** For students employed at least 20 hours per week while attending school part-time. Scholarship awarded on first-come, first-served basis. Maximum award is the lesser of the following: tuition charged at school of part-time enrollment or amount of tuition charged to Missouri undergraduate resident enrolled part-time in same class level at University of Missouri-Columbia. Employer must verify applicant's employment. Recipient may not be pursuing degree in theology or divinity.

| | |
|---|---|
| **Amount of award:** | Full tuition |
| **Number of awards:** | 179 |
| **Number of applicants:** | 246 |
| **Application deadline:** | August 1 |
| **Total amount awarded:** | $397,423 |

**Contact:**
Missouri Department of Higher Education
P.O. Box 1469
Jefferson City, MO 65102-1469
Phone: 800-473-6757, option 4
Fax: 573-751-6635
Web: www.dhe.mo.gov

## Missouri Department of Higher Education Vietnam Veteran's Survivor Grant Program

**Type of award:** Scholarship, renewable.
**Intended use:** For full-time undergraduate study at accredited vocational, 2-year or 4-year institution in United States. Designated institutions: Approved Missouri public and private schools.
**Eligibility:** Applicant must be U.S. citizen or permanent resident residing in Missouri. Applicant must be dependent of deceased veteran; or spouse of deceased veteran during Vietnam.
**Additional information:** For children and spouses of Vietnam veterans whose death was attributed to or caused by exposure to toxic chemicals during Vietnam conflict. Applicant cannot pursue degree in theology or divinity. Applications accepted in January; end date based on fund availability. Amount of award varies. Maximum amount is the lesser of actual tuition charged for twelve credit hours at school where applicant is enrolled, or

the average amount of tuition charged for twelve credit hours to undergraduate Missouri resident enrolled full-time in same class level and academic major at regional four-year public Missouri institutions.

**Number of awards:** 6
**Number of applicants:** 6
**Total amount awarded:** $24,614

**Contact:**
Missouri Department of Higher Education
P.O. Box 1469
Jefferson City, MO 65102-1469
Phone: 800-473-6757, option 4
Fax: 573-751-6635
Web: www.dhe.mo.gov

## Missouri Higher Education "Bright Flight" Academic Scholarship

**Type of award:** Scholarship, renewable.
**Intended use:** For full-time undergraduate study at accredited vocational, 2-year or 4-year institution in United States. Designated institutions: Approved Missouri public and private schools.
**Eligibility:** Applicant must be U.S. citizen or permanent resident residing in Missouri.
**Basis for selection:** Applicant must demonstrate high academic achievement.
**Application requirements:** Proof of eligibility. SAT/ACT scores.
**Additional information:** May only be used for first baccalaureate degree. May not be used for theology or divinity studies. SAT/ACT composite scores must be in top five percent of state students. Must achieve qualifying scores by June assessment date of senior year. GED and home-schooled students may also qualify. Application deadline is June assessment date of senior year. No paper application needed. Check with high school counselor or financial aid administrator for additional information. Also see Website.

**Amount of award:** $1,000-$3,000
**Number of awards:** 7,730
**Number of applicants:** 9,800
**Application deadline:** June 11
**Total amount awarded:** $14,819,446

**Contact:**
Missouri Department of Higher Education
P.O. Box 1469
Jefferson City, MO 6510-1469
Phone: 800-473-6757, option 4
Fax: 573-751-6635
Web: www.dhe.mo.gov

## Missouri Minority Teaching Scholarship

**Type of award:** Scholarship, renewable.
**Intended use:** For full-time undergraduate or master's study at accredited 2-year or 4-year institution in United States. Designated institutions: Missouri institutions with approved teacher education programs.
**Eligibility:** Applicant must be Alaskan native, Asian American, African American, Mexican American, Hispanic American, Puerto Rican or American Indian. Applicant must be U.S. citizen or permanent resident residing in Missouri.
**Basis for selection:** Major/career interest in education. Applicant must demonstrate high academic achievement.
**Application requirements:** Recommendations, essay, transcript, proof of eligibility.
**Additional information:** Must rank in top 25 percent of class and score in top 25 percent on ACT or SAT. If in college, may have 3.0 GPA at 30 hours to qualify. If college graduate, may receive award if returning to a master's level math or science education program. Upon graduation, recipient must teach for five years in Missouri public schools or scholarship becomes loan. Applicant may be renewed for up to 4 years.

**Amount of award:** $3,000
**Number of awards:** 100
**Number of applicants:** 53
**Application deadline:** February 15
**Total amount awarded:** $100,000

**Contact:**
Missouri Department of Higher Education
P.O. Box 1469
Jefferson City, MO 65102-1469
Phone: 800-473-6757, option 4
Fax: 573-731-6635
Web: www.dhe.mo.gov

## Missouri Public Safety Officer or Employee's Child Survivor Grant

**Type of award:** Scholarship, renewable.
**Intended use:** For full-time undergraduate study at accredited vocational, 2-year or 4-year institution in United States. Designated institutions: Approved Missouri public and private schools.
**Eligibility:** Applicant must be U.S. citizen or permanent resident residing in Missouri.
**Application requirements:** Proof of eligibility.
**Additional information:** For public safety officers who were permanently disabled in the line of duty or for children and spouses of Missouri public safety officers killed or permanently disabled in the line of duty. Children of Missouri Department of Highway and Transportation employees also eligible if parent died or was permanently disabled during performance of job. May not be used for theology or divinity studies. Award amounts vary; contact sponsor for information. Amount awarded is the lesser of 12 credit tuition hours at chosen institution or 12 credit tuition hours at University of Missouri. Applications accepted in January; end date based on fund availability.

**Number of awards:** 18
**Number of applicants:** 18
**Total amount awarded:** $71,537

**Contact:**
Missouri Department of Higher Education
P.O. Box 1469
Jefferson City, MO 65102-1469
Phone: 800-473-6757, option 4
Fax: 573-751-6635
Web: www.dhe.mo.gov

# Missouri League for Nursing

## Margo Ballard and Vivian Meinecke Memorial Scholarship

**Type of award:** Scholarship.
**Intended use:** For sophomore, junior, senior or graduate study at postsecondary institution.

**Eligibility:** Applicant must be U.S. citizen residing in Missouri.
**Basis for selection:** Major/career interest in nursing. Applicant must demonstrate financial need.
**Application requirements:** Recommendations, proof of eligibility. Names and addresses of three persons who will know the student's address for next five years.
**Additional information:** Minimum 3.0 GPA. Applications must be submitted by dean at current school. Applications submitted by students not considered.
**Contact:**
Contact deans at accredited nursing schools in Missouri.
Web: www.mlnmonursing.org

## Missouri League for Nursing Scholarship

**Type of award:** Scholarship, renewable.
**Intended use:** For full-time sophomore, junior, senior or master's study at accredited postsecondary institution. Designated institutions: Eligible institutions in Missouri.
**Eligibility:** Applicant must be U.S. citizen residing in Missouri.
**Basis for selection:** Major/career interest in nursing. Applicant must demonstrate financial need and high academic achievement.
**Application requirements:** Recommendations.
**Additional information:** Minimum 3.0 GPA. Scholarship must be used for study in Missouri. Amount of award varies. Applications can be obtained from dean of nationally recognized accredited schools of nursing in Missouri.

| | |
|---|---|
| **Amount of award:** | $2,000 |
| **Number of awards:** | 2 |
| **Number of applicants:** | 30 |
| **Application deadline:** | November 15 |

**Contact:**
Contact deans of school of nursing programs in Missouri.
Phone: 573-635-5355
Fax: 573-635-7908
Web: www.mlnmonursing.org

# Montana Board of Regents

## Honorably Discharged Veteran Fee Waiver

**Type of award:** Scholarship.
**Intended use:** For undergraduate or graduate study at postsecondary institution. Designated institutions: Montana University system institutions.
**Eligibility:** Applicant must be permanent resident residing in Montana. Applicant must be veteran.
**Application requirements:** Proof of eligibility.
**Additional information:** Must have been honorably discharged person who served with the United States forces during wartime. Must be pursuing his or her initial undergraduate degree. Must have used up all federal veterans educational assistance benefits. Contact college financial aid office.

| | |
|---|---|
| **Amount of award:** | Full tuition |

**Contact:**
Montana University System
P.O. Box 203101
Helena, MT 59620-3101
Phone: 800-537-7508
Fax: 406-444-1869
Web: www.mgslp.org

## Montana Higher Education Grant

**Type of award:** Scholarship.
**Intended use:** For undergraduate study at postsecondary institution. Designated institutions: Eligible Montana institutions.
**Eligibility:** Applicant must be residing in Montana.
**Basis for selection:** Applicant must demonstrate financial need.
**Application requirements:** FAFSA.

| | |
|---|---|
| **Number of awards:** | 1,000 |
| **Total amount awarded:** | $600,000 |

**Contact:**
Contact college financial aid office for application information.
P.O. Box 203101
Helena, MT 59620-3101
Phone: 800-537-7508
Fax: 406-444-1869
Web: www.mgslp.org

# Montana Office of the Commissioner of Higher Education

## Governor's Best and Brightest Merit Scholarship

**Type of award:** Scholarship, renewable.
**Intended use:** For full-time undergraduate study at 2-year or 4-year institution. Designated institutions: Montana University system or tribal colleges.
**Eligibility:** Applicant must be residing in Montana.
**Basis for selection:** Applicant must demonstrate high academic achievement.
**Additional information:** Applications available on Website. Must have minimum 3.0 GPA or 20 ACT score or 1440 SAT score.

| | |
|---|---|
| **Amount of award:** | $2,000 |
| **Number of awards:** | 180 |
| **Number of applicants:** | 1,500 |
| **Application deadline:** | March 15 |
| **Total amount awarded:** | $334,000 |

**Contact:**
Governor's Best and Brightest Merit Scholarship
c/o MGSLP
P.O. Box 203101
Helena, MT 59604-3101
Phone: 406-444-1869
Fax: 406-444-0638
Web: www.scholarship.mt.gov

## Governor's Best and Brightest Merit-at-Large Scholarship

**Type of award:** Scholarship, renewable.
**Intended use:** For full-time undergraduate study at 2-year or 4-year institution in United States. Designated institutions: Montana University System school or tribal college in Montana.
**Eligibility:** Applicant must be residing in Montana.
**Basis for selection:** Applicant must demonstrate high academic achievement.
**Additional information:** Applications available on Website. Applicants must be Montana high school graduate. Must have minimum 3.0 GPA or 20 ACT score or 1440 SAT score.

| | |
|---|---|
| **Amount of award:** | $2,000 |
| **Number of awards:** | 50 |
| **Number of applicants:** | 400 |
| **Application deadline:** | March 15 |
| **Total amount awarded:** | $100,000 |

**Contact:**
Montana Board of Regents
c/o MGSLP
P.O. Box 203101
Helena, MT 59604-3101
Phone: 406-444-1869
Fax: 406-444-0638
Web: www.scholarship.mt.gov

## Governor's Best and Brightest Need Based Scholarship

**Type of award:** Scholarship.
**Intended use:** For undergraduate study at 2-year institution in United States. Designated institutions: Montana University System schools or Montana tribal colleges.
**Eligibility:** Applicant must be residing in Montana.
**Basis for selection:** Applicant must demonstrate financial need.
**Application requirements:** FAFSA.
**Additional information:** Applications available through college financial aid office.

| | |
|---|---|
| **Amount of award:** | $1,000 |
| **Number of awards:** | 408 |
| **Number of applicants:** | 1,500 |
| **Total amount awarded:** | $408,000 |

**Contact:**
Montana Office of the Commissioner of Higher Education
c/o MGSLP
P.O. Box 203101
Helena, MT 59604-3101
Phone: 406-444-1869
Fax: 406-444-0638
Web: www.scholarship.mt.gov

## Montana University System Honor Scholarship

**Type of award:** Scholarship, renewable.
**Intended use:** For freshman study at 4-year institution. Designated institutions: Campuses in Montana University system, as well as Dawson, Flathead Valley, and Miles community colleges.
**Eligibility:** Applicant must be high school senior. Applicant must be U.S. citizen residing in Montana.
**Basis for selection:** Applicant must demonstrate high academic achievement.
**Application requirements:** Recommendations, transcript, proof of eligibility. College acceptance letter, SAT/ACT scores.
**Additional information:** Must be high school senior enrolled at accredited Montana high school for at least three years. Recipients ranked based on GPA and ACT or SAT score. Minimum 3.4 GPA. Must have met college preparatory requirements. Must submit completed application to high school guidance counselor. See Website for more details.

| | |
|---|---|
| **Amount of award:** | Full tuition |
| **Number of awards:** | 200 |
| **Number of applicants:** | 1,100 |
| **Application deadline:** | March 15 |

**Contact:**
Montana Board of Regents of Higher Education
P.O. Box 203101
Helena, MT 59620-3101
Phone: 800-537-7508
Fax: 406-444-1869
Web: www.scholarship.mt.gov

# Montana Trappers Association

## MTA Doug Slifka Memorial Scholarship

**Type of award:** Scholarship.
**Intended use:** For undergraduate study at postsecondary institution.
**Eligibility:** Applicant must be at least 15, no older than 25.
**Basis for selection:** Major/career interest in environmental science; life sciences; natural resources/conservation or wildlife/fisheries. Applicant must demonstrate depth of character and seriousness of purpose.
**Application requirements:** Interview, transcript. Essay or story on trapping or conservation. Recommendations by MTA members, teachers, or other pertinent individuals. Endorsement of MTA District Director (or sub-director) where applicant resides. Student involvement in activities that include MTA programs, trapping, school programs, and community service.
**Additional information:** Applicant must be member of MTA for at least one year or minor dependent of MTA member. Member must have been member of Association for one year prior to application. MTA members out of state and their families also eligible to apply. For application, complete request form on Website or contact local director, officer or committee member.

| | |
|---|---|
| **Amount of award:** | $500 |
| **Number of awards:** | 2 |
| **Application deadline:** | June 1 |
| **Total amount awarded:** | $1,000 |

**Contact:**
Montana Trappers Association MTA Scholarship Committee
c/o Gary VanHaele
P.O. Box 264
Hysham, MT 59038
Phone: 406-342-5552
Web: www.montanatrappers.org/programs/scholarship.htm

# The Moody's Foundation

## Moody's Mega Math "M3" Challenge

**Type of award:** Scholarship.
**Intended use:** For freshman, sophomore, junior or senior study at 2-year or 4-year institution.
**Eligibility:** Applicant must be high school junior or senior. Applicant must be residing in New York, Delaware, Massachusetts, Virginia, Connecticut, Vermont, Maine, Maryland, Pennsylvania, Florida, Georgia, South Carolina, District of Columbia, New Hampshire, West Virginia, New Jersey, North Carolina or Rhode Island.
**Basis for selection:** Competition/talent/interest in academics, based on responses to the assigned modeling problem.
**Additional information:** Each school may enter up to two teams of three to five students. Team prizes range from $1,000 to $20,000. Visit Website for details and to register.

| | |
|---|---|
| **Amount of award:** | $1,000-$20,000 |
| **Number of awards:** | 43 |
| **Number of applicants:** | 2,409 |
| **Application deadline:** | February 24 |
| **Notification begins:** | November 1 |
| **Total amount awarded:** | $100,000 |

**Contact:**
Society for Industrial and Applied Mathematics
3600 Market Street, 6th Floor
Philadelphia, PA 19104
Phone: 267-350-6388
Fax: 215-525-2756
Web: m3challenge.siam.org

# NAACP

## Agnes Jones Jackson Scholarship

**Type of award:** Scholarship, renewable.
**Intended use:** For full-time undergraduate or graduate study at accredited 4-year or graduate institution.
**Eligibility:** Applicant must be no older than 24. Applicant must be U.S. citizen.
**Basis for selection:** Applicant must demonstrate financial need.
**Application requirements:** Recommendations, essay, transcript, proof of eligibility. Financial aid forms or copies of parents' latest income tax forms. Send one personal reference, one academic reference, and one NAACP reference (from an officer). Proof of enrollment.
**Additional information:** Must be current regular member of NAACP. Minimum 2.5 GPA for undergraduates, 3.0 GPA for graduate students. Award amounts: $1,500 undergraduate, $2,500 graduate. Graduate students may be full-time or part-time. Applications may be requested after January 1; include business-sized SASE. Scholarship application administered by United Negro College Fund. Visit Website for application, deadline, and more information.

| | |
|---|---|
| **Amount of award:** | $1,500 |
| **Application deadline:** | March 15 |

**Contact:**
United Negro College Fund: Scholarships and Grants Administration
Attn: Kimberly Hall
8260 Willow Oaks Corporate Drive
Fairfax, VA 22301
Phone: 800-331-2244
Web: www.naacp.org/youth/scholarships

## Earl G. Graves Scholarship

**Type of award:** Scholarship.
**Intended use:** For full-time sophomore, junior or graduate study at accredited 4-year or graduate institution in United States.
**Basis for selection:** Major/career interest in business. Applicant must demonstrate high academic achievement.
**Application requirements:** Essay, transcript, proof of eligibility. One personal and two academic recommendations.
**Additional information:** Minimum 2.5 GPA. Applicants must be in top 20 percent of their class. May apply during sophomore year. Scholarship application administered by United Negro College Fund. Visit Website for application, deadline, and more information.

| | |
|---|---|
| **Amount of award:** | $5,000 |
| **Application deadline:** | March 15 |

**Contact:**
United Negro College Fund: Scholarships and Grants Administration
Attn: Kimberly Hall
8260 Willow Oaks Corporate Drive
Fairfax, VA 22031
Phone: 800-331-2244
Web: www.naacp.org/youth/scholarships

## Hubertus W.V. Wellems Scholarship for Male Students

**Type of award:** Scholarship, renewable.
**Intended use:** For full-time undergraduate or graduate study at accredited 4-year or graduate institution in United States.
**Eligibility:** Applicant must be male. Applicant must be U.S. citizen.
**Basis for selection:** Major/career interest in engineering; chemistry; physics or mathematics. Applicant must demonstrate financial need.
**Application requirements:** Essay, transcript, proof of eligibility. Two recommendations from teachers or professors in field of study. Financial aid forms. Proof of enrollment, application for admissions.
**Additional information:** Applications may be requested after January 1. Send 9x12 SASE. Minimum 2.5 GPA for undergraduates and 3.0 GPA for graduate students. Active membership in NAACP highly desirable. Award is $2,000 for undergraduates, $3,000 for graduate students. Graduate students may be enrolled part-time. Scholarship application administered by the United Negro College Fund. Visit Website for application, deadline, and more information.

| | |
|---|---|
| **Amount of award:** | $2,000-$3,000 |
| **Application deadline:** | March 15 |

**Contact:**
United Negro College Fund: Scholarships and Grants Administration
Attn: Kimberly Hall
8260 Willow Oaks Corporate Drive
Fairfax, VA 22031
Phone: 800-331-2244
Web: www.naacp.org/youth/scholarships

### Lillian and Samuel Sutton Education Scholarship

**Type of award:** Scholarship, renewable.
**Intended use:** For full-time undergraduate or graduate study at accredited 2-year, 4-year or graduate institution in United States.
**Eligibility:** Applicant must be U.S. citizen.
**Basis for selection:** Major/career interest in education; education, early childhood; education, special or education, teacher. Applicant must demonstrate leadership.
**Application requirements:** Essay, transcript, proof of eligibility. Two recommendations from teachers or professors in major field of study. Proof of enrollment, acceptance letter from college or university. Financial aid forms.
**Additional information:** Undergraduates must have minimum 2.5 GPA, graduate students must have minimum 3.0 GPA. Applications available in January. Include business-sized SASE. Graduate students may be enrolled part-time. NAACP membership and participation highly desirable. Award $1,000 for undergraduates; $2,000 for graduates. Scholarship application administered by United Negro College Fund. Visit Website for deadline, application, and more information.

| | |
|---|---|
| **Amount of award:** | $1,000 |
| **Application deadline:** | March 15 |

**Contact:**
United Negro College Fund: Scholarships and Grants Administration
Attn: Kimberly Hall
8260 Willow Oaks Corporate Drive
Fairfax, VA 22031
Phone: 800-331-2244
Web: www.naacp.org/youth/scholarships

### Roy Wilkins Scholarship

**Type of award:** Scholarship.
**Intended use:** For full-time freshman study at accredited 4-year institution in United States.
**Eligibility:** Applicant must be U.S. citizen.
**Application requirements:** Recommendations, essay, transcript, proof of eligibility. Send financial aid forms along with copy of letter of acceptance from college or university. Business-sized SASE.
**Additional information:** Must be entering college freshman. Minimum 2.5 GPA. Highly desirable that applicant be active member of NAACP. Applications may be requested after January 1. United Negro College Fund administers application process. Visit Website for deadline, application, and more information.

| | |
|---|---|
| **Amount of award:** | $1,000 |
| **Application deadline:** | March 15 |

**Contact:**
United Negro College Fund: Scholarships and Grants Administration
Attn: Kimberly Hall
8260 Willow Oaks Corporate Drive
Fairfax, VA 22031
Phone: 800-331-2244
Web: www.naacp.org/youth/scholarships

## NAACP Legal Defense and Education Fund, Inc.

### Herbert Lehman Educational Fund

**Type of award:** Scholarship, renewable.
**Intended use:** For full-time freshman or sophomore study at accredited 4-year institution in United States.
**Eligibility:** Applicant must be African American. Applicant must be high school senior. Applicant must be U.S. citizen.
**Basis for selection:** Applicant must demonstrate financial need, high academic achievement, depth of character, leadership, seriousness of purpose and service orientation.
**Application requirements:** Recommendations, essay, transcript. Standardized test scores.
**Additional information:** See Website for additional information.

| | |
|---|---|
| **Amount of award:** | $2,000 |
| **Application deadline:** | March 31 |
| **Notification begins:** | August 1 |

**Contact:**
The Herbert Lehman Fund
NAACP Legal Defense and Educational Fund, Inc
99 Hudson Street Suite 1600
New York, NY 10013
Phone: 212-965-2200 or 212-965-2225
Fax: 212-219-1595
Web: www.naacpldf.org

## NASA Alabama Space Grant Consortium

### NASA Space Grant Undergraduate Scholarship

**Type of award:** Scholarship, renewable.
**Intended use:** For full-time junior or senior study at accredited 4-year institution. Designated institutions: Alabama Space Grant member universities: University of Alabama Huntsville, Alabama A&M, University of Alabama, University of Alabama Birmingham, University of South Alabama, Auburn University, Tuskegee University.
**Eligibility:** Applicant must be U.S. citizen residing in Alabama.
**Basis for selection:** Major/career interest in aerospace; engineering or science, general. Applicant must demonstrate high academic achievement.
**Application requirements:** Recommendations, essay, transcript, nomination by faculty advisor at Alabama Space Grant Consortium member institution. Resume.
**Additional information:** Applicants must have minimum 3.0 GPA and attend Alabama University. Must be in final term of sophomore year or later when applying. The Consortium actively encourages women, minority, and physically challenged students to apply, but others not excluded.

| | |
|---|---|
| **Amount of award:** | $1,000 |
| **Number of awards:** | 40 |
| **Number of applicants:** | 45 |
| **Application deadline:** | March 1 |
| **Notification begins:** | April 15 |
| **Total amount awarded:** | $45,000 |

Scholarships

**Contact:**
NASA Alabama Space Grant Consortium
University of Alabama in Huntsville
301 Sparkman Dr. Materials Science Bldg, 205
Huntsville, AL 35899
Phone: 256-824-6800
Fax: 256-824-6061
Web: www.uah.edu/ASGC

# NASA Connecticut Space Grant Consortium

## NASA Connecticut Space Grant Undergraduate Fellowship

**Type of award:** Research grant, renewable.
**Intended use:** For full-time undergraduate study at accredited 4-year institution in United States. Designated institutions: Connecticut Space Grant Consortium member institutions.
**Eligibility:** Applicant must be U.S. citizen.
**Basis for selection:** Major/career interest in aerospace; engineering or science, general.
**Application requirements:** Recommendations, transcript, proof of eligibility, research proposal. Resume.
**Additional information:** Minimum 3.0 GPA. Consortium actively encourages women, minority, and disabled students to apply. Award amount varies; maximum is $4,500.

| | |
|---|---|
| **Amount of award:** | $4,500 |
| **Number of awards:** | 13 |
| **Number of applicants:** | 20 |
| **Application deadline:** | October 31 |
| **Total amount awarded:** | $58,500 |

**Contact:**
NASA Connecticut Space Grant Consortium
University of Hartford
200 Bloomfield Ave.
West Hartford, CT 06117
Phone: 860-768-4813
Fax: 860-768-5073
Web: www.ctspacegrant.org

# NASA Delaware Space Grant Consortium

## Delaware Space Grant Undergraduate Tuition Scholarship

**Type of award:** Scholarship, renewable.
**Intended use:** For full-time sophomore, junior or senior study at postsecondary institution. Designated institutions: University of Delaware, Delaware Technical and Community College, Swarthmore College, Delaware State University at Dover, Villanova University, Wesley College, Wilmington University, Goldey-Beacom College.
**Eligibility:** Applicant must be U.S. citizen.
**Basis for selection:** Major/career interest in aerospace; astronomy; communications; engineering; geography; geology/earth sciences; geophysics; physics or oceanography/marine studies.
**Application requirements:** Recommendations, transcript, nomination by department chair, DESGC Consortium Representative, or advisor. Applicant statement; letter from Department Chairperson.
**Additional information:** Must have proven interest in space-related studies. Recipient must currently attend Delaware Space Grant Consortium member institution. Award amounts vary and are available pending funding. Contact Consortium office for deadlines and additional information.

| | |
|---|---|
| **Amount of award:** | $2,500-$3,000 |
| **Number of awards:** | 5 |
| **Number of applicants:** | 10 |
| **Application deadline:** | April 22 |
| **Total amount awarded:** | $29,500 |

**Contact:**
Delaware Space Grant Consortium Program Office
University of Delaware
106 Sharp Lab
Newark, DE 19716
Phone: 302-831-1094
Fax: 302-831-1843
Web: www.delspace.org

# NASA District of Columbia Space Grant Consortium

## NASA District of Columbia Undergraduate Scholarship

**Type of award:** Scholarship, renewable.
**Intended use:** For full-time undergraduate or graduate study at postsecondary institution. Designated institutions: The American University, Catholic University, Gallaudet University, George Washington University, Georgetown University, Howard University, Trinity University, University of District of Columbia.
**Eligibility:** Applicant must be U.S. citizen.
**Basis for selection:** Major/career interest in science, general; mathematics; engineering or aerospace. Applicant must demonstrate high academic achievement.
**Application requirements:** Recommendations, transcript, proof of eligibility.
**Additional information:** Number of grants, amount of funding, deadlines, and application requirements vary by year and by institution. See Website for more information.
**Contact:**
DC Space Grant Consortium American University - Dept. of Physics
4400 Massachusetts Ave, NW
McKinley Building Suite 102
Washington, DC 20016-8058
Phone: 202-885-2755
Fax: 202-885-2723
Web: www.dcspacegrant.org

# NASA Georgia Space Grant Consortium

## NASA Space Grant Georgia Fellowship Program

**Type of award:** Scholarship, renewable.
**Intended use:** For full-time junior, senior, master's or doctoral study at accredited postsecondary institution in United States.

Designated institutions: Albany State University, Clark Atlanta University, Columbus State University, Fort Valley State University, Georgia Institute of Technology, Georgia State University, Kennesaw State University, Mercer University, Morehouse College, Spelman College, State University of West Georgia, University of Georgia.
**Eligibility:** Applicant must be U.S. citizen residing in Georgia.
**Basis for selection:** Major/career interest in engineering; science, general; aerospace; physics; atmospheric sciences/ meteorology; computer/information sciences; education or chemistry. Applicant must demonstrate seriousness of purpose and service orientation.
**Application requirements:** Interview, portfolio, recommendations, essay, transcript.
**Additional information:** Funding available for students in all areas of engineering and science, and many areas of social science.

| | |
|---|---|
| **Amount of award:** | $300 |

**Contact:**
Georgia Space Grant Consortium
Georgia Tech-Aerospace and Engineering
Space Science and Technology Bldg., Room 210
Atlanta, GA 30332-0150
Phone: 404-894-0521
Fax: 404-894-9313
Web: www.ae.gatech.edu/research/gsgc

# NASA Hawaii Space Grant Consortium

## NASA Space Grant Hawaii Undergraduate Fellowship and Traineeship Program

**Type of award:** Scholarship.
**Intended use:** For full-time undergraduate study at accredited postsecondary institution in United States. Designated institutions: Consortium member schools: University of Hawaii at Manoa and Hilo, community colleges in Hawaii.
**Eligibility:** Applicant must be U.S. citizen.
**Basis for selection:** Major/career interest in astronomy; geology/earth sciences; oceanography/marine studies; physics; zoology; engineering or geography.
**Application requirements:** Recommendations, transcript. Abstract, research proposal, budget, resume. Three copies of all application materials.
**Additional information:** Must be resident of Hawaii or attend school at one of the designated institutions. Must be sponsored by a faculty member willing to act as the student's mentor during the award period. Field of study must be relevant to NASA's goals, e.g. areas of math, science, engineering, computer science (concerned with utilizing or exploring space), and air transportation. Full-time undergraduates at Manoa, Hilo with major declared can apply for two-semester fellowships. Stipend of $3,000 per semester. Also up to $500 for supplies or travel. Recipients expected to work 10-15 hours per week on space-related projects. Women, under-represented minorities (specifically Native Hawaiians, other Pacific Islanders, Native Americans, Blacks, Hispanics), and physically challenged students who have interest in space-related fields are encouraged to apply. Visit Website for more information and application.

| | |
|---|---|
| **Amount of award:** | $3,000 |
| **Number of applicants:** | 20 |
| **Application deadline:** | June 15, December 1 |
| **Total amount awarded:** | $135,000 |

**Contact:**
NASA Hawaii Space Grant Consortium
Phone: 808-956-3138
Fax: 808-956-6322
Web: www.spacegrant.hawaii.edu

# NASA Idaho Space Grant Consortium

## NASA Idaho Space Grant Undergraduate Scholarship

**Type of award:** Scholarship, renewable.
**Intended use:** For full-time undergraduate study at accredited 4-year institution. Designated institutions: College of Idaho, Boise State University, College of Southern Idaho, Idaho State University, Lewis Clark State College, North Idaho College, Northwest Nazarene University, BYU-Idaho, and the University of Idaho.
**Eligibility:** Applicant must be U.S. citizen.
**Basis for selection:** Major/career interest in engineering; mathematics or science, general.
**Application requirements:** Recommendations, essay. High school and college transcripts, SAT or ACT scores.
**Additional information:** Applicants must attend Idaho Space Grant Consortium member institution in Idaho and maintain a 3.0 GPA. Women, minority students, and disabled students encouraged to apply. Application essay should not exceed 500 words. Applications available on Website.

| | |
|---|---|
| **Amount of award:** | $1,000-$2,000 |
| **Number of awards:** | 12 |
| **Number of applicants:** | 50 |
| **Application deadline:** | March 1 |
| **Notification begins:** | June 1 |
| **Total amount awarded:** | $49,000 |

**Contact:**
NASA Space Grant Idaho Space Grant Consortium
University of Idaho
P.O. Box 441011
Moscow, ID 83844-1011
Phone: 208-885-6438
Fax: 208-885-1399
Web: www.id.spacegrant.org

# NASA Illinois Space Grant Consortium

## NASA Space Grant Illinois Undergraduate Scholarship

**Type of award:** Scholarship, renewable.
**Intended use:** For full-time undergraduate study at postsecondary institution. Designated institutions: Illinois Space Grant Consortium member institutions.
**Eligibility:** Applicant must be U.S. citizen.

**Basis for selection:** Major/career interest in engineering or aerospace. Applicant must demonstrate high academic achievement.
**Application requirements:** Recommendations, essay, transcript.
**Additional information:** Minimum 2.5 GPA. Contact sponsor for deadline information.

| | |
|---|---|
| **Amount of award:** | $3,000 |
| **Number of awards:** | 15 |
| **Number of applicants:** | 62 |
| **Total amount awarded:** | $50,000 |

**Contact:**
Associate Director/ Illinois Space Grant Consortium
U of Illinois-Urbana, 306 Talbot Lab
104 S. Wright Street
Urbana, IL 61801-2935
Phone: 217-244-8048
Fax: 217-244-0720
Web: www.ae.illinois.edu/ISGC



# NASA Kentucky Space Grant Consortium

## NASA Space Grant Kentucky Undergraduate Scholarship

**Type of award:** Scholarship, renewable.
**Intended use:** For full-time undergraduate study at accredited 4-year institution in United States. Designated institutions: Consortium member institutions.
**Eligibility:** Applicant must be U.S. citizen.
**Basis for selection:** Major/career interest in aerospace; astronomy; education; engineering or physics. Applicant must demonstrate high academic achievement.
**Application requirements:** Interview, recommendations, essay, transcript, nomination by professor/mentor at participating institution. Research proposal, written with mentor.
**Additional information:** Stipend for materials and travel up to $1500. Preference given to schools that waive tuition for recipient. Consortium actively encourages women, minority students, and physically challenged students to apply. Applicants doing work related to space exploration may qualify for funding, whatever their field of study may be.

| | |
|---|---|
| **Amount of award:** | $6,000 |
| **Number of applicants:** | 10 |

**Contact:**
NASA/Kentucky Space Grant Consortium
University of Kentucky- Coll. Of Eng.
112 Robotics Building
Lexington, KY 40506-0108
Phone: 859-218-6272
Fax: 859-257-3304
Web: nasa.engr.uky.edu

# NASA Maine Space Grant Consortium

## NASA Space Grant Maine Consortium Annual Scholarship and Fellowship Program

**Type of award:** Research grant, renewable.
**Intended use:** For full-time undergraduate or graduate study at accredited 4-year or graduate institution. Designated institutions: University of Maine (Orono), University of Maine (Presque Isle), University of Southern Maine, University of New England, Maine Maritime Academy, College of the Atlantic, Bowdoin College, Colby College, Bates College.
**Eligibility:** Applicant must be U.S. citizen.
**Basis for selection:** Major/career interest in astronomy; geology/earth sciences; geophysics; engineering; aerospace; biology or medicine.
**Additional information:** Applicants from out of state who attend one of the designated institutions are eligible. Research project must be in an aerospace-related field. Applications from academic institutions in Maine other than those designated will be reviewed for consideration. Visit Website for additional details.

| | |
|---|---|
| **Amount of award:** | $3,000-$6,000 |
| **Total amount awarded:** | $135,000 |

**Contact:**
Maine Space Grant Consortium
87 Winthrop Street
Suite 200
Augusta, ME 04330
Phone: 877-397-7223
Fax: 207-622-4548
Web: www.msgc.org

# NASA Michigan Space Grant Consortium

## MSGC Undergraduate Underrepresented Minority Fellowship Program

**Type of award:** Research grant.
**Intended use:** For full-time undergraduate study at 4-year institution in United States. Designated institutions: Michigan Space Grant Consortium member institutions.
**Eligibility:** Applicant must be African American, Hispanic American, American Indian or Native Hawaiian/Pacific Islander. Applicant must be U.S. citizen residing in Michigan.
**Basis for selection:** Major/career interest in aerospace; engineering; science, general or mathematics. Applicant must demonstrate high academic achievement.
**Application requirements:** Recommendations, essay, transcript, research proposal. Description of project expectations and specifications; 150-word abstract.
**Additional information:** Offers support in form of undergraduate research and public service fellowships to students in aerospace, space science, Earth system science and other related science, engineering, or math fields. Students working on educational research topics in math, science, or technology also eligible to apply. Preference given to projects directly related to aerospace, space science, earth system science, and directly related educational efforts. Students required to identify a mentor with whom they intend to work. Underrepresented minority students who have a GPA below 3.0, but have strong mentorship, do qualify for an award. Visit Website for more information.

| | |
|---|---|
| **Amount of award:** | $2,500 |
| **Application deadline:** | November 20 |
| **Notification begins:** | February 28 |
| **Total amount awarded:** | $14,000 |

**Contact:**
NASA Michigan Space Grant Consortium
University of Michigan
1320 Beal Ave., 1216-C FXB
Ann Arbor, MI 48109-2140
Phone: 734-764-9508
Fax: 734-763-6904
Web: www.umich.edu/~msgc

## NASA Space Grant Michigan Undergraduate Fellowship

**Type of award:** Research grant, renewable.
**Intended use:** For undergraduate study at accredited 4-year institution. Designated institutions: Michigan Space Grant Consortium member institutions.
**Eligibility:** Applicant must be U.S. citizen.
**Basis for selection:** Major/career interest in aerospace; engineering; science, general or mathematics. Applicant must demonstrate high academic achievement.
**Application requirements:** Essay, transcript. Two letters of recommendation; description of project expectations and specifications; 150-word abstract.
**Additional information:** Offers support in form of undergraduate research and public service fellowships to students in aerospace, space science, Earth system science and other related science, engineering, or math fields. Students working on educational research topics in math, science, or technology also eligible to apply. Preference given to projects directly related to aerospace, space science, Earth system science, and directly related educational efforts. Announcements for next funding interval can be found on Website.

| | |
|---|---|
| **Amount of award:** | $2,500-$5,000 |
| **Application deadline:** | November 20 |
| **Notification begins:** | February 28 |
| **Total amount awarded:** | $100,000 |

**Contact:**
NASA Space Grant Michigan Space Grant Consortium
University of Michigan
1320 Beal Ave., 1216-C FXB
Ann Arbor, MI 48109-2140
Phone: 734-764-9508
Fax: 734-763-6904
Web: www.umich.edu/~msgc

# NASA Minnesota Space Grant Consortium

## NASA Minnesota Space Grant Consortium Wide Scholarship

**Type of award:** Scholarship, renewable.
**Intended use:** For full-time undergraduate study at accredited 2-year or 4-year institution in United States. Designated institutions: Augsburg College, Bethel University, Bemidji State University, Carleton College, Concordia College, Fond du Lac Tribal and Community College, Leech Lake Tribal College, Macalester College, Southwest Minnesota State University, St. Catherine University, University of Minnesota - Duluth, University of Minnesota - Twin Cities, University of St. Thomas.
**Eligibility:** Applicant must be U.S. citizen.
**Basis for selection:** Major/career interest in aerospace; astronomy; atmospheric sciences/meteorology; mathematics; engineering, mechanical; chemistry; engineering, electrical/electronic; engineering, chemical; engineering, civil or engineering, computer.
**Application requirements:** Recommendations, essay, transcript. Letter of intent.
**Additional information:** Minimum 3.2 GPA. Women, minority, and physically challenged students encouraged to apply. Applicant must be attending a Minnesota Space Grant Consortium school but does not have to be a resident of the state. Must major in aerospace, astronomy, physics, geology, chemistry, mathematics, computer science, or engineering. Visit Website for application.

| | |
|---|---|
| **Amount of award:** | $500-$2,500 |
| **Number of awards:** | 15 |
| **Number of applicants:** | 40 |
| **Application deadline:** | May 15 |

**Contact:**
NASA Minnesota Space Grant Consortium
U of M: Dept of Aerospace Engineering
107 Akerman Hall, 110 Union St. SE
Minneapolis, MN 55455
Phone: 612-626-9295
Web: www.aem.umn.edu/mnsgc

# NASA Missouri Space Grant Consortium

## NASA Missouri State Space Grant Undergraduate Scholarship

**Type of award:** Scholarship, renewable.
**Intended use:** For full-time undergraduate study at accredited 4-year institution in United States. Designated institutions: Missouri State University, University of Missouri - Columbia, University of Missouri - Kansas City, Missouri University of Science and Technology, University of Missouri - St. Louis, and Washington University in St. Louis.
**Eligibility:** Applicant must be U.S. citizen residing in Missouri.
**Basis for selection:** Major/career interest in aerospace; astronomy; engineering; geology/earth sciences; physics; mathematics or engineering, mechanical.
**Application requirements:** Recommendations, essay, transcript.
**Additional information:** Program encourages applications from eligible space science students. Awardees must attend Missouri Space Grant Consortium affiliate institution. Women, minority students, and physically challenged students are actively encouraged to apply. Deadline varies but is usually the first week in April. Check sponsor for exact date. Awards normally granted sometime in May.

| | |
|---|---|
| **Amount of award:** | $1,500-$3,500 |
| **Number of awards:** | 45 |
| **Number of applicants:** | 43 |
| **Total amount awarded:** | $140,000 |

Scholarships

**Contact:**
NASA Missouri Space Grant Consortium
Missouri University of Science and Technology
137 Toomey Hall
Rolla, MO 65409-0050
Phone: 573-341-4887
Fax: 573-341-4607
Web: www.mst.edu/~spaceg

# NASA Montana Space Grant Consortium

## NASA Space Grant Montana Undergraduate Scholarship Program

**Type of award:** Scholarship, renewable.
**Intended use:** For full-time undergraduate study at accredited 2-year or 4-year institution in United States. Designated institutions: Montana Space Grant Consortium member institutions.
**Eligibility:** Applicant must be U.S. citizen.
**Basis for selection:** Major/career interest in aerospace; biology; chemistry; geology/earth sciences; physics; astronomy; computer/information sciences; engineering, chemical; engineering, civil or engineering, electrical/electronic. Applicant must demonstrate depth of character and leadership.
**Application requirements:** Recommendations, essay, transcript.
**Additional information:** Must attend Montana Space Grant Consortium member institution, but does not need to be Montana resident. Awards for one year, renewable on a competitive basis. Recipients must agree to provide MSGC with information about studies and employment beyond period of award. Visit Website for more information.

| | |
|---|---|
| **Amount of award:** | $1,500 |
| **Number of awards:** | 24 |
| **Number of applicants:** | 45 |
| **Application deadline:** | April 1 |
| **Total amount awarded:** | $24,000 |

**Contact:**
NASA Space Grant Montana Space Grant Consortium
Montana State University
416 Cobleigh Hall, P.O. Box 173835
Bozeman, MT 59717-3835
Phone: 406-994-4223
Fax: 406-994-4452
Web: www.spacegrant.montana.edu

# NASA Nevada Space Grant Consortium

## NASA Space Grant Nevada Undergraduate Scholarship

**Type of award:** Scholarship.
**Intended use:** For full-time undergraduate or graduate study at accredited postsecondary institution in United States. Designated institutions: Nevada System of Higher Education institutions.
**Eligibility:** Applicant must be U.S. citizen.
**Basis for selection:** Major/career interest in aerospace; astronomy; biology; chemistry; computer/information sciences; geology/earth sciences; engineering; mathematics; science, general or physics.
**Application requirements:** Transcript. Resume. Career goal statement, including applicant's motivation toward aerospace career.
**Additional information:** Applicant must attend school in Nevada. Math, science, engineering, or majors in relevant fields eligible to apply. Application available on Website. Contact institution of interest for more information. Application deadline usually in mid-April.

| | |
|---|---|
| **Amount of award:** | $5,000 |
| **Number of awards:** | 13 |
| **Number of applicants:** | 45 |
| **Total amount awarded:** | $150,000 |

**Contact:**
Nevada Space Grant Consortium Program Coordinator
Desert Research Institute
2215 Raggio Parkway
Reno, NV 89512
Phone: 775-673-7674
Fax: 775-673-7485
Web: www.nvspacegrant.org

# NASA New Mexico Space Grant Consortium

## NASA Space Grant New Mexico Undergraduate Scholarship

**Type of award:** Research grant, renewable.
**Intended use:** For full-time sophomore, junior, senior or graduate study at accredited 4-year institution in United States. Designated institutions: New Mexico Space Grant Consortium institutions.
**Eligibility:** Applicant must be U.S. citizen.
**Basis for selection:** Major/career interest in astronomy; biology; chemistry; computer/information sciences; engineering, chemical; engineering, civil; engineering, electrical/electronic; engineering, mechanical; physics or mathematics.
**Application requirements:** Transcript, research proposal, nomination by faculty mentor.
**Additional information:** Minimum 3.0 GPA. Geology, earth science, environmental science, agriculture, range science, and fishery and wildlife science majors also eligible. Preference given to applicants who can show nonfederal matching funds. Women, minority students, and physically challenged students encouraged to apply. Visit Website for application and more information.

| | |
|---|---|
| **Amount of award:** | $5,000 |
| **Number of applicants:** | 20 |
| **Application deadline:** | March 15 |
| **Notification begins:** | March 30 |
| **Total amount awarded:** | $100,000 |

**Contact:**
NASA New Mexico Space Grant Consortium
Program Office, New Mexico State University
3050 Knox St, Sugarman Space Grant Building
Las Cruces, NM 88003-0001
Phone: 575-646-6414
Fax: 575-646-7791
Web: spacegrant.nmsu.edu

# NASA North Carolina Space Grant Consortium

## Undergraduate Research Scholarship

**Type of award:** Scholarship.
**Intended use:** For full-time junior or senior study at postsecondary institution. Designated institutions: North Carolina Space Grant Consortium member institutions.
**Eligibility:** Applicant must be returning adult student. Applicant must be U.S. citizen.
**Basis for selection:** Major/career interest in science, general; engineering; aerospace; mathematics or technology. Applicant must demonstrate high academic achievement and leadership.
**Application requirements:** Recommendations, transcript, research proposal.
**Additional information:** Minimum 3.0 GPA. Visit Website for more information and application.

| | |
|---|---|
| **Amount of award:** | $3,000-$7,000 |
| **Number of awards:** | 25 |
| **Number of applicants:** | 40 |
| **Application deadline:** | February 15 |
| **Notification begins:** | April 15 |
| **Total amount awarded:** | $100,000 |

**Contact:**
NASA North Carolina Space Grant
NCSU Box 7515
Raleigh, NC 27695-7515
Phone: 919-515-4240
Fax: 919-515-5934
Web: www.ncspacegrant.org/fs/

## Undergraduate Scholarship Program

**Type of award:** Scholarship, renewable.
**Intended use:** For full-time freshman or sophomore study at 4-year institution. Designated institutions: North Carolina Space Grant Consortium Member Institutions.
**Eligibility:** Applicant must be U.S. citizen.
**Basis for selection:** Major/career interest in science, general; engineering or aerospace. Applicant must demonstrate high academic achievement and leadership.
**Application requirements:** Recommendations, essay, transcript.
**Additional information:** Minimum 3.0 GPA. May be new or returning adult student. Visit Website for application and more information.

| | |
|---|---|
| **Amount of award:** | $1,000-$2,000 |
| **Number of awards:** | 10 |
| **Number of applicants:** | 15 |
| **Application deadline:** | February 15 |
| **Notification begins:** | April 15 |
| **Total amount awarded:** | $10,000 |

**Contact:**
NASA North Carolina Space Grant
NCSU Box 7515
Raleigh, NC 27695-7515
Phone: 919-515-4240
Fax: 919-515-5934
Web: www.ncspacegrant.org/fs/

# NASA North Dakota Space Grant Consortium

## NASA Space Grant North Dakota Consortium Lillian Goettler Scholarship

**Type of award:** Scholarship.
**Intended use:** For full-time undergraduate study at accredited postsecondary institution in United States. Designated institutions: North Dakota State University.
**Eligibility:** Applicant must be female. Applicant must be U.S. citizen.
**Basis for selection:** Major/career interest in engineering; mathematics or science, general.
**Additional information:** Must have minimum 3.5 GPA and ideally be involved in research project of interest to NASA. Must be enrolled on campus at NDSGC institution; long distance learning programs not eligible. Contact coordinator for deadline information.

| | |
|---|---|
| **Amount of award:** | $2,500 |

**Contact:**
North Dakota Space Grant Consortium
U of North Dakota, Space Studies Dept.
P.O. Box 9008
Grand Forks, ND 58202-9008
Phone: 701-777-4856
Web: www.nd.spacegrant.org

## NASA Space Grant North Dakota Undergraduate Scholarship

**Type of award:** Scholarship, renewable.
**Intended use:** For full-time undergraduate study at 2-year or 4-year institution. Designated institutions: Tribal or public NDSGC member institutions.
**Eligibility:** Applicant must be U.S. citizen.
**Basis for selection:** Major/career interest in biology; chemistry; engineering; geology/earth sciences; computer/information sciences or mathematics.
**Application requirements:** Recommendations, transcript, nomination by participating North Dakota Space Grant Consortium member institution.
**Additional information:** Minimum 3.0 GPA. Must be enrolled on campus at NDSGC institution; long distance learning programs not eligible. Consortium actively encourages women, minority students, and physically challenged students to apply. Deadlines vary. Contact financial aid office at institutions directly.

| | |
|---|---|
| **Amount of award:** | $500-$750 |

**Contact:**
Financial Aid office at eligible institutions.
Web: www.nd.spacegrant.org

### Pearl I. Young Scholarship

**Type of award:** Scholarship.
**Intended use:** For full-time undergraduate study at accredited postsecondary institution in United States. Designated institutions: University of North Dakota.
**Eligibility:** Applicant must be female. Applicant must be U.S. citizen or permanent resident.
**Basis for selection:** Major/career interest in biology; chemistry; engineering; geology/earth sciences; computer/information sciences or mathematics.
**Additional information:** Applicants must have minimum 3.5 GPA and ideally be involved in research project of interest to NASA. Must be enrolled on campus at NDSGC institution; long distance learning programs not eligible. Contact coordinator for deadline information.

| | |
|---|---|
| **Amount of award:** | $2,500 |
| **Number of awards:** | 1 |

**Contact:**
NASA Space Grant North Dakota Space Grant Consortium
U of North Dakota, Space Studies Dept.
P.O. Box 9008
Grand Forks, ND 58202-9008
Phone: 701-777-4856
Web: www.nd.spacegrant.org

## NASA Ohio Space Grant Consortium

### NASA Ohio Space Grant Junior/Senior Scholarship Program

**Type of award:** Scholarship, renewable.
**Intended use:** For full-time junior or senior study at accredited 4-year institution. Designated institutions: Ohio Space Grant Consortium members.
**Eligibility:** Applicant must be U.S. citizen.
**Basis for selection:** Major/career interest in science, general; engineering; aerospace or mathematics.
**Application requirements:** Recommendations, essay, transcript. Proposal of research project.
**Additional information:** Applications available at OSGC office at Consortium member institutions. Awardees required to participate in research projects and present results at annual OSGC Research Symposium.

| | |
|---|---|
| **Amount of award:** | $3,000-$4,000 |
| **Number of awards:** | 50 |
| **Number of applicants:** | 75 |
| **Application deadline:** | March 1 |
| **Notification begins:** | April 30 |
| **Total amount awarded:** | $130,000 |

**Contact:**
OSGC campus representative.
Phone: 800-828-6742
Web: www.osgc.org/scholarship.html

## NASA Oregon Space Grant Consortium

### NASA Space Grant Oregon Undergraduate Scholarship

**Type of award:** Scholarship.
**Intended use:** For undergraduate or graduate study at accredited 2-year or 4-year institution in United States. Designated institutions: Oregon State University, University of Oregon, Portland State University, Eastern Oregon University, Southern Oregon University, Oregon Institute of Technology, Western Oregon University, George Fox University, Portland Community Colleges (Sylvania, Rock Creek and Cascades Campuses), Lane Community College, and Pacific University.
**Eligibility:** Applicant must be U.S. citizen residing in Oregon.
**Basis for selection:** Major/career interest in science, general; engineering; aerospace; mathematics; physical sciences or education. Applicant must demonstrate high academic achievement.
**Application requirements:** Recommendations, essay, transcript.
**Additional information:** Contact Space Grant Consortium representative on campus or see Website for application deadlines and more information.

| | |
|---|---|
| **Amount of award:** | $1,000-$5,000 |
| **Number of awards:** | 22 |
| **Number of applicants:** | 125 |
| **Application deadline:** | April 15 |
| **Notification begins:** | August 1 |
| **Total amount awarded:** | $124,000 |

**Contact:**
Oregon NASA Space Grant Consortium
Oregon State University
92 Kerr Administration Bldg.
Corvallis, OR 97331-2103
Phone: 541-737-2414
Fax: 541-737-9946
Web: spacegrant.oregonstate.edu

## NASA Pennsylvania Space Grant Consortium

### NASA Pennsylvania Space Grant Undergraduate Scholarship

**Type of award:** Scholarship.
**Intended use:** For full-time junior or senior study at accredited 4-year institution in United States. Designated institutions: Pennsylvania universties and colleges.
**Eligibility:** Applicant must be U.S. citizen.
**Basis for selection:** Major/career interest in science, general; mathematics; engineering; education; aerospace or astronomy. Applicant must demonstrate high academic achievement.
**Application requirements:** Recommendations, essay, transcript. Resume, SAT scores, description of research project and plan of study.
**Additional information:** Contact campus Space Grant Consortium representative for details. Consortium actively

encourages women, minority, and physically challenged students to apply.

**Amount of award:** $4,000
**Number of awards:** 2
**Number of applicants:** 12
**Application deadline:** April 1
**Total amount awarded:** $8,000

**Contact:**
NASA Pennsylvania Space Grant Consortium
Penn State, University Park
2217 Earth-Engineering Sciences Building
University Park, PA 16802
Phone: 814-865-2535
Fax: 814-863-9563
Web: www.pa.spacegrant.org

# NASA Rhode Island Space Grant Consortium

## NASA Space Grant Rhode Island Undergraduate Research Scholarship

**Type of award:** Scholarship.
**Intended use:** For sophomore, junior or senior study at postsecondary institution. Designated institutions: Rhode Island Space Grant Consortium member institutions: Brown University, Bryant College, Community College of Rhode Island, Providence College, Roger Williams University, Rhode Island College, Rhode Island School of Design, Salve Regina University, University of Rhode Island, Wheaton College.
**Eligibility:** Applicant must be U.S. citizen.
**Basis for selection:** Major/career interest in aerospace; biology; engineering; geology/earth sciences or physics. Applicant must demonstrate high academic achievement.
**Application requirements:** Interview, recommendations, essay, transcript. Research proposal, resume.
**Additional information:** Awardees expected to work full-time with 75 percent of time devoted to research and the other 25 percent to science education outreach. Applications due in late February; call sponsor for exact dates. Number of awards may vary. Topics of study in space sciences also funded. Students should contact campus representative or the Rhode Island Space Grant office.

**Amount of award:** $4,500
**Number of awards:** 4
**Number of applicants:** 15

**Contact:**
NASA Rhode Island Space Grant Consortium
Brown University
Box 1846
Providence, RI 02912
Phone: 401-863-1151
Fax: 401-863-3978
Web: ri.spacegrant.org

## Summer Undergraduate Scholarship

**Type of award:** Scholarship, renewable.
**Intended use:** For sophomore, junior or senior study at postsecondary institution. Designated institutions: Rhode Island Space Grant Consortium member institutions: Brown University, Bryant College, Community College of Rhode Island, Providence College, Roger Williams University, Rhode Island College, Rhode Island School of Design, Salve Regina University, University of Rhode Island, Wheaton College.
**Eligibility:** Applicant must be U.S. citizen.
**Basis for selection:** Major/career interest in aerospace; biology; engineering; geology/earth sciences or physics. Applicant must demonstrate high academic achievement.
**Application requirements:** Interview, recommendations, essay, transcript. Research proposal, resume.
**Additional information:** Awardees expected to devote four hours per week to science education outreach. Application deadline in late February; call sponsor for exact dates. Number of awards may vary. Topics of study in space sciences also funded. Students should contact their campus representative or the Rhode Island Space Grant office.

**Amount of award:** $3,000
**Number of awards:** 3
**Number of applicants:** 5

**Contact:**
NASA Rhode Island Space Grant Consortium
Brown University
Box 1846
Providence, RI 02912
Phone: 401-863-1151
Fax: 401-863-3978
Web: ri.spacegrant.org

# NASA Rocky Mountain Space Grant Consortium

## NASA Rocky Mountain Space Grant Consortium Undergraduate Scholarship

**Type of award:** Scholarship, renewable.
**Intended use:** For full-time undergraduate or graduate study at accredited postsecondary institution in United States. Designated institutions: Brigham Young University, Dixie State College, Salt Lake Community College, Snow College, Southern Utah University, Utah College of Applied Technology, Utah Science Center, Utah State University, Utah Valley University, University of Utah, Weaver State University, Weber State University, and Westminster College.
**Eligibility:** Applicant must be U.S. citizen.
**Basis for selection:** Major/career interest in science, general; mathematics; engineering or technology. Applicant must demonstrate high academic achievement.
**Application requirements:** Recommendations, transcript, research proposal. Resume.
**Additional information:** Award varies from year to year. Contact sponsor for deadline information. Must be used at Rocky Mountain Space Grant Consortium member institution. Award amounts are per month during academic year.

**Amount of award:** $500-$1,500
**Number of awards:** 20
**Number of applicants:** 60
**Total amount awarded:** $22,000

**Contact:**
Rocky Mountain NASA Space Grant Consortium
Utah State University
4140 Old Main Hill
Logan, UT 84322-4140
Phone: 435-797-3666
Fax: 435-797-3382
Web: utahspacegrant.com

# NASA South Carolina Space Grant Consortium

## Kathryn D. Sullivan Science and Engineering Fellowship

**Type of award:** Scholarship, renewable.
**Intended use:** For full-time senior study at 4-year institution. Designated institutions: SCSGC member institutions.
**Eligibility:** Applicant must be high school senior. Applicant must be U.S. citizen.
**Basis for selection:** Major/career interest in science, general; engineering; mathematics or aerospace. Applicant must demonstrate high academic achievement.
**Application requirements:** Recommendations, essay, transcript. Faculty sponsorship. Resume.
**Additional information:** Applicants must attend South Carolina member institution. Applicants must have sponsorship from faculty advisor. The Consortium actively encourages women, minority, and disabled students to apply. Application deadline usually in January.

| | |
|---|---|
| **Amount of award:** | $7,000 |
| **Number of awards:** | 1 |

**Contact:**
NASA South Carolina Space Grant Consortium Tara B. Scozzaro, MPA
College of Charleston
66 George Street
Charleston, SC 29424
Phone: 843-953-5463
Fax: 843-953-5446
Web: www.cofc.edu/~scsgrant/scholar/overview.html

## NASA Space Grant South Carolina Undergraduate Student Research Fellowship

**Type of award:** Research grant, renewable.
**Intended use:** For full-time sophomore, junior or senior study at accredited 4-year institution in United States. Designated institutions: SCSGC member institutions.
**Eligibility:** Applicant must be U.S. citizen.
**Basis for selection:** Major/career interest in aerospace; astronomy; atmospheric sciences/meteorology; engineering; environmental science; geophysics; mathematics or science, general. Applicant must demonstrate high academic achievement.
**Application requirements:** Recommendations, essay, transcript, research proposal. Faculty sponsorship. Resume.
**Additional information:** Applicants must attend South Carolina Space Grant Consortium member institution. Applicants must have sponsorship from a faculty advisor. Applicants may have a field of study or interest related to any NASA enterprise. Presentation and written report on project findings due within one year of completion. Consortium actively encourages women, minority, and disabled students to apply. See Website for application and more information.

| | |
|---|---|
| **Amount of award:** | $5,000 |

**Contact:**
NASA South Carolina Space Grant Consortium Tara B. Scozzaro MPA
College of Charleston
66 George Street
Charleston, SC 29424
Phone: 843-953-5463
Fax: 843-953-5446
Web: www.cofc.edu/~scsgrant/scholar/overview.html

# NASA Texas Space Grant Consortium

## NASA Space Grant Texas Columbia Crew Memorial Undergraduate Scholarships

**Type of award:** Scholarship.
**Intended use:** For sophomore, junior or senior study at accredited 2-year or 4-year institution in United States. Designated institutions: Texas Space Grant member institutions.
**Eligibility:** Applicant must be U.S. citizen.
**Basis for selection:** Major/career interest in engineering; mathematics; science, general or technology. Applicant must demonstrate high academic achievement and leadership.
**Application requirements:** Recommendations, essay, transcript, proof of eligibility.
**Additional information:** First or second year medical school students also eligible. Must attend Texas Space Grant Consortium member institution. Online application. Deadline in late March; visit Website for exact dates.

| | |
|---|---|
| **Amount of award:** | $1,000 |
| **Number of awards:** | 15 |
| **Number of applicants:** | 40 |
| **Total amount awarded:** | $15,000 |

**Contact:**
Texas Space Grant Consortium
3925 W. Braker Lane
Suite 200
Austin, TX 78759-5321
Phone: 800-248-8742
Web: www.tsgc.utexas.edu

## STEM Scholarship

**Type of award:** Scholarship.
**Intended use:** For sophomore, junior or senior study at 2-year or 4-year institution in United States. Designated institutions: Texas Space Grant Consortium member institutions.
**Eligibility:** Applicant must be U.S. citizen.
**Basis for selection:** Major/career interest in science, general; technology; engineering or mathematics. Applicant must demonstrate high academic achievement.
**Application requirements:** Recommendations, transcript.
**Additional information:** First and second year medical students also eligible. Check Website for application deadline.

**Amount of award:** $1,500
**Number of awards:** 30
**Number of applicants:** 100
**Total amount awarded:** $45,000

**Contact:**
NASA Texas Space Grant Consortium
University of Texas at Austin
3925 West Braker Lane
Austin, TX 78759-5321
Phone: 800-248-8742
Web: www.tsgc.utexas.edu

# NASA Vermont Space Grant Consortium

## NASA Space Grant Vermont Consortium Undergraduate Scholarships

**Type of award:** Scholarship, renewable.
**Intended use:** For full-time undergraduate study at accredited postsecondary institution in United States. Designated institutions: Vermont institutions.
**Eligibility:** Applicant must be high school senior. Applicant must be U.S. citizen residing in Vermont.
**Basis for selection:** Major/career interest in science, general; engineering; mathematics; aerospace or physics.
**Application requirements:** Recommendations, essay, transcript.
**Additional information:** Open to high school seniors in Vermont who intend to be enrolled full-time in the following year. Applicant must be enrolled in program relevant to NASA's goals at a Vermont institution. Minimum 3.0 GPA. Three awards designated for Native American applicants; three scholarships designated for Burlington Technical Center Aviation & Technical Center, Aerospace Work Force Development, and Aviation Technical School. Can be used at any accredited Vermont institution of higher education. Application deadline in June. Check website for details.

**Amount of award:** $2,500
**Number of awards:** 10
**Number of applicants:** 15
**Total amount awarded:** $18,000

**Contact:**
Vermont Space Grant Consortium
Votey Hall, College of Engineering and Math
University of Vermont
Burlington, VT 05405-0156
Phone: 802-656-1429
Web: www.cems.uvm.edu/VSGC

# NASA Virginia Space Grant Consortium

## Aerospace Undergraduate Research Scholarship Program

**Type of award:** Scholarship.
**Intended use:** For full-time undergraduate study at accredited 4-year institution in United States. Designated institutions: Space Grant Consortium schools.
**Eligibility:** Applicant must be U.S. citizen.
**Basis for selection:** Major/career interest in aerospace; astronomy; chemistry; computer/information sciences; engineering; geology/earth sciences; mathematics or physics. Applicant must demonstrate high academic achievement.
**Application requirements:** Recommendations, essay, transcript, research proposal. Resume. Budget proposal.
**Additional information:** Any undergraduate major that includes coursework related to an understanding of aerospace is eligible. Minimum 3.0 GPA. Awards can include $3,000 stipend plus $1,000 travel/research during the academic year, and $3,500 stipend plus $1,000 travel/research during the summer (ten weeks). Awardees must attend a Virginia Space Grant Consortium member institution and participate in USGC's Annual Student Research Conference. The consortium actively encourages women, minorities, and students with disabilities to apply.

**Amount of award:** $1,000-$3,500
**Notification begins:** April 15

**Contact:**
Virginia Space Grant Consortium
600 Butler Farm Road, Suite 2253
Hampton, VA 23666
Phone: 757-766-5210
Fax: 757-766-5205
Web: www.vsgc.odu.edu

## NASA Space Grant Virginia Community College STEM Scholarship

**Type of award:** Scholarship.
**Intended use:** For full-time sophomore study at accredited 2-year institution in United States. Designated institutions: Virginia community colleges.
**Eligibility:** Applicant must be U.S. citizen.
**Basis for selection:** Major/career interest in aerospace; computer/information sciences; electronics; engineering; mathematics; science, general or technology.
**Application requirements:** Recommendations, essay, transcript. Resume, photograph and biographical information.
**Additional information:** Must apply during freshman year and be majoring in STEM program of study. Minimum 3.0 GPA. Scholarship is open to students at all community colleges in Virginia. Application deadline may vary. Women, minorities, and students with disabilities are encouraged to apply. Visit Website for application.

**Amount of award:** $1,500
**Notification begins:** April 1

**Contact:**
Virginia Space Grant Consortium
600 Butler Farm Road, Suite 2253
Hampton, VA 23666
Phone: 757-766-5210
Fax: 757-766-5205
Web: www.vsgc.odu.edu

## Teacher Education STEM Scholarship

**Type of award:** Scholarship.
**Intended use:** For full-time undergraduate or graduate study at 2-year, 4-year or graduate institution in United States. Designated institutions: VSGC member institutions.
**Eligibility:** Applicant must be U.S. citizen.
**Basis for selection:** Major/career interest in computer/information sciences; education; engineering; environmental

Scholarships

science; geology/earth sciences; mathematics; science, general or technology.
**Application requirements:** Recommendations, essay, transcript. Resume.
**Additional information:** Applicants must be enrolled in course of study leading to precollege teacher certification. Priority given to technology education, mathematics, and earth/space/environmental science majors. Minimum 3.0 GPA. High school seniors eligible. See Website for application and additional information.

| | |
|---|---|
| **Amount of award:** | $1,000 |
| **Notification begins:** | April 1 |
| **Total amount awarded:** | $10,000 |

**Contact:**
Virginia Space Grant Consortium
600 Butler Farm Road, Suite 2253
Hampton, VA 23666
Phone: 757-766-5210
Fax: 757-766-5205
Web: www.vsgc.odu.edu

# NASA West Virginia Space Grant Consortium

## NASA West Virginia Space Grant Undergraduate Research Fellowship

**Type of award:** Scholarship.
**Intended use:** For full-time undergraduate study at accredited 4-year institution in United States. Designated institutions: West Virgina Space Grant Consortium member institutions.
**Eligibility:** Applicant must be U.S. citizen.
**Basis for selection:** Major/career interest in aerospace; science, general; engineering or mathematics. Applicant must demonstrate high academic achievement and seriousness of purpose.
**Application requirements:** Recommendations, essay, research proposal. Resume. One recommendation must be from research advisor. Proposal must include statement of purpose, methodology, expected results, and timeline.
**Additional information:** Visit Website for more information and application. Female and minority students encouraged to apply.

| | |
|---|---|
| **Amount of award:** | $4,500-$5,000 |
| **Notification begins:** | April 1 |

**Contact:**
NASA West Virginia Space Grant Consortium, West Virginia University
G-68 Engineering Sciences Building
P.O. Box 6070
Morgantown, WV 26506-6070
Phone: 304-293-4099 ext. 3738
Fax: 304-293-4970
Web: www.nasa.wvu.edu

# NASA Wisconsin Space Grant Consortium

## NASA Space Grant Wisconsin Consortium Undergraduate Research Program

**Type of award:** Research grant.
**Intended use:** For full-time undergraduate study at 2-year or 4-year institution. Designated institutions: WSGC colleges and universities.
**Eligibility:** Applicant must be U.S. citizen.
**Basis for selection:** Major/career interest in aerospace; astronomy; engineering; science, general; architecture; law; business or medicine. Applicant must demonstrate high academic achievement and seriousness of purpose.
**Application requirements:** Recommendations, transcript, research proposal. Project proposal with budget.
**Additional information:** Funding for qualified students to create and implement a research project related to aerospace, space science, or other interdisciplinary space-related studies. For academic year or summer term use. Minimum 3.0 GPA and above-average SAT/ACT scores required. Consortium encourages applications from women, minorities, and students with disabilities. For more information, see Website.

| | |
|---|---|
| **Amount of award:** | $3,500-$4,000 |
| **Number of awards:** | 8 |
| **Application deadline:** | February 1 |
| **Notification begins:** | March 30 |
| **Total amount awarded:** | $28,000 |

**Contact:**
Wisconsin Space Grant Consortium
University of Wisconsin, Green Bay
2420 Nicolet Drive
Green Bay, WI 54311-7001
Phone: 608-785-8431
Fax: 608-785-8403
Web: www.uwgb.edu/wsgc

## NASA Space Grant Wisconsin Consortium Undergraduate Scholarship

**Type of award:** Scholarship, renewable.
**Intended use:** For full-time undergraduate study at accredited 4-year institution in United States. Designated institutions: WSGC colleges and universities.
**Eligibility:** Applicant must be U.S. citizen.
**Basis for selection:** Major/career interest in aerospace; astronomy; engineering; physics or science, general. Applicant must demonstrate high academic achievement.
**Application requirements:** Recommendations, essay, transcript.
**Additional information:** Applicant must attend Wisconsin Space Grant Consortium member institution and reside in Wisconsin during school year. Minimum 3.0 GPA and above-average SAT/ACT scores required. Qualified students may also apply for summer session's Undergraduate Research Award. Consortium actively encourages women, minorities, and students with disabilities to apply. See Website for application and details.

| | |
|---|---|
| **Amount of award:** | $1,500 |
| **Application deadline:** | February 1 |
| **Notification begins:** | March 30 |

**Contact:**
Wisconsin Space Grant Consortium
University of Wisconsin, Green Bay
2420 Nicolet Drive
Green Bay, WI 54311-7001
Phone: 920-465-2108
Web: www.uwgb.edu/wsgc

# National Academy for Nuclear Training

## Scholarship Educational Assistance Program

**Type of award:** Scholarship, renewable.
**Intended use:** For full-time junior or senior study at accredited 4-year institution in United States.
**Eligibility:** Applicant must be U.S. citizen.
**Basis for selection:** Major/career interest in engineering, chemical; engineering, mechanical; engineering, electrical/electronic or engineering, nuclear. Applicant must demonstrate high academic achievement, depth of character, leadership, seriousness of purpose and service orientation.
**Application requirements:** Recommendations, transcript, proof of eligibility, nomination by INPO member utility.
**Additional information:** Minimum 3.0 GPA. Renewal for eligible students. Additional field of study: power generation health physics. Study of chemical engineering must include nuclear or power option. Applicant should be considering career in nuclear utility industry. For additional information and application deadline, contact by e-mail or visit Website. Application deadline in mid-June.

| | |
|---|---|
| **Amount of award:** | $1,250-$2,500 |
| **Number of awards:** | 76 |
| **Number of applicants:** | 81 |
| **Notification begins:** | August 1 |
| **Total amount awarded:** | $300,000 |

**Contact:**
National Academy for Nuclear Training Scholarship Program
101 ACT Drive
P.O. Box 4030
Iowa City, IA 52243-4030
Phone: 800-294-7492
Fax: 319-337-1204
Web: www.nei.org/nantscholarships

# National Amateur Baseball Federation, Inc.

## National Amateur Baseball Federation Scholarship

**Type of award:** Scholarship, renewable.
**Intended use:** For undergraduate study at accredited postsecondary institution in United States or Canada.
**Basis for selection:** Competition/talent/interest in athletics/sports. Major/career interest in athletic training. Applicant must demonstrate financial need and high academic achievement.
**Application requirements:** Recommendations, transcript, proof of eligibility, nomination by National Amateur Baseball Federation member association. Written statement. Documentation of previous awards received from sponsoring association, nomination by president or director of franchised member team.
**Additional information:** Amount of award determined annually. Applicant must have participated in National Amateur Baseball Federation event in the current season and be sponsored by National Amateur Baseball Federation member association. Send SASE for application packet.

| | |
|---|---|
| **Amount of award:** | $500-$1,000 |
| **Number of awards:** | 10 |
| **Number of applicants:** | 11 |
| **Application deadline:** | October 1 |
| **Notification begins:** | January 1 |
| **Total amount awarded:** | $5,000 |

**Contact:**
National Amateur Baseball Federation
Attn: Chairman Awards Committee
P.O. Box 705
Bowie, MD 20718
Phone: 410-721-4727
Fax: 410-721-4940
Web: www.nabf.com

# National Art Materials Trade Association

## NAMTA Foundation Visual Arts Major Scholarship

**Type of award:** Scholarship.
**Intended use:** For undergraduate study at accredited vocational, 2-year or 4-year institution.
**Eligibility:** Applicant or parent must be member/participant of National Art Materials Trade Association.
**Basis for selection:** Major/career interest in arts, general; arts management or art/art history. Applicant must demonstrate financial need and high academic achievement.
**Application requirements:** Essay, transcript. Proof of acceptance, two to three examples of work via electronic means only (CD or email).
**Additional information:** Applicant must major in visual arts or visual arts education. Applicants judged primarily on artistic talent/potential, however financial need and GPA may also be considered.

| | |
|---|---|
| **Amount of award:** | $2,500 |
| **Number of awards:** | 8 |
| **Number of applicants:** | 57 |
| **Application deadline:** | March 1 |
| **Notification begins:** | April 15 |
| **Total amount awarded:** | $10,000 |

**Contact:**
Karen Brown, National Art Materials Trade Association
15806 Brookway Drive
Suite 300
Huntersville, NC 28078
Phone: 704-892-6244
Fax: 704-892-6247
Web: www.namtafoundation.org

# National Association of Black Accountants Inc.

## NABA National Scholarship Program

**Type of award:** Scholarship.
**Intended use:** For full-time undergraduate or master's study at 4-year or graduate institution.

Scholarships

**Eligibility:** Applicant must be Alaskan native, Asian American, African American, Mexican American, Hispanic American, Puerto Rican or American Indian.
**Basis for selection:** Major/career interest in accounting; business; finance/banking or technology. Applicant must demonstrate depth of character, leadership and service orientation.
**Application requirements:** Recommendations, essay, transcript, proof of eligibility. Resume.
**Additional information:** Must be active National Association of Black Accountants member. Applicants must have minimum 2.5 GPA for some awards, 3.3 GPA for others. Applicants must join association by December 31.

| | |
|---|---|
| **Amount of award:** | $1,000-$10,000 |
| **Number of applicants:** | 350 |
| **Application deadline:** | January 31 |
| **Notification begins:** | April 30 |
| **Total amount awarded:** | $175,000 |

**Contact:**
National Association of Black Accountants Inc.
National Scholarship Program
7474 Greenway Center Drive, #1120
Greenbelt, MD 20770
Phone: 301-474-6222
Fax: 301-474-3114
Web: www.nabainc.org

# National Association of Black Journalists

## Allison E. Fisher Scholarship

**Type of award:** Scholarship.
**Intended use:** For undergraduate or graduate study at postsecondary institution.
**Eligibility:** Applicant must be U.S. citizen, permanent resident or international student.
**Basis for selection:** Major/career interest in journalism. Applicant must demonstrate service orientation.
**Application requirements:** Essay, transcript. Resume. Applicants must submit minimum of five samples of published work in print, radio, television, photography, slideshows, website, or flash animation. Must send four copies of all application materials.
**Additional information:** Minimum 3.0 GPA. Must be a print or broadcast journalism major and a member of NABJ.

| | |
|---|---|
| **Number of awards:** | 1 |
| **Total amount awarded:** | $2,500 |

**Contact:**
National Association of Black Journalists
100 Knight Hall, Suite 3100
College Park, MD 20742
Phone: 301-405-0248
Fax: 301-314-1714
Web: www.nabj.org

## Carole Simpson Scholarship

**Type of award:** Scholarship.
**Intended use:** For undergraduate or graduate study at accredited 4-year or graduate institution.
**Eligibility:** Applicant must be U.S. citizen, permanent resident or international student.
**Basis for selection:** Major/career interest in journalism or radio/television/film.
**Application requirements:** Essay, transcript. Resume, cover letter. Applicants must submit minimum of five samples of published work in print, radio, television, photography, slideshows, website, or flash animation.
**Additional information:** Minimum 2.5 GPA. Must be member of National Association of Black Journalists and major in broadcast journalism.

| | |
|---|---|
| **Amount of award:** | $2,500 |
| **Number of awards:** | 1 |
| **Total amount awarded:** | $2,500 |

**Contact:**
National Association of Black Journalists
1100 Knight Hall, Suite 3100
College Park, MD 20742
Phone: 301-405-0248
Fax: 301-314-1714
Web: www.nabj.org

## Larry Whiteside Scholarship

**Type of award:** Scholarship.
**Intended use:** For junior or senior study at accredited 4-year institution.
**Eligibility:** Applicant must be African American.
**Basis for selection:** Major/career interest in journalism.
**Application requirements:** Portfolio, recommendations, essay, transcript. Resume, cover letter. Must submit three samples of work.
**Additional information:** Minimum 2.5 GPA in major and 2.0 major overall. Must be member of National Association of Black Journalists and be pursuing career in sports journalism.

| | |
|---|---|
| **Amount of award:** | $2,500 |
| **Number of awards:** | 1 |
| **Total amount awarded:** | $2,500 |

**Contact:**
National Association of Black Journalists
1100 Knight Hall, Suite 3100
College Park, MD 20742
Phone: 301-405-0248
Fax: 301-314-1714
Web: www.nabj.org

## Visual Task Force (VTF) Scholarship

**Type of award:** Scholarship.
**Intended use:** For sophomore, junior, senior or graduate study at 4-year or graduate institution.
**Eligibility:** Applicant must be African American.
**Basis for selection:** Major/career interest in journalism.
**Application requirements:** Portfolio, recommendations, essay, transcript. Resume, cover letter. Applicants must submit minimum of five samples of published work in print, radio, television, photography, slideshows, Website, or flash animation.
**Additional information:** Minimum 2.75 GPA. Must be member of National Association of Black Journalists and have declared a concentration in visual journalism. Must have experience working on campus newspaper or TV studio and have had one internship.

| | |
|---|---|
| **Amount of award:** | $1,250 |
| **Number of awards:** | 2 |
| **Total amount awarded:** | $2,500 |

**Contact:**
National Association of Black Journalists
1100 Knight Hall, Suite 3100
College Park, MD 20742
Phone: 301-405-0248
Fax: 301-314-1714
Web: www.nabj.org

# National Association of Letter Carriers

## Costas G. Lemonopoulos Scholarship

**Type of award:** Scholarship, renewable.
**Intended use:** For full-time undergraduate study at accredited 4-year institution. Designated institutions: St. Petersburg Junior College or four-year public Florida university.
**Eligibility:** Applicant must be high school senior.
**Basis for selection:** Applicant must demonstrate high academic achievement.
**Application requirements:** Transcript. SAT/ACT scores and NALC form.
**Additional information:** Applicant must be child of National Association of Letter Carriers member in good standing (active, retired, or deceased). Preliminary application available on Website; required for further details and primary application form. Notification published in March issue of Postal Record magazine.

| | |
|---|---|
| **Number of awards:** | 20 |
| **Number of applicants:** | 150 |
| **Application deadline:** | June 1 |

**Contact:**
National Association of Letter Carriers
Costas G. Lemonopoulos Scholarship Trust
100 Indiana Avenue NW
Washington, DC 20001-2144
Phone: 202-393-4695
Fax: 202-737-1540
Web: www.nalc.org/nalc/members/scholarships.html

## William C. Doherty - John T. Donelon Scholarships

**Type of award:** Scholarship, renewable.
**Intended use:** For full-time undergraduate study at accredited 4-year institution.
**Eligibility:** Applicant must be high school senior.
**Basis for selection:** Applicant must demonstrate financial need and high academic achievement.
**Application requirements:** Recommendations, essay, transcript, proof of eligibility. SAT/ACT scores.
**Additional information:** Applicant must be child of National Association of Letter Carriers member in good standing (active, retired, or deceased) for at least one year. Preliminary application on Website due December 31; supporting materials due March 31. Notification published in July issue of Postal Record magazine.

| | |
|---|---|
| **Amount of award:** | $1,000-$4,000 |
| **Number of awards:** | 5 |
| **Number of applicants:** | 5 |
| **Application deadline:** | December 31 |
| **Total amount awarded:** | $21,000 |

**Contact:**
National Association of Letter Carriers
Scholarship Committee
100 Indiana Avenue NW
Washington, DC 20001-2144
Phone: 202-393-4695
Fax: 202-737-1540
Web: www.nalc.org/nalc/members/scholarships.html

# National Association of Water Companies (NJ Chapter)

## Water Companies (NJ Chapter) Scholarship

**Type of award:** Scholarship.
**Intended use:** For freshman, sophomore, junior, senior or graduate study at accredited 2-year, 4-year or graduate institution in United States. Designated institutions: New Jersey colleges and universities.
**Eligibility:** Applicant must be U.S. citizen residing in New Jersey.
**Basis for selection:** Major/career interest in hydrology; natural resources/conservation; science, general; engineering, environmental; finance/banking; communications; accounting; business; computer/information sciences or law. Applicant must demonstrate financial need, high academic achievement, depth of character, leadership, seriousness of purpose and service orientation.
**Application requirements:** Recommendations, essay, transcript. Essay must illustrate interest in water utility industry or related field.
**Additional information:** Applicant must have interest in fields of study related to water industry. Acceptable fields of study also include consumer affairs and human resources. At least five years residence in New Jersey required. Minimum 3.0 GPA.

| | |
|---|---|
| **Amount of award:** | $2,500 |
| **Number of awards:** | 1 |
| **Number of applicants:** | 80 |
| **Application deadline:** | April 1 |
| **Notification begins:** | June 1 |
| **Total amount awarded:** | $2,500 |

**Contact:**
Nat'l Assn. of Water Companies (NJ Chapter)
Gail P. Brady
49 Howell Drive
Verona, NJ 07044
Phone: 973-669-5807

# National Association of Women in Construction

## NAWIC Founders' Construction Trades Scholarship

**Type of award:** Scholarship.
**Intended use:** For undergraduate study at postsecondary institution.

Scholarships

**Basis for selection:** Major/career interest in construction or construction management.
**Application requirements:** Resume, list of extracurricular activities.
**Additional information:** Must be currently enrolled in construction-related training program approved by the Bureau of Apprenticeship Training or home state's Postsecondary Education Commission. Visit Website for application.

| | |
|---|---|
| **Amount of award:** | $500-$2,500 |
| **Application deadline:** | March 15 |
| **Total amount awarded:** | $25,000 |

**Contact:**
National Association of Women in Construction
327 South Adams
Fort Worth, TX 76104
Web: www.nawic.org

### NAWIC Founders' Undergraduate Scholarship

**Type of award:** Scholarship.
**Intended use:** For full-time undergraduate study at accredited 2-year or 4-year institution in United States or Canada.
**Eligibility:** Applicant must be U.S. citizen.
**Basis for selection:** Major/career interest in construction; construction management; engineering, construction or architecture. Applicant must demonstrate financial need and high academic achievement.
**Application requirements:** Interview, recommendations, essay, transcript. Resume.
**Additional information:** Number and amount of awards vary. Interest in construction, extracurricular activities, and employment experience also taken into consideration. Applicants must have completed three terms of study in construction-related field. Minimum 3.0 GPA. Only semifinalists will be interviewed. Visit Website for additional information and application.

| | |
|---|---|
| **Amount of award:** | $500-$2,500 |
| **Application deadline:** | March 15 |
| **Notification begins:** | April 1 |
| **Total amount awarded:** | $25,000 |

**Contact:**
National Association of Women in Construction
327 South Adams Street
Fort Worth, TX 76104
Web: www.nawic.org

## National Athletic Trainers' Association Research & Education Foundation

### Athletic Trainers' Entry Level Scholarship

**Type of award:** Scholarship.
**Intended use:** For full-time junior, senior, master's or doctoral study at 4-year or graduate institution.
**Basis for selection:** Major/career interest in athletic training. Applicant must demonstrate high academic achievement.
**Application requirements:** Recommendations, essay, transcript, proof of eligibility, nomination by BOC certified trainer.
**Additional information:** Must be National Athletic Trainers' Association member. Minimum 3.2 GPA. Intention to pursue the profession of athletic training as career required. Must be sponsored by a certified athletic trainer. Must be enrolled in Commission on Accreditation of Athletic Training Education (CAATE)-accredited undergraduate or master's program. See complete guidelines on Website.

| | |
|---|---|
| **Amount of award:** | $2,300 |
| **Number of awards:** | 50 |
| **Number of applicants:** | 203 |
| **Notification begins:** | April 15 |
| **Total amount awarded:** | $150,000 |

**Contact:**
National Athletic Trainers' Association
Research & Education Foundation
2952 Stemmons Freeway
Dallas, TX 75247
Phone: 800-879-6282 ext. 121
Fax: 214-637-2206
Web: www.natafoundation.org

## National Black Nurses Association

### Black Nurses Scholarship

**Type of award:** Scholarship.
**Intended use:** For undergraduate or graduate study at postsecondary institution.
**Eligibility:** Applicant must be African American.
**Basis for selection:** Major/career interest in nursing or nurse practitioner. Applicant must demonstrate leadership, seriousness of purpose and service orientation.
**Application requirements:** Recommendations, essay, transcript. Evidence of participation in both student nursing activities and the African-American community.
**Additional information:** Must be member of National Black Nurses Association and member of local chapter if one exists. Must be currently enrolled in a nursing program and have at least one full year of school left. Must be in good academic standing. Call association for current information on program.

| | |
|---|---|
| **Amount of award:** | $500-$2,000 |
| **Application deadline:** | April 15 |
| **Notification begins:** | July 1 |

**Contact:**
National Black Nurses Association
8630 Fenton Street
Room 330
Silver Spring, MD 20910
Phone: 301-589-3200
Fax: 301-589-3223
Web: www.nbna.org

## National Commission for Cooperative Education

### National Co-op Scholarship

**Type of award:** Scholarship, renewable.
**Intended use:** For undergraduate study at postsecondary institution. Designated institutions: Drexel University, Johnson

& Wales University, Kettering University, Pace University, Rochester Institute of Technology, University of Cincinnati, University of Toledo, Wentworth Institute of Technology.
**Eligibility:** Applicant must be high school senior. Applicant must be residing in Washington or U.S. Territories.
**Application requirements:** One-page essay on decision to pursue a college cooperative education program.
**Additional information:** Applicants must be accepted to and attend one of the ten participating institutions. Minimum 3.5 GPA. Visit Website for more information and application.

| | |
|---|---|
| **Amount of award:** | $6,000 |
| **Number of awards:** | 170 |
| **Number of applicants:** | 2,251 |
| **Application deadline:** | February 15 |
| **Total amount awarded:** | $4,500,000 |

**Contact:**
National Commission for Cooperative Education
360 Huntington Avenue, 384 CP
Boston, MA 02115-5096
Phone: 617-373-3406
Fax: 617-373-3463
Web: www.co-op.edu

# National Dairy Shrine

## Core Scholarship

**Type of award:** Scholarship, renewable.
**Intended use:** For full-time freshman study at accredited 4-year institution.
**Eligibility:** Applicant must be U.S. citizen.
**Basis for selection:** Major/career interest in agriculture; animal sciences or dairy. Applicant must demonstrate high academic achievement, leadership and seriousness of purpose.
**Application requirements:** Recommendations, essay, transcript.
**Additional information:** Minimum 2.5 GPA. Student must have commitment to career in dairy.

| | |
|---|---|
| **Amount of award:** | $1,000 |
| **Number of awards:** | 1 |
| **Number of applicants:** | 12 |
| **Application deadline:** | April 15 |
| **Notification begins:** | August 1 |
| **Total amount awarded:** | $1,000 |

**Contact:**
National Dairy Shrine
P.O. Box 725
Denmark, WI 54208
Phone: 920-863-6333
Fax: 920-863-6333
Web: www.dairyshrine.org

## Dairy Student Recognition Program

**Type of award:** Scholarship.
**Intended use:** For senior study at postsecondary institution.
**Basis for selection:** Major/career interest in agriculture; business; dairy; environmental science; food production/management/services; food science/technology; law; manufacturing; marketing or veterinary medicine. Applicant must demonstrate leadership.
**Application requirements:** Recommendations, essay, transcript, nomination by college or university dairy-science department.
**Additional information:** Applicant must be recommended by university department. Cash awards for graduating seniors planning career in dairy cattle. Two candidates eligible per institution. First-place winner receives $2,000; second, $1,500; third through seventh, $1,000. National Dairy Shrine chooses final winners. Students who placed in top five in previous years not eligible for further competition.

| | |
|---|---|
| **Amount of award:** | $1,000-$2,000 |
| **Number of awards:** | 9 |
| **Number of applicants:** | 22 |
| **Application deadline:** | April 15 |
| **Notification begins:** | August 1 |
| **Total amount awarded:** | $9,500 |

**Contact:**
National Dairy Shrine
P.O. Box 725
Denmark, WI 54208
Phone: 920-863-6333
Fax: 920-863-6333
Web: www.dairyshrine.org

## DMI Milk Marketing Scholarships

**Type of award:** Scholarship.
**Intended use:** For sophomore or junior study at postsecondary institution.
**Eligibility:** Applicant must be U.S. citizen.
**Basis for selection:** Major/career interest in agriculture; animal sciences; dairy; dietetics/nutrition or education.
**Application requirements:** Recommendations, essay, transcript.
**Additional information:** For students interested in careers marketing milk or dairy products. Minimum 2.5 GPA. Visit Website for more details.

| | |
|---|---|
| **Amount of award:** | $1,000-$1,500 |
| **Number of awards:** | 8 |
| **Number of applicants:** | 24 |
| **Application deadline:** | April 15 |
| **Notification begins:** | August 1 |
| **Total amount awarded:** | $8,500 |

**Contact:**
National Dairy Shrine
Attn: Maurice E. Core
P.O. Box 725
Denmark, WI 54208
Phone: 920-863-6333
Fax: 920-863-6333
Web: www.dairyshrine.org

## Iager Dairy Scholarship

**Type of award:** Scholarship.
**Intended use:** For undergraduate study at 2-year institution.
**Eligibility:** Applicant must be U.S. citizen.
**Basis for selection:** Major/career interest in food production/management/services; food science/technology or dairy. Applicant must demonstrate high academic achievement and leadership.
**Application requirements:** Recommendations, essay, transcript.
**Additional information:** Must be second-year college student in two-year agricultural college. Minimum 2.5 GPA. May request application from Website or National Dairy Shrine.

**Amount of award:** $1,000
**Number of awards:** 1
**Number of applicants:** 4
**Application deadline:** April 15
**Notification begins:** August 1
**Total amount awarded:** $1,000

**Contact:**
National Dairy Shrine
P.O. Box 725
Denmark, WI 54208
Phone: 920-863-6333
Fax: 920-863-6333
Web: www.dairyshrine.org



## Klussendorf Scholarship

**Type of award:** Scholarship.
**Intended use:** For sophomore, junior or senior study at 2-year or 4-year institution.
**Basis for selection:** Major/career interest in animal sciences or dairy.
**Application requirements:** Recommendations, essay, transcript.
**Additional information:** For dairy or animal science majors in second, third, or fourth year of college. Must plan to become dairy cattle breeder, owner, herdsperson, or fitter. May request application from Website or National Dairy Shrine.

**Amount of award:** $2,000
**Number of awards:** 6
**Number of applicants:** 40
**Application deadline:** April 15
**Notification begins:** August 1
**Total amount awarded:** $12,000

**Contact:**
National Dairy Shrine
P.O. Box 725
Denmark, WI 54208
Phone: 920-863-6333
Fax: 920-863-6333
Web: www.dairyshrine.org

## Marshall E. McCullough Undergraduate Scholarship

**Type of award:** Scholarship.
**Intended use:** For full-time undergraduate study at accredited 4-year institution in United States.
**Eligibility:** Applicant must be high school senior. Applicant must be U.S. citizen.
**Basis for selection:** Major/career interest in animal sciences; dairy; communications or journalism.
**Application requirements:** Recommendations, essay, transcript.
**Additional information:** Finalists will be asked to submit video responding to specific questions about the dairy industry. Two awards: one for $2,500; one for $1,000. Must major in dairy/animal science with communications emphasis or agricultural journalism with dairy/animal science emphasis.

**Amount of award:** $1,000-$2,500
**Number of awards:** 2
**Number of applicants:** 8
**Application deadline:** April 15
**Notification begins:** August 1
**Total amount awarded:** $3,500

**Contact:**
National Dairy Shrine
P.O. Box 725
Denmark, WI 54208
Phone: 920-863-6333
Fax: 920-863-6333
Web: www.dairyshrine.org

## National Dairy Shrine Kildee Scholarship

**Type of award:** Scholarship.
**Intended use:** For junior, senior or graduate study at postsecondary institution.
**Eligibility:** Applicant must be U.S. citizen.
**Basis for selection:** Major/career interest in animal sciences; dairy; food production/management/services or food science/technology. Applicant must demonstrate high academic achievement and leadership.
**Application requirements:** Recommendations, essay, transcript.
**Additional information:** Applicant must have placed in top 25 in National 4-H, FFA or National Intercollegiate Judging Contests. Platinum winners from National Dairy Challenge are eligible to compete for graduate study scholarships. Up to two $3,000 scholarships for graduate study and one $2,000 scholarship for undergraduate study awarded. May request application from Website or National Dairy Shrine.

**Amount of award:** $2,000-$3,000
**Number of awards:** 3
**Number of applicants:** 7
**Application deadline:** April 15
**Notification begins:** August 1
**Total amount awarded:** $8,000

**Contact:**
National Dairy Shrine
P.O. Box 725
Denmark, WI 54208
Phone: 920-863-6333
Fax: 920-863-6333
Web: www.dairyshrine.org

# National Eagle Scout Association

## Hall/McElwain Merit Scholarship

**Type of award:** Scholarship.
**Intended use:** For undergraduate study at postsecondary institution.
**Eligibility:** Applicant must be male.
**Basis for selection:** Applicant must demonstrate leadership.
**Application requirements:** Recommendations, proof of eligibility.
**Additional information:** Applicant must be Eagle Scout. Must have strong record of participation in activities outside of scouting. Visit Website for more information and application.

**Amount of award:** $1,000
**Number of awards:** 84
**Number of applicants:** 2,500
**Application deadline:** January 31
**Notification begins:** July 1
**Total amount awarded:** $84,000

**Contact:**
NESA, Sum 322
1325 W. Walnut Hill Lane
P.O. Box 152079
Irving, TX 75015-2079
Phone: 972-580-2032
Web: www.nesa.org

### NESA Academic Scholarships

**Type of award:** Scholarship.
**Intended use:** For freshman study at accredited 4-year institution.
**Eligibility:** Applicant must be male, high school senior.
**Basis for selection:** Applicant must demonstrate financial need, high academic achievement and leadership.
**Application requirements:** Recommendations, transcript.
**Additional information:** Applicant must be Eagle Scout. Award may not be used at military institution. Minimum 1200 SAT or 28 ACT score.

| | |
|---|---|
| **Amount of award:** | $2,500-$48,000 |
| **Number of awards:** | 66 |
| **Number of applicants:** | 2,500 |
| **Application deadline:** | January 31 |
| **Notification begins:** | July 1 |
| **Total amount awarded:** | $300,000 |

**Contact:**
NESA, Sum 322
1325 West Walnut Hill Lane
P.O. Box 152079
Irving, TX 75015-2079
Phone: 972-580-2032
Web: www.nesa.org

## National Environmental Health Association/ American Academy of Sanitarians

### NEHA/AAS Scholarship

**Type of award:** Scholarship.
**Intended use:** For full-time junior, senior or graduate study at accredited 4-year or graduate institution.
**Basis for selection:** Major/career interest in environmental science or public health. Applicant must demonstrate financial need, high academic achievement and seriousness of purpose.
**Application requirements:** Transcript, proof of eligibility. Three letters of recommendation (one from active NEHA member, two from faculty members at applicant's school).
**Additional information:** Undergraduates must be enrolled in an Environmental Health Accreditation Council accredited school or National Environmental Health Association Institutional/Educational or sustaining member school (list available at sponsor Website). Graduates must be enrolled in environmental health science and/or public health program. Visit Website for further information and updates.

| | |
|---|---|
| **Amount of award:** | $1,000-$1,500 |
| **Number of awards:** | 3 |
| **Number of applicants:** | 100 |
| **Application deadline:** | February 1 |
| **Total amount awarded:** | $3,500 |

**Contact:**
National Environmental Health Association
NEHA/AAS Scholarship
720 South Colorado Boulevard., 1000-N
Denver, CO 80246-1925
Phone: 303-756-9090
Fax: 303-691-9490
Web: www.neha.org

## National Federation of the Blind

### Charles and Melva T. Owen Memorial Scholarship

**Type of award:** Scholarship, renewable.
**Intended use:** For full-time undergraduate or graduate study at postsecondary institution.
**Eligibility:** Applicant must be visually impaired.
**Basis for selection:** Applicant must demonstrate financial need, high academic achievement and service orientation.
**Application requirements:** Recommendations, essay, transcript. Interview with NFB affiliate president, SAT/ACT scores (high school seniors only), proof of legal blindness.
**Additional information:** Applicant must be legally blind in both eyes. Field of study should be directed toward attaining financial independence. Excludes study of religion and those seeking only to further general or cultural education. Recipients of Federation scholarships need not be members of National Federation of the Blind. Visit Website for application.

| | |
|---|---|
| **Amount of award:** | $3,000-$10,000 |
| **Number of awards:** | 23 |
| **Application deadline:** | March 31 |
| **Notification begins:** | June 1 |
| **Total amount awarded:** | $10,000 |

**Contact:**
National Federation of the Blind Scholarship Committee
NFB at Jernigan Place
200 East Wells Street
Baltimore, MD 21230
Phone: 410-659-9314 ext. 2415
Fax: 410-685-5653
Web: www.nfb.org/scholarships

### Kenneth Jernigan Memorial Scholarship

**Type of award:** Scholarship, renewable.
**Intended use:** For full-time undergraduate or graduate study at postsecondary institution.
**Eligibility:** Applicant must be visually impaired.
**Basis for selection:** Applicant must demonstrate financial need, high academic achievement and service orientation.
**Application requirements:** Recommendations, essay, transcript. Proof of blindness, interview with NFB affiliate president, SAT/ACT scores (high school seniors only).
**Additional information:** Applicant must be legally blind in both eyes. Recipients of Federation scholarships need not be members of Federation. Must participate in NFB Annual Convention and all scheduled scholarship activities. Visit Website for application.

**Amount of award:** $12,000
**Number of awards:** 1
**Application deadline:** March 31
**Notification begins:** June 1
**Total amount awarded:** $12,000

**Contact:**
National Federation of the Blind Scholarship Committee
NFB at Jernigan Place
200 East Wells Street
Baltimore, MD 21230
Phone: 410-659-9314 ext. 2415
Fax: 410-685-5653
Web: www.nfb.org/scholarships



### National Federation of the Blind Scholarships

**Type of award:** Scholarship, renewable.
**Intended use:** For full-time undergraduate or graduate study at postsecondary institution.
**Eligibility:** Applicant must be visually impaired.
**Basis for selection:** Major/career interest in humanities/liberal arts. Applicant must demonstrate financial need, high academic achievement and service orientation.
**Application requirements:** Recommendations, essay, transcript. Interview with NFB affiliate president, SAT/ACT scores (high school seniors only), proof of legal blindness.
**Additional information:** Applicant must be legally blind in both eyes. Recipients of Federation scholarships need not be members of National Federation of the Blind. Visit Website for application.

**Amount of award:** $5,000-$7,000
**Number of awards:** 27
**Application deadline:** March 31
**Notification begins:** June 1

**Contact:**
National Federation of the Blind Scholarship Committee
NFB at Jernigan Place
200 East Wells Street
Baltimore, MD 21230
Phone: 410-659-9314 ext. 2415
Fax: 410-685-5653
Web: www.nfb.org/scholarships

## National FFA

### National FFA Collegiate Scholarship Program

**Type of award:** Scholarship.
**Intended use:** For undergraduate study at postsecondary institution.
**Additional information:** Open to FFA members as well as a small number of qualifying non-members. Visit Website for more information and application.

**Amount of award:** $1,000-$10,000
**Application deadline:** February 15
**Notification begins:** June 1
**Total amount awarded:** $2,000,000

**Contact:**
National FFA
Attn: Scholarship Office
P.O. Box 68960
Indianapolis, IN 46268-0960
Web: www.ffa.org

## National Ground Water Research and Education Foundation

### NGWREF Len Assante Scholarship Fund

**Type of award:** Scholarship.
**Intended use:** For full-time undergraduate study at accredited 2-year or 4-year institution.
**Basis for selection:** Applicant must demonstrate financial need, high academic achievement, depth of character, leadership, patriotism, seriousness of purpose and service orientation.
**Application requirements:** Essay, transcript, proof of eligibility. Essay should be one-page biography.
**Additional information:** Applicant must be studying in a ground water-related field. Students in two-year well drilling associate degree program also eligible. Minimum 2.5 GPA. Amount and number of awards vary annually. Application available on Website.

**Amount of award:** $1,000-$2,500
**Number of awards:** 10
**Number of applicants:** 102
**Application deadline:** January 15
**Notification begins:** May 1
**Total amount awarded:** $17,500

**Contact:**
NGWREF Len Assante Scholarship Fund
601 Dempsey Road
Westerville, OH 43081
Phone: 800-551-7379
Fax: 614-898-7786
Web: www.ngwa.org

## National Inventors Hall of Fame

### Collegiate Inventors Competition

**Type of award:** Scholarship.
**Intended use:** For full-time undergraduate or graduate study at postsecondary institution in United States or Canada.
**Basis for selection:** Competition/talent/interest in science project, based on invention's potential for society and scope of use.
**Application requirements:** Advisor letter; four copies of application and any supplementary material; personal essay describing invention, including a title page and one-paragraph overview of invention.
**Additional information:** Amount of awards varies. Entry must include summary of current literature and patent search, test

data and invention's benefit. Entry must be original idea that has not been made available to public as a commercial product/process. Must not have been patented or published more than one year prior to date of submission. Competition accepts individual and team entries. Students must be (or have been) enrolled full-time at least part of 12-month period prior to date entry submitted. For teams, at least one member must meet full-time eligibility criteria. Other team members must have been enrolled on part-time basis (at minimum) sometime during 24-month period prior to date entry submitted. Deadline varies. See Website for more information.

| | |
|---|---|
| **Amount of award:** | $10,000-$15,000 |
| **Number of awards:** | 3 |

**Contact:**
The Collegiate Inventors Competition
The National Inventors Hall of Fame
520 South Main Street, Suite 2423
Akron, OH 44311
Phone: 800-968-4332 ext. 5
Web: www.invent.org/collegiate

# National Italian American Foundation

## Emanuele and Emilia Inglese Memorial Scholarship

**Type of award:** Scholarship.
**Intended use:** For undergraduate study at accredited postsecondary institution.
**Eligibility:** Applicant must be Italian. Applicant must be U.S. citizen or permanent resident.
**Basis for selection:** Applicant must demonstrate financial need and high academic achievement.
**Application requirements:** Essay, transcript. Teacher Evaluation Form, Student Aid Report from FAFSA.
**Additional information:** Applicant must be first generation of family to attend college. Must be able to trace lineage to Lombardy region in Italy. Minimum 3.0 GPA. Applications must be submitted online. See Website for details and application.

| | |
|---|---|
| **Amount of award:** | $2,500 |
| **Number of awards:** | 1 |
| **Number of applicants:** | 5 |
| **Application deadline:** | March 2 |
| **Total amount awarded:** | $2,500 |

**Contact:**
The Inglese Memorial Scholarship c/o NIAF
1860 19th Street NW
Washington, DC 20009
Phone: 202-387-0600
Web: www.niaf.org/scholarships

## National Italian American Foundation Scholarship Program

**Type of award:** Scholarship.
**Intended use:** For full-time undergraduate or graduate study at accredited 4-year or graduate institution in United States.
**Eligibility:** Applicant must be U.S. citizen or permanent resident.
**Basis for selection:** Applicant must demonstrate high academic achievement, depth of character, leadership, seriousness of purpose and service orientation.
**Application requirements:** Recommendations, transcript. FAFSA (optional).
**Additional information:** Completed application and teacher evaluation submitted online. Awards in two categories. General Category I Awards: Open to Italian-American students who demonstrate outstanding potential and high academic achievement. General Category II Awards: Open to those students majoring or minoring in Italian Language, Italian studies, Italian American Studies, or related fields. Awards not applicable for summer study. Minimum 3.5 GPA.

| | |
|---|---|
| **Amount of award:** | $2,000-$12,000 |
| **Number of awards:** | 150 |
| **Number of applicants:** | 6,000 |
| **Application deadline:** | March 2 |

**Contact:**
The National Italian American Foundation
1860 19th Street NW
Washington, DC 20009
Phone: 202-387-0600
Web: www.niaf.org/scholarships

# National Jewish Committee on Scouting

## Rick Arkans Eagle Scout Scholarship

**Type of award:** Scholarship.
**Intended use:** For undergraduate study at postsecondary institution.
**Eligibility:** Applicant must be high school senior.
**Basis for selection:** Applicant must demonstrate financial need.
**Application requirements:** Recommendation from a volunteer or professional scout leader. FAFSA.
**Additional information:** Applicant must be registered, active member of a Boy Scout troop, Varsity Scout team, or Venturing crew. Must have received Eagle Scout Award. Must be active member of synagogue and have received Ner Tamid or Etz Chaim emblem. Contact National Jewish Committee on Scouting to request application form. Visit Website for more information.

| | |
|---|---|
| **Amount of award:** | $1,000 |
| **Number of awards:** | 1 |
| **Number of applicants:** | 15 |
| **Application deadline:** | February 28 |
| **Notification begins:** | May 1 |
| **Total amount awarded:** | $1,000 |

**Contact:**
National Jewish Committee on Scouting
1325 W. Walnut Hill Lane
P.O. Box 152079
Irving, TX 75015-2079
Phone: 972-580-2119
Fax: 972-580-2535
Web: www.jewishscouting.org

# National Jewish Committee on Scouting, Boy Scouts of America

## Chester M. Vernon Memorial Eagle Scout Scholarship

**Type of award:** Scholarship, renewable.
**Intended use:** For full-time undergraduate study at accredited 2-year or 4-year institution.
**Eligibility:** Applicant must be male, high school senior. Applicant must be Jewish. Applicant must be U.S. citizen or permanent resident.
**Basis for selection:** Applicant must demonstrate financial need, depth of character, leadership and service orientation.
**Application requirements:** Recommendation from a volunteer or professional scout leader. FAFSA.
**Additional information:** Applicant must be registered, active member of a Boy Scout troop, Varsity Scout team, or Venturing crew. Must have received Eagle Scout Award. Must be active member of synagogue and have received Ner Tamid or Etz Chaim emblem. Award renewable for four years. Contact National Jewish Committee on Scouting to request application form. Recipients receive $1,000 per year for four years. Visit Website for more information.

| | |
|---|---|
| **Amount of award:** | $1,000 |
| **Number of awards:** | 1 |
| **Number of applicants:** | 15 |
| **Application deadline:** | February 28 |
| **Notification begins:** | May 1 |
| **Total amount awarded:** | $1,000 |

**Contact:**
National Jewish Committee on Scouting, BSA
1325 W. Walnut Hill Lane
P.O. Box 152079
Irving, TX 75015-2079
Phone: 972-580-2119
Fax: 972-580-2535
Web: www.jewishscouting.org

## Frank L. Weil Memorial Eagle Scout Scholarship

**Type of award:** Scholarship.
**Intended use:** For full-time undergraduate study at accredited 2-year or 4-year institution.
**Eligibility:** Applicant must be male, high school senior. Applicant must be Jewish. Applicant must be U.S. citizen or permanent resident.
**Basis for selection:** Applicant must demonstrate depth of character, leadership and service orientation.
**Application requirements:** Recommendation from volunteer or professional scout leader. FAFSA.
**Additional information:** Recipient of scholarship receives $1,000. Two $500 second-place scholarship awards also given. Applicant must be registered, active member of a Boy Scout troop, Varsity Scout team, or Venturing crew. Must have received Eagle Scout Award. Must be active member of synagogue and have received Ner Tamid or Etz Chaim emblem. Contact National Jewish Committee on Scouting to request application form. Visit Website for more information.

| | |
|---|---|
| **Amount of award:** | $500-$1,000 |
| **Number of awards:** | 3 |
| **Number of applicants:** | 15 |
| **Application deadline:** | February 28 |
| **Notification begins:** | May 1 |
| **Total amount awarded:** | $2,000 |

**Contact:**
National Jewish Committee on Scouting, BSA
1325 West Walnut Hill Lane
P.O. Box 152079
Irving, TX 75015-2079
Phone: 972-580-2119
Fax: 972-580-2535
Web: www.jewishscouting.org

# National Junior Classical League

## Latin Honor Society Scholarship

**Type of award:** Scholarship.
**Intended use:** For full-time freshman study at 2-year or 4-year institution.
**Eligibility:** Applicant must be high school senior.
**Basis for selection:** Major/career interest in classics or education. Applicant must demonstrate high academic achievement.
**Application requirements:** Recommendations, essay, transcript.
**Additional information:** Must have been member in good standing of NJCL for at least three years and must be member of NJCL Latin Honor Society for current academic year and at least one preceding year. Must be planning to major in and teach Latin, Greek, or classics. Application available online.

| | |
|---|---|
| **Amount of award:** | $1,500 |
| **Number of awards:** | 1 |
| **Number of applicants:** | 7 |
| **Application deadline:** | May 1 |
| **Total amount awarded:** | $1,500 |

**Contact:**
National Junior Classical League Attn: Scholarships
Miami University
422 Wells Mill Drive
Oxford, OH 45056
Phone: 513-529-7741
Fax: 513-529-7742
Web: www.aclclassics.org

## National Junior Classical League Scholarship

**Type of award:** Scholarship.
**Intended use:** For full-time freshman study at 2-year or 4-year institution.
**Eligibility:** Applicant must be high school senior.
**Basis for selection:** Major/career interest in classics; education or humanities/liberal arts. Applicant must demonstrate financial need, high academic achievement, leadership, seriousness of purpose and service orientation.
**Application requirements:** Recommendations, essay, transcript. List of awards and activities.
**Additional information:** Must be NJCL member. Preference given to applicants who intend to teach Latin, Greek, or classical humanities.

**Amount of award:** $1,000-$2,000
**Number of awards:** 9
**Number of applicants:** 12
**Application deadline:** May 1
**Contact:**
National Junior Classical League Attn: Scholarships
Miami University
422 Wells Mill Drive
Oxford, OH 45056
Phone: 513-529-7741
Fax: 513-529-7742
Web: www.aclclassics.org

# National Merit Scholarship Corporation

## National Achievement Scholarships

**Type of award:** Scholarship.
**Intended use:** For full-time undergraduate study at accredited postsecondary institution in United States.
**Eligibility:** Applicant must be African American. Applicant must be enrolled in high school. Applicant must be U.S. citizen or permanent resident.
**Basis for selection:** Applicant must demonstrate high academic achievement and leadership.
**Application requirements:** Recommendations, essay.
**Additional information:** A privately financed academic competition for Black American high school students. To enter, students must meet published participation requirements and request consideration in program when they take PSAT/NMSQT and enter National Merit Program. Entry requirements published each year in PSAT/NMSQT Official Student Guide, sent to schools for distribution to students before October test administration, and on NMSC's Website. Some 1,600 of highest scoring participants named Semifinalists on regional representation basis. Semifinalists must meet additional requirements and advance to Finalist standing to compete for about 800 National Achievement Scholarships offered annually. There are 700 National Achievement $2,500 Scholarships for which all Finalists compete and about 100 corporate-sponsored scholarships for Finalists who meet specified criteria of sponsoring organization.
**Number of awards:** 800
**Number of applicants:** 1,600
**Notification begins:** February 15
**Total amount awarded:** $2,500,000
**Contact:**
National Achievement Scholarship Program
1560 Sherman Avenue
Suite 200
Evanston, IL 60201-4897
Phone: 847-866-5100
Web: www.nationalmerit.org

## National Merit Scholarships

**Type of award:** Scholarship.
**Intended use:** For full-time undergraduate study at accredited postsecondary institution in United States.
**Eligibility:** Applicant must be enrolled in high school. Applicant must be U.S. citizen or permanent resident.
**Basis for selection:** Applicant must demonstrate high academic achievement and leadership.
**Application requirements:** Recommendations, essay.
**Additional information:** Open to U.S. high school students who take PSAT/NMSQT in specified year in high school and meet other entry requirements. Entry requirements published each year in PSAT/NMSQT Official Student Guide, sent to schools for distribution to students before October test administration, and on NMSC's Website. Some 16,000 high-scoring participants designated Semifinalists on state representational basis. Applications sent to students through their schools. Semifinalists must meet additional requirements and advance to Finalist standing to be considered for National Merit Scholarships. About 8,200 awards of three types offered annually: 2,500 National Merit $2,500 Scholarships for which all Finalists compete; about 1,100 corporate-sponsored Merit Scholarship awards for Finalists who meet criteria of sponsoring corporate organization; and over 4,600 college-sponsored Merit Scholarship awards for Finalists who will attend sponsor college/university. Corporate organizations also provide about 1,500 Special Scholarships for other high performers in competition who are not Finalists. Permanent residents eligible if in process of becoming U.S. citizen.
**Number of awards:** 9,700
**Number of applicants:** 19,500
**Notification begins:** March 1
**Total amount awarded:** $52,000,000
**Contact:**
National Merit Scholarship Program
1560 Sherman Avenue
Suite 200
Evanston, IL 60201-4897
Phone: 847-866-5100
Web: www.nationalmerit.org

# National Poultry & Food Distributors Association

## NPFDA Scholarship

**Type of award:** Scholarship, renewable.
**Intended use:** For full-time junior or senior study at 4-year institution in United States.
**Basis for selection:** Major/career interest in dietetics/nutrition; agriculture; agricultural economics; agribusiness or food science/technology. Applicant must demonstrate high academic achievement.
**Application requirements:** Essay, transcript, proof of eligibility. Recommendation by dean.
**Additional information:** Poultry science, animal science, or related agricultural business majors also eligible.
**Amount of award:** $1,500-$2,000
**Number of awards:** 4
**Number of applicants:** 80
**Application deadline:** May 31
**Notification begins:** January 1
**Total amount awarded:** $6,500
**Contact:**
National Poultry & Food Distributors Association
2014 Osborne Road
St. Mary's, GA 31558
Phone: 770-535-9901
Fax: 770-535-7385
Web: www.npfda.org

# National Press Photographers Foundation

## Bob Baxter Scholarship

**Type of award:** Scholarship.
**Intended use:** For full-time undergraduate or graduate study at postsecondary institution in United States or Canada.
**Basis for selection:** Major/career interest in journalism. Applicant must demonstrate financial need.
**Application requirements:** Recommendations, essay. Portfolio of six slides (digital formats also accepted), statement of financial need.
**Additional information:** Applicants must be studying photojournalism. Visit Website for more information and application.

| | |
|---|---|
| **Amount of award:** | $2,000 |
| **Number of awards:** | 1 |
| **Application deadline:** | March 1 |

**Contact:**
Danielle Richards
Phone: 201-646-4130
Web: www.nppf.org

## Bob East Scholarship Fund

**Type of award:** Scholarship.
**Intended use:** For undergraduate or graduate study at postsecondary institution in United States or Canada.
**Eligibility:** Applicant must be U.S. citizen or permanent resident residing in Florida.
**Basis for selection:** Major/career interest in journalism. Applicant must demonstrate financial need.
**Application requirements:** Portfolio, recommendations, essay. Portfolio must include at least five single images in addition to picture story. Digital portfolios accepted; see Website for instructions.
**Additional information:** Open to students studying photojournalism for newspapers. Must be undergraduate in first three and one half years of college, or be planning to pursue postgraduate work and offer indication of acceptance in such program.

| | |
|---|---|
| **Amount of award:** | $2,000 |
| **Number of awards:** | 1 |
| **Application deadline:** | March 1 |
| **Total amount awarded:** | $2,000 |

**Contact:**
The Miami Herald
Attn: Chuck Fadely
Web: www.nppf.org

## College Photographer of the Year Competition

**Type of award:** Scholarship.
**Intended use:** For undergraduate study at 4-year institution in United States or Canada.
**Basis for selection:** Major/career interest in journalism. Applicant must demonstrate financial need and high academic achievement.
**Application requirements:** Portfolio, recommendations, proof of eligibility. Portfolio must include five single images in addition to picture story. Digital portfolios accepted; see Website for instructions.
**Additional information:** Contest recognizes outstanding work of student photojournalists. NPPF Booster club provides $1,000 Col. William Lookadoo Award and $500 Milton Frier Award.

| | |
|---|---|
| **Amount of award:** | $500-$1,000 |
| **Number of awards:** | 2 |
| **Application deadline:** | October 1 |
| **Total amount awarded:** | $1,500 |

**Contact:**
University of Missouri School of Journalism
Rita Reed, CPOY Dir., University of Missouri
106 Lee Hills Hall
Columbia, MO 65211
Phone: 573-882-4442
Web: www.nppf.org

## Jimi Lott Scholarship

**Type of award:** Scholarship.
**Intended use:** For undergraduate study in United States or Canada.
**Eligibility:** Applicant must be U.S. citizen or permanent resident.
**Basis for selection:** Major/career interest in journalism.
**Application requirements:** Portfolio, recommendations, essay, transcript. GPA must be submitted. Portfolio must include six to twelve entries. Portfolio may consist of single photographs, multiple picture stories, or multimedia stories. Should include at least one multimedia entry.
**Additional information:** Applicants must be studying photojournalism. Visit Website for more information and application.

| | |
|---|---|
| **Amount of award:** | $2,000 |
| **Number of awards:** | 1 |
| **Total amount awarded:** | $2,000 |

**Contact:**
National Press Photographers Foundation
Web: www.nppf.org

## National Press Photographers Foundation Still and Multimedia Scholarship

**Type of award:** Scholarship.
**Intended use:** For sophomore, junior or senior study at 4-year institution in United States or Canada.
**Basis for selection:** Major/career interest in journalism. Applicant must demonstrate financial need and high academic achievement.
**Application requirements:** Portfolio, proof of eligibility. Portfolio must include five single images in addition to picture story. Digital portfolios accepted; see Website for instructions.
**Additional information:** Awards aimed at those with journalism potential, but with little opportunity and great need. Must have completed one year at recognized four-year college or university with courses in photojournalism. Must be continuing in program leading to bachelor's degree.

| | |
|---|---|
| **Amount of award:** | $2,000 |
| **Number of awards:** | 1 |
| **Application deadline:** | March 1 |
| **Total amount awarded:** | $2,000 |

**Contact:**
Bill Sanders
Web: www.nppf.org

## National Press Photographers Foundation Television News Scholarship

**Type of award:** Scholarship.
**Intended use:** For undergraduate study at 4-year institution in United States or Canada.
**Basis for selection:** Major/career interest in radio/television/film or journalism. Applicant must demonstrate financial need and high academic achievement.
**Application requirements:** Portfolio, recommendations, essay. Videotape containing no more than three complete stories no longer than six minutes total with voice narration and natural sound. One-page biographical sketch including personal statement addressing professional goals.
**Additional information:** Must be enrolled in recognized four-year college or university with courses in TV news photojournalism. Must be continuing program leading to bachelor's degree.

| | |
|---|---|
| **Amount of award:** | $2,000 |
| **Number of awards:** | 1 |
| **Application deadline:** | March 1 |
| **Total amount awarded:** | $2,000 |

**Contact:**
Dr. James W. Brown
Phone: 781-861-6062
Web: www.nppf.org

## Reid Blackburn Scholarship

**Type of award:** Scholarship.
**Intended use:** For undergraduate study at 4-year institution in United States or Canada.
**Basis for selection:** Major/career interest in journalism. Applicant must demonstrate financial need, high academic achievement and seriousness of purpose.
**Application requirements:** Portfolio, essay, proof of eligibility. Statement of philosophy and goals. Portfolio must include at least five single images in addition to picture story. Digital portfolios accepted; see Website for instructions.
**Additional information:** Must have completed at least one year at recognized four-year college or university with courses in photojournalism and must have at least half-year of undergraduate schooling remaining at time of award. Program must be leading to bachelor's degree.

| | |
|---|---|
| **Amount of award:** | $2,000 |
| **Number of awards:** | 1 |
| **Application deadline:** | March 1 |
| **Total amount awarded:** | $2,000 |

**Contact:**
The Columbian
Attn: Fay Blackburn
Web: www.nppf.org

# National Restaurant Association Educational Foundation

## Academic Scholarship for High School Seniors and GED Graduates

**Type of award:** Scholarship.
**Intended use:** For undergraduate study at vocational, 2-year or 4-year institution.
**Eligibility:** Applicant must be U.S. citizen or permanent resident.
**Basis for selection:** Major/career interest in food science/technology; hotel/restaurant management; food science/technology; culinary arts or marketing.
**Application requirements:** Transcript. One to three letters of recommendation verifying work hours, on business or school letterhead, from current or previous employer in the restaurant or food service industry, paystubs, two essays: one stating food service background and career goals, the other discussing what person or experience influenced you to select food industry and how this will help you reach your career goals.
**Additional information:** Must be first-time freshman accepted into accredited culinary school, or in college or university majoring in food service related major. Must plan to enroll in minimum of two terms for following school year. Must have minimum 250 hours of food-service-related work experience. Deadline in August. Visit Website for application.

| | |
|---|---|
| **Amount of award:** | $2,500 |

**Contact:**
National Restaurant Association Educational Foundation
Scholarships and Mentoring Initiative
175 West Jackson Boulevard, Suite 1500
Chicago, IL 60604-2702
Phone: 800-765-2122 ext. 6738
Fax: 312-566-9733
Web: www.nraef.org/scholarships

## Academic Scholarship for Undergraduate Students

**Type of award:** Scholarship.
**Intended use:** For undergraduate study at accredited vocational, 2-year or 4-year institution in United States.
**Eligibility:** Applicant must be U.S. citizen or permanent resident.
**Basis for selection:** Major/career interest in food production/management/services; culinary arts; hotel/restaurant management; hospitality administration/management or food science/technology. Applicant must demonstrate high academic achievement.
**Application requirements:** Recommendations, transcript. Copy of college curriculum. Letter from current or previous employer in the restaurant or food service industry, with paychecks or paystubs verifying restaurant employment. Two essays: One discussing food service background and career goals, the other discussing how either sustainability, food safety, or nutrition affect the industry and what you would do to address this issue.
**Additional information:** Applicant must have completed at least one term of two- or four-year degree program. Must be enrolled in food service related program for minimum of nine credit hours per semester. Must have performed minimum 750 hours foodservice-related work. Visit Website for application and more information.

| | |
|---|---|
| **Amount of award:** | $2,500 |
| **Application deadline:** | March 31 |

**Contact:**
National Restaurant Association Educational Foundation
Attn: Scholarships Program
175 West Jackson Boulevard, Suite 1500
Chicago, IL 60604-2702
Phone: 800-765-2122 ext. 6738
Fax: 312-566-9733
Web: www.nraef.org/scholarships

## Al Schuman Ecolab First-Time Freshman Entrepeneurial Scholarship

**Type of award:** Scholarship.
**Intended use:** For full-time freshman study at postsecondary institution. Designated institutions: California State Polytechnic University-Pomona, Cornell University, Culinary Institute of America, DePaul University, Johnson & Wales University, Kendall College, Lynn University, Michigan State University, New York University, Pennsylvania State University, Purdue University, University of Denver, University of Houston, University of Nevada-Las Vegas, University of Massachussetts-Amherst.
**Eligibility:** Applicant must be U.S. citizen or permanent resident.
**Basis for selection:** Major/career interest in culinary arts or food production/management/services.
**Application requirements:** Recommendations, essay, transcript.
**Additional information:** Must be first-time college freshman planning to remain in school for at least two consecutive terms. Minimum 3.0 GPA. Targeted to students who show entrepreneurial spirit through written essay. Must be enrolled in food service related program.

| | |
|---|---|
| **Amount of award:** | $3,000-$3,500 |
| **Number of awards:** | 2 |

**Contact:**
National Restaurant Association Educational Foundation
Attn: Scholarship Program
175 West Jackson Boulevard, Suite 1500
Chicago, IL 60604-2702
Phone: 800-765-2122, ext. 6738
Web: www.nraef.org

## Al Schuman Ecolab Undergraduate Entrepeneurial Scholarship

**Type of award:** Research grant.
**Intended use:** For undergraduate study at postsecondary institution. Designated institutions: California State Polytechnic University-Pomona, Cornell University, Culinary Institute of America, DePaul University, Johnson & Wales University, Kendall College, Lynn University, Michigan State University, New York University, Pennsylvania State University, Purdue University, University of Denver, University of Houston, University of Nevada-Las Vegas, University of Massachussetts-Amherst.
**Eligibility:** Applicant must be U.S. citizen or permanent resident.
**Basis for selection:** Major/career interest in culinary arts or food production/management/services.
**Application requirements:** Recommendations, essay, transcript.
**Additional information:** Minimum 3.0 GPA. Targeted to students who show entrepreneurial spirit through written essay. Must be enrolled in food service related program. Must have completed at least one grading term of postsecondary program. Must be enrolled for at least two consecutive terms, but not entering last semester before graduating.

| | |
|---|---|
| **Amount of award:** | $3,000-$5,500 |
| **Number of awards:** | 2 |

**Contact:**
National Restaurant Educational Foundation
175 West Jackson Blvd., Suite 1500
Attn: Scholarship Program
Chicago, IL 60604-2702
Phone: 800-756-2122, ext. 6738
Web: www.nreaf.org

## ManageFirst Program Scholarship

**Type of award:** Scholarship.
**Intended use:** For undergraduate study at accredited vocational, 2-year or 4-year institution in United States.
**Eligibility:** Applicant must be U.S. citizen or permanent resident.
**Basis for selection:** Major/career interest in culinary arts or food production/management/services.
**Application requirements:** Recommendations, essay, transcript. Topical essay. ManageFirst Certificate (optional).
**Additional information:** Must be enrolled in food service-related program and completed at least one grading term at an accredited culinary school, college, or university. Must have food-industry related experience (paid or unpaid). Deadlines are March 31, July 31, and October 1. Visit Website for application.

| | |
|---|---|
| **Amount of award:** | $2,500 |
| **Application deadline:** | March 31, July 31 |

**Contact:**
National Restaurant Association
Attn: Scholarships Program
175 West Jackson Boulevard, Suite 1500
Chicago, IL 60604-2702
Phone: 800-765-2122 ext. 6738
Web: www.nraef.org/scholarships

# National Rifle Association

## Jeanne E. Bray Law Enforcement Dependents Scholarship

**Type of award:** Scholarship.
**Intended use:** For full-time undergraduate or graduate study at accredited 2-year, 4-year or graduate institution in United States.
**Eligibility:** Applicant must be U.S. citizen. Applicant's parent must have been killed or disabled in work-related accident as police officer.
**Basis for selection:** Applicant must demonstrate high academic achievement and service orientation.
**Application requirements:** Recommendations, transcript, proof of eligibility. Letter from employing law enforcement agency; 500-700 word essay on the Second Amendment.
**Additional information:** Number of awards varies. Parent must be member of National Rifle Association. Parent must be active, disabled, deceased, discharged, or retired peace officer. Minimum 2.5 GPA, SAT score of 950 or ACT score of 25. Award given for up to four years or until applicable monetary cap is reached, as long as student maintains eligibility. Applications accepted on continuous basis.

| | |
|---|---|
| **Amount of award:** | $500-$2,000 |
| **Number of applicants:** | 35 |
| **Application deadline:** | November 15 |
| **Notification begins:** | February 15 |

**Contact:**
National Rifle Association, Attn: Sandy S. Elkin
Jeanne E. Bray Memorial Scholarship
11250 Waples Mill Road
Fairfax, VA 22030
Phone: 703-267-1131
Fax: 703-267-1083
Web: www.nrahq.org/law/lebenefits.asp

# National Science Teachers Association

## Toshiba/NSTA ExploraVision Award

**Type of award:** Scholarship.
**Intended use:** For undergraduate or non-degree study at postsecondary institution in United States or Canada.
**Eligibility:** Applicant must be no older than 21, enrolled in high school.
**Basis for selection:** Competition/talent/interest in science project, based on scientific accuracy, creativity, communication and feasibility of vision. Major/career interest in science, general.
**Application requirements:** Essay. Abstract, written description of research and design project, five graphics simulating Web pages.
**Additional information:** Applicants must apply as teams of two, three, or four students and a coach. Applicant must attend public, private, or home school. Must be full-time student, no older than 21. Technology study project. Open to grades K-12. Members of first-place team receive $10,000 savings bond. Members of second-place team receive $5,000 savings bond. Regional winners receive Toshiba products. Contact sponsor for entry kit, and visit Website to download application.

| | |
|---|---|
| **Amount of award:** | $5,000-$10,000 |
| **Number of applicants:** | 4,500 |
| **Application deadline:** | February 1 |
| **Notification begins:** | March 1 |
| **Total amount awarded:** | $240,000 |

**Contact:**
Toshiba/NSTA ExploraVision Awards
1840 Wilson Boulevard
Arlington, VA 22201-3000
Phone: 800-EXPLOR9
Web: www.exploravision.org

# National Sculpture Society

## Sculpture Society Scholarship

**Type of award:** Scholarship.
**Intended use:** For undergraduate, master's or doctoral study at postsecondary institution in United States.
**Eligibility:** Applicant must be U.S. citizen or permanent resident.
**Basis for selection:** Competition/talent/interest in visual arts, based on images of figurative or representational sculpture created by applicant. Major/career interest in arts, general. Applicant must demonstrate financial need.
**Application requirements:** Recommendations, essay, proof of eligibility. Brief letter of application including biography and background in sculpture; six to fifteen images of at least three works submitted on CD; list of works shown on CD; proof of financial need; SASE.
**Additional information:** Must be studying figurative or representational sculpture. Work inspired by nature, or figurative or realistic sculpture, preferred.

| | |
|---|---|
| **Amount of award:** | $2,000 |
| **Number of awards:** | 4 |
| **Number of applicants:** | 35 |
| **Application deadline:** | June 1 |
| **Total amount awarded:** | $8,000 |

**Contact:**
National Sculpture Society
c/o ANS
75 Varick Street, 11th Floor
New York, NY 10013
Phone: 212-764-5645
Fax: 212-764-5651
Web: www.nationalsculpture.org



# National Security Agency

## National Security Agency Stokes Educational Scholarship Program

**Type of award:** Scholarship, renewable.
**Intended use:** For full-time undergraduate study in United States.
**Eligibility:** Applicant must be U.S. citizen.
**Basis for selection:** Major/career interest in computer/information sciences; engineering, computer or engineering, electrical/electronic. Applicant must demonstrate high academic achievement, depth of character, leadership, patriotism, seriousness of purpose and service orientation.
**Application requirements:** Interview, recommendations, essay, transcript, proof of eligibility. Resume.
**Additional information:** Current applications available September 1st- November 30th of each year. Preference given to those with minimum 3.0 GPA, 1600 SAT score (reading and math) and/or 25 ACT score. Must undergo polygraph and security screening. Freshmen must major in computer science or electrical or computer engineering. Awardees must work at NSA in area related to major for 12 weeks in summer and after graduation for at least one and a half times length of study. If work debt not repaid, scholarship reverts to debt. Scholarship covers tuition, fees, and includes a book allowance of $1500. See Website for current program information.

| | |
|---|---|
| **Amount of award:** | Full tuition |
| **Number of awards:** | 20 |
| **Number of applicants:** | 600 |
| **Application deadline:** | November 30 |
| **Notification begins:** | May 1 |

**Contact:**
National Security Agency Stokes Scholars Program
9800 Savage Road
Suite 6779
Fort Meade, MD 20755-6779
Phone: 410-854-4725 or 866-NSA-HIRE
Fax: 410-854-3002
Web: www.nsa.gov

# National Society of Accountants Scholarship Foundation

## National Society of Accountants Scholarship

**Type of award:** Scholarship.
**Intended use:** For sophomore, junior or senior study at accredited vocational, 2-year or 4-year institution in United States.
**Eligibility:** Applicant must be U.S. citizen or Canadian citizen.
**Basis for selection:** Major/career interest in accounting. Applicant must demonstrate financial need, high academic achievement and leadership.
**Application requirements:** Transcript. Appraisal form.
**Additional information:** Minimum 3.0 GPA. Student must be enrolled in undergraduate accounting program at time of application. Visit Website for more information and application.

| | |
|---|---|
| **Amount of award:** | $500-$2,000 |
| **Number of applicants:** | 1,200 |
| **Application deadline:** | March 10 |
| **Total amount awarded:** | $40,000 |

**Contact:**
National Society of Accountants Scholarship Program
Web: www.nsacct.org

# National Society of Black Engineers

## NSBE Scholarship Program

**Type of award:** Scholarship.
**Intended use:** For undergraduate or graduate study at vocational, 2-year or 4-year institution in United States.
**Eligibility:** Applicant must be African American.
**Basis for selection:** Major/career interest in engineering; engineering, civil; engineering, electrical/electronic; engineering, industrial; technology; computer/information sciences; science, general or mathematics.
**Application requirements:** Transcript.
**Additional information:** NSBE membership required. All eligible applicants must apply online through their membership account.

| | |
|---|---|
| **Amount of award:** | $500-$10,000 |

**Contact:**
National Society of Black Engineers
205 Daingerfield Road
Alexandria, VA 22314
Phone: 703-549-2207
Fax: 703-683-5312
Web: www.nsbe.org

# National Society of the Sons of the American Revolution

## Arthur M. and Berdena King Eagle Scout Scholarship

**Type of award:** Scholarship.
**Intended use:** For undergraduate study at postsecondary institution.
**Eligibility:** Applicant must be male, no older than 18.
**Basis for selection:** Applicant must demonstrate depth of character, leadership and patriotism.
**Application requirements:** Essay, proof of eligibility. Essay should be 500 words on Revolutionary War, subject of applicant's choice. Four generation ancestor chart.
**Additional information:** Open to all Eagle Scouts currently registered in active unit who will not reach 19th birthday during year of application. Competition conducted in three phases: Chapter (local), Society (state), and National. Applicants need only apply at Chapter level. Winners at local level entered into state competition; state winners used in National contest. Number of awards varies. Awards may also be available at chapter and state level. See Website for more information and application.

| | |
|---|---|
| **Amount of award:** | $2,000-$8,000 |
| **Number of awards:** | 3 |
| **Application deadline:** | December 31 |
| **Total amount awarded:** | $14,000 |

**Contact:**
National Society of the Sons of the American Revolution
1000 South Fourth Street
Louisville, KY 40203
Phone: 502-589-1776
Web: www.sar.org/youth/eagle.html

# National Speakers Association

## National Speakers Association Scholarship

**Type of award:** Scholarship.
**Intended use:** For full-time junior, senior or graduate study at 4-year or graduate institution.
**Basis for selection:** Applicant must demonstrate financial need, high academic achievement, leadership and seriousness of purpose.
**Application requirements:** Recommendations, essay, transcript.
**Additional information:** Applicant must have above-average academic record and desire to be professional speaker. Application available on Website.

| | |
|---|---|
| **Amount of award:** | $5,000 |
| **Number of awards:** | 4 |
| **Number of applicants:** | 100 |
| **Application deadline:** | June 1 |
| **Notification begins:** | September 1 |
| **Total amount awarded:** | $20,000 |

**Contact:**
National Speakers Association
1500 South Priest Drive
Tempe, AZ 85281
Phone: 480-968-2552
Fax: 480-968-0911
Web: www.nsafoundation.org

# National Stone, Sand & Gravel Association

## Barry K. Wendt Commitment Award and Scholarship

**Type of award:** Scholarship.
**Intended use:** For full-time undergraduate study in United States. Designated institutions: Engineering schools.
**Eligibility:** Applicant must be U.S. citizen or permanent resident.
**Basis for selection:** Major/career interest in engineering. Applicant must demonstrate high academic achievement.
**Application requirements:** Recommendations, essay.
**Additional information:** Must be planning career in aggregate industry. Visit Website for details and application.

| | |
|---|---|
| **Number of awards:** | 1 |

**Contact:**
Wendt Memorial Scholarship Committee
c/o NSSGA
1605 King Street
Alexandria, VA 22314
Phone: 703-525-8788
Fax: 703-525-7782
Web: www.nssga.org/careerscholarships/scholarships.cfm

## Jennifer Curtis Byler Scholarship Fund for the Study of Public Affairs

**Type of award:** Scholarship.
**Intended use:** For full-time undergraduate study in United States.
**Basis for selection:** Major/career interest in public administration/service. Applicant must demonstrate high academic achievement, seriousness of purpose and service orientation.
**Application requirements:** Recommendations, essay.
**Additional information:** Applicant must be graduating high school senior or student already enrolled in public affairs program in college. Must be child of aggregate company employee. Must demonstrate commitment to career in public affairs. Visit Website for details and application.

| | |
|---|---|
| **Number of awards:** | 1 |
| **Application deadline:** | August 31 |
| **Notification begins:** | September 30 |

**Contact:**
Jennifer Curtis Byler Scholarship
c/o NSSGA
1605 King Street
Alexandria, VA 22314
Phone: 703-526-1063
Fax: 703-525-7782
Web: www.nssga.org/careerscholarships/scholarships.cfm

# Native Daughters of the Golden West

## Native Daughters of the Golden West Scholarship

**Type of award:** Scholarship, renewable.
**Intended use:** For full-time undergraduate or graduate study at accredited postsecondary institution in United States. Designated institutions: Schools in California.
**Eligibility:** Applicant or parent must be member/participant of Native Daughters of the Golden West. Applicant must be U.S. citizen residing in California.
**Basis for selection:** Applicant must demonstrate financial need, high academic achievement, depth of character, leadership, patriotism, seriousness of purpose and service orientation.
**Application requirements:** Recommendations, essay, transcript, nomination by local club or parlor.
**Additional information:** Applicant must have been born in California. Must be sponsored by NDGW parlor.
**Contact:**
Native Daughters of the Golden West
543 Baker Street
San Francisco, CA 94117-1405
Phone: 415-563-9091
Fax: 415-563-5230
Web: www.ndgw.org

# Navy Supply Corps Foundation

## Navy Supply Corps Foundation Scholarship

**Type of award:** Scholarship, renewable.
**Intended use:** For full-time undergraduate study at accredited 2-year or 4-year institution.
**Eligibility:** Applicant must be U.S. citizen. Applicant must be dependent of veteran who served in the Navy. Applicant must be family member of active duty or enlisted Supply Corps Officer/Warrant Officer.
**Basis for selection:** Applicant must demonstrate financial need, high academic achievement, depth of character, leadership and service orientation.
**Application requirements:** Transcript, proof of eligibility.
**Additional information:** Minimum 2.5 GPA. Any family member of Foundation member or enlisted member (active duty, reservist, or retired) is eligible for consideration. Number of awards varies. Visit Website for application and more information.

| | |
|---|---|
| **Amount of award:** | $1,000-$10,000 |
| **Number of applicants:** | 200 |
| **Application deadline:** | March 26 |
| **Notification begins:** | May 10 |

**Contact:**
Navy Supply Corps Foundation
Phone: 706-354-4111
Web: www.usnscf.com

# Navy-Marine Corps Relief Society

## Gold Star Scholarship Program

**Type of award:** Scholarship, renewable.
**Intended use:** For undergraduate study at postsecondary institution.
**Eligibility:** Applicant must be dependent of deceased veteran; or spouse of deceased veteran who served in the Marines or Navy. Service member must have died on active duty, in combat situation, or after retirement.
**Basis for selection:** Applicant must demonstrate financial need.
**Application requirements:** Current military dependent ID card; DD214 and death certificate or DD1300.
**Additional information:** Minimum 2.0 GPA. Visit Website for more information and application. Must be child or spouse of Navy or Marine Corps. service member who died on active duty, in combat situation, or after retirement.

| | |
|---|---|
| **Amount of award:** | $500-$2,500 |
| **Number of applicants:** | 50 |
| **Application deadline:** | March 1 |
| **Total amount awarded:** | $132,000 |

**Contact:**
Navy-Marine Corps Relief Society
875 North Randolph Street, Suite 225
Arlington, VA 22203-1977
Phone: 703-696-4960
Web: www.nmcrs.org/education

## McAlinden Divers Scholarship

**Type of award:** Scholarship.
**Intended use:** For undergraduate study at postsecondary institution.
**Eligibility:** Must be active duty or retired Navy-Marine Corp. diver. Family of divers also eligible.
**Basis for selection:** Major/career interest in oceanography/ marine studies.
**Additional information:** Must be studying oceanography, ocean agriculture, or aqua culture.

| | |
|---|---|
| **Amount of award:** | $500-$3,000 |

**Contact:**
Navy-Marine Corps Relief Society
875 North Randolph Street
Suite 225
Arlington, VA 22203-1977
Phone: 703-696-4904
Fax: 703-696-0144
Web: www.nmcrs.org/education

## Sociey of Sponsors Scholarship Program

**Type of award:** Scholarship.
**Intended use:** For undergraduate study at 4-year institution.
**Eligibility:** Applicant must be dependent of disabled veteran who served in the Marines or Navy. Must have been wounded in combat during Iraq-Afghanistan conflict.
**Basis for selection:** Major/career interest in education.
**Additional information:** Applicants must be veteran wounded in combat during Iraq-Afghanistan conflict. Must be pursing bachelor's degree leading to teacher licensure.

| | |
|---|---|
| **Amount of award:** | $500-$3,000 |
| **Number of awards:** | 5 |
| **Total amount awarded:** | $3,000 |

**Contact:**
Navy-Marine Corps Relief Society
875 North Randolph Street
Suite 225
Arlington, VA 22203-1977
Phone: 703-696-4904
Fax: 703-696-0144
Web: www.nmcrs.org/education

# NCAA

## NCAA Division I Degree-Completion Award Program

**Type of award:** Scholarship.
**Intended use:** For senior study at 4-year institution. Designated institutions: Colleges in Division I of the NCAA.
**Basis for selection:** Competition/talent/interest in athletics/ sports. Applicant must demonstrate financial need, depth of character, leadership and service orientation.
**Application requirements:** Recommendations, essay, transcript. Endorsement and signature from dean of college or head of department and director of athletics; statement and signature from financial aid office, official tax forms, list of extracurricular activities.
**Additional information:** Program established to assist student athletes who have exhausted their eligibility for institutional financial aid (in five years). Applicants must have received athletics-related grant-in-aid at NCAA Division I institution and must be within 30 semester hours or 45 quarter hours of their degree requirements. Award will not exceed full athletics-related grant-in-aid as defined by institution and is renewable for second term, given completion of 12 hours with 2.0 GPA or better. Award covers tuition and fees plus book allowance.

| | |
|---|---|
| **Amount of award:** | Full tuition |
| **Number of applicants:** | 135 |
| **Total amount awarded:** | $950,000 |

**Contact:**
NCAA Division I Degree-Completion Program
Karen Cooper
P.O. Box 6222
Indianapolis, IN 46206-6222
Phone: 317-917-6307
Fax: 317-917-6364
Web: www.ncaa.org

# Nebraska Coordinating Commission for Postsecondary Education

## Nebraska Opportunity Grant

**Type of award:** Scholarship.
**Intended use:** For undergraduate study at postsecondary institution.
**Eligibility:** Applicant must be residing in Nebraska.

**Basis for selection:** Applicant must demonstrate financial need.
**Application requirements:** FAFSA.
**Additional information:** Award amount, application deadline, and requirements determined by individual institutions. Awards made on rolling basis. Notification begins in January preceding award year.

| | |
|---|---|
| **Number of applicants:** | 38,081 |
| **Total amount awarded:** | $14,093,053 |

**Contact:**
Contact financial aid office at eligible institution
Phone: 402-471-2847
Fax: 402-471-2886
Web: www.ccpe.state.ne.us

# Nebraska State Department of Education

## Nebraska Robert C. Byrd Honors Scholarship

**Type of award:** Scholarship, renewable.
**Intended use:** For full-time freshman study at accredited postsecondary institution in United States.
**Eligibility:** Applicant must be high school senior. Applicant must be U.S. citizen or permanent resident residing in Nebraska.
**Basis for selection:** Applicant must demonstrate high academic achievement.
**Application requirements:** Transcript. ACT scores.
**Additional information:** Renewable up to four years with good academic standing. Minimum ACT score of 30. Applications mailed to counselors at all Nebraska high schools in January. Award not available to students of U.S. military academies.

| | |
|---|---|
| **Amount of award:** | $1,500 |
| **Number of awards:** | 40 |
| **Number of applicants:** | 350 |
| **Application deadline:** | March 15 |
| **Total amount awarded:** | $234,000 |

**Contact:**
Nebraska State Department of Education Robert C. Byrd Scholarship
301 Centennial Mall South
P.O. Box 94987
Lincoln, NE 68509-4987
Phone: 402-471-3962
Web: www.education.ne.gov/byrd

# Nevada Department of Education

## Nevada Robert C. Byrd Honors Scholarship

**Type of award:** Scholarship, renewable.
**Intended use:** For undergraduate study at postsecondary institution.
**Eligibility:** Applicant must be high school senior. Applicant must be U.S. citizen or permanent resident residing in Nevada.
**Basis for selection:** Applicant must demonstrate high academic achievement, depth of character and seriousness of purpose.
**Additional information:** Applicant must be Nevada High School Scholar. Minimum 3.5 GPA and 1100 SAT (reading and math) or 25 ACT score required. Renewable up to four years.

| | |
|---|---|
| **Amount of award:** | $1,500 |
| **Number of awards:** | 40 |
| **Number of applicants:** | 300 |
| **Notification begins:** | May 1 |
| **Total amount awarded:** | $324,000 |

**Contact:**
Nevada Department of Education
700 East Fifth Street
Carson City, NV 89710
Phone: 775-687-9150
Fax: 775-687-9113
Web: www.doe.nv.gov

## Nevada Student Incentive Grant

**Type of award:** Scholarship.
**Intended use:** For undergraduate or graduate study at vocational, 2-year, 4-year or graduate institution.
**Eligibility:** Applicant must be U.S. citizen or permanent resident residing in Nevada.
**Basis for selection:** Applicant must demonstrate financial need.
**Application requirements:** FAFSA.
**Additional information:** Must apply through post-secondary financial aid office. Deadlines vary by institution. Maximum award is $5,000.

| | |
|---|---|
| **Amount of award:** | $5,000 |
| **Notification begins:** | July 1 |

**Contact:**
Nevada Department of Education
700 East Fifth Street
Carson City, NV 87910
Phone: 775-687-9150
Fax: 775-687-9123
Web: www.doe.nv.gov

# New England Board of Higher Education

## NEBHE's Tuition Break Regional Student Program

**Type of award:** Scholarship.
**Intended use:** For undergraduate or graduate study in United States. Designated institutions: New England public colleges and universities.
**Eligibility:** Applicant must be permanent resident residing in Vermont, New Hampshire, Connecticut, Maine, Massachusetts or Rhode Island.
**Additional information:** Regional Student Program provides tuition discount to New England residents who study majors not offered at public institutions in their own state at out-of-state public colleges in New England. Must be enrolling in approved major listed in annual catalog.

| | |
|---|---|
| **Amount of award:** | $7,000 |
| **Number of applicants:** | 9,000 |
| **Total amount awarded:** | $51,000,000 |

Scholarships

New England Board of Higher Education: NEBHE's Tuition Break Regional Student Program

**Contact:**
New England Board of Higher Education
45 Temple Place
Boston, MA 02111
Phone: 617-357-9620
Web: www.nebhe.org/tuitionbreak

# New England Employee Benefits Council

## NEEBC Scholarship

**Type of award:** Scholarship, renewable.
**Intended use:** For undergraduate or graduate study at accredited postsecondary institution.
**Basis for selection:** Major/career interest in business/management/administration; human resources; insurance/actuarial science or health services administration. Applicant must demonstrate high academic achievement, depth of character, leadership, seriousness of purpose and service orientation.
**Application requirements:** Recommendations, transcript. 500-word essay; minimum of two references from college professors, NEEBC members or other benefits professionals.
**Additional information:** Applicants must aspire to career in employee benefits. Applicants must reside or attend college in New England.

| | |
|---|---|
| **Amount of award:** | $2,500-$5,000 |
| **Number of applicants:** | 2 |
| **Application deadline:** | April 1 |
| **Notification begins:** | May 1 |
| **Total amount awarded:** | $5,000 |

**Contact:**
New England Benefits Council
240 Bear Hill Road
Suite 102
Waltham, MA 02451
Phone: 781-684-8700
Web: www.neebc.org

# New Hampshire Postsecondary Education Commission

## New Hampshire Incentive Program

**Type of award:** Scholarship, renewable.
**Intended use:** For undergraduate study at accredited vocational, 2-year or 4-year institution. Designated institutions: Eligible institutions in New England (Connecticut, Maine, Massachusetts, New Hampshire, Rhode Island, Vermont).
**Eligibility:** Applicant must be U.S. citizen or permanent resident residing in New Hampshire.
**Basis for selection:** Applicant must demonstrate financial need.
**Application requirements:** Proof of eligibility. FAFSA.
**Additional information:** Must not have previous bachelor's degree. Upper class applicants must have minimum 2.0 GPA. Application online at www.fafsa.org.

| | |
|---|---|
| **Amount of award:** | $125-$1,000 |
| **Number of awards:** | 4,000 |
| **Application deadline:** | May 1 |
| **Total amount awarded:** | $3,182,132 |

**Contact:**
New Hampshire Postsecondary Education Commission
Cynthia Capodestria
3 Barrell Court, Suite 300
Concord, NH 03301-8543
Phone: 603-271-2555 ext. 360
Fax: 603-271-2696
Web: www.nh.gov/postsecondary/financial

## New Hampshire Scholarship for Orphans of Veterans

**Type of award:** Scholarship, renewable.
**Intended use:** For undergraduate or graduate study at vocational, 2-year or 4-year institution. Designated institutions: New Hampshire public institutions.
**Eligibility:** Applicant must be at least 16, no older than 25. Applicant must be U.S. citizen residing in New Hampshire. Applicant must be dependent of deceased veteran during Korean War, WW I, WW II or Vietnam. Dependents of deceased veterans of Gulf War or deceased veterans awarded an armed forces expeditionary medal.
**Application requirements:** Proof of eligibility.
**Additional information:** Parent must have been legal resident of New Hampshire at time of service-related death.

| | |
|---|---|
| **Amount of award:** | $2,500 |
| **Number of applicants:** | 1 |
| **Total amount awarded:** | $3,750 |

**Contact:**
New Hampshire Postsecondary Education Commission
Judith Knapp
3 Barrell Court, Suite 300
Concord, NH 03301-8543
Phone: 603-271-2555 ext. 352
Fax: 603-271-2696
Web: www.nh.gov/postsecondary

# New Jersey Commission on Higher Education

## New Jersey Educational Opportunity Fund Grant

**Type of award:** Scholarship, renewable.
**Intended use:** For full-time undergraduate or graduate study at accredited 2-year or 4-year institution. Designated institutions: Participating New Jersey community colleges, four-year colleges and universities.
**Eligibility:** Applicant must be U.S. citizen or permanent resident residing in New Jersey.
**Basis for selection:** Applicant must demonstrate financial need.
**Application requirements:** FAFSA.
**Additional information:** For students from educationally disadvantaged backgrounds with demonstrated financial need. Must be New Jersey resident for at least 12 consecutive months prior to enrollment. Students are admitted into EOF program by college. Program includes summer sessions, tutoring, counseling, and student leadership development.

Award amounts vary; undergraduate $200-$2,500, graduate $200-$4,350. Contact EOF director at institution for specific application requirements.

**Amount of award:** $200-$4,350
**Number of awards:** 18,259
**Application deadline:** October 1
**Notification begins:** April 1
**Total amount awarded:** $26,643,935

**Contact:**
New Jersey Commission on Higher Education
P.O. Box 542
Trenton, NJ 08625-0542
Phone: 609-984-2709
Fax: 609-663-5420
Web: www.nj.gov/highereducation/EOF

# New Jersey Department of Military and Veterans Affairs

## New Jersey POW/MIA Tuition Benefit Program

**Type of award:** Scholarship, renewable.
**Intended use:** For full-time undergraduate study at accredited 4-year institution in United States. Designated institutions: New Jersey colleges and universities.
**Eligibility:** Applicant must be residing in New Jersey. Applicant must be dependent of active service person or POW/MIA. Parent must have been officially declared Prisoner of War or Missing in Action after 1/1/60 and must have been resident of New Jersey.
**Application requirements:** Proof of eligibility. Copy of DD 1300.
**Additional information:** Award does not include room, board, or expenses.

**Amount of award:** Full tuition

**Contact:**
New Jersey Department of Military and Veterans Affairs
DVS-VBB-Patty Richter
P.O. Box 340
Trenton, NJ 08625-7005
Phone: 609-530-6854
Fax: 609-530-6970
Web: www.state.nj.us/military

## New Jersey War Orphans Tuition Assistance Program

**Type of award:** Scholarship, renewable.
**Intended use:** For undergraduate or graduate study at postsecondary institution in United States.
**Eligibility:** Applicant must be at least 16, no older than 21. Applicant must be residing in New Jersey. Applicant must be veteran who served in the Army, Air Force, Marines, Navy, Coast Guard or Reserves/National Guard during Vietnam. Child of service personnel who died due to service-connected disabilities or who is officially listed as Missing In Action. Veteran must have been New Jersey resident.
**Application requirements:** Proof of eligibility.
**Additional information:** Must have been New Jersey resident for one year prior to application.

**Amount of award:** $500
**Number of applicants:** 1

**Contact:**
New Jersey Department of Military and Veterans Affairs
DVS-VBB-Patty Richter
P.O. Box 340
Trenton, NJ 08625-7005
Phone: 609-530-6854
Fax: 609-530-6970
Web: www.state.nj.us/military

# New Jersey Higher Education Student Assistance Authority

## Dana Christmas Scholarship for Heroism

**Type of award:** Scholarship.
**Intended use:** For undergraduate or graduate study at postsecondary institution.
**Eligibility:** Applicant must be U.S. citizen or permanent resident residing in New Jersey.
**Additional information:** Honors young New Jersey residents for acts of heroism. Students must be age 21 or younger at time of act of heroism. Applicant must be resident of New Jersey upon application and at time act of heroism was performed. Application can be obtained by calling HESAA or by visiting Website.

**Amount of award:** $10,000
**Number of awards:** 5
**Number of applicants:** 5
**Application deadline:** October 15
**Notification begins:** December 1
**Total amount awarded:** $50,000

**Contact:**
New Jersey Higher Education Student Assistance Authority
4 Quakerbridge Plaza
P.O. Box 540
Trenton, NJ 08625-0540
Phone: 800-792-8670
Fax: 609-588-2228
Web: www.hesaa.org

## Law Enforcement Officer Memorial Scholarship

**Type of award:** Scholarship.
**Intended use:** For full-time undergraduate study. Designated institutions: New Jersey institutions.
**Eligibility:** Applicant must be U.S. citizen residing in New Jersey. Applicant's parent must have been killed or disabled in work-related accident as police officer.
**Application requirements:** Proof of eligibility.
**Additional information:** Must be dependent of law enforcement officer killed in the line of duty. Award may cover up to the cost of attendance at any approved institution of higher education in New Jersey. Awards are renewable for up to four years.

**Amount of award:** Full tuition
**Application deadline:** October 1, March 1
**Total amount awarded:** $152,514

**Contact:**
New Jersey Higher Education Student Assistance Authority
4 Quakerbridge Plaza
P.O. Box 540
Trenton, NJ 08625-0540
Phone: 800-792-8670
Fax: 609-588-2228
Web: www.hesaa.org

## New Jeresy Student Tuition Assistance Reward Scholarship (NJSTARS)

**Type of award:** Scholarship, renewable.
**Intended use:** For full-time undergraduate study in United States. Designated institutions: New Jersey county colleges.
**Eligibility:** Applicant must be U.S. citizen or permanent resident residing in New Jersey.
**Basis for selection:** Applicant must demonstrate high academic achievement.
**Application requirements:** FAFSA.
**Additional information:** Must be resident of New Jersey for 12 months prior to high school graduation. Provides tuition and approved fees for up to 18 credits per semester for up to five semesters at a county college for students graduating in top 15 percent of high school class. To be eligible for renewal, students must have minimum 3.0 GPA.

| | |
|---|---|
| **Application deadline:** | June 1, October 1 |
| **Total amount awarded:** | $11,052,629 |

**Contact:**
New Jersey Higher Education Student Assistance Authority
4 Quakerbridge Plaza
P.O. Box 540
Trenton, NJ 08625-0540
Phone: 800-792-8670
Fax: 609-588-2228
Web: www.hesaa.org

## New Jersey STARS II

**Type of award:** Scholarship, renewable.
**Intended use:** For full-time undergraduate study at accredited 4-year institution in United States. Designated institutions: New Jersey public institutions.
**Eligibility:** Applicant must be U.S. citizen or permanent resident residing in New Jersey.
**Basis for selection:** Applicant must demonstrate financial need and high academic achievement.
**Application requirements:** FAFSA.
**Additional information:** Must be successful NJ STARS scholar receiving associate's degree with a minimum 3.25 GPA. Provides for tuition and approved fees for up to 18 credits per semester for four semesters at a New Jersey public four-year institution.

| | |
|---|---|
| **Amount of award:** | $6,000-$7,000 |
| **Application deadline:** | June 1, October 1 |
| **Total amount awarded:** | $6,032,677 |

**Contact:**
New Jersey Higher Education Student Assistance Authority
4 Quakerbridge Plaza
P.O. Box 540
Trenton, NJ 08625-0540
Phone: 800-792-8670
Fax: 609-588-2228
Web: www.hesaa.org

## New Jersey Tuition Aid Grants (TAG)

**Type of award:** Scholarship, renewable.
**Intended use:** For full-time undergraduate study in United States. Designated institutions: Approved New Jersey colleges, universities, and degree-granting proprietary institutions.
**Eligibility:** Applicant must be U.S. citizen or permanent resident residing in New Jersey.
**Basis for selection:** Applicant must demonstrate financial need.
**Application requirements:** FAFSA.
**Additional information:** Applicant must be legal New Jersey resident for at least 12 consecutive months immediately prior to enrollment. Students must maintain satisfactory academic progress. Deadline is June 1 for renewal students; October 1 for new applicants. Notification begins in March.

| | |
|---|---|
| **Number of applicants:** | 511,500 |
| **Application deadline:** | June 1, October 1 |
| **Total amount awarded:** | $311,182,687 |

**Contact:**
New Jersey Higher Education Student Assistance Authority
4 Quakerbridge Plaza
P.O. Box 540
Trenton, NJ 08625-0540
Phone: 800-792-8670
Fax: 609-558-2228
Web: www.hesaa.org

## New Jersey World Trade Center Scholarship

**Type of award:** Scholarship, renewable.
**Intended use:** For full-time undergraduate study at postsecondary institution.
**Eligibility:** Applicant must be residing in New Jersey.
**Additional information:** Must be spouse or dependent of New Jersey resident who was killed or is presumed dead as a result of the terrorist attacks of September 11, 2001. This includes first responders and rescue workers who died as a result of illness caused by attack sites.

| | |
|---|---|
| **Application deadline:** | October 1, March 1 |

**Contact:**
New Jersey Higher Education Student Assistance Authority
4 Quakerbridge Plaza
P.O. Box 540
Trenton, NJ 08625-0540
Phone: 800-792-8670
Fax: 609-588-2228
Web: www.hesaa.org

## Part-Time Tuition Aid Grant for County Colleges

**Type of award:** Scholarship, renewable.
**Intended use:** For half-time undergraduate study at postsecondary institution in United States. Designated institutions: Participating New Jersey county colleges.
**Eligibility:** Applicant must be U.S. citizen or permanent resident residing in New Jersey.
**Basis for selection:** Applicant must demonstrate financial need.
**Application requirements:** FAFSA.
**Additional information:** Must be enrolled part-time (6-11 credits). Must be legal New Jersey resident for at least 12 months prior to enrollment. Must maintain satisfactory academic progress. Renewals due June 1; new applications due

October 1. Visit Website for application and additional information.

**Application deadline:** June 1, October 1
**Total amount awarded:** $9,004,019

**Contact:**
New Jersey Higher Education Student Assistance Authority
4 Quakerbridge Plaza
P.O. Box 540
Trenton, NJ 08625-0540
Phone: 800-792-8670
Fax: 609-588-2228
Web: www.hesaa.org

# New Jersey State Golf Association

## Caddie Scholarship

**Type of award:** Scholarship, renewable.
**Intended use:** For full-time undergraduate study at accredited 2-year or 4-year institution in United States. Designated institutions: Members of Association of American Colleges and Universities.
**Basis for selection:** Applicant must demonstrate financial need and high academic achievement.
**Application requirements:** Proof of eligibility. Recommendation from golf club.
**Additional information:** Applicants must have been a caddie for at least two seasons at a member club of New Jersey State Golf Association. Must be in top half of class and have minimum 900 SAT and 2.5 GPA. Awards renewable for up to four years. Foundation also offers one full scholarship award at Rutgers University.

**Amount of award:** $2,500-$5,000
**Number of awards:** 225
**Number of applicants:** 261
**Application deadline:** March 1
**Notification begins:** June 15
**Total amount awarded:** $596,325

**Contact:**
New Jersey State Golf Association
Caddie Scholarship Foundation
P.O. Box 6947
Freehold, NJ 07728
Phone: 908-241-4653
Fax: 908-245-4696
Web: www.njsga.org

# New Mexico Commission on Higher Education

## New Mexico Competitive Scholarships

**Type of award:** Scholarship.
**Intended use:** For full-time undergraduate study at 4-year institution in United States. Designated institutions: Public New Mexico institutions.
**Basis for selection:** Applicant must demonstrate high academic achievement.
**Additional information:** Awards to encourage out-of-state students who have demonstrated high academic achievement in high school to enroll in public institutions in New Mexico. Recipients of at least $100 in competitive scholarships per semester eligible for resident tuition and fees. Applicants must meet GPA/ACT score requirements, which vary by institution. Contact financial aid office of any New Mexico public postsecondary institution or see Website.

**Contact:**
New Mexico Commission on Higher Education
Financial Aid and Student Services
2048 Galisteo Street
Santa Fe, NM 87505
Phone: 800-279-9777
Web: www.hed.state.nm.us

## New Mexico Legislative Endowment Program

**Type of award:** Scholarship, renewable.
**Intended use:** For undergraduate study at accredited postsecondary institution. Designated institutions: Public institutions in New Mexico.
**Eligibility:** Applicant must be U.S. citizen or permanent resident residing in New Mexico.
**Basis for selection:** Applicant must demonstrate financial need.
**Application requirements:** FAFSA.
**Additional information:** Contact financial aid office of any public postsecondary institution in New Mexico. Four-year public institutions may award up to $2,500 per student per academic year. Two-year public institutions may award up to $1,000 per student per year. Part-time students eligible for prorated awards. Deadlines set by institutions.

**Amount of award:** $1,000-$2,500

**Contact:**
New Mexico Commission on Higher Education
Financial Aid and Student Services
2048 Galisteo Street
Santa Fe, NM 87505
Phone: 505-476-8400
Web: www.hed.state.nm.us

## New Mexico Legislative Lottery Scholarship

**Type of award:** Scholarship.
**Intended use:** For full-time undergraduate study at postsecondary institution. Designated institutions: Eligible New Mexico public colleges and universities.
**Eligibility:** Applicant must be high school senior. Applicant must be residing in New Mexico.
**Additional information:** Must complete 12 graded credit hours with 2.5 GPA in the first regular semester immediately following graduation from New Mexico high school. Deadlines vary according to institution; see Website or apply through financial aid office.

**Amount of award:** Full tuition

**Contact:**
New Mexico Commission on Higher Education
Financial Aid and Student Services
2048 Galisteo Street
Santa Fe, NM 87505
Phone: 505-476-8400
Web: www.hed.state.nm.us

## New Mexico Scholars Program

**Type of award:** Scholarship, renewable.
**Intended use:** For full-time undergraduate study at accredited 2-year or 4-year institution. Designated institutions: Public institutions in New Mexico or the following private institutions: College of Santa Fe, St. John's College, College of the Southwest.
**Eligibility:** Applicant must be no older than 21. Applicant must be U.S. citizen or permanent resident residing in New Mexico.
**Basis for selection:** Applicant must demonstrate financial need and high academic achievement.
**Application requirements:** FAFSA.
**Additional information:** Award includes books and required fees. Number of awards based on availability of funds. Must be graduate of New Mexico high school. Must have 25 ACT score or be in top five percent of class. Must attend eligible university by end of 21st birthday. Combined family income may not exceed $30,000 per year. Contact financial aid office of New Mexico postsecondary institution of choice for information and application. Application deadline set by institution.

**Amount of award:** Full tuition

**Contact:**
New Mexico Commission on Higher Education
Financial Aid and Student Services
2048 Galisteo Street
Santa Fe, NM 87505
Phone: 505-476-8400
Web: www.hed.state.nm.us

## New Mexico Student Choice Grant

**Type of award:** Scholarship, renewable.
**Intended use:** For undergraduate study at postsecondary institution. Designated institutions: St. John's College, College of the Southwest, College of Santa Fe.
**Eligibility:** Applicant must be U.S. citizen or permanent resident residing in New Mexico.
**Basis for selection:** Applicant must demonstrate financial need.
**Application requirements:** FAFSA.
**Additional information:** Amount of award and application deadline determined by institution. Apply to financial aid office at one of designated colleges. Part-time students eligible for pro-rated awards.

**Contact:**
New Mexico Commission on Higher Education
Financial Aid and Student Services
2048 Galisteo Street
Santa Fe, NM 87505
Phone: 505-476-8400
Web: www.hed.state.nm.us

## New Mexico Student Incentive Grant

**Type of award:** Scholarship, renewable.
**Intended use:** For undergraduate study at accredited postsecondary institution. Designated institutions: College of Santa Fe, St. John's College, College of the Southwest, Institute of American Indian Art, Crownpoint Institute of Technology, Dine College, Southwestern Indian Polytechnic Institute.
**Eligibility:** Applicant must be U.S. citizen or permanent resident residing in New Mexico.
**Basis for selection:** Applicant must demonstrate financial need.
**Application requirements:** FAFSA.
**Additional information:** Must demonstrate exceptional financial need. Contact financial aid office of designated institutions for information, application, and deadline. Part-time students eligible for pro-rated awards.

**Amount of award:** $200-$2,500

**Contact:**
New Mexico Commission on Higher Education
Financial Aid and Student Services
2048 Galisteo Street
Santa Fe, NM 87505
Phone: 505-476-8400
Web: www.hed.state.nm.us

## New Mexico Vietnam Veteran's Scholarship

**Type of award:** Scholarship, renewable.
**Intended use:** For undergraduate or graduate study at postsecondary institution. Designated institutions: College of Santa Fe, St. John's College, College of the Southwest.
**Eligibility:** Applicant must be U.S. citizen residing in New Mexico. Applicant must be veteran during Vietnam. Must have been awarded Vietnam campaign medal between 9/5/64 and termination of Vietnam conflict.
**Application requirements:** Proof of eligibility.
**Additional information:** Maximum award provides tuition, fees, and book allowance on first come, first served basis. Eligibility and coursework must be certified by New Mexico Veterans Service Commission. Contact financial aid office of any New Mexico public postsecondary institution for information, deadline, and application. Must have been honorably discharged from U.S. armed forces. Must have been resident of New Mexico at original time of entry into armed forces or have lived in New Mexico for ten years or more.

**Amount of award:** Full tuition

**Contact:**
New Mexico Veteran's Service Commission
P.O. Box 2324
Santa Fe, NM 87505
Phone: 505-827-6300
Web: www.hed.state.nm.us

# New York State Education Department

## New York State Arthur O. Eve Higher Education Opportunity Program (HEOP)

**Type of award:** Scholarship.
**Intended use:** For undergraduate study at 2-year or 4-year institution. Designated institutions: Independent New York State colleges and universities.
**Eligibility:** Applicant must be residing in New York.
**Basis for selection:** Applicant must demonstrate financial need.
**Additional information:** Applicant must be resident of New York State for one year preceding entry into HEOP and be academically and economically disadvantaged. Contact college or university of interest for application and additional

information, and apply at time of admission. Support services include pre-session summer program and tutoring, counseling, and special coursework during academic year. Award amounts vary; contact sponsor for information. For general information, contact New York State Education Department.

**Number of applicants:** 5,368

**Contact:**
New York State Education Department
Collegiate and Prof. Development Prgms.
Room 1071
Albany, NY 11234
Phone: 518-474-5313
Fax: 518-486-5221
Web: www.highered.nysed.gov

### New York State Robert C. Byrd Federal Honors Scholarship

**Type of award:** Scholarship, renewable.
**Intended use:** For full-time undergraduate study at accredited 2-year or 4-year institution in United States.
**Eligibility:** Applicant must be high school senior. Applicant must be U.S. citizen or permanent resident residing in New York.
**Basis for selection:** Applicant must demonstrate high academic achievement.
**Application requirements:** Nomination by high school.
**Additional information:** Must have 1875 SAT score, minimum 95 average, or 410 GED score. Applicants will be ranked within county of legal residence based on final ranking score composed of 75 percent GPA or GED and 25 percent SAT score. Applications available in early fall at student's high school.

| | |
|---|---|
| **Amount of award:** | $1,500 |
| **Number of awards:** | 400 |
| **Number of applicants:** | 6,000 |
| **Application deadline:** | March 1 |
| **Total amount awarded:** | $700,000 |

**Contact:**
New York State Education Department
Scholarships Dept.
Room 967 EBA
Albany, NY 12234
Phone: 518-486-1319
Fax: 518-474-0060
Web: www.highered.nysed.gov

## New York State Grange

### Caroline Kark Scholarship

**Type of award:** Scholarship.
**Intended use:** For undergraduate study at postsecondary institution.
**Eligibility:** Applicant must be residing in New York.
**Basis for selection:** Major/career interest in deafness studies.
**Additional information:** Award available to Grange members preparing for a career working with the deaf or hearing impaired and to non-members who are deaf and want to further their education beyond high school. Hearing applicants must have been a Grange member for one year prior to applying. Deaf applicants must show sufficient hearing loss to receive full-time amplification.

| | |
|---|---|
| **Application deadline:** | April 15 |

**Contact:**
New York State Grange
100 Grange Place
Cortland, NY 13045
Phone: 607-756-7553
Fax: 607-756-7757
Web: www.nysgrange.org

### Grange Denise Scholarship

**Type of award:** Scholarship, renewable.
**Intended use:** For full-time undergraduate study at 2-year or 4-year institution.
**Eligibility:** Applicant must be residing in New York.
**Basis for selection:** Major/career interest in agriculture; agribusiness; agricultural education; agricultural economics or natural resources/conservation. Applicant must demonstrate financial need.
**Application requirements:** Recommendations, transcript.
**Additional information:** Send SASE for application.

| | |
|---|---|
| **Amount of award:** | $1,000 |
| **Number of awards:** | 3 |
| **Number of applicants:** | 6 |
| **Application deadline:** | April 15 |
| **Notification begins:** | June 15 |
| **Total amount awarded:** | $3,000 |

**Contact:**
New York State Grange
100 Grange Place
Cortland, NY 13045
Phone: 607-756-7553
Fax: 607-756-7757
Web: www.nysgrange.org

### Grange Susan W. Freestone Education Award

**Type of award:** Scholarship, renewable.
**Intended use:** For full-time undergraduate or graduate study at 2-year or 4-year institution in United States. Designated institutions: Approved institutions in New York state.
**Eligibility:** Applicant must be residing in New York.
**Basis for selection:** Applicant must demonstrate financial need, depth of character and service orientation.
**Application requirements:** Transcript.
**Additional information:** Applicant must be current New York State Grange member. Must have been Junior Grange member to qualify for maximum award. Send SASE for application. Activity in Grange work considered.

| | |
|---|---|
| **Amount of award:** | $1,000 |
| **Number of awards:** | 2 |
| **Number of applicants:** | 5 |
| **Application deadline:** | April 15 |
| **Notification begins:** | June 15 |
| **Total amount awarded:** | $1,000 |

**Contact:**
New York State Grange
100 Grange Place
Cortland, NY 13045
Phone: 607-756-7553
Fax: 607-756-7757
Web: www.nysgrange.org

### June Gill Nursing Scholarship

**Type of award:** Scholarship, renewable.
**Intended use:** For undergraduate study at postsecondary institution.

**Eligibility:** Applicant or parent must be member/participant of New York State Grange. Applicant must be residing in New York.
**Basis for selection:** Major/career interest in nursing. Applicant must demonstrate financial need and high academic achievement.
**Application requirements:** Transcript, proof of eligibility. Career statement.
**Additional information:** Grandchild of member of the New York State Grange also eligible. Award amounts vary.

| | |
|---|---|
| **Amount of award:** | $1,000 |
| **Number of awards:** | 2 |
| **Application deadline:** | April 15 |
| **Notification begins:** | June 1 |

**Contact:**
New York State Grange
100 Grange Place
Cortland, NY 13045
Phone: 607-756-7553
Fax: 607-756-7757
Web: www.nysgrange.org

# New York State Higher Education Services Corporation

## City University SEEK/College Discovery Program

**Type of award:** Scholarship.
**Intended use:** For undergraduate study at 2-year or 4-year institution. Designated institutions: City University of New York campuses.
**Eligibility:** Applicant must be U.S. citizen or permanent resident residing in New York.
**Basis for selection:** Applicant must demonstrate financial need.
**Application requirements:** Proof of eligibility. FAFSA, TAP.
**Additional information:** Applicant must be both academically and economically disadvantaged. Available at CUNY and community college campuses. Apply to CUNY financial aid office. For SEEK, student must have resided in New York State for at least one year; for College Discovery, student must have resided in New York City for at least one year.
**Contact:**
City University of New York
Office of Admission Services
1114 Avenue of the Americas
New York, NY 10036
Phone: 212-997-CUNY
Web: www.cuny.edu

## Flight 587 Memorial Scholarships

**Type of award:** Scholarship, renewable.
**Intended use:** For full-time undergraduate study at postsecondary institution. Designated institutions: Approved New York state institutions.
**Eligibility:** Applicant must be residing in New York.
**Application requirements:** FAFSA. TAP. Scholarship supplement. Proof of applicant's relationship to the deceased (birth certificate, marriage license, etc.)
**Additional information:** Provides financial aid to children, spouses, and financial dependents of individuals killed as a direct result of American Airlines Flight 587's crash in the Belle Harbor neighborhood of Queens, New York, on the morning of November 12, 2001. Award is full tuition for students attending public colleges and universities in New York State, and the monetary equivalent for students attending private New York schools.

| | |
|---|---|
| **Amount of award:** | Full tuition |
| **Application deadline:** | May 1 |

**Contact:**
New York State Higher Education Services Corporation
HESC Scholarship Unit
99 Washington Avenue, Room 1430A
Albany, NY 12255
Phone: 888-NYS-HESC
Web: www.hesc.com

## Military Service Recognition Scholarship (MSRS)

**Type of award:** Scholarship, renewable.
**Intended use:** For full-time undergraduate study at 2-year or 4-year institution. Designated institutions: Approved New York State institutions.
**Eligibility:** Applicant must be residing in New York. Applicant must be disabled while on active duty; or dependent of disabled veteran, deceased veteran or POW/MIA; or spouse of disabled veteran, deceased veteran or POW/MIA. Must be child, spouse, or financial dependent of member of the U.S. armed forces or state-organized militia who, at any time after August 2, 1990, while New York State resident, (1) died or became permanently disabled as a result of injury or illness in a combat theater or combat zone or during military training operations in preparation for duty in a combat theater or (2) is classified as MIA in a combat theater or combat zone of operations.
**Application requirements:** FAFSA, TAP application.
**Additional information:** At public colleges and universities (CUNY or SUNY), award covers actual tuition and mandatory educational fees; actual room and board for living on campus (or an allowance for commuters); and allowances for books, supplies, and transportation. At private institutions, award amount equals SUNY four-year college tuition and fees and allowances for room and board, books, supplies, and transportation. New York State resident family members who were enrolled in undergraduate programs at U.S. colleges or universities outside of New York State on September 11, 2001, are also eligible. See Website for more details.

| | |
|---|---|
| **Amount of award:** | Full tuition |
| **Application deadline:** | June 30 |

**Contact:**
New York State Higher Education Services Corporation
Scholarships and Grants
99 Washington Avenue
Albany, NY 12255
Phone: 888-NYS-HESC
Web: www.hesc.com

## New York State Aid for Part-Time Study Program

**Type of award:** Scholarship, renewable.
**Intended use:** For half-time undergraduate study at postsecondary institution. Designated institutions: Participating New York state institutions.

**Eligibility:** Applicant must be U.S. citizen or permanent resident residing in New York.
**Basis for selection:** Applicant must demonstrate financial need.
**Application requirements:** Proof of eligibility.
**Additional information:** Must fall within income limits. Campus-based program; recipients selected and award amount determined by school. Maximum award is $2,000. Must not have used up TAP eligibility or be in default on Federal Family Education Loan. Student must maintain minimum 2.0 GPA. Applications available from individual colleges.

**Amount of award:** $2,000

**Contact:**
New York State Higher Education Services Corporation
Scholarships and Grants
99 Washington Avenue
Albany, NY 12255
Phone: 888-NYS-HESC
Web: www.hesc.com

## New York State Memorial Scholarship for Families of Deceased Police/Volunteer Firefighters/Peace Officers and Emergency Medical Service Workers

**Type of award:** Scholarship, renewable.
**Intended use:** For full-time undergraduate study at 2-year or 4-year institution. Designated institutions: Approved New York institutions.
**Eligibility:** Applicant must be U.S. citizen residing in New York. Applicant's parent must have been killed or disabled in work-related accident as firefighter, police officer or public safety officer.
**Application requirements:** Proof of eligibility. Memorial Scholarship Supplement, FAFSA, and Express TAP Application.
**Additional information:** Spouse and/or children of police officer/firefighter/peace officer/EMS worker who died as result of injuries sustained in line of duty in service to New York State are eligible. Award will equal applicant's actual tuition cost or SUNY undergraduate tuition cost, whichever is less. Also provides funds to meet non-tuition costs, such as room and board, books, supplies, and transportation. Visit Website for additional information.

**Amount of award:** Full tuition
**Application deadline:** May 1

**Contact:**
New York State Higher Education Services Corporation
Scholarships and Grants
99 Washington Avenue
Albany, NY 12255
Phone: 888-NYS-HESC
Web: www.hesc.com

## New York State Regents Awards for Children of Deceased and Disabled Veterans

**Type of award:** Scholarship.
**Intended use:** For full-time undergraduate or non-degree study at 2-year or 4-year institution.
**Eligibility:** Applicant must be residing in New York. Applicant must be dependent of veteran, disabled veteran or deceased veteran during Korean War, Persian Gulf War, WW I, WW II or Vietnam. Student's parent must have been disabled or deceased veteran or POW, or classified as MIA. Student whose parent is a veteran of Afghanistan conflict also eligible. Student whose parent has received Armed Forces, Navy, or Marine Corps expeditionary medal for participation in operations in Lebanon, Grenada, and Panama also eligible, as are students born with spina bifida whose parent(s) served in Vietnam between 12/22/61 and 5/7/75.
**Application requirements:** Proof of eligibility. FAFSA and Express TAP Application.
**Additional information:** Student must initially establish eligibility by submitting a Child of Veteran Award Supplement before applying. Veteran must be a resident of New York state. Visit Website for additional information.

**Amount of award:** $450
**Application deadline:** June 30

**Contact:**
New York State Higher Education Services Corporation
Scholarships and Grants
99 Washington Avenue
Albany, NY 12255
Phone: 888-NYS-HESC
Web: www.hesc.com

## New York State Tuition Assistance Program

**Type of award:** Scholarship, renewable.
**Intended use:** For undergraduate or graduate study at accredited postsecondary institution in United States. Designated institutions: TAP-eligible schools in New York.
**Eligibility:** Applicant must be U.S. citizen or permanent resident residing in New York.
**Basis for selection:** Applicant must demonstrate financial need.
**Application requirements:** Proof of eligibility. FAFSA.
**Additional information:** Must fall within income limits. Submit FAFSA to receive prefilled Express TAP Application (ETA) to review, sign, and return. Award subject to budget appropriations. Must maintain at least C average. Must not be in default on a HESC-guaranteed loan. Part-time, first-time freshmen attending CUNY, SUNY, or not-for-profit independent degree-granting colleges also eligible. Visit Website for additional information.

**Amount of award:** $5,000
**Application deadline:** May 1

**Contact:**
New York State Higher Education Services Corporation
Grants and Scholarships
99 Washington Avenue
Albany, NY 12255
Phone: 888-NYS-HESC
Web: www.hesc.com

## New York State Veterans Tuition Award

**Type of award:** Scholarship, renewable.
**Intended use:** For undergraduate or graduate study at accredited vocational, 2-year, 4-year or graduate institution in United States. Designated institutions: Approved postsecondary schools in New York.
**Eligibility:** Applicant must be returning adult student. Applicant must be U.S. citizen or permanent resident residing in New York. Applicant must be veteran during Persian Gulf War or Vietnam. Must have served in armed forces in hostilities in Indochina between December 1961 and May

1975, or in Persian Gulf on or after August 2, 1990. Veterans of the conflict in Afghanistan also eligible. Must not have been dishonorably discharged.
**Application requirements:** Proof of eligibility. FAFSA. Express Tap Application (ETA). Documentation of Indochina, Persian Gulf, or Afghanistan service.
**Additional information:** Students must have also applied for TAP and Federal Pell Grant awards. Visit Website for additional information.

| | |
|---|---|
| **Amount of award:** | $4,895 |
| **Application deadline:** | June 30 |

**Contact:**
New York State Higher Education Services Corporation
Scholarships and Grants
99 Washington Avenue
Albany, NY 12255
Phone: 888-NYS-HESC
Web: www.hesc.com



### New York State World Trade Center Memorial Scholarship

**Type of award:** Scholarship, renewable.
**Intended use:** For full-time undergraduate study at 2-year or 4-year institution. Designated institutions: Approved New York colleges and universities.
**Application requirements:** Proof of eligibility. FAFSA, Express TAP Application.
**Additional information:** Must be child, spouse, or financial dependent of person who died or became severely and permanently disabled due to the September 11th attacks or rescue and recovery operation. At public colleges and universities (CUNY or SUNY), award covers actual tuition and mandatory educational fees; actual room and board for living on campus (or an allowance for commuters); and allowances for books, supplies, and transportation. At private institutions, award amount equals SUNY four-year college tuition and fees, and allowances for room and board, books, supplies, and transportation. New York State resident family members who were enrolled in undergraduate programs at U.S. colleges or universities outside of New York State on September 11, 2001, are also eligible. See Website for details.

| | |
|---|---|
| **Amount of award:** | Full tuition |
| **Application deadline:** | June 30 |

**Contact:**
New York State Higher Education Services Corporation
Grants and Scholarships
99 Washington Avenue
Albany, NY 12255
Phone: 888-NYS-HESC
Web: www.hesc.com

## New York State Office of Adult Career and Educational Services

### New York State Readers Aid Program

**Type of award:** Scholarship, renewable.
**Intended use:** For undergraduate, master's or doctoral study at 2-year, 4-year or graduate institution.
**Eligibility:** Applicant must be visually impaired or hearing impaired. Applicant must be residing in New York.
**Application requirements:** Interview, proof of eligibility.
**Additional information:** Applicant must be legally blind or deaf. Number of awards varies. Applications available at degree-granting institutions. Award provides funds for note-takers, readers, or interpreters. Applicant may be attending out-of-state institution.

| | |
|---|---|
| **Amount of award:** | $800 |
| **Number of applicants:** | 411 |
| **Application deadline:** | March 15, June 30 |
| **Total amount awarded:** | $300,000 |

**Contact:**
New York State Office of Adult Career and Educational Services
Readers Aid Program Att: Bryan Baszczuk
One Commerce Plaza, Room 1605
Albany, NY 12234
Phone: 518-474-2925
Fax: 518-473-6073
Web: www.acces.nysed.gov

## New York Women in Communications Foundation

### New York Women in Communications Foundation Scholarship

**Type of award:** Scholarship, renewable.
**Intended use:** For undergraduate or graduate study at accredited postsecondary institution.
**Eligibility:** Applicant must be U.S. citizen.
**Basis for selection:** Major/career interest in communications. Applicant must demonstrate financial need, high academic achievement, leadership and service orientation.
**Application requirements:** Interview, recommendations, essay, transcript, proof of eligibility. Resume.
**Additional information:** Minimum 3.2 GPA. Applicant must be majoring in a communications-related field or a high school senior intending to declare a major in a communications-related field. Must be attending school in New York City or be a resident of New York, New Jersey, Connecticut, or Pennsylvania. Finalists will be required to attend an in-person interview in New York City in February. Visit Website for application and additional requirements.

| | |
|---|---|
| **Amount of award:** | $2,500-$10,000 |
| **Number of awards:** | 15 |
| **Number of applicants:** | 500 |
| **Application deadline:** | January 27 |
| **Notification begins:** | April 1 |
| **Total amount awarded:** | $100,000 |

**Contact:**
New York Women in Communications Foundation Scholarship Program
355 Lexington Avenue, 15th Floor
New York, NY 10017-6603
Phone: 212-297-2133
Fax: 212-370-9047
Web: www.nywici.org

# Nisei Student Relocation Commemorative Fund

## Nisei Student Relocation Commemorative Fund

**Type of award:** Scholarship.
**Intended use:** For freshman study at vocational, 2-year or 4-year institution in United States.
**Eligibility:** Applicant must be Southeast Asian (Vietnamese, Cambodian, Hmong, Laotian, Amerasian) refugee or immigrant. Applicant must be high school senior.
**Basis for selection:** Applicant must demonstrate financial need and high academic achievement.
**Application requirements:** Recommendations, essay, transcript.
**Additional information:** Applicant must be high school senior living in city/area/region of the U.S. where scholarships are awarded, as determined annually by organization's board of directors. Location changes yearly; contact group for information. Number of awards varies.

| | |
|---|---|
| **Amount of award:** | $1,000-$2,000 |
| **Number of awards:** | 30 |
| **Number of applicants:** | 80 |
| **Total amount awarded:** | $37,500 |

**Contact:**
Nisei Student Relocation Commemorative Fund
c/o Y. Kobayashi or J. Hibino
19 Scenic Drive
Portland, CT 06480
Phone: 860-342-1731
Web: www.nsrcfund.org

# NMIA Ohio

## NMIA Ohio Scholarship Program

**Type of award:** Scholarship, renewable.
**Intended use:** For full-time junior, senior or graduate study at accredited 4-year or graduate institution in United States.
**Eligibility:** Applicant must be U.S. citizen residing in Ohio.
**Basis for selection:** Applicant must demonstrate high academic achievement.
**Additional information:** Applicant must be interested in a career in Intelligence. Funds awarded may be used for tuition, room, board, and/or laboratory fees and will be payable to the student's institution. Size and number of awards depends on funding; one to six awards will be given each year. Scholarships for full-time students will be greater than scholarships for part-time students. Applicant must not be relative of NMIA or scholarship committee members. Preference is given to students attending Ohio colleges and universities. The decision of the Scholarship Committee is final and not subject to external review.

| | |
|---|---|
| **Amount of award:** | $500-$2,000 |
| **Number of awards:** | 6 |
| **Number of applicants:** | 7 |
| **Application deadline:** | March 1 |
| **Notification begins:** | April 1 |
| **Total amount awarded:** | $3,000 |

**Contact:**
NMIA Ohio
c/o Deanne Otto
P.O. Box 341508
Beavercreek, OH 45434
Phone: 937-429-7601
Fax: 937-429-7602
Web: www.nmiaohio.org

# Non Commissioned Officers Association

## Non Commissioned Officers Association Scholarship for Children of Members

**Type of award:** Scholarship, renewable.
**Intended use:** For full-time undergraduate study in United States.
**Application requirements:** Transcript. Autobiography, ACT/SAT scores, and minimum 200-word essay on Americanism. Include two recommendation letters from school and one personal recommendation letter from adult who is not a relative.
**Additional information:** Applicant's parent must be member of Non Commissioned Officers Association.

| | |
|---|---|
| **Amount of award:** | $900-$1,000 |
| **Number of awards:** | 11 |
| **Number of applicants:** | 200 |
| **Application deadline:** | March 31 |
| **Notification begins:** | June 1 |
| **Total amount awarded:** | $21,000 |

**Contact:**
Non Commissioned Officers Association
P.O. Box 33790
San Antonio, TX 78265
Phone: 210-653-6161
Fax: 210-637-3337
Web: www.ncoausa.org

## Non Commissioned Officers Association Scholarship for Spouses

**Type of award:** Scholarship, renewable.
**Intended use:** For full-time undergraduate study in United States.
**Application requirements:** Transcript. Copy of high school diploma or GED, brief biographical background, and certificates for any training courses completed. Letter of intent describing degree course of study, plans for completion of program, and a closing paragraph on "What a College Degree Means to Me."
**Additional information:** Must be spouse of member of Non Commissioned Officers Association. Recipient must apply for auxiliary membership in Non Commissioned Officers Association.

| | |
|---|---|
| **Amount of award:** | $900 |
| **Number of awards:** | 4 |
| **Number of applicants:** | 30 |
| **Application deadline:** | March 31 |
| **Notification begins:** | June 1 |
| **Total amount awarded:** | $7,200 |

**Contact:**
Non Commissioned Officers Association
P.O. Box 33790
San Antonio, TX 78265
Phone: 210-653-6161
Fax: 210-637-3337
Web: www.ncoausa.org

# North American Limousin Foundation

## Limi Boosters National Educational Grant

**Type of award:** Scholarship.
**Intended use:** For undergraduate study at vocational, 2-year or 4-year institution.
**Basis for selection:** Major/career interest in agriculture. Applicant must demonstrate financial need, high academic achievement, depth of character, leadership, patriotism, seriousness of purpose and service orientation.
**Application requirements:** Recommendations, proof of eligibility. Recent photo. One of the three recommendations must be from active NALF member other than relative or guardian, two must be from the following: school superintendent, school principal, minister, 4-H leader, FFA instructor, county agent, or teacher.
**Additional information:** Experience with Limousin cattle preferred. Proven excellence in Limousin activities as well as leadership skills demonstrated in NALJA, 4-H, and FFA. Must be NALF Junior member.

| | |
|---|---|
| **Amount of award:** | $500-$750 |
| **Application deadline:** | May 15 |

**Contact:**
North American Limousin Junior Association
Marci Hicks
P.O. Box 4253
Midway, KY 40347
Phone: 859-576-2602
Web: www.nalf.org

## Limi Boosters Scholarship

**Type of award:** Scholarship.
**Intended use:** For undergraduate or graduate study at 2-year or 4-year institution.
**Basis for selection:** Applicant must demonstrate financial need, high academic achievement, depth of character, leadership, patriotism, seriousness of purpose and service orientation.
**Application requirements:** Transcript, proof of eligibility. Three recommendations, one of which must be from active NALF member other than relative or guardian.
**Additional information:** Must be NALF member and be active in 4H and FFA work. Must rank in top third of class.

| | |
|---|---|
| **Amount of award:** | $500-$750 |
| **Number of awards:** | 2 |
| **Application deadline:** | May 15 |
| **Total amount awarded:** | $3,000 |

**Contact:**
North American Limousin Foundation
Attn: Marci Hicks
P.O. Box 4253
Midway, KY 40347
Phone: 859-576-2602
Web: www.nalf.org

# North Carolina Community Colleges Foundation

## North Carolina Community Colleges Wells Fargo Technical Scholarship

**Type of award:** Scholarship.
**Intended use:** For full-time sophomore study at vocational or 2-year institution.
**Eligibility:** Applicant must be residing in North Carolina.
**Basis for selection:** Applicant must demonstrate financial need and high academic achievement.
**Additional information:** Scholarships distributed through the 58 community colleges in the system; apply through financial aid office of institution where enrolled.

| | |
|---|---|
| **Amount of award:** | $500 |

**Contact:**
North Carolina Community Colleges Foundation
200 West Jones Street
Raleigh, NC 27603
Phone: 919-807-7106
Fax: 919-807-7173
Web: www.ncccs.cc.nc.us

## Rodney E. Powell Memorial Scholarship

**Type of award:** Scholarship.
**Intended use:** For full-time undergraduate study at 2-year institution. Designated institutions: Community colleges in Progress Energy's service area.
**Eligibility:** Applicant must be residing in North Carolina.
**Basis for selection:** Major/career interest in engineering, electrical/electronic; electronics or technology. Applicant must demonstrate financial need and high academic achievement.
**Application requirements:** Essay.
**Additional information:** Minimum 3.0 GPA. Scholarship for students of electronic technology. Applicant must be enrolled full-time or must intend to enroll as new student at designated institution. Number of awards varies.

| | |
|---|---|
| **Amount of award:** | $1,000 |
| **Number of awards:** | 1 |

**Contact:**
North Carolina Department of Community Colleges
Attn: Lee McCollum
410 S. Wilmington Street PEB 7
Raleigh, NC 27601
Phone: 919-546-7585
Fax: 919-546-7652
Web: www.ncccs.cc.nc.us

# North Carolina Division of Veterans Affairs

## North Carolina Scholarships for Children of War Veterans

**Type of award:** Scholarship, renewable.
**Intended use:** For undergraduate or graduate study at accredited postsecondary institution.
**Eligibility:** Applicant must be no older than 24. Applicant must be residing in North Carolina. Applicant must be dependent of disabled veteran, deceased veteran or POW/MIA who served in the Army, Air Force, Marines, Navy or Coast Guard. Parent must have served during a period of war.
**Basis for selection:** Applicant must demonstrate financial need.
**Application requirements:** Interview, transcript, proof of eligibility. Birth certificate.
**Additional information:** For state schools, award is tuition waiver plus maximum of $2,200 room and board allowance for up to four years. For private schools, award is up to $4,500 per year. Parent must have been North Carolina resident at time of enlistment or child must have been born in and reside permanently in North Carolina. See Website for deadline information.

| | |
|---|---|
| **Amount of award:** | Full tuition |
| **Number of applicants:** | 555 |

**Contact:**
North Carolina Division of Veterans Affairs
1315 Mail Service Center
Albemarle Building, Suite 1065
Raleigh, NC 27699-1315
Web: www.doa.state.nc.us/vets/benefits-scholarships.htm

# North Carolina Division of Vocational Rehabilitation Services

## North Carolina Vocational Rehabilitation Award

**Type of award:** Scholarship, renewable.
**Intended use:** For full-time undergraduate study at accredited vocational, 2-year or 4-year institution.
**Eligibility:** Applicant must be physically challenged or learning disabled. Applicant must be residing in North Carolina.
**Basis for selection:** Applicant must demonstrate financial need.
**Application requirements:** Interview, proof of eligibility. Proof of mental, physical, or learning disability that is an impediment to employment.
**Additional information:** This program provides educational assistance for individuals who meet eligibility requirements and require training to reach their vocational goals.

| | |
|---|---|
| **Amount of award:** | $2,670 |

**Contact:**
North Carolina Division of Vocational Rehabilitation Services
2801 Mail Service Center
Raleigh, NC 27699-2801
Phone: 919-855-3500
Fax: 919-715-0616
Web: www.ncdhhs.gov/dvrs/

# North Carolina State Board of Refrigeration Examiners

## North Carolina State Board of Refrigeration Examiners Scholarship

**Type of award:** Scholarship.
**Intended use:** For undergraduate study at 2-year institution.
**Eligibility:** Applicant must be residing in North Carolina.
**Basis for selection:** Major/career interest in air conditioning/heating/refrigeration technology. Applicant must demonstrate financial need and high academic achievement.
**Application requirements:** Essay.
**Additional information:** Number of awards varies. Must enroll in Associate of Applied Science degree of study in commercial refrigeration or HVAC/R technology.

| | |
|---|---|
| **Number of awards:** | 2 |
| **Application deadline:** | February 1 |

**Contact:**
North Carolina State Board of Refrigeration Examiners
Suite 208
893 Highway 70 W
Garner, NC 27529
Phone: 919-779-4711
Web: www.refrigerationboard.org/wp/

# North Carolina State Education Assistance Authority

## GlaxoSmithKline Opportunity Scholarship

**Type of award:** Scholarship.
**Intended use:** For undergraduate study at vocational, 2-year or 4-year institution in United States.
**Eligibility:** Applicant must be U.S. citizen residing in North Carolina.
**Basis for selection:** Applicant must demonstrate depth of character and seriousness of purpose.
**Additional information:** Applicant must have been a permanent resident of Durham, Orange, or Wake county for one year prior to application. GlaxoSmithKline and Triangle Community Foundation employees or their families not eligible. Visit Website for application.

| | |
|---|---|
| **Amount of award:** | $5,000 |
| **Number of awards:** | 5 |
| **Application deadline:** | March 15 |

**Contact:**
Triangle Community Foundation Scholarship Program
Attn: Libby Long
324 Blackwell Street, Suite 1220
Durham, NC 27701
Phone: 919-474-8370
Fax: 919-941-9208
Web: www.trianglecf.org

## Golden LEAF Scholars Program - Two-Year Colleges

**Type of award:** Scholarship.
**Intended use:** For undergraduate study at 2-year institution. Designated institutions: Member institutions of North Carolina Community College system.
**Eligibility:** Applicant must be residing in North Carolina.
**Basis for selection:** Applicant must demonstrate financial need, high academic achievement, depth of character, leadership and service orientation.
**Application requirements:** Disclosure of other financial aid awards.
**Additional information:** Applicant must demonstrate need under federal TRIO formula. Award is up to $750 per semester (including summer) for curriculum students; up to $250 per semester for occupational education students. Finalist will undergo merit competition and be judged on academics, leadership, community service, and the effect of the tobacco industry's and economy's decline on his/her family. Must be permanent resident of one of 73 eligible counties. Visit Website for more information. Contact financial aid office for application.

| | |
|---|---|
| **Amount of award:** | $250-$750 |

**Contact:**
Contact financial aid office at local community college.
Phone: 800-700-1775 ext. 650
Fax: 919-549-8481
Web: www.cfnc.org

## Golden LEAF Scholarship - Four-Year University Program

**Type of award:** Scholarship, renewable.
**Intended use:** For undergraduate study at 4-year institution. Designated institutions: Public universities.
**Eligibility:** Applicant must be high school senior. Applicant must be residing in North Carolina.
**Basis for selection:** Applicant must demonstrate financial need.
**Application requirements:** FAFSA.
**Additional information:** Must be incoming freshman, transfer student from a North Carolina community college, or previous recipient applying for renewal. New applicants must be permanent resident of economically distressed and/or tobacco-dependent rural county. Recipients of other aid amounting to 75 percent or more of total education costs will be given low priority. Visit Website for application and more information.

| | |
|---|---|
| **Amount of award:** | $3,000 |
| **Number of awards:** | 580 |
| **Application deadline:** | March 15 |

**Contact:**
North Carolina State Education Assistance Authority
P.O. Box 14103
Research Triangle Park, NC 27709
Phone: 800-700-1775 ext. 650
Web: www.ncseaa.edu

## Jagannathan Scholarship

**Type of award:** Scholarship, renewable.
**Intended use:** For full-time freshman study at 4-year institution in United States. Designated institutions: Constituent institutions of the University of North Carolina.
**Eligibility:** Applicant must be high school senior. Applicant must be U.S. citizen or permanent resident residing in North Carolina.
**Basis for selection:** Applicant must demonstrate financial need, high academic achievement and leadership.
**Application requirements:** Proof of eligibility, nomination by high school guidance counselor, financial office of UNC institution, or Tolaram Polymers, Cookson Fibers, or related company. SAT scores, College Scholarship Service's PROFILE (register and file by February 8), and documented proof of financial need.
**Additional information:** Special consideration given to students whose parents are employees of Tolaram Polymers, Cookson Fibers, or related companies. Applications available at all North Carolina public high schools. Minimum SAT 1200 score (reading and math) or ACT equivalent. Check Website for specific details.

| | |
|---|---|
| **Amount of award:** | $3,500 |
| **Number of awards:** | 4 |
| **Number of applicants:** | 4 |
| **Notification begins:** | May 1 |
| **Total amount awarded:** | $14,000 |

**Contact:**
North Carolina State Education Assistance Authority
P.O. Box 14103
Research Triangle Park, NC 27709-3663
Phone: 800-700-1775
Web: www.cfnc.org/jag

## Latino Diamante Scholarship Fund

**Type of award:** Scholarship.
**Intended use:** For freshman or sophomore study at postsecondary institution. Designated institutions: North Carolina institutions.
**Eligibility:** Applicant must be Hispanic American. Applicant must be residing in North Carolina.
**Application requirements:** Recommendations, essay, transcript.
**Additional information:** Minimum 2.5 GPA. Visit Website for application and more information.

| | |
|---|---|
| **Amount of award:** | $750 |
| **Number of awards:** | 2 |
| **Application deadline:** | August 15 |
| **Notification begins:** | September 15 |

**Contact:**
Diamante, Inc.
315 North Academy Street
Suite 256
Cary, NC 27513
Phone: 919-852-0075
Web: www.cfnc.org

## NC Sheriff's Association Criminal Justice Scholarship

**Type of award:** Scholarship.
**Intended use:** For full-time undergraduate study in United States. Designated institutions: Appalachian State University, East Carolina University, Elizabeth City State University, Fayetteville State University, North Carolina Central University, North Carolina State University, the University of

North Carolina at Charlotte, the University of North Carolina at Pembroke, the University of North Carolina at Wilmington, Western Carolina University.
**Eligibility:** Applicant must be residing in North Carolina.
**Basis for selection:** Major/career interest in criminal justice/law enforcement.
**Application requirements:** Recommendations, essay, transcript.
**Additional information:** Application available at financial aid offices of eligible institutions. Application and supplemental material should be submitted to sheriff of county where applicant resides. First priority given to child of sheriff/law enforcement officer killed in the line of duty; second priority given to child of retired or deceased sheriff/law enforcement officer; third priority given to criminal justice students.

| | |
|---|---|
| **Amount of award:** | $2,000 |
| **Number of awards:** | 10 |
| **Number of applicants:** | 50 |
| **Total amount awarded:** | $20,000 |

**Contact:**
North Carolina State Education Assistance Authority
P.O. Box 14103
Research Triangle Park, NC 27709-3663
Phone: 800-700-1775 ext. 650
Web: www.ncseaa.edu

## North Carolina Aubrey Lee Brooks Scholarship

**Type of award:** Scholarship, renewable.
**Intended use:** For full-time undergraduate study at 4-year institution in United States. Designated institutions: North Carolina State University, University of North Carolina at Chapel Hill, University of North Carolina at Greensboro.
**Eligibility:** Applicant must be high school senior. Applicant must be U.S. citizen residing in North Carolina.
**Basis for selection:** Applicant must demonstrate financial need, depth of character, leadership and seriousness of purpose.
**Application requirements:** Proof of eligibility.
**Additional information:** Award amount varies; maximum $9,500 per year, plus one-time computer award up to $3,000. Scholarship pays additional amounts for approved summer study or internships. Applications available through high school. Applicants must reside and attend high school in one of the following counties: Alamance, Bertie, Caswell, Durham, Forsyth, Granville, Guilford, Orange, Person, Rockingham, Stokes, Surry, Swain, or Warren. One additional scholarship awarded to student from cities of Greensboro and High Point and to eligible senior at North Carolina School of Science and Mathematics.

| | |
|---|---|
| **Amount of award:** | $9,500 |
| **Number of awards:** | 17 |
| **Application deadline:** | February 1 |

**Contact:**
North Carolina State Education Assistance Authority
P.O. Box 14103
Research Triangle Park, NC 27709-3663
Phone: 800-700-1775 ext. 650
Web: www.cfnc.org

## North Carolina Legislative Tuition Grant

**Type of award:** Scholarship, renewable.
**Intended use:** For undergraduate study at accredited 2-year or 4-year institution. Designated institutions: Eligible North Carolina private institutions.
**Eligibility:** Applicant must be U.S. citizen or permanent resident residing in North Carolina.
**Additional information:** Award not applicable for theology, divinity, or religious education programs. Award amount determined by North Carolina General Assembly. Applications available from eligible institutions' financial aid offices.

| | |
|---|---|
| **Amount of award:** | $1,850 |
| **Number of awards:** | 24,078 |
| **Total amount awarded:** | $43,911,790 |

**Contact:**
North Carolina State Education Assistance Authority
P.O. Box 14103
Research Triangle Park, NC 27709-3663
Phone: 800-700-1775 ext. 650
Web: www.cfnc.org

## North Carolina Student Incentive Grant

**Type of award:** Scholarship, renewable.
**Intended use:** For full-time undergraduate study at postsecondary institution. Designated institutions: Approved institutions in North Carolina.
**Eligibility:** Applicant must be U.S. citizen residing in North Carolina.
**Basis for selection:** Applicant must demonstrate financial need.

| | |
|---|---|
| **Amount of award:** | $700 |
| **Number of awards:** | 8,110 |
| **Number of applicants:** | 395,913 |
| **Application deadline:** | March 15 |
| **Total amount awarded:** | $5,101,881 |

**Contact:**
North Carolina State Education Assistance Authority
P.O. Box 14103
Research Triangle Park, NC 27709-3663
Phone: 800-700-1775
Web: www.cfnc.org

## State Contractual Scholarship Fund

**Type of award:** Scholarship, renewable.
**Intended use:** For undergraduate study at accredited 2-year or 4-year institution. Designated institutions: Private institutions in North Carolina.
**Eligibility:** Applicant must be U.S. citizen or permanent resident residing in North Carolina.
**Basis for selection:** Applicant must demonstrate financial need.
**Application requirements:** Proof of eligibility.
**Additional information:** Theology and divinity students not eligible. Contact school's financial aid office or NCSEAA for more information. Must be enrolled in degree-seeking program. Award amount varies; check with private institution's financial aid office for current award amount.
**Contact:**
North Carolina State Education Assistance Authority
P.O. Box 14103
Research Triangle Park, NC 27709-3663
Phone: 800-700-1775 ext. 650
Web: www.cfnc.org

## Teacher Assistant Scholarship Fund

**Type of award:** Scholarship, renewable.
**Intended use:** For undergraduate study at 2-year or 4-year institution in United States. Designated institutions: North

Carolina institutions offering teacher licensure programs (visit Website for list).
**Eligibility:** Applicant must be residing in North Carolina.
**Basis for selection:** Major/career interest in education; education, early childhood; education, special or education, teacher. Applicant must demonstrate financial need.
**Application requirements:** FAFSA.
**Additional information:** Applicant must be full-time teacher assistant for at least one year at public or federal school in North Carolina. Must be enrolled in program leading toward initial teacher licensure. Minimum 3.0 GPA. Must maintain minimum 2.8 GPA to renew. Students at two-year schools receive up to $1,800 per year; those at four-year schools receive up to $3,600 per year. Students cannot receive more than $25,200 in total aid. Must not be in default on a student loan.

| | |
|---|---|
| **Amount of award:** | $600-$3,600 |
| **Application deadline:** | April 15 |

**Contact:**
North Carolina State Education Assistance Authority
P.O. Box 14103
Research Triangle Park, NC 27709-3663
Phone: 800-700-1775 ext. 650
Web: www.cfnc.org



# North Dakota University System

## North Dakota Academic Scholarships

**Type of award:** Scholarship.
**Intended use:** For freshman study at postsecondary institution. Designated institutions: North Dakota universities, colleges, and tribal colleges.
**Eligibility:** Applicant must be high school senior. Applicant must be residing in North Dakota.
**Basis for selection:** Applicant must demonstrate high academic achievement.
**Additional information:** Must be graduate of North Dakota high school. Minimum 3.0 GPA. Minimum 24 ACT score or three 5s WorkKeys assessment. Renewable for full-time students who maintain 2.75 GPA.

| | |
|---|---|
| **Amount of award:** | $6,000 |

**Contact:**
North Dakota University System
600 East Boulevard Ave., Dept. 215
Bismarck, ND 58505-0230
Phone: 701-328-4414
Fax: 701-328-2961
Web: www.ndus.edu

## North Dakota Career & Technical Education Scholarships

**Type of award:** Scholarship, renewable.
**Intended use:** For freshman study at postsecondary institution in United States. Designated institutions: North Dakota universities, colleges, and tribal colleges.
**Eligibility:** Applicant must be high school senior. Applicant must be residing in North Dakota.
**Basis for selection:** Applicant must demonstrate high academic achievement.
**Additional information:** Must be graduate of North Dakota high school. Minimum 3.0 GPA. Minimum 24 ACT score or three 5s WorkKeys assessment. Renewable for full-time students who maintain 2.75 GPA.

| | |
|---|---|
| **Amount of award:** | $6,000 |

**Contact:**
North Dakota University System
600 East Boulevard Ave. Dept 215
Bismarck, ND 58505-0230
Phone: 701-328-4414
Fax: 701-328-2961
Web: www.ndus.edu

## North Dakota Indian Scholarship Program

**Type of award:** Scholarship, renewable.
**Intended use:** For full-time undergraduate or graduate study at vocational, 2-year or 4-year institution.
**Eligibility:** Applicant must be American Indian. Must be enrolled member of Indian tribe. Applicant must be U.S. citizen residing in North Dakota.
**Basis for selection:** Applicant must demonstrate financial need.
**Application requirements:** Transcript, proof of eligibility. Budget completed by financial aid officer at institution student is attending/will attend.
**Additional information:** Minimum 2.0 GPA. Priority given to undergraduates with cumulative 3.5 GPA or higher.

| | |
|---|---|
| **Amount of award:** | $800-$2,000 |
| **Number of awards:** | 175 |
| **Number of applicants:** | 400 |
| **Application deadline:** | July 15 |
| **Total amount awarded:** | $102,000 |

**Contact:**
North Dakota University System, Indian Scholarship Program
BSC Horizon Building
1815 Schaefer Street, Suite 202
Bismarck, ND 58501
Phone: 701-224-2497
Web: www.ndus.nodak.edu

## North Dakota Scholars Program

**Type of award:** Scholarship, renewable.
**Intended use:** For full-time undergraduate study at postsecondary institution.
**Eligibility:** Applicant must be high school senior. Applicant must be residing in North Dakota.
**Basis for selection:** Applicant must demonstrate high academic achievement.
**Application requirements:** Proof of eligibility.
**Additional information:** Applicant must take ACT between October and June of junior year and score in upper five percentile of all North Dakota ACT test-takers. Numeric sum of English, math, reading, and science reasoning scores may be considered. Award is full-tuition scholarship for students attending ND's public and tribal colleges; equal to NDSU/UND tuition for students attending private institutions. Recipients must maintain 3.5 GPA for renewal. Contact sponsor for more information and deadline.

| | |
|---|---|
| **Amount of award:** | Full tuition |
| **Number of awards:** | 60 |
| **Number of applicants:** | 400 |

**Contact:**
North Dakota University System Student Financial Assistance Program
600 East Boulevard
Dept. 215
Bismarck, ND 58505-0230
Phone: 701-328-4114
Web: www.ndus.edu

### North Dakota State Student Incentive Grant

**Type of award:** Scholarship, renewable.
**Intended use:** For full-time undergraduate study at vocational, 2-year or 4-year institution. Designated institutions: North Dakota colleges.
**Eligibility:** Applicant must be U.S. citizen or permanent resident residing in North Dakota.
**Basis for selection:** Applicant must demonstrate financial need.
**Application requirements:** Proof of eligibility. FAFSA.
**Additional information:** Application automatic with FAFSA. Applicant must be first-time undergraduate student. Must not be in default on any federal loans or owe refund on any Title IV grants or loans.

| | |
|---|---|
| **Amount of award:** | $800-$1,500 |
| **Number of awards:** | 8,200 |
| **Number of applicants:** | 28,000 |
| **Application deadline:** | March 15 |
| **Total amount awarded:** | $2,220,000 |

**Contact:**
North Dakota University System Student Financial Assistance Program
600 East Boulevard
Dept. 215
Bismarck, ND 58505-0230
Phone: 701-328-4114
Web: www.ndus.edu

## Northern Cheyenne Tribal Education Department

### Northern Cheyenne Higher Education Program

**Type of award:** Scholarship, renewable.
**Intended use:** For undergraduate study at postsecondary institution.
**Eligibility:** Applicant must be American Indian. Must be enrolled with Northern Cheyenne Tribe. Applicant must be U.S. citizen.
**Basis for selection:** Applicant must demonstrate financial need.
**Application requirements:** Recommendations, essay, transcript, proof of eligibility. FAFSA.
**Additional information:** Award amount varies, depends on unmet need. Deadlines: October 1 for spring, April 1 for summer, and March 1 for fall.

| | |
|---|---|
| **Amount of award:** | $6,000 |
| **Number of awards:** | 84 |
| **Number of applicants:** | 349 |
| **Application deadline:** | March 1, April 1 |
| **Total amount awarded:** | $284,853 |

**Contact:**
Northern Cheyenne Tribal Education Department
Attn: Norma Bixby
Box 307
Lame Deer, MT 59043
Phone: 406-477-6602
Fax: 406-477-8150
Web: www.cheyennenation.com

## Northwest Danish Association

### The Kaj Christensen Scholarship for Vocational Training

**Type of award:** Scholarship, renewable.
**Intended use:** For undergraduate or graduate study at postsecondary institution in or outside United States.
**Eligibility:** Applicant must be at least 17. Applicant must be U.S. citizen or permanent resident.
**Basis for selection:** Applicant must demonstrate depth of character and service orientation.
**Application requirements:** Recommendations, transcript. Personal essay on educational goals, two references.
**Additional information:** Must be member of Northwest Danish Association. Must demonstrate some connection to Denmark via life experience, travel, heritage, etc. Must be resident of Oregon or Washington. Must have interest in vocational training.

| | |
|---|---|
| **Amount of award:** | $500 |
| **Number of awards:** | 1 |
| **Application deadline:** | March 31 |
| **Notification begins:** | May 1 |
| **Total amount awarded:** | $500 |

**Contact:**
Northwest Danish Association
1833 North 105th Street
Suite 101
Seattle, WA 98133-8973
Phone: 800-564-7736
Fax: 206-729-6997
Web: www.northwestdanishfoundation.org

### Northwest Danish Association Scholarship

**Type of award:** Scholarship.
**Intended use:** For undergraduate or graduate study at postsecondary institution in United States.
**Eligibility:** Applicant must be residing in Oregon or Washington.
**Additional information:** Studies must be related to Danish community. Must be of Danish descent or married to someone of Danish descent, who actively participates in Danish community. Consideration given to those of non-Danish descent who show exceptional involvement with Danish community. Must be resident of Oregon or Washington. Those training for artistic careers also considered.

| | |
|---|---|
| **Number of awards:** | 6 |
| **Application deadline:** | March 31 |

Scholarships

**Contact:**
Northwest Danish Association
1833 North 105th Street
Suite 101
Seattle, WA 98133
Phone: 206-523-3263
Fax: 206-729-6997
Web: www.northwestdanishfoundation.org

### Scan/Design Foundation by Inger and Jens Bruun Scholarship for Study in Denmark

**Type of award:** Scholarship.
**Intended use:** For undergraduate study at postsecondary institution.
**Eligibility:** Applicant must be at least 18. Applicant must be residing in Oregon or Washington.
**Application requirements:** Essay on why you wish to study in Denmark, written statement on what has prepared you to take full advantage of your study experience, two references.
**Additional information:** Open to current residents of Washington or Oregon who wish to study in Denmark.

| | |
|---|---|
| **Amount of award:** | $5,000 |
| **Number of awards:** | 1 |
| **Application deadline:** | March 31 |
| **Total amount awarded:** | $5,000 |

**Contact:**
Northwest Danish Association
1833 North 105 Street
Suite 101
Seattle, WA 98133-8973
Phone: 800-564-7736
Fax: 206-729-6997
Web: www.northwestdanishfoundation.org

## OCA

### OCA-AXA Achievement Scholarships

**Type of award:** Scholarship.
**Intended use:** For freshman study at postsecondary institution.
**Eligibility:** Applicant must be Asian American or Native Hawaiian/Pacific Islander. Applicant must be U.S. citizen or permanent resident.
**Basis for selection:** Applicant must demonstrate high academic achievement, leadership and service orientation.
**Application requirements:** Recommendations, essay. Resume.
**Additional information:** Minimum 3.0 GPA. Number of awards varies. Visit Website for more information and deadline.

| | |
|---|---|
| **Amount of award:** | $2,000 |
| **Total amount awarded:** | $20,000 |

**Contact:**
OCA
1322 18th Street, NW
Washington, DC 20036
Phone: 202-223-5500
Fax: 202-296-0540
Web: www.ocanational.org

### OCA/UPS Foundation Gold Mountain College Scholarship

**Type of award:** Scholarship.
**Intended use:** For full-time freshman study in United States.
**Eligibility:** Applicant must be Asian American or Native Hawaiian/Pacific Islander. Applicant must be U.S. citizen or permanent resident.
**Basis for selection:** Applicant must demonstrate financial need.
**Application requirements:** Recommendations, essay. Resume, FAFSA.
**Additional information:** Minimum 3.0 GPA. Applicant must be Asian Pacific American and first person in family to go to college in the United States. Visit Website for deadline.

| | |
|---|---|
| **Amount of award:** | $2,000 |
| **Number of awards:** | 12 |
| **Number of applicants:** | 250 |
| **Total amount awarded:** | $24,000 |

**Contact:**
OCA
1322 18th Street, NW
Washington, DC 20036
Phone: 202-223-5500
Fax: 202-296-0540
Web: www.ocanational.org

### OCA/Verizon Foundation College Scholarship

**Type of award:** Scholarship.
**Intended use:** For full-time sophomore, junior or senior study at 4-year institution.
**Eligibility:** Applicant must be Asian American. Applicant must be U.S. citizen or permanent resident.
**Basis for selection:** Major/career interest in accounting; business/management/administration; electronics; engineering; education; engineering, electrical/electronic; finance/banking; human resources; marketing or engineering, mechanical. Applicant must demonstrate financial need.
**Application requirements:** Recommendations, essay. FAFSA.
**Additional information:** Minimum 3.0 GPA. Visit Website for full list of eligible majors and deadline.

| | |
|---|---|
| **Amount of award:** | $2,000 |
| **Number of awards:** | 10 |
| **Number of applicants:** | 10 |
| **Total amount awarded:** | $20,000 |

**Contact:**
OCA
1322 18th Street, NW
Washington, DC 20036
Phone: 202-223-5500
Fax: 202-296-0540
Web: www.ocanational.org

## Ohio Board of Regents

### Ohio College Opportunity Grant

**Type of award:** Scholarship, renewable.
**Intended use:** For freshman study at accredited 2-year or 4-year institution. Designated institutions: Ohio and select Pennsylvania schools.
**Eligibility:** Applicant must be residing in Ohio.

**Basis for selection:** Applicant must demonstrate financial need.
**Application requirements:** FAFSA.
**Additional information:** Must be pursuing associates degree, bachelor's degree, or nursing diploma. Amount of award varies. Visit Website for more information.

| | |
|---|---|
| **Number of awards:** | 66,779 |
| **Application deadline:** | October 1 |
| **Total amount awarded:** | $76,301,177 |

**Contact:**
Ohio Board of Regents
30 E. Broad St.
36th Floor
Columbus, OH 43215-3414
Phone: 888-833-1133
Fax: 614-752-5903
Web: www.regents.ohio.gov/sgs/ocog/

## Ohio Safety Officers College Memorial Fund

**Type of award:** Scholarship, renewable.
**Intended use:** For undergraduate study at accredited 2-year or 4-year institution. Designated institutions: Ohio institutions.
**Eligibility:** Applicant must be U.S. citizen or permanent resident residing in Ohio. Applicant's parent must have been killed or disabled in work-related accident as firefighter, police officer or public safety officer.
**Application requirements:** Proof of eligibility.
**Additional information:** Applicant whose spouse was killed in the line of duty as a firefighter, police officer, or public safety officer also eligible. Visit Website for more information.

| | |
|---|---|
| **Number of applicants:** | 54 |
| **Total amount awarded:** | $339,262 |

**Contact:**
Ohio Board of Regents
30 E. Broad Street
36th Floor
Columbus, OH 43215-3414
Phone: 888-833-1133
Fax: 614-752-5903
Web: www.regents.ohio.gov/sgs/oso/

## Ohio War Orphans Scholarship

**Type of award:** Scholarship, renewable.
**Intended use:** For full-time undergraduate study at accredited 2-year or 4-year institution. Designated institutions: Ohio institutions.
**Eligibility:** Applicant must be at least 16. Applicant must be U.S. citizen or permanent resident residing in Ohio. Applicant must be dependent of veteran, disabled veteran, deceased veteran or POW/MIA. Child of disabled veteran who has combined disability rating of 60% or more.
**Application requirements:** Proof of eligibility.
**Additional information:** Visit Website for more information.

| | |
|---|---|
| **Number of applicants:** | 803 |
| **Application deadline:** | July 1 |
| **Notification begins:** | August 1 |
| **Total amount awarded:** | $3,969,912 |

**Contact:**
Ohio Board of Regents
30 E. Broad Street
36th Floor
Columbus, OH 43215-3414
Phone: 888-833-1133
Fax: 614-752-5903
Web: www.regents.ohio.gov/sgs/war_orphans

# Ohio National Guard

## Ohio National Guard Scholarship Program

**Type of award:** Scholarship, renewable.
**Intended use:** For undergraduate study at accredited postsecondary institution. Designated institutions: Degree-granting institutions in Ohio approved by Ohio Board of Regents.
**Eligibility:** Applicant must be in military service in the Reserves/National Guard. Must enlist, re-enlist, or extend current enlistment to equal six years with Ohio National Guard. Must remain in good standing.
**Application requirements:** Proof of eligibility.
**Additional information:** Minimum three credit hours per semester or quarter. Award covers 100 percent of instructional and general fees for state-assisted institutions; average of state-assisted university fees for proprietary/private institutions. Application deadlines: July 1 (fall), November 1 (winter quarter/spring semester), February 1 (spring quarter), April 1 (summer). Must not already possess bachelor's degree. Lifetime maximum of 12 full-time quarters or eight full-time semesters. Number of awards varies.

| | |
|---|---|
| **Amount of award:** | Full tuition |
| **Number of awards:** | 6,400 |
| **Number of applicants:** | 5,940 |
| **Total amount awarded:** | $16,200,000 |

**Contact:**
Adjutant General's Department
Ohio National Guard Scholarship Program
2825 West Dublin Granville Road
Columbus, OH 43235
Phone: 888-400-6484 or 614-336-7032
Fax: 614-336-7318
Web: www.ongsp.org

# Ohio Newspapers Foundation

## Harold K. Douthit Scholarship

**Type of award:** Scholarship.
**Intended use:** For sophomore, junior or senior study at postsecondary institution. Designated institutions: Ohio institutions.
**Eligibility:** Applicant must be U.S. citizen residing in Ohio.
**Basis for selection:** Major/career interest in communications or journalism. Applicant must demonstrate financial need and high academic achievement.
**Application requirements:** Essay, transcript. Two letters of recommendation from faculty members.
**Additional information:** Applicant must be resident of one of the following Ohio counties: Cuyahoga, Lorain, Huron, Erie, Wood, Geauga, Sandusky, Ottawa, or Lucas. Minimum 3.0 GPA. Student may provide up to two published writing samples.

**Amount of award:** $1,500
**Number of awards:** 1
**Number of applicants:** 14
**Application deadline:** March 31
**Notification begins:** May 15
**Total amount awarded:** $1,500

**Contact:**
Ohio Newspapers Foundation Douthit Scholarship
1335 Dublin Road
Suite 216-B
Columbus, OH 43215
Web: www.ohionews.org

Scholarships

## Ohio Newspapers Minority Scholarship

**Type of award:** Scholarship.
**Intended use:** For full-time freshman study at postsecondary institution. Designated institutions: Ohio institutions.
**Eligibility:** Applicant must be Asian American, African American, Hispanic American or American Indian. Applicant must be high school senior. Applicant must be residing in Ohio.
**Basis for selection:** Major/career interest in journalism. Applicant must demonstrate high academic achievement.
**Application requirements:** Recommendations, essay, transcript, proof of eligibility. Up to two writing samples or published articles.
**Additional information:** Minimum 2.5 GPA.

**Amount of award:** $1,500
**Number of awards:** 1
**Number of applicants:** 8
**Application deadline:** March 31
**Notification begins:** May 15
**Total amount awarded:** $4,500

**Contact:**
Ohio Newspapers Foundation Minority Scholarship
1335 Dublin Road
Suite 216-B
Columbus, OH 43215
Web: www.ohionews.org

## Ohio Newspapers Women's Scholarship

**Type of award:** Scholarship.
**Intended use:** For junior or senior study at postsecondary institution. Designated institutions: Ohio institutions.
**Eligibility:** Applicant must be residing in Ohio.
**Basis for selection:** Major/career interest in communications or journalism.
**Application requirements:** Recommendations, transcript. Three or four newspaper clippings demonstrating applicant's writing skills. Answers to questions: Who or what was your inspiration to get involved in the field of journalism and why did you select print journalism as your area of interest? Why do you need a scholarship? What do you think qualifies you for a scholarship? What do you hope to accomplish during your career as a professional journalist?
**Additional information:** Applicants may be male or female.

**Amount of award:** $1,500
**Number of awards:** 1
**Application deadline:** March 31

**Contact:**
Ohio Newspapers Foundation Women's Scholarship
1335 Dublin Road
Suite 216-B
Columbus, OH 43215
Web: www.ohionews.org

## University Journalism Scholarship

**Type of award:** Scholarship.
**Intended use:** For sophomore, junior or senior study at 2-year or 4-year institution. Designated institutions: Ohio institutions.
**Eligibility:** Applicant must be residing in Ohio.
**Basis for selection:** Major/career interest in communications or journalism.
**Application requirements:** Essay, transcript. Two letters of recommendation from faculty members and published writing samples.
**Additional information:** Minimum 2.5 GPA. Preference given to applicants demonstrating career commitment to newspaper journalism.

**Amount of award:** $1,500
**Number of awards:** 3
**Number of applicants:** 6
**Application deadline:** March 31
**Notification begins:** May 15

**Contact:**
Ohio Newspaper Foundation University Journalism Scholarship
1335 Dublin Road
Suite 216-B
Columbus, OH 43215
Web: www.ohionews.org

# Oklahoma City Community Foundation

## Carolyn Watson Opportunities Scholarship

**Type of award:** Scholarship, renewable.
**Intended use:** For undergraduate study at accredited 2-year or 4-year institution in United States.
**Eligibility:** Applicant must be residing in Oklahoma.
**Basis for selection:** Major/career interest in arts, general; science, general or engineering. Applicant must demonstrate financial need, high academic achievement, leadership and service orientation.
**Application requirements:** Nomination by teacher or professional who can document applicant's ability or commitment to excellence. Nomination form, Invitation form, Applicant's plan for educational or professional goals.
**Additional information:** Minimum 3.5 GPA. Applicant must be senior or graduate of rural Oklahoma high schools (except Lawton, Oklahoma City, and Tulsa metropolitan statistical areas as defined by the U.S. Census Bureau). Award amount varies; up to $10,000 per academic year. Renewable 4 years if requirements met.

**Amount of award:** $10,000
**Application deadline:** March 1

**Contact:**
Oklahoma City Community Foundation
P.O. Box 1146
Oklahoma City, OK 73101-1146
Phone: 405-235-5603
Web: occf.org/watsonaward.html

### Hal W. Almen - West OKC Rotary Scholarship Fund

**Type of award:** Scholarship.
**Intended use:** For freshman study at accredited 2-year or 4-year institution in United States.
**Eligibility:** Applicant must be high school senior. Applicant must be residing in Oklahoma.
**Application requirements:** Essay.
**Additional information:** Minimum 2.75 GPA. Maximum family income of $100,000. Must be current year graduate of high school in Oklahoma.

| | |
|---|---|
| **Amount of award:** | $2,000-$4,000 |
| **Application deadline:** | February 28 |

**Contact:**
Scholarship Coordinator
Oklahoma City Community Foundation
P.O. Box 1146
Oklahoma City, OK 73101-1146
Phone: 405-235-5603
Web: occf.org/scholarships/almen.html

## Oklahoma Engineering Foundation

### Oklahoma Engineering Foundation Scholarship

**Type of award:** Scholarship, renewable.
**Intended use:** For undergraduate study at accredited 4-year institution in United States. Designated institutions: Oklahoma Christian University of Science & Arts, Oklahoma State University, University of Oklahoma, University of Central Oklahoma, Oral Roberts University, University of Tulsa.
**Eligibility:** Applicant must be high school senior. Applicant must be U.S. citizen residing in Oklahoma.
**Basis for selection:** Major/career interest in engineering. Applicant must demonstrate depth of character, leadership and service orientation.
**Application requirements:** Interview, essay, transcript.
**Additional information:** Minimum 3.0 GPA, ACT composite score of 24-29, and ACT Math component score of 28 or above. Applicants eligible for National Merit or Oklahoma Regents Scholarships not eligible for this award. Visit Website for pre-qualification form.

| | |
|---|---|
| **Amount of award:** | $1,000 |
| **Number of awards:** | 12 |
| **Number of applicants:** | 52 |
| **Application deadline:** | February 15 |
| **Notification begins:** | May 15 |
| **Total amount awarded:** | $12,000 |

**Contact:**
Oklahoma Engineering Foundation Executive Director
201 Northeast 27th Street
Room 125
Oklahoma City, OK 73105
Phone: 405-528-1435
Web: www.ospe.org

## Oklahoma State Department of Education Professional Services Division

### Robert C. Byrd Honors Scholarship Program

**Type of award:** Scholarship, renewable.
**Intended use:** For full-time undergraduate study at postsecondary institution.
**Eligibility:** Applicant must be high school senior. Applicant must be U.S. citizen or permanent resident residing in Oklahoma.
**Basis for selection:** Applicant must demonstrate high academic achievement.
**Application requirements:** Recommendations, essay, transcript.
**Additional information:** Students receive award for first year of study at eligible postsecondary institutions. Scholarships renewable up to three additional years of study provided students continue to meet eligibility requirements as defined by the institution they are attending. Award amount varies based on funding. Deadlines vary; check Website for details. Must have minimum ACT composite score of 32 and/or minimum SAT combined score of 2130 or GED score of 700.
**Contact:**
Oklahoma State Department of Education
Oliver Hodge Building
2500 N. Lincoln Boulevard, Room 212
Oklahoma City, OK 73105-4599
Phone: 405-521-4527
Web: www.sde.state.ok.us

## Oklahoma State Regents for Higher Education

### Academic Scholars Program

**Type of award:** Scholarship, renewable.
**Intended use:** For full-time undergraduate study at postsecondary institution. Designated institutions: Oklahoma institutions.
**Eligibility:** Applicant must be residing in Oklahoma.
**Basis for selection:** Applicant must demonstrate high academic achievement.
**Application requirements:** Transcript, proof of eligibility.
**Additional information:** Applicant must be National Merit Scholar or Finalist; Presidential Scholar; have SAT/ACT in

Scholarships

99.5 percentile for Oklahoma residents. Application deadline varies.

**Amount of award:** $1,800-$5,500

**Contact:**
Oklahoma State Regents for Higher Education
P.O. Box 108850
Oklahoma City, OK 73101-8850
Phone: 800-858-1840
Web: www.okhighered.org

## Future Teachers Scholarship

**Type of award:** Scholarship, renewable.
**Intended use:** For undergraduate or graduate study at accredited 2-year or 4-year institution.
**Eligibility:** Applicant must be U.S. citizen or permanent resident residing in Oklahoma.
**Basis for selection:** Major/career interest in education, early childhood or education. Applicant must demonstrate high academic achievement.
**Application requirements:** Essay, transcript, proof of eligibility, nomination by college. SAT/ACT scores.
**Additional information:** Application deadline varies; visit Website for more information. Priority given to full-time students. Minimum 2.5 GPA. Recipient must agree to teach in shortage area in Oklahoma public schools for at least three years after graduation and licensure. Must apply for renewal. Visit Website for list of shortage areas.

**Amount of award:** $500-$1,500
**Number of awards:** 85

**Contact:**
Oklahoma State Regents for Higher Education
P.O. Box 108850
Oklahoma City, OK 73101-8850
Phone: 800-858-1840
Web: www.okhighered.org

## George and Donna Nigh Public Service Scholarship

**Type of award:** Scholarship.
**Intended use:** For full-time undergraduate study at 4-year institution in United States.
**Eligibility:** Applicant must be U.S. citizen or permanent resident residing in Oklahoma.
**Basis for selection:** Major/career interest in public administration/service. Applicant must demonstrate high academic achievement.
**Application requirements:** Nomination by Presidents of Oklahoma colleges and universities.
**Additional information:** Scholarship provides opportunities to outstanding students preparing for careers in public service. Winners must participate in seminars on public service offered by Nigh Institute. Eligible colleges may nominate one scholarship per year. For information, contact the Nigh Institute.

**Amount of award:** $1,000

**Contact:**
Nigh Institute, Attn: Carl F. Reherman
Kilpatrick Bank
3001 E. Memorial Road
Edmond, OK 73013
Phone: 405-818-0414
Web: www.okcollegestart.org

## Independent Living Act (Department of Human Services Tuition Waiver)

**Type of award:** Scholarship.
**Intended use:** For undergraduate study at vocational, 2-year or 4-year institution.
**Eligibility:** Applicant must be no older than 21. Applicant must be residing in Oklahoma.
**Application requirements:** Proof of eligibility.
**Additional information:** Awards tuition waivers to eligible individuals who have been or are in the Oklahoma Department of Human Services foster care program. Applicant must have been in DHS custody for at least nine months between the ages of 16 and 18. Within last three years, applicant must have graduated from State Board of Education-accredited high school, the Oklahoma School of Science and Mathematics, or approved school in a bordering state, or have attained GED. Tuition waivers available to eligible students up to age 26 or completion of baccalaureate degree or program certificate, whichever comes first.

**Amount of award:** Full tuition

**Contact:**
Oklahoma State Regents for Higher Education
P.O. Box 108850
Oklahoma City, OK 73101-8850
Phone: 800-858-1840
Web: www.okhighered.org

## National Guard Tuition Waiver

**Type of award:** Scholarship.
**Intended use:** For undergraduate study at 2-year or 4-year institution.
**Eligibility:** Applicant must be residing in Oklahoma. Applicant must be bona fide member in good standing of Oklahoma National Guard.
**Application requirements:** Proof of eligibility. Statement of Understanding and Certificate of Basic Eligibility.
**Additional information:** Applicant must be enrolled in degree-granting program. Applicant cannot currently have a bachelor's or graduate degree. Waivers not awarded for certificate-granting courses, continuing education courses, or career technology courses.

**Amount of award:** Full tuition

**Contact:**
Oklahoma State Regents for Higher Education
P.O. Box 108850
Oklahoma City, OK 73101-8850
Phone: 800-858-1840 or 800-464-8273
Web: www.okhighered.org or www.ok.ngb.army.mil

## Oklahoma Tuition Aid Grant

**Type of award:** Scholarship, renewable.
**Intended use:** For undergraduate study at vocational, 2-year or 4-year institution. Designated institutions: Approved Oklahoma institutions.
**Eligibility:** Applicant must be residing in Oklahoma.
**Basis for selection:** Applicant must demonstrate financial need.
**Application requirements:** Proof of eligibility. FAFSA.
**Additional information:** Award is $1,000 for public schools and $1,300 for private non-profit institutions. For best consideration, apply as soon as possible after January 1.

| | |
|---|---|
| **Amount of award:** | $1,000-$1,300 |
| **Number of awards:** | 26,000 |
| **Number of applicants:** | 50,000 |
| **Total amount awarded:** | $19,750,576 |

**Contact:**
Oklahoma Tuition Aid Grant Program
P.O. Box 108850
Oklahoma City, OK 73101-8850
Phone: 800-858-1840
Web: www.okhighered.org

## Oklahoma's Promise - Oklahoma Higher Learning Access Program

**Type of award:** Scholarship.
**Intended use:** For undergraduate study at 2-year or 4-year institution.
**Eligibility:** Applicant must be residing in Oklahoma.
**Basis for selection:** Applicant must demonstrate financial need, high academic achievement and seriousness of purpose.
**Additional information:** Scholarship for students in families earning less than $100,000 per year. Student must enroll in the program in eighth, ninth, or tenth grade and demonstrate commitment to academic success in high school; homeschooled students must be age 13, 14, or 15. Deadline for homeschooled students must occur before student's 16th birthday. Minimum 2.5 GPA. Award amount varies; full tuition at public institutions or portion of tuition at private institutions in OK. See counselor or visit Website for details.

| | |
|---|---|
| **Number of awards:** | 19,000 |
| **Number of applicants:** | 9,334 |
| **Application deadline:** | June 30 |
| **Total amount awarded:** | $54,000,000 |

**Contact:**
Oklahoma State Regents for Higher Education
P.O. Box 108850
Oklahoma City, OK 73101-8850
Phone: 800-858-1840
Web: www.okpromise.org

## Regional University Baccalaureate Scholarship

**Type of award:** Scholarship.
**Intended use:** For full-time undergraduate study at postsecondary institution. Designated institutions: Oklahoma regional universities.
**Eligibility:** Applicant must be residing in Oklahoma.
**Basis for selection:** Applicant must demonstrate high academic achievement.
**Additional information:** Must have ACT score of at least 30 or be National Merit Semifinalist or Commended Student. Award is $3,000 plus resident tuition waiver. Application deadlines vary by institution.

| | |
|---|---|
| **Amount of award:** | $3,000 |

**Contact:**
Oklahoma State Regents for Higher Education
P.O. Box 108850
Oklahoma City, OK 73101-8850
Phone: 800-858-1840
Web: www.okhighered.org

## SREB Academic Common Market

**Type of award:** Scholarship, renewable.
**Intended use:** For undergraduate or graduate study at 2-year, 4-year or graduate institution in United States.
**Eligibility:** Applicant must be U.S. citizen or permanent resident residing in Oklahoma.
**Application requirements:** Proof of eligibility. Copy of letter of acceptance into specific program, completed application and residency certification form, curricular information about the program.
**Additional information:** Academic Common Market allows Oklahoma residents to pay in-state tuition rates at a non-Oklahoma college or university in the South while studying in select programs not available at Oklahoma public institutions. Visit Website for eligible programs, application, more information.
**Contact:**
ACM State Coordinator for Oklahoma, Academic Common Market Program
Oklahoma State Regents for Higher Education
P.O. Box 108850
Oklahoma City, OK 73101-8850
Phone: 405-225-9170

# OMNE/Nursing Leaders of Maine

## OMNE/Nursing Leaders of Maine Scholarship

**Type of award:** Scholarship.
**Intended use:** For undergraduate or graduate study at accredited 4-year or graduate institution. Designated institutions: Maine institutions.
**Eligibility:** Applicant must be U.S. citizen residing in Maine.
**Basis for selection:** Major/career interest in nursing. Applicant must demonstrate high academic achievement, seriousness of purpose and service orientation.
**Application requirements:** Recommendations, transcript, proof of eligibility. Brief note explaining how scholarship would help applicant.
**Additional information:** Applicant must be enrolled in baccalaureate or graduate nursing program. Minimum 2.0 GPA.

| | |
|---|---|
| **Amount of award:** | $500 |
| **Number of awards:** | 2 |
| **Number of applicants:** | 30 |
| **Application deadline:** | May 1 |
| **Notification begins:** | June 30 |
| **Total amount awarded:** | $1,000 |

**Contact:**
Diane York, RN, MS Chair, OMNE Scholarship Subcommittee
Rumford Hospital
420 Franklin Street
Rumford, ME 04276
Web: www.omne.org

# ONS Foundation

## Bachelor's Scholarships

**Type of award:** Scholarship.
**Intended use:** For undergraduate study at accredited 4-year institution in United States. Designated institutions: Schools

accredited by National League for Nursing or Commission on Collegiate Nursing Education.
**Basis for selection:** Major/career interest in nursing or oncology. Applicant must demonstrate high academic achievement, depth of character, leadership and service orientation.
**Application requirements:** $5 application fee. Essay, transcript, proof of eligibility.
**Additional information:** Must be currently enrolled in bachelor's nursing degree program. At the end of each year of scholarship participation, recipient shall submit a summary of education activities in which he/she participated.

| | |
|---|---|
| **Amount of award:** | $2,000 |
| **Number of applicants:** | 37 |
| **Application deadline:** | February 1 |
| **Notification begins:** | April 15 |
| **Total amount awarded:** | $26,000 |

**Contact:**
ONS Foundation
125 Enterprise Drive
Pittsburgh, PA 15275-1214
Phone: 412-859-6100
Fax: 412-859-6163
Web: www.onsfoundation.org

# OP Loftbed

## OP Loftbed $500 Scholarship Award

**Type of award:** Scholarship.
**Intended use:** For undergraduate or graduate study at accredited postsecondary institution in United States.
**Eligibility:** Applicant must be U.S. citizen.
**Additional information:** Must submit application online. Applications first accepted in February for summer scholarship and August for winter scholarship. Recipients selected based on creativity of answers to a given set of questions. Guidelines and additional information available on Website.

| | |
|---|---|
| **Amount of award:** | $500 |
| **Number of awards:** | 2 |
| **Number of applicants:** | 2 |
| **Application deadline:** | January 31, July 31 |
| **Notification begins:** | February 21, August 15 |

**Contact:**
OP Loftbed
7324 Farmbrook Place
Thomasville, NC 27360
Phone: 866-567-5638
Web: www.oploftbed.com

# Oregon Collectors Association

## Hasson-Newman Memorial Scholarship Fund Essay

**Type of award:** Scholarship.
**Intended use:** For full-time freshman study at vocational, 2-year or 4-year institution. Designated institutions: Oregon institutions.
**Eligibility:** Applicant must be high school senior. Applicant must be U.S. citizen or permanent resident residing in Oregon.
**Application requirements:** Transcript. FAFSA. 1,000- to 1,500-word essay: "Credit in the 21st Century." Applicant's name/address/phone number, parent name/telephone number, and high school name/telephone number must be included.
**Additional information:** Must enroll in Oregon college within 12 months of high school graduation. Children and grandchildren of owners and officers of collection agencies in Oregon not eligible. Finalists must read their essays at Association's annual spring meeting. Essays may be printed/published at discretion of Association. Apply by mailing essays or submitting online. Visit Website for details and application.

| | |
|---|---|
| **Amount of award:** | $1,000-$3,000 |
| **Number of awards:** | 3 |
| **Application deadline:** | March 1 |
| **Total amount awarded:** | $6,000 |

**Contact:**
ORCA Scholarship Fund
c/o Doug Jones
1814 NE 123rd Ave.
Vancouver, WA 98684
Phone: 503-201-0858
Web: www.orcascholarshipfund.com

# Oregon Student Assistance Commission

## Ahmad-Sehar Saleha Ahmad and Abrahim Ekramullah Zafar Foundation

**Type of award:** Scholarship, renewable.
**Intended use:** For undergraduate study at accredited 4-year institution in United States. Designated institutions: Oregon institutions.
**Eligibility:** Applicant must be female, high school senior. Applicant must be U.S. citizen or permanent resident residing in Oregon.
**Basis for selection:** Major/career interest in English. Applicant must demonstrate high academic achievement.
**Application requirements:** Essay, transcript. FAFSA.
**Additional information:** Must be graduating from Oregon high school. GED recipients and home-schooled seniors in Oregon are also eligible. Minimum 3.8 GPA. Visit Website for details and application.

| | |
|---|---|
| **Application deadline:** | March 1 |

**Contact:**
Oregon Student Assistance Commission
Grants and Scholarship Division
1500 Valley River Drive, Suite 100
Eugene, OR 97401
Phone: 800-452-8807
Web: www.osac.state.or.us

## Albina Fuel Company Scholarship

**Type of award:** Scholarship.
**Intended use:** For undergraduate study in United States.
**Eligibility:** Applicant must be residing in Oregon or Washington.
**Application requirements:** Essay, transcript.

Scholarships

**Additional information:** Applicant must be dependent child of current Albina Fuel Company employee who has been employed by Albina for at least one year by October 1 prior to application deadline. Early bird deadline mid-February. Visit Website for more details.

**Application deadline:** March 1

**Contact:**
Oregon Student Assistance Commission
Grants and Scholarship Division
1500 Valley River Drive, Suite 100
Eugene, OR 97401
Phone: 800-452-8807
Web: www.osac.state.or.us

## Allcott/Hunt Share It Now II Scholarship

**Type of award:** Scholarship.
**Intended use:** For undergraduate study in United States.
**Eligibility:** Applicant must be residing in Oregon.
**Basis for selection:** Applicant must demonstrate financial need.
**Application requirements:** Transcript. Names, addresses, and phone numbers of two community or school references. FAFSA strongly recommended. Essay (250-350 words): Describe why you might be the best candidate for the Share It Now II Scholarship and your experience living or working in diverse environments.
**Additional information:** Preference given to first- or second-generation immigrants to the U.S. Early bird deadline mid-February. Visit Website for details.

**Application deadline:** March 1

**Contact:**
Oregon Student Assistance Commission
Grants and Scholarship Division
1500 Valley River Drive, Suite 100
Eugene, OR 97401
Phone: 800-452-8807
Web: www.osac.state.or.us

## Alpha Delta Kappa/Harriet Simmons Scholarship

**Type of award:** Scholarship, renewable.
**Intended use:** For full-time senior or graduate study at accredited postsecondary institution in United States. Designated institutions: Oregon institutions.
**Eligibility:** Applicant must be U.S. citizen or permanent resident residing in Oregon.
**Basis for selection:** Major/career interest in education. Applicant must demonstrate financial need and high academic achievement.
**Application requirements:** Transcript. FAFSA. Two essays.
**Additional information:** Applicants must be elementary or secondary education majors. Visit Website for details and application.

**Application deadline:** March 1

**Contact:**
Oregon Student Assistance Commission
Grants and Scholarship Division
1500 Valley River Drive, Suite 100
Eugene, OR 97401
Phone: 800-452-8807
Web: www.osac.state.or.us

## American Council of Engineering Companies of Oregon Scholarship

**Type of award:** Scholarship, renewable.
**Intended use:** For freshman study at 4-year institution. Designated institutions: Oregon colleges offering ABET-accredited programs.
**Eligibility:** Applicant must be U.S. citizen or permanent resident residing in Oregon.
**Basis for selection:** Major/career interest in engineering, chemical; engineering, civil; engineering, electrical/electronic or engineering, mechanical.
**Application requirements:** Transcript. Essay (500-700 words): Describe why you are interested in a career in consulting engineering and how you expect your career to contribute to society.
**Additional information:** Minimum 3.3 GPA. Minimum 1800 combined SAT or 28 ACT. Applicant must be graduating high school senior or have had no previous college education. Preference given to applicants interested in the consulting engineering profession. Visit Website for details and application.

**Application deadline:** March 1

**Contact:**
Oregon Student Assistance Commission
Grants and Scholarship Division
1500 Valley River Drive, Suite 100
Eugene, OR 97401
Phone: 800-452-8807
Web: www.osac.state.or.us

## American Federation of State, County, and Municipal Employees (AFSCME) Oregon Council #75

**Type of award:** Scholarship, renewable.
**Intended use:** For undergraduate or graduate study at 4-year or graduate institution in United States.
**Eligibility:** Applicant must be U.S. citizen or permanent resident.
**Application requirements:** Transcript. FAFSA. Essay: What is the importance of organizing political action and contract bargaining for workers?
**Additional information:** Applicant, spouse (including life partner), parent, or grandparent must be member (active, laid-off, retired, or disabled) of Oregon AFSCME Council. Must have been member for at least one year prior to scholarship deadline or for one year prior to death, layoff, disability, or retirement. Part-time enrollment (minimum six credit hours) considered for active members and spouses or laid-off members. Early bird deadline mid-February. Visit Website for application and details.

**Application deadline:** March 1

**Contact:**
Oregon Student Assistance Commission
Grants and Scholarship Division
1500 Valley River Drive, Suite 100
Eugene, OR 97401
Phone: 800-452-8807
Web: www.osac.state.or.us

## Bandon Submarine Cable Council Scholarship

**Type of award:** Scholarship, renewable.
**Intended use:** For freshman study at postsecondary institution in United States.
**Eligibility:** Applicant must be high school senior. Applicant must be residing in Oregon.
**Basis for selection:** Applicant must demonstrate financial need.
**Application requirements:** Essay, transcript.
**Additional information:** First preference given to members of the Bandon Submarine Cable Council or their dependent children. Second preference given to commercial fishermen or their family members residing in Coos County. Third preference given to any commercial fishermen or family member. Fourth preference given to postsecondary students residing in Clatsop, Coos, Curry, Lane, Lincoln, or Tillamook counties. Fifth preference to any postsecondary student in Oregon. Early bird deadline mid-February. Visit Website for essay topic.

**Application deadline:** March 1

**Contact:**
Oregon Student Assistance Commission
Grants and Scholarship Division
1500 Valley River Drive, Suite 100
Eugene, OR 97401
Phone: 800-452-8807
Web: www.osac.state.or.us

## Ben Selling Scholarship

**Type of award:** Scholarship, renewable.
**Intended use:** For sophomore, junior or senior study at postsecondary institution in United States.
**Eligibility:** Applicant must be U.S. citizen or permanent resident residing in Oregon.
**Basis for selection:** Applicant must demonstrate financial need and high academic achievement.
**Application requirements:** Essay, transcript. FAFSA.
**Additional information:** Minimum 3.5 GPA. Early bird deadline in mid-February. Visit Website for details and application.

**Amount of award:** $500
**Application deadline:** March 1

**Contact:**
Oregon Student Assistance Commission
Grants and Scholarship Division
1500 Valley River Drive, Suite 100
Eugene, OR 97401
Phone: 800-452-8807
Web: www.osac.state.or.us

## Benjamin Franklin/Edith Green Scholarship

**Type of award:** Scholarship.
**Intended use:** For full-time undergraduate study at accredited 4-year institution. Designated institutions: Oregon public colleges.
**Eligibility:** Applicant must be high school senior. Applicant must be U.S. citizen or permanent resident residing in Oregon.
**Basis for selection:** Applicant must demonstrate financial need and high academic achievement.
**Application requirements:** Essay, transcript. FAFSA.
**Additional information:** Minimum 3.45 GPA. Must show improvements in grades from freshman year. Early bird deadline mid-February. Visit Website for details and application.

**Application deadline:** March 1

**Contact:**
Oregon Student Assistance Commission
Grants and Scholarship Division
1500 Valley River Drive, Suite 100
Eugene, OR 97401
Phone: 800-452-8807
Web: www.osac.state.or.us

## Bertha P. Singer Scholarship

**Type of award:** Scholarship, renewable.
**Intended use:** For full-time undergraduate or graduate study at accredited postsecondary institution. Designated institutions: Oregon institutions.
**Eligibility:** Applicant must be U.S. citizen or permanent resident residing in Oregon.
**Basis for selection:** Major/career interest in nursing.
**Application requirements:** Essay, transcript, proof of eligibility. FAFSA.
**Additional information:** Employees of U.S. Bank, their children, or near relatives not eligible. Minimum 3.0 GPA. Must be a graduate of Oregon high school. Must be enrolling as a second-year student in two-year program or third-year student in a four-year program. Visit Website for details and application.

**Application deadline:** March 1

**Contact:**
Oregon Student Assistance Commission
Grants and Scholarship Division
1500 Valley River Drive, Suite 100
Eugene, OR 97401
Phone: 800-452-8807
Web: www.osac.state.or.us

## Blacktail Deer-Oregon Foundation for Blacktail Deer Scholarship

**Type of award:** Scholarship.
**Intended use:** For undergraduate study at postsecondary institution. Designated institutions: Oregon institutions.
**Eligibility:** Applicant must be residing in Oregon.
**Basis for selection:** Major/career interest in forestry; biology; wildlife/fisheries or zoology. Applicant must demonstrate financial need and seriousness of purpose.
**Application requirements:** Transcript. FAFSA. Essay (250 words) discussing the challenges of wildlife management in the coming ten years. Copy of previous year's hunting license.
**Additional information:** Must have serious commitment to career in wildlife management. Early bird deadline mid-February. Visit Website for details.

**Application deadline:** March 1

**Contact:**
Oregon Student Assistance Commission
Grants and Scholarship Division
1500 Valley River Drive, Suite 100
Eugene, OR 97401
Phone: 800-452-8807
Web: www.osac.state.or.us

## Chafee Education and Training Grant

**Type of award:** Scholarship, renewable.
**Intended use:** For undergraduate or graduate study in United States.
**Eligibility:** Applicant must be at least 14, no older than 20. Applicant must be residing in Oregon.
**Basis for selection:** Applicant must demonstrate financial need and service orientation.
**Application requirements:** Transcript. Two essays, FAFSA.
**Additional information:** Applicant must currently be in or previously been in foster care placement with the Oregon Department of Human Services or federally recognized Oregon Tribes; be a former foster youth with 180 days of substitute care after age 14 with Oregon DHS or an Oregon Tribe; and exited substitute care at age 16 or older. Deadline for fall, August 1; spring, February 1; summer, May 1; winter, November 1. Students may continue receiving award until age 23, but first-time recipients must be no older than 20. May apply for fall after deadline, but all funds may already be allocated. Visit Website for details and supplemental information form.

**Amount of award:** $3,000
**Application deadline:** August 1, February 1

**Contact:**
Oregon Student Assistance Commission
Chafee Program
1500 Valley River Drive, Suite 100
Eugene, OR 97401
Phone: 800-452-8807 ext. 7443
Fax: 541-687-7414
Web: www.osac.state.or.us/chafeetv.html

## Clark-Phelps Scholarship

**Type of award:** Scholarship.
**Intended use:** For undergraduate or graduate study at 4-year or graduate institution. Designated institutions: Oregon public institutions.
**Eligibility:** Applicant must be U.S. citizen or permanent resident residing in Oregon or Alaska.
**Basis for selection:** Major/career interest in dentistry; medicine or nursing. Applicant must demonstrate financial need.
**Application requirements:** Essay, transcript. FAFSA.
**Additional information:** Preference given to Oregon Health and Science University students and graduates of Oregon and Alaskan high schools. Award amount varies. Early bird application deadline is mid-February. Visit Website for details and application.

**Application deadline:** March 1

**Contact:**
Oregon Student Assistance Commission
Grants and Scholarship Division
1500 Valley River Drive, Suite 100
Eugene, OR 97401
Phone: 800-452-8807
Web: www.osac.state.or.us

## Connacher - Peter Connacher Memorial Scholarship

**Type of award:** Scholarship, renewable.
**Intended use:** For full-time undergraduate or graduate study at postsecondary institution in United States.
**Eligibility:** Applicant must be U.S. citizen or permanent resident. Must be former American prisoner of war or descendant.
**Basis for selection:** Applicant must demonstrate financial need and high academic achievement.
**Application requirements:** Transcript, proof of eligibility. FAFSA, two essays, copy of POW's military discharge papers and proof of POW status, if selected as a semifinalist. State relationship to POW on supporting documents.
**Additional information:** Preference given to Oregon residents and their dependents. Visit Website for details and application.

**Application deadline:** March 1

**Contact:**
Oregon Student Assistance Commission
Grants and Scholarship Division
1500 Valley River Drive, Suite 100
Eugene, OR 97401
Phone: 800-452-8807
Web: www.osac.state.or.us

## Darfur Humanitarian Essay

**Type of award:** Scholarship.
**Intended use:** For undergraduate study in United States.
**Eligibility:** Applicant must be no older than 21. Applicant must be residing in Oregon.
**Basis for selection:** Competition/talent/interest in writing/journalism, based on 350-500 word essay exploring the meaning and global significance of the humanitarian crisis in Darfur.
**Application requirements:** Transcript.
**Additional information:** Early bird deadline mid-February. Visit Website for more details.

**Application deadline:** March 1

**Contact:**
Oregon Student Assistance Commission
Grants and Scholarship Division
1500 Valley River Drive, Suite 100
Eugene, OR 97401
Phone: 800-452-8807
Web: www.osac.state.or.us

## Darlene Hooley for Oregon Veterans Scholarship

**Type of award:** Scholarship.
**Intended use:** For undergraduate or graduate study at postsecondary institution in United States. Designated institutions: Oregon institutions.
**Eligibility:** Applicant must be U.S. citizen or permanent resident residing in Oregon. Applicant must be veteran who served in the Army, Air Force, Marines, Navy, Coast Guard or Reserves/National Guard. Must have served in armed services during Global War on Terror.
**Basis for selection:** Applicant must demonstrate financial need.
**Application requirements:** Essay, transcript, proof of eligibility. FAFSA.
**Additional information:** Award amount varies. Early bird application deadline is mid-February. Visit Website for details and application.

**Application deadline:** March 1

**Contact:**
Oregon Student Assistance Commission
Grants and Scholarship Division
1500 Valley River Drive, Suite 100
Eugene, OR 97401
Phone: 800-452-8807
Web: www.osac.state.or.us

## David Family Scholarship

**Type of award:** Scholarship, renewable.
**Intended use:** For sophomore, junior, senior or graduate study at postsecondary institution in United States. Designated institutions: Public or nonprofit institutions.
**Eligibility:** Applicant must be U.S. citizen or permanent resident residing in Oregon.
**Basis for selection:** Major/career interest in health-related professions; health education; health sciences; education or health services administration. Applicant must demonstrate financial need and high academic achievement.
**Application requirements:** Essay, transcript. FAFSA.
**Additional information:** Minimum 2.5 GPA. Intended for residents of Benton, Clackamas, Lane, Multnomah, and Washington counties. Preference given to applicants enrolling at least half-time in upper-division or graduate health- or education-related programs at four-year colleges. Visit Website for details and application.

**Application deadline:** March 1

**Contact:**
Oregon Student Assistance Commission
Grants and Scholarship Division
1500 Valley River Drive, Suite 100
Eugene, OR 97401
Phone: 800-452-8807
Web: www.osac.state.or.us

## Dorothy Campbell Memorial Scholarship

**Type of award:** Scholarship, renewable.
**Intended use:** For full-time undergraduate study at accredited 4-year institution. Designated institutions: Oregon institutions.
**Eligibility:** Applicant must be female, high school senior. Applicant must be U.S. citizen or permanent resident residing in Oregon.
**Basis for selection:** Applicant must demonstrate financial need and high academic achievement.
**Application requirements:** Transcript. FAFSA. Essay (one page): Describe strong continuing interest in golf and contribution the sport has made to applicant's development.
**Additional information:** Must have strong interest in golf. Minimum 2.75 GPA. Early bird deadline in mid-February. Visit Website for details and application.

**Application deadline:** March 1

**Contact:**
Oregon Student Assistance Commission
Grants and Scholarship Division
1500 Valley River Drive, Suite 100
Eugene, OR 97401
Phone: 800-452-8807
Web: www.osac.state.or.us

## Eugene Bennet Visual Arts Scholarship

**Type of award:** Scholarship.
**Intended use:** For undergraduate or graduate study in United States. Designated institutions: Public and nonprofit institutions.
**Eligibility:** Applicant must be residing in Oregon.
**Basis for selection:** Major/career interest in arts, general. Applicant must demonstrate financial need.
**Application requirements:** Interview, essay, transcript. FAFSA.
**Additional information:** Applicants must be graduates of a Jackson County high school, or GED recipients or home-schooled graduates from Jackson County. Minimum 2.75 GPA. Career interest should be in fine/visual arts, not performing arts. Early bird deadline mid-February. Visit Website for details.

**Application deadline:** March 1

**Contact:**
Oregon Student Assistance Commission
Grants and Scholarship Division
1500 Valley River Drive, Suite 100
Eugene, OR 97401
Phone: 800-452-8807
Web: www.osac.state.or.us

## Ford Opportunity Program

**Type of award:** Scholarship, renewable.
**Intended use:** For full-time undergraduate study at accredited 2-year or 4-year institution. Designated institutions: Public or nonprofit Oregon institutions.
**Eligibility:** Applicant must be single. Applicant must be U.S. citizen or permanent resident residing in Oregon.
**Basis for selection:** Applicant must demonstrate financial need and high academic achievement.
**Application requirements:** Essay, transcript. FAFSA.
**Additional information:** Minimum 3.0 GPA or 2650 GED score, unless application is accompanied by special recommendation form from counselor or OSAC. Must be single head of household with custody of dependent child/children. Interviews required of all semifinalists. Visit Website for details and application.

**Number of awards:** 30
**Application deadline:** March 1

**Contact:**
Oregon Student Assistance Commission
Grants and Scholarship Division
1500 Valley River Drive, Suite 100
Eugene, OR 97401
Phone: 800-452-8807
Web: www.osac.state.or.us

## Ford Scholars Program

**Type of award:** Scholarship, renewable.
**Intended use:** For full-time undergraduate study at accredited 2-year or 4-year institution. Designated institutions: Public or nonprofit Oregon institutions.
**Eligibility:** Applicant must be U.S. citizen or permanent resident residing in Oregon.
**Basis for selection:** Applicant must demonstrate financial need and high academic achievement.
**Application requirements:** Interview, essay, transcript. FAFSA.
**Additional information:** Minimum 3.0 GPA or 2650 GED score, unless application accompanied by special

recommendation form from counselor or OSAC. Intended for high school graduates who have not yet been full-time undergraduates, or for individuals who have completed two years at Oregon community college and are entering junior year at Oregon four-year college. Visit Website for details and application.

**Application deadline:** March 1

**Contact:**
Oregon Student Assistance Commission
Grants and Scholarship Division
1500 Valley River Drive, Suite 100
Eugene, OR 97401
Phone: 800-452-8807
Web: www.osac.state.or.us

## Frank Stenzel M.D. and Kathryn Stenzel II Scholarship

**Type of award:** Scholarship, renewable.
**Intended use:** For undergraduate or graduate study at postsecondary institution in United States.
**Eligibility:** Applicant must be U.S. citizen or permanent resident residing in Oregon.
**Basis for selection:** Applicant must demonstrate financial need.
**Application requirements:** Transcript. FAFSA.
**Additional information:** Not open to graduating high school seniors. Not open to medicine, nursing, or physician assistant majors. Preference given to nontraditional students, first-generation college students, and students approaching final year of program. Minimum 2.5 GPA. Award amount varies. Early bird application deadline mid-February. Visit Website for details and application.

**Application deadline:** March 1

**Contact:**
Oregon Student Assistance Commission
Grants and Scholarship Division
1500 Valley River Drive, Suite 100
Eugene, OR 97401
Phone: 800-452-8807
Web: www.osac.state.or.us

## Glenn Jackson Scholars

**Type of award:** Scholarship, renewable.
**Intended use:** For full-time undergraduate study at postsecondary institution in United States. Designated institutions: Public and nonprofit institutions.
**Eligibility:** Applicant must be high school senior. Applicant must be U.S. citizen or permanent resident residing in Oregon.
**Basis for selection:** Applicant must demonstrate financial need.
**Application requirements:** Essay, transcript. FAFSA.
**Additional information:** For dependents of employees/retirees of Oregon Department of Transportation or Parks and Recreation Department. Parent must have been employed by their department at least three years. Financial need not required, but considered. Early bird deadline mid-February. Visit Website for details and application.

**Application deadline:** March 1

**Contact:**
Oregon Student Assistance Commission
Grants and Scholarship Division
1500 Valley River Drive, Suite 100
Eugene, OR 97401
Phone: 800-452-8807
Web: www.osac.state.or.us

## Ida M. Crawford Scholarship

**Type of award:** Scholarship, renewable.
**Intended use:** For full-time undergraduate study at accredited postsecondary institution in United States.
**Eligibility:** Applicant must be U.S. citizen or permanent resident residing in Oregon.
**Basis for selection:** Applicant must demonstrate financial need and high academic achievement.
**Application requirements:** Essay, transcript, proof of eligibility. FAFSA.
**Additional information:** Minimum 3.5 GPA. Must be graduate of accredited Oregon high school. Not available to students majoring in law, medicine, music, theology, or education. U.S. Bank employees, their children, and near relatives not eligible. Visit Website for details and application.

**Application deadline:** March 1

**Contact:**
Oregon Student Assistance Commission
Grants and Scholarship Division
1500 Valley River Drive, Suite 100
Eugene, OR 97401
Phone: 800-452-8807
Web: www.osac.state.or.us

## Jackson Foundation Journalism Scholarship

**Type of award:** Scholarship, renewable.
**Intended use:** For full-time undergraduate study at postsecondary institution. Designated institutions: Public and nonprofit Oregon institutions.
**Eligibility:** Applicant must be U.S. citizen or permanent resident residing in Oregon.
**Basis for selection:** Major/career interest in journalism. Applicant must demonstrate financial need and high academic achievement.
**Application requirements:** Essay, transcript. FAFSA.
**Additional information:** Must be graduate of an Oregon high school. Preference given to applicants who have strong SAT writing scores. Early bird deadline mid-February. Visit Website for details and application.

**Application deadline:** March 1

**Contact:**
Oregon Student Assistance Commission
Grants and Scholarship Division
1500 Valley River Drive, Suite 100
Eugene, OR 97401
Phone: 800-452-8807
Web: www.osac.state.or.us

## James Carlson Memorial Scholarship

**Type of award:** Scholarship.
**Intended use:** For full-time senior or graduate study at accredited 4-year institution in United States.
**Eligibility:** Applicant must be U.S. citizen or permanent resident residing in Oregon.
**Basis for selection:** Major/career interest in education; education, teacher; education, special or education, early childhood. Applicant must demonstrate financial need and high academic achievement.
**Application requirements:** Essay, transcript. FAFSA.
**Additional information:** Available to elementary or secondary education majors entering senior year or fifth year of study, or to graduate students in fifth year for elementary or secondary

certificate. Preference given to students with experience living or working in diverse environments (250-350 word essay describing this experience required for applicants qualifying under this preference); dependents of Oregon Education Association members; and students committed to teaching autistic children. Early bird deadline in mid-February. Visit Website for details and application.

**Application deadline:** March 1

**Contact:**
Oregon Student Assistance Commission
Grants and Scholarship Division
1500 Valley River Drive, Suite 100
Eugene, OR 97401
Phone: 800-452-8807
Web: www.osac.state.or.us



## Jeffrey Alan Scoggins Memorial Scholarship

**Type of award:** Scholarship.
**Intended use:** For junior or senior study at 4-year institution. Designated institutions: Oregon public and nonprofit institutions.
**Eligibility:** Applicant must be U.S. citizen or permanent resident residing in Oregon.
**Basis for selection:** Major/career interest in engineering. Applicant must demonstrate financial need.
**Application requirements:** Essay, transcript. FAFSA.
**Additional information:** Minimum 3.0 GPA. Preference given to applicants attending Oregon State University and to members of Sigma Chi fraternity. Award amount varies. Early bird application deadline mid-February. Visit Website for details and application.

**Application deadline:** March 1

**Contact:**
Oregon Student Assistance Commission
Grants and Scholarship Division
1500 Valley River Drive, Suite 100
Eugene, OR 97401
Phone: 800-452-8807
Web: www.osac.state.or.us

## Jerome B. Steinbach Scholarship

**Type of award:** Scholarship.
**Intended use:** For full-time sophomore, junior or senior study at accredited postsecondary institution in United States.
**Eligibility:** Applicant must be U.S. citizen residing in Oregon.
**Basis for selection:** Applicant must demonstrate financial need and high academic achievement.
**Application requirements:** Essay, transcript, proof of eligibility. FAFSA.
**Additional information:** Minimum 3.5 GPA. U.S. Bank employees, their children, and near relatives not eligible. Early bird deadline in mid-February. Visit Website for details and application.

**Application deadline:** March 1

**Contact:**
Oregon Student Assistance Commission
Grants and Scholarship Division
1500 Valley River Drive, Suite 100
Eugene, OR 97401
Phone: 800-452-8807
Web: www.osac.state.or.us

## Laurence R. Foster Memorial Scholarship

**Type of award:** Scholarship, renewable.
**Intended use:** For undergraduate or graduate study at accredited 4-year institution in United States. Designated institutions: Public and nonprofit institutions.
**Eligibility:** Applicant must be U.S. citizen or permanent resident residing in Oregon.
**Basis for selection:** Major/career interest in nursing; medical specialties/research; physician assistant; public health; medical assistant; health-related professions or nurse practitioner. Applicant must demonstrate financial need and service orientation.
**Application requirements:** Essay, transcript. FAFSA. Two additional essays.
**Additional information:** Applicant must be seeking career in public health, not private practice. General preference given to applicants of diverse cultures. Preference also given to persons working in (or graduate students majoring in) public health and to undergraduates entering junior/senior-year health programs. Early bird deadline in mid-February. Visit Website for essay topic and application.

**Application deadline:** March 1

**Contact:**
Oregon Student Assistance Commission
Grants and Scholarship Division
1500 Valley River Drive, Suite 100
Eugene, OR 97401
Phone: 800-452-8807
Web: www.osac.state.or.us

## Maria C. Jackson-General George A. White Scholarship

**Type of award:** Scholarship, renewable.
**Intended use:** For full-time undergraduate or graduate study at postsecondary institution. Designated institutions: Oregon institutions.
**Eligibility:** Applicant must be U.S. citizen or permanent resident residing in Oregon. Applicant must be veteran; or dependent of active service person or veteran in the Army, Air Force, Marines, Navy or Coast Guard. Must have been Oregon resident at time of enlistment.
**Basis for selection:** Applicant must demonstrate financial need and high academic achievement.
**Application requirements:** Essay, transcript, proof of eligibility. FAFSA.
**Additional information:** Minimum 3.75 GPA for undergraduates; no GPA requirement for graduate students or students at technical schools. U.S. Bank employees, children, and near relatives not eligible. Early bird deadline in mid-February. Visit Website for details and application.

**Application deadline:** March 1

**Contact:**
Oregon Student Assistance Commission
Grants and Scholarship Division
1500 Valley River Drive, Suite 100
Eugene, OR 97401
Phone: 800-452-8807
Web: www.osac.state.or.us

## Neil Hamilton Memorial Scholarship

**Type of award:** Scholarship.
**Intended use:** For undergraduate study at 2-year institution. Designated institutions: Oregon community colleges.
**Eligibility:** Applicant must be U.S. citizen or permanent resident residing in Oregon.
**Basis for selection:** Major/career interest in fire science/ technology.
**Application requirements:** Transcript. FAFSA.
**Additional information:** Minimum 2.5 GPA or 2500 GED. Award amount varies. Early bird application deadline mid-February. Visit Website for details and application.
**Application deadline:** March 1
**Contact:**
Oregon Student Assistance Commission
Grants and Scholarship Division
1500 Valley River Drive, Suite 100
Eugene, OR 97401
Phone: 800-452-8807
Web: www.osac.state.or.us

## Oregon Dungeness Crab Commission

**Type of award:** Scholarship.
**Intended use:** For full-time undergraduate study at postsecondary institution in United States.
**Eligibility:** Applicant must be no older than 23. Applicant must be U.S. citizen or permanent resident residing in Oregon.
**Basis for selection:** Major/career interest in wildlife/fisheries or environmental science. Applicant must demonstrate financial need and high academic achievement.
**Application requirements:** Essay, transcript. Identify name of vessel in place of "worksite" on item 16 of application.
**Additional information:** Major/career interest restrictions do not apply to high school seniors. For dependents of licensed Oregon Dungeness Crab fishermen or crew. Early bird deadline in mid-February. Visit Website for details and application.
**Application deadline:** March 1
**Contact:**
Oregon Student Assistance Commission
Grants and Scholarship Division
1500 Valley River Drive, Suite 100
Eugene, OR 97401
Phone: 800-452-8807
Web: www.osac.state.or.us

## Oregon Occupational Safety and Health Division Workers Memorial Scholarship

**Type of award:** Scholarship, renewable.
**Intended use:** For full-time undergraduate or graduate study at postsecondary institution in United States.
**Eligibility:** Applicant must be U.S. citizen or permanent resident residing in Oregon.
**Basis for selection:** Applicant must demonstrate financial need and high academic achievement.
**Application requirements:** Essay, transcript. FAFSA. Additional 500-word essay: "How has the injury or death of your parent or spouse affected or influenced your decision to further your education?" Must provide name, last four digits of social security number, or workers compensation claim number of worker permanently disabled or fatally injured; date of death or injury; location of incident; and exact relationship to applicant.
**Additional information:** Applicant must be dependent or spouse of Oregon worker permanently disabled on the job or be the recipient of fatality benefits as dependent or spouse of worker fatally injured in Oregon. Early bird deadline in mid-February. Visit Website for details and application.
**Application deadline:** March 1
**Contact:**
Oregon Student Assistance Commission
Grants and Scholarship Division
1500 Valley River Drive, Suite l00
Eugene, OR 97401
Phone: 800-452-8807
Web: www.osac.state.or.us

## Oregon Robert C. Byrd Honors Scholarship

**Type of award:** Scholarship, renewable.
**Intended use:** For full-time freshman study at accredited postsecondary institution in United States.
**Eligibility:** Applicant must be U.S. citizen or permanent resident residing in Oregon.
**Basis for selection:** Applicant must demonstrate high academic achievement.
**Application requirements:** Essay, transcript.
**Additional information:** Minimum 3.85 GPA or Oregon GED of 3300. Minimum 1300 on SAT (Math and Reading) or 29 on ACT. Must be graduating senior of Oregon high school, homeschooled senior, or GED recipient. New awards contingent on federal funding. Early bird deadline in mid-February. Visit Website for details and application.
**Application deadline:** March 1
**Contact:**
Oregon Student Assistance Commission
Grants and Scholarship Division
1500 Valley River Drive, Suite l00
Eugene, OR 97401
Phone: 800-452-8807
Web: www.osac.state.or.us

## Oregon Scholarship Fund Community College Student Award Programs

**Type of award:** Scholarship, renewable.
**Intended use:** For undergraduate study at accredited 2-year institution. Designated institutions: Oregon community colleges.
**Eligibility:** Applicant must be high school senior. Applicant must be U.S. citizen or permanent resident residing in Oregon.
**Basis for selection:** Applicant must demonstrate financial need.
**Application requirements:** Essay, transcript. FAFSA.
**Additional information:** Early bird deadline in mid-February. Visit Website for details and application.
**Application deadline:** March 1
**Contact:**
Oregon Student Assistance Commission
Grants and Scholarship Division
1500 Valley River Drive, Suite 100
Eugene, OR 97401
Phone: 800-452-8807
Web: www.osac.state.or.us

## Professional Land Surveyors of Oregon Scholarship

**Type of award:** Scholarship, renewable.
**Intended use:** For full-time undergraduate study at 2-year or 4-year institution. Designated institutions: Public and nonprofit Oregon institutions.
**Eligibility:** Applicant must be U.S. citizen or permanent resident residing in Oregon.
**Basis for selection:** Major/career interest in surveying/mapping. Applicant must demonstrate financial need.
**Application requirements:** Essay, transcript. FAFSA. Names, addresses, and phone numbers of two references (do not submit letters).
**Additional information:** Students must be enrolled in curricula leading to land-surveying career. Community college applicants must intend to transfer to eligible four-year schools. Four-year applicants must intend to take Fundamentals of Land Surveying (FLS) exam. Maximum award based on year in school. Early bird deadline mid-February. Visit Website for details and application.
**Application deadline:** March 1
**Contact:**
Oregon Student Assistance Commission
Grants and Scholarship Division
1500 Valley River Drive, Suite 100
Eugene, OR 97401
Phone: 800-452-8807
Web: www.osac.state.or.us

## Richard F. Brentano Memorial Scholarship

**Type of award:** Scholarship, renewable.
**Intended use:** For full-time undergraduate study at postsecondary institution in United States.
**Eligibility:** Applicant must be U.S. citizen or permanent resident.
**Basis for selection:** Applicant must demonstrate high academic achievement.
**Application requirements:** Essay, transcript.
**Additional information:** Intended for children or IRS-legal dependents of employees of Waste Control Systems, Inc., and subsidiaries. Parent must have been employed by Waste Control Systems one year as of deadline. Early bird deadline mid-February. Visit Website for details and application.
**Application deadline:** March 1
**Contact:**
Oregon Student Assistance Commission
Grants and Scholarship Division
1500 Valley Drive, Suite 100
Eugene, OR 97401
Phone: 800-452-8807
Web: www.osac.state.or.us

## Roger W. Emmons Memorial Scholarship

**Type of award:** Scholarship, renewable.
**Intended use:** For full-time undergraduate study at accredited postsecondary institution in United States. Designated institutions: Public and nonprofit institutions.
**Eligibility:** Applicant must be high school senior. Applicant must be U.S. citizen or permanent resident.
**Basis for selection:** Applicant must demonstrate high academic achievement.
**Application requirements:** Essay, transcript, proof of eligibility.
**Additional information:** Parent(s) or grandparent(s) must have been solid waste company owner(s) or employee(s) for at least three years and member(s) of Oregon Refuse & Recycling Association. Early bird deadline in mid-February. Visit Website for details and application.
**Application deadline:** March 1
**Contact:**
Oregon Student Assistance Commission
Grants and Scholarship Division
1500 Valley River Drive, Suite l00
Eugene, OR 97401
Phone: 800-452-8807
Web: www.osac.state.or.us

## Teamsters Clyde C. Crosby/Joseph M. Edgar Memorial Scholarship

**Type of award:** Scholarship, renewable.
**Intended use:** For full-time undergraduate study at postsecondary institution in United States.
**Eligibility:** Applicant must be high school senior. Applicant must be U.S. citizen or permanent resident residing in Oregon.
**Basis for selection:** Applicant must demonstrate financial need and high academic achievement.
**Application requirements:** Essay, transcript. FAFSA.
**Additional information:** Minimum 3.0 cumulative GPA. Must be child or dependent stepchild of active, retired, disabled, or deceased member of local unions affiliated with Joint Council of Teamsters #37. Qualifying members must have been active at least one year. Early bird deadline in mid-February. Visit Website for details and application.
**Application deadline:** March 1
**Contact:**
Oregon Student Assistance Commission
Grants and Scholarship Division
1500 Valley River Drive, Suite 100
Eugene, OR 97401
Phone: 800-452-8807
Web: www.osac.state.or.us

## Teamsters Council #37 Federal Credit Union Scholarship

**Type of award:** Scholarship.
**Intended use:** For undergraduate or graduate study at postsecondary institution in United States.
**Eligibility:** Applicant must be U.S. citizen or permanent resident residing in Oregon.
**Basis for selection:** Applicant must demonstrate financial need and high academic achievement.
**Application requirements:** Essay, transcript. FAFSA.
**Additional information:** For members (or dependents) of Council #37 credit union. Members must have been active in local affiliated with the Joint Council of Teamsters #37 for at least one year. Applicant must have cumulative GPA between 2.0 and 3.0. Early bird deadline mid-February. Visit Website for details and application.
**Application deadline:** March 1
**Contact:**
Oregon Student Assistance Commission
Grants and Scholarship Division
1500 Valley River Drive, Suite 100
Eugene, OR 97401
Phone: 800-452-8807
Web: www.osac.state.or.us

## Teamsters Local 305 Scholarship

**Type of award:** Scholarship, renewable.
**Intended use:** For full-time undergraduate study at postsecondary institution in United States.
**Eligibility:** Applicant must be high school senior. Applicant must be U.S. citizen or permanent resident.
**Basis for selection:** Applicant must demonstrate high academic achievement.
**Application requirements:** Essay, transcript.
**Additional information:** Must be child or dependent stepchild of active, retired, disabled, or deceased member of Local 305 of the Joint Council of Teamsters #37. Member must have been active at least one year. Early bird deadline in mid-February. Visit Website for details and application.

**Application deadline:** March 1

**Contact:**
Oregon Student Assistance Commission
Grants and Scholarship Division
1500 Valley River Drive, Suite 100
Eugene, OR 97401
Phone: 800-452-8807
Web: www.osac.state.or.us

## Walter and Marie Schmidt Scholarship

**Type of award:** Scholarship, renewable.
**Intended use:** For undergraduate study at postsecondary institution in United States.
**Eligibility:** Applicant must be U.S. citizen or permanent resident residing in Oregon.
**Basis for selection:** Major/career interest in nursing or gerontology. Applicant must demonstrate financial need and high academic achievement.
**Application requirements:** Essay, transcript. FAFSA. Additional essay describing desire to pursue nursing career in geriatric healthcare.
**Additional information:** Available to students enrolling in programs to become registered nurses and intending to pursue careers in geriatric healthcare. Priority given to students: 1) attending Lane Community College; 2) enrolled in another two-year nursing program. U.S. Bank employees, children, and near relatives not eligible. Early bird deadline in mid-February. Visit Website for details and application.

**Application deadline:** March 1

**Contact:**
Oregon Student Assistance Commission
Grants and Scholarship Division
1500 Valley River Drive, Suite 100
Eugene, OR 97401
Phone: 800-452-8807
Web: www.osac.state.or.us

# The Orthotic and Prosthetic Education and Development Fund

## Chester Haddan Scholarship Program

**Type of award:** Scholarship.
**Intended use:** For undergraduate or post-bachelor's certificate study at accredited 2-year or 4-year institution in United States.
**Eligibility:** Applicant must be U.S. citizen.
**Basis for selection:** Major/career interest in orthotics/prosthetics or medical specialties/research. Applicant must demonstrate financial need, depth of character, leadership, seriousness of purpose and service orientation.
**Application requirements:** Recommendations, transcript. A 200-word essay on why student wants to work in orthotics or prosthetics. Recent W-2 or letter from current employer.
**Additional information:** Students may apply directly or professors may nominate them. Applicants must be willing to financially contribute to their education.

| | |
|---|---|
| **Amount of award:** | $1,000 |
| **Number of awards:** | 1 |
| **Application deadline:** | January 29 |

**Contact:**
The Orthotic and Prosthetic Education and Development Fund
c/o The Academy
1331 H Street, NW, Suite 501
Washington, DC 20005
Phone: 202-380-3663 ext. 206
Web: www.oandp.org/education

## Dan McKeever Scholarship Program

**Type of award:** Scholarship.
**Intended use:** For senior study at accredited 4-year institution in United States. Designated institutions: American Academy of Orthotists and Prosthetists-accredited institutions.
**Eligibility:** Applicant must be U.S. citizen.
**Basis for selection:** Major/career interest in orthotics/prosthetics or medical specialties/research. Applicant must demonstrate financial need, leadership, seriousness of purpose and service orientation.
**Application requirements:** Recommendations, transcript. A 200-word essay on why student wants to work in orthotics or prosthetics. Recent W-2 or letter from current employer.
**Additional information:** Students may apply directly or professors may nominate them. Must maintain minimum 3.0 GPA. Applicants must be willing to financially contribute to their education.

| | |
|---|---|
| **Amount of award:** | $1,000 |
| **Number of awards:** | 3 |
| **Application deadline:** | May 30 |

**Contact:**
Orthotic and Prosthetic Education and Development Fund
The Academy
1331 H Street, NW, Suite 501
Washington, DC 20005
Phone: 202-380-3663 ext. 206
Web: www.oandp.org/education

## Ken Chagnon Scholarship

**Type of award:** Scholarship.
**Intended use:** For undergraduate study at accredited 2-year or 4-year institution in United States.
**Eligibility:** Applicant must be U.S. citizen.
**Basis for selection:** Major/career interest in orthotics/prosthetics or medical specialties/research. Applicant must demonstrate financial need, leadership and seriousness of purpose.
**Application requirements:** Recommendations, transcript. A 200-word essay on why student wants to work in orthotics or prosthetics. Recent W-2 or letter from current employer.
**Additional information:** Students may apply directly or professors may nominate them. Applicants must be willing to financially contribute to their education. Applicants must be

enrolled in technician program and show exceptional technical aptitude.

**Amount of award:** $500
**Number of awards:** 1
**Application deadline:** January 29

**Contact:**
Orthotic and Prosthetic Education and Development Fund
The Academy
1331 H Street, NW, Suite 501
Washington, DC 20005
Phone: 202-380-3663 ext. 206
Web: www.oandp.org/education



# Osage Tribal Education Committee

## Osage Tribal Education Scholarship

**Type of award:** Scholarship, renewable.
**Intended use:** For undergraduate or graduate study at accredited postsecondary institution in United States.
**Eligibility:** Applicant must be American Indian. Must be a member of the Osage Nation. Applicant must be U.S. citizen.
**Application requirements:** Proof of Osage Indian blood.
**Additional information:** Must maintain 2.0 GPA. Award amount varies.

**Application deadline:** July 1, December 31

**Contact:**
Osage Tribal Education Committee
Oklahoma Area Education Office
200 Northwest 4th, Suite 4049
Oklahoma City, OK 73102
Phone: 405-605-6051 ext. 304
Fax: 405-605-6057

# Papercheck.com

## Papercheck.com Charles Shafae' Scholarship Fund

**Type of award:** Scholarship.
**Intended use:** For undergraduate study at accredited 4-year institution in United States.
**Eligibility:** Applicant must be U.S. citizen or permanent resident.
**Basis for selection:** Competition/talent/interest in writing/journalism. Applicant must demonstrate high academic achievement.
**Application requirements:** Transcript. Minimum 1,000-word essay in MLA format. Include "works cited" page with at least two sources.
**Additional information:** Minimum 3.2 GPA. Applicant must be in good standing at institution. Visit Website for essay questions, guidelines, and deadline. Complete entry form online. Contact via e-mail.

**Amount of award:** $500
**Number of awards:** 2

**Contact:**
Papercheck.com
Charles Shafae' Scholarship
P.O. Box 642
Half Moon Bay, CA 94019
Phone: 866-693-EDIT
Web: www.papercheck.com

# Par Aide

## Par Aide's Joseph S. Garske Collegiate Grant Program

**Type of award:** Scholarship, renewable.
**Intended use:** For undergraduate study at vocational, 2-year or 4-year institution.
**Eligibility:** Applicant must be high school senior.
**Basis for selection:** Applicant must demonstrate high academic achievement, leadership and service orientation.
**Application requirements:** Transcript. A 500-word essay evaluating a significant experience, achievement, or risk and its effect on the student.
**Additional information:** Minimum 2.0 GPA. Applicant's parent or stepparent must be Golf Course Superintendents Association of America member for five or more consecutive years in one of the following classifications: A, Superintendent Member, C, Retired-A, Retired-B, or AA life. Children or stepchildren of deceased members eligible if member was active for five years at time of death. Children of Par Aide employees, the Environmental Institute for Golf's Board of Trustees, the GCSAA Board of Directors, and GCSAA staff not eligible. First place award is $2,500; second place, $1,500; third place, $1,000. First-place awardees eligible for one-year renewal.

**Amount of award:** $1,000-$2,500
**Number of awards:** 3
**Application deadline:** March 15
**Notification begins:** May 15
**Total amount awarded:** $7,500

**Contact:**
Golf Course Superintendents Association of America
Garske Grant Program
1421 Research Park Drive
Lawrence, KS 66049-3859
Phone: 785-832-4445
Web: www.gcsaa.org

# Patient Advocate Foundation

## Scholarships for Survivors

**Type of award:** Scholarship.
**Intended use:** For full-time undergraduate or graduate study at accredited 2-year, 4-year or graduate institution.
**Eligibility:** Applicant must be no older than 25.
**Basis for selection:** Applicant must demonstrate financial need, depth of character, leadership and service orientation.

**Application requirements:** Recommendations, essay, transcript, proof of eligibility. Previous year's tax returns. Written documentation from physician stating medical history.
**Additional information:** Must be survivor of life-threatening, chronic, or debilitating disease. Must maintain 3.0 overall GPA. Must complete 20 hours of community service in year scholarship will be dispensed. Check Website for application deadline.

| | |
|---|---|
| **Amount of award:** | $3,000 |
| **Number of awards:** | 12 |
| **Number of applicants:** | 150 |
| **Total amount awarded:** | $36,000 |

**Contact:**
Patient Advocate Foundation
421 Butler Farm Rd.
Hampton, VA 23666
Web: www.patientadvocate.org

# Peacock Productions, Inc.

## Audria M. Edwards Scholarship Fund

**Type of award:** Scholarship, renewable.
**Intended use:** For full-time undergraduate study at accredited vocational, 2-year or 4-year institution in United States.
**Eligibility:** Applicant must be U.S. citizen residing in Oregon or Washington.
**Basis for selection:** Major/career interest in arts, general. Applicant must demonstrate financial need, depth of character and leadership.
**Application requirements:** Recommendations, essay, transcript, proof of eligibility.
**Additional information:** Applicant must be gay, lesbian, bisexual, or transgendered; or the child of gay, lesbian, bisexual, or transgendered parents. Applicant must be pursuing degree in academic field, trade, vocation, or the arts. Applicants living in Washington must reside in Clark, Cowlitz, Lewis, Pacific, Skamania, or Wahkiakum counties. Visit Website for application information.

| | |
|---|---|
| **Amount of award:** | $1,000-$10,000 |
| **Application deadline:** | May 1 |
| **Total amount awarded:** | $5,000 |

**Contact:**
Peacock Productions, Inc.
Audria M. Edwards Scholarship Fund
P.O. Box 8854
Portland, OR 97207-8854
Web: www.peacockinthepark.com

# Penguin Putnam, Inc.

## Signet Classic Student Scholarship Essay Contest

**Type of award:** Scholarship.
**Intended use:** For undergraduate study at postsecondary institution.
**Eligibility:** Applicant must be high school junior or senior. Applicant must be U.S. citizen or permanent resident.
**Basis for selection:** Competition/talent/interest in writing/journalism, based on style, content, grammar, and originality; judges look for clear, concise writing that is articulate, logically organized, and well-supported. Major/career interest in English or literature.
**Application requirements:** Proof of eligibility, nomination by high school English teacher. Entrant must read designated book and answer one of several book-related questions in two- to three-page essay. Cover letter on school letterhead from teacher. Only one junior and one senior essay may be submitted per teacher. Parent or legal guardian must submit essay for home-schooled students.
**Additional information:** Home-schooled entrants must be between ages 16 and 18. Immediate relatives of employees of Penguin Group (USA) Inc. and its affiliates ineligible. Visit Website for details and application. Winner also receives Signet Classic library for school (or for public library in the case of home-schooled winner). Deadline in mid-April.

| | |
|---|---|
| **Amount of award:** | $1,000 |
| **Number of awards:** | 5 |
| **Notification begins:** | June 15 |
| **Total amount awarded:** | $5,000 |

**Contact:**
Penguin Group Signet Classic Student Scholarship Essay Contest
Academic Marketing Department
375 Hudson Street
New York, NY 10014
Web: us.penguingroup.com/static/pages/services-academic/essayhome.html

# Pennsylvania Higher Education Assistance Agency

## Chafee Education and Training Grant (ETG) Program

**Type of award:** Scholarship, renewable.
**Intended use:** For undergraduate study at accredited vocational, 2-year or 4-year institution. Designated institutions: Institutions approved by U.S. Department of Education for Title IV student assistance programs.
**Eligibility:** Applicant must be residing in Pennsylvania.
**Basis for selection:** Applicant must demonstrate financial need.
**Application requirements:** FAFSA.
**Additional information:** Must be eligible for services under the Commonwealth's Chafee Foster Care Independence Program. Must be in foster care or adopted from foster care after age 16. Must participate in ETG program on 21st birthday until age 23. Must maintain satisfactory academic progress. Visit Website for details and application.

| | |
|---|---|
| **Amount of award:** | $4,000 |

**Contact:**
PHEAA State Grant and Special Programs
P.O. Box 8157
Harrisburg, PA 17105-8157
Phone: 800-692-7392
Web: www.pheaa.org

Scholarships

## Gaining Early Awareness and Readiness for Undergraduate Programs (GEAR UP) Scholarship

**Type of award:** Scholarship.
**Intended use:** For freshman study at postsecondary institution in United States.
**Eligibility:** Applicant must be no older than 22. Applicant must be U.S. citizen residing in Pennsylvania.
**Application requirements:** FAFSA.
**Additional information:** Must have graduated within 2008 through 2013 from one of the following high schools in the Philadelphia or Harrisburg school districts: Young Women's Leadership School at E.W. Rhodes High School, John Bartram Main High School, Martin Luther King High School, Strawberry Mansion High School, or Harrisburg High School (including SciTech High School, William Penn High School, ACTS, and CTA). Must be deemed scholarship-eligible through participation in college readiness activities. Must be eligible for a Federal Pell Grant each year. Must meet all federal student aid requirements. Annual maximum GEAR UP scholarship is equal to the maximum Federal Pell Grant for the same academic year. GEAR UP scholarship may be reduced based on enrollment status, Expected Family Contribution (EFC), fund availability, or unmet cost as determined by the school's financial aid office. Awards contingent upon federal funding and are not guaranteed.
**Contact:**
PHEAA State Grant and Special Programs
P.O. Box 8157
Harrisburg, PA 17105-8157
Phone: 800-692-7392
Web: www.pheaa.org

## Partnership for Access to Higher Education (PATH)

**Type of award:** Scholarship, renewable.
**Intended use:** For undergraduate study at postsecondary institution in United States. Designated institutions: Pennsylvania State Grant-approved postsecondary institutions in Pennsylvania.
**Eligibility:** Applicant must be U.S. citizen residing in Pennsylvania.
**Basis for selection:** Applicant must demonstrate financial need and high academic achievement.
**Application requirements:** Nomination by participating PATH organization (visit PHEAA Website for list). FAFSA.
**Additional information:** Must receive a scholarship from participating PHEAA PATH organization for the academic year that PATH aid is requested. Must be Pennsylvania State Grant recipient for academic year or period for which PHEAA PATH aid is requested. Amount of award varies, and is up to $2,500 per academic year.
**Contact:**
PHEAA State Grant and Special Programs
P.O. Box 8157
Harrisburg, PA 17105-8157
Phone: 800-692-7392
Web: www.pheaa.org

## Pennsylvania Robert C. Byrd Honors Scholarship

**Type of award:** Scholarship, renewable.
**Intended use:** For full-time at accredited postsecondary institution in United States.
**Eligibility:** Applicant must be high school senior. Applicant must be U.S. citizen or permanent resident residing in Pennsylvania.
**Basis for selection:** Applicant must demonstrate high academic achievement.
**Application requirements:** Transcript. SAT/ACT or GED scores.
**Additional information:** Applicant must rank in top five percent of class, have minimum 3.5 GPA, 1150 SAT (Math and Reading) or 25 ACT, or 3550 GED. Must graduate from high school same year scholarship is awarded. Information available from high school guidance office.
**Application deadline:** April 1
**Contact:**
Pennsylvania Higher Education Assistance Agency
Robert C. Byrd Scholarship
P.O. Box 8157
Harrisburg, PA 17105-8157
Phone: 800-692-7392
Web: www.pheaa.org

## Pennsylvania State Grant Program

**Type of award:** Scholarship, renewable.
**Intended use:** For undergraduate study at accredited vocational, 2-year or 4-year institution in United States.
**Eligibility:** Applicant must be residing in Pennsylvania.
**Basis for selection:** Applicant must demonstrate financial need.
**Application requirements:** Proof of eligibility. FAFSA.
**Additional information:** Applicant must be high school graduate or GED recipient enrolled in PHEAA-approved program. Applicant must not already have four-year undergraduate degree. Grants are portable to approved institutions in other states. Number and amount of awards vary. Deadlines: August 15 for first-time applicants in business, trade, technical, or nursing schools or terminal two-year programs; May 1 for other applicants.
**Application deadline:** May 1, August 15
**Contact:**
PHEAA State Grant and Special Programs Division
P.O. Box 8157
Harrisburg, PA 17105-8157
Phone: 800-692-7392
Web: www.pheaa.org

## Pennsylvania Work-Study Program

**Type of award:** Scholarship, renewable.
**Intended use:** For undergraduate, master's, doctoral or first professional study at accredited postsecondary institution. Designated institutions: PHEAA-approved institutions.
**Eligibility:** Applicant must be U.S. citizen or permanent resident residing in Pennsylvania.
**Basis for selection:** Applicant must demonstrate financial need.
**Application requirements:** Interview, proof of eligibility. Proof of state grant or subsidized Stafford loan.
**Additional information:** Student must demonstrate ability to benefit from career-related high-tech or community service work experience. Applicant must be state grant or subsidized federal loan recipient and not owe state grant refund or be in

default on student loan. Recipient must secure a job with PHEAA-approved on or off-campus SWSP employer. Amount and number of awards vary. Deadlines: Fall term only and academic year, October 1; spring term only, January 31; summer, May 31.

**Application deadline:** October 1, January 31

**Contact:**
PHEAA State Grant and Special Programs Division
P.O. Box 8157
Harrisburg, PA 17105-8157
Phone: 800-692-7392
Web: www.pheaa.org

## Postsecondary Educational Gratuity Program

**Type of award:** Scholarship, renewable.
**Intended use:** For full-time undergraduate study at 2-year or 4-year institution. Designated institutions: Pennsylvania public institutions.
**Eligibility:** Applicant must be no older than 25. Applicant must be residing in Pennsylvania. Applicant must be dependent of deceased veteran. Applicant's parent must have been killed or disabled in work-related accident as firefighter, police officer or public safety officer.
**Application requirements:** Record of application for other financial aid. Certified copy of birth certificate.
**Additional information:** Applicant must be: child by birth or adoption of deceased police officer, firefighter, rescue or ambulance squad member, corrections facility employee, or active National Guard member who died after January 1, 1976 as direct result of performing official duties; or child by birth or adoption of deceased sheriff, deputy sheriff, National Guard member, or certain other individual on federal or state active military duty who died since September 11, 2001 as direct result of performing official duties. Award may include waiver of tuition, fees, and room and board costs. Must apply for other available financial aid prior to application to this program. Visit Website for application.

**Amount of award:** Full tuition

**Contact:**
PHEAA State Grant and Special Programs
P.O. Box 8157
Harrisburg, PA 17105-8157
Phone: 800-692-7392
Web: www.pheaa.org

## SciTech Scholarship

**Type of award:** Scholarship, renewable.
**Intended use:** For full-time sophomore, junior or senior study at 4-year institution in United States. Designated institutions: Approved Pennsylvania institutions.
**Eligibility:** Applicant must be residing in Pennsylvania.
**Basis for selection:** Major/career interest in science, general; technology or health-related professions.
**Additional information:** Must apply for Federal Pell and Pennsylvania State Grants. Minimum 3.0 GPA at time of application; must maintain to be eligible for renewal. Must complete approved internship or relevant work experience with Pennsylvania company prior to graduation. Must begin employment in state within one year of graduation and work one year for each year scholarship was awarded. Must provide employment verification every six months. Students pursuing full-time graduate study within one year of receiving bachelor's may request deferment of work obligation. Award is renewable for maximum of three years (some exceptions made for approved five-year programs). Scholarship converts to loan if student fails to satisfy work obligation.

**Amount of award:** $3,000

**Contact:**
PHEAA State Grant and Special Programs
P.O. Box 8157
Harrisburg, PA 17105-8157
Phone: 800-692-7392
Web: www.pheaa.org

## Technology Scholarship

**Type of award:** Scholarship, renewable.
**Intended use:** For undergraduate study at vocational, 2-year or 4-year institution. Designated institutions: PHEAA-approved institutions.
**Eligibility:** Applicant must be residing in Pennsylvania.
**Additional information:** Applicant must apply for Federal Pell Grant and Pennsylvania State Grant. Must be a high school graduate with minimum 3.0 GPA. Must be enrolled in approved program. Applicant must begin employment in Pennsylvania within one year of graduation and work one year for each year scholarship was awarded. Employment verification must be provided every six months. Deferment of work obligation possible if student begins full-time graduate study within one year of receiving bachelor's. Scholarship converts to loan if student fails to satisfy work obligation. Award is up to $1,000 or 20% of tuition or mandatory fees—whichever is less.

**Amount of award:** $1,000

**Contact:**
PHEAA State Grant and Special Programs
P.O. Box 8157
Harrisburg, PA 17105-8157
Phone: 800-692-7392
Web: www.pheaa.org

# Pennsylvania State System of Higher Education Foundation, Inc.

## Dr. & Mrs. Arthur William Phillips Scholarship

**Type of award:** Scholarship.
**Intended use:** For full-time freshman study at 4-year institution in United States. Designated institutions: Pennsylvania State System of Higher Education universities.
**Eligibility:** Applicant must be residing in Pennsylvania.
**Basis for selection:** Applicant must demonstrate financial need and high academic achievement.
**Additional information:** Must be resident of Butler, Clarion, Forest, Jefferson, Lawrence, Mercer, or Venango counties. Visit Website for deadline and other information.

**Amount of award:** $500-$1,000
**Number of applicants:** 1
**Notification begins:** May 31
**Total amount awarded:** $1,000

**Contact:**
Pennsylvania State System of Higher Education Foundation, Inc.
2896 N. 2nd Street
Harrisburg, PA 17110
Phone: 717-720-4065
Fax: 717-720-7082
Web: www.thepafoundation.org

## Fitz Dixon Memorial Scholarship

**Type of award:** Scholarship.
**Intended use:** For undergraduate or graduate study at 4-year or graduate institution in United States. Designated institutions: Pennsylvania State System of Higher Education (PASSHE) universities.
**Basis for selection:** Applicant must demonstrate financial need, high academic achievement and service orientation.
**Application requirements:** Recommendations, essay. Community/University service form.
**Additional information:** Undergraduate applicants must have passed 45 credits at a PASSHE university with a minimum GPA of 3.0. Graduate students must have passed nine credits at a PASSHE university with a minimum GPA of 3.5.

| | |
|---|---|
| **Amount of award:** | $500 |
| **Number of awards:** | 1 |
| **Number of applicants:** | 1 |
| **Application deadline:** | April 30 |
| **Notification begins:** | June 1 |
| **Total amount awarded:** | $500 |

**Contact:**
Pennsylvania State System of Higher Education Foundation, Inc.
2896 N. 2nd St.
Harrisburg, PA 17110
Phone: 717-720-4065
Fax: 717-720-7082
Web: www.thepafoundation.org

## Harry & Lorraine Ausprich Endowed Scholarship for the Arts

**Type of award:** Scholarship.
**Intended use:** For full-time undergraduate study at 4-year institution in United States. Designated institutions: Pennsylvania State System of Higher Education universities.
**Basis for selection:** Major/career interest in music; theater arts; arts, general or dance.
**Application requirements:** Recommendations, essay.
**Additional information:** Pre-architecture students also eligible. Minimum 3.0 GPA. One to two scholarships are awarded yearly dependent on available funds. Amount of award varies. Visit Website for deadline.

| | |
|---|---|
| **Number of applicants:** | 1 |
| **Application deadline:** | April 30 |
| **Notification begins:** | June 1 |
| **Total amount awarded:** | $500 |

**Contact:**
Pennsylvania State System of Higher Education Foundation, Inc.
2896 N. 2nd St.
Harrisburg, PA 17110
Phone: 717-720-4065
Fax: 717-720-7082
Web: www.thepafoundation.org

## Highmark Scholarship

**Type of award:** Scholarship.
**Intended use:** For full-time freshman study at postsecondary institution in United States. Designated institutions: Pennsylvania State System of Higher Education universities.
**Basis for selection:** Major/career interest in biology; health education; health sciences; health services administration; health-related professions; nursing or physical therapy.
**Additional information:** Must be attending one of the Pennsylvania State System of Higher Education universities. Visit Website for list of PASSHE universities. Other healthcare majors including pre-physician assistant, pre-medicine, medical imagery, and exercise science also eligible. Contact university for requirements.

| | |
|---|---|
| **Amount of award:** | $1,000 |
| **Number of awards:** | 140 |
| **Number of applicants:** | 140 |
| **Total amount awarded:** | $140,000 |

**Contact:**
Pennsylvania State System of Higher Education Foundation, Inc.
2896 N. 2nd Street
Harrisburg, PA 17110
Phone: 717-720-4065
Fax: 717-720-7082
Web: www.thepafoundation.org

## Wayne G. Failor Scholarship

**Type of award:** Scholarship.
**Intended use:** For full-time freshman study at postsecondary institution in United States. Designated institutions: Pennsylvania State System of Higher Education universities.
**Eligibility:** Applicant must be high school senior. Applicant must be residing in Pennsylvania.
**Basis for selection:** Major/career interest in business. Applicant must demonstrate financial need and high academic achievement.
**Additional information:** Number of awards varies yearly. Scholarship awarded to graduating senior of a West Shore School District high school. Eligible applicants are selected by district. Must have "B" average or better by the end of junior year. Visit Website for information.

| | |
|---|---|
| **Amount of award:** | $500 |
| **Number of awards:** | 1 |
| **Total amount awarded:** | $500 |

**Contact:**
Pennsylvania State System of Higher Education Foundation, Inc.
2986 N. 2nd Street
Harrisburg, PA 17110
Phone: 717-720-4065
Fax: 717-720-7082
Web: www.thepafoundation.org

# The Persian Scholarship Foundation

## The Persian Scholarship Recognition Award

**Type of award:** Scholarship.
**Intended use:** For undergraduate or graduate study in United States.

**Application requirements:** Transcript. Cover letter, digital copy of valid student ID, scanned copy of published article, MS Word copy of article, scanned copy of official transcript.
**Additional information:** Applicant must be of Iranian descent. Must have published an essay or article in a school, local, or national newspaper discussing the positive achievements of Iranian people and society. One winner each will be selected from high school, undergraduate, and graduate levels. Visit Website for deadline and more information.

| | |
|---|---|
| **Amount of award:** | $500-$1,000 |
| **Number of awards:** | 3 |
| **Total amount awarded:** | $2,500 |

**Contact:**
The Persian Scholarship Foundation
1434 Westwood Boulevard, #5
Los Angeles, CA 90024
Web: www.persianscholarship.org

# PFLAG National Office

## PFLAG National Scholarship Program

**Type of award:** Scholarship.
**Intended use:** For full-time freshman study at 2-year or 4-year institution.
**Eligibility:** Applicant must be high school senior.
**Additional information:** Applicants who graduated within last year also eligible. Must self-identify as gay, lesbian, bisexual, transgender, or ally/supporter of LGBT people who has worked on behalf of the LGBT community or overcome odds because of identity. Deadline in early March. Applications and full details available online in December.

| | |
|---|---|
| **Amount of award:** | $1,000-$5,000 |
| **Number of awards:** | 16 |
| **Number of applicants:** | 300 |
| **Application deadline:** | March 11 |
| **Notification begins:** | May 11 |
| **Total amount awarded:** | $35,000 |

**Contact:**
PFLAG National Office
1828 L. St. NW, Suite 660
Washington, DC 20036
Phone: 202-467-8180, ext. 212
Web: www.pflag.org

# The Phillips Foundation

## Ronald Reagan College Leaders Scholarship Program

**Type of award:** Scholarship, renewable.
**Intended use:** For full-time junior or senior study at accredited 4-year institution in United States.
**Eligibility:** Applicant must be U.S. citizen.
**Basis for selection:** Applicant must demonstrate high academic achievement, depth of character, leadership, patriotism, seriousness of purpose and service orientation.
**Application requirements:** Recommendations, essay. Proof of full-time enrollment in good standing; proof of leadership activities.
**Additional information:** Number of awards varies based on merit. Recipients will be notified in late March/early April. Visit Website for application and more information.

| | |
|---|---|
| **Amount of award:** | $1,000-$10,000 |
| **Number of awards:** | 93 |
| **Number of applicants:** | 430 |
| **Application deadline:** | January 15 |
| **Total amount awarded:** | $217,000 |

**Contact:**
The Phillips Foundation
Attn: Jeff Hollingsworth
1 Massachusetts Avenue NW, Suite 620
Washington, DC 20001
Phone: 202-250-3887, ext. 628
Web: www.thephillipsfoundation.org

# Plumbing-Heating-Cooling Contractors Educational Foundation

## A.O. Smith Water Heaters Scholarship

**Type of award:** Scholarship.
**Intended use:** For full-time undergraduate study at accredited vocational, 2-year or 4-year institution in United States.
**Eligibility:** Applicant must be U.S. citizen or Canadian citizen.
**Basis for selection:** Major/career interest in air conditioning/heating/refrigeration technology; business/management/administration; construction management or engineering, mechanical.
**Application requirements:** Recommendations, essay, transcript. SAT/ACT scores. List of extracurricular activities.
**Additional information:** Students enrolled or planning to enroll in PHCC-approved apprenticeship program also eligible. Other eligible majors include mechanical CAD design, plumbing or HVACR installation, and others directly related to the plumbing-heating-cooling profession. Must be working full-time for an active member of PHCC National Association. Minimum 2.0 GPA. Visit Website for details and application.

| | |
|---|---|
| **Amount of award:** | $2,500 |
| **Number of awards:** | 2 |
| **Application deadline:** | May 1 |

**Contact:**
PHCC-EF Scholarships
180 South Washington St.
P.O. Box 6808
Falls Church, VA 22046
Phone: 800-533-7694
Fax: 703-237-7442
Web: www.foundation.phccweb.org/Scholarships

## Bradford White Scholarship

**Type of award:** Scholarship.
**Intended use:** For full-time undergraduate study at accredited vocational, 2-year or 4-year institution in United States.
**Eligibility:** Applicant must be U.S. citizen or Canadian citizen.
**Basis for selection:** Major/career interest in air conditioning/heating/refrigeration technology; business/management/administration; construction management or engineering, mechanical.

**Application requirements:** Recommendations, essay, transcript. SAT/ACT scores. List of extracurricular activities.
**Additional information:** Students enrolled or planning to enroll in PHCC-approved apprenticeship program also eligible. Other eligible majors include mechanical CAD design, plumbing or HVACR installation, and others directly related to the plumbing-heating-cooling profession. Must be sponsored by active member of PHCC National Association. Minimum 2.0 GPA. Visit Website for details and application.

| | |
|---|---|
| **Amount of award:** | $2,500 |
| **Number of awards:** | 3 |
| **Application deadline:** | May 1 |

**Contact:**
PHCC-EF Scholarships
180 South Washington St.
P.O. Box 6808
Falls Church, VA 22046
Phone: 800-533-7694
Fax: 703-237-7442
Web: www.foundation.phccweb.org/scholarships

## Delta Faucet Company Scholarship

**Type of award:** Scholarship.
**Intended use:** For full-time undergraduate study at accredited vocational, 2-year or 4-year institution in United States.
**Eligibility:** Applicant must be U.S. citizen or Canadian citizen.
**Basis for selection:** Major/career interest in air conditioning/heating/refrigeration technology; business/management/administration; construction management or engineering, mechanical.
**Application requirements:** Recommendations, essay, transcript. SAT/ACT scores, list of extracurricular activities.
**Additional information:** Applicants must pursue studies in major related to plumbing-heating-cooling industry or apprentice in a PHCC-approved program. Must be sponsored by active member of PHCC National Association. Minimum 2.0 GPA. Visit Website for application.

| | |
|---|---|
| **Amount of award:** | $2,500 |
| **Number of awards:** | 6 |
| **Number of applicants:** | 45 |
| **Application deadline:** | May 1 |
| **Total amount awarded:** | $15,000 |

**Contact:**
PHCC-EF Scholarships
180 South Washington St.
P.O. Box 6808
Falls Church, VA 22046
Phone: 800-533-7694
Fax: 703-237-7442
Web: www.foundation.phccweb.org/scholarships

## PHCC Auxiliary of Texas Scholarship

**Type of award:** Scholarship.
**Intended use:** For full-time undergraduate study at accredited 2-year or 4-year institution in United States.
**Eligibility:** Applicant must be high school senior. Applicant must be U.S. citizen residing in Texas.
**Application requirements:** Recommendations, essay, transcript. SAT/ACT scores. List of extracurricular activities.
**Additional information:** Must be sponsored by active member of PHCC National Auxiliary residing in TX. Minimum 2.0 GPA. Visit Website for details and application.

| | |
|---|---|
| **Amount of award:** | $1,500 |
| **Number of awards:** | 1 |
| **Application deadline:** | May 1 |

**Contact:**
PHCC-EF Scholarships
180 South Washington St.
P.O. Box 6808
Falls Church, VA 22046
Phone: 800-533-7694
Fax: 703-237-7442
Web: www.foundation.phccweb.org/scholarships

## The PHCC Educational Foundation & The South Jersey Mechanical Contractors Association

**Type of award:** Scholarship, renewable.
**Intended use:** For full-time undergraduate study at accredited vocational, 2-year or 4-year institution in United States.
**Eligibility:** Applicant must be U.S. citizen or Canadian citizen.
**Basis for selection:** Major/career interest in air conditioning/heating/refrigeration technology; architecture; business; engineering, construction or construction management. Applicant must demonstrate high academic achievement.
**Application requirements:** Recommendations, transcript. SAT/ACT scores, list of extracurricular activities.
**Additional information:** Applicants must pursue studies in major related to plumbing-heating-cooling industry or apprentice in a PHCC-approved program. Must be sponsored by active member of PHCC National Association. Must maintain minimum 2.0 GPA.

| | |
|---|---|
| **Amount of award:** | $2,500-$5,000 |
| **Number of awards:** | 5 |
| **Application deadline:** | May 1 |
| **Notification begins:** | August 1 |

**Contact:**
PHCC-EF Scholarships
180 South Washington St.
P.O. Box 6808
Falls Church, VA 22046
Phone: 800-533-7694
Fax: 703-237-7442
Web: www.foundation.phccweb.org/scholarships

## PHCC Educational Foundation Need-Based Scholarship

**Type of award:** Scholarship.
**Intended use:** For full-time undergraduate study at accredited vocational, 2-year or 4-year institution in United States.
**Eligibility:** Applicant must be U.S. citizen or Canadian citizen.
**Basis for selection:** Major/career interest in air conditioning/heating/refrigeration technology; business/management/administration; construction management or engineering, mechanical. Applicant must demonstrate financial need.
**Application requirements:** Recommendations, essay, transcript. SAT/ACT scores. List of extracurricular activities.
**Additional information:** Students enrolled or planning to enroll in PHCC-approved apprenticeship program also eligible. Other eligible majors include mechanical CAD design, plumbing or HVACR installation, and others directly related to the plumbing-heating-cooling profession. Must be sponsored by active member of PHCC National Association. Minimum 2.0 GPA. Visit Website for details and application.

| | |
|---|---|
| **Amount of award:** | $2,500 |
| **Number of awards:** | 1 |
| **Application deadline:** | May 1 |

**Contact:**
PHCC Educational Foundation Need-Based Scholarship Program
P.O. Box 6808
Falls Church, VA 22040
Phone: 800-533-7694
Fax: 703-237-7442
Web: www.foundation.phccweb.org/scholarships

# Point Foundation

## Point Scholarship

**Type of award:** Scholarship.
**Intended use:** For undergraduate or graduate study at accredited 4-year institution in United States.
**Basis for selection:** Competition/talent/interest in gay/lesbian. Applicant must demonstrate financial need, high academic achievement, depth of character, leadership, seriousness of purpose and service orientation.
**Application requirements:** Essay, transcript. Two or three letters of recommendation, two of them from a teacher or professor. Applicants who have been out of school five years or more may substitute a reference from a supervisor for one letter.
**Additional information:** Applicants should have a history of leadership in the lesbian, gay, bisexual, and transgendered community and plan to be a LGBT leader in the future (not necessarily in a career). Award amount varies based on available funds; average award $13,600. Scholars must be willing to speak publicly at Foundation events, provide the Foundation with transcripts, remain in contact with Foundation, and do an individual community service project with the LGBT community. Deadline occurs in February; visit Website for exact date and application.

| | |
|---|---|
| **Number of awards:** | 28 |

**Contact:**
Point Foundation
5757 Wilshire Blvd., Suite #370
Los Angeles, CA 90036
Phone: 323-933-1234
Web: www.pointfoundation.org

# Presbyterian Church (USA)

## National Presbyterian Scholarship

**Type of award:** Scholarship, renewable.
**Intended use:** For full-time undergraduate study in United States. Designated institutions: Presbyterian-affiliated colleges.
**Eligibility:** Applicant must be high school senior. Applicant must be Presbyterian.
**Basis for selection:** Applicant must demonstrate financial need and high academic achievement.
**Application requirements:** Transcript. Recommendation from church pastor, biographical questionnaire, and record from high school guidance counselor.
**Additional information:** SAT/ACT must be taken no later than December 15 of senior year of high school. Must re-apply annually.

| | |
|---|---|
| **Amount of award:** | $500-$1,500 |
| **Number of awards:** | 130 |
| **Number of applicants:** | 177 |
| **Application deadline:** | March 1 |
| **Notification begins:** | May 1 |

**Contact:**
Presbyterian Church (USA)
Financial Aid for Studies
100 Witherspoon Street
Louisville, KY 40202-1396
Phone: 888-728-7228 ext. 5735
Fax: 502-569-8766
Web: www.pcusa.org/financialaid

## Native American Education Grant

**Type of award:** Scholarship.
**Intended use:** For full-time undergraduate study at accredited postsecondary institution in United States.
**Eligibility:** Applicant must be Alaskan native or American Indian.
**Basis for selection:** Applicant must demonstrate financial need.
**Additional information:** Minimum 2.5 GPA. Must demonstrate Cost of Attendance with preference given to students demonstrating financial need. Preference is given to members of Presbyterian Church (USA). Native American students from all faith traditions are encouraged to apply. Award is renewable up to first degree; after first degree dependent upon availability of funds. Visit Website to request application.

| | |
|---|---|
| **Amount of award:** | $500-$1,500 |
| **Application deadline:** | June 15 |

**Contact:**
Presbyterian Church (USA)
100 Witherspoon Street
Louisville, KY 40202-1396
Phone: 888-728-7228 ext. 5735
Fax: 502-569-8766
Web: www.pcusa.org/financialaid

## Presbyterian Student Opportunity Scholarship

**Type of award:** Scholarship, renewable.
**Intended use:** For full-time junior or senior study at accredited 4-year institution in United States.
**Eligibility:** Applicant must be Presbyterian. Applicant must be U.S. citizen or permanent resident.
**Basis for selection:** Applicant must demonstrate financial need.
**Application requirements:** Recommendations, essay, transcript, proof of eligibility.
**Additional information:** Preference given to students of African American, Asian American, Hispanic American, Alaskan Native, and Native American descent. Minimum 2.5 GPA. Must reapply annually for renewal.

| | |
|---|---|
| **Amount of award:** | $200-$2,000 |
| **Number of awards:** | 120 |
| **Number of applicants:** | 67 |
| **Application deadline:** | June 15 |
| **Notification begins:** | August 1 |
| **Total amount awarded:** | $175,000 |

**Contact:**
Presbyterian Church (USA)
Financial Aid for Studies
100 Witherspoon Street
Louisville, KY 40202-1396
Phone: 888-728-7228 ext. 5735
Fax: 502-569-8766
Web: www.pcusa.org/financialaid

### Samuel Robinson Award

**Type of award:** Scholarship.
**Intended use:** For full-time junior or senior study at 4-year institution. Designated institutions: One of 69 colleges affiliated with Presbyterian Church (USA).
**Eligibility:** Applicant must be Presbyterian.
**Application requirements:** A 2,000-word essay on assigned topic related to the Catechism.
**Additional information:** Applicant must successfully recite answers of the Westminster Shorter Catechism. Amount of award based on annual funds.

| | |
|---|---|
| **Amount of award:** | $200-$5,000 |
| **Number of awards:** | 12 |
| **Number of applicants:** | 27 |
| **Application deadline:** | April 1 |
| **Notification begins:** | May 15 |
| **Total amount awarded:** | $32,000 |

**Contact:**
Presbyterian Church (USA)
Financial Aid for Studies
100 Witherspoon Street
Louisville, KY 40202-1396
Phone: 888-728-7228 ext. 5776
Fax: 502-569-8766
Web: www.pcusa.org/financialaid

## Press Club of Houston Educational Foundation

### Press Club of Houston Scholarship

**Type of award:** Scholarship.
**Intended use:** For full-time junior or senior study at accredited 4-year institution in United States.
**Eligibility:** Applicant must be U.S. citizen.
**Basis for selection:** Major/career interest in journalism; radio/television/film or communications. Applicant must demonstrate financial need and high academic achievement.
**Application requirements:** Interview, recommendations, transcript. Writing samples, statement from college financial aid office about current financial aid package, personal statement outlining career goal and reasons behind that goal.
**Additional information:** Applicant must have permanent residence in greater Houston area (Harris, Brazoria, Chambers, Fort Bend, Galveston, Liberty, Montgomery, and Waller counties) or, if residing elsewhere, must be attending a college or university in greater Houston area. Relatives of members of the Press Club of Houston board of directors, Press Club of Houston Educational Foundation board of directors, or of the Scholarship Committee are ineligible. Applications available after January 1. Total amount available for awards depends on proceeds from annual Gridiron Show. Deadline varies; visit Website for details and application.

| | |
|---|---|
| **Amount of award:** | $500-$3,000 |
| **Application deadline:** | June 30 |
| **Total amount awarded:** | $10,000 |

**Contact:**
Press Club of Houston Educational Foundation
Scholarship Chairman
4343 Elgin
Houston, TX 77204-0887
Phone: 713-743-1822
Web: www.houstonpressclub.com

## Pride of the Greater Lehigh Valley

### Rainbow Scholarship

**Type of award:** Scholarship.
**Intended use:** For undergraduate study at postsecondary institution.
**Eligibility:** Applicant must be residing in Pennsylvania.
**Application requirements:** Recommendations, transcript.
**Additional information:** Three awards available to students who identify as gay, lesbian, bisexual, transgender, or intersex. Queer Student of the Year, awarded to a queer teen who is a positive force in the GBLTI community through involvement and participation in community activities; Rainbow Award, awarded to a queer teen for academic excellence; Diversity Essay Contest, open to all college-bound youth, regardless of sexual orientation or gender identity. Must live in Berks, Bucks, Carbon, Lehigh, Monroe, Montgomery, Northampton, Schuylkill, or Warren counties. Visit Website for more information and application.

| | |
|---|---|
| **Amount of award:** | $200-$500 |
| **Number of awards:** | 3 |
| **Number of applicants:** | 2 |
| **Application deadline:** | June 1 |

**Contact:**
The Rainbow Scholarship
c/o Pride-GLV
1101 West Hamilton Street
Allentown, PA 18101-1043
Phone: 610-770-6200
Web: www.prideglv.org

## The Princess Grace Foundation USA

### Princess Grace Award for Dance

**Type of award:** Scholarship.
**Intended use:** For sophomore, junior or senior study in United States. Designated institutions: Non-profit institutions.
**Eligibility:** Applicant must be U.S. citizen or permanent resident.
**Basis for selection:** Major/career interest in dance.
**Application requirements:** Nomination by dean or department head.
**Additional information:** Award amount varies.

| | |
|---|---|
| **Number of awards:** | 6 |
| **Application deadline:** | April 30 |

**Contact:**
Princess Grace Foundation USA
150 E. 58th Street
25th Floor
New York, NY 10155
Phone: 212-317-1470
Fax: 212-317-1473
Web: www.pgfusa.org

## Princess Grace Award For Film

**Type of award:** Scholarship.
**Intended use:** For senior or graduate study at accredited 4-year or graduate institution. Designated institutions: Eligible film schools.
**Eligibility:** Applicant must be U.S. citizen or permanent resident.
**Basis for selection:** Major/career interest in film/video.
**Application requirements:** Nomination by dean or department head.
**Additional information:** Award amount varies. Scholarships to help produce thesis projects. Only students of invited film schools are eligible to apply.

| | |
|---|---|
| **Number of awards:** | 6 |
| **Application deadline:** | June 1 |

**Contact:**
The Princess Grace Foundation USA
150 E. 58th Street
25th Floor
New York, NY 10155
Phone: 212-317-1470
Fax: 212-317-1473
Web: www.pgfusa.org

## Princess Grace Award For Playwriting

**Type of award:** Scholarship.
**Intended use:** For undergraduate study in United States.
**Eligibility:** Applicant must be U.S. citizen or permanent resident.
**Basis for selection:** Major/career interest in playwriting/ screenwriting.
**Application requirements:** One unproduced play.
**Additional information:** Award given directly to individual through residency at New Dramatists, Inc. in New York. Applicant must not have had any professional productions. Readings, workshops, and Equity showcases are admissible. See Website for application.

| | |
|---|---|
| **Amount of award:** | $7,500 |
| **Number of awards:** | 1 |
| **Application deadline:** | March 31 |

**Contact:**
The Princess Grace Foundation USA
150 E. 58th Street
25th Floor
New York, NY 10155
Phone: 212-317-1470
Fax: 212-317-1473
Web: www.pgfusa.org

## Princess Grace Award For Theater

**Type of award:** Scholarship.
**Intended use:** For senior or master's study at accredited 4-year or graduate institution.
**Eligibility:** Applicant must be U.S. citizen or permanent resident.
**Basis for selection:** Major/career interest in theater arts or theater/production/technical.
**Application requirements:** Nomination by dean or department head.
**Additional information:** Scholarships awarded to students for their last year (undergraduate or graduate) of professional training in acting; directing; or scenic, lighting, sound, costume design, projection design. Award amount varies.

| | |
|---|---|
| **Number of awards:** | 6 |
| **Application deadline:** | March 31 |

**Contact:**
The Princess Grace Foundation USA
150 E. 58th Street
25th Floor
New York, NY 10155
Phone: 212-317-1470
Fax: 212-317-1473
Web: www.pgfusa.org

# Print and Graphics Scholarship Foundation

## PGSF Annual Scholarship Competition

**Type of award:** Scholarship, renewable.
**Intended use:** For full-time undergraduate study at 2-year or 4-year institution.
**Eligibility:** Applicant must be U.S. citizen.
**Basis for selection:** Major/career interest in graphic arts/ design; printing or publishing. Applicant must demonstrate high academic achievement.
**Application requirements:** Recommendations, transcript. Biographical information including extracurricular activities and academic honors. Photocopy of intended course of study. High school students must submit SAT, PSAT/NMSQT, or ACT scores.
**Additional information:** To renew, recipients must maintain 3.0 GPA and continue as graphic arts/printing technology major. Application deadline March 1 for high school seniors and high school graduates not currently attending college and April 1 for current undergraduates. Application requirements and criteria may vary by trust fund member institution. Visit Website for application.

| | |
|---|---|
| **Amount of award:** | $1,000-$5,000 |
| **Number of awards:** | 300 |
| **Number of applicants:** | 1,200 |
| **Application deadline:** | March 1, April 1 |
| **Notification begins:** | June 30 |
| **Total amount awarded:** | $375,000 |

**Contact:**
Print and Graphics Scholarship Foundation
200 Deer Run Road
Sewickley, PA 15143-2600
Phone: 800-910-4283 or 412-259-1740
Fax: 412-741-2311
Web: www.pgsf.org

# Professional Association of Georgia Educators Foundation, Inc.

## PAGE Foundation Scholarships

**Type of award:** Scholarship.
**Intended use:** For junior, senior or post-bachelor's certificate study at accredited 4-year or graduate institution in United States.
**Eligibility:** Applicant must be U.S. citizen or permanent resident residing in Georgia.
**Basis for selection:** Major/career interest in education. Applicant must demonstrate high academic achievement and service orientation.
**Application requirements:** Recommendations, essay, transcript.
**Additional information:** Minimum 3.0 GPA. Must be PAGE or SPAGE member. Intended for future teachers and certified teachers seeking advanced degrees. Must agree to teach in Georgia for three years. Applications available from September to April. Visit Website for additional information, deadline, and application procedures.

| | |
|---|---|
| **Amount of award:** | $1,000 |
| **Number of awards:** | 15 |
| **Number of applicants:** | 125 |
| **Application deadline:** | April 30 |
| **Notification begins:** | July 1 |
| **Total amount awarded:** | $15,000 |

**Contact:**
PAGE Foundation
P.O. Box 942270
Atlanta, GA 31141-2270
Phone: 800-334-6861
Fax: 770-216-9672
Web: www.pagefoundation.org

# Proof-Reading.com

## Proof-Reading.com Scholarship Program

**Type of award:** Scholarship.
**Intended use:** For full-time at postsecondary institution in United States.
**Eligibility:** Applicant must be U.S. citizen or permanent resident.
**Application requirements:** Essay answering topical question.
**Additional information:** Minimum 3.5 GPA. Visit Website for essay topic and online application.

| | |
|---|---|
| **Amount of award:** | $1,500 |
| **Number of awards:** | 1 |
| **Number of applicants:** | 185 |
| **Application deadline:** | June 1 |
| **Notification begins:** | July 1 |
| **Total amount awarded:** | $1,500 |

**Contact:**
Proof-Reading.com Scholarship Program
12 Geary Street
San Francisco, CA 91403
Web: www.proof-reading.com/proof-reading_scholarship_program.asp

# Quill and Scroll Foundation

## Edward J. Nell Memorial Scholarship

**Type of award:** Scholarship.
**Intended use:** For full-time freshman study at accredited 2-year or 4-year institution in United States.
**Eligibility:** Applicant must be high school senior. Applicant must be U.S. citizen.
**Basis for selection:** Major/career interest in journalism. Applicant must demonstrate seriousness of purpose.
**Application requirements:** Recommendations, essay, transcript. Statement of intent to major in journalism. Three selections of student's journalistic work. One color photo of applicant.
**Additional information:** Open only to winners of Quill and Scroll's Annual National Yearbook Excellence or International Writing/Photo Contests at any time during high school career.

| | |
|---|---|
| **Amount of award:** | $500-$1,500 |
| **Number of awards:** | 6 |
| **Number of applicants:** | 50 |
| **Application deadline:** | May 10 |
| **Notification begins:** | June 1 |
| **Total amount awarded:** | $5,000 |

**Contact:**
Scholarship Committee Quill and Scroll Foundation
E346 Adler Journalism Building
University of Iowa
Iowa City, IA 52242-1401
Phone: 319-335-3457
Fax: 319-335-3989
Web: www.uiowa.edu/~quill-sc

# Radio-Television News Director Foundation (RTNDF)

## Carole Simpson Scholarship

**Type of award:** Scholarship.
**Intended use:** For full-time sophomore, junior or senior study at 4-year institution.
**Basis for selection:** Major/career interest in communications; film/video; journalism or radio/television/film. Applicant must demonstrate depth of character and seriousness of purpose.
**Application requirements:** Recommendations, essay, proof of eligibility. Resume. One to three samples (audio or video cassettes or CD, maximum 15 minutes) showing journalistic skills, accompanied by script.
**Additional information:** Must be preparing for career in electronic journalism. Preference given to students of color. Visit Website for deadline and application.

**Amount of award:** $2,000
**Number of awards:** 1
**Number of applicants:** 20
**Total amount awarded:** $2,000

**Contact:**
RTNDF Scholarships
4121 Plank Road, #512
Fredericksburg, VA 22407
Phone: 202-662-7158
Web: www.rtndf.org

## Ed Bradley Scholarship

**Type of award:** Scholarship.
**Intended use:** For full-time sophomore, junior, senior or graduate study at 4-year institution.
**Basis for selection:** Major/career interest in communications; film/video; journalism or radio/television/film. Applicant must demonstrate seriousness of purpose.
**Application requirements:** Recommendations, essay, proof of eligibility. Resume. One to three samples (audio or video cassettes or CD, maximum 15 minutes) showing journalistic skills, accompanied by script.
**Additional information:** Must have at least one full year of school remaining. Must be preparing for career in electronic journalism. Preference given to undergraduate students of color. Visit Website for deadline and application.

**Amount of award:** $10,000
**Number of awards:** 1
**Number of applicants:** 47
**Total amount awarded:** $10,000

**Contact:**
RTNDF Scholarships
4121 Plank Road, #512
Fredericksburg, VA 22407
Phone: 202-662-7158
Web: www.rtndf.org

## The George Foreman Tribute to Lyndon B. Johnson Scholarship

**Type of award:** Scholarship.
**Intended use:** For full-time sophomore, junior, senior or graduate study at 4-year institution in United States. Designated institutions: University of Texas at Austin.
**Eligibility:** Applicant must be U.S. citizen or permanent resident residing in Texas.
**Basis for selection:** Major/career interest in communications; film/video; journalism or radio/television/film.
**Application requirements:** Recommendations, essay, proof of eligibility. Resume. One to three samples (audio or video cassettes or CD, maximum 15 minutes) showing journalistic skills, accompanied by script.
**Additional information:** Must be preparing for career in electronic journalism. Visit Website for deadline and application.

**Amount of award:** $6,000
**Number of awards:** 1
**Number of applicants:** 9
**Total amount awarded:** $6,000

**Contact:**
RTNDF Scholarships
4121 Plank Road, #512
Fredericksburg, VA 22407
Phone: 202-662-7158
Web: www.rtndf.org

## Ken Kashiwahara Scholarship

**Type of award:** Scholarship.
**Intended use:** For full-time sophomore, junior, senior or graduate study at postsecondary institution in United States.
**Eligibility:** Applicant must be U.S. citizen or permanent resident.
**Basis for selection:** Major/career interest in communications; film/video; journalism or radio/television/film.
**Application requirements:** Recommendations, essay, proof of eligibility. Resume. One to three samples (audio or video cassettes or CD, maximum 15 minutes) showing journalistic skills, accompanied by script.
**Additional information:** Applicant must be in good standing and preparing for a career in electronic journalism. Preference given to undergraduate students of color. Visit Website for deadline and application.

**Amount of award:** $2,500
**Number of awards:** 1
**Number of applicants:** 27
**Total amount awarded:** $2,500

**Contact:**
RTNDF Scholarships
4121 Plank Road, #512
Fredericksburg, VA 22407
Phone: 202-662-7158
Web: www.rtndf.org

## Lou and Carole Prato Sports Reporting Scholarship

**Type of award:** Scholarship.
**Intended use:** For full-time sophomore, junior or senior study at postsecondary institution.
**Basis for selection:** Major/career interest in communications; film/video; journalism; radio/television/film or sports/sports administration.
**Application requirements:** Recommendations, essay, proof of eligibility. Resume. One to three samples (audio or video cassettes or CD, maximum 15 minutes) showing journalistic skills, accompanied by script.
**Additional information:** Must be planning career as sports reporter in television or radio. Visit Website for deadline and application.

**Amount of award:** $1,000
**Number of awards:** 1
**Number of applicants:** 15
**Total amount awarded:** $1,000

**Contact:**
RTNDF Scholarships
4121 Plank Road, #512
Fredericksburg, VA 22407
Phone: 202-662-7158
Web: www.rtndf.org

## Pete Wilson Journalism Scholarship

**Type of award:** Scholarship.
**Intended use:** For full-time undergraduate or graduate study at accredited 4-year or graduate institution. Designated institutions: San Francisco Bay area institutions.
**Eligibility:** Applicant must be residing in California.
**Basis for selection:** Major/career interest in communications; film/video; journalism or radio/television/film.
**Application requirements:** Recommendations, essay, proof of eligibility. Resume. One to three samples (audio or video cassettes or CD, maximum 15 minutes) showing journalistic skills, accompanied by script.

**Additional information:** Must be preparing for career in electronic journalism. Must have one full year of school left to be eligible. Visit Website for deadline and application.

**Amount of award:** $2,000

**Contact:**
RTNDF Scholarships
4121 Plank Road, #512
Fredericksburg, VA 22407
Phone: 202-662-7158
Web: www.rtndf.org

### Presidents' $2,500 Scholarships

**Type of award:** Scholarship.
**Intended use:** For full-time junior, senior or graduate study at 2-year, 4-year or graduate institution.
**Basis for selection:** Major/career interest in communications; film/video; journalism or radio/television/film. Applicant must demonstrate high academic achievement and seriousness of purpose.
**Application requirements:** Recommendations, essay, proof of eligibility. Resume. One to three samples (audio or video cassettes or CD, maximum 15 minutes) showing journalistic skills, accompanied by script.
**Additional information:** Must be preparing for career in electronic journalism. Visit Website for deadline and application.

**Amount of award:** $1,000
**Number of awards:** 2
**Number of applicants:** 79
**Total amount awarded:** $2,000

**Contact:**
RTNDF Scholarships
4121 Plank Road, #512
Fredericksburg, VA 22407
Phone: 202-662-7158
Web: www.rtndf.org

## Recording for the Blind and Dyslexic

### Marion Huber Learning Through Listening Award

**Type of award:** Scholarship.
**Intended use:** For undergraduate study at vocational, 2-year or 4-year institution.
**Eligibility:** Applicant must be learning disabled. Applicant must be high school senior.
**Basis for selection:** Applicant must demonstrate high academic achievement, leadership and service orientation.
**Application requirements:** Recommendations, essay, transcript. List of honors, achievements, and activities.
**Additional information:** Winners may be asked to represent RFB&D as spokesperson and advocate at various events, with costs funded by RFB&D. Winners must be present at celebratory event to receive award. Must have 3.0 GPA or better in grades 10-12. Applications due in March.

**Amount of award:** $2,000-$6,000
**Number of awards:** 6
**Total amount awarded:** $24,000

**Contact:**
Recording for the Blind and Dyslexic LTL Awards
c/o Melissa Greenwald
20 Roszel Road
Princeton, NJ 08540
Phone: 609-243-7087 or 866-732-3585
Web: www.rfbd.org

### Mary P. Oenslager Scholastic Achievement Award

**Type of award:** Scholarship.
**Intended use:** For senior, master's or doctoral study at accredited 4-year or graduate institution in United States.
**Eligibility:** Applicant must be visually impaired.
**Basis for selection:** Applicant must demonstrate high academic achievement, leadership and service orientation.
**Application requirements:** Recommendations, essay, transcript. List of honors, achievements, and community activities.
**Additional information:** Must receive degree during the current year. Minimum 3.0 GPA on 4.0 scale or equivalent. Winners may be asked to represent RFB&D as spokesperson and advocate at various events, with cost funded by RFB&D. Winners must be present at celebratory event to receive award. Continuing education beyond bachelor's degree not required. Applications due in March.

**Amount of award:** $1,000-$6,000
**Number of awards:** 9
**Total amount awarded:** $30,000

**Contact:**
Recording for the Blind and Dyslexic SAA Awards
c/o Melissa Greenwald
20 Roszel Road
Princeton, NJ 08540
Phone: 609-243-7087 or 866-732-3585
Web: www.rfbd.org

## Red River Valley Fighter Pilots Association

### Red River Valley Fighter Pilots Association (RRVA) Scholarship Program

**Type of award:** Scholarship, renewable.
**Intended use:** For undergraduate or graduate study at accredited vocational, 2-year, 4-year or graduate institution in United States.
**Eligibility:** Applicant must be U.S. citizen.
**Basis for selection:** Applicant must demonstrate financial need, high academic achievement and service orientation.
**Application requirements:** Transcript, proof of eligibility. SAT/ACT scores.
**Additional information:** Applicants are eligible if they are one of the following: 1) Dependent (legal son, daughter, or spouse) of deceased veteran, dependent of POW/MIA, dependent of member of any branch of the U.S. Armed Forces listed as KIA or MIA since August 1964, dependent of military aircrew members killed in combat or non-combat military missions, or dependent of current or deceased RRVA member in good standing; 2) pursuing a career in field related to aviation/space. See Website for application and more information.

**Amount of award:** $500-$3,500
**Number of awards:** 32
**Number of applicants:** 42
**Application deadline:** May 15
**Total amount awarded:** $67,000

**Contact:**
Red River Valley Fighter Pilots Association
P.O. Box 1553
Front Royal, VA 22630
Phone: 540-636-9798
Fax: 540-636-9776
Web: www.river-rats.org

# Reserve Officers Association

## Henry J. Reilly Memorial College Scholarship

**Type of award:** Scholarship, renewable.
**Intended use:** For full-time undergraduate or graduate study at accredited 4-year or graduate institution in United States.
**Eligibility:** Applicant must be U.S. citizen.
**Basis for selection:** Applicant must demonstrate high academic achievement, depth of character and leadership.
**Application requirements:** Essay, transcript, proof of eligibility. SAT or ACT scores.
**Additional information:** Must be ROA member or child/grandchild of ROA member. Minimum SAT score of 1875 for applicants who took the SAT on or after March 2005; minimum SAT score of 1250 for applicants who took the SAT prior to March 2005. Minimum 3.0 GPA for applicants already attending college; minimum 3.3 GPA for applicants still attending high school. Must have registered for the draft if eligible. Number of awards and award amounts vary. Visit Website for more information.

**Amount of award:** $1,000
**Number of awards:** 30
**Number of applicants:** 30
**Application deadline:** May 15
**Notification begins:** June 30
**Total amount awarded:** $30,000

**Contact:**
Reserve Officers Association
Mr. Keith Weller
One Constitution Avenue, NE
Washington, DC 20002-5655
Phone: 800-809-9448 or 202-646-7718
Web: www.roa.org/scholarships

# Restaurant Association of Maryland Education Foundation

## Letitia B. Carter Scholarship

**Type of award:** Scholarship.
**Intended use:** For undergraduate study in United States.
**Eligibility:** Applicant must be enrolled in high school. Applicant must be U.S. citizen residing in Maryland.
**Basis for selection:** Major/career interest in hospitality administration/management. Applicant must demonstrate high academic achievement.
**Application requirements:** Recommendations, essay. Paystub from most recent employer in industry-related work. Two typed and double-spaced essays: 1) Describe any personal skills and characteristics that will help you meet the future challenges of the food service/hospitality industry; 2) Which person was most influential in helping you choose a career in the food service/hospitality industry?
**Additional information:** Applicant must have applied to an RAMEF-recognized professional development program in hospitality or enrolled in a RAMEF-recognized food service/hospitality program. Any high school or college student applying for scholarship must have a minimum 3.0 cumulative GPA and a minimum of 400 hours documented industry experience. Any teachers or instructors applying must have a minimum of 1,500 hours documented industry experience. Visit Website for more information.

**Amount of award:** $500-$2,000
**Number of applicants:** 10
**Application deadline:** April 1
**Notification begins:** May 11
**Total amount awarded:** $5,000

**Contact:**
Restaurant Association of Maryland Education Foundation
6301 Hillside Court
Columbia, MD 21046
Phone: 410-290-6800
Fax: 410-290-6882
Web: www.ramef.org

## Marcia S. Harris Legacy Fund Scholarship

**Type of award:** Scholarship.
**Intended use:** For undergraduate study at postsecondary institution.
**Eligibility:** Applicant must be residing in Maryland.
**Basis for selection:** Major/career interest in culinary arts; food production/management/services; food science/technology; hospitality administration/management or hotel/restaurant management. Applicant must demonstrate financial need and high academic achievement.
**Application requirements:** Interview. Proof of employment in culinary or hospitality industry. Three essays.
**Additional information:** Selection based on grades in food service coursework, essays, and work experience. Number and amount of award varies.

**Number of applicants:** 11
**Application deadline:** April 1
**Notification begins:** May 11
**Total amount awarded:** $2,000

**Contact:**
Restaurant Association of Maryland Education Foundation
6301 Hillside Court
Columbia, MD 21046
Phone: 410-290-6800 ext. 1015
Fax: 410-290-6882
Web: www.ramef.org

# Rhode Island Higher Education Assistance Authority

## College Bound Fund Academic Promise Scholarship

**Type of award:** Scholarship, renewable.
**Intended use:** For full-time undergraduate study at vocational, 2-year or 4-year institution. Designated institutions: Institutions participating in at least one Title IV financial aid program.
**Eligibility:** Applicant must be U.S. citizen or permanent resident residing in Rhode Island.
**Basis for selection:** Applicant must demonstrate financial need and high academic achievement.
**Application requirements:** FAFSA. SAT or ACT scores.
**Additional information:** Initial eligibility based on SAT/ACT scores and expected family contribution; renewal subject to maintenance of specified GPA. Dependent applicant's parent must reside in Rhode Island. Award notification begins in late spring.

| | |
|---|---|
| **Amount of award:** | $2,500 |
| **Number of awards:** | 100 |
| **Number of applicants:** | 1,450 |
| **Application deadline:** | March 1 |
| **Total amount awarded:** | $1,000,000 |

**Contact:**
Rhode Island Higher Education Assistance Authority
560 Jefferson Boulevard
Warwick, RI 02886
Phone: 401-736-1170
Fax: 401-732-3541
Web: www.riheaa.org

## Rhode Island State Grant

**Type of award:** Scholarship, renewable.
**Intended use:** For undergraduate study at vocational, 2-year or 4-year institution in or outside United States or Canada. Designated institutions: U.S., Canadian, or Mexican institutions that participate in at least one federal financial aid program.
**Eligibility:** Applicant must be U.S. citizen or permanent resident residing in Rhode Island.
**Basis for selection:** Applicant must demonstrate financial need.
**Application requirements:** FAFSA.
**Additional information:** Must meet all Title IV eligibility requirements. Dependent applicant's parent must reside in Rhode Island. Award notification begins in late spring.

| | |
|---|---|
| **Amount of award:** | $250-$900 |
| **Number of awards:** | 15,000 |
| **Number of applicants:** | 54,298 |
| **Application deadline:** | March 1 |
| **Total amount awarded:** | $12,689,572 |

**Contact:**
Rhode Island Higher Education Assistance Authority
560 Jefferson Boulevard
Warwick, RI 02886
Phone: 401-736-1170
Fax: 401-736-1178
Web: www.riheaa.org

# Rocky Mountain Coal Mining Institute

## RCMI Technical/Trade School Scholarship

**Type of award:** Scholarship.
**Intended use:** For sophomore study at vocational or 2-year institution.
**Eligibility:** Applicant must be U.S. citizen residing in Wyoming, Utah, Texas, Montana, New Mexico, Colorado, North Dakota or Arizona.
**Basis for selection:** Major/career interest in engineering, mining or geology/earth sciences.
**Additional information:** Applicant must be first-year student at a two-year technical school in good standing. Must be studying an applicable trade and be interested in coal as a career path.

| | |
|---|---|
| **Amount of award:** | $1,000 |
| **Number of awards:** | 8 |
| **Number of applicants:** | 4 |
| **Application deadline:** | February 1 |
| **Notification begins:** | March 1 |
| **Total amount awarded:** | $3,000 |

**Contact:**
Rocky Mountain Coal Mining Institute
3500 S. Wadsworth Blvd., Ste. 211
Lakewood, CO 80235
Phone: 303-948-3300
Fax: 303-954-9004
Web: www.rmcmi.org

## Rocky Mountain Coal Mining Institute Scholarship

**Type of award:** Scholarship, renewable.
**Intended use:** For full-time junior or senior study in United States. Designated institutions: Mining schools approved by Rocky Mountain Coal Mining Institute.
**Eligibility:** Applicant must be U.S. citizen residing in Wyoming, Utah, Texas, Montana, New Mexico, Colorado, Arizona or North Dakota.
**Basis for selection:** Major/career interest in engineering; engineering, mining or geology/earth sciences. Applicant must demonstrate high academic achievement.
**Application requirements:** Interview, recommendations.
**Additional information:** Must have career interest in western coal mining. Recommended 3.0 GPA or higher. One new award per Rocky Mountain Coal Mining Institute member state per year. Can be renewed as senior or post-graduate.

| | |
|---|---|
| **Amount of award:** | $2,500 |
| **Number of awards:** | 8 |
| **Number of applicants:** | 25 |
| **Application deadline:** | February 1 |
| **Notification begins:** | March 1 |
| **Total amount awarded:** | $32,000 |

**Contact:**
Rocky Mountain Coal Mining Institute
3500 S. Wadsworth Blvd. Ste. 211
Lakewood, CO 80235
Phone: 303-948-3300
Fax: 303-954-9004
Web: www.rmcmi.org

# Ronald McDonald House Charities

## RMHC Scholarship Programs

**Type of award:** Scholarship.
**Intended use:** For full-time undergraduate study at accredited vocational, 2-year or 4-year institution.
**Eligibility:** Applicant must be high school senior. Applicant must be U.S. citizen or permanent resident.
**Basis for selection:** Applicant must demonstrate financial need, high academic achievement, leadership and service orientation.
**Application requirements:** Recommendations, essay, transcript, proof of eligibility. IRS Form 1040.
**Additional information:** Intended for those who live within geographic boundaries of RMHC chapter that offers scholarships. Geographic areas listed on Website. Some requirements include: RMHC/ASIA: Applicant must have at least one parent of Asian heritage; RMHC/Future African American Achievers: Applicant must have at least one parent of African American or Black/Caribbean heritage; RMHC/HACER: Applicant must have at least one parent of Hispanic heritage; RMHC/Scholars: No race restrictions. Number of awards varies. Minimum award $1000. Award notification begins in May. See Website for contact information and application.

| | |
|---|---|
| **Application deadline:** | January 27 |
| **Notification begins:** | May 1 |
| **Total amount awarded:** | $2,800,000 |

**Contact:**
Ronald McDonald House Charities Scholarship Program Administrators
One Kroc Drive
Oak Brook, IL 60523
Phone: 630-623-7048
Fax: 630-623-7488
Web: www.rmhc.org

# The Rotary Foundation

## Academic-Year Ambassadorial Scholarship

**Type of award:** Scholarship.
**Intended use:** For full-time undergraduate, graduate, postgraduate or non-degree study at postsecondary institution in another country where there are Rotary Clubs.
**Eligibility:** Applicant must be citizen of country that has Rotary Clubs.
**Basis for selection:** Competition/talent/interest in study abroad. Applicant must demonstrate high academic achievement, leadership, seriousness of purpose and service orientation.
**Application requirements:** Interview, recommendations, essay, transcript, proof of eligibility. Proof of language ability.
**Additional information:** Deadlines set by the local Rotary Clubs and fall between March and August of year prior to when studies begin. Must have interest in international understanding and peace. Scholarship provides funding for one academic year of study in another country and is intended to defray costs associated with tuition, room and board, round-trip transportation, and one month of language training (if necessary). Need not be current student but must have completed two years of postsecondary work or have equivalent professional experience and be proficient in the language of the proposed host country. Number of awards varies from year to year. Spouses or descendants of Rotarians ineligible. Visit Website or check with local Rotary Club for more information and scholarship availability.

| | |
|---|---|
| **Amount of award:** | $27,000 |

**Contact:**
The Rotary Foundation
One Rotary Center
1560 Sherman Avenue
Evanston, IL 60201-3698
Phone: 866-9ROTARY
Web: www.rotary.org

# ROTC/Air Force

## ROTC/Air Force Four-Year Scholarship (Types 1, 2, and 7)

**Type of award:** Scholarship.
**Intended use:** For freshman study at accredited 4-year institution in United States.
**Eligibility:** Applicant must be at least 17, no older than 25, high school senior. Applicant must be U.S. citizen.
**Basis for selection:** Applicant must demonstrate high academic achievement.
**Application requirements:** Interview, recommendations, transcript. SAT/ACT scores, physical fitness assessment, resume.
**Additional information:** Recipients agree to serve four years' active duty. Minimum 3.0 GPA. At least 24 ACT or 1100 SAT. Opportunities available in any major. Applicants must not be enrolled in college full-time prior to application. Type 1 provides full tuition, most fees, $900 for textbooks, and $300-$500 monthly stipend during academic year. Type 2 provides tuition, most fees up to $18,000 per year, $900 for textbooks, and $300-$500 monthly stipend. Type 7 provides tuition and fees up to the equivalent of the in-state rate, $900 for books, and $300-$500 monthly stipend. Scholarship board decides which type is offered. For all scholarships, amount of stipend is based on student's academic year. To contact a local ROTC recruiter, visit www.afrotc.com/admissions/locateRep.php.

| | |
|---|---|
| **Amount of award:** | Full tuition |
| **Application deadline:** | December 1 |

**Contact:**
Contact local ROTC recruiter.
Phone: 866-423-7682
Web: www.afrotc.com

# ROTC/United States Army

## Four-Year Nursing Scholarship

**Type of award:** Scholarship.
**Intended use:** For freshman study at accredited 4-year institution in United States.
**Eligibility:** Applicant must be at least 17, no older than 26. Applicant must be U.S. citizen.

**Basis for selection:** Major/career interest in military science or nursing. Applicant must demonstrate high academic achievement and depth of character.
**Application requirements:** Interview, transcript.
**Additional information:** Must enlist to serve in the Army on Active Duty or in a Reserve Component for eight years. Minimum 920 SAT (Math and Reading) or 19 ACT. Must maintain minimum 2.5 GPA in college. Scholarships offered at different levels, providing college tuition and educational fees. All applicants considered for each level. Includes living allowance (increasing each year) for each year of scholarship, plus allowance for books and other educational items. Travel expenses not included. Limited number of three- and two-year scholarships available once student is on campus; check with school's professor of military science or contact local Army ROTC recruiter.

| | |
|---|---|
| **Amount of award:** | Full tuition |
| **Application deadline:** | January 1 |

**Contact:**
Army ROTC Scholarship
U.S. Army Cadet Command
Fort Monroe, VA 23651-1052
Phone: 800-USA-ROTC
Web: www.goarmy.com/rotc/nurse_program.jsp

## Four-Year Scholarship

**Type of award:** Scholarship, renewable.
**Intended use:** For freshman study at accredited 4-year institution in United States.
**Eligibility:** Applicant must be at least 17, no older than 26. Applicant must be U.S. citizen. Must enlist in Army on active duty or in Army Reserve or Army National Guard for minimum eight years.
**Basis for selection:** Major/career interest in military science. Applicant must demonstrate high academic achievement and depth of character.
**Application requirements:** Interview, recommendations, transcript. SAT/ACT scores. Proof of high school class rank.
**Additional information:** Recipient receives living allowance (increasing each year) for each year of scholarship, plus allowance for books and other educational items. Minimum 920 SAT (Math and Reading) or 19 ACT. Minimum 2.5 GPA. Limited number of three- and two-year scholarships available once student is on campus; check with professor of military science once enrolled. Contact local Army ROTC recruiter or visit Website for application.

| | |
|---|---|
| **Amount of award:** | Full tuition |
| **Application deadline:** | January 10 |

**Contact:**
Army ROTC Scholarship
U.S. Army Cadet Command
Fort Monroe, VA 23651-1052
Phone: 800-USA-ROTC
Web: www.goarmy.com/rotc or www.rotc.monroe.army.mil

# Sachs Foundation

## Sachs Foundation Undergraduate Grant

**Type of award:** Scholarship, renewable.
**Intended use:** For full-time undergraduate study at accredited 2-year or 4-year institution.
**Eligibility:** Applicant must be African American. Applicant must be high school senior. Applicant must be U.S. citizen or permanent resident residing in Colorado.
**Basis for selection:** Applicant must demonstrate financial need, high academic achievement, depth of character and leadership.
**Application requirements:** Interview, recommendations, transcript, proof of eligibility. Financial statement and parents' tax returns. Small recent photo. One-page personal biography. A copy of Colorado School Enrollment form.
**Additional information:** Must have been resident of Colorado for at least five years. Minimum 3.4 GPA. Must maintain at least 2.5 GPA throughout college for renewal consideration.

| | |
|---|---|
| **Amount of award:** | $4,000-$5,000 |
| **Number of awards:** | 125 |
| **Application deadline:** | March 15 |

**Contact:**
Sachs Foundation
90 South Cascade Avenue
Suite 1410
Colorado Springs, CO 80903
Phone: 719-633-2353
Web: www.sachsfoundation.org

# SAE International

## BMW/SAE Engineering Scholarships

**Type of award:** Scholarship, renewable.
**Intended use:** For full-time freshman study at accredited 4-year institution in United States. Designated institutions: ABET-accredited engineering schools.
**Eligibility:** Applicant must be high school senior. Applicant must be U.S. citizen.
**Basis for selection:** Major/career interest in engineering or computer/information sciences. Applicant must demonstrate high academic achievement, depth of character and leadership.
**Application requirements:** Transcript. SAT or ACT scores.
**Additional information:** Must have 3.75 GPA and rank in 90th percentile on ACT composite or SAT I (Math and Reading). Must maintain 3.0 GPA to renew scholarship. Renewable for four years. Visit Website for more information. For list of ABET-accredited schools, visit www.abet.org.

| | |
|---|---|
| **Amount of award:** | $1,500 |
| **Number of awards:** | 1 |
| **Application deadline:** | January 15 |
| **Notification begins:** | June 30 |

**Contact:**
SAE International
SAE Engineering Scholarships
400 Commonwealth Drive
Warrendale, PA 15096-0001
Phone: 724-776-4841
Web: www.sae.org/scholarships

## Edward D. Hendrickson/SAE Engineering Scholarship

**Type of award:** Scholarship, renewable.
**Intended use:** For undergraduate study at accredited postsecondary institution. Designated institutions: ABET-accredited institutions.

**Eligibility:** Applicant must be high school senior. Applicant must be U.S. citizen.
**Basis for selection:** Major/career interest in engineering. Applicant must demonstrate high academic achievement.
**Application requirements:** Essay, transcript. SAT or ACT scores, list of extracurricular activities.
**Additional information:** Minimum 3.75 GPA. Must rank in 90th percentile on SAT (Math and Reading) or composite ACT. Award renewable for three years if student maintains 3.0 GPA. Visit Website for application. For list of ABET-accredited schools, visit www.abet.org.

| | |
|---|---|
| **Amount of award:** | $1,000 |
| **Number of awards:** | 1 |
| **Application deadline:** | January 15 |
| **Notification begins:** | June 30 |

**Contact:**
SAE International
SAE Engineering Scholarships
400 Commonwealth Drive
Warrendale, PA 15096-0001
Phone: 724-776-4841
Web: www.sae.org/scholarships

## Fred M. Young, Sr./SAE Engineering Scholarship

**Type of award:** Scholarship, renewable.
**Intended use:** For undergraduate study at accredited postsecondary institution. Designated institutions: ABET-accredited institutions.
**Eligibility:** Applicant must be high school senior. Applicant must be U.S. citizen.
**Basis for selection:** Major/career interest in engineering. Applicant must demonstrate high academic achievement.
**Application requirements:** Transcript. SAT or ACT scores.
**Additional information:** Minimum 3.75 GPA. Applicants must rank in the 90th percentile on SAT (Math and Reading) or ACT. Award renewable for three years if student maintains 3.0 GPA. Visit Website for application. For list of ABET-accredited schools, visit www.abet.org.

| | |
|---|---|
| **Amount of award:** | $1,000 |
| **Number of awards:** | 1 |
| **Application deadline:** | January 15 |
| **Notification begins:** | June 30 |

**Contact:**
SAE International
SAE Engineering Scholarships
400 Commonwealth Drive
Warrendale, PA 15096-0001
Phone: 724-776-4841
Web: www.sae.org/scholarships

## Ralph K. Hillquist Honorary SAE Scholarship

**Type of award:** Scholarship.
**Intended use:** For full-time junior study at accredited 4-year institution in United States. Designated institutions: ABET-accredited engineering schools.
**Eligibility:** Applicant must be U.S. citizen.
**Basis for selection:** Major/career interest in engineering, mechanical. Applicant must demonstrate high academic achievement.
**Application requirements:** College transcript.
**Additional information:** Minimum 3.0 GPA. Any automotive-related engineering majors are eligible. Preference given to those with areas of expertise related to noise and vibration (statics, dynamic, physics, vibration). Award is given every other year at the SAE Noise & Vibration Conference. For list of ABET-accredited schools, visit www.abet.org.

| | |
|---|---|
| **Amount of award:** | $1,000 |
| **Number of awards:** | 1 |
| **Application deadline:** | January 15 |
| **Notification begins:** | June 30 |

**Contact:**
SAE Engineering Scholarships
400 Commonwealth Drive
Warrendale, PA 15096-0001
Phone: 724-776-4841
Web: www.sae.org/scholarships

## SAE Detroit Section Technical Scholarship

**Type of award:** Scholarship, renewable.
**Intended use:** For freshman study at accredited 2-year or 4-year institution. Designated institutions: ABET-accredited schools.
**Eligibility:** Applicant must be high school senior. Applicant must be U.S. citizen.
**Basis for selection:** Major/career interest in engineering or computer/information sciences. Applicant must demonstrate financial need.
**Application requirements:** Recommendations, transcript. FAFSA, SAT or ACT scores.
**Additional information:** Applicant must be child or grandchild of current SAE Detroit Section member. Minimum 3.0 GPA. Must maintain 2.5 GPA to renew scholarship. Renewable and transferable up to three consecutive years. Visit Website for application. For list of ABET-accredited schools, visit www.abet.org.

| | |
|---|---|
| **Amount of award:** | $5,000 |
| **Number of awards:** | 2 |
| **Application deadline:** | January 15 |
| **Notification begins:** | June 30 |

**Contact:**
SAE International
SAE Engineering Scholarships
400 Commonwealth Drive
Warrendale, PA 15096-0001
Phone: 724-776-4841
Web: www.sae.org/scholarships

## SAE Long-Term Member Sponsored Scholarship

**Type of award:** Scholarship.
**Intended use:** For full-time senior study at 4-year institution.
**Basis for selection:** Major/career interest in engineering. Applicant must demonstrate leadership.
**Application requirements:** Recommendations.
**Additional information:** Applicant must be active SAE student member. Must demonstrate support for SAE activities and programs. Must be junior in college at time of application. Number of awards varies. Apply online.

| | |
|---|---|
| **Amount of award:** | $1,000 |
| **Application deadline:** | February 15 |
| **Notification begins:** | June 30 |

**Contact:**
SAE International
SAE Engineering Scholarships
400 Commonwealth Drive
Warrendale, PA 15096-0001
Phone: 724-776-4841
Web: www.sae.org/scholarships

## SAE Women Engineers Committee Scholarship

**Type of award:** Scholarship.
**Intended use:** For freshman study. Designated institutions: ABET-accredited engineering schools.
**Eligibility:** Applicant must be female, high school senior. Applicant must be U.S. citizen.
**Basis for selection:** Major/career interest in engineering.
**Application requirements:** Transcript. SAT or ACT scores.
**Additional information:** Minimum 3.0 GPA. Visit Website for application. For list of ABET-accredited schools, visit www.abet.org.

| | |
|---|---|
| **Amount of award:** | $2,000 |
| **Number of awards:** | 1 |
| **Application deadline:** | January 15 |
| **Notification begins:** | June 30 |

**Contact:**
SAE International
SAE Engineering Scholarships
400 Commonwealth Drive
Warrendale, PA 15096-0001
Phone: 724-776-4841
Web: www.sae.org/scholarships

## SAE/David Hermance Hybird Technologies Scholarship

**Type of award:** Scholarship.
**Intended use:** For junior study at accredited 2-year or 4-year institution in United States. Designated institutions: ABET-accredited engineering schools.
**Eligibility:** Applicant must be U.S. citizen.
**Basis for selection:** Major/career interest in engineering.
**Application requirements:** High school and college transcripts. SAT/ACT scores.
**Additional information:** Minimum 3.5 GPA. For list of ABET-accredited schools, visit www.abet.org.

| | |
|---|---|
| **Amount of award:** | $2,500 |
| **Number of awards:** | 1 |
| **Application deadline:** | February 15 |
| **Notification begins:** | June 30 |

**Contact:**
SAE Engineering Scholarships
400 Commonwealth Drive
Warrendale, PA 15096-0001
Phone: 724-776-4841
Web: www.sae.org/scholarships

## SAE/Ford Partnership for Advanced Studies Scholarship

**Type of award:** Scholarship.
**Intended use:** For full-time freshman study at accredited 4-year institution in United States. Designated institutions: ABET-accredited engineering schools.
**Eligibility:** Applicant must be high school senior. Applicant must be U.S. citizen.
**Application requirements:** Recommendations, transcript.
**Additional information:** Minimum 3.0 GPA. Must rank in the 90th percentile in both math and critical reading on SAT I or the composite ACT scores. Must be past or present student of Ford PAS program at their high school or in a Ford PAS afterschool/weekend/summer/college program. For list of ABET-accredited schools, visit www.abet.org.

| | |
|---|---|
| **Amount of award:** | $5,000 |
| **Number of awards:** | 1 |
| **Application deadline:** | January 15 |
| **Notification begins:** | June 30 |

**Contact:**
SAE International
SAE Engineering Scholarships
400 Commonwealth Drive
Warrendale, PA 15096-0001
Phone: 724-776-4841
Web: www.sae.org/scholarships

## Siegel Service Technology Scholarships

**Type of award:** Scholarship, renewable.
**Intended use:** For sophomore study at 4-year institution in United States. Designated institutions: University of Montana-Helena, University of Montana-Missoula, Montana State University-Billings, Montana State University-Great Falls, Montana State University-Northern Havre, Montana Tech-Butte.
**Eligibility:** Applicant must be U.S. citizen residing in Montana.
**Basis for selection:** Major/career interest in automotive technology or agriculture. Applicant must demonstrate high academic achievement.
**Application requirements:** Recommendations. College transcript.
**Additional information:** Minimum 3.0 GPA. Other eligible service technology fields are aircraft, heavy truck, auto body repair and refinishing, off-highway equipment, and related mobility technology. Award is renewable with a 2.5 GPA.

| | |
|---|---|
| **Amount of award:** | $1,000 |
| **Number of awards:** | 6 |
| **Application deadline:** | May 15 |
| **Total amount awarded:** | $6,000 |

**Contact:**
SAE International
SAE Engineering Scholarships
400 Commonwealth Drive
Warrendale, PA 15096-0001
Phone: 724-776-4841
Web: www.sae.org/scholarships

## Tau Beta Pi/SAE Engineering Scholarship

**Type of award:** Scholarship.
**Intended use:** For freshman study at accredited postsecondary institution. Designated institutions: ABET-accredited engineering schools.
**Eligibility:** Applicant must be high school senior. Applicant must be U.S. citizen.
**Basis for selection:** Major/career interest in engineering. Applicant must demonstrate high academic achievement.
**Application requirements:** Transcript. SAT or ACT scores.
**Additional information:** Minimum 3.75 GPA. Applicant must rank in 90th percentile on SAT (Math and Reading) or composite ACT. Visit Website for application. For list of ABET-accredited schools, visit www.abet.org.

**Amount of award:** $1,000
**Number of awards:** 6
**Application deadline:** January 15
**Notification begins:** June 30
**Total amount awarded:** $6,000

**Contact:**
SAE International
SAE Engineering Scholarships
400 Commonwealth Drive
Warrendale, PA 15096-0001
Phone: 724-776-4841
Web: www.sae.org/scholarships

## TMC/SAE Donald D. Dawson Technical Scholarship

**Type of award:** Scholarship, renewable.
**Intended use:** For undergraduate study. Designated institutions: ABET-accredited engineering schools.
**Eligibility:** Applicant must be U.S. citizen.
**Basis for selection:** Major/career interest in engineering.
**Application requirements:** Transcript. Essay showing evidence of hands-on automotive experience or activity, SAT or ACT scores.
**Additional information:** Graduating high school seniors must have minimum 3.25 GPA, 600 SAT (Math) and 550 SAT (Reading), 27 ACT. Transfer students from four-year schools with 3.0 GPA, and students/graduates of technical/vocational schools with 3.5 GPA also eligible. Award renewable for four years as long as a 3.0 GPA maintained. Visit Website for application. For list of ABET-accredited schools, visit www.abet.org.

**Amount of award:** $1,500
**Number of awards:** 1
**Application deadline:** January 15
**Notification begins:** June 30

**Contact:**
SAE International
SAE Engineering Scholarships
400 Commonwealth Drive
Warrendale, PA 15096-0001
Phone: 724-776-4841
Web: www.sae.org/scholarships

## Yanmar/SAE Scholarship

**Type of award:** Scholarship, renewable.
**Intended use:** For full-time senior or graduate study at accredited 4-year institution. Designated institutions: ABET-accredited engineering schools.
**Eligibility:** Applicant must be U.S. citizen or Canadian or Mexican citizen.
**Basis for selection:** Major/career interest in engineering. Applicant must demonstrate high academic achievement and leadership.
**Application requirements:** College transcript.
**Additional information:** Must pursue course of study or research related to conservation of energy in transportation, agriculture and construction, or power generation. Emphasis placed on research or study related to internal combustion engine. Must be junior in college at time of application. Scholarship renewable for one additional year if in good standing with university and minimum 2.5 GPA. Visit Website for application. For list of ABET-accredited schools, visit www.abet.org.

**Amount of award:** $1,000
**Number of awards:** 1
**Application deadline:** February 15
**Notification begins:** June 30

**Contact:**
SAE International
SAE Scholarship & Award Program
400 Commonwealth Drive
Warrendale, PA 15096-0001
Phone: 724-776-4841
Web: www.sae.org/scholarships

# Salute to Education, Inc.

## Salute to Education Scholarship

**Type of award:** Scholarship.
**Intended use:** For undergraduate study at postsecondary institution.
**Eligibility:** Applicant must be high school senior. Applicant must be U.S. citizen residing in Florida.
**Basis for selection:** Applicant must demonstrate financial need, high academic achievement, depth of character, leadership, seriousness of purpose and service orientation.
**Additional information:** Minimum 3.0 GPA. Number of awards varies from 140 to 200 per year. Applicant must be a resident of and attend an accredited public or private high school in Miami-Dade or Broward County. Scholarships in following categories: athletics, language arts and foreign languages, leadership/service, mathematics/computer science, natural science, performing arts, and visual arts. Visit Website for application and deadline.

**Amount of award:** $1,000
**Number of awards:** 140
**Number of applicants:** 1,400
**Notification begins:** April 15
**Total amount awarded:** $140,000

**Contact:**
Salute to Education, Inc.
P.O. Box 833425
Miami, FL 33283
Phone: 305-799-6726
Fax: 786-515-9864
Web: www.stescholarships.org

# Scarlett Family Foundation Scholarship Program

## Scarlett Family Foundation Scholarship

**Type of award:** Scholarship, renewable.
**Intended use:** For full-time undergraduate study at postsecondary institution. Designated institutions: Not-for-profit institutions.
**Eligibility:** Applicant must be residing in Tennessee.
**Basis for selection:** Major/career interest in accounting; business; business, international; business/management/administration or finance/banking. Applicant must demonstrate financial need.

**Application requirements:** Essay, transcript. FAFSA.
**Additional information:** Minimum award is $2500. Amount of award varies based on need. Applicant's minimum high school or college GPA must be 2.5. Applicant must be from one of 39 counties in Tennessee. Visit Website for details.

| | |
|---|---|
| **Amount of award:** | $2,500-$15,000 |
| **Number of awards:** | 18 |
| **Number of applicants:** | 770 |
| **Application deadline:** | December 15 |
| **Notification begins:** | September 15 |
| **Total amount awarded:** | $457,000 |

**Contact:**
Scarlett Family Foundation Scholarship Program
c/o ISTS, Inc.
P.O. Box 23737
Nashville, TN 37202-3737
Phone: 615-320-3149
Fax: 615-627-9685
Web: www.scarlettfoundation.org

# Screen Actors Guild Foundation

## John L. Dales Standard Scholarship

**Type of award:** Scholarship, renewable.
**Intended use:** For full-time undergraduate or graduate study at accredited 2-year, 4-year or graduate institution in United States.
**Eligibility:** Applicant or parent must be member/participant of Screen Actor's Guild.
**Basis for selection:** Applicant must demonstrate financial need.
**Application requirements:** Recommendations, essay, transcript, proof of eligibility. Most recent federal income tax return and additional financial information. SAT/ACT scores.
**Additional information:** Member under the age of 22 must have been a member for five years and have lifetime earnings of $30,000. Parent of applicant must have ten vested years of pension credits or lifetime earnings of $150,000. Consult office or Website for more information. Number and amount of awards vary.

| | |
|---|---|
| **Number of awards:** | 81 |
| **Number of applicants:** | 135 |
| **Application deadline:** | March 15 |
| **Notification begins:** | July 7 |
| **Total amount awarded:** | $282,000 |

**Contact:**
Screen Actors Guild Foundation
John L. Dales Scholarship Fund
5757 Wilshire Boulevard, Suite 124
Los Angeles, CA 90036
Phone: 323-549-6649
Fax: 323-549-6710
Web: www.sagfoundation.org

## John L. Dales Transitional Scholarship

**Type of award:** Scholarship, renewable.
**Intended use:** For full-time undergraduate or graduate study at accredited postsecondary institution in United States.
**Basis for selection:** Applicant must demonstrate financial need.
**Application requirements:** Recommendations, essay, transcript, proof of eligibility. Most recent federal income tax return and additional financial information. SAT/ACT scores.
**Additional information:** Must be member of Screen Actors Guild. Applicant must have ten vested years of pension credits with SAG or lifetime earnings of $150,000. Consult office or visit Website for more information. Number and amount of awards vary.

| | |
|---|---|
| **Number of awards:** | 7 |
| **Number of applicants:** | 15 |
| **Application deadline:** | March 15 |
| **Notification begins:** | July 7 |
| **Total amount awarded:** | $24,000 |

**Contact:**
Screen Actors Guild Foundation
John L. Dales Scholarship Fund
5757 Wilshire Boulevard, Suite 124
Los Angeles, CA 90036
Phone: 323-549-6649
Fax: 323-549-6710
Web: www.sagfoundation.org

# Seabee Memorial Scholarship Association, Inc.

## Seabee Memorial Scholarship

**Type of award:** Scholarship, renewable.
**Intended use:** For full-time undergraduate study at accredited 4-year institution in United States.
**Eligibility:** Applicant must be U.S. citizen. Applicant must be descendant of veteran who served in the Navy. Applicant must be child or grandchild of a currently enlisted, honorably discharged, or deceased member of Naval Construction FORCE (Seabees) or Navy CEC (Civil Engineer Corps).
**Basis for selection:** Applicant must demonstrate financial need, high academic achievement, depth of character, leadership, patriotism, seriousness of purpose and service orientation.
**Application requirements:** Essay, transcript, proof of eligibility. IRS Form 1040. Official document (DD214, reenlistment certificate, transfer orders, etc.) that verifies rate/rank of sponsor.
**Additional information:** Not available for part-time or graduate students. Not available for great-grandchildren of members of Seabees or Navy CEC. Award is renewable for up to four years. Download application from Website.

| | |
|---|---|
| **Amount of award:** | $1,900 |
| **Number of awards:** | 100 |
| **Number of applicants:** | 415 |
| **Application deadline:** | April 15 |
| **Notification begins:** | June 15 |

**Contact:**
Scholarship Committee
P.O. Box 6574
Silver Spring, MD 20916
Phone: 301-570-2850
Fax: 301-570-2873
Web: www.seabee.org

# Seattle Jaycees

## Seattle Jaycees Scholarship

**Type of award:** Scholarship, renewable.
**Intended use:** For undergraduate or graduate study at accredited vocational, 2-year, 4-year or graduate institution. Designated institutions: Institutions in Washington state.
**Eligibility:** Applicant must be residing in Washington.
**Basis for selection:** Applicant must demonstrate depth of character, leadership and service orientation.
**Application requirements:** $5 application fee. Recommendations, essay, transcript. List of community service, civic, and other extra-curricular activities.
**Additional information:** Scholarships granted for exemplary civic involvement, volunteerism, and community service. Renewable one time. Visit Website for application and more information.

| | |
|---|---|
| **Amount of award:** | $1,000 |
| **Number of awards:** | 20 |
| **Number of applicants:** | 480 |
| **Application deadline:** | April 1 |
| **Notification begins:** | June 1 |

**Contact:**
Seattle Jaycees
Scholarship Committee
P.O. Box 9640
Seattle, WA 98109
Phone: 206-286-2014
Web: www.seattlejaycees.org

# Second Marine Division Association

## Second Marine Division Association Scholarship Fund

**Type of award:** Scholarship, renewable.
**Intended use:** For full-time undergraduate study at accredited vocational, 2-year or 4-year institution.
**Eligibility:** Must be dependent child or grandchild of person who serves or served in Second Marine Division, U.S. Marine Corps, or unit attached to the division.
**Basis for selection:** Applicant must demonstrate financial need.
**Application requirements:** Recommendations, essay, transcript, proof of eligibility.
**Additional information:** Family's adjusted gross income should not exceed $65,000 for the taxable year prior to application. Exceptions may be made for larger families. Minimum 2.75 GPA. Must reapply for renewal. Include SASE when requesting application. Parent or grandparent who served in the Second Marine Division must join SMDA, if not already a member, once scholarship is awarded.

| | |
|---|---|
| **Amount of award:** | $1,200 |
| **Number of awards:** | 38 |
| **Number of applicants:** | 44 |
| **Application deadline:** | April 1, July 1 |
| **Notification begins:** | September 15 |
| **Total amount awarded:** | $43,200 |

**Contact:**
Second Marine Division Association Memorial Scholarship Fund
Phone: 910-451-3167
Web: www.2Dmardiv.com

# Senator George J. Mitchell Scholarship Research Institute

## Senator George J. Mitchell Scholarship

**Type of award:** Scholarship, renewable.
**Intended use:** For freshman study at accredited 2-year or 4-year institution in United States.
**Eligibility:** Applicant must be high school senior. Applicant must be U.S. citizen residing in Maine.
**Basis for selection:** Applicant must demonstrate financial need and service orientation.
**Application requirements:** Essay, transcript, proof of eligibility. Letter from guidance counselor, SAR, copy of financial aid award from college student plans to attend.
**Additional information:** Applicant must display academic achievement. One award made to graduating senior from every public high school in Maine. Renewable for up to four years. Award total is $5,000 ($1,250 per year for four years). Scholarship to be applied to spring semester bill. Application due April 1, supporting materials due May 1.

| | |
|---|---|
| **Amount of award:** | $1,250-$5,000 |
| **Number of awards:** | 130 |
| **Number of applicants:** | 1,000 |
| **Application deadline:** | April 1 |
| **Notification begins:** | June 1 |
| **Total amount awarded:** | $650,000 |

**Contact:**
Senator George J. Mitchell Scholarship Research Institute
22 Monument Square
Suite 200
Portland, ME 04101
Phone: 207-773-7700
Fax: 207-773-1133
Web: www.mitchellinstitute.org

# Seneca Nation and BIA

## Seneca Nation Higher Education Program

**Type of award:** Scholarship, renewable.
**Intended use:** For undergraduate or graduate study at accredited 2-year, 4-year or graduate institution.
**Eligibility:** Applicant must be American Indian. Must be an enrolled member of Seneca Nation of Indians. Applicant must be U.S. citizen.
**Basis for selection:** Applicant must demonstrate financial need.

**Application requirements:** Essay, transcript, proof of eligibility. Proof of tribal enrollment, letter of reference from non-relative.
**Additional information:** Amount and number of awards vary. Residency requirements: Level 1- New York State residents living on reservation; Level 2- New York State residents living in New York; Level 3- Enrolled members living outside New York. Application deadlines: fall, July 1; spring, December 1; summer, May 1. Contact sponsor or see Website for more information.

| | |
|---|---|
| **Application deadline:** | July 1, December 1 |

**Contact:**
Seneca Nation of Indians
Higher Education Program
P.O. Box 231
Salamanca, NY 14779
Phone: 716-945-1790 ext. 3103
Web: www.sni.org

# Sertoma

## Sertoma Scholarships for Students Who are Hard of Hearing or Deaf

**Type of award:** Scholarship, renewable.
**Intended use:** For full-time undergraduate study at 4-year institution in United States.
**Eligibility:** Applicant must be hearing impaired. Applicant must be U.S. citizen or permanent resident.
**Basis for selection:** Applicant must demonstrate high academic achievement, depth of character and seriousness of purpose.
**Application requirements:** Transcript. Statement of purpose, two letters of recommendation, documentation of hearing impairment in form of recent audiogram or signed statement by hearing-health professional.
**Additional information:** Applicant must have minimum of 40 dB bilateral hearing loss. Must have minimum 3.2 GPA. Visit Website for application and more information.

| | |
|---|---|
| **Amount of award:** | $1,000 |
| **Number of awards:** | 40 |
| **Number of applicants:** | 160 |
| **Application deadline:** | May 1 |
| **Notification begins:** | June 1 |
| **Total amount awarded:** | $40,000 |

**Contact:**
Sertoma
Attn: Scholarships
1912 East Meyer Boulevard
Kansas City, MO 64132-1174
Web: www.sertoma.org

# Shoshone Tribe

## Shoshone Tribal Scholarship

**Type of award:** Scholarship, renewable.
**Intended use:** For undergraduate or graduate study at accredited vocational, 2-year or 4-year institution in United States.
**Eligibility:** Applicant must be American Indian. Must be enrolled member of Eastern Shoshone Tribe.
**Basis for selection:** Applicant must demonstrate financial need.
**Application requirements:** Transcript, proof of eligibility.
**Additional information:** Must first apply for Pell Grant and appropriate campus-based aid. Minimum 2.5 GPA. Award renewable for maximum ten semesters. Application deadlines: academic year, June 1; spring, November 15; summer, April 15. Number of awards varies.

| | |
|---|---|
| **Amount of award:** | $50-$15,000 |
| **Number of awards:** | 60 |
| **Number of applicants:** | 100 |
| **Application deadline:** | June 1, November 15 |
| **Total amount awarded:** | $300,000 |

**Contact:**
Eastern Shoshone Tribe
PL102-447 Program
104 Washakie Street, P.O. Box 1210
Fort Washakie, WY 82514
Phone: 307-332-8052
Fax: 307-332-8055

# Sid Richardson Memorial Fund

## Sid Richardson Scholarship

**Type of award:** Scholarship, renewable.
**Intended use:** For full-time undergraduate or graduate study at accredited postsecondary institution.
**Basis for selection:** Applicant must demonstrate financial need and high academic achievement.
**Application requirements:** Essay, transcript, proof of eligibility. SAT or ACT scores.
**Additional information:** Must be direct descendant (child or grandchild) of persons who qualified for early retirement, normal retirement, disability retirement, or death benefits from The Retirement Plan for Employees of Bass Enterprises Production Co.; or direct descendant of persons presently employed with a minimum of three years' full-time service with any of the following employers: Sid Richardson Carbon and Energy Co. (Sid Richardson Carbon and Gasoline Company or Sid Richardson Carbon Company) and SRCE, L.P.; Bass Enterprises Production Co.; BEPCO, L.P.; Bass Brothers Enterprises, Inc.; Richardson Oils, Inc.; Perry R. Bass, Inc. (Sid W. Richardson, Inc.); Chisholm Trail Ventures, L.P.; Sid W. Richardson Foundation; San Jose Cattle Company (Fairview Farms); City Center Development Co.; Richardson Aviation; Sid Richardson Carbon, Ltd.; SRCG Aviation, Inc.; Leapartners, L.P.; Barbnet Investments Co.; City Club of Fort Worth (City Center Development Co.); City Center Development Co., L.P. (DBA City Center Development Co. and City Center Executive Suite); Sundance Square; Sundance Square Partners, L.P. (DBA Sundance Square, the Cassidy, and Sundance Square Development); Sundance Square Management, L.P. (DBA Sundance Square Management Co. and Sundance Square Management); BOPCO, L.P., Sid Richardson Energy Services, Ltd. (Sid Richardson Energy Services Co., Sid Richardson Gasoline, Ltd., or Sid Richardson Gasoline Co.) and Richardson Energy Marketing, Ltd. (Richardson Products II, Ltd.). Apply by mail, email, or fax. Must include student name, address, qualifying employee name, Social Security number of employee, qualifying company name, and dates of employment.

**Amount of award:** $500-$7,000
**Number of applicants:** 87
**Application deadline:** March 31
**Notification begins:** May 15
**Total amount awarded:** $252,000

**Contact:**
Sid Richardson Memorial Fund
309 Main Street
Fort Worth, TX 76102
Phone: 817-336-0494
Fax: 817-332-2176

# Siemens Foundation

## Siemens Awards for Advanced Placement

**Type of award:** Scholarship.
**Intended use:** For full-time freshman study at accredited 4-year institution.
**Eligibility:** Applicant must be enrolled in high school.
**Basis for selection:** Competition/talent/interest in academics, based on the most scores of "5" on AP tests in eight subjects: Calculus BC, Computer Science A, Statistics, Chemistry, Biology, Environmental Science, Physics C: Mechanics, and Physics C: Electricity.
**Additional information:** A $2,000 college scholarship awarded each spring to up to one male and one female student from each of the 50 states. No application for award. Two additional national winners (one male, one female) will be awarded $5,000 college scholarship. Students must still be in high school in the spring when the award is announced. Must attain a score of 5 on at least two of the aforementioned exams. Composite exams used as tiebreaker if multiple students attain same number of 5's. All U.S. high school students who have taken an AP exam in year prior to applying are eligible, as well as homeschooled students. Students may be awarded state or national award only once, but state winners may be considered for national award in subsequent years. See Website for more details.

**Amount of award:** $2,000-$5,000
**Number of awards:** 102
**Notification begins:** December 1
**Total amount awarded:** $210,000

**Contact:**
The College Board
Attn: Siemens Awards for AP
11955 Democracy Drive
Reston, VA 20190
Phone: 877-358-6777
Fax: 703-935-7795
Web: www.collegeboard.com/saap or www.siemens-foundation.org/en/advanced_placement.htm

## Siemens Competition in Math, Science and Technology

**Type of award:** Scholarship.
**Intended use:** For full-time undergraduate or graduate study at accredited 4-year or graduate institution.
**Eligibility:** Applicant must be enrolled in high school. Applicant must be U.S. citizen or permanent resident.
**Basis for selection:** Competition/talent/interest in science project, based on originality, scientific importance, validity, creativity, academic rigor, clarity of expression, comprehensiveness, experimental work, field knowledge. Major/career interest in biology; chemistry; engineering; environmental science; materials science; mathematics; physics; computer/information sciences or medicine.
**Application requirements:** Proof of eligibility, research proposal. An 18-page (maximum) research report followed by poster and oral presentations for Regional Finalists. Confirmation page signed by school administrator. Completed supplemental form and project advisor or mentor comments form.
**Additional information:** Competition to encourage students to do research in math, science, or technology, giving young scientists the opportunity to present their research to leading scientists in their field. Regional Finalists awarded trip to compete at one of six regional competitions. At regional event, after presenting poster, oral presentation, and participating in Q&A session, student or team of students will qualify for $1,000 or $3,000 scholarship. National Finalists qualify for $10,000 to $100,000 scholarship. Individual applicants must be seniors; team applicants may be freshmen, sophomores, juniors, or seniors. Register at Website.

**Amount of award:** $1,000-$100,000
**Number of awards:** 60
**Number of applicants:** 1,677
**Application deadline:** October 3
**Notification begins:** October 21
**Total amount awarded:** $600,000

**Contact:**
The Collage Board
Attn: Siemens Competition
11955 Democracy Drive
Reston, VA 20190
Phone: 877-358-6777
Fax: 703-935-7795
Web: www.collegeboard.com/siemens

## Siemens Merit Scholarship

**Type of award:** Scholarship.
**Intended use:** For full-time senior study at 4-year institution in United States.
**Eligibility:** Applicant must be high school junior. Applicant must be U.S. citizen or permanent resident.
**Basis for selection:** Applicant must demonstrate financial need and high academic achievement.
**Application requirements:** Proof of eligibility. PSAT/NMSQT scores.
**Additional information:** Award is $6,000 distributed at $1,500 each year for up to four years of undergraduate study or until baccalaureate degree requirements are completed, whichever comes first. High school students who are sons and daughters of employees of Siemens or its designated operating companies are eligible. Students must also meet all requirements for participation in the National Merit Scholarship Program that are published in the Official Student Guide to the PSAT/NMSQT which is updated annually and distributed to students through their high schools. Number of awards varies. Visit Website for deadline and more details.

**Amount of award:** $6,000

**Contact:**
Siemens Foundation c/o Kiesha Boykins
170 Wood Avenue South
Iselin, NJ 08830
Phone: 732-321-3150 or 877-822-5233
Fax: 732-603-5890
Web: www.siemens-foundation.org

Scholarships

Scholarships

# Slovak Gymnastic Union Sokol, USA

## Milan Getting Scholarship

**Type of award:** Scholarship, renewable.
**Intended use:** For full-time undergraduate study at accredited 4-year institution.
**Eligibility:** Applicant must be high school junior or senior. Applicant must be U.S. citizen.
**Basis for selection:** Applicant must demonstrate high academic achievement, depth of character, leadership, patriotism and seriousness of purpose.
**Application requirements:** Recommendations, transcript.
**Additional information:** Applicant must be member in good standing of Slovak Gymnastic Union Sokol, USA, for at least three years. Minimum scholastic average of C+ or equivalent required. Award renewable for four years. Number of awards varies. Deadline in March. Contact sponsor for application form and more information.

| | |
|---|---|
| **Amount of award:** | $500 |
| **Number of awards:** | 2 |
| **Number of applicants:** | 6 |
| **Total amount awarded:** | $7,500 |

**Contact:**
Slovak Gymnastic Union Sokol, USA
P.O. Box 189
East Orange, NJ 07019
Phone: 973-676-0280

# Slovenian Women's Union of America

## Slovenian Women's Union Scholarship For Returning Adults

**Type of award:** Scholarship.
**Intended use:** For undergraduate certificate or non-degree study at vocational, 2-year or 4-year institution in United States.
**Eligibility:** Applicant must be returning adult student.
**Basis for selection:** Applicant must demonstrate financial need, depth of character, leadership and service orientation.
**Application requirements:** Resume and/or personal statement or autobiography.
**Additional information:** Applicant must be member of Slovenian Women's Union or active participant of organization's activities for three years. Open to men and women with interest in promoting Slovene culture. Contact Mary Turvey at SWUA for more information.

| | |
|---|---|
| **Amount of award:** | $500 |
| **Number of awards:** | 2 |
| **Application deadline:** | March 1 |
| **Total amount awarded:** | $1,000 |

**Contact:**
Slovenian Women's Union of America
Scholarship Director
4 Lawrence Drive
Marquette, MI 49855
Phone: 906-249-4288
Web: www.swua.org

## Slovenian Women's Union Scholarship Foundation

**Type of award:** Scholarship.
**Intended use:** For full-time undergraduate study at accredited 2-year or 4-year institution in United States.
**Basis for selection:** Applicant must demonstrate financial need, depth of character, leadership and service orientation.
**Application requirements:** Recommendations, essay, transcript. FAFSA, resume, and photograph.
**Additional information:** Applicant must be member of Slovenian Women's Union or active participant of organization's activities for three years. Open to women and men with interest in promoting Slovene culture. Recommendation must be from SWUA branch officer and instructor. Number of awards varies. Contact Mary Turvey at SWUA for more information.

| | |
|---|---|
| **Amount of award:** | $1,000-$2,000 |
| **Number of awards:** | 8 |
| **Number of applicants:** | 18 |
| **Application deadline:** | March 1 |
| **Notification begins:** | April 1 |
| **Total amount awarded:** | $10,000 |

**Contact:**
Slovenian Women's Union of America
Scholarship Director
4 Lawrence Drive
Marquette, MI 49855
Phone: 906-249-4288
Web: www.swua.org

# SME Education Foundation

## Albert E. Wischmeyer Memorial Scholarship Award

**Type of award:** Scholarship, renewable.
**Intended use:** For full-time undergraduate study at accredited 4-year institution. Designated institutions: Institutions located in the state of New York.
**Eligibility:** Applicant must be U.S. citizen or permanent resident residing in New York.
**Basis for selection:** Major/career interest in manufacturing; engineering or technology. Applicant must demonstrate high academic achievement.
**Application requirements:** Recommendations, essay, transcript. Resume, SAT or ACT scores for current high school students.
**Additional information:** Applicants must reside in New York State west of Interstate 81. Minimum 2.5 GPA. Must reapply for renewal. Application available on Website.

| | |
|---|---|
| **Amount of award:** | $1,000-$5,000 |
| **Application deadline:** | February 1 |

**Contact:**
SME Education Foundation
One SME Drive, P.O. Box 930
Dearborn, MI 48121-0930
Phone: 313-425-3300
Web: www.smeef.org

## Albuquerque Scholarship

**Type of award:** Scholarship.
**Intended use:** For undergraduate study at accredited 2-year or 4-year institution in United States. Designated institutions: Colleges and universities in New Mexico.
**Basis for selection:** Major/career interest in engineering. Applicant must demonstrate high academic achievement.
**Application requirements:** Recommendations, transcript. Resume.
**Additional information:** Minimum 2.5 GPA. Must be pursuing manufacturing engineering or manufacturing technology. Scholarship may be used toward books, fees, or tuition. First preference goes to applicant who is child/grandchild/stepchild or current Chapter 93 member. Second preference given to SME student member attending a New Mexico university. Third preference given to applicants residing in New Mexico. Fourth preference given to scholarship applicants planning to attend engineering college or university in New Mexico. Fifth preference given to applicants pursuing associate's degree.

| | |
|---|---|
| **Amount of award:** | $1,000 |
| **Number of awards:** | 1 |
| **Application deadline:** | February 1 |

**Contact:**
SME Education Foundation
One SME Drive, P.O. Box 930
Dearborn, MI 48121-0930
Phone: 313-425-3300
Web: www.smeef.org

## Allen and Loureena Weber Scholarship

**Type of award:** Scholarship.
**Intended use:** For sophomore, junior or senior study at 2-year or 4-year institution in United States.
**Eligibility:** Applicant must be U.S. citizen or permanent resident residing in Kentucky.
**Basis for selection:** Major/career interest in manufacturing; engineering, mechanical; engineering, industrial or technology. Applicant must demonstrate high academic achievement.
**Application requirements:** Recommendations, transcript. Resume.
**Additional information:** Must be attending University of Northern Kentucky or seeking associate's degree or bachelor's degree in manufacturing, mechanical, industrial engineering, engineering technology, or industrial technology, and have satisfactory GPA. First preference given to students who are graduates of Dayton High School (Dayton, KY). Second preference given to other high schools in Dayton, KY area. Must have technical aptitude and desire for education and practical learning. Scholarship may be used toward books, fees, or tuition.

| | |
|---|---|
| **Amount of award:** | $1,000 |
| **Number of awards:** | 1 |
| **Application deadline:** | February 1 |

**Contact:**
SME Education Foundation
One SME Drive, P.O. Box 930
Dearborn, MI 48121-0630
Phone: 313-425-3300
Web: www.smeef.org

## Alvin and June Sabroff Manufacturing Engineering Scholarship

**Type of award:** Scholarship.
**Intended use:** For undergraduate study at accredited 4-year institution in United States or Canada.
**Eligibility:** Applicant must be U.S. citizen.
**Basis for selection:** Major/career interest in manufacturing; engineering or technology.
**Application requirements:** Recommendations, transcript. Resume.
**Additional information:** Minimum 3.0 GPA. Must be seeking degree in manufacturing engineering, technology, or closely related field. First preference given to applicants attending college or university in Ohio.

| | |
|---|---|
| **Amount of award:** | $1,000 |
| **Number of awards:** | 1 |
| **Application deadline:** | February 1 |

**Contact:**
SME Education Foundation
One SME Drive, P.O. Box 930
Dearborn, MI 48121-0930
Phone: 313-425-3300
Web: www.smeef.org

## Arthur and Gladys Cervenka Scholarship

**Type of award:** Scholarship, renewable.
**Intended use:** For full-time sophomore, junior or senior study at accredited 4-year institution in United States or Canada.
**Basis for selection:** Major/career interest in manufacturing; engineering or technology. Applicant must demonstrate high academic achievement.
**Application requirements:** Recommendations, essay, transcript. Resume.
**Additional information:** Must be residing in the U.S. or Canada. Applicant must have completed minimum of 30 college credit hours. Minimum 3.0 GPA. Preference given to students attending institutions in Florida.

| | |
|---|---|
| **Amount of award:** | $1,000-$5,000 |
| **Number of awards:** | 1 |
| **Application deadline:** | February 1 |

**Contact:**
SME Education Foundation
One SME Drive, P.O. Box 930
Dearborn, MI 48121-0930
Phone: 313-425-3300
Web: www.smeef.org

## Caterpillar Scholars Award

**Type of award:** Scholarship, renewable.
**Intended use:** For full-time undergraduate study at 4-year institution in United States or Canada.
**Basis for selection:** Major/career interest in manufacturing or engineering. Applicant must demonstrate high academic achievement.
**Application requirements:** Recommendations, essay, transcript. Resume.
**Additional information:** Must be residing in the U.S. or Canada. Freshmen must supply SAT or ACT scores. Applicants must be enrolled in manufacturing engineering degree program and have completed minimum 30 college credit hours. Minority applicants may apply as incoming freshmen. Minimum 3.0 GPA. Preference will be given to students who

Scholarships

have participated in a STEPS camp. Scholarship can be used toward tuition, fees, or books. Applicants must reapply for renewal. Application available on Website.

**Amount of award:** $1,000-$5,000
**Number of awards:** 5
**Application deadline:** February 1

**Contact:**
SME Education Foundation
One SME Drive, P.O. Box 930
Dearborn, MI 48121-0930
Phone: 313-425-3300
Web: www.smeef.org



## Chapter 17 St. Louis Scholarship

**Type of award:** Scholarship, renewable.
**Intended use:** For sophomore, junior or senior study at accredited 2-year or 4-year institution.
**Basis for selection:** Major/career interest in manufacturing; engineering; engineering, mechanical or technology. Applicant must demonstrate high academic achievement, depth of character and seriousness of purpose.
**Application requirements:** Recommendations, essay, transcript. Resume.
**Additional information:** Must be residing in the U.S. or Canada. Applicants must be enrolled in manufacturing engineering, industrial technology, or related degree program. Preference given to applicants residing in boundaries of St. Louis Chapter 17. Second preference given to applicants living in Missouri. Minimum 2.5 GPA. Must reapply for renewal. Application available on Website.

**Amount of award:** $1,000-$5,000
**Number of awards:** 2
**Application deadline:** February 1

**Contact:**
SME Education Foundation
One SME Drive, P.O. Box 930
Dearborn, MI 48121-0930
Phone: 313-425-3300
Web: www.smeef.org

## Chapter 198 - Downriver Detroit Scholarship

**Type of award:** Scholarship.
**Intended use:** For full-time undergraduate or graduate study at accredited 2-year, 4-year or graduate institution.
**Basis for selection:** Major/career interest in manufacturing; engineering, mechanical; engineering; technology or mathematics.
**Application requirements:** Recommendations, essay, transcript. Resume, SAT or ACT scores for current high school students.
**Additional information:** Must be residing in the U.S. or Canada. First preference given to children or grandchildren of current SME Downriver Chapter 198 members. Second preference given to members of student SME chapters sponsored by Chapter 198 or Ann Arbor Area Chapter 079. Third preference given to residents of Michigan. Fourth preference given to applicants planning to attend college/ university in Michigan. Not restricted to Michigan. Minimum 2.5 GPA.

**Amount of award:** $1,000-$5,000
**Number of awards:** 1
**Application deadline:** February 1

**Contact:**
SME Education Foundation
One SME Drive, P.O. Box 930
Dearborn, MI 48121-0930
Phone: 313-425-3300
Web: www.smeef.org

## Chapter 198 and Chapter 079 Ann Arbor Area Endowment Fund

**Type of award:** Scholarship.
**Intended use:** For undergraduate study at accredited 2-year, 4-year or graduate institution.
**Basis for selection:** Major/career interest in technology; engineering; mathematics or manufacturing. Applicant must demonstrate high academic achievement.
**Application requirements:** Recommendations, transcript. Resume.
**Additional information:** Minimum 2.5 GPA. First preference given to applicants who are children, grandchildren, or related dependants of current SME Downriver Chapter No. 198 or Ann Arbor Area Chapter No. 079 member. Second preference given to SME members of student chapters sponsored by SME Downriver Chapter No. 198 or Ann Arbor Area Chapter 079. Third preference given to scholarship applicants residing in the state of Michigan. Fourth preference given to scholarship applicants planning to attend college or university located in Michigan. Not restricted to Michigan residents or students.

**Number of awards:** 1
**Application deadline:** February 1
**Total amount awarded:** $1,000

**Contact:**
SME Education Foundation
One SME Drive, P.O. Box 930
Dearborn, MI 48121-0930
Phone: 313-425-3300
Web: www.smeef.org

## Chapter 23 - Quad Cities Iowa/ Illinois Scholarship

**Type of award:** Scholarship.
**Intended use:** For undergraduate study at 4-year institution.
**Basis for selection:** Major/career interest in manufacturing. Applicant must demonstrate high academic achievement.
**Application requirements:** Recommendations, transcript. Resume.
**Additional information:** Minimum 2.5 GPA. Scholarship may be used toward books, fees, or tuition. First preference given to applicant who is a child, grandchild, or stepchild of registered SME member or student member. Second preference given to applicant who is resident of Iowa or Illinois and attending an Iowa or Illinois college or university. Third preference given to students who are residents of Iowa or Illinois. Fourth preference will be given to applicants who attend a college or university located in Iowa or Illinois.

**Amount of award:** $1,000
**Number of awards:** 1
**Application deadline:** February 1

**Contact:**
SME Education Foundation
One SME Drive, P.O. Box 930
Dearborn, MI 48121-0930
Phone: 313-425-3300
Web: www.smeef.org

## Chapter 311 - Tri City Scholarship

**Type of award:** Scholarship.
**Intended use:** For undergraduate study at 4-year institution.
**Basis for selection:** Major/career interest in manufacturing; engineering or engineering, industrial. Applicant must demonstrate high academic achievement.
**Application requirements:** Recommendations, transcript. Resume.
**Additional information:** Manufacturing engineering technology or closely related majors also eligible. Minimum 3.0 GPA. First preference given to scholarship applicants who are residents of Michigan. Second preference given to applicants seeking education from college or university in Michigan.

| | |
|---|---|
| **Amount of award:** | $1,000 |
| **Number of awards:** | 1 |
| **Application deadline:** | February 1 |

**Contact:**
SME Education Foundation
One SME Drive, P.O. Box 930
Dearborn, MI 48121-0930
Phone: 313-425-3300
Web: www.smeef.org

## Chapter 4 - Lawrence A. Wacker Memorial Scholarship

**Type of award:** Scholarship, renewable.
**Intended use:** For undergraduate study at accredited 4-year institution in United States. Designated institutions: Wisconsin institutions.
**Basis for selection:** Major/career interest in manufacturing; engineering, industrial or engineering, mechanical. Applicant must demonstrate high academic achievement.
**Application requirements:** Recommendations, essay, transcript. Resume, SAT or ACT scores for current high school students.
**Additional information:** Applicants must be seeking bachelor's degree in manufacturing, mechanical, or industrial engineering. Minimum 3.0 GPA. One scholarship granted to graduating high school senior, one to current undergraduate. First preference given to SME Chapter 4 members or spouses, children, or grandchildren of members. Second preference given to residents of Milwaukee, Ozaukee, Washington, and Waukesha counties. Third preference given to Wisconsin residents. Application available on Website.

| | |
|---|---|
| **Amount of award:** | $1,000-$5,000 |
| **Number of awards:** | 2 |
| **Application deadline:** | February 1 |

**Contact:**
SME Education Foundation
One SME Drive, P.O. Box 930
Dearborn, MI 48121-0930
Phone: 313-425-3300
Web: www.smeef.org

## Chapter 52 - Wichita Scholarship

**Type of award:** Scholarship.
**Intended use:** For sophomore, junior, senior or graduate study at accredited 2-year, 4-year or graduate institution in United States. Designated institutions: Kansas, Oklahoma, or Missouri institutions.
**Eligibility:** Applicant must be residing in Oklahoma, Kansas or Missouri.
**Basis for selection:** Major/career interest in engineering or engineering, mechanical.
**Application requirements:** Recommendations, essay, transcript. Resume.
**Additional information:** Must be residing in the U.S. or Canada. First preference given to children, grandchildren, or other relatives of current SME Wichita Chapter 52 members. Second preference given to residents of Kansas, Oklahoma, and Missouri. Third preference given to applicants attending colleges or universities in Kansas. Minimum 2.5 GPA.

| | |
|---|---|
| **Amount of award:** | $1,000-$5,000 |
| **Number of awards:** | 1 |
| **Application deadline:** | February 1 |

**Contact:**
SME Education Foundation
One SME Drive, P.O. Box 930
Dearborn, MI 48121-0930
Phone: 313-425-3300
Web: www.smeef.org

## Chapter 56 - Fort Wayne Scholarship

**Type of award:** Scholarship.
**Intended use:** For undergraduate or graduate study at 2-year, 4-year or graduate institution. Designated institutions: Indiana institutions.
**Eligibility:** Applicant must be residing in Indiana.
**Basis for selection:** Major/career interest in engineering or engineering, mechanical.
**Application requirements:** Recommendations, essay, transcript. Resume, SAT or ACT scores for high school students.
**Additional information:** Must be residing in the U.S. or Canada. First preference given to children or grandchildren of current members of SME Fort Wayne Chapter 56. Second preference given to members of SME student chapters sponsored by Chapter 56. Third preference given to residents of Indiana. Fourth preference given to applicants attending or planning to attend Indiana institutions. Minimum 2.5 GPA.

| | |
|---|---|
| **Amount of award:** | $1,000-$5,000 |
| **Number of awards:** | 3 |
| **Application deadline:** | February 1 |

**Contact:**
SME Education Foundation
One SME Drive, P.O. Box 930
Dearborn, MI 48121-0930
Phone: 313-425-3300
Web: www.smeef.org

## Chapter 6 - Fairfield County Scholarship

**Type of award:** Scholarship.
**Intended use:** For full-time undergraduate study in United States or Canada.
**Basis for selection:** Major/career interest in engineering; manufacturing or technology.
**Application requirements:** Recommendations, essay, transcript. Resume, SAT or ACT scores for current high school students.
**Additional information:** Must be residing in the U.S. or Canada. Minimum 3.0 GPA. Preference given to residents of the eastern United States.

| | |
|---|---|
| **Amount of award:** | $1,000-$5,000 |
| **Number of awards:** | 1 |
| **Application deadline:** | February 1 |

Scholarships

**Contact:**
SME Education Foundation
One SME Drive, P.O. Box 930
Dearborn, MI 48121-0930
Phone: 313-425-3300
Web: www.smeef.org

## Chapter 67 - Phoenix Scholarship

**Type of award:** Scholarship, renewable.
**Intended use:** For full-time undergraduate study. Designated institutions: Arizona institutions.
**Eligibility:** Applicant must be residing in Arizona.
**Basis for selection:** Major/career interest in engineering or manufacturing.
**Application requirements:** Recommendations, essay, transcript. Resume, SAT or ACT scores for current high school students.
**Additional information:** Minimum 2.5 overall GPA; maintain 3.0 in manufacturing courses to continue eligibility in future years.

| | |
|---|---|
| **Amount of award:** | $1,000-$5,000 |
| **Number of awards:** | 2 |
| **Application deadline:** | February 1 |

**Contact:**
SME Education Foundation
One SME Drive, P.O. Box 930
Dearborn, MI 48121-0930
Phone: 313-425-3300
Web: www.smeef.org

## Clarence & Josephine Myers Scholarship

**Type of award:** Scholarship.
**Intended use:** For undergraduate or graduate study at 2-year, 4-year or graduate institution. Designated institutions: Indiana institutions.
**Eligibility:** Applicant must be residing in Indiana.
**Basis for selection:** Major/career interest in engineering, mechanical; engineering or manufacturing.
**Application requirements:** Recommendations, essay, transcript. Resume, SAT or ACT scores for current high school students.
**Additional information:** Preference given to students planning to attend or currently attending college or university in Indiana, students who attend Arsenal Technological High School in Indianapolis, members of SME student chapters sponsored by SME Chapter 37, and children or grandchildren of current SME Chapter 37 members. Minimum 3.0 GPA.

| | |
|---|---|
| **Amount of award:** | $1,000-$5,000 |
| **Number of awards:** | 1 |
| **Application deadline:** | February 1 |

**Contact:**
SME Education Foundation
One SME Drive, P.O. Box 930
Dearborn, MI 48121-0930
Phone: 313-425-3300
Web: www.smeef.org

## Clinton J. Helton Manufacturing Scholarship Award

**Type of award:** Scholarship.
**Intended use:** For full-time sophomore, junior or senior study at accredited 4-year institution. Designated institutions: Colorado State University and all University of Colorado campuses.
**Eligibility:** Applicant must be residing in Colorado.
**Basis for selection:** Major/career interest in manufacturing; engineering or technology. Applicant must demonstrate high academic achievement and depth of character.
**Application requirements:** Recommendations, essay, transcript. Resume.
**Additional information:** Applicants must be enrolled in manufacturing engineering or technology degree program and must have completed at least 30 credit hours. Minimum 3.0 GPA. Applicants must reapply for renewal. Application available on Website.

| | |
|---|---|
| **Amount of award:** | $1,000-$5,000 |
| **Application deadline:** | February 1 |

**Contact:**
SME Education Foundation
One SME Drive, P.O. Box 930
Dearborn, MI 48121-0930
Phone: 313-425-3300
Web: www.smeef.org

## Connie and Robert T. Gunter Scholarship

**Type of award:** Scholarship.
**Intended use:** For full-time sophomore, junior or senior study at accredited 4-year institution.
**Basis for selection:** Major/career interest in manufacturing; engineering or technology. Applicant must demonstrate high academic achievement, depth of character and seriousness of purpose.
**Application requirements:** Recommendations, essay, transcript. Resume.
**Additional information:** Must be residing in the U.S. or Canada. Applicants must be enrolled in manufacturing engineering degree program and must have completed at least 30 credit hours. Minimum 3.5 GPA. Applicants must reapply for renewal. Application available on Website.

| | |
|---|---|
| **Amount of award:** | $1,000-$5,000 |
| **Number of awards:** | 1 |
| **Application deadline:** | February 1 |

**Contact:**
SME Education Foundation
One SME Drive, P.O. Box 930
Dearborn, MI 48121-0930
Phone: 313-425-3300
Web: www.smeef.org

## Detroit Chapter One - Founding Chapter Scholarship Award

**Type of award:** Scholarship, renewable.
**Intended use:** For undergraduate or graduate study at accredited 2-year, 4-year or graduate institution. Designated institutions: Wayne State University, Lawrence Technological University, University of Detroit Mercy, Focus: HOPE Center for Advanced Technologies, Henry Ford Community College, Macomb Community College, University of Michigan.
**Basis for selection:** Major/career interest in manufacturing or engineering. Applicant must demonstrate high academic achievement, depth of character and leadership.
**Application requirements:** Recommendations, essay, transcript. Resume.
**Additional information:** Awarded to one student each at associate, baccalaureate, and graduate levels. Applicants must be enrolled in manufacturing engineering, manufacturing

engineering technology, or closely related degree or certificate program. Student must be member of SME student chapter sponsored by Detroit Chapter 1. Minimum 3.0 GPA. Applicants must reapply for renewal. Financial need considered only between two otherwise equal applicants. Application available on Website.

**Amount of award:** $1,000-$5,000
**Number of awards:** 3
**Application deadline:** February 1

**Contact:**
SME Education Foundation
One SME Drive, P.O. Box 930
Dearborn, MI 48121-0930
Phone: 313-425-3300
Web: www.smeef.org

## E. Wayne Kay Co-op Scholarship

**Type of award:** Scholarship, renewable.
**Intended use:** For full-time sophomore, junior or senior study at accredited postsecondary institution in United States or Canada.
**Basis for selection:** Major/career interest in manufacturing; engineering or technology. Applicant must demonstrate high academic achievement.
**Application requirements:** Essay, transcript, proof of eligibility. Letter of recommendation from employer and letter of support from faculty member at college or university.
**Additional information:** Must be residing in the U.S. or Canada. Applicants must be enrolled in manufacturing engineering or technology degree program and working through co-op program in a manufacturing-related environment. Applicants must have completed minimum 30 college credit hours. Must provide evidence of demonstrated excellence related to manufacturing engineering or technology which may include project completed for employer. Minimum 3.0 GPA. Applicants must reapply for renewal. Application available on Website.

**Amount of award:** $1,000-$5,000
**Number of awards:** 2
**Application deadline:** February 1

**Contact:**
SME Educational Foundation
One SME Drive, P.O. Box 930
Dearborn, MI 48121-0930
Phone: 313-425-3300
Web: www.smeef.org

## E. Wayne Kay Community College Scholarship

**Type of award:** Scholarship, renewable.
**Intended use:** For full-time freshman or sophomore study at accredited vocational or 2-year institution in United States or Canada. Designated institutions: Community colleges and trade schools.
**Basis for selection:** Major/career interest in manufacturing or technology. Applicant must demonstrate high academic achievement.
**Application requirements:** Recommendations, essay, transcript. Resume, SAT or ACT scores.
**Additional information:** Must be residing in the U.S. or Canada. Applicants must be enrolled in manufacturing engineering or closely related degree program at a two-year community college or trade school in the U.S. or Canada. Entering freshman or sophomore students with 60 or fewer college credits are also eligible. Minimum 3.0 GPA. Must reapply for renewal. Application available on Website.

**Amount of award:** $1,000-$5,000
**Number of awards:** 3
**Application deadline:** February 1

**Contact:**
SME Education Foundation
One SME Drive, P.O. Box 930
Dearborn, MI 48121-0930
Phone: 313-425-3300
Web: www.smeef.org

## E. Wayne Kay High School Scholarship

**Type of award:** Scholarship, renewable.
**Intended use:** For full-time freshman study at accredited 4-year institution in United States or Canada.
**Eligibility:** Applicant must be high school senior.
**Basis for selection:** Major/career interest in manufacturing or engineering. Applicant must demonstrate high academic achievement.
**Application requirements:** Recommendations, essay, transcript. Resume, SAT or ACT scores.
**Additional information:** Must be residing in the U.S. or Canada. Applicant must commit to enrolling in manufacturing engineering or technology degree program. Minimum 3.0 GPA. Application available on Website.

**Amount of award:** $1,000-$5,000
**Number of awards:** 2
**Application deadline:** February 1

**Contact:**
SME Foundation
One SME Drive, P.O. Box 930
Dearborn, MI 48121-0930
Phone: 313-425-3300
Web: www.smeef.org

## E. Wayne Kay Scholarship

**Type of award:** Scholarship, renewable.
**Intended use:** For full-time undergraduate study at accredited 4-year institution in United States or Canada.
**Basis for selection:** Major/career interest in manufacturing or engineering. Applicant must demonstrate high academic achievement.
**Application requirements:** Recommendations, essay, transcript. Resume.
**Additional information:** Must be residing in the U.S. or Canada. Applicants must be enrolled in manufacturing engineering or technology degree program or closely related field. Minimum 3.0 GPA. Must reapply for renewal. Application available on Website.

**Amount of award:** $1,000-$5,000
**Number of awards:** 2
**Application deadline:** February 1

**Contact:**
SME Education Foundaiton
One SME Drive, P.O. Box 930
Dearborn, MI 48121-0930
Phone: 313-425-3300
Web: www.smeef.org

## Edward S. Roth Manufacturing Engineering Scholarship

**Type of award:** Scholarship, renewable.
**Intended use:** For full-time undergraduate or graduate study at accredited 4-year institution in United States. Designated

institutions: California State Polytechnic University; University of Miami, FL; Bradley University, IL; Central State University, OH; Miami University, OH; Boston University; Worcester Polytechnic Institute, MA; University of Massachusetts; St. Cloud State University, MN; University of Texas-Pan American; Brigham Young University, UT; Utah State University.
**Eligibility:** Applicant must be U.S. citizen.
**Basis for selection:** Major/career interest in manufacturing or engineering. Applicant must demonstrate high academic achievement, depth of character and seriousness of purpose.
**Application requirements:** Recommendations, essay, transcript. Resume.
**Additional information:** Applicants must be enrolled in manufacturing engineering degree program. Minimum 3.0 GPA. Preference given to students demonstrating financial need, minority students, and students participating in co-op program. Must reapply for renewal. Application available on Website.

| | |
|---|---|
| **Amount of award:** | $1,000-$5,000 |
| **Number of awards:** | 1 |
| **Application deadline:** | February 1 |

**Contact:**
SME Education Foundation
One SME Drive, P.O. Box 930
Dearborn, MI 48121-0930
Phone: 313-425-3300
Web: www.smeef.org

## Future Leaders of Manufacturing Scholarships

**Type of award:** Scholarship.
**Intended use:** For full-time undergraduate or graduate study at postsecondary institution.
**Basis for selection:** Major/career interest in manufacturing; engineering or technology.
**Application requirements:** Recommendations, transcript, nomination by SME student chapter faculty advisor. Resume.
**Additional information:** Must be residing in the U.S. or Canada. Applicant must be current SME student member. Faculty advisors may only nominate one student from the chapter. Visit Website for nomination form and application.

| | |
|---|---|
| **Amount of award:** | $1,000-$5,000 |
| **Number of awards:** | 10 |
| **Application deadline:** | February 1 |

**Contact:**
SME Education Foundation
One SME Drive, P.O. Box 930
Dearborn, MI 48121-0930
Phone: 313-425-3300
Web: www.smeef.org

## Giuliano Mazzetti Scholarship

**Type of award:** Scholarship, renewable.
**Intended use:** For full-time sophomore, junior or senior study at accredited 4-year institution in United States or Canada.
**Basis for selection:** Major/career interest in manufacturing; engineering or technology. Applicant must demonstrate high academic achievement.
**Application requirements:** Recommendations, essay, transcript. Resume.
**Additional information:** Must be residing in the U.S. or Canada. Applicants must be enrolled in manufacturing engineering, technology, or closely related degree program and must have completed minimum 30 college credit hours. Minimum 3.0 GPA. Must reapply for renewal. Financial need considered only between two otherwise equal applicants. Application available on Website.

| | |
|---|---|
| **Amount of award:** | $1,000-$5,000 |
| **Number of awards:** | 3 |
| **Application deadline:** | February 1 |

**Contact:**
SME Education Foundation
One SME Drive, P.O. Box 930
Dearborn, MI 48121-0930
Phone: 313-425-3300
Web: www.smeef.org

## Lucile B. Kaufman Women's Scholarship

**Type of award:** Scholarship, renewable.
**Intended use:** For full-time sophomore, junior or senior study at 4-year institution in United States or Canada.
**Eligibility:** Applicant must be female.
**Basis for selection:** Major/career interest in manufacturing or engineering. Applicant must demonstrate high academic achievement.
**Application requirements:** Recommendations, essay, transcript. Resume.
**Additional information:** Must be residing in the U.S. or Canada. Applicants must be enrolled in manufacturing engineering or manufacturing engineering technology degree program and must have completed minimum 30 credits. Minimum 3.0 GPA. Must reapply for renewal. Application available on Website.

| | |
|---|---|
| **Amount of award:** | $1,000-$5,000 |
| **Number of awards:** | 2 |
| **Application deadline:** | February 1 |

**Contact:**
SME Education Foundation
One SME Drive, P.O. Box 930
Dearborn, MI 48121-0930
Phone: 313-425-3300
Web: www.smeef.org

## Myrtle and Earl Walker Scholarship

**Type of award:** Scholarship, renewable.
**Intended use:** For full-time undergraduate study at accredited 4-year institution in United States or Canada.
**Basis for selection:** Major/career interest in manufacturing or engineering. Applicant must demonstrate high academic achievement.
**Application requirements:** Recommendations, essay, transcript. Resume.
**Additional information:** Must be residing in the U.S. or Canada. Applicants must be enrolled in manufacturing engineering degree or technology program and must have completed minimum 15 credits. Minimum 3.0 GPA. Must reapply for renewal. Application available on Website.

| | |
|---|---|
| **Amount of award:** | $1,000-$5,000 |
| **Number of awards:** | 20 |
| **Application deadline:** | February 1 |

**Contact:**
SME Education Foundation
One SME Drive, P.O. Box 930
Dearborn, MI 48121-0930
Phone: 313-425-3300
Web: www.smeef.org

## North Central Region Scholarship

**Type of award:** Scholarship.
**Intended use:** For full-time undergraduate study at 2-year or 4-year institution. Designated institutions: Institutions in Iowa, Minnesota, Nebraska, North Dakota, South Dakota, Wisconsin, or the upper peninsula of Michigan.
**Eligibility:** Applicant must be residing in Michigan, Wisconsin, Iowa, South Dakota, Minnesota, Nebraska or North Dakota.
**Basis for selection:** Major/career interest in manufacturing; engineering or engineering, mechanical.
**Application requirements:** Recommendations, essay, transcript. Resume, SAT or ACT scores for current high school students.
**Additional information:** Must be residing in the U.S. or Canada. First preference given to applicants from the North Central Region who are SME members, spouses of members, or children or grandchildren of members. Second preference given to residents of Iowa, Minnesota, Nebraska, North Dakota, South Dakota, Wisconsin, and the upper peninsula of Michigan. Minimum 3.0 GPA.

**Amount of award:** $1,000-$5,000
**Number of awards:** 1
**Application deadline:** February 1

**Contact:**
SME Education Foundation
One SME Drive, P.O. Box 930
Dearborn, MI 48121-0930
Phone: 313-425-3300
Web: www.smeef.org

## SME Directors Scholarship

**Type of award:** Scholarship, renewable.
**Intended use:** For full-time sophomore, junior or senior study at accredited 4-year institution in United States or Canada.
**Basis for selection:** Major/career interest in manufacturing. Applicant must demonstrate high academic achievement and leadership.
**Application requirements:** Recommendations, essay, transcript. Resume.
**Additional information:** Must be residing in the U.S. or Canada. Applicants must have completed minimum 30 college credit hours. Minimum 3.5 GPA. Applicants must reapply for renewal. Preference given to applicants who demonstrate leadership skills in a community, academic, or professional environment. Application available on Website.

**Amount of award:** $1,000-$5,000
**Number of awards:** 2
**Application deadline:** February 1

**Contact:**
SME Education Foundation
One SME Drive, P.O. Box 930
Dearborn, MI 48121-0930
Phone: 313-425-3300
Web: www.smeef.org

## SME Education Foundation Family Scholarship

**Type of award:** Scholarship.
**Intended use:** For full-time freshman or sophomore study in United States or Canada.
**Basis for selection:** Major/career interest in engineering or manufacturing. Applicant must demonstrate high academic achievement, leadership and seriousness of purpose.
**Application requirements:** Recommendations, essay, transcript. Resume. High school seniors must submit SAT/ACT scores.
**Additional information:** Must be residing in the U.S. or Canada. Applicant must have parent or grandparent who has been SME member in good standing for at least two years. Graduating high school seniors and current undergraduates with fewer than 30 credit hours are eligible. Minimum 3.0 GPA. Minimum 1000 SAT or 21 ACT.

**Amount of award:** $1,000-$5,000
**Number of awards:** 3
**Application deadline:** February 1

**Contact:**
SME Education Foundation
One SME Drive, P.O. Box 930
Dearborn, MI 48121-0930
Phone: 313-425-3300
Web: www.smeef.org

## Walt Bartram Memorial Education Award (Region 12 and Chapter 119)

**Type of award:** Scholarship, renewable.
**Intended use:** For full-time undergraduate study at accredited 2-year or 4-year institution. Designated institutions: Schools with manufacturing engineering programs within Desert Pacific Region 12 (Arizona, New Mexico, Southern California).
**Eligibility:** Applicant must be high school senior. Applicant must be residing in California, New Mexico or Arizona.
**Basis for selection:** Major/career interest in manufacturing or engineering. Applicant must demonstrate high academic achievement, depth of character and seriousness of purpose.
**Application requirements:** Recommendations, essay, transcript. Resume, SAT or ACT scores for current high school students.
**Additional information:** Applicant must be enrolled in manufacturing engineering or closely related degree program. Minimum 3.5 GPA. Application available on Website.

**Amount of award:** $1,000-$5,000
**Number of awards:** 1
**Application deadline:** February 1

**Contact:**
SME Foundation
One SME Drive, P.O. Box 930
Dearborn, MI 48121-0930
Phone: 313-425-3300
Web: www.smeef.org

## William E. Weisel Scholarship

**Type of award:** Scholarship, renewable.
**Intended use:** For full-time sophomore, junior or senior study at 4-year institution in United States or Canada.
**Basis for selection:** Major/career interest in manufacturing; engineering; robotics or technology. Applicant must demonstrate high academic achievement.
**Application requirements:** Recommendations, essay, transcript. Resume.
**Additional information:** Must be residing in the U.S. or Canada. Applicant must be enrolled in manufacturing engineering degree program and must have completed minimum 30 credits. Preference given to applicants seeking career in robotics or automated systems used in manufacturing. Consideration given to students who intend to apply knowledge to career in medical robotics. Minimum 3.0 GPA. Applicants must reapply for renewal. Financial need considered only between two otherwise equal applicants. Application available on Website.

**Amount of award:** $1,000-$5,000
**Number of awards:** 1
**Application deadline:** February 1
**Contact:**
SME Education Foundation
One SME Drive, P.O. Box 930
Dearborn, MI 48121-0930
Phone: 313-425-3300
Web: www.smeef.org

# Sociedad Honoraria Hispanica

## Joseph S. Adams Scholarship

**Type of award:** Scholarship.
**Intended use:** For full-time freshman study in United States.
**Eligibility:** Applicant must be high school senior.
**Basis for selection:** Major/career interest in Latin American studies or foreign languages. Applicant must demonstrate high academic achievement, depth of character, leadership, patriotism, seriousness of purpose and service orientation.
**Application requirements:** Recommendations, essay, transcript, proof of eligibility, nomination by local high school chapter sponsor.
**Additional information:** Applicant must be active senior member of Sociedad Honoraria Hispanica. Applicant must be presently enrolled in high school Spanish or Portuguese class. SHH members should contact their sponsor, not the national director, regarding application before December 31. All majors eligible; strong interest in Latin American Studies, Spanish, Portuguese preferred. Only one member per chapter may apply.
**Amount of award:** $1,000-$2,000
**Number of awards:** 52
**Number of applicants:** 200
**Application deadline:** February 15
**Notification begins:** April 15
**Total amount awarded:** $64,000
**Contact:**
Upakar c/o Mukunda
10237 Nolan Drive
Rockville, MD 20850
Phone: 847-550-0455
Fax: 847-550-0460
Web: www.sociedadhonorariahispanica.org

# Society for Range Management

## Masonic Range Science Scholarship

**Type of award:** Scholarship, renewable.
**Intended use:** For full-time freshman or sophomore study at postsecondary institution. Designated institutions: Colleges or universities with range science programs.
**Basis for selection:** Major/career interest in range science. Applicant must demonstrate high academic achievement and leadership.
**Application requirements:** Recommendations, essay, transcript, nomination by member of Society for Range Management, National Association of Conservation Districts, or Soil and Water Conservation Society. SAT/ACT scores.
**Additional information:** Award amount varies. Renewable for maximum of eight semesters. Student must maintain 2.5 GPA first two semesters, 3.0 GPA any subsequent semesters. Visit Website for more information and application.
**Number of awards:** 1
**Number of applicants:** 24
**Application deadline:** January 15
**Notification begins:** March 1
**Total amount awarded:** $6,200
**Contact:**
Society for Range Management
Paul Loeffler, Texas General Land Office
500 West Avenue H, Suite 101, Box 2
Alpine, TX 79830-6008
Phone: 303-986-3309
Fax: 303-986-3892
Web: www.rangelands.org

# Society of Daughters of the United States Army

## Society of Daughters of United States Army Scholarship Program

**Type of award:** Scholarship, renewable.
**Intended use:** For full-time undergraduate study at accredited postsecondary institution.
**Eligibility:** Applicant must be female. Applicant must be daughter or granddaughter (including step or adopted) of a career warrant (WO 1-5) or commissioned officer (2nd & 1st LT, CPT, MAJ, LTC, COL, or General) of U.S. Army who (1) is currently on active duty; (2) retired from active duty after at least 20 years of service; (3) was medically retired before 20 years of active service; (4) died while on active duty; or (5) died after retiring from active duty with 20 or more years of service.
**Basis for selection:** Applicant must demonstrate high academic achievement, depth of character, leadership, patriotism and seriousness of purpose.
**Additional information:** Minimum 3.0 GPA. Scholarships cover academic expenses only. Request for application must include parent or grandparent's name, rank, component (Active, Regular, Reserve), inclusive dates of active service, and relationship to applicant. Number of awards varies annually. Send business-size SASE and one letter of request only. Do not send birth certificate or original documents. Do not use registered/certified mail. All application submissions become property of DUSA. Application request deadline is March 1. Completed applications due from March 15 to March 31.
**Amount of award:** $1,000
**Number of applicants:** 150
**Application deadline:** March 31
**Notification begins:** June 1
**Total amount awarded:** $12,000
**Contact:**
Society of Daughters of the United States Army
Mary P. Maroney, Scholarship Chairman
11804 Grey Birch Place
Reston, VA 20191-4223

# Society of Exploration Geophysicists

## SEG Foundation Scholarship

**Type of award:** Scholarship, renewable.
**Intended use:** For undergraduate or graduate study in or outside United States.
**Basis for selection:** Major/career interest in physics; mathematics; geology/earth sciences or geophysics. Applicant must demonstrate high academic achievement and seriousness of purpose.
**Application requirements:** Recommendations, essay, transcript, proof of eligibility.
**Additional information:** Applicant must pursue college course directed toward career in geophysics or a closely related field and must possess an interest in and aptitude for geosciences. Amount and number of awards vary. Visit Website for more information and application.

| | |
|---|---|
| **Amount of award:** | $500-$14,000 |
| **Number of applicants:** | 524 |
| **Application deadline:** | March 1 |
| **Notification begins:** | May |
| **Total amount awarded:** | $434,150 |

**Contact:**
Phone: 918-497-4618
Fax: 918-497-5560
Web: www.seg.org/scholarships

## Society of Exploration Geophysicists Scholarship

**Type of award:** Scholarship, renewable.
**Intended use:** For full-time undergraduate or graduate study at accredited 4-year or graduate institution.
**Basis for selection:** Major/career interest in geophysics; geology/earth sciences; physics or environmental science. Applicant must demonstrate high academic achievement.
**Application requirements:** Recommendations, essay, transcript. SAT or ACT scores for high school and undergraduate students, GRE or TOEFL scores for graduate students.
**Additional information:** Number of scholarships available yearly depends on the number of sponsors and the amount they contribute. Applicants must intend to pursue career in exploration geophysics (graduate students in operations, teaching, or research). Visit Website for more information.

| | |
|---|---|
| **Amount of award:** | $500-$14,000 |
| **Application deadline:** | March 1 |
| **Notification begins:** | September 1 |
| **Total amount awarded:** | $434,150 |

**Contact:**
SEG Foundation
Scholarship Committee
P.O. Box 702740
Tulsa, OK 74170-2740
Phone: 918-497-5500
Web: www.seg.org

# Society of Physics Students

## Society of Physics Students Leadership Scholarship

**Type of award:** Scholarship.
**Intended use:** For full-time junior or senior study at 2-year or 4-year institution.
**Basis for selection:** Major/career interest in physics. Applicant must demonstrate high academic achievement and seriousness of purpose.
**Application requirements:** Transcript. Letters of recommendation from at least two full-time faculty members.
**Additional information:** Awards payable in equal installments at the beginning of each semester or quarter of full-time study in final year of baccalaureate degree. Applicants in two-year schools should apply after completing one semester of physics. Must be active participant in Society of Physics Students. Must show intention for continued scholastic development in physics. Number of awards varies. Obtain application from Website or SPS Chapter Adviser.

| | |
|---|---|
| **Amount of award:** | $2,000-$5,000 |
| **Application deadline:** | February 15 |
| **Notification begins:** | April 1 |
| **Total amount awarded:** | $39,500 |

**Contact:**
SPS Scholarships Committee
One Physics Ellipse
College Park, MD 20740
Phone: 301-209-3007
Fax: 301-209-0839
Web: www.spsnational.org

# Society of Plastics Engineers

## Extrusion Division/Lew Erwin Memorial Scholarship

**Type of award:** Scholarship.
**Intended use:** For full-time senior or master's study at 4-year or graduate institution.
**Basis for selection:** Major/career interest in chemistry; engineering; engineering, chemical; engineering, materials; engineering, mechanical or physics. Applicant must demonstrate financial need.
**Application requirements:** Research proposal. One- to two-page typed statement explaining reasons for application, qualifications, and educational/career goals in the plastics industry. Recommendation letter from faculty adviser associated with project.
**Additional information:** All applicants must be in good academic standing and have a demonstrated interest in the plastics industry. Applicants must be working on senior or MS research project in polymer extrusion that the scholarship will help support. The project must be described in writing, including background, objective, and proposed experiments. Recipient will be expected to furnish final research summary report. Visit Website for more information.

**Amount of award:** $2,500
**Number of awards:** 1
**Application deadline:** March 1
**Total amount awarded:** $2,500

**Contact:**
Society of Plastics Engineers
13 Church Hill Road
Newtown, CT 06470
Phone: 203-740-5447
Fax: 203-775-8490
Web: www.4spe.org

## Fleming/Blaszcak Scholarship

**Type of award:** Scholarship.
**Intended use:** For full-time undergraduate or graduate study at 4-year or graduate institution.
**Eligibility:** Applicant must be Mexican American. Applicant must be U.S. citizen or permanent resident.
**Basis for selection:** Major/career interest in chemistry; engineering; engineering, chemical; engineering, materials; engineering, mechanical or physics. Applicant must demonstrate financial need.
**Application requirements:** Transcript. One- to two-page typed statement explaining reasons for application, qualifications, and educational/career goals in the plastics industry. Three recommendation letters: two from teachers or school officials and one from an employer or non-relative.
**Additional information:** All applicants must be in good standing and have a demonstrated interest in the plastics industry. Visit Website for more information.

**Amount of award:** $2,000
**Number of awards:** 1
**Application deadline:** January 15
**Total amount awarded:** $2,000

**Contact:**
Society of Plastics Engineers
13 Church Hill Road
Newtown, CT 06470
Phone: 203-740-5447
Fax: 203-775-8490
Web: www.4spe.org

## Gulf Coast Hurricane Scholarships

**Type of award:** Scholarship.
**Intended use:** For full-time undergraduate or graduate study at 2-year, 4-year or graduate institution in United States.
**Eligibility:** Applicant must be residing in Texas, Mississippi, Alabama, Louisiana or Florida.
**Basis for selection:** Major/career interest in chemistry; engineering; engineering, chemical; engineering, materials; engineering, materials or physics. Applicant must demonstrate financial need and high academic achievement.
**Application requirements:** Recommendations, essay, transcript. A listing of employment history, including description of work with plastics/polymers. A list of current and past school activities and community activities and honors.
**Additional information:** Applicants must have a demonstrated or expressed interest in the plastics industry. Applicants must be majoring in or taking courses that are beneficial to a career in the plastics/polymer industry. One four-year university scholarship of $6,000 (funds distributed on a yearly basis) and two two-year junior or technical institute scholarships of $2,000 (funds distributed on a yearly basis) are available. Applicants must be a resident of, and attending college in, a Gulf Coast State (Florida, Alabama, Mississippi, Louisiana, and Texas).

**Amount of award:** $2,000-$6,000
**Number of awards:** 3
**Application deadline:** January 15

**Contact:**
Society of Plastics Engineers
13 Church Hill Road
Newtown, CT 06470
Phone: 203-740-5447
Fax: 203-740-8490
Web: www.4spe.org/spe-foundation

## K. K. Wang Scholarship

**Type of award:** Scholarship.
**Intended use:** For full-time undergraduate or graduate study at 2-year, 4-year or graduate institution.
**Basis for selection:** Major/career interest in chemistry; engineering; engineering, chemical; engineering, materials; engineering, mechanical or physics. Applicant must demonstrate financial need and high academic achievement.
**Application requirements:** Recommendations, essay, transcript. A listing of employment history, including description of work in the plastics/polymers industry. A list of current and past school activities, community activities, and honors.
**Additional information:** Applicants must have a demonstrated or expressed interest in the plastics industry, and must be majoring or taking courses that are beneficial to a career in the plastics/polymer industry. Applicants must have experience in injection molding and computer-aided engineering (CAE), such as courses taken, research conducted, or jobs held.

**Amount of award:** $2,000
**Number of awards:** 1
**Application deadline:** January 15
**Total amount awarded:** $2,000

**Contact:**
Society of Plastics Engineers
13 Church Hill Road
Newtown, CT 06470
Phone: 203-740-5447
Fax: 203-775-8490
Web: www.4spe.org/spe-foundation

## Pittsburgh Scholarship

**Type of award:** Scholarship, renewable.
**Intended use:** For full-time undergraduate or graduate study at 2-year, 4-year or graduate institution.
**Eligibility:** Applicant must be residing in Pennsylvania.
**Basis for selection:** Major/career interest in chemistry; engineering, chemical; engineering, mechanical; physics or engineering, industrial. Applicant must demonstrate financial need.
**Application requirements:** Recommendations, essay, transcript, proof of eligibility. List of current and past school and community activities and honors. List of employment history with detailed description of any involvement in plastics/polymers.
**Additional information:** All applicants must be in good standing with their colleges and must have a demonstrated or expressed interest in the plastics industry. Plastics engineering and polymer science majors also eligible. Must be resident of one of the following Pennsylvania counties: Allegheny, Armstrong, Beaver, Bedford, Blair, Brooke, Butler, Cambria, Clarion, Clearfield, Fayette, Greene, Hancock, Indiana, Jefferson, Lawrence, Mercer, Somerset, Venango, Washington, or Westmoreland. Visit Website for more information.

| | |
|---|---|
| **Number of awards:** | 2 |
| **Application deadline:** | January 15 |
| **Total amount awarded:** | $4,000 |

**Contact:**
Society of Plastics Engineers
13 Church Hill Road
Newtown, CT 06470
Phone: 203-740-5447
Fax: 203-775-8490
Web: www.4spe.org/spe-foundation

## Plastics Pioneers Scholarships

**Type of award:** Scholarship, renewable.
**Intended use:** For full-time undergraduate study at 2-year or 4-year institution.
**Basis for selection:** Major/career interest in chemistry; engineering, chemical; engineering, mechanical; physics or engineering, industrial. Applicant must demonstrate financial need.
**Application requirements:** Recommendations, essay, transcript. List of current and past school activities and community activities and honors. List of employment history with detailed description of any involvement in plastics/ polymers.
**Additional information:** All applicants must be in good standing with their colleges and must have a demonstrated or expressed interest in the plastics industry. Must be committed to becoming "hands on" worker in the plastics industry as plastics technician or engineer. Plastics engineering and polymer science majors also eligible. Visit Website for more information.

| | |
|---|---|
| **Amount of award:** | $3,000 |
| **Number of awards:** | 10 |
| **Application deadline:** | January 15 |
| **Total amount awarded:** | $30,000 |

**Contact:**
Society of Plastics Engineers
13 Church Hill Road
Newtown, CT 06470
Phone: 203-740-5447
Fax: 203-775-8490
Web: www.4spe.org/spe-foundation

## Society of Plastics Engineers General Scholarships

**Type of award:** Scholarship, renewable.
**Intended use:** For full-time undergraduate or graduate study at vocational, 2-year, 4-year or graduate institution.
**Basis for selection:** Major/career interest in chemistry; engineering; engineering, chemical; engineering, mechanical; engineering, materials or physics. Applicant must demonstrate financial need and seriousness of purpose.
**Application requirements:** Transcript. One- to two-page typed statement explaining reasons for application, qualifications, and educational/career goals in the plastics industry. Three recommendation letters: two from teachers or school officials and one from an employer or non-relative.
**Additional information:** All applicants must be in good standing with their colleges and must have a demonstrated interest in the plastics industry. Recipients must re-apply for renewal, for up to three additional years. Visit Website for more information.

| | |
|---|---|
| **Amount of award:** | $1,000-$4,000 |
| **Application deadline:** | February 15 |
| **Total amount awarded:** | $107,500 |

**Contact:**
Society of Plastics Engineers
13 Church Hill Road
Newtown, CT 06470
Phone: 203-740-5447
Fax: 203-775-8490
Web: www.4spe.org

## The SPE Foundation Blow Molding Division Memorial Scholarships

**Type of award:** Scholarship.
**Intended use:** For junior study at 4-year institution.
**Basis for selection:** Major/career interest in engineering. Applicant must demonstrate financial need.
**Application requirements:** Recommendations, transcript. Essay on the importance of blow molding to the technical parts and packing industries.
**Additional information:** Applicants must be members of a Society of Plastics Engineers Student Chapter and be in second year of four-year undergraduate plastics engineering program. Award is $8,000, payable over two years.

| | |
|---|---|
| **Amount of award:** | $8,000 |
| **Number of awards:** | 2 |
| **Application deadline:** | January 15 |
| **Total amount awarded:** | $12,000 |

**Contact:**
Society of Plastics Engineers
13 Church Hill Road
Newtown, CT 06470
Phone: 203-740-5447
Fax: 203-775-8490
Web: www.4spe.org

## Thermoforming Division Memorial Scholarship

**Type of award:** Scholarship.
**Intended use:** For full-time undergraduate or graduate study at vocational, 2-year, 4-year or graduate institution.
**Basis for selection:** Major/career interest in chemistry; engineering; engineering, chemical; engineering, materials; engineering, mechanical or physics. Applicant must demonstrate financial need.
**Application requirements:** Transcript. One- to two-page typed statement explaining reasons for application, qualifications, and educational/career goals. Statement detailing exposure to the thermostat industry, including courses, research conducted, or jobs held. Three recommendation letters: two from teachers or school officials, and one from an employer or other non-relative.
**Additional information:** All applicants must be in good standing and have a demonstrated interest in the plastics industry. Visit Website for more information.

| | |
|---|---|
| **Amount of award:** | $5,000 |
| **Number of awards:** | 2 |
| **Application deadline:** | January 15 |
| **Total amount awarded:** | $10,000 |

**Contact:**
Society of Plastics Engineers
13 Church Hill Road
Newtown, CT 06470
Phone: 203-740-5447
Fax: 203-775-8490
Web: www.4spe.org

## Thermoset Division/James I. MacKenzie Memorial Scholarship

**Type of award:** Scholarship.
**Intended use:** For full-time undergraduate or graduate study at vocational, 2-year or 4-year institution.
**Basis for selection:** Major/career interest in chemistry; engineering; engineering, chemical; engineering, materials; engineering, mechanical or physics. Applicant must demonstrate financial need.
**Application requirements:** Transcript. One- to two-page typed statement explaining reasons for application, qualifications, and educational/ career goals. Statement detailing exposure to the thermoset industry. Three recommendation letters: two from teachers or school officials and one from an employer or non-relative.
**Additional information:** All applicants must be in good academic standing and have a demonstrated interest in the plastics industry. Must have experience in the thermoset industry, such as courses taken, research conducted, or jobs held. Visit Website for more information.

| | |
|---|---|
| **Amount of award:** | $2,500 |
| **Number of awards:** | 2 |
| **Application deadline:** | January 15 |
| **Total amount awarded:** | $5,000 |

**Contact:**
Society of Plastics Engineers
13 Church Hill Road
Newtown, CT 06470
Phone: 203-740-5447
Fax: 203-775-8490
Web: www.4spe.org

## Western Plastics Pioneers Scholarship

**Type of award:** Scholarship, renewable.
**Intended use:** For full-time undergraduate study at 2-year or 4-year institution. Designated institutions: Institutions in Arizona, California, Oregon, or Washington state.
**Basis for selection:** Major/career interest in chemistry; engineering, chemical; engineering, mechanical; physics or engineering, industrial. Applicant must demonstrate financial need.
**Application requirements:** Recommendations, essay, transcript. List of current and past school activities and community activities and honors. List of employment history with detailed description of any involvement in plastics/ polymers.
**Additional information:** All applicants must be in good standing with their colleges and must have a demonstrated or expressed interest in the plastics industry. Plastics engineering and polymer science majors also eligible. Visit Website for more information.

| | |
|---|---|
| **Amount of award:** | $2,000 |
| **Number of awards:** | 1 |
| **Application deadline:** | January 15 |
| **Total amount awarded:** | $2,000 |

**Contact:**
Society of Plastics Engineers
13 Church Hill Road
Newtown, CT 06470
Phone: 203-740-5447
Fax: 203-775-8490
Web: www.4spe.org/spe-foundation

# The Society of the Descendants of the Signers of the Declaration of Independence

## Annual Scholarship

**Type of award:** Scholarship, renewable.
**Intended use:** For full-time undergraduate or graduate study at accredited vocational, 2-year, 4-year or graduate institution in or outside United States.
**Basis for selection:** Applicant must demonstrate high academic achievement, depth of character, leadership, patriotism, seriousness of purpose and service orientation.
**Application requirements:** Recommendations, essay, transcript, proof of eligibility. Resume.
**Additional information:** Applicant must be member of the Society of the Descendants of the Signers of the Declaration of Independence. Applicant must reapply for renewal. Number and amount of awards vary. See Website for application deadline and more information.

| | |
|---|---|
| **Number of applicants:** | 90 |
| **Total amount awarded:** | $200,000 |

**Contact:**
Descendants of the Signers of the Declaration of Independence
Scholarship Committee
P.O. Box 8223
Savannah, GA 31412
Web: www.dsdi1776.com

# Society of Women Engineers

## Ada I. Pressman Memorial Scholarship

**Type of award:** Scholarship.
**Intended use:** For full-time sophomore, junior, senior or graduate study at accredited 4-year institution.
**Eligibility:** Applicant must be female. Applicant must be U.S. citizen.
**Basis for selection:** Major/career interest in engineering. Applicant must demonstrate high academic achievement.
**Application requirements:** Recommendations, essay, transcript, proof of eligibility.
**Additional information:** Applicants must be enrolled or plan to be enrolled in ABET- or CSAB-accredited program. Minimum 3.0 GPA. Visit www.abet.org for list of ABET-accredited schools. Visit Website for application. Award amount varies.

| | |
|---|---|
| **Application deadline:** | February 15 |
| **Notification begins:** | June 15 |

**Contact:**
Phone: 312-596-5237
Web: www.societyofwomenengineers.swe.org

## Admiral Grace Murray Hopper Scholarship

**Type of award:** Scholarship.
**Intended use:** For full-time freshman study at accredited 4-year institution in United States.
**Eligibility:** Applicant must be female, high school senior. Applicant must be U.S. citizen or permanent resident.
**Basis for selection:** Major/career interest in engineering or engineering, computer. Applicant must demonstrate high academic achievement.
**Application requirements:** Recommendations, essay, transcript, proof of eligibility.
**Additional information:** Minimum 3.5 GPA. Must not be receiving fulll education funding from another organization. Applicants must plan to enroll in ABET- or CSAB-accredited program or SWE-approved school. Preference given to computer-related engineering majors. Visit www.abet.org for list of ABET-accredited schools. Deadline in mid-May. Visit Website for application. Award amount varies.

**Notification begins:** September 15

**Contact:**
Phone: 312-596-5237
Web: www.societyofwomenengineers.swe.org

## Anne Maureen Whitney Barrow Memorial

**Type of award:** Scholarship.
**Intended use:** For full-time undergraduate study at accredited 4-year institution in United States.
**Eligibility:** Applicant must be female. Applicant must be U.S. citizen or permanent resident.
**Basis for selection:** Major/career interest in engineering.
**Application requirements:** Recommendations, essay, transcript, proof of eligibility.
**Additional information:** Must not be receiving full funding from any other organization. Minimum 3.0 GPA. Applicants must plan to enroll in an ABET- or CSAB-accredited program. Visit www.abet.org for list of ABET-accredited schools. Visit Website for application. Amount of award varies.

**Contact:**
Phone: 312-596-5237
Web: www.societyofwomenengineers.swe.org

## B. K. Krenzer Re-entry Scholarship

**Type of award:** Scholarship.
**Intended use:** For undergraduate or graduate study at accredited 4-year or graduate institution in United States.
**Eligibility:** Applicant must be female, returning adult student. Applicant must be U.S. citizen or permanent resident.
**Basis for selection:** Major/career interest in engineering. Applicant must demonstrate high academic achievement.
**Application requirements:** Recommendations, essay, transcript, proof of eligibility.
**Additional information:** Eligibility restricted to women who have been out of school and the engineering or technology workforce for at least two years prior to re-entry. Applicants must be enrolled or plan to be enrolled in an ABET- or CSAB-accredited program. Visit www.abet.org for list of ABET-accredited schools. Visit Website for application. Amount of award varies.

**Contact:**
Phone: 312-596-5237
Web: www.societyofwomenengineers.swe.org

## Baker Hughes Scholarship

**Type of award:** Scholarship.
**Intended use:** For full-time sophomore, junior, senior or graduate study at accredited 4-year or graduate institution in United States.
**Eligibility:** Applicant must be female. Applicant must be U.S. citizen or permanent resident.
**Basis for selection:** Major/career interest in engineering, chemical; engineering, electrical/electronic; engineering, mechanical or engineering, petroleum. Applicant must demonstrate high academic achievement.
**Application requirements:** Recommendations, essay, transcript, proof of eligibility.
**Additional information:** Underrepresented groups preferred. Must be SWE member. Must not be receiving full funding from any other organization. Applicants must be enrolled or plan to enroll in ABET- or CSAB-accredited program. Minimum 3.0 GPA. Visit www.abet.org for list of ABET-accredited schools. Visit Website for application. Award amount varies.

**Application deadline:** February 15
**Notification begins:** June 15

**Contact:**
Phone: 312-596-5237
Web: www.societyofwomenengineers.swe.org

## Bechtel Foundation Scholarship

**Type of award:** Scholarship.
**Intended use:** For full-time sophomore, junior or senior study at accredited 4-year institution in United States.
**Eligibility:** Applicant must be female. Applicant must be U.S. citizen or permanent resident.
**Basis for selection:** Major/career interest in engineering, civil; engineering, electrical/electronic; engineering, environmental; engineering, mechanical; engineering or architecture. Applicant must demonstrate high academic achievement.
**Application requirements:** Recommendations, essay, transcript, proof of eligibility.
**Additional information:** Must not be receiving full funding from any other organization. Applicant must be member of SWE. Architectural engineering technology majors also eligible. Applicants must be enrolled or plan to be enrolled in an ABET- or CSAB-accredited program. Minimum 3.0 GPA. Visit www.abet.org for list of ABET-accredited schools. Visit Website for application. Award amount varies.

**Application deadline:** February 15
**Notification begins:** June 15

**Contact:**
Phone: 312-596-5237
Web: www.societyofwomenengineers.swe.org

## Bertha Lamme Memorial Scholarship

**Type of award:** Scholarship.
**Intended use:** For full-time freshman study at 4-year institution in United States.
**Eligibility:** Applicant must be female. Applicant must be U.S. citizen.
**Basis for selection:** Major/career interest in engineering, electrical/electronic.
**Application requirements:** Recommendations, transcript, proof of eligibility.
**Additional information:** Minimum 3.5 GPA. Must not be receiving full funding from any other organization. Applicants must plan to enroll in an ABET- or CSAB-accredited program.

Scholarships

Visit www.abet.org for list of ABET-accredited schools. Deadline mid-May. Visit Website for application. Award amount varies.

**Notification begins:** September 15

**Contact:**
Phone: 312-596-5237
Web: www.societyofwomenengineers.swe.org

## B.J. Harrod Scholarships

**Type of award:** Scholarship.
**Intended use:** For full-time freshman study at accredited 4-year institution in United States.
**Eligibility:** Applicant must be female, high school senior. Applicant must be U.S. citizen or permanent resident.
**Basis for selection:** Major/career interest in engineering. Applicant must demonstrate high academic achievement.
**Application requirements:** Essay, transcript, proof of eligibility. Two letters of reference: one from a high school teacher, one from a person who knows the applicant but is not a family member.
**Additional information:** Minimum 3.5 GPA. Must not be receiving full funding from any other organization. Applicants must plan to enroll in an ABET- or CSAB-accredited program. Visit www.abet.org for list of ABET-accredited schools. Deadline in mid-May. Visit Website for application. Amount of award varies.

**Notification begins:** September 15

**Contact:**
Phone: 312-596-5237
Web: www.societyofwomenengineers.swe.org

## Boston Scientific Scholarship

**Type of award:** Scholarship.
**Intended use:** For full-time senior study at 4-year institution in United States. Designated institutions: SWE-approved schools (contact sponsor for list).
**Eligibility:** Applicant must be female. Applicant must be U.S. citizen or permanent resident.
**Basis for selection:** Major/career interest in computer/information sciences; engineering, chemical; engineering, computer; engineering, electrical/electronic; engineering, materials; engineering, mechanical or engineering, industrial. Applicant must demonstrate high academic achievement.
**Application requirements:** Recommendations, essay, transcript, proof of eligibility.
**Additional information:** Manufacturing engineering majors also eligible. Minimum 3.5 GPA. Applicants must be enrolled in an ABET- or CSAB-accredited program. Visit www.abet.org for list of ABET-accredited schools. Must not be receiving full funding from another organization. Visit Website for application. Amount of award varies.

**Application deadline:** February 15
**Notification begins:** June 15

**Contact:**
Phone: 312-596-5237
Web: www.societyofwomenengineers.swe.org

## Brill Family Scholarship

**Type of award:** Scholarship.
**Intended use:** For full-time sophomore, junior or senior study at accredited 4-year institution in United States.
**Eligibility:** Applicant must be female. Applicant must be U.S. citizen or permanent resident.
**Basis for selection:** Major/career interest in biomedical; aerospace or engineering. Applicant must demonstrate high academic achievement.
**Application requirements:** Recommendations, essay, transcript, proof of eligibility.
**Additional information:** Must not be receiving full funding from another organization. Must be aerospace engineering or biomedical engineering major. Applicants must be enrolled or plan to enroll in ABET- or CSAB-accredited program. Minimum 3.0 GPA. Visit www.abet.org for list of ABET-accredited schools. Visit Website for application. Award amount varies.

**Application deadline:** February 15
**Notification begins:** June 15

**Contact:**
Phone: 312-596-5237
Web: www.societyofwomenengineers.swe.org

## Caterpillar Inc. Scholarship

**Type of award:** Scholarship.
**Intended use:** For full-time sophomore, junior, senior or graduate study at 4-year or graduate institution in United States.
**Eligibility:** Applicant must be female.
**Basis for selection:** Major/career interest in engineering, agricultural; engineering, chemical; engineering, electrical/electronic; engineering, materials; engineering, mechanical; engineering or engineering, industrial.
**Application requirements:** Recommendations, essay, transcript, proof of eligibility.
**Additional information:** Manufacturing engineering majors also eligible. Minimum 3.0 GPA. Must not be receiving full funding from any other organization. Applicants must be enrolled in or plan to enroll in ABET- or CSAB-accredited program. Non-U.S. citizens must be eligible to work in U.S. Visit www.abet.org for list of ABET-accredited schools. Visit Website for application. Amount of award varies.

**Application deadline:** February 15
**Notification begins:** June 15

**Contact:**
Phone: 312-596-5237
Web: www.societyofwomenengineers.swe.org

## Central New Mexico Scholarship

**Type of award:** Scholarship, renewable.
**Intended use:** For sophomore, junior, senior or graduate study at 4-year institution. Designated institutions: New Mexico engineering or technology institutions.
**Eligibility:** Applicant must be female. Applicant must be U.S. citizen or permanent resident residing in New Mexico.
**Basis for selection:** Major/career interest in engineering.
**Application requirements:** Recommendations, transcript, proof of eligibility.
**Additional information:** Applicants must be enrolled or plan to enroll in ABET- or CSAB-accredited program. Must not be receiving full funding from another organization. One scholarship available for applicant re-entering the workforce. Minimum 3.0 GPA. Visit www.abet.org for list of ABET-accredited schools. Visit Website for deadline. Amount of award varies.

**Application deadline:** February 15
**Notification begins:** June 15

**Contact:**
Phone: 312-596-5237
Web: www.societyofwomenengineers.swe.org

## Chevron Corporation Scholarship

**Type of award:** Scholarship.
**Intended use:** For full-time sophomore study at accredited 4-year institution in United States.
**Eligibility:** Applicant must be female. Applicant must be U.S. citizen.
**Basis for selection:** Major/career interest in engineering, environmental; engineering, chemical; engineering, petroleum; engineering, mechanical; engineering, electrical/electronic; computer/information sciences or engineering, computer. Applicant must demonstrate high academic achievement.
**Application requirements:** Recommendations, essay, transcript, proof of eligibility.
**Additional information:** Applicant must be active SWE student member. Underrepresented groups preferred. Must not be receiving full funding from another organization. Applicants must be enrolled or plan to be enrolled in ABET- or CSAB-accredited program. Minimum 3.0 GPA. Visit www.abet.org for list of ABET-accredited schools. Visit SWE Website for application. Award amount varies.

**Application deadline:** February 15
**Notification begins:** June 15

**Contact:**
Phone: 312-596-5237
Web: www.societyofwomenengineers.swe.org

## Cummins Scholarship

**Type of award:** Scholarship.
**Intended use:** For full-time sophomore, junior, senior or graduate study at accredited 4-year or graduate institution in United States.
**Eligibility:** Applicant must be female. Applicant must be U.S. citizen.
**Basis for selection:** Major/career interest in engineering; engineering, chemical; engineering, computer; engineering, electrical/electronic; engineering, industrial or engineering, mechanical. Applicant must demonstrate high academic achievement.
**Application requirements:** Recommendations, essay, transcript, proof of eligibility.
**Additional information:** Must not be receiving full funding from another organization. Underrepresented groups preferred. Automotive engineering, manufacturing engineering, and materials science/engineering majors are also eligible. Applicants must be enrolled or plan to enroll in ABET- or CSAB-accredited program. Minimum 3.5 GPA. Visit www.abet.org for list of ABET-accredited schools. Visit SWE Website for deadline. Award amount varies.

**Application deadline:** February 15
**Notification begins:** June 15

**Contact:**
Phone: 312-596-5237
Web: www.societyofwomenengineers.swe.org

## Dell Inc. Scholarship

**Type of award:** Scholarship.
**Intended use:** For full-time junior or senior study at 4-year institution in United States.
**Eligibility:** Applicant must be female. Applicant must be U.S. citizen or permanent resident.
**Basis for selection:** Major/career interest in engineering, electrical/electronic; engineering, computer; engineering, mechanical or computer/information sciences. Applicant must demonstrate financial need.
**Application requirements:** Recommendations, essay, transcript, proof of eligibility.
**Additional information:** Must not be receiving full funding from another organization. Minimum 3.0 GPA. Applicants must be enrolled in an ABET- or CSAB-accredited program. Visit www.abet.org for list of ABET-accredited schools. Visit Website for application. Amount of award varies.

**Application deadline:** February 15
**Notification begins:** June 15

**Contact:**
Phone: 312-596-5237
Web: www.societyofwomenengineers.swe.org

## Dorothy Lemke Howarth Scholarship

**Type of award:** Scholarship.
**Intended use:** For full-time sophomore study at accredited 4-year institution.
**Eligibility:** Applicant must be female. Applicant must be U.S. citizen.
**Basis for selection:** Major/career interest in engineering. Applicant must demonstrate high academic achievement.
**Application requirements:** Recommendations, essay, transcript, proof of eligibility.
**Additional information:** Must not be receiving full funding from another organization. Applicants must be enrolled or plan to enroll in ABET- or CSAB-accredited program. Minimum 3.0 GPA. Visit www.abet.org for list of ABET-accredited schools. Visit Website for application. Award amount varies.

**Application deadline:** February 15
**Notification begins:** June 15

**Contact:**
Phone: 312-596-5237
Web: www.societyofwomenengineers.swe.org

## Dorothy M. & Earl S. Hoffman Scholarship

**Type of award:** Scholarship, renewable.
**Intended use:** For full-time freshman study at accredited 4-year institution in United States. Designated institutions: Bucknell University and Rensselaer Polytechnic University.
**Eligibility:** Applicant must be female, high school senior. Applicant must be U.S. citizen or permanent resident.
**Basis for selection:** Major/career interest in engineering. Applicant must demonstrate high academic achievement.
**Application requirements:** Recommendations, essay, transcript, proof of eligibility.
**Additional information:** Must not be receiving full funding from another organization. Applicants must plan to enroll in ABET- or CSAB-accredited program. Visit www.abet.org for list of ABET-accredited schools. Deadline in mid-May. Visit Website for application. Award amount varies.

**Application deadline:** May 15
**Notification begins:** September 15

**Contact:**
Phone: 312-596-5237
Web: www.societyofwomenengineers.swe.org

## Dorothy P. Morris Scholarship

**Type of award:** Scholarship.
**Intended use:** For full-time sophomore, junior or senior study at 4-year institution in United States.
**Eligibility:** Applicant must be female. Applicant must be U.S. citizen.

**Basis for selection:** Major/career interest in engineering.
**Application requirements:** Recommendations, essay, transcript, proof of eligibility.
**Additional information:** Must not be receiving full funding from any other organization. Minimum 3.0 GPA. Applicants must be enrolled or plan to enroll in an ABET- or CSAB-accredited program. Visit www.abet.org for list of ABET-accredited schools. Visit Website for application. Amount of award varies.

**Application deadline:** February 15
**Notification begins:** June 15

**Contact:**
Phone: 312-596-5237
Web: www.societyofwomenengineers.swe.org

## DuPont Company Scholarship

**Type of award:** Scholarship.
**Intended use:** For full-time sophomore, junior or senior study at 4-year institution in United States. Designated institutions: Eastern and midwestern U.S. institutions.
**Eligibility:** Applicant must be female. Applicant must be U.S. citizen or permanent resident.
**Basis for selection:** Major/career interest in engineering, chemical or engineering, mechanical.
**Application requirements:** Recommendations, transcript, proof of eligibility.
**Additional information:** Must not be receiving full funding from another organization. Minimum 3.0 GPA. Applicants must be enrolled or plan to enroll in ABET- or CSAB-accredited program. Visit www.abet.org for list of ABET-accredited schools. Visit Website for application. Award amount varies.

**Application deadline:** February 15
**Notification begins:** June 15

**Contact:**
Phone: 312-596-5237
Web: www.societyofwomenengineers.swe.org

## Electronics for Imaging Scholarship

**Type of award:** Scholarship.
**Intended use:** For sophomore, junior, senior or graduate study at 4-year or graduate institution in United States. Designated institutions: Approved institutions (contact sponsor for list).
**Eligibility:** Applicant must be female. Applicant must be U.S. citizen or permanent resident.
**Basis for selection:** Major/career interest in engineering.
**Application requirements:** Recommendations, transcript, proof of eligibility.
**Additional information:** Minimum 3.0 GPA. Must not be receiving full funding from any other organization. Applicants must be enrolled in ABET- or CSAB-accredited program. Visit Website for application. Award amount varies.

**Application deadline:** February 15

**Contact:**
Phone: 312-596-5237
Web: www.societyofwomenengineers.swe.org

## Elizabeth McLean Memorial Scholarship

**Type of award:** Scholarship.
**Intended use:** For full-time sophomore, junior or senior study at accredited 4-year institution in United States.
**Eligibility:** Applicant must be female. Applicant must be U.S. citizen or permanent resident.
**Basis for selection:** Major/career interest in engineering, civil.
**Application requirements:** Recommendations, transcript, proof of eligibility.
**Additional information:** Minimum 3.0 GPA. Must not be receiving full funding from any other organization. Applicant must be enrolled in an ABET- or CSAB-accredited degree program. Visit www.abet.org for list of ABET-accredited schools. Visit Website for application. Award amount varies.

**Application deadline:** February 15
**Notification begins:** June 15

**Contact:**
Phone: 312-596-5237
Web: www.societyofwomenengineers.swe.org

## Exelon Scholarship

**Type of award:** Scholarship.
**Intended use:** For full-time freshman study at 4-year institution in United States.
**Eligibility:** Applicant must be female, high school senior. Applicant must be U.S. citizen or permanent resident.
**Basis for selection:** Major/career interest in engineering, electrical/electronic or engineering, mechanical.
**Application requirements:** Recommendations, transcript, proof of eligibility.
**Additional information:** Minimum 3.5 GPA. Applicants must plan to enroll in an ABET- or CSAB-accredited program. Must not be receiving full funding from any other foundation. Visit www.abet.org for list of ABET-accredited schools. Visit Website for application. Deadline in mid-May. Award amount varies.

**Notification begins:** September 15

**Contact:**
Phone: 312-596-5237
Web: www.societyofwomenengineers.swe.org

## Ford Motor Company Scholarship

**Type of award:** Scholarship.
**Intended use:** For full-time sophomore or junior study at accredited 4-year institution.
**Eligibility:** Applicant must be female. Applicant must be U.S. citizen or permanent resident.
**Basis for selection:** Major/career interest in engineering, electrical/electronic; engineering, mechanical; automotive technology; manufacturing or engineering, industrial. Applicant must demonstrate high academic achievement and leadership.
**Application requirements:** Recommendations, transcript, proof of eligibility.
**Additional information:** Manufacturing engineering majors also eligible. Minimum 3.5 GPA. Applicants must be enrolled or plan to enroll in ABET- or CSAB-accredited program. Must not be receiving full funding through another organization. Visit www.abet.org for list of ABET-accredited schools. Visit Website for application. Award amount varies.

**Application deadline:** February 15
**Notification begins:** June 15

**Contact:**
Phone: 312-596-5237
Web: www.societyofwomenengineers.swe.org

## General Electric Women's Network Queretaro, Mexico Scholarship

**Type of award:** Scholarship.
**Intended use:** For full-time freshman, sophomore, junior or senior study at 4-year institution in United States. Designated institutions: Visit Website for list of eligible Mexican universities in Queretaro, Mexico.

**Eligibility:** Applicant must be female, high school senior.
**Basis for selection:** Major/career interest in engineering, electrical/electronic; engineering, mechanical or engineering, industrial.
**Application requirements:** Recommendations, transcript, proof of eligibility.
**Additional information:** Minimum 3.0 GPA. Applicants must plan to enroll in an ABET- or CSAB-accredited program. Must not be receiving full funding from another organization. Visit www.abet.org for list of ABET-accredited schools. Visit Website for application and deadline. Award amount varies.
**Contact:**
Phone: 312-596-5237
Web: www.societyofwomenengineers.swe.org

## General Electric Women's Network Scholarship

**Type of award:** Scholarship.
**Intended use:** For full-time sophomore or junior study at accredited 4-year institution in United States. Designated institutions: Preferred schools (contact sponsor for list).
**Eligibility:** Applicant must be female. Applicant must be U.S. citizen.
**Basis for selection:** Major/career interest in engineering.
**Additional information:** Minimum 3.0 GPA. Must be SWE member. Must not be receiving full funding from any other organization. Visit Website for application. Award amount varies.

**Application deadline:** February 15
**Notification begins:** June 15

**Contact:**
Phone: 312-596-5237
Web: www.societyofwomenengineers.swe.org

## General Motors Foundation Scholarships

**Type of award:** Scholarship, renewable.
**Intended use:** For full-time sophomore or junior study at accredited 4-year institution in United States. Designated institutions: Approved institutions (contact sponsor for list).
**Eligibility:** Applicant must be female. Applicant must be U.S. citizen.
**Basis for selection:** Major/career interest in engineering; automotive technology; engineering, electrical/electronic; engineering, mechanical; manufacturing or engineering, industrial. Applicant must demonstrate high academic achievement and leadership.
**Application requirements:** Recommendations, essay, transcript, proof of eligibility.
**Additional information:** Must not be receiving full funding from another organization. Manufacturing engineering majors also eligible. Applicants must be enrolled or plan to enroll in ABET- or CSAB-accredited program. Applicants should have career interest in automotive industry or manufacturing. Minimum 3.5 GPA. Visit www.abet.org for list of ABET-accredited schools. Visit Website for application. Award amount varies.

**Application deadline:** February 15
**Notification begins:** June 15

**Contact:**
Phone: 312-596-5237
Web: www.societyofwomenengineers.swe.org

## Goldman Sachs Scholarship

**Type of award:** Scholarship.
**Intended use:** For full-time junior or senior study at accredited 4-year institution in United States.
**Eligibility:** Applicant or parent must be member/participant of Society of Women Engineers. Applicant must be female. Applicant must be U.S. citizen or permanent resident.
**Basis for selection:** Major/career interest in engineering, computer; engineering, electrical/electronic or computer/information sciences.
**Application requirements:** Recommendations, transcript, proof of eligibility.
**Additional information:** Minimum 3.2 GPA. Applicants must be enrolled in ABET- or CSAB-accredited program. SWE membership required. Includes travel stipend to annual conference. Must not be receiving full funding from any other organization. Visit www.abet.org for list of ABET-accredited schools. Visit Website for deadline. Award amount varies.

**Application deadline:** February 15
**Notification begins:** June 15

**Contact:**
Phone: 312-596-5237
Web: www.societyofwomenengineers.swe.org

## Honeywell International Inc. Scholarship

**Type of award:** Scholarship.
**Intended use:** For full-time undergraduate study at accredited 4-year institution in United States.
**Eligibility:** Applicant must be female. Applicant must be U.S. citizen.
**Basis for selection:** Major/career interest in engineering, chemical; engineering, computer; engineering, electrical/electronic; engineering, mechanical; engineering, materials; computer/information sciences; aerospace; architecture; manufacturing or engineering, industrial. Applicant must demonstrate financial need and high academic achievement.
**Application requirements:** Recommendations, transcript, proof of eligibility.
**Additional information:** Minimum 3.5 GPA. Architectural and manufacturing engineering majors also eligible. Some state restrictions. Underrepresented groups preferred. Must not be receiving funding from any other organization. Applicants must be enrolled or plan to enroll in ABET- or CSAB-accredited program. Visit www.abet.org for list of ABET-accredited schools. Visit Website for application and deadline. Award amount varies.
**Contact:**
Phone: 312-596-5237
Web: www.societyofwomenengineers.swe.org

## IBM Corporation Scholarship

**Type of award:** Scholarship.
**Intended use:** For full-time sophomore or junior study at accredited 4-year institution in United States.
**Eligibility:** Applicant must be female. Applicant must be U.S. citizen.
**Basis for selection:** Major/career interest in engineering, electrical/electronic; engineering, computer or computer/information sciences.
**Application requirements:** Recommendations, transcript, proof of eligibility.
**Additional information:** Underrepresented groups preferred. Must not be receiving full funding from another organization. Applicants must be enrolled or plan to enroll in ABET- or

Scholarships

CSAB-accredited program. Minimum 3.4 GPA. Visit www.abet.org for list of ABET-accredited schools. Visit Website for application. Award amount varies.

**Application deadline:** February 15
**Notification begins:** June 15

**Contact:**
Phone: 312-596-5237
Web: www.societyofwomenengineers.swe.org

## ITT Scholarship

**Type of award:** Scholarship, renewable.
**Intended use:** For full-time junior, senior or graduate study at accredited 4-year or graduate institution in United States. Designated institutions: Contact sponsor for list of preferred institutions.
**Eligibility:** Applicant must be female. Applicant must be U.S. citizen or permanent resident.
**Basis for selection:** Major/career interest in engineering, chemical; engineering, civil; computer/information sciences; engineering, environmental; engineering, industrial; engineering, mechanical or engineering, electrical/electronic. Applicant must demonstrate high academic achievement.
**Application requirements:** Recommendations, essay, transcript, proof of eligibility.
**Additional information:** Manufacturing engineering, aerospace engineering, and electronic engineering technology majors also eligible. Must not be receiving full funding from another organization. Applicants must be enrolled or plan to enroll in ABET- or CSAB-accredited program. Minimum 3.5 GPA. Visit www.abet.org for list of ABET-accredited schools. Visit Website for application. Award amount varies.

**Application deadline:** February 15
**Notification begins:** June 15

**Contact:**
Phone: 312-596-5237
Web: www.societyofwomenengineers.swe.org

## Ivy Parker Memorial Scholarship

**Type of award:** Scholarship.
**Intended use:** For full-time junior or senior study at accredited 4-year institution in United States.
**Eligibility:** Applicant must be female. Applicant must be U.S. citizen or permanent resident.
**Basis for selection:** Major/career interest in engineering. Applicant must demonstrate financial need and high academic achievement.
**Application requirements:** Recommendations, essay, transcript, proof of eligibility.
**Additional information:** Applicants must be enrolled in ABET- or CSAB-accredited program. Minimum 3.0 GPA. Must not be receiving full funding from any other organization. Visit www.abet.org for list of ABET-accredited schools. Visit Website for application. Award amount varies.

**Application deadline:** February 15
**Notification begins:** June 15

**Contact:**
Phone: 312-596-5237
Web: www.societyofwomenengineers.swe.org

## Jill S. Tietjen P.E. Scholarship

**Type of award:** Scholarship.
**Intended use:** For full-time sophomore, junior or senior study at accredited 4-year institution in United States.
**Eligibility:** Applicant must be female. Applicant must be U.S. citizen.
**Basis for selection:** Major/career interest in engineering.
**Application requirements:** Recommendations, transcript, proof of eligibility.
**Additional information:** Applicants must be enrolled or plan to enroll in ABET- or CSAB-accredited program. Minimum 3.0 GPA. Must not be receiving full funding from any other organization. Visit www.abet.org for list of ABET-accredited schools. Visit Website for application. Award amount varies.

**Application deadline:** February 15
**Notification begins:** June 15

**Contact:**
Phone: 312-596-5237
Web: www.societyofwomenengineers.swe.org

## Judith Resnik Memorial Scholarship

**Type of award:** Scholarship.
**Intended use:** For full-time sophomore, junior or senior study at accredited 4-year institution.
**Eligibility:** Applicant must be female. Applicant must be U.S. citizen or permanent resident.
**Basis for selection:** Major/career interest in engineering or aerospace. Applicant must demonstrate high academic achievement.
**Application requirements:** Recommendations, essay, transcript, proof of eligibility.
**Additional information:** Must be aeronautical/aerospace engineering or astronautical engineering major. Applicants must be enrolled or plan to enroll in ABET- or CSAB-accredited program. Applicant must be SWE student member. Minimum 3.0 GPA. Must not be receiving full funding from another organization. Visit www.abet.org for list of ABET-accredited schools. Visit Website for application. Award amount varies.

**Application deadline:** February 15
**Notification begins:** June 15

**Contact:**
Phone: 312-596-5237
Web: www.societyofwomenengineers.swe.org

## Lillian Moller Gilbreth Scholarship

**Type of award:** Scholarship.
**Intended use:** For full-time junior or senior study at accredited 4-year institution in United States.
**Eligibility:** Applicant must be female. Applicant must be U.S. citizen or permanent resident.
**Basis for selection:** Major/career interest in engineering. Applicant must demonstrate high academic achievement.
**Application requirements:** Recommendations, essay, transcript, proof of eligibility.
**Additional information:** Renewable for continuing undergraduate study only. Applicants must be enrolled in ABET- or CSAB-accredited program. Minimum 3.0 GPA. Must not be receiving full funding from any other organization. Visit www.abet.org for list of ABET-accredited schools. Visit Website for application. Award amount varies.

**Application deadline:** February 15
**Notification begins:** June 15

**Contact:**
Phone: 312-596-5237
Web: www.societyofwomenengineers.swe.org

## Lockheed Martin Freshman Scholarships

**Type of award:** Scholarship.
**Intended use:** For full-time freshman study at accredited 4-year institution in United States.
**Eligibility:** Applicant must be female, high school senior. Applicant must be U.S. citizen or permanent resident.
**Basis for selection:** Major/career interest in engineering. Applicant must demonstrate high academic achievement.
**Application requirements:** Recommendations, essay, transcript, proof of eligibility.
**Additional information:** Minimum 3.5 GPA. Must not be receiving full funding from any other organization. Includes travel grant for SWE National Conference. Applicants must plan to enroll in an ABET- or CSAB-accredited program. Visit www.abet.org for list of ABET-accredited schools. Deadline in mid-May. Visit Website for application. Award amount varies.

**Notification begins:** September 15

**Contact:**
Phone: 312-596-5237
Web: www.societyofwomenengineers.swe.org

## Lydia I. Pickup Memorial Scholarship

**Type of award:** Scholarship.
**Intended use:** For full-time sophomore, junior, senior or graduate study at accredited 4-year or graduate institution in United States.
**Eligibility:** Applicant must be female. Applicant must be U.S. citizen or permanent resident.
**Basis for selection:** Major/career interest in engineering. Applicant must demonstrate high academic achievement.
**Application requirements:** Recommendations, essay, transcript, proof of eligibility.
**Additional information:** Graduate students are preferred, but undergraduate sophomores, juniors, and seniors are encouraged to apply. Applicants must be enrolled or plan to enroll in ABET- or CSAB-accredited program. Minimum 3.0 GPA. Must not be receiving full funding from another organization. Visit www.abet.org for list of ABET-accredited schools. Visit Website for application. Amount of award varies.

**Application deadline:** February 15
**Notification begins:** June 15

**Contact:**
Phone: 312-596-5237
Web: www.societyofwomenengineers.swe.org

## Mary V. Munger Scholarship

**Type of award:** Scholarship.
**Intended use:** For full-time sophomore, junior or senior study at accredited 4-year institution in United States.
**Eligibility:** Applicant must be female. Applicant must be U.S. citizen.
**Basis for selection:** Major/career interest in engineering. Applicant must demonstrate high academic achievement.
**Application requirements:** Recommendations, essay, transcript, proof of eligibility.
**Additional information:** Applicants must be enrolled or plan to enroll in ABET- or CSAB-accredited program. Minimum 3.0 GPA. Must be SWE member. Must not be receiving full funding through any other organization. Visit www.abet.org for list of ABET-accredited schools. Visit Website for application. Amount of award varies.

**Application deadline:** February 15
**Notification begins:** June 15

**Contact:**
Phone: 312-596-5237
Web: www.societyofwomenengineers.swe.org

## MASWE Scholarships

**Type of award:** Scholarship.
**Intended use:** For full-time sophomore, junior or senior study at accredited 4-year institution in United States.
**Eligibility:** Applicant must be female. Applicant must be U.S. citizen or permanent resident.
**Basis for selection:** Major/career interest in engineering. Applicant must demonstrate financial need and high academic achievement.
**Application requirements:** Recommendations, essay, transcript, proof of eligibility.
**Additional information:** Applicants must be enrolled or plan to enroll in ABET- or CSAB-accredited program. Minimum 3.0 GPA. Must not be receiving full funding from any other organization. Visit www.abet.org for list of ABET-accredited schools. Visit Website for application. Award amount varies.

**Application deadline:** February 15
**Notification begins:** June 15

**Contact:**
Phone: 312-596-5237
Web: www.societyofwomenengineers.swe.org

## Meridith Thoms Memorial Scholarships

**Type of award:** Scholarship.
**Intended use:** For full-time sophomore, junior or senior study at accredited 4-year institution in United States.
**Eligibility:** Applicant must be female. Applicant must be U.S. citizen or permanent resident.
**Basis for selection:** Major/career interest in engineering. Applicant must demonstrate high academic achievement.
**Application requirements:** Recommendations, essay, transcript, proof of eligibility.
**Additional information:** Minimum 3.0 GPA. Applicants must be enrolled or plan to enroll in an ABET- or CSAB-accredited program. Must not be receiving full funding from any other organization. Visit www.abet.org for list of ABET-accredited schools. Visit Website for application. Award amount varies.

**Application deadline:** February 15
**Notification begins:** June 15

**Contact:**
Phone: 312-596-5237
Web: www.societyofwomenengineers.swe.org

## New Jersey Scholarship

**Type of award:** Scholarship.
**Intended use:** For full-time freshman study at accredited 4-year institution in United States.
**Eligibility:** Applicant must be female, high school senior. Applicant must be U.S. citizen or permanent resident residing in New Jersey.
**Basis for selection:** Major/career interest in engineering. Applicant must demonstrate high academic achievement.
**Application requirements:** Recommendations, essay, transcript, proof of eligibility.
**Additional information:** Minimum 3.5 GPA. Must not be receiving full funding from any other scholarship. Applicants must plan to enroll in an ABET- or CSAB-accredited program. Visit www.abet.org for list of ABET-accredited schools.

Deadline mid-May. Visit Website for application. Amount of award varies.

**Notification begins:** September 15

**Contact:**
Phone: 312-596-5237
Web: www.societyofwomenengineers.swe.org

## Northrop Grumman Corporation Scholarship

**Type of award:** Scholarship.
**Intended use:** For full-time sophomore, junior or senior study at accredited 4-year institution in United States.
**Eligibility:** Applicant must be female. Applicant must be U.S. citizen.
**Basis for selection:** Major/career interest in engineering, materials; engineering, civil; engineering, computer; computer/information sciences; engineering, electrical/electronic or engineering, industrial. Applicant must demonstrate high academic achievement.
**Application requirements:** Recommendations, essay, transcript, proof of eligibility.
**Additional information:** Systems engineering and aerospace engineering majors also eligible. Minimum 3.0 GPA. Applicants must plan to enroll in ABET- or CSAB-accredited program. Application forms available through deans of engineering at eligible schools, through SWE sections, SWE student sections, SWE headquarters, or on Website. Visit www.abet.org for list of ABET-accredited schools.

**Amount of award:** $5,000
**Number of awards:** 5
**Application deadline:** February 15
**Notification begins:** June 15

**Contact:**
Phone: 312-596-5237
Web: www.societyofwomenengineers.swe.org

## Olive Lynn Salembier Re-entry Scholarship

**Type of award:** Scholarship.
**Intended use:** For undergraduate or graduate study at accredited 4-year or graduate institution in United States.
**Eligibility:** Applicant must be female, returning adult student. Applicant must be U.S. citizen or permanent resident.
**Basis for selection:** Major/career interest in engineering.
**Application requirements:** Recommendations, essay, transcript, proof of eligibility.
**Additional information:** Minimum 3.0 GPA. Must not be receiving full funding from any other organization. Must have been out of school or engineering workforce at least two years prior to re-entry. Applicants must be enrolled or plan to enroll in ABET- or CSAB-accredited program. Visit www.abet.org for list of ABET-accredited schools. Upperclassman deadline February 15; freshman deadline mid-May. Visit Website for application. Amount of award varies.

**Application deadline:** February 15
**Notification begins:** June 15, September 15

**Contact:**
Phone: 312-596-5237
Web: www.societyofwomenengineers.swe.org

## Rockwell Automation Scholarships

**Type of award:** Scholarship.
**Intended use:** For full-time junior or senior study at accredited 4-year institution in United States.
**Eligibility:** Applicant must be female. Applicant must be U.S. citizen or permanent resident.
**Basis for selection:** Major/career interest in engineering; engineering, computer; engineering, electrical/electronic; engineering, mechanical; computer/information sciences; manufacturing or engineering, industrial. Applicant must demonstrate leadership.
**Application requirements:** Recommendations, essay, transcript, proof of eligibility.
**Additional information:** Must not be receiving full funding from another organization. Software engineering and manufacturing engineering majors also eligible. Applicants must be enrolled in ABET- or CSAB-accredited program. Minimum 3.0 GPA. Visit www.abet.org for list of ABET-accredited schools. Visit Website for application. Amount of award varies.

**Application deadline:** February 15
**Notification begins:** June 15

**Contact:**
Phone: 312-596-5237
Web: www.societyofwomenengineers.swe.org

## Susan Miszkowitz Memorial Scholarship

**Type of award:** Scholarship.
**Intended use:** For full-time sophomore, junior or senior study at accredited 4-year institution in United States.
**Eligibility:** Applicant must be female. Applicant must be U.S. citizen or permanent resident.
**Basis for selection:** Major/career interest in engineering. Applicant must demonstrate high academic achievement.
**Application requirements:** Recommendations, transcript, proof of eligibility.
**Additional information:** Minimum 3.0 GPA. Applicants must be enrolled or plan to enroll in an ABET- or CSAB-accredited program. Visit www.abet.org for list of ABET-accredited schools. Visit website for application. Award amount varies.

**Application deadline:** February 15
**Notification begins:** June 15

**Contact:**
Phone: 312-596-5237
Web: www.societyofwomenengineers.swe.org

## The SWE Past Presidents Scholarships

**Type of award:** Scholarship.
**Intended use:** For full-time sophomore, junior, senior or graduate study at accredited 4-year or graduate institution in United States.
**Eligibility:** Applicant must be female. Applicant must be U.S. citizen.
**Basis for selection:** Major/career interest in engineering. Applicant must demonstrate high academic achievement.
**Application requirements:** Recommendations, essay, transcript, proof of eligibility.
**Additional information:** Must not be receiving funding from another organization. Minimum 3.0 GPA. Applicants must be enrolled or plan to enroll in an ABET- or CSAB-accredited program. Visit www.abet.org for list of ABET-accredited schools. Visit Website for application. Amount of award varies.

**Application deadline:** February 15
**Notification begins:** June 15

**Contact:**
Phone: 312-596-5237
Web: www.societyofwomenengineers.swe.org

### The SWE Phoenix Section Scholarship

**Type of award:** Scholarship.
**Intended use:** For full-time freshman study at accredited 4-year institution in United States.
**Eligibility:** Applicant must be high school senior. Applicant must be U.S. citizen or permanent resident residing in Arizona.
**Basis for selection:** Major/career interest in engineering. Applicant must demonstrate high academic achievement.
**Application requirements:** Recommendations, essay, transcript, proof of eligibility.
**Additional information:** Minimum 3.5 GPA. Non-residents attending school in Arizona also eligible. Applicants must plan to enroll in an ABET- or CSAB-accredited program. Visit www.abet.org for list of ABET-accredited schools. Deadline in mid-May. Visit Website for application. Amount of award varies.

**Notification begins:** September 15

**Contact:**
Phone: 312-596-5237
Web: www.societyofwomenengineers.swe.org

## Sodexo Foundation

### STOP Hunger Scholarships

**Type of award:** Scholarship.
**Intended use:** For undergraduate, graduate, postgraduate or non-degree study at accredited postsecondary institution in United States.
**Eligibility:** Applicant must be U.S. citizen or permanent resident.
**Basis for selection:** Applicant must demonstrate service orientation.
**Application requirements:** Recommendations.
**Additional information:** Awards open to applicants from kindergarten through graduate school who have performed unpaid, U.S. hunger-related volunteer services within the last 12 months. Added consideration for applicants fighting childhood hunger. Employees of Sodexo and previous recipients not eligible to apply, but previous regional STOP Hunger Honorees may apply. Award recipients will receive a $5,000 scholarship and a $5,000 grant to the local hunger-related charity of their choice. Deadline in mid-February. Visit Website for date, application and details. Apply via email.

| | |
|---|---|
| **Amount of award:** | $5,000 |
| **Number of awards:** | 5 |
| **Number of applicants:** | 7,000 |
| **Total amount awarded:** | $25,000 |

**Contact:**
Phone: 800-763-3946 ext. 44848
Web: www.sodexofoundation.org/hunger_us/scholarships/scholarships.asp

## Soil and Water Conservation Society

### Melville H. Cohee Student Leader Conservation Scholarship

**Type of award:** Scholarship.
**Intended use:** For full-time junior, senior or graduate study at accredited 4-year or graduate institution.
**Eligibility:** Applicant or parent must be member/participant of Soil and Water Conservation Society.
**Basis for selection:** Major/career interest in natural resources/conservation.
**Additional information:** Must have been member of SWCS for at least 1 year. Family members of the Professional Development Committee not eligible. Visit Website for application and deadline.

| | |
|---|---|
| **Amount of award:** | $500 |
| **Number of awards:** | 1 |

**Contact:**
SWCS-Scholarship
945 SW Ankeny Rd.
Ankeny, IA 50023
Phone: 515-289-2331
Fax: 515-289-1227
Web: www.swcs.org

## Sons of Italy Foundation

### Charles Evans Scholarship

**Type of award:** Scholarship.
**Intended use:** For undergraduate or graduate study at accredited 4-year or graduate institution in United States.
**Eligibility:** Applicant must be Italian. Applicant must be U.S. citizen.
**Application requirements:** $30 application fee. Recommendations, essay, transcript. Standardized test scores, resume.
**Additional information:** Must have at least one Italian or Italian American grandparent. $30 processing fee includes a one-year national at-large membership to the Order Sons of Italy in America and a subscription to Italian America magazine.

**Application deadline:** February 28

**Contact:**
Sons of Italy Foundation
219 E Street, NE
Washington, DC 20002
Phone: 202-547-2900
Web: www.osia.org

### General Scholarship

**Type of award:** Scholarship.
**Intended use:** For undergraduate or graduate study at accredited 4-year institution.
**Eligibility:** Applicant must be Italian. Applicant must be U.S. citizen.
**Application requirements:** $30 application fee. Recommendations, essay, transcript. Resume, cover letter. SAT/ACT scores.
**Additional information:** Must have at least one Italian or Italian-American grandparent. Visit Website for application.

**Application deadline:** February 28

**Contact:**
Sons of Italy Foundation
219 E Street NE
Washington, DC 20002
Phone: 202-547-2900
Web: www.osia.org

Scholarships

## Henry Salvatori Scholarship

**Type of award:** Scholarship.
**Intended use:** For full-time undergraduate study.
**Eligibility:** Applicant must be high school senior. Applicant must be Italian. Applicant must be U.S. citizen.
**Basis for selection:** Applicant must demonstrate high academic achievement, depth of character, leadership, patriotism, seriousness of purpose and service orientation.
**Application requirements:** $30 application fee. Essay, transcript, proof of eligibility. SAT/ACT scores. Cover letter, resume. Two letters of recommendation from public figures who have demonstrated the ideals of liberty, freedom, and equality in their work.
**Additional information:** Must have at least one Italian or Italian-American grandparent. Visit Website for application.

| | |
|---|---|
| **Amount of award:** | $5,000 |
| **Number of awards:** | 1 |
| **Number of applicants:** | 200 |
| **Application deadline:** | February 28 |
| **Notification begins:** | April 15 |
| **Total amount awarded:** | $5,000 |

**Contact:**
Sons of Italy Foundation
219 E Street NE
Washington, DC 20002
Phone: 202-547-2900
Web: www.osia.org

## Italian Language Scholarship

**Type of award:** Scholarship.
**Intended use:** For junior or senior study.
**Eligibility:** Applicant must be Italian. Applicant must be U.S. citizen.
**Basis for selection:** Major/career interest in Italian.
**Application requirements:** $30 application fee. Recommendations, essay, transcript. Resume, cover letter. SAT/ACT scores. Essay must be in Italian.
**Additional information:** Must have at least one Italian or Italian-American grandparent. Visit Website for application.

| | |
|---|---|
| **Application deadline:** | February 28 |

**Contact:**
Sons of Italy Foundation
219 E Street NE
Washington, DC 20002
Phone: 202-547-2900
Web: www.osia.org

## National Leadership Grant

**Type of award:** Scholarship.
**Intended use:** For full-time undergraduate, master's, doctoral or first professional study at accredited 4-year or graduate institution in United States.
**Eligibility:** Applicant must be Italian. Applicant must be U.S. citizen.
**Basis for selection:** Applicant must demonstrate high academic achievement, depth of character, leadership, seriousness of purpose and service orientation.
**Application requirements:** $30 application fee. Recommendations, essay, transcript, proof of eligibility. SAT/ACT scores, resume.
**Additional information:** Must have at least one Italian or Italian-American grandparent. Amount and number of awards vary. Visit Website for application.

| | |
|---|---|
| **Amount of award:** | $5,000-$25,000 |
| **Number of awards:** | 12 |
| **Number of applicants:** | 600 |
| **Application deadline:** | February 28 |
| **Notification begins:** | April 15 |

**Contact:**
Sons of Italy Foundation
219 E Street NE
Washington, DC 20002
Phone: 202-547-2900
Web: www.osia.org

## Sorrento Lingue Scholarship

**Type of award:** Scholarship.
**Intended use:** For junior, senior or graduate study at accredited postsecondary institution outside United States.
**Eligibility:** Applicant must be Italian. Applicant must be U.S. citizen.
**Basis for selection:** Major/career interest in Italian.
**Application requirements:** $30 application fee. Recommendations, essay, transcript. Essay must be submitted in Italian. SAT/ACT scores. Resume, cover letter.
**Additional information:** Scholarship for study abroad in Sorrento, Italy from January to June. Must have at least one Italian or Italian-American grandparent. Basic knowledge of Italian language preferred. Visit Website for application and more information.

| | |
|---|---|
| **Application deadline:** | February 28 |

**Contact:**
Sons of Italy Foundation
219 E Street NE
Washington, DC 20002
Phone: 202-547-2900
Web: www.osia.org

# Sons of Norway Foundation

## Astrid G. Cates Scholarship Fund and Myrtle Beinhauer Scholarship

**Type of award:** Scholarship.
**Intended use:** For undergraduate study at postsecondary institution.
**Eligibility:** Applicant or parent must be member/participant of Sons of Norway. Applicant must be U.S. citizen.
**Basis for selection:** Applicant must demonstrate financial need, high academic achievement, depth of character and service orientation.
**Application requirements:** Recommendations, transcript, proof of eligibility.
**Additional information:** Applicant, parent, or grandparent must be current member of Sons of Norway District 1-6. Student must include the following information with application: GPA, what type of study is intended, where and when. Related fees must be specified, as well as long-term career goals, Sons of Norway involvement, extracurricular activities and financial need. The Cates Scholarship is $1,000; Beinhauer Scholarship awards $3,000 to the most qualified of all candidates. Student can be awarded maximum two scholarships within five-year period. Visit Website for application.

**Amount of award:** $1,000-$3,000
**Number of awards:** 8
**Number of applicants:** 99
**Application deadline:** March 1
**Notification begins:** May 1

**Contact:**
Sons of Norway Foundation
Attn: Cates/Beinhauer Scholarship
1455 West Lake Street
Minneapolis, MN 55408-2666
Web: www.sonsofnorway.com/foundation

## King Olav V Norwegian-American Heritage Fund

**Type of award:** Scholarship.
**Intended use:** For full-time undergraduate or graduate study at accredited postsecondary institution in United States.
**Eligibility:** Applicant must be at least 18.
**Basis for selection:** Major/career interest in Scandinavian studies/research. Applicant must demonstrate financial need, high academic achievement, depth of character, leadership and service orientation.
**Application requirements:** Recommendations, transcript, proof of eligibility. SAT or ACT scores. Essay of maximum 500 words about reasons for application; course of study to be pursued; length of the course; name, tuition, and other costs of institution; amount of financial assistance desired; and how the applicant's course of study will benefit his or her community and accord with the goals and objectives of the Sons of Norway Foundation.
**Additional information:** Open to Americans who have demonstrated keen and sincere interest in Norwegian heritage or Norwegians who have demonstrated interest in American heritage and have desire to further study heritage (arts, crafts, literature, history, music, folklore, etc.) at recognized educational institution. Number and amount of awards varies. Visit Website for application.

**Amount of award:** $1,000-$1,500
**Number of awards:** 7
**Number of applicants:** 100
**Application deadline:** March 1
**Notification begins:** May 1

**Contact:**
Sons of Norway Foundation
Attn: King Olav Fund
1455 West Lake Street
Minneapolis, MN 55408-2666
Web: www.sonsofnorway.com/foundation

## Nancy Lorraine Jensen Memorial Scholarship

**Type of award:** Scholarship, renewable.
**Intended use:** For full-time undergraduate study.
**Eligibility:** Applicant or parent must be member/participant of Sons of Norway. Applicant must be female, at least 17, no older than 35. Applicant must be U.S. citizen.
**Basis for selection:** Major/career interest in chemistry; physics; engineering, electrical/electronic; engineering, mechanical or engineering, chemical. Applicant must demonstrate high academic achievement, depth of character and seriousness of purpose.
**Application requirements:** Recommendations, essay, transcript, proof of eligibility. SAT/ACT scores.
**Additional information:** Applicant or applicant's parent or grandparent must have been a member of Sons of Norway for at least three years. Must have completed at least one semester of undergraduate study in current program. Award is no less than 50 percent of one semester's tuition and no more than full tuition for one year. Minimum 1800 SAT (or at least 600 Math) or 26 ACT. Must apply each year. Visit Website for application.

**Number of awards:** 6
**Application deadline:** April 1

**Contact:**
Sons of Norway Foundation
Attn: Nancy L. Jensen Memorial Scholarship
1455 West Lake Street
Minneapolis, MN 55408-2666
Web: www.sonsofnorway.com/foundation

# Sons of the Republic of Texas

## Texas History Essay Scholarship

**Type of award:** Scholarship.
**Intended use:** For undergraduate study at 4-year institution.
**Eligibility:** Applicant must be high school senior.
**Basis for selection:** Competition/talent/interest in research paper, based on depth of research in Texas history, originality of thought and expression, and organization.
**Application requirements:** Four photocopies of essay (total of 5 copies) including a CD copy with contestant's name, address, phone number and year of contest.
**Additional information:** Graduating seniors of any high school or home school may enter. Must follow Chicago Manual of Style or Turabian's Manual for Writers. Visit Website for yearly topic and more information.

**Amount of award:** $1,000-$3,000
**Number of awards:** 3
**Application deadline:** January 31
**Total amount awarded:** $6,000

**Contact:**
Sons of the Republic of Texas
1717 8th Street
Bay City, TX 77414
Phone: 979-245-6644
Web: www.srttexas.org/essay.html

# South Carolina Commission on Higher Education

## Dayco Scholarship Program

**Type of award:** Scholarship, renewable.
**Intended use:** For full-time freshman study at 4-year institution in United States. Designated institutions: South Carolina institutions.
**Eligibility:** Applicant must be high school senior. Applicant must be U.S. citizen or permanent resident residing in South Carolina.
**Basis for selection:** Applicant must demonstrate financial need and high academic achievement.
**Application requirements:** Transcript, proof of eligibility. Need analysis, affidavit documenting that student has never

been convicted of felonies or alcohol- or drug-related misdemeanor offenses.
**Additional information:** Must be either an employee or dependent of an employee of a branch of Dayco Products, Inc. in South Carolina. Employee must be employed by Dayco for at least four calendar years. In the event that there are no eligible dependents meeting above criteria, the award will be given to a resident of one of the counties of Walterboro, Williston, or Easley. Minimum 3.25 GPA. Must rank in top 20% of graduating high school class. Must have completed 12 credit hours at time of scholarship disbursement. Must not owe refund or repayment to a grant program or be under default on a loan. Must not have criminal record. Must reapply and meet eligibility requirements annually. Amount of award varies.
**Contact:**
South Carolina Commission on Higher Education
1333 Main Street, Suite 200
Columbia, SC 29201
Phone: 803-737-2260
Fax: 803-737-2297
Web: www.che.sc.gov

## LIFE Scholarship Program

**Type of award:** Scholarship, renewable.
**Intended use:** For full-time freshman study at vocational, 2-year or 4-year institution. Designated institutions: Eligible institutions in South Carolina.
**Eligibility:** Applicant must be U.S. citizen or permanent resident residing in South Carolina.
**Basis for selection:** Applicant must demonstrate high academic achievement.
**Application requirements:** Transcript. SAT/ACT scores.
**Additional information:** First-time entering freshmen at four-year institutions must meet two of three criteria: 3.0 high school GPA on Uniform Grading Policy (UGP); minimum 1100 SAT or 24 ACT; rank in top 30 percent of graduating class. First-time entering freshmen at two-year institution must have 3.0 high school GPA on UGP. Applicant must graduate from high school as South Carolina resident. No application required; college/university will determine eligibility based on transcript and will notify student directly. Maximum award $5,000 for four-year schools, average in-state tuition for two-year schools, and up to full in-state tuition at technical schools, not to exceed $5,000. Students in approved math and science programs could earn an additional $2,500.

| | |
|---|---|
| **Amount of award:** | $5,000 |
| **Number of awards:** | 31,004 |
| **Total amount awarded:** | $150,595,333 |

**Contact:**
South Carolina Commission on Higher Education
1333 Main Street, Suite 200
Columbia, SC 29201
Phone: 803-737-2260
Fax: 803-737-2297
Web: www.che.sc.gov

## Lottery Tuition Assistance Program

**Type of award:** Scholarship, renewable.
**Intended use:** For undergraduate study at vocational or 2-year institution. Designated institutions: Eligible South Carolina institutions.
**Eligibility:** Applicant must be U.S. citizen or permanent resident residing in South Carolina.
**Application requirements:** FAFSA or FAFSA waiver.
**Additional information:** Award may not exceed cost of tuition. Award based on lottery revenue and number of applicants. Amount varies by semester. All federal grants and need-based grants must be awarded first before determining amount for which student is eligible. Student must be degree-seeking and enrolled in minimum six credit hours. Visit Website for more information.

| | |
|---|---|
| **Number of awards:** | 45,628 |
| **Number of applicants:** | 59,486 |
| **Total amount awarded:** | $47,641,997 |

**Contact:**
South Carolina Commission on Higher Education
1333 Main Street, Suite 200
Columbia, SC 29201
Phone: 803-737-2262
Fax: 803-737-2297
Web: www.che.sc.gov

## Palmetto Fellows Scholarship Program

**Type of award:** Scholarship, renewable.
**Intended use:** For full-time undergraduate study at 4-year institution. Designated institutions: Eligible South Carolina institutions.
**Eligibility:** Applicant must be high school senior. Applicant must be U.S. citizen or permanent resident residing in South Carolina.
**Basis for selection:** Applicant must demonstrate high academic achievement.
**Application requirements:** Transcript. ACT/SAT scores. Must apply through guidance counselor.
**Additional information:** Minimum 1200 SAT (Math and Reading) or 27 ACT, 3.5 GPA on the SC Uniform Grading Policy, and rank in top six percent of class. Class ranking requirement waived for students with 1400 SAT (Math and Reading) or 32 ACT and 4.0 GPA. High school graduates or students who have completed home-school program as prescribed by law may be eligible. For more information, contact guidance counselor or S.C. Commission.

| | |
|---|---|
| **Amount of award:** | $6,700-$7,500 |
| **Application deadline:** | December 15, June 15 |
| **Notification begins:** | February 15, August 15 |
| **Total amount awarded:** | $44,035,892 |

**Contact:**
South Carolina Commission on Higher Education
1333 Main Street, Suite 200
Columbia, SC 29201
Phone: 877-349-7183 or 803-787-2286
Fax: 803-737-2297
Web: www.che.sc.gov

## South Carolina HOPE Scholarships

**Type of award:** Scholarship.
**Intended use:** For freshman study at 4-year institution. Designated institutions: Eligible South Carolina institutions.
**Eligibility:** Applicant must be U.S. citizen or permanent resident residing in South Carolina.
**Basis for selection:** Applicant must demonstrate high academic achievement.
**Application requirements:** Transcript, proof of eligibility.
**Additional information:** No application necessary. College or university will determine eligibility based on official high school transcript and will notify students directly. Minimum 3.0 cumulative GPA upon high school graduation. Student must certify that he/she has not been convicted of any felonies or any second drug/alcohol misdemeanors within past academic year. Contact institution's financial aid office for more information.

**Amount of award:** $2,800
**Number of awards:** 2,724
**Total amount awarded:** $7,037,260

**Contact:**
South Carolina Commission on Higher Education
1333 Main Street, Suite 200
Columbia, SC 29201
Phone: 803-737-2260
Fax: 803-737-2297
Web: www.che.sc.gov

### South Carolina Need-Based Grants Program

**Type of award:** Scholarship.
**Intended use:** For undergraduate study at vocational, 2-year or 4-year institution. Designated institutions: Eligible South Carolina public institutions.
**Eligibility:** Applicant must be U.S. citizen or permanent resident residing in South Carolina.
**Basis for selection:** Applicant must demonstrate financial need.
**Application requirements:** FAFSA.
**Additional information:** May receive award for maximum eight full-time equivalent terms or until degree is earned, whichever is less. Must enroll in at least 12 credit hours per semester if full-time or six if part-time. Visit Website for more information.

**Amount of award:** $1,250-$2,500
**Number of awards:** 28,051
**Number of applicants:** 28,507
**Total amount awarded:** $26,989,583

**Contact:**
South Carolina Commission on Higher Education
1333 Main Street, Suite 200
Columbia, SC 29201
Phone: 803-737-2262
Fax: 803-737-2297
Web: www.che.sc.gov

## South Carolina Higher Education Tuition Grants Commission

### South Carolina Tuition Grants

**Type of award:** Scholarship, renewable.
**Intended use:** For full-time undergraduate study at accredited 2-year or 4-year institution in United States. Designated institutions: SACS-accredited South Carolina private, nonprofit institutions (visit Website for list).
**Eligibility:** Applicant must be U.S. citizen residing in South Carolina.
**Basis for selection:** Applicant must demonstrate financial need.
**Application requirements:** FAFSA.
**Additional information:** Award amount varies. Recipient may reapply for up to four years. Incoming freshmen must score 900 SAT (Math and Reading) or 19 ACT, graduate in top three-fourths of high school class, or graduate from South Carolina high school with 2.0 GPA. Upperclassmen must complete 24 semester hours and meet college's satisfactory progress requirements. Application is automatic with FAFSA; submit to federal processor and list eligible college in college choice section. All eligible applicants funded if deadline is met. Contact campus financial aid office for details.

**Amount of award:** $2,350-$2,600
**Number of awards:** 14,200
**Number of applicants:** 27,206
**Application deadline:** June 30
**Total amount awarded:** $37,948,782

**Contact:**
South Carolina Higher Education Tuition Grants Commission
800 Dutch Square Blvd., Suite 260A
Columbia, SC 29210-7317
Phone: 803-896-1120
Fax: 803-896-1126
Web: www.sctuitiongrants.com

Scholarships

## South Dakota Board of Regents

### South Dakota Annis I. Fowler/Kaden Scholarship

**Type of award:** Scholarship.
**Intended use:** For freshman study at postsecondary institution. Designated institutions: University of South Dakota, Black Hills State University, Dakota State University, and Northern State University.
**Eligibility:** Applicant must be high school senior. Applicant must be U.S. citizen residing in South Dakota.
**Basis for selection:** Major/career interest in education, early childhood. Applicant must demonstrate high academic achievement, depth of character, leadership, seriousness of purpose and service orientation.
**Application requirements:** Recommendations, essay, transcript, proof of eligibility. ACT scores.
**Additional information:** Open to high school seniors who have a cumulative GPA of 3.0 after three years. Applicants must select elementary education as major field. Special consideration given to applicants with demonstrated motivation or disability, or who are self-supporting. Transcript must include class rank, cumulative GPA, and list of courses to be taken during senior year. Deadline in late February.

**Amount of award:** $1,000
**Number of awards:** 2
**Number of applicants:** 30
**Notification begins:** April 15

**Contact:**
South Dakota Board of Regents
Scholarship Committee
306 E. Capitol Avenue, Suite 200
Pierre, SD 57501-3159
Phone: 605-773-3455
Web: www.sdbor.edu

### South Dakota Ardell Bjugstad Scholarship

**Type of award:** Scholarship.
**Intended use:** For freshman study at postsecondary institution in United States.
**Eligibility:** Applicant must be American Indian. Must be member of federally recognized Indian tribe whose reservation is in North Dakota or South Dakota. Applicant must be high

school senior. Applicant must be U.S. citizen residing in South Dakota or North Dakota.
**Basis for selection:** Major/career interest in agribusiness; agriculture; natural resources/conservation or environmental science. Applicant must demonstrate high academic achievement, depth of character, leadership and seriousness of purpose.
**Application requirements:** Recommendations, transcript. Verification of tribal enrollment.
**Additional information:** Transcript must include class rank and cumulative GPA.

| | |
|---|---|
| **Amount of award:** | $500 |
| **Number of awards:** | 1 |
| **Number of applicants:** | 3 |
| **Notification begins:** | April 15 |

**Contact:**
South Dakota Board of Regents
Scholarship Committee
306 E. Capitol Avenue, Suite 200
Pierre, SD 57501-3159
Phone: 605-773-3455
Web: www.sdbor.edu

## South Dakota Haines Memorial Scholarship

**Type of award:** Scholarship.
**Intended use:** For full-time sophomore, junior or senior study at accredited 4-year institution in United States. Designated institutions: University of South Dakota, Black Hills State University, Dakota State University, Northern State University, South Dakota State University.
**Eligibility:** Applicant must be residing in South Dakota.
**Basis for selection:** Major/career interest in education; education, early childhood; education, special or education, teacher. Applicant must demonstrate depth of character, leadership, seriousness of purpose and service orientation.
**Application requirements:** Proof of eligibility. Resume. Two two-page essays: one describing personal philosophy and another describing philosophy of education.
**Additional information:** Minimum 2.5 GPA. Deadline in late February.

| | |
|---|---|
| **Amount of award:** | $2,150 |
| **Number of awards:** | 1 |
| **Number of applicants:** | 20 |
| **Notification begins:** | April 15 |

**Contact:**
South Dakota Board of Regents Scholarship Committee
306 E. Capitol, Suite 200
Pierre, SD 57501-3159
Phone: 605-773-3455
Web: www.sdbor.edu

## South Dakota Marlin R. Scarborough Memorial Scholarship

**Type of award:** Scholarship.
**Intended use:** For full-time junior study at accredited 4-year institution in United States. Designated institutions: Public institutions in South Dakota.
**Eligibility:** Applicant must be residing in South Dakota.
**Basis for selection:** Applicant must demonstrate high academic achievement, depth of character, leadership, seriousness of purpose and service orientation.
**Application requirements:** Nomination by participating South Dakota public university. Essay explaining leadership and academic qualities, career plans, and educational interests.
**Additional information:** Must be sophomore at time of application. Submit application to school financial aid office. Minimum 3.5 GPA. Must have completed three full semesters at same university. Each South Dakota public university may nominate one student. Application deadlines vary by university; visit Website for dates and application.

| | |
|---|---|
| **Amount of award:** | $1,000 |
| **Number of awards:** | 1 |
| **Notification begins:** | April 15 |

**Contact:**
South Dakota Board of Regents Scholarship Committee
306 East Capitol, Suite 200
Pierre, SD 57501-3159
Phone: 605-773-3455
Web: www.sdbor.edu

## South Dakota Opportunity Scholarship Program

**Type of award:** Scholarship.
**Intended use:** For undergraduate study at accredited vocational, 2-year or 4-year institution in United States. Designated institutions: Augustana College, Colorado Technical University, Dakota Wesleyan University, Lake Area Technical Institute, Mitchell Technical Institute, Northern State University, South Dakota School of Mines & Technology, Southeast Technical Institute, University of Sioux Falls, Black Hills State University, Dakota State University, Kilian Community College, Mount Mary College, National American University, Presentation College, South Dakota State University, University of South Dakota, Western Dakota Technical Institute.
**Eligibility:** Applicant must be U.S. citizen or permanent resident residing in South Dakota.
**Basis for selection:** Applicant must demonstrate high academic achievement.
**Application requirements:** Transcript. SAT/ACT scores.
**Additional information:** Award is distributed bi-annually over four academic years. Minimum 1090 SAT (Verbal and Math) and 24 ACT. Minimum 3.0 GPA. See Website for specific high school curriculum requirements, which must be completed with no final grade below a 2.0. Completed applications must be submitted directly to the institution to which applicant is applying. Visit Website for detailed credit hour requirements.

| | |
|---|---|
| **Amount of award:** | $5,000 |
| **Application deadline:** | September 1, January 15 |

**Contact:**
South Dakota Board of Regents c/o Dr. Paul D. Turman
306 E. Capitol Ave., Suite 200
Pierre, SD 57501-2545
Phone: 605-773-3455
Web: www.sdbor.edu

# South Dakota Department of Education

## South Dakota Robert C. Byrd Honors Scholarship

**Type of award:** Scholarship, renewable.
**Intended use:** For full-time undergraduate study in United States.

**Eligibility:** Applicant must be high school senior. Applicant must be U.S. citizen or permanent resident residing in South Dakota.
**Basis for selection:** Applicant must demonstrate high academic achievement.
**Application requirements:** Transcript. ACT scores.
**Additional information:** Minimum 3.5 GPA. Must have at least 30 ACT score.

| | |
|---|---|
| **Amount of award:** | $1,500 |
| **Number of awards:** | 72 |
| **Number of applicants:** | 123 |
| **Application deadline:** | March 18 |
| **Notification begins:** | February 4 |
| **Total amount awarded:** | $113,250 |

**Contact:**
South Dakota Department of Education
800 Governors Drive
Pierre, SD 57501-2291
Phone: 605-773-3248
Fax: 605-773-6139
Web: www.doe.sd.gov/scholarships/byrd

# Southern Nursery Organization

## Southern Nursery Organization Sidney B. Meadows Scholarship

**Type of award:** Scholarship.
**Intended use:** For full-time junior, senior, master's or doctoral study at accredited 4-year or graduate institution.
**Eligibility:** Applicant must be U.S. citizen residing in Tennessee, Louisiana, Virginia, Mississippi, Alabama, Kentucky, Missouri, Texas, Arkansas, Maryland, Florida, Georgia, South Carolina, Oklahoma, West Virginia or North Carolina.
**Basis for selection:** Major/career interest in horticulture.
**Application requirements:** Recommendations, transcript. Resume, cover letter.
**Additional information:** Must be enrolled in ornamental horticulture or related discipline in good standing. Minimum 2.75 GPA for undergraduates, 3.0 for graduates. Must be resident of one of 16 states in Southern Nursery Organization, but matriculation in these states is not mandatory. Preference given to applicants who plan to work in the horticulture industry after graduation, and for those who demonstrate financial need. Visit Website for application and additional information.

| | |
|---|---|
| **Amount of award:** | $2,500 |
| **Number of awards:** | 7 |
| **Application deadline:** | May 31 |
| **Notification begins:** | July 1 |
| **Total amount awarded:** | $17,500 |

**Contact:**
Sidney B. Meadows Scholarship Endowment Fund
1827 Powers Ferry Road SE, Ste. 4-100
Atlanta, GA 30339-8422
Phone: 770-953-3311
Fax: 703-953-4411
Web: www.sna.org/education.cfm

# Southern Scholarship Foundation

## Southern Scholarship Foundation Scholarships

**Type of award:** Scholarship, renewable.
**Intended use:** For undergraduate or graduate study in United States. Designated institutions: Florida State University, Florida A&M, University of Florida, Florida Gulf Coast University.
**Basis for selection:** Applicant must demonstrate financial need, high academic achievement, depth of character and service orientation.
**Application requirements:** Interview, recommendations, essay, transcript, proof of eligibility. Resume, FAFSA, SAR, recent photograph.
**Additional information:** Number of awards varies. Minimum 3.0 GPA. Applicants encouraged to submit early in spring semester. Graduating high school students and students currently attending community college and universities are eligible to apply. Awards given in the form of housing at one of 25 Florida-based scholarship houses. Awardees do not pay rent, but are responsible for basic household expenses. Each student contributes approximately $950/semester. Florida Gulf Coast University awards are for females only.

| | |
|---|---|
| **Number of awards:** | 80 |
| **Number of applicants:** | 300 |

**Contact:**
Southern Scholarship Foundation
Attn: Barby Moro
322 Stadium Drive
Tallahassee, FL 32304
Phone: 850-222-3833
Fax: 850-222-6750
Web: www.southernscholarship.org

# SPIE - The International Society for Optical Engineering

## SPIE Educational Scholarship in Optical Science and Engineering

**Type of award:** Scholarship, renewable.
**Intended use:** For undergraduate, graduate or non-degree study in or outside United States.
**Basis for selection:** Major/career interest in engineering or physics. Applicant must demonstrate seriousness of purpose.
**Application requirements:** Recommendations, essay.
**Additional information:** Open only to SPIE student members; nonmembers may submit SPIE student membership application and dues with scholarship application. High school and pre-university students may receive one-year complimentary membership. Applicant must be enrolled in optics, photonics, imaging, optoelectronics, or related program at accredited institution for year in which award will be used (unless high school student). Award amount and number of awards varies. Students must reapply for renewal. Visit Website for application and deadline.

**Amount of award:** $1,000-$11,000
**Number of applicants:** 360
**Application deadline:** February 15
**Notification begins:** May 1

**Contact:**
SPIE Scholarship Committee
Web: www.spie.org/scholarships

# Spina Bifida Association

## Spina Bifida Association One-Year Scholarship

**Type of award:** Scholarship.
**Intended use:** For undergraduate study at postsecondary institution in United States.
**Basis for selection:** Applicant must demonstrate financial need, high academic achievement, leadership, seriousness of purpose and service orientation.
**Application requirements:** Recommendations, essay, transcript, proof of eligibility. SAT, ACT, or GRE scores. Statement verifying disability from physician. Verification of high school diploma or GED; verification of acceptance at school/college. FAFSA or financial aid forms.
**Additional information:** Must be a high school graduate or possess G.E.D. Open to all persons with spina bifida. Applicant must be enrolled in/accepted by college, junior college, graduate program, or approved trade or vocational program. Number of awards varies. Immediate family members of SBA Board, scholarship committee, or staff are not eligible. Visit Website for deadline and more information.

**Amount of award:** $2,000
**Number of awards:** 6

**Contact:**
Spina Bifida Association, Attn: Scholarship Committee
4590 MacArthur Boulevard, NW
Suite 250
Washington, DC 20007-4226
Phone: 202-944-3285 or 800-621-3141
Fax: 202-944-3295
Web: www.spinabifidaassociation.org

# Staples

## Staples Associates Annual Scholarships Plan

**Type of award:** Scholarship, renewable.
**Intended use:** For undergraduate, graduate or non-degree study at vocational, 2-year, 4-year or graduate institution.
**Application requirements:** Proof of eligibility.
**Additional information:** Applicants must have worked at Staples for 90 days, averaging at least 18 hours per week. Contact Human Resources for complete details and application. Number of awards granted depends on funding.

**Amount of award:** $750-$2,000
**Number of applicants:** 3,000
**Application deadline:** September 30
**Notification begins:** November 15
**Total amount awarded:** $2,500,000

**Contact:**
Staples
500 Staples Drive
Framingham, MA 01702
Phone: 888-490-4747

# State Council of Higher Education for Virginia

## Virginia Academic Common Market

**Type of award:** Scholarship.
**Intended use:** For full-time undergraduate or graduate study at 4-year or graduate institution. Designated institutions: Eligible public institutions in 15 southern states.
**Eligibility:** Applicant must be U.S. citizen or permanent resident residing in Virginia.
**Additional information:** Awards Virginia residents in-state tuition at participating out-of-state institutions in the South. Institution must offer program unavailable at Virginia public institutions. Applicant must be domiciled in Virginia. Deadlines vary by institution.

**Contact:**
Academic Common Market/SCHEV
James Monroe Building
101 North Fourteenth Street
Richmond, VA 23219
Phone: 877-516-0138
Fax: 804-225-2604
Web: www.schev.edu

## Virginia Tuition Assistance Grant

**Type of award:** Scholarship, renewable.
**Intended use:** For full-time undergraduate, master's, doctoral or first professional study at accredited postsecondary institution. Designated institutions: Private, nonprofit institutions in Virginia.
**Eligibility:** Applicant must be residing in Virginia.
**Application requirements:** Proof of eligibility.
**Additional information:** Must be in eligible degree program in participating Virginia private college. Graduate students must be enrolled in health-related major. Applicant must be domiciled in Virginia. Theology and divinity majors not eligible. Award is $3200 for undergraduates; $1900 for graduate students. If funding is insufficient, priority given first to renewals, then to new applicants who apply prior to deadline. Interested students should contact financial aid office of qualifying postsecondary institution.

**Amount of award:** $1,900-$3,200
**Number of awards:** 20,000
**Application deadline:** July 31
**Total amount awarded:** $60,000,000

**Contact:**
Web: www.schev.edu

# State of Alabama

## Alabama Scholarship for Dependents of Blind Parents

**Type of award:** Scholarship, renewable.
**Intended use:** For undergraduate study at vocational, 2-year or 4-year institution. Designated institutions: Alabama public institutions.
**Eligibility:** Parent must be visually impaired. Applicant must be U.S. citizen or permanent resident residing in Alabama.
**Basis for selection:** Applicant must demonstrate financial need.
**Application requirements:** Proof of eligibility.
**Additional information:** Award waives instructional fees and tuition costs and pays for portion of books. Parent must be head of household and legally blind, and family income must be at or below 1.3 times the federal poverty guidelines. Applicant must have been Alabama resident for five years prior to application. Must reapply for renewal. Award available for all eligible applicants.

| | |
|---|---|
| **Amount of award:** | Full tuition |
| **Application deadline:** | June 30, September 30 |

**Contact:**
Alabama Department of Rehabilitation Services
Attn: Debra Culver
4 Medical Office Park
Talladega, AL 35160
Phone: 334-293-7315
Fax: 256-362-6387

# State Student Assistance Commission of Indiana

## Frank O'Bannon Grant

**Type of award:** Scholarship, renewable.
**Intended use:** For full-time undergraduate study at 2-year or 4-year institution. Designated institutions: Eligible Indiana schools.
**Eligibility:** Applicant must be U.S. citizen or permanent resident residing in Indiana.
**Basis for selection:** Applicant must demonstrate financial need.
**Application requirements:** FAFSA.
**Additional information:** Submitting FAFSA automatically fulfills application requirement. All eligible students offered an award. Amount of award varies. Visit Website for list of eligible schools.

| | |
|---|---|
| **Number of awards:** | 50,000 |
| **Number of applicants:** | 54,554 |
| **Application deadline:** | March 10 |
| **Notification begins:** | July 1 |
| **Total amount awarded:** | $196,838,902 |

**Contact:**
State Student Assistance Commission of Indiana
W462 Indiana Government Center South
402 West Washington Street
Indianapolis, IN 46204
Phone: 317-232-2350
Web: www.in.gov/ssaci

## Indiana Minority Teacher & Special Education Services Scholarship

**Type of award:** Scholarship, renewable.
**Intended use:** For full-time undergraduate or graduate study at accredited 4-year or graduate institution.
**Eligibility:** Applicant must be African American, Mexican American, Hispanic American or Puerto Rican. Applicant must be U.S. citizen or permanent resident residing in Indiana.
**Basis for selection:** Major/career interest in education; education, special; occupational therapy or physical therapy. Applicant must demonstrate financial need and high academic achievement.
**Application requirements:** Proof of eligibility. FAFSA.
**Additional information:** Minimum 2.0 GPA. Applicant must be black or Latino, unless applicant is entering field of special education, or occupational/physical therapy. Graduate students must be seeking a teaching certificate. Number of awards varies. Application deadline established by school. Schools responsible for selecting and notifying eligible applicants. Applications available online. Must be submitted to institution's financial aid department. Contact college financial aid office for more information.

| | |
|---|---|
| **Amount of award:** | $1,000-$4,000 |
| **Number of applicants:** | 214 |
| **Total amount awarded:** | $240,000 |

**Contact:**
State Student Assistance Commission of Indiana
Phone: 317-232-2350
Fax: 317-232-3260
Web: www.in.gov/ssaci

## Indiana National Guard Supplemental Grant

**Type of award:** Scholarship, renewable.
**Intended use:** For undergraduate study at 2-year or 4-year institution. Designated institutions: Indiana state-funded colleges and universities.
**Eligibility:** Applicant must be residing in Indiana. Applicant must be member of Indiana Air and Army National Guard. Applicant must be in active drilling status and be certified by Indiana National Guard (ING).
**Application requirements:** FAFSA.
**Additional information:** Room, board, and textbooks not covered. Contact unit commander with eligibility and certification questions.

| | |
|---|---|
| **Amount of award:** | Full tuition |
| **Number of applicants:** | 726 |
| **Application deadline:** | March 10 |
| **Notification begins:** | September 1 |
| **Total amount awarded:** | $2,509,489 |

**Contact:**
State Student Assistance Commission of Indiana
W462 Indiana Government Center
402 West Washington St.
Indianapolis, IN 46204
Phone: 317-232-2350
Web: www.in.gov/ssaci

## Indiana Nursing Scholarship

**Type of award:** Scholarship, renewable.
**Intended use:** For undergraduate study at accredited vocational, 2-year or 4-year institution. Designated institutions: Eligible Indiana schools.
**Eligibility:** Applicant must be U.S. citizen residing in Indiana.

**Basis for selection:** Major/career interest in nursing. Applicant must demonstrate financial need and high academic achievement.
**Application requirements:** Proof of eligibility. FAFSA.
**Additional information:** Minimum 2.0 GPA. Must be admitted to eligible Indiana school. Must commit to work two years as nurse in specific Indiana health care settings. Application available online. Submit completed application to financial aid department at the institution. Schools select eligible recipients. Number of awards varies. Deadline varies by institution.

| | |
|---|---|
| **Amount of award:** | $50-$5,000 |
| **Number of applicants:** | 330 |
| **Total amount awarded:** | $224,661 |

**Contact:**
State Student Assistance Commission of Indiana
Web: www.in.gov/ssaci



### Indiana Robert C. Byrd Honors Scholarship

**Type of award:** Scholarship, renewable.
**Intended use:** For full-time undergraduate study at accredited 2-year or 4-year institution in United States.
**Eligibility:** Applicant must be high school senior. Applicant must be U.S. citizen residing in Indiana.
**Basis for selection:** Applicant must demonstrate high academic achievement.
**Application requirements:** Transcript, proof of eligibility.
**Additional information:** Minimum 1940 SAT, 29 ACT, or 620 GED. Minimum 3.0 GPA. Cannot be in debt to federal government or have been sentenced for drug offense. Number of awards varies. Award cannot exceed $6,000 over four years. Visit Website for application. Contact high school guidance counselor for information.

| | |
|---|---|
| **Amount of award:** | $1,500 |
| **Number of applicants:** | 592 |
| **Application deadline:** | April 29 |
| **Notification begins:** | June 1 |
| **Total amount awarded:** | $888,000 |

**Contact:**
State Student Assistance Commission of Indiana
Web: www.in.gov/ssaci

### Indiana Twenty-First Century Scholars Program

**Type of award:** Scholarship.
**Intended use:** For full-time undergraduate study at accredited 2-year or 4-year institution. Designated institutions: Participating Indiana schools.
**Eligibility:** Applicant must be high school senior. Applicant must be U.S. citizen or permanent resident residing in Indiana.
**Basis for selection:** Applicant must demonstrate financial need.
**Application requirements:** FAFSA.
**Additional information:** Minimum 2.0 high school GPA. Must enroll in 6th, 7th, or 8th grade by taking pledge to remain drug, alcohol, and crime free. Must file affirmation that pledge was fulfilled in high school senior year. Full tuition waiver after other financial aid applied. Number and amount of awards varies. Visit Website for details.

| | |
|---|---|
| **Number of awards:** | 9,875 |
| **Number of applicants:** | 9,875 |
| **Application deadline:** | March 10 |
| **Notification begins:** | July 1 |
| **Total amount awarded:** | $22,787,104 |

**Contact:**
State Student Assistance Commission of Indiana
150 West Market Street, Suite 500
Indianapolis, IN 46204
Phone: 317-233-2100
Fax: 317-232-3260

## Stephen T. Marchello Scholarship Foundation

### Legacy of Hope

**Type of award:** Scholarship.
**Intended use:** For undergraduate study at accredited vocational, 2-year or 4-year institution in United States.
**Eligibility:** Applicant must be high school senior. Applicant must be U.S. citizen residing in Montana or Colorado.
**Application requirements:** Interview, recommendations, essay, transcript, proof of eligibility. SAT/ACT scores (when available).
**Additional information:** Some awards renewable depending on fund availability; all others are one-time grants. Applicant must be survivor of childhood cancer. Visit Website for more information. Submit application online or send SASE to address below. Number and amount of awards vary.

| | |
|---|---|
| **Amount of award:** | $1,000-$1,500 |
| **Number of awards:** | 6 |
| **Number of applicants:** | 20 |
| **Application deadline:** | March 15 |
| **Total amount awarded:** | $9,500 |

**Contact:**
Stephen T. Marchello Scholarship Foundation
1170 East Long Place
Centennial, CO 80122
Phone: 303-886-5018
Web: www.stmfoundation.org

## Studio Art Centers International

### Anna K. Meredith Fund Scholarship

**Type of award:** Scholarship.
**Intended use:** For undergraduate study in Florence, Italy. Designated institutions: Studio Art Centers International (SACI).
**Basis for selection:** Competition/talent/interest in study abroad. Major/career interest in arts, general or art/art history. Applicant must demonstrate financial need and high academic achievement.
**Application requirements:** Portfolio. SAR/FAFSA.
**Additional information:** Must demonstrate artistic talent. Must be accepted to study with Studio Art Centers International. Number of awards varies depending on budget.

| | |
|---|---|
| **Amount of award:** | $2,000 |
| **Application deadline:** | March 15, October 15 |
| **Notification begins:** | April 15, November 15 |

**Contact:**
Studio Art Centers International
50 Broad Street
Suite 1617
New York, NY 10004-2372
Phone: 212-248-7225 or 877-257-7225
Fax: 212-248-7222
Web: www.saci-florence.org

## Clare Brett Smith Scholarship

**Type of award:** Scholarship.
**Intended use:** For undergraduate or graduate study in Florence, Italy. Designated institutions: Studio Art Centers International (SACI).
**Basis for selection:** Competition/talent/interest in study abroad. Major/career interest in arts, general. Applicant must demonstrate financial need.
**Application requirements:** Portfolio. SAR/FAFSA.
**Additional information:** Must be accepted to study with Studio Art Centers International. Applicant must be studying photography.

| | |
|---|---|
| **Amount of award:** | $1,000 |
| **Number of awards:** | 2 |
| **Application deadline:** | March 15, October 15 |
| **Notification begins:** | April 15, November 15 |

**Contact:**
Studio Art Centers International
50 Broad Street
Suite 1617
New York, NY 10004-2372
Phone: 212-248-7225 or 877-257-7225
Fax: 212-248-7222
Web: www.saci-florence.org

## Elizabeth A. Sackler Museum Educational Trust

**Type of award:** Scholarship.
**Intended use:** For undergraduate study in Florence, Italy. Designated institutions: Studio Art Centers International (SACI).
**Eligibility:** Applicant must be female.
**Basis for selection:** Major/career interest in arts, general or art/art history. Applicant must demonstrate financial need and high academic achievement.
**Application requirements:** Portfolio, recommendations. FAFSA/SAR, statement of intent.
**Additional information:** Must be accepted to study with Studio Art Centers International. Must attend SACI for one full academic year. Must exhibit exceptional artistic talent in painting, drawing, printmaking, sculpture, ceramics, photography, art history, or art conservation. Must maintain a 3.0 to retain scholarship in the spring. Visit Website for application and more information.

| | |
|---|---|
| **Amount of award:** | $7,500 |
| **Number of awards:** | 1 |
| **Application deadline:** | March 15 |
| **Notification begins:** | May 1 |
| **Total amount awarded:** | $15,000 |

**Contact:**
Studio Art Centers International
50 Broad Street
Suite 1617
New York, NY 10004-2372
Phone: 212-248-7225 or 877-257-7225
Fax: 212-248-7222
Web: www.saci-florence.org/admissions/sackler.htm

## Florence Travel Stipend

**Type of award:** Scholarship.
**Intended use:** For undergraduate study. Designated institutions: Studio Art Centers International (SACI) institutions.
**Basis for selection:** Major/career interest in arts, general or art/art history.
**Application requirements:** $60 application fee. Portfolio. FAFSA.
**Additional information:** Award is two free roundtrip tickets to SACI Florence, Italy. Must be attending SACI in the spring term. Valid only on SACI's spring term group flight from New York.

| | |
|---|---|
| **Number of awards:** | 2 |
| **Application deadline:** | October 15 |

**Contact:**
Studio Art Centers International
50 Broad Street
Suite 1617
New York, NY 10004-2372
Phone: 212-248-7225
Fax: 212-248-7222
Web: www.saci-florence.org

## The Gillian Award

**Type of award:** Scholarship.
**Intended use:** For undergraduate study. Designated institutions: Studio Art Centers International (SACI).
**Eligibility:** Applicant must be female.
**Basis for selection:** Major/career interest in arts, general.
**Application requirements:** $60 application fee. Portfolio. FAFSA.
**Additional information:** Award is open to a female artist with demonstrated artistic achievement who will be attending in both fall and spring terms. Award offers opportunity for aspiring fine artist to live and work in Florence, utilizing all the resources of SACI.

| | |
|---|---|
| **Number of awards:** | 1 |
| **Application deadline:** | March 15, October 15 |
| **Total amount awarded:** | $3,000 |

**Contact:**
Studio Art Centers International
50 Broad Street
Suite 1617
New York, NY 10004-2372
Phone: 212-248-7225
Fax: 212-248-7222
Web: www.saci-florence.org

## International Incentive Awards

**Type of award:** Scholarship.
**Intended use:** For junior or senior study in Florence, Italy. Designated institutions: Studio Art Centers International (SACI).
**Basis for selection:** Competition/talent/interest in study abroad. Major/career interest in arts, general or art/art history. Applicant must demonstrate financial need and high academic achievement.
**Application requirements:** Portfolio. SAR/FAFSA.
**Additional information:** Must be accepted to study with Studio Art Centers International. Minimum 3.0 GPA. Special efforts made to encourage applications from minorities and underrepresented groups. Number of awards varies depending on budget.

**Amount of award:** $1,500
**Application deadline:** March 15, October 15
**Notification begins:** April 15, November 15
**Contact:**
Studio Art Centers International
50 Broad Street
Suite 1617
New York, NY 10004-2372
Phone: 212-248-7225 or 877-257-7225
Fax: 212-248-7222
Web: www.saci-florence.org



## Jules Maidoff Scholarship

**Type of award:** Scholarship.
**Intended use:** For undergraduate or graduate study in Florence, Italy. Designated institutions: Studio Art Centers International (SACI).
**Basis for selection:** Competition/talent/interest in study abroad. Major/career interest in arts, general or art/art history. Applicant must demonstrate financial need.
**Application requirements:** Portfolio. FAFSA/SAR.
**Additional information:** Must be accepted to study with Studio Art Centers International. Awarded to students exhibiting both exceptional artistic talent and financial need. Number of awards varies depending on budget.
**Amount of award:** $2,500
**Application deadline:** March 15, October 15
**Notification begins:** April 15, November 15
**Contact:**
Studio Art Centers International
50 Broad Street
Suite 1617
New York, NY 10004-2372
Phone: 212-248-7225 or 877-257-7225
Fax: 212-248-7222
Web: www.saci-florence.org

## Lele Cassin Scholarship

**Type of award:** Scholarship.
**Intended use:** For undergraduate or graduate study in Florence, Italy. Designated institutions: Studio Art Centers International (SACI).
**Basis for selection:** Competition/talent/interest in study abroad. Major/career interest in film/video. Applicant must demonstrate financial need.
**Application requirements:** Video (no longer than 15 minutes) of own work. SAR/FAFSA.
**Additional information:** Must be accepted to study with Studio Art Centers International. Number of awards offered varies yearly according to budget.
**Amount of award:** $1,000
**Application deadline:** March 15, October 15
**Notification begins:** April 15, November 15
**Contact:**
Studio Art Centers International
50 Broad Street
Suite 1617
New York, NY 10004-2372
Phone: 212-248-7225 or 877-257-7225
Fax: 212-248-7222
Web: www.saci-florence.org

## SACI Alumni Heritage Scholarship

**Type of award:** Scholarship.
**Intended use:** For undergraduate or graduate study at postsecondary institution in Florence, Italy. Designated institutions: Studio Art Centers International (SACI).
**Basis for selection:** Major/career interest in arts, general or art/art history. Applicant must demonstrate financial need and high academic achievement.
**Application requirements:** Portfolio. FAFSA/SAR. Statement indicating the name of parent who attended SACI and dates of attendance.
**Additional information:** Must be accepted to study with Studio Art Centers International and have a parent who attended SACI. Applicants for late spring or summer terms must submit materials by the admissions deadline of the term they wish to enroll. Number of awards varies depending on budget.
**Amount of award:** $500-$2,500
**Application deadline:** March 15, October 15
**Notification begins:** April 15, November 15
**Contact:**
Studio Art Centers International
50 Broad Street
Suite 1617
New York, NY 10004-2372
Phone: 212-248-7225 or 877-257-7225
Fax: 212-248-7222
Web: www.saci-florence.com

## SACI Consortium Scholarship

**Type of award:** Scholarship.
**Intended use:** For undergraduate or graduate study in Florence, Italy. Designated institutions: Studio Art Centers International (SACI) consortium institutions.
**Basis for selection:** Competition/talent/interest in study abroad. Major/career interest in arts, general or art/art history. Applicant must demonstrate financial need.
**Application requirements:** Portfolio, nomination by SACI consortium school. FAFSA/SAR.
**Additional information:** Must be accepted to study with Studio Art Centers International. Each consortium school may submit one nominee. Award for one semester; one award available per semester. See Website for list of eligible institutions.
**Amount of award:** Full tuition
**Number of awards:** 2
**Application deadline:** March 15, October 15
**Notification begins:** April 15, November 15
**Contact:**
Studio Art Centers International
50 Broad Street
Suite 1617
New York, NY 10004-2372
Phone: 212-248-7225 or 877-257-7225
Fax: 212-248-7222
Web: www.saci-florence.org

## SACI ICFAD Full Tuition Scholarship

**Type of award:** Scholarship.
**Intended use:** For freshman study at 4-year institution. Designated institutions: Eligible ICFAD member institutions.
**Basis for selection:** Applicant must demonstrate high academic achievement.

**Additional information:** Award covers tuition for a full semester at SACI for talented or academically gifted student. May be used for first semester of study at SACI during fall or spring terms. Must be attending a school that is a member institution of International Council of Fine Arts Deans (ICFAD). Scholarship applicants attending ICFAD schools are automatically reviewed for this award.

**Application deadline:** March 15, October 15

**Contact:**
Studio Art Centers International
50 Broad Street
Suite 1617
New York, NY 10004-2372
Phone: 212-248-7225
Fax: 212-248-7222
Web: www.saci-florence.org

# Sunkist Growers

## A.W. Bodine Sunkist Memorial Scholarship

**Type of award:** Scholarship, renewable.
**Intended use:** For full-time undergraduate study at accredited 2-year or 4-year institution.
**Basis for selection:** Applicant must demonstrate financial need, high academic achievement, depth of character, leadership, seriousness of purpose and service orientation.
**Application requirements:** Recommendations, essay, transcript, proof of eligibility. SAT or ACT scores, tax return (or parents' tax return for applicants younger than 21).
**Additional information:** Applicant or someone in immediate family must have derived majority of income from California- or Arizona-based agriculture. All majors eligible. Award renewable up to four years based on annual review. Must maintain 2.7 GPA and carry 12 credits per semester to qualify for renewal. Number of awards varies. Visit Website for application.

**Amount of award:** $2,000
**Number of applicants:** 300
**Application deadline:** April 30

**Contact:**
A.W. Bodine Sunkist Memorial Scholarship
Sunkist Growers
P.O. Box 7888
Van Nuys, CA 91409-7888
Web: www.sunkist.com/about/bodine_scholarship.aspx

# Supreme Guardian Council, International Order of Job's Daughters

## The Grotto Scholarships

**Type of award:** Scholarship.
**Intended use:** For full-time undergraduate study at 2-year or 4-year institution.
**Eligibility:** Applicant must be single, female, no older than 30.
**Basis for selection:** Major/career interest in dentistry. Applicant must demonstrate financial need, high academic achievement, depth of character, leadership and seriousness of purpose.
**Application requirements:** Recommendations, transcript, proof of eligibility. Personal letter.
**Additional information:** Applicant must be member of Job's Daughters. Job's Daughters activities, financial self-help, and achievements outside of Job's Daughters are also factors in awarding scholarships. Training in the handicapped field is preferred. Minimum 2.5 GPA. Visit Website for more information.

**Amount of award:** $1,500
**Application deadline:** April 30

**Contact:**
International Order of Job's Daughters
Phone: 402-592-7987
Web: www.iojd.org

## Supreme Guardian Council, International Order of Job's Daughters Scholarship

**Type of award:** Scholarship.
**Intended use:** For full-time undergraduate study at vocational, 2-year or 4-year institution.
**Eligibility:** Applicant must be single, female, no older than 30.
**Basis for selection:** Applicant must demonstrate financial need, high academic achievement, depth of character, leadership, seriousness of purpose and service orientation.
**Application requirements:** Recommendations, transcript, proof of eligibility. Personal letter.
**Additional information:** Applicant must be member of Job's Daughters. Job's Daughters activities, applicant's financial self-help, and achievements outside of Job's Daughters are also factors in awarding scholarships. Number of awards varies. Visit Website for more information.

**Amount of award:** $750
**Number of applicants:** 100
**Application deadline:** April 30

**Contact:**
Supreme Guardian Council
Phone: 402-592-7987
Web: www.iojd.org

## Susie Holmes Memorial Scholarship

**Type of award:** Scholarship.
**Intended use:** For full-time undergraduate study at vocational, 2-year or 4-year institution.
**Eligibility:** Applicant must be single, female, no older than 30.
**Basis for selection:** Applicant must demonstrate financial need, depth of character and seriousness of purpose.
**Application requirements:** Recommendations, transcript, proof of eligibility. Personal letter.
**Additional information:** Applicant must be member of Job's Daughters. Must be high school graduate with 2.5 GPA; show dedicated, continuous, joyful service to Job's Daughters; and regularly attend Grand and/or Supreme Session and participate in competitions. Job's Daughter's activities, applicant's financial self-help, and achievements outside of Job's Daughters are also factors in awarding scholarships. Visit Website for more details.

**Amount of award:** $1,000
**Application deadline:** April 30

**Contact:**
Supreme Guardian Council, International Order of Job's Daughters
Phone: 402-592-7987
Web: www.iojd.org

# SWCS-Scholarship

## Donald A. Williams Soil Conservation Scholarship

**Type of award:** Scholarship.
**Intended use:** For undergraduate study at postsecondary institution.
**Basis for selection:** Major/career interest in natural resources/conservation. Applicant must demonstrate financial need, depth of character and seriousness of purpose.
**Application requirements:** Recommendations, essay.
**Additional information:** Applicant must have been member of Soil and Water Conservation Society for at least one year at time of application. Must demonstrate competence in line of work. Must have completed at least one year of full-time employment and be currently employed in a natural resource conservation endeavor. Number of awards varies. Visit Website for application and deadline.

| | |
|---|---|
| **Amount of award:** | $1,000 |
| **Number of awards:** | 1 |

**Contact:**
SWCS-Scholarship
945 SW Ankeny Road
Ankeny, IA 50023
Phone: 515-289-2331
Fax: 515-289-1227
Web: www.swcs.org

# Swiss Benevolent Society of New York

## Sonia Streuli Maguire Outstanding Scholastic Achievement Award

**Type of award:** Scholarship.
**Intended use:** For full-time senior, post-bachelor's certificate, master's, doctoral or first professional study at accredited 4-year or graduate institution in United States.
**Eligibility:** Applicant must be Swiss. Applicant must be permanent resident residing in New York, Connecticut, Delaware, New Jersey or Pennsylvania.
**Basis for selection:** Applicant must demonstrate high academic achievement.
**Application requirements:** Recommendations, transcript, proof of eligibility. SAT/GRE results.
**Additional information:** Applicant or parent must be Swiss national. Must have minimum 3.8 GPA. Visit Website for application.

| | |
|---|---|
| **Application deadline:** | March 31 |
| **Notification begins:** | June 1 |

**Contact:**
Swiss Benevolent Society Scholarship Committee
500 Fifth Avenue
Room 1800
New York, NY 10110
Phone: 212-246-0655
Fax: 212-246-1366
Web: www.sbsny.org/sbs_scholarships.html

## Swiss Benevolent Society Medicus Student Exchange

**Type of award:** Scholarship.
**Intended use:** For full-time junior, senior, post-bachelor's certificate, master's, doctoral or first professional study in universities and polytechnic institutes in Switzerland.
**Eligibility:** Applicant must be Swiss. Applicant must be U.S. citizen or permanent resident.
**Basis for selection:** Competition/talent/interest in study abroad. Applicant must demonstrate financial need and high academic achievement.
**Application requirements:** Recommendations, transcript, proof of eligibility. SAT or GRE scores. Letter of acceptance from Swiss institution. Statement of funding. Proof of fluency in language of instruction.
**Additional information:** Provides partial financial support for U.S. students accepted to Swiss post-secondary institutions. Applicant or parent must be Swiss national. Visit Website for application.

| | |
|---|---|
| **Application deadline:** | March 31 |
| **Notification begins:** | June 1 |

**Contact:**
Swiss Benevolent Society Scholarship Committee
500 Fifth Avenue
Room 1800
New York, NY 10110
Phone: 212-246-0655
Fax: 212-246-1366
Web: www.sbsny.org/sbs_scholarships.html

## Swiss Benevolent Society Pellegrini Scholarship

**Type of award:** Scholarship, renewable.
**Intended use:** For undergraduate, graduate or non-degree study at accredited postsecondary institution in United States.
**Eligibility:** Applicant must be Swiss. Applicant must be permanent resident residing in New York, Connecticut, Delaware, New Jersey or Pennsylvania.
**Basis for selection:** Applicant must demonstrate financial need and high academic achievement.
**Application requirements:** Recommendations, transcript, proof of eligibility. SAT or GRE scores. Proof of Swiss parentage and tax return. Copy of bursar's bill. Incoming freshmen should provide figures of anticipated cost.
**Additional information:** Applicant or parent must be Swiss national. Minimum 3.0 GPA. Visit Website for application.

| | |
|---|---|
| **Application deadline:** | March 31 |
| **Notification begins:** | June 1 |

**Contact:**
Swiss Benevolent Society Scholarship Committee
500 Fifth Avenue
Room 1800
New York, NY 10110
Phone: 212-246-0655
Fax: 212-246-1366
Web: www.sbsny.org/sbs_scholarships.html

# TAG Education Collaborative

## Web Challenge Contest

**Type of award:** Scholarship.
**Intended use:** For full-time undergraduate study.
**Eligibility:** Applicant must be enrolled in high school. Applicant must be U.S. citizen or permanent resident residing in Georgia.
**Basis for selection:** Competition/talent/interest in web-site design, based on use of technology to create a theme-based project. Major/career interest in computer/information sciences or computer graphics. Applicant must demonstrate seriousness of purpose.
**Application requirements:** Proof of eligibility.
**Additional information:** Applicants work in teams of up to four members to create projects using free and/or open source technologies. Team must be sponsored by faculty adviser. Total amount awarded varies. Visit Website for registration information, deadline, and contest information and theme.

| | |
|---|---|
| **Number of awards:** | 25 |
| **Number of applicants:** | 100 |
| **Total amount awarded:** | $21,100 |

**Contact:**
TAG Education Collaborative
75 Fifth Street, NW
Suite 625
Atlanta, GA 30308
Web: www.tagedonline.org

# Taglit-Birthright Israel

## Taglit-Birthright Israel Gift

**Type of award:** Scholarship.
**Intended use:** For undergraduate or graduate study at postsecondary institution.
**Eligibility:** Applicant must be at least 18, no older than 26. Applicant must be Jewish.
**Application requirements:** Proof of eligibility. Passport.
**Additional information:** Applicant must be out of high school. All eligible applicants receive free trip to Israel under the auspices of Aish HaTorah, Hillel, and other organizations. Round-trip airfare and ten days of program activity (including hotel, transportation, and most meals) are funded. Must not have visited Israel previously on an educational peer-group trip or study program. Must not have lived in Israel past age 12. Visit Website or contact sponsor for current offerings.

| | |
|---|---|
| **Number of awards:** | 20,000 |

**Contact:**
Phone: 888-99-ISRAEL
Web: www.birthrightisrael.com

# Tennessee Student Assistance Corporation

## Dual Enrollment Grant

**Type of award:** Scholarship, renewable.
**Intended use:** For undergraduate study at postsecondary institution.
**Eligibility:** Applicant must be high school junior or senior. Applicant must be residing in Tennessee.
**Additional information:** Student must meet dual enrollment requirements for high school and postsecondary institution. Must be a Tennessee resident for at least one year prior to enrollment. Visit Website for designated institutions. Application deadline is 9/15 for fall; 2/1 for spring; 5/1 for summer.

| | |
|---|---|
| **Amount of award:** | $600 |
| **Number of awards:** | 14,700 |
| **Application deadline:** | September 15, February 1 |
| **Total amount awarded:** | $6,400,000 |

**Contact:**
Tennessee Student Assistance Corporation
Parkway Towers, Suite 1510
404 James Robertson Parkway
Nashville, TN 37243-0820
Phone: 800-342-1663
Fax: 615-741-6101
Web: www.tn.gov/collegepays

## Helping Heroes Grant

**Type of award:** Scholarship, renewable.
**Intended use:** For undergraduate study at 2-year or 4-year institution.
**Eligibility:** Applicant must be residing in Tennessee. Applicant must be veteran who served in the Army, Air Force, Marines, Navy or Reserves/National Guard. Must be a veteran who was honorably discharged and was awarded the Iraq Campaign Medal, Afghanistan Campaign Medal, or Global War on Terrorism Expeditionary Medal.
**Additional information:** Award amount is up to $2,000. Fall application deadline is 9/1; spring deadline is 2/1; summer deadline is 5/1. Scholarships are given on a first-come, first-served basis, with up to $750,000 awarded per academic year.

| | |
|---|---|
| **Amount of award:** | $2,000 |
| **Number of awards:** | 367 |
| **Application deadline:** | September 1, February 1 |
| **Total amount awarded:** | $513,000 |

**Contact:**
Tennessee Student Assistance Corporation
Parkway Towers, Suite 1510
404 James Robertson Parkway
Nashville, TN 37243-0820
Phone: 800-342-1633
Fax: 615-741-6101
Web: www.tn.gov/collegepays

## Hope Foster Child Tuition Grant

**Type of award:** Scholarship, renewable.
**Intended use:** For undergraduate study at 2-year or 4-year institution.
**Eligibility:** Applicant must be residing in Tennessee.
**Application requirements:** Proof of eligibility.
**Additional information:** Must meet the academic requirements for the HOPE Scholarship or HOPE Access Grant. Must have

been in custody of Tennessee Department of Children's Services for at least one year after age 14.

**Amount of award:** Full tuition
**Number of awards:** 30
**Application deadline:** September 1
**Notification begins:** January 1
**Total amount awarded:** $126,300

**Contact:**
Tennessee Student Assistance Corporation
Parkway Towers, Suite 1510
404 James Robertson Parkway
Nashville, TN 37243-0820
Phone: 800-342-1663
Fax: 615-741-6101
Web: www.tn.gov/collegepays

## HOPE-Aspire Award

**Type of award:** Scholarship.
**Intended use:** For freshman or sophomore study at postsecondary institution. Designated institutions: Eligible Tennessee institutions.
**Eligibility:** Applicant must be residing in Tennessee.
**Basis for selection:** Applicant must demonstrate financial need.
**Application requirements:** FAFSA.
**Additional information:** Applicant must be eligible for HOPE. Entering freshman must have a minimum 21 ACT or 980 SAT or 3.0 GPA. Parent's or student's income must be $36,000 or less. Applicant must be a Tennessee resident for one year prior to enrollment.

**Amount of award:** $1,500
**Number of awards:** 16,724
**Application deadline:** September 1
**Notification begins:** January 1
**Total amount awarded:** $78,900,000

**Contact:**
Tennessee Student Assistance Corporation
Parkway Towers, Suite 1510
404 James Robertson Parkway
Nashville, TN 37243-0820
Phone: 800-342-1663
Fax: 615-741-6101
Web: www.tn.gov/collegepays

## Hope-General Assembly Merit Scholarship

**Type of award:** Scholarship, renewable.
**Intended use:** For undergraduate study at postsecondary institution. Designated institutions: Eligible Tennessee institutions.
**Eligibility:** Applicant must be residing in Tennessee.
**Basis for selection:** Applicant must demonstrate high academic achievement.
**Application requirements:** FAFSA.
**Additional information:** Supplement to HOPE Scholarship. Entering freshman must have minimum 3.75 weighted GPA and 29 ACT or 1280 SAT. Applicant must be a resident of Tennessee for one year prior to enrollment.

**Amount of award:** $1,000
**Number of awards:** 5,562
**Application deadline:** September 1
**Notification begins:** January 1
**Total amount awarded:** $26,900,000

**Contact:**
Tennessee Student Assistance Corporation
Parkway Towers, Suite 1510
404 James Robertson Parkway
Nashville, TN 37243-0820
Phone: 800-342-1663
Fax: 614-741-6101
Web: www.tn.gov/collegepays

## Tennessee Dependent Children Scholarship Program

**Type of award:** Scholarship, renewable.
**Intended use:** For full-time undergraduate study at accredited postsecondary institution.
**Eligibility:** Applicant must be U.S. citizen residing in Tennessee. Applicant's parent must have been killed or disabled in work-related accident as firefighter or police officer.
**Basis for selection:** Applicant must demonstrate financial need.
**Application requirements:** Proof of eligibility. FAFSA.
**Additional information:** Applicant must be enrolled in a degree-granting program. Applicant's parent may also be emergency medical technician killed or disabled in work-related accident. Award based on student's financial aid package.

**Amount of award:** Full tuition
**Number of awards:** 28
**Number of applicants:** 75
**Application deadline:** July 15
**Total amount awarded:** $157,955

**Contact:**
Tennessee Student Assistance Corporation
Parkway Towers, Suite 1510
404 James Robertson Parkway
Nashville, TN 37243-0820
Phone: 800-342-1663
Fax: 615-741-6101
Web: www.tn.gov/collegepays

## Tennessee HOPE Access Grant

**Type of award:** Scholarship.
**Intended use:** For freshman study at 2-year or 4-year institution. Designated institutions: Eligible Tennessee institutions.
**Eligibility:** Applicant must be residing in Tennessee.
**Basis for selection:** Applicant must demonstrate financial need.
**Application requirements:** FAFSA.
**Additional information:** Award amount is $2,750 for four-year institutions or $1,750 for two-year institutions. Minimum 2.75 GPA. Minimum 18 ACT, 860 SAT. Parents' or independent student and spouse's adjusted gross income must be $36,000 or less on IRS tax form. Applicant must be a Tennessee resident for one year prior to enrollment.

**Amount of award:** $1,750-$2,750
**Number of awards:** 408
**Application deadline:** September 1
**Notification begins:** January 1
**Total amount awarded:** $895,000

**Contact:**
Tennessee Student Assistance Corporation
Parkway Towers, Suite 1510
404 James Robertson Parkway
Nashville, TN 37243-0820
Phone: 800-342-1663
Fax: 615-741-6101
Web: www.tn.gov/collegepays

## Tennessee HOPE Scholarship

**Type of award:** Scholarship.
**Intended use:** For undergraduate study at postsecondary institution. Designated institutions: Eligible Tennessee institutions.
**Eligibility:** Applicant must be residing in Tennessee.
**Application requirements:** FAFSA.
**Additional information:** Applicant must be a Tennessee resident for one year prior to enrollment. Award amount is $4,000 for four-year institutions, $2,000 for two-year institutions. Minimum 3.0 GPA or 21 ACT/980 SAT.

| | |
|---|---|
| **Amount of award:** | $2,000-$4,000 |
| **Number of awards:** | 43,056 |
| **Application deadline:** | September 1 |
| **Notification begins:** | January 1 |
| **Total amount awarded:** | $147,700,000 |

**Contact:**
Tennessee Student Assistance Corporation
Parkway Towers, Suite 1510
404 James Robertson Parkway
Nashville, TN 37243-0820
Phone: 800-342-1663
Fax: 615-741-6101
Web: www.tn.gov/collegepays

## Tennessee Ned McWherter Scholars Program

**Type of award:** Scholarship, renewable.
**Intended use:** For full-time freshman study at accredited 2-year or 4-year institution.
**Eligibility:** Applicant must be high school senior. Applicant must be U.S. citizen residing in Tennessee.
**Basis for selection:** Applicant must demonstrate high academic achievement and leadership.
**Application requirements:** Transcript, proof of eligibility. List of leadership activities.
**Additional information:** Applicant must score at 95th percentile on ACT/SAT. Minimum 3.5 cumulative GPA. Difficulty of high school courses considered.

| | |
|---|---|
| **Amount of award:** | $6,000 |
| **Number of awards:** | 188 |
| **Number of applicants:** | 1,426 |
| **Application deadline:** | February 15 |
| **Total amount awarded:** | $541,500 |

**Contact:**
Tennessee Student Assistance Corporation
Parkway Towers, Suite 1510
404 James Robertson Parkway
Nashville, TN 37243-0820
Phone: 800-342-1663
Fax: 615-741-6101
Web: www.tn.gov/collegepays

## Tennessee Robert C. Byrd Honors Scholarship Program

**Type of award:** Scholarship, renewable.
**Intended use:** For full-time freshman study at accredited vocational, 2-year or 4-year institution in United States.
**Eligibility:** Applicant must be high school senior. Applicant must be U.S. citizen or permanent resident residing in Tennessee.
**Basis for selection:** Applicant must demonstrate high academic achievement.
**Application requirements:** Transcript, proof of eligibility.
**Additional information:** Minimum 3.5 GPA. May also qualify with 3.0 GPA and 24 ACT or 1090 SAT. At least 570 GED also accepted.

| | |
|---|---|
| **Amount of award:** | $1,500 |
| **Number of awards:** | 519 |
| **Number of applicants:** | 5,573 |
| **Application deadline:** | March 1 |
| **Total amount awarded:** | $754,593 |

**Contact:**
Tennessee Student Assistance Corporation
Parkway Towers, Suite 1510
404 James Robertson Parkway
Nashville, TN 37243-0820
Phone: 800-342-1663
Fax: 615-741-6101
Web: www.tn.gov/collegepays

## Tennessee Student Assistance Award Program

**Type of award:** Scholarship, renewable.
**Intended use:** For undergraduate study at postsecondary institution.
**Eligibility:** Applicant must be U.S. citizen residing in Tennessee.
**Basis for selection:** Applicant must demonstrate financial need.
**Application requirements:** FAFSA.
**Additional information:** Applicant's expected family contribution must be $2,100 or less. Award is up to $4,000 for private institutions; up to $2,000 for public, based on funding.

| | |
|---|---|
| **Number of awards:** | 24,616 |
| **Number of applicants:** | 419,149 |
| **Application deadline:** | February 15 |
| **Total amount awarded:** | $53,904,938 |

**Contact:**
Tennessee Student Assistance Corporation
Parkway Towers, Suite 1510
404 James Robertson Parkway
Nashville, TN 37243-0820
Phone: 800-342-1663
Fax: 615-741-6101
Web: www.tn.gov/collegepays

## Wilder-Naifeh Technical Skills Grant

**Type of award:** Scholarship.
**Intended use:** For freshman or sophomore study at vocational institution. Designated institutions: Tennessee Technology Centers.
**Eligibility:** Applicant must be residing in Tennessee.
**Application requirements:** FAFSA.

**Additional information:** Applicant must be Tennessee resident for one year prior to enrollment. Application deadline varies. See Website for details.

| | |
|---|---|
| **Amount of award:** | $2,000 |
| **Number of awards:** | 13,435 |
| **Notification begins:** | January 1 |
| **Total amount awarded:** | $15,900,000 |

**Contact:**
Tennessee Student Assistance Corporation
Parkway Towers, Suite 1510
404 James Robertson Parkway
Nashville, TN 37243-0820
Phone: 800-342-1663
Fax: 615-741-6101
Web: www.tn.gov/collegepays



# Texas 4-H Club

## Texas 4-H Opportunity Scholarships

**Type of award:** Scholarship, renewable.
**Intended use:** For undergraduate study at accredited 4-year institution in United States. Designated institutions: Colleges and universities in Texas.
**Eligibility:** Applicant must be high school senior. Applicant must be U.S. citizen residing in Texas.
**Basis for selection:** Applicant must demonstrate financial need and high academic achievement.
**Application requirements:** Recommendations, essay, transcript. SAT/ACT scores.
**Additional information:** Must be current Texas 4-H member in good standing. Must graduate from Texas public/private high school or home school in top fourth of class. Must have minimum 1350 SAT or 19 ACT score. Cannot have applied for scholarship though state FFA or state FCCLA.

| | |
|---|---|
| **Amount of award:** | $500-$16,000 |
| **Number of awards:** | 245 |
| **Number of applicants:** | 350 |
| **Application deadline:** | January 31 |
| **Notification begins:** | June 1 |
| **Total amount awarded:** | $2,250,000 |

**Contact:**
Texas 4-H Club
P.O. Box 11020
College Station, TX 77842
Phone: 979-845-1212
Fax: 979-845-6495
Web: texas4-h.tamu.edu

# Texas Association, Family Career and Community Leaders of America

## Blue Bell Scholarship

**Type of award:** Scholarship.
**Intended use:** For full-time undergraduate study at accredited postsecondary institution in United States. Designated institutions: Colleges and universities in Texas.
**Eligibility:** Applicant must be high school senior. Applicant must be U.S. citizen residing in Texas.
**Basis for selection:** Applicant must demonstrate financial need, high academic achievement, depth of character and leadership.
**Application requirements:** Recommendations, essay, transcript. SAT/ACT scores.
**Additional information:** Must be active member of Family Career and Community Leaders of America in good standing. Must have passed TAKS Mastery/Exit Level exam and be in top fourth of graduating class.

| | |
|---|---|
| **Amount of award:** | $1,000 |
| **Number of awards:** | 5 |
| **Number of applicants:** | 112 |
| **Application deadline:** | March 1 |
| **Notification begins:** | April 15 |
| **Total amount awarded:** | $5,000 |

**Contact:**
Texas Association, Family Career and Community Leaders of America
6513 Circle S Road
TX 78745
Phone: 512-306-0099
Fax: 512-442-7100
Web: www.texasfccla.org

## C. J. Davidson Scholarship

**Type of award:** Scholarship, renewable.
**Intended use:** For undergraduate study at accredited postsecondary institution in United States. Designated institutions: Texas colleges with family and consumer sciences departments.
**Eligibility:** Applicant must be high school senior. Applicant must be U.S. citizen residing in Texas.
**Basis for selection:** Major/career interest in education. Applicant must demonstrate financial need and high academic achievement.
**Application requirements:** Recommendations, essay, transcript. SAT/ACT scores.
**Additional information:** Must graduate from a Texas high school with 85 average. Must be active member of Family Career and Community Leaders of America for at least one year. Must major in and receive a teaching certificate for family/consumer sciences.

| | |
|---|---|
| **Amount of award:** | $4,000 |
| **Number of awards:** | 10 |
| **Number of applicants:** | 101 |
| **Application deadline:** | March 1 |
| **Notification begins:** | April 15 |
| **Total amount awarded:** | $160,000 |

**Contact:**
Texas Association, Family Career and Community Leaders of America
6513 Circle S Road
Austin, TX 78745
Phone: 512-306-0099
Fax: 512-442-7100
Web: www.texasfccla.org

## Houston Livestock Show and Rodeo Scholarships

**Type of award:** Scholarship, renewable.
**Intended use:** For full-time undergraduate study at accredited 4-year institution in United States. Designated institutions: Colleges and universities in Texas.

**Eligibility:** Applicant must be high school senior. Applicant must be U.S. citizen residing in Texas.
**Basis for selection:** Applicant must demonstrate financial need, high academic achievement, depth of character and leadership.
**Application requirements:** Recommendations, essay, transcript. SAT/ACT scores.
**Additional information:** Must be current member of Family Career and Community Leaders of America in good standing. Must graduate from Texas public high school in top fourth of class and have minimum 1350 SAT or 19 ACT score. Cannot have applied for scholarship through Texas 4-H or FFA.

| | |
|---|---|
| **Amount of award:** | $3,750 |
| **Number of awards:** | 10 |
| **Number of applicants:** | 91 |
| **Application deadline:** | March 1 |
| **Notification begins:** | April 15 |
| **Total amount awarded:** | $150,000 |

**Contact:**
Texas Association, Family Career and Community Leaders of America
6513 Circle S Road
Austin, TX 78745
Phone: 512-306-0099
Fax: 512-442-7100
Web: www.texasfccla.org

### Texas Farm Bureau Scholarship

**Type of award:** Scholarship.
**Intended use:** For full-time undergraduate study at accredited postsecondary institution in United States. Designated institutions: Texas colleges and universities with family and consumer sciences departments.
**Eligibility:** Applicant must be high school senior. Applicant must be U.S. citizen residing in Texas.
**Basis for selection:** Applicant must demonstrate financial need, high academic achievement, depth of character and leadership.
**Application requirements:** Recommendations, essay, transcript. SAT/ACT scores, two copies of autobiography.
**Additional information:** Must be active Family Career and Community Leaders of America member in good standing for at least one year. Must be FFCLA regional or state officer. Must be a graduate of Texas high school with minimum 85 average. Must major in family/consumer sciences.

| | |
|---|---|
| **Amount of award:** | $1,000 |
| **Number of awards:** | 1 |
| **Number of applicants:** | 5 |
| **Application deadline:** | March 1 |
| **Notification begins:** | April 15 |
| **Total amount awarded:** | $1,000 |

**Contact:**
Texas Association, Family Career and Community Leaders of America
6513 Circle S Road
Austin, TX 78745
Phone: 512-306-0099
Fax: 512-442-7100
Web: www.texasfccla.org

## Texas Future Farmers of America

### FFA Scholarships

**Type of award:** Scholarship, renewable.
**Intended use:** For undergraduate study at accredited 4-year institution in United States. Designated institutions: Colleges and universities in Texas.
**Eligibility:** Applicant must be high school senior. Applicant must be U.S. citizen residing in Texas.
**Basis for selection:** Applicant must demonstrate financial need and high academic achievement.
**Application requirements:** Interview, recommendations, essay, transcript. SAT/ACT scores.
**Additional information:** Must be current member of Texas FFA in good standing. Must have graduated from Texas public high school in top half of class. Must have minimum 1350 SAT or 19 ACT score. Cannot have applied for scholarship through Texas 4-H or FCCLA. Preliminary deadlines vary based on area; visit Website for more information.

| | |
|---|---|
| **Amount of award:** | $2,000-$16,000 |
| **Number of awards:** | 135 |
| **Number of applicants:** | 700 |
| **Notification begins:** | June 10 |
| **Total amount awarded:** | $2,000,000 |

**Contact:**
Texas FFA Association
614 East 12th Street
Austin, TX 78701
Phone: 512-480-8045
Fax: 512-476-2894
Web: www.texasffa.org

## Texas Higher Education Coordinating Board

### Competitive Scholarship Waiver

**Type of award:** Scholarship.
**Intended use:** For undergraduate study at 4-year institution in United States. Designated institutions: Public institutions.
**Eligibility:** Applicant must be U.S. citizen, permanent resident or international student residing in Texas.
**Additional information:** Program enables public institutions to grant waiver of nonresident tuition charges to individuals who receive scholarships totaling at least $1,000 awarded by their institution in competition open both to residents and to nonresidents. Students must have competed with other students, including Texas residents, for the award. Student may receive a waiver of nonresident tuition for the period of time covered by the scholarship, not to exceed 12 months. Process for applying for waivers varies from college to college.
**Contact:**
Texas Higher Education Coordinating Board
Phone: 800-242-3062
Web: www.collegeforalltexans.com

## Concurrent Enrollment Waiver (Enrollment in Two Texas Community Colleges)

**Type of award:** Scholarship.
**Intended use:** For undergraduate study at 2-year or 4-year institution in United States. Designated institutions: Texas public colleges or universities.
**Eligibility:** Applicant must be residing in Texas.
**Application requirements:** Proof of eligibility. Proof of concurrent enrollment.
**Additional information:** Waiver provides a break in tuition charges to students enrolled at two public Texas community colleges at the same time. Award is reduced tuition at second institution of enrollment (student pays minimum tuition rate at second institution). No funds may be used to pay tuition for continuing education classes for which the college receives no state tax support. For more information, contact registrar at second college in which you are enrolled.
**Contact:**
Texas Higher Education Coordinating Board
Phone: 800-242-3062
Web: www.collegeforalltexans.com

## Engineering Scholarship Program

**Type of award:** Scholarship, renewable.
**Intended use:** For sophomore study at 4-year institution in United States. Designated institutions: Texas public or private universities.
**Eligibility:** Applicant must be residing in Texas.
**Basis for selection:** Major/career interest in engineering.
**Additional information:** Minimum 3.5 high school GPA in mathematics and science. Must have graduated in top 20 percent of graduating high school class. Minimum 3.0 college GPA. Must have registered for Selective Service or be exempt from this requirement. Depending on funding, recipients may receive up to $5,000 per year. Contact engineering department in which student is enrolled.
**Contact:**
Texas Higher Education Coordinating Board
Phone: 800-242-3062
Web: www.collegeforalltexans.com

## Exemption for Peace Officers Disabled in the Line of Duty

**Type of award:** Scholarship.
**Intended use:** For undergraduate study at postsecondary institution in United States. Designated institutions: Texas public colleges and universities.
**Eligibility:** Applicant must be residing in Texas.
**Application requirements:** Proof of eligibility. Satisfactory evidence of status as a disabled peace officer as required by institution.
**Additional information:** Award for persons injured in the line of duty while serving as peace officers in Texas. Must enroll in classes for which college receives tax support. Maximum award is exemption from payment of tuition and fees for not more than 12 semesters or sessions. Contact college for additional information.

**Amount of award:** Full tuition

**Contact:**
Texas Higher Education Coordinating Board
Phone: 800-242-3062
Web: www.collegeforalltexans.com

## Exemption for the Surviving Spouse and Dependent Children of Certain Deceased Public Servants (Employees)

**Type of award:** Scholarship.
**Intended use:** For full-time undergraduate study at postsecondary institution in United States. Designated institutions: Texas public colleges and universities.
**Eligibility:** Applicant must be residing in Texas.
**Application requirements:** Proof of eligibility.
**Additional information:** Exemption for surviving spouse and/or dependent children of certain public employees (defined by Texas Government Code 615.003) killed in the line of duty. Public employee must have died on or after September 1, 2000. Program covers cost of tuition and fees, textbooks, and possibly room and board. Visit Website for link to list of eligible public servants. Contact registrar's office at college/university for information on claiming this exemption.

**Amount of award:** Full tuition

**Contact:**
Texas Higher Education Coordinating Board
Phone: 800-242-3062
Web: www.collegeforalltexans.com

## Federal Supplemental Educational Opportunity Grant

**Type of award:** Scholarship.
**Intended use:** For undergraduate study at vocational, 2-year, 4-year or graduate institution in United States.
**Eligibility:** Applicant must be U.S. citizen or permanent resident.
**Basis for selection:** Applicant must demonstrate financial need and high academic achievement.
**Application requirements:** FAFSA.
**Additional information:** Must have valid Social Security Number. Expected Family Contribution must be lower than the federal cut-off rate set each year. Must have high school diploma, GED Certificate, pass test approved by the U.S. Department of Education or meet other standards approved by U.S. Department of Education. Must register for the Selective Service.

**Amount of award:** $100-$4,000

**Contact:**
Texas Higher Education Coordinating Board
Phone: 800-242-3062
Web: www.collegeforalltexans.com

## Professional Nursing Scholarships

**Type of award:** Scholarship.
**Intended use:** For undergraduate or graduate study at accredited vocational, 2-year, 4-year or graduate institution. Designated institutions: Texas public colleges and universities.
**Eligibility:** Applicant must be U.S. citizen or permanent resident residing in Texas.
**Basis for selection:** Major/career interest in nursing or health-related professions. Applicant must demonstrate financial need and high academic achievement.
**Application requirements:** Proof of eligibility.
**Additional information:** A variety of scholarships for vocational or professional nursing students. Award amount varies; maximum is $2,500. Must register for the Selective Service (unless exempt). Contact institutional financial aid office to apply.

**Amount of award:** $2,500

**Contact:**
Texas Higher Education Coordinating Board
Phone: 800-242-3062
Web: www.collegeforalltexans.com

## Reduction in Tuition Charges for Students Taking 15 or More Semester Credit Hours Per Term

**Type of award:** Scholarship.
**Intended use:** For full-time undergraduate study at postsecondary institution. Designated institutions: Texas public colleges and universities.
**Eligibility:** Applicant must be residing in Texas.
**Application requirements:** Proof of eligibility.
**Additional information:** Applicant must be enrolled in at least 15 credit hours at institution during semester/term for which reduction is offered. Must be making satisfactory progress toward completion of a degree program. Contact registrar's office at college/university to inquire whether they offer reduction.
**Contact:**
Texas Higher Education Coordinating Board
Phone: 800-242-3062
Web: www.collegeforalltexans.com

## Robert C. Byrd Honors Scholarship

**Type of award:** Scholarship, renewable.
**Intended use:** For undergraduate study at vocational, 2-year or 4-year institution.
**Eligibility:** Applicant must be high school senior. Applicant must be U.S. citizen or permanent resident residing in Texas.
**Basis for selection:** Applicant must demonstrate high academic achievement.
**Application requirements:** Transcript, nomination by high school guidance counselor, home school instructor, or GED-center director.
**Additional information:** Applicants completing GED certification or a secondary school program in a home school setting during award year also eligible. Must be in top ten percent of class. Students attending a U.S. Military Academy not eligible. Visit Website for deadline. For more information, contact high school guidance office or GED center director.

**Amount of award:** $1,500
**Number of awards:** 3,839

**Contact:**
Texas Higher Education Coordinating Board
Phone: 800-242-3062 or 512-427-6340
Web: www.collegeforalltexans.com

## Senior Citizen, 65 or Older, Free Tuition for Up to 6 Credit Hours

**Type of award:** Scholarship.
**Intended use:** For half-time undergraduate or graduate study at 2-year or 4-year institution in United States. Designated institutions: Participating Texas public colleges and universities.
**Eligibility:** Applicant must be at least 65, returning adult student.
**Application requirements:** Proof of eligibility.
**Additional information:** Program allows senior citizens to take up to 6 credit hours per semester, tuition-free. Texas institutions not required to offer program; applicants should check with registrar. Classes must not already be filled with students paying at full price and must use tax support for some of their cost. Contact college for additional information.
**Contact:**
Texas Higher Education Coordinating Board
Phone: 800-242-3062
Web: www.collegeforalltexans.com

## Texas Armed Services Scholarship Program

**Type of award:** Scholarship.
**Intended use:** For freshman study at 4-year institution.
**Eligibility:** Applicant must be high school senior. Applicant must be U.S. citizen or permanent resident residing in Texas.
**Basis for selection:** Applicant must demonstrate high academic achievement.
**Application requirements:** Nomination by the governor, lieutenant governor, state senator, or state representative.
**Additional information:** Must meet two of four following criteria: Minimum 3.0 GPA. Minimum 1590 (SAT) or 23 (ACT). Must be ranked in top third of high school graduating class or be on track to graduate high school with the Distinguished Achievement Program (DAP) or the International Baccalaureate Program (IB). Must enroll in Reserve Officers' Training Corps, agree to four years of ROTC training, and graduate no later than five years after date first enrolled. After graduation, must enter into four-year commitment to Texas Army or Texas Air Force National Guard, contract to serve as commissioned officer in branch in the U.S., or repay scholarship if requirements not met. See Website for additional criteria.

**Amount of award:** $15,000

**Contact:**
Texas Higher Education Coordinating Board
Phone: 800-242-3062
Web: www.collegeforalltexans.com

## Texas Career Opportunity Grant Program

**Type of award:** Scholarship.
**Intended use:** For undergraduate study at vocational institution in United States. Designated institutions: Eligible Texas institutions meeting requirements set out in Texas labor Code, Title 4, Chapter 305, Section 305.002(3).
**Eligibility:** Applicant must be U.S. citizen or permanent resident residing in Texas.
**Basis for selection:** Applicant must demonstrate financial need.
**Additional information:** Must be required to pay more tuition and required fees than amount charged at a public technical institution. Must be charged not less than regular tuition and required fees paid by other students enrolled at the institution the person attends. Must register for Selective Service, unless exempt. Must not be in default on federal or state student loan and not owe refund on grant received under federal Pell Grant Program or federal Supplemental Education Opportunity Grant program. Contact career school or college's financial aid office for information on applying.
**Contact:**
Texas Higher Education Coordinating Board
Phone: 800-242-3062
Web: www.collegeforalltexans.com

## Texas Fifth-Year Accounting Student Scholarship Program

**Type of award:** Scholarship.
**Intended use:** For senior, post-bachelor's certificate or master's study at accredited postsecondary institution in United States. Designated institutions: Texas institutions.
**Eligibility:** Applicant must be residing in Texas.
**Basis for selection:** Major/career interest in accounting. Applicant must demonstrate financial need and high academic achievement.
**Application requirements:** Proof of eligibility. Signed statement of intent to take CPA exam in Texas. FAFSA.
**Additional information:** Must be enrolled as fifth-year accounting student who has completed at least 120 credit hours, including 15 hours of accounting. Must register for selective service or be exempt from this requirement. Contact college financial aid office for application.

**Amount of award:** $5,000

**Contact:**
Texas Higher Education Coordinating Board
Phone: 800-242-3062
Web: www.collegeforalltexans.com

## Texas Foster Care Students Exemption

**Type of award:** Scholarship, renewable.
**Intended use:** For undergraduate or graduate study at accredited vocational, 2-year or 4-year institution in United States. Designated institutions: Texas public colleges and universities.
**Eligibility:** Applicant must be no older than 21. Applicant must be U.S. citizen or permanent resident residing in Texas.
**Application requirements:** Proof of eligibility from the Department of Family and Protective Services.
**Additional information:** Applicants must have been either in the care or conservatorship of Texas Department of Family and Protective Services on the day before their 18th birthday, the day of their graduation from high school, or the day of receipt of GED or the day preceding; or in the care or conservatorship of the TDFS on 14th birthday and then adopted. Must enroll in college before 25th birthday. Program awards tuition and fees; once student determined eligible for the benefit, it continues indefinitely. Contact college's financial aid office for application.

**Amount of award:** Full tuition

**Contact:**
Texas Higher Education Coordinating Board
Phone: 800-242-3062
Web: www.collegeforalltexans.com

## Texas Good Neighbor Scholarship

**Type of award:** Scholarship.
**Intended use:** For undergraduate or graduate study at accredited 2-year, 4-year or graduate institution in United States. Designated institutions: Texas public colleges and universities.
**Eligibility:** Applicant must be native-born citizen of any Western Hemisphere country other than Cuba. Applicant must be residing in Texas.
**Application requirements:** Proof of eligibility.
**Additional information:** Must plan to return to native country. Contact institution's financial aid office or the international student affairs office for application. Award covers one year of tuition.

**Amount of award:** Full tuition
**Application deadline:** March 15

**Contact:**
College For All Texans
Phone: 800-242-3062
Web: www.collegeforalltexans.com

## TEXAS Grant (Toward Excellence, Access, and Success)

**Type of award:** Scholarship, renewable.
**Intended use:** For undergraduate study at vocational, 2-year or 4-year institution. Designated institutions: Texas public colleges or universities.
**Eligibility:** Applicant must be U.S. citizen or permanent resident residing in Texas.
**Basis for selection:** Applicant must demonstrate financial need and high academic achievement.
**Application requirements:** Selective Service registration or exemption from requirement. FAFSA.
**Additional information:** Applicant must have completed Recommended High School Program or Distinguished Achievement Program, enroll in college at least 3/4-time (unless granted hardship waiver) within 16 months of high school graduation, and must receive first award prior to completing 30 hours on campus. Also eligible are students with associate degrees from public technical or community colleges in Texas, who enroll in public Texas universities within 12 months of receiving associate's. Expected Family Contribution (EFC) to education must be less than $4,000. Minimum 2.5 GPA required to renew award. Applicant must not have been convicted of felony or crime involving controlled substance. Award not to exceed student's need or public institution tuition and fees. Must register for Selective Service or be exempt from this requirement. Contact financial aid office at specific college/university for application deadline and procedures.

**Amount of award:** Full tuition

**Contact:**
Texas Higher Education Coordinating Board
Phone: 800-242-3062
Web: www.collegeforalltexans.com

## Texas Hazlewood Act Tuition Exemption: Veterans

**Type of award:** Scholarship, renewable.
**Intended use:** For undergraduate or graduate study at accredited 2-year, 4-year or graduate institution. Designated institutions: Texas public colleges and universities.
**Eligibility:** Applicant must be U.S. citizen residing in Texas. Applicant must be veteran; or dependent of disabled veteran or deceased veteran. Must have served at least 181 days of active military duty, excluding basic training. Must have received honorable discharge or general discharge under honorable conditions. If dependent of disabled veteran, parent must be totally disabled for purposes of employability as result of service-related injury or illness.
**Application requirements:** Proof of eligibility.
**Additional information:** Must have tuition and fee charges that exceed all federal education benefits. Veteran must have been resident of Texas prior to enlistment. Award amount includes all dues, fees, and charges, excluding property deposit, student services, and lodging/board/clothing fees. Must be enrolled in courses receiving state tax support. For a child of eligible veteran to receive benefits, child must be 25 or younger on first day of semester that exemption is claimed, must make satisfactory progress, must be biological, stepchild,

adopted or claimed as dependent in current or previous tax year. Applicants should contact specific school's financial aid office for more information.

**Amount of award:** Full tuition

**Contact:**
Texas Higher Education Coordinating Board
Phone: 800-242-3062
Web: www.collegeforalltexans.com

## Texas Highest Ranking High School Graduate Tuition Exemption

**Type of award:** Scholarship.
**Intended use:** For freshman study at accredited postsecondary institution. Designated institutions: Texas public colleges and universities.
**Eligibility:** Applicant must be residing in Texas.
**Basis for selection:** Applicant must demonstrate high academic achievement.
**Application requirements:** Proof of eligibility. Valedictorian certificate issued by Texas Education Agency.
**Additional information:** Must be highest-ranking graduate of accredited public or private Texas high school. Award covers tuition during both semesters of first regular session immediately following the student's high school graduation; fees not included. Deadline varies. Contact college/university financial aid office to apply.

**Amount of award:** Full tuition
**Number of awards:** 1,000

**Contact:**
College For All Texans
Phone: 800-242-3062 or 512-427-6100
Web: www.collegeforalltexans.com

## Texas National Guard Tuition Assistance Program

**Type of award:** Scholarship.
**Intended use:** For undergraduate or graduate study at postsecondary institution in United States. Designated institutions: Texas institutions.
**Eligibility:** Applicant must be residing in Texas.
**Application requirements:** Proof of eligibility.
**Additional information:** Program provides tuition exemption to active, drilling members of Texas National Guard, Texas Air Guard, or State Guard. Must be registered for Selective Service or exempt from this requirement. Awards at public colleges/universities are for student's tuition charges up to 12 credit hours per semester. Awards for private, non-profit institutions are based on public university amount. For more information, visit Texas National Guard Website at www.agd.state.tx.us. Applicants may also contact the commander of their National Guard, Air Guard, or State Guard unit, or the education officer via information below.

**Amount of award:** Full tuition

**Contact:**
State Adjutant General's Office
P.O. Box 5218/AGTX-PAE
Austin, TX 78763-5218
Phone: 512-782-5515
Web: www.collegeforalltexans.com

## Texas Public Educational Grant

**Type of award:** Scholarship.
**Intended use:** For undergraduate or graduate study at accredited vocational, 2-year or 4-year institution. Designated institutions: Texas public colleges and universities.
**Eligibility:** Applicant must be residing in Texas.
**Basis for selection:** Applicant must demonstrate financial need.
**Application requirements:** FAFSA.
**Additional information:** Award amount varies; may not exceed student's financial need. Deadline varies. Applicant must register for Selective Service, unless exempt. Contact financial aid office at college/university for more information.

**Contact:**
Texas Higher Education Coordinating Board
Phone: 800-242-3062
Web: www.collegeforalltexans.com

## Texas Tuition Exemption for Blind or Deaf Students

**Type of award:** Scholarship, renewable.
**Intended use:** For undergraduate or graduate study at accredited 2-year or 4-year institution in United States. Designated institutions: Texas public colleges and universities.
**Eligibility:** Applicant must be visually impaired or hearing impaired. Applicant must be U.S. citizen or permanent resident residing in Texas.
**Basis for selection:** Applicant must demonstrate depth of character.
**Application requirements:** Recommendations, transcript, proof of eligibility. Certification of disability. Written statement indicating which certificate, degree program, or professional enhancement applicant intends to pursue.
**Additional information:** Must be certified by Texas Department of Assistive and Rehabilitative Services and have high school diploma or equivalent. Applicant must enroll in classes for which the college receives tax support. Award does not include fees or charges for lodging, board, or clothing. Application deadline varies. Contact financial aid office at college/university for more information.

**Amount of award:** Full tuition

**Contact:**
Texas Higher Education Coordinating Board
Phone: 800-242-3062
Web: www.collegeforalltexans.com

## Tuition Equalization Grant (TEG)

**Type of award:** Scholarship.
**Intended use:** For full-time undergraduate or graduate study at accredited 2-year or 4-year institution in United States. Designated institutions: Private, non-profit Texas colleges and universities.
**Eligibility:** Applicant must be U.S. citizen or permanent resident residing in Texas.
**Basis for selection:** Applicant must demonstrate financial need.
**Application requirements:** Proof of eligibility. Selective Service registration or exemption from requirement. FAFSA.
**Additional information:** Non-resident National Merit Finalists also eligible. Not open to athletic scholarship recipients. Award cannot exceed difference between applicant's tuition at private institution and what applicant would pay at public institution. Award amount varies; maximum is $3,518, but students with exceptional need may receive up to $5,277. Applicants should

contact the financial aid office at the Texas private college/university they plan to attend for more information.

**Number of awards:** 28,000

**Contact:**
Texas Higher Education Coordinating Board
Phone: 800-242-3062
Web: www.collegeforalltexans.com

## Tuition Exemption for Children of Disabled or Deceased Firefighters, Peace Officers, Game Wardens, and Employees of Correctional Institutions

**Type of award:** Scholarship, renewable.
**Intended use:** For undergraduate or graduate study at 2-year or 4-year institution in United States. Designated institutions: Texas public colleges and universities.
**Eligibility:** Applicant must be no older than 21. Applicant must be residing in Texas. Applicant's parent must have been killed or disabled in work-related accident as firefighter, police officer or public safety officer.
**Application requirements:** Proof of eligibility.
**Additional information:** Applicant must be child of paid or volunteer firefighter; paid municipal, county or state peace officer; custodial employee of Department of Corrections; or game warden disabled or killed in Texas in the line of duty. Persons eligible to participate in a school district's special education program under section 29.003 at age 22 may also apply. Applicant must enroll in courses that use tax support to cover some of their cost. Applicant must obtain certification form from Texas Higher Education Coordinating Board, have parent's former employer complete it, and submit to Texas Higher Education Coordinating Board. The Board will notify applicant's institution of eligibility. Students may be exempted from tuition and fees for the first 120 semester credits or until age 26, whichever comes first.

**Amount of award:** Full tuition

**Contact:**
Texas Higher Education Coordinating Board
Student Services Division
P.O. Box 12788
Austin, TX 78711-2788
Phone: 800-242-3062
Web: www.collegeforalltexans.com

## Tuition Exemption for Children of U.S. Military POW/MIAs from Texas

**Type of award:** Scholarship, renewable.
**Intended use:** For undergraduate study at accredited 2-year or 4-year institution. Designated institutions: Texas public colleges or universities.
**Eligibility:** Applicant must be no older than 25. Applicant must be U.S. citizen or permanent resident residing in Texas. Applicant must be dependent of POW/MIA.
**Application requirements:** Proof of eligibility. Documentation from Department of Defense that a parent, classified as Texas resident, is MIA or a POW. FAFSA.
**Additional information:** Applicants 22 to 25 years of age must receive most of their support from a parent. Applicant must enroll in courses that use tax support to cover some of their cost. Award does not include room, board, clothing, or property deposits. Applicants should contact the registrar at the college/university they plan to attend for more information.

**Amount of award:** Full tuition

**Contact:**
Texas Higher Education Coordinating Board
Phone: 800-242-3062
Web: www.collegeforalltexans.com

## Tuition Rebate for Certain Undergraduates

**Type of award:** Scholarship.
**Intended use:** For full-time undergraduate study at postsecondary institution in United States. Designated institutions: Texas public colleges and universities.
**Eligibility:** Applicant must be residing in Texas.
**Additional information:** Program provides tuition rebates for students who efficiently acquire their bachelor's degrees. Students must graduate in a timely manner to receive rebate: within four years for four-year degree, five years for five-year degree. Student must have taken all coursework at Texas public institutions, and must have been entitled to pay in-state tuition at all times while pursuing degree. Student must complete bachelor's degree with no more than 3 hours in excess of degree plan, excluding up to 9 hours of credit by examination. Students must apply for tuition rebate prior to receiving bachelor's degree. Contact business office at college/university for more information.

**Amount of award:** $1,000

**Contact:**
Texas Higher Education Coordinating Board
Phone: 800-242-3062
Web: www.collegeforalltexans.com

## Tuition Reduction for Students Taking More Than 15 Hours

**Type of award:** Scholarship.
**Intended use:** For full-time undergraduate study at 4-year institution in United States. Designated institutions: Texas public colleges or universities.
**Additional information:** Award is reduced tuition. Must be enrolled in at least 15 semester credit hours at institution during semester or term for which reduction is offered. College governing board determines whether institution will offer reduction. Contact registrar's office to find out if college is offering this reduction.

**Contact:**
Texas Higher Education Coordinating Board
Phone: 800-242-3062
Web: www.collegeforalltexans.com

# Third Marine Division Association

## Memorial Scholarship Fund

**Type of award:** Scholarship, renewable.
**Intended use:** For undergraduate study at accredited 2-year or 4-year institution in United States or Canada.
**Eligibility:** Applicant must be U.S. citizen. Applicant must be dependent of active service person or deceased veteran who serves or served in the Marines or Navy during Vietnam. Must

be dependent child of qualified member or deceased member (Marine or Navy Corpsman) of the Third Marine Division Association, or dependent child of any military personnel who served in any Third Marine Division (Reinf) unit and who died as result of combat actions while serving in Vietnam between March 8, 1965 and November 27, 1969, or in operations Desert Shield, Desert Storm, or any other qualified Persian Gulf operations after August 2, 1990. Dependent children of deceased Third Marine Division personnel who served in above operations whose post-service deaths have been certified by the Department of Veterans Affairs to have been the result of combat-related wounds or other disabilities incurred during the period of eligible combat service, and were not the result of any misconduct by the veteran, are also eligible.
**Basis for selection:** Applicant must demonstrate financial need.
**Application requirements:** Proof of eligibility. Financial aid form.
**Additional information:** Minimum 2.0 GPA. Number of awards varies. Eligible dependent children participating automatically receive renewal application forms.

| | |
|---|---|
| **Amount of award:** | $500-$1,500 |
| **Number of applicants:** | 16 |
| **Application deadline:** | April 15 |
| **Notification begins:** | June 15 |
| **Total amount awarded:** | $11,250 |

**Contact:**
MGySgt James G. Kyser USMC (Ret)
Secretary, Memorial Scholarship Fund
15727 Vista Drive
Dumfries, VA 22025-1810
Web: www.caltrap.com

# Thurgood Marshall College Fund

## Thurgood Marshall Scholarship Award

**Type of award:** Scholarship, renewable.
**Intended use:** For full-time undergraduate or graduate study at 4-year or graduate institution in United States. Designated institutions: One of 47 designated historically black public universities.
**Eligibility:** Applicant must be U.S. citizen.
**Basis for selection:** Applicant must demonstrate financial need, high academic achievement and service orientation.
**Application requirements:** Recommendations, essay, transcript. Resume, headshot or personal photograph.
**Additional information:** Must have high school or current GPA of 3.0 or higher, and must maintain throughout duration of scholarship. Must have minimum 1650 SAT or 25 ACT score. Contact university's Thurgood Marshall College Fund campus coordinator directly for more information, or visit Website.

| | |
|---|---|
| **Amount of award:** | $4,400 |
| **Number of awards:** | 200 |
| **Number of applicants:** | 2,270 |
| **Application deadline:** | August 15 |
| **Total amount awarded:** | $1,200,000 |

**Contact:**
Thurgood Marshall College Fund
80 Maiden Lane
Suite 2204
New York, NY 10038
Phone: 212-573-8888
Web: www.thurgoodmarshallfund.net

# Tourism Cares

## Alexander Harris Scholarship

**Type of award:** Scholarship.
**Intended use:** For sophomore, junior or senior study at accredited 4-year institution in United States.
**Eligibility:** Applicant must be U.S. citizen or permanent resident.
**Basis for selection:** Major/career interest in hospitality administration/management or tourism/travel. Applicant must demonstrate high academic achievement.
**Application requirements:** Essay, transcript. Resume. U.S. passport or U.S. Alien Registration Card. Two evaluations and letters of recommendation (one from hospitality/tourism-related faculty member, one from hospitality/tourism professional).
**Additional information:** Minimum 3.0 GPA. Must be entering the second year of a two-year school, junior or senior year of a four-year school. Visit Website for application, deadline, additional criteria.

| | |
|---|---|
| **Amount of award:** | $1,000 |
| **Number of awards:** | 1 |

**Contact:**
Tourism Cares
275 Turnpike Street
Suite 307
Canton, MA 02021
Phone: 781-821-5990
Fax: 781-821-8949
Web: www.tourismcares.org/scholarships

## ASTA A.J. Spielman Scholarship

**Type of award:** Scholarship, renewable.
**Intended use:** For undergraduate certificate or non-degree study at vocational institution in United States.
**Eligibility:** Applicant must be returning adult student. Applicant must be U.S. citizen or permanent resident.
**Basis for selection:** Major/career interest in tourism/travel.
**Application requirements:** Essay. Resume. U.S. passport or Alien Registration Card. Evaluation and letter of recommendation from faculty member or tourism professional.
**Additional information:** Visit Website for application and deadline date. Must be entering or working in travel and tourism industry. Must have successfully completed and fully paid for a travel and tourism certificate program at a U.S. state-licensed school no more than 12 months prior to application deadline.

| | |
|---|---|
| **Amount of award:** | $1,000 |
| **Number of awards:** | 1 |

Scholarships

**Contact:**
Tourism Cares
275 Turnpike Street
Suite 307
Canton, MA 02021
Phone: 781-821-5990
Fax: 781-821-8949
Web: www.tourismcares.org/scholarships

## ASTA Alaska Airlines Scholarship

**Type of award:** Scholarship.
**Intended use:** For sophomore, junior or senior study at accredited 2-year or 4-year institution in United States or Canada.
**Eligibility:** Applicant must be U.S. citizen, permanent resident or Canadian citizen or resident.
**Basis for selection:** Major/career interest in tourism/travel or hospitality administration/management.
**Application requirements:** Essay, transcript. Resume, copy of U.S. or Canadian Passport or Alien Registration Card. Two evaluations and letters of recommendation (one from hospitality/tourism-related faculty member, one from hospitality/tourism professional).
**Additional information:** Minimum 3.0 GPA. Must be entering the second year of a two-year school, third year of a three-year school (for Quebec), junior or senior year of a four-year school, any year of graduate study. Check Website for deadline and additional criteria.

| | |
|---|---|
| **Amount of award:** | $1,000 |
| **Number of awards:** | 1 |

**Contact:**
Tourism Cares
275 Turnpike Street
Suite 307
Canton, MA 02021
Phone: 781-821-5990
Fax: 781-821-8949
Web: www.tourismcares.org/scholarships

## ASTA American Express Travel Scholarship

**Type of award:** Scholarship, renewable.
**Intended use:** For full-time freshman study at accredited 2-year or 4-year institution in United States or Canada.
**Eligibility:** Applicant must be high school senior. Applicant must be U.S. citizen or permanent resident.
**Basis for selection:** Major/career interest in hospitality administration/management or tourism/travel.
**Application requirements:** Essay, transcript. Resume. U.S. Passport or U.S. Alien Registration Card. Two evaluations and letters of recommendation (one from hospitality/tourism-related faculty member, one from hospitality/tourism professional).
**Additional information:** Minimum 3.0 GPA. Visit Website for deadline, application, additional criteria.

| | |
|---|---|
| **Amount of award:** | $1,000 |
| **Number of awards:** | 1 |

**Contact:**
Tourism Cares
275 Turnpike Street
Suite 307
Canton, MA 02021
Phone: 781-821-5990
Fax: 781-821-8949
Web: www.tourismcares.org/scholarships

## ASTA Arizona Chapter Dependent Scholarship

**Type of award:** Scholarship, renewable.
**Intended use:** For undergraduate study at accredited vocational institution in United States.
**Eligibility:** Applicant or parent must be member/participant of ASTA Arizona Chapter. Applicant must be U.S. citizen or permanent resident.
**Application requirements:** Essay. ASTA Chapter Professional Development Scholarship Application Board Officer Approval Form. Either ASTA Chapter Professional Development Two-Year Employment verification form or ASTA Chapter Professional Development Scholarship Two-Year Self-Employment verification form. Proof of course completion. U.S. Passport or Alien Registration Card.
**Additional information:** Must be working travel agent who is individual member of the ASTA Arizona Chapter or employed at an office where at least one travel agent is a member of that ASTA chapter. Minimum two year experience in travel and tourism industry. Must have successfully completed and fully paid for a self-directed study (not online) Educational Program offered by ASTA or The Travel Institute or have attended and fully paid for the ASTA International Destination Expo no more than 12 months prior to application date. Amount of award varies.

| | |
|---|---|
| **Number of awards:** | 1 |

**Contact:**
Tourism Cares
275 Turnpike Street
Suite 307
Canton, MA 02021
Phone: 781-821-5990
Fax: 781-821-8949
Web: www.tourismcares.org/scholarships

## ASTA Arizona Scholarship

**Type of award:** Scholarship, renewable.
**Intended use:** For sophomore, junior or senior study at accredited 2-year or 4-year institution in United States. Designated institutions: Colleges and universities in Arizona.
**Eligibility:** Applicant must be U.S. citizen, permanent resident or Canadian citizen/resident. Applicant must be residing in Arizona.
**Basis for selection:** Major/career interest in tourism/travel.
**Application requirements:** Transcript. Resume. U.S. or Canadian passport or U.S. or Canadian Alien Registration Card. Two evaluations and letters of recommendation (one from hospitality/tourism-related faculty member, one from hospitality/tourism professional).
**Additional information:** Minimum 3.0 GPA. Applicants attending two-year schools must be entering second year of program; students attending four-year schools must be entering junior or senior years. Visit Website for application, deadline, additional criteria.

| | |
|---|---|
| **Amount of award:** | $2,000 |
| **Number of awards:** | 1 |

**Contact:**
Tourism Cares
275 Turnpike Street
Suite 307
Canton, MA 02021
Phone: 781-821-5990
Fax: 781-821-8949
Web: www.tourismcares.org/scholarships

## ASTA George Reinke Scholarship

**Type of award:** Scholarship.
**Intended use:** For undergraduate study at vocational institution in United States or Canada.
**Eligibility:** Applicant must be returning adult student. Applicant must be U.S. citizen, permanent resident or Canadian citizen or permanent resident.
**Basis for selection:** Major/career interest in tourism/travel.
**Application requirements:** Essay. Resume. U.S. or Canadian passport or Alien Registration Card. Evaluation and letter of recommendation from tourism faculty member or tourism professional.
**Additional information:** See Website for application and deadline date. Must be entering or working in the travel and tourism industry. Must have successfully completed and fully paid for a travel and tourism certificate program at a state-licensed school in the United States or Canada no more than 12 months prior to application deadline date.

| | |
|---|---|
| **Amount of award:** | $1,500 |
| **Number of awards:** | 2 |
| **Total amount awarded:** | $3,000 |

**Contact:**
Tourism Cares
275 Turnpike Street
Suite 307
Canton, MA 02021
Phone: 781-821-5990
Fax: 781-821-8949
Web: www.tourismcares.org/scholarships

## ASTA Holland American Line Undergraduate Scholarship

**Type of award:** Scholarship.
**Intended use:** For sophomore, junior or senior study at 2-year or 4-year institution in United States or Canada.
**Eligibility:** Applicant must be U.S. citizen, permanent resident or Canadian citizen or resident.
**Basis for selection:** Major/career interest in tourism/travel or hospitality administration/management.
**Application requirements:** Essay, transcript. Resume. U.S. or Canadian passport or U.S. or Canadian Alien Registration Card. Two evaluations and letters of recommendation (one from hospitality/tourism-related faculty member, one from hospitality/tourism professional).
**Additional information:** Minimum 3.0 GPA. Applicants attending two-year schools must be entering second year of program; students attending four-year schools must be entering junior or senior years. Visit Website for application, deadline, additional criteria.

| | |
|---|---|
| **Amount of award:** | $1,500 |
| **Number of awards:** | 1 |

**Contact:**
Tourism Cares
275 Turnpike Street, Suite 307
Canton, MA 02021
Phone: 781-821-5990
Fax: 781-821-8949
Web: www.tourismcares.org/scholarships

## ASTA Northern California Chapter - Richard Epping Scholarship

**Type of award:** Scholarship, renewable.
**Intended use:** For sophomore, junior or senior study at accredited 2-year or 4-year institution in United States. Designated institutions: Colleges and universities in California.
**Eligibility:** Applicant must be U.S. citizen or permanent resident residing in California.
**Basis for selection:** Major/career interest in hospitality administration/management or tourism/travel.
**Application requirements:** Essay, transcript. Resume. U.S. passport or Alien Registration Card, California driver's license. Two evaluations and letters of recommendation (one from hospitality/tourism-related faculty member, one from hospitality/tourism professional).
**Additional information:** Minimum 3.0 GPA. Must be entering second year at two-year school, junior or senior year at four-year school. Visit Website for application, deadline, additional criteria.

| | |
|---|---|
| **Amount of award:** | $2,000 |
| **Number of awards:** | 1 |

**Contact:**
Tourism Cares
275 Turnpike Street
Suite 307
Canton, MA 02021
Phone: 781-821-5990
Fax: 781-821-8949
Web: www.tourismcares.org/scholarships

## ASTA Pacific Northwest Chapter/ William Hunt Scholarship

**Type of award:** Scholarship.
**Intended use:** For sophomore, junior or senior study at accredited 2-year or 4-year institution in United States or Canada.
**Eligibility:** Applicant must be U.S. citizen or permanent resident residing in Oregon, Montana, Alaska, Idaho or Washington.
**Basis for selection:** Major/career interest in tourism/travel or hospitality administration/management.
**Application requirements:** Essay, transcript. Resume. U.S. Passport or U.S. Alien Registration card. U.S. driver's license as proof of state residency. Two evaluations and letters of recommendation (one from hospitality/tourism-related faculty member, one from hospitality/tourism professional).
**Additional information:** Minimum 3.0 GPA. Must be entering the second year of a two-year school, or junior or senior year of a four-year school. Submit all items in electronic form except transcript, which should be sent directly from school. Visit Website for deadline and additional eligibility criteria.

| | |
|---|---|
| **Amount of award:** | $1,500 |
| **Number of awards:** | 2 |
| **Total amount awarded:** | $3,000 |

**Contact:**
Tourism Cares
275 Turnpike Street
Suite 307
Canton, MA 02021
Phone: 781-821-5990
Fax: 781-821-8949
Web: www.tourismcares.org/scholarships

## ASTA Princess Cruises Scholarship

**Type of award:** Scholarship, renewable.
**Intended use:** For sophomore, junior or senior study at accredited 2-year or 4-year institution in United States or Canada.
**Eligibility:** Applicant must be U.S. citizen, permanent resident or Canadian citizen/resident.
**Basis for selection:** Major/career interest in hospitality administration/management or tourism/travel.
**Application requirements:** Recommendations, essay, transcript. Resume. U.S. or Canadian passport or U.S. or Canadian Alien Registration Card. Two evaluations and letters of recommendation (one from hospitality/tourism-related faculty member, one from hospitality/tourism professional).
**Additional information:** Minimum 3.0 GPA. Must be entering the second year of a two-year school, third year of a three-year school (Quebec), junior or senior year of a four-year school. Visit Website for application, deadline, additional criteria.

**Amount of award:** $2,500
**Number of awards:** 1

**Contact:**
Tourism Cares
275 Turnpike Street
Suite 307
Canton, MA 02021
Phone: 781-821-5990
Fax: 781-821-8949
Web: www.tourismcares.org/scholarships

## ASTA Stan and Leone Pollard Scholarship

**Type of award:** Scholarship, renewable.
**Intended use:** For sophomore study at accredited 2-year institution in United States or Canada.
**Eligibility:** Applicant must be returning adult student. Applicant must be U.S. citizen, permanent resident or Canadian citizen/resident.
**Basis for selection:** Major/career interest in hospitality administration/management or tourism/travel.
**Application requirements:** Essay, transcript. Resume. U.S. passport or U.S. Alien Registration Card. Two evaluations and letters of recommendation (one from hospitality/tourism-related faculty member, one from hospitality/tourism professional).
**Additional information:** Minimum 3.0 GPA. Check Website for deadline, application, additional criteria. Amount of award varies.

**Number of awards:** 1

**Contact:**
Tourism Cares
275 Turnpike Street
Suite 307
Canton, MA 02021
Phone: 781-821-5990
Fax: 781-821-8949
Web: www.tourismcares.org/scholarships

## Dr. William C. Wright Scholarship

**Type of award:** Scholarship.
**Intended use:** For full-time junior or senior study at accredited 4-year institution in United States. Designated institutions: University of Houston, Conrad N. Hilton College of Hotel and Restaurant.
**Basis for selection:** Major/career interest in tourism/travel or hospitality administration/management. Applicant must demonstrate leadership.
**Additional information:** Must be in good standing at the University of Houston. Minimum 3.0 GPA. Apply online through the University of Houston, Conrad N. Hilton College of Hotel and Restaurant Management Website.

**Amount of award:** $1,500
**Number of awards:** 1

**Contact:**
Tourism Cares
275 Turnpike Street, Suite 307
Canton, MA 02021
Phone: 781-821-5990
Fax: 781-821-8949
Web: www.hrm.uh.edu/form/scholoarshipForm.asp

## IATAN Ronald A. Santana Memorial Scholarship

**Type of award:** Scholarship.
**Intended use:** For sophomore, junior or senior study at 2-year or 4-year institution in United States in Guam, Puerto Rico.
**Eligibility:** Applicant must be U.S. citizen, permanent resident or Guam or Puerto Rico citizens/residents.
**Basis for selection:** Major/career interest in tourism/travel or hospitality administration/management.
**Application requirements:** Essay, transcript. Resume. U.S. passport or Alien Registration Card. Two evaluations and letters of recommendation (one from hospitality/tourism-related faculty member, one from hospitality/tourism professional).
**Additional information:** Minimum 3.0 GPA. Applicants attending two-year schools must be entering second year of program; students attending four-year schools must be entering junior or senior year. Visit Website for application, deadline, additional criteria.

**Amount of award:** $1,000
**Number of awards:** 5
**Total amount awarded:** $5,000

**Contact:**
Tourism Cares
275 Turnpike Street, Suite 307
Canton, MA 02021
Phone: 781-821-5990
Fax: 781-821-8949
Web: www.tourismcares.org/scholarships

## NTA Canada Scholarship

**Type of award:** Scholarship.
**Intended use:** For full-time sophomore, junior, senior or graduate study at accredited 2-year or 4-year institution in United States or Canada.
**Eligibility:** Applicant must be permanent resident of Canada.
**Basis for selection:** Major/career interest in tourism/travel or hospitality administration/management.
**Application requirements:** Essay, transcript. Resume. Canadian passport or Canadian Alien Registration Card. Two evaluations and letters of recommendation from hospitality/tourism-related faculty, one from a professional in the hospitality/tourism industry.
**Additional information:** Minimum 3.0 GPA. Must demonstrate focus and commitment to tourism. Must be entering the second year of a two-year school, third year of a three-year school (Quebec), senior year of a four-year school, any year of graduate school. Visit Website for application, deadline, additional criteria.

**Amount of award:** $1,000
**Number of awards:** 1

**Contact:**
Tourism Cares
275 Turnpike Street
Suite 307
Canton, MA 02021
Phone: 781-821-5990
Fax: 781-821-8949
Web: www.tourismcares.org/scholarships

## NTA Connecticut Scholarship

**Type of award:** Scholarship.
**Intended use:** For full-time junior or senior study at accredited 4-year institution in United States.
**Eligibility:** Applicant must be U.S. citizen or permanent resident residing in Connecticut.
**Basis for selection:** Major/career interest in hospitality administration/management or tourism/travel. Applicant must demonstrate high academic achievement.
**Application requirements:** Essay, transcript. Resume. U.S. passport or Alien Registration Card, Connecticut driver's license. Two evaluations and letters of recommendation (one from hospitality/tourism-related faculty member, one from hospitality/tourism professional).
**Additional information:** Minimum 3.0 GPA. Visit Website for application, deadline, additional criteria.

| | |
|---|---|
| **Amount of award:** | $1,000 |
| **Number of awards:** | 1 |

**Contact:**
Tourism Cares
275 Turnpike Street
Suite 307
Canton, MA 02021
Phone: 781-821-5990
Fax: 781-821-8949
Web: www.tourismcares.org/scholarships

## NTA Dave Herren Memorial Scholarship

**Type of award:** Scholarship.
**Intended use:** For full-time junior, senior or graduate study at accredited 4-year institution in United States.
**Eligibility:** Applicant must be U.S. citizen or permanent resident.
**Basis for selection:** Major/career interest in hospitality administration/management or tourism/travel. Applicant must demonstrate high academic achievement.
**Application requirements:** Essay, transcript. Resume. U.S. passport or U.S. Alien Registration Card. Two evaluations and letters of recommendation (one from hospitality/tourism-related faculty member, one from hospitality/tourism professional).
**Additional information:** Minimum 3.0 GPA. Visit Website for application, deadline, additional criteria.

| | |
|---|---|
| **Amount of award:** | $1,000 |
| **Number of awards:** | 1 |

**Contact:**
Tourism Cares
275 Turnpike Street
Suite 307
Canton, MA 02021
Phone: 781-821-5990
Fax: 781-821-8949
Web: www.tourismcares.org/scholarships

## NTA Florida Scholarship

**Type of award:** Scholarship.
**Intended use:** For junior or senior study at accredited 2-year or 4-year institution in United States.
**Eligibility:** Applicant must be U.S. citizen or permanent resident residing in Florida.
**Basis for selection:** Major/career interest in hospitality administration/management or tourism/travel. Applicant must demonstrate high academic achievement.
**Application requirements:** Essay, transcript. Resume. U.S. passport or Alien Registration Card, Florida driver's license. Two evaluations and letters of recommendation (one from hospitality/tourism-related faculty member, one from hospitality/tourism professional).
**Additional information:** Minimum 3.0 GPA. Must be entering the second year of a two-year school, junior or senior year of a four-year school. Visit Website for application, deadline, additional criteria.

| | |
|---|---|
| **Amount of award:** | $1,500 |
| **Number of awards:** | 1 |

**Contact:**
Tourism Cares
275 Turnpike Street
Suite 307
Canton, MA 02021
Phone: 781-821-5990
Fax: 781-821-8949
Web: www.tourismcares.org/scholarships

## NTA Hawaii Chuck Yim Gee Scholarship

**Type of award:** Scholarship.
**Intended use:** For junior or senior study at accredited 4-year institution in United States or Canada.
**Eligibility:** Applicant must be U.S. citizen or permanent resident residing in Hawaii.
**Basis for selection:** Major/career interest in hospitality administration/management or tourism/travel. Applicant must demonstrate high academic achievement.
**Application requirements:** Essay, transcript. Resume. U.S. Passport or Alien Registration Card, Hawaii driver's license. Two evaluations and letters of recommendation (one from hospitality/tourism-related faculty member, one from hospitality/tourism professional).
**Additional information:** Minimum 3.0 GPA. Visit Website for application, deadline, additional criteria.

| | |
|---|---|
| **Amount of award:** | $1,500 |
| **Number of awards:** | 1 |

**Contact:**
Tourism Cares
275 Turnpike Street
Suite 307
Canton, MA 02021
Phone: 781-821-5990
Fax: 781-821-8949
Web: www.tourismcares.org/scholarships

## NTA LaMacchia Family Scholarship

**Type of award:** Scholarship.
**Intended use:** For full-time junior or senior study at 4-year institution. Designated institutions: Wisconsin institutions.
**Eligibility:** Applicant must be U.S. citizen or permanent resident.
**Basis for selection:** Major/career interest in tourism/travel or hospitality administration/management.

**Application requirements:** Essay, transcript. Resume. U.S. passport or Alien Registration Card. Two evaluations and letters of recommendation (one from hospitality/tourism-related faculty member, one from hospitality/tourism professional).
**Additional information:** Must have minimum 3.0 GPA. Visit Website for application, deadline, additional criteria.

| | |
|---|---|
| **Amount of award:** | $1,000 |
| **Number of awards:** | 1 |

**Contact:**
Tourism Cares
275 Turnpike Street
Suite 307
Canton, MA 02021
Phone: 781-821-5990
Fax: 781-821-8949
Web: www.tourismcares.org/scholarships

## NTA Massachusetts Scholarship

**Type of award:** Scholarship.
**Intended use:** For sophomore, junior or senior study at accredited 2-year or 4-year institution in United States. Designated institutions: Massachusetts institutions.
**Eligibility:** Applicant must be U.S. citizen or permanent resident residing in Massachusetts.
**Basis for selection:** Major/career interest in hospitality administration/management or tourism/travel. Applicant must demonstrate high academic achievement.
**Application requirements:** Essay, transcript. Resume. U.S. passport or Alien Registration Card, Massachusetts driver's license. Two evaluations and letters of recommendation (one from hospitality/tourism-related faculty member, one from hospitality/tourism professional).
**Additional information:** Minimum 3.0 GPA. Applicants attending two-year schools must be entering second year of program; students attending four-year schools must be entering junior or senior years. Visit Website for application, deadline, additional criteria.

| | |
|---|---|
| **Amount of award:** | $1,000 |
| **Number of awards:** | 1 |

**Contact:**
Tourism Cares
275 Turnpike Street
Suite 307
Canton, MA 02021
Phone: 781-821-5990
Fax: 781-821-8949
Web: www.tourismcares.org/scholarships

## NTA New Horizons - Kathy LeTarte Scholarship

**Type of award:** Scholarship.
**Intended use:** For junior or senior study at accredited 4-year institution in United States or Canada.
**Eligibility:** Applicant must be U.S. citizen or permanent resident residing in Michigan.
**Basis for selection:** Major/career interest in tourism/travel or hospitality administration/management.
**Application requirements:** Essay, transcript. Resume. U.S. passport or U.S. Alien Registration Card. Michigan driver's license. Two evaluations and letters of recommendation (one from hospitality/tourism-related faculty and one from a professional in hospitality/tourism industry).
**Additional information:** Minimum 3.0 GPA. Must be entering third year of three-year school (Quebec), or junior, senior year of four-year school. Visit Website for application, deadline, additional criteria.

| | |
|---|---|
| **Amount of award:** | $1,000 |
| **Number of awards:** | 1 |

**Contact:**
Tourism Cares
275 Turnpike Street
Suite 307
Canton, MA 02021
Phone: 781-821-5990
Fax: 781-821-8949
Web: www.tourismcares.org/scholarships

## NTA New Jersey Scholarship

**Type of award:** Scholarship.
**Intended use:** For sophomore, junior or senior study at accredited 2-year or 4-year institution in United States. Designated institutions: New Jersey institutions.
**Eligibility:** Applicant must be U.S. citizen or permanent resident residing in New Jersey.
**Basis for selection:** Major/career interest in hospitality administration/management or tourism/travel. Applicant must demonstrate high academic achievement.
**Application requirements:** Essay, transcript. Resume. U.S. passport or U.S. Alien Registration Card. New Jersey driver's license. Two evaluations and letters of recommendation (one from hospitality/tourism-related faculty member, one from hospitality/tourism professional).
**Additional information:** Minimum 3.0 GPA. Applicant must be entering the second year of a two-year school, or junior or senior year of a four-year school. Visit Website for application, deadline, additional criteria.

| | |
|---|---|
| **Amount of award:** | $1,000 |
| **Number of awards:** | 1 |

**Contact:**
Tourism Cares
275 Turnpike Street
Suite 307
Canton, MA 02021
Phone: 781-821-5990
Fax: 781-821-8949
Web: www.tourismcares.org/scholarships

## NTA New York Scholarship

**Type of award:** Scholarship.
**Intended use:** For full-time sophomore, junior or senior study at accredited 2-year or 4-year institution in United States. Designated institutions: New York institutions.
**Eligibility:** Applicant must be U.S. citizen or permanent resident residing in New York.
**Basis for selection:** Major/career interest in hospitality administration/management or tourism/travel. Applicant must demonstrate high academic achievement.
**Application requirements:** Essay, transcript. Resume. U.S. passport or U.S. Alien Registration Card. New York driver's license. Two evaluations and letters of recommendation (one from hospitality/tourism-related faculty member, one from hospitality/tourism professional).
**Additional information:** Minimum 3.0 GPA. Applicants attending two-year schools must be entering second year of program; students at four-year schools must be entering junior or senior years. Visit Website for application, deadline, additional criteria.

| | |
|---|---|
| **Amount of award:** | $1,000 |
| **Number of awards:** | 1 |

**Contact:**
Tourism Cares
275 Turnpike Street
Suite 307
Canton, MA 02021
Phone: 781-821-5990
Fax: 781-821-8949
Web: www.tourismcares.org/scholarships

## NTA North America Scholarship

**Type of award:** Scholarship.
**Intended use:** For sophomore, junior, senior or graduate study at 2-year, 4-year or graduate institution in United States or Canada.
**Eligibility:** Applicant must be U.S. citizen, permanent resident or Canadian citizen/resident.
**Basis for selection:** Major/career interest in tourism/travel or hospitality administration/management.
**Application requirements:** Essay, transcript. Resume. U.S. or Canadian passport or U.S. or Canadian Alien Registration Card. Two evaluations and letters of recommendation (one from hospitality/tourism-related faculty member, one from hospitality/tourism professional).
**Additional information:** Minimum 3.0 GPA. Applicants attending two-year schools must be entering second year of program; students attending four-year schools must be entering junior or senior year. Visit Website for application, deadline, additional criteria.

| | |
|---|---|
| **Amount of award:** | $1,000 |
| **Number of awards:** | 13 |
| **Total amount awarded:** | $13,000 |

**Contact:**
Tourism Cares
275 Turnpike Street, Suite 307
Canton, MA 02021
Phone: 781-821-5990
Fax: 781-821-8949
Web: www.tourismcares.org/scholarships

## NTA Ohio Scholarship

**Type of award:** Scholarship.
**Intended use:** For sophomore, junior or senior study at accredited 2-year or 4-year institution in United States. Designated institutions: Ohio institutions.
**Eligibility:** Applicant must be U.S. citizen or permanent resident residing in Ohio.
**Basis for selection:** Major/career interest in hospitality administration/management or tourism/travel. Applicant must demonstrate high academic achievement.
**Application requirements:** Essay, transcript. Resume. U.S. passport or Alien Registration Card, Ohio driver's license. Two evaluations and letters of recommendation (one from hospitality/tourism-related faculty member, one from hospitality/tourism professional).
**Additional information:** Minimum 3.0 GPA. Applicants attending two-year schools must be entering second year of program; students at four-year schools must be entering junior or senior years. Visit Website for application, deadline, additional criteria.

| | |
|---|---|
| **Amount of award:** | $1,000 |
| **Number of awards:** | 1 |

**Contact:**
Tourism Cares
275 Turnpike Street
Suite 307
Canton, MA 02021
Phone: 781-821-5990
Fax: 781-821-8949
Web: www.tourismcares.org/scholarships

## NTA Pat & Jim Host Scholarship

**Type of award:** Scholarship.
**Intended use:** For full-time sophomore, junior, senior or graduate study at accredited 4-year institution.
**Eligibility:** Applicant must be U.S. citizen or permanent resident residing in Kentucky.
**Basis for selection:** Major/career interest in tourism/travel or hospitality administration/management. Applicant must demonstrate high academic achievement.
**Application requirements:** Essay, transcript. Resume. U.S. passport or U.S. Alien Registration Card. Copy of Kentucky driver's license. Two evaluations and letters of recommendation (one from hospitality/tourism-related faculty member; other from hospitality/tourism industry professional).
**Additional information:** Minimum 3.0 GPA. Must demonstrate a clear focus on and commitment to tourism. Visit Website for application, deadline, additional criteria.

| | |
|---|---|
| **Amount of award:** | $1,000 |
| **Number of awards:** | 1 |

**Contact:**
Tourism Cares
275 Turnpike Street
Suite 307
Canton, MA 02021
Phone: 781-821-5990
Fax: 781-821-8949
Web: www.tourismcares.org/scholarships

## NTA Quebec Scholarship

**Type of award:** Scholarship.
**Intended use:** For full-time senior or graduate study at accredited 4-year institution in United States or Canada.
**Eligibility:** Applicant must be permanent resident of Quebec or Canada.
**Basis for selection:** Major/career interest in tourism/travel or hospitality administration/management.
**Application requirements:** Essay, transcript. Resume. Canadian passport or Alien Registration Card, Quebec driver's license. Two evaluations and letters of recommendation (one from hospitality/tourism-related faculty, other from a professional in the hospitality/tourism industry).
**Additional information:** Students may also attend three-year schools in Quebec. Minimum 3.0 GPA. Visit Website for application, deadline, additional criteria.

| | |
|---|---|
| **Amount of award:** | $1,500 |
| **Number of awards:** | 1 |

**Contact:**
Tourism Cares
275 Turnpike Street
Suite 307
Canton, MA 02021
Phone: 781-821-5990
Fax: 781-821-8949
Web: www.tourismcares.org/scholarships

## NTA Rene Campbell - Ruth McKinney Scholarship

**Type of award:** Scholarship.
**Intended use:** For junior or senior study at accredited 4-year institution in United States or Canada.
**Eligibility:** Applicant must be U.S. citizen or permanent resident residing in North Carolina.
**Basis for selection:** Major/career interest in tourism/travel or hospitality administration/management.
**Application requirements:** Essay, transcript. Resume. U.S. Passport or U.S. Alien Registration Card, North Carolina driver's license. Two evaluations and letters of recommendation (one from hospitality/tourism-related faculty member, one from hospitality/tourism professional).
**Additional information:** Minimum 3.0 GPA. Must be entering the second year of a two-year school, third year of a three-year school (Quebec), junior or senior year of a four-year school. Visit Website for application, deadline, additional criteria.

| | |
|---|---|
| **Amount of award:** | $1,000 |
| **Number of awards:** | 1 |

**Contact:**
Tourism Cares
275 Turnpike Street
Suite 307
Canton, MA 02021
Phone: 781-821-5990
Fax: 781-821-8949
Web: www.tourismcares.org/scholarships

## NTA Texas - Doug Harman Scholarship

**Type of award:** Scholarship.
**Intended use:** For undergraduate study at accredited 2-year institution in United States. Designated institutions: Tarrant County College Southeast Campus.
**Eligibility:** Applicant must be U.S. citizen or permanent resident residing in Texas.
**Basis for selection:** Major/career interest in tourism/travel or hospitality administration/management.
**Application requirements:** Essay, transcript. Resume, signed application form. U.S. passport or U.S. Alien Registration Card. Texas driver's license. Two evaluations and letters of recommendation (one from hospitality/tourism-related faculty member, one from hospitality/tourism professional).
**Additional information:** Minimum 3.0 GPA. Must be pursuing an Associate of Applied Science Degree in Hospitality Management at Tarrant County College Southeast Campus. Minimum 30 credit hours completed and minimum nine semester hours currently enrolled. Visit Tarrant County College Foundation Website for application.

| | |
|---|---|
| **Amount of award:** | $1,000 |
| **Number of awards:** | 1 |

**Contact:**
Tourism Cares
275 Turnpike Street, Suite 307
Canton, MA 02021
Phone: 781-821-5990
Fax: 781-821-8949
Web: www.tccd.edu/x6404.xml

## NTA Utah Keith Griffall Scholarship

**Type of award:** Scholarship.
**Intended use:** For junior or senior study at accredited 2-year or 4-year institution in United States. Designated institutions: Utah institutions.
**Eligibility:** Applicant must be U.S. citizen or permanent resident residing in Utah.
**Basis for selection:** Major/career interest in hospitality administration/management or tourism/travel. Applicant must demonstrate high academic achievement.
**Application requirements:** Essay, transcript. Resume. U.S Passport or Alien Registration Card, Utah driver's license. Two evaluations and letters of recommendation (one from hospitality/tourism-related faculty member, one from hospitality/tourism professional).
**Additional information:** Minimum 3.0 GPA. Must be entering the second year of a two-year school, junior or senior year of a four-year school. Visit Website for application, deadline, additional criteria.

| | |
|---|---|
| **Amount of award:** | $1,000 |
| **Number of awards:** | 1 |

**Contact:**
Tourism Cares
275 Turnpike Street
Suite 307
Canton, MA 02021
Phone: 781-821-5900
Fax: 781-821-8949
Web: www.tourismcares.org/scholarships

## NTA Yellow Ribbon Scholarship

**Type of award:** Scholarship.
**Intended use:** For sophomore, junior, senior or graduate study at accredited postsecondary institution in United States or Canada.
**Eligibility:** Applicant must be visually impaired, hearing impaired or physically challenged. Applicant must be U.S. citizen, permanent resident or Canadian citizen or resident.
**Basis for selection:** Major/career interest in tourism/travel; hospitality administration/management or hotel/restaurant management. Applicant must demonstrate high academic achievement.
**Application requirements:** Essay, transcript, proof of eligibility. Two evaluations and recommendation letters (one from hospitality/tourism-related faculty member, one from hospitality/tourism industry professional). U.S. or Canadian passport or Alien Registration Card. Letter from an accredited physician attesting to applicant's disability. Resume.
**Additional information:** Minimum 2.5 GPA. Must be entering the second year of a two-year school, third year of a three-year school (for Quebec), junior or senior year of a four-year school, any year of graduate study. Visit Website for additional criteria, application, deadline.

| | |
|---|---|
| **Amount of award:** | $5,000 |
| **Number of awards:** | 1 |

**Contact:**
Tourism Cares
275 Turnpike Street
Suite 307
Canton, MA 02021
Phone: 781-821-5990
Fax: 781-821-8949
Web: www.tourismcares.org/scholarships

# Transportation Clubs International

## Alice Glaisyer Warfield Memorial Scholarship

**Type of award:** Scholarship.
**Intended use:** For undergraduate or graduate study at accredited postsecondary institution.
**Basis for selection:** Major/career interest in transportation. Applicant must demonstrate financial need, high academic achievement, depth of character and service orientation.
**Application requirements:** Recommendations, essay, transcript. Small current photograph (for publication).
**Additional information:** Minimum 3.0 GPA.

| | |
|---|---|
| **Amount of award:** | $1,500 |
| **Number of awards:** | 1 |
| **Application deadline:** | May 31 |
| **Total amount awarded:** | $1,500 |

**Contact:**
Transportation Clubs International Scholarships
Attn: Bill Blair, A B Plant USA LLC
14614 Falling Creek, Suite 132
Houston, TX 77068
Web: www.transportationclubsinternational.com

## Charlotte Woods Memorial Scholarship

**Type of award:** Scholarship.
**Intended use:** For undergraduate or graduate study.
**Eligibility:** Applicant or parent must be member/participant of Transportation Clubs International.
**Basis for selection:** Major/career interest in transportation. Applicant must demonstrate financial need, high academic achievement, depth of character and service orientation.
**Application requirements:** Recommendations, essay, transcript. Small current photograph (for publication).
**Additional information:** Minimum 3.0 GPA.

| | |
|---|---|
| **Amount of award:** | $1,500 |
| **Number of awards:** | 1 |
| **Application deadline:** | May 31 |
| **Total amount awarded:** | $1,500 |

**Contact:**
Transportation Clubs International Scholarships
Attn: Bill Blair, A B Plant Shipping USA LLC
14614 Falling Creek, Suite 132
Houston, TX 77068
Web: www.transportationclubsinternational.com

## Denny Lydic Scholarship

**Type of award:** Scholarship.
**Intended use:** For undergraduate or graduate study at accredited vocational, 4-year or graduate institution.
**Basis for selection:** Major/career interest in transportation. Applicant must demonstrate financial need, high academic achievement, depth of character and service orientation.
**Application requirements:** Recommendations, essay, transcript. Small current photograph (for publication).
**Additional information:** Minimum 3.0 GPA. Award amount varies; up to $1,000.

| | |
|---|---|
| **Amount of award:** | $1,000 |
| **Number of awards:** | 1 |
| **Application deadline:** | May 31 |
| **Total amount awarded:** | $1,000 |

**Contact:**
Transportation Clubs International Scholarships
Attn: Bill Blair, A B Plant Shipping USA LLC
14614 Falling Creek, Suite 132
Houston, TX 77068
Web: www.transportationclubsinternational.com

## Ginger and Fred Deines Canada Scholarship

**Type of award:** Scholarship.
**Intended use:** For undergraduate or graduate study in United States or Canada.
**Eligibility:** Applicant must be Canadian citizen.
**Basis for selection:** Major/career interest in transportation. Applicant must demonstrate financial need, high academic achievement, depth of character and service orientation.
**Application requirements:** Recommendations, essay, transcript. Small current photograph (for publication).
**Additional information:** Minimum 3.0 GPA.

| | |
|---|---|
| **Amount of award:** | $2,000 |
| **Number of awards:** | 1 |
| **Application deadline:** | May 31 |
| **Total amount awarded:** | $2,000 |

**Contact:**
Transportation Clubs International Scholarships
Attn: Bill Blair, A B Plant Shipping USA LLC
14614 Falling Creek, Suite 132
Houston, TX 77068
Web: www.transportationclubsinternational.com

## Ginger and Fred Deines Mexico Scholarship

**Type of award:** Scholarship.
**Intended use:** For undergraduate or graduate study. Designated institutions: Institutions in U.S. or Mexico.
**Eligibility:** Applicant must be Mexican citizen.
**Basis for selection:** Major/career interest in transportation. Applicant must demonstrate financial need, high academic achievement, depth of character and service orientation.
**Application requirements:** Recommendations, essay, transcript. Small current photograph (for publication).
**Additional information:** Minimum 3.0 GPA.

| | |
|---|---|
| **Amount of award:** | $2,000 |
| **Number of awards:** | 1 |
| **Application deadline:** | May 31 |
| **Total amount awarded:** | $2,000 |

**Contact:**
Transportation Clubs International Scholarships
Attn: Bill Blair, A B Plant Shipping USA LLC
14614 Falling Creek, Suite 132
Houston, TX 77032
Web: www.transportationclubsinternational.com

## Hooper Memorial Scholarship

**Type of award:** Scholarship.
**Intended use:** For undergraduate or graduate study.
**Basis for selection:** Major/career interest in transportation. Applicant must demonstrate financial need, high academic achievement, depth of character and service orientation.

**Application requirements:** Recommendations, essay, transcript. Small current photograph (for publication).
**Additional information:** Minimum 3.0 GPA.

| | |
|---|---|
| **Amount of award:** | $2,000 |
| **Number of awards:** | 1 |
| **Application deadline:** | May 31 |
| **Total amount awarded:** | $2,000 |

**Contact:**
Transportation Clubs International Scholarships
Attn: Bill Blair, A B Plant Shipping USA LLC
14614 Falling Creek, Suite 132
Houston, TX 77068
Web: www.transportationclubsinternational.com

### Texas Transportation Scholarship

**Type of award:** Scholarship.
**Intended use:** For undergraduate or graduate study.
**Basis for selection:** Major/career interest in transportation. Applicant must demonstrate financial need, high academic achievement, depth of character and service orientation.
**Application requirements:** Recommendations, essay, transcript. Small current photograph (for publication).
**Additional information:** Applicant must have been enrolled in a Texas school for some phase of elementary through high school education. Minimum 3.0 GPA.

| | |
|---|---|
| **Amount of award:** | $1,500 |
| **Number of awards:** | 1 |
| **Application deadline:** | May 31 |
| **Total amount awarded:** | $1,500 |

**Contact:**
Transportation Clubs International Scholarships
Attn: Bill Blair, A B Plant Shipping USA LLC
14614 Falling Creek, Suite 132
Houston, TX 77068
Web: www.transportationclubsinternational.com

## Treacy Company

### Treacy Company Scholarship

**Type of award:** Scholarship, renewable.
**Intended use:** For full-time freshman or sophomore study at postsecondary institution.
**Eligibility:** Applicant must be residing in Montana, Idaho or North Dakota.
**Basis for selection:** Applicant must demonstrate financial need, leadership, seriousness of purpose and service orientation.
**Application requirements:** Transcript. Letter stating reason for applying, including personal information.
**Additional information:** Student may attend school outside of ND, ID, and MT. Must write for application; applications available from January to end of May.

| | |
|---|---|
| **Amount of award:** | $1,000 |
| **Number of awards:** | 25 |
| **Number of applicants:** | 55 |
| **Application deadline:** | June 15 |
| **Notification begins:** | July 31 |
| **Total amount awarded:** | $28,000 |

**Contact:**
Treacy Company
P.O. Box 1479
Helena, MT 59624

## Trinity Episcopal Church

### Shannon Scholarship

**Type of award:** Scholarship, renewable.
**Intended use:** For undergraduate study at postsecondary institution.
**Eligibility:** Applicant must be female. Applicant must be Episcopal. Applicant must be residing in Pennsylvania.
**Basis for selection:** Applicant must demonstrate financial need.
**Application requirements:** Proof of eligibility.
**Additional information:** Only open to daughters of Episcopal clergy in state of Pennsylvania. Must apply for state and federal financial assistance first. Previous recipients may reapply. Number of awards varies. For more information, contact church office.

| | |
|---|---|
| **Amount of award:** | $500-$7,500 |
| **Number of applicants:** | 3 |
| **Application deadline:** | April 30 |
| **Total amount awarded:** | $20,000 |

**Contact:**
Trinity Episcopal Church
200 South Second Street
Pottsville, PA 17901
Phone: 570-622-8720

## Two Ten Footwear Foundation

### Two Ten Footwear Design Scholarship

**Type of award:** Scholarship, renewable.
**Intended use:** For undergraduate or graduate study in or outside United States.
**Eligibility:** Applicant must be U.S. citizen or permanent resident.
**Basis for selection:** Based on design talent. Major/career interest in design. Applicant must demonstrate financial need.
**Application requirements:** Portfolio, recommendations, essay, transcript.
**Additional information:** Rolling deadline. Individual must be attending recognized design program. Must be interested in pursuing career in footwear design.

| | |
|---|---|
| **Amount of award:** | $1,000-$5,000 |

**Contact:**
Two Ten Footwear Foundation
Scholarship Department
1466 Main Street
Waltham, MA 02451
Phone: 800-346-3210 ext. 1510
Fax: 781-736-1555
Web: www.twoten.org

### Two Ten Footwear Foundation Scholarship

**Type of award:** Scholarship, renewable.
**Intended use:** For undergraduate study at accredited vocational, 2-year or 4-year institution.

**Eligibility:** Applicant or parent must be employed by Footwear/Leather Industry. Applicant must be U.S. citizen or permanent resident.
**Basis for selection:** Applicant must demonstrate financial need and high academic achievement.
**Application requirements:** Recommendations, essay, transcript, proof of eligibility.
**Additional information:** Top-ranking applicant is candidate for $15,000 super-scholarship, renewable up to four years. Additional information and application available on Website.

| | |
|---|---|
| **Amount of award:** | $500-$15,000 |
| **Application deadline:** | February 16 |
| **Notification begins:** | June 15 |
| **Total amount awarded:** | $700,000 |

**Contact:**
Two Ten Footwear Foundation
Attn: Scholarship Department
1466 Main Street
Waltham, MA 02451-1623
Phone: 800-346-3210 ext. 1512
Fax: 781-736-1555
Web: www.twoten.org

# UCB Pharma Inc.

## Keppra Family Epilepsy Scholarship Program

**Type of award:** Scholarship.
**Intended use:** For undergraduate or graduate study at vocational, 2-year, 4-year or graduate institution in United States.
**Eligibility:** Applicant must be U.S. citizen or permanent resident.
**Basis for selection:** Applicant must demonstrate high academic achievement, leadership and service orientation.
**Application requirements:** Transcript. Essay or artistic presentation explaining why applicant should be selected for scholarship (awards received, community involvement, etc.) and how epilepsy has impacted his or her life. Photograph. Three letters of recommendation: one from a school official, one from a community member, and one from applicant's epilepsy healthcare team.
**Additional information:** Scholarships are awarded to people with epilepsy, and to caregivers and family members of epilepsy patients. Visit Website for deadline and application.

| | |
|---|---|
| **Amount of award:** | $5,000 |
| **Number of awards:** | 30 |
| **Total amount awarded:** | $200,000 |

**Contact:**
UCB Pharma Inc.
Phone: 866-825-1920
Web: www.keppra.com

# Unico Foundation, Inc.

## Alphonse A. Miele Scholarship

**Type of award:** Scholarship.
**Intended use:** For undergraduate study at postsecondary institution.
**Eligibility:** Applicant must be high school senior. Applicant must be Italian.
**Basis for selection:** Applicant must demonstrate financial need, high academic achievement, depth of character and leadership.
**Application requirements:** Recommendations, essay, transcript, proof of eligibility. SAT/ACT scores.
**Additional information:** Applications must be acquired from and submitted through a participating local UNICO chapter. Must be of Italian heritage. Award is $1,500 per year for four years.

| | |
|---|---|
| **Amount of award:** | $6,000 |
| **Number of awards:** | 1 |
| **Application deadline:** | April 15 |

**Contact:**
Unico Foundation, Inc.
271 US Highway, 46 #A108
Fairfield, NJ 07004
Phone: 973-808-0035
Web: www.unico.org

## Major Don S. Gentile Scholarship

**Type of award:** Scholarship.
**Intended use:** For undergraduate study at postsecondary institution.
**Eligibility:** Applicant must be high school senior. Applicant must be Italian.
**Basis for selection:** Applicant must demonstrate financial need, high academic achievement, depth of character and leadership.
**Application requirements:** Recommendations, essay, transcript, proof of eligibility. SAT/ACT scores.
**Additional information:** Applications must be acquired from and submitted through a participating local UNICO chapter. Must be of Italian heritage. Award is $1,500 per year for four years.

| | |
|---|---|
| **Amount of award:** | $6,000 |
| **Number of awards:** | 1 |
| **Application deadline:** | April 15 |

**Contact:**
Unico Foundation, Inc.
271 US Highway 46 #A108
Fairfield, NJ 07004-2458
Phone: 973-808-0035
Web: www.unico.org

## Theodore Mazza Scholarship

**Type of award:** Scholarship.
**Intended use:** For undergraduate study at postsecondary institution.
**Eligibility:** Applicant must be high school senior. Applicant must be Italian.
**Basis for selection:** Applicant must demonstrate financial need, high academic achievement, depth of character and leadership.
**Application requirements:** Recommendations, essay, transcript, proof of eligibility. SAT/ACT scores.
**Additional information:** Applications must be acquired from and submitted through a participating local UNICO chapter. Must be of Italian heritage. Award is $1,500 per year for four years.

| | |
|---|---|
| **Amount of award:** | $6,000 |
| **Number of awards:** | 1 |
| **Application deadline:** | April 15 |

**Contact:**
Unico Foundation, Inc.
271 US Highway 46 #A108
Fairfield, NJ 07004-2458
Web: www.unico.org

### William C. Davini Scholarship

**Type of award:** Scholarship.
**Intended use:** For undergraduate study at postsecondary institution.
**Eligibility:** Applicant must be high school senior. Applicant must be Italian.
**Basis for selection:** Applicant must demonstrate financial need, high academic achievement, depth of character and leadership.
**Application requirements:** Recommendations, essay, transcript, proof of eligibility. SAT/ACT scores.
**Additional information:** Applications must be acquired from and submitted through a participating local UNICO chapter. Must be of Italian heritage. Award is $1,500 per year for four years.

| | |
|---|---|
| **Amount of award:** | $6,000 |
| **Number of awards:** | 1 |
| **Application deadline:** | April 15 |

**Contact:**
Unico Foundation, Inc.
271 US Highway 46 #A108
Fairfield, NJ 07004-2458
Web: www.unico.org

## Union Plus

### Union Plus Scholarship

**Type of award:** Scholarship.
**Intended use:** For undergraduate or graduate study at accredited vocational, 2-year, 4-year or graduate institution.
**Basis for selection:** Applicant must demonstrate financial need, high academic achievement, depth of character and leadership.
**Application requirements:** Recommendations, essay, proof of eligibility.
**Additional information:** Open to current or retired members, and dependents and spouses of current or retired members, of unions that participate in Union Plus programs.

| | |
|---|---|
| **Amount of award:** | $500-$4,000 |
| **Number of awards:** | 108 |
| **Number of applicants:** | 4,237 |
| **Application deadline:** | January 31 |
| **Notification begins:** | May 31 |
| **Total amount awarded:** | $150,000 |

**Contact:**
Union Plus Education Foundation c/o Union Privilege
1125 15th St., NW
Suite 300
Washington, DC 20005
Fax: 202-293-5311
Web: www.unionplus.org

## Unitarian Universalist Association

### Stanfield and D'Orlando Art Scholarship

**Type of award:** Scholarship.
**Intended use:** For full-time undergraduate or graduate study in United States.
**Eligibility:** Applicant must be Unitarian Universalist.
**Basis for selection:** Major/career interest in arts, general. Applicant must demonstrate financial need, depth of character and service orientation.
**Application requirements:** Portfolio, recommendations, essay, transcript, proof of eligibility.
**Additional information:** Number of awards varies; on average, five are given. Applicant must be preparing for fine arts career in fields such as painting, drawing, sculpture, or photography. Art therapy and performing arts majors not eligible. Returning adult students also eligible. See Website for application and more information.

| | |
|---|---|
| **Amount of award:** | $1,000-$4,500 |
| **Number of awards:** | 5 |
| **Number of applicants:** | 15 |
| **Application deadline:** | March 1 |
| **Notification begins:** | March 31 |
| **Total amount awarded:** | $22,500 |

**Contact:**
Unitarian Universalist Funding Program
P.O. Box 301149
Jamaica Plain, MA 02130
Phone: 617-971-9600
Fax: 617-971-0029
Web: www.uua.org/giving/awardsscholarships/

## United Food and Commercial Workers International Union

### United Food and Commercial Workers International Union Scholarship Program

**Type of award:** Scholarship.
**Intended use:** For undergraduate or graduate study at accredited postsecondary institution.
**Eligibility:** Applicant or parent must be member/participant of United Food and Commerical Workers.
**Basis for selection:** Applicant must demonstrate high academic achievement and service orientation.
**Application requirements:** Essay, transcript. Complete biographical questionnaire.
**Additional information:** Award is $2,000 per year for up to four years; 14-20 awards are available yearly. Open to current and prospective high school graduates and GED recipients. Applicant or applicant's parent must be member of United Food and Commercial Workers International Union for one year prior to application. Dependents of members must be under age 20.

| | |
|---|---|
| **Amount of award:** | $8,000 |
| **Number of awards:** | 14 |
| **Number of applicants:** | 3,500 |
| **Application deadline:** | April 15 |
| **Notification begins:** | July 1 |
| **Total amount awarded:** | $112,000 |

**Contact:**
United Food and Commercial Workers International Union
1775 K Street, N.W.
Washington, DC 20006
Phone: 202-223-3111
Web: www.ufcw.org/scholarship

# United Methodist Church General Board of Higher Education and Ministry

## United Methodist Scholarships

**Type of award:** Scholarship, renewable.
**Intended use:** For full-time undergraduate or graduate study at accredited 2-year, 4-year or graduate institution in United States.
**Eligibility:** Applicant must be United Methodist.
**Basis for selection:** Applicant must demonstrate seriousness of purpose.
**Application requirements:** Recommendations, essay, transcript. Online application.
**Additional information:** Sponsor administers more than 60 scholarship programs. All recipients must be full active members of United Methodist Church for minimum of one year prior to application and maintain minimum 2.5 GPA. Deadlines vary. Some scholarships are renewable. Visit Website for more information.

| | |
|---|---|
| **Notification begins:** | January 5 |

**Contact:**
United Methodist Church General Board of Higher Education and Ministry
Office of Loans and Scholarships
P.O. Box 340007
Nashville, TN 37203-0007
Phone: 615-340-7344
Web: www.gbhem.org

# United Methodist Communications

## Leonard M. Perryman Communications Scholarship for Ethnic Minority Students

**Type of award:** Scholarship.
**Intended use:** For full-time junior or senior study at accredited 4-year institution in United States.
**Eligibility:** Applicant must be Alaskan native, Asian American, African American, Mexican American, Hispanic American, Puerto Rican, American Indian or Native Hawaiian/Pacific Islander. Applicant must be United Methodist.
**Basis for selection:** Major/career interest in journalism; communications; radio/television/film or religion/theology. Applicant must demonstrate seriousness of purpose.
**Application requirements:** Recommendations, essay, transcript. Three examples of journalistic work in any medium; photograph (appropriate for publicity purposes).
**Additional information:** Must plan to pursue career in religious journalism or religious communication. Application forms may be downloaded from Website.

| | |
|---|---|
| **Amount of award:** | $2,500 |
| **Number of awards:** | 1 |
| **Number of applicants:** | 6 |
| **Application deadline:** | March 15 |
| **Total amount awarded:** | $2,500 |

**Contact:**
United Methodist Communications
Communications Ministry Team
P.O. Box 320, 810 12th Avenue South
Nashville, TN 37202-0320
Phone: 888-278-4862
Web: www.umcom.org

# United Negro College Fund

## Carnival/Miami HEAT Scholarship

**Type of award:** Scholarship, renewable.
**Intended use:** For full-time undergraduate study at 4-year institution.
**Eligibility:** Applicant must be U.S. citizen or permanent resident.
**Basis for selection:** Applicant must demonstrate financial need and high academic achievement.
**Application requirements:** Recommendations, essay, transcript.
**Additional information:** Minimum 2.8 GPA. Award is up to $5,000 per academic year. Must have completed the Carnival or Miami HEAT School to Work Mentoring Program.

| | |
|---|---|
| **Amount of award:** | $5,000 |

**Contact:**
United Negro College Fund
8260 Willow Oaks Corporate Drive
P.O. Box 10444
Fairfax, VA 22031-8044
Phone: 800-331-2244
Web: www.uncf.org

## Earl & Patricia Armstrong Scholarship

**Type of award:** Scholarship.
**Intended use:** For full-time undergraduate or graduate study at accredited 4-year institution in United States. Designated institutions: UNCF member institutions.
**Eligibility:** Applicant must be U.S. citizen or permanent resident.
**Basis for selection:** Major/career interest in medicine; biology or health sciences. Applicant must demonstrate financial need and high academic achievement.
**Application requirements:** Recommendations, essay, transcript, proof of eligibility. FAFSA and SAR.
**Additional information:** Minimum 3.0 GPA. Visit Website for application.

| | |
|---|---|
| **Amount of award:** | $3,000 |

**Contact:**
United Negro College Fund
8260 Willow Oaks Corporate Drive
P.O. Box 10444
Fairfax, VA 22031-8044
Phone: 800-331-2244
Web: www.uncf.org

## Gates Millennium Scholars Program

**Type of award:** Scholarship, renewable.
**Intended use:** For full-time freshman or graduate study at accredited 4-year or graduate institution in United States.
**Eligibility:** Applicant must be Alaskan native, Asian American, African American, Mexican American, Hispanic American, Puerto Rican, American Indian or Native Hawaiian/Pacific Islander. Applicant must be U.S. citizen or permanent resident.
**Basis for selection:** Major/career interest in education; engineering; library science; mathematics; public health or computer/information sciences. Applicant must demonstrate financial need, high academic achievement, leadership and service orientation.
**Application requirements:** Recommendations, transcript, nomination by high school principal, teacher, counselor, college president, professor, or dean. Nominee Personal Information Form, FAFSA, GMS information sheet, admission letter.
**Additional information:** Must be eligible for Pell Grant. Must participate in community service, volunteer work, or extracurricular activities. Minimum 3.3 GPA. Scholarship provides tuition, room, materials, and board not covered by existing financial aid. Eliminates loans, work-study, and outside jobs for scholarship recipients. Funded by Bill and Melinda Gates Foundation. Visit Website for application and deadline.

| | |
|---|---|
| **Number of awards:** | 1,000 |
| **Number of applicants:** | 13,350 |
| **Total amount awarded:** | $61,415,141 |

**Contact:**
Gates Millenium Scholars
P.O. Box 1434
Alexandria, VA 22313
Phone: 877-690-4677
Fax: 703-205-2079
Web: www.uncf.org or www.gmsp.org

## Greyhound Lines Scholarship Program

**Type of award:** Scholarship.
**Intended use:** For full-time undergraduate study at accredited 4-year institution.
**Basis for selection:** Applicant must demonstrate financial need.
**Application requirements:** Essay.
**Additional information:** Minimum 3.0 GPA. Visit Website for deadline and application.

**Amount of award:** $2,750

**Contact:**
United Negro College Fund
8260 Willow Oaks Corporate Drive
P.O. Box 10444
Fairfax, VA 22031-8044
Phone: 800-331-2244
Web: www.uncf.org

## John W. Anderson Foundation Scholarship

**Type of award:** Scholarship, renewable.
**Intended use:** For full-time undergraduate study at accredited 4-year institution in United States. Designated institutions: UNCF member institutions.
**Eligibility:** Applicant must be U.S. citizen or permanent resident residing in Indiana.
**Basis for selection:** Applicant must demonstrate financial need and high academic achievement.
**Application requirements:** FAFSA and SAR.
**Additional information:** Minimum 2.5 GPA. See Website for more information.

**Amount of award:** $3,000

**Contact:**
United Negro College Fund
8260 Willow Oaks Corporate Drive
P.O. Box 10444
Fairfax, VA 22031-8044
Phone: 800-331-2244
Web: www.uncf.org

## Maya Angelou/Vivian Baxter Scholarship

**Type of award:** Scholarship, renewable.
**Intended use:** For full-time undergraduate study at accredited 4-year institution in United States. Designated institutions: UNCF member institutions.
**Eligibility:** Applicant must be residing in North Carolina.
**Basis for selection:** Applicant must demonstrate financial need, high academic achievement, leadership and service orientation.
**Application requirements:** FAFSA and SAR.
**Additional information:** Minimum 2.5 GPA. Visit Website for details.

**Amount of award:** $2,500

**Contact:**
United Negro College Fund
8260 Willow Oaks Corporate Drive
P.O. Box 10444
Fairfax, VA 22031-8044
Phone: 800-331-2244
Web: www.uncf.org

# United States Association of Blind Athletes

## Arthur and Helen Copeland Scholarship for Females

**Type of award:** Scholarship.
**Intended use:** For full-time undergraduate study at 2-year or 4-year institution.
**Eligibility:** Applicant must be visually impaired. Applicant must be U.S. citizen.
**Basis for selection:** Applicant must demonstrate high academic achievement and service orientation.
**Application requirements:** Transcript, proof of eligibility. Autobiographical sketch outlining USABA involvement, academic goals, and objective for which scholarship funds will be used.

**Additional information:** Applicants must be legally blind. Priority given applicants participating in a sport who are also USABA members. $500 award may be split into two $250 scholarships if there are two qualified applicants.

| | |
|---|---|
| **Amount of award:** | $250-$500 |
| **Number of awards:** | 2 |
| **Application deadline:** | August 15 |
| **Notification begins:** | November 1 |
| **Total amount awarded:** | $500 |

**Contact:**
U.S. Association of Blind Athletes
33 North Institute Street
Colorado Springs, CO 80903
Phone: 719-630-0422
Fax: 719-630-0616
Web: www.usaba.org

### Arthur E. Copeland Scholarship

**Type of award:** Scholarship.
**Intended use:** For full-time undergraduate study at 2-year or 4-year institution.
**Eligibility:** Applicant must be visually impaired. Applicant must be U.S. citizen.
**Basis for selection:** Applicant must demonstrate high academic achievement and service orientation.
**Application requirements:** Transcript, proof of eligibility. Autobiographical sketch outlining community service and academic goals. References.
**Additional information:** Applicant must be legally blind. Must be high school senior or in college. Must be current United States Association of Blind Athletes member. Must have participated in USABA sports programs or plan on participating in future programs; preference given to athletes.

| | |
|---|---|
| **Amount of award:** | $500 |
| **Number of awards:** | 1 |
| **Application deadline:** | August 15 |
| **Notification begins:** | November 1 |

**Contact:**
Mark Lucas
33 North Institute Street
Colorado Springs, CO 80903
Phone: 719-630-0422
Fax: 719-630-0616
Web: www.usaba.org

## United States Institute of Peace

### National Peace Essay Contest

**Type of award:** Scholarship.
**Intended use:** For undergraduate study at postsecondary institution.
**Eligibility:** Applicant must be enrolled in high school. Applicant must be U.S. citizen or permanent resident.
**Basis for selection:** Competition/talent/interest in writing/ journalism. Major/career interest in international relations.
**Application requirements:** Three-part maximum 1500-word essay on topic chosen by the Institute. Student form and coordinator form.
**Additional information:** Home-schooled students, foreign exchange students, or those enrolled in correspondence programs also eligible. Non-International Relations majors are also eligible and encouraged to submit essay. Applicant must submit essay to contest coordinator before deadline; the coordinator will submit essay to the Institute. State-level winners receive $1,000 and will compete for national awards of $10,000, $5,000, and $2,500 (national amount includes state award). Also invited to attend awards program in Washington, DC. Visit Website for more information.

| | |
|---|---|
| **Amount of award:** | $1,000-$10,000 |
| **Number of awards:** | 53 |
| **Number of applicants:** | 1,200 |
| **Application deadline:** | February 1 |
| **Notification begins:** | May 1 |
| **Total amount awarded:** | $67,500 |

**Contact:**
United States Institute of Peace
1200 17th Street NW
Suite 200
Washington, DC 20036-3011
Phone: 202-429-4710
Fax: 202-429-6063
Web: www.usip.org/npec

## United Transportation Union Insurance Association

### United Transportation Union Insurance Association Scholarship

**Type of award:** Scholarship, renewable.
**Intended use:** For full-time undergraduate study at accredited vocational, 2-year or 4-year institution in or outside United States.
**Eligibility:** Applicant or parent must be member/participant of United Transportation Union. Applicant must be no older than 25. Applicant must be permanent resident.
**Application requirements:** Proof of eligibility.
**Additional information:** Scholarships awarded by lottery. Applicant must be accepted to or enrolled in an eligible institution. Members and direct descendants of living or deceased members eligible. Notification takes place prior to fall enrollment.

| | |
|---|---|
| **Amount of award:** | $500 |
| **Number of awards:** | 50 |
| **Number of applicants:** | 900 |
| **Application deadline:** | March 31 |

**Contact:**
United Transportation Union Insurance Association
24950 Country Club Blvd., Ste. 340
North Olmsted, OH 44070-5333
Phone: 216-228-9400
Web: www.utu.org

## University Film and Video Association

### Carole Fielding Video Grant

**Type of award:** Research grant.
**Intended use:** For undergraduate or graduate study at accredited 2-year or 4-year institution.

**Basis for selection:** Major/career interest in film/video.
**Application requirements:** Resume, budget, research/production proposal.
**Additional information:** Project categories include narrative, documentary, experimental, multimedia/installation, animation, and research. Applicant must be sponsored by faculty member who is active member of University Film and Video Association. Number of awards varies. Visit Website for application.

| | |
|---|---|
| **Amount of award:** | $500-$4,000 |
| **Application deadline:** | December 15 |
| **Notification begins:** | March 31 |

**Contact:**
Prof. Adrianne Carageorge, UFVA Carole Fielding Student Grants Chair
Rochester Inst. Of Tech., Bldg. 7B, Rm. 2270
70 Lomb Memorial Dr.
Rochester, NY 14623-5604
Web: www.ufva.org

# Upakar

## Indian American Scholarship

**Type of award:** Scholarship, renewable.
**Intended use:** For freshman study.
**Eligibility:** Applicant must be Asian American. Applicant must be U.S. citizen or permanent resident.
**Basis for selection:** Applicant must demonstrate financial need and high academic achievement.
**Application requirements:** Recommendations, essay.
**Additional information:** Applicant must have either been born or have one grandparent/parent who was born in the Republic of India. Applicant must have cumulative, unadjusted GPA over 3.6. Applicant's family must have Adjusted Gross Income of less than $75,000. Must have green card or be American citizen.

| | |
|---|---|
| **Amount of award:** | $2,000 |
| **Number of awards:** | 20 |
| **Number of applicants:** | 250 |
| **Application deadline:** | April 30 |
| **Notification begins:** | June 1 |
| **Total amount awarded:** | $60,000 |

**Contact:**
Upakar c/o M. Mukunda
10237 Nolan Drive
Rockville, MD 20850
Web: www.upakar.org

# U.S. Army Recruiting Command

## Montgomery GI Bill (MGIB)

**Type of award:** Scholarship.
**Intended use:** For undergraduate or graduate study at accredited postsecondary institution in United States.
**Eligibility:** Applicant must be at least 17, no older than 35. Applicant must be U.S. citizen. Applicant must be in military service in the Army.
**Basis for selection:** Applicant must demonstrate depth of character, leadership, patriotism, seriousness of purpose and service orientation.
**Application requirements:** Interview. Armed Services Vocational Aptitude Battery.
**Additional information:** Award amount varies depending on type of service. Visit Website for award amounts and service requirements.
**Contact:**
U.S. Army Recruiting Command
Phone: 888-550-ARMY
Web: www.goarmy.com

## Selected Reserve Montgomery GI Bill

**Type of award:** Scholarship.
**Intended use:** For undergraduate or graduate study at accredited postsecondary institution.
**Eligibility:** Applicant must be at least 17, no older than 35. Applicant must be U.S. citizen. Applicant must be veteran who served in the Army or Reserves/National Guard.
**Basis for selection:** Applicant must demonstrate depth of character, leadership, patriotism, seriousness of purpose and service orientation.
**Application requirements:** Interview. Armed Services Vocational Aptitude Battery.
**Additional information:** Award amount varies. Visit Website for award amounts and service requirements.
**Contact:**
U.S. Army Recruiting Command
Phone: 888-550-ARMY
Web: www.goarmy.com

## Student Loan Repayment Program

**Type of award:** Scholarship.
**Intended use:** For at 2-year or 4-year institution.
**Eligibility:** Applicant must be at least 17, no older than 35. Applicant must be U.S. citizen or permanent resident.
**Basis for selection:** Applicant must demonstrate depth of character.
**Additional information:** Program is part of ECS program, allowing students to defer from mobilization and deployment to finish college degree. Maximum benefit of $50,000. Must be high school graduate or graduating senior. Must score 50 or higher on Armed Services Vocational Aptitude Battery. Minimum 2.0 GPA must be maintained. Must be healthy, in good physical condition, in good moral standing. Must attend scheduled monthly training assemblies and required annual training.
**Contact:**
U.S. Army Recruiting Command
Phone: 888-550-ARMY
Web: www.goarmy.com

## Tuition Assistance (TA)

**Type of award:** Scholarship.
**Intended use:** For at 2-year or 4-year institution.
**Eligibility:** Applicant must be at least 17, no older than 35. Applicant must be U.S. citizen or permanent resident.
**Basis for selection:** Applicant must demonstrate depth of character.
**Additional information:** Award is $4,500 per academic year. Program is part of ECS program, allowing students to defer from mobilization and deployment to finish college degree. Must be high school graduate or graduating senior. Must score

50 or higher on Armed Services Vocational Aptitude Battery. Minimum 2.0 GPA must be maintained. Must be healthy, in good physical condition, in good moral standing. Must attend scheduled monthly training assemblies and required annual training.

**Contact:**
U.S. Army Recruiting Command
Phone: 888-550-ARMY
Web: www.goarmy.com

# U.S. Department of Agriculture

## USDA/1890 National Scholars Program

**Type of award:** Scholarship, renewable.
**Intended use:** For full-time freshman study at 4-year institution in United States. Designated institutions: One of the 1890 Historically Black Land-Grant Institutions: Alabama A&M University, Alcorn State University (MS), Delaware State University, Florida A&M University, Fort Valley State University (GA), Kentucky State University, Lincoln University (MO), Langston University (OK), North Carolina A&T University, Prairie View A&M University (TX), South Carolina State University, Southern University (LA), Tennessee State University, Tuskegee University (AL), University of Arkansas at Pine Bluff, University of Maryland at Eastern Shore, Virginia State University, and West Virginia State University.
**Eligibility:** Applicant must be high school senior. Applicant must be U.S. citizen.
**Basis for selection:** Major/career interest in agriculture; agribusiness; agricultural education; agricultural economics; animal sciences; botany; food science/technology; wildlife/fisheries; forestry or horticulture. Applicant must demonstrate high academic achievement, leadership and service orientation.
**Application requirements:** Transcript. One recommendation from school counselor and one recommendation from high school teacher. SAT/ACT scores.
**Additional information:** Must be seeking bachelor's degree in agriculture, food, natural resource sciences, or related disciplines. Scholarship covers full tuition and fees, plus room and board, for four years, up to $120,000. Upon completion of academic degree program, recipient has obligation of one year of service to USDA for each year of financial support. Number of awards varies depending on funding. Minimum 1000 SAT (Math and Reading; 1500 Math/Reading/Writing) or minimum 21 ACT and 3.0 GPA. Program includes summer employment. Upon successful completion of summer program, students are eligible for non-competitive transition as permanent employees. Contact designated institutions for more information and application.

| | |
|---|---|
| **Amount of award:** | Full tuition |
| **Number of applicants:** | 421 |
| **Application deadline:** | February 1 |
| **Notification begins:** | May 1 |
| **Total amount awarded:** | $2,280,000 |

**Contact:**
U.S. Department of Agriculture
Web: www.usda.gov

# U.S. Department of Education

## Academic Competitiveness Grant

**Type of award:** Scholarship, renewable.
**Intended use:** For freshman or sophomore study at 2-year or 4-year institution in United States.
**Eligibility:** Applicant must be U.S. citizen or permanent resident.
**Basis for selection:** Applicant must demonstrate high academic achievement.
**Additional information:** Must be a Federal Pell Grant recipient. If first-year student, must not have been previously enrolled in an ACG-eligible program while at or below age of compulsory school attendance. If a second-year student, must have at minimum 3.0 GPA at end of first year. Must meet "rigorous secondary school program of study" requirement. See Website for details.

| | |
|---|---|
| **Amount of award:** | $750-$1,300 |

**Contact:**
Federal Student Aid Information Center
P.O. Box 84
Washington, DC 20044-0084
Phone: 800-4-FED AID
Web: www.studentaid.ed.gov

## Federal Pell Grant Program

**Type of award:** Scholarship, renewable.
**Intended use:** For undergraduate study at 2-year or 4-year institution.
**Eligibility:** Applicant must be U.S. citizen or permanent resident.
**Basis for selection:** Applicant must demonstrate financial need.
**Application requirements:** Proof of eligibility. FAFSA.
**Additional information:** Grant based on financial need, costs to attend school, and enrollment status. Must not have previously earned baccalaureate or professional degree. Amount of award varies; the maximum amount is $5,550. Visit Website for more information.

| | |
|---|---|
| **Application deadline:** | June 30 |

**Contact:**
Federal Student Aid Information Center
P.O. Box 84
Washington, DC 20044-0084
Phone: 800-4-FED-AID or 800-730-8913
Web: www.studentaid.ed.gov

## Federal Supplemental Educational Opportunity Grant Program

**Type of award:** Scholarship, renewable.
**Intended use:** For undergraduate study at accredited vocational, 2-year or 4-year institution in United States.
**Eligibility:** Applicant must be U.S. citizen or permanent resident.
**Basis for selection:** Applicant must demonstrate financial need.
**Application requirements:** Proof of eligibility. FAFSA.
**Additional information:** Priority given to Federal Pell Grant recipients with exceptional financial need. Must not have defaulted on federal grant or educational loan. Awards not

generally made to students enrolled less than half-time. Check with institution's financial aid office for deadline.

**Amount of award:** $100-$4,000

**Contact:**
Federal Student Aid Information Center
P.O. Box 84
Washington, DC 20044-0084
Phone: 800-4-FED-AID
Web: www.studentaid.ed.gov

### Federal Work-Study Program

**Type of award:** Scholarship.
**Intended use:** For undergraduate or graduate study at accredited postsecondary institution in United States.
**Eligibility:** Applicant must be U.S. citizen or permanent resident.
**Basis for selection:** Applicant must demonstrate financial need.
**Application requirements:** Proof of eligibility. FAFSA.
**Additional information:** Part-time on-campus and off-campus jobs based on class schedule and academic progress. Students earn at least federal minimum wage. Visit Website for more information.

**Application deadline:** June 30

**Contact:**
Federal Student Aid Information Center
P.O. Box 84
Washington, DC 20044-0084
Phone: 800-4-FED-AID
Web: www.studentaid.ed.gov

### Iraq and Afghanistan Service Grant

**Type of award:** Scholarship.
**Intended use:** For undergraduate study at 4-year institution in United States.
**Eligibility:** Applicant must be no older than 24. Applicant must be U.S. citizen or permanent resident. Applicant must be dependent of deceased veteran.
**Additional information:** Grant is for students whose parent or guardian was a member of the U.S. Armed Forces and died as a result of service performed in Iraq or Afghanistan after September 11, 2001. Must not be eligible for Pell Grant. Must be enrolled in college at least part-time at time of parent's or guardian's death.

**Contact:**
Federal Student Aid Information Center
P.O. Box 84
Washington, DC 20044-0084
Phone: 800-4-FED-AID
Web: www.studentaid.ed.gov

### The National Science and Mathematics Access to Retain Talent Grant (National SMART Grant)

**Type of award:** Scholarship, renewable.
**Intended use:** For junior or senior study at 4-year institution in United States.
**Eligibility:** Applicant must be U.S. citizen or permanent resident.
**Basis for selection:** Major/career interest in computer/information sciences; life sciences; physical sciences; mathematics; technology; engineering or foreign languages. Applicant must demonstrate high academic achievement.
**Additional information:** Minimum 3.0 GPA. Nonmajor single liberal arts programs majors also eligible. Must be Pell Grant-eligible. Award amount varies, maximum amount of $4,000.

**Amount of award:** $4,000

**Contact:**
Federal Student Aid Center
P.O. Box 84
Washington, DC 20044-0084
Phone: 800-4-FED AID
Web: www.studentaid.ed.gov

### Robert C. Byrd Honors Scholarship Program

**Type of award:** Scholarship, renewable.
**Intended use:** For full-time undergraduate study at postsecondary institution in United States.
**Eligibility:** Applicant must be high school senior. Applicant must be U.S. citizen or permanent resident.
**Basis for selection:** Applicant must demonstrate high academic achievement.
**Application requirements:** Proof of eligibility.
**Additional information:** Merit-based. Renewable up to three years. Selections by state education agencies (SEAs) supervising public elementary/secondary schools. Awards made in all 50 states, District of Columbia, Puerto Rico, and insular areas. Deadlines vary by state; contact high school guidance counselor or SEA for details.

**Amount of award:** $1,500

**Contact:**
Federal Student Aid Information Center
P.O. Box 84
Washington, DC 20044
Phone: 800-4-FED-AID
Web: www.studentaid.ed.gov

## U.S. Department of Education Rehabilitation Services Administration

### Vocational Rehabilitation Assistance

**Type of award:** Scholarship, renewable.
**Intended use:** For undergraduate or graduate study at postsecondary institution in United States.
**Additional information:** Number of awards varies; amount varies depending on institution. Applicant must have a disability. Award applicable to many fields/majors, but must be consistent with applicant's abilities, interest, and informed choice. Must contact state vocational rehabilitation agency to become eligible. See Website for more information.

**Contact:**
Rehabilitation Services Administration
400 Maryland Ave SW
PCP Room 5014
Washington, DC 20202-2800
Web: www.ed.gov/about/offices/list/osers/rsa/index.html

# U.S. Department of Health and Human Services

## National Health Service Corps Scholarship

**Type of award:** Scholarship.
**Intended use:** For full-time undergraduate or graduate study at accredited 4-year or graduate institution in United States.
**Eligibility:** Applicant must be U.S. citizen.
**Basis for selection:** Major/career interest in dentistry; nursing; nurse practitioner; physician assistant or midwifery. Applicant must demonstrate depth of character, seriousness of purpose and service orientation.
**Application requirements:** Interview, recommendations, essay, transcript, proof of eligibility. Resume, tuition bill, W-4.
**Additional information:** Students pursuing degree in allopathic or osteopathic medicine also eligible. Doctorate nurse training and "pre-professional" students ineligible. Awardees commit to providing health-care services in a National Health Service Corps approved site. One year of service owed for every year of scholarship support. Minimum service commitment two years; maximum four years. Award includes monthly stipend. Must be in training program. Number of awards varies. Visit Website for deadline and application.

| | |
|---|---|
| **Amount of award:** | Full tuition |
| **Number of applicants:** | 1,400 |

**Contact:**
Web: www.nhsc.hrsa.gov

# U.S. Environmental Protection Agency

## EPA National Network for Environmental Management Studies Fellowship

**Type of award:** Research grant.
**Intended use:** For undergraduate or graduate study.
**Eligibility:** Applicant must be U.S. citizen or permanent resident.
**Basis for selection:** Major/career interest in environmental science; public relations; communications; computer/information sciences or law. Applicant must demonstrate leadership and seriousness of purpose.
**Application requirements:** Transcript. Resume. One-page work-plan proposal. Letter of reference from faculty member or department head familiar with student's work and qualifications; letter must discuss student's aptitude and/or experience for project.
**Additional information:** Program provides students with research opportunities and experience at EPA locations nationwide. NNEMS develops and distributes annual catalog listing available research opportunities for coming year. Selected students receive stipend for performing research project. Projects also available in environmental management/administration and environmental policy, regulation, and law. Undergraduate applicants must: 1) be enrolled in program directly related to pollution control or environmental protection; 2) have 3.0 GPA; 3) have already completed four courses related to environmental field. Seniors who graduate prior to completion of advertised NNEMS fellowship period ineligible unless admitted to graduate school with submittable verification. Visit Website for award information and deadline. Catalog of available research opportunities available at www.epa.gov/education/students.html.

| | |
|---|---|
| **Number of awards:** | 32 |
| **Number of applicants:** | 345 |
| **Total amount awarded:** | $316,087 |

**Contact:**
Web: www.epa.gov/enviroed/students.html

## Greater Research Opportunities Undergraduate Student Fellowships

**Type of award:** Scholarship.
**Intended use:** For full-time junior or senior study at accredited 4-year institution in United States.
**Eligibility:** Applicant must be U.S. citizen or permanent resident.
**Basis for selection:** Major/career interest in life sciences; environmental science; engineering; social/behavioral sciences; physical sciences; mathematics; computer/information sciences or economics. Applicant must demonstrate financial need, high academic achievement and seriousness of purpose.
**Application requirements:** Recommendations, essay, transcript, proof of eligibility. Pre-application form. Resident Aliens must include green card number. EPA may verify number with the Immigration and Naturalization Service.
**Additional information:** Award provides funding for last two years of four-year education. Students must apply before beginning of junior year. Applicant must attend a four-year institution or be in the second year at a two-year school at the time of applying, with the intent of transferring to a four-year institution. Minimum 3.0 GPA. Fellowship provides up to $19,700 per year for two years to cover tuition and fees as well as $9,500 of internship support for a three month period. Stipends and expense allowance also provided. Recipient must complete summer internship at EPA facility between funded junior and senior years. Preference given to applicants attending academic institutions that are not highly funded for development of environmental research. See Website for link to list. Applicants must submit preapplication form first; following a merit review, top-ranked applicants will be asked to submit formal application. See Website for application and deadline.

| | |
|---|---|
| **Amount of award:** | $48,900 |
| **Number of awards:** | 40 |
| **Total amount awarded:** | $1,956,000 |

**Contact:**
U.S. Environmental Protection Agency
Peer Review Division (8725F)
1200 Pennsylvania Avenue, NW
Washington, DC 20460
Phone: 800-490-9194
Web: www.epa.gov/ncer/fellow

# U.S. Navy/Marine NROTC College Scholarship Program

## ROTC/Navy Nurse Corps Scholarship Program

**Type of award:** Scholarship.
**Intended use:** For full-time freshman study at accredited 4-year institution in United States. Designated institutions: NROTC-approved nursing schools.

**Eligibility:** Applicant must be at least 17, no older than 23. Applicant must be U.S. citizen.
**Basis for selection:** Major/career interest in nursing. Applicant must demonstrate high academic achievement and leadership.
**Application requirements:** Interview, recommendations, transcript, proof of eligibility.
**Additional information:** Scholarships are highly competitive and based on individual merit. Scholarships pay for college tuition, fees, books, uniforms, and offer $250 monthly allowance, which increases yearly. Electronic application is first step in application process. Number of awards varies. Applicant must be medically qualified for the NROTC Scholarship Program. Minimum 530 SAT (Reading), 520 (Math); minimum 22 ACT (English), 21 (Math). Participation in extracurricular activities and work experience required. Applicants must have fewer than 30 hours college credit. Obligation of eight years commissioned service, four of which must be active duty. Contact local recruiter for more details.

| | |
|---|---|
| **Amount of award:** | Full tuition |
| **Number of applicants:** | 500 |
| **Application deadline:** | January 31 |

**Contact:**
Contact local recruitment officer.
Phone: 800-NAV-ROTC
Web: www.navy.com/joining/education-opportunities/nrotc.html

## ROTC/Navy/Marine Four-Year Scholarship

**Type of award:** Scholarship.
**Intended use:** For full-time freshman study at accredited 4-year institution in United States. Designated institutions: Colleges and universities hosting NROTC program.
**Eligibility:** Applicant must be at least 17, no older than 23. Applicant must be U.S. citizen.
**Basis for selection:** Applicant must demonstrate high academic achievement and leadership.
**Application requirements:** Interview, recommendations, transcript, proof of eligibility.
**Additional information:** Scholarships are highly competitive and based on individual merit. Provide full tuition, fees, book allowance, and $250 monthly allowance, which increases annually. Number of awards varies. Applicant must be medically qualified for NROTC Scholarship. Minimum 530 SAT (Reading), 520 (Math); minimum 22 ACT (English), 21 (Math). Participation in extracurricular activities and work experience required. Applicant must have fewer than 30 hours college credit. Obligation of eight years commissioned service, five of which must be active duty. Contact nearest NROTC unit for more information. Visit Website to fill out electronic application.

| | |
|---|---|
| **Amount of award:** | Full tuition |
| **Number of applicants:** | 5,900 |
| **Application deadline:** | January 31 |

**Contact:**
Contact your local recruitment officer.
Phone: 800-NAV-ROTC
Web: www.navy.com/joining/education-opportunities/nrotc.html

## ROTC/Navy/Marine Two-Year Scholarship

**Type of award:** Scholarship.
**Intended use:** For full-time junior or senior study at 4-year institution in United States. Designated institutions: Colleges and universities hosting NROTC programs.
**Eligibility:** Applicant must be at least 17, no older than 23. Applicant must be U.S. citizen.
**Basis for selection:** Applicant must demonstrate high academic achievement and leadership.
**Application requirements:** Interview, recommendations, transcript, proof of eligibility.
**Additional information:** Scholarships are highly competitive and based on individual merit. Scholarships open to students who have completed sophomore year, or third year in a five-year curriculum. NROTC scholarships pay for college tuition, fees, book allowance, uniforms, and $250 monthly allowance, which increases annually. Minimum 530 SAT (Reading), 520 (Math); minimum 22 ACT (English), 21 ACT (Math). Participation in extracurricular activities and work experience required. Total military service obligation is eight years, five of which must be active duty. Contact local NROTC unit of university you wish to attend for more information.

| | |
|---|---|
| **Amount of award:** | Full tuition |
| **Number of applicants:** | 50 |
| **Application deadline:** | March 15 |

**Contact:**
Contact local recruitment officer.
Phone: 800-NAV-ROTC
Web: www.navy.com/joining/education-opportunities/nrotc.html

# USTA Tennis and Education Foundation

## USTA Scholarships

**Type of award:** Scholarship, renewable.
**Intended use:** For full-time undergraduate study at accredited 2-year or 4-year institution.
**Eligibility:** Applicant must be high school senior.
**Basis for selection:** Applicant must demonstrate financial need, high academic achievement, leadership and seriousness of purpose.
**Application requirements:** Interview, recommendations, essay, transcript. Photograph, FAFSA or SAR, ACT/SAT scores.
**Additional information:** Applicant must have participated in USTA or other organized youth tennis program. The USTA offers six scholarship programs. Amount and number of awards vary. Applications available online and must be mailed to local USTA Section office. Visit Website for application, deadline, and individual scholarship requirements.

| | |
|---|---|
| **Amount of award:** | $1,000-$15,000 |
| **Number of awards:** | 76 |
| **Total amount awarded:** | $379,000 |

**Contact:**
United States Tennis Association
Phone: 914-696-7000
Web: www.usta.com

# Utah Higher Education Assistance Authority (UHEAA)

## Leveraging Educational Assistance Partnership (LEAP)

**Type of award:** Scholarship, renewable.
**Intended use:** For undergraduate study in United States. Designated institutions: Participating Utah public institutions.

**Eligibility:** Applicant must be residing in Utah.
**Basis for selection:** Applicant must demonstrate financial need.
**Application requirements:** FAFSA.
**Additional information:** Allocations made to participating Utah institutions. Contact participating institution's financial aid office. Amount of award varies. Awards given on first-come-first-served basis to eligible participants.

| | |
|---|---|
| **Number of awards:** | 3,252 |
| **Number of applicants:** | 3,252 |
| **Total amount awarded:** | $1,928,157 |

**Contact:**
Contact institution's financial aid office.

### Utah Centennial Opportunity Program for Education (UCOPE)

**Type of award:** Scholarship, renewable.
**Intended use:** For undergraduate study at postsecondary institution.
**Eligibility:** Applicant must be residing in Utah.
**Basis for selection:** Applicant must demonstrate financial need.
**Application requirements:** FAFSA.
**Additional information:** Allocations are made to participating Utah institutions. Contact participating institution's financial aid office.

| | |
|---|---|
| **Amount of award:** | $300-$5,000 |
| **Number of awards:** | 7,375 |
| **Number of applicants:** | 6,288 |
| **Total amount awarded:** | $5,257,309 |

**Contact:**
Utah Higher Education Assistance Authority (UHEAA)
Web: www.uheaa.org

## Utah State Office of Education

### Utah Robert C. Byrd Honors Scholarship

**Type of award:** Scholarship, renewable.
**Intended use:** For full-time undergraduate study in United States.
**Eligibility:** Applicant must be high school senior. Applicant must be U.S. citizen residing in Utah.
**Basis for selection:** Applicant must demonstrate high academic achievement.
**Application requirements:** Transcript. SAT or ACT scores. Proof of U.S. citizenship and Utah residency. College or university acceptance letter.
**Additional information:** Minimum 3.7 GPA. Minimum 25 ACT score or 1940 SAT score. Home-schooled students also eligible. Contact high school counselor or financial aid adviser after January for application, or see Website. Deadline in late March.

| | |
|---|---|
| **Amount of award:** | $1,500 |
| **Number of awards:** | 62 |
| **Number of applicants:** | 500 |
| **Notification begins:** | June 30 |
| **Total amount awarded:** | $384,000 |

**Contact:**
The Robert C. Byrd Scholarship
Utah State Office of Education
250 East 500 South, P.O. Box 144200
Salt Lake City, UT 84114-4200
Web: www.schools.utah.gov/curr/Early_College/Byrd.htm

## The Vegetarian Resource Group

### The Vegetarian Resource Group College Scholarships

**Type of award:** Scholarship.
**Intended use:** For freshman study at postsecondary institution in United States.
**Eligibility:** Applicant must be high school senior. Applicant must be U.S. citizen.
**Application requirements:** Essay.
**Additional information:** Award for graduating high school students who have promoted vegetarianism or veganism in their schools or communities. Students will be judged on having shown compassion, courage and a strong commitment to promoting a peaceful world through a vegetarian or vegan diet/lifestyle. Visit Website for application information.

| | |
|---|---|
| **Amount of award:** | $5,000 |
| **Number of awards:** | 2 |
| **Number of applicants:** | 200 |
| **Application deadline:** | February 20 |
| **Notification begins:** | June 1 |
| **Total amount awarded:** | $10,000 |

**Contact:**
The Vegetarian Resource Group
P.O. Box 1463
Baltimore, MD 21203
Phone: 410-366-8343
Web: www.vrg.org

## Ventura County Japanese-American Citizens League

### Ventura County Japanese-American Citizens League Scholarships

**Type of award:** Scholarship.
**Intended use:** For freshman study at vocational, 2-year, 4-year or graduate institution in United States.
**Eligibility:** Applicant must be high school senior. Applicant must be Japanese. Applicant must be U.S. citizen residing in California.
**Application requirements:** Recommendations, essay, transcript, proof of eligibility. SAT scores.
**Additional information:** Applicant must be a Ventura County high school senior and a member of the Japanese American Citizens League. Amount and number of awards depend on available funding. Visit Website for application.

| | |
|---|---|
| **Application deadline:** | April 1 |
| **Total amount awarded:** | $10,000 |

**Contact:**
Ventura County JACL Scholarship Committee
P.O. Box 1092
Camarillo, CA 93011
Phone: 805-498-0764
Web: www.vcjacl.org

# Vermont Golf Association Scholarship Fund, Inc.

## Vermont Golf Association Scholarship

**Type of award:** Scholarship, renewable.
**Intended use:** For full-time undergraduate study at 2-year or 4-year institution.
**Eligibility:** Applicant must be high school senior. Applicant must be permanent resident residing in Vermont.
**Application requirements:** Interview, recommendations, transcript. FAFSA.
**Additional information:** Must be graduate of Vermont high school and in top 40 percent of class or have GPA of 3.0 and 1500 SAT. Students of Hanover High School, NH, Riverdell Interstate School District, NH, and Grandville High School, NY, are also eligible. Applicant must have valid connection to golf.

| | |
|---|---|
| **Amount of award:** | $1,000 |
| **Number of awards:** | 10 |
| **Number of applicants:** | 38 |
| **Application deadline:** | April 20 |
| **Total amount awarded:** | $10,000 |

**Contact:**
Vermont Golf Association Scholarship Fund
P.O. Box 1612
Station A
Rutland, VT 05701
Phone: 802-775-7837
Fax: 802-773-7182
Web: www.vtga.org

# Vermont Student Assistance Corporation

## AIWF Culinary Scholarship

**Type of award:** Scholarship.
**Intended use:** For undergraduate study at accredited postsecondary institution. Designated institutions: Institutions approved for federal Title IV funding.
**Eligibility:** Applicant must be U.S. citizen or permanent resident residing in Vermont.
**Basis for selection:** Major/career interest in culinary arts. Applicant must demonstrate financial need.
**Application requirements:** Recommendations, essay. Personal interview (if necessary).
**Additional information:** Must attend school at least three-quarters time. Must have been Vermont resident for at least ten years. Deadline in early March.

| | |
|---|---|
| **Amount of award:** | $2,500 |
| **Number of awards:** | 1 |
| **Number of applicants:** | 18 |

**Contact:**
VSAC Scholarships Program
10 East Allen Street
P.O. Box 2000
Winooski, VT 05404
Phone: 888-253-4819
Web: www.vsac.org/scholarships

## Alfred T. Granger Student Art Fund Scholarship

**Type of award:** Scholarship.
**Intended use:** For undergraduate or graduate study at accredited postsecondary institution. Designated institutions: Institutions approved for federal Title IV funding.
**Eligibility:** Applicant must be U.S. citizen or permanent resident residing in Vermont.
**Basis for selection:** Major/career interest in architecture; interior design; arts, general or design. Applicant must demonstrate financial need and high academic achievement.
**Application requirements:** Portfolio, recommendations.
**Additional information:** Architectural engineering, lighting design, and mechanical drawing (CAD) majors also eligible. Four awards of $2,500 each for undergraduates and two $5,000 awards for graduate students. Deadline in early March.

| | |
|---|---|
| **Amount of award:** | $2,500-$5,000 |
| **Number of awards:** | 6 |
| **Number of applicants:** | 57 |

**Contact:**
VSAC Scholarships Program
10 East Allen Road
P.O. Box 2000
Winooski, VT 05404
Phone: 888-253-4819
Web: www.vsac.org/scholarships

## Calvin Coolidge Memorial Foundation Scholarship

**Type of award:** Scholarship.
**Intended use:** For undergraduate study at accredited postsecondary institution. Designated institutions: Institutions approved for federal Title IV funding.
**Eligibility:** Applicant must be U.S. citizen or permanent resident residing in Vermont.
**Basis for selection:** Major/career interest in archaeology; anthropology; criminal justice/law enforcement; economics; geography; history; international relations; philosophy; political science/government or psychology. Applicant must demonstrate high academic achievement and service orientation.
**Application requirements:** Recommendations, essay.
**Additional information:** Must be enrolled at least three-quarters time. Social work, sociology, urban studies, and other social science majors also eligible. Deadline in early March.

| | |
|---|---|
| **Amount of award:** | $1,000 |
| **Number of awards:** | 1 |
| **Number of applicants:** | 195 |

**Contact:**
VSAC Scholarships Program
10 East Allen Street
P.O. Box 2000
Winooski, VT 05404
Phone: 888-253-4819
Web: www.vsac.org/scholarships

## Champlain Valley Kennel Club Scholarship

**Type of award:** Scholarship.
**Intended use:** For full-time undergraduate or graduate study at accredited postsecondary institution. Designated institutions: Institutions approved for federal Title IV funding.
**Eligibility:** Applicant must be residing in Vermont.
**Basis for selection:** Major/career interest in veterinary medicine. Applicant must demonstrate financial need and high academic achievement.
**Application requirements:** Recommendations, essay, transcript. FAFSA, tax return.
**Additional information:** Graduating high school seniors also eligible. Applicant must have been Vermont resident for at least five years at time of application.

| | |
|---|---|
| **Amount of award:** | $250 |
| **Number of awards:** | 1 |
| **Number of applicants:** | 20 |
| **Application deadline:** | May 10 |

**Contact:**
Pamela Parshall CVKC Scholarship Chair
77 Range Road
Underhill, VT 05489-9410
Phone: 802-899-2994
Web: www.vsac.org/scholarships

## Charles E. Leonard Memorial Scholarship

**Type of award:** Scholarship.
**Intended use:** For undergraduate or graduate study at accredited postsecondary institution. Designated institutions: Institutions approved for federal Title IV funding.
**Eligibility:** Applicant of parent must be visually impaired. Applicant must be U.S. citizen or permanent resident residing in Vermont.
**Basis for selection:** Applicant must demonstrate financial need and high academic achievement.
**Application requirements:** Essay.
**Additional information:** Applicants pursuing career in education/rehabilitation of blind or visually impaired people also eligible. Deadline in early March.

| | |
|---|---|
| **Amount of award:** | $500 |
| **Number of awards:** | 3 |
| **Number of applicants:** | 8 |

**Contact:**
VSAC Scholarships Program
10 East Allen Street
P.O. Box 2000
Winooski, VT 05404
Phone: 888-253-4819
Web: www.vsac.org/scholarships

## Emily Lester Vermont Opportunity Scholarship

**Type of award:** Scholarship, renewable.
**Intended use:** For undergraduate study at accredited postsecondary institution. Designated institutions: Vermont schools approved for federal Title IV funding.
**Eligibility:** Applicant must be residing in Vermont.
**Basis for selection:** Applicant must demonstrate financial need.
**Application requirements:** Proof of eligibility.
**Additional information:** Applicant must be under the custody of the Vermont commissioner of social and rehabilitation services or be between the ages of 18 and 24 and have been under the custody of the commissioner for at least six months between ages 16 and 18. Graduating high school seniors also eligible. Deadline in early March.

| | |
|---|---|
| **Amount of award:** | $1,000-$3,000 |
| **Total amount awarded:** | $22,500 |

**Contact:**
VSAC Scholarship Program
10 East Allen Street
P.O. Box 2000
Winooski, VT 05404
Phone: 888-253-4819
Web: www.vsac.org/scholarships

## Jedidiah Zabrosky Scholarship

**Type of award:** Scholarship.
**Intended use:** For full-time undergraduate study at 2-year or 4-year institution in United States. Designated institutions: Castleton State College, Lyndon State College, Johnson State College, Community College of Vermont, Vermont Technical College, University of Vermont.
**Eligibility:** Applicant must be residing in Vermont.
**Basis for selection:** Major/career interest in business or education. Applicant must demonstrate financial need, high academic achievement and service orientation.
**Application requirements:** Recommendations, essay.
**Additional information:** Minimum 2.5 GPA. Applicant must be employed at time of application working minimum ten hours per week. Deadline in early March.

| | |
|---|---|
| **Amount of award:** | $2,000 |
| **Number of awards:** | 1 |
| **Number of applicants:** | 40 |

**Contact:**
VSAC Scholarships Progam
10 East Allen Street
P.O. Box 2000
Winooski, VT 05404
Phone: 888-253-4819
Web: www.vsac.org/scholarships

## Kittredge Coddington Memorial Scholarship

**Type of award:** Scholarship.
**Intended use:** For undergraduate study at accredited postsecondary institution. Designated institutions: Vermont institutions approved for federal Title IV funding.
**Eligibility:** Applicant must be enrolled in high school. Applicant must be U.S. citizen or permanent resident residing in Vermont.
**Basis for selection:** Major/career interest in business; business, international or business/management/administration.
**Application requirements:** Recommendations, essay.
**Additional information:** Must be planning career in business or industry. One award to female, one to male. Deadline in early March.

| | |
|---|---|
| **Amount of award:** | $500 |
| **Number of awards:** | 1 |
| **Number of applicants:** | 55 |

**Contact:**
VSAC Scholarships Program
10 East Allen Street
P.O. Box 2000
Winooski, VT 05404
Phone: 888-253-4819
Web: www.vsac.org/scholarships

## Lee A. Lyman Memorial Music Scholarship

**Type of award:** Scholarship.
**Intended use:** For undergraduate or graduate study at accredited postsecondary institution. Designated institutions: Institutions approved for federal Title IV funding.
**Eligibility:** Applicant must be U.S. citizen or permanent resident residing in Vermont.
**Basis for selection:** Major/career interest in music. Applicant must demonstrate financial need and high academic achievement.
**Application requirements:** Recommendations, essay.
**Additional information:** Must demonstrate participation in music-related activities, performances, or groups. Deadline in early March.

| | |
|---|---|
| **Amount of award:** | $1,000 |
| **Number of awards:** | 4 |
| **Number of applicants:** | 34 |
| **Total amount awarded:** | $4,000 |

**Contact:**
VSAC Scholarships Program
10 East Allen Street
P.O. Box 2000
Winooski, VT 05404
Phone: 888-253-4819
Web: www.vsac.org/scholarships

## Patrick and Judith McHugh Scholarship

**Type of award:** Scholarship.
**Intended use:** For undergraduate or graduate study at accredited postsecondary institution. Designated institutions: Institutions approved for federal Title IV funding.
**Eligibility:** Applicant must be U.S. citizen or permanent resident residing in Vermont.
**Basis for selection:** Major/career interest in health-related professions; dentistry; medicine; mental health/therapy; nursing; pharmacy/pharmaceutics/pharmacology or psychology. Applicant must demonstrate financial need.
**Application requirements:** Recommendations, essay.
**Additional information:** Must be enrolled at least three-quarters time. Deadline in early March.

| | |
|---|---|
| **Amount of award:** | $1,000 |
| **Number of awards:** | 1 |
| **Number of applicants:** | 260 |

**Contact:**
VSAC Scholarships Program
10 East Allen Street
P.O. Box 2000
Winooski, VT 05404
Phone: 888-253-4819
Web: www.vsac.org/scholarships

## People's United Bank Scholarship

**Type of award:** Scholarship, renewable.
**Intended use:** For full-time freshman study at accredited 2-year or 4-year institution in United States. Designated institutions: Vermont postsecondary schools approved for federal Title IV funding.
**Eligibility:** Applicant must be high school senior. Applicant must be residing in Vermont.
**Basis for selection:** Applicant must demonstrate financial need, high academic achievement and service orientation.
**Application requirements:** Recommendations, essay.
**Additional information:** Minimum 3.0 GPA. Deadline in early March.

| | |
|---|---|
| **Amount of award:** | $2,500 |
| **Number of awards:** | 2 |
| **Number of applicants:** | 305 |

**Contact:**
VSAC Scholarships Program
10 East Allen Street
P.O. Box 2000
Winooski, VT 05404
Phone: 888-253-4819
Web: www.vsac.org/scholarships

## Philip and Alice Angell Eastern Star Scholarship

**Type of award:** Scholarship.
**Intended use:** For undergraduate study at accredited 2-year or 4-year institution. Designated institutions: Postsecondary institutions approved for federal Title IV funding.
**Eligibility:** Applicant must be residing in Vermont.
**Basis for selection:** Major/career interest in business or education. Applicant must demonstrate financial need and high academic achievement.
**Application requirements:** Recommendations, essay.
**Additional information:** Minimum 3.5 GPA. Graduating high school seniors eligible. Deadline in early March.

| | |
|---|---|
| **Amount of award:** | $500 |
| **Number of awards:** | 1 |
| **Number of applicants:** | 118 |

**Contact:**
VSAC Scholarships Program
10 East Allen Street
P.O. Box 2000
Winooski, VT 05404
Phone: 888-253-4819
Web: www.vsac.org/scholarships

## RehabGYM Scholarship

**Type of award:** Scholarship.
**Intended use:** For undergraduate study at accredited postsecondary institution. Designated institutions: Institutions approved for federal Title IV funding.
**Eligibility:** Applicant must be physically challenged. Applicant must be U.S. citizen or permanent resident residing in Vermont.
**Basis for selection:** Applicant must demonstrate financial need.
**Application requirements:** Essay.
**Additional information:** Must be enrolled at least three-quarters time. Must have overcome significant physical challenge or illness. Deadline in early March.

| | |
|---|---|
| **Amount of award:** | $1,000 |
| **Number of awards:** | 1 |
| **Number of applicants:** | 47 |

**Contact:**
VSAC Scholarships Program
10 East Allen Street
P.O. Box 2000
Winooski, VT 05404
Phone: 888-253-4819
Web: www.vsac.org/scholarships

## Samara Foundation of Vermont Scholarship

**Type of award:** Scholarship.
**Intended use:** For undergraduate study at vocational, 2-year or 4-year institution.
**Eligibility:** Applicant must be high school senior. Applicant must be residing in Vermont.
**Basis for selection:** Competition/talent/interest in gay/lesbian.
**Application requirements:** Recommendations, essay.
**Additional information:** Applicant must demonstrate, through personal experience and/or public commitment, dedication to the interests of the gay, lesbian, bisexual, transgendered, and questioning community. Up to $5,000 is awarded annually. Deadline in early March.

| | |
|---|---|
| **Number of awards:** | 3 |
| **Number of applicants:** | 15 |

**Contact:**
VSAC Scholarships Programs
10 East Allen Street
P.O. Box 2000
Winooski, VT 05404
Phone: 888-253-4819
Web: www.vsac.org/scholarships

## Students With Disabilities Endowed Scholarship Honoring Elizabeth Daley Jeffords

**Type of award:** Scholarship.
**Intended use:** For undergraduate study at accredited postsecondary institution. Designated institutions: Institutions approved for federal Title IV funding.
**Eligibility:** Applicant must be visually impaired, hearing impaired, physically challenged or learning disabled. Applicant must be U.S. citizen or permanent resident residing in Vermont.
**Basis for selection:** Applicant must demonstrate financial need and seriousness of purpose.
**Application requirements:** Recommendations, essay, proof of eligibility. Personal interview (if necessary).
**Additional information:** Number of awards varies. Deadline in early March.

| | |
|---|---|
| **Amount of award:** | $1,500 |
| **Number of awards:** | 1 |
| **Number of applicants:** | 58 |

**Contact:**
VSAC Scholarships Program
10 East Allen Street
P.O. Box 2000
Winooski, VT 05404
Phone: 888-253-4819
Web: www.vsac.org/scholarships

## Vermont Alliance for Arts Education (VAEE) Scholarship

**Type of award:** Scholarship.
**Intended use:** For undergraduate study at accredited postsecondary institution. Designated institutions: Institutions approved for federal Title IV funding.
**Eligibility:** Applicant must be high school senior. Applicant must be U.S. citizen or permanent resident residing in Vermont.
**Basis for selection:** Major/career interest in arts, general; dance; music or theater arts. Applicant must demonstrate financial need and high academic achievement.
**Application requirements:** Portfolio, recommendations, essay.
**Additional information:** Recipients may be invited to perform and/or exhibit at VAAE functions. Deadline in early March.

| | |
|---|---|
| **Amount of award:** | $500 |
| **Number of awards:** | 4 |
| **Number of applicants:** | 35 |

**Contact:**
VSAC Scholarships Program
10 East Allen Street
P.O. Box 2000
Winooski, VT 05404
Phone: 888-253-4819
Web: www.vsac.org/scholarships

## Vermont Incentive Grant

**Type of award:** Scholarship.
**Intended use:** For full-time undergraduate study in United States.
**Eligibility:** Applicant must be U.S. citizen or permanent resident residing in Vermont.
**Basis for selection:** Applicant must demonstrate financial need.
**Application requirements:** Proof of eligibility. FAFSA.
**Additional information:** Must not yet have bachelor's degree. Vermont residents who attend Vermont College of Medicine or who are enrolled in Doctor of Veterinary Science program also eligible. Application may be completed online. Grant applications considered on first-come, first-served basis while funding is available.
**Contact:**
Grant Department
VSAC
P.O. Box 2000
Winooski, VT 05404
Phone: 800-882-4166 or 802-654-3750
Web: www.vsac.org

## Vermont John H. Chafee Education and Training Scholarship

**Type of award:** Scholarship.
**Intended use:** For undergraduate study at accredited vocational, 2-year or 4-year institution. Designated institutions: Institutions approved for federal Title IV funding.
**Eligibility:** Applicant must be no older than 21. Applicant must be U.S. citizen or permanent resident residing in Vermont.
**Basis for selection:** Applicant must demonstrate financial need.
**Additional information:** Must be under custody of Vermont Commissioner of the Department for Children and Families (DCF) through eighteenth birthday or be adopted after age 16. Deadline in early March.

| | |
|---|---|
| **Amount of award:** | $1,000-$5,000 |

**Contact:**
VSAC Scholarships Program
10 East Allen Street
P.O. Box 2000
Winooski, VT 05404
Phone: 888-253-4819
Web: www.vsac.org/scholarships

## Vermont Non-Degree Program

**Type of award:** Scholarship.
**Intended use:** For non-degree study at postsecondary institution in United States.
**Eligibility:** Applicant must be permanent resident residing in Vermont.
**Basis for selection:** Applicant must demonstrate financial need.
**Application requirements:** Proof of eligibility.
**Additional information:** Award amount varies. Applicants must be enrolled in non-degree course that will improve employability or encourage further study. Applications available at Vermont Department of Employment and Training offices, schools and vocation centers, and VSAC. Grant applications considered on a first-come, first-served basis as long as funding is available.

| | |
|---|---|
| **Number of applicants:** | 1,290 |
| **Total amount awarded:** | $645,732 |

**Contact:**
Grant Department
VSAC
P.O. Box 2000
Winooski, VT 05404
Phone: 800-882-4166 or 802-654-3750
Web: www.vsac.org

## Vermont Part-Time Grant

**Type of award:** Scholarship.
**Intended use:** For half-time undergraduate study at vocational, 2-year or 4-year institution in United States.
**Eligibility:** Applicant must be permanent resident residing in Vermont.
**Basis for selection:** Applicant must demonstrate financial need.
**Application requirements:** Proof of eligibility. FAFSA.
**Additional information:** Must be taking fewer than 12 credits and not yet received bachelor's degree. Award amounts vary according to number of credits.

| | |
|---|---|
| **Number of applicants:** | 3,743 |
| **Total amount awarded:** | $1,016,909 |

**Contact:**
Grant Department
VSAC
P.O. Box 2000
Winooski, VT 05404
Phone: 800-882-4166 or 802-654-3750
Web: www.vsac.org

# Veterans of Foreign Wars

## Voice of Democracy Scholarship

**Type of award:** Scholarship.
**Intended use:** For undergraduate or graduate study at postsecondary institution in United States.
**Eligibility:** Applicant must be enrolled in high school.
**Application requirements:** Audiotape or CD of essay. Participants are judged by tape or CD, not written essay script.
**Additional information:** Student must be 19 or younger to apply. Must apply through high school or local Veterans of Foreign Wars post. Not all VFW posts participate in program. Any entry submitted to VFW National Headquarters will be returned to sender. Selection based on interpretation of assigned patriotic theme, content, and presentation of recorded 3-5 minute audio-essay. Visit Website for additional information and application form. Award is non-renewable.

| | |
|---|---|
| **Amount of award:** | $1,000-$30,000 |
| **Number of awards:** | 54 |
| **Number of applicants:** | 50,000 |
| **Application deadline:** | November 1 |
| **Total amount awarded:** | $151,000 |

**Contact:**
Veterans of Foreign Wars National Headquarters
Voice of Democracy Program
406 West 34 Street
Kansas City, MO 64111
Phone: 816-968-1117
Fax: 816-968-1149
Web: www.vfw.org

# Virgin Islands Board of Education

## Virgin Islands Leveraging Educational Assistance Partnership Program

**Type of award:** Scholarship, renewable.
**Intended use:** For full-time undergraduate or graduate study at postsecondary institution.
**Eligibility:** Applicant must be U.S. citizen or permanent resident residing in Virgin Islands.
**Basis for selection:** Applicant must demonstrate financial need.
**Application requirements:** Transcript. Acceptance letter from institution for first-time applicants or transfer students.
**Additional information:** Minimum 2.0 GPA. Number of awards varies.

| | |
|---|---|
| **Amount of award:** | $500-$5,000 |
| **Number of applicants:** | 50 |
| **Application deadline:** | May 1 |

**Contact:**
Virgin Islands Board of Education Financial Aid Office
P.O. Box 11900
St. Thomas, VI 00801
Phone: 340-774-4546
Web: www.myviboe.com

## Virgin Islands Music Scholarship

**Type of award:** Scholarship, renewable.
**Intended use:** For full-time undergraduate study at accredited 2-year or 4-year institution in United States.
**Eligibility:** Applicant must be high school senior. Applicant must be U.S. citizen or permanent resident residing in Virgin Islands.
**Basis for selection:** Major/career interest in music. Applicant must demonstrate financial need.
**Application requirements:** Transcript. Acceptance letter from college or university if first-time applicant.
**Additional information:** Minimum 2.0 GPA.

| | |
|---|---|
| **Amount of award:** | $2,000 |
| **Number of awards:** | 8 |
| **Number of applicants:** | 20 |
| **Application deadline:** | May 1 |
| **Total amount awarded:** | $16,000 |

**Contact:**
Virgin Islands Board of Education Financial Aid Office
P.O. Box 11900
St. Thomas, VI 00801
Phone: 340-774-4546
Web: www.myviboe.com

## Virginia Department of Education

### Virginia Lee-Jackson Scholarship

**Type of award:** Scholarship.
**Intended use:** For full-time freshman study at accredited 2-year or 4-year institution in United States.
**Eligibility:** Applicant must be high school junior or senior. Applicant must be residing in Virginia.
**Basis for selection:** Competition/talent/interest in writing/journalism.
**Application requirements:** Essay demonstrating appreciation for virtues exemplified by General Robert E. Lee or General "Stonewall" Jackson.
**Additional information:** Award amount varies depending on essay. Additional awards for exceptional essays. Students must submit essay and application form to high school principal or guidance counselor. Application deadline is generally in mid-February. Community college awardees must plan to enroll in their college's transfer program. See Website for more information.

| | |
|---|---|
| **Amount of award:** | $1,000-$10,000 |
| **Number of awards:** | 27 |
| **Total amount awarded:** | $44,000 |

**Contact:**
The Lee-Jackson Foundation
P.O. Box 8121
Charlottesville, VA 22906
Web: www.lee-jackson.org

### Virginia Robert C. Byrd Honors Scholarship

**Type of award:** Scholarship, renewable.
**Intended use:** For full-time undergraduate study at accredited postsecondary institution in United States.
**Eligibility:** Applicant must be high school senior. Applicant must be U.S. citizen or permanent resident residing in Virginia.
**Basis for selection:** Applicant must demonstrate high academic achievement and service orientation.
**Application requirements:** Recommendations, transcript, nomination by high school. SAT/ACT scores. Must file a Statement of Selective Service Registration Status.
**Additional information:** Students with a GED are also eligible. Application and information sent to principals of public and private high schools in February. Number of awards varies. Award renewable for three years during first four years of higher education. Visit Website for application. Deadline in early April.

| | |
|---|---|
| **Amount of award:** | $1,500 |
| **Number of applicants:** | 320 |
| **Total amount awarded:** | $1,027,750 |

**Contact:**
Robert C. Byrd Scholarships
CTE Resource Center
2002 Bremo Road, Lower Level
Richmond, VA 23226
Phone: 804-255-3370
Web: www.doe.virginia.gov

## Virginia Department of Health

### Mary Marshall Nursing LPN Scholarship

**Type of award:** Scholarship.
**Intended use:** For full-time undergraduate study. Designated institutions: Virginia nursing schools.
**Eligibility:** Applicant must be U.S. citizen or permanent resident residing in Virginia.
**Basis for selection:** Major/career interest in nursing. Applicant must demonstrate financial need.
**Application requirements:** Recommendations, transcript. FAFSA.
**Additional information:** Award amount varies. Provides awards to students who agree to work in nursing profession in Virginia at rate of one month for every $100 of aid received. Must reside in Virginia at least one year prior to application. Recipient may reapply for up to four succeeding years. Applications and guidelines available from dean or financial aid office at applicant's nursing school, or from address listed.

| | |
|---|---|
| **Amount of award:** | $200-$500 |
| **Number of awards:** | 91 |
| **Application deadline:** | June 30 |

**Contact:**
Virginia Department of Health
109 Governor Street
Suite 1016-E
Richmond, VA 23219
Phone: 804-864-7435
Fax: 804-864-7440
Web: www.vdh.virginia.gov

### Mary Marshall Nursing RN Scholarship

**Type of award:** Scholarship.
**Intended use:** For undergraduate study at postsecondary institution in United States.
**Eligibility:** Applicant must be U.S. citizen residing in Virginia.
**Basis for selection:** Major/career interest in nursing.
**Additional information:** Award amount varies. Provides awards to students who agree to work in nursing profession in Virginia at rate of one month for every $100 of aid received. Must reside in Virginia at least one year prior to application. Recipient may reapply for up to four succeeding years. Applications and guidelines available from dean or financial aid office at applicant's nursing school, or from address listed.

| | |
|---|---|
| **Amount of award:** | $1,500-$2,000 |
| **Number of awards:** | 52 |
| **Application deadline:** | June 30 |
| **Total amount awarded:** | $100,000 |

**Contact:**
Virginia Department of Health
109 Governor Street
Suite 1016-E
Richmond, VA 23219
Phone: 804-864-7435
Fax: 804-864-7440
Web: www.vdh.virginia.gov

### Nurse Pracitioner Nurse Midwife Scholarship

**Type of award:** Scholarship.
**Intended use:** For full-time undergraduate study at postsecondary institution. Designated institutions: Institutions in Virginia.
**Eligibility:** Applicant must be residing in Virginia.
**Basis for selection:** Major/career interest in nurse practitioner. Applicant must demonstrate high academic achievement and depth of character.
**Application requirements:** Recommendations, transcript.
**Additional information:** Applicant must commit to post-graduate employment in a medically underserved area of Virginia, in a setting that provides services to persons unable to pay and participates in all government-sponsored insurance programs. Employment must last for number of years equal to the number of annual scholarships received. If work commitment is not fulfilled or student does not complete studies, the award amount converts to loan. Minimum 3.0 GPA. Award amount and number of awards varies.

| | |
|---|---|
| **Amount of award:** | $5,000 |
| **Number of awards:** | 5 |
| **Application deadline:** | July 31 |
| **Notification begins:** | September 15 |
| **Total amount awarded:** | $25,000 |

**Contact:**
Virginia Department of Health
109 Governor Street
Suite 1016-E
Richmond, VA 23219
Phone: 804-864-7435
Fax: 804-864-7440
Web: www.vdh.virginia.gov

## Virginia Department of Rehabilitative Services

### Virginia Rehabilitative Services College Program

**Type of award:** Scholarship.
**Intended use:** For undergraduate study at postsecondary institution.
**Eligibility:** Applicant must be visually impaired, hearing impaired, physically challenged or learning disabled. Applicant must be residing in Virginia.
**Basis for selection:** Applicant must demonstrate financial need.
**Application requirements:** Proof of eligibility. Proof must be furnished at least 60 days before start of school or educational program.
**Additional information:** Applicant must have a disability and an employment goal. This program is not a true scholarship, but rather a source of funding for eligible individuals if need remains after other federal, state, and private sources are used. Program provides vocational rehabilitation and related services to Virginians with disabilities in order to foster the skills necessary to achieve greater self-sufficiency, independence, and employment. Contact nearest Department of Rehabilitative Services office or visit Website for numbers.
**Contact:**
Virginia Department of Rehabilitative Services
8004 Franklin Farms Drive
Richmond, VA 23229
Phone: 804-662-7000
Web: www.vadrs.org

## Virginia Museum of Fine Arts

### Virginia Museum of Fine Arts Fellowship

**Type of award:** Scholarship, renewable.
**Intended use:** For full-time undergraduate or graduate study at accredited 4-year or graduate institution.
**Eligibility:** Applicant must be U.S. citizen or permanent resident residing in Virginia.
**Basis for selection:** Major/career interest in arts, general; film/video or art/art history. Applicant must demonstrate financial need.
**Application requirements:** Portfolio, transcript. Eight images on CD representing recent work or three of the following: 16mm or video format films, videos, DVD, research papers, or published articles. References.
**Additional information:** May apply in one of the following categories on the undergraduate or graduate level: crafts, drawing, sculpture, filmmaking, painting, photography, printmaking. Candidates in art history may apply on the graduate level only. Visit Website for guidelines and application.

| | |
|---|---|
| **Amount of award:** | $2,000-$8,000 |
| **Number of awards:** | 43 |
| **Number of applicants:** | 642 |
| **Application deadline:** | November 10 |
| **Notification begins:** | February 1 |
| **Total amount awarded:** | $258,000 |

**Contact:**
Virginia Museum of Fine Arts Fellowships
Statewide Partnerships
200 N. Boulevard
Richmond, VA 23220-4007
Phone: 804-204-2685 or 804-204-2685
Fax: 804-204-2675
Web: www.vmfa.museum

## Wal-Mart Foundation

### Higher REACH Scholarship

**Type of award:** Scholarship.
**Intended use:** For undergraduate study at accredited 2-year or 4-year institution in United States.

**Eligibility:** Applicant must be U.S. citizen or permanent resident.
**Basis for selection:** Applicant must demonstrate financial need and leadership.
**Additional information:** Awarded to nontraditional students who have been employed by Wal-Mart Stores, Inc. for at least six months. Award amount varies depending on part-time or full-time enrollment. Students enrolled in a two-year program receive up to $2,000; students enrolled in a four-year program receive up to $3,000. Applicants must be out of high school for one year. Must maintain 2.0 GPA to renew. Visit Website for application and deadline.

| | |
|---|---|
| **Amount of award:** | $500-$3,000 |

**Contact:**
Higher Reach Scholarship, Wal-Mart Scholarship Program
301 ACT Drive
P.O. Box 4030
Iowa City, IA 52243-4030
Phone: 877-333-0284
Fax: 319-337-1204
Web: www.walmartstores.com/communitygiving

## Sam Walton Community Scholarship

**Type of award:** Scholarship.
**Intended use:** For full-time freshman study at accredited 2-year or 4-year institution in United States.
**Eligibility:** Applicant must be high school senior. Applicant must be U.S. citizen or permanent resident.
**Basis for selection:** Applicant must demonstrate financial need, high academic achievement and leadership.
**Application requirements:** Transcript, proof of eligibility. ACT/SAT scores, list of school/community/extracurricular involvement and work experience.
**Additional information:** Applicant must not be an employee of Wal-Mart Stores, Inc., or child/dependent of an employee. Applications available first week of November on Website. Minimum 2.5 GPA. Student must have his/her local Sam's Club or Wal-Mart store's 4-digit location number to apply. Deadline varies, visit Website for details.

| | |
|---|---|
| **Amount of award:** | $3,000 |
| **Number of awards:** | 2,500 |
| **Number of applicants:** | 42,564 |

**Contact:**
Sam Walton Community Scholarship, Wal-Mart Scholarship Program
301 ACT Drive
P.O. Box 4030
Iowa City, IA 52243-4030
Phone: 887-333-0284
Web: www.walmartstores.com/communitygiving

## Wal-Mart Dependent Scholarship

**Type of award:** Scholarship.
**Intended use:** For full-time undergraduate study at accredited 2-year or 4-year institution in United States.
**Eligibility:** Applicant or parent must be employed by Wal-Mart Stores, Inc. Applicant must be high school senior. Applicant must be U.S. citizen or permanent resident.
**Basis for selection:** Applicant must demonstrate financial need and high academic achievement.
**Application requirements:** Transcript, proof of eligibility. SAT/ACT scores and financial data.
**Additional information:** Award for Wal-Mart employees and their dependents who are not eligible for the Walton Foundation Scholarship. Employee must have been working at Wal-Mart for at least six consecutive months. Minimum 2.5 GPA. Minimum 18 ACT or 800 SAT. Visit Website for application and deadline information.

| | |
|---|---|
| **Amount of award:** | $3,000 |
| **Number of awards:** | 26 |
| **Number of applicants:** | 2,600 |

**Contact:**
Wal-Mart Associate Scholarship, Wal-Mart Scholarship Program
301 ACT Drive
P.O. Box 4030
Iowa City, IA 52243-4030
Phone: 877-333-0284
Web: www.walmartstores.com/communitygiving

## Walton Family Foundation Scholarship

**Type of award:** Scholarship.
**Intended use:** For full-time undergraduate study at accredited 2-year or 4-year institution.
**Eligibility:** Applicant must be high school senior. Applicant must be U.S. citizen or permanent resident.
**Basis for selection:** Applicant must demonstrate financial need and high academic achievement.
**Application requirements:** Transcript, proof of eligibility. SAT/ACT scores and financial data.
**Additional information:** Award is $13,000 payable over four years. Applicant's parent or guardian must have been employed with Wal-Mart full-time (32 hours/week) for at least one year. Minimum 22 ACT or 1030 SAT. Maintenance of 3.0 GPA required for renewal. Recipients attending two-year institutions must agree to transfer to four-year institution by beginning of third academic year. Visit Website for application and deadline.

| | |
|---|---|
| **Amount of award:** | $13,000 |
| **Number of awards:** | 150 |
| **Number of applicants:** | 800 |
| **Total amount awarded:** | $960,000 |

**Contact:**
Walton Family Foundation Scholarship, Wal-Mart Scholarship Program
301 ACT Drive
P.O. Box 4030
Iowa City, IA 52243-4030
Phone: 877-333-0284
Web: www.walmartstores.com/communitygiving

# Washington Crossing Foundation

## Washington Crossing Foundation Scholarship

**Type of award:** Scholarship.
**Intended use:** For full-time undergraduate study at accredited 4-year institution.
**Eligibility:** Applicant must be high school senior. Applicant must be U.S. citizen residing in Pennsylvania.
**Basis for selection:** Major/career interest in political science/government or public administration/service. Applicant must demonstrate high academic achievement, depth of character, leadership, patriotism, seriousness of purpose and service orientation.

**Application requirements:** Recommendations, transcript. Essay on why student is planning a career in government service, including any inspiration derived from Washington's famous crossing of the Delaware. SAT/ACT scores.
**Additional information:** Number of awards varies. Visit Website for more information.

| | |
|---|---|
| **Amount of award:** | $1,000-$5,000 |
| **Application deadline:** | January 15 |
| **Notification begins:** | June 30 |
| **Total amount awarded:** | $42,000 |

**Contact:**
Washington Crossing Foundation
Attn: Vice Chairman
P.O. Box 503
Levittown, PA 19058
Phone: 215-949-8841
Web: www.gwcf.org



# Washington State Higher Education Coordinating Board

## Washington State Need Grant

**Type of award:** Scholarship, renewable.
**Intended use:** For undergraduate study at accredited vocational, 2-year or 4-year institution. Designated institutions: Eligible postsecondary institutions in Washington.
**Eligibility:** Applicant must be U.S. citizen or permanent resident residing in Washington.
**Basis for selection:** Applicant must demonstrate financial need.
**Application requirements:** Proof of eligibility. FAFSA.
**Additional information:** Grants are given only to students from low-income families. Family income must be equal to or less than 70 percent of the state median. Must meet qualifications every year for renewal, up to five years. Contact institution's financial aid office for additional requirements and deadlines. Must not be pursuing a degree in theology. Number of awards varies. Visit Website for family income requirements and more information.

| | |
|---|---|
| **Amount of award:** | $845-$7,717 |
| **Total amount awarded:** | $182,735,778 |

**Contact:**
Washington State Higher Education Coordinating Board
917 Lakeridge Way
P.O. Box 43430
Olympia, WA 98504-3430
Phone: 360-753-7850
Web: www.hecb.wa.gov

## Washington State Scholars Program

**Type of award:** Scholarship.
**Intended use:** For undergraduate study at accredited vocational, 2-year or 4-year institution. Designated institutions: Eligible colleges and universities in Washington state.
**Eligibility:** Applicant must be high school senior. Applicant must be U.S. citizen or permanent resident residing in Washington.
**Basis for selection:** Applicant must demonstrate high academic achievement, depth of character, leadership, seriousness of purpose and service orientation.
**Application requirements:** Nomination by high school principal or guidance counselor. SAT/ACT scores.
**Additional information:** Four-year award based on tuition, which may be prorated. Must rank in top one percent of class. May not defer enrollment. Eligible high school seniors should contact their high school counselors for more information. Must not pursue a degree in theology.

| | |
|---|---|
| **Amount of award:** | $2,633-$7,168 |
| **Number of awards:** | 147 |
| **Application deadline:** | January 18 |
| **Notification begins:** | March 15 |
| **Total amount awarded:** | $2,300,000 |

**Contact:**
Washington State Higher Education Coordinating Board
917 Lakeridge Way
P.O. Box 43430
Olympia, WA 98504-3430
Phone: 360-753-7843
Fax: 360-704-6243
Web: www.hecb.wa.gov

# Washington State PTA

## Washington State Scholarship Program

**Type of award:** Scholarship.
**Intended use:** For full-time freshman study at accredited vocational, 2-year or 4-year institution.
**Eligibility:** Applicant must be residing in Washington.
**Basis for selection:** Applicant must demonstrate financial need, high academic achievement, depth of character, leadership, seriousness of purpose and service orientation.
**Application requirements:** Recommendations, essay, transcript, proof of eligibility.
**Additional information:** Must be graduate of a Washington State public high school. Grant administered according to college's determination. Not transferable to another institution if already enrolled in classes. Visit Website for additional information and application.

| | |
|---|---|
| **Amount of award:** | $1,000-$2,000 |
| **Number of awards:** | 60 |
| **Number of applicants:** | 2,000 |
| **Application deadline:** | March 1 |
| **Total amount awarded:** | $65,000 |

**Contact:**
Washington State Scholarship Program
2003 65 Avenue West
Tacoma, WA 98466-6215
Phone: 253-565-2153
Fax: 253-565-7753
Web: www.wastatepta.org

# Wells Fargo

## CollegeSTEPS Program

**Type of award:** Scholarship.
**Intended use:** For undergraduate study at postsecondary institution.

**Eligibility:** Applicant must be high school freshman, sophomore, junior or senior. Applicant must be U.S. citizen.
**Additional information:** Awardees selected via random drawing. Visit Website to apply. Employees of Wells Fargo and immediate family members not eligible for tuition prize.

| | |
|---|---|
| **Amount of award:** | $1,000 |
| **Number of awards:** | 20 |
| **Total amount awarded:** | $20,000 |

**Contact:**
Education Financial Services
Wells Fargo
P.O. Box 5185
Sioux Falls, SD 57117-5185
Phone: 888-511-7302
Web: www.wellsfargo.com/collegesteps

# Welsh Society of Philadelphia

## Undergraduate Scholarship

**Type of award:** Scholarship.
**Intended use:** For full-time undergraduate study at accredited 2-year or 4-year institution in United States.
**Eligibility:** Applicant must be Welsh. Applicant must be residing in Delaware, New Jersey, Maryland or Pennsylvania.
**Basis for selection:** Applicant must demonstrate high academic achievement, leadership, seriousness of purpose and service orientation.
**Application requirements:** Recommendations, essay, transcript, proof of eligibility.
**Additional information:** Applicant must be of Welsh descent. Must live or attend school within 125 miles of Philadelphia. Must rank in top third of class.

| | |
|---|---|
| **Amount of award:** | $500-$1,000 |
| **Number of awards:** | 7 |
| **Number of applicants:** | 40 |
| **Application deadline:** | May 1 |
| **Total amount awarded:** | $5,000 |

**Contact:**
Welsh Society of Philadelphia Scholarship Committee
c/o Dr. Donald Marcus
P.O. Box 7287
Saint Davids, PA 19087-7287
Web: www.philadelphiawelsh.org

## Welsh Heritage Scholarship

**Type of award:** Scholarship, renewable.
**Intended use:** For full-time undergraduate study at accredited 2-year or 4-year institution.
**Eligibility:** Applicant must be Welsh.
**Basis for selection:** Applicant must demonstrate high academic achievement and seriousness of purpose.
**Application requirements:** Recommendations, essay, transcript. Statement of purpose.
**Additional information:** Applicant must be of Welsh descent. Applicant must live or attend college within 100 miles of Philadelphia. Participation in Welsh/Welsh-American organizations or events preferred.

| | |
|---|---|
| **Amount of award:** | $500-$1,000 |
| **Number of awards:** | 5 |
| **Number of applicants:** | 50 |
| **Application deadline:** | May 1 |
| **Total amount awarded:** | $5,000 |

**Contact:**
Welsh Society of Philadelphia c/o Dr. Donald Marcus
Scholarship Committee Chairman
P.O. Box 7287
St. David's, PA 19087-7287
Web: www.philadelphiawelsh.com

# West Pharmaceutical Services, Inc.

## Herman O. West Foundation Scholarship Program

**Type of award:** Scholarship, renewable.
**Intended use:** For full-time undergraduate study at accredited 2-year or 4-year institution.
**Eligibility:** Applicant or parent must be employed by West Pharmaceutical Services, Inc. Applicant must be high school senior. Applicant must be U.S. citizen.
**Basis for selection:** Applicant must demonstrate high academic achievement.
**Application requirements:** Recommendations, essay, transcript, proof of eligibility. List of extracurricular activities.
**Additional information:** Parent must be employee of West Pharmaceutical Services, Inc. Award is renewable annually for maximum of four years.

| | |
|---|---|
| **Amount of award:** | $2,500 |
| **Number of awards:** | 7 |
| **Number of applicants:** | 26 |
| **Application deadline:** | February 28 |
| **Notification begins:** | May 1 |
| **Total amount awarded:** | $50,000 |

**Contact:**
H.O. West Foundation
101 Gordon Drive
Lionville, PA 19341
Phone: 610-594-2945

# West Virginia Division of Veterans Affairs

## West Virginia War Orphans Educational Assistance

**Type of award:** Scholarship, renewable.
**Intended use:** For undergraduate, graduate or non-degree study in United States.
**Eligibility:** Applicant must be at least 16, no older than 25. Applicant must be U.S. citizen residing in West Virginia. Applicant must be dependent of deceased veteran who served in the Army, Air Force, Marines, Navy, Coast Guard or Reserves/National Guard. Applicant's parent must be veteran who was killed while on active duty during wartime or who died of injury or illness resulting from wartime service.

**Application requirements:** Proof of eligibility.
**Additional information:** Award is waiver of tuition and registration fees for West Virginia residents attending a West Virginia school. If attending a private school in West Virginia or out of state college, may only receive a maximum of $2,000 for academic year. Non-West Virginia residents exempt.

| | |
|---|---|
| **Amount of award:** | Full tuition |
| **Number of awards:** | 23 |
| **Number of applicants:** | 8 |
| **Application deadline:** | July 1, December 1 |
| **Notification begins:** | July 15, December 15 |
| **Total amount awarded:** | $15,000 |

**Contact:**
West Virginia Division of Veterans Affairs
Attn: Angela S. Meadows
1321 Plaza East, Suite 109
Charleston, WV 25301
Phone: 304-558-3661 or 866-984-8387
Fax: 304-558-3662
Web: www.wvs.state.wv.us/va

Scholarships

# West Virginia Higher Education Policy Commission

## PROMISE Scholarship

**Type of award:** Scholarship, renewable.
**Intended use:** For undergraduate study at 2-year or 4-year institution.
**Eligibility:** Applicant must be U.S. citizen or permanent resident residing in West Virginia.
**Basis for selection:** Applicant must demonstrate high academic achievement.
**Application requirements:** FAFSA.
**Additional information:** Merit-based scholarship; all eligible applicants will receive award up to $4,750. Minimum 22 composite ACT, with scores of at least 20 in math, science, English, and reading, or 1020 SAT (Math and Reading) with minimum 480 Math and 490 Reading. Minimum 3.0 GPA. GED/home-schooled students must maintain a 2500 minimum score on the GED. Tuition waiver only for public institutions. Students attending private institutions will receive tuition assistance based on average cost of public college tuition and fees. See Website for more information.

| | |
|---|---|
| **Amount of award:** | $4,750 |
| **Number of awards:** | 10,000 |
| **Number of applicants:** | 8,000 |
| **Application deadline:** | March 1 |
| **Notification begins:** | April 1 |
| **Total amount awarded:** | $30,000,000 |

**Contact:**
West Virginia Higher Education Policy Commission
1018 Kanawha Boulevard East
Suite 700
Charleston, WV 25301
Phone: 877-987-7664 or 304-558-4618
Fax: 304-558-5719
Web: www.cfwv.com

## West Virginia Engineering, Science, and Technology Scholarship

**Type of award:** Scholarship, renewable.
**Intended use:** For full-time undergraduate study at 2-year or 4-year institution in United States. Designated institutions: Eligible West Virginia institutions.
**Eligibility:** Applicant must be U.S. citizen or permanent resident residing in West Virginia.
**Basis for selection:** Major/career interest in science, general; engineering; engineering, civil; engineering, computer; engineering, electrical/electronic; engineering, mechanical; computer/information sciences; life sciences; physical sciences or natural sciences. Applicant must demonstrate high academic achievement and seriousness of purpose.
**Application requirements:** Essay, transcript.
**Additional information:** Recipients should obtain degree/certificate in engineering, science, or technology and pursue career in West Virginia. Recipient must, within one year after ceasing to be a full-time student, work full-time in engineering, science, or technology field in West Virginia, or begin a program of community service relating to these fields in West Virginia for a duration of one year for each year scholarship was received. If work requirement fails to be met, recipient must repay scholarship plus interest and any required collection fees. Interested high school students should apply through high school counselor; currently enrolled college/university students should apply through their institution. Minimum 3.0 GPA. Application available on Website.

| | |
|---|---|
| **Amount of award:** | $3,000 |
| **Number of awards:** | 100 |
| **Number of applicants:** | 400 |
| **Application deadline:** | March 1 |
| **Total amount awarded:** | $395,802 |

**Contact:**
West Virginia Higher Education Policy Commission
Engineering, Science, and Technology Program
1018 Kanawha Boulevard East, Suite 700
Charleston, WV 25301-2800
Phone: 304-558-4614
Web: www.cfwv.com

## West Virginia Higher Education Adult Part-time Student (HEAPS) Grant Program

**Type of award:** Scholarship, renewable.
**Intended use:** For half-time undergraduate certificate, freshman, sophomore, junior or senior study at postsecondary institution.
**Eligibility:** Applicant must be returning adult student. Applicant must be U.S. citizen or permanent resident residing in West Virginia.
**Basis for selection:** Applicant must demonstrate financial need.
**Application requirements:** FAFSA and any supplemental materials required by individual institutions.
**Additional information:** Applicant must be out of high school for at least two years and plan to continue education on part-time basis. Must either be enrolled in college with cumulative 2.0 GPA (for renewal applicants), or be accepted for enrollment by intended institution (for first-time applicants); must have complied with Military Selective Service Act; must qualify as independent student according to federal financial aid criteria; must not be in default on higher education loan; and must not be incarcerated in correctional facility. At public

colleges/universities, award is actual amount of tuition and fees. At independent colleges/universities and vocational/technical schools, award is based upon average per credit/term hours tuition and fee charges assessed by all public undergraduate institutions. Contact school's financial aid office, or visit Website for additional information.

**Contact:**
West Virginia Higher Education Policy Commission
1018 Kanawha Boulevard East, Fifth Floor
Charleston, WV 25301
Phone: 304-558-4618
Web: www.cfwv.com

## West Virginia Higher Education Grant

**Type of award:** Scholarship, renewable.
**Intended use:** For full-time undergraduate study at accredited 2-year or 4-year institution. Designated institutions: West Virginia or Pennsylvania institutions.
**Eligibility:** Applicant must be U.S. citizen or permanent resident residing in West Virginia or Pennsylvania.
**Basis for selection:** Applicant must demonstrate financial need and high academic achievement.
**Application requirements:** Transcript. FAFSA. ACT/SAT scores.
**Additional information:** Applicants must fill out common application for state-level financial aid programs. Visit Website for application.

| | |
|---|---|
| **Amount of award:** | $350-$2,100 |
| **Number of awards:** | 9,800 |
| **Number of applicants:** | 34,000 |
| **Application deadline:** | April 15 |
| **Total amount awarded:** | $34,600,000 |

**Contact:**
West Virginia Higher Education Grant Program
Office of Financial Aid and Outreach Services
1018 Kanawha Boulevard East, Suite 700
Charleston, WV 25301-2800
Phone: 304-558-4618 or 877-987-7664
Fax: 304-558-5719
Web: www.cfwv.com

## West Virginia Robert C. Byrd Honors Scholarship

**Type of award:** Scholarship, renewable.
**Intended use:** For full-time freshman study at vocational, 2-year or 4-year institution in United States.
**Eligibility:** Applicant must be high school senior. Applicant must be U.S. citizen or permanent resident residing in West Virginia.
**Basis for selection:** Applicant must demonstrate high academic achievement.
**Application requirements:** Transcript, proof of eligibility, nomination by high school. SAT or ACT scores.
**Additional information:** Because of limited funding, high schools with senior class enrollment of 1-199 may submit one application for consideration and high schools with senior class of 200+ may submit two applications for consideration. Students should apply through their high school counselor.

| | |
|---|---|
| **Amount of award:** | $1,500 |
| **Number of awards:** | 36 |
| **Number of applicants:** | 400 |
| **Total amount awarded:** | $211,500 |

**Contact:**
West Virginia Higher Education Policy Commission
Robert C. Byrd Honors Scholarship Program
1018 Kanawha Boulevard East, Suite 700
Charleston, WV 25301-2800
Phone: 304-558-4614
Web: www.cfwv.com

## West Virginia Underwood-Smith Teacher Scholarship

**Type of award:** Scholarship, renewable.
**Intended use:** For full-time junior, senior or graduate study at 4-year or graduate institution.
**Eligibility:** Applicant must be U.S. citizen or permanent resident residing in West Virginia.
**Basis for selection:** Major/career interest in education; education, early childhood; education, special or education, teacher. Applicant must demonstrate high academic achievement.
**Application requirements:** Essay, proof of eligibility.
**Additional information:** Undergraduate applicants must have cumulative 3.25 GPA; graduate students must rank in top 10 percent of class or have 3.5 GPA. Number of applicants varies. Recipients must agree to teach at the public school level in West Virginia for two years for each year the scholarship is received or be willing to repay the scholarship on a pro rata basis. Visit Website for details and application.

| | |
|---|---|
| **Amount of award:** | $5,000 |
| **Number of awards:** | 54 |
| **Number of applicants:** | 100 |
| **Total amount awarded:** | $235,000 |

**Contact:**
West Virginia Higher Education Policy Commission
Underwood-Smith Teacher Scholarship Program
1018 Kanawha Boulevard East, Suite 700
Charleston, WV 25301-2800
Phone: 304-558-4614
Web: www.cfwv.com

# Western European Architecture Foundation

## Gabriel Prize

**Type of award:** Research grant.
**Intended use:** For non-degree study at postsecondary institution.
**Eligibility:** Applicant must be U.S. citizen.
**Basis for selection:** Major/career interest in architecture. Applicant must demonstrate seriousness of purpose.
**Application requirements:** Portfolio, recommendations, research proposal. Resume.
**Additional information:** Award to encourage personal investigative and critical studies of French architectural compositions completed between 1630 and 1930. Work is expected to be executed in France under supervision of foundation's European representative. Winner is required to begin studies in France by May 1, keep a traveling sketchbook, and prepare three large colored drawings within three months. Must use stipend for travel and study. Send SASE for return of materials. Visit Website for application and deadline.

**Amount of award:** $20,000
**Number of awards:** 1
**Number of applicants:** 24
**Total amount awarded:** $20,000

**Contact:**
Western European Architecture Foundation
306 West Sunset, Suite 115
San Antonio, TX 78209
Phone: 210-829-4040
Fax: 210-829-4049
Web: www.gabrielprize.org

# Western Golf Association/ Evans Scholars Foundation

## Chick Evans Caddie Scholarship

**Type of award:** Scholarship, renewable.
**Intended use:** For full-time undergraduate study at accredited 4-year institution in United States.
**Eligibility:** Applicant must be high school senior.
**Basis for selection:** Competition/talent/interest in athletics/ sports, based on consistent caddie record at Western Golf Association-affiliated club. Applicant must demonstrate financial need, high academic achievement, depth of character and leadership.
**Application requirements:** Recommendations, transcript, proof of eligibility. Tax returns, financial aid profile.
**Additional information:** Scholarship for full tuition, plus housing. Must have caddied minimum two years at Western Golf Association-affiliated club and maintain at least B average in college prep classes. Must have strong caddie record and work at sponsoring club during summer of application. Most recipients attend one of 14 universities where Evans Scholars Foundation owns and operates chapter house. Approximately 200 new Evans Scholarships awarded each year. Renewable up to four years. See Website for designated institutions.

**Amount of award:** Full tuition
**Number of awards:** 200
**Number of applicants:** 678
**Application deadline:** September 30
**Total amount awarded:** $8,000,000

**Contact:**
Scholarship Committee
Western Golf Assoc./Evans Scholars Foundation
1 Briar Road
Golf, IL 60029
Phone: 847-724-4600
Fax: 847-724-7133
Web: www.evansscholarsfoundation.com

# William Randolph Hearst Foundation

## Hearst Journalism Award

**Type of award:** Scholarship.
**Intended use:** For undergraduate study at accredited 4-year institution. Designated institutions: Institutions accredited by Accrediting Council on Education in Journalism and Mass Communication.
**Basis for selection:** Competition/talent/interest in writing/ journalism, based on newsworthiness, research, excellence of journalistic writing, photojournalism, or broadcast news. Major/ career interest in journalism; radio/television/film or communications.
**Additional information:** Field of study may also include photojournalism or broadcast news. Applicants must be actively involved in campus media and submit work that has been published or aired. Competition consists of monthly contests and one championship. Scholarships awarded to student winners with matching grants awarded to their departments of journalism. Entries must be submitted by journalism department. For additional information and deadlines, applicants should contact journalism department chair or visit Website. Only two applicants per competition per school.

**Amount of award:** $1,000-$2,600
**Number of awards:** 14
**Total amount awarded:** $500,000

**Contact:**
Hearst Journalism Awards Program
90 New Montgomery Street
Suite 1212
San Francisco, CA 94105-4504
Phone: 415-908-4560 or 800-841-7048 ext. 4560
Web: www.hearstfdn.org

## United States Senate Youth Program

**Type of award:** Scholarship.
**Intended use:** For undergraduate study at accredited 2-year or 4-year institution in United States.
**Eligibility:** Applicant must be high school junior or senior. Applicant must be U.S. citizen or permanent resident.
**Basis for selection:** Applicant must demonstrate leadership and service orientation.
**Application requirements:** Nomination by high school principal or teacher.
**Additional information:** Applicant must be permanent resident of and currently enrolled in public or private secondary school located in the state (including District of Columbia) in which parent or guardian legally resides. Must be currently serving in elected capacity as student body officer; class officer; student council representative; or student representative to district, regional, or state-level civic or educational organization. Selection process managed by state-level department of education. Scholarship includes all-expenses-paid week in Washington, D.C., in March. Application deadline is in early fall for most states; application available from high school principal or teacher. Visit Website for more information.

**Amount of award:** $5,000
**Number of awards:** 104
**Notification begins:** December 1
**Total amount awarded:** $520,000

**Contact:**
Rayne Guilford, Program Director William Randolph Hearst Foundation
90 New Montgomery Street
Suite 1212
San Francisco, CA 94105-4504
Phone: 800-841-7048 ext. 4540
Fax: 415-243-0760
Web: www.ussenateyouth.org

# Wilson Ornithological Society

## George A. Hall/Harold F. Mayfield Award

**Type of award:** Research grant.
**Intended use:** For non-degree study at postsecondary institution.
**Basis for selection:** Major/career interest in ornithology.
**Application requirements:** Recommendations, research proposal. Budget. Research proposal must be no longer than three pages.
**Additional information:** Research proposal must not exceed three pages. Award restricted to amateur researchers, including high school students, without access to funds and facilities of academic institutions or governmental agencies. Willingness to report research results as oral or poster paper is condition of award. Applicants whose first language is not English may also submit proposal in their first language. Award should be used for equipment, supplies, travel, or living expenses. Visit Website for contact information and application.

| | |
|---|---|
| **Amount of award:** | $1,000 |
| **Number of awards:** | 1 |
| **Number of applicants:** | 4 |
| **Application deadline:** | February 1 |
| **Total amount awarded:** | $1,000 |

**Contact:**
Web: www.wilsonsociety.org/awards

## Paul A. Stewart Award

**Type of award:** Research grant.
**Intended use:** For undergraduate, master's, doctoral, postgraduate or non-degree study at postsecondary institution.
**Basis for selection:** Major/career interest in ornithology.
**Application requirements:** Recommendations, research proposal. Research budget.
**Additional information:** Research proposal should not exceed three pages. Preference given to proposals studying bird movements based on banding, analysis of recoveries, and returns of banded birds, with an emphasis on economic ornithology. Willingness to report research results as oral or poster paper is condition of award. Applicants whose first language is not English may also submit proposal in their first language. Visit Website for contact information and application.

| | |
|---|---|
| **Amount of award:** | $1,000 |
| **Number of awards:** | 8 |
| **Number of applicants:** | 18 |
| **Application deadline:** | February 1 |
| **Total amount awarded:** | $8,000 |

**Contact:**
Web: www.wilsonsociety.org/awards

# Wisconsin Department of Veterans Affairs

## Wisconsin Veterans Affairs Retraining Grant

**Type of award:** Scholarship.
**Intended use:** For undergraduate study at accredited vocational institution. Designated institutions: Wisconsin technical colleges; occupational/technical schools approved by the Wisconsin Educational Approval Board; Wisconsin on-the-job training programs.
**Eligibility:** Applicant must be residing in Wisconsin. Applicant must be veteran. Must have served two years of continuous active duty during peacetime or 90 days of active duty during designated wartime period.
**Basis for selection:** Applicant must demonstrate financial need.
**Additional information:** Applicant must be recently unemployed or underemployed and registered for or enrolled in education program that will lead to re-employment and be completed within two years. Must have been involuntarily laid off within a period beginning one year before WDVA receives application. Must have been employed for six consecutive months with same employer or in the same or similar occupation. Must have been a resident of Wisconsin on entry into military service or a continuous resident of Wisconsin for at least five years after separation from military service. Apply year-round at local county Veterans Service Office to establish eligibility.

| | |
|---|---|
| **Amount of award:** | $3,000 |

**Contact:**
Wisconsin Department of Veterans Affairs
P.O. Box 7843
30 West Mifflin Street
Madison, WI 53707-7843
Phone: 800-947-8387
Web: www.WisVets.com/RetrainingGrants

## Wisconsin Veterans Education GI Bill Tuition Remission Program

**Type of award:** Scholarship, renewable.
**Intended use:** For undergraduate study at vocational, 2-year or 4-year institution. Designated institutions: University of Wisconsin system schools, Wisconsin Technical College system schools.
**Eligibility:** Applicant must be residing in Wisconsin. Applicant must be veteran; or dependent of veteran, disabled veteran or deceased veteran; or spouse of veteran, disabled veteran or deceased veteran.
**Basis for selection:** Applicant must demonstrate financial need.
**Application requirements:** Proof of eligibility. Federal tax return or proof of annual income.
**Additional information:** Veteran must have been Wisconsin resident at time of entry into active duty; children of veterans must be between ages 17-25; widowed spouse of veteran must not be remarried. Veterans and spouses of veterans rated by the federal VA with a combined service-connected disability rating of 30% or greater are also eligible. Family income limit of $50,000; limit increases by $1,000 for each independent child. Veterans may receive up to 100 percent reimbursement of cost of tuition and fees. May receive reimbursement for up to eight semesters of full-time study. Visit Website for list of eligible schools, further requirements, and deadlines.

**Contact:**
Wisconsin Department of Veterans Affairs
P.O. Box 7843
30 West Mifflin Street
Madison, WI 53707-7843
Phone: 800-947-8387
Web: www.WisVets.com/WisGIBill

Scholarships

# Wisconsin Higher Educational Aids Board

## Wisconsin Academic Excellence Scholarship

**Type of award:** Scholarship, renewable.
**Intended use:** For full-time undergraduate study at vocational, 2-year or 4-year institution. Designated institutions: Wisconsin non-profit colleges or universities.
**Eligibility:** Applicant must be high school senior. Applicant must be residing in Wisconsin.
**Basis for selection:** Applicant must demonstrate high academic achievement.
**Application requirements:** Nomination by high school guidance counselor.
**Additional information:** Awarded to Wisconsin high school seniors who have the highest grade point average in each public and private high school throughout Wisconsin. Must be registered with Selective Service, unless exempt. 3.0 GPA must be maintained for renewal.

| | |
|---|---|
| **Amount of award:** | $2,250 |
| **Number of awards:** | 2,670 |
| **Application deadline:** | March 1 |
| **Total amount awarded:** | $2,894,469 |

**Contact:**
Higher Educational Aids Board
Attn: Nancy Wilkison
131 West Wilson, Suite 902
Madison, WI 53707-7885
Phone: 608-267-2213
Web: www.heab.state.wi.us/programs.html

## Wisconsin Hearing & Visually Handicapped Student Grant

**Type of award:** Scholarship, renewable.
**Intended use:** For undergraduate study at postsecondary institution. Designated institutions: Non-profit Wisconsin institutions; some out-of-state schools.
**Eligibility:** Applicant must be visually impaired or hearing impaired. Applicant must be residing in Wisconsin.
**Basis for selection:** Applicant must demonstrate financial need.
**Application requirements:** Proof of eligibility. FAFSA.

| | |
|---|---|
| **Amount of award:** | $250-$1,800 |
| **Number of awards:** | 54 |
| **Total amount awarded:** | $85,910 |

**Contact:**
Higher Educational Aids Board
Attn: Cindy Cooley
P.O. Box 7885
Madison, WI 53707-7885
Phone: 608-266-0888
Web: www.heab.state.wi.us

## Wisconsin Higher Education Grant

**Type of award:** Scholarship, renewable.
**Intended use:** For undergraduate study at vocational or 4-year institution. Designated institutions: University of Wisconsin, Wisconsin Technical College, Tribal institutions. Some exceptions for hard of hearing or visually handicapped students.
**Eligibility:** Applicant must be residing in Wisconsin.
**Basis for selection:** Applicant must demonstrate financial need.
**Application requirements:** Proof of eligibility. FAFSA.
**Additional information:** Apply with FAFSA through high school guidance counselor or financial aid office of institution. Must be registered with Selective Service, unless exempt. Rolling deadline.

| | |
|---|---|
| **Amount of award:** | $250-$3,000 |
| **Number of awards:** | 37,172 |
| **Total amount awarded:** | $35,060,586 |

**Contact:**
Higher Educational Aids Board
Attn: Cindy Cooley
P.O. Box 7885
Madison, WI 53707-7885
Phone: 608-266-0888
Web: www.heab.state.wi.us

## Wisconsin Indian Student Assistance Grant

**Type of award:** Scholarship, renewable.
**Intended use:** For undergraduate or graduate study at postsecondary institution. Designated institutions: University of Wisconsin, Wisconsin Technical College, independent colleges and universities, tribal colleges, proprietary institutions in Wisconsin.
**Eligibility:** Applicant must be American Indian. Must be at least one-quarter Native American. Applicant must be residing in Wisconsin.
**Basis for selection:** Applicant must demonstrate financial need.
**Application requirements:** Proof of eligibility. FAFSA.
**Additional information:** Must be at least 25% Native American. Must be registered with Selective Service, unless exempt.

| | |
|---|---|
| **Amount of award:** | $250-$1,100 |
| **Number of awards:** | 837 |
| **Total amount awarded:** | $784,857 |

**Contact:**
Higher Educational Aids Board
Attn: Cindy Cooley
P.O. Box 7885
Madison, WI 53707-7885
Phone: 608-266-0888
Web: www.heab.state.wi.us

## Wisconsin Minority Undergraduate Retention Grant

**Type of award:** Scholarship, renewable.
**Intended use:** For sophomore, junior or senior study at vocational, 2-year or 4-year institution. Designated institutions: Wisconsin technical colleges, independent colleges and universities, or tribal colleges.
**Eligibility:** Applicant must be Asian American, African American, Mexican American, Hispanic American, Puerto Rican or American Indian. Asian American applicants must be former citizens or children of former citizens of Laos, Vietnam, or Cambodia admitted to United States after 12/31/75. Applicant must be U.S. citizen or permanent resident residing in Wisconsin.
**Basis for selection:** Applicant must demonstrate financial need.
**Application requirements:** FAFSA and nomination by Financial Aid Office.

**Amount of award:** $250-$2,500
**Number of awards:** 913
**Number of applicants:** 915
**Total amount awarded:** $687,596

**Contact:**
Higher Educational Aids Board
Attn: May Lou Kuzdas
P.O. Box 7885
Wisconsin, WI 53707-7885
Phone: 608-267-2212
Web: www.heab.state.wi.us

### Wisconsin Talent Incentive Program Grant

**Type of award:** Scholarship, renewable.
**Intended use:** For freshman study at postsecondary institution. Designated institutions: Non-profit Wisconsin institutions.
**Eligibility:** Applicant must be residing in Wisconsin.
**Basis for selection:** Applicant must demonstrate financial need.
**Application requirements:** Nomination by financial aid department or Wisconsin Educational Opportunity Programs. FAFSA.
**Additional information:** Applicant must meet at least one of non-traditional/economically disadvantaged criteria. Visit Website for list. Eligibility cannot exceed ten semesters.

**Amount of award:** $250-$1,800
**Number of awards:** 4,146
**Total amount awarded:** $5,489,498

**Contact:**
Higher Educational Aids Board
Attn: Colette Brown
P.O. Box 7885
Madison, WI 53707-7885
Phone: 608-266-1665
Web: www.heab.state.wi.us

### Wisconsin Tuition Grant

**Type of award:** Scholarship, renewable.
**Intended use:** For undergraduate study at postsecondary institution. Designated institutions: Independent, nonprofit institutions in Wisconsin.
**Eligibility:** Applicant must be residing in Wisconsin.
**Basis for selection:** Applicant must demonstrate financial need.
**Application requirements:** FAFSA.
**Additional information:** Minimum award $250; maximum award amount set annually by HEAB. Must be registered for Selective Service, unless exempt.

**Number of awards:** 12,343
**Total amount awarded:** $23,247,820

**Contact:**
Higher Educational Aids Board
Attn: Mary Lou Kuzdas
P.O. Box 7885
Madison, WI 53707-7885
Phone: 608-267-2212
Web: www.heab.state.wi.us

## Women Grocers of America

### Mary Macey Scholarship

**Type of award:** Scholarship, renewable.
**Intended use:** For sophomore, junior, senior or graduate study at accredited 2-year, 4-year or graduate institution in United States.
**Basis for selection:** Major/career interest in food production/management/services.
**Application requirements:** Recommendations, essay, transcript.
**Additional information:** Must plan on a career in the independent sector of the grocery industry. Majors in public health and hotel management are not eligible. Minimum 2.0 GPA. Minimum of two $1000 awards each year.

**Number of applicants:** 15
**Application deadline:** June 30
**Notification begins:** July 31
**Total amount awarded:** $5,000

**Contact:**
Women Grocers of America
1005 North Glebe Road
Suite 250
Arlington, VA 22201-5758
Phone: 703-516-0700
Fax: 703-516-0115
Web: www.nationalgrocers.org

## Women in Defense, A National Security Organization

### Horizons Scholarship

**Type of award:** Scholarship.
**Intended use:** For junior, senior or graduate study at accredited 4-year institution in United States.
**Eligibility:** Applicant must be female. Applicant must be U.S. citizen.
**Basis for selection:** Major/career interest in science, general; engineering; mathematics; computer/information sciences; physics; business; law; international relations or political science/government. Applicant must demonstrate financial need and high academic achievement.
**Application requirements:** Recommendations, essay, transcript.
**Additional information:** Scholarship intended to provide financial assistance to women either employed or planning careers in defense or national security areas. Minimum 3.25 GPA. Studies must be aimed at national defense/national security. Visit Website for details and application (no phone calls).

**Amount of award:** $500-$2,000
**Number of awards:** 5
**Number of applicants:** 40
**Application deadline:** July 1
**Total amount awarded:** $10,000

**Contact:**
Women in Defense
2111 Wilson Blvd., Suite 400
Arlington, VA 22201-3061
Phone: 703-522-1820
Fax: 703-522-1885
Web: wid.ndia.org

# Women's Western Golf Foundation

## Women's Western Golf Foundation Scholarship

**Type of award:** Scholarship, renewable.
**Intended use:** For full-time freshman study at accredited 4-year institution in United States.
**Eligibility:** Applicant must be female, high school senior. Applicant must be U.S. citizen.
**Basis for selection:** Competition/talent/interest in athletics/sports. Applicant must demonstrate financial need, high academic achievement, depth of character, leadership and seriousness of purpose.
**Application requirements:** Essay, transcript, proof of eligibility. SAT/ACT scores, FAFSA. Personal recommendation required from high school teacher or counselor. List of high school activities.
**Additional information:** Must be in top 15 percent of class. 3.5 GPA is recommended. Must demonstrate involvement in golf, but skill not criterion. Deadline to request application is March 1; SASE required. Awards renew for each of four years, assuming scholarship terms are fulfilled (financial need, GPA above 3.0). About 20 new awards each year, plus 50 renewals.

| | |
|---|---|
| **Amount of award:** | $2,000 |
| **Number of awards:** | 22 |
| **Number of applicants:** | 500 |
| **Application deadline:** | April 5 |
| **Notification begins:** | May 20 |
| **Total amount awarded:** | $150,000 |

**Contact:**
Director of Scholarship
Women's Western Golf Foundation
393 Ramsay Road
Deerfield, IL 60015

# Woodrow Wilson National Fellowship Foundation

## Thomas R. Pickering Foreign Affairs Fellowship

**Type of award:** Scholarship.
**Intended use:** For full-time senior or graduate study at accredited 4-year or graduate institution in United States. Designated institutions: Institutions affiliated with Association of Professional Schools of International Affairs (graduate portion of fellowship).
**Eligibility:** Applicant must be U.S. citizen.
**Basis for selection:** Major/career interest in international relations; communications; history; economics; political science/government; foreign languages or business/management/administration. Applicant must demonstrate financial need, high academic achievement, depth of character, leadership, seriousness of purpose and service orientation.
**Application requirements:** Recommendations, essay, transcript, proof of eligibility. Resume, SAT or ACT scores, SAR, if applicable.
**Additional information:** Award is up to $40,000 toward tuition, mandatory fees, books, travel, and living stipend. Undergraduates must apply as juniors; applicants for graduate fellowship must be seeking admission to graduate school for the following academic year. Must have interest in career as Foreign Service officer. Number of fellowships determined by available funding. Finalists will attend interview session in Washington, D.C.; transportation to interview site paid. Orientation in Washington, D.C. Medical and security clearances required for program participation. Applicants must have minimum 3.2 GPA at time of application and maintain GPA throughout fellowship. Women and members of minority groups historically underrepresented in the Foreign Service encouraged to apply. Successful applicants obligated to a minimum of three years as a Foreign Service officer. Must register and apply online. Deadline varies; visit Website for details.
**Contact:**
Dr. Richard O. Hope, Pickering Foreign Affairs Fellowship Program
Woodrow Wilson National Fellowship Foundation
P.O. Box 2437
Princeton, NJ 08543-2437
Phone: 609-452-7007
Web: www.woodrow.org

# Worldstudio Foundation

## Worldstudio AIGA Scholarship

**Type of award:** Scholarship.
**Intended use:** For full-time undergraduate or graduate study at accredited 2-year or 4-year institution in United States.
**Eligibility:** Applicant must be U.S. citizen or permanent resident.
**Basis for selection:** Major/career interest in graphic arts/design or arts, general. Applicant must demonstrate financial need, seriousness of purpose and service orientation.
**Application requirements:** Portfolio, recommendations, transcript. Statement of purpose and self-portrait.
**Additional information:** Illustration, art direction for advertising, interactive design/motion graphics, and photography majors also eligible. The foundation's primary aim is to increase diversity in the creative professions and to foster social and environmental responsibility in the artists, designers, and studios of tomorrow. Applicants must be enrolled in courses related to or planning a career in design arts professions, and must demonstrate a social agenda in their work. Students with minority status given preference. Minimum 2.0 GPA. Visit Website for guidelines and application. Deadline in early April. Awards not offered for performing arts.

| | |
|---|---|
| **Amount of award:** | $200-$6,000 |
| **Number of awards:** | 20 |
| **Number of applicants:** | 400 |

**Contact:**
Worldstudio Foundation AIGA Scholarships
164 Fifth Avenue
New York, NY 10010
Phone: 212-807-1990
Fax: 212-807-1799
Web: scholarships.worldstudioinc.com

# Wyzant Tutoring

## Wyzant College Scholarship

**Type of award:** Scholarship.
**Intended use:** For undergraduate study at 4-year institution.
**Basis for selection:** Competition/talent/interest in writing/journalism.
**Application requirements:** Essay describing most influential tutor, teacher or coach; must not exceed 300 words.
**Additional information:** First place winner receives $3,000 to school of choice; second place, $2,000; third place, $1,000. See website for application and details.

| | |
|---|---|
| **Amount of award:** | $1,000-$3,000 |
| **Number of awards:** | 3 |
| **Application deadline:** | May 1 |

**Contact:**
Wyzant College Scholarship
1714 N. Damen Ave
Suite 3N
Chicago, IL 60647
Phone: 877-999-2681
Fax: 773-345-5525
Web: www.wyzant.com/scholarships/v1/apply.aspx

# Xerox

## Technical Minority Scholarship

**Type of award:** Scholarship.
**Intended use:** For full-time undergraduate or graduate study in United States.
**Eligibility:** Applicant must be Alaskan native, Asian American, African American, Mexican American, Hispanic American, Puerto Rican, American Indian or Native Hawaiian/Pacific Islander. Applicant must be U.S. citizen or permanent resident.
**Basis for selection:** Major/career interest in chemistry; engineering; science, general; information systems; physics or computer/information sciences. Applicant must demonstrate high academic achievement, leadership, patriotism and seriousness of purpose.
**Application requirements:** Resume and cover letter.
**Additional information:** Minimum 3.0 GPA. Spouses and children of Xerox employees not eligible. Visit Website for application and more information.

| | |
|---|---|
| **Amount of award:** | $1,000-$10,000 |
| **Number of awards:** | 99 |
| **Number of applicants:** | 1,524 |
| **Application deadline:** | September 30 |
| **Notification begins:** | December 31 |
| **Total amount awarded:** | $160,000 |

**Contact:**
Xerox
Technical Minority Scholarship Program
150 State Street, 4th Floor
Rochester, NY 14614
Web: www.xeroxstudentcareers.com

# Yakama Nation Higher Education Program

## Yakama Nation Tribal Scholarship

**Type of award:** Scholarship.
**Intended use:** For undergraduate, master's or doctoral study at accredited 2-year, 4-year or graduate institution.
**Eligibility:** Must be enrolled member of Yakama Nation.
**Application requirements:** Transcript. High school or GED score sheet. Tribal ID card copy. Enrollment verification, FAFSA, college acceptance letter.
**Additional information:** Maximum $3,000 awarded to undergraduate students; maximum $6,000 awarded to graduate students. Recipients notified two weeks prior to the start of semester to which aid will be applied.

| | |
|---|---|
| **Amount of award:** | $3,000-$6,000 |
| **Number of awards:** | 300 |
| **Number of applicants:** | 299 |
| **Application deadline:** | July 1 |
| **Notification begins:** | July 10 |
| **Total amount awarded:** | $200,000 |

**Contact:**
Yakama Nation Higher Education Program
P.O. Box 151
Toppenish, WA 98948
Phone: 509-865-5121
Fax: 509-865-6994

# Internships

## Academy of Television Arts & Sciences Foundation

### Student Internship Program

**Type of award:** Internship.
**Intended use:** For full-time undergraduate or graduate study in United States.
**Eligibility:** Applicant must be U.S. citizen, permanent resident or international student.
**Basis for selection:** Major/career interest in film/video or radio/television/film.
**Application requirements:** Recommendations, essay, transcript. Resume.
**Additional information:** Designed to expose students to professional TV production, techniques, and practices. Opportunities available in many fields; see Website for categories and special requirements. Internships are full-time for eight weeks. Interns responsible for housing, transportation, and living expenses. Interns must have car for transportation in Los Angeles. International students must be authorized to work in the United States. Apply online.

| | |
|---|---|
| **Amount of award:** | $4,000 |
| **Number of awards:** | 41 |
| **Number of applicants:** | 1,200 |
| **Application deadline:** | March 15 |
| **Notification begins:** | May 15 |

**Contact:**
Academy of Television Arts & Sciences Foundation
Nancy Robinson, Student Internship Program
5220 Lankershim Boulevard
North Hollywood, CA 91601-3109
Phone: 818-754-2800
Web: www.emmysfoundationintern.org

## Accuracy in Media/ American Journalism Center

### Accuracy in Media Internships

**Type of award:** Internship.
**Intended use:** For undergraduate or graduate study.
**Basis for selection:** Major/career interest in journalism; marketing; public relations; political science/government or history.
**Application requirements:** Cover letter and resume. Writing sample.
**Additional information:** Accuracy in Media is a nonprofit media watchdog group that reports on media bias. Internships open to applicants from all majors, though some positions require experience in a particular field. Internships pay $50 per day. High school students may apply, as well as recent college graduates. Applications are processed on rolling basis; send early for best chance and to allow time to find housing. Deadlines: April 1 for summer, August 15 for fall, December 15 for spring. See Website for application and more information.

| | |
|---|---|
| **Amount of award:** | $3,000 |
| **Number of awards:** | 15 |
| **Application deadline:** | April 1, August 15 |

**Contact:**
Accuracy in Media/American Journalism Center
Internship Coordinator
4455 Connecticut Avenue, NW, Suite 330
Washington, DC 20008
Phone: 202-364-4401 ext. 110
Fax: 202-364-4098
Web: www.aimajc.org

## Allstate

### Allstate Internships

**Type of award:** Internship, renewable.
**Intended use:** For full-time undergraduate study at accredited 4-year institution.
**Basis for selection:** Major/career interest in insurance/actuarial science; accounting; marketing; business; business/ management/administration; computer/information sciences; finance/banking; mathematics or statistics. Applicant must demonstrate high academic achievement.
**Application requirements:** Resume and cover letter.
**Additional information:** In addition to salary, eligible interns receive subsidized transportation to and from Allstate Home Office in Northbrook, IL, at beginning and end of internship; daily transportation; and subsidized housing. Please respond directly to position posted on Website.
**Contact:**
Allstate Insurance Company
2775 Sanders Road
Northbrook, IL 60062
Web: www.allstate.jobs

## American Association of Advertising Agencies

### Multicultural Advertising Intern Program

**Type of award:** Internship, renewable.
**Intended use:** For full-time senior or graduate study at accredited 4-year or graduate institution.
**Eligibility:** Applicant must be Asian American, African American, Mexican American, Hispanic American, Puerto Rican, American Indian or Native Hawaiian/Pacific Islander. Applicant must be U.S. citizen or permanent resident.

**Basis for selection:** Major/career interest in advertising. Applicant must demonstrate seriousness of purpose.
**Application requirements:** Recommendations, essay, transcript. Resume, work samples (if applying for creative internship).
**Additional information:** Applicants must have completed at least junior year of college and have strong interest in advertising. Minimum 3.0 GPA. Applicants with lower GPA (2.7-2.9) must complete additional essay question on application. Students are placed in member agency offices for ten weeks during the summer. $10/hour. MAIP interns requesting travel/housing assistance will be responsible for paying $1,000 to the 4A's toward summer housing and transportation cost. Can apply for following departments: account management, digital/interactive technologies, media planning/buying, broadcast/print production, traffic, art direction, copywriting, public relations, or strategic/account planning. Agency professionals interview semifinalists before selection. Application deadline is second Friday in November; notification in late December. Number of awards varies. See Website for more information.

| | |
|---|---|
| **Number of applicants:** | 486 |

**Contact:**
American Association of Advertising Agencies
405 Lexington Avenue, 18th Floor
New York, NY 10174-1801
Phone: 800-676-9333
Fax: 212-682-8391
Web: maipmatters.aaaa.org



# American Bar Foundation

## Summer Research Diversity Fellowships in Law and Social Sciences for Undergraduate Students

**Type of award:** Internship.
**Intended use:** For sophomore or junior study at 4-year institution.
**Eligibility:** Applicant must be U.S. citizen or permanent resident.
**Basis for selection:** Major/career interest in law; social/behavioral sciences; criminal justice/law enforcement; public administration/service or humanities/liberal arts. Applicant must demonstrate high academic achievement.
**Application requirements:** Recommendations, essay, transcript.
**Additional information:** Interns work eight 35-hour weeks as research assistants at American Bar Foundation in Chicago. Fellowships are intended for, but not limited to, persons who are African American, Hispanic/Latino, Native American, or Puerto Rican. Applicants must have minimum 3.0 GPA and intend to pursue academic major in social sciences or humanities. See Website for application deadline.

| | |
|---|---|
| **Amount of award:** | $3,600 |
| **Number of awards:** | 4 |
| **Application deadline:** | February 15 |
| **Notification begins:** | April 1 |

**Contact:**
American Bar Foundation - Summer Diversity Fellowships
750 North Lake Shore Drive, Fourth Floor
Chicago, IL 60611
Phone: 312-988-6560
Fax: 312-988-6579
Web: www.americanbarfoundation.org

# American Conservatory Theater

## American Conservatory Theater Production Internships

**Type of award:** Internship.
**Intended use:** For undergraduate, graduate or non-degree study.
**Eligibility:** Applicant must be U.S. citizen or permanent resident.
**Basis for selection:** Major/career interest in performing arts; theater arts or theater/production/technical.
**Application requirements:** Recommendations, essay. Resume. Writing sample, if required by specific internship.
**Additional information:** Provides intern with practical experience in many areas of theater production. Departments include costume rentals, costume shop, properties, and stage management. Fellowships are full-time for duration of entire season (September to June). A small weekly stipend is available. Visit Website for more information.

| | |
|---|---|
| **Number of awards:** | 9 |
| **Number of applicants:** | 200 |
| **Application deadline:** | April 1 |
| **Notification begins:** | June 11 |

**Contact:**
American Conservatory Theater
Fellowship Coordinator
30 Grant Avenue, 6th Floor
San Francisco, CA 94108-5834
Phone: 415-834-3200
Web: www.act-sf.org/fellowships

## Artistic and Administrative Internships

**Type of award:** Internship.
**Intended use:** For undergraduate, graduate or non-degree study.
**Eligibility:** Applicant must be U.S. citizen or permanent resident.
**Basis for selection:** Major/career interest in theater arts; theater/production/technical; arts management; performing arts; public relations; marketing; English or literature.
**Application requirements:** Recommendations, essay. Resume. Writing sample if required by specific internship.
**Additional information:** Provides intern with opportunity to work in dramaturgy, publications, arts management, development, literary or marketing/public relations departments. Fellowship is full-time for duration of entire season (September to June). A weekly stipend is available. Visit Website for more information.

**Number of awards:** 6
**Number of applicants:** 200
**Application deadline:** April 1
**Notification begins:** June 11
**Contact:**
American Conservatory Theater
Fellowship Coordinator
30 Grant Avenue, 6th Floor
San Francisco, CA 94108-5834
Phone: 415-834-3200
Web: www.act-sf.org/fellowships

# American Federation of State, County and Municipal Employees

## AFSCMA/UNCF Union Scholars Program

**Type of award:** Internship.
**Intended use:** For junior or senior study at 4-year institution.
**Eligibility:** Applicant must be Alaskan native, Asian American, African American, Mexican American, Hispanic American, Puerto Rican, American Indian or Native Hawaiian/Pacific Islander.
**Basis for selection:** Major/career interest in ethnic/cultural studies; women's studies; sociology; anthropology; history; political science/government; psychology; social work; economics or public administration/service.
**Application requirements:** Recommendations.
**Additional information:** Labor studies and American studies majors also eligible. Minimum 2.5 GPA. Must demonstrate interest in working for social and economic justice through the labor movement. Must have a driver's license. Award is a ten-week summer field placement to participate in union organizing campaign in one of several U.S. locations. Includes on-site housing and week-long orientation and training. Scholars receive up to $4,000 stipend and up to $5,000 academic scholarship for upcoming school year.
**Amount of award:** $4,000-$9,000
**Number of awards:** 10
**Application deadline:** February 28
**Notification begins:** September 15
**Contact:**
AFSCME
Attn: Education Department
1625 L Street, NW
Washington, DC 20036
Phone: 202-429-1025
Web: www.afscme.org

# American Museum of Natural History

## Anthropology Internship Program

**Type of award:** Internship.
**Intended use:** For undergraduate or graduate study.
**Basis for selection:** Major/career interest in anthropology; archaeology or museum studies.
**Application requirements:** Essay, transcript. Resume, contact information of academic advisor.
**Additional information:** Must specify whether applying for paid, academic credit, or unpaid internship. Deadlines: April 1 for summer; August 27 for fall; December 1 for spring. Internships may range from three to six months. Number of awards varies.
**Application deadline:** April 1, December 1
**Contact:**
American Museum of Natural History
Attn: Anita Caltabiano
Central Park West at 79th Street
New York, NY 10024-5192
Phone: 212-769-5375
Web: www.research.amnh.org/anthropology/about/internship

## Research Experiences for Undergraduates in the Physical Sciences

**Type of award:** Internship.
**Intended use:** For undergraduate study at accredited postsecondary institution in United States.
**Eligibility:** Applicant must be U.S. citizen or permanent resident.
**Basis for selection:** Major/career interest in physical sciences; astronomy or geophysics. Applicant must demonstrate high academic achievement and seriousness of purpose.
**Application requirements:** Essay, transcript. List of courses. List of references. Ranking of first two choices among summer projects listed on Website and explanation of why applicant chose them.
**Additional information:** Nearby university dormitory housing provided, as well as travel to and from New York City, as per need. Visit Website for updated list of projects offered and application. Application must be submitted electronically. Contact Dr. James Webster (jdw@amnh.org) for more information on the Earth and Planetary Science program or Dr. Charles Liu (cliu@amnh.org) for the Astrophysics program. Amount and number of award varies. Check Website for deadline.
**Contact:**
Richard Gilder Graduate School, REU Program in Physical Sciences
American Museum of Natural History
Central Park West at 79th Street
New York, NY 10024-5192
Phone: 212-769-5055
Web: www.research.amnh.org/physsci/reu.html

# American Society of International Law

## American Society of International Law Internships

**Type of award:** Internship.
**Intended use:** For undergraduate or graduate study at accredited postsecondary institution.

**Basis for selection:** Major/career interest in accounting; communications; international relations; law; public administration/service or public relations.
**Application requirements:** Cover letter, resume.
**Additional information:** Positions require a minimum commitment of 15 hours per week during fall and spring semesters, and 20 hours per week during summer semester. All internships unpaid; students may arrange academic credit. Address application to one of the following departments: communications and development, finance office, or legal research. See Website for more information. Applications accepted on rolling basis.
**Contact:**
American Society of International Law
Internship Coordinator
2223 Massachusetts Avenue, NW
Washington, DC 20008
Phone: 202-939-6000
Fax: 202-797-7133
Web: www.asil.org/asil-internships.cfm

# Americans for the Arts

## Arts & Business Council of New York Internship

**Type of award:** Internship.
**Intended use:** For undergraduate or graduate study.
**Basis for selection:** Major/career interest in nonprofit administration; arts, general or arts management.
**Application requirements:** Cover letter, resume.
**Additional information:** Ten-week internship available on part-time basis for winter/spring and fall terms, and full-time basis for summer. $500 stipend for winter/spring, $1000 stipend for summer. Recent college graduates also eligible. Application deadlines are in March for summer, July for fall, and December for winter/spring. Visit Website for details and deadlines. Internship takes place in New York City. Candidates should have a passion for the arts, knowledge of Microsoft Office, and be able to multi-task and work with minimal supervision. Internship not always available for all seasons.

| | |
|---|---|
| **Amount of award:** | $500-$1,000 |
| **Number of awards:** | 1 |

**Contact:**
Americans for the Arts
Attn: John Cloys
1000 Vermont Avenue, NW, 6th Floor
Washington, DC 20005
Phone: 202-371-2830
Fax: 202-371-0424
Web: www.americansforthearts.org

## Arts Action Fund Internship

**Type of award:** Internship.
**Intended use:** For undergraduate or graduate study at postsecondary institution.
**Basis for selection:** Major/career interest in arts management; nonprofit administration or political science/government.
**Application requirements:** Cover letter, resume.
**Additional information:** Applicant may also be recent college graduate. Ten-week positions available part-time for winter/spring and fall and full-time for summer. Application deadlines are March for summer, July for fall, and December for winter/spring. Internship not always available for all seasons. Check Website for more details and deadlines. $500 stipend for winter/spring, $1000 stipend for summer. Must have excellent written and organizational skills, some experience in campaigns or political activities, strong computer skills (including proficiency in Adobe Creative Suite), and interest in basic Website management. Download application from Website or apply online.

| | |
|---|---|
| **Amount of award:** | $500-$1,000 |
| **Number of awards:** | 1 |

**Contact:**
Americans for the Arts
Attn: John Cloys
1000 Vermont Avenue NW, 6th Floor
Washington, DC 20005
Phone: 202-371-2830
Fax: 202-371-0424
Web: www.americansforthearts.org

## Arts Policy Internship

**Type of award:** Internship.
**Intended use:** For undergraduate or graduate study.
**Basis for selection:** Major/career interest in arts management; arts, general or nonprofit administration.
**Application requirements:** Cover letter, resume.
**Additional information:** Internship takes place in New York City office. Recent college graduates may apply. Positions available part-time for winter/spring and fall and full-time for summer. Application deadlines are March for summer, July for fall, and December for winter/spring. Internship not always available for all seasons. Check Website for details and deadlines. $500 stipend for winter/spring, $1000 stipend for summer. Must know MS office (especially Excel), be able to work independently, have good communication skills, and an interest in arts and culture policy.

| | |
|---|---|
| **Amount of award:** | $500-$1,000 |
| **Number of awards:** | 1 |

**Contact:**
Americans for the Arts
Attn: John Cloys
1000 Vermont Avenue NW, 6th Floor
Washington, DC 20005
Phone: 202-371-2830
Fax: 202-371-0424
Web: www.americansforthearts.org

## Government and Public Affairs Internship

**Type of award:** Internship.
**Intended use:** For undergraduate or graduate study at postsecondary institution.
**Basis for selection:** Major/career interest in arts management; arts, general; education; governmental public relations; public administration/service or nonprofit administration.
**Application requirements:** Cover letter, resume.
**Additional information:** Recent college graduates may apply. Ten-week positions available part-time for winter/spring and fall and full-time for summer. Application deadlines are March for summer, July for fall, and December for winter/spring. Internship not always available for all seasons. Check Website for details and deadlines. $500 stipend for winter/spring, $1000 stipend for summer. Must know MS Office and have good communication skills. Download application from Website or apply online.

| | |
|---|---|
| **Amount of award:** | $500-$1,000 |
| **Number of awards:** | 1 |

**Contact:**
Americans for the Arts
Attn: John Cloys
1000 Vermont Avenue NW, 6th Floor
Washington, DC 20005
Phone: 202-371-2830
Fax: 202-371-0424
Web: www.americansforthearts.org

## Leadership Alliances Internship

**Type of award:** Internship.
**Intended use:** For undergraduate or graduate study at postsecondary institution.
**Basis for selection:** Major/career interest in arts, general or nonprofit administration.
**Application requirements:** Cover letter, resume.
**Additional information:** Recent college graduates may apply. Ten-week positions available part-time for winter/spring and fall and full-time for summer. Application deadlines are March for summer, July for fall, and December for winter/spring. Internship not always available for all seasons. Check Website for details and deadlines. $500 stipend for winter/spring, $1000 stipend for summer. Must know MS Office and have good communication skills. Must know Word and Excel, especially mail merge and data sorting. Good communication skills and gregarious personality preferred. Download application from Website or apply online.

| | |
|---|---|
| **Amount of award:** | $500-$1,000 |
| **Number of awards:** | 1 |

**Contact:**
Americans for the Arts
Attn: Human Resources Associate
1000 Vermont Avenue NW, 6th Floor
Washington, DC 20005
Phone: 202-371-2830
Fax: 202-371-0424
Web: www.americansforthearts.org

## Local Arts Advancement Services Internship

**Type of award:** Internship.
**Intended use:** For undergraduate or graduate study at postsecondary institution.
**Basis for selection:** Major/career interest in arts management; arts, general; communications or nonprofit administration.
**Application requirements:** Cover letter, resume.
**Additional information:** Recent college graduates may apply. Ten-week position available part-time for winter/spring and fall and full-time for summer. Application deadlines are March for summer, July for fall, and December for winter/spring. Internship not always available for all seasons. $500 stipend for fall/spring, $1000 stipend for summer. Must know Microsoft Office and Outlook, and have exceptional written and verbal communication skills. Check Website for details, deadlines and application.

| | |
|---|---|
| **Amount of award:** | $500-$1,000 |
| **Number of awards:** | 1 |

**Contact:**
Americans for the Arts
Attn: John Cloys
1000 Vermont Avenue NW, 6th Floor
Washington, DC 20005
Phone: 202-371-2830
Fax: 202-371-0424
Web: www.americansforthearts.org

## Marketing and Communications Internship

**Type of award:** Internship.
**Intended use:** For undergraduate or graduate study at postsecondary institution.
**Basis for selection:** Major/career interest in public relations; marketing; communications or nonprofit administration.
**Application requirements:** Cover letter, resume.
**Additional information:** Recent college graduates may apply. Ten-week positions available part-time for winter/spring and fall and full-time for summer. Application deadlines are March for summer, July for fall, and December for winter/spring. Internship not always available for all seasons. Check Website for details and deadlines. $500 stipend for winter/spring, $1000 stipend for summer. Must know MS Office and have good phone manner. Experience with database software, HTML, and proofreading/editing a plus. Download application from Website or apply online.

| | |
|---|---|
| **Amount of award:** | $500-$1,000 |
| **Number of awards:** | 1 |

**Contact:**
Americans for the Arts
Attn: John Cloys
1000 Vermont Avenue NW, 6th Floor
Washington, DC 20005
Phone: 202-371-2830
Fax: 202-371-0424
Web: www.americansforthearts.org

## Meetings and Events/Executive Office Internship

**Type of award:** Internship.
**Intended use:** For undergraduate study.
**Basis for selection:** Major/career interest in hospitality administration/management; hotel/restaurant management; communications; public relations or nonprofit administration.
**Application requirements:** Cover letter, resume.
**Additional information:** Recent college graduates also eligible. Ten-week internship available on part-time basis for winter/spring and fall terms and full-time for summer. $500 stipend for fall/spring, $1000 stipend for summer. Application deadlines are in March for summer, July for fall, and December for winter/spring. Internship not always available for all seasons. Must have strong knowledge of Microsoft Office. Candidate should have interest in event planning and/or nonprofit sector. Visit Website for details and deadlines.

| | |
|---|---|
| **Amount of award:** | $500-$1,000 |
| **Number of awards:** | 1 |

**Contact:**
Americans for the Arts
Attn: John Cloys
1000 Vermont Avenue, NW, 6th Floor
Washington, DC 20005
Phone: 202-371-2830
Fax: 202-371-0424
Web: www.americansforthearts.org

## Membership Internship

**Type of award:** Internship.
**Intended use:** For undergraduate or graduate study.
**Basis for selection:** Major/career interest in nonprofit administration; arts management; arts, general or marketing.
**Application requirements:** Cover letter, resume.

Internships

**Additional information:** Recent college graduates also eligible. Ten-week internship available part-time for winter/spring and fall and full-time for summer. $500 stipend for winter/spring, $1000 stipend for summer. Application deadlines are in March for summer, July for fall, and December for winter/spring. Internship not always available for all seasons. Check Website for details and deadlines. Must have knowledge of Microsoft Office; experience using database software a plus. Ideal candidate has interest and experience in marketing, membership, or arts administration.

**Amount of award:** $500-$1,000
**Number of awards:** 1

**Contact:**
Americans for the Arts
Attn: John Cloys
1000 Vermont Avenue, NW, 6th Floor
Washington, DC 20005
Phone: 202-371-2830
Fax: 202-371-0424
Web: www.americansforthearts.org

### Private-Sector Initiatives Internship

**Type of award:** Internship.
**Intended use:** For undergraduate or graduate study at postsecondary institution.
**Basis for selection:** Major/career interest in business; arts, general; arts management or nonprofit administration.
**Application requirements:** Cover letter, resume.
**Additional information:** Recent college graduates may apply. Position is based in New York, NY. Major/career interest in program management, research, and development. Ten-week internship available part-time for winter/spring and fall and full-time for summer. Application deadlines are in March for summer, July for fall, and December for winter/spring. Internship not always available for all seasons. Check Website for details and deadlines. $500 stipend for winter/spring, $1000 stipend for summer. Must have excellent writing and research skills, know MS Office (especially Excel), and have interest in the business value of the arts. Download application from Website or apply online.

**Amount of award:** $500-$1,000
**Number of awards:** 1

**Contact:**
Americans for the Arts
Attn: John Cloys
1000 Vermont Avenue NW, 6th Floor
Washington, DC 20005
Phone: 202-371-2830
Fax: 202-371-0424
Web: www.americansforthearts.org

### Research Services Internship

**Type of award:** Internship.
**Intended use:** For undergraduate or graduate study.
**Basis for selection:** Major/career interest in nonprofit administration; arts management or arts, general.
**Application requirements:** Cover letter, resume.
**Additional information:** Recent college graduates also eligible. Ten-week positions available part-time for winter/spring and fall and full-time for summer. Application deadlines are March for summer, July for fall, and December for winter/spring. $500 stipend for fall/spring, $1000 stipend for summer. Must have knowledge of Microsoft Office and be able to work independently. Commitment to serve the nonprofit arts field required. Internship may not be available every year, check Website for details and deadlines.

**Amount of award:** $500-$1,000
**Number of awards:** 1

**Contact:**
Americans for the Arts
Attn: John Cloys
1000 Vermont Avenue, NW, 6th Floor
Washington, DC 20005
Phone: 202-371-2830
Fax: 202-371-0424
Web: www.americansforthearts.org

## Applied Arts

### Applied Arts Internships

**Type of award:** Internship.
**Intended use:** For undergraduate study at postsecondary institution.
**Basis for selection:** Major/career interest in arts, general; public administration/service; marketing; education or arts management.
**Application requirements:** Resume, cover letter.
**Additional information:** Internships are for college credit and are open to all high school/college/international students or graduates. Available in the following fields: education TA in fine arts (painting, drawing, sculpture, digital media, and photography); arts management; events management; office assistant; public service; youth program assistant; marketing/promotion. Rolling application deadline and open duration. E-mail applications preferred.

**Number of awards:** 10
**Number of applicants:** 100

**Contact:**
Applied Arts
Attn: Internship Coordinator
P.O. Box 1336
Amagansett, NY 11930
Phone: 631-267-2787
Fax: 631-267-3428
Web: www.appliedartsschool.com/internships.html

### Elizabeth Dow Ltd. Internships

**Type of award:** Internship.
**Intended use:** For undergraduate or graduate study.
**Basis for selection:** Major/career interest in arts, general; interior design; marketing; design or arts management.
**Application requirements:** Recommendations. Resume, cover letter.
**Additional information:** High school students and recent college graduates also eligible to apply. Internship is unpaid, but college credit available. Program has rolling admission; duration of internship is flexible.

**Number of awards:** 30
**Number of applicants:** 100

**Contact:**
Elizabeth Dow Ltd.
Attn: Internship Coordinator
P.O. Box 2310
Amagansett, NY 11930
Phone: 631-267-3401
Fax: 631-267-3428
Web: www.appliedartsschool.com/internships.html

# Applied Materials

## Internship and Co-op Program

**Type of award:** Internship.
**Intended use:** For undergraduate or graduate study at accredited postsecondary institution.
**Basis for selection:** Major/career interest in accounting; business; business/management/administration; computer/information sciences; engineering, chemical; engineering, electrical/electronic; engineering, mechanical; finance/banking; materials science or physics. Applicant must demonstrate high academic achievement.
**Application requirements:** Resume.
**Additional information:** Applicant should have interest in semi-conductor industry. Summer and year-round internships and co-op positions based in Texas and California. Visit Website to submit resume and to find out when internship interviews will be held at college campuses. Minimum 3.0 GPA.
**Contact:**
Applied Materials, Attn: Global College Programs
3050 Bowers Avenue
P.O. Box 58039
Santa Clara, CA 95054-3299
Web: www.appliedmaterials.com/careers

# Arts and Business Council of New York

## Multicultural Arts Management Internship Program

**Type of award:** Internship.
**Intended use:** For sophomore, junior or senior study at 2-year or 4-year institution.
**Basis for selection:** Major/career interest in arts management.
**Application requirements:** Interview, recommendations, essay, transcript. Resume, cover letter.
**Additional information:** Interns spend ten weeks (June to August) working full-time at a New York City arts organization. Preference given to African-American, Asian-American, Latino/a, and Native American students. Must have taken arts, business, or marketing courses, or been involved in similar extracurricular activities. Application available online.

| | |
|---|---|
| **Amount of award:** | $2,500 |
| **Application deadline:** | February 17 |
| **Notification begins:** | April 8 |

**Contact:**
Arts and Business Council of New York
Attn: Internship Program
One East 53rd Street, 3rd Floor
New York, NY 10022
Phone: 212-279-5910
Fax: 212-279-5915
Web: www.artsandbusiness-ny.org

# Bernstein-Rein Advertising

## Advertising Internship

**Type of award:** Internship.
**Intended use:** For junior study.
**Basis for selection:** Major/career interest in advertising; communications or marketing.
**Application requirements:** Interview. Resume, cover letter, three reference names, one-page writing sample.
**Additional information:** Internship runs for eight weeks in summer. Applicant must have one or two semesters left before graduation. Pay is $10 per hour. Two positions each in account management, media, and creative. Application available online.

| | |
|---|---|
| **Number of awards:** | 6 |
| **Number of applicants:** | 149 |
| **Application deadline:** | March 15 |
| **Notification begins:** | May 1 |

**Contact:**
Bernstein-Rein
Human Resources
4600 Madison, Suite 1500
Kansas City, MO 64112
Phone: 816-756-0640
Fax: 816-399-6000
Web: www.bernstein-rein.com

# Black & Veatch Corporation

## Summer Internship Program

**Type of award:** Internship.
**Intended use:** For full-time junior or senior study in United States.
**Eligibility:** Applicant must be U.S. citizen or permanent resident.
**Basis for selection:** Major/career interest in architecture; engineering, nuclear; engineering, civil; engineering, electrical/electronic; engineering, mechanical; technology or construction management. Applicant must demonstrate high academic achievement.
**Application requirements:** Resume.
**Additional information:** Internship compensation varies by discipline. Additional acceptable majors/career interests include construction management and mechanical, electrical or civil technicians. Minimum 2.75 GPA. Positions offered across the U.S. Students should apply for internships as soon as the fall career fairs, and positions will be posted online until filled.
**Contact:**
Web: www.bv.com/collegecareers

# Board of Governors of the Federal Reserve System

## Economic Research Division Project Internships

**Type of award:** Internship, renewable.
**Intended use:** For undergraduate or graduate study at postsecondary institution.

**Eligibility:** Applicant must be U.S. citizen or permanent resident.
**Basis for selection:** Major/career interest in economics; statistics; computer/information sciences; mathematics or finance/banking. Applicant must demonstrate high academic achievement.
**Application requirements:** Recommendations, transcript. Resume, cover letter.
**Additional information:** Paid internship lasts from June to September. Submit application by e-mail.

**Application deadline:** April 1

**Contact:**
Board of Governors of the Federal Reserve System
20th Street and Constitution Avenue NW
Washington, DC 20551
Phone: 202-452-3880
Web: www.federalreserve.gov/careers/intern_research.htm

# Boeing Company

## Boeing Internships

**Type of award:** Internship.
**Intended use:** For undergraduate or graduate study in United States.
**Eligibility:** Applicant must be U.S. citizen or permanent resident.
**Basis for selection:** Major/career interest in aerospace; computer/information sciences; statistics; human resources; manufacturing; economics; science, general; engineering; mathematics or business.
**Application requirements:** Resume.
**Additional information:** Internships available in Alabama, Arizona, California, Florida, Illinois, Kansas, Missouri, Oklahoma, Pennsylvania, Texas, Washington, D.C. (Metro) and Washington state. Deadlines, eligibility requirements, and compensation vary depending on position. See Website for detailed information on available positions and to submit resume.

**Number of awards:** 1,200

**Contact:**
Web: www.boeing.com/collegecareers

# Boston Globe

## Boston Globe Summer Internship

**Type of award:** Internship.
**Intended use:** For junior, senior or graduate study at 4-year or graduate institution.
**Basis for selection:** Major/career interest in journalism.
**Application requirements:** Interview, recommendations. Writing samples/clips.
**Additional information:** Full-time, 12-week summer internship at approximately $700 per week. Current undergraduate students in any major may apply, as well as journalism graduate students without professional experience as newspaper reporter. Applicants must have had at least one previous internship at daily newspaper. Must have driver's license and be able to type 30 words per minute. Application available online in September.

**Number of awards:** 10
**Number of applicants:** 500
**Application deadline:** November 1
**Notification begins:** December 31

**Contact:**
The Boston Globe
Attn: Mary Rourke
P.O. Box 55819
Boston, MA 02205-5819
Phone: 617-929-3120
Web: www.bostonglobe.com/newsintern

# Chevron Corporation

## Chevron Internship Program

**Type of award:** Internship.
**Intended use:** For full-time sophomore, junior, senior, master's or doctoral study at postsecondary institution.
**Basis for selection:** Major/career interest in business; business/management/administration; computer/information sciences; engineering; finance/banking; geology/earth sciences; human resources; information systems; marketing or political science/government.
**Application requirements:** Transcript. Resume and cover letter.
**Additional information:** Paid, full-time internships, terms vary. International students must be qualified to work in U.S. Apply through campus visits or special recruiting events, or for those attending non-recruited schools, apply for internships posted online. Visit Website for more details. Application deadline is rolling.

**Number of awards:** 300

**Contact:**
Web: careers.chevron.com/students/

# Citizens for Global Solutions

## Citizens for Global Solutions Internship

**Type of award:** Internship, renewable.
**Intended use:** For undergraduate or graduate study at postsecondary institution.
**Basis for selection:** Major/career interest in international relations; international studies; information systems; journalism; nonprofit administration; political science/government or web design.
**Application requirements:** Resume, cover letter, three- to five- page writing sample.
**Additional information:** Recent graduates also eligible. Internship includes $10 per day stipend. Application deadlines are April 1 for summer, August 1 for fall, and December 1 for spring. Visit Website for more information.

**Application deadline:** April 1, August 1

**Contact:**
Citizens for Global Solutions
418 7th Street SE
Washington, DC 20003-2796
Phone: 202-546-3950 ext. 100
Fax: 202-546-3749
Web: www.globalsolutions.org/about/internships

# Congressional Hispanic Caucus Institute

## CHCI Congressional Internship

**Type of award:** Internship.
**Intended use:** For full-time undergraduate study at accredited 2-year or 4-year institution.
**Eligibility:** Applicant must be U.S. citizen or permanent resident.
**Basis for selection:** Applicant must demonstrate high academic achievement, leadership and service orientation.
**Application requirements:** Recommendations, transcript. Three personal essays, resume.
**Additional information:** Spring (12 week), fall (12 week) and summer (eight week) internship in Washington, D.C. congressional offices. Transportation, housing, and stipend provided; $2,500 for eight week program, and $3,750 for 12 week program. Must have excellent writing and analytical skills and active participation in community service activities. Work experience is complemented by leadership development sessions. Minimum 3.0 GPA preferred. Visit Website for deadline information and application.

| | |
|---|---|
| **Number of awards:** | 62 |
| **Number of applicants:** | 396 |

**Contact:**
CHCI Internship Program
911 Second Street, NE
Washington, DC 20002
Phone: 202-543-1771
Fax: 202-546-2143
Web: www.chci.org/internships

# Congressional Institute, Inc.

## Congressional Institute Internships

**Type of award:** Internship.
**Intended use:** For undergraduate study at accredited 2-year or 4-year institution in United States.
**Eligibility:** Applicant must be U.S. citizen.
**Basis for selection:** Major/career interest in political science/government; public administration/service; law or communications. Applicant must demonstrate high academic achievement.
**Application requirements:** Recommendations. Resume and writing samples.
**Additional information:** Paid internships available throughout the year on flexible terms. Must have interest in public policy or legislative policy issues. Visit Website for application and additional information.

**Contact:**
Congressional Institute, Inc.
1700 Diagonal Road
Suite 730
Alexandria, VA 22314
Phone: 703-837-8812
Fax: 703-837-8817
Web: www.conginst.org

# Creede Repertory Theatre

## CRT Internship Program

**Type of award:** Internship.
**Intended use:** For undergraduate study at postsecondary institution.
**Eligibility:** Applicant must be at least 18.
**Basis for selection:** Major/career interest in business; design; humanities/liberal arts; performing arts; theater arts; theater/production/technical; education or marketing.
**Application requirements:** Recommendations. Statement of intent. Resume.
**Additional information:** Potential internship positions available depending on seasons' needs/limitations: wardrobe, prop assistant, stage management, actors, box office/front of house, or business/marketing. Interns receive $125 weekly stipend and free housing. Application deadline on rolling basis. See Website for more information or e-mail with questions.
**Contact:**
CRT Internship Program Attn: Renee Stynchula
Creede Repertory Theatre
P.O. Box 269
Creede, CO 81130
Phone: 719-658-2540 ext. 27
Web: www.creederep.org

# Cushman School

## Cushman School Internship

**Type of award:** Internship, renewable.
**Intended use:** For undergraduate or graduate study.
**Basis for selection:** Major/career interest in education.
**Application requirements:** Resume, cover letter.
**Additional information:** Internship is 17 weeks on Cushman School campus for fall and spring semesters. Interns assist staff in grading papers, supervising students, and performing administrative work. Internships are full-time, 8 a.m. to 4 p.m., Monday to Friday. Stipend of $2,000 for U.S. students and $3,000 for international students awarded each semester. International students must have J1 visa. Rolling application deadline. Number of internships varies.

| | |
|---|---|
| **Amount of award:** | $2,000-$3,000 |

**Contact:**
Cushman School
592 Northeast 60th Street
Miami, FL 33137
Phone: 305-757-1966
Fax: 305-757-1632
Web: www.cushmanschool.org

Internships

# Denver Rescue Mission

## Denver Rescue Mission Center for Mission Studies Internships

**Type of award:** Internship.
**Intended use:** For junior, senior or graduate study at postsecondary institution in United States.
**Basis for selection:** Major/career interest in social work; religion/theology; ministry; nonprofit administration; health services administration; public relations; marketing or information systems. Applicant must demonstrate service orientation.
**Application requirements:** Interview. Background check.
**Additional information:** Denver Rescue Mission is a nondenominational Christian charity offering internships in the following areas: child development, family studies, human services, management information systems, medical office administration, public relations/marketing, social work, volunteer relations, counseling, family therapy, shelter management, and nonprofit administration. Internships vary in length, and some may have gender, age, level-of-study, or other requirements. Full-time interns earn $400 per month, and are held to a minimum work commitment of four months. See Website for details and to apply.
**Contact:**
Denver Rescue Mission
3501 E. 46th Ave.
Denver, CO 80216
Phone: 303-953-3956
Web: www.denverrescuemission.org



# Dow Jones News Fund

## Business Reporting Intern Program

**Type of award:** Internship.
**Intended use:** For full-time junior, senior or graduate study.
**Eligibility:** Applicant must be U.S. citizen, permanent resident or international student.
**Basis for selection:** Major/career interest in journalism or business. Applicant must demonstrate high academic achievement and seriousness of purpose.
**Application requirements:** Interview, essay, transcript. Resume, three to five recently published clips, reporting test.
**Additional information:** May have any major, but must plan to pursue journalism career. Special interest in business a plus. Applications available online August to October 30. All applicants notified by January 31. Applicants must take reporting test administered by designated professor on applicant's campus. Telephone interview required for finalists. Paid summer internships as business reporters at daily newspapers last at least 10 weeks. Interns returning to school receive scholarship at end of summer to apply toward following year. All interns attend pre-internship training that lasts one week. International students must have work visa.

| | |
|---|---|
| **Amount of award:** | $1,000 |
| **Number of awards:** | 12 |
| **Application deadline:** | November 1 |
| **Notification begins:** | January 15 |
| **Total amount awarded:** | $12,000 |

**Contact:**
Dow Jones News Fund
Business Reporting Intern Program
P.O. Box 300
Princeton, NJ 08543-0300
Phone: 609-452-2820
Web: www.newsfund.org

## Multimedia Intern Program

**Type of award:** Internship.
**Intended use:** For full-time junior, senior or graduate study in United States.
**Eligibility:** Applicant must be U.S. citizen, permanent resident or international student.
**Basis for selection:** Major/career interest in journalism. Applicant must demonstrate high academic achievement and seriousness of purpose.
**Application requirements:** Essay, transcript. Resume, exam.
**Additional information:** May have any major but must intend to pursue journalism career. Common application form for all editing programs available online starting in August. Must take editing test administered by designated professor on applicant's campus. Finalists undergo telephone interview. Paid 10 to 12-week summer internships as editors at daily newspapers, online newspapers, or news services. Must attend one-week pre-internship training. Interns returning to school receive scholarship. International students must have work visa.

| | |
|---|---|
| **Amount of award:** | $1,000 |
| **Number of awards:** | 12 |
| **Number of applicants:** | 600 |
| **Application deadline:** | November 1 |
| **Notification begins:** | December 15 |
| **Total amount awarded:** | $12,000 |

**Contact:**
Dow Jones News Fund
Multimedia Editing Intern Program
P.O. Box 300
Princeton, NJ 08543-0300
Phone: 609-452-2820
Web: www.newsfund.org

## News Copy Editing Intern Program

**Type of award:** Internship.
**Intended use:** For full-time junior, senior or graduate study in United States.
**Eligibility:** Applicant must be U.S. citizen, permanent resident or international student.
**Basis for selection:** Major/career interest in journalism. Applicant must demonstrate high academic achievement and seriousness of purpose.
**Application requirements:** Essay, transcript. Resume, editing test.
**Additional information:** May have any major but must plan to pursue journalism career. Common application form for all editing programs available online starting in August. All applicants notified by December 31. Editing test administered by designated professor on applicant's campus. Telephone interview required for finalists. Paid summer internships, as editors at daily newspapers, online newspapers, or real-time financial news services, last 10 to 12 weeks. Interns returning to school receive scholarship at end of summer to apply toward following year. All interns attend pre-internship training that lasts one week. International students must have work visa.

**Amount of award:** $1,000
**Number of awards:** 100
**Number of applicants:** 600
**Application deadline:** November 1
**Notification begins:** December 15
**Total amount awarded:** $70,000

**Contact:**
Dow Jones News Fund
News Copy Editing Intern Program
P.O. Box 300
Princeton, NJ 08543-0300
Phone: 609-452-2820
Web: www.newsfund.org

### Sports Copy Editing Intern Program

**Type of award:** Internship.
**Intended use:** For full-time junior, senior or graduate study.
**Eligibility:** Applicant must be U.S. citizen, permanent resident or international student.
**Basis for selection:** Major/career interest in journalism.
**Application requirements:** Essay, transcript. Editing exam, resume.
**Additional information:** Applicants may have any major but must plan to pursue career in journalism. Interns will work on sports copy desks at daily newspapers and attend training at the University of Nebraska at Lincoln, taught by Dr. Charlyne Berens. Seminars last two weeks. Applicants may apply for sports, online, and/or news copy editing programs using common application form beginning in August. International students must have work visa.

**Amount of award:** $1,000
**Number of awards:** 12
**Application deadline:** November 1
**Notification begins:** December 15
**Total amount awarded:** $12,000

**Contact:**
Dow Jones News Fund
Sports Copy Editing Intern Program
P.O. Box 300
Princeton, NJ 08543-0300
Phone: 609-452-2820
Web: www.newsfund.org

## DuPont Company

### DuPont Co-ops

**Type of award:** Internship.
**Intended use:** For full-time sophomore, junior or senior study at accredited 4-year institution in United States.
**Eligibility:** Applicant must be U.S. citizen or permanent resident.
**Basis for selection:** Major/career interest in accounting; engineering, chemical; engineering, electrical/electronic; engineering, mechanical; finance/banking; marketing or science, general.
**Application requirements:** Resume and cover letter.
**Additional information:** Co-ops available at DuPont company sites throughout U.S. Participants alternate work assignments and academic terms. Applicants can start no earlier than after completion of freshman year and work a minimum of three industrial work periods. Preference given to juniors and seniors. Must be registered with school's co-op office. Competitive compensation. Minimum 3.0 GPA. Must apply through Website.

**Contact:**
Phone: 302-774-1000
Web: www.dupont.com/careers

### DuPont Internships

**Type of award:** Internship.
**Intended use:** For full-time sophomore, junior, senior or master's study at accredited 4-year institution in United States.
**Eligibility:** Applicant must be U.S. citizen or permanent resident.
**Basis for selection:** Major/career interest in accounting; engineering, chemical; engineering, electrical/electronic; engineering, mechanical; finance/banking; marketing or science, general.
**Application requirements:** Resume and cover letter.
**Additional information:** Interns normally work in summer between junior and senior years at DuPont company sites throughout U.S. May apply for extended internship. Minimum 3.0 GPA. Number and amount of awards vary. Must apply through Website.

**Contact:**
Phone: 302-774-1000
Web: www.dupont.com/careers

## Eastman Kodak Company

### Cooperative Internship Programs

**Type of award:** Internship.
**Intended use:** For full-time sophomore, junior, senior or graduate study.
**Basis for selection:** Major/career interest in accounting; business; chemistry; computer/information sciences; engineering; finance/banking; manufacturing; marketing; physics or graphic arts/design.
**Application requirements:** Resume and cover letter.
**Additional information:** Internship must be minimum ten consecutive weeks during summer. Positions offered in Rochester, NY and Dayton, OH. Internship includes competitive salary based upon discipline and education level, and travel expenses. Applicant must be drug-screened as condition of employment. Minimum 3.0 GPA highly desired. Apply online. Number of available internships varies.

**Contact:**
Web: www.kodak.com/go/careers

## Entergy

### Entergy Jumpstart Co-ops and Internships

**Type of award:** Internship, renewable.
**Intended use:** For full-time undergraduate or graduate study at accredited 4-year or graduate institution in United States.
**Eligibility:** Applicant must be U.S. citizen or permanent resident.
**Basis for selection:** Major/career interest in engineering, civil; business; accounting; human resources; finance/banking; engineering, electrical/electronic; engineering, mechanical;

engineering, nuclear or information systems. Applicant must demonstrate high academic achievement and depth of character.
**Additional information:** Paid co-ops and internships available. Minimum 3.0 GPA. Apply online. Visit Website for application deadline and current openings. Must have work experience and give graduation date.
**Contact:**
Phone: 504-576-4000
Web: www.entergy.com/careers

# Entertainment Weekly

## Entertainment Weekly Internship Program

**Type of award:** Internship.
**Intended use:** For junior, senior or postgraduate study at postsecondary institution.
**Application requirements:** Resume, cover letter, and five clips/writing samples.
**Additional information:** Internships in editorial department last 12-18 weeks and pay $10 per hour. Summer internships open to rising seniors and recent graduates. Fall and spring internships for recent college graduates only. Application deadlines are Feb. 15 for summer, Jun. 15 for fall, and Oct. 15 for winter. Number of internships varies.

| | |
|---|---|
| **Number of applicants:** | 200 |
| **Application deadline:** | February 15, June 15 |
| **Notification begins:** | March 1, July 1 |

**Contact:**
Entertainment Weekly Internship Program
Attn: Tina Jordan
135 W. 50th Street, 3rd Floor
New York, NY 10020
Phone: 212-522-2332
Fax: 212-522-6104
Web: www.ew.com

# ESPN Inc.

## ESPN Internship

**Type of award:** Internship.
**Intended use:** For full-time junior study.
**Eligibility:** Applicant must be U.S. citizen or permanent resident.
**Basis for selection:** Major/career interest in sports/sports administration; communications; computer/information sciences; statistics; graphic arts/design; journalism; marketing or radio/television/film. Applicant must demonstrate high academic achievement.
**Application requirements:** Resume and cover letter.
**Additional information:** Applicants should be current students within 12 months of graduation during the internship. Other majors welcome to apply. Internships last ten weeks at 40 hours per week. Most positions based in Bristol, CT or New York, NY, with limited opportunities at other locations. CT and NY interns may qualify for subsidized housing. Previous internship experience a plus. Competitive pay. Course credit offered based on college requirements. Limited internships offered in spring and fall; majority of internships offered in summer. Applications processed on rolling basis; apply online. Check Website for deadline.

| | |
|---|---|
| **Number of applicants:** | 10,000 |

**Contact:**
ESPN Inc.
Phone: 860-766-2000
Web: www.espncareers.com/campus

# Essence Magazine

## Essence Summer Internship

**Type of award:** Internship, renewable.
**Intended use:** For undergraduate or graduate study at accredited 4-year institution in United States.
**Basis for selection:** Major/career interest in advertising; business; fashion/fashion design/modeling; graphic arts/design; journalism; marketing; public relations or publishing.
**Application requirements:** Resume and writing sample or digital portfolio.
**Additional information:** Must be authorized to work in U.S. Nine-week summer internships available in several departments: sales and marketing, Essence.com, fashion and beauty, art/photo, public relations, business office, and editorial. Interns responsible for finding their own housing. Receive bi-weekly paycheck. Must have appreciation for magazine industry; be self-motivated and detail-oriented. Visit Website for application and more information. Number of internships varies.

| | |
|---|---|
| **Number of applicants:** | 300 |
| **Application deadline:** | January 15 |
| **Notification begins:** | April 15 |

**Contact:**
Essence Internship Program, Attn: Human Resources
1271 Avenue of the Americas
7th Floor
New York, NY 10020
Phone: 212-522-1212
Fax: 212-467-2357
Web: www.hr.timeinc.com/campusrecruiting

# Federal Reserve Bank of New York

## Undergraduate Summer Internship

**Type of award:** Internship.
**Intended use:** For full-time junior or senior study at postsecondary institution.
**Basis for selection:** Major/career interest in finance/banking; economics; business; computer/information sciences; accounting or public administration/service. Applicant must demonstrate high academic achievement.
**Application requirements:** Interview, transcript. Cover letter, resume.
**Additional information:** Paid internships begin in late May/early June. Applicants must have completed sophomore year of college before beginning internship. Applicants must be available for in-person interviews in March/April. Housing not provided. International students must be legally authorized to

work in U.S. on a multi-year basis for other than practical training purposes. Submit resume online.

**Application deadline:** January 15

**Contact:**
Federal Reserve Bank of New York
Summer Internship Coordinator
33 Liberty Street
New York, NY 10045
Phone: 212-720-5000
Web: www.ny.frb.org/careers/summerintern.html

# Feminist Majority Foundation

## Feminism & Leadership Internship

**Type of award:** Internship.
**Intended use:** For undergraduate study at accredited 4-year institution.
**Basis for selection:** Major/career interest in women's studies or political science/government. Applicant must demonstrate high academic achievement and leadership.
**Application requirements:** Resume, cover letter, writing sample.
**Additional information:** Recent graduates may also apply. Full-time or part-time internships for a minimum of two months available year-round in the Washington, DC, area and Los Angeles. Interns have various responsibilities, such as monitoring press conferences and coalition meetings, researching, attending rallies, and organizing events. Internships unpaid, but students may be able to earn small stipend in exchange for administrative work. Applicants with experience working on women's issues preferred. People of color, people with disabilities, and math/science majors encouraged to apply. Application deadlines for DC office are March 31 for summer, June 30 for fall, and September 30 for spring. Applications processed on rolling basis for LA office. See Website for more information.

**Application deadline:** March 31, June 30

**Contact:**
Feminist Majority Foundation
Attn: Internship Coordinator
1600 Wilson Boulevard, Suite 801
Arlington, VA 22209
Phone: 703-522-2214
Fax: 703-522-2219
Web: www.feminist.org/intern

# Filoli Center

## Filoli Center Garden Internships and Apprenticeships

**Type of award:** Internship.
**Intended use:** For undergraduate, graduate or non-degree study at postsecondary institution. Designated institutions: Filoli Center.
**Basis for selection:** Major/career interest in horticulture; landscape architecture or botany. Applicant must demonstrate high academic achievement, depth of character, leadership and seriousness of purpose.
**Application requirements:** Recommendations, transcript. Resume and cover letter outlining interests.
**Additional information:** Also for students pursuing careers in public garden management and landscape maintenance. Students paid $8 per hour and may earn college credit for ten-week internship program or six-month apprenticeship program. Applicants must have at least 12 units of horticulture classes and 3.0 GPA. Ability to work well with public and work teams essential. Maximum five students per internship. Visit Website for deadlines and application.

**Amount of award:** $2,300-$8,320
**Number of awards:** 12
**Number of applicants:** 9
**Total amount awarded:** $32,000

**Contact:**
Filoli Center
Filoli Garden Internships
86 Canada Road
Woodside, CA 94062
Phone: 650-364-8300 ext. 214
Fax: 650-366-7836
Web: www.filoli.org/education/garden-internships.html

# Florida Department of Education

## Florida Work Experience Program

**Type of award:** Internship, renewable.
**Intended use:** For undergraduate study at vocational, 2-year or 4-year institution. Designated institutions: Eligible Florida postsecondary institutions.
**Eligibility:** Applicant must be U.S. citizen or permanent resident residing in Florida.
**Basis for selection:** Applicant must demonstrate financial need.
**Application requirements:** Proof of eligibility. FAFSA.
**Additional information:** Minimum 2.0 GPA. Provides students with opportunity to be employed off-campus in jobs related to their academic major or area of career interest. Applications available from participating schools' financial aid offices. Amount of award determined by institution and may not exceed student's financial need.

**Contact:**
Office of Student Financial Assistance
325 West Gaines Street
Suite 1314
Tallahassee, FL 32399-0400
Phone: 888-827-2004
Web: www.floridastudentfinancialaid.org

# Fox Group

## Fox Internship

**Type of award:** Internship.
**Intended use:** For junior, senior or graduate study at accredited 4-year or graduate institution.

**Eligibility:** Applicant must be International students eligible to work in United States.
**Application requirements:** Resume.
**Additional information:** Internships are available in all departments within Film, Television and Digital Media. Applicants must be eligible to receive college credit. Some internships are paid. Apply via Website.
**Contact:**
Web: www.foxcareers.com

# Franklin D. Roosevelt Library

## Roosevelt Archival Internships

**Type of award:** Internship.
**Intended use:** For undergraduate or graduate study at postsecondary institution.
**Basis for selection:** Major/career interest in library science; computer/information sciences; museum studies; history; political science/government or education.
**Application requirements:** Transcript.
**Additional information:** Interns work at FDR library with other interns and staff organizing and automating archival materials, making indices, finding aids and databases, digitizing documents and photographs, and assisting with other projects. Internship can last up to eight weeks and must take place during summer break (mid-May through end of August). Housing not provided. Work Monday through Friday, 9 a.m. to 5 p.m. Stipend of $400 per week. Number of awards depends on funding. Familiarity with FDR presidency helpful. Visit Website for application.

| | |
|---|---|
| **Number of awards:** | 3 |
| **Number of applicants:** | 75 |
| **Application deadline:** | April 1 |
| **Notification begins:** | April 15 |

**Contact:**
Franklin D. Roosevelt Library
Roosevelt Archival Internship Program
4079 Albany Post Road
Hyde Park, NY 12538
Phone: 845-486-7745
Fax: 845-486-1147
Web: www.fdrlibrary.marist.edu/getinvolved.html

# Garden Club of America

## GCA Internship in Garden History and Design

**Type of award:** Internship.
**Intended use:** For undergraduate or graduate study.
**Basis for selection:** Major/career interest in botany; horticulture; landscape architecture or museum studies.
**Application requirements:** Recommendations, essay, transcript. Two letters of recommendation (one from professor in major, one from advisor).
**Additional information:** May apply to Archives of American Gardens in Washington, DC or at other eligible institutions (contact sponsor to verify). Interns at Archives of American Gardens, Smithsonian Institutes work for 10 to 16 weeks and receive stipends of $360/week for undergraduates, $420 for graduate students; GCA funds act as supplement.

| | |
|---|---|
| **Amount of award:** | $2,000 |
| **Number of awards:** | 1 |
| **Application deadline:** | February 15 |

**Contact:**
Garden Club of America
Ms. Connie Yates
14 East 60th Street
New York, NY 10022-1002
Phone: 212-753-8287
Fax: 212-753-0134
Web: www.gcamerica.org

# Genentech, Inc.

## Genentech, Inc. Internship Program

**Type of award:** Internship, renewable.
**Intended use:** For full-time undergraduate or graduate study at accredited 4-year institution.
**Basis for selection:** Major/career interest in biology; business; chemistry; computer/information sciences; engineering; engineering, biomedical; engineering, chemical; law; life sciences or medicine. Applicant must demonstrate high academic achievement.
**Application requirements:** Resume and cover letter.
**Additional information:** Paid summer internships last 10-12 weeks and are available in various research and business areas. International students must have work authorization. Apply online or check Website for campus recruiting schedule.

| | |
|---|---|
| **Number of awards:** | 250 |

**Contact:**
Genentech, Inc.
1 DNA Way
South San Francisco, CA 94080-4990
Phone: 650-225-1000
Fax: 650-225-6000
Web: www.gene.com/gene/careers

# Hannaford Bros Co.

## Hannaford Internships

**Type of award:** Internship.
**Intended use:** For undergraduate or master's study at postsecondary institution.
**Eligibility:** Applicant must be U.S. citizen, permanent resident or international student.
**Basis for selection:** Major/career interest in pharmacy/pharmaceutics/pharmacology.
**Application requirements:** Cover letter and resume.
**Additional information:** Twelve week paid summer internship, beginning early June. Interns at Hannaford are exposed to a multicultural organization with support systems and training opportunities. Internships available at Hannaford's corporate office, distribution centers, and retail locations. Pharmacy internships also available. Inquire at campus placement office to schedule recruiting interview or e-mail for additional information. Minimum 3.0 GPA. Must be legally authorized to work in United States. Amount of payment or

course credit awarded varies. International students must have work authorization. Visit Website for more information. Applications accepted online only.

**Application deadline:** February 15

**Contact:**
Hannaford Brothers Company Employment Department
Phone: 800-442-6049
Fax: 207-885-2859
Web: www.hannaford.com

# Hispanic Association of Colleges and Universities

## HACU National Internship Program

**Type of award:** Internship.
**Intended use:** For sophomore, junior, senior or graduate study at 2-year, 4-year or graduate institution. Designated institutions: Institutions with significant number of Hispanic students.
**Eligibility:** Applicant must be U.S. citizen or permanent resident.
**Basis for selection:** Applicant must demonstrate high academic achievement and service orientation.
**Application requirements:** Essay, transcript. Resume.
**Additional information:** Paid internships provide opportunities for students from institutions with significant numbers of Hispanic students to explore potential careers with federal agencies and private corporations. Interns work in Washington, DC, area and field sites throughout country. Some internships require U.S. citizenship to participate. Applicants must have 3.0 GPA and have completed freshman year of college before internship begins. Weekly pay varies according to class level: $450 for sophomores and juniors, $480 for seniors and $550 for graduates. Must be active in college and community service. Fall and spring internships last 15 weeks; summer internships last ten weeks. Deadlines: November for spring, February for summer, June for fall. Visit Website for more information.

**Contact:**
Hispanic Association of Colleges and Universities
One Dupont Circle, NW
Suite 430
Washington, DC 20036
Phone: 202-833-8361
Fax: 202-261-5082
Web: www.hacu.net/hnip

# Hoffman-La Roche Inc.

## Hoffman-La Roche Inc. Student Internship

**Type of award:** Internship.
**Intended use:** For full-time freshman, sophomore, junior or graduate study at postsecondary institution.
**Basis for selection:** Major/career interest in pharmacy/pharmaceutics/pharmacology; engineering; computer/information sciences; science, general; business; business/management/administration; biology; chemistry or biochemistry.
**Application requirements:** Interview. Cover letter, resume.
**Additional information:** Applicant must be authorized to work in the United States. Internship fields, topics, and amount of compensation vary. Send materials to address provided. If deadline is missed, application will be considered after those students who have met deadline. Visit Website for more information and internship descriptions.

**Contact:**
University Relations Department Hoffman-La Roche, Inc.
340 Kingsland Street
Nutley, NJ 07110-1199
Phone: 973-235-4035 or 973-235-5000
Web: www.rocheusa.com

# IBM

## IBM Co-op and Intern Program

**Type of award:** Internship.
**Intended use:** For full-time sophomore, junior, senior or graduate study at accredited 4-year or graduate institution in United States.
**Basis for selection:** Major/career interest in computer/information sciences; engineering, computer; engineering, electrical/electronic; information systems; accounting or finance/banking. Applicant must demonstrate high academic achievement and leadership.
**Application requirements:** Interview.
**Additional information:** Applicants chosen on competitive basis, based on relevant work or research experience, communication, team skills, and high evaluation during interview process. Most awardees are undergraduate juniors or first year master's students. Competitive salary based on number of credits completed towards degree. Applicants hired on semester basis. Must submit resume via IBM Website.

**Contact:**
IBM Co-op and Intern Program
Web: www.ibm.com/employment/us/

# The Indianapolis Star

## Pulliam Journalism Fellowship

**Type of award:** Internship.
**Intended use:** For junior, senior, graduate or postgraduate study at postsecondary institution.
**Basis for selection:** Competition/talent/interest in writing/journalism. Major/career interest in humanities/liberal arts or journalism. Applicant must demonstrate high academic achievement, depth of character, leadership and seriousness of purpose.
**Application requirements:** Recommendations, transcript, proof of eligibility. Writing samples. Recent photograph.
**Additional information:** Paid fellowship lasts ten weeks during summer. Ten recipients work for The Indianapolis Star, ten for The Arizona Republic in Phoenix. Early deadline in November. Some candidates may be accepted post-deadline. Visit Website for application and more information.

| | |
|---|---|
| **Amount of award:** | $6,500 |
| **Number of awards:** | 20 |
| **Number of applicants:** | 175 |
| **Application deadline:** | November 1 |

**Contact:**
Russell B. Pulliam, Director
The Pulliam Fellowship
P.O. Box 145
Indianapolis, IN 46206-0145
Phone: 317-444-6001
Web: www.indystar.com/pjf

# INROADS, Inc.

## INROADS Internship

**Type of award:** Internship, renewable.
**Intended use:** For full-time freshman or sophomore study.
**Eligibility:** Applicant must be Alaskan native, Asian American, African American, Mexican American, Hispanic American, Puerto Rican or American Indian. Applicant must be high school senior. Applicant must be U.S. citizen or permanent resident.
**Basis for selection:** Major/career interest in engineering; business; computer/information sciences; communications; retailing/merchandising or health-related professions. Applicant must demonstrate high academic achievement, leadership and service orientation.
**Application requirements:** Interview, transcript. Resume. National College Component Application.
**Additional information:** Applicant must have minimum high school 3.0 GPA or college 2.8 GPA; minimum 1000 SAT or 20 ACT. Internship duration and compensation varies, and deadlines vary according to local affiliate office. Visit Website for additional information.

| | |
|---|---|
| **Number of awards:** | 4,000 |
| **Number of applicants:** | 20,000 |
| **Application deadline:** | March 31 |

**Contact:**
INROADS, Inc.
10 S. Broadway
Suite 300
St. Louis, MO 63102
Phone: 314-241-7488
Fax: 314-241-9325
Web: www.inroads.org

# International Radio and Television Society Foundation

## International Radio and Television Society Foundation Summer Fellowship Program

**Type of award:** Internship.
**Intended use:** For junior, senior or graduate study at postsecondary institution.
**Basis for selection:** Major/career interest in communications.
**Additional information:** Nine week internship. Applicants must have prior internship experience and demonstrated interest in the field of communications. Fellows are awarded travel and housing expenses and small stipend. Visit Website for deadlines, information, and application.

| | |
|---|---|
| **Number of awards:** | 25 |
| **Application deadline:** | December 1 |

**Contact:**
International Radio and Television Society Foundation
420 Lexington Avenue, Suite 1601
New York, NY 10170
Phone: 212-867-6650 ext. 303
Fax: 212-867-6653
Web: www.irts.org

# J. Paul Getty Trust

## Multicultural Undergraduate Summer Internships at the Getty Center

**Type of award:** Internship.
**Intended use:** For full-time undergraduate study at 4-year institution.
**Eligibility:** Applicant must be Asian American, African American, Mexican American, Hispanic American, Puerto Rican, American Indian or Native Hawaiian/Pacific Islander. Applicant must be U.S. citizen.
**Basis for selection:** Major/career interest in arts management; communications; humanities/liberal arts; architecture; museum studies/administration or art/art history.
**Application requirements:** Interview, recommendations. Supplemental application (plus three copies), all official transcripts (plus three copies), and SASE.
**Additional information:** Ten-week internship in specific departments of Getty Museum and other programs located at the Getty Center in Los Angeles. Interns receive $3500 stipend. Limited to students attending school in or residing in Los Angeles County. Intended for outstanding students who are members of groups currently underrepresented in museum professions and fields related to visual arts and humanities. Applicants must have completed at least one semester of college by June and not be graduating before December. Housing and transportation not included. Applications accepted in December, and applicants notified of acceptance in early May.

| | |
|---|---|
| **Amount of award:** | $3,500 |
| **Number of applicants:** | 124 |
| **Application deadline:** | February 1 |

**Contact:**
Multicultural Undergraduate Internships at the Getty Center
The Getty Foundation
1200 Getty Center Dr., Suite 800
Los Angeles, CA 90049-1685
Phone: 310-440-7320
Fax: 310-440-7703
Web: www.getty.edu/grants/education

# John Deere

## John Deere Student Training Programs

**Type of award:** Internship.
**Intended use:** For full-time sophomore, junior, senior or graduate study at accredited 2-year, 4-year or graduate institution.

**Eligibility:** Applicant must be U.S. citizen or permanent resident.
**Basis for selection:** Major/career interest in accounting; finance/banking; human resources; health services administration; engineering; information systems or marketing. Applicant must demonstrate high academic achievement.
**Application requirements:** Recommendations.
**Additional information:** Deere and Company offers paid internships, course credit, and academic scholarships through Student Training Program. Applicants may also be interested/ majoring in supply management and credit. Open to undergraduates; graduate students may also be eligible. Minimum 3.0 GPA. Apply through Career Section on Website. Co-op applicants must be enrolled undergraduates and meet academic requirement. Number and amount of awards vary. For co-ops, students must apply through and be recommended by Cooperative Education Office at college or university.
**Contact:**
Recruitment Coordinator
Deere and Company
One John Deere Place
Moline, IL 61265
Phone: 309-765-8000
Web: www.deere.com

# The John F. Kennedy Center for the Performing Arts

## Kennedy Center Arts Management Internship

**Type of award:** Internship.
**Intended use:** For junior, senior or post-bachelor's certificate study at accredited 4-year or graduate institution.
**Basis for selection:** Major/career interest in arts management.
**Application requirements:** Interview, transcript. Cover letter stating career goals. Two letters of recommendation. Resume and writing sample.
**Additional information:** Arts education majors also eligible. Three- to four-month full-time internship in areas such as advertising, development, education, National Symphony Orchestra, press relations, production, programming, technology, volunteer management, and finance. Interns receive $225 stipend per week to defray housing and transportation costs. College credit may be available. Interns attend weekly sessions led by executives of Kennedy Center and other major arts institutions in Washington, D.C. Interns may attend performances, workshops, classes, and courses presented by center, free of charge (space available), during their internship. Visit Website for application, deadline, and more information.

| | |
|---|---|
| **Number of awards:** | 60 |
| **Number of applicants:** | 800 |

**Contact:**
Vilar Institute for Arts Management/Internships
2700 F Street N.W
Washington, DC 20566
Phone: 202-416-8800
Web: www.kennedy-center.org/education/artsmanagement/internships

# John F. Kennedy Library Foundation

## Kennedy Library Archival Internship

**Type of award:** Internship.
**Intended use:** For undergraduate or graduate study at postsecondary institution. Designated institutions: John F. Kennedy Presidential Library.
**Eligibility:** Applicant must be U.S. citizen or permanent resident.
**Basis for selection:** Major/career interest in history; political science/government; library science; English; journalism; communications or museum studies. Applicant must demonstrate high academic achievement.
**Application requirements:** Interview, recommendations, transcript.
**Additional information:** Minimum 12 hours per week, $12.50 per hour. Provides intern with opportunity to work on projects such as digitizing papers of Kennedy and his administration. Interns given career-relevant archival experience. Internships open up as vacancies occur. Library considers proposals for unpaid internships, independent study, work-study, and internships undertaken for academic credit. See Website for application and more information.

| | |
|---|---|
| **Notification begins:** | April 1 |

**Contact:**
Archival Internships c/o Intern Coordinator
John F. Kennedy Presidential Library & Museum
Columbia Point
Boston, MA 02125-3313
Fax: 617-514-1629
Web: www.jfklibrary.org

# John Wiley and Sons, Inc.

## John Wiley and Sons, Inc. Internship Program

**Type of award:** Internship.
**Intended use:** For full-time junior or senior study at 4-year institution.
**Basis for selection:** Major/career interest in marketing; publishing; information systems or public relations.
**Application requirements:** Resume. Letter addressing why applicant would like to be selected for the program and listing areas of interest.
**Additional information:** Summer internship programs available for students who have completed junior year; program runs from mid-June through mid-August. Internships available in marketing, editorial, production, information technology, new media, and publicity; based at corporate offices in Hoboken and Somerset in NJ, Indianapolis, San Francisco, and Malden, MA. Interns receive weekly stipend. Those interested in interning in Hoboken, NJ, Somerset, NJ, San Francisco, CA, Indianapolis, IN, and Malden, MA should visit www.wiley.com for more information. Application address varies by city. See Website for details.

| | |
|---|---|
| **Application deadline:** | April 1 |

**Contact:**
John Wiley and Sons, Inc. Attn: Internship Program
Human Resources Department
111 River Street
Hoboken, NJ 07030-5774
Fax: 201-748-6049
Web: www.wiley.com

# Johnson Controls

## Johnson Controls Co-op and Internship Programs

**Type of award:** Internship, renewable.
**Intended use:** For full-time undergraduate or graduate study at accredited 4-year institution in United States.
**Basis for selection:** Major/career interest in engineering; law; business/management/administration; manufacturing or automotive technology. Applicant must demonstrate high academic achievement.
**Application requirements:** Proof of eligibility. Resume, cover letter.
**Additional information:** Johnson Controls offers several co-op and internship programs in locations throughout the U.S. and abroad. The Engineering Co-op Program develops and trains students in all aspects of the Automotive Systems Group at Johnson Controls. Over a period of two to five years, mechanical and design engineering students alternate between work terms at Johnson Controls and school terms at college or university. Paid summer internships and positions in most other company divisions also available. Visit Website for complete program descriptions and application.
**Contact:**
Johnson Controls
Human Resources
5757 N. Green Bay Ave.
Glendale, WI 53209
Phone: 414-524-1200
Web: www.johnsoncontrols.com

# J.W. Saxe Memorial Fund

## J.W. Saxe Memorial Prize for Public Service

**Type of award:** Internship.
**Intended use:** For undergraduate, graduate or non-degree study at accredited postsecondary institution in United States.
**Basis for selection:** Major/career interest in public administration/service. Applicant must demonstrate financial need, depth of character, leadership, seriousness of purpose and service orientation.
**Application requirements:** Resume, letter of support from faculty member, two additional recommendations, and an essay on short- and long-term goals.
**Additional information:** Award enables public-service-minded college or university students to gain practical experience working no-pay or low-pay public service job or internship during summer or other term. Preference given to applicants who have already found public service-oriented position, but require additional funds. Interns receive $2000 stipend. Number of awards varies.

| | |
|---|---|
| **Amount of award:** | $2,000 |
| **Number of applicants:** | 200 |
| **Application deadline:** | March 15 |
| **Notification begins:** | May 1 |
| **Total amount awarded:** | $24,000 |

**Contact:**
J.W. Saxe Memorial Fund
1524 31 St. N.W.
Washington, DC 20007-3074
Web: www.jwsaxefund.org

# Kentucky Higher Education Assistance Authority (KHEAA)

## Kentucky Work-Study Program

**Type of award:** Internship, renewable.
**Intended use:** For undergraduate, master's, doctoral, first professional or postgraduate study at vocational, 2-year, 4-year or graduate institution. Designated institutions: Approved Kentucky institutions.
**Eligibility:** Applicant must be U.S. citizen residing in Kentucky.
**Application requirements:** Interview, proof of eligibility.
**Additional information:** Job must be related to major course of study. Work-study wage is at least federal minimum wage. May also be enrolled in technical schools. Visit Website for additional information.

| | |
|---|---|
| **Number of awards:** | 880 |
| **Number of applicants:** | 880 |
| **Total amount awarded:** | $568,000 |

**Contact:**
Kentucky Higher Education Assistance Authority (KHEAA)
KHEAA Work-Study Program
P.O. Box 798
Frankfort, KY 40602-0798
Phone: 800-928-8926
Fax: 502-696-7373
Web: www.kheaa.com

# KIMT

## KIMT Weather/News Internships

**Type of award:** Internship.
**Intended use:** For undergraduate study.
**Eligibility:** Applicant must be at least 18.
**Basis for selection:** Major/career interest in atmospheric sciences/meteorology; journalism; radio/television/film or sports/sports administration.
**Application requirements:** Interview. Resume.
**Additional information:** Applicant must be majoring in field directly related to the department of internship. All internships for college credit only. Student must arrange to receive college credit. Internships available year-round. Hours are flexible.

**Contact:**
KIMT
Attn: Human Resources Coordinator
112 North Pennsylvania
Mason City, IA 50401
Phone: 641-423-2540

# Louis Carr Internship Foundation (LCIF)

## Louis Carr Summer Internship

**Type of award:** Internship.
**Intended use:** For full-time freshman, sophomore or junior study in United States.
**Eligibility:** Applicant must be Asian American, African American, Mexican American, Hispanic American, Puerto Rican, American Indian or Native Hawaiian/Pacific Islander. Applicant must be U.S. citizen.
**Basis for selection:** Major/career interest in advertising; marketing or communications. Applicant must demonstrate high academic achievement, depth of character, leadership and seriousness of purpose.
**Application requirements:** Recommendations, essay, transcript. Resume.
**Additional information:** Paid, ten-week summer internship in New York, Chicago, Detroit, or Washington D.C.

| | |
|---|---|
| **Amount of award:** | $4,000 |
| **Number of awards:** | 10 |
| **Number of applicants:** | 16 |
| **Application deadline:** | March 1 |
| **Notification begins:** | April 15 |
| **Total amount awarded:** | $84,000 |

**Contact:**
Louis Carr Internship Foundation
P.O. Box 81859
Chicago, IL 60681-0589
Phone: 312-819-8617
Fax: 312-540-1109
Web: www.louiscarrfoundation.org

# Macy's, Inc.

## Internships at Macy's and Bloomingdale's

**Type of award:** Internship, renewable.
**Intended use:** For full-time undergraduate study.
**Basis for selection:** Applicant must demonstrate high academic achievement.
**Application requirements:** Resume.
**Additional information:** Eight- to ten-week paid internships offered in buying, planning, store management, product development, design, and macys.com. Apply online or visit Website for campus recruiting schedule.

| | |
|---|---|
| **Number of awards:** | 350 |

**Contact:**
Macy's, Inc.
Web: www.macysjobs.com/college/internships

# Makovsky & Company Inc.

## Public Relations Internship

**Type of award:** Internship.
**Intended use:** For senior study at 4-year institution in United States or Canada.
**Basis for selection:** Major/career interest in public relations; communications; English or political science/government. Applicant must demonstrate high academic achievement.
**Application requirements:** Interview. Resume, cover letter, writing sample.
**Additional information:** Two to four full- or part-time (20 hours minimum) paid positions offered in summer. Compensation $10/hr. Must major in public relations or related subject. Applicant must be responsible, diligent, and energetic. Provides opportunity to receive hands-on experience in all facets of public relations under direction of forums staff.

| | |
|---|---|
| **Number of awards:** | 4 |
| **Number of applicants:** | 200 |
| **Application deadline:** | March 15 |

**Contact:**
Makovsky & Company, Inc. Internship Coordinator
16 East 34th Street
New York, NY 10016
Phone: 212-508-9670
Fax: 212-751-9710
Web: www.makovsky.com

# Massachusetts Democratic Party

## John Joseph Moakely Democratic Internship

**Type of award:** Internship.
**Intended use:** For junior or senior study at accredited 4-year institution.
**Eligibility:** Applicant must be at least 18, no older than 23. Applicant must be U.S. citizen or permanent resident residing in Massachusetts.
**Basis for selection:** Major/career interest in political science/ government or public administration/service. Applicant must demonstrate financial need, high academic achievement, leadership, seriousness of purpose and service orientation.
**Additional information:** Preference given to registered Democrats. Eleven-week summer internship at Massachusetts Democratic State Convention Headquarters. Interns receive $3,500 stipend. Visit Website for more program information and important dates.

| | |
|---|---|
| **Amount of award:** | $3,500 |
| **Number of awards:** | 1 |
| **Number of applicants:** | 10 |
| **Application deadline:** | April 13 |

**Contact:**
Massachusetts Democratic Party
MDP Office, Attn: Stacy Monahan
56 Roland St., Suite 203
Boston, MA 02129
Phone: 617-776-2676
Fax: 617-776-2579
Web: www.massdems.org

# MCC Theater

## MCC Theater Internships

**Type of award:** Internship.
**Intended use:** For undergraduate study at vocational institution.
**Eligibility:** Applicant must be residing in New York.
**Basis for selection:** Major/career interest in theater arts; theater/production/technical; performing arts; design; business/management/administration or arts management.
**Application requirements:** Resume.
**Additional information:** Rolling application deadlines, negotiable schedule. Internships available in general management/theater administration, development, marketing, production, and literary and arts education. College credit available. E-mail resume to apply.
**Contact:**
MCC Theater
311 West 43rd Street, Suite 302
New York, NY 10036
Phone: 212-727-7722
Fax: 212-727-7780
Web: www.mcctheater.org/jobs

# Metropolitan Museum of Art

## The Cloisters Summer Internship Program

**Type of award:** Internship.
**Intended use:** For undergraduate study at postsecondary institution.
**Basis for selection:** Major/career interest in art/art history; history; museum studies or museum studies/administration.
**Application requirements:** $50 application fee. Recommendations, essay, transcript. Resume and list of art history courses taken.
**Additional information:** Must be currently enrolled college student at time of internship. First- and second-year students especially encouraged to apply. Interns receive $2,750 stipend. Interest in medieval history appreciated. Nine-week full-time internship from mid-June to mid-August. Five-day, 35-hour work week.

| | |
|---|---|
| **Amount of award:** | $2,750 |
| **Number of awards:** | 8 |
| **Notification begins:** | April 10 |

**Contact:**
The Cloisters
College Internship Program
Fort Tryon Park
New York, NY 10040
Phone: 212-650-2280
Web: www.metmuseum.org/education

## Mentoring Program for College Juniors

**Type of award:** Internship.
**Intended use:** For sophomore or junior study at postsecondary institution.
**Application requirements:** $35 application fee. Recommendations, transcript.
**Additional information:** Interns work full-time for 6 weeks over the summer. Designed to encourage college juniors from diverse backgrounds to pursue museum careers. Participants work in one of the Museum's departments (curatorial, administrative, or educational). Includes a two-week orientation of the Museum, meetings with Museum professionals, a Museum mentor, and field trips to other institutions. Visit Website for deadline and application details.

| | |
|---|---|
| **Amount of award:** | $3,250 |

**Contact:**
Metropolitan Museum of Art
1000 Fifth Avenue
New York, NY 10028
Phone: 212-570-3710
Web: www.metmuseum.org/education

## Six-Month Internship

**Type of award:** Internship.
**Intended use:** For senior, graduate or non-degree study at 4-year or graduate institution.
**Eligibility:** Applicant must be U.S. citizen or international student.
**Basis for selection:** Major/career interest in art/art history; museum studies or history.
**Application requirements:** $50 application fee. Recommendations, transcript, proof of eligibility. Resume. List of art history and other relevant courses taken and foreign languages spoken. 500-word essay describing career goals, interest in museum work, specific areas of interest within the museum, and reasons for applying to the program.
**Additional information:** Interns work full-time from early June to early December and participate in summer orientation program. Interns receive $11,000 stipend. International students must have permission to earn stipend in U.S. Visit Website for more information.

| | |
|---|---|
| **Amount of award:** | $11,000 |

**Contact:**
Metropolitan Museum of Art
1000 Fifth Avenue
New York, NY 10028-0198
Phone: 212-570-3710
Web: www.metmuseum.org/education

## Summer Internship Program

**Type of award:** Internship.
**Intended use:** For junior, senior, graduate or non-degree study at postsecondary institution.
**Eligibility:** Applicant must be U.S. citizen or international student.
**Basis for selection:** Major/career interest in art/art history; arts management or museum studies/administration. Applicant must demonstrate seriousness of purpose.
**Application requirements:** $50 application fee. Typed paper indicating desired internship and include name, home and school addresses and phone numbers. Resume. Two academic recommendations. Transcripts. Separate list with art history or relevant courses taken and knowledge of foreign languages. 500-word (maximum) essay describing career goals, interest in museum work, specific areas of interest within the museum, and reason for applying.
**Additional information:** Ten-week program for college students, recent college graduates who have not yet entered graduate school, and graduate students who have completed at least one year of graduate work in art history or related field.

Interns work full-time. International students must have permission to work in U.S. Applicants should have broad background in art history. Program begins in June with two-week orientation, ends in August, and includes $3,250 honorarium for college interns and recent graduates and $3,500 for graduate interns. Visit Website for more information.

**Amount of award:** $3,250-$3,500
**Number of awards:** 15

**Contact:**
Attn: Internship Programs
Metropolitan Museum of Art
1000 Fifth Avenue
New York, NY 10028-0198
Phone: 212-570-3710
Web: www.metmuseum.org/education

# Minnesota Office of Higher Education

## Minnesota Work-Study Program

**Type of award:** Internship.
**Intended use:** For undergraduate or graduate study.
**Eligibility:** Applicant must be U.S. citizen or permanent resident residing in Minnesota.
**Basis for selection:** Applicant must demonstrate financial need.
**Application requirements:** Interview.
**Additional information:** This is a work-study program, but it may be applied to internships. Work placement must be approved by school or nonprofit agency. Must be used at Minnesota college or for internship with nonprofit or private sector employer located in Minnesota. Must be enrolled for at least six credit hours. Apply to financial aid office of school. Award maximum set at cost of attendance minus EFC and other financial aid.

**Number of applicants:** 11,094
**Total amount awarded:** $14,128,804

**Contact:**
Minnesota Office of Higher Education
1450 Energy Park Drive, Suite 350
St. Paul, MN 55108-5227
Phone: 800-657-3866
Web: www.getreadyforcollege.org

# Morris Arboretum of the University of Pennsylvania

## Arboriculture Internship

**Type of award:** Internship.
**Intended use:** For undergraduate or graduate study at postsecondary institution.
**Basis for selection:** Major/career interest in horticulture; forestry or landscape architecture.
**Application requirements:** Recommendations, transcript. Letter of intent, resume.
**Additional information:** Applicant should have interest in arboriculture. Internships train students in most up-to-date tree care techniques. Interns work 40 hours per week at hourly rate of $9.75 for full year. Intern works with Chief Arborist in all aspects of tree care, including tree assessment, pruning, cabling, and removal. Safety-conscious techniques are emphasized, and recent innovations in climbing and rigging are demonstrated and put into practice. Other opportunities include assisting with outreach activities including workshops and off-site consulting. Benefits include health insurance and dental plan. Must have solid academic background in arboriculture and horticulture. Tree climbing ability helpful. Driver's license required. Academic credit given.

**Application deadline:** February 15

**Contact:**
Morris Arboretum of the University of Pennsylvania
Jan McFarlan, Education Coordinator
100 Northwestern Avenue
Philadelphia, PA 19118
Phone: 215-247-5777 ext. 156
Web: www.upenn.edu/arboretum

## Morris Arboretum Education Internship

**Type of award:** Internship.
**Intended use:** For undergraduate or graduate study at postsecondary institution.
**Basis for selection:** Major/career interest in education; botany; horticulture; ecology or education, teacher.
**Application requirements:** Recommendations, transcript. Letter of intent, resume.
**Additional information:** Interns work 40 hours/week at hourly wage of $9.75 for full year. Interns develop workshops for experienced guides, training sessions for new guides, occasionally lead tours. Other responsibilities include supervising the school tour program, running special programs for the public, helping to prepare the adult education course brochure, and writing promotional copy including a newsletter for volunteer guides. Benefits include insurance, dental plan, and tuition benefits. Academic background or experience in education or educational programming preferred. Knowledge of plant-related subjects helpful. Strong writing and interpersonal skills essential. Academic credit given.

**Application deadline:** February 15

**Contact:**
Morris Arboretum of the University of Pennsylvania
Jan McFarlan, Education Coordinator
100 Northwestern Avenue
Philadelphia, PA 19118
Phone: 215-247-5777 ext. 156
Web: www.upenn.edu/arboretum

## Morris Arboretum Horticulture Internship

**Type of award:** Internship.
**Intended use:** For undergraduate or graduate study at postsecondary institution.
**Basis for selection:** Major/career interest in horticulture.
**Application requirements:** Recommendations, transcript. Letter of intent, resume.
**Additional information:** Intern assists in all phases of garden development and care of collections. Specific emphasis on refining practical horticultural skills. Supervisory skills are developed by directing activities of volunteers and part-time staff. Other activities include developing Integrated Pest Management skills, arboricultural techniques, and the operation and maintenance of garden machinery. Special projects will be assigned to develop individual skills in garden planning and

management. Must have strong academic background in horticulture or closely related field. Interns work 40 hours per week at hourly wage of $9.75 for full year. Benefits include health insurance, dental plan, and tuition benefits. Some internships require travel. Driver's license required. Academic credit given.

**Application deadline:** February 15

**Contact:**
Morris Arboretum of the University of Pennsylvania
Jan McFarlan, Education Coordinator
100 Northwestern Avenue
Philadelphia, PA 19118
Phone: 215-247-5777 ext. 156
Web: www.upenn.edu/arboretum

## Plant Propagation Internship

**Type of award:** Internship.
**Intended use:** For undergraduate or graduate study at postsecondary institution.
**Basis for selection:** Major/career interest in botany or horticulture.
**Application requirements:** Recommendations, transcript. Letter of intent, resume.
**Additional information:** Strong background in woody landscape plants, plant propagation, nursery management, and plant physiology required. Interns work 40 hours/week at hourly rate of $9.75 for full year. Benefits include health insurance, dental plan, and tuition benefits. Academic credit given. Intern assists propagator in the development of plant propagation and production schemes for arboretum. Emphasis is placed on the refinement of skills in traditional methods of plant propagation, nursery production, and greenhouse management. Other duties include management of the field nursery and data collection for ongoing research projects.

**Application deadline:** February 15

**Contact:**
Morris Arboretum of the University of Pennsylvania
Jan McFarlan, Education Coordinator
100 Northwestern Avenue
Philadelphia, PA 19118
Phone: 215-247-5777 ext. 156
Web: www.upenn.edu/arboretum

## Plant Protection Internship

**Type of award:** Internship.
**Intended use:** For undergraduate or graduate study at postsecondary institution.
**Basis for selection:** Major/career interest in horticulture; entomology or botany.
**Application requirements:** Recommendations, transcript. Letter of intent, resume.
**Additional information:** Interns work 40 hours per week at hourly wage of $9.75 for full year. Course work in entomology or plant pathology required. Intern assists arboretum's plant pathologist with the Integrated Pest Management program, which includes regular monitoring of the living collection and communicating information on pests and diseases to staff members. Related projects include establishing threshold levels for specific plant pests and evaluating the effectiveness of control measures. Modern laboratory facilities are available for identifying plant pests and pathogens. Intern also participates in Plant Clinic's daily operations, providing diagnostic services to the public about horticultural problems. Benefits include health insurance, dental plan, and tuition benefits. Strong writing skills essential. Academic credit given.

**Application deadline:** February 15

**Contact:**
Morris Arboretum of the University of Pennsylvania
Jan McFarlan, Education Coordinator
100 Northwestern Avenue
Philadelphia, PA 19118
Phone: 215-247-5777 ext. 156
Web: www.upenn.edu/arboretum

## Rose and Flower Garden Internship

**Type of award:** Internship.
**Intended use:** For undergraduate or graduate study at postsecondary institution.
**Basis for selection:** Major/career interest in horticulture. Applicant must demonstrate seriousness of purpose.
**Application requirements:** Recommendations, transcript. Letter of intent, resume.
**Additional information:** Intern assists Rosarian in garden development, management, and care of collections. Emphasis on mastering skills used in the culture of modern and antique roses, developing pest management skills, and refining horticulture skills including formal garden maintenance. Other duties include plant record keeping, support for volunteer gardeners, operation of garden machinery, and supervision of part-time staff. Interns work 40-hour week at hourly rate of $9.75 for full year. Benefits include health insurance, dental plan, and tuition benefits. Applicant should have strong academic background in horticulture with course work in herbaceous and woody landscape plants. Driver's license required. Academic credit given.

**Application deadline:** February 15

**Contact:**
Morris Arboretum of the University of Pennsylvania
Jan McFarlan, Education Coordinator
100 Northwestern Avenue
Philadelphia, PA 19118
Phone: 215-247-5777 ext. 156
Web: www.upenn.edu/arboretum

## Urban Forestry Internship

**Type of award:** Internship.
**Intended use:** For undergraduate study at postsecondary institution.
**Basis for selection:** Major/career interest in forestry; horticulture; landscape architecture or ecology.
**Application requirements:** Recommendations, transcript. Letter of intent, resume.
**Additional information:** Intern will engage in urban forestry and natural resources programs and strategies for public gardens, government agencies, and educational and community organizations; learn and teach stewardship concepts and practical applications through riparian and woodland restoration projects; develop community partnership, urban vegetation analysis, and management planning skills. Interns work 40 hours per week at hourly wage of $9.75 for full year. Benefits include health insurance, dental plan, and tuition benefits. Academic background in urban forestry, horticulture, landscape design, or related field. Communication skills essential. Car required; mileage reimbursed. Academic credit given.

**Application deadline:** February 15

**Contact:**
Morris Arboretum of the University of Pennsylvania
Jan McFarlan, Education Coordinator
100 Northwestern Avenue
Philadelphia, PA 19118
Phone: 215-247-5777 ext. 156
Web: www.upenn.edu/arboretum

# Mother Jones

## Mother Jones Ben Bagdikian Fellowship Program

**Type of award:** Internship.
**Intended use:** For junior, senior, graduate or non-degree study at postsecondary institution.
**Basis for selection:** Major/career interest in political science/government; communications; journalism or publishing. Applicant must demonstrate high academic achievement.
**Application requirements:** Interview, recommendations. Resume with cover letter; contact information for two references; writing samples.
**Additional information:** Deadlines are rolling. Internships are full-time and run six months with stipend of $1,000/month with seven-day vacation allowance. After six months, interns may apply for fellowship program which also runs six months with $1,400/month stipend. Hours vary according to magazine production schedule. No course credit offered. Reporting, writing, and research skills preferred. See Website for more information. Application deadlines occur twice a year: April 1st and October 1st.

| | |
|---|---|
| **Number of awards:** | 10 |
| **Application deadline:** | April 1, October 1 |

**Contact:**
Mother Jones
Attn: Ben Bagdikian Fellowship Program
222 Sutter Street, Suite 600
San Francisco, CA 94108
Web: www.motherjones.com

# Museum of Modern Art

## Museum of Modern Art Internship

**Type of award:** Internship.
**Intended use:** For junior, senior, graduate or non-degree study at postsecondary institution.
**Eligibility:** Applicant must be U.S. citizen, permanent resident or international student.
**Application requirements:** Interview, essay, transcript. Resume and one recommendation.
**Additional information:** Course credit available, but not required. Fall, spring, summer, and 12-month internships. Twelve-month internships are paid, full-time programs for recent college graduates. Fall, spring, and summer internships are part-time and unpaid. Fields of study encompass broad spectrum of topics. Visit Website for complete list of departments, applications, and deadline information.

| | |
|---|---|
| **Number of awards:** | 110 |
| **Number of applicants:** | 1,600 |

**Contact:**
The Museum of Modern Art
Internship Coordinator, Dept. of Education
11 W. 53rd Street
New York, NY 10019
Web: www.moma.org

# NASA Arizona Space Grant Consortium

## NASA Space Grant Arizona Undergraduate Research Internship

**Type of award:** Internship, renewable.
**Intended use:** For full-time sophomore, junior or senior study at accredited 2-year or 4-year institution in United States. Designated institutions: Arizona Space Grant Consortium (AZSGC) Colleges and Universities.
**Eligibility:** Applicant must be U.S. citizen residing in Arizona.
**Basis for selection:** Major/career interest in aerospace; astronomy; engineering; physics; geology/earth sciences; science, general; journalism or education.
**Additional information:** Approximately 100 students will be employed for 10-20 hours per week for the academic year in research programs, working alongside upper-level graduate students and practicing scientists. Hourly wage offered. Awardees must attend Arizona Space Grant Consortium member institution. Availability of internships varies. Some internships are renewable. Current announcements/application posted on Website.

| | |
|---|---|
| **Number of applicants:** | 350 |

**Contact:**
NASA Space Grant Arizona Space Grant Consortium
Lunar and Planetary Laboratory, Room 349
U of Arizona, 1629 E. University Blvd.
Tucson, AZ 85721-0092
Phone: 520-621-8556
Web: spacegrant.arizona.edu

# NASA Delaware Space Grant Consortium

## Delaware Space Grant Undergraduate Research Internship

**Type of award:** Internship, renewable.
**Intended use:** For full-time sophomore, junior or senior study at postsecondary institution. Designated institutions: University of Delaware, Delaware Technical and Community College, Swarthmore College, Delaware State University at Dover, Villanova University, Wesley College, Wilmington University, Goldey-Beacom College.
**Eligibility:** Applicant must be U.S. citizen.
**Basis for selection:** Major/career interest in geography; mathematics; science, general or technology.
**Application requirements:** Recommendations, transcript. Description of proposed research project.
**Additional information:** Must have proven interest in space science-related studies. Recipient must attend a Delaware Space Grant Consortium member institution. Stipend offered. Contact Consortium office for deadlines and additional information.

| | |
|---|---|
| **Amount of award:** | $3,500 |
| **Number of awards:** | 5 |
| **Number of applicants:** | 5 |
| **Application deadline:** | April 22 |
| **Total amount awarded:** | $19,500 |

Internships

**Contact:**
Delaware Space Grant Consortium Program Office
University of Delaware
106 Sharp Lab
Newark, DE 19716
Phone: 302-831-1094
Fax: 302-831-1843
Web: www.delspace.org

# NASA New Jersey Space Grant Consortium

## Undergraduate Summer Fellowships in Engineering and Science

**Type of award:** Internship, renewable.
**Intended use:** For junior or senior study at accredited 4-year institution in United States. Designated institutions: Georgian Court University, New Jersey Institute of Technology, Princeton University, Raritan Valley Community College, Rutgers University, Stevens Institute of Technology, University of Medicine and Dentistry of NJ, New Jersey City University, Rowan University, Seton Hall, College of New Jersey.
**Eligibility:** Applicant must be U.S. citizen.
**Basis for selection:** Major/career interest in aerospace; biology; computer/information sciences; engineering, computer; engineering, chemical; engineering, electrical/electronic; engineering, mechanical; materials science; natural sciences or physical sciences.
**Application requirements:** Recommendations, essay. Biographical sketch, statement that describes career goals and what applicant hopes to accomplish as Space Grant Fellow, plan for immediate future and reference letter from faculty advisor.
**Additional information:** Applicants must have completed at least two but preferably three years of college. Consortium actively encourages women, minority students, and physically challenged students to apply. Awardees must attend NJSGC member institution. Academic year ($2,000 stipend) and summer fellowships ($5,500 stipend) offered. Summer fellowship deadline in April. Academic year fellowship has ongoing deadline, although applications preferred in fall. Visit Website for important dates and additional information.

| | |
|---|---|
| **Amount of award:** | $2,000-$5,500 |
| **Number of awards:** | 45 |
| **Number of applicants:** | 75 |
| **Total amount awarded:** | $175,000 |

**Contact:**
Program Director New Jersey Space Grant Consortium
Rutgers University, College of Engineering
Room B213, 98 Brett Road
Piscataway, NJ 08854
Phone: 201-216-8964
Web: www.njsgc.rutgers.edu

# NASA Pennsylvania Space Grant Consortium

## NASA Academy Internship

**Type of award:** Internship.
**Intended use:** For full-time junior, senior or graduate study at accredited 4-year or graduate institution in United States. Designated institutions: Pennsylvania colleges and universities.
**Eligibility:** Applicant must be U.S. citizen or permanent resident residing in Pennsylvania.
**Basis for selection:** Major/career interest in engineering; science, general; mathematics; aerospace or astronomy. Applicant must demonstrate high academic achievement and leadership.
**Application requirements:** Recommendations, essay, transcript.
**Additional information:** Awards are for ten-week internships at participating NASA centers. Minimum B average required. Stipend, plus room and board and travel expenses. Earth science students also eligible. Awardees must attend Pennsylvania institution or be a full-time resident. Interns receive $5,000 stipend. Consortium actively encourages women, minority, and physically challenged students to apply. Visit the NASA Academy Website for application information.

| | |
|---|---|
| **Amount of award:** | $5,000 |
| **Number of awards:** | 3 |
| **Number of applicants:** | 24 |
| **Application deadline:** | January 15 |
| **Total amount awarded:** | $15,000 |

**Contact:**
NASA Pennsylvania Space Grant Consortium
Penn State, University Park
2217 Earth-Engineering Sciences Building
University Park, PA 16802
Phone: 814-865-2535
Fax: 814-863-9563
Web: www.pa.spacegrant.org or www.academyapp.com

# National Association of Black Journalists

## NABJ Internships

**Type of award:** Internship.
**Intended use:** For full-time undergraduate study at postsecondary institution.
**Eligibility:** Applicant must be African American.
**Basis for selection:** Major/career interest in journalism or radio/television/film.
**Application requirements:** Portfolio, recommendations, essay. Resume, cover letter. Applicants must submit minimum of five samples of published work in print, radio, television, photography, slideshows, website, or flash animation.
**Additional information:** Ten-week paid internship in print, broadcast, online, sports, or photojournalism. Must have prior experience in collegiate or professional media. Must be member of National Association of Black Journalists. Weekly stipend varies between $400 and $600. Some internships are unpaid. Visit Website for more information.

**Contact:**
National Association of Black Journalists
1100 Knight Hall, Suite 3100
College Park, MD 20742
Phone: 301-405-0248
Fax: 301-314-1714
Web: www.nabj.org

# National Geographic Society

## Geography Students Internship

**Type of award:** Internship.
**Intended use:** For junior, senior or master's study at 4-year or graduate institution in United States.
**Basis for selection:** Major/career interest in geography or cartography.
**Application requirements:** Recommendations, essay, transcript. Resume.
**Additional information:** Spring, summer, and fall internships for 14 to 16 weeks in Washington, D.C., at $400 per week. Application deadline for all internships in the fall. Emphasis on editorial and cartographic research. Students should contact their school's geography department chair or call internship hotline for more information.

| | |
|---|---|
| **Number of awards:** | 30 |
| **Number of applicants:** | 100 |

**Contact:**
National Geographic Society
Robert E. Dulli
1145 17 Street, NW
Washington, DC 20036-4688
Phone: 202-857-7134
Web: www.nationalgeographic.com

# National Museum of the American Indian

## National Museum of the American Indian Internship

**Type of award:** Internship.
**Intended use:** For undergraduate, graduate or non-degree study at postsecondary institution.
**Basis for selection:** Major/career interest in museum studies.
**Application requirements:** Recommendations, essay, transcript. Resume.
**Additional information:** Provides educational work/research experience for students in museum practice and related programming using resources of museum and other Smithsonian offices. Internships available at NMAI in Suitland, MD; Washington, DC; and New York City. Applicants must have minimum 3.0 GPA. Four 10-week internships, deadlines as follows: February 6 for summer; July 12 for fall; October 10 for winter; and November 20 for spring. Selection based on professional and educational goals of student; needs of museum. Students receiving stipends must work full-time; other interns must work at least 20 hours per week. Museum will grant academic credit if student makes arrangements with school. Visit Website or contact via e-mail for more information.

| | |
|---|---|
| **Number of awards:** | 20 |
| **Number of applicants:** | 40 |
| **Application deadline:** | November 20, February 6 |

**Contact:**
Internship Program, National Museum of the American Indian
Cultural Resources Center- Community Services
4220 Silver Hill Road
Suitland, MD 20746-2863
Phone: 301-238-1541
Fax: 301-238-3200
Web: www.nmai.si.edu

# National Museum of Women in the Arts

## Museum Coca-Cola Internship

**Type of award:** Internship.
**Intended use:** For junior, senior, graduate or non-degree study in United States.
**Basis for selection:** Major/career interest in public relations; advertising; library science; journalism; museum studies; art/art history; museum studies/administration; accounting; education or retailing/merchandising. Applicant must demonstrate high academic achievement and seriousness of purpose.
**Application requirements:** Recommendations, transcript. Resume, cover letter, and one- to two-page writing sample.
**Additional information:** Internship available to students interested in pursuing careers in museum environments. Minimum 3.25 GPA. Interns receive $1500 stipend. Full-time internship lasts 12 weeks; application deadline for spring is October 15; summer is March 15; fall is June 15.

| | |
|---|---|
| **Amount of award:** | $1,500 |
| **Number of awards:** | 3 |
| **Number of applicants:** | 50 |
| **Application deadline:** | October 15, March 15 |
| **Total amount awarded:** | $1,500 |

**Contact:**
National Museum of Women in the Arts
Manager of Public Programs Education Dept.
1250 New York Avenue, NW
Washington, DC 20005-3970
Phone: 202-783-7996
Fax: 202-393-3234
Web: www.nmwa.org

## Southern California Council Endowed Internship

**Type of award:** Internship, renewable.
**Intended use:** For junior, senior or graduate study at postsecondary institution. Designated institutions: Art and design institutions in Los Angeles County area.
**Eligibility:** Applicant must be residing in California.
**Basis for selection:** Major/career interest in art/art history; arts management; arts, general; museum studies or museum studies/administration.
**Application requirements:** Recommendations, essay, transcript. Cover letter, brief writing sample, resume.
**Additional information:** Full-time, twelve-week internship. $2,000 stipend. Applicant must be resident of Los Angeles

Internships

County. Minimum 3.25 GPA. Application deadline for spring is October 15; summer is March 15; fall is June 15.

| | |
|---|---|
| **Amount of award:** | $2,000 |
| **Number of awards:** | 1 |
| **Number of applicants:** | 1 |
| **Application deadline:** | March 15, June 15 |

**Contact:**
National Museum of Women in the Arts
Manager of Public Programs Education Dept.
1250 New York Avenue, NW
Washington, DC 20005-3970
Phone: 202-783-7996
Fax: 202-393-3234
Web: www.nmwa.org

# National Science Foundation

## Research Experiences for Undergraduates - Maria Mitchell Observatory

**Type of award:** Internship.
**Intended use:** For undergraduate study at 4-year institution. Designated institutions: Maria Mitchell Observatory, Nantucket, MA.
**Eligibility:** Applicant must be U.S. citizen or permanent resident.
**Basis for selection:** Major/career interest in astronomy. Applicant must demonstrate high academic achievement.
**Application requirements:** Recommendations, essay, transcript.
**Additional information:** Positions provide chance for students to conduct independent research and to participate in common project. Students expected to develop their ability to communicate with the public. Furnished housing is available at no cost. Partial travel funds available. Internship runs from June through August, with $1,700 monthly stipend. Applicant must demonstrate motivation in research. Minimum of one year undergraduate physics required.

| | |
|---|---|
| **Number of awards:** | 6 |
| **Number of applicants:** | 100 |
| **Application deadline:** | February 15 |
| **Notification begins:** | March 1 |

**Contact:**
Maria Mitchell Observatory
4 Vestal Street
Nantucket, MA 02554
Phone: 508-228-9273
Fax: 508-228-1031
Web: www.mmo.org

# NCR Corporation

## NCR Summer Internships

**Type of award:** Internship.
**Intended use:** For full-time undergraduate study at accredited 4-year institution.
**Basis for selection:** Major/career interest in accounting; computer/information sciences; engineering, computer; finance/banking; human resources; information systems or marketing.
**Application requirements:** Interview, proof of eligibility. Resume.
**Additional information:** Minimum 3.0 GPA. Must have at least one semester or two quarters remaining before graduation. Interns paid hourly wage. Applicants must complete personal profile, including resume, on Website before applying for positions. Applicants encouraged to visit Website frequently during spring to review newly added offerings and important information.
**Contact:**
Visit Website for more information.
Web: www.ncr.com/careers

# New Dramatists

## Bernard B. Jacobs Internship Program

**Type of award:** Internship.
**Intended use:** For undergraduate or graduate study at postsecondary institution.
**Basis for selection:** Major/career interest in theater arts; performing arts or arts management.
**Application requirements:** Interview, recommendations, essay. Resume.
**Additional information:** Must have passion for new plays and playwrights. Twelve- to twenty-week internships, three to five days per week. Internships run September to December, January to May, and June to August. Stipend is $25 per week for three days, $50 per week for five days. College credit may be available. Computer and writing skills essential. Applications must be filled out online.

| | |
|---|---|
| **Application deadline:** | December 1, March 31 |

**Contact:**
New Dramatists
Internship Coordinator
424 West 44th Street
New York, NY 10036
Phone: 212-757-6960
Fax: 212-265-4738
Web: www.newdramatists.org

# New Mexico Commission on Higher Education

## New Mexico Work-Study Program

**Type of award:** Internship, renewable.
**Intended use:** For undergraduate study at postsecondary institution. Designated institutions: College of Santa Fe, St. John's College, College of the Southwest, Institute of American Indian Art, Crownpoint Institute of Technology, Diné College, Southwestern Indian Polytechnic Institute.
**Eligibility:** Applicant must be U.S. citizen or permanent resident residing in New Mexico.
**Basis for selection:** Applicant must demonstrate financial need.

**Application requirements:** FAFSA.
**Additional information:** Awards vary. Limit of 20 hours per week, on-campus or off-campus in federal, state, or local public agency. New Mexico residents receive state portion of funding. Contact financial aid office of New Mexico public postsecondary institutions for information, deadlines, and application.
**Contact:**
New Mexico Commission on Higher Education
Financial Aid and Student Services
2048 Galisteo Street
Santa Fe, NM 87505
Phone: 505-476-8400
Web: www.hed.state.nm.us

# The New Republic

## The New Republic Internships

**Type of award:** Internship.
**Intended use:** For undergraduate, graduate or non-degree study at postsecondary institution.
**Eligibility:** Applicant must be U.S. citizen.
**Basis for selection:** Major/career interest in journalism. Applicant must demonstrate depth of character and seriousness of purpose.
**Application requirements:** Cover letter, resume.
**Additional information:** Visit Website for list of available internships. Past internships include social media, literary, reporter-researcher, editorial web, and business associate. Provides intern with opportunity to gain editorial experience at leading opinion magazine located in Washington, D.C.
**Contact:**
The New Republic
Phone: 202-508-4444
Web: www.tnr.com

# New York State Assembly

## New York State Assembly Session Internship Program

**Type of award:** Internship, renewable.
**Intended use:** For full-time junior, senior or graduate study at accredited postsecondary institution in United States.
**Basis for selection:** Applicant must demonstrate high academic achievement.
**Application requirements:** Recommendations, essay, transcript, proof of eligibility. Writing sample. Letter from college endorsing candidate and outlining course credit arrangements.
**Additional information:** All majors eligible. Interns assigned to work with assembly members or assembly staff. Program runs from January to May. Undergraduate interns receive $4,140 stipend. Graduate interns receive $11,500 stipend. Applications accepted on an ongoing basis until deadline. Extensions granted upon request. Housing not provided, but offers assistance in finding apartments and roommates. Visit Website for deadline information.

| | |
|---|---|
| **Amount of award:** | $4,140-$11,500 |
| **Number of awards:** | 150 |
| **Number of applicants:** | 200 |
| **Application deadline:** | November 1 |

**Contact:**
Kathleen McCarty, Director New York State Assembly
Assembly Intern Committee
Legislative Office Building, Room 104A
Albany, NY 12248
Phone: 518-455-4704
Fax: 518-455-4705
Web: www.assembly.state.ny.us/internship/

# New York Times

## David E. Rosenbaum Reporting Internship in Washington, D.C.

**Type of award:** Internship.
**Intended use:** For senior or graduate study at postsecondary institution.
**Basis for selection:** Major/career interest in journalism.
**Application requirements:** Essay. Cover letter, resume, 8-10 clips from daily professional or college newspapers.
**Additional information:** Ten-week summer internship at the Washington Bureau for aspiring reporters with interest in government and policy. Portion of first week spent in New York for orientation. Salary is $900/week. Applications via mail only. No telephone calls.

| | |
|---|---|
| **Number of awards:** | 1 |
| **Application deadline:** | November 15 |

**Contact:**
New York Times
Attn: Susan Keller, Assistant News Editor
1627 Eye Street, NW, Seventh Floor
Washington, DC 20006
Web: www.nytco.com/careers

## New York Times James Reston Reporting Fellowships

**Type of award:** Internship.
**Intended use:** For senior, graduate or non-degree study at postsecondary institution.
**Basis for selection:** Major/career interest in journalism. Applicant must demonstrate seriousness of purpose.
**Application requirements:** Portfolio. Cover letter, resume, eight to ten writing samples.
**Additional information:** Ten-week summer internship available. All applicants must have had at least one previous internship, preferably on a daily newspaper. Visit Website for internship descriptions and more information.

| | |
|---|---|
| **Application deadline:** | November 15 |

**Contact:**
The New York Times
Dana Canedy
620 8th Avenue
New York, NY 10018
Web: www.nytco.com/careers/internships/summer.html

### Thomas Morgan Internships in Visual Journalism

**Type of award:** Internship.
**Intended use:** For junior or senior study at postsecondary institution.
**Basis for selection:** Major/career interest in design or graphic arts/design.
**Application requirements:** Portfolio. Photography: resume, portfolio. Design: portfolio including dummies, layouts, and typography. Graphics: cover letter, resume, writing and graphic design work samples.
**Additional information:** Internships in photography, design, and graphics. Must have newspaper experience. Students from University of Missouri will be given preference for one of the internships each year.

**Application deadline:** November 15

**Contact:**
New York Times
Dana Canedy, Senior Editor
620 Eighth Avenue
New York, NY 10018
Web: www.nytco.com/careers

## NextEra Energy

### NextEra Energy Internship Program

**Type of award:** Internship, renewable.
**Intended use:** For full-time undergraduate study at accredited vocational or 4-year institution in United States.
**Eligibility:** Applicant must be U.S. citizen or permanent resident.
**Basis for selection:** Major/career interest in engineering; engineering, nuclear; engineering, mechanical; engineering, electrical/electronic; engineering, civil; engineering, industrial; finance/banking; accounting; computer/information sciences or business. Applicant must demonstrate high academic achievement.
**Application requirements:** Resume.
**Additional information:** Positions are paid. Minimum 3.0 GPA. Apply online or check Website for campus recruiting calendar.

**Contact:**
NextEra Energy
Attn: Human Resources
P.O. Box 14000
Juno Beach, FL 33408-0420
Web: www.nexteraenergy.com/careers/college.shtml

## Oak Ridge Institute for Science and Education

### Department of Commerce Internship for Postsecondary Students

**Type of award:** Internship.
**Intended use:** For undergraduate or graduate study at 4-year or graduate institution in United States. Designated institutions: Department of Commerce headquarters, division offices and field centers.
**Eligibility:** Applicant must be U.S. citizen.
**Basis for selection:** Major/career interest in business; communications; computer/information sciences; engineering; graphic arts/design; health sciences; life sciences; mathematics or physical sciences.
**Application requirements:** Recommendations, transcript.
**Additional information:** Provides opportunities to participate in hands-on education and training related to Department of Commerce. Minimum 2.5 GPA. Ten-week internship in summer; 15-week internship for fall or spring semesters. Weekly stipend of $500 for undergraduates, $600 for graduate students; housing allowance of $150 per week based on appointment location; limited travel reimbursement; accidental medical expense coverage provided. Summer deadline is January 31. Number of awards varies. See Website for application.

**Application deadline:** July 1, December 1

**Contact:**
Web: see.orau.org

### Department of Energy Community College Institute at Oak Ridge National Laboratory

**Type of award:** Internship.
**Intended use:** For full-time undergraduate study at accredited 2-year institution in United States. Designated institutions: Oak Ridge National Laboratory (Oak Ridge, TN).
**Eligibility:** Applicant must be at least 18. Applicant must be U.S. citizen or permanent resident.
**Basis for selection:** Major/career interest in computer/information sciences; science, general; engineering; environmental science; life sciences; mathematics or physical sciences.
**Application requirements:** Recommendations, transcript. Proof of health insurance.
**Additional information:** Applicant must be student at community college. Provides opportunities to participate in research in a broad range of science and engineering activities related to basic sciences, energy, and the environment. Applicant must have passed at least 12 credit hours of coursework toward a degree (with at least six credit hours in science, math, engineering, or technology courses) at community college. Ten-week summer internship. Bi-weekly stipend. Limited travel reimbursement and limited housing allowance. Visit Website for application and deadlines.

**Contact:**
Web: see.orau.org or www.orau.gov/orise/edu/ornl/doeprog

### DOE Pre-Service Teacher Internships

**Type of award:** Internship.
**Intended use:** For undergraduate or graduate study. Designated institutions: Oak Ridge National Laboratory (Oak Ridge, TN).
**Eligibility:** Applicant must be at least 18. Applicant must be U.S. citizen or permanent resident.
**Basis for selection:** Major/career interest in science, general; mathematics or education. Applicant must demonstrate high academic achievement.
**Application requirements:** Recommendations, transcript. List of courses, research paper, proof of health insurance.
**Additional information:** Provides opportunities to participate in educational training and research relating to preparation for teaching K-12 science, math, and technology. Ten-week

summer program. Bi-weekly stipend with limited travel reimbursement and limited housing allowance. Must have completed a minimum of two math classes above college algebra or at least two laboratory science classes. Application available online. Visit Website for deadline.
**Contact:**
Web: see.orau.org

## DOE Scholars Program

**Type of award:** Internship.
**Intended use:** For undergraduate certificate, graduate or postgraduate study at accredited 4-year or graduate institution.
**Eligibility:** Applicant must be U.S. citizen.
**Basis for selection:** Major/career interest in business; communications; graphic arts/design; mathematics; computer graphics; physical sciences; science, general or engineering.
**Application requirements:** Recommendations, essay. Resume.
**Additional information:** DOE Scholars Program provides opportunities at various Department of Energy sites throughout the U.S. Up to $650 stipend per week depending on academic status. Travel to and from appointment site will be paid when distance is over 60 miles one-way.
**Application deadline:** January 31
**Contact:**
Web: http://see.orau.org

## DOE Science Undergraduate Laboratory Internships at Oak Ridge National Laboratory

**Type of award:** Internship.
**Intended use:** For undergraduate study at postsecondary institution. Designated institutions: Oak Ridge National Laboratory (Oak Ridge, TN).
**Eligibility:** Applicant must be U.S. citizen or permanent resident.
**Basis for selection:** Major/career interest in computer/information sciences; physical sciences; mathematics; life sciences; engineering; science, general or environmental science.
**Application requirements:** Recommendations, transcript. Proof of health insurance.
**Additional information:** Applicant must have intention to teach. Internship program provides opportunity to participate in research in a broad range of science and engineering activities related to basic sciences, energy, and the environment. Bi-weekly stipend; limited travel reimbursement and housing allowance. Internship lasts ten weeks in the summer. See Website for more information and deadlines.
**Contact:**
Web: see.orau.org or www.orau.gov/orise/edu/ornl/doeprog/

## Environmental Management Participation at the U.S. Army Environmental Command (USAEC)

**Type of award:** Internship, renewable.
**Intended use:** For undergraduate or graduate study at 2-year, 4-year or graduate institution. Designated institutions: U.S. Army Environmental Center (Aberdeen Proving Ground, MD) and other approved locations.
**Eligibility:** Applicant must be U.S. citizen.
**Basis for selection:** Major/career interest in archaeology; biology; chemistry; computer/information sciences; ecology; engineering; entomology; environmental science; forestry or zoology.
**Application requirements:** Recommendations, transcript. Resume, proof of health insurance.
**Additional information:** Provides opportunities to participate in research in environmental programs involving cultural and natural resources, restoration, compliance, conservation, pollution prevention, validation, demonstration, technology transfer, quality assurance and quality control, training, information management and reporting, and related programs. Up to one year; full-time or part-time appointments. Stipend based on research area and academic classification. Minimum 2.5 GPA. Applications accepted year-round. Number of awards varies. Visit Website for application.
**Contact:**
Web: see.orau.org

## Global Change Education Program

**Type of award:** Internship, renewable.
**Intended use:** For junior, senior or graduate study at 4-year or graduate institution in United States.
**Eligibility:** Applicant must be U.S. citizen.
**Basis for selection:** Major/career interest in physical sciences; geology/earth sciences; environmental science or ecology.
**Additional information:** Program offers opportunities to participate in research areas related to global change in various U.S Department of Energy facilities (undergraduates) and U.S. Department of Energy facilities and universities (graduates) across the U.S. Undergraduates are awarded a $475/week stipend, plus travel. Graduates are awarded a $1,500/month stipend. Tuition and fees not to exceed $10,000 per academic year. Duration is 10 to 12 weeks in the summer for undergraduates, and three years for graduates, with the option to renew annually. Number of awards varies. For more information, visit www.atmos.anl.gov/GCEP/.
**Application deadline:** December 31
**Contact:**
Web: see.orau.org

## Higher Education Research Experiences at Oak Ridge National Laboratory for Students

**Type of award:** Internship.
**Intended use:** For undergraduate or graduate study in United States. Designated institutions: Oak Ridge National Laboratory (Oak Ridge, TN).
**Eligibility:** Applicant must be at least 18. Applicant must be U.S. citizen or permanent resident.
**Basis for selection:** Major/career interest in computer/information sciences; environmental science; engineering, environmental; health sciences; life sciences; medicine; physical sciences or mathematics.
**Application requirements:** Recommendations, transcript. Two academic references.
**Additional information:** Provides opportunities to participate in research in a broad range of science and engineering activities related to basic sciences, energy, and the environment. Terms vary with academic level; full- or part-time positions available. Minimum 2.5 GPA. Weekly stipend varies with academic level. One round-trip travel reimbursement and housing allowance. Number of awards varies. Deadlines for undergraduates: February 1 for summer, June 1 for fall, and October 1 for spring. Deadline for freshmen is February 1. See Website for application and more information.

**Application deadline:** February 1, June 1

**Contact:**
Web: see.orau.org or www.orau.gov/hereatornl

## Laboratory Technology Program

**Type of award:** Internship, renewable.
**Intended use:** For undergraduate or graduate study at postsecondary institution. Designated institutions: Oak Ridge National Laboratory (Oak Ridge, TN).
**Eligibility:** Applicant must be U.S. citizen or permanent resident residing in Tennessee.
**Basis for selection:** Major/career interest in engineering; engineering, electrical/electronic; engineering, mechanical; computer/information sciences or physical sciences.
**Application requirements:** Recommendations, transcript.
**Additional information:** Applicant must be attending a regionally-accredited college or university. Provides opportunity to receive hands-on experience in technical areas via long-term assignment. Minimum 2.5 GPA. Internship duration varies with academic level; full-time or part-time appointments of up to one year, renewable up to two additional years. Applications accepted year-round. Stipend available; amount based on academic level or degree. Interns also receive benefits of full-time or part-time employees. Depending on fund availability, participants may be eligible for 100% tuition reimbursement.

**Contact:**
Web: see.orau.org

## National Energy Technology Laboratory Professional Internship Program

**Type of award:** Internship, renewable.
**Intended use:** For undergraduate or graduate study at accredited 2-year, 4-year or graduate institution in United States. Designated institutions: National Energy Technology Laboratory (Pittsburgh, PA, Albany, OR, and Morgantown, WV).
**Eligibility:** Applicant must be at least 18.
**Basis for selection:** Major/career interest in chemistry; computer/information sciences; engineering; environmental science; geology/earth sciences; mathematics; physics; physical sciences or statistics.
**Application requirements:** Transcript. Proof of health insurance. Two references; at least one academic reference.
**Additional information:** Provides opportunities to participate in energy-related research. Three to 24 consecutive months, full-time or part-time appointments. Weekly stipend. Limited travel reimbursement (round-trip transportation expenses between facility and home or campus). Off-campus tuition and fees may be paid. Deadline for summer is February 15. Number of awards varies. Visit Website for application.

**Number of applicants:** 80
**Application deadline:** June 1, October 1

**Contact:**
Web: see.orau.org

## Nuclear Engineering Science Laboratory Synthesis

**Type of award:** Internship.
**Intended use:** For undergraduate study at 4-year institution in United States.
**Basis for selection:** Major/career interest in engineering or physical sciences. Applicant must demonstrate high academic achievement.
**Additional information:** Program is a cooperative research initiative geared toward students in physics and nuclear engineering. Minimum 3.0 GPA. 2/1 deadline is for 10-week summer appointment. Limited number of fall and spring appointments. Weekly stipend varies with academic level. One round-trip travel reimbursement; housing allowance.

**Application deadline:** March 1

**Contact:**
Web: http://see.orau.org

## Nuclear Regulatory Commission Historically Black Colleges and Universities Student Research Participation

**Type of award:** Internship.
**Intended use:** For undergraduate or graduate study at accredited postsecondary institution in United States. Designated institutions: Laboratories conducting NRC research; some appointments on HBCU campuses; some appointments at host universities under the guidance of principal investigators who have NRC research grants.
**Eligibility:** Applicant must be U.S. citizen or permanent resident.
**Basis for selection:** Major/career interest in computer/information sciences; engineering; biology; mathematics; geophysics; physics; materials science; physical sciences; health sciences or statistics.
**Application requirements:** Recommendations, transcript. Resume.
**Additional information:** Provides opportunities for students from historically black colleges to participate in ongoing NRC research and development. Minimum 2.5 GPA. Ten to 12 weeks during the summer; some part-time appointments of one year. Weekly stipend of $500 to $600. Limited travel reimbursement (round-trip transportation expenses between facility and home or campus). Funded by U.S. Nuclear Regulatory Commission. Visit Website for application.

**Contact:**
Web: see.orau.org

## Oak Ridge National Laboratory Undergraduate Student Cooperative Education Program

**Type of award:** Internship.
**Intended use:** For sophomore, junior or senior study at accredited 4-year institution in United States.
**Basis for selection:** Major/career interest in computer/information sciences; science, general; engineering; life sciences; mathematics or physical sciences.
**Application requirements:** Recommendations.
**Additional information:** Co-op program provides opportunities for qualified undergraduate students to receive hands-on experience in real-world setting. Must be available for more than one term at ORNL alternating with terms at academic institution. Fall, winter/spring, and summer terms available; apply three months before requested start date. Stipends vary by discipline and academic status and range from $530 to $900 per week. Students from the outside area may qualify for $105/week housing allowance and travel reimbursement.

**Contact:**
Web: http://see.orau.org

## Oak Ridge Science Semester

**Type of award:** Internship.
**Intended use:** For full-time junior or senior study at accredited 4-year institution in United States. Designated institutions: Oak Ridge National Laboratory (Oak Ridge, TN).
**Basis for selection:** Major/career interest in astronomy; computer/information sciences; engineering; environmental science; health sciences; physics; biology; geology/earth sciences or mathematics.
**Application requirements:** Recommendations, transcript.
**Additional information:** Provides opportunities to participate in research in a broad range of scientific research areas. Program is 16 weeks in the fall (late August through mid-December). $6,800 stipend and $2,200 housing allowance. Academic credit offered for combination of research, coursework, and seminar series. Minimum 3.0 GPA. Visit Website for application deadline.
**Amount of award:** $9,000
**Contact:**
Web: www.denison.edu/oakridge

## Research Participation at the Centers for Disease Control and Prevention/Agency for Toxic Substances and Disease Registry

**Type of award:** Internship.
**Intended use:** For undergraduate or graduate study at accredited 2-year, 4-year or graduate institution in United States. Designated institutions: Centers for Disease Control and Prevention (Atlanta, GA and other domestic and international locations) and Agency for Toxic Substances and Disease Registry (Atlanta, GA).
**Basis for selection:** Major/career interest in economics; environmental science; epidemiology; health sciences; life sciences; medicine; physical sciences or science, general.
**Application requirements:** Recommendations, transcript. Resume, proof of health insurance.
**Additional information:** Provides opportunities to participate in research on infectious diseases, environmental health, epidemiology, or occupational safety and health. Minimum 2.5 GPA. One month to one year; full-time or part-time appointments. Stipend based on research area(s) and academic classification. Applications accepted year-round. See Website for application.
**Contact:**
Web: see.orau.org or www.orau.gov/cdc

## Research Participation at the National Center for Toxicological Research

**Type of award:** Internship, renewable.
**Intended use:** For undergraduate or graduate study at accredited 2-year, 4-year or graduate institution in United States. Designated institutions: National Center for Toxicological Research (Jefferson, AK).
**Basis for selection:** Major/career interest in biology; chemistry; computer/information sciences; mathematics; pharmacy/pharmaceutics/pharmacology; science, general or medicine.
**Application requirements:** Recommendations, transcript. Resume, proof of health insurance.
**Additional information:** Provides opportunities to participate in research on biological effects of potentially toxic chemicals and solutions to toxicology problems that have a major impact on human health and the environment. One month to one year; full-time or part-time appointments. Stipend based on research area and academic classification. Applications accepted year-round for academic year appointments. Number of awards varies. Visit Website for application.
**Number of applicants:** 100
**Contact:**
Web: see.orau.org

## Research Participation at the U.S. Food and Drug Administration

**Type of award:** Internship, renewable.
**Intended use:** For undergraduate or graduate study at accredited 4-year or graduate institution.
**Basis for selection:** Major/career interest in life sciences; health sciences; bioengineering; physical sciences; veterinary medicine; epidemiology; food science/technology; materials science or statistics.
**Application requirements:** Recommendations. Resume.
**Additional information:** Program provides opportunities to participate in research related to the mission of the U.S. Food and Drug Administration. Appointments available at the Center for Biologics Evaluation and Research, Center for Devices and Radiological Health, Center for Drug Evaluation and Research, Center for Food Safety and Applied Nutrition, Center for Veterinary Medicine, and Office of the Commissioner. Program is from one month to one year, up to four years maximum, full-time or part-time appointments available. Stipend based on research area(s) and educational level. Applications accepted year-round.
**Contact:**
Web: http://see.orau.org

## Research Participation Program for the U.S. Army Medical Research Institute of Chemical Defense

**Type of award:** Internship, renewable.
**Intended use:** For undergraduate or graduate study at 2-year, 4-year or graduate institution in United States. Designated institutions: U.S. Army Medical Research Institute of Chemical Defense (Aberdeen Proving Ground, MD).
**Eligibility:** Applicant must be U.S. citizen.
**Basis for selection:** Major/career interest in biochemistry; biology; medicine or physical sciences.
**Application requirements:** Recommendations, transcript. Resume.
**Additional information:** Provides opportunities to participate in development of medical countermeasures to chemical warfare agents. Internship lasts up to one year; full- and part-time appointments available. Stipend based on research area and academic classification. Number of awards varies. Minimum 2.5 GPA. Applications accepted year-round. Visit Website for application and details.
**Contact:**
Web: see.orau.org or www.orau.org/maryland

## Research Participation Program for the U.S. Army Research Laboratory

**Type of award:** Internship.
**Intended use:** For undergraduate or graduate study at 2-year, 4-year or graduate institution in United States. Designated institutions: U.S. Army Research Laboratory (Adelphi and Aberdeen Proving Ground, MD) and other approved locations.
**Eligibility:** Applicant must be U.S. citizen.
**Basis for selection:** Major/career interest in biology; medicine; physical sciences; computer/information sciences; materials science or engineering.
**Application requirements:** Recommendations, transcript.
**Additional information:** Provides opportunities to participate in research and technology development in areas such as engineering, mechanics, chemistry, survivability & lethality analysis, sensors & electron devices, and weapons & materials research related to enhancing the technologies and analytical support to assure supremacy of America's ground forces. Internship lasts up to one year; up to a total of four years; full- or part-time appointments available. Stipend based on research area and classification. Number of awards varies. Minimum 2.5 GPA. Applications accepted year-round. Visit Website for application.
**Contact:**
Web: see.orau.org

## Savannah River Site Professional Internship Program

**Type of award:** Internship.
**Intended use:** For undergraduate or graduate study at 2-year, 4-year or graduate institution in United States. Designated institutions: Savannah River Site (Aiken, SC).
**Eligibility:** Applicant must be U.S. citizen.
**Basis for selection:** Major/career interest in business; chemistry; computer/information sciences; engineering; environmental science; geology/earth sciences; mathematics or physics.
**Application requirements:** Recommendations, transcript. Proof of health insurance.
**Additional information:** Provides opportunities to participate in energy-related and environmental research. Three to 24 consecutive months; full-time or part-time appointments. Weekly stipend; limited travel reimbursement (round-trip transportation expenses between facility and home or campus). Minimum 2.5 GPA. Funded by Savannah River Site. Visit Website for application.
**Contact:**
Web: see.orau.org

## Student Internship Program at the U.S. Army Center for Health Promotion and Preventive Medicine

**Type of award:** Internship, renewable.
**Intended use:** For undergraduate or graduate study at postsecondary institution in United States. Designated institutions: U.S. Army Center for Health Promotion and Preventive Medicine (Aberdeen Proving Ground, MD) and other approved locations.
**Eligibility:** Applicant must be U.S. citizen.
**Basis for selection:** Major/career interest in biology; chemistry; entomology; engineering; environmental science; physical sciences; science, general or health sciences.
**Application requirements:** Recommendations, transcript. Resume, proof of insurance.
**Additional information:** Provides opportunities to participate in applied clinical research in areas such as occupational and environmental health engineering, entomology, ionizing and non-ionizing radiation, health promotion, industrial hygiene and worksite hazards, ergonomics, environmental sanitation and hygiene, laboratory science, chemistry, biology, toxicology, health physics, environmental health risk assessment and risk communication, and related projects. Up to one year; full-time or part-time appointments. Minimum 2.5 GPA. Stipend based on research area and academic classification. Number of awards varies. Applications accepted year-round. Visit Website for application.
**Contact:**
Web: see.orau.org

## Student Research at the U.S. Army Edgewood Chemical Biological Center

**Type of award:** Internship, renewable.
**Intended use:** For undergraduate or graduate study at accredited 4-year or graduate institution in United States. Designated institutions: U.S. Army Edgewood Chemical Biological Center (Aberdeen Proving Ground, MD).
**Eligibility:** Applicant must be U.S. citizen.
**Basis for selection:** Major/career interest in biology; computer/information sciences; engineering; environmental science; physical sciences; science, general or mathematics.
**Application requirements:** Transcript. Resume.
**Additional information:** Provides opportunities to participate in research and development in support of military missions. Three months to one year; full-time or part-time appointments. Stipend based on research area and academic classification. Applications accepted year-round. Award amount and number vary. Visit Website for application.
**Contact:**
Phone: 410-306-9205 or 410-306-9204
Web: see.orau.org

## U.S. Department of Homeland Security Scholarship Program

**Type of award:** Internship.
**Intended use:** For full-time sophomore or junior study at accredited 4-year or graduate institution in United States.
**Eligibility:** Applicant must be U.S. citizen.
**Basis for selection:** Major/career interest in biology; engineering; social/behavioral sciences; physical sciences; mathematics; computer/information sciences; life sciences; physical sciences or agriculture. Applicant must demonstrate high academic achievement.
**Application requirements:** Recommendations, essay, transcript. Test scores.
**Additional information:** Opportunity to participate in educational program intended to ensure diverse and highly talented science and technology human resource base to meet mission, goals, and objectives of U.S. Department of Homeland Security. Appointments are two years for undergraduates and three years for graduate students, given satisfactory progress. Successful applicants will receive full-tuition scholarship and monthly stipend. Summer internship following first year of award required. One year of full-time service in relevant HS-STEM field required. Minimum 3.3 GPA. Visit Website for application and more information.

**Amount of award:** Full tuition
**Number of applicants:** 157
**Contact:**
Web: www.orau.gov/dhsed

# Ohio Newspapers Foundation

## AdOhio Advertising Internship

**Type of award:** Internship.
**Intended use:** For junior or senior study at postsecondary institution. Designated institutions: Ohio institutions.
**Eligibility:** Applicant must be residing in Ohio.
**Basis for selection:** Major/career interest in journalism or advertising.
**Application requirements:** Resume, writing samples, and cover letter.
**Additional information:** Ten-week internship in Columbus office of this trade association, which represents 83 daily newspapers, more than 180 weekly newspapers, and more than 150 Websites in Ohio. Duties include writing and layout for sales presentation sheets and client mailings, assistance with newspaper ad bid sheets, newspaper tear sheets, and research. Negotiable start date after June 1. Salary is $350 per week. Finalists will be contacted for interviews.
**Application deadline:** March 31
**Notification begins:** May 1
**Contact:**
Ohio Newspapers Foundation
Walt Dozier, AdOhio
1335 Dublin Road, Suite 216-B
Columbus, OH 43215
Web: www.ohionews.org

## Ohio Newspaper Association Publications/Public Relations Internship

**Type of award:** Internship.
**Intended use:** For sophomore, junior or senior study at postsecondary institution. Designated institutions: Ohio institutions.
**Eligibility:** Applicant must be residing in Ohio.
**Basis for selection:** Major/career interest in communications or journalism.
**Application requirements:** Resume, writing samples, and cover letter.
**Additional information:** Ten-week internship at this trade association, which represents 83 daily newspapers, more than 180 weekly newspapers, and more than 150 Websites in Ohio. Duties include writing and assisting in production of newsletter, miscellaneous flyers and mailings, meeting planning, and research. Negotiable start date after June 1. Salary of $350 per week. Finalists will be contacted for interviews.
**Application deadline:** March 31
**Notification begins:** May 1
**Contact:**
Ohio Newspapers Foundation
Dennis Hetzel, Executive Director
1335 Dublin Road, Suite 216-B
Columbus, OH 43215
Web: www.ohionews.org

# Oracle Corporation

## Product Development Summer Internship Program

**Type of award:** Internship.
**Intended use:** For full-time sophomore, junior, senior or graduate study at accredited 4-year or graduate institution in United States.
**Basis for selection:** Major/career interest in computer/information sciences. Applicant must demonstrate high academic achievement.
**Application requirements:** Resume.
**Additional information:** Foreign student must have unrestricted permission to work in United States. Interns are offered excellent compensation and fully furnished corporate apartments are provided. Car/bike rentals and round-trip travel expenses are paid for, as well as a helicopter ride under the Golden Gate Bridge. Visit Website to submit resume and sign up to search for current openings.
**Application deadline:** January 1
**Notification begins:** February 28
**Contact:**
Oracle Corporation
500 Oracle Parkway
Redwood Shores, CA 94065
Phone: 800-633-0738
Web: www.oracle.com/us/corporate/careers/college/internships/index.html

# Owens Corning

## Owens Corning Internships

**Type of award:** Internship.
**Intended use:** For full-time junior, senior, master's or doctoral study at accredited 4-year institution.
**Eligibility:** Applicant must be U.S. citizen or permanent resident.
**Basis for selection:** Major/career interest in engineering; accounting; environmental science; information systems; marketing; materials science; technology or finance/banking. Applicant must demonstrate high academic achievement and leadership.
**Application requirements:** Proof of eligibility.
**Additional information:** Variety of internships offered with housing assistance, competitive salary. Summer programs last thirteen weeks. Positions throughout the U.S. See Website for more information.

**Contact:**
Owens Corning
One Owens Corning Parkway
Toledo, OH 43659
Phone: 1-800-GET-PINK
Web: www.owenscorningcareers.com

# Pacific Gas and Electric Company

## Pacific Gas and Electric Summer Intern Program

**Type of award:** Internship.
**Intended use:** For full-time undergraduate or graduate study in United States.
**Eligibility:** Applicant must be U.S. citizen or permanent resident.
**Basis for selection:** Major/career interest in business; chemistry; statistics; computer/information sciences; economics; engineering; geology/earth sciences; marketing; engineering, mechanical or public administration/service. Applicant must demonstrate high academic achievement and seriousness of purpose.
**Application requirements:** Interview. Resume, cover letter.
**Additional information:** Paid internships available throughout northern and central California, including company headquarters in San Francisco. Deadline is rolling, but early applications are encouraged. Resume may be submitted online; format specifications available online. Visit Website or call sponsor for openings and campus recruitment dates. Must be eligible to work in the United States. Number and amount of awards vary. Most internships are summer only and typically last 10-12 weeks. Internships include a competitive salary and paid company holidays.
**Contact:**
Web: www.pge.com/about/careers/college/intern

# PBS

## PBS Internships

**Type of award:** Internship.
**Intended use:** For undergraduate or graduate study at postsecondary institution.
**Application requirements:** Resume and cover letter.
**Additional information:** Various internships are available in different departments. All paid, except for internship in General Counsel's office. Internships also offered for graduate students seeking an MBA. Internships change on a semester basis. Visit Website for internship listings, application forms, and more information.
**Contact:**
PBS Internship Program
2100 Crystal Dr.
Arlington, VA 22202
Phone: 703-739-5088
Web: www.pbs.org/jobs

# PGA Tour

## PGA Tour Diversity Intern Program

**Type of award:** Internship.
**Intended use:** For sophomore, junior, senior or master's study at postsecondary institution.
**Eligibility:** Applicant must be U.S. citizen.
**Basis for selection:** Major/career interest in marketing; business/management/administration; communications; information systems; journalism; radio/television/film; sports/sports administration or public relations. Applicant must demonstrate high academic achievement, depth of character, leadership, seriousness of purpose and service orientation.
**Application requirements:** Interview, recommendations, essay, transcript.
**Additional information:** Non-citizens eligible to work in U.S. may also apply. Internship lasts ten weeks at $440 per week with $200 per month deducted for housing (if needed). Internship sites located in Florida. Minimum 3.0 GPA. Visit Website to apply.

| | |
|---|---|
| **Amount of award:** | $4,400 |
| **Number of awards:** | 18 |
| **Number of applicants:** | 1,450 |
| **Application deadline:** | February 28 |
| **Notification begins:** | May 1 |
| **Total amount awarded:** | $132,000 |

**Contact:**
PGA Tour Diversity Intern Program
Attn: Jim Clarke
100 PGA Tour Boulevard
Ponte Vedra Beach, FL 32082
Phone: 904-273-3209
Fax: 904-543-2046
Web: www.pgatour.com

# Phipps Conservatory and Botanical Gardens

## Phipps Conservatory and Botanical Gardens Internships

**Type of award:** Internship.
**Intended use:** For junior, senior or graduate study at accredited 2-year or 4-year institution.
**Eligibility:** Applicant must be U.S. citizen.
**Basis for selection:** Major/career interest in horticulture; landscape architecture; environmental science or botany. Applicant must demonstrate high academic achievement.
**Application requirements:** Recommendations. Resume and cover letter.
**Additional information:** Interns paid $8 per hour. Related majors, such as environmental education, also eligible. Internships may be full- or part-time. Four to six positions available in summer; one to two positions available during academic year. Application deadline is rolling. Contact sponsor or visit Website for more information.

| | |
|---|---|
| **Number of awards:** | 8 |
| **Number of applicants:** | 7 |
| **Application deadline:** | February 15 |
| **Notification begins:** | March 15 |

**Contact:**
Phipps Conservatory and Botanical Gardens Human Resources
1059 Shady Avenue
Pittsburgh, PA 15232
Phone: 412-441-4442 x3229
Fax: 412-665-2368
Web: www.phipps.conservatory.org

# Princeton Plasma Physics Laboratory

## Plasma Physics National Undergraduate Fellowship Program

**Type of award:** Internship.
**Intended use:** For junior study at 4-year institution in United States.
**Eligibility:** Applicant must be U.S. citizen or permanent resident.
**Basis for selection:** Major/career interest in engineering; physics; mathematics or computer/information sciences. Applicant must demonstrate high academic achievement, depth of character, leadership, seriousness of purpose and service orientation.
**Application requirements:** Recommendations, essay, transcript.
**Additional information:** Minimum 3.5 GPA. Internship paid and lasts ten weeks in the summer. Application due in mid-February.

| | |
|---|---|
| **Amount of award:** | $4,800 |
| **Number of awards:** | 25 |
| **Number of applicants:** | 100 |
| **Application deadline:** | February 29 |
| **Notification begins:** | March 15 |

**Contact:**
Princeton Plasma Physics Laboratory
P.O. Box 451
Princeton, NJ 08543-0451
Phone: 609-243-2116
Web: science-education.pppl.gov

# Random House

## Random House Summer Internship Program

**Type of award:** Internship.
**Intended use:** For undergraduate study at 4-year institution.
**Basis for selection:** Major/career interest in publishing. Applicant must demonstrate seriousness of purpose.
**Application requirements:** Resume, cover letter expressing interest in specific publishing group.
**Additional information:** Ten-week internship beginning in early June open to rising college seniors for New York program; Westminster program open to all undergrads. All majors encouraged to apply. Internships are for college credit and unpaid. If invited, applicant must travel to New York City or Westminster, Maryland, at own expense for interview in late February through mid-April. See Website for application, deadline, and more information.

| | |
|---|---|
| **Number of awards:** | 40 |
| **Number of applicants:** | 2,400 |

**Contact:**
Random House Internship Coordinator
Human Resources, 25th Floor
1745 Broadway
New York, NY 10019
Web: www.careers.randomhouse.com

# Rhode Island State Government

## Rhode Island State Government Internship Program

**Type of award:** Internship, renewable.
**Intended use:** For undergraduate or postgraduate study at postsecondary institution.
**Eligibility:** Applicant must be residing in Rhode Island.
**Basis for selection:** Major/career interest in governmental public relations or public administration/service. Applicant must demonstrate high academic achievement, depth of character, leadership, seriousness of purpose and service orientation.
**Application requirements:** Interview, recommendations, transcript, proof of eligibility. Writing sample (for law students only).
**Additional information:** Minimum 2.5 GPA. Summer program lasts eight weeks; spring and fall programs last entire semester. Fall application deadline is rolling. Compensation for summer interns only, at $100 per week. Spring and fall interns earn academic credit or work-study, if eligible. All placements in Rhode Island.

| | |
|---|---|
| **Number of awards:** | 243 |
| **Number of applicants:** | 450 |

**Contact:**
Rhode Island State Government
State Capitol, Room 8AA
Providence, RI 02903
Phone: 401-222-6782
Fax: 401-222-4447
Web: www.rilin.state.ri.us

# Simon and Schuster Inc.

## Simon and Schuster Internship Program

**Type of award:** Internship, renewable.
**Intended use:** For full-time undergraduate or graduate study at accredited vocational, 4-year or graduate institution.
**Basis for selection:** Major/career interest in publishing. Applicant must demonstrate high academic achievement and leadership.
**Application requirements:** Interview. Resume. Cover letter.
**Additional information:** Internship program is designed to train and recruit a diverse group of students interested in exploring careers in publishing. Summer, spring, fall, and year-round programs are available. Student must register for academic credit with their college or university and provide

official documentation confirming this information. During spring/fall semesters, intern works a minimum 16 hours to a maximum 20 hours per week. During summer semester, office hours are 9 to 5 p.m. Applicants must have well-rounded extracurricular interests and work experience. Visit Website for application.

**Contact:**
Simon and Schuster, Inc.
Web: www.simonandschuster.biz/careers/internships

# Smithsonian Environmental Research Center

## Smithsonian Environmental Research Center Internship Program

**Type of award:** Internship, renewable.
**Intended use:** For undergraduate or master's study at 4-year or graduate institution.
**Basis for selection:** Major/career interest in biology; chemistry; environmental science; physics; mathematics or education. Applicant must demonstrate seriousness of purpose.
**Application requirements:** Recommendations, essay, transcript.
**Additional information:** Projects are 40 hours per week, lasting from 10 to 16 weeks. Stipend is $450 per week and available winter/spring, summer, and fall. Dorm space is available for $85 per week on limited basis. Several application deadlines: spring, November 15; summer, February 1; fall, June 1. Applicants should demonstrate academic credentials, relevant experience, and the congruence of expressed goals with those of internship program. Open to all undergraduates, recent college graduates (within six months), and beginning Master's students.

| | |
|---|---|
| **Number of awards:** | 30 |
| **Number of applicants:** | 250 |
| **Application deadline:** | November 15, February 1 |
| **Notification begins:** | December 15, March 15 |
| **Total amount awarded:** | $144,000 |

**Contact:**
Smithsonian Environmental Research Center
Internship Program
647 Contees Wharf Road
Edgewater, MD 21037
Phone: 443-428-2217
Fax: 443-428-2380
Web: www.serc.si.edu/pro_training/internships.aspx

# Smithsonian Institution

## James E. Webb Internship Program for Minority Undergraduate Seniors and Graduate Students in Business and Public Administration

**Type of award:** Internship.
**Intended use:** For senior or graduate study at 4-year or graduate institution. Designated institutions: Smithsonian Institution.
**Eligibility:** Applicant must be Alaskan native, Asian American, African American, Mexican American, Hispanic American, Puerto Rican, American Indian or Native Hawaiian/Pacific Islander. Applicant must be U.S. citizen or permanent resident.
**Basis for selection:** Major/career interest in business/management/administration or public administration/service. Applicant must demonstrate high academic achievement.
**Application requirements:** Recommendations, essay, transcript. Resume.
**Additional information:** Minimum 3.0 GPA. Applicant must be minority student enrolled as undergraduate senior or graduate student in business or public administration program. Selection based on relevance of internship at the Smithsonian to student's academic and career goals. Internships are full-time, 40 hours per week for ten weeks. Stipend is $550 per week, with additional travel allowances offered in some cases. Deadlines: February 1 for summer and fall; October 1 for spring. Contact sponsor or visit Website for more information and application.

| | |
|---|---|
| **Application deadline:** | February 1, October 1 |

**Contact:**
Smithsonian Institution Office of Fellowships
470 L'Enfant Plaza, SW, Suite 7102, MRC 902
P.O. Box 37012
Washington, DC 20013-7012
Phone: 202-633-7070
Web: www.si.edu/ofg

## Smithsonian Minority Internship

**Type of award:** Internship.
**Intended use:** For undergraduate or graduate study at postsecondary institution. Designated institutions: Smithsonian Institution.
**Basis for selection:** Major/career interest in anthropology; archaeology; ecology; environmental science; art/art history; museum studies; zoology or natural sciences.
**Application requirements:** Recommendations, essay, transcript. Resume.
**Additional information:** Research internships at Smithsonian Institution in anthropology/archaeology; astrophysics and astronomy; earth sciences/paleontology; ecology; environmental, behavioral (tropical animals), evolutionary, and systematic biology; history of science and technology; history of art (including American contemporary, African, Asian); 20th-century American crafts; social and cultural history and folk life of America. Applicants must have major/career interest in research or museum-related activity pursued by the Smithsonian Institution. Stipend of $550 per week for ten weeks. February 1 deadline for summer session and for fall; October 1 deadline for spring. Intended for U.S. minority groups under-represented in Smithsonian scholarly programs. Contact sponsor for minority requirements. Minimum 3.0 GPA. Visit Website for more information.

| | |
|---|---|
| **Application deadline:** | February 1, October 1 |

**Contact:**
Smithsonian Institution Office of Fellowships
470 L'Enfant Plaza, SW, Suite 7102, MRC 902
P.O. Box 37012
Washington, DC 20013-7012
Phone: 202-633-7070
Web: www.si.edu/ofg

### Smithsonian Native American Internship

**Type of award:** Internship.
**Intended use:** For undergraduate or graduate study at postsecondary institution. Designated institutions: Smithsonian Institution.
**Eligibility:** Applicant must be Alaskan native or American Indian.
**Basis for selection:** Major/career interest in Native American studies.
**Application requirements:** Recommendations, essay, transcript. Resume.
**Additional information:** Internship at Smithsonian Institution in research or museum activities related to Native American studies. Stipend of $550 a week for ten weeks. Deadline for summer and fall is February 1; spring is October 1. American Indian students encouraged to apply. Contact Office of Fellowships for application procedures or visit Website.

| | |
|---|---|
| **Application deadline:** | February 1, October 1 |

**Contact:**
Smithsonian Institution Office of Fellowships
470 L'Enfant Plaza, SW, Suite 7102, MRC 902
P.O. Box 37012
Washington, DC 20013-7012
Phone: 202-633-7070
Web: www.si.edu/ofg

## Society of Physics Students

### Society of Physics Students Summer Internship Program

**Type of award:** Internship.
**Intended use:** For full-time undergraduate study.
**Eligibility:** Applicant or parent must be member/participant of Society of Physics Students.
**Basis for selection:** Major/career interest in physics. Applicant must demonstrate high academic achievement.
**Application requirements:** Transcript. Resume and cover letter. Two letters of recommendation (one should be written by SPS advisor).
**Additional information:** Offers nine-and-a-half-week internships in science policy and research for undergraduate physics majors. Internships include $4,200 stipend, paid housing, and transportation supplement. Internships are based in Washington, DC. Applicants must be active SPS members with excellent scholastic record and experience in science outreach events or science research. See Website for application and deadline.

| | |
|---|---|
| **Amount of award:** | $4,200 |
| **Number of awards:** | 12 |
| **Number of applicants:** | 483 |
| **Application deadline:** | February 1 |
| **Notification begins:** | March 15 |
| **Total amount awarded:** | $33,300 |

**Contact:**
SPS Summer Internship Program
One Physics Ellipse
College Park, MD 20740
Phone: 301-209-3007
Fax: 301-209-0839
Web: www.spsnational.org/programs/internships

## Solomon R. Guggenheim Museum

### Guggenheim Museum Internship

**Type of award:** Internship.
**Intended use:** For junior, senior or graduate study at postsecondary institution.
**Basis for selection:** Major/career interest in art/art history; arts, general; arts management; communications; education; finance/banking; graphic arts/design; library science; museum studies or museum studies/administration. Applicant must demonstrate high academic achievement.
**Application requirements:** Interview, recommendations. Cover letter, resume, writing sample.
**Additional information:** Potential internships available in Conservation, Curatorial, Education, Development, Director's Office, Exhibition Development, Exhibition Management, Finance, Graphic Design, Human Resources, Information Technology, Legal, Library Archives, Marketing, Photography, Public Affairs, Publications, Registrar, Special Events, Special Projects, and Visitor Services. International students must have J-1 visa. Internships during academic year are for college credit; some stipends available in summer. Application deadlines are January 18 for summer, May 3 for fall and academic year, November 1 for spring. Spring, fall, and academic year internships are full- or part-time, with minimum commitment of 16 hours/week for three months. Summer internships are full-time.

| | |
|---|---|
| **Number of awards:** | 40 |
| **Number of applicants:** | 300 |
| **Application deadline:** | January 18, May 3 |

**Contact:**
Solomon R. Guggenheim Museum
Education Coordinator—Internship Program
1071 Fifth Avenue
New York, NY 10128-0173
Phone: 212-360-4287
Web: www.guggenheim.org

### Peggy Guggenheim Internship

**Type of award:** Internship.
**Intended use:** For undergraduate or graduate study at postsecondary institution.
**Basis for selection:** Major/career interest in arts, general; art/art history; education; museum studies or museum studies/administration. Applicant must demonstrate high academic achievement, depth of character, leadership and seriousness of purpose.
**Application requirements:** Recommendations, essay, transcript. Resume.
**Additional information:** One- to three-month internship at Peggy Guggenheim Collection in Venice, Italy. Two deadlines: October 15 for internships in January-April; December 1 for internships in May-December. Must be fluent in English with knowledge of spoken Italian. Interns receive a monthly stipend. Request further information and application forms from the Peggy Guggenheim Collection. Visit Website for details.

| | |
|---|---|
| **Number of applicants:** | 1,400 |
| **Application deadline:** | October 15, December 1 |
| **Notification begins:** | December 1, February 15 |

**Contact:**
Peggy Guggenheim Collection Internship Coodinator
701 Dorsoduro
30123 Venice, Italy
Phone: 39-41-240-5401
Web: www.guggenheim.org or www.guggenheim-venice.it

# Sony Music Entertainment

## Sony Credited Internship

**Type of award:** Internship.
**Intended use:** For undergraduate or graduate study at accredited postsecondary institution.
**Eligibility:** Applicant must be U.S. citizen or permanent resident.
**Basis for selection:** Major/career interest in accounting; business; finance/banking; communications; computer/information sciences; law; music; music management or marketing.
**Application requirements:** Interview, transcript, proof of eligibility. Resume and cover letter.
**Additional information:** Unpaid internship. Applicant must be available to work at least 15 hours a week. Internships are available in various departments throughout company. Must possess excellent computer skills (Word, Excel and Outlook) and strong organizational skills. Applicant must be enrolled at accredited university and provide verification of course credit. Visit Website for available internship listings.

| | |
|---|---|
| **Number of awards:** | 60 |
| **Number of applicants:** | 200 |

**Contact:**
Phone: 212-833-8000
Web: www.sonymusic.com

# Southface Energy Institute

## Southface Internship

**Type of award:** Internship.
**Intended use:** For undergraduate or graduate study at accredited 2-year, 4-year or graduate institution in United States.
**Eligibility:** Applicant must be U.S. citizen, permanent resident or international student.
**Basis for selection:** Major/career interest in architecture; business/management/administration; engineering, civil; engineering, environmental; engineering, mechanical; environmental science; graphic arts/design; landscape architecture; public relations or urban planning. Applicant must demonstrate high academic achievement.
**Application requirements:** Statement of intent. Names of references with contact information. Resume.
**Additional information:** Internships cover variety of interests: sustainable building, community design, water-efficient landscaping, smart growth, environmental event planning, energy policy and tech assistance, non-profit marketing, and public relations. Six- to twelve-month positions available. Students work 40 hours per week; weekly stipend of $100. Shared housing available if space permits. Transportation assistance available. Applications accepted year-round. International students must have work authorization.

**Contact:**
Phone: 404-604-3595
Web: www.southface.org

# Spoleto Festival USA

## Spoleto Festival USA Apprenticeship Program

**Type of award:** Internship, renewable.
**Intended use:** For undergraduate, graduate or non-degree study in United States.
**Basis for selection:** Major/career interest in arts management; arts, general; music; public relations or theater/production/technical. Applicant must demonstrate seriousness of purpose.
**Application requirements:** Recommendations. Writing sample (media applicants only). Resume, cover letter.
**Additional information:** Four-week full-time apprenticeship with arts professionals producing and operating international arts festival. Posts available in media relations, development, box office, production, orchestra management, finance and accounting, artist services/facilities management, and office administration. Weekly stipend may be provided; housing and travel allowance provided. See Website for details and deadlines.

| | |
|---|---|
| **Number of awards:** | 50 |

**Contact:**
Spoleto Festival USA
Apprentice Program
14 George Street
Charleston, SC 29401
Web: www.spoletousa.org

# Sports Journalism Institute

## Aspiring Sports Journalist Internship

**Type of award:** Internship.
**Intended use:** For sophomore or junior study at postsecondary institution.
**Basis for selection:** Major/career interest in journalism; communications; publishing; English or sports/sports administration. Applicant must demonstrate high academic achievement and seriousness of purpose.
**Application requirements:** Recommendations, essay, transcript. Professional-style photo, up to seven writing samples.
**Additional information:** The Sports Journalism Institute is a nine-week, paid summer training and internship program for undergraduates interested in sports journalism. Applicants need not be journalism majors. Scholarship available for students returning to college upon successful completion of program. Visit Website for more information, application, and deadline.

**Contact:**
Gregory Lee
The Boston Globe
135 Morrissey Blvd.
Boston, MA 02125
Web: www.sportsjournalisminstitute.org

# Staples

## Staples Summer Internship Program

**Type of award:** Internship.
**Intended use:** For undergraduate study at 4-year institution in United States.
**Basis for selection:** Major/career interest in advertising; marketing; accounting; technology; information systems or finance/banking.
**Application requirements:** Resume.
**Additional information:** Internships located at corporate headquarters in Framingham, MA. Other eligible majors include supply chain, corporate strategy, customer service, merchandising/brand management, and sales. Visit Website to see openings and apply online.
**Contact:**
Staples
500 Staples Drive
Framingham, MA 01702
Web: www.staples.com/sbd/cre/resources/jobs/college_intern.html

# Student Conservation Association

## SCA Conservation Internships

**Type of award:** Internship, renewable.
**Intended use:** For undergraduate or graduate study at accredited postsecondary institution in United States.
**Basis for selection:** Major/career interest in archaeology; ecology; forestry; natural resources/conservation; history; education; wildlife/fisheries; biology or communications.
**Application requirements:** Resume.
**Additional information:** Travel and housing is provided, and a weekly stipend is given for food. Positions at various locations in United States. Applicants are advised to apply three months prior to position start date. Rolling admissions process—seven application deadlines per year. Applicants with interest in environmental education, interpretation, marine biology, and wilderness preservation also eligible. See Website for application.

| | |
|---|---|
| **Amount of award:** | $1,000-$4,725 |

**Contact:**
Admissions Department Student Conservation Association
P.O. Box 550
Charlestown, NH 03603
Phone: 603-543-1700
Fax: 603-543-1828
Web: www.thesca.org

# Texas Historical Commission

## Preservation Fellows Program

**Type of award:** Internship.
**Intended use:** For sophomore, junior, senior or graduate study at 2-year, 4-year or graduate institution in United States.
**Eligibility:** Applicant must be Alaskan native, Asian American, African American, Mexican American, Hispanic American, Puerto Rican, American Indian or Native Hawaiian/Pacific Islander. Applicant must be U.S. citizen.
**Basis for selection:** Applicant must demonstrate high academic achievement.
**Application requirements:** Recommendations, transcript. Resume or CV, list of previous experience with the Texas Historical Commission.
**Additional information:** Minimum 3.0 GPA. Applicants must either attend institutions in Texas, or be Texas residents attending school out-of-state are eligible to apply. Preservation Fellows receive a $5,000 stipend for eight weeks of 40-hour-week employment under the supervision of the THC, either at its headquarters in Austin or "in the field" with an associated preservation organization.

| | |
|---|---|
| **Amount of award:** | $5,000 |
| **Number of awards:** | 2 |
| **Number of applicants:** | 9 |
| **Application deadline:** | December 31 |
| **Notification begins:** | September 1 |
| **Total amount awarded:** | $10,000 |

**Contact:**
Preservation Fellows c/o Friends of the Texas Historical Commission
P.O. Box 13497
Austin, TX 78711-3497
Phone: 512-936-2241
Fax: 512-936-0237
Web: www.thc.state.tx.us

# Time Inc.

## Time Inc. Internship Program

**Type of award:** Internship.
**Intended use:** For undergraduate or graduate study at accredited 4-year or graduate institution.
**Basis for selection:** Major/career interest in finance/banking; advertising; communications; graphic arts/design; information systems; journalism or marketing. Applicant must demonstrate high academic achievement.
**Application requirements:** Essay. Cover letter and resume.
**Additional information:** Spring and fall academic year internships are offered on an as-needed basis, with available positions and magazines/Websites varying each semester. Most positions require a minimum of 14 hours per week and are based in NYC. Nine- to ten-week paid summer internship programs include the Consumer Marketing and Sales Internship Program, the Corporate Program, the Editorial Internship Program, the Essence Internship Program and the Finance Internship Program.
**Contact:**
Time Inc.
1271 Avenue of the Americas
New York, NY 10020
Phone: 212-522-1212
Web: www.timeinc.com/careers/campusrecruiting.php

# Tourism Cares

## ASTA David J. Hallissey Memorial Internship

**Type of award:** Internship.
**Intended use:** For sophomore, junior, senior or graduate study at accredited 4-year or graduate institution in United States.
**Eligibility:** Applicant must be U.S. citizen, permanent resident or international student.
**Basis for selection:** Major/career interest in tourism/travel or marketing.
**Application requirements:** Essay, transcript. Passport or Alien Registration Card. Two evaluations and letters of recommendation (one from hospitality/tourism-related faculty member, one from hospitality/tourism professional).
**Additional information:** Minimum 3.0 GPA. Applicant must have strong written and verbal communication skills as well as interpersonal skills and a basic understanding of Microsoft Excel. Preference given to applicants with knowledge of Microsoft Access and SBSS software. The intern will be working in the Washington, D.C. area. Visit Website for deadline, additional criteria.

| | |
|---|---|
| **Amount of award:** | $2,000 |
| **Number of awards:** | 1 |

**Contact:**
Tourism Cares
275 Turnpike Street
Suite 307
Canton, MA 02021
Phone: 781-821-5990
Fax: 781-821-8949
Web: www.tourismcares.org/scholarships

## NTA Mayflower Tours - Patrick Murphy Internship

**Type of award:** Internship.
**Intended use:** For sophomore, junior, senior or graduate study in United States or Canada.
**Eligibility:** Applicant must be U.S. citizen, permanent resident or international student.
**Basis for selection:** Major/career interest in tourism/travel or political science/government. Applicant must demonstrate high academic achievement.
**Application requirements:** Essay, transcript. Resume. Passport or Alien Registration Card. Two evaluations and letters of recommendation (one from hospitality/tourism-related faculty member, one from hospitality/tourism professional).
**Additional information:** Minimum 3.0 GPA. Applicants pursuing political science degree with an interest in travel and tourism are preferred. Intern will be assigned to work in Washington, D.C. area during fall semester. Must have excellent written, oral, and interpersonal skills. Visit Website for application, deadline, additional criteria.

| | |
|---|---|
| **Amount of award:** | $2,000 |
| **Number of awards:** | 1 |

**Contact:**
Toursim Cares
275 Turnpike Street
Suite 307
Canton, MA 02021
Phone: 781-821-5990
Fax: 781-821-8949
Web: www.tourismcares.org/scholarships

# Tyson Foods, Inc.

## Tyson Foods Intern Program

**Type of award:** Internship.
**Intended use:** For full-time undergraduate study at accredited vocational, 2-year or 4-year institution.
**Basis for selection:** Major/career interest in agribusiness; agriculture; computer/information sciences; engineering; food production/management/services; food science/technology; health-related professions; law; marketing or science, general. Applicant must demonstrate high academic achievement.
**Application requirements:** Proof of eligibility. Resume and cover letter.
**Additional information:** Various paid internships include but not limited to computer programming, industrial engineering, livestock procurement, quality assurance, carcass sales, and production. Program locations across the United States. Must be eligible to work in the U.S. Visit Website for job descriptions and list of campus recruiting events, or to submit resume and cover letter. Summer and academic-year internships available.

| | |
|---|---|
| **Number of awards:** | 50 |

**Contact:**
Tyson Foods, Inc.
Web: www.tysonfoodscareers.com

# United States Holocaust Memorial Museum

## United States Holocaust Memorial Museum Internship

**Type of award:** Internship, renewable.
**Intended use:** For freshman, sophomore, junior, senior or graduate study at postsecondary institution.
**Eligibility:** Applicant must be U.S. citizen, permanent resident or international student.
**Basis for selection:** Major/career interest in museum studies/administration; history; English; foreign languages; communications; geography; graphic arts/design or communications.
**Additional information:** Semester-long internships available during summer, fall, and spring in Holocaust research and museum studies. Phone interviews conducted with top qualified candidates. Most positions unpaid. Applicants interested in German or Eastern European studies also eligible. Application deadline is March 1 for summer; July 1 for fall; October 15 for spring. Apply online. All applicants subject to criminal background check. International students must have work authorization. Award notification begins at the end of March.

| | |
|---|---|
| **Number of awards:** | 70 |
| **Number of applicants:** | 500 |
| **Application deadline:** | March 1 |
| **Notification begins:** | April 1 |

**Contact:**
Internship Coordinator, Office of Volunteer and Intern Services
United States Holocaust Memorial Museum
100 Raoul Wallenburg Place, SW
Washington, DC 20024-2150
Phone: 202-479-9737
Fax: 202-488-6568
Web: www.ushmm.org

# United States Senate

## U.S. Senate Member Internships

**Type of award:** Internship.
**Intended use:** For full-time undergraduate study at accredited 4-year institution.
**Eligibility:** Applicant must be U.S. citizen or permanent resident.
**Basis for selection:** Major/career interest in political science/government; law; communications; public relations; public administration/service or economics. Applicant must demonstrate high academic achievement.
**Application requirements:** Resume, cover letter, writing sample.
**Additional information:** Senate member interns generally reside or attend college in senator's state. Positions available in Washington, D.C., or member's state. Internships may be unpaid or paid (less common), but generally offer assistance obtaining college credit. Term of service, eligibility vary. Some internships restricted to upper-level undergraduates. Senators administer their own internship programs. Contact individual senator's office directly. Visit Website for links to member sites, e-mail addresses, and telephone numbers.
**Contact:**
Office of (name of senator)
United States Senate
Washington, DC 20510
Web: www.senate.gov

# U.S. Department of Agriculture

## USDA Summer Intern Program

**Type of award:** Internship.
**Intended use:** For undergraduate or graduate study at postsecondary institution.
**Eligibility:** Applicant must be U.S. citizen.
**Application requirements:** Transcript. Resume, U.S. government forms.
**Additional information:** Internships last approximately four months (May to August). Stipends are based on level of education, prior experience, and position. Various internships available at different agencies. Also open to high school graduates entering college. Applications available in late December. All majors encouraged to apply. Deadline varies. See Website for more information.
**Contact:**
Contact individual agencies or see Website.
Web: www.usda.gov

# U.S. Department of State

## U.S. Department of State Internship

**Type of award:** Internship.
**Intended use:** For junior, senior or graduate study at accredited 4-year or graduate institution.
**Eligibility:** Applicant must be U.S. citizen.
**Basis for selection:** Major/career interest in political science/government; foreign languages; governmental public relations; business; public administration/service; social work; economics; information systems; journalism or science, general. Applicant must demonstrate high academic achievement.
**Application requirements:** Transcript. Statement of interest.
**Additional information:** Provides opportunities working in varied administrative branches of the Department of State, both abroad and in Washington, D.C. Internships are generally unpaid, but many institutions provide academic credit and/or financial assistance for overseas assignments. Paid internships primarily granted to students in financial need. Must be able to work a minimum of ten weeks. Selected students must undergo background investigation to receive security clearance. Random drug testing performed. Internships available year-round. Visit Website for more information.
**Contact:**
U.S. Department of State
Web: www.careers.state.gov/students

# U.S. House of Representatives

## House Member Internships

**Type of award:** Internship, renewable.
**Intended use:** For full-time undergraduate study.
**Eligibility:** Applicant must be U.S. citizen or permanent resident.
**Basis for selection:** Major/career interest in political science/government; public administration/service; public relations or communications. Applicant must demonstrate high academic achievement.
**Additional information:** Members of the United Stated House of Representatives use undergraduate interns for a variety of jobs including constituent contact, research, and correspondence. Positions are based in Congressional District Offices and in Washington, DC. Internships generally facilitate course credit, but offer no stipend. Some paid internships are funded through private nonprofit organizations. Information about the individual House member intern programs can usually be found online. A complete set of links to representatives' sites is available at www.house.gov. In general, applicants residing in the member's home district and enrolled in the same political party are favored. Typically, many Washington, D.C.-based internships are filled by students from outside the member district. Applicants may also be interested in working for congressperson serving on committee (i.e. Agriculture, Financial Services) relevant to their major. Interested parties should contact the representative with whom they are interested in working.

Internships

**Contact:**
Contact individual congressman/congresswoman's office
Phone: 202-224-3121
Web: www.house.gov

# U.S. National Arboretum

## Summer Horticultural Internship

**Type of award:** Internship.
**Intended use:** For undergraduate or graduate study at postsecondary institution.
**Basis for selection:** Major/career interest in botany; horticulture or landscape architecture.
**Application requirements:** Transcript. Resume, cover letter.
**Additional information:** Interns work on independent projects supervised by arboretum staff. Pay is $11.91 per hour. Must work two days per week or 16 hours, usually between 7 a.m. and 3:30 p.m. College credit available. Must have completed course work or have acquired practical experience in horticulture or related field. Must have basic gardening or laboratory skills, interest in plants, and ability to work independently. Visit Website for more information and application.
**Contact:**
Internship Coordinator
U.S. National Arboretum
3501 New York Avenue, NE
Washington, DC 20002-1958
Phone: 202-245-4563
Fax: 202-245-4575
Web: www.usna.usda.gov

## Summer Research Internship

**Type of award:** Internship.
**Intended use:** For undergraduate or graduate study at postsecondary institution.
**Eligibility:** Applicant must be U.S. citizen.
**Basis for selection:** Major/career interest in agriculture; botany; education; forestry; horticulture or public administration/service.
**Application requirements:** Transcript. Resume and cover letter.
**Additional information:** Internships pay stipend of $11.91 per hour. Average workday for most interns: Monday through Friday, 7 a.m. to 3:30 p.m. Provides opportunity to gain experience in plant research in premier horticultural collection. Applicants need to have completed 24 hours of coursework or have acquired practical experience in horticulture or related field. Basic gardening or laboratory skills, interest in plants, strong communication skills, and ability to work independently preferred. Course credit may be arranged. See Website for deadline, application, and more information.
**Contact:**
Internship Coordinator
U.S. National Arboretum
3501 New York Avenue, NE
Washington, DC 20002-1958
Phone: 202-245-4563
Fax: 202-245-4575
Web: www.usna.usda.gov

## Ten-Month-Long Horticultural Internship

**Type of award:** Internship.
**Intended use:** For undergraduate or graduate study at postsecondary institution.
**Basis for selection:** Major/career interest in botany; horticulture or landscape architecture.
**Additional information:** Interns participate in educational programs and field trips and work on independent projects supervised by arboretum staff. Pay is $16.33 per hour. Most interns work Tuesday through Saturday, 7 a.m. to 3:30 p.m. College credit is available. Must have completed 24 hours of relevant course work or have one year practical working experience in horticulture or related field. Must have basic gardening or laboratory skills, interest in plants, and ability to work independently. Visit Website for deadline, application, and more information.
**Contact:**
U.S. National Arboretum
3501 New York Avenue, NE
Washington, DC 20002-1958
Phone: 202-245-4563
Fax: 202-245-4575
Web: www.usna.usda.gov

# Wachovia

## Finance Undergraduate Internships

**Type of award:** Internship.
**Intended use:** For full-time junior or senior study at accredited 4-year institution.
**Eligibility:** Applicant must be U.S. citizen or permanent resident.
**Basis for selection:** Major/career interest in finance/banking; accounting; business/management/administration; economics or real estate. Applicant must demonstrate high academic achievement and leadership.
**Application requirements:** Resume and cover letter.
**Additional information:** Ten- to twelve-week program consists of work assignments and professional development opportunities related to corporate and investment banking. Number of awards varies. Locations in major cities throughout the U.S. Visit Website to search for internship and to create a profile and apply online. Minimum 3.0 GPA.
**Contact:**
Wachovia Corporation
Web: www.wachovia.com

# The Wall Street Journal

## The Wall Street Journal Asia Internship

**Type of award:** Internship.
**Intended use:** For undergraduate or graduate study at postsecondary institution.
**Basis for selection:** Major/career interest in journalism.
**Application requirements:** Cover letter, resume and six to eight writing samples.

**Additional information:** Internships available in the U.S., Europe, and Asia. Selection process strongly emphasizes submitted clips and journalistic experience. Roundtrip airfare allowance included. Pay is $700 per week. Candidate should be fluent in one or more Asian languages,—preferably Mandarin, Japanese or Korean—a strong interest in business reporting in Asia, and experience living or working in the region.

**Number of awards:** 1
**Application deadline:** November 1

**Contact:**
The Wall Street Journal Asia
Almar Latour, Editor-in-Chief
25/F Central Plaza, 18 Harbour Road
Wanchai, Hong Kong
Web: www.dowjones.com/careers-interns.asp

## The Wall Street Journal Europe Internship

**Type of award:** Internship.
**Intended use:** For undergraduate or graduate study at postsecondary institution.
**Basis for selection:** Major/career interest in journalism.
**Application requirements:** Cover letter, resume and six to eight writing samples. Proof of health insurance.
**Additional information:** Reporting interns will work in WSJ news bureau in Europe. Must be fluent in one or more of the following languages: French, German, Dutch, or Russian. Must demonstrate interest in Europe and willingness and ability to work in overseas environment. Selection process strongly emphasizes submitted clips and journalistic experience. Successful applicants must pay own roundtrip airfare. Pay is $700 per week. Include email address and expected month and year of graduation at top of cover letter.

**Number of awards:** 1
**Application deadline:** November 1

**Contact:**
The Wall Street Journal Europe
Attn: Tim Hanrahan, Managing Editor
10 Fleet Place
London, EC4M 7QN
Web: www.dowjones.com/careers-interns.asp

## The Wall Street Journal Journalism Internship

**Type of award:** Internship.
**Intended use:** For undergraduate or graduate study at postsecondary institution.
**Basis for selection:** Major/career interest in journalism.
**Application requirements:** Cover letter, resume, and six to eight writing samples.
**Additional information:** Full-time summer internship lasts ten weeks. Interns work in one of news bureaus. Previous journalism or college newspaper experience required. Interns paid $700 a week. All majors encouraged to apply. Currently enrolled students only.

**Number of awards:** 15
**Number of applicants:** 335
**Application deadline:** November 1
**Notification begins:** February 28

**Contact:**
The Wall Street Journal, WSJ Intern Application (U.S.)
Deborah Brewster Dep. Managing Editor
1211 Avenue of the Americas
New York, NY 10036
Web: www.dowjones.com/careers-interns.asp

# The Walt Disney Company

## Disney Theme Parks & Resorts Professional Internships

**Type of award:** Internship.
**Intended use:** For junior or senior study at 2-year or 4-year institution in United States.
**Eligibility:** Applicant must be U.S. citizen, permanent resident or currently studying in the U.S. under an F-1 visa.
**Basis for selection:** Major/career interest in animal sciences; architecture; construction management; engineering; finance/banking; communications; human resources; hospitality administration/management; marketing or computer/information sciences. Applicant must demonstrate high academic achievement, seriousness of purpose and service orientation.
**Application requirements:** Interview. Resume and cover letter.
**Additional information:** Internships available in a variety of fields. Offerings vary by season. Certain roles only open to alumni participants of the Disney College Program. For most positions, applicants must be enrolled in college/university during spring/fall semester prior to participation. Pay rates and schedules vary by location. Must have valid driver's license. Housing may be available, with the exception of management internships. Visit Website for more information, application deadline, and to search for openings.

**Contact:**
Disney Professional Recruiting
P.O. Box 10000
Lake Buena Vista, FL 32830
Phone: 800-722-2930
Web: www.disneyinterns.com

# Walt Disney World and Disneyland

## Disney College Program

**Type of award:** Internship.
**Intended use:** For undergraduate study at postsecondary institution.
**Eligibility:** Applicant must be U.S. citizen, permanent resident or currently studying in the U.S. under an F-1 visa.
**Application requirements:** Interview, recommendations. Online application and Web-based interview required.
**Additional information:** Disney College Program is a semester-long paid internship at the Walt Disney World® Resort near Orlando, FL or the Disneyland® Resort in Anaheim, CA, in which students work in a front-line role at theme parks and resorts, participate in college-level coursework, and live in company-sponsored housing with other students from around the globe. Applicant must be enrolled in a college/university during the spring/fall semester prior to participation. Must view the Disney College Program presentation (online or on campus) to apply for program. Work schedules and pay rates vary by role. College credit may be available. Must have strong communication skills, understanding of Guest Service principles, ability to work independently and/or with large team. Program terms vary; are at least one semester in length. See Website for application and more information.

**Number of awards:** 10,000

**Contact:**
Disney College Recruiting
P.O. Box 10090
Lake Buena Vista, FL 32830
Phone: 800-722-2930
Web: www.disneycollegeprogram.com

# Washington Internships for Students of Engineering

## Washington Internships for Students of Engineering

**Type of award:** Internship.
**Intended use:** For junior, senior or graduate study at postsecondary institution.
**Eligibility:** Applicant must be U.S. citizen or permanent resident.
**Basis for selection:** Major/career interest in computer/information sciences; engineering; engineering, chemical; engineering, electrical/electronic or engineering, mechanical.
**Application requirements:** Recommendations, essay, transcript. Reference forms.
**Additional information:** Nine-week summer internship learning about technological issues and public policy available to students who have completed three years of study. Internship located in Washington, D.C. Interns write required research paper as part of process. Lodging expenses covered. Must be member of and sponsored by ANS, ASCE, ASME, IEEE, or SAE. IEEE will sponsor computer science majors. Graduate students beginning Masters study in technology policy-related degree also eligible. $2,100 stipend provided to assist with intern's living and travel expenses. Apply directly to sponsoring organization; application forms and sponsor contact information available on Website.

| | |
|---|---|
| **Amount of award:** | $2,100 |
| **Number of awards:** | 12 |
| **Total amount awarded:** | $25,200 |

**Contact:**
Washington Internships for Students of Engineering
c/o IEEE - USA
2001 L Street, N.W. Suite 700
Washington, DC 20036-4910
Phone: 202-785-0017
Fax: 202-785-0835
Web: www.wise-intern.org

# Wolf Trap Foundation for the Performing Arts

## Wolf Trap Foundation for the Performing Arts Internship

**Type of award:** Internship.
**Intended use:** For sophomore, junior, senior or graduate study in United States.
**Eligibility:** Applicant must be U.S. citizen, permanent resident or international student.
**Basis for selection:** Major/career interest in performing arts or arts management. Applicant must demonstrate seriousness of purpose.
**Application requirements:** Recommendations. Cover letter outlining career goals and specifying internship desired; resume. Two writing samples (except technical, scenic painting, costuming, stage management, accounting, graphic design, photography, or information systems applicants). Graphic design applicants must submit three design samples. Refer to individual internship descriptions for additional required materials.
**Additional information:** Deadline for full-time summer internships is March 1; deadline for part-time fall internships is July 1; deadline for part-time spring internships is November 1. Stipend provided to help offset housing and travel expenses. College credit available. Applicant must have own transportation. Internships available in the following areas: opera (directing, administrative, stage management, technical, costume, scenic/prop painting); education; development; communications and marketing (advertising, marketing, graphic design, publications, public relations, photography, Web design, multimedia); human resources; ticket services; information systems; planning and initiatives; accounting; production and sound; program and production. Two letters of recommendation needed in application. International students must meet INS I-9 requirement. Internships vary by season; visit Website for details. Also available to recent college graduates.

| | |
|---|---|
| **Application deadline:** | March 1, July 1 |

**Contact:**
Wolf Trap Foundation for the Performing Arts
Internship Program
1645 Trap Road
Vienna, VA 22182
Phone: 800-404-8461
Fax: 703-255-1924
Web: www.wolftrap.org

# Women's Sports Foundation

## Women's Sports Foundation Internship

**Type of award:** Internship, renewable.
**Intended use:** For undergraduate or graduate study in United States.
**Basis for selection:** Major/career interest in communications; humanities/liberal arts; public relations; publishing or sports/sports administration. Applicant must demonstrate high academic achievement.
**Application requirements:** Interview. Resume and two letters of recommendation.
**Additional information:** Internship set up to provide sports management students with exposure to sports industry. Open to students or women in career change. Hourly rate of $7.25. Minimum six-month term and a maximum length of one year. Internships available in two sessions: January to June and June to December. Most internships located at headquarters in East Meadow, NY, or Manhattan office. Writing samples required for some positions. Visit Website for application.

| | |
|---|---|
| **Number of awards:** | 20 |
| **Number of applicants:** | 50 |

**Contact:**
Women's Sports Foundation
1899 Hempstead Turnpike
Suite 400
East Meadow, NY 11554
Phone: 800-227-3988
Fax: 516-542-4716
Web: www.womenssportsfoundation.org

# The World Food Prize

## George Washington Carver Internship

**Type of award:** Internship.
**Intended use:** For undergraduate or graduate study at 4-year or graduate institution.
**Basis for selection:** Major/career interest in agriculture; science, general; business; education; political science/ government; communications or journalism. Applicant must demonstrate high academic achievement, seriousness of purpose and service orientation.
**Application requirements:** Resume and cover letter. Reference letter and writing samples suggested but not required.
**Additional information:** Interns come from variety of academic disciplines, and roles are often specialized to individual's background or interest. Interns learn first-hand both public and private side of operating an international non-profit organization and increase their understanding of the international fight against hunger, malnutrition, and poverty. Unpaid internship; course credit available. Twelve-hour/week minimum. Internships seasonal.
**Contact:**
The World Food Prize
Phone: 515-245-3731
Web: www.worldfoodprize.org

# World Security Institute

## World Security Institute Internship

**Type of award:** Internship.
**Intended use:** For undergraduate or graduate study at postsecondary institution.
**Basis for selection:** Major/career interest in political science/ government; military science; international relations; communications or computer/information sciences. Applicant must demonstrate high academic achievement, depth of character, leadership, seriousness of purpose and service orientation.
**Application requirements:** Recommendations, transcript. Resume, cover letter stating interest and reasons for wanting to work at WSI.
**Additional information:** Intended for graduates and highly-qualified undergraduates. Highly competitive internships are full-time paid positions in research, television, computer/web editing, communications, and more in Washington, D.C. office. U.S. citizenship not required; must be able to provide proof that they may work legally in the U.S.
**Contact:**
World Security Institute
1779 Massachusetts Avenue, NW
Washington, DC 20036
Phone: 202-332-0900
Fax: 202-462-4559
Web: worldsecurityinstitute.org/jobs.cfm

# Loans

## Alaska Commission on Postsecondary Education

### Alaska Family Education Loan

**Type of award:** Loan, renewable.
**Intended use:** For full-time undergraduate or graduate study at vocational, 4-year or graduate institution.
**Eligibility:** Applicant must be U.S. citizen or permanent resident residing in Alaska.
**Application requirements:** Proof of eligibility.
**Additional information:** Borrower may apply for 7.3 percent interest rate loan on behalf of family member if the borrower is an AK resident of at least one year, is credit-worthy or has a cosigner, and does not have status at time of loan that would prevent repayment. Both borrower and student must not be past due on child support, must comply with selective service, may not have had student loan written off unless discharged in bankruptcy in the last five years, and may not have been delinquent or defaulted on prior student loans. Must apply annually. Award amounts: $6,500/year for career training program; $8,500 for undergraduate; $9,500 for graduate. Maximum for undergraduate is $42,500; graduate student, $47,500; total per student, $60,000; total per borrower, $102,000.

| | |
|---|---|
| **Amount of award:** | $6,500-$9,500 |

**Contact:**
Alaska Commission on Postsecondary Education
Alaska Family Education Loan
P.O. Box 110505
Juneau, AK 99811-0505
Phone: 907-465-2962
Fax: 907-465-5316
Web: www.alaskadvantage.state.ak.us

### Alaska Teacher Education Loan

**Type of award:** Loan, renewable.
**Intended use:** For full-time undergraduate or post-bachelor's certificate study at accredited 4-year institution.
**Eligibility:** Applicant must be U.S. citizen or permanent resident residing in Alaska.
**Basis for selection:** Major/career interest in education. Applicant must demonstrate high academic achievement.
**Application requirements:** Recommendations, proof of eligibility, nomination by rural school district. Statement of intent for teaching career.
**Additional information:** Must be enrolled in program in elementary or secondary school teacher education. May borrow up to $37,500 in total. Must reapply each year. Applicant must meet requirements for teachers set by student's local school board. Must be graduate of AK high school. May not have past-due child support or status at application that will prevent repayment. Must be credit-worthy or have cosigner. Must comply with selective service. Eligible for forgiveness of percentage of loan and interest in each of first five years borrower teaches in rural AK elementary or secondary school: 15 percent for years one to three; 25 percent for year four; and 30 percent for five years and beyond.

| | |
|---|---|
| **Amount of award:** | $7,500 |
| **Application deadline:** | July 1 |

**Contact:**
Alaska Commission on Postsecondary Education
Alaska Teacher Education Loan
P.O. Box 110505
Juneau, AK 99811-0505
Phone: 907-465-2962
Fax: 907-465-5316
Web: www.alaskadvantage.state.ak.us

### A.W. "Winn" Brindle Memorial Education Loan

**Type of award:** Loan, renewable.
**Intended use:** For full-time undergraduate or graduate study at accredited postsecondary institution.
**Eligibility:** Applicant must be U.S. citizen or permanent resident residing in Alaska.
**Basis for selection:** Major/career interest in wildlife/fisheries.
**Application requirements:** Proof of eligibility.
**Additional information:** Five percent-interest loan may not exceed cost of tuition, fees, books and supplies, room and board, and limited transportation. Loan may not be for more than eight years of undergraduate/graduate study. Availability of loans is subject to annual funding levels. Preference to applicants nominated by private donors to memorial education loan account. Recipients qualify for forgiveness up to ten percent of loan for each of first five years employed in fishery-related field. Must be current in repayment. No past-due child support. Must be creditworthy or have cosigner. Must comply with selective service.
**Contact:**
Alaska Commission on Postsecondary Education
Winn Brindle Loan Program
P.O. Box 110505
Juneau, AK 99811-0505
Phone: 907-465-2962
Fax: 907-465-5316
Web: www.alaskadvantage.state.ak.us

## American Legion Kentucky Auxiliary

### Mary Barrett Marshall Student Loan Fund

**Type of award:** Loan, renewable.
**Intended use:** For undergraduate study at vocational, 2-year or 4-year institution. Designated institutions: Eligible postsecondary institutions in Kentucky.
**Eligibility:** Applicant or parent must be member/participant of American Legion Auxiliary. Applicant must be female. Applicant must be residing in Kentucky. Applicant must be

descendant of veteran; or dependent of veteran; or spouse of veteran or deceased veteran during Grenada conflict, Korean War, Lebanon conflict, Panama conflict, Persian Gulf War, WW I, WW II or Vietnam.
**Basis for selection:** Applicant must demonstrate financial need.
**Application requirements:** SASE.
**Additional information:** Maximum $800 per year, payable monthly without interest after graduation or upon securing employment; 6% interest after five years.

| | |
|---|---|
| **Amount of award:** | $800 |
| **Application deadline:** | April 1 |

**Contact:**
American Legion Auxiliary, Department of Kentucky
Chairman Lois Smith
812 Madison Street
Rockport, IN 47635
Phone: 812-649-2163
Web: www.kyamlegionaux.org

# American Legion South Dakota

## American Legion South Dakota Educational Loan

**Type of award:** Loan, renewable.
**Intended use:** For undergraduate study at vocational, 2-year or 4-year institution.
**Eligibility:** Applicant must be residing in South Dakota. Applicant must be veteran or descendant of veteran; or dependent of veteran.
**Additional information:** Up to $1,500 per year; $3,000 maximum; 3% interest on unpaid balance.

| | |
|---|---|
| **Amount of award:** | $1,500-$3,000 |
| **Application deadline:** | November 1, May 1 |

**Contact:**
American Legion South Dakota
Department Adjutant
P.O. Box 67
Watertown, SD 57201-0067
Phone: 605-886-3604

# ASME Auxiliary, Inc.

## ASME Auxiliary Student Loan Fund

**Type of award:** Loan.
**Intended use:** For junior, senior or graduate study at accredited 4-year or graduate institution in United States. Designated institutions: Schools with ABET-accredited mechanical engineering or engineering technology curricula.
**Eligibility:** Applicant must be U.S. citizen.
**Basis for selection:** Major/career interest in engineering, mechanical. Applicant must demonstrate financial need.
**Application requirements:** Recommendations.
**Additional information:** Loans are interest-free until graduation. No application deadline. Must be American Society of Mechanical Engineers member. Number of loans available varies. Visit Website for more information application or send SASE to address.

| | |
|---|---|
| **Amount of award:** | $5,000 |
| **Number of applicants:** | 76 |
| **Application deadline:** | April 15, October 15 |
| **Total amount awarded:** | $192,509 |

**Contact:**
Susan Hawthorne
White Horse Village, S#121
535 Gradyville Road
Newtown Square, PA 19073-2814
Web: www.asme.org/Education/College/FinancialAid/

# ASME Foundation

## ASME Student Loan Program

**Type of award:** Loan, renewable.
**Intended use:** For full-time undergraduate or graduate study. Designated institutions: North American institutions.
**Basis for selection:** Major/career interest in engineering, mechanical. Applicant must demonstrate financial need.
**Additional information:** Applicant must be student member of American Society of Mechanical Engineers in United States, Canada or Mexico, and enrolled in mechanical engineering or mechanical engineering technology program/courses. Minimum 2.2 GPA for undergraduates; minimum 3.2 GPA for graduates. Award is up to $3,000 per year with $9,000 maximum for undergraduate degree and additional $3,000 for graduate students. Visit Website for application.

| | |
|---|---|
| **Amount of award:** | $3,000 |
| **Number of applicants:** | 76 |
| **Application deadline:** | April 15, October 15 |
| **Total amount awarded:** | $192,509 |

**Contact:**
ASME
Ann-Marie Beck
22 Law Drive, MS: NO1
Fairfield, NJ 07007-2900
Phone: 973-244-2319
Web: www.asme.org/education/college/financialaid/Student_Loan_Funds.cfm

# California Student Aid Commission

## Assumption Program of Loans for Education (APLE)

**Type of award:** Loan, renewable.
**Intended use:** For junior or senior study at accredited 4-year institution. Designated institutions: California postsecondary institutions with Commission on Teacher Credential-approved programs.
**Eligibility:** Applicant must be U.S. citizen or permanent resident residing in California.
**Basis for selection:** Major/career interest in education; education, early childhood; education, special or education, teacher. Applicant must demonstrate financial need and high academic achievement.

Loans

**Application requirements:** Proof of eligibility, nomination by participating institution.
**Additional information:** June 30 is priority deadline. Must have received educational loan and not be in default of said loan. Must agree to teach in California public school in teacher shortage area for at least four years. Loans assumed up to $2,000 for first year, and up to $3,000 for second, third, and fourth years of consecutive service. Those who agree to teach math, science, or special education may receive up to $1,000 of additional loan assumption benefits each year. Another annual $1,000 of benefits may be received by those teaching math, science, or education specialist instruction in schools ranked in API lowest 20 percentile, for a maximum of $19,000. Applicants must be pursuing teaching credentials for K-12. Credentialed teachers may also apply.

| | |
|---|---|
| **Amount of award:** | $19,000 |
| **Number of awards:** | 7,400 |
| **Number of applicants:** | 50,000 |
| **Application deadline:** | June 30 |

**Contact:**
California Student Aid Commission
Specialized Programs Operations Branch
P.O. Box 419029
Rancho Cordova, CA 95741-9029
Phone: 888-224-7268 opt. 3
Fax: 916-464-7977
Web: www.csac.ca.gov

# Connecticut Higher Education Supplemental Loan Authority

## CHESLA Loan Program

**Type of award:** Loan.
**Intended use:** For undergraduate or graduate study in United States. Designated institutions: Non-profit institutions (non-residents must attend Connecticut non-profit institutions to be eligible).
**Application requirements:** Alien registration receipt card (I-151 or I-551) for non-citizens.
**Additional information:** Applicant must be a resident of or attending school in Connecticut. Loan amount ranges from $2,000 to full cost of education minus aid. Visit Website for application.

| | |
|---|---|
| **Amount of award:** | $2,000 |
| **Number of applicants:** | 2,308 |
| **Total amount awarded:** | $20,880,670 |

**Contact:**
Connecticut Higher Education Supplemental Loan Authority (CHESLA)
21 Talcott Notch Road
Suite 1
Farmington, CT 06032
Phone: 800-252-FELP (CT) or 860-678-7788 (out of state)
Web: www.chesla.org

# Delaware Higher Education Commission

## Christa McAuliffe Teacher Incentive Program

**Type of award:** Loan, renewable.
**Intended use:** For undergraduate study at accredited 4-year institution.
**Eligibility:** Applicant must be U.S. citizen or permanent resident residing in Delaware.
**Basis for selection:** Major/career interest in education. Applicant must demonstrate high academic achievement.
**Application requirements:** Essay, transcript. SAT scores.
**Additional information:** Applicant must be high school senior with combined score of 1570 on the SAT and rank in top half of class, or undergraduate with minimum 2.75 GPA. Preference given to applicants planning to teach in critical need area as defined by DE Department of Education. Though award is for full-time students, it may be prorated for part-time students in a qualifying program. Loan not to exceed cost of tuition, fees, and other direct educational expenses. Loan forgiveness provision at rate of one year of teaching in a DE public school for one year of loan. Visit Website for deadline information.

| | |
|---|---|
| **Number of applicants:** | 69 |

**Contact:**
Delaware Higher Education Commission
820 North French Street
Wilmington, DE 19801
Phone: 302-577-5240
Fax: 302-577-6765
Web: www.doe.k12.de.us/programs/dhec/how_to_apply/financial_aid

## Delaware Nursing Incentive Program

**Type of award:** Loan, renewable.
**Intended use:** For undergraduate study at accredited vocational, 2-year or 4-year institution in United States. Designated institutions: Colleges with accredited nursing programs that lead to RN, LPN, or BSN certification.
**Eligibility:** Applicant must be U.S. citizen or permanent resident residing in Delaware.
**Basis for selection:** Major/career interest in nursing. Applicant must demonstrate high academic achievement.
**Application requirements:** Essay, transcript.
**Additional information:** Loan-forgiveness for practicing nursing at state-owned hospital or clinic, one year for each year of loan. High school seniors must rank in top half of class and have at least 2.5 GPA. Though award generally for full-time students who are residents of DE, current state employees do not have to be DE residents and may be considered for part-time enrollment. RNs with five or more years of state service may enroll in BSN program full or part time. Loan not to exceed cost of tuition, fees, and other direct educational expenses. Visit Website for deadline information.

| | |
|---|---|
| **Number of applicants:** | 84 |
| **Total amount awarded:** | $35,000 |

**Contact:**
Delaware Higher Education Commission
820 North French Street
Wilmington, DE 19801
Phone: 302-577-5240
Fax: 302-577-6765
Web: www.doe.k12.de.us/programs/dhec/how_to_apply/financial_aid

# Franklin Lindsay Student Aid Fund

## Franklin Lindsay Student Aid Loan

**Type of award:** Loan, renewable.
**Intended use:** For full-time sophomore, junior, senior or graduate study at accredited 4-year or graduate institution in United States. Designated institutions: Texas colleges accredited by the Southern Association of Colleges and Schools Commission on Colleges.
**Eligibility:** Applicant must be U.S. citizen.
**Basis for selection:** Applicant must demonstrate financial need.
**Application requirements:** Interview.
**Additional information:** Minimum 2.0 GPA for undergraduates and 3.0 for graduates. Must have co-signer who is U.S. citizen. Upon graduation or termination from school, loan goes to repayment structure at four percent, with maximum payment term of seven years. Visit Website for application and more information.

| | |
|---|---|
| **Amount of award:** | $7,000 |
| **Number of applicants:** | 97 |
| **Application deadline:** | June 1 |
| **Total amount awarded:** | $723,550 |

**Contact:**
The Franklin Lindsay Student Aid Fund
c/o JPMorgan Chase Bank, N.A.
P.O. Box 227237
Dallas, TX 75222-7237
Phone: 866-300-6222
Web: www.franklinlindsay.org

# Grand Encampment of Knights Templar of the USA

## Knights Templar Educational Foundation Loan

**Type of award:** Loan, renewable.
**Intended use:** For junior, senior or first professional study at accredited vocational, 4-year or graduate institution in United States.
**Basis for selection:** Applicant must demonstrate high academic achievement and depth of character.
**Application requirements:** Recommendations.
**Additional information:** Student should request application from Grand Encampment of Knights Templar in state of residence. Available loan amount varies by state division.

**Contact:**
Grand Encampment of Knights Templar of the USA
5909 West Loop South
Suite 495
Belaire, TX 77401-2402
Phone: 713-349-8700
Fax: 713-349-8710
Web: www.knightstemplar.org

# Jewish Family and Children's Services (JFCS)

## JFCS Scholarship Fund

**Type of award:** Scholarship.
**Intended use:** For undergraduate or graduate study at postsecondary institution.
**Eligibility:** Applicant must be Jewish. Applicant must be residing in California.
**Basis for selection:** Applicant must demonstrate financial need and high academic achievement.
**Additional information:** Minimum 2.75 GPA for grants. Applicants must demonstrate connection to Jewish community. High school seniors, undergraduates, and graduate students may apply. Applicants may also be high school students traveling to Israel. Grants available for residents of Sonoma, Marin, San Francisco, San Mateo, or Santa Clara counties; loans available for all nine Bay area counties. Deadline is for consideration for school year; applicants for Israel travel, Holocaust study, and vocational study may apply any time. Organization has several scholarships and loans; see Website for more details.

| | |
|---|---|
| **Amount of award:** | $1,000-$1,500 |
| **Number of awards:** | 100 |
| **Application deadline:** | August 1 |

**Contact:**
Jewish Family and Children's Services
Attn: Eric Singer
2150 Post Street
San Francisco, CA 94115
Phone: 415-449-1226
Fax: 415-449-1229
Web: www.jfcs.org

# Maine Educational Loan Authority

## The Maine Loan

**Type of award:** Loan.
**Intended use:** For undergraduate or graduate study at accredited vocational, 2-year, 4-year or graduate institution in United States or Canada.
**Eligibility:** Applicant must be residing in Maine.
**Application requirements:** Proof of eligibility. Income information/credit analysis.
**Additional information:** Loans available to Maine residents attending approved schools and out-of-state students attending Maine schools. May borrow full cost of education minus other financial aid. May be used to pay prior balance up to one

academic year. Applicant has 5-15 years to repay, depending on amount owed. See Website for interest rates, payment options, and additional information. Applications accepted year round. Minimum loan amount is $1,000.

| | |
|---|---|
| **Number of applicants:** | 2,510 |
| **Total amount awarded:** | $30,000,000 |

**Contact:**
Maine Educational Loan Authority
131 Presumpscot Street
Portland, ME 04103
Phone: 800-922-6352
Fax: 207-791-3616
Web: www.mela.net

# Massachusetts Board of Higher Education

## Massachusetts No Interest Loan

**Type of award:** Loan.
**Intended use:** For full-time undergraduate study at accredited vocational, 2-year or 4-year institution.
**Eligibility:** Applicant must be U.S. citizen or permanent resident residing in Massachusetts.
**Basis for selection:** Applicant must demonstrate financial need.
**Application requirements:** FAFSA.
**Additional information:** No Interest Loan (NIL) Program offers no interest loans to those who meet requirements; students have 10 years to repay NIL loans and a borrowing limit of $20,000 ($4,000/year). Must not have received prior bachelor's degree.

| | |
|---|---|
| **Amount of award:** | $1,000-$4,000 |
| **Number of applicants:** | 2,200 |
| **Total amount awarded:** | $6,000,000 |

**Contact:**
Office of Student Financial Assistance
Massachusetts Board of Higher Education
454 Broadway, Suite 200
Revere, MA 02151
Phone: 617-727-9420
Fax: 617-727-0667
Web: www.osfa.mass.edu

# Military Officers Association of America

## MOAA Interest-Free Loan and Grant Program

**Type of award:** Loan, renewable.
**Intended use:** For full-time undergraduate study at accredited 2-year or 4-year institution in United States.
**Eligibility:** Applicant must be no older than 23. Applicant must be U.S. citizen. Applicant must be dependent of active service person, veteran or deceased veteran who serves or served in the Army, Air Force, Marines, Navy, Coast Guard or Reserves/National Guard. Applicant must be child of MOAA member or active-duty, Reserve, National Guard, or retired enlisted military personnel.
**Basis for selection:** Applicant must demonstrate financial need, high academic achievement, depth of character, leadership, patriotism, seriousness of purpose and service orientation.
**Application requirements:** Essay, transcript, proof of eligibility. SAT/ACT score. Parent or sponsor's military status and/or MOAA number.
**Additional information:** Minimum 3.0 GPA. Applicant must be child of active-duty or retired enlisted personnel. Must be under 24; however, if applicant served in Uniformed Service before completing college, maximum age for eligibility increases by number of years served, up to five years. Parent must sign promissory note before funds can be disbursed. Military academy cadets not eligible. Application available on Website.

| | |
|---|---|
| **Amount of award:** | $5,500 |
| **Number of awards:** | 1,600 |
| **Number of applicants:** | 2,000 |
| **Application deadline:** | March 1 |
| **Notification begins:** | June 1 |
| **Total amount awarded:** | $8,800,000 |

**Contact:**
MOAA Scholarship Fund
Educational Assistance Program
201 North Washington Street
Alexandria, VA 22314-2529
Phone: 800-234-6622
Web: www.moaa.org/education

# Minnesota Office of Higher Education

## Minnesota Student Educational Loan Fund (SELF)

**Type of award:** Loan.
**Intended use:** For undergraduate or graduate study at vocational, 2-year, 4-year or graduate institution. Designated institutions: Minnesota and eligible out-of-state institutions.
**Additional information:** Applicant must be enrolled at least half-time in eligible Minnesota school, or be Minnesota resident enrolled in eligible school outside Minnesota. Must seek aid from certain other sources before applying, except federal unsubsidized and subsidized Stafford loans, National Direct Student loans, HEAL loans, and other private loans. Institution must approve application. Must have a creditworthy cosigner.

| | |
|---|---|
| **Amount of award:** | $500-$10,000 |
| **Number of applicants:** | 22,681 |
| **Total amount awarded:** | $118,316,074 |

**Contact:**
Minnesota Office of Higher Education
1450 Energy Park Drive, Suite 350
St. Paul, MN 55108-5227
Phone: 800-657-3866
Web: www.selfloan.org

# Mississippi Office of Student Financial Aid

## Critical Needs Teacher Loan/Scholarship

**Type of award:** Loan, renewable.
**Intended use:** For junior or senior study at 4-year institution in United States. Designated institutions: Mississippi institutions.
**Eligibility:** Applicant must be U.S. citizen residing in Mississippi.
**Basis for selection:** Major/career interest in education; education, early childhood; education, special or education, teacher.
**Application requirements:** Signed CNTP Rules and Regulations.
**Additional information:** Minimum 2.5 GPA or must rank in top 50 percent of class. Must be enrolled in program of study leading to Class "A" teacher educator license. Must agree to full-time employment in Mississippi public school located in critical teacher shortage or subject area. Must participate in Entrance Counseling. Award covers tuition, fees, and housing plus book allowance. Students at private institutions receive award equivalent to costs at nearest comparable public institution. Interested non-Mississippi residents may apply if they have been accepted to Mississippi school. See Website for application and more information.

| | |
|---|---|
| **Amount of award:** | $4,000 |
| **Application deadline:** | March 31 |

**Contact:**
Mississippi Office of Student Financial Aid
3825 Ridgewood Road
Jackson, MS 39211-6453
Phone: 800-327-2980
Web: www.mississippi.edu/riseupms

## Mississippi Health Care Professions Loan/Scholarship

**Type of award:** Loan, renewable.
**Intended use:** For full-time junior or senior study at accredited 4-year or graduate institution. Designated institutions: Mississippi institutions.
**Eligibility:** Applicant must be residing in Mississippi.
**Basis for selection:** Major/career interest in physical therapy; occupational therapy; speech pathology/audiology or psychology. Applicant must demonstrate high academic achievement.
**Application requirements:** Transcript, proof of eligibility. Mississippi tax return.
**Additional information:** Loan forgiveness for service in Mississippi health care institution: one year for each year of financial assistance, with a maximum of two years. Undergraduates must major in speech pathology/audiology, psychology, or occupational therapy; graduates must major in physical therapy or occupational therapy at University of Mississippi Medical Center. Visit Website for application and further information.

| | |
|---|---|
| **Amount of award:** | $1,500-$6,000 |
| **Number of awards:** | 3 |
| **Application deadline:** | March 31 |
| **Notification begins:** | August 1 |
| **Total amount awarded:** | $7,500 |

**Contact:**
Susan Eckels, Program Manager
Mississippi Office of Student Financial Aid
3825 Ridgewood Road
Jackson, MS 39211-6453
Phone: 800-327-2980
Fax: 601-432-6527
Web: www.mississippi.edu/riseupms

## Mississippi William Winter Teacher Scholar Loan Program

**Type of award:** Loan, renewable.
**Intended use:** For full-time junior or senior study at 4-year institution. Designated institutions: Mississippi institutions.
**Eligibility:** Applicant must be U.S. citizen residing in Mississippi.
**Basis for selection:** Major/career interest in education; education, early childhood; education, special or education, teacher. Applicant must demonstrate high academic achievement.
**Application requirements:** Proof of eligibility.
**Additional information:** Must be studying towards a Class A teacher educator license. Minimum 2.5 GPA or must rank in top 50 percent of class. Loan forgiveness for teaching service in Mississippi public school or public school district: one year for each year of financial assistance, for a maximum of two years. Apply online.

| | |
|---|---|
| **Amount of award:** | $4,000 |
| **Application deadline:** | March 31 |
| **Notification begins:** | August 1 |
| **Total amount awarded:** | $1,921,658 |

**Contact:**
Mississippi Office of Student Financial Aid
3825 Ridgewood Road
Jackson, MS 39211-6453
Phone: 800-327-2980
Fax: 601-432-6527
Web: www.mississippi.edu/riseupms

# Navy-Marine Corps Relief Society

## Vice Admiral E.P. Travers Loan

**Type of award:** Loan, renewable.
**Intended use:** For full-time undergraduate study.
**Eligibility:** Applicant must be U.S. citizen. Applicant must be dependent of active service person; or spouse of active service person in the Marines or Navy.
**Basis for selection:** Applicant must demonstrate financial need.
**Application requirements:** Proof of eligibility. Current military ID of service member.
**Additional information:** Minimum 2.0 GPA. Applicant must be dependent child of an active duty or retired service member of Navy or Marine Corp (including Reservists on active duty) or a spouse of active duty service member. Loan must be repaid in allotments over 24-month period (minimum monthly repayment is $50). Must reapply to renew.

| | |
|---|---|
| **Amount of award:** | $500-$3,000 |
| **Number of applicants:** | 1,200 |
| **Application deadline:** | March 1 |
| **Total amount awarded:** | $800,000 |

**Contact:**
Navy-Marine Corps Relief Society
875 North Randolph Street, Suite 225
Arlington, VA 22203
Phone: 703-696-4960
Web: www.nmcrs.org/education

# New Hampshire Postsecondary Education Commission

## Workforce Incentive Program

**Type of award:** Loan, renewable.
**Intended use:** For full-time undergraduate or graduate study at accredited 2-year, 4-year or graduate institution.
**Eligibility:** Applicant must be U.S. citizen or permanent resident residing in New Hampshire.
**Basis for selection:** Major/career interest in education, special; foreign languages or nursing. Applicant must demonstrate financial need.
**Additional information:** Program assists in loan repayment. Contact financial aid office at New Hampshire institution. Maximum $10,000 over five years. Number of awards varies. Visit Website for more information.

| | |
|---|---|
| **Amount of award:** | $1,500-$10,000 |
| **Number of applicants:** | 139 |
| **Application deadline:** | September 30 |
| **Total amount awarded:** | $210,018 |

**Contact:**
Postsecondary Education Commission
WIP Repayment Program
3 Barrell Court, Suite 300
Concord, NH 03301-8543
Phone: 603-271-2555 ext. 360
Fax: 603-271-2696
Web: www.nh.gov/postsecondary

# New Jersey Higher Education Student Assistance Authority

## New Jersey Class Loan Program

**Type of award:** Loan.
**Intended use:** For undergraduate or graduate study at accredited vocational, 2-year, 4-year or graduate institution in United States. Designated institutions: Approved institutions. Proprietary institutions also eligible.
**Eligibility:** Applicant must be U.S. citizen or permanent resident.
**Application requirements:** Proof of eligibility. Income and credit history, FAFSA, school certification.
**Additional information:** All New Jersey residents may apply, as may out-of-state students attending school in New Jersey. Must demonstrate credit-worthiness or provide co-signer. Parent or other eligible family member may borrow on behalf of student. Maximum loan amount may not exceed education cost less all other financial aid. Minimum loan amount $500. Low fixed interest rate loans available for both undergraduate and graduate students. Two percent administrative fee deducted from approved loan amount. Apply online for instant credit approval.

| | |
|---|---|
| **Total amount awarded:** | $341,272,644 |

**Contact:**
New Jersey Higher Education Student Assistance Authority
4 Quakerbridge Plaza
P.O. Box 540
Trenton, NJ 08625-0540
Phone: 800-792-8670
Fax: 609-588-2228
Web: www.hesaa.org

# New Mexico Commission on Higher Education

## New Mexico Allied Health Student Loan-for-Service Program

**Type of award:** Loan, renewable.
**Intended use:** For undergraduate or graduate study at accredited postsecondary institution. Designated institutions: Public postsecondary institutions in New Mexico.
**Eligibility:** Applicant must be U.S. citizen or permanent resident residing in New Mexico.
**Basis for selection:** Major/career interest in health-related professions; occupational therapy; mental health/therapy; physical therapy; pharmacy/pharmaceutics/pharmacology; dietetics/nutrition or speech pathology/audiology. Applicant must demonstrate financial need.
**Application requirements:** FAFSA.
**Additional information:** Loan forgiveness offered to those who practice in medically underserved areas in New Mexico. Must be accepted by or enrolled in approved programs at accredited New Mexico public postsecondary institution. Call sponsor number or visit Website for application and more information.

| | |
|---|---|
| **Amount of award:** | $12,000 |
| **Application deadline:** | July 1 |

**Contact:**
New Mexico Higher Education Department
Financial Aid and Student Services
2048 Galisteo Street
Santa Fe, NM 87505
Phone: 505-476-8400
Web: www.hed.state.nm.us

## New Mexico Nursing Student Loan-for-Service

**Type of award:** Loan, renewable.
**Intended use:** For undergraduate or graduate study at accredited 2-year or 4-year institution. Designated institutions: New Mexico public colleges and universities.
**Eligibility:** Applicant must be U.S. citizen or permanent resident residing in New Mexico.
**Basis for selection:** Major/career interest in nursing. Applicant must demonstrate financial need.
**Application requirements:** FAFSA.
**Additional information:** Loan forgiveness for New Mexico resident to practice in medically underserved areas in New Mexico. Part-time students eligible for prorated awards.

**Amount of award:** $12,000
**Application deadline:** July 1

**Contact:**
New Mexico Commission on Higher Education
Financial Aid and Student Services
2048 Galisteo Street
Santa Fe, NM 87505
Phone: 505-476-8400
Web: www.hed.state.nm.us

### New Mexico Teacher's Loan-for-Service

**Type of award:** Loan.
**Intended use:** For undergraduate or post-bachelor's certificate study at accredited postsecondary institution. Designated institutions: Public college or university.
**Eligibility:** Applicant must be physically challenged. Applicant must be U.S. citizen or permanent resident residing in New Mexico.
**Basis for selection:** Major/career interest in education, teacher. Applicant must demonstrate financial need.
**Application requirements:** FAFSA.
**Additional information:** Must be accepted by undergraduate, graduate, or alternative licensure teacher preparation program approved by State Board of Education. Must provide one year of teaching service for each year of award at a public school in New Mexico.

**Amount of award:** $4,000
**Application deadline:** July 1

**Contact:**
New Mexico Commission on Higher Education
Financial Aid and Student Services
2048 Galisteo Street
Santa Fe, NM 87505
Phone: 505-476-8400
Web: www.hed.state.nm.us

## New York State Grange

### Grange Student Loan Fund

**Type of award:** Loan, renewable.
**Intended use:** For full-time undergraduate or graduate study at postsecondary institution.
**Eligibility:** Applicant must be residing in New York.
**Basis for selection:** Applicant must demonstrate financial need.
**Additional information:** Must have been member of New York State Grange for at least 6 months at time of application. Must send SASE for application. Loanee may borrow a maximum of $10,000. May apply for less than the maximum award. Loan repayment at five percent annual interest.

**Amount of award:** $2,000
**Number of awards:** 11
**Number of applicants:** 11
**Application deadline:** April 15
**Notification begins:** June 15
**Total amount awarded:** $22,000

**Contact:**
New York State Grange
100 Grange Place
Cortland, NY 13045
Phone: 607-756-7553
Fax: 607-756-7757
Web: www.nysgrange.org

## North Carolina Community Colleges Foundation

### Community College Grant & Loan

**Type of award:** Loan.
**Intended use:** For undergraduate study at 2-year institution.
**Eligibility:** Applicant must be residing in North Carolina.
**Basis for selection:** Applicant must demonstrate financial need.
**Application requirements:** FAFSA.
**Additional information:** Value of grants and loans vary. Applicant must qualify for Federal Pell Grant. Provides financial assistance to credit and occupational extension students who enroll in low-enrollment programs that prepare students for high-demand occupations.

**Total amount awarded:** $762,806

**Contact:**
North Carolina Community Colleges Foundation
200 West Jones Street
Raleigh, NC 27603
Phone: 919-807-7106
Fax: 919-807-7173
Web: www.ncccs.cc.nc.us

## North Carolina State Education Assistance Authority

### North Carolina Nurse Scholars Program

**Type of award:** Loan, renewable.
**Intended use:** For full-time undergraduate study at accredited postsecondary institution. Designated institutions: North Carolina institutions.
**Eligibility:** Applicant must be U.S. citizen residing in North Carolina.
**Basis for selection:** Major/career interest in nursing. Applicant must demonstrate high academic achievement, leadership and service orientation.
**Application requirements:** Recommendations, essay, transcript, proof of eligibility.
**Additional information:** Minimum 3.0 GPA. Candidates for associate's degree in nursing and hospital diploma in nursing will receive $3,000. Candidates for bachelor's in nursing will receive $5,000 or $3,000 per year. Also, $2,500 per year scholarship/loan is available for an RN seeking a BSN degree. Recipient agrees to work full-time as RN in North Carolina; 12 months of work results in forgiveness of one year of loan support. Visit Website for more information.

**Amount of award:** $2,500-$5,000
**Number of awards:** 450
**Application deadline:** February 28, May 3

**Contact:**
North Carolina Nurse Scholars Program
P.O. Box 14223
Research Triangle Park, NC 27709-4223
Phone: 800-700-1775 ext. 313
Web: www.cfnc.org

### North Carolina Student Loans for Health/Science/Mathematics

**Type of award:** Loan, renewable.
**Intended use:** For full-time undergraduate or graduate study at accredited postsecondary institution in United States. Designated institutions: North Carolina postsecondary institutions and eligible out-of-state schools.
**Eligibility:** Applicant must be U.S. citizen residing in North Carolina.
**Basis for selection:** Major/career interest in health-related professions; mathematics; science, general; dentistry; optometry/ophthalmology; social work or nursing. Applicant must demonstrate financial need.
**Application requirements:** Transcript, proof of eligibility. FAFSA.
**Additional information:** Loan obligation may be forgiven through approved employment within the state of North Carolina, provided the recipient works in the field for which he/she was funded. May not be used for religion or theology studies. Application available on Website.

**Amount of award:** $3,000-$8,500
**Application deadline:** May 1

**Contact:**
North Carolina Student Loan Program
Health, Science and Mathematics
P.O. Box 14223
Research Triangle Park, NC 27709-4223
Phone: 800-700-1775
Web: www.cfnc.org

## Ohio Board of Regents

### Ohio Nurse Education Assistance Loan Program

**Type of award:** Loan, renewable.
**Intended use:** For undergraduate, post-bachelor's certificate or master's study at 4-year or graduate institution. Designated institutions: Eligible Ohio institutions.
**Eligibility:** Applicant must be U.S. citizen or permanent resident residing in Ohio.
**Basis for selection:** Major/career interest in nursing. Applicant must demonstrate financial need.
**Application requirements:** Proof of eligibility. FAFSA.
**Additional information:** Future nurse applicants must demonstrate financial need. Future nurse instructor applicants awarded on first-come, first-served basis. Award amount varies; up to $3,000 for future nurses, and at least $5,000 for future nurse instructors. Up to 100% loan cancellation if borrower meets cancellation requirements and practices nursing in Ohio after graduation. Debt cancellation rate of 20% per year for maximum of five years for future nurse recipients; 25% per year for maximum of four years for future nurse instructor recipients. Must not be in default or owe refund to any federal financial aid programs. Visit Website for application and more information.

**Number of awards:** 241
**Application deadline:** July 15
**Total amount awarded:** $388,152

**Contact:**
Ohio Board of Regents
30 E. Broad Street
36th Floor
Columbus, OH 43215-3414
Phone: 888-833-1133
Fax: 614-752-5903
Web: www.regents.ohio.gov/sgs/nealp

## Pickett and Hatcher Educational Fund, Inc.

### Pickett and Hatcher Educational Loan

**Type of award:** Loan, renewable.
**Intended use:** For full-time undergraduate study at 4-year institution.
**Eligibility:** Applicant must be U.S. citizen.
**Basis for selection:** Applicant must demonstrate financial need and high academic achievement.
**Additional information:** Not available to law, medicine, or ministry students. Loans renewed up to $40,000. Applications accepted year-round.

**Amount of award:** $1,000-$10,000
**Number of awards:** 550
**Number of applicants:** 539
**Total amount awarded:** $2,869,434

**Contact:**
Pickett and Hatcher Educational Fund, Inc.
Loan Program
P.O. Box 8169
Columbus, GA 31908-8169
Phone: 706-327-6586
Fax: 706-324-6788
Web: www.phef.org

## Presbyterian Church (USA)

### Presbyterian Undergraduate and Graduate Loan

**Type of award:** Loan, renewable.
**Intended use:** For full-time undergraduate or graduate study at accredited 2-year, 4-year or graduate institution in United States.
**Eligibility:** Applicant must be Presbyterian. Applicant must be U.S. citizen or permanent resident.
**Basis for selection:** Applicant must demonstrate financial need and high academic achievement.
**Additional information:** Must establish and maintain minimum 2.0 GPA. Contact office for current interest rates and deferment policies. Must give evidence of financial reliability.

Undergraduates and graduates can apply for up to $15,000, spread out over length of undergraduate and graduate studies.

**Amount of award:** $200-$3,000
**Number of awards:** 150
**Number of applicants:** 200
**Application deadline:** July 30
**Notification begins:** August 15
**Total amount awarded:** $400,000

**Contact:**
Presbyterian Church (USA)
Financial Aid for Studies
100 Witherspoon Street
Louisville, KY 40202-1396
Phone: 888-728-7228 ext. 5735
Fax: 502-569-8766
Web: www.pcusa.org/financialaid

# South Carolina Student Loan Corporation

## South Carolina Teacher Loans

**Type of award:** Loan, renewable.
**Intended use:** For undergraduate or graduate study at accredited 2-year, 4-year or graduate institution.
**Eligibility:** Applicant must be U.S. citizen or permanent resident residing in South Carolina.
**Basis for selection:** Major/career interest in education; education, early childhood; education, special or education, teacher. Applicant must demonstrate high academic achievement.
**Additional information:** Freshmen and sophomores may borrow up to $2,500 per year; juniors, seniors, and graduate students may borrow up to $5,000 per year. Graduate study eligible only if required for initial teacher certification. Entering freshmen must have SAT score equal to South Carolina state average for year of high school graduation, and rank in top 40 percent of high school class. Undergraduate and entering graduate applicants must have 2.75 GPA and have passed PRAXIS 1 Examination. Graduate applicants who have completed at least one semester must have 3.5 GPA. Applicants with SAT score of 1100 or greater (1650 or greater for exams taken on or after March 1, 2005) or ACT score of 24 or greater are exempt from PRAXIS 1 requirement. Loan forgiveness for service in teacher shortage area in South Carolina public schools: 20 percent or $3,000, whichever is greater, for each year of service, 33 percent or $5,000, whichever is greater, if service in geographic and subject shortage area. Apply early.

**Amount of award:** $2,500-$5,000
**Application deadline:** April 15
**Notification begins:** July 15
**Total amount awarded:** $5,000,000

**Contact:**
South Carolina Student Loan Corporation
P.O. Box 21487
Columbia, SC 29221
Phone: 803-798-0916 or 800-347-2752
Web: www.scstudentloan.org

# Student Aid Foundation

## Student Aid Foundation Loan

**Type of award:** Loan, renewable.
**Intended use:** For full-time undergraduate, master's, doctoral or first professional study at accredited vocational, 2-year, 4-year or graduate institution in United States.
**Eligibility:** Applicant must be female. Applicant must be U.S. citizen residing in Georgia.
**Basis for selection:** Applicant must demonstrate financial need, high academic achievement and seriousness of purpose.
**Application requirements:** Recommendations, essay, transcript.
**Additional information:** Non-Georgia residents attending Georgia institutions can qualify. Loan not forgivable. Must have financially responsible endorser. Minimum 2.5 GPA. Send SASE with request for application, or download it from Website.

**Amount of award:** $3,500-$7,500
**Number of awards:** 40
**Number of applicants:** 89
**Application deadline:** May 1
**Notification begins:** June 1

**Contact:**
Student Aid Foundation
#312
2550 Sandy Plains Road, Suite 225
Marietta, GA 30066
Phone: 770-973-7077
Fax: 770-973-2220
Web: www.studentaidfoundation.org

# Tennessee Student Assistance Corporation

## Tennessee Minority Teaching Fellows Program

**Type of award:** Loan, renewable.
**Intended use:** For full-time undergraduate study at accredited 2-year or 4-year institution.
**Eligibility:** Applicant must be Alaskan native, Asian American, African American, Hispanic American, American Indian or Native Hawaiian/Pacific Islander. Applicant must be U.S. citizen residing in Tennessee.
**Basis for selection:** Major/career interest in education. Applicant must demonstrate high academic achievement.
**Application requirements:** Recommendations, essay, transcript. List of extracurricular activities.
**Additional information:** Entering freshmen applicants have priority and must have minimum 2.75 GPA, rank in top 25 percent of class, or score at least 18 on ACT (860 SAT). Undergraduate applicants must have minimum 2.5 GPA. Must make commitment to teaching. Loan can be forgiven by teaching in Tennessee public pre K-12 schools, one year for each year of funding.

**Amount of award:** $5,000
**Number of awards:** 113
**Number of applicants:** 312
**Application deadline:** April 15
**Total amount awarded:** $543,010

**Contact:**
Tennessee Student Assistance Corporation
404 James Robertson Parkway
Parkway Towers, Suite 1510
Nashville, TN 37243-0820
Phone: 800-342-1663
Fax: 615-741-6101
Web: www.tn.gov/collegepays

### Tennessee Student Assistance Corporation/Math And Science Teachers Loan Forgiveness Program

**Type of award:** Loan, renewable.
**Intended use:** For undergraduate certificate, graduate or postgraduate study at postsecondary institution.
**Eligibility:** Applicant must be residing in Tennessee.
**Basis for selection:** Major/career interest in mathematics; science, general or education.
**Additional information:** Must be admitted to post-secondary institution seeking advanced degree in math/science, or a certificate to teach math/science, and be a tenured Tennessee public school teacher. Application deadline is September 1 for students beginning the academic year in the fall, February 1 for spring, and May 1 for summer.

| | |
|---|---|
| **Amount of award:** | $2,000 |
| **Number of awards:** | 25 |
| **Application deadline:** | September 1, February 1 |
| **Total amount awarded:** | $47,000 |

**Contact:**
Tennessee Student Assistance Corporation
404 James Robertson Parkway
Suite 1510, Parkway Towers
Nashville, TN 37243-0820
Phone: 800-342-1663
Web: www.tn.gov/collegepays

### Tennessee Teaching Scholars Program

**Type of award:** Loan, renewable.
**Intended use:** For junior, senior, post-bachelor's certificate or master's study at accredited 4-year or graduate institution.
**Eligibility:** Applicant must be U.S. citizen residing in Tennessee.
**Basis for selection:** Major/career interest in education; education, teacher; education, special or education, early childhood. Applicant must demonstrate high academic achievement.
**Application requirements:** Recommendations, transcript, proof of eligibility. Verification of standardized test score and acceptance into Teacher Licensure Program.
**Additional information:** Loan can be forgiven for teaching in Tennessee public schools, K-12. Minimum 2.75 cumulative GPA and a standardized test score adequate for admission to the Teacher Education Program in Tennessee schools. Amount of award based on funding.

| | |
|---|---|
| **Amount of award:** | $4,500 |
| **Number of awards:** | 145 |
| **Number of applicants:** | 381 |
| **Application deadline:** | April 15 |
| **Total amount awarded:** | $571,125 |

**Contact:**
Tennessee Student Assistance Corporation
404 James Robertson Parkway
Parkway Towers, Suite 1510
Nashville, TN 37243-0820
Phone: 800-342-1663
Fax: 615-741-6101
Web: www.tn.gov/collegepays

## Texas Higher Education Coordinating Board

### College Access Loan (CAL)

**Type of award:** Loan.
**Intended use:** For undergraduate or graduate study at 2-year, 4-year or graduate institution in United States.
**Eligibility:** Applicant must be U.S. citizen or permanent resident residing in Texas.
**Additional information:** Texas colleges and universities have a limited number of CAL loans. Applicants need not show financial need. The loan may be used to cover the family's expected contribution (EFC). Co-signers must have good credit and meet other program criteria. Loans will not be sold to another lender and will be serviced by the THECB until paid in full. Apply online.
**Contact:**
Texas Higher Education Coordinating Board
Phone: 800-242-3062
Web: www.collegeforalltexans.com and www.hhloans.com

### William D. Ford Direct Student Loans

**Type of award:** Loan.
**Intended use:** For undergraduate study at vocational, 2-year or 4-year institution in United States.
**Eligibility:** Applicant must be U.S. citizen or permanent resident.
**Basis for selection:** Applicant must demonstrate financial need and high academic achievement.
**Application requirements:** FAFSA.
**Additional information:** Borrowers must not be in default or delinquent on any federal student loan. Contact college financial aid office for more information.

| | |
|---|---|
| **Amount of award:** | $2,625-$18,500 |

**Contact:**
Texas Higher Education Coordinating Board
Phone: 800-242-3062
Web: www.collegeforalltexans.com

## United Methodist Church

### United Methodist Loan Program

**Type of award:** Loan, renewable.
**Intended use:** For undergraduate or graduate study at accredited postsecondary institution in United States.
**Eligibility:** Applicant must be United Methodist.
**Additional information:** Must be active member of United Methodist Church one year prior to application. Must maintain

Loans

"C" average. May reapply for loan to maximum of $30,000. Interest rate 5 percent; cosigner required. Ten years permitted to repay loan after graduation or withdrawal from school. Qualified applicants are chosen on a first-come, first-served basis.

**Amount of award:** $5,000

**Contact:**
United Methodist Church/Board of Higher Education and Ministry
Office of Loans and Scholarships
P.O. Box 340007
Nashville, TN 37203-0007
Phone: 615-340-7346
Web: www.gbhem.org

# UPS

## United Parcel Service Earn & Learn Program Loans

**Type of award:** Loan.
**Intended use:** For undergraduate study at accredited vocational, 2-year or 4-year institution in United States.
**Application requirements:** Proof of eligibility.
**Additional information:** Must be UPS employee. Award for part-time employees is $3,000 per year in student loans with $15,000 lifetime maximum. Award for part-time management employees is $4,000 per year with a $20,000 lifetime maximum. Visit Website for participating locations and job listings.

**Amount of award:** $3,000-$20,000

**Contact:**
UPS
Phone: 888-WORK-UPS
Web: www.upsjobs.com

# U.S. Department of Education

## Federal Direct Stafford Loans

**Type of award:** Loan, renewable.
**Intended use:** For undergraduate or graduate study at postsecondary institution.
**Eligibility:** Applicant must be U.S. citizen or permanent resident.
**Basis for selection:** Applicant must demonstrate financial need.
**Application requirements:** Proof of eligibility. FAFSA and promissory note.
**Additional information:** Some loans subsidized, based on need eligibility. Loan amount depends on grade level in school and student type. Telecommunications Device for the Deaf at 800-730-8913. FAFSA available online. Visit Website for interest rates.

**Amount of award:** $5,500-$20,500

**Contact:**
Federal Student Aid Information Center
Phone: 800-4-FED-AID
Web: www.studentaid.ed.gov

## Federal Family Education Loan Program (FFEL)

**Type of award:** Loan, renewable.
**Intended use:** For undergraduate or graduate study at accredited postsecondary institution in or outside United States or Canada.
**Eligibility:** Applicant must be U.S. citizen or permanent resident.
**Basis for selection:** Applicant must demonstrate financial need.
**Application requirements:** Proof of eligibility. FAFSA.
**Additional information:** Subsidized and unsubsidized loans. First-year dependent undergraduates eligible for up to $3,500; independent first-year undergraduates eligible for $7,500. Visit Website for interest rates and more information.

**Application deadline:** June 30

**Contact:**
Federal Student Aid Information Center
P.O. Box 84
Washington, DC 20044-0084
Phone: 800-4-FED-AID
Web: www.studentaid.ed.gov

## Federal Perkins Loan

**Type of award:** Loan, renewable.
**Intended use:** For undergraduate or graduate study at accredited postsecondary institution in United States.
**Eligibility:** Applicant must be U.S. citizen or permanent resident.
**Basis for selection:** Applicant must demonstrate financial need.
**Application requirements:** Proof of eligibility. FAFSA.
**Additional information:** Maximum annual loan amount: $5,500 for undergraduates, $8,000 for graduates. Five percent interest rate. Applicant must demonstrate exceptional financial need. Repayment begins nine months after graduation, leaving school, or dropping below half-time status. Visit Website for more information.

**Application deadline:** June 30

**Contact:**
Federal Student Aid Information Center
P.O. Box 84
Washington, DC 20044-0084
Phone: 800-4-FED AID
Web: www.studentaid.ed.gov

## Federal Plus Loan

**Type of award:** Loan.
**Intended use:** For undergraduate or graduate study at accredited postsecondary institution in or outside United States or Canada.
**Eligibility:** Applicant must be U.S. citizen or permanent resident.
**Basis for selection:** Applicant must demonstrate financial need.
**Application requirements:** PLUS loan application and promissory note. FAFSA.
**Additional information:** Unsubsidized loans for parents of undergraduate students, or for graduate students. Must pass credit check. Interest rate is 7.9 percent. Award amount varies. Loan is equal to cost of attendance minus any other financial aid. Generally, repayment must begin 60 days after the loan is fully disbursed. Visit Website for more information.

**Application deadline:** June 30

**Contact:**
Federal Student Aid Information Center
P.O. Box 84
Washington, DC 20044-0084
Phone: 800-4-FED-AID
Web: www.studentaid.ed.gov

## Utah State Office of Education

### Utah Career Teaching Scholarship/ T.H. Bell Teaching Incentive Loan

**Type of award:** Loan, renewable.
**Intended use:** For full-time undergraduate study at accredited 4-year institution. Designated institutions: Utah institutions.
**Eligibility:** Applicant must be high school junior or senior. Applicant must be U.S. citizen residing in Utah.
**Basis for selection:** Major/career interest in education, teacher; education; education, early childhood or education, special.
**Application requirements:** Transcript. SAT/ACT scoresheet.
**Additional information:** Must have completed requirements for Early Graduation Program (including ACT). Awardees must teach in Utah public school for term equal to number of years loan was received in order to have loans forgiven. Visit Website for application.

| | |
|---|---|
| **Amount of award:** | Full tuition |
| **Number of applicants:** | 110 |
| **Application deadline:** | March 30 |

**Contact:**
Utah State Office of Education Teaching and Learning
Linda Alder, Educator Quality and Licensing
250 East 500 South/P.O. Box 144200
Salt Lake City, UT 84114-4200
Web: www.schools.utah.gov/cert/loans-and-scholarships.aspx

## Virgin Islands Board of Education

### Virgin Islands Territorial Grants/ Loans Program

**Type of award:** Loan, renewable.
**Intended use:** For full-time undergraduate or graduate study at accredited postsecondary institution.
**Eligibility:** Applicant must be U.S. citizen or permanent resident residing in Virgin Islands.
**Basis for selection:** Applicant must demonstrate financial need.
**Application requirements:** Transcript. Acceptance letter from institution for first-time applicants or transfer students.
**Additional information:** Minimum 2.0 GPA. Must agree to accept one year of employment in Virgin Islands government for every year of award upon completion of studies. Number and amount of awards vary. Six percent interest on repayment, additional 2 percent if delinquent. Number and amount of award varies.

| | |
|---|---|
| **Number of applicants:** | 625 |
| **Application deadline:** | May 1 |

**Contact:**
Virgin Islands Board of Education
Scholarship Committee
P.O. Box 11900
St. Thomas, VI 00801
Phone: 340-774-4546
Web: www.myviboe.com

## Wisconsin Department of Veterans Affairs

### Wisconsin Veterans Affairs Personal Loan Program

**Type of award:** Loan.
**Intended use:** For undergraduate or graduate study at postsecondary institution in United States.
**Eligibility:** Applicant must be residing in Wisconsin. Applicant must be veteran; or dependent of veteran or deceased veteran; or spouse of veteran or deceased veteran. Must meet WDVA service requirements. Must have 90 days of active duty during wartime and/or two years of continuous active duty.
**Application requirements:** Proof of eligibility. Credit report.
**Additional information:** Applicant must have been resident of Wisconsin upon entry into military service or a continuous resident of Wisconsin for at least one year immediately preceding the application date. Maximum loan of $25,000 available. Loan must be secured by a mortgage on the applicant's property or with a guarantor. Subsidized annual interest rate varies; loan term varies depending on amount borrowed. Apply to local county veterans service officer to establish eligibility. Adult children of veterans must be under 26 years old and attending school full-time.
**Contact:**
Wisconsin Department of Veterans Affairs
P.O. Box 7843
30 West Mifflin Street
Madison, WI 53707-7843
Phone: 800-947-8387
Web: www.dva.state.wi.us



## Wisconsin Higher Educational Aids Board

### Wisconsin Minority Teacher Loan Program

**Type of award:** Loan, renewable.
**Intended use:** For junior, senior or graduate study at accredited 4-year institution. Designated institutions: Wisconsin colleges and universities offering teaching degree.
**Eligibility:** Applicant must be Asian American, African American, Mexican American, Hispanic American, Puerto Rican or American Indian. Asian American applicants must be either former citizens or descendants of former citizens of Laos, Vietnam, or Cambodia admitted to the U.S. after 12/31/1975. Applicant must be residing in Wisconsin.

**Basis for selection:** Major/career interest in education; education, special or education, teacher. Applicant must demonstrate financial need.
**Application requirements:** Nomination by financial aid office. FAFSA.
**Additional information:** Recipient must agree to teach in Wisconsin school district where minority students constitute at least 29 percent of enrollment or in school district participating in the inter-district pupil transfer (Chapter 220) program. For each year student teaches in eligible district, 25 percent of loan is forgiven; otherwise loan must be repaid at interest rate of 5 percent. Must be registered with Selective Service, unless exempt.

| | |
|---|---|
| **Amount of award:** | $250-$2,500 |
| **Number of awards:** | 109 |
| **Total amount awarded:** | $238,662 |

**Contact:**
Higher Educational Aids Board
Attn: Mary Lou Kuzdas
P.O. Box 7885
Madison, WI 53707-7885
Phone: 608-267-2212
Web: www.heab.state.wi.us

# Sponsor Index

Sponsor Index

Sponsor Index

# Program Index

Program Index

Program Index

# More College Planning Resources from the College Board

**College Handbook 2012**

The only guide listing all accredited universities, two-year and four-year colleges, and technical schools in the United States — more than 3,900 in total.

2,300 pages, paperback
ISBN: 978-0-87447-967-6
**$29.99**

**Book of Majors 2012**

Explore in-depth descriptions of 200 majors, and see where over 1,100 majors are offered at colleges nationwide.

1,350 pages, paperback
ISBN: 978-0-87447-968-3
**$26.99**

## COLLEGE ADMISSION

**The Official SAT Study Guide™: Second Edition**

*The Official SAT Study Guide*™ is the only book that features 10 official practice tests created by the test maker. The No. 1 best-selling guide is packed with valuable test-taking approaches and focused sets of practice questions — just like those on the actual SAT® — to help students get ready for the test.

998 pages, trade paper
ISBN: 978-0-87447-852-5
**$21.99**

**The College Application Essay**
*By Sarah Myers McGinty*

These strategies help students craft a college essay that stands out from the crowd.

160 pages, paperback
ISBN: 978-0-87447-711-5
**$15.95**

**Campus Visits & College Interviews**
*By Zola Dincin Schneider*

Get the most out of college campus visits and make a good impression during interviews.

160 pages, paperback
ISBN: 978-0-87447-675-0
**$12.95**

## PAYING FOR COLLEGE

**Getting Financial Aid 2012**

A must-have book in today's economy, this is the perfect resource for families managing the high cost of college. This easy step-by-step guide shows why, when and how to apply for financial aid.

1,050 pages, paperback
978-0-87447-970-6
**$21.99**

**Scholarship Handbook 2012**

The most complete and comprehensive guide to help families tap into the more than 1.7 million scholarships, internships and loans available to students each year.

624 pages, paperback
ISBN: 978-0-87447-971-3
**$28.99**

Available wherever books are sold. Distributed by Macmillan

©2011 The College Board. College Board, SAT and the acorn logo are registered trademarks of the College Board. inspiring minds and The Official SAT Study Guide are trademarks owned by the College Board.
Visit the College Board on the Web: www.collegeboard.org.

CLEP®

Achieve College Success with CLEP!

Earn college credit for what you already know

Average cost of a course at a 4-year public college: $600*

Cost of a CLEP exam: $77

A passing score on a 90-minute CLEP® exam can earn you between 3 and 12 credits toward your college degree. Exams are offered in over 30 different subjects and accepted at more than 2,900 colleges.

2012 CLEP Official Study Guide

The ONLY CLEP guide written by the test developer!

978-0-87447-976-8

$24.95

Get started today!
Find out more about CLEP at:
**www.collegeboard.org/clep**

*The College Board. *Trends in College Pricing* 2010

© The College Board.

Showcase your achievements with

# SAT Subject Tests™!

Get ready for test day with the only study guides developed by the Test Maker!

## The Official Study Guide for ALL SAT Subject Tests™ 2nd Edition

$22.99

**The new edition includes:**

- NEW detailed answer explanations for all test questions
- Full-length, previously administered tests for all 20 SAT Subject Tests
- Exclusive test-taking tips and approaches
- The most up-to-date versions of the instructions, background questions and answer sheets
- Two audio CDs for all six Language with Listening Tests

The Official SAT Subject Tests in U.S. and World History Study Guide™
$18.99

The Official SAT Subject Tests in Mathematics Levels 1 & 2 Study Guide™
$18.99

## History and Mathematics guides also available.

**Each guide includes:**

Recently updated, each of these guides provides four full-length practice tests, detailed answer explanations, and the most up-to-date tips and approaches to help students feel better prepared on test day.

Order today at store.collegeboard.org

© 2011 The College Board.

# Applying to College?

Know what to do, how to do it, and when — with the new edition of

# Get it together for College

**Packed with:**

- **Checklists** to know what to do
- **Journal pages** to record what you learn
- **Tips** to keep it simple
- **Timelines** to keep on track
- **PLUS:** special tips for art portfolios, music auditions, student athletes and home-schooled applicants

240 pages, paperback | ISBN: 978-0-87447-974-4 | $15.99

**Don't get overwhelmed — get organized.**

oard. College Board and the acorn logo are registered trademarks of the College Board.
demark owned by the College Board. Visit the College Board on the Web: www.collegeboard.org.